Published by DJhistory.com

www.djhistory.com

ISBN: 978-0-9561896-0-8

A CIP catalogue record for this book is available from the British Library.

THE DISCO FILES 1973-78
New York's Underground, Week by Week

by Vince Aletti

Smoking dancefloor at New York, NY © **Toby Old**

❝Discos have opened in any place you could stick a mirrored ball, two turntables and a DJ. In a recession economy, they're a bargain❞

Buy this book direct from www.djhistory.com/books

Credits

Written by Vince Aletti
Editors Frank Broughton & Bill Brewster
Impossible without Matthew Higgs, Tony Harriss & Mark Lamb

Cover Leo Elstob
Design John Meikle
Layout Frank Broughton & Dave Barlow
Copy Editor Miranda Morton
Copy editing Christopher Moss, Susannah Gowers
Scanning & library research Emma Spertus, Ryan Foerster, Andrew Henry, Ryan Evans, Amie Scally, Catherine Nguyen

Photography Toby Old, Peter Hujar

Printed by Pyramid Press

Big thanks to

Everyone at White Columns Gallery; Amanda Green & Richard Tennant at Globe Business Publishing; Richard Tuffs at Pyramid Press; Kenny Carpenter; Brian Chin; Michael Gomes; Danny Krivit; Tony Smith; Sarah Lazin; Jasen Emmons & Erynn Summers at Experience Music Project; Ed Cartwright & Leo Greenslade at Darling Dept; Mark McQuillan & Andy Singh at Republic of Music; Karen Tate at Soul Jazz; Paul Williams; Stephen Koch and Matthew Israel at the Peter Hujar Archive; Philip Tan at Matthew Marks Gallery, B. George at the ARChive of Contemporary Music; Anne Marie Basanese at *Rolling Stone*, Christina Pettit at *Village Voice*.

A quick note on the text

We've kept it all as close to the original sources as possible, so styles vary. We corrected a few spelling errors in artists, labels and titles, and put all titles in a consistent style. For space we sadly had to lose the formats from the charts (ie "album cut," "disco disc," etc), though we kept references to imports. There were minor cuts in some of the articles to avoid repetition. Whereas Vince ran a Top 20 chart every week, we only had space to include one roughly every month (it moves slowly), and we had to lose four or five club charts when they all got too damn long. Don't worry though, we always cut the least interesting one.

DJhistory.com

14 Jack's Place
6 Corbet Place
London E1 6NN
tel + 44 (0)20 7247 6232
email info@djhistory.com
www.djhistory.com

Contents

Vince Aletti © **Peter Hujar Archive**

Vince Aletti was disco's greatest chronicler, the first writer to cover the emerging scene. From 1974-78 he wrote the weekly Disco File column in Record World, *which became required reading in US clubland. Born in Philadelphia in 1945, Vince began his career on sixties underground music mags* The Rat, Fusion, Crawdaddy, Creem *and* Rolling Stone. *He quickly became their most knowledgeable black music critic and when this music became the soundtrack to a new club scene in New York, he was entranced. An integral part of the disco industry that emerged, Vince helped launch the Record Pool and was head of A&R for Ray Caviano's RFC Records. He went on to become a senior editor at the* Village Voice, *and today is the photography critic at the* New Yorker. *He donated his record collection to the Experience Music Project, but still has one of the greatest collection of fashion magazines in the world.*

Introduction

I'd been writing about music for five or six years before arriving at *Record World*, but I'd never written for one of the music trades and had always taken a skeptical, if not adversarial, view of the music business. Suddenly, I was not just writing from inside that business, I was an integral part of a booming scene. For most record companies, disco was a puzzlement and an annoyance, but mainly an opportunity to make money – if they could only figure out what it was. Within my first year on the job, most of the old-school promo men and women I met when I started had been replaced with or supplemented by disco promo guys, nearly all of them gay part-time or former DJs who understood the music and didn't have a problem staying out until 4 in the morning promoting it.

Although I didn't go out to clubs more than one or two nights a week, I usually spent time in the DJ booths asking about the songs I hadn't heard before. I'd listen to all the promo records that were sent to me free each week, supplementing them with records I bought from specialty stores or test pressings DJs passed on to me. It was important to me to be as *au courant* as the jocks I was writing for.

Disco was making money and the record companies were throwing it around, but no one could make a bad record a hit. The disco dance floor was the ultimate proving ground: if people screamed, you had it made; if they cleared the floor, you had better go back to the studio.

Disco File was influential, but it wasn't about me, it was about the music and the people who played it. Especially early on, the music had no dominant style, and that's what made it so interesting: it was coming from all over, but mainly underground, and a lot of the most successful club records never made it to radio. And when they did, they were over as far as most hard-core clubgoers were concerned. They had already moved on to the next left-field record. The serious disco crowd didn't care about mainstream popularity; they were happy to have the hits to themselves. But when radio discovered disco could draw listeners that their old formats couldn't, club exclusivity became harder and harder. Club records became bestsellers and before the column had run its course, I'd accumulated 12 gold records for albums and singles that I'd only written about. I'm grateful to *Record World* for the opportunity to write Disco File and the freedom to do it just as I wanted. But I'm most indebted to the DJs for taking my phone calls and letting me share their knowledge and their passion. Big thanks, too, to Matthew Higgs and his White Columns team for reviving Disco File in a limited edition collection in 2008 and to Frank Broughton and Bill Brewster for taking that project several giant steps further with this more complete and illustrated edition. Music Is the Message. Always.

– Vince Aletti

Upside Down at Les Mouches © **Toby Old**

❝Discotheques never died; they just went back underground where the hardcore dance crowd was – blacks, Latins, gays❞

Discotheque rock '73: Paaaaarty!

By Vince Aletti

Paar-ty! Paar-ty! You hear the chant at concerts, rising like a tribal rallying cry on a shrill wave of whistles and hard-beaten tambourines. It's at once a call to get down and party, a statement that there's a party going on and an indication that discotheques, where the chant originated, are back in force after their virtual disappearance with the flashbulb pop of the Sixties.

Actually, discotheques never died; they just went back underground where the hardcore dance crowd – blacks, Latins, gays – was. But in the last year they've returned, not only as a rapidly spreading social phenomenon (via juice bars, after-hours clubs, private lofts open on weekends to members only, floating groups of party-givers who take over the ballrooms of old hotels from midnight to dawn), but as a strong influence on the music people listen to and buy.

The best discotheque DJs are underground stars, discovering previously ignored albums, foreign imports, album cuts and obscure singles with the power to make the crowd scream, and playing them overlapped, non-stop so you dance until you drop. Because these DJs are much closer to the minute-to-minute changes in people's listening/dancing taste, they are the first to reflect these changes in the music they play, months ahead of trade magazine charts and all but a few radio station playlists.

Records like the O'Jays' "Love Train," Eddie Kendricks' "Girl You Need A Change of Mind," the Intruders' "I'll Always Love My Mama," the Pointer Sisters' "Yes We Can Can" and the Temptations' "Papa Was A Rolling Stone" were broken or made in discotheques but with few exceptions, their acceptance above ground was nothing compared to their popularity with the dance crowd. Other records – many of those noted here – live and die in discotheques, like exotic hothouse flowers. Typically, the music nurtured in the new discotheques is Afro-Latin in sound or instrumentation, heavy on the drums, with minimal lyrics, sometimes in a foreign language, and a repetitive, chant-like chorus. The most popular cuts are usually the longest and the most instrumental, performed by black groups who are, frequently, not American.

One of the most spectacular discotheque records in recent months is a perfect example of the genre: Manu Dibango's "Soul Makossa." Originally a French pressing on the Fiesta label, the 45 was being largely undistributed by an African import company in Brooklyn when a friend brought it to the attention of DJ Frankie Crocker. Crocker broke it on the air on New York's WBLS-FM, a black station highly attuned to the disco sound, but the record was made in discotheques where its hypnotic beat and mysterious African vocals drove people crazy. Within days "Soul Makossa" was *the* underground record and when copies of the original 45 disappeared at $3 and $4, cover versions (many unlicensed and one a pirated copy put out under another group's name) were rushed out. Atlantic Records stepped into this confusion, bought the US rights and had both the single and an album out on their own label days later.

❝ Several of these records have disappeared from the turntables at clubs, but they all revive rather remarkably given the right atmosphere at home ❞

The album, Soul Makossa (Atlantic SD 7267), far from being a package of waste filler cushioning the title single, is one of the best to emerge from the new discotheque scene. Recorded in Paris, Manu Dibango and his group of expatriates from formerly French West Africa put together a heady Afro-jazz blend, using horns and electric guitars but in an utterly African way. Their "Soul Makossa" is still the gutsiest, most compelling of all the versions that followed and no one has matched the strange, slightly echoed quality of the lead vocal. The other cuts are more instrumental than vocal and several are at least as good as dance music, particularly "New Bell" and "Oboso." Perfect for a sub-tropical evening in the jungle of the cities.

The only group to get a version of "Soul Makossa" on the charts before Atlantic picked up Dibango's original was a 13-man congregation of studio musicians called Afrique. Their "Makossa" is exactly as long as the original (4:30) but has a hard-edged, over-slick feel and vocals that sound somehow more Latin than African. Their album, Soul Makossa (Mainstream MRL 394), features guitarists David T. Walker and Arthur Wright and Chuck Rainey on Fender bass and is about as Afrique as the Temptations. Not for dancing.

A third Soul Makossa album (Paramount PAS 6061) is considerably more interesting, if only as the first LP from African drummer Babatutunde Olatunji in four years. At nearly seven minutes, his version of "Soul Makossa" is the longest I know of, but its length is its undoing. It lacks the concentrated energy of the original and though far from boring, it's entirely too rambling and overworked. But it's only a minor disappointment in an otherwise fine album. Being much more drum-based, the sound is denser than Manu Dibango's, but the structure of the cuts is looser, more improvisatory. The horns are not as integrated into the texture of the music as they might be and most tracks don't achieve any tightness or intensity until they are halfway through, yet the music is always rich and exciting. Though it's hard to sit still for any of this, "Takuta" and "O-Wa" are especially good for dancing. Still largely undiscovered, this album could be very big once the word gets out.

The following albums form a sort of basic discotheque library supplemental to the selected works of War, Eddie Kendricks, the O'Jays, Earth, Wind & Fire, the Temptations, James Brown, Stevie Wonder *et al.*, but vital to any house party for the moment at least. Several of these records are fading fast or have disappeared from the turntables at clubs, but they all revive rather remarkably given the right atmosphere at home.

DOING IT TO DEATH – The J.B.'s (People)
James Brown & Co. in another one of their many permutations. The title cut is a little more than ten minutes, twice the length of the 45, and *smokes* from Brown's opening words, "Hit it!" to a fade-out on flute. The funk band at their best. The remainder of the album is less exciting, even a little laid-back. Nearly the entire lyric content of the repeated theme track, "You Can Have Watergate, Jus' Gimme Some Bucks And I'll Be Straight," is right there in the title, and much of the rest is basic black jazz and very loose.

COMPOSITE TRUTH – Mandrill (Polydor)
The third and most successful album by a seven-man New York group, Composite Truth focuses a wide range of black, Latin and rock influences into several tracks. Side one, with "Hang Loose," "Fencewalk" and its Latin extension "Hagalo," is the party side, a hard-whipped combination of horns, nervous guitar, organ and Latin percussion with tough, deep vocals.

BARRABAS – Barrabas (RCA)
On the basis of two tracks, "Wild Safari" and "Woman," Barrabas broke in discotheques when it was still an import record. The group, oddly enough, is

from Spain, including among its six members one from Cuba, one from Portugal and two from the Philippines. Where they got such a hard Afro-rock sound, I don't know, but at their best they're fantastic. "Wild Safari" crackles with electricity and Latin percussion that makes it impossible to sit down.

EVERYDAY PEOPLE (Paramount)

This one's even weirder than Barrabas: an album more than a year old by a white Canadian group identified only as Bruce, Chris, Pam, etc. whose one good cut is so hot no one seems to mind all the waste tracks. "I Like What I Like" is the track – more than six minutes long and quite extraordinary. A completely strange production that builds from a jungle-drum and throbbing bass introduction with an echoed jumble of vocals that sounds like bird cries, to a basic rock song with just the sort of minimal message you can connect with when you're dancing: "I like what I like/Because I like it."

LET'S DO IT AGAIN – the Fatback Band (Perception)

Another album with a lot of filler. But "Street Dance," Fatback's big single, is such a fine house party record it deserves a note. A nasty bit of funk, "Street Dance" rides along on an insinuating bass and guitar line, highly spiced with horns, tambourines, flute and the sort of yelled-out comments that loud party music invites.

THE MACK – Willie Hutch (Motown)

The only primarily vocal soundtrack to come up to the standards set by Superfly, The Mack has already spawned two excellent dance singles. The first, "Brother's Gonna Work It Out," is given a sweetly contrasting flute intro on the album so that the song's opening seconds – hard-pounded drums and a delicious ripple of harps – hits you with even more force. "Slick," the current single, is lighter, brighter and sounds more like Marvin Gaye; again, the production is tight and irresistible. Very slick.

CYMANDE, and SECOND TIME AROUND – Cymande (Janus)

A group of West Indians living in England, Cymande hasn't made any great impact on the discotheque scene, but their free-style Afro mood music is very attractive. The group vocals and the productions are relaxed and pleasant but they have little impact. The first album's two popular cuts, "Bra" and "The Message," are nicely understated, for dancing in a quieter mood, but much of the rest fades away.

WOYAYA – Osibisa (Decca)

More Afro rock, but with high impact. Another London-based band of expatriates, this time from Africa as well as the West Indies, Osibisa has the drive and hard upbeat Cymande lack, yet they are frequently without much substance. But "Survival" on *Woyaya* is impressive: Beginning with a beautiful segment of African drumming and chanting, it breaks suddenly into American drumming and electric guitar, then fills in with bright horns and cooks on for more than six minutes. ✪

Drag queens mugging © **Peter Hujar Archive**

❝ Discos and what has come to be known as disco music have turned out to be, if not the Next Big Thing everyone in the music business was waiting for, then the closest thing to it in years ❞

Dancing Madness

By Vince Aletti

NEW YORK – It's not easy to pin down the disco craze with figures. As one independent mixer of disco singles explained, "The numbers are growing so fast. Every day I get four or five invitations to grand openings of new clubs." But even the rough estimates of disco scene observers are revealing: 2000 discos from coast to coast, 200 to 300 in New York alone – the uncrowned capital of dancing madness, where an estimated 200,000 dancers make the weekly club pilgrimage. And when disco people like a record, it can become a hit regardless of radio play. Take Consumer Rapport's "Ease On down The Road." Released on tiny Wing and a Prayer Records, it sold more than 100,000 copies in New York in its first two weeks before it was picked up on the radio.

Discos and what has come to be known as disco music have turned out to be, if not the Next Big Thing everyone in the music business was waiting for, then the closest thing to it in years. Discos have opened in old warehouses, steak restaurants, unused hotel ballrooms and singles bars... any place you could stick a ceiling full of flashing, colored lights, a mirrored ball, two turntables, a battery of speakers, a mixer and a DJ. In a recession economy, they're a bargain both for the club owner – who has few expenses after his initial setup investment and an average $50-a-night salary to the DJ – and the patrons, who can dance nonstop all night for a fraction of the cost of a concert ticket.

But the spread of disco music, especially in the last year and a half has outpaced even the growth of discos themselves. Though the new disco music evolved from the hard dance records of the Sixties – primarily Motown and James Brown – the direction has been away from the basic, hard-edged brassy style and toward a sound that is more complex, polished and sweet. If one style dominates now, it's the Philadelphia Sound, which is rich and elegant, highly sophisticated and tightly structured but full of punch. The Philadelphia producers are the masters at using strings energetically, to boost as well as soften the arrangements, and they've perfected the glossy sound with Harold Melvin and the Bluenotes, the O'Jays, the Trammps, the Three Degrees and Blue Magic. Gamble & Huff and the other busy producers working out of Philly have also excelled in keeping their songs lyrically sharp and involving, while much other disco music has reduced lyrics to repeated words or simple verses. But disco music now includes so many different performers – from the Jackson 5 to Frankie Valli – and so many different styles, tied together only by a consistent danceable beat, that its definition has to be a broad one.

The discos' most obvious influence on music has been the length of records. The best disco music is full of changes and breaks, which allow for several shifts of mood or pace within one song and usually open up long instrumental passages. If the break works, it becomes the pivot and anticipated peak of the song – like the sudden stop and gradual rebuild, instrument by instrument, in Eddie Kendricks's "Girl You Need A Change Of Mind," still one of the best dance records ever made. It's hard to develop an effective build and break within a short record. As long as the beat is tight and involving and the texture of the changes rich and diverting, a song may run up to ten minutes, given the indulgent mood on dance floors.

❝ There are so many young producers hooked up into the disco sound that the ready-made formulas may fall by the side ❞

So "disco version" or "disco mix" means primarily that the record is longer than the version released for radio play, though it may also mean that the cut is specifically mixed for a "hotter," brighter sound. Disco DJs are much more concerned with the technical quality of the records they play than their radio counterparts, rejecting otherwise danceable singles because of the deadness of their mix or their loss of distinction at high volumes. This passion for quality has had its effect: Both Atlantic and Scepter have put selected single cuts on 12-inch discs at 33⅓ for best reproduction at top volume.

In New York, record firms are demonstrating acute interest in promoting their disco products by supporting the Record Pool, a no-cost record distribution arrangement that services the area's DJs. The 40-plus participating companies deliver their latest singles and albums to the pool, and the almost 200 member DJs pick them up at their convenience. During a recent week, according to Steve D'Acquisto, a DJ and one of the founders of the pool, more than 10,000 records were handed out.

All this attention has meant recognition for some performers who had been trapped in the disco underground, as well as for jazz artists like Grover Washington, Hubert Laws, Donald Byrd and Herbie Mann (who had the most successful single of his career with a glossy cover of Barrabas's "Hijack" before his *Discotheque* album betrayed a nearly total lack of comprehension of disco music). It's also meant that much new "disco music" is merely a replay of several set formulas, established for or by Barry White, George McCrae and Gloria Gaynor. White's sound is heavy on the strings, light on the vocals, with an emphasis on pillow talk. McCrae's features an insistent but more laid back beat with sweet, cooled out vocals. And Gaynor, whose *Never Can Say Goodbye* mixed "Honey Bee," the title song and "Reach Out, I'll Be There" into the only album-length disco blend to date, revised the Sixties "girl group" sound with tough, sharp vocals and relentless drumming, to become the "Queen of the Disco" – a title coveted by a number of young men on the scene – before flopping with a follow-up formula version of "Walk On By."

Even if the disco scene eventually self-destructs on its own success, it remains diverse and open enough to revitalize and redirect itself. Disco DJs – the people who made all the musical connections in the first place, pulling together the different sounds that make up the total disco sound – are too adventurous to be pinned down to music biz definitions of "disco." Already they've gotten heavily into European imports like Banzai's "Chinese Kung-Fu" and Bimbo Jet's "El Bimbo." And there are so many young producers hooked up into the disco sound that the ready-made formulas may fall by the side. ✆

David Mancuso © **Peter Hujar Archive**

❝Because a soundless second in a discotheque is like an hour in the real world, the new DJs blend all-night seamless musical environments, flights that may last eight hours from peak to ecstatic peak**❞**

The Loft

By Vince Aletti

Listening to the radio spots or reading the leaflets pressed into your hand outside blow-your-whistle concerts you might think they were new bands or star performers. "The tropical Sounds of Maboya," "The Enchanting dreamwaves of Rip and Cliff," "The Vibrant Sounds of Flowers," "Shockwaves Conceived and Regulated by the Smith Brothers." But "Maboya," "Flowers," Rip and Cliff and a growing number of others known like models and graffiti artists by a single name, are discotheque disc jockeys. These wizard/technicians in the raised booths are the underground stars of the discotheque boom that began three years ago and is now approaching the turning point from genuine phenomenon to media fad. No longer just human jukeboxes, discotheque DJs talk about creating "total evenings" or turning the night into "a whole big song, a trip," and worry as much about their artistry as they do about new turntables that won't slip cue like the old ones. Like hair stylists a few years back (another first-name-only group), disco DJs are emerging as the new pop professionals, holding down the up-from-the-ranks glamour jobs of the moment.

Because a soundless second in a discotheque is like an hour in the real world, the new DJs blend all-night seamless musical environments, flights that may last eight hours from peak to ecstatic peak, while the lights flash and the crowd screams. But it's not as master mixers or mood magicians that club DJs have gotten a sudden snap-to of attention from the music business. Major record companies have begun to recognize the best discotheque DJs as tastemakers with an avid and often affluent following. Unlike their radio station counterparts, discotheque DJs don't wait to see sales figures, tipsheets or activity reports from other parts of the country. They're used to tracking down new albums, singles and imports even before they're reported in the music trades (often spending as much as $50 a week to keep their collections up to date), and pride themselves on being the first to introduce records hot off the presses to their crowd. Record company promo men are finding they may have to fend off anxious disco DJs before they can hype them, but they're also discovering

....

that the DJs usually have the first reports on what records are going to make it big – weeks, sometimes months, before they show up on radio station playlists.

Broadly speaking the typical New York discotheque DJ is young (between 18 and 30), Italian and gay. The prime variable is "Italian" because there are a large number of black and Latin DJs; "gay" is less variable, but here it is more a description of sensibility than sexual preference. He (there are women DJs but few of them) plays between two and six nights a week, making an average of $50 a night, sometimes supplemented by a full- or part-time day job. Because discotheques tend to be highly unstable, blowing on the whims of their crowd and subject to sudden shutdown by often-shady managements, most DJs, even the youngest, have played at a lengthy string of clubs.

Given this sketchy profile, David Mancuso is hardly "typical." In fact though he does fit in a few key categories, it may be wrong to even label him a discotheque DJ since he's never played anywhere but in his own living space,."When people ask me what I do," he says, "I tell them, 'I have parties'." Starting in 1970, his "parties" were held every Saturday night, from just before midnight to six or seven the following morning, at his loft on lower Broadway which, though purposely unnamed and unpublicized, quickly became known as "the Loft." Open only to invited "guests" – friends of Mancuso's who were issued numbered cards and allowed to bring a limited number of their own friends – the Loft was more like a weekly house party than a discotheque. The ceiling was hung with colored streamers and balloons, other balloons bobbed around on the floor and in the next room there were tables covered with bowls of fruit punch, nuts and raisins, bananas, small candies, and gum – once you paid your $3 (in the final year, $4) and stepped in the door, it was like being at someone's – everyone's – birthday party. In the center, in a small enclosed booth filled with records and equipment, was David Mancuso at double turntables, blending records end-to-end (Rule #1: Never let the music stop") and playing the lights until the crowd screamed and swooned and begged for more.

Mancuso began the Loft as a rent party after he "got kind of bored with the nine to five thing" which he'd been at since he dropped out of school at 15. An orphan on his own in Utica, New York, he'd worked as a shoeshine boy and a dishwasher before he visited New York City on Labor Day the year he was 17, decided he liked it and moved here a month later. The last jobs he can remember were in an employment agency and designing towels. The first parties weren't successful; they were completely open, but no one showed up, the feeling wasn't right. David started all over again with a new group of people, and this time he was playing the records, "It was the last thing in the world I wanted to do," he recalls. "Socially, I'm an introvert, I'm very shy. But I had to do it – no one else was going to."

Loft invitation **Collection of Vince Aletti**

"Broadly speaking the typical New York discotheque DJ is young (between 18 and 30), Italian and gay. Given this sketchy profile, David Mancuso is hardly "typical""

....

If Mancuso is an introvert, he's also capable of drawing people – the Loft inner circle and a warmly loyal crowd of dancers – with an intensity that approaches the charismatic, and he was able to translate this quite unselfconscious magnetism into his music. Once he started playing, he says, "I got inspired by the fact that people would dance, that things would happen," and he began to develop a style. "It was all dancing music," Mancuso begins tentatively, trying to define his approach, "but you had to get the feeling of it, to take all this energy and kind of disperse it – like you would sound with acoustics – and work your way through the course of the evening, You can't burn out all the energy in the first two or three hours."

Mancuso drifts off for a moment, then resumes with the intensity level a little lower. "I spent a lot of time in the country, listening to birds, lying next to a spring and listening to water go across the rocks. And suddenly one day, I realized: What perfect music, Like with the sunrise and sunset, how things would build up into midday. There were times when it would be intense and times it would be very soft and at sunset, it would get quiet and then the crickets would come in. I took this sense of rhythm, this sense of feeling... "

It's all a matter of tuning into what Mancuso calls "that natural rhythm, that three-billion-year-old dance – I just applied it through these artificial means which were amplifiers and records." Though this style of structuring the evening around a natural ebb and flow of energy was arrived at independently by a number of other disco DJs and has become a standard approach for the new wave of discotheques, Mancuso was one of the first to perfect it and make it work for him. Dancing at the Loft was like riding waves of music, being carried along as one song after another built relentlessly to a brilliant crest and broke, bringing almost involuntary shouts of approval from the crowd, then smoothed out, softened, and slowly began welling up to another peak.

While other private clubs that opened in the years after the Loft's success established their own styles (the Tenth Floor, for instance, leaned toward the cool, sweet, heavily stylized Philadelphia sound with some tropical accents), Mancuso's reputation was for hard, driving, heavily percussive numbers and frantic jungle music. He was one of the first to introduce Barrabas, a Spanish rock group whose "Wild Safari" and "Woman" helped to whet the disco crowd's appetite for off-beat European imports. Later, he played Willie Henderson's eccentric "Dance Master" when it, too, was only available as an import single. These records weren't unique to the Loft, but they were characteristic of the Loft's dominant style, which tended to veer sharply off the beaten path. What was unique was the total blend of music, especially Mancuso's introduction of rock material that much of his crowd had never heard in a discotheque context before. Chicago, the Doobie Brothers and unexpected surprises like Bonnie Bramlett's "Crazy 'Bout My Baby."

David admits that in the beginning the Loft had some problems, mainly getting over the first unsuccessful few months when it was public, but "once it was strictly a private thing and the people who were getting on the mailing list were people that I knew," it began settling down into a smoothly run operation. The crowd was a rich mix of classes, colors and sexual tastes with two things in common: they were hard-core dancers and they were utterly devoted to the Loft. Their high spirits preserved the Loft's house-party atmosphere and helped establish its reputation. In the more than four years it was running, Mancuso reports (and repeats), with obvious pride, the Loft never had a "disturbance" of any sort and he could count only three small items stolen from the house. But in the Loft's last year a tenant of the building began making regular complaints about noise and the police would show up once or twice a month, shutting off the music for a time, sauntering through the still-vibrating rooms, then leaving, as Mancuso puts it, "in peace and friendship," so the party could resume. But eventually the complaints and some unexpected publicity in the Times ("Weekly Parties for 500 Chill Tenants") forced Mancuso to close the Loft to parties, though he continues to live there himself. The Loft crowd formed such a tight grapevine that when Mancuso received a vacate notice from the city on a Friday he was able to call off the following night's regular party with only twenty phone calls. On Saturday only fifteen out of the usual 500 showed up at the door.

When Mancuso announced an afternoon party for this past Easter, his first in sprawling new quarters at 99 Prince Street and the first Loft gathering since the old location closed nearly a year before, mailing-list regulars were ecstatic with anticipation. Some called to say they'd be flying in from Detroit or Chicago, others offered 100 pounds of potato salad, 50 pounds of macaroni salad, and sacks of sugar. For the Loft crowd, the Easter party was the official first day of Spring and they arrived as if to a family reunion, bringing bakery boxes of cake, pastries, and cookies that were stacked precariously high behind the food counter, Mancuso stood in his new booth high above the main dance floor, nervous about his music – "re-entry is very delicate," he said – but beaming at the vibrant crowd below. "People get together and it's like a Ouija board," he says, and the messages never fail to excite him. ✪

(Originally published as part of a news story entitled 'SoHo vs Disco'.)

Back row, L-R: Barry Lederer, Tom Savarese, Don Findlay, Vincent Cafiso, Jimmy Stuard, Nicky Siano; Front row Tony Smith, Larry Sanders © **Eric Stephen Jacobs**

❝One is famous for his drum collages – his hot pulsing evocation of the urban jungle. Another has a trademark sound that's cool, loose and sweetly ecstatic❞

The Men In The Glass Booth

By Vince Aletti

He's there each night from ten to closing time,
With sights and sounds to help the crowds unwind,
And from the booth each night he blows your mind,
With his mix and tricks

Forget – for the moment at least – Donna Summer, Silver Convention, Brass Construction, Gloria Gaynor, Bohannon, Love Unlimited – that endless ever-changing, slippery starstream of names shooting through disco heaven. The real stars of the seventies disco boom aren't on records, they're spinning them.

Discotheque DJs have become tastemakers, record-breakers (several have received gold records in recognition of their influence on sales), mood magicians, performers with personal styles. The new DJ doesn't just change records, he creates a musical "journey," blending records into "one continuous song, one story." As Tom Savarese, one of New York's top DJs puts it, "From the moment I go in there to the moment I leave – that's my canvas."

To conjure up this kind of vibrant, volatile aural landscape the DJ has to be part artist (the medium: musical collage), part technician, part crowd psychologist. Some would say a total madmen. You have to know your records inside out, they say: the intros, the fades, the breaks, the changes, then maybe you'll understand why disco DJs talk about "my music." This intimate knowledge allows them to weave record into record, making one seamless tapestry. Like any artist, a talented DJ develops an individual, idiosyncratic style. One is famous for his drum collages – his hot pulsing evocation of the urban jungle. Another has a trademark sound that's cool, loose and sweetly ecstatic. Still another will purposely break the floor "like a billiard table," shifting the crowd for a record he feels they should hear, nudging them into unfamiliar music. Others are abrasive or frenzied or cheerfully crowd-pleasing, but they all stamp the music with their personal taste. The best inspire passionately loyal followings that trail them from club to club. (In New York, where discos open and close at the drop of a Thorens tonearm, most experienced DJs can reel off a list of past jobs – Sanctuary, the Haven, Machine I, Machine II, Tambourlaine, Limelight, the Ice Palace, Le Jardin, Make-Believe Ballroom – that reads like an index to the city's underground high and low life for the past ten years.)

But if disco DJing is an art, it's solidly based on technology – not only on the mastery of elaborate systems of turntables, mixers, speakers, amps, filters, headphones and lightboards but on a sensitivity to the technical pluses and minuses of the records. DJs quickly develop a sharp critical ear for the quality of a mix or a pressing, if only because disco equipment is sure to exaggerate flaws. When record companies realized that a muddy studio mix or a drastically reduced sound level was keeping their records off disco turntables they snapped to with special pressings "For Disco DJs Only," usually single long tracks on limited edition, high-quality twelve-inch discs. This past spring, a number of companies began commercially marketing these discs – the first new record format in decades – and found them selling briskly to people eager for the same full length and quality they had heard in the clubs. (Appropriately, the first "disco disc" in the stores, Double Exposure's stunning "Ten Percent," was "disco blended" by New York DJ Walter Gibbons, one of a small but increasing number of spinners crossing over to the production side of the music.) Not only was the disco DJ the impetus behind the creation of the "disco disc" but he was the key factor in the development of the entire specialized disco market that record and equipment manufacturers are now turning into a goldmine.

Another necessary talent of the successful disco DJ is a subtle, spontaneous, sure understanding of crowd control. Even when he's removed, often elevated above the dance floor, absorbed in the next blend, the next switching of knobs and flashing of lights, the DJ has to be simultaneously on the floor, in the midst of the crowd, anticipating its mood at the same time he's channeling it. It isn't a matter of simply playing a hot record. Anyone can do that. The DJ must sense the moment when it will have its greatest impact: when the crowd wants it the most and when they least expect it; when they'll burst into delirious screams on hearing the first three notes. The DJ has to know how long to run them, when to ease up and smooth out, when to hit a peak and keep pushing, when to slip in something new so they'll love it and not clear the floor. It's an intuitive science. David Mancuso, famous for the private disco parties at his Loft in New York, describes his approach this way: "I can't program myself to what happens because it all gets so spontaneous. I don't plan it, I don't feel I have any control over it. I'm only a part of the whole, a part of the dance."❷

Onlookers at Roseland © **Toby Old**

❝ The first issue of Punk magazine put it most blatantly – suggesting that readers commit suicide before exposing themselves to "the epitome of all that's wrong with Western Civilization" ❞

Village Voice April 26, 1976

I Won't Dance, Don't Ask Me

By Vince Aletti

White rock critics find disco music banal and false because they don't partake of the music's ritual; they aren't ready to get down.

If there is any common stance among rock critics these days, it's a shared hostility toward what has become known in the past year as "disco." The "Death to Disco Shit" editorial in the first issue of Punk magazine put it most blatantly – suggesting that readers commit suicide before exposing themselves to "the epitome of all that's wrong with Western Civilization" – but the attitude had already been set through countless snide asides in the rock press where disco music was regarded as silly yet somehow subversive drivel worth only a passing sneer.

Since music publishers and record companies have seized upon ready-made disco formulas as a way of recycling old songs ("Baby Face," "Night and Day," "Exodus," "Volare," "Theme From 'A Summer Place'") and old singers (Al Martino, Frankie Avalon, Bobby Rydell, Monti Rock, Teresa Brewer), a lot of the ridicule is well deserved. Disco, the only major pop trend to hit the music business in years, has been treated like a sell-out line on Seventh Avenue. Cheap knock-offs – "disco versions" often just a step above elevator Muzak – are everywhere. But the rock press's aversion to disco isn't restricted to the genre's formulaic rip-offs; in fact it's so generalized that it bears closer examination.

Because disco evolved quite naturally out of rhythm & blues and more technically advanced soul, this attitude springs first of all from a widespread critical unease and unfamiliarity with black popular music. There are some exceptions of course – Al Green, Aretha Franklin, Stevie Wonder, Smokey Robinson, or Sly Stone; Millie Jackson, Bobby Womack, or Natalie Cole – but the average rock critic's taste in black music was fixed in the '60s with the Motown and Stax/Volt sound, recognizing only modern extensions of those styles – tight, hard-edged, and "black" – as valid. But even those critics with a wide-ranging interest in and sympathy for black music in general tend to view disco as predictable ("It all sounds alike"), alienated from its r&b roots, anonymous, and studio-slick. Dave Marsh's recent dismissal in *Rolling Stone* of "Dance Your Troubles Away," Archie Bell & the Drells' total-disco comeback album, is almost a model of the anti-disco stance. Marsh describes the album as "a nearly perfect Philadelphia formula record, executed with neither flaws nor feeling" on which "five of the seven tracks are locked into a mechanical disco beat that won't quit even when you wish it would." Of course the "won't-quit" factor is part of the record's design, but when he echoes the prevailing notion that studio sophistication has replaced "feeling" in disco records, Marsh just isn't listening.

"Dance Your Troubles Away" is, in movie terms, an "entertainment" – an album not just for dancing but *about* dancing, a celebration of release and shared ecstasy. The message, plain and simple: "Music was designed for the body/It's the perfect remedy/So if you wanna feel better/Come on out here and get down with me." But Marsh isn't ready to get down; even a grudging acknowledgement of several "fine dance cuts" is taken back immediately with the comment that "they aren't anything more than that." What more, exactly, do they have to be?

Marsh looks back to the old Archie Bell & the Drells, especially "There's Gonna Be a Showdown," produced by Kenny Gamble and Leon Huff, who supervised the new album. "Showdown," like "Tighten Up," "I Can't Stop Dancing," and the group's other singles from the late '60s, is brash, bright, and fun; a perfect pop record, inconsequential and of the moment yet delightful enough to stick and last. What is puzzling here is that Marsh, and nearly every other critic with a fondness for the r&b trivia of the past, fails to see "Let's Groove" – the most successful of the new Archie Bell cuts – as the exact equivalent of "Showdown" for 1976.

But "Let's Groove" cuts deeper than early Archie Bell because here he's captured the mood of a time in which the dance floor has become a focus for the social life and energy of so many of us. Like "I Love Music," "Fly, Robin, Fly," "Get Down Tonight," and Bobby Womack's "Daylight," "Let's Groove" is an anthem for the middle '70s, creating and invoking the sustained, expansive spirit of the Party. "Let the music take your mind/It'll soothe you every time": Submerge yourself, "dance your troubles away," get down, get higher. Do it any way you wanna. There's a naive belief here that dancing – the movement, the release, and the utter submission to the power of the music – can cure all ills (not unlike the belief that rock & roll could "set you free"). So maybe it isn't the music itself but the demands of the music – the pressure of the beat and the lyrics: "dance, dance, dance," "get down, get down" – that arouses critical resistance. Marsh's review is headlined "Do You Wanna Dance?" and the obvious answer is no. I won't dance, don't ask me. This is part of a general refusal to see disco partying as anything but mindless escapism when, in fact, a good case could be made for it as a vital tribal rite, an affirmation of high spirits and shared delight, a coming together to let loose that in no way ignores the problems of everyday life ("Bad Luck" was one of the biggest disco records last year), but relieves them. Maybe we need a whole new aesthetics for the disco, one that includes the ritual as well as the music.

The emotion of much recent disco music isn't the romantic love/lost love of basic soul; instead it's a kind of joyous, out-of-your-head ecstasy, often explicitly sexual (prime example: Donna Summer's "Love To Love You Baby" in its full 17-minute version), drawn out over a series of changes designed to prolong, heighten, and vary the mood. Long cuts must be better for dancing, Marsh writes, "because they're awful to listen to." Several of the Archie Bell cuts (especially "Let's Go Disco," the only one produced by Gamble & Huff alone) are indefensible in this respect; they do become monotonous, even on the dance floor. But "Let's Groove" (6:21) and the best extended disco music is texturally rich and inventive – it has to be to keep the dancers not only on their feet but involved and excited.

If nothing else, this is supremely functional music. Disco producers create a structure of repetitive, flowing patterns and peaks, waves that shift, crest, and break, carrying the spirits of the dancers with them. But breaks that cause screams in discos – and if you haven't heard a roomful of people erupt in spontaneous yells and squeals to a particularly stunning change, you haven't begun to appreciate the disco phenomenon – slip by unnoticed on the radio (where bite-sized chunks are easier to digest) or on a record player at home (unless you're ready to dance around the living room). Silver Convention's "Fly, Robin, Fly," one of last year's most exhilarating, appealing and off-the-wall disco records, turned into a surprise number-one hit, but a lot of the most advanced, hard-core disco music doesn't survive translation from the dance floor to the radio.

Although it's been the main crossover music of the past few years – and the first substantial bridge between white performers and the black audience since jazz-rock – disco music has also begin to draw certain social lines more clearly than before, defining two audiences, each in near-total ignorance of the other's music save for what gets through on the radio. That this ignorance should be wilfully shared by a large part of the rock press is pretty dismaying, and it suggests not only a critical hardening of the arteries, as John Rockwell wrote in the Times, but a desperate attempt at shoring up the bastions of rock & roll against the first wave of a Third World assault. ●

A Dialogue Between Two Editors: Vince Aletti
& Michael Gomes, Summer 1 9 7 8
Transcribed by Judy Weinstein, set into print
by Alan Bell.

A MIX/MASTER Publication

" To me, the disc jockey is the paramount of everything. He holds the destiny of so many people in his hands "

A Dialogue Between Two Editors

By Vince Aletti & Michael Gomes

VA: Who are the DJ legends?
MG: Well in the very first issue of *MixMaster* I listed the legends.

VA: (Reading) David Mancuso, Nicky Siano, Richie Kaczor.
MG: Those are the ones who are still working...

VA: (Reading) Bobby DJ, David Rodriguez, Walter Gibbons.
MG: The others I don't consider them an influence on the scene. They work too infrequently and to be a real legend you have to have other DJs hear you and talk about you, good, bad or indifferent. There are more new DJs this year who are really, really good and who are really going to replace all of these people. I think out of all of them David Mancuso will last the longest. The others, it's like rise and fall. They build themselves up and get very grand and then they go. It's like being America's Number One DJ and not working anywhere. And right now, I can count ten of them who are really good and not people from the past. Richie Pampinella, who I think is an excellent DJ and has not gotten the publicity he deserves.

VA: Who else?
MG: New people now, alphabetically, I don't want to commit myself by listing. I would say John Benitez, who is young and is very good. I think to be a legend you have to have a personality. You have to be more than just a good DJ. You have to have a personality that will stand up. You could be the best mixer and be so dull. It could be a tape playing. These people have personality, if nothing else. John Benitez, who is very nice and we are wondering whether he's gay or not. He's like 20 years old. He's probably the youngest of this whole group. He has a vigorous sound, very energetic and this kid doesn't do a lot of drugs. I'm really surprised at him, for somebody who's only been playing for about a year or more and this kid is good. He plays around, pardon the expression. Jerry Bossa,

at the Barefoot Boy, he's good. He has an old following of people who come to see him. He has a personality. Jonathan Fearing, who has-suddenly blossomed rapidly. The success story of the year. I called him the new Richie Kaczor and he said, "I'm not the new anyone, I'm Jonathan Fearing."

VA: Well, he has his lines together.

MG: From discovering him on a one night affair at the Ice Palace and then finally getting the job at Cockring on Sundays and then to Xenon. It's like a Lana Turner story. Danny Krivit, who if nothing else, gets by on just being cute. Billy Carroll, who really impressed me, who gets away with murder at his club and has a real following who come to hear him. These kids are playing new records and they all have a distinctive sound, while this older group, they all have the same sound, a downtown sound. The older DJs, especially those who have a name, play it safe. They will play new records but they will play old records, things that have been out two to three months. They don't want to lose their audience. DJs underestimate their audience a lot. They figure that these people are coming and they want to hear this thing over and over after weekend after weekend, and it's not true. People want to hear new records.

If you want to make it in this business, you've got to put out a little. It's a question of, as one DJ said, "Stay straight and struggle or have greatness thrust upon you." In the end – under the pressure of home-cooked Italian meals or ethyl chloride, barbituates, quaaludes, dust, grass, being able to stand in the booth of a famous DJ, in a famous club, and look down upon this wide world of audience – in the end you are going to crumble. They get corrupted and then, since there's so many fish in the sea, they get dumped.

VA: Don't you think the life of a DJ can be very lonely?

MG: Oh yeah, that's why they play all these sad songs and I think the dance floor should only be a happy place. There should be a law against sad songs. The dance floor is somewhere where you should ask, "Could heaven ever be like this?" It should be a place of bliss, just happiness and joy. When people go out, they have problems, broken hearts. It should be a sanctuary, a retreat that is somewhere wonderful. Some places I have been, god, the things I hear on that dance floor, the music that comes out. Oh, those women are so bitchy. And some DJs will follow it record after record this way and I flee from clubs this way. You can't take it after a while.

VA: What songs do you mean?

MG: Of course, the example this year, which I think is the rudest, is "Runaway Love." No wonder she can't keep that man, honey, with an attitude like that, I would run away too. "You could leave if you want to."

VA: That was a lot of people's favorite record.

MG: If there is nothing else I have learned about the dance floor, it is built on bondage and discipline. We have no records per se from men where they take this attitude which women are taking, what man is ever saying "Oh baby, you can leave if you want to?"

VA: Only Teddy Pendergrass.

MG: Women keep coming out with these things, and then they literally push the guy out of the door and they then wonder what it is that makes "a man leave a girl so all alone." I asked Linda Clifford, "How can you, after making a record a year ago saying from now on things are going to be so different, so wonderful, you come up a year later telling him he can leave if he wants to?" She said, "Sometimes it be that way."

VA: Of the discos that are now no longer in existence, which was your favorite?

MG: I had ties between the Grand Ballroom. Late 1973-1974. There was nothing like it in the city. It was very grand and pleasant. I liked old Gallery on 22nd Street. It was wild and frantic. That wildness has gone out of the scene completely. Where do you think this whole scene is going? I interviewed you in 1975 and you at that time told me that you thought the scene had peaked.

VA: To me, it's like peaks in an evening at a club. But there are successive peaks and it doesn't mean that one prevents another one from coming up. I think it did peak at a certain point of really being a high point of the scene and then sort of levelled off and peaked again in another form, commercially.

MG: I think it's spreading itself too thin. Now everything is disco. Life is now an endless disco party. I see disco suspenders!

VA: When there are so many disco TV shows and things like that, I begin to wonder now, it is spreading itself too thin.

MG: You, yourself, must remember in the sixties, people began to be aware of a very new sound of music, which was all the San Francisco sound. It had been there as a culture but suddenly broke loose and then everything was swamped with beads and everything became very hippie-ish. When you start identifying a scene with a look or clothes, people get tired of it.

VA: Disco has already been through that phase. It's been faddish several times already, but spreading to wider and wider groups of people.

MG: Do you think eventually that in music everything will have this beat and will absorb everything, and even say, rock, will unconsciously have this beat?

VA: No, I think that rock and roll people are going to be using the disco style more often, but I don't think there is any way that it will encompass all rock and roll.

MG: So the beat will just go on and on and on...

VA: But in its own way, I think it's going to end up being influential. I don't think soul music ended when disco started.

MG: The thing that makes this whole scene so different from anything else in the music industry – I remember in the sixties, it was a scene either created by the industry or by managers or by agents; here it was something created by the kids in clubs. It's something that's not divorced from club life. Before, it was something you could only hear through the radio or see in a live concert. Now in a way it is independent of radio play, of what the industry says. So in a way perhaps that's its survival. I think the future of the scene lies in the hands of young DJs coming up who have a real love for it.

   And this is another thing – the whole scene has become a business. Even DJs I know, who would just get really, really bombed, just have a good time with their audience, just to get as high as their audience. They may still get bombed but it's like a serious business, which is good, but a lot of the fun has gone out of the scene.

VA: Well, I think everybody's much more conscious of well, maybe Ray Caviano is going to come by the booth tonight or maybe so and so is going to drop a record off.

MG: So they can't be passed out over the turntable? I have stories I could tell you! I'm *MixMaster*, I'm a repository. For some reason it's like DJs have a need to confess these things to me. The stories that are passed on to me are unbelievable. A lot of those things that have made a legend have gone. Everyone is so normal now.

VA: You think so?

MG: To a great extent, they are just human beings, before they were bizarre. It's like the twilight of the idols. That whole old group, who did legendary things, who made a legend, it's like their legends are fading.

VA: Most of the names that you named as the people who are coming up are all kind of aggressive, together kids, in a way, who know what

The men's room at G.G. Barnums © **Toby Old**

"The personal person we know is obliterated and an unconscious self is playing the records"

they are doing, who are very straightforward about what they want
to do and they are not heavy drug users.

MG: It's hard to divorce the scene from drugs; disco drugs. I've been collecting a
whole archive. I've been collecting every sort of drug that I have taken in a club.
I have a sample of everything you could imagine. I have 26 different drugs you
could have taken at a club. It's like a whole pharmaculture. It's amazing.

**VA: Speaking of disco drugs, how have the drugs changed over
the years?**

MG: Let's see, now there are two schools. If you're straight you do ups, if you're not,
you do downs. Listen to this trick, people who used to get so bombed on downs will
now get really bombed on downs but at the same time take liquid speed, which will
still keep them standing up, but at the same time really bombed.

**VA: For the dance floor, people who go out dancing, do you think the
drugs have changed?**

MG: The thing that has become popular recently is dust, which has come and
gone. Everything has remained the same. I myself am sorry that we couldn't have
had as many hallucinogenics as in the sixties.

**VA: To get to performers, who would you consider the disco pantheon
from the past to today?**

MG: I would say David Mancuso because he remains the only disc jockey who
has his own club. This is the thing that makes him distinctive, where he has
complete freedom. Others may have that freedom, but lurking in the back of your
mind, you still have a boss over you. He has complete freedom, which in a way
entails a certain responsibility. Of course, Nicky Siano, who's survived, who I used
to go out to hear when I was a teenager, just growing up. Richie Kaczor who has
become very successful, but who I enjoyed more when he was at Hollywood.

**"I have a sample of
26 different drugs
you could have taken
at a club. It's a whole
pharmaculture.
It's amazing"**

VA: I really meant by that question, in terms of people, like Cerrone, the actual performers, not the DJs.

MG: I still think it's the disc jockey who makes it. The producers are there, but to me, the disc jockey is the paramount of everything. He holds the destiny of so many people in his hands. It used to be that way, it's slipping away now. At one time that's where the power lay. They could make or break hits. Now the formula is so well known. We know that between so many beats per minute, this is acceptable, this is not acceptable.

VA: If you were to make a list of the most important producers or performers who would they be?

MG: It would not be what is commercially applicable. It would just be my personal taste. I would choose people who to me were creative and often the most creative people are not the most successful financially. Cerrone, I think is really, really a talent. I think Constandinos is, to make "Romeo and Juliet" so successful. Gamble and Huff – it's the people we all know about.

VA: Who are some of the better neglected people?

MG: I would say Rene Geyer who had an album on Polydor produced by Frank Wilson, who had a beautiful voice and just made a slight comeback because Walter put her on his last album. Other than that, the majority of people are OK, but they're products of the studio. They are not voices that can stand by themselves. They are the product of a producer or an engineer and you don't have to have a good voice to make it on a record. You have to have a good producer or a good engineer because so many people we hear are just elevated background singers. There are very few records I like anymore.

VA: Well I notice generally that you are not writing as much about records recently and you seem to be more down on disco.

MG: I'm just tired of it. I hear it everywhere I go. It's like everybody plays the same records. I would be happy, I would give half my kingdom to the DJ who would play something out of the ordinary. I want to be shocked, I want to be shocked out of the complacency of just hearing the same thing that I can hear from club A, club B, club C. One night I made a tour of clubs and I swear, I left one club on one record and made it to the other club on the same record. In a way it's good and bad: it's a certain standardization, everyone gets the same records in the mail, everything comes at the same time, which is what record pools were formed for. It was to stamp out this trend where one person was getting an acetate four months early and so-and-so wasn't getting it. Now everybody gets it at the same time.

....

VA: More or less.

MG: There has never been a *MixMaster* past the middle of August simply because there is nothing to write about until November.

VA: September last year was very, very hot.

MG: People are not innovative enough. They don't care enough, they play it safe. The dance floor has become a very depressing place. It has become a cesspool of desire. It has become a cesspool! It is nothing but a backroom. The formula for love has changed. Remember in the past love was like an idealized love? It was the Gamble and Huff version of love. That universal love, like "Love Train," "Peace and Love," "One Day Of Peace." Can you imagine how embarrassed people would be if you heard "America, We Need the Light" by Billy Paul which we used to hear on the dance floor? Records like that are no longer possible because the formula for love has changed. It's "You Plus Me Equals Love," right? It's become a very personal thing because of that. That's why you have all these records about people breaking up and running away. I think we may have a comeback of the sound of Philadelphia. Literally, if you make an analysis percentage wise of what's being played, almost 40 percent are negative records, especially of women being bitchy; 30 percent is male vocals. For some reason the male records deal with jogging, running and moving around. Men are moving around this time of year. The last 30 percent is still that ray of hope. You still have Donna who has always made her claim to fame by being very much into love. In that 30 percent of like very positive records, one percent is a spiritual record – "Law and Order."

VA: What was the first disco record?

MG: "What's Going On" by Marvin Gaye, simply because it used the formula that is not in use now, it has a human concern, it was not a soul record, it was the beginning, at the turn of the Seventies. But before that, there were other records that paved the way, for instance like "Flying" by the Beatles, from Magical Mystery Tour, the overlay of sounds.

VA: A record you can dance to?

MG: "Papa Was A Rolling Stone," is one of the earliest I can remember. "Girl, You Need a Change of Mind." When I went out dancing, the first record I can vaguely remember is "Yes I Can Can," by the Pointer Sisters. We danced to a record by the J Geils Band called "Give It to Me" on red vinyl.

When I first came to New York I started going out to clubs and became captivated by these DJs. I was held in bondage on the dance floor, and of course the ones who played the sweetest love songs I became more and more attached to over the years, until it became a very personal thing. Admittantly, I was captivated by certain DJs. They would play me the sweetest love songs. But then things changed: "Hey baby, where are you going, you can't leave yet." These sad or bitchy records broke up my happy home. That's why I'm so against them. The dance floor was my office, my home was the dance floor. Every year they come and they break up my happy home. You don't know the agony I went through with "Runaway," and now she sings she's a victim, she's doing the best she can.

VA: I always identify with that song, "victim of the very songs I sing."
MG: I'm sorry, I'm getting ready for the future. I have developed so many feelings about the dance floor that may just be my own projections, that are really unusual. For instance, going through the year certain records come up at certain times. Between November and April you do not get these sad records, they pop up starting April, then one or two records where she leaves, and by November this wonderful happy note comes along, like Donna saying I love you. And things get very happy until Valentine's Day. It's like a whole relationship. In songs it's the women who always complain. You never hear men complaining. They are always so much in love. It's the woman who is always dissatisfied with the relationship. She is always jealous, she thinks he's running around. Like Lenny Williams says, he's running. It ends up with a bust-up.

VA: Where do you think the scene is headed?
MG: This whole disco movement is DJs to me – I've seen remarkable things night after night. It happens to DJs who get so bombed that their regular waking personality completely disappears. The personal person we know is obliterated and an unconscious self is playing the records, not the person we know, who is getting an unconscious feedback from the audience and it's like a rapport back and forth and keeps building this theme and when they come down, they are almost like mediums. So *MixMaster* has become a repository for this information. In a way it's written for some future historian 20 to 30 years from now. I think all of us are too close to this thing to see what it actually means. It really has little to do with the sales of records. It's a remarkable phenomenon that's unlike anything before. ⬤

1974

Boys at Les Mouches © **Toby Old**

NOVEMBER 16, 1974

Beginning a regular report on the state of the dance floor.

ALBUM OF THE MOMENT: "Do It ('Til You're Satisfied)" by **B.T. Express** (Scepter). Their steamy: "Express," running just over 5 minutes on the album, is the cut – and, for nearly everyone polled, the most immediate answer to the question, "What's the hottest record in your club right now?" but just about everything is getting played. "That's What I Want For You Baby" got special mention, but Wayne Thorberg in Los Angeles says he's playing the whole first side, including that cut (6:47), the still-popular title song, "Do You Like It," and the terrifically raucous "This House Is Smokin'."

The five-foot shelf of essential discotheque albums is suddenly full of records on which nearly every cut gets played, After **B.T. Express**, **Creative Source's** "Migration" (on Sussex, with 5 of its 7 cuts being played; the title song, "Keep on Movin'," "Harlem," "Corazon," "I'm Gonna Get There") and **First Choice's** "The Player" (Philly Groove) were the most frequently mentioned. "The Player" (in its 7:10 lp length), "Guilty" (both the vocal and instrumental versions) and "Hustler Bill" spread First Choice across three top ten lists (below); they're dancing to "Guess What Mary Jones Did," too. "Lady Marmalade" (just out as a 45) and "What Can I Do For You?" are the top choices from **LaBelle's** soaring "Nightbirds" (Epic). A tip from "Tee" Scott at Better Days: "What Can I Do For You?" and the **J5's** "What You Don't Know" (from their "Dancing Machine" lp on Motown) make an irresistible combination back-to-back.

The next essential album: "Hot City" **Gene Page's** delicious Big Band debut on Atlantic, produced by **Barry White**. Again, you'll be hearing nearly every track, but "Gene's Theme." "Don't Play That Song" and "Satin Soul" (already being played In its **Love Unlimited Orchestra** version) sound the most

attractive right now. Other lp cuts to watch: "Hey Girl, Come And Get It" by **The Stylistics** (from "Heavy" on Avco), **Hot Chocolate's** "Makin' Music" (from "Cicero Park" on Big Tree), **Popcorn Wylie's** "Georgia's After Hours" (from "Extrasensory Perception" on ABC), and "African Symphony" by **Van McCoy and the Soul City Orchestra** (from "Love Is The Answer" on Avco).

My current obsession is the B-side of Aretha Franklin's latest Atlantic single, an extraordinary transformation of an old Bacharach-David song called "Don't Go Breaking My Heart." While the A-side, "Without Love." is merely brilliant, the flip is quite unlike anything Aretha's done in some time: very fast, very audacious and, it seems to me, discotheque material. The only DJ I spoke to who'd played – or even heard – the song, Thorberg in L.A., warned that "the changes sort of throw the kids off," but with a sophisticated crowd and equally sophisticated programming, "Don't Go Breaking My Heart" could move.

RED HOT: **Jimmy Ruffin's** "Tell Me What You Want" (Chess). Originally released on Polydor in England last spring, the song has been a top New York disco record since the summer – both Richie Kaczor and Tom Savarese have been playing the import 45 for months now. With its American release on Chess, it's already picking up requests and should crossover fast.

UPCOMING: "Harlem," a surprise from the **5th Dimension** (Bell); "Second Best (Is Never Enough)" by **Finishing Touch** (Philly Groove); "Just Got to Be More Careful" by **Carolyn Crawford** (Philadelphia International); **The Invitations'** "Look on the Good Side" (Silver Blue); "Each Morning I Wake Up" by **The Major Harris Boogie Blues Band** (Atlantic) and "Walk Of Life" by (get this) **Fessor Funk & The Queens 8th Street Funk Band** (Roxbury). ◉

“Beginning a regular report on the state of the dance floor ”

BETTER DAYS, NEW YORK
DJ: Toraino "Tee" Scott

EVERLASTING LOVE – Carl Carlton (Back Beat)
EXPRESS – B.T. Express (Scepter)
GET DANCIN' – Disco Tex & the Sex-O-Lettes (Chelsea)
HUSTLER BILL – First Choice (Philly Groove)
NEVER CAN SAY GOODBYE – Gloria Gaynor (MGM)
PHILADELPHIA – B.B. King (ABC)
SUGAR PIE GUY PARTS 1 & 2 – Joneses (Mercury)
WHAT CAN I DO FOR YOU? – LaBelle (Epic)
WHO GOT THE MONSTER – Rimshots (Astroscope)
YOU'RE THE FIRST, THE LAST, MY EVERYTHING
– Barry White (20th Century)

HOLLYWOOD, NEW YORK
DJ: Richie Kaczor

DOCTOR'S ORDERS – Carol Douglas
(Midland International)
EXPRESS – B.T. Express (Scepter)
GET DANCIN' – Disco Tex & the Sex-O-Lettes (Chelsea)
GUILTY – First Choice (Philly Groove)
I CAN'T FIGHT YOUR LOVE – Modulations (Buddah)
NEVER CAN SAY GOODBYE – Gloria Gaynor (MGM)
PHILADELPHIA – B.B. King (ABC)
ROCKIN' SOUL – Hues Corporation (RCA)
TELL ME WHAT YOU WANT – Jimmy Ruffin (Chess)
YOU'RE THE FIRST, THE LAST, MY EVERYTHING
– Barry White (20th Century)

PHAROAHS, LOS ANGELES
DJ: Wayne Thorberg

DOCTOR'S ORDERS – Carol Douglas
(Midland International)
EXPRESS – B.T. Express (Scepter)
GET DANCIN' – Disco Tex & the Sex-O-Lettes (Chelsea)
HEY GIRL, COME AND GET IT – Stylistics (Avco)
I FEEL SANCTIFIED – Commodores (Motown)
LADY MARMALADE – LaBelle (Epic)
NEVER CAN SAY GOODBYE – Gloria Gaynor (MGM)
STOP IN THE NAME OF LOVE – Donnie Elbert (Trip)
ROCK ME AGAIN AND AGAIN – Lyn Collins (People)
VOO-DOO MAGIC – Rhodes Kids (GRC)

SOUND MACHINE, NEW YORK
DJ: Tom Savarese

ASK ME – Ecstasy, Passion & Pain (Roulette)
DOCTOR'S ORDERS – Carol Douglas
(Midland International)
EXPRESS – B.T. Express (Scepter)
GET DANCIN' – Disco Tex & the Sex-O-Lettes (Chelsea)
I CAN'T FIGHT YOUR LOVE – Modulations (Buddah)
NEVER CAN SAY GOODBYE – Gloria Gaynor (MGM)
TELL ME WHAT YOU WANT – Jimmy Ruffin (Chess)
THAT'S WHAT I WANT FOR YOU BABY – B.T. Express
(Scepter)
THE PLAYER – First Choice (Philly Groove)
YOU'RE THE FIRST, THE LAST, MY EVERYTHING – Barry
White (20th Century)

"WHO GOT THE MONSTER"
(H. Ray, A. Goodman)

ASTROSCOPE
Distributed Nationally by All Platinum
Record Company, Inc.

AS-118B
AS-131-GM
Time : 3:05
Gambi BMI
Prod. by
H. Ray,
A. Goodman

RIMSHOTS
℗ All Platinum
Record Co. 1974

CANCER VIRGO TAURUS GEMINI ARIES SCORPIO

While the albums that everyone was scrambling to get this week – the latest from **Eddie Kendricks**, the **Blackbyrds**, **Willie Hutch**, **David Ruffin** and the **Hues Corporation** – were still being sorted out, the club deejays polled started talking about their old stand-bys. **Hamilton Bohannon's** largely instrumental "Keep On Dancing" (Dakar), out since April, is still one of the essentials, with "South African Man," sparked perhaps by its recent release as a single, turning up on two of the top 10 lists (below) in its full 7 minute album length. Other tracks – "Keep On Dancing," "Truck Stop" and "The Fat Man"– remain popular, especially at basically black clubs like Pippins; but many people are not aware that the single release of "Keep On Dancing," rather than being cut, was lengthened to more than 7 minutes (in a two-part format) and punched up with some new vocals. Definitely worth investigating. Another stand-by: **George McCrae's** "Rock Your Baby" album on T.K., getting play on nearly all its cuts, but especially "Look At You," "I Can't Leave You Alone" and "You Got My Heart."

There was only one point of consensus among the deejays this week: everyone's still excited about "Express" by **B.T. Express** (Scepter). But it's the idiosyncrasies that fascinate me and help to define the particular taste of a deejay and his crowd. For instance: Bobby Guttadaro at Le Jardin is playing the **Rolling Stones'** complex, long (6:31) "Time Waits For No One" (from "It's Only Rock 'N Roll" on Rolling Stones) and Tyrone "DJ" Hollywood at Pippins finds that **Fela Ransome Kuti's** "Shakara Oloje" and the Lafayette Afro-Rock Band's "Hihache" and "Voodounon" (both albums on the African import label, Editions Makossa) are "doin' it" for his crowd. But if Pippins leans toward African rhythms, it's also among the first clubs to report solid success with the **Average White Band's** finely polished "Pick Up The Pieces" (Atlantic).

Also reported this week: **Isaac Hayes'** exciting 9-minute "Pursuit of the Pimpmobile" (from the "Truck Turner" soundtrack on Enterprise), "Sex Trip" by **Crown Heights Affair** (from "Crown Heights Affair," RCA), **Paul Kelly's** delicious "Take It Away From Him (Put It On Me)" (on "Hooked, Hogtied & Collared," Warner Bros.) Ready to take off: "Get Ready For The Get Down" by **Willie Hutch** (from "The Mark Of The Beast," Motown), the **Blackbyrds'** "Walking in Rhythm" and "I Need You" (on "Flying Start," Fantasy), "Let Yourself Go" and "Shoeshine Boy" by **Eddie Kendricks** (the "For You" album, on Tamla).

The version of the **Tymes'** "You Little Trustmaker" that Bobby Guttadaro and a number of other New York deejays are playing was taken from an unreleased acetate recorded in Philadelphia with backing vocals by the **Three Degrees** and is slightly longer than the final 45 released on RCA. Guttadaro is also playing an as-yet-unreleased cut from **Jimmy Castor's** next album for Atlantic, not yet finished or scheduled for release. Hot from the studio, the track, "He-Man Boogie," has gotten "incredible reaction – whistles, screams – from the first time I played it," according to Guttadaro. Both Howard Metz at Studio One and Artie Feldman at Our Den like "Party Is A Groovy Thing" by **People's Choice** (TSOP), but in Chicago, it "turns the whole floor around."

Also moving up: "Wanna Be Where You Are" by **Zulema** (RCA), **Love Committee's** "One Day Of Peace" (Golden Fleece), "Do You Wanna Dance" by **Five Easy Pieces** (Claridge), "How Have You Been" by **Blood Hollins** (RCA) and the **Peppers'** "Do It, Do It" (Event). Left Field: "Geisha Girl," a fascinating 4 minutes by the **Lords of Percussion** (the B side of the gimmicky-but-great "The Kung-Fu" on Old Town); **Lalo Schifrin's** unexpected "Ape Shuffle" (20th Century); and "Disposable Society" by **Esther Phillips** (Kudu), which has the intelligence and feel of **Gil Scott-Heron's** successful "The Bottle" and could just take off the same way. ✪

> **" It's the idiosyncracies that fascinate me and help to define the particular taste of a deejay and his crowd. While DJ Hollywood leans toward African rhythms, Bobby Guttadaro is playing The Rolling Stones "**

OUR DEN, CHICAGO
DJ: Artie Feldman

ASK ME – Ecstasy, Passion & Pain (Roulette)
DO IT ('TIL YOU'RE SATISFIED) – B.T. Express
(Scepter)
EVERLASTING LOVE – Carl Carlton (Back Beat)
EXPRESS – B.T. Express (Scepter)
GET DANCIN' – Disco Tex & The Sex-O-lettes
(Chelsea)
NEVER CAN SAY GOODBYE – Gloria Gaynor (MGM)
PARTY IS A GROOVY THING – People's Choice (TSOP)
SOUTH AFRICAN MAN – Bohannon (Dakar)
THE PLAYER – First Choice (Philly Groove)
YOU'RE THE FIRST, THE LAST, MY EVERYTHING
– Barry White (20th Century)

PIPPINS, NEW YORK
DJ: Tyrone 'DJ' Hollywood

CAN'T GET ENOUGH – Barry White (20th Century)
DO IT ('TIL YOU'RE SATISFIED) – B.T. Express
(Scepter)
EXPRESS – B.T. Express (Scepter)
I FEEL SANCTIFIED – Commodores (Motown)
LIVE IT UP – Isley Brothers (T-Neck)
PHILADELPHIA – B. B. King (ABC)
PICK UP THE PIECES – AWB (Atlantic)
SHAKARA OLOJE – Fela Ransome Kuti & Afro '70
(Editions Makossa)
WICKI WACKY – Fatback Band (Event)

LE JARDIN, NEW YORK
DJ: Bobby Guttadaro

DOCTOR'S ORDERS – Carol Douglas
(Midland International)
EXPRESS – B.T. Express (Scepter)
GET DANCIN' – Disco Tex & The Sex-O-Lettes
(Chelsea)
GUT LEVEL – Blackbyrds (Fantasy)
I CAN'T FIGHT YOUR LOVE – Modulations (Buddah)
NEVER CAN SAY GOODBYE – Gloria Gaynor (MGM)
SUGAR PIE GUY (PARTS 1 & 2) – The Joneses (Mercury)
TELL ME WHAT YOU WANT – Jimmy Ruffin (Chess)
WHAT CAN I DO FOR YOU? – LaBelle (Epic)
YOU LITTLE TRUSTMAKER – The Tymes (RCA)

STUDIO ONE, LOS ANGELES
DJ: Howard Metz

ASK ME – Ecstasy, Passion & Pain (Roulette)
BROTHER – Mary McCreary (Shelter)
EXPRESS – B.T. Express (Scepter)
GET DANCIN' – Disco Tex & The Sex-O-Lettes
(Chelsea)
LADY MARMALADE – LaBelle (Epic)
NEVER CAN SAY GOODBYE – Gloria Gaynor (MGM)
SMOKE MY PEACE PIPE – Wild Magnolias (Polydor)
PHILADELPHIA – B. B. King (ABC)
WHERE ARE ALL MY FRIENDS – Harold Melvin and The
Bluenotes (Philadelphia International)
YOU'RE THE FIRST, THE LAST, MY EVERYTHING
– Barry White (20th Century)

DECEMBER 14, 1974

Though there are bound to be challenges to Gary Broaddus' claim to be "the only black deejay who can have black people dancing to rock music," it's obvious from his top 10 list this week (below) that he's into something rather unique. Gary, now at New York's Leviticus after a series of club jobs stretching back to 1968, and his brother "Tank," who plays at the after-hours Liquid Smoke, both report playing **Loggins & Messina's** long (8:35), largely instrumental "Pathway to Glory" (from their "Full Sail" album) and **Chicago's** crackling "Woman Don't Want to Love Me" (on "Chicago VII"– both Columbia lps) to strong response from mostly black crowds. Loggins & Messina are hardly standard discotheque fare, but the Broaddus brothers' enthusiasm for the group (Gary also plays "Good Friend" from the "Loggins & Messina" album) has spread to their crowds and Gary says "Pathway" is now "by far the number one choice" at his club. A likely follow-up: the 7-minute-plus "Move On" from L&M's latest album, "Mother Lode."

Gary Broaddus is also unusual in that he very rarely plays singles – and didn't put any on his top 10 – feeling that it "keeps me away from the top 40" and avoids discotheque cliches. His picks right this moment: the mysterious "Summer Madness" from **Kool & the Gang's** most sophisticated album yet, "Light Of Worlds" (De-Lite); "Earth Juice" by **Return to Forever**, featuring Chick Corea on Polydor (on "Where Have I Known You Before" and as an uncut 45); and nearly everything from the new **Blackbyrds** album, "Flying Start" (Fantasy), but especially "The Baby," "Walking In Rhythm," "Future Children, Future Hopes" and "Spaced Out." **Roy Ayers**, whose vibes lead the group Ubiquity, is also a Broaddus favorite because his music is perfect for the spirit and pulse Gary is after. From Ayers' new "Change Up The Groove" album (Polydor), Broaddus is

playing "When Is Real Real?" and "The Boogie Back," with "MASH Theme" his closing record each night.

Tim Zerr at San Francisco's Cabaret After Dark is already playing the Album Cut of the Moment – "Blue Eyed Soul," a terrific 4:49 instrumental from **Carl Douglas's** "Kung Fu Fighting" lp (20th Century); who says the west coast is always weeks behind New York? Wayne Thorberg, who reported from Pharoahs in L.A. a few weeks back, called to say the **Spinners'** "I've Got To Make It On My Own" (from their Atlantic album, "New and Improved") was going over very big and announced that Pharoahs was changing its name to Disco 1984 immediately. Don't ask me why. Other cuts to watch: "Put Out My Fire" from **Lamont Dozier's** "Black Bach" (ABC); "Midnight Flyer" (6:02) by **Trapeze** (from "Hot Wire" on Warner Bros.) and, for the more adventurous (or crazy?), **Caston & Majors'** joyous "Let There Be Love" taken from about the middle of its more than 7 minutes (from "Caston & Majors" on Motown).

Avco Records has sent 45s of the Stylistics' fine "Hey Girl, Come And Get It" imprinted "for DISCO use only" to discotheque deejays across the country with a note acknowledging the clubs' "power to break records and create hits." The record, untrimmed from its album-cut length (on "Heavy"), has not and will not be made available to radio stations or record stores and Avco insists it will never be a commercially-released single – at least not an A-side. So... watch for it on the B-side of the next Stylistics single.

Rich Pampinella at Hippopotamus is excited about "Crystal World" by **Crystal Grass** (or is it the other way around? he wonders), a mostly instrumental import on the Phillips label not scheduled for release here. Pampinella, who says the record sounds like a

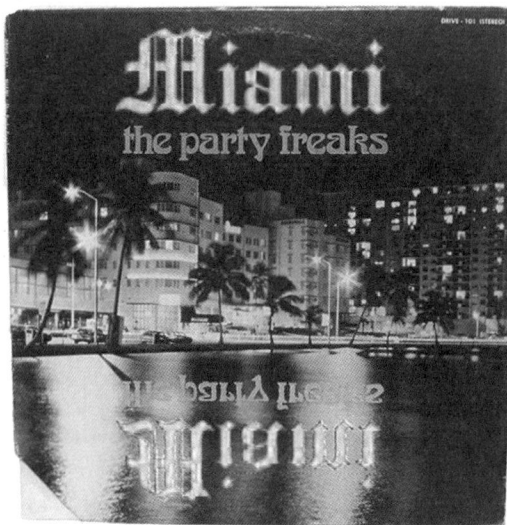

HIPPOPOTAMUS, NEW YORK
DJ: Rich Pampinella

CRYSTAL WORLD – Crystal Grass (Phillips Import)
DOCTOR'S ORDERS – Carol Douglas
(Midland International)
DON'T KNOCK MY LOVE – Marvin Gaye & Diana Ross
(Motown)
EVERLASTING LOVE – Carl Carlton (Back Beat)
EXPRESS – B.T. Express (Scepter)
GET DANCIN' – Disco Tex & the Sex-O-Lettes (Chelsea)
I'LL BE HOLDING ON – AL Downing (Chess)
LA LA PEACE SONG – O. C. Smith (Columbia)
LOVE DON'T YOU GO THROUGH NO CHANGES ON ME –
Sister Sledge (Atco)
NEVER CAN SAY GOODBYE – Gloria Gaynor (MGM)

CABARET AFTER DARK, SAN FRANCISCO
DJ: Tim Zerr

ASK ME – Ecstasy, Passion & Pain (Roulette)
BLUE EYED SOUL – Carl Douglas (20th Century)
DOCTOR'S ORDERS – Carol Douglas
(Midland International)
EXPRESS – B.T. Express (Scepter)
GET DANCIN' – Disco Tex & the Sex-O-Lettes (Chelsea)
I'LL BE HOLDING ON – Al Downing (Chess)
LADY MARMALADE – LaBelle (Epic)
PARTY FREAKS – Miami (Drive)
TELL ME WHAT YOU WANT – Jimmy Ruffin (Chess)
YOU'RE THE FIRST, THE LAST, MY EVERYTHING – Barry
White (20th Century)

LEVITICUS, NEW YORK
DJ: Gary Broaddus

EXPRESS – B.T. Express (Scepter)
GOOD FRIEND – Loggins & Messina (Columbia)
IF IT DON'T TURN YOU ON – B.T. Express (Scepter)
JELLY ROLL – Power of Attorney (Polydor)
MIGRATION – Creative Source (Sussex)
PATHWAY TO GLORY – Loggins & Messina (Columbia)
SMOKE MY PEACE PIPE – Wild Magnolias (Polydor)
WE FEEL THE SAME – Miracles (Tamla)
WHAT'S IT ALL ABOUT – Sylvers (MGM)
WOMAN DON'T WANT TO LOVE ME – Chicago (Columbia)

LIQUID SMOKE, NEW YORK
DJ: James "Tank" Broaddus

ASK ME – Ecstasy, Passion & Pain (Roulette)
EXPRESS – B.T. Express (Scepter)
FIRE – Ohio Players (Mercury)
GUT LEVEL – Blackbyrds (Fantasy)
MIRRORS OF MY MIND – Jackson 5 (Motown)
PATHWAY TO GLORY – Loggins & Messina (Columbia)
PHILADELPHIA – B.B. King (ABC)
PICK UP THE PIECES – AWB (Atlantic)
PUT THE MUSIC WHERE YOUR MOUTH IS – Olympic
Runners (London)
WOMAN DON'T WANT TO LOVE ME – Chicago
(Columbia)

> **" Gary Broaddus claims to be the only black deejay who can have black people dancing to rock music. It's obvious from his top 10 list that he's into something rather unique "**

cross between the **African Music Machine's** "Black
Water Gold" and **James Brown's** "Give It Up Or Turnit
A Loose" (oh yeah?), has been playing a dub and
waiting anxiously for more copies to arrive. Another
popular import at Hippo: "Angel Face" by the **Glitter
Band** on Bell. Tim Zerr says he's mixing **Carol Douglas'**
"Doctor's Orders" (Midland International) with the
original version of the song by **Sunny** (released last
June by Epic and now hard to find) and getting good
response to both. He's also pulling for one of my
favorite singles from this past Summer, Baker, Harris
& Young's energetic Philadelphia production for **Robert
Upchurch**, "The Devil Made Me Do It" (Golden Fleece),
sadly neglected on its release but still hot.

Hot, Hotter, Hottest: **The Temptations'** first work
without Norman Whitfield in years, a just-right "Happy
People" (Gordy); "La-La-Love Chains" by a girl group
called **Silver, Platinum & Gold** (Warner Bros.); the
Miracles' "Don't Cha Love It" (Tamla); "Kung Fu Man"
by **Ultrafunk**, a 6:25 instrumental already a disco
success in England (Contempo); and **Polly Brown's**
great "Up In A Puff Of Smoke" (GTO), bound to hit if
only because it sounds so Diana Ross 1968 with a disco
up-date. ✪

DECEMBER 21, 1974

Murray Brooks is upsetting the crowd at Act I in New York with a track off the new, import-only **Barrabas** album, "Release" (on the Ariola label), which a friend brought back from Venezuela. According to Brooks, the cut, titled "Hijack," has the feel of the group's discotheque classic, "Woman," runs about eight minutes and is so powerful he had to play it four times in a row the night he introduced it before the crowd was satisfied (and exhausted). Since "Woman" and the incredible "Wild Safari" broke nearly two years ago – first as imports, snatched up at ridiculous prices in New York, then on an RCA album – Barrabas, a six-man Spanish group, has had only one other album released in this country and RCA has no plans to release a third. Its very unavailability – and its inevitable spread among the disco freaks, who're willing to pay almost any price for the right record – should turn "Hijack" into an underground sensation. And after repeated raids by radio stations on discotheque territory club deejays will be only too delighted to have a piece of exclusive property again.

Brooks and his crowd were also very excited about the long, sensuous title cut from **Ramsey Lewis'** "Sun Goddess" album (Columbia). If the eight-minute instrumental has a familar sound, that's because it was written and produced by Maurice White and performed by his group, **Earth, Wind & Fire**, with Lewis on keyboards – in fact, it sounds very much like an extension of "Caribou" from EW&F's "Open Our Eyes" album (Columbia). Since Brooks was the only deejay I've spoken to who mentioned playing slow records, I got a list of Act I favorites from him for a glimpse at the more languid side of the disco sound. At the top of the list: **LaBelle's** knockout "You Turn Me On" (from "Nightbirds" on Epic), which makes for a pretty steamy dance floor. Among the others: "I Belong To You" and "Share A Little Love In Your Heart" by **Love Unlimited** (on "In Heat," 20th Century), "Barry's Love (Parts I & II)" and "Dreaming" by **Love Unlimited Orchestra** (on "White Gold," 20th Century), **Ace Spectrum's** "Moving On" (from "Inner Spectrum" on Atlantic) and the first half of the **Jackson 5's** long (7:30) "I Am Love" ("Dancing Machine," on Motown). And, yes, there are 11 cuts listed on Brook's top 10-the **Gene Page** and **Love Unlimited Orchestra** versions of **Barry White's** "Satin Soul" are neck-and-neck at Act I. (I suspect there was a kind of photo finish at Outer Limits in L.A., but there Paul Dougan decided in favor of Gene Page.) Even people, like me, who resisted **Carl Douglas'** aggressive "Kung Fu Fighting," are falling for his album of the same name (20th Century). In addition to "Blue Eyed Soul," reported last week, and the title cut, "Dance The Kung Fu" and "I Want To Give You My Everything" are reported picking up play this week. And of course, from the new Blue Magic album, "The Magic Of The Blue" (Atlantic): "Let Me Be The One," "Love Has Found Its Way To Me" and, though it is difficult, "Never Get Over You."

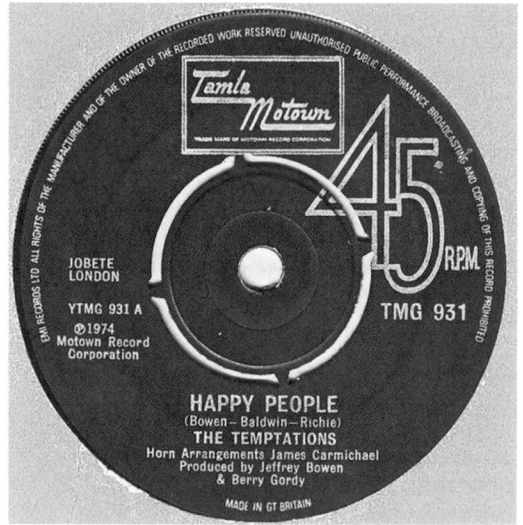

Ray Mastracchio at Nite Life in New York is pushing "How Have You Been" by **Blood Hollins** (both the vocal and instrumental sides, on RCA) almost as hard as Paul Dougan is pushing **Gino Vannelli's** single, "People Gotta Move" (A&M) in L.A. – and both are picking up. Bob Evans, at D.C.'s Sundown, is blending both sides of **Lalo Schifrin's** new single – "Escape From Tomorrow," which has proved to be the more popular, and "Ape Shuffle" (20th Century). And some people are flipping **Lea Roberts'** lovely "Laughter In The Rain" (UA), which came out at the end of the summer, and playing her terrific version of Jerry Butler's "She Will Break Your Heart" (arrangement by **Gene Page**).

Recommended: "Waitin' For The Rain" by the **Philly Sound** (Phil-L.A. of Soul), the instrumental track from last year's disco hit of the same name by the **Fantastic Johnny C** – production is by Philadelphia's **Baker, Harris & Young** so we can assume key elements of

> ## " The disco freaks are willing to pay almost any price for the right record "

ACT I, NEW YORK
DJ: Murray Brooks

EXPRESS – B.T. Express (Scepter)
FIRE – Ohio Players (Mercury)
GET DANCIN' – Disco Tex & the Sex-O-Lettes (Chelsea)
LOVE YOU JUST AS LONG AS I CAN – Free Spirit (Chess)
MIGHTY CLOUD OF JOY – Mighty Clouds of Joy (Dunhill)
MIRRORS OF MY MIND – Jackson 5 (Motown)
PARTY FREAKS – Miami (Drive)
PHILADELPHIA – B.B. King (ABC)
SUGAR PIE GUY – Joneses (Mercury)
SATIN SOUL – Gene Page (Atlantic)
SATIN SOUL – Love Unlimited Orchestra (20th Century)

SUNDOWN, WASHINGTON, D.C.
DJ: Bob Evans

DOCTOR'S ORDERS – Carol Douglas
(Midland International)
EXPRESS – B.T. Express (Scepter)
GET DANCIN' – Disco Tex & the Sex-O-Lettes (Chelsea)
HAPPY PEOPLE – Temptations (Gordy)
I'LL BE HOLDING ON – Al Downing (Chess)
KUNG FU FIGHTING – Carl Douglas (20th Century)
LADY MARMALADE – LaBelle (Epic)
NEVER CAN SAY GOODBYE – Gloria Gaynor (MGM)
TELL ME WHAT YOU WANT – Jimmy Ruffin (Chess)
YOU'RE THE FIRST, THE LAST, MY EVERYTHING – Barry
White (20th Century)

OUTER LIMITS, LOS ANGELES
DJ: Paul Dougan

ASK ME – Ecstasy, Passion & Pain (Roulette)
DOCTOR'S ORDERS – Carol Douglas
(Midland International)
EXPRESS – B.T. Express (Scepter)
GET DANCIN' – Disco Tex & the Sex-O-Lettes (Chelsea)
I'LL BE HOLDING ON – Al Downing (Chess)
KEEP ON MOVIN' – Creative Source (Sussex)
LADY MARMALADE – LaBelle (Epic)
NEVER CAN SAY GOODBYE – Gloria Gaynor (MGM)
SATIN SOUL – Gene Page (Atlantic)
YOU'RE THE FIRST, THE LAST, MY EVERYTHING – Barry
White (20th Century)

NITE LIFE, NEW YORK
DJ: Ray Mastracchio

BLUE EYED SOUL – Carl Douglas (20th Century)
DOCTOR'S ORDERS – Carol Douglas
(Midland International)
EACH MORNING I WAKE UP – Major Harris Boogie
Blues Band (Atlantic)
ESCAPE FROM TOMORROW – Lalo Schifrin
(20th Century)
EXPRESS – B.T. Express (Scepter)
GUILTY – First Choice (Philly Groove)
HEY GIRL, COME AND GET IT – Stylistics (Avco)
I'LL BE HOLDING ON – Al Downing (Chess)
TELL ME WHAT YOU WANT – Jimmy Ruffin (Chess)
WHAT CAN I DO FOR YOU? – LaBelle (Epic)

MFSB are present, and don't ignore the B side, also the track from the original "Don't Depend on Me;" **Johnny Rivers'** very up "Get It Up For Love" (Atlantic); "Just as Long As We're Together," a **Barry White** production for **Gloria Scott** (Casablanca); **Ronnie Walker's** sharply-produced "You've Got To Try Harder (Times Are Bad)" (Event) and "Getting It On '75," a **Dennis Coffey** instrumental (Sussex).

FLASH: Rich Pampinella, who reported from Hippopotamus last week, is so excited about "Shame, Shame, Shame" by **Shirley (And Company)** (Vibration), which is very "Rock Your Baby" with screaming vocals, that he's making wild predictions about it – number one by next week? We'll see, we'll see. ◐

DECEMBER 28, 1974

"Flamingo, a huge, superbly-designed new private discotheque, opened in New York last week and even with the rugs rolled and stacked at one end it looked like the hottest space in town"

Flamingo, a huge, superbly-designed new private discotheque (for members and their guests only) opened in New York last week and even with the rugs rolled and stacked at one end and a ladder still standing at the other, it looked like the best space in town. Armando Galvez, who has done occasional parties and some incredible tapes, was the opening night deejay, so the pace was, in his word, "hectic." Wonderfully hectic. Among Armando's favorites, aside from those listed in his first-night top 10 (below), were **Barry Manilow's** "It's A Miracle" (from "Barry Manilow II" on Bell), **Jay Dee's** "Come On In love" (from the album of the same name on Warner Bros.) and one of this past Summer's great – and largely undiscovered – singles, "Dirty Feet" by **Jenny's Daughters** (Paramount) (sample lyric: "You got dirty feet – who you been walkin' with? You got dirty mouth – who you been talkin' with?"). Galvez, who has been known to play records at the wrong speed for the right effect, also played a number of records that had never sounded quite so terrific before. Specifically: "Keep An Eye On Your Close Friends" by the Newcomers (Truth), **Carolyn Crawford's** biting "Just Got To Be More Careful" (Phila. Intl.) and, most impressive of all, "Don't Depend On Me," with the new instrumental by the **Philly Sound** and the vocal by the **Fantastic Johnny C** (both on Phil-L.A. of Soul) played back-to-back.

The fastest-breaking single this week: "Happy People" by the **Temptations** (Gordy), spurred by the added attraction of an instrumental B side (credited to "The Temptations Band") which brings the song, neatly segued, to a comfortable 6:23 altogether. Hot off the presses: **Joe Bataan's** Latin-flavored instrumental version of **Gil Scott-Heron's** "The Bottle," appropriately sub-titled "La Botella" and due out this week as the first release on Bataan's new Salsoul label (an album will follow in January). Both Raymond Goynes at La Martinique and Douglas Riddick at Opus I report immediate response to advance copies made available last weekend and Riddick, who had to play it seven times the first night it broke at his club, is already predicting a gold record for Bataan, whose work has always been a rich blend of Latin and black urban sounds – "salsa" and soul – sharpens "The Bottle" with horns, adds an unexpected sweep of strings and runs it very up-tempo for nearly four minutes. With Scott-Heron's song something of a disco standard already, this re-cycling should pick up very fast.

More Latin spice: Mitch Schatsky at Pier 9 in D.C is enthusiastic about **Tito Puente's** fine instrumental "Watu Wasuri," a fast-paced Latin jazz piece available as the B side of his recent single, "Borinquen," or on the album "Tito Unlimited" (Tico). With the exception of "Baby Don't Let This Good Love Die," the B side of Carol Douglas' hit, "Doctor's Orders" (Midland International) – which Mitch claims all the Washington deejays are playing but no one in New York will touch, and with good reason – Schatsky has most of the best tips this week: **Dooley Silverspoon's** "Bump Me Baby," another two-part George McCrae imitation, but a good one (on Ottion); **Louise Freeman's** gutsy "I Can Do It (If I See It)" (Shout) and "The Whole Damn World's Gone Crazy" by **John Gary Williams** (Stax), which he says has been very big in D.C. and Philadelphia (as my Philly correspondent confirms) but quite unknown in New York. He also points out that one of his top 10 choices, "Voo-Doo Magic" by the **Rhodes Kids** – some white children who pretend to be the Jackson 5 and almost make it (on GRC)-has yet to have the success in New York that it now enjoys in D.C and Los Angeles. Already we're having regional discotheque hits? ✦

FLAMINGO, NEW YORK
DJ: Armando Galvez

BLUE EYED SOUL – Carl Douglas (20th Century)
GET' DANCIN' – Disco Tex & The Sex-O-Lettes (Chelsea)
HAPPY PEOPLE – Temptations (Gordy)
HEY GIRL, COME AND GET IT – Stylistics (Avco)
LOVE DON'T YOU GO THROUGH NO CHANGES ON ME –
Sister Sledge (Atlantic)
NEVER SAY GOODBYE – Gloria Gaynor (MGM)
REMEMBER ME – Laura lee (Invictus)
SATIN SOUL – Gene Page (Atlantic)
SOMETHING FISHY GOING ON – Universal Mind (Red Coach)
WHAT CAN I DO FOR YOU?' – LaBelle (Epic)

OPUS I, NEW YORK
DJ: Douglas Riddick

ASK ME – Ecstasy, Passion & Pain (Roulette)
THE BOTTLE (LA BOTELLA) – Joe Bataan (Salsoul)
**DOCTOR'S ORDERS/BABY DON'T LET THIS GOOD
LOVE DIE** – Carol Douglas (Midland International)
DON'T LEAVE ME – Lamont Dozier (Invictus)
EVERLASTING LOVE – Carl Carlton (Back Beat)
GUT LEVEL – Blackbyrds (Fantasy lp cut)
HAPPY PEOPLE – Temptations (Gordy)
I'LL BE HOLDING ON – Al Downing (Chess)
SOON, EVERYTHING IS GONNA BE ALRIGHT – Third
Time Around (Denine)
YOU'RE THE FIRST, THE LAST, MY EVERYTHING – Barry
White (20th Century)

PIER 9, WASHINGTON, D.C.
DJ: Mitch Schatsky

**DOCTOR'S ORDERS/BABY DON'T LET THIS GOOD
LOVE DIE** – Carol Douglas (Midland International)
E-MAN BOOGIE – Jimmy Castor Bunch (Atlantic)
EACH MORNING I WAKE UP – Major Harris Boogie
Blues Band (Atlantic)
EXPRESS – B.T. Express (Scepter)
HAPPY PEOPLE – Temptations (Gordy)
I'LL BE HOLDING ON – Al Downing (Chess)
LOVE DON'T YOU GO THROUGH NO CHANGES ON ME –
Sister Sledge (Atlantic)
SHAME, SHAME, SHAME – Shirley And Company (Vibration)
VOO-DOO MAGIC – Rhodes Kids (GRC)
YOU'RE THE SONG (I'VE ALWAYS WANTED TO SING) –
Timmy Thomas (Glades)

LA MARTINIQUE, NEW YORK
DJ: Raymond Goynes

EXPRESS – B.T. Express (Scepter)
FUNKY PRESIDENT – James Brown (Polydor)
GUT LEVEL – Blackbyrds (Fantasy)
LIVE IT UP – Isley Brothers (T-Neck)
THE MIRRORS OF MY MIND – Jackson Five (Motown)
PHILADELPHIA – B.B. King (ABC)
PICK UP THE PIECES – AWB (Atlantic)
PUT THE MUSIC WHERE YOUR MOUTH IS – Olympic
Runners (London)
SATIN SOUL – Gene Page (Atlantic)
SATIN SOUL – Love Unlimited Orchestra (20th Century)

1975

Two couples dancing © **Peter Hujar Archive**

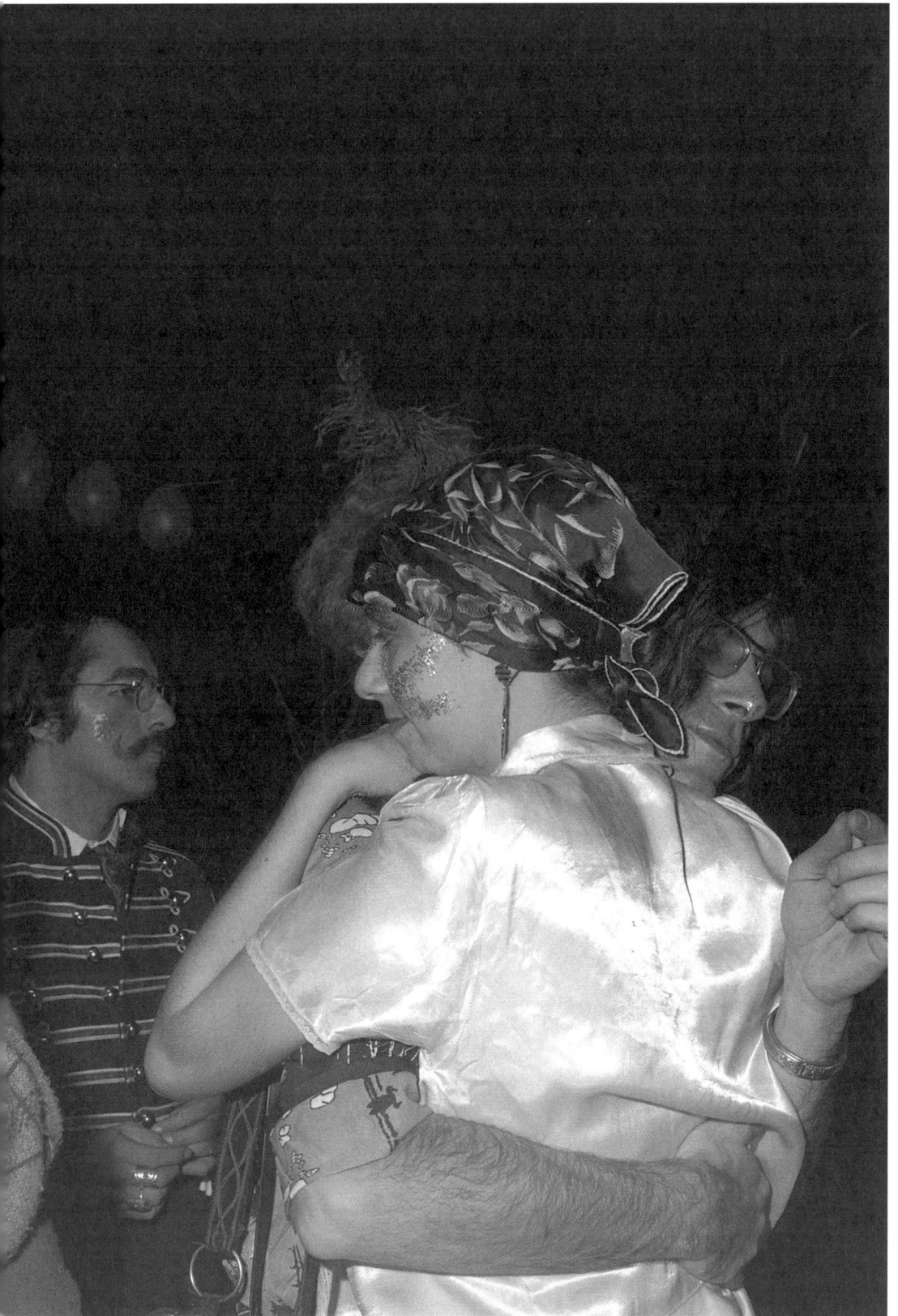

JANUARY 4, 1975

"Release," that new **Barrabas** album Act I deejay Murray Brooks was so enthusiastic about two columns back (December 21) turns out to be MGM's. Now an import, the album was originally scheduled to late January, preceded a week or two by the release of a shortened 45 version of its prime cut, "Hijack." Only "Hijack" has already been hijacked – to Atlantic by **Herbie Mann**. Mann, who's been planning a flow-through discotheque album for his next release, seized on a copy of the Barrabas original that Brooks had made available to Atlantic's head of a&r, Jim Delehant. A few days later, Mann's cover version – featuring **Ray Barretto** on congas and vocals by the **Sweet Inspirations** with **Cissy Houston** – was finished and cut in two lengths: 3:00 for radio stations, 5:32 for discotheques (and everybody else).

In a few more days – barely a week after the Brooks report appeared in print – the record had been pressed and shipped. Mann's "Hijack" is airier and more upbeat than the Barrabas cut, but it lacks that group's, hard-edged lead vocals. Come January, this could turn into a very interesting battle, but right now Herbie Mann's taken over.

But why should MGM worry when they have the **Gloria Gaynor** album coming out the first Week of January? One side of the album – "Honeybee," "Never Can Say Goodbye" and a wonderful version of 'the Four Tops' classic, "Reach Out I'll Be There," all running about six minutes and blended together – has been made available to a few New York deejays including David Rodriguez at Limelight and Michael Cappello at Le Jardin. Both report a predictably knock-out response, especially when the pressing is played straight through ("It gives me a chance to take a break, too," Rodriguez adds). "Honeybee," I'm glad to report, is a return to the very buzzy version first released on Columbia rather than the toned-down, cut-down record MGM put out at the beginning of the year; and it goes

on and on. Hector Reyes at the Stardust Ballroom is playing "The Warrior," a four-minute cut from the album of the same name, by a South African group called **Ipi 'N Tombia** (Stax). Though most of the album sounds like the Singing Nun gone native, this one cut has such fine drumming that the whole record's been selling on its strength alone, and picking up steadily since its release this past summer. At the Monastery, Paul Casella and his crowd are getting into a cut from **David Barretto's** album "Para Mis Hermanos" (Mercury), the raspy, driving "On And On."

Recommended: **Carl Carlton's** version of "Our Day Will Come," on his "Everlasting Love" album (ABC), and these new 45s: "Just Can't Say Goodbye" by the **Philly Devotions**, with an instrumental B side (Columbia); **Johnny Hammond's** instrumental "Yesterday Was Cool," condensed to 3 :45 from his nearly seven-minute album cut on "Gambler's Life" (Salvation) – a Ronald Coles pick; "Inspiration Information" by **Shuggie Otis** (Epic), which is not for hard dancing or for every taste, but Murray Brooks says he plays it coming out of a slow set; and an edited, re-mixed "Living, Loving, Laughing," now even more irresistible, by **Jesus** (Vibration). ❂

> **❝ Why should MGM worry when they have the Gloria Gaynor album coming out in January? One side of the album, with the songs blended together, has been made available to a few New York deejays ❞**

STARDUST BALLROOM, NY (BRONX)
DJ: Hector Reyes

BLUE EYED SOUL – Carl Douglas (20th Century)
THE BOTTLE (LA BOTELLA) – Joe Bataan (Salsoul)
DOCTOR'S ORDERS – Carol Douglas
(Midland International)
E-MAN BOOGIE – Jimmy Caster Bunch (Atlantic)
EXPRESS – B.T. Express (Scepter)
GIRLS (PARTS I & II) – Moments and Whatnauts (Stang)
HEY GIRL, COME AND GET IT Stylistics (Avco)
I'LL BE HOLDING ON – Al Downing (Chess)
NEVER CAN SAY GOODBYE – Gloria Gaynor (MGM)
SATIN SOUL – Gene Page (Atlantic)

LE JARDIN, NEW YORK
DJ: Michael Cappello

ASK ME – Ecstasy, Passion & Pain (Roulette)
DOCTOR'S ORDERS – Carol Douglas
(Midland International)
DO IT ('TIL YOU'RE SATISFIED) – B.T. Express (Scepter)
EXPRESS – B.T. Express (Scepter)
GET DANCIN' – Disco Tex & the Sex-O-Lettes (Chelsea)
LADY MARMALADE – LaBelle (Epic)
NEVER CAN SAY GOODBYE – Gloria Gaynor (MGM)
SHAME, SHAME, SHAME – Shirley And Company
(Vibration)
TELL ME WHAT YOU WANT – Jimmy Ruffin (Chess)
WHAT CAN I DO FOR YOU? – LaBelle (Epic)

LIMELIGHT, NEW YORK
DJ: David Rodriguez

ASK ME – Ecstasy, Passion & Pain (Roulette)
BUMP ME BABY – Dooley Silverspoon (Cotton)
EXPRESS – B.T. Express (Scepter)
HEY GIRL, COME AND GET IT – Stylistics (Avco)
I'LL BE HOLDING ON – Al Downing (Chess)
LADY MARMALADE – LaBelle (Epic)
MIRRORS OF MY MIND – Jackson 5 (Motown)
SHAME, SHAME, SHAME – Shirley And Company
(Vibration)
TELL ME WHAT YOU WANT – Jimmy Ruffin (Chess)
WHAT CAN I DO FOR YOU? – LaBelle (Epic)

THE MONASTERY, NY (QUEENS)
DJ: Paul Casella

BLUE EYED SOUL – Carl Douglas (20th Century)
THE BOTTLE LA BOTELLA) – Joe Bataan (Salsoul)
DOCTOR'S ORDERS – Carol Douglas
(Midland International)
E-MAN BOOGIE – Jimmy Caster Bunch (Atlantic)
EXPRESS – B.T. Express (Scepter)
I'LL BE HOLDING ON – Al Downing (Chess)
JUST AS LONG AS WE'RE TOGETHER – Gloria Scott
(Casablanca)
LET ME BE THE ONE – Blue Magic (Atco)
SHOORAH! SHOORAH! – Betty Wright (Alston)
YOU'VE BROKEN MY HEART – Sound Experience
(Soulville)

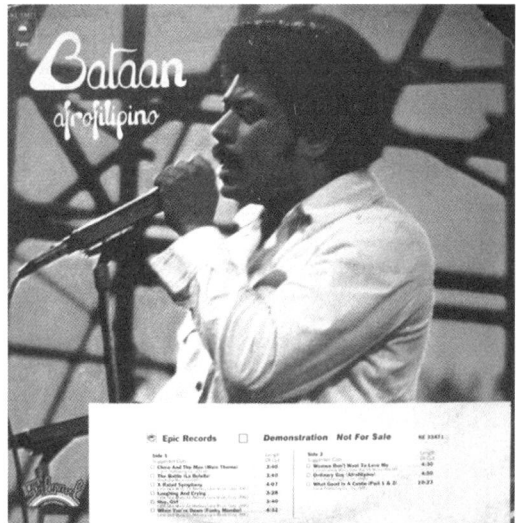

JANUARY 11, 1975

Out of a dull week, these notes: Doug Douglas called from South Carolina to ask were we ever going to cover discotheques in the South? And I said yes, so here he is (and Miami, too). Douglas, who says he's been playing records at clubs and dances since 1957, gave me a top 10 list "based on request, demand and response" which includes two rather obscure items: (1) "Rockin' Chair" by **Clarence Reid**, put out as the B side of a single called "When My Daddy Rode The West," which had been released only in the Miami test market by Dash, one of TK's small, local-release labels. Though it was short-lived in Miami and never released nationally, Douglas says "Rockin' Chair" is taking off very fast right at his regular club, Zig Zag. (2) "Hot Grits!!!" by **Elijah and the Ebonies** (Capsoul), a pumping, wild-party instrumental that Douglas admits is by a local group but certainly deserves to get beyond South Carolina. It's loud and brassy and Elijah, one assumes, shouts the title throughout.

In addition, Douglas had two of the most common complaints expressed by club deejays outside of New York and L.A. First, he finds it difficult to get serviced with records; then, once he starts playing a record, too often local stores won't stock it. "Many times," he says, "I've broken records that no one can find." In the same way, a good deal of the potential sales impact of discotheques around the country is blunted or cut off altogether by stores that are ignoring the market.

Wayne Thorberg, who previously reported from Pharoahs in L.A., is now also playing at Donkin's Inn in the suburb of Marina del Rey where he's been introducing the years-old **Brenda & the Tabulations** beauty, "Little Bit Of Love" (Epic/Memory Lane), to crowds largely unfamiliar with the record. A "lost" record everywhere except in the discotheques, "Little Bit Of Love" remains one of the great disco discoveries and its more recent, still scattered reappearance in California could signal a general revival, maybe even a more serious reissue... Tony Gioe, who works at Hollywood and declines to pronounce his last name, is "in love with" **Gene Page's** "I Am Living In A World Of Gloom" (from the "Hot City" album on Atlantic) and while we are not quite so ardent, we agree it's very attractive. Gioe also warns that the mix of "Crystal World" by **Crystal Grass** which Polydor plans to release this month is not the same as that being played around New York as a Philips import... The **Stylistics** have a new single, "Star On A TV Show" (Avco). Relegated to the B side: "Hey Girl, Come And Get It." Go and get it.

Left field report of the moment: Wayne Thorberg insists that one of his more popular new records is by **Rod McKuen**, or maybe it's the Rod McKuen Orchestra. The record's a single version of an instrumental called "Love Conquers All" (Stanyan), originally the opening cut on a live, in-concert album. Thorberg says it's reminiscent of "Love's Theme" (isn't everything?) and is getting "excellent response." Almost as left-field is his report of

> **"Doug Douglas called from South Carolina to ask were we ever going to cover discotheques in the South. And I said yes, so here he is (and Miami too). His top 10 list includes two rather obscure items"**

HOLLYWOOD, NEW YORK
DJ: Tony Gioe

BLUE EYED SOUL – Carl Douglas (20th Century)
DOCTOR'S ORDERS – Carol Douglas
(Midland International)
EXPRESS – B.T. Express (Scepter)
GIRLS (PARTS I & II) – Moments and Whatnauts (Stang)
HEY GIRL, COME AND GET IT – Stylistics (Avco)
I'LL BE HOLDING ON – Al Downing (Chess)
LOVE DON'T YOU GO THROUGH NO CHANGES ON ME –
Sister Sledge (Atco)
SHAME, SHAME, SHAME – Shirley And Company
(Vibration)
THAT'S WHAT I WANT FOR YOU BABY – B.T. Express
(Scepter)
WHAT CAN I DO FOR YOU? – LaBelle (Epic)

LOVE, MIAMI BEACH
DJ: Aristides Jacobs

BLUE EYED SOUL – Carl Douglas (20th Century)
DOCTOR'S ORDERS – Carol Douglas
(Midland International)
EACH MORNING I WAKE UP – Major Harris Boogie
Blues Band (Atlantic)
EXPRESS – B.T. Express (Scepter)
I'LL BE HOLDING ON – Al Downing (Chess)
IT'S A MIRACLE – Barry Manilow (Bell)
JUST AS LONG AS WE'RE TOGETHER – Gloria Scott
(Casablanca)
LADY MARMALADE – LaBelle (Epic)
LOVE DON'T YOU GO THROUGH NO CHANGES ON ME –
Sister Sledge (Atco)
NEVER CAN SAY GOODBYE – Gloria Gaynor (MGM)

DONKIN'S INN, MARINA DEL REY, C.A.
DJ: Wayne Thorberg

BOOGIE DOWN – Van McCoy (Avco)
EACH MORNING I WAKE UP – Major Harris Boogie
Blues Band (Atlantic)
FIRE – Ohio Players (Mercury)
GETTING IT ON '75 – Dennis Coffey (Sussex)
HAPPY PEOPLE – Temptations (Gordy)
LITTLE BIT OF LOVE – Brenda & the Tabulations
(Epic/Memory Lane)
LOVE DON'T YOU GO THROUGH NO CHANGES ON ME –
Sister Sledge (Atco)
THE TWIST – James Brown (Polydor)
UP IN A PUFF OF SMOKE – Polly Brown (GTO)
WAITIN' FOR THE RAIN – Philly Sound (Phil-L.A. of Soul)

ZIG ZAG, ANDERSON, SOUTH CAROLINA
DJ: Doug Douglas

EXPRESS – B.T. Express (Scepter)
FIRE – Ohio Players (Mercury)
HEY GIRL, COME AND GET IT – Stylistics (Avco)
HEY POCKY-A-WAY – Meters (Reprise)
HOT GRITS – Elijah and the Ebonies (Capsoul)
I WANT TO BE FREE – Ohio Players (Mercury)
PHILADELPHIA – B.B. King (ABC)
PICK UP THE PIECES – AWB (Atlantic)
ROCKIN' CHAIR – Clarence Reid (Dosh)
SEXY IDA – Ike & Tina Turner (UA)

James Brown's 1975 version of **Hank Ballard's** 1959 song, "The Twist" (from "Reality" on Polydor); needless to say, it's hardly recognizable. Let's twist again?... In Miami, Aristides Jacobs is playing an overlooked cut from the "Act I" album (Spring), "It's The Same Old Story," a personal favorite... TV Guide: That black girl trio that sings "Hold the pickle, hold the lettuce" behind the counter in the Burger King commercials is the underground group of 1974, **Jenny's Daughters**, whose song "Dirty Feet" (Paramount), disappeared during the Paramount-ABC merger only to surface in a few tastemaking discos.

Get Ready: Among the performers with albums scheduled for release during the next four to five weeks are **Ecstasy, Passion & Pain** (Roulette), **Zulema** (RCA), **Intruders, Soul Survivors** (both TSOP), **Billy Paul, Harold Melvin & the Bluenotes, O'Jays, MFSB** (all on Philadelphia International), **Temptations, Undisputed Truth** (both Gordy) **Miracles** (Tamla), **Michael Jackson** (Motown), **Gil Scott-Heron** (Arista) **Gloria Gaynor** (MGM), **Sister Sledge** (Atco), **Major Harris Boogie Blues Band, Jimmy Castor** (Atlantic), **Futures, Barbara Mason** (Buddah) **Tower of Power** (Warner Bros.) and **Bonnie Bramlett** (Capricorn). ✪

JANUARY 18, 1975

For some time now, the singles counter of New York's Colony Records has not only been a sort of action central for the city's discotheque DJs – a source for the most danceable new records as well as a clearing house for club gossip, hot tips and inside reports on what's being played where – but, for the guys who work there, it's been a crash course education in discotheque music that many of them eventually take out into the field. Though Colony is now only one of a number of stores giving special attention to the disco dance masters (the new favorite is Downstairs Records in the Sixth Avenue subway arcade at 42nd Street), more DJs have come from behind its counters than from anywhere else. The latest is Ronald Coles, who works at Colony nights until two and then runs downtown on Friday and Saturday to play at Private Party, a membership club that doesn't really start happening until he gets there at three. Very after hours.

At Colony, Coles keeps meticulous lists of singles and album cuts that would appeal to any discotheque taste – from obscure cuts by the **Sweet Inspirations** to unlikely items like **Pleasure's** "Midnight At The Oasis" (Fantasy) which he says is going over well at some straight clubs in Queens – and he prides himself on being able to separate the "garbage" from the "stuff that has potential," no matter how marginal, and pitch it to the right deejay. But at his weekend parties, he plays only what excites him, whether it be **Minnie Riperton's** lovely, languid "Lovin' You" (Epic) or **Patti Jo's** neglected "Make Me Believe In You," a **Curtis Mayfield** production and composition originally released in April of 1973 on Wand and worth looking for if you're at all interested in tough girl r&b. Ronald Coles is a walking tipsheet and will be consulted by this column from time to time.

> **❝Colony Records is action central for the city's discotheque DJs – a source for the most danceable new records, as well as a clearing house for club gossip, hot tips and inside reports on what's being played where❞**

BETTER DAYS, NEW YORK
DJ: Toraino "Tee" Scott

EXPRESS – B.T. Express (Scepter)
I'LL BE HOLDING ON – Al Downing (Chess)
LANSANA'S PRIESTESS – Donald Byrd (Blue Note)
LOVE DON'T YOU GO THROUGH NO CHANGES ON ME – Sister Sledge (Atco)
SATIN SOUL – Gene Page (Atlantic)
SHAME, SHAME, SHAME – Shirley And Company (Vibration)
VOO-DOO MAGIC – Rhodes Kids (GRC)
WHAT CAN I DO FOR YOU? – LaBelle (Epic)
WHATEVER'S YOUR SIGN YOU'VE GOT TO BE MINE – Hustlers (Effie)

PRIVATE PARTY, NEW YORK
DJ: Ronald Coles

THE BOTTLE (LA BOTELLA) – Bataan (Salsoul)
E-MAN BOOGIE – Jimmy Castor Bunch (Atlantic)
EXPRESS – B.T. Express (Scepter)
HEY GIRL, COME AND GET IT – Stylistics (Avco)
HONEYBEE/NEVER CAN SAY GOODBYE/ REACH OUT I'LL BE THERE – Gloria Gaynor (MGM)
JUST AS LONG AS WE'RE TOGETHER – Gloria Scott (Casablanca)
LOVIN' YOU – Minnie Riperton (Epic)
MAKE ME BELIEVE IN YOU – Patti Jo (Wand)
SATIN SOUL – Gene Page (Atlantic)
YESTERDAY WAS COOL – Johnny Hammond (Salvation)

STUDIO ONE, LOS ANGELES
DJ: Howard Metz

GET DANCIN' – Disco Tex & the Sex-O-Lettes (Chelsea)
GOT TO GET YOU BACK – Sons of Robin Stone (Atco)
HAPPY PEOPLE – Temptations (Gordy)
HEY GIRL, COME AND GET IT – Stylistics (Avco)
I'LL BE HOLDING ON – Al Downing (Chess)
LADY MARMALADE – LaBelle (Epic)
LOVE DON'T YOU GO THROUGH NO CHANGES ON ME – Sister Sledge (Atco)
PICK UP THE PIECES – AWB (Atlantic)
YOU'RE THE FIRST, THE LAST, MY EVERYTHING – Barry White (20th Century)
YOU'RE THE SONG I'VE ALWAYS WANTED TO SING – Timmy Thomas (Glades)

LE TWINKIE ZONE, NEW YORK
DJ: Aris Rodrigues

BLUE EYED SOUL – Carl Douglas (20th Century)
DOCTOR'S ORDERS – Carol Douglas (Midland International)
EXPRESS – B.T. Express (Scepter)
HAPPY PEOPLE – Temptations (Gordy)
HEY GIRL, COME AND GET IT – Stylistics (Avco)
I'LL BE HOLDING ON – Al Downing (Chess)
LADY MARMALADE – LaBelle (Epic)
SHAME, SHAME, SHAME – Shirley And Company (Vibration)
TELL ME WHAT YOU WANT – Jimmy Ruffin (Chess)
YOU'RE THE FIRST, THE LAST, MY EVERYTHING – Barry White (20th Century)

Other new entries on the Top 10 lists this week: **Donald Byrd's** breezy instrumental "Lansana's Priestess," the 7:16 opening cut from his "Street Lady" album (Blue Note), which "Tee" Scott at Better Days has been playing about two weeks now and feels could be very big. "Whatever's Your Sign, You've Got To Be Mine," by the **Hustlers** (Effie) also on Scott's list, was brought to his attention by Ronald Coles, who also passed this obscure single on to several other DJs before his supply ran out and the supplier disappeared. With no more copies available at the moment, this could become another "lost" disco hit unless someone picks it up. Also, you'll note from Howard Metz's Studio One list that "Got To Get You Back," the **Sons of Robin Stone** record (on Atco) that was so successful on the east coast during the Summer of last year, is just getting out west. Metz, who complained that he just couldn't find it in L.A., mail-ordered it from Downstairs in New York.

Recommended: **Ben E. King's** excellent, two-part "Supernatural Thing" (Atlantic) with a pumping, sharp-edged production by **Tony Sylvester**, ex-**Main Ingredient**, and **Bert DeCoteaux**; a mix of the two parts runs just over seven minutes – so why didn't Atlantic mail out both sides on their promotion copies to discos? Too many companies are servicing only half a record of the increasingly frequent Part I/Part II disco format singles which is both a frustration to the deejay and a disservice to the record. Also: the **Jackson 5's** "I Am Love – Part II" (Motown), taken from their last album and edited into two parts so that the second half of the song, the upbeat part, stands on its own; and "Movin' In The Right Direction" by Wiz kid, **Stephanie Mills**, a 16-year-old with an incredible voice (ABC). ☻

JANUARY 25, 1975

When Douglas Riddick from New York's Opus I woke me up with a phone call Saturday morning (well, it was almost noon) to tell me about a new record he'd played at the club the night before, I was barely paying attention. But, as it turns out, Riddick's call was the first word on what may be the most interesting new disco album this year. The record, three cuts of which were put on high-quality dubs and given to Riddick, is by a young percussionist and singer from Ghana named **Buari**, whose music is one of the most exciting African imports since "Soul Makossa." But, like **Manu Dibango's** work, this is not an entirely African product, having been recorded in New York with the aid of some of the city's top studio musicians (among them, **Bernard Purdie**), who provide a sharp, finely polished edge without losing the rawness and life of Buari's sound. Of the three tracks being played at Opus I, "Karam Bani," "Iro Epa" and "Coqua Maria," the first, with a heavy, relentless percussion and a chorus of women chanting the title, sounds the best to me. Though dubs are being placed at selected discotheques in New York, the album as a whole was finished only weeks ago and has not yet been sold to a label. If the reaction at the companies is anything like the enthusiasm at the clubs, Buari should be picked up very soon. Watch for it.

Suzanne, who plays at a Long Island club called the Square Lemon (I thought names like that went out with the '60s) and reports her top 10 this week, is not exactly

– "I open up a new bottle every week" – and this week it includes "Rice 'N' Ribs" from the **Fred Wesley & the New J.B.'s** album, "Breakin' Bread" (People), a densely brassy four-minute instrumental that would seem rather left-field because of its rhythm changes, but which Johnson says was an "instant hit." **Norman Connors'** "Back On The Street," a nice, chugging instrumental from his Buddah album, "Slewfoot," is much more accessible.

Tim Zerr from Cabaret After Dark in San Francisco recommends two attractive, comfortably upbeat cuts from the recent **Al Green** album ("Explores Your Mind" on Hi Records): "Take Me To The River," "One Nite Stand." Other album notes: **Gloria Gaynor's** lp, "Never Can Say Goodbye" (MGM) is finally out and we should begin hearing several of the shorter side two cuts as well as the pre-released (and, I hear, already bootlegged) side one rush-through of "Honeybee," "Never Can Say Goodbye" and "Reach Out, I'll Be There." Of the five new tracks, "All I Need Is Your Sweet Lovin'" and "False Alarm" sound best right now. The **Bataan** (he's dropped the Joe) album is also out, on his new label, Salsoul. Titled "Afrofilpino," it contains a surprisingly interesting version of "Chico & The Man," an uneven but spicy cut called "X-Rated Symphony," a version of **Chicago's** "Woman Don't Want To Love Me" and, of course, "The Bottle (La Botella)." "The Mexican," from **Babe Ruth's** two-year-old debut album, "First Base"

> **❝ I asked his assistant Mimi why Perry Johnson was called "Doctor," she said without a moment's hesitation, "Cause he makes you feel *so good!*" ❞**

your typical DJ. She's the mother of two children (one of whom burst into the room in the middle of the list-giving and had to be firmly hustled out again), teaches second graders during the week and turns DJ weekend nights for the crowd at the Lemon. Of the newer things she's playing, Suzanne's particularly enthusiastic about "Rasha (Part II)," an instrumental by **Garry Davis and the Vendors** (20th Century), which I suppose is of West Indian derivation but sounds like African bluegrass music. Suzanne and her crowd also enjoy the "tremendous camp" of hearing the spoken intro to "Doctor's Orders" at 33 1/3, at which speed **Carol Douglas** sounds quite like a young man.

Also reporting for the first time this week is "Doctor" Perri Johnson, DJ at International Astrodisc discotheque and radio station WDAS-FM in Philadelphia. When I asked Johnson's assistant and alternate DJ, Mimi, why he was called "Doctor," she said without a moment's hesitation, "Cause he makes you feel *so good*!" Johnson calls his particular blend of music Antiwallflowerserum

INTERNATIONAL ASTRODISC, PHILA.
DJ: "Doctor" Perri Johnson

BACK ON THE STREET – Norman Connors (Buddah)
DO YOU LIKE IT – B.T. Express (Scepter)
FIRE – Ohio Players (Mercury)
KEEP ON DANCING – Bohannan (Dakar)
PHILADELPHIA – B.B. King (ABC)
PICK UP THE PIECES – AWB (Atlantic)
PUT THE MUSIC WHERE YOUR MOUTH IS – Olympic Runners (London)
RELEASE YOURSELF – Graham Central Station (Warner Bros.)
RICE 'N' RIBS – Fred Wesley & the New J.B.'s (People)
STREET CORNER SYMPHONY – Kool & the Gang (De-Lite)

CABARET AFTER DARK, SAN FRANCISCO
DJ: Tim Zerr

BLUE EYED SOUL – Carl Douglas (20th Century)
EXPRESS – B.T. Express (Scepter)
HAPPY PEOPLE – Temptations (Gordy)
HIJACK – Herbie Mann (Atlantic)
I'LL BE HOLDING ON – Al Downing (Chess)
JUST AS LONG AS WE'RE TOGETHER – Gloria Scott (Casablanca)
LADY MARMALADE – LaBelle (Epic)
SATIN SOUL – Gene Page (Atlantic)
SHAME, SHAME, SHAME – Shirley And Company (Vibration)
WHAT CAN I DO FOR YOU? – LaBelle (Epic)

PIPPINS, NEW YORK
DJ: Tyrone "DJ" Hollywood

DO YOU LIKE IT – B.T. Express (Scepter)
EXPRESS – B.T. Express (Scepter)
FIRE – Ohio Players (Mercury)
HAPPY PEOPLE – Temptations (Gordy)
I DON'T KNOW IF I CAN MAKE IT – Dawson Smith (Scepter)
LADY MARMALADE – LaBelle (Epic)
PICK UP THE PIECES – AWB (Atlantic)
SATIN SOUL – Gene Page (Atlantic)
SHAKARA OLOJE – Fela Ransome Kuti and the African 70 (Editions Makossa)
WHAT CAN I DO FOR YOU? – LaBelle (Epic)

SQUARE LEMON, NEW YORK (QUEENS)
DJ: Suzanne

BLUE EYED SOUL – Carl Douglas (20th Century)
DOCTOR'S ORDERS – Carol Douglas (Midland International)
EXPRESS – B.T. Express (Scepter)
HEY GIRL, COME AND GET IT – Stylistics (Avco)
I'LL BE HOLDING ON – Al Downing (Chess)
LOVE DON'T YOU GO THROUGH NO CHANGES ON ME – Sister Sledge (Atlantic)
NEVER CAN SAY GOODBYE – Gloria Gaynor (MGM)
SATIN SOUL – Gene Page (Atlantic)
SHAME, SHAME, SHAME – Shirley And Company (Vibration)
TELL ME WHAT YOU WANT – Jimmy Ruffin (Chess)

(Harvest), has been picking up discotheque play in New York at clubs willing to try something unusual and unexpected. The group's latest album, simply "Babe Ruth" (Harvest), contains a cut with a similar feel, a tight version of the instrumental "A Fistful Of Dollars" which should blend very well with the equally Latin-flavored "Mexican." And from the new **Zulema** album ("Zulema" on RCA): a terrific "Standing In The Back Row Of Your Heart" and her excellent version of "Wanna Be Where You Are."

Recommended singles: "Deeper And Deeper" by **Bobby Wilson** (Buddah); **Jay & the Techniques'** version of **Barry White's** "I Feel Love Coming On," played faithfully by a few DJs since its release on Silver Blue last August and now, happily, re-released on Event; and the mostly instrumental B side (Part 2) of the **Dawson Smith** record Tyrone "DJ" Hollywood put on his list, a recession lament called "I Don't Know If I Can Make It" (Scepter). ☻

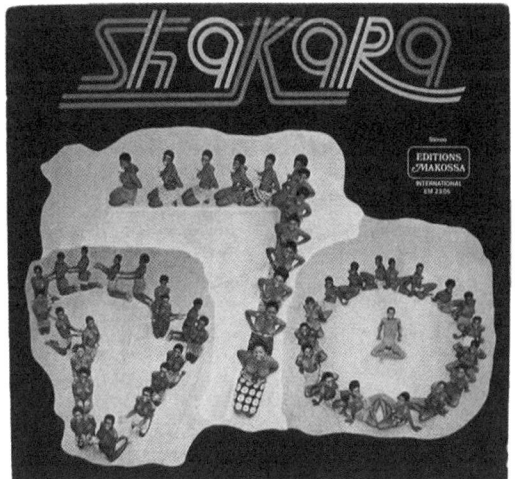

FEBRUARY 1, 1975

Hijack (Continued): The Spanish "Wild Safari" group, **Barrabas**, has left MGM for Atlantic, bringing with them their current import album titled "Release" (Ariola) and containing that "Hijack" cut **Herbie Mann** covered so successfully (on Atlantic). The album is being re-designed, re-titled and scheduled for release here sometime in February. (It's coincidental but appropriate that Murray Brooks, the DJ at Act I in New York who provided the first installment to this continuing story with his report on Barrabas' "Hijack" five weeks ago, is back this week with that original version now planted firmly in his Top 10.) Other albums coming out in the next few weeks: new releases by **Barry White** (20th Century), **Tribe** (ABC) and **George McCrae** (TK).

Far Left Field Alert: Trying to weed out a ridiculous accumulation of albums recently, I discovered a September 1974 release called "The **George Clinton Band** Arrives" (ABC) which contains the most bizarre assortment of music I've come across in some time. Except for the fact that he was born in Chattanooga, Tennessee, George Clinton remains a mystery to me (he is not, however, the George Clinton who produces and writes for **Parliament** and **Funkadelic** – that's another sort of strangeness), and very little is revealed on the album cover, which features those somehow surreal N.A.S.A. photographs of the first footsteps on the moon. Production is credited to **Jerry Fuller**, but his work with **Al Wilson** and others would hardly prepare you for the brilliant flashes of insanity here.

> **❝I discovered "The George Clinton Band Arrives" which contains the most bizarre assortment of music I've come across in some time. He is not the George Clinton who writes for Funkadelic❞**

Most insane: "Jungle Love," which goes through more changes in its six minutes than most albums do in 30. Though the lyrics, concerning the unhappy love affair of a chimpanzee and a cockatoo "under the black Congo sky," tend to slide into cuteness, they are more than made up for in the music, which slides into a little of everything. Animal sounds, bird calls, "native" chanting and synthesizer groans are sprinkled here and there but the killer segment comes about two-thirds of the way through when the band suddenly breaks into a strong chant, elephant calls are heard and the hard pounding of drums takes over. This is interrupted by a rush of brassy big band music which then fades in to back the drumming and a false ending – well, you get the point.

Altogether, it's oddly reminiscent of **Everyday People's** stunning "I Like What I Like" (Paramount) and some of that beautifully off-the-wall feeling is preserved on a few of the other **George Clinton Band** cuts, notably, "Hold On To Your Lady," "Please Don't Run From Me" and the chilling "Free Lover." This is definitely not for most tastes, but Wayne Thorberg (Donkin's Inn, Los Angeles) and Luis Romero (Flamingo, New York) have been springing "Jungle Love" on unsuspecting people whenever they feel like confusing the dance floor. Worth investigating, if only for a rush.

And from the new albums: **Vernon Burch's** fine debut, containing "Frame Of Mind," "And You Call That Love," "Changes" (also released as a 45), "Ain't Gonna Tell Nobody" and the title cut "I'll Be Your Sunshine" (on United Artists); "Don't Close the Book," "Do Unto Others" and especially the nearly eight-minute "Castles" on the **Future's** debut, "Castles In The Sky" (Buddah); "What Am I Gonna Do" (up to a certain point) on **Barbara Mason's** "Love's The Thing" (Buddah); **Joel Webster's** "Sing My Song For You" on his "Elixir" album (Crossover); "Can't Live This Way" by **Barnaby Bye**, a Ronald Coles pick from their new "Touch" album (Atlantic) and "Everyone's A Star" (where have I heard that before?) on the **Intruders** album, "Energy of love" (TSOP), which also contains a rather left field pick of Murray Brooks', "Be On Time."

Notes on 45s: **Dooley Silverspoon's** great "Bump Me Baby" (Cotton) has been picked up for distribution by Arista, which means it should be more widely available soon. The **Blackbyrds'** new single, "Walking In Rhythm"/"The Baby" has been pressed in special copies marked "For Discos Only" and containing the album-cut length "Rhythm" and a 4:30 version of "The Baby." For its commercial release, "Rhythm" was cut to 2:54.

Recommended: "Shining Star," the latest from **Earth, Wind & Fire** (Columbia); **Greg Perry's** "Come On Down (Get Your Head Out Of The Clouds)" (Casablanca); the long version (4:15) of "Love Is Everywhere" by

ACT I, NEW YORK
DJ: Murray Brooks

THE BABY – Blackbyrds (Fantasy)

TELL ME WHAT YOU WANT – Jimmy Ruffin (Chess)

HIJACK – Barrabas (Ariola import)

I AM LOVE (PART II) – Jackson 5 (Motown)

I JUST CAN'T SAY GOODBYE – Philly Devotions (Columbia)

SATIN SOUL – Gene Page (Atlantic)

STREET CORNER SYMPHONY – Kool & the Gang (De-Lite)

SUPERNATURAL THING – Ben E. King (Atlantic)

WAITIN' FOR THE RAIN – Philly Sound (Phil-L.A. of Soul)

WHAT CAN I DO FOR YOU? – LaBelle (Epic)

EXODUS, PHILADELPHIA
DJ: Ray Collazo

THE BOTTLE – Gil Scott-Heron (Strata East)

DEVOTION – Earth, Wind & Fire (Columbia)

DO IT 'TIL YOU'RE SATISFIED – B.T. Express (Scepter)

DO IT FLUID – Blackbyrds (Fantasy)

FIRE – Ohio Players (Mercury)

LADY MARMALADE – LaBelle (Epic)

PAPA DON'T TAKE NO MESS – James Brown (Polydor)

RELEASE YOURSELF – Graham Central Station (Warner)

SMOKE – Ohio Players (Mercury)

SUN GODDESS – Ramsey Lewis (Columbia)

SOUND MACHINE, NEW YORK
DJ: Joe Palminteri

E-MAN BOOGIE – Jimmy Castor Bunch (Atlantic)

EXPRESS – B.T. Express (Scepter)

HIJACK – Herbie Mann (Atlantic)

HONEYBEE/NEVER CAN SAY GOODBYE/ REACH OUT I'LL BE THERE – Gloria Gaynor (MGM)

JUST AS LONG AS WE'RE TOGETHER – Gloria Scott (Casablanca)

LA-LA-LOVE CHAINS – Silver, Platinum & Gold (Warner Bros.)

LOVE DON'T YOU GO THROUGH NO CHANGES ON ME – Sister Sledge (Atco)

PAIN RELIEVER – Sister Sledge (Atco)

SHAME, SHAME, SHAME – Shirley And Company (Vibration)

WHAT CAN I DO FOR YOU? – LaBelle (Epic)

LA DIRECTOIRE, NEW ORLEANS
DJ: David Wolf

FIRE – Ohio Players (Mercury)

GET DANCIN' – Disco Tex & the Sex-O-Lettes (Chelsea)

GET DOWN – Kay Gees (Bang)

HEY POCKY-A-WAY – Meters (Reprise)

I'M A PUSHOVER – K.C. & the Sunshine Band (TK)

LADY MARMALADE – LaBelle (Epic)

PICK UP THE PIECES – AWB (Atlantic)

SHOORAH SHOORAH – Betty Wright (Alston)

SOUL SISTER – Wet Willie (Capricorn)

YOU'RE THE FIRST, THE LAST, MY EVERYTHING – Barry White (20th Century)

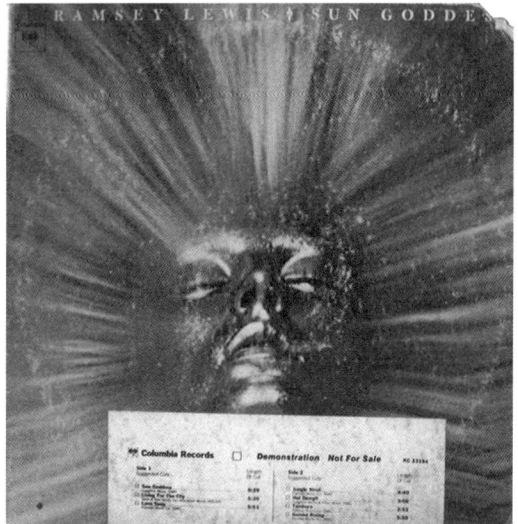

City Limits (TSOP) which my west coast correspondent is crazy about; Isis' about-time knock-out "Bobbi & Maria," a two-part (vocal/instrumental) song about the love between "a woman and a lady" (on Buddah); **Carl Carlton's** "Smokin' Room" (ABC); **Eddie Harris'** "I Need Some Money," another recession lament (the chorus: "Everything is so damn high") (Atlantic); and, for those of us who had previously ignored the album cut, **Van McCoy and The Soul City Symphony's** nicely-turned "Boogie Down" (Avco). And Joe Palminteri, DJ at the recently redecorated Sound Machine in New York, says **Donny Beaumont's** "Look But Don't Touch" (Mercury), with a **Stylistics** feel, went over very well with his more-than-capacity re-opening night crowd. ✪

FEBRUARY 8, 1975

Latin music – even hot New York *salsa*, which is the steamiest dance music outside of Africa – may not be everyone's idea of discotheque music, but an increasing number of clubs in New York and other cities with large Latin, primarily Puerto Rican, communities are scattering records by **Eddie Palmieri**, **Larry Harlow**, **Tito Puente** and others in between **B. T. Express**, **Carl Douglas** and **LaBelle**. Because Latin is an abrupt change of pace (and rhythm) from the predominant disco sound and because it dictates a different and more formalized style of dancing, its popularity on a discotheque level is restricted to Latin dancers and fans. But in New York, especially at largely black or black-and-Latin clubs, there are plenty of both, with the DJs themselves often the biggest Latin fans of all. Though maybe only six or seven Latin cuts are played in a night – usually in groups of two or three back-to-back and most often at the request of dancers who "can Latin" – the music turns on the dance floor in a whole new way. Even if there're only 10 couples out there, they generate the kind of electricity that even the observers can enjoy.

The following is a list of some of the popular Latin cuts played in discotheque right now. Some are new, some are classics; nearly all of them run 5 minutes or more, with Eddie Palmieri's "Un Dia Bonito" reaching 14:20 (though only the last half is really danceable). The list was compiled with the help of the following DJs, each of whom was asked to contribute his favorites: Gary Broaddus (Leviticus), Murray Brooks (Act I), Paul Casella (The Monastery), Joe Palminteri (Sound Machine), Hector Reyes (formerly at the Stardust Ballroom) and Aris Rodrigues (Twinkie Zone) – all in New York – and Ray Collazo from Exodus in Philadelphia who also has a Latin show on radio station WIBF-FM there.

PUERTO RICO – Eddie Palmieri
(Mango: from the "Sentido" lp)
IQUI CON IQUI – Ricardo Ray
(Tico/Alegre: from the "Jala Jala Boogaloo" lp)
CHANCHULLO – Fania All Stars
(Fania: from the "Latin-Soul-Rock" lp)
PICADILLO – Cal Tjader & Eddie Palmieri
(Fantasy: from the "El Sonido Nuevo"lp)
TORO MATA and CANTO A LA HABANA – Celia Cruz & Johnny Pacheco (Vaya: from the "Celia & Johnny" lp)
NO HAY AMIGO – Orchestra Harlow (Fania: from the "Salsa" lp)

VIBE MAMBO – Tito Puente
(Tico: from the "Tico Unlimited" lp)
NADA DE TI and UN DIA BONITO – Eddie Palmieri
(Coco: from "The Sun of Latin Music" lp)
NO, QUE VA A LLORAR – Andy Harlow
(Vaya: from the "Sorpresa La Flauta" lp)
EL NEGRO Y RAY – Ray Barretto
(Riverside: from the "Latino" lp)
LA HIJA DE LOLA – Charlie Palmieri
(Alegre: from the "El Gigante Del Teclado" lp)

Speaking of Latin, you might add to that list a new single by **Willie Colon**, one of the youngest of the Latin stars, who seems headed in the "Salsoul" direction **Bataan** has taken. Check out the instrumental B side of his 45, titled "MC^2 (Theme Realidades)" and a surprising blend of old and new Latin and soul/jazz styles (on Fania). And for those DJs having difficulty getting Latin product, Alex Masucci at Fania in New York suggests you call him.

Buari, the African performer whose album was getting advance exposure in some New York discos while he was shopping for a label, has found one. He's been signed to RCA.

Notes on the Top 10 lists: David Todd from the Adam's Apple in New York is so enthusiastic about "Handle It," a nicely upbeat cut from the **Sylvers'** 1973 "The Sylvers II" album (MGM/Pride), that he's trying to get MGM to bring it back as a single. "Aggravation," a strong, brassy, rock-styled cut by **Martha Velez**, is on Vincent Carleo's list this week, though it, too, is from 1973. The song, from Velez' "Matinee Weepers" album (Sire), is apparently a favorite of Flamingo DJs and their crowd.

The essential new cuts: Of an astonishingly good batch, my favorite is "Bad Luck" by **Harold Melvin & the Bluenotes** (from "To Be True" on Philadelphia International), which pumps for more than 6 minutes and ends with the best rap on record since ''I'll Always Love My Mama." Also on the Bluenotes album: "Where Are All My Friends" and "Nobody Could Take My Place." Just as Hot: "Glasshouse" and "Shakey Ground" by the **Temptations** (from "A Song For You" on Gordy); **Michael Jackson's** beautiful "We're Almost There" and "Just A Little Bit Of You" (from "Forever, Michael," with the heart throb cover on Motown); "Pain Reliever,"

> **❝ Hot New York salsa, the steamiest dance music outside of Africa, may not be everyone's idea of discotheque music, but an increasing number of clubs are scattering records by Latin artists ❞**

THE ALLEY, NEW YORK (QUEENS)
DJ: Frank Strivelli

BLUE EYED SOUL – Carl Douglas (20th Century)
DOCTOR'S ORDERS – Carol Douglas
(Midland International)
EXPRESS – B.T. Express (Scepter)
HAPPY PEOPLE – Temptations (Gordy)
HIJACK – Herbie Mann (Atlantic)
**HONEYBEE/NEVER CAN SAY GOODBYE/ REACH OUT I'LL
BE THERE** – Gloria Gaynor (MGM)
LOVE DON'T YOU GO THROUGH NO CHANGES ON ME –
Sister Sledge (Atco)
SHAME, SHAME, SHAME – Shirley And Company
(Vibration)
WHAT CAN I DO FOR YOU? – LaBelle (Epic)
WHERE IS THE LOVE? – Betty Wright (Alston)

ADAM'S APPLE, NEW YORK
DJ: David Todd

GLASSHOUSE – Temptations (Gordy)
HANDLE IT – Sylvers (MGM)
**HONEYBEE/NEVER CAN SAY GOODBYE/ REACH OUT
I'LL BE THERE** – Gloria Gaynor (MGM)
I JUST CAN'T SAY GOODBYE – Philly Devotions
(Columbia)
JUST AS LONG AS WE'RE TOGETHER – Gloria Scott
(Casablanca)
LOVE CORPORATION – Hues Corporation (RCA)
POTENTIAL – Jimmy Castor Bunch (Atlantic)
PROTECT OUR LOVE – Sister Sledge (Atco)
SHAME, SHAME, SHAME – Shirley And Company
(Vibration)
THAT'S WHAT I WANT FOR YOU BABY – B.T. Express
(Scepter)

DIAMOND HORSESHOE, LOS ANGELES
DJ: "RC" Michaels

EXPRESS – B.T. Express (Scepter)
LOVE YOU JUST AS LONG AS I CAN – Free Spirit (Chess)
MIGHTY CLOUD OF JOY – Mighty Clouds of Joy (ABC)
NEVER CAN SAY GOODBYE – Gloria Gaynor (MGM)
PICK UP THE PIECES – AWB (Atlantic)
SOME KIND OF WONDERFUL – Grand Funk (Capitol)
WHAT A WONDERFUL THING WE HAVE – Fabulous
Rhinestones (Just Sunshine)
WHEN WILL I SEE YOU AGAIN – Three Degrees
(Phila. Intl.)
WHERE'S YOUR LOVE BEEN – Sandra Rhodes (Fantasy)
YOU GOT THE LOVE – Rufus (ABC)

FLAMINGO, NEW YORK
DJ: Vincent Carleo

AGGRAVATION – Martha Velez (Sire)
THE BOTTLE (LA BOTELLA) – Bataan (Salsoul)
CRYSTAL WORLD – Crystal Grass (Philips import)
E-MAN BOOGIE – Jimmy Castor Bunch (Atlantic)
I'LL BE HOLDING ON – Al Downing (Chess)
NEVER CAN SAY GOODBYE – Gloria Gaynor (MGM)
REACH OUT, I'LL BE THERE – Gloria Gaynor (MGM)
SATIN SOUL – Gene Page (Atlantic)
WHAT CAN I DO FOR YOU? – Labell (Epic)
WHERE IS THE LOVE? – Betty Wright (Alston)

"Protect Our Love" and the title song from the debut **Sister Sledge** album, "Circle of Love" (Atco); and, of course, "E-Man Boogie," now out on **Jimmy Castor Bunch's** "Butt of Course... " (Atlantic). Left field: **American Gypsy's** "Angel Eyes," another bizarre, full-of-changes cut that's exciting if only because it's a change from the too-often-predictable disco ready-mades that are coming out. The cut has been out in Europe nearly half a year, made in Holland by an American group that sounds like **Sly**, **Hendrix** and a lot of other people, but puts the influences together very neatly. Now their album, "American Gypsy," is out here on Chess and is well worth looking into.

Singles: The **Hues Corporation's** new "Love Corporation" sounds even better than "Rock The Boat" and should go just as far (on RCA). And a young man named **Valentino** has put out a two-sided record on the Gaiee label, "I Was Born This Way" /"Liberation," that's already causing a sensation and is as essential right this minute as the Hues Corporation. Also: "Let's Get Into Something" by **Richmond Extension**, a **Van McCoy** production on Polydor; the **Al Foster Band's** Latin-flavored instrumental, "The Night Of The Wolf" (long version: 3:55, on Roulette); the instrumental side of **Leon Collins'** "I Just Wanna Say I Love You" (Elf). ✍

FEBRUARY 15, 1975

RCA left four tracks from the forthcoming **Carol Douglas** album on Midland International at a small sampling of New York discotheques last week, two weeks in advance of their commercial release. The cuts, pressed on a one-sided record marked "Specially Prepared for Disco Use," include a 5:25 version of "Doctor's Orders" which injects a rather thin instrumental break just before the song's second spoken segment. The other cuts are much more successful, especially "I Fell In Love With Love," which has a wonderful '60s girl group edge to it: the **Chiffons** with a disco production. "All Night Long," the song that asks the question, "Will we make it tonight?" also has a '60s feel, if only because of its shouted choruses and innocent obsession with sex. And the fourth track, "A Hurricane is Coming Tonite," has its ups and downs in four minutes but at its best – when Douglas is shouting "Tornado warnings are out" – it'll stir up any dance floor. Watch out for Hurricane Carol.

Another Midland International release dropped off for reaction at several discotheques in advance of its release this week was "Save Me" by a German group called **Silverbird**. Basically an instrumental with a girl chorus that drifts in on gorgeous waves of strings, every once in a while singing, "Save me, save me, I am falling in love," it's one of the sweetest records I've heard since "Love's Theme" and is the Disco File pick for the Single of the Moment.

> **" Steak, at Newark's Highest Peak is trying the Temptations' long homage to Kahlil Gibran, "The Prophet," on a slightly speeded up turntable because the track itself is so beautifully produced "**

While I'm picking favorites, here are three from far left field: "I Fell In Love With God," a Philadelphia-style gospel song by **Nat Townsley, Jr.** (Peacock/ABC) that is so passionate it doesn't matter that you can't dance to it. The B side is more high-spirited, though: a strong shout version of "Old Time Religion" which uses a number of disco tricks in its production and could be this year's "I Got It." The **21st Century's** "Remember the Rain?" (RCA) is the sort of pure, falsetto-led, adolescent love song I find irresistible – the best in

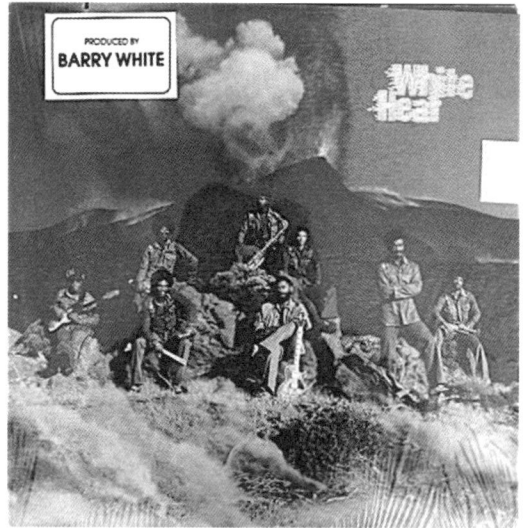

the genre since "Love Jones" by **Brighter Side of Darkness** – but, again, it's not disco material. Instead, try the B side here too, a somewhat gimmicky version of "You're My Only World," a cut from the **George Clinton Band** album mentioned here two weeks ago. Finally, there's a single that's been out since late last year called "The Joneses" by **S.O.U.L.** (Musicor), a two-part record (total time: 7:44) about drug addiction (the ironic chorus: "Try it, you'll like it") that has the sort of Latin beat that may not go over everywhere but should be heard anyway.

And if you think those are off-the-wall, here are some of the new reports from DJs this week: Bobby Guttadaro at Le Jardin played **Walter Heath's** "I Thought You Might Like To Know" – a pleasant, very laid-back cut from his album "You Know You're Wrong, Don't Ya Brother" (Buddah) – to what he described as a "wow" response and now feels the cut is "going to be very big." Guttadaro is also playing **Swamp Dogg's** 7:20 "The Mind Does The Dancing While The Body Pulls The Strings" (from his new Island album, "Have You Heard This Story??") which doesn't entirely live up to its title, but should serve as introduction to this bizarre man's work. "Steak" at Newark's Highest Peak is trying the **Temptations'** long homage to Kahlil Gibran, "The Prophet" (from the "A Song For You" album, Gordy), on a slightly speeded-up turntable because the track itself is so beautifully produced. And he's revived "Super Rod" by **Crown Heights Affair** (RCA) because

LE JARDIN, NEW YORK
DJ: Bobby Guttadaro

BAD LUCK – Harold Melvin & the Bluenotes
(Phila. Intl.)
E-MAN BOOGIE – Jimmy Castor Bunch (Atlantic)
FRAME OF MIND – Vernon Burch(UA)
GLASSHOUSE – Temptations (Gordy)
HIJACK – Herbie Mann (Atlantic)
LOVE CORPORATION – Hues Corporation (RCA)
ONCE YOU GET STARTED – Rufus (ABC)
PROTECT OUR LOVE – Sister Sledge (Atco)
WHAT CAN I DO FOR YOU? – LaBelle (Epic)
WHERE IS THE LOVE? – Betty Wright (Alston)

HIGHEST PEAK, NEWARK, NEW JERSEY
DJ: "Steak"

BLUE EYED SOUL – Carl Douglas (20th Century)
BOOGIE OOGIE – Hot Ice (Atlantic)
E-MAN BOOGIE – Jimmy Castor Bunch (Atlantic)
HIJACK – Herbie Mann (Atlantic)
HONEYBEE/NEVER CAN SAY GOODBYE/REACH OUT –
Gloria Gaynor (MGM)
JUST AS LONG AS WE'RE TOGETHER – Gloria Scott
(Casablanca)
KUNG FU MAN – Ultrafunk (Contempo)
MIRRORS OF MY MIND – Jacksons (Motown)
THE ROAD TO LOVE – Mandrill (Polydor)
SATIN SOUL – Gene Page (Atlantic)

SUNDOWN and ZANZIBAR, WASHINGTON
DJ: Bob Evans

THE BOTTLE (LA BOTELLA) – Bataan (Salsoul)
DISCO QUEEN – Hot Chocolate (Big Tree)
DOCTOR'S ORDERS – Carol Douglas
(Midland International)
E-MAN BOOGIE – Jimmy Castor Bunch (Atlantic)
EXPRESS – B.T. Express (Scepter)
FIRE – Ohio Players (Mercury)
HIJACK – Herbie Mann (Atlantic)
HONEYBEE/NEVER CAN SAY GOODBYE/REACH OUT –
Gloria Gaynor (MGM)
LOVE CORPORATION – Hues Corporation (RCA)
SHAME, SHAME, SHAME – Shirley And Company
(Vibration)

LEVITICUS, NEW YORK
DJ: Gary Broaddus

GEMINI – Miracles (Tamla)
GET READY FOR THE GET DOWN – Willie Hutch
(Motown)
IF THAT'S THE WAY YOU FEEL – White Heat (RCA)
I'M A WOMAN – Rufus (ABC)
ONCE YOU GET STARTED – Rufus (ABC)
SHAKEY GROUND – Temptations (Gordy)
SUN GODDESS – Ramsey Lewis (Columbia)
THAT'S WHAT I WANT FOR YOU BABY – B.T. Express
(Scepter)
TRY IT, YOU'LL LIKE IT – Willie Hutch (Motown)
WOMAN DON'T WANT TO LOVE ME – Bataan (Salsoul)

he finds the instrumental perfect for the Hustle, a
dance I'm already tired of hearing about. Gary Broaddus
at Levitucus in New York was talking about two fine
Bobbi Humphrey cuts, "Fun House" (now a single)
and "New York Times" (from "Satin Doll" on Blue
Note), which seem rather too loose for disco dancing,
but then he seems capable of getting his crowd to
dance to practically anything.

Among the new albums, the surprise of the week was
Melissa Manchester's rich "Melissa" (Arista), with a
strong, sexy version of **Stevie Wonder's** "Love Havin'
You Around;" a special tribute to Wonder called
"Stevie's Wonder" and done in his style; "Party Music"
and "Just Too Many People." There are elements of
Laura Nyro, **Dusty Springfield** and Wonder here but
for the first time Manchester is strong enough to both
support and overcome her influences with a glowing
personal style – and the help of producer **Vini Ponda**.
Catching Up: **Betty Wright's** "High Voltage" album
(Alston) just arrived, several months late, but anyone
who hasn't picked up on her nearly-five-minute
"Where Is The Love" is missing, as I have for too
long, one of the hottest album cuts out now.

Recommended: **Ecstasy, Passion & Pain's** new single,
"One Beautiful Day" (Roulette), the trademark EP&P
sound continued under the production of **Bobby
Martin**; "Sweeter" a **Major Lance** song in a whole
new style, produced by Lance and Philadelphia's
Stan Watson (on Playboy); "Back From The Dead"
by **Bobby Byrd**, formerly with the **James Brown**
entourage, now working with the Miami Sound people
(producer: **Clarence Reid**) and definitely in top shape,
if a little morbid ("You gave me a new start/like pulling
the stake from my heart," he sings) – also check out
the powerful B side, "The Way To Get Down"
(International Brothers/T.K.); "Smokin'," a driving,
two-part record by **Metropolis** (Ebony Sounds) and, at
the other extreme, **Del Shannon's** "Runaway" as done
by the **Rhodes Kids** (GRC), truly bubblegum disco or is
it disco bubblegum? And **John Gary Williams'** "The
Whole Damn World Is Going Crazy," just reissued on
Stax nearly a year after its original appearance, is highly
recommended. It's a message we can all believe in. ◐

Atlantic Records is pulling back their **Gene Page** single, "All Our Dreams Coming True"/"Cream Corner," and re-issuing it with "Satin Soul," cut from its album length of 4:23 to 2:56, as the record's B side. The **Love Unlimited Orchestra** version of this **Barry White** instrumental is, of course, already on a single (time: 3:25, on 20th Century), but Page's track is the one most reported by discotheques. 20th already has a giant-step lead on the charts, but Atlantic, better late than never, could do some quick catching up with this new combination.

Epic Records is re-releasing one of the great disco singles, **Brenda & the Tabulations'** knockout "Little Bit Of Love." The song became an underground disco hit after its release three years ago but was probably ahead of its time for the general public, whatever that is. Now, however, it's very much on time and Brenda shouldn't have much trouble following **Carol Douglas** and **Gloria Gaynor** up the charts.

Mimi, who plays at Philadelphia's International Astra Disc and has the sexiest telephone voice I know (after Hector Reyes), reports two very new records on her top 10 this week. One is yet another version of **Gil Scott-Heron's** durable "The Bottle" by a group called **Brute** who are, as yet, not signed to any label. Mimi says a dub of the record was left at the club last week and it caught on immediately. It is, according to Philadelphia's "Disco Queen," "dynamite," "very funky," about seven minutes long and a mix of vocals and instrumental. The other record is by **Edwin Birdsong**, who has been around for some time and whose "Survival" is also about a week old at IAD. The cut, approximately eight minutes as an album track and cut to nearly six for a planned single release (on Bamboo), is apparently super upbeat and, Mimi assured me, "the best thing you ever heard in your entire life." That remains to be seen – or heard.

Also reported and recommended: "Get Down" by the **Kay-Gees** (Gang) which appears on Mimi's list; "Run And Hide" by the **Philadelphia Flyers**, picked up in England by Casablanca and available in a Part I/Part II format or on promotional copies with the total 5:55 length on one side – mentioned in glowing terms by both Bob Gordon of Nepentha and Doug Riddick of Opus I, both in New York; "Nefertiti," a long (4:07) Afro-Latin style instrumental by a group called **Wisdom** (Adelia) and **Al Green's** delightful new single "L-O-V-E (Love)" (Hi) – both brought to my attention by Richie Kaczor at New York's popular Hollywood; and **Betty Everett's** "Keep It Up" (Fantasy), a **Gene & Billy Page** production now available "For Discos Only" in a longer 3:23 version and very fine – DJ Artie Feldman couldn't wait to get to his turntables at Our Den in Chicago to play it some more.

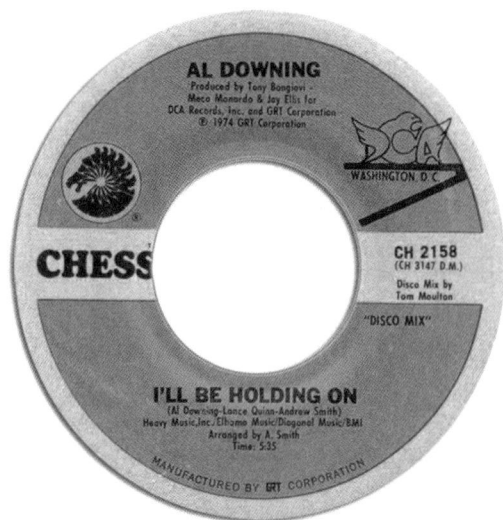

NEPENTHA, NEW YORK
DJ: Bob Gordon

AND YOU CALL THAT LOVE – Vernon Burch (UA)
BAD LUCK – Harold Melvin & the Bluenotes (Phila. Intl.)
BLUE EYED SOUL – Carl Douglas (20th Century)
HIJACK – Herbie Mann (Atlantic)
A HURRICANE IS COMING TONITE – Carol Douglas (Midland International lp cut)
GLASSHOUSE – Temptations (Gordy)
LOVE CORPORATION – Hues Corporation (RCA)
PAIN RELIEVER – Sister Sledge (Atco)
REAL GOOD PEOPLE – Gloria Gaynor (MGM)
WHERE IS THE LOVE? – Betty Wright (Alston)

INTERNATIONAL ASTRO DISC, PHILA.
DJ: Mimi

THE BOTTLE – Brute (not commercially available)
BUS STOP – Oliver Sain (Abet)
DO YOU LIKE IT – B.T. Express (Scepter)
E-MAN BOOGIE – Jimmy Castor Bunch (Atlantic)
HIJACK – Herbie Mann (Atlantic)
GET DOWN – Kay Gees (Gang)
LOPSY LU – Stanley Clarke (Nemperor)
SHACKIN' UP – Barbara Mason (Buddah)
SHINING STAR – Earth, Wind & Fire (Columbia)
SURVIVAL – Edwin Birdsong (Bamboo)

OUR DEN, CHICAGO
DJ: Artie Feldman

THE BOTTLE (LA BOTELLA) – Bataan (Salsoul)
EXPRESS – B.T. Express (Scepter)
FIRE – Ohio Players (Mercury)
GET DANCIN' – Disco Tex & the Sex-O-Lettes (Chelsea)
HONEYBEE/NEVER CAN SAY GOODBYE/ REACH OUT – Gloria Gaynor (MGM lp cuts)
I JUST CAN'T SAY GOODBYE – Philly Devotions (Columbia)
LADY MARMALADE – LaBelle (Epic)
SATIN SOUL – Gene Page (Atlantic)
SHAME, SHAME, SHAME – Shirley And Company (Vibration)
THAT'S THE KIND OF LOVE I'VE GOT FOR YOU – Rita Jean Bodine (20th Century)

HOLLYWOOD, NEW YORK
DJ: Richie Kaczor

BAD LUCK – Harold Melvin & the Bluenotes (Phila. Intl.)
BLUE EYED SOUL – Carl Douglas (20th Century)
HEY THERE SEXY LADY – Hank Ballard (Stang)
HIJACK – Herbie Mann (Atlantic)
HIJACK – Barrabas (Ariola import)
I'LL BE HOLDING ON – Al Downing (Chess)
LANSANA'S PRIESTESS – Donald Byrd (Blue Note)
SHAME, SHAME, SHAME – Shirley And Company (Vibration)
WALKING IN RHYTHM – Blackbyrds (Fantasy)
WHAT CAN I DO FOR YOU? – LaBelle (Epic)
WHERE IS THE LOVE? – Betty Wright (Alston)

Shopping List: "Dynomite" by **Tony Camillo's Bazuka** (A&M), a disco instrumental whose long version runs to 5:10; another instrumental, this time more in the lush **Barry White** mold and quite beautiful, by **LeRoy Hutson** and titled "All Because Of You" (Curtom – vocal on the A side); "Hook It Up," a great **Van McCoy** production for the **Choice Four** (RCA); **Hot Line's** "How Funky Do You Do It" in two parts (Red Coach); **Innervision's** bouncy "Honey Baby (Be Mine)" (Private Stock) and a brightened, re-mixed version of **Barry Manilow's** "It's A Miracle," already getting some disco play as an album cut and now a 3:15 single (Arista). Note: The name of the group performing last week's highly recommended "Save Me" (with an even longer B side, "Save Me Again") has been changed from **Silverbird**, which already belonged to an American group, to **Silver Convention** – and will appear that way on subsequent pressings of the single. ◉

> **" Brenda & the Tabulations became an underground disco hit but was probably ahead of its time for the general public, whatever that is. Now, however, it's very much on time "**

News & Notes: **Bataan's** Salsoul Records has been picked up for distribution by Epic, so his current single, "The Bottle (La Botella)," and the "Afrofilipino" album on which it appears, will soon be more widely available on an Epic/Salsoul label, already being shipped... Cotton Records (distributed by Arista) has pressed a 4-minute version of **Dooley Silverspoon's** ecstatic "Bump Me Baby" on a specially designed disco DJ label marked "prepared for Discos only" and also shipping immediately.

Titanic, the French rock group which has had considerable success on the discotheque level, is showing up in a number of stores on a Canadian import album titled "Macumba!" (Columbia Canada) which includes "Rain 2000," "Sultana" and the title cut – all in versions longer than their previous American single releases. "Sultana," in particular, is a classic disco instrumental and is in itself worth any trouble you may have locating the album... Producer **Norman Harris** (for W.M.O.T. Productions) is working with **Blue Magic** on a long re-make of **Ultra High Frequency's** great "We're On The Right Track" for inclusion on their next Atlantic album, tentatively titled "13 Blue Magic Lane." Harris produced the original UHF single (on Wand) with **Stan Watson**.

The Broaddus brothers can always be depended on for an out-of-the-ordinary (if not off-the-wall) list, and James, known at New York's Liquid Smoke as "Tank," reports cuts by **Grand Funk**, **Loggins & Messina** and the **Doobie Brothers** this week along with the more familiar disco fare. The most interesting of his unexpected selections, however, is **Honk's** "Hesitation" (Epic), a light, attractive song which doesn't quite sustain its fine instrumental opening but comes through nicely nevertheless. The song, which has a kind of **Average White Band** feeling, is available on a single but "Tank" prefers its album length (4:05) for the saxophone solo toward the end. Speaking of **AWB**, Broaddus is also playing "Person To Person" (from their Atlantic album) which Charles Richardson at Extension 225 in Stockton California, put on his top 10 along with "Pick Up The Pieces." Richardson says people at the club come up to him as "Pieces" is ending and ask him to leave the needle where it is so they can slide right into the following cut, "Person to Person" – a natural follow-up. "The **Carol Douglas** Album" (Midland International)

is out now and, in addition to the cuts already made available on that DJ pressing – "A Hurricane Is Coming Tonite," "I Fell In Love With Love" and "Will We Make It Tonight" – I'd recommend "A Friend In Need," a bright, 4-mlnute tribute to the pleasures and satisfactions of friendship. And from **Dionne Warwicke's** "Then Came You" album (Warner Bros.), a beautifully high-spirited track called "Take It From Me" has become my favorite of the moment. A few lines (by writer/producer **Jerry Ragovoy**): "I'm jumping inside with expectation/I feel it throughout my circulation/ I never felt such anticipation." Wonderful.

Recommended 45s: Obviously, **Barry White's** latest "What Am I Gonna Do With you" (20th Century) heads the list, especially because it's more pumping and up than his recent releases – listen for his scream about midway through; **Gwen McCrae's** new mid-tempo "Rockin' Chair" (Cat), originally made by **Clarence Reid** (who co-produced here) and mentioned in this column a few weeks back by South Carolina DJ Doug Douglas – this version features Gwen's husband **George McCrae** on the backgrounds; the **Temptations** "Shakey Ground" (Gordy), taken from their recent album; and the B side of **Jimmy Jackson's** "Footsteps In The Shadows" (Buddah), an instrumental version of that song credited to the **Kantlose Orchestra and Chorus** (arranged and conducted by **Gene Page**). ✪

❝ Cotton Records has pressed a 4-minute version of Dooley Silverspoon's ecstatic "Bump Me Baby" on a specially designed disco DJ label marked "prepared for Discos only" ❞

PLAYERS, UNION CITY, N.J.
DJ: Steve Santoro
BAD LUCK – Harold Melvin & the Bluenotes (Phila. Intl.)
BLUE EYED SOUL – Carl Douglas (20th Century)
GIRLS – Moments & Whatnauts (Stang)
HIJACK – Herbie Mann (Atlantic)
HONEYBEE/NEVER CAN SAY GOODBYE/ REACH OUT – Gloria Gaynor (MGM)
I JUST CAN'T SAY GOODBYE – Philly Devotions (Columbia)
I'LL BE HOLDING ON – Al Downing (Chess)
LOVE DON'T YOU GO THROUGH NO CHANGES ON ME – Sister Sledge (Atco)
ONE BEAUTIFUL DAY – Ecstasy, Passion & Pain (Roulette)
SHAME, SHAME, SHAME – Shirley And Company (Vibration)

LIQUID SMOKE, NEW YORK
DJ: James "Tank" Broaddus
BAD LUCK – Harold Melvin & the Bluenotes (Phila. Intl.)
EYES OF SILVER – Doobie Brothers (Warner Bros.)
GET A HOLD – Loggins & Messina (Columbia)
HESITATION – Honk (Epic)
HIJACK – Herbie Mann (Atlantic)
ONCE YOU GET STARTED – Rufus (ABC)
RUFUSIZED – Rufus (ABC)
SATIN SOUL – Gene Page (Atlantic)
SOME KIND OF WONDERFUL – Grand Funk (Capitol)
SUPERNATURAL THING – Ben E. King (Atlantic)

BON SOIR, NEW YORK
DJ: Lee Pineiro
BAD LUCK – Harold Melvin & the Bluenotes (Phila. Intl.)
CASTLES – Futures (Buddah)
E-MAN BOOGIE – Jimmy Castor Bunch (Atlantic)
HIJACK – Herbie Mann (Atlantic)
IT'S A MIRACLE – Barry Manilow (Arista)
LANSANA'S PRIESTESS – Donald Byrd (Blue Note)
PAIN RELIEVER – Sister Sledge (Atco)
PURSUIT OF THE PIMPMOBILE – Isaac Hayes (Enterprise)
WHAT CAN I DO FOR YOU? – LaBelle (Epic)
WHERE IS THE LOVE? – Betty Wright (Alston)

EXTENSION 225, STOCKTON, C.A.
DJ: Charles Richardson
BAD LUCK – Harold Melvin & the Bluenotes (Phila. Intl.)
BUS STOP – Oliver Sain (Abet)
FIRE – Ohio Players (Mercury)
PERSON TO PERSON – AWB (Atlantic)
PICK UP THE PIECES – AWB (Atlantic)
SHAKEY GROUND – Temptations (Gordy)
SHINING STAR – Earth, Wind & Fire (Columbia)
SIGN FOR ME DAD – Bloodstone (London)
SUN GODDESS – Ramsey Lewis (Columbia)
SUPERNATURAL THING – Ben E. King (Atlantic)

MARCH 8, 1975

This week – mostly out of plain curiosity but partly in an effort to find out, albeit on a small scale, if increased record company interest in the discotheque DJ had changed things – I asked the four DJs polled whether they're still buying records and, if so, exactly what they'd bought most recently. Since DJs outside of New York and Los Angeles are usually the last to be added to promotional mailing lists and the first to complain about both the lack of attention from companies and the absence of disco-oriented record stores in their area, I was surprised that the only person who said he didn't buy records was Lynn Cook, who plays at a club called Bayou Landing in Atlanta. He said that what records he didn't get in the mail he picked up from cooperative distributors in Atlanta.

At the other end of the spectrum, there's Howard Metz at Studio One in L.A. who gets a great many records from the companies (both by pick-up and by mail) but still finds himself spending about $15 a week to get everything he needs. On the day we spoke, he'd just put out $16.09 for a wide variety of records new and old ranging from the Mickey Mouse Club theme song to the new **Carol Douglas** album. Metz estimates that at least half the records he actually plays at Studio One are records he bought. Included in his purchases this past week: "Let's Get Into Something" by **Richmond Extension** (Polydor); the **Truth** album (Roulette); **Honey Cone's** "Girls It Ain't Easy" (Hot Wax) and **Steely Dan's** "Do It Again" (ABC), both old singles; and two copies of the new **Harold Melvin & The Bluenotes** two-part 45, "Bad Luck" (Phila. Intl.). (Note: While some promotion departments are now beginning to make the increasingly frequent two-part singles available in their entirety – there is nothing more dismaying than getting a 45 that says "Part I" on both sides – even more enlightened people are sending out two copies of such records, realizing – and this should be painfully obvious – that DJs need two separate records in order to make a Part I/Part II or vocal/instrumental blend from one turntable to the other. It may be a special service, but it's greatly appreciated.)

In New York, where DJs have easier access to record companies, people still buy records but their purchases are more likely to be releases on hard-to-get labels, imports or material not generally thought of as discotheque music. For instance, Rich Pampinella at Hippopotamus just bought a batch of albums by **Frank Sinatra**, **Billie Holiday**, **Glenn Miller**, **Barbra Streisand** and an old release by **Getz, Gilberto & Jobim**, all of which he insists he plays at the club to change the mood around, along with a number of rock & roll oldies. Then there's Rafael Charres at the new Rouge et Blanc who guesses most New York DJs buy between 20 and 30 percent of their records, especially if they're interested in anything out-of-the-ordinary as he apparently is. On his last run to Downstairs, Charres picked up: the **Trammps** oldie, "Zing Went The Strings Of My Heart" (Buddah) (watch for an expanded, up-dated re-make of "Zing" under a different title on the Trammps always-forthcoming album, now due at the end of the month); and two rather unusual singles on

Contempo (Downstairs said they came in from Canada) – a typically driving, insistent **Titanic** cut called "Santa Fe" (not included on the "Macumba!" album mentioned here last week) backed with the original English version of "Black Skin Blue Eyed Boys" by **Tony Morgan**, and a terrific, loud **Jackson Sisters** cut, "I Believe In Miracles," backed with "Rain," an equally loud, gutsy gospel-style song by **Dorothy Morrison**. The Contempo singles were $2 each, but worth it.

Conclusions? I hesitate to draw too many from such a small survey, but even if promotional record service – most of which has come about only in the last nine months – seems to be keeping disco DJs supplied with most of the essentials, a large percentage of records, especially at the trend-setting, adventurous clubs, continue to be sought out and bought by DJs. Anyone interested in more than the run-of-the-mill, increasingly cliched "disco hit" doesn't depend on what the companies decide to feed him, so he goes out of his way to find the surprises. Which is exactly why the discotheque field is so vital and rich and will, I expect, remain that way.

Notes: Pampinella says "the heavy of the week" is **Randy Pie's** Highway Driver" (Polydor), which has that rock & soul sound of **Chicago** or the **Doobie Brothers** and is quite a knockout. Rich is also playing two Contempo imports (from England) by the **Armada Orchestra**, instrumental versions of "Do Me Right" (the **Detroit Emeralds** song) and "It's the Same Old Song" (**Four Tops**), both of which he says are getting "hot reaction." Rafael Charres is "really high about" **Billy Paul's** "July July July July" (5:30 and on his "Got My Head on Straight" album, Philadelphia International) which is very laid-back and also a favorite of my west coast correspondents. Lynn Cook, who emphasizes that "If it's danceable, I'll play it, rock or soul," included **Lon**

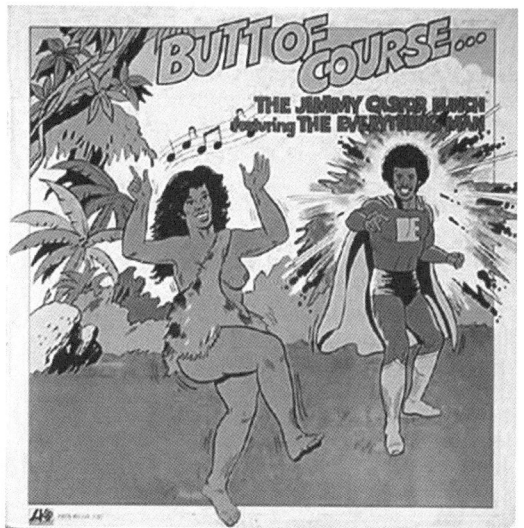

ROUGE ET BLANC, NEW YORK
DJ: Rafael Charres

ALL BECAUSE OF YOU (Instrumental) – LeRoy Hutson (Curtom)
BAD LUCK – Harold Melvin & the Bluenotes (Phila. Intl.)
BLUE EYED SOUL – Carl Douglas (20th Century)
CASTLES – Futures (Buddah)
HIJACK – Herbie Mann/Barrabas (Atlantic/Ariola import)
LOVE IS EVERYWHERE – City Limits (TSOP)
NEFERTITI – Wisdom (Adelia)
ONCE YOU GET STARTED – Rufus (ABC)
REAL GOOD PEOPLE – Gloria Gaynor (MGM)
WHERE IS THE LOVE? – Betty Wright (Alston)

HIPPOPOTAMUS, NEW YORK
DJ: Rich Pampinella

BAD LUCK – Harold Melvin & the Bluenotes (Phila. Intl.)
DO YOU LIKE IT – B.T. Express (Scepter)
HIJACK – Barrabas (Ariola import)
HONEYBEE/NEVER CAN SAY GOODBYE/REACH OUT – Gloria Gaynor (MGM)
I'LL BE HOLDING ON – Al Downing (Chess)
LADY MARMALADE – LaBelle (Epic)
SAVE ME – Silver Convention (Midland Intl.)
SHAME, SHAME, SHAME – Shirley And Company (Vibration)
SMOKIN' (Part 2) – Metropolis (Ebony Sounds)
WHERE IS THE LOVE? – Betty Wright (Alston)

STUDIO ONE, LOS ANGELES
DJ: Howard Metz

THE BOTTLE (LA BOTELLA) – Bataan (Salsoul)
E-MAN BOOGIE – Jimmy Castor Bunch (Atlantic)
GLASSHOUSE – Temptations (Gordy)
HAPPY PEOPLE – Temptations (Gordy)
HIJACK – Herbie Mann (Atlantic)
I'LL BE HOLDING ON – Al Downing (Chess)
LADY MARMALADE – LaBelle (Epic)
LOVE DON'T YOU GO THROUGH NO CHANGES ON ME – Sister Sledge (Atco)
REACH OUT, I'LL BE THERE – Gloria Gaynor (MGM)
SHAME, SHAME, SHAME – Shirley And Company (Vibration)

BAYOU LANDING, ATLANTA
DJ: Lynn Cook

BUMP ME BABY – Dooley Silverspoon (Cotton)
EXPRESS – B.T. Express (Scepter)
FIRE – Ohio Players (Mercury)
HIJACK – Herbie Mann (Atlantic)
LADY MARMALADE – LaBelle (Epic)
ONCE YOU GET STARTED – Rufus (ABC)
PICK UP THE PIECES – AWB (Atlantic)
SHAME, SHAME, SHAME – Shirley And Company (Vibration)
YOU'RE NO GOOD – Linda Ronstadt (Capitol)
WILDFIRE – Lon & Derek (A&M)

& Derrek's "Wildfire" (formerly a single, now the opening cut of their new "Who Do You Out Do" album, A&M) on his top 10 – it's brassy and builds well and should be checked out.

Album of the week: **Earth, Wind & Fire's** "That's the Way of the World" (Columbia), with the beautiful, high-spirited "Happy Feelin'," "Shining Star" and the full-of-changes instrumental "Africano." Best thing on the new **Tribe** album ("Tribal Bumpin'" on ABC) is, annoyingly, the shortest, "Montezuma's Revenge" (1:52), which is also the closest thing to "Koke;" but you might also try: "Solid" and "Tribal Bumpin'."

Recommended singles: **Moment of Truth's** fine "Helplessly" (Roulette); **Elliot Lurie's** light, diverting "Disco (Where You Gonna Go)" (Epic), which dissects the dance scene; **First Choice's** sudden new one, "Love Freeze" (Philly Groove), yet another biting recession lament; **Return to Forever's** steamy "Jungle Waterfall" (Polydor – also on their just-out album, "No Mystery"); "Funky Love Song" by **Quad** (Leo Mini) and very tough. Left field: **Universal Mind's** unusual version of the **Bacharach-David** "Reach Out For Me" (Red Coach). ◐

MARCH 22, 1975

The dance floors surveyed this week are mostly in Fort Lauderdale, Florida, with Flamingo, New York's chic private club, thrown in as an attempt at perspective (although Luis Romero's list is so idiosyncratic – **Martha Velez, Buddy Miles, Ipi 'N Tombia** – that his is hardly a "typical" New York Top 10). I went to high school down here (Fort Lauderdale High – a dump that I passed through in something of a haze; the football team was called the Flying L's) and my family still lives here – part of it at least – in a house not far from the beach. So I know how postcard pretty Lauderdale can be and how tired it really is deep down. And I figured it might make a good semirepresentative non-cosmopolitan center for a small-scale investigation of just how far urban disco music and discotheque style had spread from the coasts to the hinterlands.

"Small-scale" not so much by choice as by necessity: Fort Lauderdale (pop: 156,000) has only two full-time discotheques that I could discover – the Poop Deck and the Village Zoo, both on the beach – and only a couple of part-time – one of these, The Button, a popular beach-front bar with a one-night-a-week disco and records between live band sets other nights, is included here. The Zoo, which also features live entertainment from time to time, has been open the longest – two years. The Poop Deck has been open about 16 months and it recently expanded into larger, sleeker quarters to accomodate its mostly male crowd. And disco nights at The Button started only half a year ago, but are more and more packed each week.

Though all the DJs were somewhat apologetic about their lists pointing out that they had to play for a constantly-shifting crowd, many of whom are tourists from parts of the country even less in touch with the disco sound than Fort Lauderdale – they all proved to be far more up-to-date than I'd expected, perhaps because radio is spreading disco music faster than ever before. But Frank Heber at the Poop Deck says he still finds it hard to get his crowd into new cuts like "Hijack" and "Bad Luck"until they've heard them a number of times on the radio. Both Rich Catalano at the Village Zoo and John Terry at The Bottom say they try to stick to disco songs – mostly the standards with a few interesting exceptions – but crowd requests often run

KOKOMO
I CAN UNDERSTAND IT
(Part II)
B. Womack Taken From The Columbia
Lp: "KOKOMO" PC 33442
Produced by Chris Thomas

COLUMBIA
® "Columbia." Marcas Reg.

STEREO
4:39

45 RPM
3-10145
ZSS 160597
℗ 1975 CBS
Records

❝ The DJs in Fort Lauderdale all proved to be far more up-to-date than I expected, perhaps because radio is spreading disco music faster than ever before ❞

OIL CAN HARRY'S, LOS ANGELES
DJ: Terry Ponce

BAD LUCK – Harold Melvin & the Bluenotes (Phila. Intl.)
GLASSHOUSE – Temptations (Gordy)
HAPPY PEOPLE – Temptations (Gordy)
I'LL BE HOLDING ON – Al Downing (Chess)
I'M READY – Commodores (Motown)
LOOK BUT DON'T TOUCH – Donny Beaumont (Mercury)
SHAME, SHAME, SHAME – Shirley And Company (Vibration)
SISTERS & BROTHERS – Rita Fortune (Columbia)
TELL ME WHAT YOU WANT – Jimmy Ruffin (Chess)
VOO-DOO MAGIC Rhodes Kids (GRC)

ADAM'S APPLE, NEW YORK
DJ: David Todd

BAD LUCK – Harold Melvin & the Bluenotes (Phila. Intl.)
CRYSTAL WORLD – Crystal Grass (Philips import/Polydor)
EASE ON DOWN THE ROAD – Consumer Report (A Wing & A Prayer)
HIJACK – Barrabas (Ariola import/Atco)
I CAN UNDERSTAND IT – Kokomo (Columbia)
LOVE CORPORATION – Hues Corporation (RCA)
ONCE YOU GET STARTED – Rufus (ABC)
ROLLING DOWN A MOUNTAINSIDE – Main Ingredient (RCA)
SAVE ME AGAIN – Silver Convention (Midland Intl.)
WHERE IS THE LOVE? – Betty Wright (Alston)

OPUS I, NEW YORK
DJ: Douglas Riddick

BERBERBIAN WOOD – Les Variations (Buddah)
THE BOTTLE – Bataan (Epic)
BUMP YOUR BOOTY – Bobby Marchan (Mercury)
DANCE, DANCE, DANCE – Liquid Smoke (Roulette)
GUT LEVEL – Blackbyrds (Fantasy)
HELPLESSLY– Moment of Truth (Roulette)
HIJACK – Barrabas (Ariola import/Atco)
LOVE HAS SO MANY MEANINGS – Lily Fields (Sunburst)
QUESTIONS & CONCLUSIONS – Black Heat (Atlantic)
TAKE IT FROM ME – Dionne Warwick (Warner Bros.)

HOLLYWOOD, NEW YORK
DJ: Tony Gioe

AND YOU CAN CALL THAT LOVE – Vernon Burch (UA)
BAD LUCK – Harold Melvin & the Bluenotes (Phila. Intl.)
HELPLESSLY – Moment of Truth (Roulette)
HIJACK – Barrabas/Herbie Mann (Atco/Atlantic)
I'LL BE HOLDING ON – Al Downing (Chess)
LANSANA'S PRIESTESS – Donald Byrd (Blue Note)
PROTECT OUR LOVE – Sister Sledge (Atco)
REACH OUT, I'LL BE THERE – Gloria Gaynor (MGM)
SHAME, SHAME, SHAME – Shirley And Company (Vibration)
WHERE IS THE LOVE? – Betty Wright (Alston)

to rock: **Led Zeppelin**, **Elton John**, **Wet Willie**. The night I visited The Button, it was overflowing with a young college crowd – DJ Terry took the microphone to welcome the Universities of Michigan and West Virginia, to great cheers from each contingent – which wanted nothing so much as Led Zeppelin. So Terry sandwiched "Whole Lotta Love" between "Do It ('Til You're Satisfied)" and "Shame, Shame, Shame." When it comes to soul, Button people prefer the funky, familiar stuff – **Sly**, **War**, **Stevie Wonder** or **Doctor John**'s still-popular "Right Place, Wrong Time" – but Terry says **Barry White**'s "What Am I Gonna Do With You," **Graham Central Station**'s "Feel The Need," "Satin Soul" by **Love Unlimited Orchestra** (he didn't have the **Gene Page** version) and cuts from **Herbie Hancock**'s "Thrust" album are going over well.

Rich Catalano at the Zoo is into more soft-core, sweet-soul stuff and lists among his personal favorites "Girls" by the **Moments & Whatnauts**, **Gloria Scott**'s "Just As Long As We're Together," the **Sons of Robin Stone**'s "Got To Get You Back" (still popular) and, especially, **Ebb Tide**'s "Gimme Your Best Shot Baby" (Sound Gems). Catalano, who used to play in New York, mentioned that he gets particularly dismayed when he hears people talking about disco music as a "fad" – he's sure it's here to stay.

Back in New York, Luis Romero says he feels **Sister Sledge**'s "Circle Of Love" (from their Atlantic album) is picking up over the album's other, initially more popular cuts. Also catching on more surely: "Castles" by the **Futures** (on the Buddah album), **Melissa Manchester**'s version of **Stevie Wonder**'s "Love Havin' You Around" ("Melissa," on Arista), **Carol Douglas**' "A Friend In Need" (on "The Carol Douglas Album," Midland International).

Out this week: "Kokomo," an album by an eight-man, two-woman English group of the same name, who sound like the best white r&b group out of Great Britain since the **Average White Band**. Included on the album (from Columbia) is a 7:45 version of the **Bobby Womack/ New Birth** song, "I Can Understand It" which is slightly down-paced and quite terrific. And try the opening cut, too, an almost five-minute "Kitty Sittin' Pretty." ◐

Beginning this week, Disco File is adding a Top 20 list of the most popular discotheque records, appearing alongside this column, and compiled from DJ Top 10 records for this and the past four weeks. **Harold Melvin & the Bluenotes'** powerful "Bad Luck" came in at number one by such a wide margin that it should remain there quite comfortably for some time. Second place was a tie between the **Herbie Mann** and **Barrabas** versions of "Hijack," now running neck-and-neck after Mann's initial lead. Oldest cut on the list: "Gut Level," from the **Blackbyrds'** debut album released about a year ago but still going strong, primarily on requests (Ray Goynes at La Martinique put it on his Top 10 this week and at the Sound Machine, Joe Palminteri says it remains one of his "biggest records," played two or three times a night). Newest cuts on the list: **Kokomo's** "I Can Understand It" and "Ease On Down The Road" by **Consumer Report**, both getting strong initial reaction and moving up fast. Watch for: **Frankie Valli's** long, flow-through "Swearin' To God," which continues to astound. Palminteri reports it's his most requested record, and Steve D'Acquisto at Broadway in Brooklyn says more people have asked him about Valli's album track than about any other record since the club opened four months ago.

Also picking up: "Love Has So Many Meanings" by **Lily Fields** (Sunburst), which appeared on Doug Riddick's Opus I list last week and again this week on Palminteri's Top 10. Though it's one of those songs that doesn't quite live up to its instrumental intro, it's pleasant enough in an **Ecstasy, Passion & Pain** mold and features an instrumental B side. Richie Conte, one of the DJs at Hadaar on Staten Island, chose three cuts from as yet unreleased albums for his Top 10 – two from the forthcoming **Van McCoy** "Disco Baby" album (Avco), "Turn This Mother Out," which is going to be upsetting a lot of dance floors this Spring, and "The Hustle." The other cut is from an album titled "Disco Soul" by **The Brothers** (RCA) which, like Van McCoy's record, contains largely instrumental selections from the current disco hit catalogue ("Fire," "Get Dancin'," "Never Can Say Goodbye," "Doctor's Orders," "You're The First, The Last, My Everything") plus a few originals. Conte's choice is one of the latter, "Everybody Loves A Winner;" I much prefer "In the Pocket" or "Are You Ready For This," the track recently released as a single (long version: 4:16). "Disco Soul" should be out and available this week.

Harold Wheeler's "Black Cream" (RCA) is yet another instrumental album, this one with discotheque leanings rather than a total disco concept, but enough danceable cuts to make it attractive. Wheeler, who arranged **Gloria Gaynor's** "Never Can Say Goodbye" and co-produced **Consumer Report's** "Ease On Down The Road," produced and arranged here, coming up with a surprising version of "Mack The Knife," a nice "Then Came You" and a sexy composition of his own, the title cut, "Black Cream."

Rap on, Mr. DJ: Bobby Guttadaro of Le Jardin called to recommend "Think Twice" from the new **Donald Byrd** album, "Stepping Into Tomorrow" (Blue Note), a six-minute-plus vocal-and-instrumental cut he feels is another "Lansana's Priestess." "Stepping Into Tomorrow," the title cut, feels somewhat like "Walking In Rhythm" and the entire album is recommended for your extra quiet night at home and in some condition. Other Bobby DJ tips: "Trampled Underfoot," a pounding, loud cut from **Led Zeppelin's** "Physical Graffiti" album (Swan Song), **Bobby Womack's** predictable but hard-to-resist "Check It Out" (UA) and **Lulu's** "Take Your Mama For A Ride" (Chelsea). Disco File Recommends: The title cut from **Greg Perry's** debut album, "One For The Road" (Casablanca) and that album's instrumental cut, "Love Is

> ## " Beginning this week, Disco File is adding a Top 20 list of the most popular discotheque records, compiled from DJ Top 10 records for this and the past four weeks "

HADAAR, STATEN ISLAND, NEW YORK
DJ: Richie Conte

BAD LUCK – Harold Melvin & the Bluenotes
(Phila. Intl.)
EVERYBODY LOVES A WINNER – The Brothers (RCA)
FREE AND EASY – Satyr (RCA)
HELPLESSLY – Moment of Truth (Roulette)
HIJACK – Barrabas (Atco)
I CAN UNDERSTAND IT – Kokomo (Columbia)
SAVE ME – Silver Convention (Midland Intl.)
TAKE IT FROM ME – Dionne Warwick
(Warner Bros.)
TURN THIS MOTHER OUT/THE HUSTLE – Van McCoy
(Avco)
WHERE IS THE LOVE? – Betty Wright (Alston)

SOUND MACHINE, NEW YORK
DJ: Joe Palminteri

ALL RIGHT NOW – Lea Roberts (UA)
BAD LUCK – Harold Melvin & the Bluenotes
(Phila. Intl.)
CASTLES – Futures (Buddah)
CRYSTAL WORLD – Crystal Grass (Polydor)
EASE ON DOWN THE ROAD – Consumer Report
(A Wing & a Prayer)
HIJACK – Barrabas (Atco)
I CAN UNDERSTAND IT – Kokomo (Columbia)
LOVE HAS SO MANY MEANINGS – Lily Fields
(Sunburst)
SWEARIN' TO GOD – Frankie Valli (Private Stock)
WHERE IS THE LOVE? – Betty Wright (Alston)

BROADWAY, BROOKLYN, NEW YORK
DJ: Steve D'Acquisto

AND YOU CALL THAT LOVE – Vernon Burch (UA)
BAD LUCK – Harold Melvin & the Bluenotes
(Phila. Intl.)
EASE ON DOWN THE ROAD – Consumer Report
(A Wing & A Prayer)
HELPLESSLY – Moment of Truth (Roulette)
HIJACK – Herbie Mann (Atlantic)
LOVE CORPORATION – Hues Corporation (RCA)
SAVE ME AGAIN – Silver Convention (Midland Intl.)
SWEARIN' TO GOD – Frankie Valli (Private Stock)
WHAT CAN I DO FOR YOU? – LaBelle (Epic)
WHERE IS THE LOVE? – Betty Wright (Alston)

LA MARTINQUE, NEW YORK
DJ: Raymond Goynes

BAD LUCK – Harold Melvin & the Bluenotes
(Phila. Intl.)
DO YOU LIKE IT – B.T. Express (Scepter)
EXPRESS – B.T. Express (Scepter)
FIRE – Ohio Players (Mercury)
GUT LEVEL – Blackbyrds (Fantasy)
HIJACK – Barrabas (Atco)
LADY MARMALADE – LaBelle (Epic)
ONCE YOU GET STARTED – Rufus (ABC)
PHILADELPHIA – B.B. King (ABC)
PICK UP THE PIECES – AWB (Atlantic)

Magic;" **Eddie Harris'** "Get On Down," which has **Bohannon** overtones, from his new "I Need Some Money" album (Atlantic), and the following singles: "Spirit of the Boogie" by **Kool & the Gang** with "Summer Madness" on the other side (De-Lite); **KC & the Sunshine Band's** terrific "Get Down Tonight" (TK); **Buddy Miles'** "Pull Yourself Together," from his last album and produced by **Johnny Bristol** (Columbia); "Touch Me," a wonderfully torchy, very sexy **Brian Holland** production for **Eloise Laws** (Invictus) and **Destiny's** joyous "So Much Love," produced by **Van McCoy** (RCA).

Not for everyone, but worth a try: "God Made Me Funky" by the **Headhunters**, **Herbie Hancock's** group featuring some background vocals from the **Pointer Sisters** (Arista); "Out Of My Mind" by **Rhodes, Chalmers & Rhodes** (Warner Bros.) and **Christopher Bond's** "A Good Love" (DiscReet), both interesting productions; "Voodoo Doll," a rocker by **Wild Cherry** (A&M); "Mighty Love Man (Part 1)," female vocals from **Black Stash** (Contempo) and **Saundra Phillips'** funny, low-down nasty "Miss Fatback," a fat woman's liberation song (Brown Dog). And Stang has released a rather redundant "More Shame," by **Seldon Powell and Company**, adding a sax to the instrumental version of "Shame, Shame, Shame" and trotting it out in hopes of a little extra action behind the first record's enormous success. ◙

DISCO FILE TOP 20

1. **BAD LUCK** – Harold Melvin & The Bluenotes (Phila. Intl.)
2. **HIJACK** – Herbie Mann (Atlantic)
   HIJACK – Barrabas (Atco)
3. **SHAME, SHAME, SHAME** – Shirley and Company (Vibration)
4. **WHERE IS THE LOVE** – Betty Wright (Alston)
5. **I'LL BE HOLDING ON** – Al Downing (Chess)
6. **ONCE YOU GET STARTED** – Rufus (ABC)
7. **REACH OUT, I'LL BE THERE** – Gloria Gaynor (MGM)
8. **LADY MARMALADE** – LaBelle (Epic)
9. **FIRE** – Ohio Players (Mercury)
10. **PICK UP THE PIECES** – AWB (Atlantic)
11. **HELPLESSLY** – Moment Of Truth (Roulette)
12. **EXPRESS** – B. T. Express (Scepter)
13. **SAVE ME/SAVE ME AGAIN** – Silver Convention (Midland Intl.)
14. **DO YOU LIKE IT** – B.T. Express (Scepter)
15. **CASTLES** – Futures (Buddah)
16. **I CAN UNDERSTAND IT** – Kokomo (Columbia)
17. **EASE ON DOWN THE ROAD** – Consumer Rapport (Wing And A Prayer)
18. **GUT LEVEL** – Blackbyrds (Fantasy)
19. **I JUST CAN'T SAY GOODBYE** – Philly Devotions (Columbia)
20. **LOVE DON'T YOU GO THROUGH NO CHANGES ON ME** – Sister Sledge (Atco)

APRIL 5, 1975

Most essential new album: **Van McCoy's** stunning "Disco Baby," now available on Avco and containing the two cuts that were pulled for an equally essential single – "The Hustle," tightened down to 3:27 from the 4:05 album cut and backed with a re-vamped instrumental version of "Hey Girl, Come And Get It." "The Hustle" is cute, light-weight but irresistible and already appears on two Top 10 lists this week – reported by Spike at the recently re-opened private club, Buttermilk Bottom in New York, and by Hector Lebron at Limelight, also in New York. But the cuts that knock me out – I think my screams and the ever-increasing volume alarmed the neighbors late last night – are "Turn This Mother Out," as strong as its title, and "Spanish Boogie," *con sabor Latino* and one of the hottest horn lines I know of. Both are Van McCoy compositions, as is "The Hustle," and both far outweigh any of the borrowed material here, though "Pick Up The Pieces," "Shakey Ground," "Hey Girl" and "Fire" – all done Van McCoy-style – are excellent. All together, McCoy's best work so far and the first great album of the Spring.

News & Notes: **Bunny Jones'** Gaiee Records, designed as an outlet for openly gay performers – an idea whose time has certainly come – has been picked up for distribution by Motown. Gaiee already has something of an underground hit on its hands in **Valentino's** "I Was Born This Way," and Motown will begin by working that single further... **Consumer Report's** wizbang "Ease On Down The Road," which Ronald Coles at Colony Records says is "selling like crazy – 50 copies in one night," has moved to Atlantic for distribution. The label, Wing And A Prayer, will remain the same but the group's name will be changed to **Consumer Rapport**... My west coast correspondent reports the release of "Hold On (Just A Little Bit Longer)" by **Anthony and the Imperials** (no longer "Little" – on Avco) has prompted some Los Angeles DJs to revive the original **Persuaders** version of that song (on their Atco album, "Best Thing That Ever Happened to Me") and play them back-to-back. Both were produced in Philadelphia by **Phil Hurtt & Tony Bell**, part of the Young Professionals team.

DJ Tom Savarese, who played at Fire Island's Ice Palace all last Summer, is reporting from a new club, Casablanca, which has opened an ambitious disco/bar/restaurant in the former Nepenthe II in New York. Also playing at Casablanca: former Nepenthe DJ Bob Gordon... Angel Burgos at Time Machine in Westchester and his friend Spike from Buttermilk Bottom both mentioned getting strong response to a dub of an unreleased single by **J.J. Jackson** (remember "But It's Alright?") called "Let Me Try Again." Written and produced by **Bobby Flax** and **Lanny Lambert**, who are represented by a song on both the **Carol Douglas** and **Gloria Gaynor** albums, the song has some nice, gritty **Jimmy Ruffin** overtones and runs to 4:48 in its long version. Flax and Lambert had a number of dubs made and distributed to key clubs in New York for reaction; they are still shopping for a label

"I think my screams and the ever-increasing volume alarmed the neighbors last night"

BUTTERMILK BOTTOM, NEW YORK
DJ: Spike (Fernando Oquendo)

BAD LUCK – Harold Melvin & the Bluenotes
(Phila. Intl.)
HELPLESSLY – Moment of Truth (Roulette)
HIJACK – Barrabas (Ariola import/Atco)
HIJACK – Herbie Mann (Atlantic)
HONEYBEE/NEVER CAN SAY GOODBYE – Gloria Gaynor
(MGM)
THE HUSTLE – Van McCoy (Avco)
I'LL BE HOLDING ON – Al Downing (Chess)
SWEARIN' TO GOD – Frankie Valli (Private Stock)
TAKE IT FROM ME – Dionne Warwick (Warner Bros.)
WHERE IS THE LOVE? – Betty Wright (Alston)

CASABLANCA, NEW YORK
DJ: Tom Savarese

BAD LUCK – Harold Melvin & the Bluenotes
(Phila. Intl.)
EASE ON DOWN THE ROAD – Consumer Report
(A Wing & A Prayer)
GLASSHOUSE – Temptations (Gordy)
I CAN UNDERSTAND IT – Kokomo (Columbia)
LADY MARMALADE – LaBelle (Epic)
ONCE YOU GET STARTED – Rufus (ABC)
REAL GOOD PEOPLE – Gloria Gaynor (MGM)
SUN GODDESS – Ramsey Lewis (Columbia)
WALKING IN RHYTHM – Blackbyrds (Fantasy)
WHERE IS THE LOVE? – Betty Wright (Alston)

TIME MACHINE, WESTCHESTER, NY
DJ: Angel Burgos

BAD LUCK – Harold Melvin & the Bluenotes
(Phila. Intl.)
CASTLES – Futures (Buddah)
CRYSTAL WORLD – Crystal Grass Philips (Polydor)
FRAME OF MIND – Vernon Burch (UA)
GLASSHOUSE – Temptations (Gordy)
HIJACK – Herbie Mann/ Barrabas
(Atco/Ariola import)
ONCE YOU GET STARTED – Rufus (ABC)
SAVE ME/SAVE ME AGAIN – Silver Convention
(Midland Intl.)
SWEARIN' TO GOD – Frankie Valli (Private Stock)
WHERE IS THE LOVE? – Betty Wright (Alston)

LIMELIGHT, NEW YORK
DJ: Hector Lebron

ARE YOU READY FOR THIS – The Brothers (RCA)
BAD LUCK – Harold Melvin & the Bluenotes
(Phila. Intl.)
EASE ON DOWN THE ROAD – Consumer Report
(A Wing & A Prayer)
GLASSHOUSE – Temptations (Gordy)
HELPLESSLY – Moment of Truth (Roulette)
HIJACK – Herbie Mann/ Barrabas
(Ariola import/Atco)
THE HUSTLE –Van McCoy (Avco)
TAKE IT FROM ME – Dionne Warwick (Warner Bros.)
THAT'S THE KIND OF LOVE I'VE GOT FOR YOU – Rita Jean
Bodine (20th Century)
WHERE IS THE LOVE? – Betty Wright (Alston)

deal. Worth a Try: "Stoned Out Of My Mind" and "Got To Get Your Own," instrumentals from the album "Got To Get Your Own" by **Reuben Wilson and the Cost of Living** (Cadet); "Moe, Let's Have A Party," "Chi-Town Theme" and "All Your Love, All Day, All Night" (which is 9:27) from **Cleveland Eaton's** mostly instrumental album "Plenty Good Eaton" (Black Jazz/Ovation); "Feeling the Magic" from the new **Johnny Bristol** album of the same name (MGM); "Love Do Me Right," which reminds me of **Babe Ruth**, on the "Rockin' Horse" album (RCA).

Recommended 45s: "We're Not Getting Any Younger" a **Baker-Harris-Young** production for **Kaleidoscope** and the best new single this week (TSOP); **American Gypsy's** great "Angel Eyes," now out as a 45 (Chess); "Cut the Cake" and "Person To Person" back-to-back **AWB** (Atlantic); a driving, two-part "Peace And Love" by **Ron Butler and the Ramblers** (Playboy); **Jeree Palmer's** "Flattery," produced by **Tony Silvester** and **Bert DeCoteaux** and sounding like a winning combination of **Gloria Gaynor** and **Sister Sledge** (Columbia); and "Oh Baby," the up B side of the **Ebony Rhythm Funk Campaign** record whose A side, "How's Your Wife (And My Child)," is my favorite real-life soap opera song this month (Innovation II). "I Wanna Dance Wit' Choo (Doo Dat Dance)" is the new **Disco Tex & the Sex-O-Lettes** single and more of the same (Chelsea). ◗

APRIL 12, 1975

Notes & Feedback: **Van McCoy's** single, "The Hustle," jumped right into the middle of Disco File's Top 20 this week, grabbing a strong number 10 spot the first time on the list... And on the Top 10 lists there are a number of new items. Paul Casella at the Monastery includes a pounding version of **Gene Krupa's** classic "Big Noise From Winnetka" by a group with the rather off-putting name of **Spaghetti Head** (Private Stock) – recommended for its sensational percussion and eerie whistling, though one wishes it were longer than 2:44. Casella, whose non-stop schedule now includes nights at New Rochelle's Second Floor as well as the Monastery, also lists an instrumental cut from the elusive **Crystal Grass** album called "Love To Dance This One With You." The album, titled "Dedicated To Philadelphia" (on Philips), is apparently available in Canada but so rare and so sought-after here that New York's ever-alert Downstairs Records is able to sell their occasional import copy at $20.

Another sought-after import appears on Mitch Schatsky's list from Pier 9 in Washington. Though "El Bimbo" by **Bimbo Jet**, a back-to-back vocal/instrumental import 45 on the Parise label, has been mentioned in passing by a number of DJs over the past month or two (including Larry Saunders, reporting this week from Wonderland), Schatsky is the first to elevate it to his Top 10. "El Bimbo" is also a Downstairs find; Schatsky says he paid $6 for it on one of his recent visits there and the store sells out its limited supply almost immediately. **Simon Said's** whip-creamy "Love Song"

(Roulette), recommended here a few weeks back, also entered the Pier 9 Top 10 this week after an enthusiastic reception by Schatsky and his crowd.

Sam Meyer at Barbary Coast in Houston echoed many of the comments I heard from DJs in Fort Lauderdale when he pointed out that his list reflected the often conservative taste of his crowd, which tends to resist a new record until it's been broken in on the radio. But among the new things getting over are "Get Down Tonight" **by K.C. & the Sunshine Band** (TK) – the group's best disco single so far, also on Schatsky's Top 10 – and a lovely left field choice by **Juan Carlos Calderon** called "Bandolero" (Epic), a Spanish-flavored instrumental that's an odd combination of the bouncy and the lush.

After a number of delays, **Barry White's** album, "Just Another Way To Say I Love You" (20th Century), is finally here, and while it contains few surprises, his formula seems almost fail-safe. "I'll Do For You Anything You Want Me To," already on Mitch Schatsky's list, is the obvious choice cut but "Heavenly, That's What You Are To Me" – though White has a way of running out of words after his titles – is just as nice. Also out: **Herbie Mann's** much-discussed "Discotheque" album (Atlantic) which hardly lives up to its title – only a few of the cuts are disco-danceable – but is quite attractive nevertheless. I saw Mann and his group battling awful sound problems at the Beacon Theatre last week but he managed to put across superb versions of "Lady Marmalade" (sparked by

BIMBO JET

DISTRIBUTED BY CBS RECORDS   MADE IN ENGLAND

Philadelphia International Records

Not for sale

S PIR 4351
Side A
S PIR 4351 A
Gamble-Huff
Music Ltd./
Carlin Music
Corp.
℗ 1975 CBS Inc.
4.17
(Long
Version)
45
STEREO

CITY LIMITS
Original sound recording made by CBS Inc. CBS Records are the exclusive licensees for the UK

ALL RIGHTS OF THE MANUFACTURER AND OF THE OWNER OF THE RECORDED WORK RESERVED · UNAUTHORISED PUBLIC PERFORMANCE BROADCASTING AND COPYING OF THIS RECORD PROHIBITED

LOVE IS EVERYWHERE
(B. Hawes/J. Jefferson/C. Simmons)
Arranged by Jack Faith Produced by Bruce Hawes and Joseph Jefferson

❝A group with the rather off-putting name of Spaghetti Head, recommended for its sensational percussion and eerie whistling❞

THE MONASTERY, NY (QUEENS)
DJ: Paul Casella

AND YOU CALL THAT LOVE – Vernon Burch (UA)
BAD LUCK – Harold Melvin & the Bluenotes (Phila. Intl.)
BIG NOISE FROM WINNETKA – Spaghetti Head
(Private Stock)
DISCO BABY – Van McCoy (Avco)
EASE ON DOWN THE ROAD – Consumer Rapport
(A Wing & A Prayer)
HELPLESSLY – Moment of Truth (Roulette)
THE HUSTLE – Van McCoy (Avco)
LOVE IS EVERYWHERE – City Limits (TSOP)
LOVE TO DANCE THIS ONE WITH YOU – Crystal Grass
(Philips import)
ROLLING DOWN A MOUNTAINSIDE – Main Ingredient (RCA)

BARBARY COAST, HOUSTON
DJ: Sam Meyer

CHANGES (MESSIN' WITH MY MIND) – Vernon Burch (UA)
EXPRESS – B.T. Express (Scepter)
GET DANCIN' – Disco Tex & the Sex-O-Lettes (Chelsea)
GET DOWN – Kay-Gees (Gang)
GET DOWN TONIGHT – K.C. & the Sunshine Band (TK)
LADY MARMALADE – LaBelle (Epic)
SHAME, SHAME, SHAME – Shirley And Company
(Vibration)
SHINING STAR – Earth, Wind & Fire (Columbia)
SUPERNATURAL THING – Ben E. King (Atlantic)
WHAT AM I GONNA DO WITH YOU – Barry White
(20th Century)

PIER 9, WASHINGTON, D.C.
DJ: Mitch Schatsky

BAD LUCK – Harold Melvin & the Bluenotes (Phila. Intl.)
EASE ON DOWN THE ROAD – Consumer Rapport
(A Wing & A Prayer)
EL BIMBO – Bimbo Jet (Parise import)
GET DANCIN' – Van McCoy (Avco lp cut)
GET DOWN TONIGHT – K.C. & the Sunshine Band (TK)
HELPLESSLY – Moment of Truth (Roulette)
THE HUSTLE – Van McCoy (Avco)
I'LL DO FOR YOU ANYTHING YOU WANT ME TO – Barry
White (20th Century lp cut)
I WANNA DANCE WIT 'CHOO – Disco Tex & the
Sex-O-Lettes (Chelsea)
LOVE SONG – Simon Said (Roulette)

WONDERLAND, NEW YORK
DJ: Larry Sanders

BAD LUCK – Harold Melvin & the Bluenotes (Phila. Intl.)
EASE ON DOWN THE ROAD – Consumer Rapport
(A Wing & A Prayer)
HIJACK – Herbie Mann/Barrabas (Atlantic/Atco)
A HURRICANE IS COMING TONIGHT – Carol Douglas
(Midland Intl.)
THE HUSTLE – Van McCoy (Avco)
I CAN'T LIVE A DREAM – Frankie Valli (Private Stock)
LOVE FREEZE – First Choice (Philly Groove)
TAKE IT FROM ME – Dionne Warwick (Warner Bros.)
WHAT AM I GONNA DO WITH YOU – Barry White
(20th Century)
WHERE IS THE LOVE? – Betty Wright (Alston)

vocals from a great back-up group including **Cissy Houston**), "Pick Up The Pieces" and an original composition called "Mediterranean:' all included on the album and worth checking into.

Other notable albums: "California Sunset," marking a welcome return for the **Originals** (on Motown), produced by **Lamont Dozier** (stepping back into the old Berry Gordy fold) and containing four fine tracks: "Let Me Live In Your Life," "Financial Affair," "Why'd You Lie" and "Good Lovin' Is Just a Dime Away;" **Mandrill's** new "Solid" (their first for UA) with a complex, rich cut called "Wind on Horseback," running more than six minutes; and, for left field tastes, **Amon Duul II's** long, strange "Da Guadeloop" (from their "Hijack" album, not to be confused with the Herbie Mann/Barrabas cuts, on Atco). Steve D'Acquisto, DJ at Broadway, called to point out a cut we'd missed –"I Can Feel Your Jones," a sexy, flowing cut from the **Rasputin Stash** album (Gemigo) – which he says has been going over well at his club and does just fine in my living room, too.

Recommended singles: "Karam Bani:' the first release by **Buari**, the Ghanian performer we wrote about some time back – Afro-jazz and quite terrific (on RCA, with a long version of 4:27); "Everybody Hustle" by **Funky People**, which is not a hustle number but smokes anyway – again, there's a long version, at 4:11 (Roulette); "Lost Time," the instrumental from **Popcorn Wylie's** album cut to 3:17 for the single (ABC), and **Zulema's** hot "Standing In The Back Row Of Your Heart" (RCA). ●

DISCO FILE TOP 20

1. **BAD LUCK** – Harold Melvin & The Bluenotes (Phila. Intl.)
2. **HIJACK** – Barrabas (Atco)
3. **WHERE IS THE LOVE** – Betty Wright (Alston)
4. **EASE ON DOWN THE ROAD** – Consumer Rapport (Wing And A Prayer)
5. **HELPLESSLY** – Moment Of Truth (Roulette)
6. **HIJACK** – Herbie Mann (Atlantic)
7. **SHAME, SHAME, SHAME** – Shirley and Company (Vibration)
8. **ONCE YOU GET STARTED** – Rufus (ABC)
9. **I'LL BE HOLDING ON** – Al Downing (Chess)
10. **THE HUSTLE** – Van McCoy (Avco)
11. **TAKE IT FROM ME** – Dionne Warwick (Warner Bros.)
12. **LADY MARMALADE** – LaBelle (Epic)
13. **SAVE ME/SAVE ME AGAIN** – Silver Convention (Midland Intl.)
14. **SWEARIN' TO GOD** – Frankie Valli (Private Stock)
15. **GLASS HOUSE** – Temptations (Gordy)
16. **I CAN UNDERSTAND IT** – Kokomo (Columbia)
17. **EXPRESS** – B. T. Express (Scepter)
18. **REACH OUT, I'LL BE THERE** – Gloria Gaynor (MGM)
19. **CRYSTAL WORLD** – Crystal Grass (Polydor)
20. **FIRE** – Ohio Players (Mercury)

APRIL 19, 1975

The Shape of Things To Come? A rather appalling little item appeared recently about a chain of steak restaurants that were turning themselves into discotheques. The chain's headquarters in Rockville, Maryland (disco central, right?), makes up a weekly list of 30 records which are supplied to DJs at each location, supplemented by basic collections of another 100 current "disco" records and 100 "oldie" dance cuts. The DJs, who are trained by the parent company, can play only those records on the lists and are expected to program the top 30 two or three times in the course of the night. Records by specially-spotlighted "artists of the month" – also chosen in Rockville – are programmed every 45 or 60 minutes in each of the locations in the chain. Clearly, disco DJing is the glamor, noexperience-necessary profession of the year, but is this what it's coming to? The best DJs – a number of whom were making record-to-record collages and brilliant musical connections years before the media discovered the disco phenomenon, years before many of us were ready to hear them – are artists, tastemakers, shaping the immediate environment with their music. God knows all those people out there at their double turntables are not cruising the same heights of creativity but, until now, they haven't been reduced to playlist automatons. With discotheques becoming Big Business, the "disco" chain, run like a fast-food empire or a string of laundromats, could be the next major move. If it is, count me out.

> ## " With discotheques becoming Big Business, the "disco" chain, run like a fast-food empire or a string of laundromats, could be the next major move. If it is, count me out "

Michael Cappello points out that the version of **Frankie Valli's** "Swearin' To God" which appears on his list from Le Jardin is a disco re-mix by producer **Bob Crewe** which brings the cut up slightly, giving it a nicer, more attractive beat without changing the length substantially. Crewe left a few copies of this new mix with a number of New York DJs on his recent visit here – he was also sneak-previewing the new **Disco Tex** album, due out this month – but special promotional pressings should be generally available to clubs this week. **Love Committee's** "One Day Of Peace," also on Cappello's list, is another re-mix, this one almost doubling the length of the original **Golden Fleece** single but, as yet, not commercially released.

Louis Schneider and a few other New York DJs who have been given acetates, are excited about **Bobbi Martin's** "Man Was Made To Love Woman," an up-beat women's lib message with a **Gloria Gaynor** sound in spite of country-type vocals. Arrangement is by Harold Wheeler, production by Henry Jerome who is bringing it out this week on the Green Menu label and hoping it'll be snatched up by one of the majors. Schneider plays at New York's Casablanca, a Latin club on West 73rd Street which features live entertainment and disco, and should be distinguished from Club Casablanca downtown, from which Tom Savarese reported two weeks back for Disco File.

Our first Boston report comes this week from John Luongo who: plays at a club called Rhinoceros; runs a weekly disco program called "The Right Track" on Boston's WGBS-FM; produces occasional records (last effort: **Leon Collins'** "I Just Wanna Say I Love You" on the Elf label; coming up: a new version of **Gentle Persuasion's** "Dynamite Explodes") and has just started a bi-weekly disco newsletter called Night Fall, for which he compiles a top 12 from the Boston area (note: disco newsletters are proliferating like crazy – I'll have a report in an upcoming column). Luongo has this week's surprise tip: check out "Clap Your Hands" on the just-out **Manhattan Transfer** album (Atlantic), a terrific, high-spirited number as irresistible as anything I've heard this month.

The new essential albums: "**Trammps**" *finally* available (though copies have been floating around New York for the past few weeks, as prized as first-edition books) and including the familiar "Love Epidemic," "Where Do We Go From Here" and "Shout," plus the original, better version of "Trusting Heart" (previously only available on a one-sided promotional sampler of Philadelphia International material), "Trammps Disco Theme," "Stop And Think," "I Know That Feeling" and "Save A Place" – all varying degrees of greatness; not a bad cut here and well worth the wait (on Golden Fleece). The O'Jays "Survival" (Philadelphia International) has just barely been absorbed here, but three cuts stand out immediately: "Give The People What They Want," also released as a 45, "Rich Get Richer" and "Survival,"

LE JARDIN, NEW YORK
DJ: Michael Cappello

AND YOU CALL THAT LOVE – Vernon Burch (UA)
ARE YOU READY FOR THIS – The Brothers (RCA)
BAD LUCK – Harold Melvin & the Bluenotes
(Phila. Intl.)
EASE ON DOWN THE ROAD – Consumer Rapport
(A Wing & A Prayer)
HELPLESSLY – Moment of Truth (Roulette)
ONE DAY OF PEACE – Love Committee (Golden Fleece)
SWEARIN' TO GOD – Frankie Valli (Private Stock)
TAKE IT FROM ME – Dionne Warwick
(Warner Bros.)
TRAMMP'S DISCO THEME/STOP AND THINK – Trammps
(Golden Fleece)
WHERE IS THE LOVE? – Betty Wright (Alston)

CABARET, LOS ANGELES
DJ: Howard Metz

BAD LUCK – Harold Melvin & the Bluenotes (Phila. Intl.)
E-MAN BOOGIE – Jimmy Castor Bunch (Atlantic)
FIRE – Van McCoy (Avco)
GLASSHOUSE – Temptations (Gordy)
HIJACK – Herbie Mann (Atlantic)
I WANNA DANCE WIT 'CHOO – Disco Tex & the
Sex-O-Lettes (Chelsea)
SAVE ME AGAIN – Silver Convention (Midland Intl.)
SHAME, SHAME, SHAME – Shirley And Company
(Vibration)
WHAT CAN I DO FOR YOU? – LaBelle (Epic)
WHERE IS THE LOVE? – Betty Wright (Alston)

RHINOCEROS, BOSTON
DJ: John Luongo

AFRICANO – Earth, Wind & Fire (Columbo)
ARE YOU READY FOR THIS – The Brothers (RCA)
BAD LUCK – Harold Melvin & the Bluenotes
(Phila. Intl.)
CRYSTAL WORLD – Crystal Grass (Polydor)
DYNOMITE – Tony Camillo's Bazuka (A&M)
E-MAN BOOGIE – Jimmy Castor Bunch (Atlantic)
HIJACK – Herbie Mann/ Barrabas (Atlantic/Atco)
I WANNA DANCE WIT 'CHOO – Disco Tex & the
Sex-O-Lettes (Chelsea)
LOVE IS EVERYWHERE – City Limits (TSOP)
POTENTIAL – Jimmy Castor Bunch (Atlantic)

CASABLANCA, NEW YORK
DJ: Louis Schneider

BAD LUCK – Harold Melvin & the Bluenotes
(Phila. Intl.)
CRYSTAL WORLD – Crystal Grass (Polydor)
E-MAN BOOGIE – Jimmy Castor Bunch (Atlantic)
EASE ON DOWN THE ROAD – Consumer Rapport
(A Wing & A Prayer)
FRAME OF MIND – Vernon Burch (UA)
HELPLESSLY – Moment of Truth (Roulette)
HIJACK – Barrabas (Atco)
MAN WAS MADE TO LOVE WOMAN – Bobbi Martin
(Green Menu)
SWEARIN' TO GOD – Frankie Valli (Private Stock)
WHERE IS THE LOVE? – Betty Wright (Alston)

all tough, down-to-earth messages on the order of their own "For The Love Of Money" and **Stevie Wonder's** "You Haven't Done Nothing." With only one exception, the cuts on **Hamilton Bohannon's** "Insides Out" album (Dakar) are all over five minutes in length – the best, "Foot Stompin Music," runs 7:15 – it's not as consistently danceable as his last album, but this is the best of the new mood music.

Also recommended: "Sign Of The Times," which blends with a version of **Carole King's** "Believe In Humanity," and "I Can't Move No Mountain" from **Margie Joseph's** excellent new album, "Margie," produced by **Arif Mardin** (Atlantic). And these singles: a fiery "Super Kumba" by **Manu Dibango** (Atlantic); "Slippery When Wet" by the **Commodores** (Motown); **Boby Franklin's** "Whatever's Your Sign (You Got to Be Mine)" in a long version (4:51) which even this astrology cynic likes (Babylon); "Honey Baby Theme" with vocals by the **Friends of Distinction** and featuring **Blood Hollins** and **Weldon Irvine** (RCA), and, for a taste of nostalgia, an interesting version of **Kim Weston's** classic "Take Me In Your Arms (Rock Me a Little While)" by **Charity Brown** (A&M). ✺

APRIL 26, 1975

About a month ago, CTI Records sent out a number of unlabeled 45s to its discotheque DJ mailing list, each record bearing only a small white sticker rubber-stamped "SUPERSHIP" and accompanied by a letter asking for the DJ's reaction. The response, according to CTI, has been sufficiently overwhelming – if only in the volume of calls that the company now feels encouraged to go beyond the immediate release of the single (scheduled in the next two weeks) to a more serious involvement in the disco field. "Supership," which takes the "Love Train" metaphor to sea with a pleasant, churning upbeat, turns out to be by **George Benson**, whose pop departure from his usual jazz work CTI wanted to test in the disco market. The reactions I've heard range from shrug-offs to raves like "to die over," with a large middle ground of solid enthusiasm. Watch for this one.

Records, We Get Records: Rich Pampinella from Hippopotamus dropped off a copy of the **Armada Orchestra's** instrumental version of "Do Me Right," a British import on the Contempo label so good it should be picking up some American distribution soon, and another instrumental by the **Sunshine Band** called "Shotgun Shuffle" (TK), which has that light "Rock Your Baby" feel but with some additional hard-edged instrumentation, mainly horns. Both recommended... The Sound Machine's Joe Palminteri sent me a copy of the French "Lady Marmalade" everyone was talking about a week or two ago. It's by someone named **Nanette Workman**, on the Pacha label, and while it does work an interesting variation on the **LaBelle** hit – the singer here takes on the persona of Lady Marmalade, singing "Je suis Lady Marmalade" – it lacks any real original punch. A nice diversion, but disappointing. Thanks anyway, Joe. **Mongo Santamaria** has also put out a version of "Lady Marmalade" (Vaya), this one an instrumental with Latin flavoring, though not enough for my taste. A little hotter, please... And Ronald Coles, the dance master at Colony Records in New York, was good enough to get me a copy of **Lulu's** "Take Your Mama For A Ride, Part 2" (Chelsea), the longer B side of the commercial copy which runs to 5:26 and includes a fine instrumental break that really makes the record. Now I understand what everyone was excited about.

Best New Single This Week (Maybe This Month): "Free Man" by **South Shore Commission** (Wand), produced and written by **Bunny Sigler**, arranged by **Norman Harris** and superhot. The "Disco Mix" version is 5:35 and breaks down-to-basics, soul-shouting dialogue between the male and female lead singers with a driving instrumental segment toward the end. Already on the Top 10 supplied by Armondo Galvez at Flamingo, "Free Man" is the most essential new record right now.

Also recommended: "Hey Baby" by **Anthony White** (Phila. Intl.) and **T.U.M.E.'s** "Love Shortage" (MGM), both Philadelphia productions; **Peter Nero's** lush instrumental, "Soul Ballet," produced by **Tony Silvester** and **Bert DeCoteaux** (Arista); **Oliver Sain's** "London Express," which picks up where his "Bus Stop" left off (Abet) and "Hypertension Part 2," the mostly instrumental side of a song by **Calendar** (Pi Kappa). For more left field tastes, there's a pair of French imports on Mainstream, one the eerily electronic "Dr. Beezar" (Bizarre?) by **Captain Dax** which includes some great demonic laughter, the other an Afro-Latin chant by **Black Blood** called "A.I.E. (A Mwana)" that sounds like slicked-up jungle music. On the other end of the spectrum, but still in left field, there's "Shakedown" by **Elephants Memory** (Atlantic) which builds into some very interesting knockout drumming and chanting and **Little Feat's** "Spanish Moon" (Warner Bros.), a tight production with a sound reminiscent of the **Doobie Brothers** which Wayne Thorberg at Disco 1985 in Los Angeles says is going over well with his crowd.

Album cuts: "Your Lovin' Ain't Good Enough" from **Ben E. King's** "Supernatural" album (Atlantic); the surging instrumental "Tornado" from "The Wiz" original cast recording (Atlantic); "Sneakin' Up Behind You," very **AWB** and sharp on "**The Brecker Brothers**" (Arista) and the full-length "All Because Of You" on **LeRoy Hutson's** "Hutson" album, a very classy release on Curtom, recommended for a relaxed night at home. Not alone. ❷

❝CTI Records sent out a number of unlabeled 45s to its discotheque DJ mailing list, each bearing only a small white sticker rubber-stamped SUPERSHIP❞

FLAMINGO, NEW YORK
DJ: Armondo Galvez

BAD LUCK – Harold Melvin & the Bluenotes (Phila. Intl.)
EASE ON DOWN THE ROAD – Consumer Rapport (A Wing & A Prayer)
FREE MAN – South Shore Commission (Wand)
HELPLESSLY – Moment of Truth (Roulette)
HIJACK – Barrabas (Atco)
HONEY BABY (BE MINE) – Innervision (Private Stock)
THE HUSTLE – Van McCoy (Avco)
PULL YOURSELF TOGETHER – Buddy Miles (Columbia)
TAKE IT FROM ME – Dionne Warwick (Warner Bros.)
WHERE IS THE LOVE? – Betty Wright (Alston)

DISCO 1985, LOS ANGELES
DJ: Wayne Thorberg

CHANGES – Vernon Burch (UA)
DYNOMITE – Tony Camillo's Bazuka (A&M)
E-MAN BOOGIE – Jimmy Castor Bunch (Atlantic)
FIRE – Van McCoy (Avco)
GIVE THE PEOPLE WHAT THEY WANT – O'Jays (Phila. Intl.)
HIJACK – Barrabas (Atco)
I WANNA DANCE WIT 'CHOO – Disco Tex & the Sex-O-Lettes (Chelsea)
LET ME LIVE MY LIFE LOVIN' YOU BABE – Barry White (20th Century)
SPIRIT OF THE BOOGIE – Kool & the Gang (De-Lite)
SWEARIN' TO GOD – Frankie Valli (Private Stock)

ZANZIBAR, WASHINGTON, D.C.
DJ: Bob Evans

AND YOU CALL THAT LOVE – Vernon Burch (UA)
BAD LUCK – Harold Melvin & the Bluenotes (Phila. Intl.)
DISCO BABY – Van McCoy (Avco)
DISCO STOMP – Bohannon (Dakar)
EASE ON DOWN THE ROAD – Consumer Rapport (A Wing & A Prayer)
THE HUSTLE – Van McCoy (Avco)
I CAN UNDERSTAND IT – Kokomo (Columbia)
I WANNA DANCE WIT 'CHOO – Disco Tex & the Sex-O-Lettes (Chelsea)
SWEARIN' TO GOD – Frankie Valli (Private Stock)
TURN THIS MOTHER OUT – Van McCoy (Avco)

DIRECTOIRE, NEW YORK
DJ: Aris Rodriguez

CASTLES – Futures (Buddah)
EASE ON DOWN THE ROAD – Consumer Rapport (A Wing & A Prayer)
HELPLESSLY – Moment of Truth (Roulette)
HIJACK – Barrabas (Atco)
THE HUSTLE – Van McCoy (Avco)
I'LL DO FOR YOU ANYTHING YOU WANT ME TO – Barry White (20th Century)
I WANNA DANCE WIT 'CHOO – Disco Tex & the Sex-O-Lettes (Chelsea)
STOP AND THINK – Trammps (Golden Fleece)
SWEARIN' TO GOD – Frankie Valli (Private Stock)
WHERE IS THE LOVE? – Betty Wright (Alston)

Just Another Way To Say I Love You
Barry White

MAY 3, 1975

Record of the Week: "El Bimbo," which has been surfacing as one of the most popular imports of recent weeks, is suddenly available here in two different versions. One, the original version by **Bimbo Jet**, has been picked up by Scepter which is bringing out the song in its original length (2:25) and a longer, nearly four-minute "disco version" mixing vocal and instrumental sides and scheduled for release later this week. Salsoul Records has released the Spanish version of "El Bimbo" by **Georgie Dann** and re-mixed here to nearly twice its original length, stretching it to 4:40. Both versions, instrumentals with some vocal underlining, have an ecstatic quality reminiscent of **Nino Rota's** scores for Fellini films: airy, a little sentimental, with a particularly European blend of violins and electronics. The Georgie Dann version is slightly more upbeat and tighter, but the Bimbo Jet original, already riding high on the European charts, Top 10 in France and Spain, also has the edge here because of its current play as an import (on the EMI or Pathé labels, depending on the country of origin): Mainly as a result of this week's Top 10 reports, Bimbo Jet entered the Disco File Top 20 (at number 13) before its release on an American label and before Georgie Dann's entrance into the competition. The race is just beginning.

"El Bimbo" is one of the records that Paul Salari and Jay Negron, who calls their operation the PJ Collection and play alternate nights at the Playhouse in the Bronx, have helped introduce to New York. Working with retailer Peter Frost in Toronto, Canada, Salari and Negron bring in batches of disco-oriented imports, distributing them to their own network of DJs and making them available to disco specialists like Downstairs Records. A number of the records they've imported are simply Canadian or European pressings of American releases which they, and many other quality-conscious DJs, feel are technically superior to American copies (e.g.: "Shame, Shame, Shame" and "Girls" by the **Moments and the Whatnauts** in stereo). A few of the records on their joint Top 10 list this week are PJ Collection imports, including "El Bimbo," the **Armada Orchestra's** "Do Me Right," "Love To Dance This One With You" from the **Crystal Grass** album (which Polydor plans to release in June) and a Canadian pressing of **Silver Convention's** "Save Me" which Negron says is different from the American release and features a better stereo separation.

News & Notes: Atlantic Records has hired Douglas Riddick, DJ at New York's Opus I, to handle national discotheque promotion for the label beginning this week. To my knowledge, Riddick is the first disco DJ hired to do promotion in his own field – hopefully, this will signal the move toward more serious disco promotion by the major labels and encourage others to make use of the talents of the many knowledgeable DJs currently at work... PIP Records has picked up an excellent master in "7-6-5-4-3-2-1 (Blow Your Whistle)" by a group called **Gary Tom's Empire**, a hard party record with a lot of whistle blowing, now turning up as an acetate on some New York club turntables and commercially available next week... Franklin Robinson, a friend and sometime disco DJ, suggests speeding up the turntable and playing **Percy Sledge's** "I Believe In You" (on his Capricorn album, "I'll Be Your Everything") which sounds just luscious with the adjustment... And Hector Reyes passed on a Paul Casella discovery: play "Jungle Man" by the **Meters** (on their Reprise album, "Rejuvenation") at 45 rpm instead of 33 1/3-the vocals may sound chipmunkish, but the beat is hot. Recommended: Two albums for international tastes,

"Atlantic has hired Douglas Riddick, DJ at Opus I, to handle national discotheque promotion for the label. To my knowledge he is the first disco DJ hired to do promotion in his own field "

CLUB CASABLANCA, NEW YORK
DJ: Bob Gordon

BAD LUCK – Harold Melvin & the Bluenotes
(Phila. Intl.)
EASE ON DOWN THE ROAD – Consumer Rapport
(A Wing & A Prayer)
EL BIMBO – Bimbo Jet (Pathé/EMI import)
HIJACK – Barrabas (Atco)
THE HUSTLE – Van McCoy (Avco)
SAVE ME/SAVE ME AGAIN – Silver Convention
(Midland Intl.)
SUN GODDESS – Ramsey Lewis (Columbia)
SWEARIN' TO GOD – Frankie Valli (Private Stock)
TAKE IT FROM ME – Dionne Warwick (Warner Bros.)
WHERE IS THE LOVE? – Betty Wright (Alston)

STUDIO ONE, LOS ANGELES
DJ: Tim Zerr

BAD LUCK – Harold Melvin & the Bluenotes (Phila. Intl.)
DYNOMITE – Tony Camillo's Bazuka (A&M)
EASE ON DOWN THE ROAD – Consumer Rapport
(A Wing & A Prayer)
GET DOWN TONIGHT – KC & the Sunshine Band (TK)
GLASSHOUSE – Temptations (Gordy)
THE HUSTLE – Van McCoy (Avco)
I WANNA DANCE WIT 'CHOO – Disco Tex & the
Sex-O-Lettes (Chelsea)
KEEP ON BUMPIN' – Kay-Gees (Gang)
STOP AND THINK/TRAMMPS DISCO THEME – Trammps
(Golden Fleece)
YEARNIN LEARNIN' – Earth, Wind & Fire (Columbia)

THE PLAYHOUSE, NY (BRONX)
DJs: Paul Salari & Jay Negron

BAD LUCK – Harold Melvin & the Bluenotes
(Phila. Intl.)
DO ME RIGHT – Armada Orchestra (Contempo import)
EASE ON DOWN THE ROAD – Consumer Rapport
(A Wing & A Prayer)
EL BIMBO – Bimbo Jet (Pathé/EMI import)
FREE MAN – South Shore Commission (Wand)
GET DOWN TONIGHT – KC & the Sunshine Band (TK)
LOVE TO DANCE THIS ONE WITH YOU – Crystal Grass
(Philips import)
RICH GET RICHER – O'Jays (Phila. Intl.)
SAVE ME – Silver Convention (Columbia import)
STOP AND THINK – Trammps (Golden Fleece)

LOST AND FOUND, WASHINGTON, D.C.
DJ: Frannie DeSantis

BAD LUCK – Harold Melvin & the Bluenotes (Phila. Intl.)
DISCO BABY/THE HUSTLE – Van McCoy (Avco)
DISCO STOMP – Bohannon (Dakar)
EASE ON DOWN THE ROAD – Consumer Rapport
(A Wing & A Prayer)
EL BIMBO – Bimbo Jet (Pathé/EMI import)
GET DOWN TONIGHT – KC & the Sunshine Band (TK)
I WANNA DANCE WIT 'CHOO – Disco Tex & the
Sex-O-Lettes (Chelsea)
LOVE IS EVERYWHERE – City Limits (TSOP)
ONCE YOU GET STARTED – Rufus (ABC)
SWEARIN' TO GOD – Frankie Valli (Private Stock)

the new Editions Makossa release by **Fela Ransome
Kuti & Africa '70**, "Roforofo Fight," containing one cut
to a side, both steamy, exciting Afro-jazz; and **Elkin &
Nelson**, a Spanish brother team with an album just out
on Caytronics all of which I like but particularly notable
for "Samba Samba" and its continuation, "Chevere,"
which are both terrifically driving Latin cuts. And these
singles: "Stone Cold Love Affair" by **The Real Thing** an
English production by **Gerry Shury & Ron Raker** with
very strong Philly-styled vocals (20th Century); **Tapestry's**
light-weight "Life Is What You Make It" with a **Spinners**
sound; and "Getting Off" (B side: "Getting On"), an
instrumental by **Hot Butter** (Dynamo). ◙

DISCO FILE TOP 20

1. **BAD LUCK** – Harold Melvin & The Bluenotes
   (Phila. Intl.)
2. **EASE ON DOWN THE ROAD** – Consumer Rapport
   (Wing And A Prayer)
3. **HIJACK** – Barrabas (Atco)
4. **WHERE IS THE LOVE** – Betty Wright (Alston)
5. **THE HUSTLE** – Van McCoy (Avco)
6. **SWEARIN' TO GOD** – Frankie Valli (Private Stock)
7. **I WANNA DANCE WIT' CHOO** – Disco Tex & The
   Sex-O-Lettes (Chelsea)
8. **HELPLESSLY** – Moment Of Truth (Roulette)
9. **TAKE IT FROM ME** – Dionne Warwick
   (Warner Bros.)
10. **HIJACK** – Herbie Mann (Atlantic)
11. **GET DOWN TONIGHT** – KC & the Sunshine
    Band (TK)
12. **GLASS HOUSE** – Temptations (Gordy)
13. **EL BIMBO** – Bimbo Jet (Pathe/EMI import)
14. **STOP AND THINK** – Trammps (Golden Fleece)
15. **E-MAN BOOGIE** – Jimmy Castor Bunch (Atlantic)
16. **CRYSTAL WORLD** – Crystal Grass (Polydor)
17. **AND YOU CALL THAT LOVE** – Vernon Burch (UA)
18. **SAVE ME/SAVE ME AGAIN** – Silver Convention
    (Midland Intl.)
19. **ARE YOU READY FOR THIS** – The Brothers (RCA)
20. **LOVE IS EVERYWHERE** – City Limits (TSOP)

MAY 10, 1975

Atlantic's innovative "Disco Disc" series – a group of non-commercial singles specially chosen for and serviced exclusively to discotheques – began last week with the release of "Mad Love" by **Barrabas** and **Hot Chocolate's** "Disco Queen" (both cuts from the groups' current albums), and continues this week with the much-anticipated longer version (6:23) of **Consumer Rapport's** "Ease On Down The Road" and a previously unannounced long versions of "Tornado," the surging instrumental from "The Wiz" original cast recording, expanded to 6:39. A few advance copies of the long "Ease On Down" were leaked to certain DJs and immediately became the talk of the town. The new version – which, like "Tornado," was re-worked in New York's Soundtek studio by **Stephen Schaeffer** and **Harold Wheeler** – adds some rich **MFSB**-style instrumental breaks and plays around with repeated fragments of music and vocals which give the song an exciting texture. Atlantic already feels it's gotten a strong enough response to the Hot Chocolate cut to follow it up with a commercial release of "Disco Queen," but how will they deal with the inevitable commercial demand – if only from avid disco-goers – for the 6:23 "Ease On Down," which was released, like the other records, in the "Disco Disc" series, on a special 7-inch, 33 1/3 rpm disc and would probably resist the compression of a regular 45? Tune in next week.

Warner Brothers will probably be faced with a similar question following their special disco release of a record called "Dance, Dance, Dance" by **Calhoon**, which should appear later this week on 10-inch, 33 1/3 rpm pressings that run about 6:30. A wonderfully up, high-spirited record with some hot instrumental breaks (especially the first time the strings come flowing in), "Dance, Dance, Dance" (not to be confused with **Liquid Smoke's** single with the same title) is one of the best singles to come our way this week. Added attraction: a version of **Titanic's** powerful "Rain 2000" on the B side. A regular commercial release of "Dance, Dance, Dance"/"Rain 2000" will be available in two or three weeks on the Warner Spector label, but the A side will be cut nearly in half and the longer version kept for a future album cut.

One of the best instrumentals I've heard in a while comes, unexpectedly, from Chicago or, more precisely, Oak Park, Illinois, where two brothers named **Don** and **Ken Marier** have written, produced and arranged a luxurious, lush number called "Lady, Lady, Lady" by a group they named the **Boogie Man Orchestra**. The Mariers released the record on their own label, Boogie Man Records (this is their first release), going one step at a time from an initial shipment to Chicago discotheques, to retailers in a tri-state area and, through special mailings, to interested parties around the country. My mailing came from Rufus Smith, publisher of a monthly disco newsletter in Chicago called "Disco-Tech," which is one of the most informative and well-organized of those I've seen so far (Note: I'd appreciate seeing copies of any other newsletters currently being published for the disco market for review in a future column). Smith says "Lady, Lady, Lady" is among the top 15 records in the Chicago area and, as a result, has started to hit the radio there. The instrumental, which draws from the styles of **Isaac Hayes**, **Gene Page** and **Van McCoy** for maximum effect, was pressed in two lengths, 3:19 and 4:11, and would, I think, make a wise master purchase.

In my rush to congratulate Douglas Riddick on his new position at Atlantic last week, I wrote that he was the "first disco DJ hired to do promotion in his own field." I was wrong. My apologies to David Todd, DJ at New York's Adams Apple, who has been doing an excellent job in disco promotion at RCA for some time now and who knows what I like... That sold-out night of **LaBelle's** week at the Harkness Theater in New York – Thursday, May 8 – was bought by Flamingo discotheque for its members and guests, with a party to follow at the club. Very classy... Best studio news this week: **Van McCoy** is in the studio with **Faith, Hope & Charity** (a trio which used to include **Zulema**) polishing up a 7-minute version of "Little Bit Of Love," which he originally wrote and produced for **Brenda & the Tabulations**. This one for RCA.

Just out of curiosity, I asked the four DJs polled this week to tell me what records they would recommend to anyone who wanted to buy just two of the best new records available, This is the sort of question I'm often asked, so I decided to pass it on. Their responses: Eddie Rivera from Cork & Bottle suggests "Think Twice" from the **Donald Byrd** album, "Stepping Into Tomorrow" (Blue Note), and "Stop And Think" on the **Trammps** album (Golden Fleece); Chuck Parsons, in Washington

> **❝I was wrong. My apologies to David Todd, DJ at Adam's Apple, who has been doing an excellent job at disco promotion at RCA for some time now, and who knows what I like❞**

SOUND MACHINE, NEW YORK
DJ: Joe Palminteri

ARE YOU READY FOR THIS – The Brothers (RCA)
BAD LUCK – Harold Melvin & the Bluenotes (Phila. Intl.)
EASE ON DOWN THE ROAD – Consumer Rapport
(A Wing & A Prayer long version)
EL BIMBO – Bimbo Jet /Georgie Dann (Scepter/Salsoul)
FREE MAN – South Shore Commission (Wand)
THE HUSTLE – Van McCoy (Avco)
LOVE DO ME RIGHT – Rockin' Horse (RCA)
PEACE AND LOVE – Ron Butler & the Ramblers (Playboy)
STOP AND THINK/SAVE A PLACE – Trammps
(Golden Fleece)
SUN GODDESS – Ramsey Lewis (Columbia)

HADAAR, NEW YORK (STATEN ISLAND)
DJ: Richard Conte

BAD LUCK – Harold Melvin & the Bluenotes (Phila. Intl.)
EASE ON DOWN THE ROAD – Consumer Rapport
(A Wing & A Prayer)
FORGET THAT GIRL – De-lightful (Vigor)
FREE MAN – South Shore Commission (Wand)
HELPLESSLY – Moment of Truth (Roulette)
THE HUSTLE –Van McCoy (Roulette)
PEACE AND LOVE – Ron Butler & the Ramblers (Playboy)
STOP AND THINK – Trammps (Golden Fleece)
SUN GODDESS – Ramsey Lewis (Columbia)
SWEARIN' TO GOD – Frankie Valli (Private Stock)

CORK & BOTTLE, NEW YORK
DJ: Eddie Rivera

BAD LUCK – Harold Melvin & the Bluenotes
(Phila. Intl.)
EASE ON DOWN THE ROAD – Consumer Rapport
(A Wing & A Prayer)
EL BIMBO – Chocolate Boys (Disques Elver import)
FOOTSTEPS IN THE SHADOWS – Kantlose Orchestra &
Chorus (Buddah)
HELPLESSLY – Moment of Truth (Roulette)
HIJACK – Barrabas/Herbie Mann (Atco/Atlantic)
THE HUSTLE – Van McCoy (Avco)
I JUST CAN'T SAY GOODBYE – Philly Devotions
(Columbia)
ONE DAY OF PEACE – Love Committee (TSOP)
ROLLING DOWN A MOUNTAINSIDE – Main Ingredient
(RCA)

GRAND CENTRAL, WASHINGTON, D.C.
DJ: Chuck Parsons

BAD LUCK – Harold Melvin & the Bluenotes (Phila. Intl.)
CASTLES – Futures (Buddah)
EASE ON DOWN THE ROAD – Consumer Rapport
(A Wing & A Prayer)
EL BIMBO – Bimbo Jet (Scepter)
FOOT STOMPIN' MUSIC/DISCO STOMP – Bohannon
(Dakar)
HIJACK – Barrabas/Herbie Mann (Atco/Atlantic)
HONEYBEE/REACH OUT, I'LL BE THERE – Gloria Gaynor
(MGM)
THE HUSTLE – Van McCoy (Avco)
WHAT CAN I DO FOR YOU – LaBelle (Epic)
WHERE IS THE LOVE? – Betty Wright (Alston)

at Grand Central, chose "El Bimbo" by **Bimbo Jet** (Scepter) and the whole **Bohannon** album, "Insides Out" (Dakar); Richie Conte from Hadaar picked "Free Man" by **South Shore Commission** (Wand) and **Frankie Valli's** album cut, "Swearin' To God" (Private Stock); and the Sound Machine's Joe Palminteri also chose "Free Man" along with "7-6-5-4-3-2-1 (Blow Your Whistle)" by **Gary Toms Empire** (PIP). Additional suggestions: Rivera says **Mary McCreary's** "Singing The Blues" (on her "Jezebel" album and the B side of her last single on Shelter) is going over very well with its tasty **Leon Russell** rockin' soul feel, and Palminteri raved about an All Platinum release (already out in England) called "Sending Out An SOS" by **Retta Young**, which sounded good and snappy even over the phone – due out here soon.

Disco file Recommends: "Run Johnny" by **Jimmy Maelen** (Epic), the surprise of the week – for anyone who liked "Highway Driver," another tough record that builds and builds; "Three Steps From True Love" by the **Reflections** (Capitol), which sounds very much like "Do Me Right" and, at its best, approaches gospel strength; another surprise, though more left field, in "Jive Talkin' " by the **Bee Gees** (RSO); "Jungle Fever '75" by **Chakachas** (Polydor), basically a re-release with a suggestive climax break at the end which expands the original to 4:15, but this may be just in time to catch rising temperatures and pick up all over again; "Action Speaks Louder Than Words," a pointed message song by **Chocolate Milk** with an **Allen Toussaint** production (RCA); the new **Love Unlimited Orchestra** opus, "Forever In Love" (20th Century); **Ujima's** long version of "A Shoulder To Lean On," 5:22 and produced by **Hurtt** and **Bell** (Epic); and for sexy slow, **Solomon Burke's** "Everlasting Love," a composition and co-production of his own with some **Gene Page** touches for a little of that sugary (**Barry**) White frosting. ❂

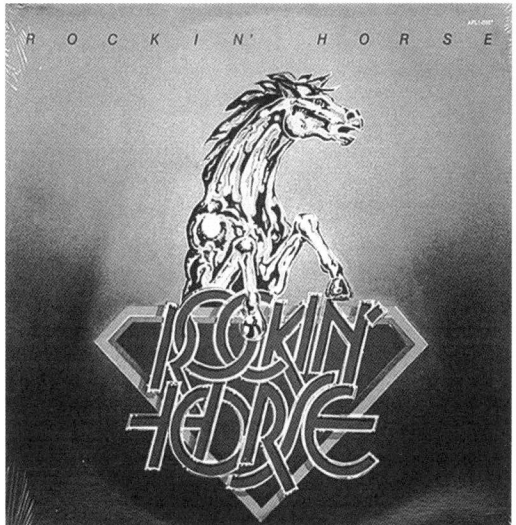

Motown has always produced some of the best dance music around, but at the end of this week, they're bringing out three albums specially designed for what is now known as the Disco Market. Two of the albums are essentially traditional re-package collections under the titles "Disc-O-Tech #1" and "Disc-O-Tech #2," initial installments in a projected series of releases devoted to the company's most danceable records. The first collection is basic history: **Stevie Wonder's** "Uptight," **Junior Walker's** "Roadrunner," "Dancing In The Street," "ABC," "Going To A Go-Go" and a few unexpected selections like **Shorty Long's** "Function At The Junction" and **Gladys Knight and the Pips'** version of "You Need Love Like I Do (Don't You)." Also included: the unsatisfying single version of **Eddie Kendricks'** brilliant "Girl You Need A Change of Mind;" an automatic 10-point deduction. Package #2 is more current and less predictable, including "Bad Weather" by the **Supremes**; **G. C. Cameron's** overlooked single, "No Matter Where;" "It's All Over But The Shoutin' " by **Gladys Knight and the Pips**; "Law Of The Land" by the **Temptations**; **Willie Hutch's** "You Sure Know How To Love Your Man;" **Kendricks'** consistently popular "Date with the Rain" and others. Although the first collection is put together like any other Motown re-pack (and they do have a certain genius in the re-cycling field), "Disc-O-Tech #2" attempts to blend the cuts into one another, non-stop disco style, making it one of the more successful house party records in some time.

The third album in the Motown release is called "Magic Disco Machine" and is the most interesting of the three because it's all instrumental and all previously unreleased material (with the exception of the instrumental version of "You Don't Know How Hard It Is To Make It," which was re-mixed slightly from the B side of the **Devastating Affair** single from last year). The tracks are the work of a number of producers in the Motown stable, some old material, some created just for this package. The best is the opening cut, "Control Tower," produced by **Frank Wilson** (whose work with Eddie Kendricks has been outstanding) and running, with the addition of a "reprise" cut, a total of 7:12. Other cuts average three minutes and the standouts include "(I Could Never Make) A Better Man Than You" with some vocals by **Sisters Love**, "Let's Go Back to Day One" and "Window Shopping," both **Hal Davis** productions.

The most talked-about new record this week is **Hubert Laws'** "The Chicago Theme," which has been leaking out of CTI in advance of its commercial release and getting ecstatic reaction everywhere it's played (one of the places: The Alley in Queens, where DJ Roy Thode has been pushing it). The album's title cut is the one that's exciting all the comment – it's light and lush but with plenty of sharp edges to keep it from turning into one of those Reddi-whip extravaganzas we've had so much of. A **Bob James** composition that runs 5:37, "The Chicago Theme" sounds like the next big instrumental and should be available early next week. Tom Savarese, who's playing at the new private club everyone's talking about, New York's 12 West, reports getting good reaction to a potentially difficult "Alvin Stone (The Birth and Death of a Gangster)," the long (7:50) title cut from the new **Fantastic Four** album (Westbound/20th Century). An ambitious and tough short story of a song, "Alvin Stone" may be the sort of thing that won't go over everywhere but deserves the attention of the more adventurous DJ... Bobby Guttadaro of Le Jardin is definitely one of the more adventurous DJs, and among the records he reports playing this week are: "How Long" by **Ace** (Anchor), which does sound deceptively

> ## ❝ Motown is bringing out three albums specially designed for what is now known as the Disco market ❞

12 WEST, NEW YORK
DJ: Tom Savarese

BAD LUCK – Harold Melvin & the Bluenotes
(Phila. Intl.)
EASE ON DOWN THE ROAD – Consumer Rapport
(A Wing & A Prayer long version)
EL BIMBO – Bimbo Jet (Scepter)
FOOT STOMPIN' MUSIC/DISCO STOMP – Bohannon
(Dakar)
FREE MAN – South Shore Commission (Wand)
HELPLESSLY – Moment of Truth (Roulette)
LOVE DO ME RIGHT – Rockin' Horse (RCA)
SUN GODDESS – Ramsey Lewis (Columbia)
TAKE IT FROM ME – Dionne Warwick (Warner Bros.)
WHERE IS THE LOVE? – Betty Wright (Alston)

LE JARDIN, NEW YORK
DJ: Bobby Guttadaro

BAD LUCK – Harold Melvin & the Bluenotes
(Phila. Intl.)
EASE ON DOWN THE ROAD – Consumer Rapport
(A Wing & A Prayer long version)
FOOT STOMPIN' MUSIC – Bohannon (Dakar)
FREE MAN – South Shore Commission (Wand)
LOVE DO ME RIGHT – Rockin' Horse (RCA)
SURVIVAL – O'Jays (Phila. Intl.)
SWEARIN' TO GOD – Frankie Valli (Private Stock)
THREE STEPS FROM TRUE LOVE – Reflections
(Capitol)
TORNADO – 'The Wiz' Original Cast (Atlantic)
WHERE IS THE LOVE? – Betty Wright (Alston)

INTERNATIONAL ASTRO DISC, PHILA.
DJ: Mimi

BUS STOP – Oliver Sain (Abet)
CRYSTAL WORLD – Crystal Grass (Polydor)
EAST COAST GROOVE – Bohannon (Dakar)
GET DOWN – Kaygees (Gang)
HAPPY FEELIN' – Earth, Wind & Fire (Columbia)
IF YOU'VE GOT IT, YOU'LL GET IT – Headhunters
(Arista)
KEEP ON BUMPIN' – Kaygees (Gang)
PECK YA NECK – Mandrill (UA)
SPIRIT OF THE BOOGIE – Kool & the Gang (De-Lite)
WHAT'S YOUR SIGN – Edwin Birdsong (Bamboo)

THE ALLEY, NY (QUEENS)
DJ: Roy Thode

ARE YOU READY FOR THIS – Brothers (RCA)
BAD LUCK – Harold Melvin & the Bluenotes
(Phila. Intl.)
CRYSTAL WORLD – Crystal Grass (Polydor)
DISCO STOMP – Bohannon (Dakar)
EASE ON DOWN THE ROAD – Consumer Rapport
(A Wing & A Prayer)
EL BIMBO – Bimbo Jet (Scepter)
HELPLESSLY – Moment of Truth (Roulette)
THE HUSTLE – Van McCoy (Avco)
TRAMMPS DISCO THEME – Trammps
(Golden Fleece)
WHERE IS THE LOVE? – Betty Wright (Alston)

491 WEST STREET, NYC
TELEPHONE 924-6855

Philadelphia; **Martha Reeves'** first single for Arista, "Love Blind," her own composition with a production by **Tony Silvester** and **Bert DeCoteaux**, which sounds like a cop of their own production for **Ben E. King** on "Supernatural Thing" (Bobby suggests speeding "Love Blind" up for maximum effect); and, from Latin left field (a favorite hang-out), the very sexy "Salsa Na' Ma'" by **Azuquita**, which one-ups "Jungle Fever" (the B side of their Vaya single, "Coco De Maria").

Recommended: "Cool It," a fine instrumental from **The 3 Pieces** album (Fantasy), and "Spaced," "Naked As The Day I Was Born" and "You're My Baby," more glowing instrumentals from **Stanley Turrentine's** excellent "In the Pocket" album (Fantasy), produced by **Gene & Billy Page** and Turrentine – all for slow, cool-off periods. And these singles: **Ike & Tina Turner's** raunchy, rocking "Baby – Get It On" (LJA) and **Ripple's** on-time message, "This Ain't No Time To Be Giving Up" (GRC). ◐

MAY 24, 1975

❝ Retta Young is just missin' her man, but she's not relying on a phone call to get her delightful desperation across ❞

The two best singles this week are **Retta Young's** "(Sending Out An) S.O.S." (All Platinum) and "Sexy," a tantalizing preview of the long-awaited (too long) new **MFSB** album (Philadelphia International). "S.O.S.," which Joe Palminteri gave us excited advance word on two weeks back, has a high-gloss **Carol Douglas** sound, punctuated by bursts of sharp telegraph beeps and the familiar crackling guitar. Like Douglas, Retta Young is just missin' her man, but she's not relying on a phone call to get her delightful desperation across. On the B side: an instrumental version with chorus vocals called, predictably, "More S.O.S."; together, they make All Platinum's hottest release since "Shame, Shame, Shame." "Sexy," all instrumental, is only a fast-food bite compared to the usual MFSB feast and it does start out somewhat hesitantly. But once the whole orchestra jumps in, and a little later, when the sax solo begins, you're carried away in that great, soaring Philadelphia sound all over again. Written and produced by **Gamble & Huff**, arranged by **Bobby Martin**.

Other recommended singles: "I Could Dance All Night," which brings **Archie Bell & the Drells** back in top form (on TSOP), probably because they're also back in Philadelphia where they did most of their best work – produced by **Bunny Sigler**, arranged by **Ronnie Baker** and reminiscent of a speeded-up "Together" by the **Intruders**; **Chuck Jackson**, also back, with a surprising, building "Love Lights" (All Platinum, on their handsome new label); and Motown has re-issued **Junior Walker & the All Stars'** great "What Does It Take (To Win Your Love)" (from 1969) because of a movie tie-in ("Aloha, Bobby & Rose") – a lot of Walker's work has gotten richer with age and this one could make an interesting revival. From country rock left field: The feminist counterpart to **Randy Pie** ("Highway Driver") and **Jimmy Maelen** ("Run Johnny") is **Debbie Burgan**, who tears out an angry song called "Cabin Fever" (A&M). Sample lines: "The kids climb the curtains and I climb the walls/And he's with the boys havin' fun." At which club?

More left field (if only because their changes are so disconcerting): **Barbara Hall's** tasty "You Brought It On Yourself" (Innovation II), produced in part by **Major Lance**, who combines 1965 style with 1975 style for some interesting results (this is the B side of "Drop My Heart Off at the Door"), and "I Know Where You're Coming From" on **Loleatta Holloway's** "Cry to Me"

album (Aware) (on the same album, listen to "The World Don't Owe You Nothing" – very **Staple Singers** – and her version of **Ruby Andrews'** classic "Casanova").

Recommended in spite of an overwhelming sense of deja vu: "Out Among 'Em," a studio album by a group called **Love Childs Afro Cuban Blues Band** (Roulette), dedicated to disco DJs and including versions of "Where Do We Go From Here," "Life And Death In G&A," "Black Skin Blue Eyed Boys," "Once You Get Started," "Ask Me" and **Joe Cuba's** "Bang Bang" – all somewhat uneven but most brightened by terrific instrumental highlights. The best cuts: "Black Skin Blue Eyed Boys," "Once You Get Started" and "Ask Me" after the vocals. More satisfying: the **Choice Four's** new album, produced by **Van McCoy** ("The Choice Four" on RCA) and containing three fine upbeat cuts – "You're My Happiness," "Is It Love" and "Until We Said Goodbye" – as well as a longer version of "Hook It Up."

Feedback: Bill Vos at Reflections in New York recommends two jazz cuts – **Lonnie Liston Smith's** solid, glowing "Expansions" (Signature – Vos says he prefers the 45 version, though it also appears on an album of the same name) and **Cleveland Eaton's** overlooked "Chi Town Theme," recommended here some time back and the opening cut of the "Plenty Good Eaton" album (Black Jazz)... Artie Feldman in Chicago at Our Den puts "Lady, Lady, Lady," that lush instrumental by the **Boogie Man Orchestra**; on his Top 10 this week and points out that he's been playing it for months. But the Chicago breakout is already hitting New York with some force – Steve D'Acquisto at Broadway and a number of other DJs who have gotten the record are reporting strong response.

Coming Up: An album by Motown's gutsy **Yvonne Fair** called "The Bitch Is Black" (also in the same release: new albums from the **Supremes**, whoever they are this time around, and the **Jackson 5**); an **Esther Phillips** transformation of **Jerry Butler's** "One Night Affair" (on Kudu); and an update of **Betty Everett's** "Shoop Shoop Song," produced by **Tony Silvester** and **Bert deCoteaux** for England's challenge to **Minnie Riperton**, **Linda Lewis** (on Arista)... And an open meeting for all New York area disco DJs to discuss DJ – record company relations and other taking-care-of-business matters – to be held Monday, June 2, at 3:00 in the afternoon at David Mancuso's 99 Prince Street. Be there. ◗

BROADWAY, NEW YORK (BROOKLYN)
DJ: Steve D'Acquisto

ARE YOU READY FOR THIS – The Brothers (RCA)
BAD LUCK – Harold Melvin & the Bluenotes (Phila. Intl.)
EASE ON DOWN THE ROAD – Consumer Rapport
(A Wing & A Prayer disco version)
EL BIMBO – Bimbo Jet (Scepter)
FOOT STOMPIN' MUSIC – Bohannon (Dakar)
FREE MAN – South Shore Commission (Wand)
THE HUSTLE – Van McCoy (Avco)
I WANNA DANCE WIT 'CHOO – Disco Tex & the
Sex-O-Lettes (Chelsea)
STOP AND THINK – Trammps (Golden Fleece)
SWEARIN' TO GOD – Frankie Valli (Private Stock)

REFLECTIONS, NEW YORK
DJ, Bill Vos

BAD LUCK – Harold Melvin & the Bluenotes
(Phila. Intl.)
EASE ON DOWN THE ROAD – Consumer Rapport
(A Wing & A Prayer)
EL BIMBO – Bimbo Jet (Scepter)
FOOT STOMPIN' MUSIC – Bohannon (Dakar)
FREE MAN – South Shore Commission (Wand)
THE HUSTLE – Van McCoy (Avco)
I CAN UNDERSTAND IT – Kokomo (Columbia)
MISTER MAGIC – Grover Washington, Jr. (Kudu)
PEACE AND LOVE – Ron Butler & the Ramblers (Playboy)
SWEARIN' TO GOD – Frankie Valli (Private Stock)

BETTER DAYS, NEW YORK
DJ: Toraino "Tee" Scott

AND YOU CALL THAT LOVE – Vernon Burch (UA)
EASE ON DOWN THE ROAD – Consumer Rapport
(A Wing & A Prayer)
FOOT STOMPIN' MUSIC/DISCO STOMP – Bohannon
(Dakar)
FREE MAN – South Shore Commission (Wand)
HONEY BABY (BE MINE) – Innervision (Private Stock)
I CAN UNDERSTAND IT /KITTY SITTIN' PRETTY –
Kokomo (Columbia)
LOVE DO ME RIGHT – Rockin' Horse (RCA)
STOP AND THINK – Trammps (Golden Fleece)
SWEARIN' TO GOD – Frankie Valli (Private Stock)
TORNADO – 'The Wiz' Original Cast (Atlantic)

OUR DEN, CHICAGO
DJ: Artie Feldman

ARE YOU READY FOR THIS – The Brothers (RCA)
BAD LUCK – Harold Melvin & the Bluenotes (Phila. Intl.)
BUS STOP/LONDON EXPRESS – Oliver Sain (Abet)
EASE ON DOWN THE ROAD – Consumer Rapport
(A Wing & A Prayer)
FREE MAN – South Shore Commission (Wand)
THE HUSTLE – Van McCoy (Avco)
I WANNA DANCE WIT 'CHOO – Disco Tex & the
Sex-O-Lettes (Chelsea)
LADY, LADY, LADY – Boogie Man Orchestra (Boogie Man)
TURN THIS MOTHER OUT – Van McCoy (Avco)
WHERE IS THE LOVE? – Betty Wright (Alston)

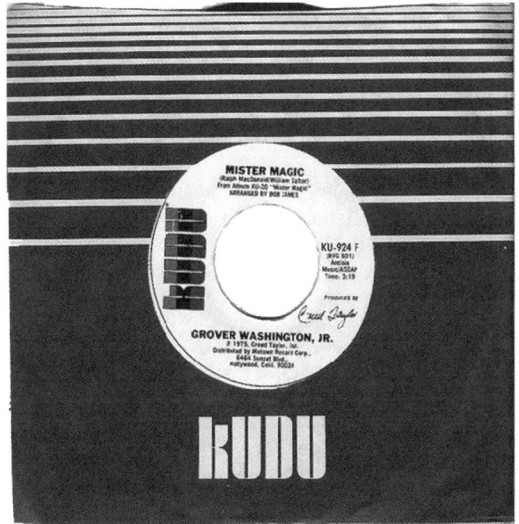

MAY 31, 1975

Knockout of the Week: The cut everybody's talking about is "Forever Came Today," the six-minute-plus opener on the new **Jackson 5** album, "Moving Violation" (Motown) – Kenn Friedman, my dedicated west coast correspondent, reports it was the sensation of the re-opening of newly-remodeled Studio One in L.A. and David Todd, DJ at New York's Adams Apple, has already slipped it onto his forward-looking top 10 this week. The Jackson 5 have been full of surprises the past few years; no one was quite prepared for the brilliance of their "Get It Together" album, and this is another giant step. Producer **Brian Holland** has re-thought the **Holland-Dozier-Holland Supremes** classic (1968) in entirely new terms and the results, as interpreted by the J5, are stunning, surely one of the finest productions this year. Best part: the beginning, repeated throughout, when the group sings, "Ever, forever, ever and ever and ever," a chant that sounds like echoes in a deep canyon, the voices bouncing from speaker to speaker. The rest of "Moving Violation" is almost totally upbeat, but these cuts stand out: "(You Were Made) Especially for Me" and "Honey Love," both Brian Holland productions, and "Body Language," produced by **Hal Davis**, who was responsible for "Get It Together."

Another powerful up-date job was done by producers **Tony Silvester** and **Bert deCoteaux** on "The Shoop Shoop Song," which has been transformed disco-style for **Linda Lewis** and renamed with the original's parenthetical title, "It's In His Kiss" (Arista). Lewis, who sounds something like early Michael Jackson, carries the song away with two beautifully sustained wails over two of the record's many breaks. Knockout number two.

Two records that must be heard to be believed: John Luongo reports that one of the most off-the-wall records being played in Boston right now is **George Fischoff's** wildly eccentric "King Kingston" (Pickwick International), an outrageous melange of piano styles run together and underlined by a heavy, constant bass beat. Though the record is certainly far left field, Luongo says that when the bass is brought way up, it gets over; even reminds him of **The Baronet's** obscure "Pelican Dance." And in an entirely different vein, there's the **Cuff Links'** "Some Girls Do (Some Girls Don't)" (Roulette), which has a chirpy girl chorus singing, "Some girls do, some girls don't/ Some girls will and some girls won't/you can't force a person to do it." It ends with a guy singing, "Some guys do, some guys don't, etc." a line I'm more familiar with, though here he's talking about marriage. Very 1962 white rock, but a wonderful anachronism.

Feedback: Both Danae Jacovidis from Styx in Boston and Flamingo's Vincent Carleo were talking about **Bimbo Jet's** "La Palanga" this week, an import on the Pathé label that reportedly blends very well with that group's successful "El Bimbo." "It has that same Italian wedding dance feeling," says Jacovidis, and if it's mixed in after "El Bimbo," "at first, they don't realize it's a different song"... John Iozia, who often does the lights at Flamingo, alerted me that the B side of **The Bee Gees'** "Jive Talkin'," titled "Wind Of Change" and running 4:54, is also pretty extraordinary and in a very different style... Rafael Charres, DJ at New York's Rouge et Blanc, was the first of a number of people to rave about the new **Crown Heights Affair** single, "Dreaming A Dream" (De-Lite), another attractive instrumental from the group that made "Super Rod." The A side adds vocals, but the "disco version" on the B side (3:45) concentrates on the production and reduces the vocals to a bright break in the center. Recommended, and another cool instrumental for hot Summer nights.

Also recommended: **Fay Hauser**, who gives you flashes of **Dionne Warwicke** in "You Bring The Sun In The Morning" (Satellite Music International), singing about how fine her man is – the "disco mix" is 5:10 long and awfully good – watch it get picked up by a larger label soon; **Demis Roussos'** **Barry White**-styled "Midnight Is the Time I Need You" (Big Tree); **Loleatta Holloway's** "I Know Where You're Coming From," the record I fell in love with last week, now out on a single (Aware); "Let Me Try Again" the

> **" The six-minute-plus opener on the new Jackson 5 album, "Forever Came Today," was the sensation of the re-opening of newly-remodeled Studio One in L.A "**

ADAMS APPLE, NEW YORK
DJ: David Todd

CHICAGO THEME – Hubert Laws (CTI)
EXPANSIONS – Lonnie Liston Smith
(Flying Dutchman)
FOREVER CAME TODAY – Jackson Five (Motown)
FREE MAN – South Shore Commission (Wand)
THE HUSTLE – Van McCoy (Avco)
LOVE DO ME RIGHT – Rockin' Horse (RCA)
MAN WAS MADE TO LOVE WOMAN – Bobbi Martin
(Green Menu)
SEXY – MFSB (Phila. Intl.)
SUPERSHIP – George Benson (CTI)
SWEARIN' TO GOD – Frankie Valli (Private Stock)

ROUGE ET BLANC, NEW YORK
DJ: Rafael Charres

CAN'T LIVE THIS WAY – Barnaby Bye (Atlantic)
CHICAGO THEME – Hubert Laws (CTI)
EASE ON DOWN THE ROAD – Consumer Rapport
(A Wing & A Prayer)
EL BIMBO – Bimbo Jet (Scepter)
FREE MAN – South Shore Commission (Wand)
LADY, LADY, LADY – Boogie Man Orchestra
(Boogie Man)
MISTER MAGIC – Grover Washington, Jr. (Kudu)
SWEARIN' TO GOD – Frankie Valli (Private Stock)
THREE STEPS FROM TRUE LOVE – Reflections
(Capitol)
YOU'VE BROKEN MY HEART – Sound Experience
(Soundville)

STYX, BOSTON
DJ: Danae Jacovidis

EASE ON DOWN THE ROAD – Consumer Rapport
(A Wing & A Prayer)
EL BIMBO – Bimbo Jet (Scepter)
FOOT STOMPIN' MUSIC – Bohannon (Dakar)
FRAME OF MIND – Vernon Burch (UA)
FREE MAN – South Shore Commission (Wand)
GET DOWN TONIGHT – KC & the Sunshine Band (TK)
HAPPY FEELIN' – Earth, Wind & Fire (Columbia)
THE HUSTLE – Van McCoy (Avco)
STOP AND THINK – Trammps (Golden Fleece)
TORNADO – 'The Wiz' Original Cast (Atlantic)

FLAMINGO, NEW YORK
DJ: Vincent Carleo

ARE YOU READY FOR THIS – The Brothers (RCA)
EASE ON DOWN THE ROAD – Consumer Rapport
(A Wing & A Prayer)
EL BIMBO – Bimbo Jet (Scepter)
FOOT STOMPIN' MUSIC – Bohannon (Dakar)
FREE MAN – South Shore Commission (Wand)
GEORGIA'S AFTER HOURS – Popcorn Wylie (ABC)
JUST A LITTLE BIT OF YOU – Michael Jackson
(Motown)
STOP AND THINK/SAVE A PLACE – Trammps
(Golden Fleece)
TAKE IT FROM ME – Dionne Warwick (Warner Bros.)
THREE STEPS FROM TRUE LOVE – Reflections
(Capitol)

J.J. Jackson record that was circulating on dubs a few months back, now out on MagnaGlide (through London) with a more than five-minute version on the B side that reminds me of "I'll Be Holding On;" and the B side of **Barry White's** new single, "Anything You Want Me To," the instrumental version of the A side, "I'll Do For You Anything You Want Me To" (20th Century).

Left field: The B side of a new Chess single by **Tony Gregory & Family Child**, called "Gimme Gimme" (the A side is a ballad, "One More Time"), one of those records you're not sure about until the end (begun here by some Latin percussion) which is so nice you pick the needle up and start it from the beginning again – unlikely, but interesting; and "Ain't Gonna Be A Next Time," a **Patrick Adams** job for a group named **Magnetic Touch** (Cheryl).

Footnotes: Now available: those three Motown anthology albums under the "Disc-O-Tech" logo – volumes #1 and #2 and the excellent "Magic Disco Machine" containing the new batch of instrumentals... And for those of you who have just gotten into **Popcorn Wylie's** powerful, driving "Georgia's After Hours" (from his ABC album, "Extrasensory Perception"), let me point out, in all immodesty, that the cut was recommended in the first installment of DISCO FILE (November 16, 1974), along with **Hot Chocolate's** "Makin' Music," as an "album cut to watch." ✏

DISCO FILE TOP 20
1. **EASE ON DOWN THE ROAD** – Consumer Rapport (Wing And A Prayer)
2. **BAD LUCK** – Harold Melvin & The Bluenotes (Phila. Intl.)
3. **FREE MAN** – South Shore Commission (Wand)
4. **THE HUSTLE** – Van McCoy (Avco)
5. **EL BIMBO** – Bimbo Jet (Pathe/EMI import)
6. **SWEARIN' TO GOD** – Frankie Valli (Private Stock)
7. **STOP AND THINK** – Trammps (Golden Fleece)
8. **FOOT STOMPIN' MUSIC** – Bohannon (Dakar)
9. **HIJACK** – Barrabas (Atco)
10. **WHERE IS THE LOVE** – Betty Wright (Alston)
11. **DISCO STOMP** – Bohannon (Dakar)
12. **LOVE DO ME RIGHT** – Rockin' Horse (RCA)
13. **ARE YOU READY FOR THIS** – The Brothers (RCA)
14. **SUN GODDESS** – Ramsey Lewis (Columbia)
15. **GET DOWN TONIGHT** – KC & the Sunshine Band (TK)
16. **I WANNA DANCE WIT' CHOO** – Disco Tex & The Sex-O-Lettes (Chelsea)
17. **HELPLESSLY** – Moment Of Truth (Roulette)
18. **THREE STEPS FROM TRUE LOVE** – Reflections (Capitol)
19. **TAKE IT FROM ME** – Dionne Warwick (Warner Bros.)
20. **TORNADO** – "The Wiz" original cast (Atlantic)

JUNE 7, 1975

Martin Ragusa and George Cucuzzella, two DJs who play at a Montreal club called the Tube, dropped in at the office this past week, prepared an impromptu Top 10 and pulled a few records out of a brown paper bag for us to hear. The most interesting was a French single they say is without question the number one record in their club, a fascinating oddity called "Chinese Kung Fu" by **Banzai** (Disques Fleche), which has just begun filtering into New York. It's an instrumental punctuated by kung fu shouts and threaded with a bright line of Moog music, sounding like "Kung Fu Fighting" as it might be interpreted by the **Chakachas**. The reverse of "Chinese Kung Fu" is "Rhythm Kung Fu," which cuts out the Moog for a sparer effect. Both are worth looking for. Other items on the Tube Top 10 are "La Balanga," the carbon-copy follow-up to "El Bimbo" by **Bimbo Jet** (an import on Pathé which Scepter plans to release later this Summer) and another record in the same mold, "Ninas," by an Italian group named **Los Bomberos** (Joker), who offer a further variation on that fluid European sound (the A side of "Ninas" is yet another version of "El Bimbo," this one Italian-made).

Ragusa and Cucuzzella say the Montreal discotheque scene includes many elements of New York disco music, as evidenced by their list, but with strong European influence because of their easy access to imports, especially from France. "El Bimbo" peaked for them in February when early copies from France were all over Montreal, and they've moved on to more recent arrivals in that vein. Other records they report are doing very well – all instrumentals with an international appeal: "Foot Stompin' Music" by **Bohannon**, the **Armada Orchestra's** "Do Me Right," "Shotgun Shuffle" by the **Sunshine Band** and **Juan Carlos Calderon's** "Bandolero."

Other feedback: Howard Metz at Cabaret in Los Angeles reports that "Honey Trippin'," a breezy instrumental by

> **"The Montreal discotheque scene includes many elements of New York disco music, but with a strong European influence because of their easy access to imports"**

the **Mystic Moods** is doing very well there. Previously available as a cut on the group's overlooked "Erogenous" album, originally released on Warner Brothers a year ago, "Honey Trippin'" is now out as a single on Soundbird Records, which has also re-issued the album and the rest of the Mystic Moods catalogue... Joe Carvello, who plays in Boston at a dub called Yesterday, prompted me to go out and buy a copy of the new **Philly Devotions** single so I could hear the B side, which he and several other DJs had mentioned. It's called "I Was A Lonely Man" and was worth the trip; upbeat and bouncy in a **Trammps** style, it's hidden on the other side of the group's current ballad release, "We're Gonna Make It" (Columbia).

An overload of albums this week. Most essential: **MFSB's** longed-for "Universal Love" album (Philadelphia Intl.), not quite up to its advance word, but, like **Bohannon**, a perfect example of the new mood music: loose, luxurious and fine for dancing or vibrant atmospheric tapes. "Sexy" has already been

CABARET, LOS ANGELES
DJ: Howard Metz

CRYSTAL WORLD – Crystal Grass (Polydor)
EASE ON DOWN THE ROAD – Consumer Rapport
(Wing & A Prayer)
FOOT STOMPIN' MUSIC – Bohannon (Dakar)
HELPLESSLY – Moment of Truth (Roulette)
HONEY TRIPPIN' – Mystic Moods (Soundbird)
THE HUSTLE/FIRE – Van McCoy (Avco)
PEACE AND LOVE – Ron Butler & the Ramblers (Playboy)
STOP AND THINK – Trammps (Golden Fleece)
THREE STEPS FROM TRUE LOVE – Reflections (Capitol)
WHERE IS THE LOVE? – Betty Wright (Alston)

YESTERDAY, BOSTON
DJ: Joe Carvello

BAD LUCK – Harold Melvin & the Bluenotes (Phila. Intl.)
CRYSTAL WORLD – Crystal Grass (Polydor)
GET DOWN TONIGHT – KC & the Sunshine Band (TK)
THE HUSTLE – Van McCoy (Avco)
PEACE AND LOVE – Ron Butler & the Ramblers (Playboy)
7-6-5-4-3-2-1 (BLOW YOUR WHISTLE) – Gary Toms
Empire (PIP)
SEXY – MFSB (Phila. Intl.)
SPIRIT OF THE BOOGIE – Kool & the Gang (De-Lite)
STOP AND THINK/TRAMMPS DISCO THEME – Trammps
(Golden Fleece)
SWEARIN' TO GOD – Frankie Valli (Private Stock)

LE TUBE, MONTREAL, CANADA
DJs: Martin Ragusa & George Cucuzzella

A.I.E. (A MWANA) – Black Blood (Mainstream)
BAD LUCK – Harold Melvin & the Bluenotes (Phila. Intl.)
CHINESE KUNG FU – Banzai
(Discues Fleche, French import)
EASE ON DOWN THE ROAD – Consumer Rapport
(Wing & A Prayer)
THE HUSTLE – Van McCoy (Avco)
LA BAIANGA – Bimbo Jet (Pathé, French Import)
NINAS – Los Bomberos (Joker, Italian Import)
PEACE AND LOVE – Ron Butler & the Ramblers (Playboy)
STOP 'AND THINK – Trammps (Golden Fleece)
SWEARIN' TO GOD – Frankie Valli (Private Stock)

BAREFOOT BOY, NEW YORK
DJ: Larry Sanders

CHICAGO THEME – Hubert Laws (CTI)
EASE ON DOWN THE ROAD – Consumer Rapport
(Wing & A Prayer)
FOREVER CAME TODAY – Jackson 5 (Motown)
FREE MAN – South Shore Commission (Wand)
LADY, LADY, LADY – Boogie Man Orchestra
(Boogie Man)
LOVE DO ME RIGHT – Rockin' Horse (RCA)
(SENDING OUT AN) S.O.S. – Retta Young (All Platinum)
SEXY/MFSB – MFSB (Phila. Intl.)
TRAMMPS DISCO THEME – Trammps (Golden fleece)
WHERE DO I GO FROM HERE – Supremes (Motown)

established as a single – picked up instantly everywhere – and the next best thing here is "T.L.C. (Tender Lovin' Care)," though it's only 3:41. "Let's Go Disco" would be more acceptable if the vocals were dropped out and "K-Jee" is difficult in points for an easy dance-through but is finally a diamond-sharp orchestration of the **Nite-Liters'** instrumental from a few years back. Note: a number of people have pointed out to me this week that MFSB's previous album, the already classic "Love Is The Message," has just been made available in quadraphonic and is, reportedly, great.

Other recommended albums: "**The Supremes**" on Motown, highlighted by "Where Do I Go From Here" (already on Larry Sanders' list from Barefoot Boy, a new club in New York), "He's My Man" and a sexy "Early Morning Love;" "The Legendary Zing Album," a collector's item from Buddah that includes the material the **Trammps** produced for that label, notably "Zing Went The Strings Of My Heart," mixed here with the instrumental "Penguin at the Big Apple," which is sort of an interpretation/progression of "Zing" just as "Trammps Disco Theme" is a further progression of "Penguin" – also great: "Pray All You Sinners," like the others, a **Baker**, **Harris** & **Young** production; "International" by the **Three Degrees** (Phila. Intl.), which is generally softer than their last album but includes their just-released single, "Take Good Care Of Yourself" – in the spirit and style of "When Will I See You Again" but a little more up – "Long Lost Lover" and the full vocal version of "TSOP;" and, from "Feel It," the new **Black Ivory** album (Buddah), the title cut, with a nice "Rock Your Baby" feel, and the instrumental version of "Daily News."

Recommended singles: "Scaredycat" by the **Doyley Brothers** (Atco), a terrific, unexpected record that has nearly made my week but is not for everyone – previously released in England and sent over a while back to tantalize a few New York DJs, it's now available and worth investigating; **Ronnie Limar's** attractive, medium-tempo "Love Came," with an instrumental Part 2 (BRC); the **Rhythm Makers'** sexy "Touch" (Vigor), for **Ohio Players** and **B.T. Express** fans; and **Gloria Gaynor's** reading of "Walk On By" (MGM) has its moments. ❂

A group of 60 New York area discotheque disc jockeys representing virtually every major club in the city and its immediate vicinity, have announced the formation of an independent, non-profit distribution center called the "Record Pool" which would act as a point of exchange between record companies and the participating DJs. The result of a series of meetings among the DJs involved, the Record Pool is designed to provide record companies with "a direct and efficient means of distributing their product to the discotheque DJs": a self-service center manned by volunteers that would receive new product and hold it for pick-up by member DJs, each of whom would have his own box. According to the group's "Declaration of Intent," the Pool will be strictly self-regulating and "take responsibility for establishing the absolute legitimacy of the DJs involved."

A record company's main commitment to the Pool, should it decide to get involved, would be to service its entire membership – so that if one DJ had a record, they would all have the record, cutting out a lot of wasteful competitiveness – and this is the step companies are most hesitant about. But representatives from Atlantic, RCA, Scepter, ABC, Roulette and Curtom/Gemigo have expressed initial willingness to participate in the Pool and Billy Smith, east coast representative for 20th Century Records and a pioneer in the field of discotheque promotion, prepared a covering letter to accompany the Pool's first mailing to record companies expressing 20th's support for the project. Smith said he feels the formation of the Record Pool is "another indication of progress" in the discotheque field. Because the central distribution point for the New York area would eliminate the need to keep up an extensive mailing list that was in need of regular up-dating. Smith sees the Pool as a way to "cut down costs and help the company get a faster reaction" to new releases. Instead of separate mailings to 100 different DJs, one mailing or one delivery to the Pool would reach them all. "This cuts time spent in my mailing room," Smith says, "and it cuts down the running around to clubs to make sure everybody has my records." The members of the Pool stress that they hope personal contact between individual DJs and record company representatives will continue and point out that the Pool itself grew out of a desire to improve that contact rather than eliminate it. DJs see the Pool as an answer to their problem of getting records quickly without having to wait for frequently-delayed mail or make often-fruitless trips to the companies themselves. But the Pool is also a response to the record companies' problems of how to regulate the flow of DJs anxious for new product and how to make sure the people who show up in their offices are legitimate. Though the Pool's membership is open to all legitimate discotheque DJs in the New York area – a number that is expected to go to 100 and includes several members from outlying cities like Hartford, Connecticut,

> ** The Record Pool is designed to provide record companies with "a direct and efficient means of distributing their product to the discotheque DJs." **

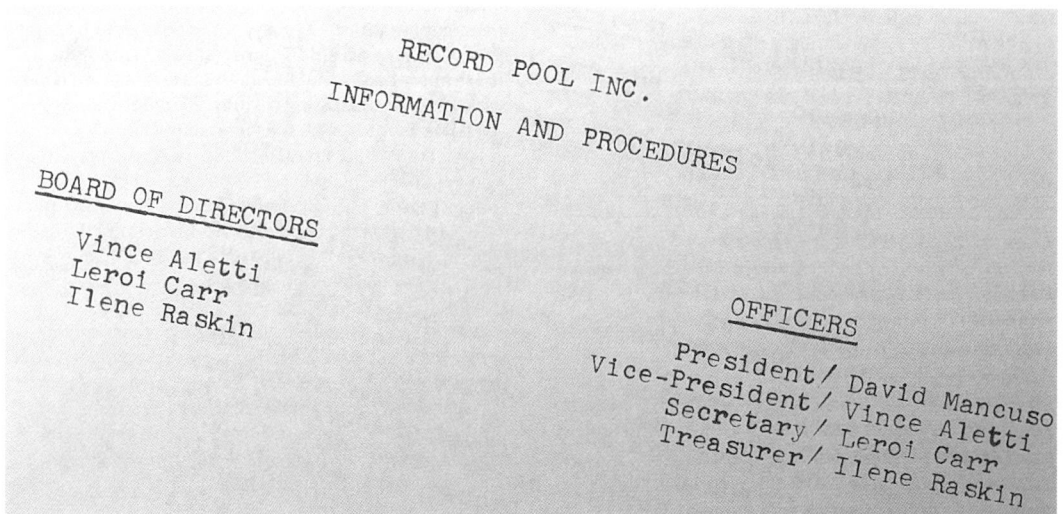

RECORD POOL INC.
INFORMATION AND PROCEDURES

BOARD OF DIRECTORS
Vince Aletti
Leroi Carr
Ilene Raskin

OFFICERS
President / David Mancuso
Vice-President / Vince Aletti
Secretary / Leroi Carr
Treasurer / Ilene Raskin

LE COCU, NEW YORK
DJ: David Chrysostomos

BAD LUCK – Harold Melvin & the Bluenotes (Phila. Intl.)

CAN'T GIVE YOU ANYTHING (BUT MY LOVE)
– Stylistics (Avco)

DREAMING A DREAM – Crown Heights Affair (De-Lite)

EL BIMBO – Bimbo Jet (Scepter)

FREE MAN – South Shore Commission (Wand)

THE HUSTLE – Van McCoy (Avco)

(SENDING OUT AN) S.O.S. – Retta Young (All Platinum)

SEXY – MFSB (Philadelphia Intl.)

SWEARIN' TO GOD – Frankie Valli (Private Stock)

THREE STEPS FROM TRUE LOVE – Reflections (Capitol)

HADAAR, NY (STATEN ISLAND)
DJ: Michael Pace

CAN'T GIVE YOU ANYTHING (BUT MY LOVE)
– Stylistics (Avco)

CHICAGO THEME – Hubert Laws (CTI)

FOREVER CAME TODAY – Jackson 5 (Motown)

GLASSHOUSE – Temptations (Gordy)

HAPPY FEELIN' – Earth, Wind & Fire (Columbia)

HELPLESSLY – Moment of Truth (Roulette)

I'LL DO FOR YOU ANYTHING YOU WANT ME TO – Barry White (20th Century)

SAVE ME/SAVE ME AGAIN – Silver Convention (Midland Intl.)

STOP AND THINK – Trammps (Golden Fleece)

SWEARIN' TO GOD – Frankie Valli (Private Stock)

STUDIO ONE, LOS ANGELES
DJ: Tim Zerr

AND YOU CALL THAT LOVE – Vernon Burch (UA)

CRYSTAL WORLD – Crystal Grass (Polydor)

EASE ON DOWN THE ROAD – Consumer Rapport (A Wing & A Prayer)

FIGHT THE POWER – Isley Brothers (T-Neck)

FOREVER CAME TODAY – Jackson 5 (Motown)

FOOT STOMPIN' MUSIC – Bohannon (Dakar)

FREE MAN – South Shore Commission (Wand)

THE HUSTLE – Van McCoy (Avco)

SEXY – MFSB (Phila. Intl.)

WALK ON BY – Gloria Gaynor (MGM)

WATU WAZURI, NY (BROOKLYN)
DJ: Phil Euphoria

CHICAGO THEME – Hubert Laws (CTI)

DO YOU WANT MY LOVE – Barrett Strong (Capitol)

EASE ON DOWN THE ROAD – Consumer Rapport (A Wing & A Prayer)

FOREVER CAME TODAY – Jackson 5 (Motown)

GEORGIA'S AFTER HOURS – Popcorn Wylie (ABC)

I WAS A LONELY MAN – Philly Devotions (Columbia)

IT'S IN HIS KISS – Linda Lewis (Arista)

LOVE DO ME RIGHT – Rockin' Horse (RCA)

LOVE SONG – Simon Said (Roulette)

TURN THIS MOTHER OUT – Van McCoy (Avco)

and Princeton, New Jersey, who depend on the city as their source of new material – members will be regularly checked by a committee to make sure they are actively spinning. Smith says that this alone is a valuable service to the record companies – "This way we know who's working and who isn't."

In a letter accompanying their "Declaration of Intent" with its list of participating DJs which was mailed to a number of record company representatives last week, the Record Pool outlined its purposes and said that, in addition to being a distribution point, it intended to "serve as a central point to exchange information about up-coming releases, present releases and who's playing what and where." A bulletin board would be set up and a turntable so new records could be reviewed on the spot. The Pool also extended an open invitation to all record company personnel interested in disco promotion to attend their next meeting, Monday, June 30, at 2 p.m. at the Pool's Soho address, 99 Prince Street in New York.

Best of the Week: **Bobby Moore's** light and lively "Call Me Your Everything Man" (Scepter), in the over-familiar **George McCrae** style but quite irresistible nevertheless. Its long disco mix runs just over six minutes and will be shipped to DJs on special 12-inch records at 33 1/3 to give it its best, hottest sound – something other record companies have been talking about doing for the disco market, but that Scepter is the first to carry out. Other recommended singles: **Major Lance's** delightful "You're Everything I Need" (Osiris), his best in some time, with an instrumental B side; and a new commercial single version of "Tornado" by the **Original Cast of "The Wiz"** (Atlantic), a re-mix of the album cut but a shortening of the Disco Disc version to 3:23.

Catching up: **The Stylistics'** "Can't Give You Anything (But My Love)," which appears on two Top 10 lists this week-those of Michael Pace at Hadaar on Staten Island and David Chrysostomas from Le Cocu in New York – is from their new album, "Thank You Baby" (Avco) and reminds everyone of "Love Is the Answer" from the group's previous album. Result: instant success; Avco plans to release the cut as a single within the month. Also check out "Sing Baby Sing" on the same album, already a hit in England.... Phil Euphoria (Phillip Gill), who plays at a Brooklyn club called Watu Wazuri, lists a long (5:31), strong cut from **Barrett Strong's** recent album, "Do You Want My Love" which we foolishly overlooked (the album: "Stronghold" on Capitol). Check it out, and "Is It True," also available as a single... And pick up the new **Hodges, James & Smith** album, "Power In Your Love" (20th Century). Though nothing can be wholeheartedly recommended here for dancing-too many changes – it's hot, particularly the sassy title cut and "Momma," "Sexy Ways," a tasty, torthy, long (5:35) version of **Ben E. King's** "I Who Have Nothing" and a version of "Nobody." Production, a superb job, is by **Mickey Stevenson**, formerly with Motown. ✪

JUNE 21, 1975

Two of the best records being passed along the New York DJ grapevine are **Esther Phillips'** excellent version of the **Dinah Washington** classic, "What A Difference A Day Makes," and a small label surprise called "Somebody's Gotta Go (Sho Ain't Me)" by a duo named **Mike & Bill**. The Phillips cut, out this week as a single, is a track from her forthcoming Kudu album (due early in July) with production by **Creed Taylor**. Though the album also contains a long remake of **Jerry Butler's** "One Night Affair" and a vocal version of **Grover Washington's** "Mister Magic," "What A Difference" was the first choice of most of the discotheque DJs who received advance copies of the record from CTI, already appearing on two New York top 10 lists this week – Tony Gioe's from Hollywood and David Rodriguez from the new Make-Believe Ballroom. In Phillips' hands, "What A Difference" is given a whole new life, pumped into it from the very beginning by a series of deep sighs over the intro which come back as a sexy punctuation during the several instrumental breaks. Phillips' voice is unique, taut and biting and combined with a very speedy arrangement, it makes the song usually sharp and tense (if the tension gets too much, ease it by slowing the turntable slightly, as some people are already doing). Altogether a knockout and the Pick of the Month by Interview's very choosy Fran Lebowitz. I agree.

Mike & Bill's "Somebody's Gotta Go (Sho Ain't Me)," also on Tony Gioe's list and mentioned by the Limelight's Hector LeBron and others this week, is on a label called Moving Up and, except for the fact that it's suddenly very hot, it's something of a mystery. Disco Discs, a Queens store specializing in disco material, is apparently one of the few retail sources for the record and their initial supply came directly from the producer who then disappeared. From all appearances, "Somebody's Gotta Go" is a piece of homemade product like the **Boogie Man Orchestra's** "Lady, Lady, Lady," put together by Mike & Bill, whoever they may be, for their own one-shot label. If that's true, it's at least as

> **❝ If the tension gets too much, ease it by slowing the turntable slightly, as some people are already doing ❞**

impressive and successful as "Lady, Lady, Lady," though in an entirely different style. Like **Kendricks'** "Girl You Need A Change Of Mind," this is one man's response to woman's liberation and a pretty bitter one: "I've given you your woman's lib/ to do the things you want to do/Tell me where did it get me, girl:/All alone without you." The message may not be to everyone's taste, but the music should be: crackling Latin soul and without the vocals on the instrumental B side (which, like the A side, is 4:15).

Speaking of "Lady, Lady, Lady," that record entered the Disco File Top 20 this week in spite of the fact that it still has no distributor outside of the Chicago area and has yet to be picked up by a larger label.

Feedback: David Finger's rather unusual list from the Black Russian in Washington, D.C. includes a record we haven't mentioned here before: "Funky Music Is The Thing," a two-part number by the **Dynamic Corvettes** (Abet) which sounds like early **Sly & the Family Stone** with a little **Kool & the Gang** thrown in, and has its moments... David Rodriguez reports his crowd is getting off on the **Pointer Sisters'** very long (7:56) version of **Alan Toussaint's** song, "Going Down Slowly," which strikes me as being too draggy for dancing but a strong production anyway. The cut is from the Pointers' new album, "Steppin'" (Blue Thumb), from which I prefer "Chainey Do" or "How Long (Betcha Got a Chick on the Side)"... Also picking up in response, according to Tony Gioe, is the **Three Degrees'** "Long Lost Lover" (from the "International" album, on Philadelphia International), and Hector LeBron is pleased with the reaction to **Barbara Hall's** "You Brought It On Yourself" (Innovation II), a personal favorite of mine as well... Steve D'Acquisto is excited about **Eric Mercury's** "Pours When It Rains" (Mercury), out and overlooked for about two months now, first as an album cut ("Eric Mercury"), then as a single (same length as the lp track, 3:17). The record starts out a little off but soon settles down into a nice, high-spirited beat with a great message.

Recommended albums: the new **George McCrae** (untitled, on TK) with a slightly different but quite familiar trademark sound, perhaps the most imitated around. The strongest cut right now – first impressions – would be "Honey I (I'll) Live My Life For You" which is very like his "I Get Lifted;" others to check out: "Baby Baby Sweet Baby," the longest at 6:25, "When I First Saw You" (at 4:45, the runner-up) and "You Treat Me Good." The **Crystal Grass** album is now available – "Crystal World" on Polydor – at their best, they remind me of **Titanic**, **Barrabas** or **American Gypsy** – that European soul/rock sound – but without the necessary toughness to sustain it very long. Side one is listenable, especially "Love To Dance This One With You," an instrumental, and a decent remake of Kiki Dee's "I've Got The Music In Me;" side two falls off sharply except for a longer version of "Crystal World," which could have been better mixed.

MAKE-BELIEVE BALLROOM, NEW YORK
DJ: David Rodriguez

ARE YOU READY FOR THIS – The Brothers (RCA)
BAD LUCK – Harold Melvin & the Bluenotes (Phila. Intl.)
DREAMING A DREAM – Crown Heights Affair (De-Lite)
EASE ON DOWN THE ROAD – Consumer Rapport
(A Wing & A Prayer)
FOOT STOMPIN' MUSIC – Bohannon (Dakar)
FOREVER CAME TODAY – Jackson 5 (Motown)
FREE MAN – South Shore Commission (Wand)
SEXY – MFSB (Phila. Intl.)
THREE STEPS FROM TRUE LOVE – Reflections (Capitol)
WHAT A DIFFERENCE A DAY MAKES – Esther Phillips
(Kudu)

BLACK RUSSIAN, WASHINGTON, D. C.
DJ: David Finger

BACK FROM THE DEAD – Bobby Byrd
(International Brothers)
BIG NOISE FROM WINNETKA – Spaghetti Head
(Private Stock)
FOOT STOMPIN' MUSIC – Bohannon (Dakar)
FUNKY MUSIC IS THE THING – Dynamic Corvettes
(Abet)
GET DOWN TONIGHT – KC & the Sunshine Band (TK)
HIJACK – Barrabas (Atco)
MACUMBA – Titanic (Epic)
POTENTIAL – Jimmy Castor Bunch (Atlantic)
7-6-5-4-3-2-1 (BLOW YOUR WHISTLE) – Gary Toms
Empire (PIP)
SLIPPERY WHEN WET – Commodores (Motown)

LIMELIGHT, NEW YORK
DJ: Hector LeBron

DREAMING A DREAM – Crown Heights Affair (De-Lite)
EASE ON DOWN THE ROAD – Consumer Rapport
(A Wing & A Prayer)
FOOT STOMPIN' MUSIC/DISCO STOMP – Bohannon
(Dakar)
FOREVER CAME TODAY – Jackson 5 (Motown)
FREE MAN – South Shore Commission (Wand)
HE'S MY MAN/WHERE DO I GO FROM HERE – Supremes
(Motown)
IT'S IN HIS KISS – Linda Lewis (Arista)
SEXY – MFSB (Phila. Intl.)
THREE STEPS FROM TRUE LOVE – Reflections (Capitol)
YOU'VE BROKEN MY HEART – Sound Experience
(Soulville)

HOLLYWOOO, NEW YORK
DJ: Tony Gioe

DREAMING A DREAM – Crown Heights Affair (De-Lite)
FOOT STOMPIN' MUSIC – Bohannon (Dakar)
FOREVER CAME TODAY – Jackson 5 (Motown)
FREE MAN – South Shore Commission (Wand)
LADY, LADY, LADY– Boogie Man Orchestra (Boogie Man)
SEXY – MFSB (Phila. Intl.)
SOMEBODY'S GOTTA GO – Mike & Bill (Moving Up)
STOP AND THINK – Trammps (Golden Fleece)
TORNADO – 'The Wiz' Original Cast (Atlantic)
WHAT A DIFFERENCE A DAY MAKES – Esther Phillips
(Kudu)

And singles: **The Joneses** don't sound as smooth as they used to (it's practically a whole new group), but just listen to the lead-in and lead-out instrumental passages on Part 1 of their new "Love Inflation" (Mercury) and the steady chug on Part 2 and you'll be won over. "(It's Not The Express) It's The JB's Monaurail" by **Fred & the New JB's** (they change their name every time) (People) is a deliberately slow take-off from the **B.T. Express** hit, but it manages to be pretty hot for such a cooled-down groove. ❂

A number of the most interesting new records this week are instrumentals – as are 10 of the cuts listed in the Disco File Top 20. "Summertime," a perfectly-timed disco update of the Gershwin classic by European MOR giant **James Last** (on the Polydor album, "Well Kept Secret"), is perhaps the most unexpected. (Though the recent **Peter Nero** album, imaginatively titled "Disco, Dance and Love Themes of the 70's" on Arista, and an upcoming **Percy Faith** album called "Disco Party" on Columbia prove that the easy listening crowd will try anything once.) Last, under Wes Farrell's direction – and it's hard to tell where Farrell's well-balanced production ends and Last begins – at least knows how to do it right. "Summertime" starts out slow and languid, a quiet wash of strings, then breaks into a steady drumbeat (almost like the beginning of **Stevie Wonder's** "Living For The City") that takes you right into the heat of a summer day. **Tom Scott** is present for a breezy flute solo and when the temperature peaks, a girl chorus enters chanting the title. The cut cools off again at the end so it will have to be carefully mixed for disco play, but at 5:14, there's plenty of hot material to work with.

The other instrumentals are singles, beginning with the sharp, solid "Do It Any Way You Wanna," a **Leon Huff** composition and production for **People's Choice** (TSOP). The title's message, "Do it any way you wanna do it," repeated at intervals by a male chorus, is just succinct enough to appeal to the dance crowd on an immediate level, and this one should pick up very fast. The other two are more left field, though in two different directions. There's "Do The Choo-Choo," the latest in an odd line of transportation tributes – the railroads may be dying but train songs will live forever – by **Jack Ashford & the Sound of New Detroit** (Blaze); this one's uneven, full of breaks, but at its best and played loud, it's tough and steamy and feels something like "Follow The Wind." Put "Choo-Choo"'s two parts together and it runs more than five minutes. On the lusher side of the instrumental field, there's "Falbala" by the **Magic Band**, a French group (on GNP Crescendo) which has a gorgeous "Lady, Lady, Lady" sound. Again, there are a lot of breaks on this one that may make dancing difficult but when it works, it works beautifully and is worth searching out. Finally, let me re-recommend the **Major Lance** record, "You're Everything I Need" (Osiris), whose instrumental side gets better all the time. The most essential new albums: "It's Rough Out Here" by the

Modulations (Buddah), featuring their successful "I Can't Fight Your Love," and "I'm Hopelessly In Love," both of which still sound good; the gritty, powerful title cut; "Head On Collision With Heartbreak," as good as its title and reminiscent of **Eddie Kendricks** (note the similar theme in the J5's "Moving Violation"); and an outstanding "Love At Last," the best of the lot (and the longest: 5:05) with tear-'em-up vocals and a chorus worth screaming along to. The whole Philadelphia crew was along on this one – Norman Harris, Earl Young, Bobby Eli, the MFSB orchestra and Vince Montana, who did most of the arrangements – and it's one of the city's nicest surprises in some time. "Get The Cream Off The Top" is the standout on the new **Eddie Kendricks** album ("The Hit Man," on Tamla), the one cut produced by **Brian Holland**, who's certainly making a strong comeback with Motown. The song's chorus: "Come get the cream off the top/ Take the best that I've got," sung in Eddie's most insinuating style. Other cuts to watch: "Body Talk," "I've Got To Be." And David Rodriguez suggests the smooth, wonderful title cut from the new **Impressions** album, "First Impressions" (Curtom).

Footnotes on the Top 10 lists: Rich Pampinella from New York's Hippopotamus can always be depended upon for some off-the-wall selections and this week they are "Save Me," a 1967 single by that English group, **Dave Dee, Dozy, Beaky, Mick & Tich** (Fontana), which Pampinella says he periodically pulls out and trys but only recently has been having some success with – as the sound changes, old things suddenly fit in again – and "Introduction," a cut from a 1971 Philips import from Brazil by **Batacuda**, an instrumental full of percussion, whistles and sudden breaks which Rich says "makes the people act like fools."... On Mitch Schatsky's list: **Banzai's** "Chinese Kung Fu" is being released on Scepter this coming week with a disco mix version combining it and "Rhythm Kung Fu," that runs 5:12 and is highly recommended even if it's a little more than you can take; "La La La" by **El Chicles** is the original Brazilian version which Schatsky and most others have only on a dub copy, so no label information is available right now; "Little Bit Of Love" and "Let's Go To The Disco" are both from the forthcoming (from RCA) **Faith, Hope & Charity** album, produced by **Van McCoy** and now advanced to disco DJs on a cherry-red vinyl pressing – I'm reserving comment on the album until next week... . The **Stylistics'** "Can't

> ** "The cut cools off again at the end so it will have to be carefully mixed for disco play, but at 5:14, there's plenty of hot material to work with "**

RHINOCEROS, BOSTON
DJ: John Luongo

CHAINEY DO/HOW LONG – Pointer Sisters (Blue Thumb)
DREAMING A DREAM – Crown Heights Affair (De-Lite)
EASE ON DOWN THE ROAD – Consumer Rapport
(Wing & A Prayer)
FIGHT THE POWER/HOPE YOU FEEL BETTER LOVE –
Isley Brothers (T-Neck)
GET DOWN TONIGHT – KC & the Sunshine Band (TK)
7-6-5-4-3-2-1 (BLOW YOUR WHISTLE) – Gary Toms
Empire (PIP)
SEXY /K-JEE – MFSB (Phila. Intl.)
SNEAKIN' UP BEHIND YOU – Brecker Brothers (Arista)
STOP AND THINK – Trammps (Golden Fleece)
THREE STEPS FROM TRUE LOVE – Reflections (Capitol)

HIPPOPOTAMUS, NEW YORK
DJ: Rich Pampinella

BAD LUCK – Harold Melvin & the Bluenotes (Phila. Intl.)
DREAMING A DREAM – Crown Heights Affair (De-Lite)
EASE ON DOWN THE ROAD – Consumer Rapport
(A Wing & A Prayer)
FREE MAN – South Shore Commission (Wand)
THE HUSTLE – Van McCoy (Avco)
INTRODUCTION – Batacuda (Philips import)
IT'S IN HIS KISS – Linda Lewis (Arista)
SAVE ME – Dave Dee, Dozy, Beaky, Mick & Tich (Fontana)
SEXY – MFSB (Phila. Intl.)
THREE STEPS FROM TRUE LOVE – Reflections (Capitol)

CASABLANCA, NEW YORK
DJ: Louis Schneider

(CALL ME YOUR) ANYTHING MAN – Bobby Moore
(Scepter)
CHICAGO THEME – Hubert Laws (CTI)
DREAMING A DREAM – Crown Heights Affair (De-Lite)
EASE ON DOWN THE ROAD – Consumer Rapport
(A Wing & A Prayer)
EL BIMBO – Bimbo Jet (Scepter)
FOREVER CAME TODAY – Jackson 5 (Motown)
HEAVENLY, THAT'S WHAT YOU ARE TO ME – Barry White
(20th Century)
(SENDING OUT AN) S.O.S. – Retta Young (All Platinum)
SEXY /K-JEE – MFSB (Phila. Intl.)
SWEARIN' TO GOD – Frankie Valli (Private Stock)

PIER 9, WASHINGTON, D.C.
DJ: Mitch Schotsky

ALVIN STONE – Fantastic Four (20th Century/Westbound)
CAN'T GIVE YOU ANYTHING (BUT MY LOVE) – Stylistics
(Avco)
CHINESE KUNG FU – Banzai (Disques Fleche import)
DREAMING A DREAM – Crown Heights Affair (De-Lite)
FOREVER CAME TODAY – Jackson 5 (Motown)
LA BALANGA – Bimbo Jet (Pathé import)
LA LA LA – El Chicles (no label available)
LITTLE BIT OF LOVE/LET'S GO TO THE DISCO – Faith,
Hope & Charity (RCA)
SEXY/K-JEE – MFSB (Phila. Intl.)
TORNADO – 'The Wiz' Original Cast (Atlantic)

Give You Anything (But My Love)," also on Schatsky's list, is, you should know, now available as a single, full-length, on Avco.

Recommended singles: **Oscar Perry's** very up "I Got What You Need" (Peri-Tone), which reminds me of **Jerry Butler** at his best; "Country John" by **Allen Toussaint** (Reprise), which has been re-done for discos with a long mix of 4:28 that takes some getting into but delivers in time; "Gimme Some," the harder side of the Miami Sound by Jimmy "Bo" Horne (Alston), in two very different parts, both exciting (added together they hit 6:01); the **Natural Four's** joyous "Love's So Wonderful" (Curtom) and "Never Get Enough Of Your Love" by **Street People** (whose lead sounds oddly like **Nick Ashford**) with a 4:39 disco version arranged by **Bert deCoteaux** (Vigor). ✪

DISCO FILE TOP 20

1. **EASE ON DOWN THE ROAD** – Consumer Rapport (Wing And A Prayer)
2. **SEXY** – MFSB (Phila. Intl.)
3. **FREE MAN** – South Shore Commission (Wand)
4. **FOREVER CAME TODAY** – Jackson 5 (Motown)
5. **FOOT STOMPIN' MUSIC** – Bohannon (Dakar)
6. **THE HUSTLE** – Van McCoy (Avco)
7. **THREE STEPS FROM TRUE LOVE** – Reflections (Capitol)
8. **STOP AND THINK** – Reflections (Capitol)
9. **DREAMING A DREAM** – Crown Heights Affair (De-Lite)
10. **SWEARIN' TO GOD** – Frankie Valli (Private Stock)
11. **CHICAGO THEME** – Hubert Lewis (CTI)
12. **BAD LUCK** – Harold Melvin & The Bluenotes (Phila. Intl.)
13. **EL BIMBO** – Bimbo Jet (Pathe/EMI import)
14. **LOVE DO ME RIGHT** – Rockin' Horse (RCA)
15. **PEACE & LOVE** – Ron Butler & the Ramblers (Playboy)
16. **TORNADO** – "The Wiz" original cast (Atlantic)
17. **LADY, LADY, LADY** – Boogie Man Orchestra (Boogie Man)
18. **K-JEE** – MFSB (Phila. Intl.)
19. **GET DOWN TONIGHT** – KC & the Sunshine Band (TK)
20. **HIJACK** – Barrabas (Atco)

Van McCoy, who already has one of the 10 best disco albums of the year so far in "Disco Baby" (Avco), has come up with another: his production for **Faith, Hope & Charity**, due for release early in July but already out to discotheque DJs in New York on special bright red vinyl pressings. If the most eagerly anticipated cut – the remake of his own song (for **Brenda & the Tabulations**), "Little Bit Of Love" turns out a disappointment (perhaps because one was hoping for something entirely new, a transformation of the sort **Brian Holland** accomplished with "Forever Came Today"), McCoy proves himself still a master of the mood and message of disco music for the '70s in the rest of the album. The two best – already listed on Richie Conte's list from Hadaar – are "To Each His Own" and "Mellow Me," both with a bright, sharp **Ecstasy, Passion & Pain** feel (though the group is a one-man, two-woman trio). "To Each His Own" reflects the attitude of the disco crowd as accurately and directly as **Everyday People's** "I Like What I Like" once did: "To each his own/that's my philosophy/I don't know what's right for you/You don't know what's right for me." Other favorites: "Don't Go Looking For Love," "Find A Way," "Let's Go To The Disco" – all over four minutes – and "Disco Dan," the first song I know of about a disco DJ: "From his booth each night he blows your mind/with his mix and his tricks."

Another much-discussed album now available: Scepter's "Disco Gold," the best of the disco repackages yet released because it contains the most hard-to-get material in specially re-mixed, re-edited and, in most cases, lengthened versions whipped up by Tom Moulton, who seems to have singlehandedly invented the profession of disco mixer. There are four cuts to a side, all over four minutes, most over five, and including a knockout, 6:34 "Make Me Believe In You" by Patti Joe (originally written and produced by **Curtis Mayfield**), **Ultra High Frequency's** classic "We're On The Right Track" expanded to 5:17, "I Love You, Yes I Do" and "Arise And Shine" by the **Independents** and **George Tindley's** "Wan Tu Wah Zuree." On the package's back cover there's a long list of over 200 names of discotheque DJs from around the country under the heading, "Thanks, For Without Your Help This Album Would Not Be Possible." Thank you, Scepter.

Also out: **Calhoon's** "(Do You Wanna) Dance Dance Dance" (Warner Spector), recommended here a few months back and then delayed for a number of reasons. Now it's available to DJs on a one-sided 12-inch disc that runs 6:19 in length, plenty of time for some fine instrumental breaks .... **Shirley (And Company)'s** album (Vibration), remarkable more for its cover – a crudely-drawn cartoon of Shirley gesturing cryptically to **Richard M. Nixon**, perhaps illustrating the title, "Shame, Shame, Shame" – than for its contents: vocal and instrumental versions of the title cut and its follow-up, "Cry Cry Cry," and seven other cuts. One of them, "I Gotta Get Next to you," includes these lines: "I gotta get next to you/Closer than one can be next to you/ If that ain't close/Then I'll eat my shoe." I'm not kidding.

Producer **Sonny Casella** is releasing **Black Rock's** "New York City Bump" (Blackwood Record's) this week, a complex, very long (nearly 9 minutes) record of a "day in the life of the city." Casella recorded live street and subway sounds that run as a background montage through the song and give it a fascinating cinema verite feel: police calls, barking dogs, confrontations, ravings, all ending with a subway conductor announcing, "42nd Street, Times Square... step lively." Casella, who wrote and produced **Dooley Silverspoon's** "Bump Me Baby," reports he also produced the **Ritchie Family's** "Brazil," previously released in France and Canada and just out on 20th Century here. Already picking up the past week or so as an import in New York, "Brazil," a new version of the pop-Latin standard, was recorded at Philadelphia's Sigma Sound and arranged by **Richard Rome**, so this is another **MFSB** combination and a good one. Although Casella claims his production credit has been unfairly taken away from him on "Brazil," the record includes this note: "Special Thanks to Sonny Casella."

"Brazil" was one of the many imports brought by the office this past week by Desi DJ from Uno's Cafe Disco in the Bronx who is one of the most active freelance importers on the New York disco scene. His speciality seems to be lush European instrumentals like those by England's **Armada Orchestra** (whose product should be available here soon, the fruits of Scepter's American release deal with Contempo) or **Love Sounds'** lovely disco-styled version of the standard "Ebb Tide" (Pye, also from England). On Desi's top 10, another import which fits into this mold, "Undecided Love" by the **Chequers** (Creole, from England), with an instrumental and a vocal side (also recommended this week by Frank Strivelli at the Alley). The rest of Desi's import batch I'll have to get to in a later column; meanwhile check him and his collection out.

"Tom Moulton seems to have singlehandedly invented the profession of disco mixer"

OIL CAN HARRY'S, LOS ANGELES
DJ: Terry Ponce

EASE ON DOWN THE ROAD – Consumer Rapport
(A Wing & A Prayer)
FIGHT THE POWER – Isley Brothers (T-Neck)
FOOT STOMPIN' MUSIC – Bohannon (Dakar)
FOREVER CAME TODAY – Jackson 5 (Motown)
GET DOWN TONIGHT – KC & the Sunshine Band (TK)
GET YA SOME – Melvin Sparks
(20th Century/Westbound)
HE'S MY MAN – Supremes (Motown)
THE HUSTLE – Van McCoy (Avco)
STOP AND THINK – Trammps (Golden Fleece)
SURVIVAL – O'Jays (Phila. Intl.)

THE ALLEY, NEW YORK (QUEENS)
DJ: Frank Strivelli

BAD LUCK – Harold Melvin & the Bluenotes (Phila. Intl.)
CHICAGO THEME – Hubert Laws (CTI)
DISCO STOMP/ FOOT STOMPIN' MUSIC – Bohannon
(Dakar)
DREAMING A DREAM – Crown Heights Affair (De-Lite)
FOREVER CAME TODAY – Jackson 5 (Motown)
FREE MAN – South Shore Commission (Wand)
LA BALANGA/EL BIMBO – Bimbo Jet (Pathé
import/Scepter)
LOVE INFLATION – Joneses (Mercury)
SEXY – MFSB (Phila. Intl.)
WHAT A DIFF'RENCE A DAY MAKES – Esther Phillips
(Kudu)

HADAAR, NEW YORK (STATEN ISLAND)
DJ: Richie Conte

CHICAGO THEME – Hubert Laws (CTI lp cut)
DANCE DANCE DANCE – Calhoon (Warner Spector)
DREAMING A DREAM – Crown Heights Affair (De-Lite)
FOREVER CAME TODAY – Jackson 5 (Motown)
I COULD DANCE ALL NIGHT – Archie Bell & the Drells
(TSOP)
LADY, LADY, LADY – Boogie Man Orchestra (Boogie Man)
STOP AND THINK – Trammps (Golden Fleece)
THREE STEPS FROM TRUE LOVE – Reflections (Capitol)
TO EACH HIS OWN/MELLOW ME – Faith, Hope & Charity
(RCA)
WHAT A DIFF'RENCE A DAY MAKES – Esther Phillips
(Kudu)

UNO'S CAFE DISCO, NY (THE BRONX)
DJ: Desi DJ

DISCO QUEEN – Hot Chocolate (Big Tree)
DISCO STOMP – Bohannon (Dakar)
DREAMING A DREAM – Crown Heights Affair (De-Lite)
FOREVER CAME TODAY – Jackson 5 (Motown)
IT'S IN HIS KISS – Linda Lewis (Arista)
STOP AND THINK – Trammps (Golden Fleece)
TORNADO – 'The Wiz' Original Cast (Atlantic)
THREE STEPS FROM TRUE LOVE – Reflections (Capitol)
UNDECIDED LOVE – Chequers (Creole import)
WHAT A DIFF'RENCE A DAY MAKES – Esther Phillips
(Kudu)

Watch for: "Makin' Love To Ya," with vocal and instrumental sides by a group called **Got-Cha** (Sterling Disc) which Frank Strivelli had dropped off at his club last week. Even over the phone it sounded real nice.

Recommended: Some instrumentals –"I Wouldn't Treat A Dog (The Way You Treated Me)," a biting version of the recent **Bobby Bland** single by **Rhythm Heritage** (ABC) which I heard and loved for the first time at New York's suddenly super-popular 12 West (DJ: Tom Savarese) this past weekend; "Doctor's Music," a typically quirky entry by **The Peppers** (who are now on the Big Tree); "I Can't Quit Your Love," the old **Four Tops** record re-done instrumentally by **Bobby Taylor** and **Thorn Bell** (as **BT** And **TB**) (Phila. Intl.) who also produced and arranged (**Gene Page** joined them lor the latter job, making quite a threesome) – and "Think Before You Stop" by the **Notations** (Gemigo), which has taken a lot of obvious elements from both the **Spinners** and **Blue Magic** but gets off into something on its own, too; a message song called "What's The Answer, Brother" by **Winner's Circle** (Casablanca) with a 5:45 disco version; "Magic's In The Air" by **Ronnie Walker** which has a very up **Stylistics** sound and a beautiful chorus (on Event); **Ralph Carter's** sweet "When You're Young And In Love" (Mercury) with a 5:04 disco version that Rich Pampinella has already called to recommend, though we both noted cops from other disco records (notably "I'll Be Holding On") and, finally, best for last, the **Persuasions** great change-of-style release, "One Thing On My Mind," the **Evie Sands** record beautifully reworked by **Tony Camillo** (A&M). ◉

JULY 12, 1975

The big news this week is the tremendous success of New York's Record Pool. The discotheque DJs involved in this independent, non-profit distribution center had their first meeting with record company representatives last Monday (30) at their 99 Prince Street headquarters and I think everyone involved was overwhelmed by the turnout: disco promotion people from over 25 companies, several in from out of town, and more than 150 DJs interested in joining the Pool who, when added to the already established membership of 75, would swell the ranks of the group to 225. Before the meeting was over, in a kind of charged, fund-raising benefit atmosphere, the Pool had gotten verbal commitments for participation from nearly all the record companies present, including Capitol, Polydor, RCA, Arista, Avco, Fania, London, Mercury, MCA, Scepter, Roulette, Private Stock, Curtom/Gemigo, Midland International and Fantasy. Each pledge, indicating the company's willingness to use the Pool as their central distribution point for disco DJs in the New York area, brought cheers from the crowd, turning what already felt like a party – there were balloons floating all over, plates of cold cuts and cheese, a huge bowl of punch and a decorated cake – into a celebration.

Before late afternoon restlessness set in, Pool members attempted to answer questions about the operation. Among other things, they reassured the companies that their membership would be carefully checked to confirm that they were active DJs and that complete membership lists would be mailed to all participating companies, with supplements as new members are added. The Pool, they said, was not designed to be a spokesperson for or a dictator to the DJs involved – every DJ will continue to have his own voice and make his own programming decisions. After the meeting broke up, Pool members were allowed to pick up batches of singles and albums from record companies

already involved – including product from 20th Century, United Artists, Blaze and the TK labels – and prospective members went about getting the necessary two references to help Pool people in verifying their legitimacy. Interested companies or disc jockeys should contact the Record Pool at 99 Prince Street, New York 10012 or call (212) 431-8187. Their rallying cry: "Everybody into the Pool!"

Best new records this week: "It Only Takes A Minute," a special disco release by **Tavares** (Capitol), available only to disco DJs on a 4:46, limited edition, small-hole 45 and the group's most powerful, driving work to date; the **Fatback Band's** tasty "Yum, Yum (Gimme Some)" (Event) available on a single (at 3:18) or as the title cut from their new album (at 4:04), sensational either way (the album also contains the group's last single, the overlooked "(Hey) I Feel Real Good," running six minutes here); and "Hollywood Hot" by the **Eleventh Hour** (20th Century), a steamy, sexy record that works in spite of its vocals because **Bob Crewe's** production on the mostly instrumental second half of the song is so varied and intense. The Eleventh Hour record has been released on a 12-inch disc at 7:28 specially for DJs and as a commercial 45 at five mintues even, with an instrumental B side, "Hollywood Hotter," of 4:26. According to west coast sources, it's already the hit of Los Angeles, where it came out first, and in New York, Le Jardin's Bobby Guttadaro, who reportedly supplied more inspiration for the song than he's willing to talk about, says he expects it to enter his club's top 10 by next week.

Some quick feedback: "One Way Street" by **Becket Brown** on Jackie McCloy's list from Penrod's on Long Island, is an English import on RCA which the label plans to release here within a week's time. Production is by **Biddu**, who did **Carl Douglas'** album, and the sound is a pleasant variation on the **George McCrae** style, vocal on one side, instrumental on the other. Also on McCloy's list, "Chi Town Theme," previously recommended here, by Cleveland Eaton (Black Jazz) and which Jackie says works best speeded up some... The new version of **Titanic's** "Rain 2000" on John Colon's list from Make Believe Ballroom is by a New Jersey Group called **Megaton** (and on a New Jersey label, Cenpro); Colon says it's even stronger than the original and runs 3:58 in the long version... Bob Lombardi's inclusion of **George McCrae's** "I Ain't Lyin'" (from his new TK album) on his list from Rumbottom's in Hollywood, Florida, prompts me to add it to my own list of recommended cuts from that album – I overlooked it on my initial run-through and review and I've been kicking myself ever since... Among the many suggestions from Bobby Guttadaro this time around: "In My Baby's Arms" on the new **Joe Simon** album, "Get Down" (Spring), which is indeed hot. Sample lines: "There's no inflation in my baby's arms/There's no recession in my baby's arms/There's no depression in my baby's arms." Another Bobby DP pick hit: "Dancin' Shoes" by **Side Effect** (Fantasy). News: **Mike & Bill's** terrific "Somebody's Gotta Go,"

PENROD'S, NEW YORK (LONG ISLAND)
DJ: Jackie McCloy

CHINESE KUNG FU – Banzai (Scepter)
CHI TOWN THEME – Cleveland Eaton (Black Jazz)
DANCE DANCE DANCE – Calhoon (Warner Spector)
DO IT ANY WAY YOU WANNA – People's Choice (TSOP)
FOREVER CAME TODAY – Jackson 5 (Motown)
GIMME SOME – Jimmy "Bo" Horne (Alston)
LOVE POWER – Willie Hutch (Motown)
ONE WAY STREET – Becket Brown (RCA import)
TO EACH HIS OWN – Faith, Hope & Charity (RCA)
YOU'RE ALL I EVER DREAMED OF – Crystal Grass
(Polydor)

MAKE BELIEVE BALLROOM, NEW YORK
DJ: John Colon

CHICAGO THEME – Hubert Laws (CTI)
DREAMING A DREAM – Crown Heights Affair (De-Lite)
FOOT STOMPIN' MUSIC – Bohannon (Dakar)
IT'S IN HIS KISS – Linda Lewis (Arista)
RAIN 2000 – Megaton (Cenpro)
SOMEBODY'S GOTTA GO – Mike & Bill (Moving Up)
STOP AND THINK – Trammps (Golden Fleece)
THREE STEPS FROM TRUE LOVE – Reflections (Capitol)
TORNADO – 'The Wiz' Original Cast (Atlantic)
WHAT A DIFF'RENCE A DAY MAKES – Esther Phillips
(Kudu)

RUMBOTTOM'S, HOLLYWOOD, FLORIDA
DJ: Bob Lombardi

BRAZIL – Ritchie Family (20th Century)
CAN'T GIVE YOU ANYTHING – Stylistics (Avco)
DANCE DANCE DANCE – Calhoon (Warner Spector)
DREAMING A DREAM – Crown Heights Affair (De-Lite)
FOREVER CAME TODAY – Jackson 5 (Motown)
I AIN'T LYIN' – George McCrae (TK)
LA BALANGA – Bimbo Jet (Pathé import)
SEXY – MFSB (Phila. Intl.)
THREE STEPS FROM TRUE LOVE – Reflections (Capitol)
YOU BRING THE SUN IN THE MORNING – Fay Hauser
(SMI)

LE JARDIN, NEW YORK
DJ: Bobby Guttadaro

BRAZIL – Ritchie Family (20th Century)
CHICAGO THEME – Hubert Laws (CTI)
DREAMING A DREAM – Crown Heights Affair (De-Lite)
EL BIMBO – Bimbo Jet (Scepter)
FOREVER CAME TODAY – Jackson 5 (Motown)
FREE MAN – South Shore Commission (Wand)
GIMME SOME – Jimmy "Bo" Horne (Alston)
SEXY – MFSB (Phila. Intl.)
SOMEBODY'S GOTTA GO – Mike & Bill (Moving Up)
WHAT A DIFF'RENCE A DAY MAKES – Esther Phillips
(Kudu)

" The big news this week is the tremendous success of New York's Record Pool. There were balloons floating all over, plates of cold cuts and cheese, a huge bowl of punch and a decorated cake "

which hit the Disco File Top 20 this week, is being picked up by Arista from its original label, Moving Up... Now available as commercial singles: "Clap Your Hands" by **Manhattan Transfer** (Atlantic), "He's My Man" by the **Supremes** (Motown), **Eddie Kendricks'** "Get The Cream Off The Top" (Tamla), the long disco version of **Consumer Rapport's** "Ease On Down The Road" (Wing & A Prayer), "Glasshouse" by the **Temptations** (Gordy), "I (Who Have Nothing)" by **Hodges, James & Smith** (20th Century) and "Spaced" backed with "Naked As The Day I Was Born," two fine **Stanley Turrentine** instrumentals on Fantasy.

Recommended: "Dance With Me," a very strong, string-swept instrumental version of **Melissa Manchester's** song, the fine disco side (5:15) of **Pat Lundi's** new single (Vigor). ✇

JULY 19, 1975

Two albums now available to disco DJs as white-cover advance pressings – both scheduled for commercial release by the end of this week – present two very different sides of the European Eclectic disco sound. From Spain (but recorded in Nueva York), there's **Barrabas**, long established as one of the hottest disco groups, now ready with their most solid album to date, "Heart of the City" '(Atco). "Mellow Blow" is the knockout cut – a loose, airy, completely hypnotic instrumental that picks up where Creative Source's "Corazon" left off. Immediately put on the new top 10s supplied this week by Tom Savarese (12 West) and Bobby Koprowski (Kenny's in Getty Square, Yonkers, New York), "Mellow Blow" is also the first single release scheduled from the album. Other cuts are in the more familiar Barrabas style (though here the sound is more consistent and attractive than ever before; in particular, check out "Family Size" and "Checkmate.") The other album out this week is Silver Convention's debut, made in Germany and titled, not surprisingly, "Save Me" (Midland International). At its best, the group, three girls identified only as Ingrid, Wilma and Monica; sounds like Love Unlimited (though they are limited to spare chorus work throughout) backed by an MFSB-styled outfit. The sound may not have a lot of variety, but it is delightfully light and ecstatic, with a fine use of strings and sweet vocals. Tom Savarese chose "Fly, Robin, Fly" – at 5:31, the album's longest cut – for his top 10 this week, and Tony Gioe from Hollywood was most enthusiastic about "Another Girl" (the next single) and "I Like It" which, with "Save' Me" (at 4:25), covers the whole first side of the album. "Tiger Baby" on the other side can also be recommended for dancing and the whole album is perfect for at-home atmosphere.

Rumor of the Week: **The Rolling Stones** are planning a version of **Shirley And Company's** "Shame, Shame, Shame" for their next album. **Mick Jagger** fell in love with the song while preparing for the group's Tour of the Americas and may yet work it into their stage act before that tour runs its course. And don't overlook **Angelo Bond's** powerful deout album, "Bondage" (ABC), beautifully written and produced by Bond and **McKinley Jackson** and containing a devastating show biz biography, "He Gained the World (But Lost His Soul)," the story of a singer from his beginning in a gospel choir ("Every Sunday he sang a solo/That made the sisters shout and cry") to his end in a hotel room ("Cause of death was unknown/At least that's what the

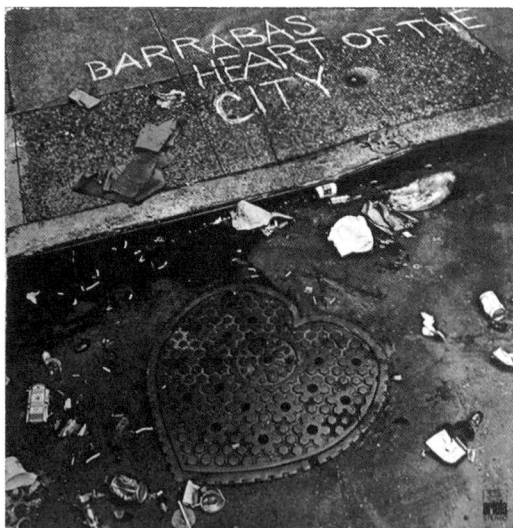

paper said"), plus the sadly overlooked but moving "Reach For The Moon." Bond's lyrics on much of the album approach **Smokey Robinson's** in intelligence and precision (and that's one of the best things I could say about any songwriter), particularly on "Man Can't Serve Two Masters," "Eve," "I Never Sang For My Baby" and the two cuts already mentioned. Even though it's more for listening than for partying, "Bondage" is this month's left field favorite.

We seem to have gotten ourselves into something of a controversy over the **Ritchie Family's** enormously successful single, "Brazil". Our report two issues back of **Sonny Casella's** claim that he was the record's producer prompted a letter from a lawyer on behalf of the credited producer **Jacque Morali**, and the French-based Can't Stop Productions, headed by **Henri Belolo**. Casella, the letter informs us, only booked studio time (at Philadelphia's Sigma Sound) for the "Brazil" session and introduced Morali to several musicians who played on the record. For this he was given the "Special Thanks" credit we noted. A talk with "Brazil's" arranger, **Richard Rome**, confirmed this basic story but pointed out the difficulty of assigning credit when a number of people are creatively involved on a single project. For our part, we regret our involvement in this whole matter to begin with and offer apologies and best wishes to all concerned.

> **" Rumor of the week: The Rolling Stones are planning a version of Shirley And Company's "Shame, Shame, Shame" for their next album "**

12 WEST, NEW YORK
DJ: Tom Savarese

BRAZIL – The Ritchie Family (20th Century)

CHINESE KUNG FU – Banzaii (Scepter)

DO IT ANY WAY YOU WANNA – People's Choice (TSOP)

DREAMING A DREAM – Crown Heights Affair (De-Lite)

FOREVER CAME TODAY – Jackson 5 (Motown)

FLY, ROBIN, FLY – Silver Convention (Midland Intl.)

MELLOW BLOW/CHECKMATE – Barrabas (Atco)

SUMMERTIME – James Last (Polydor)

WHAT A DIFF'RENCE A DAY MAKES – Esther Phillips (Kudu)

WHEN YOU'RE YOUNG AND IN LOVE – Ralph Carter (Mercury)

KENNY'S, NY (GETTY SQUARE, YONKERS)
DJ, Bobby Koprowski

BRAZIL – The Ritchie Family (20th Century)

CHINESE KUNG FU – Banzaii (Scepter)

LITTLE BIT OF LOVE/DISCO DAN – Faith Hope & Charity (RCA)

MELLOW BLOW – Barrabas (Atco)

SCAREDYCAT – Doyley Brothers (Atco)

SNEAKIN' UP BEHIND YOU – Brecker Brothers (Arista)

SOLID FUNK – Funky Boys (RCA)

SOMEBODY'S GOTTA GO – Mike & Bill (Moving Up)

UNDECIDED LOVE – Chequers (Creole Import)

WHAT A DIFF'RENCE A DAY MAKES – Esther Phillips (Kudu)

HOLLYWOOD, NEW YORK
DJ: Tony Gioe

BRAZIL – The Ritchie Family (20th Century)

DO THE CHOO-CHOO – Jock Ashford & the Sound of New Detroit (Blaze)

DREAMING A DREAM – Crown Heights Affair (De-Lite)

FOOT STOMPIN' MUSIC – Bohannon (Dakar)

FOREVER CAME TODAY – Jackson 5 (Motown)

HAPPY BRAZILIA – James Last (Polydor import)

LOVE POWER – Willie Hutch (Motown)

SEXY – MFSB (Phila. Intl.)

SOMEBODY'S GOTTA GO – Mike & Bell (Moving Up)

WHAT A DIFF'RENCE A DAY MAKES – Esther Phillips (Kudu)

OUR SIDE, LOS ANGELES
DJ: A.J. Miller

BAD LUCK – Harold Melvin & Ihe Bluenotes (Phila. Intl.)

DO IT ANY WAY YOU WANNA – People's Choice (TSOP)

DREAMING A DREAM – Crown Heights Affair (De-Lite)

EASE ON DOWN THE ROAD – Consumer Rapport (Wing & A Prayer)

FIGHT THE POWER – Isley Brothers (T-Neck)

FOOT STOMPIN' MUSIC – Bohannon (Dakar)

FOREVER CAME TODAY – Jackson 5 (Motown)

HOLLYWOOD HOT – Eleventh Hour (20th Century)

THE HUSTLE – Van McCoy (Avco)

7-6-5-4-3-2-1 (BLOW YOUR WHISTLE) – Gary Toms Empire (PIP)

Feedback: Among the new records on this week's batch of top 10s, aside from those already recommended here like "Do The Choo-Choo," "Hollywood Hot" and "Scaredycat," are "Happy Brazilia" by **James Last** (a cut on a European Polydor album called "Beach Party"), which Tony Gioe describes as "an uptempo "Gut Level" with breaks" – oh yeah? – and, on Bobby Koprowski's list, a tight little instrumental called "Solid Funk" by the **Funky Boys** (RCA), a German group which we can also recommend… Gioe was also raving about an import by someone named **Moon Williams** titled "Suspicious Love" (DJM, in England), which was first brought to my attention by Sheldon Smith, a DJ who occasionally plays at the Adams Apple. Though it may not be, in Gioe's word, "flawless," the record is sharp, well produced and to the point: "Suspicious love is the worst kind of love that you can think of." MCA has picked the record up for the American market and expects to have it out this week… Tom Savarese suggests "Take A Trip To The Islands," a wonderfully evocative cut on the new **Chi-Lites** album ("Half A Love" on Brunswick), for a refreshing change of pace. We also like "When Temptation Comes," which is more in the trademark Chi-Lites style and quite nice… Louis Schneider from Casablanca, the upper west side one in New York, brought by a copy of the only Latin single I know of that runs six minutes and is marked "For DJ and Disco Play." It's "La Batalla De Los Barrios" by **Orquesta Tipica Novel** (on TR Records), the group that won Latin NY magazine's award for the best charanga band of the past year, and should be checked out. Also for Latin lovers: the steamy, jumping "Cucula" by **Celia & Johnny** (Vaya) – Celia Cruz and Johnny Pacheco, that is – obviously a hit.

Recommended: **Revelation's** "Get Ready For This" (RSO), my favorite single this week and a **Norman Harris-Allan Felder** production, (with **Jemore Gasper**). The message, delivered with a gospel fervor: "Take a stand/Stand up strong/Help yourself/Get ready for this." Also: "You And I" by **Joe Anderson** (Buddah), who sounds pleasantly like **Al Green** on this sweet and slow hustle number; "Ain't Got No Love" by **Milt Matthews & Uprising** (Bryan), a· good combination of disco production and Memphis-style vocals (somewhat reminiscent of the **Staple Singers** sound) – arranged and mixed by **Bert deCoteaux** and **Barnaby Bye's** unusual "Can't Live This Way" (Atlantic), now out as a single. ⊘

JULY 26, 1975

The new **B.T. Express** album, "Non-Stop" (Scepter/Roadshow), is out now and, like the first, is so consistently strong that it immediately establishes them as one of the most interesting and potentially important (that is, long-lasting) black groups around. (The others? **Earth, Wind & Fire**, the **O'Jays**, **Kool & the Gang**, **LaBelle**, the **Jackson 5** and **Harold Melvin & the Bluenotes**, if only because of "Bad Luck.") The strongest cut is also the longest: "Peace Pipe," which opens the album up at just a little over six minutes and smokes hard and heavy; a "Love Train" message put on the "Express" track. We also particularly like "Happiness," "Give It What You Got" and "You Got It – I Want It." With **Barrabas'** "Heart of the City" (Atco) now available, this is the most essential new album out. "Non-Stop" is right.

Also recommended: "**KC And The Sunshine Band**" (TK), the heart of the Miami Sound, featuring a longer version of their successful "Get Down Tonight" (5:14) and an equally sharp "That's the Way (I Like It)," already on Danae Jacovidis' list from Styx in Boston, and running 5:07. Also try the two-part instrumental, "Let It Go," which opens and closes the album.

I don't usually write about concerts, but I have to make an exception here for the recent **Fania All Stars** night at Madison Square Garden, which was the most impressive and exciting show I've seen in years. The highlights: two songs from **Celia Cruz**, dressed in a long electric blue lame gown and matching turban, coming on like a combination of **Patti LaBelle** and **Tina Turner** (how's that for knockdown power?) and dancing with band leader **Johnny Pacheco** until I was in a state of shock – simply the most spectacular woman singer I've seen on a stage in some time; **Hector LaVoe**, a white-suited and obviously apprehensive Tarzan, swinging out over the audience, already in a state of delighted uproar, for the surprise ending of "Mi Gente;" **Tito Puente's** guest appearance, greeted by a howling standing ovation and worth every minute of it; and the final number, featuring **Ray Barretto** on congas, which took everyone into the heart of the jungle and left us reeling there. Don't miss them next time around.

Jeff Baugh and Ilene Raskin who report this week from the new Southampton club, Jaws, are also known as Disco On The Run, one of the many mobile discotheque teams operating in New York and across the country. They travel with their own equipment and lights (including a portable mirrored ball) and set up for parties anywhere (like the recent closing party for **Bette Midler's** "Clams On The Half-Shell Revue" and frequent late afternoons at the Promenade Cafe in Rockefeller Center). They'll also be providing the musical setting for the **Disco Tex & the Sex-O-Lettes** show at the Diplomat Hotel's Grand Ballroom coming up on August 13. Other records the Disco On The Run team are excited about: "It Only Takes A Minute" by **Tavares** (Capitol), "Dinero," a fine Latin hustle from the LTG

Exchange album, "Susie Heartbreaker" (RCA) and "The Summer Of '42," the lush **Biddu Orchestra** version of the **Michel Legrand** movie theme that's become one of the most talked-about and sought-after imports in New York in the past few weeks (it's on Epic in England but as yet they have no plans to release it here). My favorite single this week is a left field choice but the only bright spot in a rather dull batch. It's called "There'll Come A Time, There'll Come A Day" by a group with the fabulous name of **Basic Black and Pearl** with a great, gutsy lead and a updated '60s girl group sound. The record was brought to my attention by **Record World's Bob Adels** who writes the snappy singles reviews among other things and who turned it up on the B side of a Canadian import version of the **Crystals'** old "He's A Rebel." It happened to be on a Polydor label (WAM Records) in Canada, and they're bringing out advance copies for DJs this week (and commercial copies on Polydor very soon) after DJ Steve D'Acquisto (now at Le Jardin) alerted them to it. Listen and see what you think. ◗

> **❝ Disco On The Run is one of the many mobile discotheque teams operating across the country. They travel with their own equipment and lights (including a portable mirror ball) ❞**

JAWS, SOUTHAMPTON, N.Y.
DJs: Jeff Baugh & Ilene Raskin

BRAZIL – The Ritchie Family (20th Century)
CHICAGO THEME – Hubert Laws (CTI)
DIDN'T I TAKE YOU HIGHER – Steve Wright (Atec)
DOCTOR'S MUSIC – Peppers (Big Tree)
DREAMING A DREAM – Crown Heights Affair (De-Lite)
FOREVER CAME TODAY – Jackson 5 (Motown)
LADY, LADY, LADY – Boogie Man Orchestra
(Boogie Man)
SOMEBODY'S GOTTA GO – Mike & Bill (Moving Up)
UNDECIDED LOVE – Chequers (Creole import)
WHAT A DIFF'RENCE A DAY MAKES – Esther Phillips
(Kudu)

STYX, BOSTON
DJ: Danae Jacovidis

BRAZIL – The Ritchie Family (20th Century)
CHINESE KUNG FU – Banzaii (Scepter)
DANCE DANCE DANCE – Calhoon (Warner Spector)
DO IT ANY WAY YOU WANNA – People's Choice (TSOP)
FLY, ROBIN, FLY – Silver Convention (Midland Intl.)
FOREVER CAME TODAY – Jackson 5 (Motown)
LOVE INFLATION – Joneses (Mercury)
ONE WAY STREET – Becket Brown (RCA)
THAT'S THE WAY (I LIKE IT) – KC & the Sunshine Band (TK)
WHAT A DIFF'RENCE A DAY MAKES – Esther Phillips
(Kudu)

CABARET, LOS ANGELES
DJ: Howard Metz

BRAZIL – The Ritchie Family (20th Century)
CHINESE KUNG FU – Banzaii (Scepter)
DO IT ANY WAY YOU WANNA – People's Choice (TSOP)
DREAMING A DREAM – Crown Heights Affair (De-Lite)
FIGHT THE POWER – Isley Brothers (T-Neck)
FOOT STOMPIN' MUSIC – Bohannon (Dakar)
FOREVER CAME TODAY – Jackson 5 (Motown)
THE HUSTLE – Van McCoy (Avco)
PEACE AND LOVE – Ron Butler & the Ramblers (Playboy)
7-6-5-4-3-2-1 (BLOW YOUR WHISTLE) – Gary Toms
Empire (PIP)

LA MARTINIQUE, NEW YORK
DJ: Ray Goynes

DREAMING A DREAM – Crown Heights Affair (De-Lite)
FIGHT THE POWER – Isley Brothers (T-Neck)
FOOT STOMPIN' MUSIC – Bohannon (Dakar)
FREE MAN – South Shore Commission (Wand)
GET DOWN TONIGHT – KC & the Sunshine Band (TK)
I'LL DO FOR YOU ANYTHING YOU WANT ME TO – Barry
White (20th Century)
LONDON EXPRESS – Oliver Sain (Abet)
LOVE INFLATION – Joneses (Mercury)
SPIRIT OF THE BOOGIE/SUMMER MADNESS – Kool &
the Gang (De-Lite)
SWEARIN' TO GOD – Frankie Valli (Private Stock)

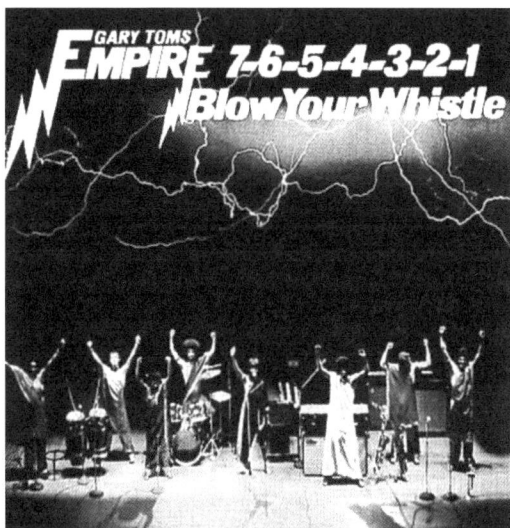

AUGUST 2, 1975

“Discotheque music has been around for several years now, but it's only in the past year that it's taken on some sort of identity and been treated as a separate genre of music”

In last week's issue, **Dede Dabney**, **Record World's** r&b editor, posed a few questions about discos and disco music that deserve some response in this column. While acknowledging the impact of disco-style music on the record industry and its increasing dominance of radio station playlists, Dede is apparently concerned that this direction is sweeping other, less aggressive styles of music aside. "What about the producer who would like to lay down a slow melodic track with sensitive lyrics?" she asks. "Is it fair to hinder him?" Certainly not, but are producers actually being "hindered" from making traditional slow records? And are they being deprived of airplay? Of the performers Dede listed as among those potentially threatened by this trend, the majority – the **Moments**, **Major Harris**, **Blue Magic**, the **Stylistics**, **Johnny Bristol**, the **Main Ingredient** – have done very well over the past year, many of them successful both in the disco field and out. Another on the list, **Smokey Robinson**, currently has his most successful album as a solo artist in "A Quiet Storm," an epitome of passionate, sweet ballad styling. And **Gladys Knight**, **Minnie Riperton** and **Al Green** haven't exactly fallen on hard times when it comes to successful ballads.

So I think it's safe to say that the popularity of disco music hasn't prevented performers and producers in other styles from breaking through and I don't think anyone is predicting an all-out disco takeover (I can see it now: program directors, like the bad guy bullies in Western movies, skimming records like bullets at people's feet, commanding them to dance or else). If record producers and radio stations are following the disco directions, it's hardly on a whim. It is, for the moment, a sound that people want to hear, with the sort of vitality and freshness many of us found lacking on the music scene in recent years.

This brings us to Dede's final question: Is the "discotheque syndrome," as she calls it, just a fad or will it last? This is a favorite music business question and a hard one to answer. First, discotheque music has been around for several years now but it's only in the past year that it's taken on some sort of identity and been treated as a separate genre of music. When producers began to hook into the resurgence of discotheques and consciously apply themselves to the new style of dance music they were nurturing, that style became more defined and, unfortunately, more predictable. So, to some extent, what started out as an underground phenomenon has been commercialized into a fad whose very popularity may kill it before long. But disco music is not hula hoops and it still remains a highly varied and largely unpredictable style – just look at the range of material and treatment represented in the Disco File Top 20. Any trend that can encompass **Hubert Laws'** "Chicago Theme," "Chinese Kung Fu," "Forever Came Today," **Esther Phillips'** "What A Diff'rence A Day Makes" and **B.T. Express'** new "Peace 'Pipe" is broad and rich enough to keep from turning stagnant and rigid in the near future. Meaning the fad may pass, discotheques may fade as a prominent social phenomenon, but the music will remain because it's too strong not to.

New items on the lists this week: **The Dynamic Superiors'** "Face The Music," a sharp, cutting, change-of-pace production by **Nick Ashford** and **Valerie Simpson** (who also wrote the song), which Paul Casella put on his Top 10 from the Monastery in the first week out. The only complaint, also voiced by Phil Gill from Watu Wazuri, is that, at 3:08, the song's not long enough. Also recommended from the Dynamic Superiors' new album (on Motown): "Deception" and a strong message song that's worth a try called "Nobody's Gonna Change Me" … **Merry Clayton's** comeback record, "Keep Your Eye On The Sparrow," an uneven but powerful production by **Gene McDaniels** (Ode) is on Casella's list as well because he reports both he and his crowd are totally knocked out by it. …Walter Gibbons, who plays at the popular new private club in New York, Galaxy 21, admits that "2 Pigs And A Hog" from the "Cooley High Original Soundtrack" (Motown) is very short (1:46) but he says he uses two copies back-to-back and they love it. The cut is essentially some very hard percussion, particularly striking because of the lack of any other instrumentation until the very end. Also on the soundtrack album: "Baby Love," "You Beat Me To The Punch," "Fingertips," "OOO Baby Baby" and other Motown classics… If Bob Gordon from Club Casablanca had his way, he'd list the whole **Silver Convention** album ("Save Me" on Midland International) but I insisted he choose two cuts. His choice: "Fly, Robin, Fly," which is shaping up as the favorite, and "I Like It." Gordon is also playing Sundays at 12 West… Paul Christy, who reports this week for the first time from the new L'Esprit in Detroit, is also the program director at W4-FM in that city. Best news I heard all week: **David Ruffin** is back in the recording studio-this time in New York with **Van McCoy** producing the sessions for Motown. Should be a winning combination. Off-the-Wall Dept.: United Artists has issued several albums of

THE MONESTARY, NY (QUEENS)
DJ: Paul Casella

BRAZIL – The Ritchie Family (20th Century)
CONTROL TOWER – Magic Disco Machine (Motown)
FACE THE MUSIC – Dynamic Superiors (Motown)
IT ONLY TAKES A MINUTE – Tavares (Capitol)
KEEP YOUR EYE ON THE SPARROW – Merry Clayton (Ode)
MELLOW BLOW – Barrabas (Atco)
PEACE PIPE – B.T. Express (Scepter/Roadshow)
SUMMER OF '42 – Biddu Orchestra (Epic import)
TO EACH HIS OWN – Faith, Hope & Charity (RCA)
WHAT A DIFF'RENCE A DAY MAKES – Esther Phillips (Kudu)

CLUB CASABLANCA, NEW YORK
DJ: Bob Gordon

BRAZIL – The Ritchie Family (20th Century)
CHINESE KUNG FU – Banzaii (Scepter)
DO IT ANY WAY YOU WANNA – People's Choice (TSOP)
DREAMING A DREAM – Crown Heights Affair (De-Lite)
FOREVER CAME TODAY – Jackson 5 (Motown)
I LIKE IT/FLY, ROBIN, FLY – Silver Convention (Midland Intl.)
IT ONLY TAKES A MINUTE – Tavares (Capitol)
PEACE PIPE – B. T. Express (Scepter/Roadshow)
SUMMERTIME – James Last (Polydor)
WHAT A DIFF'RENCE A DAY MAKES – Esther Philips (Kudu)

L'ESPRIT, DETROIT
DJ: Paul Christy

CHICAGO THEME – Hubert Laws (CTI)
DYNOMITE – Tony Camillo's Bazuka (A&M)
EASE ON DOWN THE ROAD – Consumer Rapport (Wing & A Prayer)
FIGHT THE POWER – Isley Brothers (T-Neck)
FREE MAN – South Shore Commission (Wand)
GET DOWN TONIGHT – KC & the Sunshine Band (TK)
THE HUSTLE – Van McCoy (Avco)
I COULD DANCE ALL NIGHT – Archie Bell & the Drells (TSOP)
7-6-5-4-3-2-1 (BLOW YOUR WHISTLE) – Gary Toms Empire (PIP)
SEXY – MFSB (Phila.)

GALAXY 21/NEW YORK
DJ: Walter Gibbons

BRAZIL – The Ritchie Family (20th Century)
CHI-TOWN THEME – Cleveland Eaton (Black Jazz)
DO IT ANY WAY YOU WANNA – People's Choice (TSOP)
FOREVER CAME TODAY – Jackson 5 (Motown)
IT ONLY TAKES A MINUTE – Tavares (Capitol)
ONE WAY STREET – Becket Brown (RCA)
PEACE PIPE/DISCOTIZER – B.T. Express (Scepter /Roadshow)
SOMEBODY'S GOTTA GO – Mike & Bill (Moving Up)
2 PIGS AND A HOG – 'Cooley High' Original Soundtrack (Motown)
WHAT A DIFF'RENCE A DAY MAKES – Esther Phillips (Kudu)

original motion picture scores-not, apparently, the actual soundtracks, but recently-recorded versions of the actual scores – and among them is **Max Steiner's** score for "King Kong," which turns out to be quite extraordinary. Listen in particular to "Jungle Dance/Anne Is Offered To Kong," the music that accompanied that terrific scene of the Americans' first cautious observation of the natives and their ritual dance. There's a steady drumbeat through most of the track and a pounding, driving mood is created by the orchestra. It certainly couldn't be played just anywhere in the evening, but I suspect that, placed carefully, "Jungle Dance" could upset or at least amuse some of the ready-for-anything crowds.

Recommended, but not for all tastes: **Sunny Gale's** "I Wanna Know" (on the special Disco-Soul label, available only to DJs right now, through RCA), an involving, invigorating production and arrangement by **Vince Montana**, MFS8's vibes player, also the arranger on **Black Ivory's** great "What Goes Around (Comes Around)." "I Wanna Know" is 5:58 and available on a regular 7-inch single but at 331/3 speed; on the other side is a version of **Third Time Around's** "Soon Every-thing's Gonna Be Alright" by **Schatz**. And try "Who Loves You" by the Four Seasons (Warner Bros./Curb) released as a single with a production by **Bob Gaudio** full of surprising touches, though perhaps a few too many changes for many dance floors. See what you think. ❧

DISCO FILE TOP 20

1. **FOREVER CAME TODAY** – Jackson 5 (Motown)
2. **DREAMING A DREAM** – Crown Heights Affair (De-Lite)
3. **WHAT A DIFF'RENCE A DAY MAKES** – Esther Phillips (Kudu)
4. **BRAZIL** – The Ritchie Family (Avco)
5. **DO IT ANY WAY YOU WANNA** – People's Choice (TSOP)
6. **FOOT STOMPIN' MUSIC** – Bohannon (Dakar)
7. **FIGHT THE POWER** – Isley Brothers (T-Neck)
8. **SOMEBODY'S GOTTA GO** – Mike & Bill (Moving Up)
9. **CHICAGO THEME** – Hubert Lewis (CTI)
10. **SEXY** – MFSB (Phila. Intl.)
11. **THREE STEPS FROM TRUE LOVE** – Reflections (Capitol)
12. **STOP AND THINK** – Trammps (Golden Fleece)
13. **FIGHT THE POWER** – Isley Brothers (T-Neck)
14. **FREE MAN** – South Shore Commission (Wand)
15. **THE HUSTLE** – Van McCoy (Avco)
16. **DANCE, DANCE, DANCE** – Calhoon (Warner Spector)
17. **MELLOW BLOW** – Barrabas (Atco)
18. **TO EACH HIS OWN** – Faith, Hope & Charity (RCA)
19. **IT ONLY TAKES A MINUTE** – Tavares (Capitol)
20. **PEACE PIPE** – B.T. Express (Scepter /Roadshow)

AUGUST 9, 1975

The best of the new singles: (1) "Salsoul," a sensational instrumental which sounds like it could be the best, longest (6:41) cut on the new **MFSB** album but is, in fact, by the new **Salsoul Orchestra** (Salsoul), produced, arranged and conducted by **Vince Montana** (who also wrote the song). The rhythm section was recorded in New York, the strings and horns at Sigma Sound in Philadelphia. Sounds like the next major instrumental. The other side is "Salsoul Hustle," a shorter version of the same cut that runs 3:24.

(2) "Hooked For Life," the **Trammps'** first release on Atlantic and a continuation of their trademark sound under the direction of **Baker**, **Harris & Young** – not as inspired as their best work, but attractive. Atlantic is planning to bring out a longer version on their classy 12-inch Disco Disc series in the next few weeks. And don't overlook the B side, a wonderful '50s update song called "I'm Alright" that jumps like the group's earlier version of "Shout."

(3) "Waterbed," **Herbie Mann's** slick version of the **LTG Exchange** record, also scheduled for release as an Atlantic Disco Disc, though the length is not expected to be significantly longer than the commercial release (3:50) due out this week. The vocals here are stronger than on "Hijack" and the overall sound is punched-up, steamier, not as raw as the LTG original, but just accessible enough to be the perfect follow-up to "Hijack."

(4) "Peace In The Family" by, appropriately, the **Johnson Family** (Atlantic), which is more left field than those above but it's a message a lot of people will get into and a production by **Bob Ezrin**, best known for quite different work with **Alice Cooper**.

Also recommended: "Cheer-Up Syrup" by **David "K" & the Blue Ties** (Spigot), an oddity built around a carnival-style New York radio jingle (the Palisades Amusement Park tune, written by the Park's owner **Gladys Shelley**) set in an ornate disco frame. Very cute and just the sort of novelty that could catch on, especially with an instrumental side of 4:28. "Cheer-Up Syrup" is already on Spike's list from Charisma, a new club for the young & Latin crowd in New York. To continue: "Police Stopped The Party" by **Willard King** (Raintree) is a two-part funky, loud houseparty record just right when you're feeling rowdy; **Martin Mull's** instrumental, "Do The Dog" (Capricorn), manages to be both a send-up of the **AWB** funk-for-the-seventies style and a neat cover of it at the same time; and **Charity Brown's** ultra-bright version of the great **Ruby & the Romantics'** record, "Our Day Will Come" (A&M), which is on the other side of their version of "Take Me In Your Arms (Rock Me A Little While)," recommended some time back. Now out on singles: **Isaac Hayes'** "Chocolate Chip," both vocal and instrumental (ABC), with the latter cut to a generous 4:05; **Popcorn Wylie's** excellent "Georgia's After

Hours" (ABC) and **Hubert Laws'** "Chicago Theme," which is available in its album length (5:37) or cut to 3:15 on either side of the 45 (on CTI).

Highly recommended: **Felix Cavaliere's** new album, "Destiny" (Bearsville), basically a return to and a refinement of his **Young Rascals** style with the whole first side just terrific, especially the title cut and "Never Felt Love Before." Along with the new **Dynamic Superiors** album, "Destiny" is the record I find myself listening to most often these days. Also check out **Ronnie Laws'** "Pressure Sensitive" album (Blue Note) with a fine version of "Momma," the very strong cut on the recent **Hodges, James & Smith** album, written by guitarist **Roland Bautista** who plays on both lps. Ronnie laws is Hubert's younger brother and a saxophonist; production is by **Wayne Henderson** from the **Crusaders**, who also brought along **Joe Sample** and **Wilton Felder** from the group.

Feedback: Phil Gill from Watu Wazuri in Brooklyn recommends "Flight," a striking four-minute instrumental from **David Sanborn's** first album, "Taking Off" (Warner Brothers), which reminds me of a jazzier, more Latin-styled "Lady Lady Lady," with beautiful string work and a lot of changes. Unusual and worth a try... **Calender's** "Hypertension," originally released on Pi Kappa Records, is now on Buddah; I still recommend Part 2. ❂

“ Atlantic is planning to bring out a longer version on their classy 12-inch Disco Disc series in the next few weeks ”

CHARISMA, NEW YORK
DJ: Fernando Oquendo ("Spike")

BRAZIL – The Ritchie Family (20th Century)
CHEER-UP SYRUP – David "K" & the Blue Ties (Spigot)
DREAMING A DREAM – Crown Heights Affair (De-Lite)
GIMME SOME – Jimmy "Bo" Horne (Alston)
KEEP YOUR EYE ON THE SPARROW – Merry Clayton (Ode)
SEXY – MFSB (Phila, Intl.)
SOMEBODY'S GOTTA GO – Mike & Bill (Moving Up)
STOP AND THINK – Trammps (Golden Fleece)
TO EACH HIS OWN – Faith, Hope & Charity (RCA)
WHAT A DIFF'RENCE A DAY MADE – Esther Phillips (Kudu)

SCARLETT'S, WESTHAMPTON BEACH, N.Y.
DJ: Bill Vos

BRAZIL – The Ritchie Family (20th Century)
CHECKMATE/MELLOW BLOW – Barrabas (Atco)
DO IT ANY WAY YOU WANNA – People's Choice (TSOP)
DREAMING A DREAM – Crown Heights Affair (De-Lite)
FOREVER CAME TODAY – Jackson 5 (Motown)
IT ONLY TAKES A MINUTE – Tavares (Capitol)
KEEP YOUR EYE ON THE SPARROW – Merry Clayton (Ode)
PEACE PIPE – B.T. Express (Scepter/Roadshaw)
SOMEBODY'S GOTTA GO – Mike & Bill (Moving Up)
WHAT A DIFF'RENCE A DAY MADE – Esther Phillips (Kudu)

LE CLUB, NEW YORK
DJ: Kay Beckett

BRAZIL – The Ritchie Family (20th Century)
CHECKMATE – Barrabas (Atco)
FREE MAN – South Shore Commission (Wand)
GIMME SOME – Jimmy "Bo" Harne (Alston)
MELLOW ME – Faith, Hope & Charity (RCA)
PEACE PIPE – B.T. Express (Scepter/Roadshaw)
SEXY – MFSB (Phila, Intl.)
SOMEBODY'S GOTTA GO – Mike & Bill (Moving Up)
WE'RE ON THE RIGHT TRACK – Ultra High Frequency (Scepter)
WHEN YOU'RE YOUNG AND IN LOVE – Ralph Carter (Mercury)

WATU WAZURI, NY (BROOKLYN)
DJ: Phil Gill

BRAZIL – The Ritchie Family (20th Century)
CHECKMATE/FAMILY SIZE – Barrabas (Atco)
FACE THE MUSIC – Dynamic Superiors (Motown)
I LIKE IT/ANOTHER GIRL – Silver Convention (Midland Intl.)
IT ONLY TAKES A MINUTE – Tavares (Capitol)
MAGIC'S IN THE AIR – Ronnie Walker (Event)
MR. MAGIC – Esther Phillips (Kudu)
PEACE PIPE/WHATCHA THINK ABOUT THAT? – B. T. Express (Scepter/Roadshaw)
SALSOUL – Salsoul Orchestra (Salsoul)
SOMEBODY'S GOTTA GO – Mike & Bill (Moving Up)

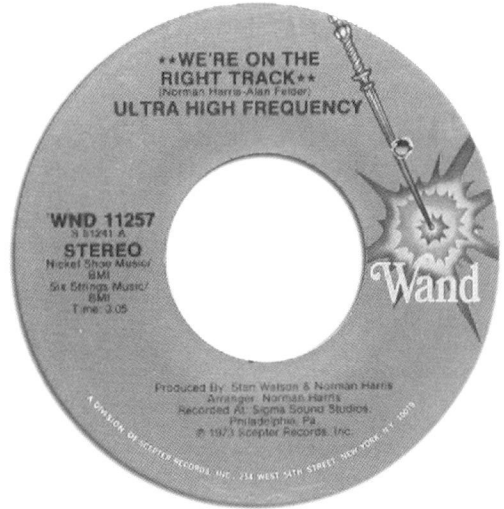

WE'RE ON THE RIGHT TRACK
(Norman Harris-Alan Felder)
ULTRA HIGH FREQUENCY

WND 11257
3) 61241 A
STEREO
Nickel Shoe Music/
BMI
Six Strings Music/
BMI
Time: 3.05

Produced By: Stan Watson & Norman Harris
Arranger: Norman Harris
Recorded At: Sigma Sound Studios,
Philadelphia, Pa.
℗ 1973 Scepter Records, Inc.

A DIVISION OF SCEPTER RECORDS, INC., 254 WEST 54TH STREET, NEW YORK, N.Y. 10019

Wand

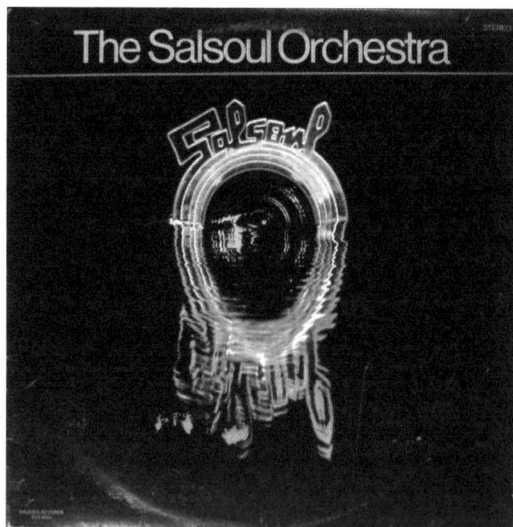

As media observers have surely noted, the Hustle is the most written about and discussed dance since the Twist and the most conspicuous product of the disco revival. Last month, the New York Times ran an article on the first page of its second section called "The 'Hustle' Restores Old Touch to Dancing," complete with a basic

dancing that means more inventiveness and excitement on the dance floor. Which leads me to a prediction of my own, considerably less portentous than Safire's but no less fervently believed-in. I don't think I'll go so far as to predict the revival of major dance marathons, but a small dance contest promotion for RCA's **Faith, Hope**

"Times columnist William Safire sees the Hustle as a return to discipline and responsibility after a long period of "frantic self-expression" and self-absorption both on the dance floor and off"

footwork diagram for beginners, but this past week Times columnist **William Safire**, hardly a noted pop culturist, got into the Hustle even more seriously in an Op Ed page essay titled, "On the Hustle." Analyzing the implications of the Hustle as a dance that (1) must be learned, as opposed to the free-form dances of the past 10 years which could be intuitively picked up; (2) requires "mental communication" with one's partner and (3) involves actual body-to-body contact, Safire draws some interesting sociological conclusions. He sees the dance as a return to discipline and responsibility after a long period of "frantic self-expression" and self-absorption both on the dance floor and off. To Safire, the Hustle is a conservative political statement, an indication that "turning inward is no longer 'in'; that personal isolationism has peaked and may already be on the decline." And as such, the Hustle's success is "the most profound political development on the American scene in recent months." I don't know about "profound" or "political," but the Hustle has meant a return to a more formalized, more involved style of

& **Charity** last week convinced me that dance contests are the next big form of entertainment in the seventies. Watching good dancers in competition was more fun than most of the concerts I've been to over the past year and as a contest it certainly beats the dreary routine of the Miss America shows. I'm looking forward to 90-minute color specials on TV with one hot couple after the other competing for big prizes. Wouldn't it be great to have star dancers with the sort of pop cultural status we now give football players and rock stars?

News & Notes: I usually don't write about records far in advance of their release, but an exception must be made for the **Armada Orchestra's** debut album for Contempo, a tape of which I heard this past week. Scheduled for release in England and America around the middle of September, the album contains lush and vibrant instrumental versions of three **Detroit Emeralds** songs: "Do Me Right," already around as an import single, "Feel The Need" and "You Want It, You Got It;" **Van McCoy's** "The Hustle;" **Jimmy Ruffin's**

VEGAS, WASHINGTON, DC
DJ: Bob Evans

BRAZIL – Ritchie Family (20th Century)
DREAMING A DREAM – Crown Heights Affair (De-Lite)
EASE ON DOWN THE ROAD – Consumer Rapport
(Wing & A Prayer)
FLY, ROBIN, FLY – Silver Convention (Midland Intl.)
FOREVER CAME TODAY – Jackson 5 (Motown)
GET DOWN TONIGHT – KC & the Sunshine Band (TK)
GIVE IT WHAT YOU GOT – B.T. Express
(Scepter/Roadshow)
IT ONLY TAKES A MINUTE – Tavares (Capitol)
THREE STEPS FROM TRUE LOVE – Reflections (Capitol)
WHAT A DIFF'RENCE A DAY MADE – Esther Phillips (Kudu)

YESTERDAYS, BOSTON
DJ: Joe Carvello

BRAZIL – Ritchie Family (20th Century)
DO IT ANY WAY YOU WANNA – People's Choice (TSOP)
DREAMING A DREAM – Crown Heights Affair (De-Lite)
IT ONLY TAKES A MINUTE – Tavares (Capitol)
LADY, LADY, LADY – Boogie Man Orchestra (Boogie Man)
ONE WAY STREET – Becket Brown (RCA)
PARTY MUSIC – Pat Lundi (Vigor)
SALSOUL HUSTLE – Salsoul Orchestra (Salsoul)
WHAT A DIFF'RENCE A DAY MADE – Esther Phillips (Kudu)
WHEN YOU'RE YOUNG AND IN LOVE – Ralph Carter
(Mercury)

CORK AND BOTTLE, NEW YORK
DJ: Eddie Rivera

AFTER YOU'VE HAD YOUR FLING – Intrepids (Columbia)
LADY, LADY, LADY – Boogie Man Orchestra (Boogie Man)
LIFE AND DEATH IN G&A – Love Childs Afro Cuban
Blues Band (Roulette)
NEVER GET ENOUGH OF YOUR LOVE – Street People
(Vigor)
PEACE AND LOVE – Ron Butler & the Ramblers (Playboy)
RAIN 2000 – Megaton (Cenpro)
SOMEBODY'S GOTTA GO – Mike & Bill (Moving Up)
SUMMER OF '42 – Biddu Orchestra (Epic import)
THINK BEFORE YOU STOP – Notations (Gemigo)
WHAT A DIFF'RENCE A DAY MADE/MR. MAGIC – Esther
Phillips (Kudu)

DISCO 1985, LOS ANGELES
DJ: Wayne Thorberg

BRAZIL – Ritchie Family (20th Century)
CHINESE KUNG FU – Banzaii (Scepter)
DO IT ANY WAY YOU WANNA – People's Choice (TSOP)
DO THE CHOO-CHOO – Jack Ashford & the Sound of
New Detroit (Blaze)
FAME – David Bowie (RCA)
FIGHT THE POWER – Isley Brothers (T-Neck)
HEADQUARTERS (AUGUSTA, GA.) – Bobby Byrd
(International Brothers)
HOLLYWOOD HOT – Eleventh Hour (20th Century)
THEME FROM THE MAGIC OF THE BLUE – Blue Magic
(Atco)
WHAT A DIFF'RENCE A DAY MADE – Esther Phillips (Kudu)

"Tell Me What You Want" and the **Four Tops'** "It's The Same Old Song," each cut better than the next. Definitely a contender for the instrumental album of the year... **The Biddu Orchestra** album is now out in England (on Epic, which has not yet scheduled it for American release) and is titled "Blue Eyed Soul" after the instrumental from the **Carl Douglas** "Kung Fu Fighting" album which Biddu produced. Included in the album is another version of the title cut, an odd but interesting disco version of the theme from the movie "Exodus," the already successful reworking of the theme from "Summer Of '42" (which Epic will release as a 45 in America later this week) and two other possible dance cuts, "Northern Dancer" and "Aranjuez Mon Amour." Bound to be a sought-after import... Midland International is putting out its first 12-inch disco-mix record featuring **Silver Convention's** "Fly, Robin, Fly" expanded to 7:39, backed with "Another Girl" (whose title will be changed to "Always Another Girl"), also lengthened to 5:33. One thousand copies are being pressed for distribution to the New York Record Pool and other disco DJs around the country... Speaking of the Record Pool, their location at 99 Prince Street is turning into a meeting place and showcase these days, with **B.T. Express** joining the member DJs this past week at the end of a meeting and performing a special set for everyone before cutting a huge cake welcoming them into the Pool. This week, Craig Bundy from Arista is bringing **Mike & Bill** down to the Pool to meet the people who broke "Somebody's Gotta Go" for them.

Recommended singles: the **Ventures'** new "Superstar Revue," a terrific instrumental with vocal touches written by **Vernon Burch** and available in a 4:28 disco version (UA) – a must; **Harlem River Drive's** pleasant **Stan Vincent** production, "Need You" (Arista); and "Charisma Road" by the **Charisma Band** (Buddah), in spite of its vocals but because of the tight production (especially that introduction) by **Cuba Gooding** and **Luther Simmons** of the **Main Ingredient**. Now out as singles: **George McCrae's** "I Ain't Lyin'" (TK), **Black Ivory's** "Feel It" (Buddah), "Love To Dance This One With You" by **Crystal Grass** (Polydor) and **Cleveland Eaton's** "Chitown Theme" (Black Jazz) in its full 5:03 length – all previously recommended here. I can't wait. (For New Yorkers who want to see what I'm so enthusiastic about, United Artists is having a dance contest to promote **War's** Madison garden concert this week, with the finals to be held in front of the garden Tuesday, the 12th.) ◓

AUGUST 23, 1975

I think a lot of times you don't realize how good an album is until you've had it for a few weeks. You may like and appreciate it immediately, but a great, lasting album is usually one that keeps getting better, keeps absorbing you into different cuts-first two favorites, then three others, until you're completely won over. I've already described the **Barrabas** album, "Heart Of The City" (Atco), as their most solid album to date, but in the month since I first wrote about it, it's proved to be even better than I thought at first. Like the **Silver Convention** album, "Heart Of The City" is one of those records DJs are tempted to list as a whole because so many cuts are being played. "Mellow Blow' "Checkmate" and "Family Size" were the first favorites, and now "Take A Wild Ride" and the long (6:06), languid "Along The Shore" are being picked up-both appear on Tom Savarese's top 10 this week from 12 West. Another album that sounds better all the time is **B.T. Express'** "Non-Stop" (Scepter/Roadshow). "Peace Pipe" is still the standout, but all of side one-"Give It What You Got" the single release, "Discotizer" and "Still Good, Still Like It," which Steve D'Acquisto at Le Jardin put on his list this week – and "Whatcha Think About That?" which closes the album are being played. All this action makes the Barrabas, Silver Convention and B.T. Express albums three of the most essential albums out right now and most likely choices for the top 10 disco albums of 1975.

"A lot of times you don't realize how good an album is until you've had it a few weeks. You may like and appreciate it immediately but a great, lasting album is one that keeps getting better"

New to the top 10 lists this week: **Gloria Gaynor's** new single, "(If You Want It) Do It Yourself" (MGM), picked by Vince Michaels from Sidestreet and Chardy's on Long Island. The single, incredibly restrained at only 2:49, breaks from the Gloria Gaynor formula somewhat without losing the exuberance and drive we're used to in her records; not exactly inspired, but solid and catchy…"Got To Keep On The Move" by **Sound Experience** with production by **Stan Watson** (Buddah), which, like the group's earlier disco success, "You've Broken My Heart,' is uneven – unconvincing vocals, great production – but interesting. It's from the new Sound Experience album, "Boogie Woogie,' which shares these same qualities, and was put on the Le Jardin top 10 by Steve D'Acquisto… **Natalie Cole's** razor-sharp debut single, "This Will Be" (Capitol), written and produced by **Chuck Jackson** and **Marvin Yancy** and listed by Artie Feldman at Den I (formerly Our Den) in Chicago. The production and the singing are strong enough to stand comparison with **Aretha Franklin** but this record sounds better to me on the radio than on the dance floor right now… And finally, **Sunny Gale's** excellent "I Wanna Know" (Disco-Soul/RCA), listed by Tom Savarese, raved about by Steve D'Acquisto and recommended to anyone who hasn't picked up on it already.

Destined for the Top 10: "Messin' With My Mind,' the first taste of the new **LaBelle** album and its best bite, available on promo copies in both long (4:37) and short (3:03) versions. The spirit is close to that in "What Can I Do For You?" with both vocals and drums pounding. The breaks are teriffic and the chorus, "If you keep it up/gonna give you up,' has you shouting along the first time you hear it. Very powerful, and bound to mess with everyone's mind. LaBelle's album, titled "Phoenix,' is due out within a week or two on Epic… Also a sure thing: **Deodato's** "Caravan/Watusi Strut" from his new album, "First Cuckoo" (MCA), which takes off from the **Duke Ellington** song for two minutes, then slips into more than nine minutes of pulsing instrumental, Deodato's best work for the dancefloor in some time, and the best new album cut this week.

Other recommended album cuts: "One More Ride," the brightest, most exciting cut from the new **Merry Clayton** album ("Keep Your Eye On The Sparrow" on Ode), produced by **Gene McDaniels**; and "Boogie Down USA,' the title instrumental cut from the new **People's Choice** album (TSOP), produced by **Gamble-Huff** and also featuring "Do It Any Way You Wanna" and "Party Is A Groovy Thing."

Recommended singles: **Sam Dees'** "Fragile, Handle With Care," superbly produced by **Tony Silvester** and **Bert deCoteaux** (Atlantic); "Rated X,' a perky instrumental by **L.T.D.** (A&M); and, more left field, **Gene Anderson's** "Your Love Must Be Voo Doo" in two parts (Hi), an unusual combination of southern funk, bluesy vocals and a very modern guitar line. ✪

12 WEST, NEW YORK
DJ: Tom Savarese

DO IT ANY WAY YOU WANNA – People's Choice (TSOP)
FLY, ROBIN, FLY/I LIKE IT – Silver Convention (Midland Intl.)
FOREVER CAME TODAY – Jackson 5 (Motown)
GIMME SOME – Jimmy "Bo" Horne (Alston)
I WANNA KNOW – Sunny Gale (Disco-Soul/RCA)
IT ONLY TAKES A MINUTE – Tavares (Capitol)
MELLOW BLOW/ALONG THE SHORE/TAKE A WILD RIDE – Barrabas (Atco)
PEACE PIPE – B. T. Express (Scepter/Roadshow)
WHEN YOU'RE YOUNG AND IN LOVE – Ralph Carter (Mercury)
YUM YUM (GIMME SOME) – Fatback Band (Event)

SIDE STREET, NY (LONG ISLAND)
DJ: Vince Michaels

BRAZIL – Ritchie Family (20th Century)
DO IT ANY WAY YOU WANNA – People's Choice (TSOP)
FLY, ROBIN, FLY/ANOTHER GIRL/I LIKE IT – Silver Convention (Midland Intl.)
GET DOWN TONIGHT/THAT'S THE WAY (I LIKE IT) – KC & the Sunshine Band (TK)
(IF YOU WANT IT) DO IT YOURSELF – Gloria Gaynor (MGM)
IT ONLY TAKES A MINUTE – Tavares (Capitol)
MELLOW BLOW /FAMILY SIZE/CHECKMATE – Barrabas (Atco)
PEACE PIPE – B.T. Express (Scepter/ Roadshow)
SOMEBODY'S GOTTA GO – Mike & Bill (Moving Up/Arista)

LE JARDIN, NEW YORK
DJ: Steve D'Acquisto

BRAZIL – Ritchie Family (20th Century)
CHITOWN THEME – Cleveland Eaton (Black Jazz)
DO IT ANY WAY YOU WANNA – People's Choice (TSOP)
DREAMING A DREAM – Crown Heights Affair (De-Lite)
FOREVER CAME TODAY – Jackson 5 (Motown)
GOT TO KEEP ON THE MOVE – Sound Express (Buddah)
IT ONLY TAKES A MINUTE – Tavares (Capitol)
PEACE PIPE/STILL GOOD, STILL LIKE IT – B.T. Express (Scepter/Roadshow)
SOMEBODY'S GOTTA GO – Mike & Bill (Moving Up/Arista)
WHAT A DIFF'RENCE A DAY MAKES –Esther Phillips (Kudu)

DEN 1, CHICAGO
DJ: Artie Feldman

BRAZIL – Ritchie Family (20th Century)
DO IT ANY WAY YOU WANNA – People's Choice (TSOP)
DREAMING A DREAM – Crown Heights Affair (De-Lite)
FIGHT THE POWER – Isley Brothers (T-Neck)
FOREVER CAME TODAY – Jackson 5 (Motown)
GIMME SOME – Jimmy "Bo" Horne (Alston)
IT ONLY TAKES A MINUTE – Tavares (Capitol)
MELLOW ME – Faith, Hope & Charity (RCA)
THIS WILL BE – Natalie Cole (Capitol)
WHEN YOU'RE YOUNG AND IN LOVE – Ralph Carter (Mercury)

AUGUST 30, 1975

FEEDBACK: John Colon, DJ at the Make-Believe Ballroom in New York, suggests flipping over the latest release from **Kaleidoscope**, "Thank You" (TSOP), and getting into the B side, "I'm A Changed Person," a pleasant, spirited number with a **Baker, Harris & Young** production similar to their work a while back with the **Whispers**. Colon is also one of a number of New York DJs who report playing "Breakaway," the instrumental side of a British Contempo import by **Ernie Bush**. According to the charts in the excellent English magazine, Blues & Soul, "Breakaway" is one of the most popular disco records in England right now,

Joe Palminteri, who's playing at The Monster on Fire Island (the Grove) for the summer, is enthusiastic about **Ace Spectrum's** "Keep Holding On" from their "Low Rent Rendezvous" album (Atlantic) and recently issued on the label's 12-inch disco series, same length (8:41) but effectively remixed. Reminiscent of the **Trammps'** more driving, optimistic material, "Keep Holding On" was produced by **Ed Zant**, a member of the group, and **Tony Silvester.** My only complaint: the long instrumental second half doesn't hold up to the powerful vocal half and interest falls off rapidly. Also on Palminteri's playlist: "Tell The People" and "Drive My Car," an interesting re-make of **The Beatles** song, from the new **Gary Toms Empire** album, "7-6-5-4-3-2-1 Blow Your Whistle" (PIP). We also like "Do Your Thing" from the same album, the cut Tom Savarese plays at 12 West... AJ Miller from the Paradise Ballroom in Los Angeles (which had been renamed Our Side until the Other Side disco across the street burned down recently) reports playing **Ray Charles'** version of **Stevie Wonder's** "Living For The City" (from his "Renaissance" album, on Crossover) but points out that he speeds it up and cuts out the rap; in any case, a very left field choice.

Silver Convention's "I Like It" (Midland Intl.) moved to 13 in the Disco File Top 20 this week, close behind the other popular Silver Convention track, "Fly, Robin Fly." Other albums represented on the list by two tracks are those by **Barrabas** ("Mellow Blow" and "Checkmate") and **KC & the Sunshine Band** ("Get Down Tonight" and "That's The Way I Like It"), but here the cuts are slotted together because they have been equally popular in the top 10 lists.

❝ According to the excellent English magazine, Blues & Soul, "Breakaway" is one of the most popular disco records in England right now, the only British product on their Disco Dozen list ❞

and the only British product on the magazine's Disco Dozen list. But a Blues & Soul article reveals that though the record is an English release, it was made in the States by a native of Bridgeport, Connecticut, more than a year ago and never put out. The vocal is interesting – a warning about the powers of black magic – but the instrumental is even better and worth searching out. (For the curious, Blues & Soul's most recent Disco Dozen also includes a few other songs doing much better over there than they are here: "Action Speaks Louder Than Words" by **Chocolate Milk**, "London Express" by **Oliver Sain**, **Bobby Moore's** "Call Me Your Anything Man" and "Monaurail" by **Fred & the New JBs**; number one was "Crystal World" and "Breakaway" was in second place.

RECOMMENDED SINGLES: **Tina Charles'** "You Set My Heart On Fire" (Columbia), a **Biddu** composition and production with a classic girl group sound (down to the "bomp-shu-bomp-shu-bomps") which is already being played as an import around New York and should go even further with its instrumental B side, "Fire" (3:15); "Hustling" by the **Hustlers** (People), a **James Brown** number that, typically, has nothing to do with the Hustle as a dance, but who cares when it's this spunky? – a steal from **Van McCoy's** "Disco Baby" cut, but wonderfully funked-up ; "Oh Baby" by **Wayne Miranda** and **Rush Release** (Roulette), with a 4:25 long version and an easy, smooth hustle sound much like **Bobby Moore's**; "All I Need" by **Anacostia** (Columbia), another fine **Baker, Harris & Young**

PARADISE BALLROOM, LOS ANGELES
DJ: AJ Miller

BRAZIL – Ritchie Family (20th Century)
CHINESE KUNG FU – Banzaii (Scepter)
DO IT ANY WAY YOU WANNA – People's Choice (TSOP)
FIGHT THE POWER – Isley Brothers (T-Neck)
FOREVER CAME TODAY – Jackson 5 (Motown)
HOLLYWOOD HOT – Eleventh Hour (20th Century)
IT ONLY TAKES A MINUTE – Tavares (Capitol)
PEACE PIPE – B.T. Express (Scepter/Roadshow)
THAT'S THE WAY (I LIKE IT) – KC & the Sunshine Band (TK)
WHAT A DIFFERENCE A DAY MADE – Esther Phillips (Kudu)

HADAAR, STATEN ISLAND, NEW YORK
DJ: Richie Conte

BRAZIL – Ritchie Family (20th Century)
DANCE DANCE DANCE – Calhoon (Warner Spector)
DREAMING A DREAM – Crown Heights Affair (De-Lite)
I LIKE IT – Silver Convention (Midland Intl.)
LOVE POWER – Willie Hutch (Motown)
MAGIC'S IN THE AIR – Ronnie Walker (Event)
PEACE PIPE – B.T. Express (Scepter/Roadshow)
SUPERSTAR REVUE – Ventures (UA)
TO EACH HIS OWN – Faith, Hope & Charity (RCA)
WHEN YOU'RE YOUNG AND IN LOVE – Ralph Carter (Mercury)

THE MONSTER, FIRE ISLAND, N.Y.
DJ: Joe Palminteri

BRAZIL – Ritchie Family (20th Century)
DO IT ANY WAY YOU WANNA – People's Choice (TSOP)
FLY, ROBIN, FLY – Silver Convention (Midland Intl.)
GIMME SOME – Jimmy "Bo" Horne (Alston)
HOOKED FOR LIFE – Trammps (Atlantic)
MESSIN' WITH MY MIND – LaBelle (Epic)
ONE WAY STREET – (instrumental) Becket Brown (RCA)
PEACE PIPE – B.T. Express (Scepter/Roadshow)
THAT'S THE WAY (I LIKE IT) – KC & the Sunshine Band (TK)
TO EACH HIS OWN/MELLOW ME – Faith, Hope & Charity (RCA)

MAKE-BELIEVE BALLROOM, NEW YORK
DJ: John Colon

BRAZIL – Ritchie Family (20th Century)
CARAVAN/WATUSI STRUT – Deadato (MCA)
DO IT ANY WAY YOU WANNA – People's Choice (TSOP)
DREAMING A DREAM – Crown Heights Affair (De-Lite)
EXODUS –Biddu Orchestra (Epic import)
FOREVER CAME TODAY – Jackson 5 (Motown)
HOOKED FOR LIFE – Trammps (Atlantic)
IT ONLY TAKES A MINUTE – Tavares (Capitol)
ONE WAY STREET – (instrumental) Becket Brown (RCA)
WHAT A DIFFERENCE A DAY MADE – Esther Phillips (Kudu)

production with a nice upbeat; **Jeanne Burton's** "(Nobody Loves Me) Like You Do Do" (Cotton), "arranged, produced and conducted under the influence of S.O.N.N.Y. (Sound of New New York)" – **Sonny Casella**, that is – and, in two parts that together run nearly five and a half minutes, an elaborate and rather impressive job-try the mostly instrumental Part 2 first; "Samson" by **Ebony, Ivory & Jade** (Columbia), a cautionary tale with a loud, over-gimmicky but finally quite terrific production by the DCA group, **Tony Bongiovi, Mew Monardo** & **Jay Ellis**; the **Ghetto Children's** "Don't Take Your Sweet Lovin' Away" (Roulette), with a tight Philly production by **Bobby Martin** and a co-producer; and, for those of your not already tired of AWB-style instrumentals, "Gimme The Key" by session man **Bobby Keys** (Ring O), released to discos in a special 4:06 version. Now available: "Summer Of '42" by the **Biddu Orchestra** (Epic) and the **Sunshine Band's** fine instrumental, "Shotgun Shuffle (TK), which had never been officially released and promoted before. ✪

DISCO FILE TOP 20

1. **BRAZIL** – The Ritchie Family (Avco)
2. **IT ONLY TAKES A MINUTE** – Tavares (Capitol)
3. **DO IT ANY WAY YOU WANNA** – People's Choice (TSOP)
4. **PEACE PIPE** – B.T. Express (Scepter /Roadshow)
5. **WHAT A DIFF'RENCE A DAY MAKES** – Esther Phillips (Kudu)
6. **DREAMING A DREAM** – Crown Heights Affair (De-Lite)
7. **FOREVER CAME TODAY** – Jackson 5 (Motown)
8. **SOMEBODY'S GOTTA GO** – Mike & Bill (Moving Up)
9. **FLY, ROBIN, FLY** – Silver Convention (Midland Intl.)
10. **WHEN YOU'RE YOUNG AND IN LOVE** – Ralph Carter (Mercury)
11. **GIMME SOME** – Jimmy "Bo" Horne (Alston)
12. **MELLOW BLOW/CHECKMATE** – Barrabas (Atco)
13. **I LIKE IT** – Silver Convention (Midland Intl.)
14. **ONE WAY STREET** – (instrumental) Beckett Brown (RCA)
15. **TO EACH HIS OWN** – Faith, Hope & Charity (RCA)
16. **GET DOWN TONIGHT/THAT'S THE WAY (I LIKE IT)** – KC & the Sunshine Band (TK)
17. **CHINESE KUNG FU** – Banzaii (Scepter)
18. **MELLOW ME** – Faith, Hope & Charity (RCA)
19. **SEXY** – MFSB (Phila. Intl.)
20. **FIGHT THE POWER** – Isley Brothers (T-Neck)

SEPTEMBER 6, 1975

66 Well, let's face it: this has been an exceptionally dull week. A week so dull that not even the arrival of the new LaBelle album could salvage it 99

Well, let's face it: this has been an exceptionally dull week. A week so dull in fact that not even the arrival of the new **LaBelle** album could salvage it. Everything seems to be on hold until mid-September and we're in the dead calm before the storm of early fall releases. Time to re-evaluate some of the better recent releases.

New York's Record Pool has set up a terrifically efficient and easy feedback system for the reactions of their nearly 200 member discotheque DJs to records received and distributed by the Pool (more than 40,000 in its first few months of operation), and I spoke to them this week to find out what records were getting the most positive reaction. Of those records currently available to the Pool, the most favorably received singles (those that got "yes" votes from more than half of the DJs involved) include: **Mike & Bill's** "Somebody's Gotta Go" (Moving Up/Arista), with the largest number of positive responses; "Salsoul" by the **Salsoul Orchestra** (Salsoul); **Gloria Gaynor's** "(If You Want It) Do It Yourself" (MGM); **Ralph Carter's** "When You're Young And In Love" (Mercury); "Get Ready For This" by **Revelation** (RSO); **Cleveland Eaton's** "Chitown Theme" (Black Jazz); "Superstar Revue" by the **Ventures** (UA); "Super Jaws" by **Seven Seas** (Glades) and "Need You" by **Harlem Rriver Drive** (Arista). Because the Pool DJs are asked to fill out the feedback books when they pick up their records, the Pool has a consistent and up-to-date survey of opinions on the records they service – certainly the most accurate reflection of the New York area DJs' reaction to new records now available. The only thing that puzzles me is why more record companies aren't taking advantage of this excellent feedback source while it's still free (the time and money put into support of the Pool and its services will, in time, force them to ask for donations or make an outright monthly charge). While the Pool is considering organizing a newsletter to put its feedback in an easily

useable form, we will check in with them every other week and present whatever relevant information they can provide in DISCO FILE.

The **Trammps'** "Hooked For Life" entered the Top 20 this week (at number 11) with a note that it's the "disco version" of the record that is being played. This is the 12-inch disc which runs 4:40 in length and is not commercially available; like the other Atlantic 12-inch releases, it's for disco DJs only. But it should be noted that a number of other records listed in the Top 20 are, of course, being played in their "disco version," which usually means a longer mix, sometimes a re-mix to play up the instrumental side of the record. The disco-mixed singles listed are "It Only Takes A Minute" by **Tavares** (Capitol), whose 4:46 version is also not available commercially; "Superstar Revue (4:28); "When You're Young And In Love" (5:04) and "Dreaming A Dream" (3:45). And, obviously, it's the "long version" (4:37) of LaBelle's "Messin' With My Mind" that's being played. Speaking of disco versions, one has now been made available of **Basic Black and Pearl's** fine "There'll Come A Time, There'll Come A Day" (Polydor), something of a cult record and even better with a longer ending and some added violins that takes it to 4:10.

RECOMMENDED: For those of us with a certain weakness for the adolescent boy group sound, there's the new **21st Century** album, "Ahead Of Our Time" (RCA) with **Jackson 5/Sylvers** overtones, especially attractive on the jumpy "Tricks Are Made For Kids," a full of changes "Ahead Of Our Time" and of course their beautiful single "Remember the Rain." And the only single worth noting this week, **Jackey Beavers'** "Trying To Get Back To You Girl" (Dade), which is bright and. easy and in two parts. My favorite title of the week: "No Rebate On Love" by the **Dramatics** which is worth a listen. ◐

JAWS, SOUTHAMPTON, NEW YORK
DJs: Jeff Baugh & Ilene Raskin
BRAZIL – Ritchie Family (20th Century)
CAN'T LIVE THIS WAY – Barnaby Bye (Atlantic)
DO IT ANY WAY YOU WANNA – People's Choice (TSOP)
FLY, ROBIN, FLY – Silver Convention (Midland Intl.)
FOREVER CAME TODAY– Jackson 5 (Motown)
HOOKED FOR LIFE – Trammps (Atlantic disco version)
IT ONLY TAKES A MINUTE – Tavares (Capitol)
MELLOW BLOW/ALONG THE SHORE – Barrabas (Atco)
PEACE PIPE – B.T. Express (Scepter/Roadshow)
WHAT A DIFFERENCE A DAY MADE – Esther Phillips (Kudu)

CLUB CASABLANCA, NEW YORK
DJ: Joseph Madonia
BRAZIL – Ritchie Family (20th Century)
CARAVAN/WATUSI STRUT – Deodato (MCA)
DREAMING A DREAM – Crown Heights Affair (De-Lite)
FLY, ROBIN, FLY/I LIKE IT – Silver Convention (Midland Intl.)
HOOKED FOR LIFE – Trammps (Atlantic)
IT ONLY TAKES A MINUTE – Tavares (Capitol)
MELLOW BLOW – Barrabas (Atco)
MESSIN' WITH MY MIND – LaBelle (Epic)
SOMEBODY'S GOTTA GO – Mike & Bill (Moving Up/Arista)
SUPERSTAR REVUE – Ventures (UA)

HOLLYWOOD, NEW YORK
DJ: Tony Gioe
BRAZIL – Ritchie Family (20th Century)
CARAVAN/WATUSI STRUT – Deodato (MCA)
FACE THE MUSIC – Dynamic Superiors (Motown)
FIRE/YOU SET MY HEART ON FIRE – Tina Charles (Columbia)
FLY, ROBIN, FLY/I LIKE IT – Silver Convention (Midland Intl.)
IT ONLY TAKES A MINUTE – Tavares (Capitol)
MELLOW BLOW/ALONG THE SHORE/CHECKMATE – Barrabas (Atco)
MESSIN' WITH MY MIND –LaBelle (Epic)
PEACE PIPE/STILL GOOD, STILL LIKE IT/WHATCHA THINK ABOUT THAT? – B. T. Express (Scepter/Roadshow)
SUPERSTAR REVUE – Ventures (UA)

PENTHOUSE, BROOKLYN, N.Y.
DJ: Rick Coscia
BRAZIL – Ritchie Family (20th Century)
CAN'T GIVE YOU ANYTHING – Stylistics (Avco)
DANCE DANCE DANCE – Calhoon (Warner Spector)
DREAMING A DREAM – Crown Heights Affair (De-Lite)
FOREVER CAME TODAY – Jackson 5 (Motown)
HOOKED FOR LIFE – Trammps (Atlantic)
(IF YOU WANT IT) DO IT YOURSELF – Gloria Gaynor (MGM)
IT ONLY TAKES A MINUTE – Tavares (Capitol)
PEACE PIPE– B. T. Express (Scepter/Roadshow)
WHAT A DIFFERENCE A DAY MADE – Esther Phillips (Kudu)

SEPTEMBER 13, 1975

The major news this week is the release of the **Gloria Gaynor** album, which should be just out in the stores but has already hit the dance floors through special advance pressings of the three-cut disco run-through side. This side opens up with "Casanova Brown," which has a strong First Choice feeling, both in subject matter (a "jive-time" lover the singer can't help but fall for – another "Player") and style, with a long, complex break containing a terrific rap underlined by quirky guitar and tambourine and ending with a squeal you can't help but echo – 6:23 altogether. "(If You Want It) Do It Yourself" comes next, expanded to 5:58 but not entirely worth it. Yet it's more than made up for in the closing track, a sensational version of the standard "How High the Moon" (6:35) that's bound to be one of the most successful of the many disco remakes this year. "How High" is given the trademark Gloria Gaynor treatment and even though we've heard it all before, it's quite irrestible, especially with a little "I'll Be Holding On" banjo interwoven with the strings another readymade touch, but it works. The title of the album is "Experience Gloria Gaynor" (MGM) and if side one is any indication, it's good enough to make the whole Queen of Disco hype believable again.

The other most impressive album just, released is **Revelation's** debut on RSO, the four-man group produced by **Norman Harris**, **Allan Felder** and **Jerome Gasper**. The sound is reminiscent of **Blue Magic** and the **Whispers** and there's not one bad cut, but especially recommended are: a very up version of "I Can't Move No Mountains," most recently done by **Margie Joseph**, an equally bright interpretation of **Melissa Manchester's** "Just Too Many people," a deliciously mellow message song called "We've Gotta Survive" and, of course, the group's two singles, "Sweet Talk And Melodies," which sounds even better than it did before, and the recent "Get Ready For This." Right now "Revelation" sounds like one of the three or four best male group albums of the year; don't miss it. Also recommended: "The Sound Of Sunshine," an all instrumental album from the **Sunshine Band**, produced by **Casey and Finch**, the wizards of the Miami Sound, and containing "Shotgun Shuffle," an instrumental "Rock Your Baby" and an attractive new cut, "Miss B (Theme)" – on TK Records.

The two most interesting new singles this week are at nearly opposite ends of the disco spectrum. One is Ronnie Spector's first release for Tom Cat Records, "You'd Be Good For Me" tough, hard, dense, almost a **Ronettes** sound with a punched-up disco production. It's been released as a 3:05 single but also made available to discos on a red vinyl 12-inch record that runs 4:20 and is even more of a knockout. A fine comeback record. The other pick is "Let's Do The Latin Hustle" by **Eddie Drennon** and **BBS Unlimited** (Friends & Co.) which has a **Van McCoy/MFSB** sound – ecstatic and exhilarating, with handclaps and girls chanting the title – and a **Bohannon**-like B side, "Get Down Do The Latin Hustle," whose beautifully cooled-out beginning heats up gradually as the chanting echoes "Get Down Tonight." Louis Schneider from New York Casablanca, who brought it to the office for me and put it on his top 10 this week, says Drennon is the violin player for the Latin band, **Tipica Novel**. Sounds like something a larger company might be interested in picking up.

Other recommended singles: "I Can't Live Without You" by **Ron Keith and Ladys** (A&M), a record I foolishly passed over on the first few listens (it's been out since July), but one of the sweetest records in some time (much like **Sam Dee's** "Fragile, Handle With Care," which I like more all the time), with rich **Lou Rawls**-like vocals; an instrumental version of "Bad Luck" by the **Atlanta Disco Band** (Scorpio), produced by **Dave Crawford** (**Mighty Clouds of Joy, Wilson Pickett**), arranged by **Earl Young** (of the **Trammps**, I assume) and featuring a lot of strings to replace the chorus-could be stronger, but it works well as it is, especially at just over four minutes; and a pleasant, mid-tempo record, "Call On Me," by a group with the inspired name of **Enchantment** (Polydor). NOTE: The single version of Bohannon's "Disco Stomp" has an entirely new "Part 2" (Dakar) that adds an organ over an extended instrumental segment which gives another dimension to the song – worth picking up even if you have the album (and who doesn't?).

SOUND EXPERIENCE

BOOGIE WOOGIE

RHINOCEROS, BOSTON
DJ: John Luongo

BRAZIL – Ritchie Family (20th Century)
CHECKMATE/FAMILY SIZE – Barrabas (Atco)
DO IT ANY WAY YOU WANNA – People's Choice (TSOP)
GET OFF YOUR ASS AND JAM – Funkadelic
(20th Century /Westbound lp cut)
GIMME THE KEY – Bobby Keys (Ring O)
IT ONLY TAKES A MINUTE – Tavares (Capitol)
IT'S ALRIGHT – Graham Central Station (Warners)
PEACE PIPE – B.T. Express (Scepter/Roadshow)
SOMEBODY'S GOTTA GO – Mike & Bill (Arista/ Moving Up)
THAT'S THE WAY (I LIKE IT) – KC & the Sunshine Band (TK)

SPEAKEASY, ISLAND PARK, N.Y.
DJ: John Fraumeni

ANOTHER GIRL – Silver Convention (Midland Intl.)
DANCE DANCE DANCE – Calhoon (Warner Spector)
DO IT ANY WAY YOU WANNA – People's Choice (TSOP)
HOLLYWOOD HOT – Eleventh Hour (20th Century)
HOOKED FOR LIFE – Trammps (Atlantic)
IT ONLY TAKES A MINUTE – Tavares (Capitol)
MELLOW BLOW/FOUR SEASON WOMAN – Borrobos
(Atco)
ONE NIGHT AFFAIR – Esther Phillips (Kudu)
PEACE PIPE – B.T. Express (Scepter/Roadshow)
SOMEBODY'S GOTTA GO – Mike & Bill (Arista/ Moving Up)

CASABLANCA, NEW YORK
DJ: Louis Schneider

BRAZIL – Ritchie Family (20th Century)
CARAVAN/WATUSI STRUT – Deodato (MCA)
DO IT ANYWAY YOU WANNA – People's Choice (TSOP)
FLY, ROBIN, FLY/I LIKE IT/ANOTHER GIRL – Silver
Convention (Midland Intl. lp cuts)
HOOKED FOR LIFE – Trammps (Atlantic)
IT ONLY TAKES A MINUTE – Tavares (Capitol)
LET'S DO THE LATIN HUSTLE – Eddie Drennon & BBS
Unlimited (Friends & Co.)
MELLOW BLOW /CHECKMATE – Barrabas (Atco)
MESSIN' WITH MY MIND – LaBelle (Epic)
WHAT A DIFFERENCE A DAY MADE – Esther Phillips
(Kudu)

OUTSIDE INN, NY (QUEENS)
DJ: Walter Gibbons

BRAZIL – Ritchie Family (20th Century)
**CASANOVA BROWN/DO IT YOURSELF/ HOW HIGH THE
MOON** – Gloria Gaynor (MGM)
FLY, ROBIN, FLY/I LIKE IT – Silver Convention
(Midland Intl.)
GIMME SOME – Jimmy "Bo" Horne (Alston)
HE'S LOOKING GOOD AND MOVING FAST – Sound
Experience (Buddah)
IT ONLY TAKES A MINUTE – Tavares (Capitol)
MAGIC OF THE BLUE/WE'RE ON THE RIGHT TRACK –
Blue Magic (Atco)
MESSIN' WITH MY MIND – LaBelle (Epic)
PEACE PI PE – B. T. Express (Scepter/Roadshow)
2 PIGS AND A HOG – 'Cooley High' Original Soundtrack
(Motown)

FEEDBACK: John Luongo reports that **Funkadelic's** raunchy "Get Off Your Ass And Jam" – a 2-minute cut from their recent "Let's Take It To The Stage" album (20th Century/Westbound) that repeats the driving chant, "S–t, goddamn, get off your ass and jam" – is doing very well in Boston. Luongo put the cut on his top 10 from Rhinoceros this week and says that he often plays it twice to make up for its short length (Mitch Schatsky in D.C. told me the same thing a while back). A friend told me that during a particularly hot instrumental break in a **Graham Central Station** set here last week, the entire audience broke into the Funkadelic chant, so it's apparently widely (wildly) popular beyond the range of any above ground indicators. Luongo also mentioned that his Boston-area magazine, Nightfall, with an emphasis on disco news and entertainment features, is expanding again to 64 pages and should be available in New York soon at key record stores... David Rodriguez writes from Mykonos, where he went to open a new discotheque and give the Greeks a taste of the New York disco style, that the "most requested record on the island" is the **Isley Brothers'** "For The love Of You," followed by "Peace Pipe" and "Do It Any Way You Wanna"... Walter Gibbons, formerly at Galaxie 21, reports this week from the Outside Inn in Queens and is also playing some nights at the Limelight. The version of **Blue Magic's** "Magic Of The Blue" (Atco) he's playing an advance copy of is not-quite-three-minute track that will be included on the first pressings of the group's new album, "Thirteen Blue Magic Lane." Atlantic says that a new, longer version, running more than five minutes has just become available and will be included on subsequent pressings. ◐

> **" Funkadelic's raunchy "Get Off Your Ass And Jam" is doing very well in Boston. John Luongo says he often plays it twice to make up for its short length "**

SEPTEMBER 20, 1975

The two most talked about album cuts in New York discos right now are **Donna Summer's** extraordinary "Love To Love You Baby," the title track and entire side (16:50!) of her debut album on Oasis (through Casablanca) and "Every Beat Of My Heart," the hottest cut from the just-out **Crown Heights Affair** album ("Dreaming A Dream" on De-Lite). Both are unpredictable, non-formula records full of changes and breaks, with the Crown Heights cut comparable only to their "Dreaming A Dream" but double the idiosyncrasies, and the Summer like nothing else I've heard before. "Love To Love You Baby" takes off from a few flimsy "Pillow Talk" style lyrics, delivered with breathy abandon by Summer, who does little else but moan passionately and repeat the title. She fades out regularly as the orchestra wells up, then falls back to reveal her in the throes of even deeper passion as the record builds wave upon wave. It's deliciously excessive and bound to be one of this year's great rush records, the sort some people hate but others

> ❝ The most talked about album cut right now is Donna Summer's extraordinary "Love To Love You Baby," the title track and entire side (16:50!) of her debut album ❞

die for. According to Casablanca's Neil Bogart, Summer is an American singer now living and recording in Germany. Bogart heard a single version of "Love To Love," also available, and suggested the producers lengthen it with these remarkable results. (Thanks to Phil Gill who brought the Donna Summer album down to the last Record Pool meeting and had everyone racing to the booth asking, "What *is* that?")

Crown Heights' "Every Beat Of My Heart" has elements of "Dreaming A Dream," especially around the central scat break and the horns that follow, but it's more complex, more interesting – not as perfect as "Dream," which sounds like one of those records I'll still want to hear years from now, but quite strong at 5:25. The Crown Heights album opens up with "Dreaming A Dream" on both sides, presented just as on the single, in a vocal and "disco" version and the cover features one of the great, instant-classic **James J. Kriegsmann** group photos.

The other pleasant surprise this week is from **Al Green's** new album, "Al Green Is Love" (Hi): a quirky, mostly instrumental "Love Ritual" (4:18) which is to say the least, different from Green's usual material. Dense Latin percussion stands out over a steady flow of strings and Green's whoops and wails and occasional lyrics. Highly recommended. Also out: **Gloria Gaynor's** "Experience Gloria Gaynor" (MGM) with a throwaway side 2 but another side 1 medley blend (reviewed last week) that has everyone excited; and the **Blue Magic** album "Thirteen Blue Magic Lane" (Atco), containing "Magic Of The Blue," a self-congratulatory ("Second to none/Our time has come") but undeniably attractive instrumental (2:56 here, but there are plans at expansion), and "We're On The Right Track," not up to the Ultra High Frequency original but, once the vocals fade, still good – production of course by **Norman Harris** (now calling himself "The Norman Harris Machine") for WMOT Productions. FOOTNOTE: **James Brown** has a new album. It's titled "Everybody's Doing The Hustle & Dead On The Double Bump" (Polydor). Oh, James, you're such a card.

Martin Ragusa was down this past week from Le Tube in Montreal to pick up some records, leave others, and discuss the disco scene in Montreal. As is clear from Le Tube's top 10, there is a deep European influence there, due primarily to Montreal's largely French population and the accessibility of imports. The import singles on Ragusa's list, most of them French, have a certain sound in common and an international feel that combines **Bimbo Jet** and **Crystal Grass** and mixes well. "Soul Dracula" by Hot Blood (Disques Carrere) has a lot of synthesizer like the **Peppers** and a bouncy style that contradicts the menacing "Dracula" bits on the vocal side; side two is all instrumental, "Sans Dracula." The **Pinkies'** "Porto Rico" (that's the way it's spelled on the label, Phillips), which writer Michael Gomes brought back from Toronto for me, is more Bimbo Jet style, with occasional lyric lines in English and a tasty instrumental

LE TUBE, MONTREAL
DJ: Martin Ragusa

BABY SOUL – Ron Nelson (Deram import)
FLY, ROBIN, FLY/TIGER BABY – Silver Convention (Midland Intl.)
GIMME SOME – Jimmy "Bo" Horne (Alston)
MESSIN' WITH MY MIND – LaBelle (Epic)
ONE WAY STREET – Becket Brown (RCA)
PORTO RICO – Pinkies-Philips (import)
RED BULLET – Performance (Able import)
SOMEBODY'S GOTTA GO – Mike & Bill (Arista/Moving Up)
SOUL DRACULA – Hot Blood (Carrere import)
UNDECIDED LOVE – Chequers (Creole)

BAREFOOT BOY, NEW YORK
DJ: Tony Smith

BRAZIL/PEANUT VENDOR – Ritchie Family (20th Century)
CARAVAN/WATUSI STRUT – Deodato (MCA)
CASANOVA BROWN/DO IT YOURSELF/HOW HIGH THE MOON – Gloria Gaynor (MGM)
CHECKMATE/MELLOW BLOW – Barrabas (Atco)
FLY, ROBIN, FLY/I LIKE IT – Silver Convention (Midland Intl.)
IT ONLY TAKES A MINUTE – Tavares (Capitol)
MESSIN' WITH MY MIND – LaBelle (Epic)
PEACE PIPE – B.T. Express – (Scepter/Roadshow)
SUMMER OF '42/EXODUS – Biddu Orchestra (Epic import)
2 PIGS & A HOG – Cooley High Soundtrack (Motown)

LIMELIGHT, NEW YORK
DJ: Hector LeBron

BRAZIL – Ritchie Family (20th Century)
CASANOVA BROWN/DO IT YOURSELF/ HOW HIGH THE MOON – Gloria Gaynor (MGM)
DO IT ANY WAY YOU WANNA – People's Choice (TSOP)
FLY, ROBIN, FLY/I LIKE IT – Silver Convention (Midland Intl.)
HOOKED FOR LIFE – Trammps (Atlantic)
MAGIC OF THE BLUE/WE'RE ON THE RIGHT TRACK – Blue Magic (Atco lp)
NOBODY LOVES ME) LIKE YOU DO DO – Jeanne Burton (Cotton)
2 PIGS & A HOG – Cooley High Soundtrack (Motown)
WATERBED – Herbie Mann (Atlantic)
WHEN YOU'RE YOUNG & IN LOVE – Ralph Carter (Mercury)

BOOMBAMAKAOO, NEW YORK
DJ: Jorge Wheeler, Jr.

BREAKAWAY (Instrumental) – Ernie Bush (Contempo import)
CASANOVA BROWN/DO IT YOURSELF/HOW HIGH THE MOON – Gloria Gaynor (MGM)
HOOKED FOR LIFE – Trammps (Atlantic)
IT ONLY TAKES A MINUTE – Tavares (Capitol)
LADY, LADY, LADY – Boogie Man Orchestra (Boogie Man)
SALSOUL – Salsoul Orchestra (Salsoul)
SOMEBODY'S GOTTA GO – Mike & Bill (Arista/Moving Up)
SUMMER OF '42/EXODUS – Biddu Orchestra (Epic)
SUPERSTAR REVUE – Ventures (UA)
YOU SET MY HEART ON FIRE/FIRE – Tina Charles (Columbia)

break. **Ron Nelson's** "Baby Soul" (Deram) has bizarre vocals that sound like they were recorded underwater but they drop out for the instrumental B side, a Philly sound with some European schmaltz touches and, of the three records, the one most likely to catch on here (though "Soul Dracula" and "Porto Rico" are already making inroads). **Performance's** "Red Bullet" (Able), also on Ragusa's list, I haven't heard but he compared it to the Peppers with added orchestration. Following the lead of the New York Record Pool, Montreal DJs are organizing what they now call a Record Center with a membership of 35 DJs and participation from most of the record companies in the city. Like the New York Pool, they have a reaction sheet for the DJs to fill out but they also combine individual top 10s to form a Montreal disco top 10 which we hope to print from time to time.

CALENDAR: Speaking of the Record Pool, Ronnie Robles and Eddie Rivera, who are handling the Latin product at the Pool, have announced a Latin Division meeting for members interested in Latin material on Monday, September 22 at 2:00 p.m. After the meeting, **Yambu** will Perform "Sunny" (see below) and other new material. The young **Philly Devotions** performed and hung out at the last Record Pool meeting this past week and Deodato and Revelation showed up to meet the pool members informally.

An overload of new singles, all of them good; quickly, pick up on these: **Touch of Class'** lush, lovely "I'm In Heaven" (Midland Intl.) with a long, cool instrumental break that makes up the single's Part 2 (Parts 1 & 2 mix up to 6:30); **Yambu's** fine Latin/**MFSB** treatment of the standard "Sunny" (Montuno), a juicy 4:35 that should be commercially available this week; "Tonight's The Night" by S.S.O. (Shadybrook), a sexy **Silver Convention/Love Unlimited Orchestra** with a spice all its own (disco version: 5:00); **Don Cornelius & Dick Griffey's** new "Soul Train" theme, just being introduced on the show and already a 45 by the **Soul Train Gang** (on Soul Train Records, through RCA) which, while no TSOP," should go far if only on its associations – out in creamy vocals, as well as all instrumental versions and as an almost 4-minute 45 on a 12-inch for discos of 5:55 – arrangements by **Gene Page**; **Ronnie Dyson's** at his best so far with a joyous **Norman Harris/Al Felder** production, "Cup (Runneth Over)" (Columbia); **Jungle Rock's** torrid "Down In The Jungle" (Sound Gems), which is just that, especially the 5:39 instrumental version; the vibrant "Life Is Funky" with a steady tom-tom beat – a change-of-pace from **Booker T** (Epic); "Make It Last," very up and optimistic from **Barbara Mason and the Futures** (Buddah); star of stage, screen and sometime Interview Small Talk item: (Paul) **Jabara's** "One Man Ain't Enough" (A&M) – uneven but with lots of nice flashes; **Gil Scott-Heron's** infectious chant, "Johannesburg" (Arista), as serious as his "In The Bottle" and as interesting; and, finally, "Afrodesia:' by **Lonnie Smith** (Groove Merchant), which may not be for dancing but is an excellent mood record (disco version: 5:00). ❧

SEPTEMBER 27, 1975

❝ The Ritchie Family's lush debut, "Brazil" features a pre-mixed run-through on the first side that even surpasses the trend-setting Gloria Gaynor medley sides in length (20:38) ❞

The one essential album this week is **The Ritchie Family's** lush debut, "Brazil" (20th Century), featuring a pre-mixed run-through on the first side of three discotized standards – "Peanut Vendor" (6:40), "Frenesi" (8:00) and a lengthened "Brazil" (4:58) – that even surpasses the trend-setting **Gloria Gaynor** medley sides in length (total time: 20:38). The spirit and style of "Brazil" prevails, but the Big Band mold with scattered sexy vocals ("Your love has got me crazy," the girls croon throughout "Peanut Vendor"). With advance pressings out in New York for a week or two, the preference seems to already be established for "Peanut Vendor," but "Frenesi," with some horn segments strongly reminiscent of **Isaac Hayes'** "Theme From 'The Men" is just as attractive, making this a remarkable solid disco medley side. The reverse side features five songs of standard length, all in a similar style but treated with less depth than the side one spectaculars; "Pinball," "Let's Pool" and "Dance With Me" stand out. The album was recorded at Philadelphia's Sigma Sound with production by **Jacques Morali** from France with assistance and arrangements from **Ritchie Rome**.

RECOMMENDED CUTS: "My Sweetheart," a spunky instrumental from "Mother Focus" (Atco), the new album by the Dutch rock group, **Focus**; "Sweet Sweetening" (4:12), produced by Isaac Hayes for the Masqueraders on the album "Everybody Wanna Live On" (ABC); "Don't It Feel Good" and an **Ohio Players**-style "Spider Man" from the latest **Ramsey Lewis** album, "Don't It Feel Good" (Columbia) and, catching up, the excellent "Love Rollercoaster" an exhilarating side from the **Ohio Players** "Honey" album (Mercury).

FEEDBACK: On Bob Lombardi's list from Rumbottoms in Hollywood, Florida, this week, there's a single from the TK family of labels called "Fools Rush In" – a disco version of the oldie by **Joey Porrello** (Drive) that is apparently only in release in the Miami area but, according to Lombardi, doing very well there. Lombardi is also enthusiastic about **Felix Cavaliere's** "Never Felt Love Before," the single released from his recent "Destiny" album (Bearsville)... Frank Strivelli at The Alley in Queens is more into imports than most DJs and he reports these are going over particularly well right now:

"You Gatta Rock & Roll" and "Fame" back-to-back by **Brand Army** (Creole, from England, also reported last week by Tony Smith from Barefoot Boy); "Brazilian Carnival" by **Chocolate Boys** (Disques Fleur, from France); another version of "Brazil" and its flip side, "Love Can" by **Crispy & Co.** (Creole and now on the English pop charts) and another record by **Tina Charles** (whose "You Set My Heart on Fire" is so hot now), "One Broken Heart for Sale" (Bell, also from England)... Coming Up Strong: "I'm in Heaven" by **Touch of Class** (Midland Intl.), **Donna Summer's** stunning "Love to Love You Baby" (Oasis/Casablanca); "I Just Can't Make It (Without You)" by the **Philly Devotions** (Columbia) and "Sunny" by **Yambu** (Montuno) which should be in the stores this week.

RECOMMENDED SINGLES: **Van McCoy's** very up message song, "Change With The Times" (Avco), more like his work with **Faith, Hope & Charity** than his material on the "Disco Baby" album, and backed with a lovely end-of-the-evening disco closing song, "Good Night, Baby," both from his new "Disco Kid" album, due this week; "Keep It Up:' super sexy and unusual from **Milton Wright** (Betty's brother) on Alston – may be a little left field for disco, but a terrific record; "Sweet Sounds Of Love" a sex manual of a song from **Fever**, also left field (Sound Gems) **Jimmy Castor's** new "King Kong" with a biting instrumental "Part II" (Atlantic); **Vivilore Jordan's** old-style funky "Put My Loving On You" also in the left field region (Sound Gems); the tough, rumbling "Theme from S.W.A.T." by **Rhythm Heritage** (ABC) and **Polly Brown's** sweet **Supremes**-styled "Special Delivery" (Ariola America, from a forthcoming album). Far Left Field: A disco version of, ah yes, "It's My Party" from our friends at Boogie Man Records and by **Karla Jayne and the Boogie Man Orchestra**.

Now available as singles: "Fly, Robin, Fly" (3:45, on Midland International); "Checkmate," the full 4:28, backed with "Mellow Blow" at 4:08 (Atco) – both sure hits – and **Kokomo's** "Kitty Sittin' Pretty" (Columbia) **MFSB's** "T.L.C." (3:17) backed with "Love Has No Time Or Place" (3:30) and **Greg Perry's** fine, fine "One For The Road," overlooked from his album (Casablanca). ◐

HOLLYWOOD, NEW YORK
DJ: Richie Kaczor

CASANOVA BROWN/DO IT YOURSELF/HOW HIGH THE MOON – Gloria Gaynor (MGM)
DO IT ANY WAY YOU WANNA – People's Choice (TSOP)
FLY, ROBIN, FLY/I LIKE IT – Silver Convention (Midland Intl.)
FOREVER CAME TODAY – Jackson 5 (Motown)
I WANNA KNOW – Sunny Gale (Disco-Soul)
IT ONLY TAKES A MINUTE – Tavares (Capitol)
LOVE POWER – Willie Hutch (Motown)
LOVE TO LOVE YOU BABY – Donna Summer (Oasis)
MESSIN' WITH MY MIND – LaBelle (Epic)
SUNNY – Yambu (Montuno)

THE ALLEY, NY (QUEENS)
DJ: Frank Strivelli

CARAVAN/WATUSI STRUT – Deodato (MCA)
CASANOVA BROWN/DO IT YOURSELF/HOW HIGH THE MOON – Gloria Gaynor (MGM)
DO IT ANY WAY YOU WANNA – People's Choice (TSOP)
FLY, ROBIN, FLY/I LIKE IT – Silver Convention (Midland Intl.)
I JUST CAN'T MAKE IT (WITHOUT YOU) – Philly Devotions (Columbia)
MESSIN' WITH MY MIND – LaBelle (Epic)
PEACE PIPE – B. T. Express (Scepter/Roadshow)
SUMMER OF '42/EXODUS – Biddu Orchestra (Epic import)
YOU SET MY HEART ON FIRE/FIRE – Tina Charles (Columbia)
WHEN YOU'RE YOUNG AND IN LOVE – Ralph Carter (Mercury)

RUM BOTTOMS, HOLLYWOOD, FLA.
DJ: Bob Lombardi

CARAVAN/WATUSI STRUT – Deodato (MCA)
DANCE DANCE DANCE – Calhoon (Warner Spector)
FLY, ROBIN, FLY/ANOTHER GIRL – Silver Convention (Midland Intl.)
FOOLS RUSH IN – Joey Porrello (Drive)
HOOKED FOR LIFE – Trammps (Atlantic)
LOVE TO LOVE YOU BABY – Donna Summer (Oasis)
NOBODY LOVES ME LIKE YOU DO – Jeanne Burton (Cotton)
THIS WILL BE – Natalie Cole (Capitol)
YOU SET MY HEART ON FIRE/FIRE – Tina Charles (Columbia)
WHEN YOU'RE YOUNG AND IN LOVE – Ralph Carter (Mercury)

REVELATION II
DJ: Bacho Mangual

BODY TALK – Eddie Kendricks (Tamla)
CASANOVA BROWN/DO IT YOURSELF/HOW HIGH THE MOON – Gloria Gaynor (MGM)
DREAMING A DREAM/EVERY BEAT OF MY HEART – Crown Heights Affair (De-Lite)
FLY, ROBIN, FLY/I LIKE IT/ANOTHER GIRL – Silver Convention (Midland Intl.)
FOREVER CAME TODAY – Jackson 5 (Motown)
LOVE TO LOVE YOU BABY – Donna Summer (Oasis)
LOVE POWER – Willie Hutch (Motown)
MELLOW BLOW/ALONG THE SHORE – Barrabas (Atco)
NADA DE TI – Eddie Palmieri (Coco)
SUMMER OF '42/EXODUS – Biddu Orchestra-Epic (import lp cuts)

DISCO FILE TOP 20

1. **FLY, ROBIN, FLY** – Silver Convention (Midland Intl.)
2. **BRAZIL** – The Ritchie Family (Avco)
3. **IT ONLY TAKES A MINUTE** – Tavares (Capitol)
4. **PEACE PIPE** – B.T. Express (Scepter /Roadshow)
5. **DO IT ANY WAY YOU WANNA** – People's Choice (TSOP)
6. **HOOKED FOR LIFE** – Trammps (Atlantic)
7. **I LIKE IT** – Silver Convention (Midland Intl.)
8. **MESSIN' WITH MY MIND** – LaBelle (Epic)
9. **CASANOVA BROWN/DO IT YOURSELF/HOW HIGH THE MOON** – Gloria Gaynor (MGM)
10. **CARAVAN/WATUSI STRUT** – Deodato (MCA)
11. **MELLOW BLOW/CHECKMATE** – Barrabas (Atco)
12. **ANOTHER GIRL** – Silver Convention (Midland Intl.)
13. **DREAMING A DREAM** – Crown Heights Affair (De-Lite)
14. **FOREVER CAME TODAY** – Jackson 5 (Motown)
15. **SUMMER OF '42/EXODUS** – Biddu Orchestra (Epic import)
16. **SOMEBODY'S GOTTA GO** – Mike & Bill (Moving Up)
17. **SUPERSTAR REVUE** – Ventures (UA)
18. **YOU SET MY HEART ON FIRE/FIRE** – Tina Charles (Columbia)
19. **WHAT A DIFF'RENCE A DAY MADE** – Esther Phillips (Kudu)
20. **WHEN YOU'RE YOUNG AND IN LOVE** – Ralph Carter (Mercury)

OCTOBER 4, 1975

Van McCoy, who deserves the title more than anyone I can think of (I'll take other nominations for a future run-off), has a new album titled "The Disco Kid" (Avco) that should clinch his position as the dance master for 1975. "Disco Kid" is "Disco Baby" – McCoy's last album with the **Soul City Symphony** – grown up and strengthened. Like that album, this one is largely instrumental (with occasional disco-chant vocals by McCoy and the members of **Faith, Hope & Charity**), but there are no remakes of disco standards here – unless you count "Keep On Hustlin'," a follow-up/copy of "The Hustle" for which McCoy has ripped himself off with such consummate style that you can't complain, only marvel. Taking this instrumental/chant formula off in all directions – from the pounding, shake-it-up "Earthquake" (at 4:44, the longest track) to the frothy, float-along "Love Child" (reminiscent of "Love Is The Answer") – McCoy doesn't make one false move. The mostly vocal "Change with the Times," released last week as a single of the same length as the album cut, and two smooth ballads, "Words Spoken Softly at Midnight" and "I'm Gonna Love You," are exceptions to the overall formula, with McCoy on lead vocals more impressive than any of his solo material so far in release. Recommended cuts: "Earthquake," "Keep On Hustlin'," "Love Child," "The Walk," "Roll With The Punches," "Words Spoken Softly At Midnight" and "Change With The Times." That's seven out of the 10 cuts on the album. A monster.

❝ After playing it for myself 10 times at top volume, I wrote, "Am I crazy or is this one of the greatest disco singles this year?" ❞

The other major knock-out this week is "I'm On Fire" by **5000 Volts** (Philips), one of the few records to arrive these days without some sort of advance word and all the more extraordinary for being so unexpected. Actually, the record's been leaping up the British pop charts (in the top five this week) and stands a good chance of doing the same here. After playing it for myself 10 times in succession at top volume last night, I wrote down, "Am I crazy or is this one of the greatest disco singles this year?" I still can't answer that question, but "I'm On Fire" approaches the impact of **Gloria Gaynor's** first, "Honeybee," and very few records that exciting come out each year. Side one features a driving, screaming female lead who has a rough-throated sound like **Rod Stewart's** with a rumbling male voice for the chorus; side two, "Still On

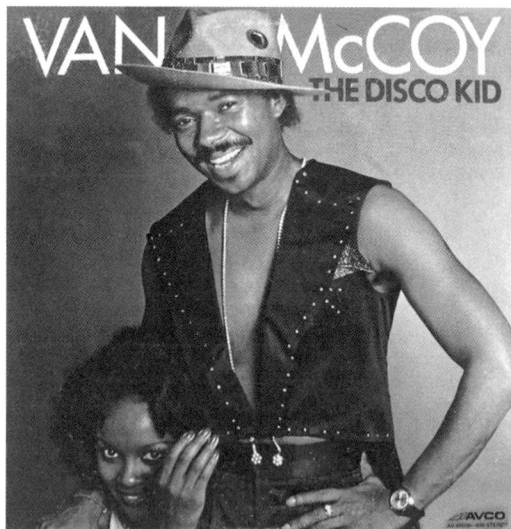

Fire," is the instrumental version. Both are almost impossibly upbeat but irresistible, and both are under three minutes (I can already hear the sighs of disappointment) but incredibly power-packed. A white-hot record. NOTE: Philips is also rush-releasing "Porto Rico" by the **Pinkies**, mentioned here a few issues back and another instant pick-up record; should be out within the week .

Several other singles came out this week with a vocal/instrumental, or Part 1/ Part 2 disco format similar to **5000 Volts**. Among the most interesting (and recommended) are: **Dooley Silverspoon's** "Let Me Be Your #1" (Cotton), which has a sound similar to that label's current success, **Jeanne Burton's** "(Nobody Loves Me) Like You Do," until the mostly instrumental Part 2 (5:14) takes it someplace even more interesting (total time of the two parts: 7:45); **Floyd Smith's** "Can't Give You Up" (Salsoul), with vocals like a roughed-up **Barry White** and a tasty instrumental side two; a perky "Name Of The Game" by **The Joneses** (Mercury), who sound like a terrific synthesis of the **O'Jays** and the **Jackson 5** (in two parts with a combined time of 6:15) and **Paul Jabara's** single, "One Man Ain't Enough" (A&M), now available with an instrumental B side which drops out his lead vocals but keeps all the girl choruses.

Other recommended singles: **Al Matthews'** "Fool" (Columbia), which doesn't quite live up to one of the nicest intros in months but is cute anyhow (and another record currently high on the charts in England); **Joe Quarterman and Free Soul's** aggressive, boasting, sexy "I'm A Young Man" (Mercury), if not a knockout at least at TKO (sample lyric: "I got the ways and means/to make you moan/to make you scream"); **Don Downing's** predictable but hard-to-resist "I'm Not Lovin'" (Roadshow), with production by the **DCA** group and a

HIPPOPOTAMUS, NEW YORK
DJ: Rich Pampinella

BRAZIL – Ritchie Family (20th Century)
DO IT ANY WAY YOU WANNA – People's Choice (TSOP)
DREAMING A DREAM – Crown Heights Affair (De-Lite)
FIRE/YOU SET MY HEART ON FIRE – Tina Charles (Columbia)
FLY, ROBIN, FLY – Silver Convention (Midland Intl.)
IT ONLY TAKES A MINUTE – Tavares (Capitol)
LOVE POWER – Willie Hutch (Motown)
LOVE TO LOVE YOU BABY – Donna Summer (Oasis)
(NOBODY LOVES ME) LIKE YOU DO – Jeanne Burton (Cotton)
ONE WAY STREET – Becket Brown (RCA instrumental)

L'ESPRIT, DETROIT
DJ: Paul Christy

DO IT ANY WAY YOU WANNA – People's Choice (TSOP)
FLY, ROBIN, FLY – Silver Convention (Midland Intl.)
I WANT A DO SOMETHING FREAKY TO YOU – Leon Haywood (20th Century)
IT ONLY TAKES A MINUTE – Tavares (Capitol)
LET'S DO THE LATIN HUSTLE – Eddie Drennon & B.B.S. Unltd. (Friends & Co.)
LOVE TO LOVE YOU BABY – Donna Summer (Oasis)
PEACE PIPE – B.T.Express (Scepter/Roadshow)
(SENDING OUT AN) S.O.S. – Retta Young (All Platinum)
(THAT'S THE WAY) I LIKE IT – KC & the Sunshine Band (TK)
THIS WILL BE – Natalie Cole (Capitol)

LE CLUB, NEW YORK
DJ: Kay Beckett

DO IT ANY WAY YOU WANNA – People's Choice (TSOP)
DO IT YOURSELF/HOW HIGH THE MOON – Gloria Gaynor (MGM)
EVERY BEAT OF MY HEART – Crown Heights Affair (De-Lite)
GET DOWN TONIGHT – KC & the Sunshine Band (TK)
I LIKE IT/ANOTHER GIRL – Silver Convention (Midland Intl.)
LET'S DO THE LATIN HUSTLE – Eddie Drennon & B.B.S. Unltd. (Friends & Co.)
(NOBODY LOVES ME) LIKE YOU DO – Jeanne Burton (Cotton)
PEACE PIPE – B.T. Express (Scepter/Roadshow)
SOMEBODY'S GOTTA GO – Mike & Bill (Arista/Moving Up)
YOU SET MY HEART ON FIRE – Tina Charles (Columbia)

DISCO 1985, LOS ANGELES
DJ: Wayne Thorberg

BAD LUCK – Atlanta Disco Band (Scorpio)
CARIBBEAN FESTIVAL – Kool & the Gang (De-Lite lp cut)
DOWN IN THE JUNGLE – Jungle Rock (Sound Gems)
DREAMING A DREAM – Crown Heights Affair (De-Lite)
FLY, ROBIN, FLY – Silver Convention (Midland Intl.)
FRENESI/PEANUT VENDOR – Ritchie Family (20th Century)
NURSERY RHYMES – People's Choice (TSOP)
[this chart is just six songs long in the original]

4:27 disco version not available before; and, finally out, **The Chequers'** "Undecided Love" (Scepter) with an entirely new disco mix on the instrumental version (5:35) that is somewhat too long but features a fine drum break for added spice (also pressed on a disco 12-inch for DJs only). LEFT FIELD: **Urszula Dudziak's** delightful, Brazilian-flavored "Papaya" (Arista), a special disco pressing (Arista's first) running 4:02 on a small-hole single at, for some reason, 33 1/3 rpm – from Dudziak's forthcoming Arista debut, "Urszula," due early in October and worth looking for unusual, diamond-bright at-home music.

ALBUM CUT OF THE WEEK: **Taj Mahal's** "Why?... And We Repeat Why?... And We Repeat!;" as gorgeous and inviting as **Ramsey Lewis'** collaboration with **Earth, Wind & Fire**, "Sungoddess," and, at 7:15, almost as long. It's from Taj's new album on Columbia, "Music Keeps Me Together," with his latest group, the **Intergalactic Soul Messengers Band**, and is unlike anything else on the album or in Taj's previous work. A welcome change of pace and one that should bring the deeper Taj Mahal to more people's attention.

Now out on an Atlantic Disco Disc: **Blue Magic's** promised extended version of their theme, "Magic Of The Blue," brought up to a fine 5:33 in length. This longer version will be added to the second pressings of the "Thirteen Blue Magic Lane" album which should be available soon. The other side of the Disco Disc contains the full-length "We're On The Right Track," which should boost both these cuts in popularity.

CORRECTION: In case my comments on the **Ritchie Family's** "Brazil" album in last week's **Record World** were a little unclear, the second sentence should have read: "The spirit and style of 'Brazil' prevail, but the other side-one cuts are even more ecstatic and loose in the **MFSB** Big Band mold with scattered sexy vocals." It's one record I don't mind repeating myself on. ◐

OCTOBER 11, 1975

I was in Boston this past weekend to attend what was advertised as the "Ultimate Disco Dance" featuring eight of the city's top discotheque DJs (each with an hour slot between 7:00 p.m. and 2:00 a.m.) in the enormous, classic Grand Ballroom of the Statler Hilton Hotel. It was reportedly the first event of its kind in Boston and it drew more than three thousand people, many of them out to see their favorite DJs perform "in concert." The turntables and other equipment were set up in the center of the Ballroom's stage, each DJ was announced by one of the radio station jocks "hosting" the event (Ron Robin from WBVF and Sonny Joe White from WILD), and there were even some encores after the night's most successful sets – John Luongo from Rhinoceros, who whipped up the most crowd-pleasing set of the night, went back for another 15 minutes of blends before turning his chair over to the next DJ on the program. Although many of the DJs were one-upping each other and mystifying the crowd with their most obscure records, once the dance floor got filled, it rarely cleared again; even when the police had the lights turned on for the last hour, the crowd stuck around until the final note.

Perhaps the most interesting thing about the Boston dance, "ultimate" or not, was the chance to observe the phenomenal spread of a new dance that apparently started in Los Angeles earlier this year, called the Roach or the L.A. Hustle (for some reason, people in Boston sometimes call it the New York Hustle), and which I usually refer to, in despair, as "that dance." That dance, call it what you will, is done in lines, row upon row across the floor, with a series of steps forward, backward and to the side, that make the dancers look like a particularly flashy marching band or drill team. It's easy to pick up and practically contagious in its appeal: in Boston, what started out as a small core of L.A. Hustlers grew and grew until by the end of the evening the entire floor seemed to be moving in a solid block. It's

> **❝It drew more than three thousand people to see their favorite DJs perform "in concert." The turntables were set up in the center of the stage, and there were even some encores❞**

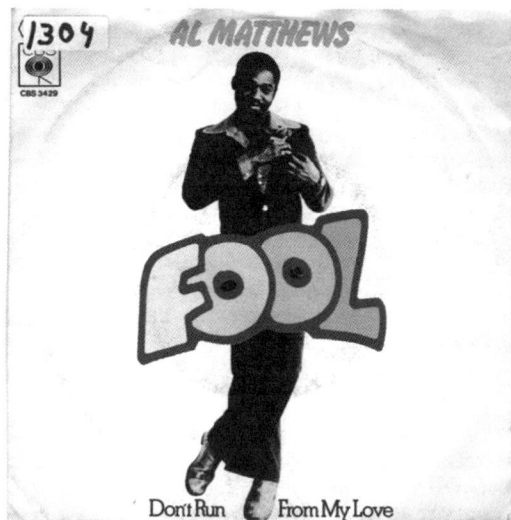

very regimented, rather stiff and quite the opposite in spirit and style from the couples-only Hustle (sociologists and pop culture watchers who saw the Hustle as a positive sign, a move away from isolation and toward community or at least contact, will now have to deal with a simultaneous trend in another direction: a mass dance with no contact, not even face-to-face). In Boston, where the crowd was a mix from all the major clubs whose DJs were playing, the L.A. Hustle acted as a way of bringing everyone together on the dance floor, picking it up from each other. But it can be hazardous, as Richard Cromelin pointed out in his recent Rolling Stone piece on the L.A. disco scene, where he described the "sudden, militaristic surge of this block of 200 people 10 feet in one direction wreaking havoc on sitting-duck couples and soloists." The L.A. Hustle hit New York during the summer, much to my alarm, taking over increasingly larger segments of some already crowded dance floors. I think I may stay home until it either blows over or moves to football fields at halftime.

New records on the top 10 lists this week: **Ron Carter's** cool and refreshing version of **Cole Porter's** "Anything Goes" (5:26), the title cut from his forthcoming Kudu album, now out on a few advance pressings and due in the stores toward the end of the month... "Baby Face," an instrumental version of the pop standard, by the **Wing & A Prayer Fife & Drum Corps**, produced by **Harold Wheeler** and **Steve Schaeffer**, and Wing & A Prayer's first release since **Consumer Rapport's** monster, "Ease On Down The Road." The single, which sounds like a "Brazil" follow-up and could go just as far, should be available within the next week or two as a commercial 45 and a longer Atlantic Disco Disc... **The Reflections'**

1270, BOSTON
DJ: Jimmy Stuard

BABY FACE – Wing & A Prayer Fife and Drum Corps (Wing & A Prayer)

CASANOVA BROWN/DO IT YOURSELF/HOW HIGH THE MOON – Gloria Gaynor (MGM)

CHANGE WITH THE TIMES – Van McCoy (Avco)

EVERY BEAT OF MY HEART – Crown Heights Affair (De-Lite)

EXODUS/ARANJUEZ MON AMOUR – Biddu Orchestra (Epic import)

FIRE/YOU SET MY HEART ON FIRE – Tina Charles (Columbia)

LOVE ON DELIVERY – Reflections (Capitol)

LOVE TO LOVE YOU BABY – Donna Summer (Oasis)

PEANUT VENDOR/FRENESI/BRAZIL – Ritchie Family (20th Century)

UNDECIDED LOVE – Chequers (Scepter)

12 WEST, NEW YORK
DJ: Tom Savarese

ANYTHING GOES – Ron Carter (Kudu)

CARAVAN/WATSUI STRUT – Deodato (MCA)

EVERY BEAT OF MY HEART – Crown Heights Affair (De-Lite)

FIRE/YOU SET MY HEART ON FIRE – Tina Charles (Columbia)

FOOL – Al Matthews (Columbia)

I AM SOMEBODY – Jimmy James & the Vagabonds (Pye)

LOVE TO LOVE YOU BABY – Donna Summer (Oasis)

NOWHERE – Hokis Pokis (Black Magic)

SUNNY – Yambu (Montuno)

WHY?... AND WE REPEAT – Taj Mahal (Columbia)

ADAMS APPLE, NEW YORK
DJ: David Todd

ANYTHING GOES – Ron Carter (Kudu lp cut)

DO IT ANY WAY YOU WANNA – People's Choice (TSOP)

EARTHQUAKE/ROLL WITH THE PUNCHES/ KEEP ON HUSTLIN' – Van McCoy (Avco)

EVERY BEAT OF MY HEART – Crown Heights Affair (De-Lite)

HOOKED FOR LIFE – Trammps (Atlantic)

I'M IN HEAVEN – Touch of Class (Midland Intl.)

FEANUT VENDOR/FRENESI/BRAZIL – Ritchie Family (20th Century)

SOMEBODY'S GOTTA GO – Mike & Bill (Arista/Moving Up)

SUNNY – Yambu (Montuno)

WHAT KIND OF PERSON ARE YOU?/ HALF OF YOUR HEART – Zulema (RCA)

MIRAGE, BOSTON
DJ: Joe Carvello

CHANGE WITH THE TIMES/EARTHQUAKE – Van McCoy (Avco)

EVERY BEAT OF MY HEART – Crown Heights Affair (De-Lite)

YOU SET MY HEART ON FIRE – Tina Charles (Columbia)

GIMME THE KEY – Bobby Keys (Ring 0)

HERE FOR THE PARTY – Bottom & Company (Motown)

HOW HIGH THE MOON – Gloria Gaynor (MGM)

IT ONLY TAKES A MINUTE – Tavares (Capitol)

LOVE ON DELIVERY – Reflections (Capitol)

SUMMER OF '42 – Biddu Orchestra (Epic)

VOLARE – Al Martino (Capitol)

follow-up to "Three Steps From True Love," a strong, gospel-flavored single called "Love On Delivery (L.O.D.)" (Capitol), with a 4:50 disco version that is apparently very hot in Boston right now; I passed on "L.O.D." the first few times around but another listening clinched it for me, too... **Bottom & Company's** "Here For The Party" (Motown) is another record I overlooked at first but one which deserves the attention Joe Carvello is giving it at Mirage in Boston where he's listed it in his top 10; it sounds very much like **Buddy Miles**, hard and rocking... "Nowhere" by **Hokis Pokis** (Black Magic) is one of those small label items that pops up every once in a while and takes everyone by surprise; this one is very strong, with a feeling somewhere between **Crown Heights Affair** and **Blackbyrds**. All the above are recommended, pretty much in the order that they appear. Then there's "Volare," **Al Martino's** re-vamp of one of those "magnifico" Italian hits they're advertising on TV right now. The new version (produced by **Mike Curb** on Capitol) uses every disco readymade device to transform the song, but schlock prevails. In spite of this, the record is reportedly number one at the Montreal Record Center and is picking up everywhere. First "Exodus," then "Volare" – what next? How about a disco version of "Beer Barrel Polka"? Or, for the Bicentennial, "America the Beautiful"?

Zulema's new album, "R.S.V.P." (RCA), is also out now on advance pressings and picking up fast. David Todd from Adams Apple picked the first two cuts, "What Kind of Person Are You?" and "Half of Your Heart," for his top 10 this week – Zulema sounds alternately like **Patti LaBelle** and **Aretha Franklin** and better comparisons could not be made. The album's first single, already getting good response in Boston, is a version of **Brenda Holloway's** old "Just Look What You've Done," sharp and snappy, especially in its long album-cut length (4:04). Should be available commercially in a week or two.

RECOMMENDED: **The Miracles'** exceptionally powerful "Love Machine" (Tamla), taken from their new album and here in a Part 1 (2:55), Part 2 (4:07) format – Part 2 is pure dynamite, a **Jackson 5**-type production that rivals "Forever Came Today" and the best from Motown this year – a must; **Frankie Valli's** new "Our Day Will Come" (Private Stock), a break with producer **Bob Crewe** (who concocted the successful "Swearin' to God") and a move to the **Gloria Gaynor** sound in a deliciously ornate arrangement of the soul classic produced by **Hank Medress** and **Dave Appell** (long version: 5:40); and **South Shore Commission's** remake with almost identical production (here, as on the original, by **Stan Watson** & **Norman Harris**) of "We're On The Right Track" (Wand) – with a "disco version" of 4:50.

CALENDAR: **Touch of Class** will perform at the next New York Record Pool meeting, Monday, October 6 at 2 p.m. ✪

> **Ever since Babe Ruth's "The Mexican" was discovered, hip DJs have been hoping they'll come up with something else that exciting on the dance floor**

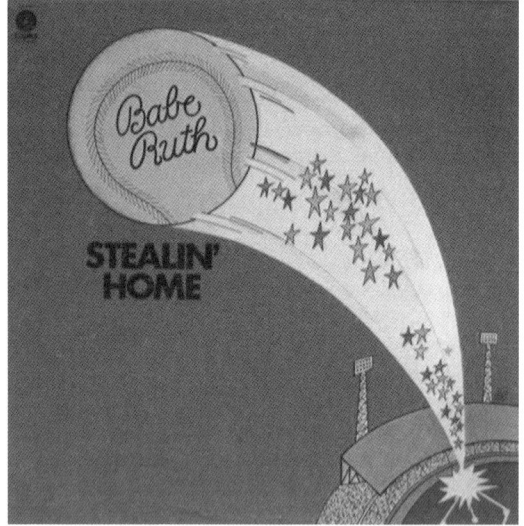

It's always nice when a week that appeared so unpromising as far as records were concerned turns out to be full of minor to above average pleasures (a thrill – a genuine thrill – is more than we expect these days). Here are some of the high spots:

Ever since "The Mexican" was discovered on **Babe Ruth's** early "First Base" album (Harvest/Capitol), hip DJs have been anxiously testing out each new album by the British group, hoping they'll come up with something else that exciting on the dance floor. They have now with a 6:40 cut on their new Capitol album called "Elusive" (the album: "Stealin' Home") that is already picking up play in New York (Phil Gill put it in his top 10 immediately and Tony Smith says it's coming on very strong at Barefoot Boy). Basically, it's hard-edged rock but with a lot of very fluid keyboard work to vary the texture and a fine instrumental second half that finishes it off beautifully: the album cut of the moment.

The Miracles' surprising "City of Angels" (Tamla) finally arrived so now I can appreciate the complete (6:52) "Love Machine," reviewed here last week as a two-part single. This is hardly the Miracles we knew and loved, but, under the production of **Freddie Perren**, the group has made a spectacular step in the same direction **Hal Davis** took the **Jackson 5** on their breakthrough "Get It Together" album. "Love Machine" clearly cops from "Dancing Machine," but when the results are this sharp you can't really carp about Motown's tendency to repeat successful formulas. The other cut already making an impact (see Tony Smith's and Phil Gill's top 10 lists) is the album's opener, an instrumental "Overture" highlighted by a exhilarating use of strings. All the cuts were written by original Miracle **Pete Moore** and **William Griffin**,

Smokey Robinson's replacement in recent years – and be sure to check out "Ain't Nobody Straight in L.A."

Another unexpected dance cut has popped up in an unlikely place – the new **Papa John Creach** album ("I'm The Fiddle Man" on Buddah). It's a racy, full-bodied instrumental (length: 4:50) called "Joyce" that pretty much buries Papa John's fiddle, which struggles out manfully here and there, but the final effect is quite nice: **MFSB** with a down-home touch.

Then there's a whole batch of recommended singles, beginning with a trio of TK studio product, my favorite being **Wildflower's** unusual, marvelously overripe "Please Don't Stop" (Dash), a sex song (the "love song" has been taken one step further so many times by now that these more explicit songs deserve a genre all to themselves) that sounds like **Love Unlimited** Miami-style, vocals appropriately roughened under the production of **Clarence Reid**. The chorus screams, "You're about to take me to paradise/Oh please don't stop." The B side is an instrumental version of roughly the same length, 3:31 – try it out first. The other TK releases are **Cashmere's** nasty "Get Down With It" (Lotta), especially because it has a "Part II" instrumental version (3:50), and **Joey Porrello's** smooth remake of "Fools Rush In" (Drive), the one Bob Lombardi from Rumbottom's in Hollywood, Florida, alerted us to a few weeks back.

To continue with the list of recommended new singles, there's: the **O'Jays'** first release from their next album, "I Love Music" (Philadelphia International), which already sounds like it might become an anthem approaching the strength of "Bad luck," though here

BAREFOOT BOY, NEW YORK
DJ: Tony Smith

ANYTHING GOES – Ron Carter (Kudu)
CARAVAN/WATUSI STRUT – Deodato (MCA)
CASANOVA BROWN/DO IT YOURSELF/ HOW HIGH THE MOON – Gloria Gaynor (MGM)
EL CARAVANERO – Chocolate Boys (Disques Elver)
EVERY BEAT OF MY HEART/FOXY – Crown Heights Affair (De-Lite)
LOVE TO LOVE YOU BABY – Donna Summer (Oasis)
MESSIN' WITH MY MIND – LaBelle (Epic)
OVERTURE – Miracles (Tamla)
PEANUT VENDOR/FRENESI/BRAZIL – Ritchie Family (20th Century)
2 PIGS & A HOG – Cooley High Soundtrack (Motown)

IRON RAIL, BROOKLYN, N.Y.
DJ: Phil Gill

ANYTHING GOES – Ron Carter (Kudu)
CHANGE WITH THE TIMES/EARTHQUAKE – Van McCoy (Avco)
ELUSIVE – Babe Ruth (Capitol)
FUNK DOWN – Mongo Santamaria (Vaya)
LET ME BE THE #1 – Dooley Silverspoon (Cotton)
LOVE TO LOVE YOU BABY – Donna Summer (Oasis)
OVERTURE/LOVE MACHINE – Miracles (Tamla)
OUR DAY WILL COME – Frankie Valli (Private Stock)
PEANUT VENDOR/FRENESI/BRAZIL – Ritchie Family (20th Century)
WHAT KIND OF PERSON ARE YOU?/HALF OF YOUR HEART/JUST LOOK WHAT YOU'VE DONE – Zulema (RCA)

PIER 9, WASHINGTON, D.C.
DJ: Mitch Schatsky

ANYTHING GOES/BARETTA'S THEME – Ron Carter (Kudu)
BREAKAWAY – Ernie Bush (Contempo import)
CASANOVA BROWN/DO IT YOURSELF/ HOW HIGH THE MOON – Gloria Gaynor (MGM)
EVERY BEAT OF MY HEART – Crown Heights Affair (De-Lite)
EXODUS/SUMMER OF '42/ARANJUEZ MON AMOUR – Biddu Orchestra (Epic import)
LET'S DO THE LATIN HUSTLE – Eddie Drennon & BBS Unltd. (Friends & Co.)
LOVE TO LOVE YOU BABY – Donna Summer (Oasis)
PEANUT VENDOR/FRENESI/BRAZIL – Ritchie Family (20th Century)
SOUL DRACULA – Hot Blood (Disques Carrere import)
WHOSE LITTLE GIRL ARE YOU – Billy Ocean (GTO import)

PENROD'S, NY (LONG ISLAND)
DJ: Jackie McCloy

CARAVAN/WATUSI STRUT – Deodato (MCA)
CASANOVA BROWN/DO IT YOURSELF/ HOW HIGH THE MOON – Gloria Gaynor (MGM)
EL CARAVANERO – Chocolate Boys (Disques Elver)
EVERY BEAT OF MY HEART – Crown Heights Affair (De-Lite)
FIRE/YOU SET MY HEART ON FIRE – Tina Charles (Columbia)
FLY, ROBIN, FLY – Silver Convention (Midland Intl.)
MAGIC OF THE BLUE – Blue Magic (Atlantic/Atco)
NOWHERE – Hokis Pokis (Black Magic)
PEANUT VENDOR/FRENESI/BRAZIL – Ritchie Family (20th Century)
SUNNY – Yambu (Montuno)

the feeling is brighter, lighter, in a tribute to music itself – doesn't cut as deep as the usual O'Jays cut, but a great **Gamble-Huff** job nevertheless (it's been released divided in two parts of which I have as yet only heard the first, 3:37); another feel-good song, "Make Some People Happy," by **Rhythm** (Polydor), with something of a **B.T. Express/Fatback Band** sound; an interesting, both sassy and deep, instrumental by the **Major Lance Revue** 'called "You Keep Me Coming to You" (Osiris); **Houston Person's** top-flight instrumental, "Disco Sax" (Westbound), which should be a big record; "Crying Crying" by **Nanette Workman**, her first release for Atco and an attractive if not totally arresting one – Mitch Schatsky says he's heard Workman's next release, "Dancer Dance," already out in France, and it's even better; **Hosanna's** excellent "Hipit," even though it does sound a bit homemade around the edges (it's on a small New Jersey label, L.H.M.A.), with a **Young Rascals**/Latin feel and an instrumental-version B side called "Any Dance Will Do;" **Sister Sledge's** pleasant, up "Love Has Found Me" (Atco), though it's not up to their best material; and, finally, though I rarely mention ballads (the last I remember was **21st Century's** definitely noteworthy "Remember the Rain"), here's one of the rare exceptions, the best I've heard in a while – "Love" by a new group called **Eon** on Scepter, a beautiful, rich production with a long version of 5:23 from an album due later this month.

LEFT FIELD: an instrumental with an African/synthesizer sound – sort of like a combination of **Bohannon** and the **Peppers**, called "Dashiki" by **Mulamba** (Editions Makossa)... **Percy Faith** has come out with a hard core disco version of "Theme from 'A Summer Place'" retitled, rather ambitiously, "Summer Place '76" – not exactly in season but, seriously folks, not half bad, certainly more into real disco styling than anything on Faith's recent "Disco Party" album (Columbia)... This item slipped out of the recommended 45s list above, but I don't want to forget **Pete Warner's** sweet, high-spirited **Patrick Adams** composition and production, "I Just Want To Spend My Life With You" (Polydor) – bet there's a terrific long version of this one in the can somewhere.

FEEDBACK: Phil Gill suggests the instrumental "Chase" (4:14) from the new "Let's Do It Again" soundtrack album, produced by **Curtis Mayfield** (Curtom), and "The Tunnel," a pounding rock instrumental from the **Graeme Edge Band** album, "Kick Off Your Muddy Boots" (Threshold/London), both worth checking out, but especially the latter in spite of its length (just over two minutes – Gill says he doubles it up as everyone does now with "2 Pigs & A Hog") … The new longer version of **Carol Douglas'** "Headline News" (Midland International) is making everyone re-evaluate the cut, primarily because the 5:16 12-inch has an entirely new intro that helps boost the song. ◐

OCTOBER 25, 1975

NEWS & NOTES: **Donna Summer's** extraordinary "Love to Love You Baby" (Oasis) is number one on the Disco File Top 20 this week after only four weeks on the chart – the fastest zoom to the top this year. The second spot is held by **Gloria Gaynor's** still powerful "Casanova Brown/Do It Yourself/How High The Moon" medley and I suspect the girls will be see-sawing back and forth in these positions for a while yet… French producer **Jaques Morali** returned to Philadelphia's Sigma Sound Studios last week to whip up a disco version of the **Ritchie Family's** next single, "Dance With Me," and came up with a frothy 6:24 track, expanding the cut to nearly twice its album length. The re-mix, which brings the song up to "Brazil" quality, will be available at the end of this week on a special 12-inch disc serviced only to discotheque DJs, but the commercial signles will not be on the market for another two to three weeks… Bob Gordon, a New York disc jockey currently playing nights at three top clubs – Galaxy 21, Hippopotamus and 12-West – is the first to list a cut from the forthcoming **Salsoul Orchestra** album, a 6-minute instrumental called "Tale Of Three Cities," written, arranged and disco-mixed by **Ronnie Baker**, produced by **Vince Montana**. "Tale" was one of three cuts made available on advance pressings to a small number of DJs, a quick, rich bite from the album which is scheduled for release on Salsoul in the last week of October… PIP has released a long (5:44) disco version of the new **Gary Toms Empire** single, that group's interpretation of the **Lennon-McCartney** song, "Drive My Car."

Small independent labels do very well in the disco field – they're one of the key elements that keeps the field strong and exciting – and two good examples of little-label success are on the Disco File Top 20 right now: **Yambu's** "Sunny," a Latin-style instrumental version of the **Bobby Hebb** song on a young New York label called Montuno, and "Nowhere" by **Hokis Pokis** on a mysterious label named Black Magic, about which I would appreciate any and all information. "Sunny" jumped from 18 to 10 on the chart this week and "Nowhere" entered at 17, trailing raves from DJs. Also moving very fast: **The O'Jays'** knockout, "I Love Music," being picked up instantly everywhere.

Only one new album cut worth talking about this week, but this one deserves the space to itself: it's

Barry Manilow's "New York City Rhythm," the opening cut (4:42) from his new Arista album, "Tryin' To Get the Feeling," and an exuberant tribute to the vibrant spirit of the city that he says keeps him (and a lot of us) going. It goes off into a Latin-flavored break toward the end with guys chanting "Nueva York, Nueva York" that might make it difficult for some dance floors but a sensation on others. Manilow's best for the discos since "It's a Miracle."

RECOMMENDED SINGLES: **Benny Troy's** "I Wanna Give You Tomorrow" (De-Lite) – although the vocals aren't especially to my taste, the production, particularly on the extended disco version (5:00) is superb; a "blue-eyed soul" sound (vocals remind me of **Boz Scaggs**) in "Delicious" by the **Duprees** (RCA), with a nice disco upsweep and a long version of 4:08, arranged by **Bobby Martin**; "Ebb Tide" (Pye) **Love Sound's** super-lush, if a bit sticky, disco restyling of the pop classic, featuring whispery female voices repeating the title in case you didn't know – just released after some success as a British disco import. LEFT FIELD: **Gail Eason's** optimstic, energetic "Love's Gonna Find You" (A&M) with my favorite chorus in weeks – written by **Melissa Manchester** and **Carole Bayer Sager**, this song could be particularly terrific in an instrumental version that smoothed out the man y tempo changes; **D.J. Rogers'** first for RCA, "It's Good To Be Alive," a spirited affirmation which should be checked out and picked up if only for its message; and another sort of message song, taking up the "Bad Luck" complaint (though without that song's special brilliance) called "It Ain't What It Used To Be" by **Randolph Brown and Company** (IX Chains) that ends by asking, "Where's the love? Where's the joy? Where's the hope? Where's the peace?"

I thought it as amusing last week when **Percy Faith** redid his own "Theme From 'A Summer Place'" as "Summer Place '76" (it's getting some very positive response already, by the way) but now we have – what next? – a disco arrangement of **Rogers and Hammerstein's** "South Pacific" tune, "Bali Hai," by **Al Allen & Co.** (Fantasy). Very bizarrre, though I must admit there is a certain attraction here, especially when the horns well up. Just as long as noone within my hearing breaks into song on the dance floor. ◐

> **" Small independent labels do very well in the disco field – they're one of the key elements that keeps the field strong and exciting "**

DEN 1, CHICAGO
DJ: Artie Feldman

BRAZIL – Ritchie Family (20th Century)
DO IT ANY WAY YOU WANNA – People's Choice (TSOP)
FIRE/YOU SET MY HEART ON FIRE – Tina Charles (Columbia)
FLY, ROBIN, FLY – Silver Convention (Midland Intl.)
I LOVE MUSIC – O'Jays (Phila. Intl.)
LOVE TO LOVE YOU BABY – Donna Summer (Oasis)
MESSIN' WITH MY MIND – LaBelle (Epic)
PEACE PIPE – B.T. Express (Scepter/Roadshow)
SOUL TRAIN '75 – Soul Train Gang (Soul Train)
TO EACH HIS OWN/MELLOW ME – Faith, Hope & Charity (RCA)

BOOMBAMAKAOO, NEW YORK
DJ: Jorge Wheeler

ANYTHING GOES – Ron Carter (Kudu)
CASANOVA BROWN/DO IT YOURSELF/ HOW HIGH THE MOON – Gloria Gaynor (MGM)
EVERY BEAT OF MY HEART – Crown Heights Affair (De-Lite)
I JUST CAN'T GIVE YOU UP – Floyd Smith (Salsoul)
LOVE TO LOVE YOU BABY – Donna Summer (Oasis)
NOWHERE – Hokis Pokis (Black Magic)
OUR DAY WILL COME – Frankie Valli (Private Stock)
PACHECO Y MASUCCI – Gonzalo, Pacheco & Pupi (Vaya)
PEANUT VENDOR/FRENESI/BRAZIL – Ritchie Family (20th Century)
SUNNY – Yambu (Montuno)

FRIENDS AGAIN, NEW YORK
DJ: John Colon

CARAVAN/WATUSI STRUT/FUNK YOURSELF – Deodato (MCA)
CASANOVA BROWN/DO IT YOURSELF/ HOW HIGH THE MOON – Gloria Gaynor (MGM)
EVERY BEAT OF MY HEART/DREAMING A DREAM – Crown Heights Affair (De-Lite)
I LOVE MUSIC – O'Jays (Phila. Intl.)
LOVE TO LOVE YOU BABY – Donna Summer (Oasis)
MESSIN' WITH MY MIND – LaBelle (Epic)
OVERTURE – Miracles (Tamla)
PEANUT VENDOR/FRENESI/BRAZIL – Ritchie Family (20th Century)
2 PIGS & A HOG – Cooley High Soundtrack (Motown)
SUNNY – Yambu (Montuno)

GALAXY 21, NEW YORK
DJ: Bob Gordon

CARAVAN/WATUSI STRUT/ – Deodato (MCA)
CASANOVA BROWN/DO IT YOURSELF/HOW HIGH THE MOON – Gloria Gaynor (MGM)
EVERY BEAT OF MY HEART – Crown Heights Affair (De-Lite)
I AM SOMEBODY – Jimmy James & the Vagabonds (Pye)
I LOVE MUSIC – O'Jays (Phila. Intl.)
LOVE TO LOVE YOU BABY – Donna Summer (Oasis)
NAME OF THE GAME – Joneses (Mercury)
NOWHERE – Hokis Pokis (Black Magic)
SUNNY – Yambu (Montuno)
TALE OF THREE CITIES – Salsoul Orchestra (Salsoul)

DISCO FILE TOP 20

1. **LOVE TO LOVE YOU BABY** – Donna Summer (Oasis)
2. **CASANOVA BROWN/DO IT YOURSELF/ HOW HIGH THE MOON** – Gloria Gaynor (MGM)
3. **EVERY BEAT OF MY HEART** – Crown Heights Affair (De-Lite)
4. **PEANUT VENDOR** – Ritchie Family (20th Century)
5. **SUNNY** – Yambu (Montuno)
6. **FRENESI** – Ritchie Family (20th Century)
7. **FIRE/YOU SET MY HEART ON FIRE** – Tina Charles (Columbia)
8. **ANYTHING GOES** – Ron Carter (Kudu)
9. **BRAZIL** – The Ritchie Family (Avco)
10. **FLY, ROBIN, FLY** – Silver Convention (Midland Intl.)
11. **CARAVAN/WATUSI STRUT** – Deodato (MCA)
12. **NOWHERE** – Hokis Pokis (Black Magic)
13. **DO IT ANY WAY YOU WANNA** – People's Choice (TSOP)
14. **PEACE PIPE** – B.T. Express (Scepter /Roadshow)
15. **I LOVE MUSIC** – O'Jays (Phila. Intl.)
16. **DREAMING A DREAM** – Crown Heights Affair (De-Lite)
17. **BABY FACE** – Wing & A Prayer Fife & Drum Corps (Wing & A Prayer)
18. **CHANGE WITH THE TIMES** – Van McCoy (Avco)
19. **MESSIN' WITH MY MIND** – LaBelle (Epic)
20. **IT ONLY TAKES A MINUTE** – Tavares (Capitol)

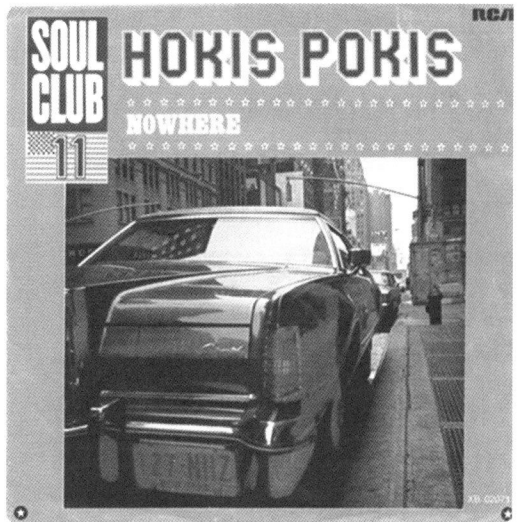

FEEDBACK: Flamingo, one of New York's classiest private clubs, reopened this past weekend for its '75/'76 season with Vincent Carleo at the turntables (he will alternate with Luis Romero), and though it took on the atmosphere of a rush-hour subway platform (complete with artificial palm trees) by 3 a.m. before I left I heard a number of new records for the first time. Two of the best were **Black Blood's** "Chicano," a pounding Afro-Latin cut by the Afro-European group (they live and record in Belgium) who made "A.I.E. (A Mwana)" – from the album "Black Blood" on Mainstream – and a long disco version of **Dionne Warwick's** "This Empty Place" by "Wiz" kid **Stephanie Mills**, reportedly re-done by **Burt Bacharach** and **Hal David** themselves for Mills' debut album on Motown, due in November. "Chicano," about four minutes long, is an exceptionally strong drum track with chanting African vocals, good enough to make the album an essential one right now; check out the "Avenue Louise" cut as well. Carleo was also pleased with the reaction to two of his favorite imports: a hard-edged "Don't Pull Your Love" by **Jimmy Helms** (Pye in England) and "Lady Bump" by **Penny McLean**, one of the singers in **Silver Convention** with that group behind her. "Lady Bump," already a success in Europe, also features a B side called "The Lady Bumps On" (4:31); Carleo's copy was on Columbia in Canada only and has been picked up for American release by Atlantic.

FEEDBACK (CONTINUED): Danae Jacovidis from Styx in Boston sent me off to find a commercial copy of **Nanette Workman's** "Crying Crying" (Atco) so I could hear the even more interesting flip side, "If It Wasn't for the Money." "Money" is worth the search – it's hard and driving and sounds very much like **Babe Ruth**, particularly in the break... Michael Nias at Othello's in New York reports that **Freddi & Henchi's** "Cartoon People" (DJM) is doing so well with his crowd that it's nearly a top 10 record already – maybe it's because the sound and theme of the song are so strongly **Norman Whitfield/Temptations** that it sounds familiar right

away... Steve D'Acquisto from Le Jardin alerted me to a fine cut on the new **Jackie Moore** album, a spirited **Brad Shapiro** production called "Heart Be Still" and the only thing on the new lp that deserves comparison to Moore's earlier "Time" or "Clean Up Your Own Yard" (the album: "Make Me Feel Like A Woman" on Kayvette, one of the TK labels)... Bobby DJ Guttadaro is enthusiastic about **Barbra Streisand's** entry into the disco field, her version of the **Four Tops'** "Shake Me, Wake Me" included on the new Streisand lp, "Lazy Afternoon" (Columbia). Though it's only 2:50, Barbra's interpretation is fairly punchy, especially with a barrage of Latin percussion adding to the density toward the end. Guttadaro will be playing at a new just-above-Soho club in New York called Infinity, opening November 1, after his summer out at Fire Island's Ice Palace.

Other notable album cuts: "A Groove Will Make You Move," the most appealing cut from the new **Jimmy Castor Bunch** album, "Supersound" (Atlantic), smoothing out some of the rough edges of the usual Castor sound (and running 5:20) – and the second, instrumental, half of the album's title cut is worth a try for its tight percussion; **Bill Withers'** "Make Love to Your Mind," a fine, fine 6:23 cut with a certain "Who Is He and What Is He to You" feeling from Withers' just-out Columbia album, "Making Friends" (the key lines: "Before I make love to your body/I wanna make love to your mind" and Withers does just that throughout the album); "Don't Be Afraid (Take My Love)" from **Creative Source's** first release for Polydor, "Pass the Feelin' On"-a very jumpy cut with a nice taste of their creamy smooth vocal blends, but not the spectacular sort of work we've come to expect from this group.

STANDOUT 45s: (1) "Baby Face" by **The Wing & A Prayer Fife & Drum Corps** (Wing & A Prayer), already on the Disco File Top 20 after a few weeks of advance play in Boston and New York, is now out as a commercial single (3:15 in length) and due soon as an extended Disco Disc on Atlantic. It's at once delightful and unbearably cute, but **Harold Wheeler** and **Steve Scheaffer**, who hit very big the first time around with "Ease On Down The Road," keep just the right balance here. Irresistible.

(2) **Al Green's** newest, "Full Of Fire" (Hi), is not on his recent album so it comes as a pleasant surprise: a joyous, top-form cut that's hotter than its title, kicked along by a steady, sharp **Willie Mitchell** production. It's commercial length is 3:25, but it's been pressed up on a special disco 10-inch record running 5:12 and quite spectacular.

(3) The B side of "What's Come Over Me" by **Margie Joseph & Blue Magic** is another collaboration called "You & Me (Got a Good Thing Going)" (Atco) which is already one of my favorite **Norman Harris** productions this year. The cut is as good or better than most of the material on the new Blue Magic album from which "What's Come Over Me" was taken and "You & Me" deserves more attention than it's likely to get as a B side. Pick it up. ✺

> ❝ Though it took on the atmosphere of a rush-hour subway platform (complete with artificial palm trees), by 3am before I left I heard a number of records for the first time ❞

STYX, BOSTON
DJ: Danae Jacovidis

ANYTHING GOES – Ron Carter (Kudu)
BABY FACE – Wing & A Prayer Fife & Drum Corps (Wing & A Prayer)
CASANOVA BROWN/DO IT YOURSELF/HOW HIGH THE MOON – Gloria Gaynor (MGM)
EVERY BEAT OF MY HEART/FOXY – Crown Heights Affair (De-Lite)
I AM SOMEBODY – Jimmy James & the Vagabonds (Pye)
LOVE TO LOVE YOU BABY – Donna Summer (Oasis)
(NOBODY LOVES ME) LIKE YOU DO DO – Jeanne Burton (Cotton)
NOWHERE – Hokis Pokis (Black Magic)
SUNNY – Yambu (Montuno)
2 PIGS & A HOG – Cooley High Soundtrack (Motown)

OTHELLO'S, NEW YORK
DJ: Michael Nias

CASANOVA BROWN/DO IT YOURSELF – Gloria Gaynor (MGM)
EVERY BEAT OF MY HEART/DREAMING A DREAM – Crown Heights Affair (De-Lite)
FACE THE MUSIC – Dynamic Superiors (Motown)
FLY, ROBIN, FLY – Silver Convention (Midland Intl.)
HOLLYWOOD HOT – Eleventh Hour (20th Century)
I LOVE MUSIC – O'Jays (Phila. Intl.)
KEEP HOLDING ON – Ace Spectrum (Atlantic)
LOVE TO LOVE YOU BABY – Donna Summer (Oasis)
MELLOW BLOW /THANK YOU LOVE – Barrabas (Atco)
SUNNY/CABALLO – Yambu (Montuno)

FLAMINGO, NEW YORK
DJ: Vincent Carleo

BABY FACE – Wing & A Prayer Fife & Drum Corps (Wing & A Prayer)
CARAVAN/WATUSI STRUT – Deodato (MCA)
CASANOVA BROWN – Gloria Gaynor (MGM)
FIRE/YOU SET MY HEART ON FIRE – Tina Charles (Columbia)
I AM SOMEBODY – Jimmy James & the Vagabonds (Pye)
LOVE TO LOVE YOU BABY – Donna Summer (Oasis)
OUR DAY WILL COME – Frankie Valli (Private Stock)
NOWHERE – Hokis Pokis (Black Magic)
SUNNY – Yambu (Montuno)
UNDECIDED LOVE – Chequers (Scepter)

BETTER DAYS, NEW YORK
DJ: Toraino Scott

ANYTHING GOES – Ron Carter (Kudu
BABY FACE – Wing & A Prayer Fife & Drum Corps (Wing & A Prayer)
CHANGE WITH THE TIMES – Van McCoy (Avco)
CHI- TOWN THEME – Cleveland Eaton (Black Jazz)
I LOVE MUSIC – O'Jays (Phila. Intl.)
LOVE TO LOVE YOU BABY – Donna Summer (Oasis)
PEACE PIPE/WHATCHA THINK ABOUT THAT? – B.T. Express (Scepter/Roadshow)
PEANUT VENDOR/FRENESI – Ritchie Family (20th Century)
SUNNY – Yambu (Montuno)
WE'RE ON THE RIGHT TRACK – South Shore Commission (Wand)

The new essential albums: Topping the list is the debut release by the **Salsoul Orchestra** (Salsoul Records), surely one of the year's best instrumental albums, produced by Philadelphia's **Vince Montana, Jr** under executive producers Joe & Ken Cayre. Though this is essentially) another variation on the **MFSB** theme, featuring Sigma Sound's most accomplished musicians (Norman Harris, Earl Young, Bobby Eli, et al.) the results here are altogether more exciting than MFSB's recent work, under **Gamble & Huff**. The variety and depth of the cuts changing moods from a carefree "Get Happy" to a more weighty "Tale of Three Cities," from "Tangerine," another classic pop song reworked disco-style, to the zip and high spirits of "Salsoul Rainbow" or "Chicago Bus Stop" or "You're Just The Right Size" (for what?) – is a total joy. Also included, of course, is the full-length "Salsoul Hustle" (6:41), the cut that started it all. This is the album of the moment and I suspect that nearly every track will be cropping up on top 10 lists for some time to come.

> **" Richard Nader is planning "The World's Biggest Disco Dance Party" for Madison Square Garden. A platform on one side will be set up for live DJs, who will do their own sort of performances in between acts "**

Another fine instrumental album, the **Armada Orchestra's** first (on Contempo/Scepter), is being released this week in the U.S. and in England where it was produced. As I wrote several months back when I had a chance to hear advance tapes, this is also a very strong disco record, though some of its impact may have been blunted by the familiarity of the material (two of the cuts, versions of "The Same Old Song" and "Do Me Right," were hits as import singles this past year). The album's first American single release is a striking version of **Jimmy Ruffin's** "Tell Me What You Want" backed with the lp's only original cut, an interesting number called "The Drifter;" versions of **Van McCoy's** "The Hustle," **Freda Payne's** "Band of Gold" and "Feel the Need in Me" and "You Want It You Got It" – both **Detroit Emeralds** songs – are also included.

Bobby Womack's new album – "Safety Zone" on UA – was produced by David Rubinson (& Friends), features guest shots by **Herbie Hancock** and the **Pointer Sisters** (both Rubinson artists), and is Womack's best in years, maybe his best period. The two longest cuts – "I Feel A Groove Comin' On" at 8:33 and "Everything's Gonna Be Alright" at 6:58 – are complete knockouts, powerhouse cuts, but my own favorite right now is "Daylight," a song that sounds like it could become an after-hours disco-goers' theme: the most attractive of laid-back tempos and great lyrics about the all-night party life. The chorus: "It looks like daylight gonna catch me up again/ Most people are getting up when I'm just getting in." The perfect end-of-the-evening song. **Donald Byrd's** new album, "Places and Spaces" (Blue Note), opens up with one of the hottest instrumentals out now: "Change (Makes You Want to Hustle)," already released on a two-part single and getting picked up very fast. The cut, a hard bump with some wonderful string touches and rough vocal segments, runs 5 :07, a little shorter than the two sides of the 45 put together, but quite compact. Also notable: **David Ruffin's** return in style with "Who I Am" (Motown), produced, arranged, conducted and largely written by **Van McCoy** and featuring his by now quite familiar sound given a little added force by Ruffin's ever-powerful voice. The standout track: "It Takes All Kind Of People To Make The World;" "Heavy Love," "Love Can Be Hazardous To Your Health" and a re-make of the **Choice Four's** "Finger Pointers" also deserve attention.

NEWS & NOTES: **Richard Nader** is planning what he likes to call "The World's Biggest Disco Dance Party" for Madison Square Garden on Friday, November 28. The entire Garden floor will be open to dancers (though each person will have his own reserved seat on the side to return to) with special platforms for featured dancers and two stages at either end for live acts so one can be setting up while the other is performing. Another platform on one side will be set up for live DJs, who will do their own sort of performances in between acts. Elaborate plans are being made to make the Garden more intimate through the use of

REFLECTIONS, NEW YORK
DJ: Aris Rodriguex

CASANOVA BROWN/DO IT YOURSELF – Gloria Gaynor (MGM)

EVERY BEAT OF MY HEART – Crown Heights Affair (De-Lite)

EXODUS/ARANJUEZ MON AMOUR – Biddu Orchestra (Epic import)

I LOVE MUSIC – O'Jays (Philadelphia Intl.)

LOVE TO LOVE YOU BABY – Donna Summer (Oasis)

NOWHERE – Hokis Pokis (Black Magic)

PEANUT VENDOR/FRENESI – Ritchie Family (20th Century)

SUNNY – Yambu (Montuno)

YOU'RE JUST THE RIGHT SIZE – Salsoul Orchestra (Salsoul)

THE ZIP – MFSB (Philadelphia Intl.)

DIMPLES, UNION, NEW JERSEY
DJ: Ralph Guida

EXODUS – Biddu Orchestra (Epic import)

HOOKED FOR LIFE – Trammps (Atlantic)

HOW HIGH THE MOON – Gloria Gaynor (MGM)

I LOVE MUSIC – O'Jays (Philadelphia Intl.)

LOVE TO LOVE YOU BABY – Donna Summer (Oasis)

MAGIC OF THE BLUE – Blue Magic (Atco)

OUR DAY WILL COME – Frankie Valli (Private Stock)

SUNNY – Yambu (Montuno)

UNDECIDED LOVE – Chequers (Scepter)

(YOU WERE MADE) ESPECIALLY FOR ME – Jackson 5 (Motown)

RHINOCEROS, BOSTON
DJ: John Luongo

BABY FACE – Wing & A Prayer Fife & Drum Corps (Wing & A Prayer)

CHANGE WITH THE TIMES – Van McCoy (Avco)

ELUSIVE – Babe Ruth (Capitol)

EVERY BEAT OF MY HEART/FOXY – Crown Heights Affair (De-Lite)

I AM SOMEBODY – Jimmy James & the Vagabonds (Pye)

I LOVE MUSIC – O'Jays (Philadelphia Intl.)

LET'S DO THE LATIN HUSTLE – Eddie Drennon & BBS Unltd. (Friends & Co.)

LOVE TO LOVE YOU BABY – Donna Summer (Oasis)

NOWHERE – Hokis Pokis (Black Magic)

SUNNY – Yambu (Montuno)

HIPPOPOTAMUS, NEW YORK
DJ: Rich Pampinella

DO IT WITH FEELING – Michael Zager & the Moon Band (Bang)

EVERY BEAT OF MY HEART – Crown Heights Affair (De-Lite)

FLY, ROBIN, FLY – Silver Convention (Midland Intl.)

I LOVE MUSIC – O'Jays (Philadelphia Intl.)

IT ONLY TAKES A MINUTE – Tavares (Capitol)

LET ME BE THE #1 – Dooley Silverspoon (Cotton)

LOVE TO LOVE YOU BABY – Donna Summer (Oasis)

(NOBODY LOVES ME) LIKE YOU DO – Jeanne Burton (Cotton)

SALSOUL RAINBOW – Salsoul Orchestra (Salsoul)

SUNNY – Yambu (Montuno)

enormous weather balloons suspended above the dance floor, all bathed in lights which will change simultaneously. Booked so far: **Gloria Gaynor**, the **Trammps** and **Crown Heights Affair**. Hot prospects: **Donna Summer** and **Silver Convention**. And Nader, smart man, is using New York's Record Pool as consultants for the whole event... Just to clear up the mystery about **Hokis Pokis**, whose "Nowhere" is doing very well wherever it's played, they're a four-man group from Long Island and Black Magic is their own label, with "Nowhere" its only product. For the many people who have been unable to get a copy of this record, help may be on the way in the form of a deal with a larger record label which would make the record more widely available. TK and Polydor are reportedly the most interested... **Crown Heights Affair's** smash "Every Beat Of My Heart" has been released in an odd assortment of single versions, all different lengths. The one that Rich Pampinella listed on his top 10 from Hippopotamus this week is 5:20 and features a slightly different beginning and a very different end; though the whole thing could have been mixed better, its variations on the album cut are interesting enough to cause a snap-to of surprise on the dance floor.

RECOMMENDED SINGLES: **Michael Zager & the Moon Band's** immediate turn-on "Do It With Feeling" (Band) which sounds almost good enough to be the new **Stevie Wonder** record (where is that, by the way?), especially when vocalist Peabo Bryson comes in – the message: "If I'm gonna do it, I'm gonna do it with feeling;" "Porto Rico" by **The Pinkies** (Philips), one of those synthesizer-laced European records but with some nice Latin breaks, now out on a U.S. label after some success as an import and much popularity in Canadian discos; **Vicki Sue Robinson's** vivacious "Never Gonna Let You Go" (RCA), with a clean, crisp production by **Warren Schatz**; the **Fatback Band's** dynamite line-dance theme, "(Are You Ready) Do The Bus Stop" (Event) – *very* good; the **Notations'** super-up "It's Alright (This Feeling)" (Gemigo), almost a gospel rave-up. NOW AVAILABLE: 45s of **Merry Clayton's** fabulous "One More Ride" (Ode), **Graham Central Station's** "It's Alright" (Warner Bros.), **Kool & the Gang's** "Caribbean Festival" (De-Lite), and the **Ohio Players'** "Love Rollercoaster (Mercury); an American pressing of **Ernie Bush's** "Breakaway" with a special disco version of 5:35 (Contempo/Scepter); and disco pressings of the complete "I Love Music" by the **O'Jays** (6:51 on a 45 at 33 1/3, from Philadelphia International) and a longer "Theme From S.W.A.T." – running 4:07 – by **Rhythm Heritage** (ABC). ◢

FEEDBACK: Tom Savarese from 12 West, who lists **Nanette Workman's** terrific "If It Wasn't for the Money" (Atco) on his top 10 this week, has also come up with a copy of the original French version, "J'ai Le Gout De Baiser" (which is, I believe, too raunchy for translation in a respectable American trade paper), an import on Pacha. One of the first to get into "I Am Somebody" by **Jimmy James & the Vagabonds**, Savarese is now on a similar gutsy message song from the recent **Rance Allen Group** album ("A Soulful Experience" on Truth) called "Talk That Talk." "Talk," which has some fine **O'Jays** overtones, is in two parts (total time: 7:31) and gets really hot with a pounding drum break in Part II. Also doing well at 12 West: **Henry Mancini's** heavy-handed version of **Van McCoy's** "African Symphony," with a too brief kalimba break (from Mancini's new "Symphonic Soul" album on RCA) and an early entry into what I'm afraid will be a popular novelty market this year – Christmas Disco – with a souped-up instrumental version of "The Little Drummer Boy" produced by the **Gary Toms Empire** guys, **Rick Bleiweiss** and **Bill Stahl**, for a group called **Moonlion** (PIP). "Drummer Boy" comes in a five-minute disco version and is already being reported by a number of DJs.

We should note that the version of **Al Martino's** "Volare," listed by Edmund Timothy of Le Cocu, is the new, longer length (4:53), now pressed on Capitol special "DISCO" label, and minus the spoken introduction... Bacha Mangual, DJ at Revelation II in Brooklyn, has put two cuts from the "Mahogany" soundtrack album (Motown) in his top 10 list this week: a bouncy cut with some flimsy **Jermaine Jackson** vocals called "She's the Ideal Girl," and "Erucu," a very short (1:23) instrumental break of a track that might pick up in the same way that "2 Pigs & A Hog" from the "Cooley High" soundtrack did. Both are the only cuts on the album produced and co-written by Jermaine – the first such credit that I know of... Moving up steadily: "Love Explosion" by **Bazuka** (A&M), even stronger than "Dynamite," on a single now (4:45) but longer on the album (5:26); "Chicano" by **Black Blood** (Mainstream), which should be out soon as a single, too; the long disco version of "Drive My Car" by **Gary Toms Empire** (PIP); and nearly all the cuts on the just-out **Salsoul Orchestra** album, but especially "Chicago Bus Stop," "Salsoul Rainbow" and "You're Just the Right Size," all of which went into the Disco File Top 20 this week.

RECOMMENDED ALBUMS: **South Shore Commission's** exciting debut on Wand, including a new long version of "Free Man," one of the year's 10 best singles, expanded to a beautifully rich 7:21 and picking up all over again; an equally knockout "Train Called Freedom" (5:16) and "I'd Rather Switch Than Fight," a rough-tough woman's song with a very funny monologue ending – shaping up as the three favorites right now – plus a complicated "Handle with Care" which is very interesting but difficult and, of course, the group's version of "We're On The Right Track"... The first album from the **Reflections** (Capitol), containing their two successful singles, "Three Steps From True Love" and "Love On Delivery" (the album's title cut), plus several up-tempo cuts very reminiscent of the **Spinners**, notably the opening tracks on both sides, "All Day, All Night" and "Day After Day (Night After Night)"... The latest from the **Blackbyrds**, "City Life" (Fantasy), not as striking as their previous releases, but worth checking out for "Happy Music," which features a fleeting vocal from **Merry Clayton**, and a delightful "Rock Creek Park"... Scepter's "Disco Gold Vol. 2," also not up to the quality of the previous volume but an essential album; **Ralph De Blanc's** sugary disco interpretation of **Maxine Brown's** "Undecided Love," "El Bimbo," "Breakaway," **Bobby Moore's** "Anything Man" and a longer version of "Waterbed" by **LTG Exchange**. Again, this volume is dedicated to spinners all over the country, with the names of hundreds of clubs and DJs filling the album cover inside and out.

RECOMMENDED SINGLES: **The Sylvers'** first release on Capitol, "Boogie Fever," a very jumpy song with an early **Jackson 5** sound and a cute production by **Freddie Perren**, who did the latest **Miracles** album; **Ralph De Blanc's** "Oh No Not My Baby" (Arista) – best parts: the intro and the end; **Dionne Warwicke's** excellent **Thom Bell** production, "Once You Hit the Road" (Warner Bros.), an overly familiar sound perhaps, but a supremely comfortable, attractive one; "The Soul City Walk," another wonderfully up song from **Archie Bell & the Drells**, reportedly already very hot in L.A. (on TSOP); "Inside America," a two-part, mostly-instrumental oddity by **Juggy Murray Jones** (Jupiter) that includes snatches of all sorts of American music in a complex, fascinating disco setting – my west coast correspondent, Kenn Friedman, suggests a new category: "Bicentennial Disco;" another unusual record,

> **❝ The original French version, "J'ai Le Gout De Baiser" (which is too raunchy for translation in a respectable American trade paper). ❞**

12 WEST, NEW YORK
DJ: Tom Savarese

BABY FACE – Wing & A Prayer Fife & Drum Corps (Wing & A Prayer)
DANCE WITH ME – Ritchie Family (20th Century)
EL CARAVANERO – Chocolat's (Aquarius import)
ELUSIVE – Babe Ruth (Capitol)
I AM SOMEBODY – Jimmy James & the Vagabonds (Pye)
IF IT WASN'T FOR THE MONEY/J'AI LE GOUT DE BAISER – Nanette Workman (Atco/ Pacha)
THE LADY BUMPS ON/LADY BUMP – Penny Mclean (Columbia import)
NEVER GONNA LET YOU GO – Vicki Sue Robinson (RCA)
RED BULLET – Performance (Polydor import)
THERE'LL COME A TIME, THERE'LL COME A DAY – Basic Black & Pearl (Polydor)

LE COCU, NEW YORK
DJ: Edmund Timothy (Juba)

BABY FACE – Wing & A Prayer Fife & Drum Corps (Wing & A Prayer)
EVERY BEAT OF MY HEART/I AM ME – Crown Heights Affair (De-Lite)
PEANUT VENDOR/BRAZIL – Ritchie Family (20th Century)
I LOVE MUSIC – O'Jays (Phila. Intl.)
JOYCE – Papa John Creach (Buddah)
LOVE TO LOVE YOU BABY – Donna Summer (Oasis)
NOWHERE – Hokis Pokis (Black Magic)
SUNNY – Yamba (Montuno)
YOU'RE JUST THE RIGHT SIZE/CHICAGO BUS STOP – Salsoul Orchestra (Salsoul)
VOLARE – Al Martino (Capitol)

HADAAR, STATEN ISLAND, N. Y.
DJ: Richie Conte

CASANOVA BROWN/HOW HIGH THE MOON – Gloria Gaynor (MGM)
CHICAGO BUS STOP/YOU'RE JUST THE RIGHT SIZE/SALSOUL RAINBOW – Salsoul Orchestra (Salsoul)
EVERY BEAT OF MY HEART – Crown Heights Affair (De-Lite)
I LOVE MUSIC – O'Jays (Phila. Intl.)
KEEP YOUR EYE ON THE SPARROW – Merry Clayton (Ode)
LOVE TO LOVE YOU BABY – Donna Summer (Oasis)
NOBODY LOVES ME LIKE YOU DO – Jeanne Burton (Cotton)
OUR DAY WILL COME – Frankie Valli (Private Stock)
SUNNY – Yambu (Montuno)
THAT'S THE WAY (I LIKE IT) – KC & the Sunshine Band (TK)

REVELATION II, BROOKLYN, N. Y.
DJ: Bacho Mangual

BABY FACE – Wing & A Prayer Fife & Drum Corps (Wing & A Prayer)
CHICAGO BUS STOP/SALSOUL RAINBOW – Salsoul Orchestra (Salsoul)
DRIVE MY CAR – Gary Toms Empire (PIP)
I LOVE MUSIC – O'Jays (Phila. Intl.)
LADY BUMP – Penny McLean (Columbia import)
OUR DAY WILL COME – Frankie Valli (Private Stock)
SHAKE ME, WAKE ME – Barbra Streisand (Columbia)
SHE'S THE IDEAL GIRL/ERUCU – "Mahogany" Soundtrack (Motown)
SUMMER PLACE '76 – Percy Faith (Columbia)
YOU & ME (GOT A GOOD THING GOING) – Margie Joseph & Blue Magic (Atco)

"You Got Me In A Whirlpool" by **Geno Washington** (Atac Internationai), interesting primarily for its instrumental side (3:16); "Funky Weekend," the nicest thing from the **Stylistics** in some time (Avco); "Sing A Song," the usual optimistic bounce from **Earth, Wind & Fire** but more than usually irresistible (Columbia).

LEFT FIELD: **Exuma's** "Africa" (Inagua), typical of the man's eccentric brand of Afro-American funk and perhaps for hard-core Exuma fans only, but worth a listen; another eccentric record, by **Cy Coleman**, called "Chloe" (RCA), started out in a strange Brazilian-tinged disco sound and ends up with some tinkly piano solo work – almost as crazy as **George Fischoff's** "King Kingston;" "Evil Woman," an interesting disco-rock number by the **Electric Light Orchestra** (UA) with some characteristically bizarre production touches; and **Rozella Johnson's** odd blend of funk and sweet soul in "(I Like Making That) Early Morning Love," which has something of a Miami sound (Columbia). ✪

DISCO FILE TOP 20

1. **LOVE TO LOVE YOU BABY** – Donna Summer (Oasis)
2. **EVERY BEAT OF MY HEART** – Crown Heights Affair (De-Lite)
3. **SUNNY** – Yambu (Montuno)
4. **I LOVE MUSIC** – O'Jays (Phila. Intl.)
5. **CASANOVA BROWN/HOW HIGH THE MOON** – Gloria Gaynor (MGM)
6. **PEANUT VENDOR** – Ritchie Family (20th Century)
7. **NOWHERE** – Hokis Pokis (Black Magic)
8. **BABY FACE** – Wing & A PrayerFife & Drum Corps (Wing And A Prayer)
9. **FRENESI** – Ritchie Family (20th Century)
10. **OUR DAY WILL COME** – Frankie Valli (Private Stock)
11. **ANYTHING GOES** – Ron Carter (Kudu)
12. **CARAVAN/WATUSI STRUT** – Deodato (MCA)
13. **BRAZIL** – The Ritchie Family (Avco)
14. **FLY, ROBIN, FLY** – Silver Convention (Midland Intl.)
15. **I AM SOMEBODY** – Jimmy James & the Vagabonds (Pye)
16. **YOU SET MY HEART ON FIRE/FIRE** – Tina Charles (Columbia)
17. **SALSOUL RAINBOW/CHICAGO BUS STOP/ YOU'RE JUST THE RIGHT SIZE** – Salsoul Orchestra (Salsoul)
18. **ELUSIVE** – Babe Ruth (Capitol)
19. **CHANGE WITH THE TIMES** – Van McCoy (Avco)
20. **EXODUS** – Biddu Orchestra (Epic import)

Most talked-about, sought-after new album: "Kickin'" by the **Mighty Clouds of Joy**, the group's first in the year and a half since producer **Dave Crawford** gave them a spectacular Philadelphia makeover with "It's Time." A few advance copies of "Kickin'," also produced by Crawford but in Atlanta this time (with special appearances by Philly musicians like **Earl Young** and **Larry Washington**), were leaked out of ABC last week and have been exploding like unexpected bombs in various clubs in the city ever since. Most explosive cut: the album's opener, "Mighty High" (4:43), high-powered gospel shouting with a churning, driving production; a celebration. "Everything Is Love" is set in a more relaxed tempo but the instrumental break is so strong and inventive that it could prove to be as popular as "Mighty High" in time. Also notable: a medley of "I Got The Music In Me" and "Superstition," an unlikely but interesting combination. "Kickin'" should be out this week on ABC and should be picked up immediately.

Other essential albums: Two new Philadelphia International releases, one of **O'Jays'** "Family Reunion," more solid than "Survival," and, already, another from **MFSB**, titled "Philadelphia Freedom" and highlighted by a fine interpretation of that **Elton John** tribute that ends with a chorus swooning, "Philadelphia, I love you." The O'Jays lp contains, of course, their smash success "I Love Music" (6:51); "Unity," the opening statement and its most forceful cut; and a lively "Livin' for the Weekend" featuring a super-hot core segment framed between two laid-back portions that function like Friday afternoon and Sunday night, buffering the raucous jump of the weekend in the center – total 6:29. Cuts to watch on the MFSB album: "Brothers and Sisters," the most danceable; "Get Down with the Philly Sound;" "The Zip," already a single (and a Polaroid commercial); and a version of **War's** "Smile Happy." **Stephanie Mills'** first album for Motown, produced by **Burt Bacharach** and **Hal David** and containing her fine re-make of **Dionne Warwicke's** "This Empty Place," is out now; the title: "For The First Time."

FEEDBACK: The instant-excitement import this week is the **Biddu Orchestra's** new British single, "I Could Have Danced All Night," a re-make of that standard, with a fabulous "Jump for Joy" which lives up to its title on the other side (Epic import). Desi, now playing at The Alley in Queens and one of the key people to introduce Biddu's imports to New York DJs, brought a copy by the office and put it on his top 10 list this week (it also popped on Bobby Guttadaro's list from the new, immediately popular Infinity in New York). Another import on Desi's list that's new to us is "Ha-Ri-Ah," an

GALAXY 21, NEW YORK
DJ: Walter Gibbons

BABY FACE – Wing & A Prayer Fife & Drum Corps (Wing & A Prayer)
CHICAGO BUS STOP/SALSOUL RAINBOW – Salsoul Orchestra (Salsoul)
DO THE BUS STOP – Fatback Band (Event)
FIND MY WAY – Cameo (Chocolate City)
FLIGHT – David Sanborn (Warner Bros.)
GET YA SOME – Melvin Sparks (Westbound)
I LOVE MUSIC – O'Jays (Phila. Intl.)
THE LADY BUMPS ON/LADY BUMP – Penny Mclean (Jupiter)
LOVE MACHINE/AIN'T NOBODY STRAIGHT IN LA – Miracles (Tamla)
SHE'S THE IDEAL GIRL/ERUCU – "Mahogany" ST (Motown)

CHARLES GALLERY, NEW YORK
DJ: Louis "Angelo" Alers

BABY FACE – Wing & A Prayer Fife & Drum Corps (Wing & A Prayer)
CHICAGO BUS STOP/TANGERINE/ YOU'RE JUST THE RIGHT SIZE – Salsoul Orchestra (Salsoul)
ELUSIVE – Babe Ruth (Capitol)
EVERY BEAT OF MY HEART/DREAMING A DREAM – Crown Heights Affair (De-Lite)
FREE MAN/TRAIN CALLED FREEDOM – South Shore Commission (Wand)
I LOVE MUSIC – O'Jays (Phila. Intl.)
LITTLE DRUMMER BOY – Moonlion (PIP)
NOWHERE – Hokis Pokis (Black Magic)
PEANUT VENDOR/FRENESI/BRAZIL – Ritchie Family (20th Century)
PICA PICA/EL BOCHINCHE – Cortijo (Coco)

INFINITY, NEW YORK
DJ: Bobby Guttadaro

BABY FACE – Wing & A Prayer Fife & Drum Corps (Wing & A Prayer)
CHLOE – Cy Coleman (RCA)
EVERY BEAT OF MY HEART – Crown Heights Affair (De-Lite)
I AM SOMEBODY – Jimmy James & the Vagabonds (Pye)
I LOVE MUSIC – O'Jays (Phila. Intl.)
JUMP FOR JOY/I COULD HAVE DANCED ALL NIGHT – Biddu Orchestra (Epic import)
THE LADY BUMPS ON/LADY BUMP – Penny Mclean (Jupiter import)
LOVE TO LOVE YOU BABY – Donna Summer (Oasis)
SUNNY-Yambu-Montuno
THIS EMPTY PLACE – Stephanie Mills (Motown)

THE ALLEY, NEW YORK (QUEENS)
DJ: Desi

BABY FACE – Wing & A Prayer Fife & Drum Corps (Wing & A Prayer)
YOU'RE JUST THE RIGHT SIZE – Salsoul Orchestra (Salsoul)
EL CARAVANERO – Chocolate Boys (Aquarius import)
HA-RI-AH – Son of Albatross (Decca import)
I AM SOMEBODY – Jimmy James & the Vagabonds (Pye)
JUMP FOR JOY – Biddu Orchestra (Epic import)
JOYCE – Papa John Creach (Buddah lp cut)
THE LADY BUMPS ON – Penny Mclean (Columbia)
NOWHERE – Hokis Pokis (Black Magic)
BRAZIL/DANCE WITH WE – Ritchie Family (20th Century)

Italian record by a group called **Son of Albatross** (Decca) with a great African chant sound that could become very popular too... **Penny McLean's** "Lady Bump/The Lady Bumps On" (available on both the Jupiter and Columbia labels, depending on the country of origin) is shaping up as the most played import right now, probably because it picks up the **Silver Convention** sound everyone's still hot for (McLean is SC's lead singer and the group back her up here). American release is scheduled by Atlantic soon... Walter Gibbons, back at Galaxy 21, lists an advance copy of the first release on Casablanca's new Chocolate City label: "Find My Way" by a group now called **Cameo** (their original name, the Players, was changed so as not to conflict with the group currently riding the "Love Rollercoaster") – very **Crown Heights Affair** but that's one of the better things you can say about a record these days – and it grows on you. Out this week... "Nowhere" by **Hokis Pokis** has been picked up by TK for the people who haven't been able to find this particular record outside of a few New York stores. It'll be out on TK's Shield label within the week... Hottest new single: "Inside America Part 1" by **Juggy Murray Jones** (Jupiter), reviewed here last week and spreading like wildfire on the DJ grapevine. One of the most surprising and invigorating instrumentals this year. ✍

"A few copies of "Kickin'" by the Mighty Clouds Of Joy leaked out and have been exploding like unexpected bombs in various clubs in the city ever since"

You're Just the Right Size: The 12-inch disc "for disco DJs only" has been established during the past year as the prime promotional device for drawing attention to new disco releases, and the number of white-sleeved records arriving in the mail seems to increase each week. The original idea behind the 12-inch was to provide a quality pressing of a single long cut, sometimes in advance of its commercial release, sometimes substantially longer than the track that was commercially available, but often just a track that the company felt (and hoped) was deserving of special attention and better reproduction than it could get as a regular lp cut or on a 45 pressing. As 12-inch releases have grown in popularity, they've become on the one hand, mere promo gimmicks (what's the use of a 12-inch pressing of an already-released single that runs under four minutes?) and, on the other, something of an art form in themselves. Atlantic, which leads the "disco disc" field in quality, design and choice of material, has one of the year's most successful records in this format with "Baby Face" by **The Wing and a Prayer Fife and Drum Corps**, expanded to a delirious 6:38 and packed with ear-catching production tricks that turn it into more than just a doubled-up version of the single. Scepter's 12-inch of the **Chequers** "Undecided Love" is another example of a record that was creatively re-worked for disco play and much of its success on a disco level can be traced directly to the quality of the long pressing.

Among the new batch of 12-inch records are a few that make fine use of the format, most especially the RCA re-mix of **Henry Mancini's** "African Symphony." The cut, from his album "Symphonic Soul," has been expanded to 4:35 and given a whole new spark with brightened and lengthened kalimba breaks and a heightened drum track that cuts the bombast of the lp version. Altogether an excellent re-working that should immediately increase its disco play. "Joyce," the **Papa John Creach** instrumental that has been getting a good response from his recent Buddah album, has also been revised on a 12-inch, Buddah's first. The new length is 5:37, giving the record a fuller beginning before Creach enters with his violin, and· the pace has been cut somewhat because the original was too racy. for most dancers. Among the other 12-inch releases this week: "Ooh What A Night" by **Linda Thompson**, who has apparently secured the right to be called the lead singer of **Silver Convention** (our apologies for referring to **Penny McLean** as the lead last week; McLean is in the chorus). The sound here is yet another extension of the Silver Convention sound, a little more forceful and vocally-oriented than their album and the change can be unsettling at first, but this one grows on you (length: 4:38; label: Midland International). Following the tremendous interest in the album cut, Pye has released **Jimmy James and the Vagabonds'** powerful "I Am Somebody" on a large disc, same length as the lp version, hoping to push it even further. Coming up: An Atlantic disco disc of "Lady Bump" (now, by the way, available as an Atco single) disco-mixed by Anita Wexler to blend "Lady Bump" and "The Lady Bumps On" into one 5:27 track; 'and a new one from **Ralph Carter** called "Extra Extra (Read All About It)" on a Mercury 12-inch (their first, too) running 5:15. Both should be out this week.

RECOMMENDED ALBUM CUTS: A fabulous synthesizer version of "Shaft" included in a quadraphonic test album called "Vector 4" (Ovation) and designed to demonstrate quadraphonic systems but fascinating enough to revive the record in some clubs, especially those with the best sound systems; "Union Man" from' the **Cate Bros.** album (Asylum), produced by Stax star **Steve Cropper** and with the same kind of non-formula spunk and drive that made **Rockin' Horse's** "Love Do Me Right" so big (also check out: "I just Wanna Sing"); "Track Of The Cat," the title cut from the beautifully realized new **Dionne Warwick** album (Warner Bros.),

> **❝ The 12-inch disc "for Disco DJs only" has been established as the prime promotional device for drawing attention to new disco releases, often a track deserving of special attention and better reproduction ❞**

FIFTEEN LANSDOWNE STREET, BOSTON
DJ: Danae Jocovidis

BABY FACE – Wing & A Prayer Fife & Drum Corps (Wing & A Prayer)
BRAZILIA CARNIVAL/EL CARAVANERO – Chocolate Boys (Aquarius import)
BROTHERS AND SISTERS – MFSB (Philadelphia Intl.)
CASANOVA BROWN/DO IT YOURSELF/ HOW HIGH THE MOON – Gloria Gaynor (MGM)
CHICANO – Black Blood (Mainstream)
I LOVE MUSIC – O'Jays (Phila. Intl.)
THE LADY BUMPS ON – Penny McLean (Columbia)
NOWHERE – Hokis Pokis (Black Magic)
SUNNY – Yambu (Montuno)
TANGERINE/YOU'RE JUST THE RIGHT SIZE/SALSOUL RAINBOW – Salsoul Orchestra (Salsoul)

CHASE, NEW YORK
DJ: Joye Madonia

CHICANO – Black Blood (Mainstream)
CHLOE – Cy Coleman (RCA)
DO IT WITH FEELING – Michael Zager & Moon Band (Bang)
ELUSIVE – Babe Ruth (Capitol)
ERUCU/SHE'S THE IDEAL GIRL – "Mahogany" Soundtrack (Motown)
I LOVE MUSIC – O'Jays (Phila. Intl)
LADY BUMP/THE LADY BUMPS ON – Penny Mclean (Columbia import)
LITTLE DRUMMER BOY – Moonlion (PIP)
SUNNY – Yambu (Montuno)
TANGERINE/SALSOUL RAINBOW /YOU'RE JUST THE RIGHT SIZE – Salsoul Orchestra (Salsoul)

THE CITY, SAN FRANCISCO
DJ: Rick Chace

CASANOVA BROWN/DO IT YOURSELF – Gloria Gaynor (MGM)
CHANGE WITH THE TIMES – Van McCoy (Avco)
DO IT ANY WAY YOU WANNA – People's Choice (TSOP)
DREAMING A DREAM – Crown Heights Affair (De-Lite)
DRIVE MY CAR – Gary Toms Empire (PIP)
FLY, ROBIN, FLY – Silver Convention (Midland Intl.)
HOLLYWOOD HOT – Eleventh Hour (20th Century)
IT ONLY TAKES A MINUTE – Tavares (Capitol)
MESSIN' WITH MY MIND – LaBelle (Epic)
THAT'S THE WAY (I LIKE IT) – KC & the Sunshine Band (TK)

WASHINGTON SQ, WASHINGTON, D.C.
DJ: Mitch Schatsky

BABY FACE – Wing & A Prayer Fife & Drum Corps (Wing & A Prayer)
DISCO SAX – Houston Person (Westbound)
DRIVE MY CAR – Gary Toms Empire (PIP)
I LOVE MUSIC – O'Jays (Phila. Intl.)
LADY BUMP/THE LADY BUMPS ON – Penny McLean (Columbia import)
LOVE TO LOVE YOU BABY – Donna Summer (Oasis)
ONE FINE DAY – Julie (Tom Cat)
SOUL CITY WALK – Archie Bell & the Drells (TSOP)
STAR TREK – Charles Randolph Green Sounde (Ranwood)
TANGERINE/SALSOUL RAINBOW/GET HAPPY – Salsoul Orchestra (Salsoul)

produced by **Thom Bell** very much in the style of his album with **Johnny Mathis** some time back – "Track" is this album's equivalent of "Life Is A Song Worth Singing," slow and sensuous; "Tell The World How I Feel About 'Cha Baby," the one cut that comes close to the feeling of "Bad Luck" on the new **Harold Melvin & the Bluenotes** album ("Wake Up Everybody" on Philadelphia International), full of tempo changes, perhaps one too many, but really involving in the end – and one of the prettiest songs in some time, **Sharon Paige's** solo track, "I'm Searching For A Love," a chance to further enjoy the voice that graced "Hope That We Can Get Together Soon" and joins the group again for another sexy, sophisticated love song we're bound to be hearing a lot of, "You Know How to Make Me Feel So Good" (5:17); and from the new **Four Seasons** album, titled "Who Loves You" (Warner Bros.) and containing a 4:22 version of that hit single (why not the full 5:28 "disco version" from the 45?). These other tracks for those who enjoyed the rapid changes of the title cut and lean toward disco-rock: "December 1963 (Oh What a Night)" and "Emily's (Salle de Danse)" (6:40)-produced and written by **Bob Gaudio** with **Frankie Valli** as one of the vocalists.

NEWS & FEEDBACK: Two of the DJs reporting this week are at brand new clubs – Rick Chace at The City in San Francisco (where he says the **Masqueraders'** "Everybody Wanna Live On" was one of the most successful records of the opening week) and Danae jacovidis at Fifteen Lansdowne Street in Boston, opened by John Addison of New York's Le Jardin (some of Danae's picks: "Chloe" by **Cy Coleman**, **Cameo's** "Find My 'Way'" and **Streisand's** "Shake Me, Wake Me")... On Mitch Schatsky's list from Washington Square in Washington, DC: a disco version of the theme from "Star Trek," quite overwrought but, he says doing very well – by the **Charles Randolph Green Sounde** on Ranwood... **Yambu's** smash version of "Sunny" has been picked up for national distribution by PIP Records and its label changed from Montuno to Montuno Gringo... Watch for the new album by **Archie Bell & The Drells** on TSOP. It will be one of the major disco albums of the year, with a cut called "Let's Groove" leading a long list of recommended tracks. Due out this week, with half of the New York contingent of DJs practically camped out on Columbia Records' doorstep waiting for its arrival.

RECOMMENDED SINGLES: Two very hot instrumentals, "The First Shot" by **Phase II** (Osiris) and **Redd Holt Unlimited's** "Gimme Some Mo" (Paula), both worth looking for; another version of "Theme From 'A Summer Place,'" this one by the **Jon-Wite Group** (Cenpro), running 3:39 and rather inventive in spots; and a re-mixed (why?) version of **Martha Velez'** terrific "Aggravation" (Sire), a track from her 1973 album that has been picked up and never put away by a number of disco DJs – the length of 3:04 won't satisfy those who are after the album cut of more than five minutes, however. ◆

This week brings the final batch of albums in Philadelphia International's overwhelming pre-Christmas release. It's been years since, the last **Archie Bell & The Drells** album, but "Dance Your Troubles Away" (TSOP) is a spectacular return, highlighted by a six-minute opener called "Let's Groove," written and produced by the Whitehead/McFadden/Carstarphen team (the trio who wrote "Bad Luck") and sure to be one of the most pervasive records of the next couple of months. Here and throughout the album, Archie Bell flashes between the classic "Tighten Up" sound ("Hi everybody, this is Archie Bell and these are the Drells – "the sort of stuff that once prompted me to write that I'd rather listen to this group than **Otis Redding**) and a variant on the **O'Jays** sound, with Bell approaching the intensity and spunk of **Eddie Levert** on the up cuts. Also included: a lyric version of "Let's Go Disco" that nearly redeems that cut from the **MFSB** "Universal Love" album (and is the only track actually produced by Gamble & Huff); "I Could Dance All Night" and "The Soul City Walk," the previous single releases; and the title cut, "Dance Your Troubles Away," at 6:21 the album's longest and another knockout. As Archie once said, "Lemme put this hamburger down. I don't want to malt – I wanna dance." Tighten Up '75.

More cause for celebration: the return of **Dee Dee Sharp**, once the "Mashed Potatoes" girl, now Mrs. Kenneth Gamble and off the record since 1967. But she's back with one of Philadelphia's most glorious productions, the title track from her comeback album, "Happy 'Bout The Whole Thing" (TSOP), which reminds me of **Jackie Moore's** "Clean Up Your Own Yard," one of the sharpest, most offbeat disco records of the past few years. Dee Dee's vocals are stunning and **Bobby Martin's** decidedly non-formula production is his best in some time – a strong contender for album cut of the month. Equally refreshing: "Share My Love."

And **Billy Paul**, who disco people had almost given up on, has some surprises on his latest release, "When Love Is New" (Philadelphia International): a trio of three solid message songs-"People Power," "America (We Need the Light)," the first bicentennial song that can be taken seriously, and "Let The Dollar Circulate" – all quite danceable though possibly not to everyone's taste ("People Power" is the first choice); plus a delightful "Let's Make A Baby" (7:11), the ultimate heterosexual love song and a real sweet hustle. This is Paul's best album, the most substantial of his career so far – produced by Gamble & Huff.

ff Everybody's talking about the latest issue of NADD's Melting Pot with its stinging "poem" to Infinity, the magazine's strongest feature to date. **JJ**

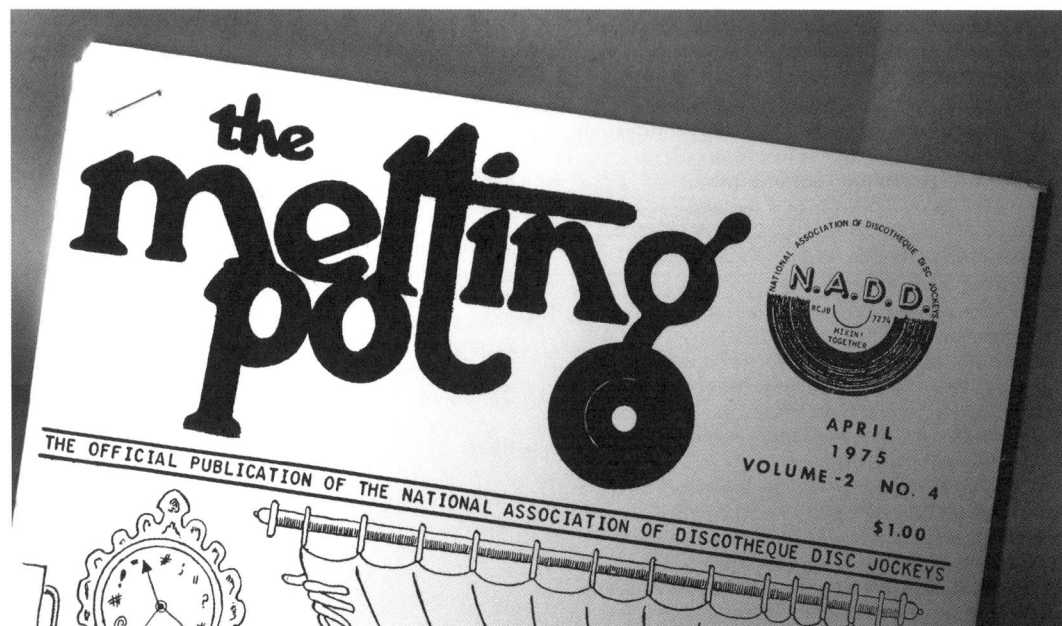

DCA CLUB, PHILADELPHIA
DJ: Kurt Borusiewicz:

BABY FACE – Wing & A Prayer Fife & Drum Corps (Wing & A Prayer)
CHICAGO BUS STOP /SALSOUL RAINBOW/TANGERINE – Salsoul Orchestra (Salsoul)
CHICANO – Black Blood (Mainstream)
I AM SOMEBODY – Jimmy James & the Vagabonds (Pye)
I LOVE MUSIC – O'Jays (Phila. Intl.)
LADY BUMP/THE LADY BUMPS ON – Penny Mclean (Atco)
MONDO DISCO – El Coco (AVI)
OH NO NOT MY BABY – De Blanc (Arista)
SUNNY – Yambu (Montuno)

CORK & BOTTLE, NEW YORK
DJ: Ed Rivera

BABY FACE – Wing & A Prayer Fife & Drum Corps (Wing & A Prayer disco version)
CHICAGO BUS STOP/YOU'RE JUST THE RIGHT SIZE – Salsoul Orchestra (Salsoul)
DO IT YOURSELF – Gloria Gaynor (MGM)
EVERY BEAT OF MY HEART – Crown Heights Affair (De-Lite)
I LOVE MUSIC – O'Jays (Phila. Intl.)
LET'S DO THE LATIN HUSTLE – Eddie Drennon & BBS Unltd. (Friends & Co.)
SOUL TRAIN '75 – Soul Train Gang (Soul Train)
SUNNY – Yambu (Montuno)
UNDECIDED LOVE – Chequers (Scepter)
VOLARE – Al Martino (Capitol)

BAREFOOT BOY, NEW YORK
DJ: Tony Smith

AFRICAN SYMPHONY – Henry Mancini (RCA)
CHICAGO BUS STOP/SALSOUL RAINBOW – Salsoul Orchestra (Salsoul)
FIND MY WAY – Cameo (Chocolate City)
FLIGHT – David Sanborn (Warner Bros.)
I LOVE MUSIC – O'Jays (Phila. Intl.)
INSIDE AMERICA – Juggy Murray Jones (Jupiter)
JUMP FOR JOY – Biddu Orchestra (Epic import)
LADY BUMP/THE LADY BUMPS ON – Penny Mclean (Atco)
MIGHTY HIGH/EVERYTHING IS LOVE – Mighty Clouds of Joy (ABC)
THAT OLD BLACK MAGIC – Softones (Avco)

RUMBOTTOMS, HOLLYWOOD, FLORIDA
DJ: Bob Lombardi

BABY FACE – Wing & A Prayer Fife & Drum Corps (Wing & A Prayer)
CASANOVA BROWN/DO IT YOURSELF/HOW HIGH THE MOON – Gloria Gaynor (MGM)
DANCE WITH ME – Ritchie Family (20th Century)
EVERY BEAT OF MY HEART – Crown Heights Affair (De-Lite)
I LOVE MUSIC – O'Jays (Phila. Intl.)
LADY BUMP/THE LADY BUMPS ON – Penny Mclean (Atco)
LET'S DO THE LATIN HUSTLE – Eddie Drennon & BBS Unltd. (Friends & Co.)
MIGHTY HIGH – Mighty Clouds of Joy (ABC)
ONE FINE DAY – Julie (Tom Cat)
SUNNY/SUNNY '76 – Yambu/Bobby Hebb (Montuno /Laurie)

MEDIA: Our favorite disco newsletter is the bi-monthly Mixmaster, because it's the only one with both style and gossip (where else can you read; "Richie Kaczor is not just another dreamy DJ," and find out that Ronald Coles was seen diamond-shopping in Cartier's?). Mixmaster was also the first to alert us to **Cameo's** "Find My Way;" the November 15 issue includes a luscious impression of **Chaka Khan's** lips and a picture of the Undecided Love of the Month. Mixmaster is available from Michael Gomes, 222 West 23rd Street, New York 10011 at one dollar a month... The Winter issue of Gentlemen's Quarterly has a double spread called "Disco to Go," featuring New York's own Bobby DJ (now at Infinity) giving advice and tips on disco tapes and blends... Everybody's talking about the latest issue of NADD's Melting Pot with its stinging "poem" to Infinity, the magazine's strongest feature to date.

FEEDBACK: Very strong response to the **Softones'** remake of the classic **Johnny Mercer-Harold Arlen** song, "That Old Black Magic," which has a **Ritchie Family** feel here (Avco). Kurt Borusiewicz from the private DCA Club in Philadelphia says it's one of the biggest records in his club in its first week out and Tony Smith put it on his top ten this week from Barefoot Boy in New York... Also drawing uniformly good comments: **Julie Budd's** revival of the **Chiffons'** oldie, "One Fine Day" (Tom Cat).

RECOMMENDED SINGLES: **Stan Watson's** first production for Warner Brothers, "Thank You Baby For Loving Me" by **The Quickest Way Out**, a terrific, classic disco sound with a 5:38 version available; "My Love Supreme" by **Milton Hamilton Crystalized** (TR), a "Sunny"-style instrumental with vocal touches by the man who arranged the **Yambu** hit (I picked this one up at the Record Pool where special pressings were being test marketed with the member DJs – the response has reportedly been so strong that TR is releasing the single commercially this week); the "disco version" of **Mary-Ann Farra and Satin Soul's** "Never Gonna Leave You" (5:35 on Brunswick) with some very cute vocals and a sound much like "Sugar Pie Guy;" and the latest in the "Do It Any Way You Wanna" – "Do It With Feeling" progression, the new one from the **Rimshots**, "Do What You Feel" (Stang), a fine, largely instrumental record that could have the same impact as the **People's Choice** and **Moon Band** records. ◉

DECEMBER 13, 1975

An exceptionally dull week for new releases (we kept ourselves satisfied with last week's records, especially Dee Dee Sharp's, which gets better all the time), so we have some space up front here for a much more diverting subject: the **MFSB** concert this past weekend at Madison Square Garden's Felt Forum. Philadelphia's magnificent Big Band, conducted by **Bobby Martin**, filled the stage-row upon row of strings (led by **Don Renaldo**), three tiers of brass (sparked-by hulking sax man **Zach Zachery**) and, in the front line, guitarists **Norman Harris** and **Bobby Eli**. Hearing that luscious, full MFSB sound live – even in Felt Forum, which is hardly acoustic heaven – was merely great until they dipped into their classic "Love Is The Message" and the whole audience swooned in delight. They swept through the song, delivering one rush after the other until, they reached the central break and Martin led the string section into a light classical diversion that had everyone tingling with anticipation, waiting for the break to be closed. When it was, with a sudden orchestral swoop, the back row of horns standing all at once, the Forum exploded in screams that lasted for a minute or two and I nearly fell backward in my seat, my greatest expectations having been met and surpassed. When "Love Is The Message" was finished, there was a long and loud standing ovation, the peak of the evening. The addition of young black dancers on several of the numbers that followed was an unnecessary distraction from the music but, happily, they cleared the stage for a strong medley that ran from "Bad Luck" to "For The Love Of Money" to "Backstabbers" to "When Will I See You Again" to " I Love Music" that was superb. The medley was repeated as an encore while nervous promoters stood at the side of the stage pointing to their watches and being very uncool. The band ignored them and the audience loved them for it. Why doesn't someone put MFSB into Carnegie Hall or Philharmonic Hall where they belong? And maybe even throw the O'Jays in to make it really irresistible? Philadelphia, I love you.

CORRECTION: Last week's Disco File Top 20 listed the **Salsoul Orchestra's** "Salsoul Rainbow" at number 5, but the typesetter left off two other album cuts in the same slot "You're Just The Right Size" and "Chicago Bus Stop." As you can see above in the Top 20, this trio has moved up one notch to the number 4. position. New chart entries include the **Mighty Clouds of Joy's** rousing "Mighty High," the **Softones'** fast-moving "That Old Black Magic" 'and "Jump for Joy"/"I Could Have Danced All Night" by the **Biddu Orchestra**, which was just released in this country by Epic.

NOTES: **Barbra Streisand's** powerful new version of "Shake Me, Wake Me" (Columbia) has been expanded from the 2:50 album length to a considerably more exciting 4:55, with a synthesizer adding depth and spice, filling in the new breaks. This longer version is due out this week as the flip side of the regular-length promotional single... Fania Records is throwing a party for the New York Record Pool this Tuesday, December 8, at the Pool, featuring one of their newer groups, **Bobby Rodriguez & Co.** Wait 'til they hear an advance pressing of a new **Louie Ramirez** instrumental cut, "Salsa"! Incredible.

RECOMMENDED: Albums: Organist **Johnny Hammond's** "Los Conquistadores Chocolates" (5:56) (from his new Milestone album, "Gears"), though it has a Spanish-spoken introduction and an undanceable ending, the core is one of the raciest, up, jazzy instrumentals since Deodato's "Caravan/Watusi Strut" – produced by **Larry** and **Fonce Mizell**, and as attractive as their recent work with **Bobbi Humphrey** and **Donald Byrd**; a longer (4:37) version of **Redd Holt Unlimited's** instrumental "Gimme Some Mo," on the album "The Other Side of the Moon" (Paula), which also included instrumental versions of "Do It Baby," "I Shot The Sheriff" and "Nothing from Nothing" and a very mellow side two; and a longer disco version of "Tonight's The Night" by Belgian group **S.S.O.** on their debut album of the same name (Shadybrook).

Singles: Beginning with two Motown remakes, one **Donny Beaumont's** very nice version of "This Old Heart of Mine" (4:58) (for an interesting comparison, listen to **Rod Stewart's** rendition of this same song, just out on a 45 from Warners), the other Retta Young's up-date of the **Mary Wells** classic "You Beat Me To The Punch" (All Platinum), which hardly comes up to the heights of the original but, slowed down some, is quite respectable; then two instrumentals, a sweet "Girl You Better Wake Up" by **Liberty** (BASF) with a kind of "Lady, Lady, Lady" feel and the six-minute instrumental version of the new **Originals** song, "Everybody's Got To Do Something" (Motown), which bumps along pleasantly enough. ◗

> **❝ Hearing that luscious, full MFSB sound live was merely great until they dipped into their classic "Love Is The Message" and the whole audience swooned in delight ❞**

BOOMBAMAKAOO, NEW YORK
DJ: Jorge Wheeler

AFRICAN SYMPHONY – Henry Mancini (RCA)
CHICAGO BUS STOP /TANGERINE/ YOU'RE JUST THE RIGHT SIZE – Salsoul Orchestra (Salsoul)
ELUSIVE – Babe Ruth (Capitol)
I LOVE MUSIC – O'Jays (Phila. Intl.)
INSIDE AMERICA – Juggy Murray Jones (Jupiter)
JOYCE – Papa John Creach (Buddah)
LADY BUMP/THE LADY BUMPS ON – Penny McLean (Atco)
LET'S GROOVE – Archie Bell & the Drells (TSOP)
MONDO DISCO – El Coco (AVI)
PAPAYA – Urszula Dudziak (Arista)

HIPPOPOTAMUS, NEW YORK
DJ: Rich Pampinella

BABY FACE – Wing & A Prayer Fife & Drum Corps (Wing & A Prayer)
CHICAGO BUS STOP /TANGERINE/ YOU'RE JUST THE RIGHT SIZE – Salsoul Orchestra (Salsoul)
ERUCU – "Mahogany" Soundtrack (Motown)
I AM SOMEBODY – Jimmy James & the Vagabonds (Pye)
I LOVE MUSIC – O'Jays (Phila. Intl.)
LADY BUMP/THE LADY BUMPS ON – Penny McLean (Atco)
LOVE TO LOVE YOU BABY – Donna Summer (Oasis)
(NOBODY LOVES ME) LIKE YOU DO – Jeanne Burton (Cotton)
SUNNY – Yambu (Montuno Gringo)
THAT OLD BLACK MAGIC – Softones (Avco)

1270, BOSTON
DJ: Jimmy Stuard

BABY FACE – Wing & A Prayer Fife & Drum Corps (Wing & A Prayer)
CASANOVA BROWN/HOW HIGH THE MOON – Gloria Gaynor (MGM)
I LOVE MUSIC – O'Jays (Phila. Intl.)
LADY BUMP/THE LADY BUMPS ON – Penny McLean (Atco)
LOVE TO LOVE YOU BABY – Donna Summer (Oasis)
MIGHTY HIGH – Mighty Clouds of Joy (ABC)
NOWHERE – Hokis Pokis (Shield)
SUNNY – Yambu (Montuno Gringo)
TANGERINE/SALSOUL RAINBOW – Salsoul Orchestra (Salsoul)
THAT OLD BLACK MAGIC – Softones (Avco)

OMEGA, NEW YORK
DJ: Robert Aquino

CARAVAN/WATUSI STRUT – Deodato (MCA)
CHICANO – Black Blood (Mainstream)
EVERY BEAT OF MY HEART – Crown Heights Affair (De-Lite)
I LOVE MUSIC – O'Jays (Phila. Intl.)
JUMP FOR JOY/I COULD HAVE DANCED ALL NIGHT – Biddu Orchestra (Epic)
LADY BUMP/THE LADY BUMPS ON – Penny McLean (Atco)
LOVE TO LOVE YOU BABY – Donna Summer (Oasis)
MIGHTY HIGH – Mighty Clouds of Joy (ABC)
THAT OLD BLACK MAGIC – Softones (Avco)
YOU'RE JUST THE RIGHT SIZE/SALSOUL RAINBOW/TALE OF THREE CITIES – Salsoul Orchestra (Salsoul)

DISCO FILE TOP 20

1. I LOVE MUSIC – O'Jays (Phila. Intl.)
2. LADY BUMP/THE LADY BUMPS ON – Penny McLean (Atco)
3. BABY FACE – Wing & A Prayer Fife & Drum Corps (Wing & A Prayer)
4. SALSOUL RAINBOW/YOU'RE JUST THE RIGHT SIZE/CHICAGO BUS STOP – Salsoul Orchestra (Salsoul)
5. SUNNY – Yambu (Montuno Gringo)
6. TANGERINE – Salsoul Orchestra (Salsoul)
7. EVERY BEAT OF MY HEART – Crown Heights Affair (De-Lite)
8. LOVE TO LOVE YOU BABY – Donna Summer (Oasis)
9. NOWHERE – Hokis Pokis (Shield)
10. I AM SOMEBODY – Jimmy James & the Vagabonds (Pye)
11. CASANOVA BROWN/HOW HIGH THE MOON – Gloria Gaynor (MGM)
12. CHICANO – Black Blood (Mainstream)
13. ELUSIVE – Babe Ruth (Capitol)
14. MIGHTY HIGH – Mighty Clouds of Joy (ABC)
15. THAT OLD BLACK MAGIC – Softones (Avco)
16. ERUCU – "Mahogany" Soundtrack (Motown)
17. JUMP FOR JOY/I COULD HAVE DANCED ALL NIGHT – Biddu Orchestra (Epic)
18. DANCE WITH ME – Ritchie Family (20th Century)
19. DRIVE MY CAR – Gary Toms Empire (PIP)
20. DREAMING A DREAM – Crown Heights Affair (De-Lite)

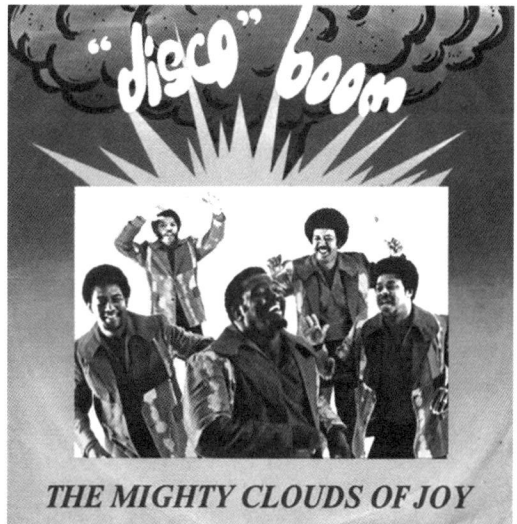

"disco" boom

THE MIGHTY CLOUDS OF JOY

DECEMBER 20, 1975

NEWS & NOTES: Patrick Jenkins, a writer and disco DJ in Los Angeles, called with news about a west coast blossoming of the Record Pool idea. The LA area group, calling itself the Southern California Disco DJs Association and already with "a little over 100 members, had two meetings in recent weeks and is now trying to decide on several alternative locations for a record distribution center. SCDDA's main difference in policy from New York's Pool is that it's collected $20 yearly dues from each member, giving them a tidy working sum for expenses. Jenkins reports the initial reaction of local record companies has been favorable, with Casablanca bringing **Donna Summer** to the group's founding meeting, but few commitments have been made as yet. Debbie Backus, DJ at the New York Experience private club and one of SCDDA's five-member central committee (along with Jenkins, AJ Miller, Jane Brinton and Jim Walters), says that most members are from the immediate LA area but some are travelling from as far away as Tijuana and two are planning to fly in every two weeks from New Zealand for new releases... Speaking of Donna Summer, her "Love To Love You Baby" album is reported to have gone "gold" and it's still just getting started at the radio level. Watch it turn platinum before too long.

Hot Blood's "Soul Dracula/Sans Dracula" has been released in this country after some success as a French import. It's on the Era label and already on Debbie Backus' list from the New York Experience, along with another Era release, yet another version of "Little Drummer," this one 4:20 in length and by **Clifton Ridgewood**... Ariola America has picked up the **Atlanta Disco Band's** instrumental, "Bad Luck," and even put it out on a 12-inch disc to get it into areas the original pressing didn't reach. An Atlanta Disco Band album, produced by **Dave Crawford** (who's done so well with the **Mighty Clouds of Joy**), is scheduled for release before the end of the year... Atlantic's latest disco disc is a longer version of the **Spinners'** wonderful "Love Or Leave," expanded by producer **Thom Bell** to 4:50 and given a whole new lease on life... **Reid Whitelaw**,

Ralph Carter's co-producer/ co-writer on the latest "Extra, Extra (Read All About It)," called to point out that the record's 5:15 disco version has been released as the B side of the commercial single on Mercury as well as on the previously mentioned (and now heartily recommended) 12-inch pressing... My favorite import in recent weeks has been **Crystal Grass'** double-sided single, "Lemme See Ya Gitchyer Thing Off Baby (Hustle)" and "Fio Maravilha/Taj Mahal" (on Philips from France). "Lemme See" is a rough, rousing vocal side and the reverse is a combination of two songs by

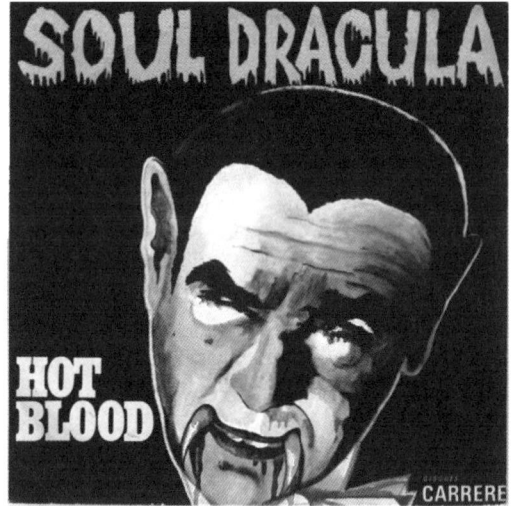

Brazilian singer **Jorge Ben**, an underground favorite who deserves an American release of his own. Oddly enough, Polydor, which had the American rights option on the record, passed it up so it may be some time before we see a U.S. release of this fine single.

Hamilton Bohannon's new album – "Bohannon" on Dakar – which should be in the stores this week, is, unfortunately, not new ground for this talented writer/arranger/producer/musician. The two most attractive cuts for the dance floor, "Bohannon's Beat (Part I)" (7:49 – and there is no Part II) and "The Bohannon Walk" (4:49), are very much in the pattern of "Disco Stomp" and "Foot Stompin' Music" from his previous album – the music isn't taken any deeper than before but it retains its unusual fascination. What is new on the album is the greater richness and delicacy of the slow mood numbers on the record's second side: three cuts ranging between six and nine minutes for this talented writer/arranger/producer/musician. The two most to relax to and luxuriate in the best of the

REVELATION III, BROOKLYN, N.Y.
DJ: Joel Sal

BABY FACE – Wing & A Prayer Fife & Drum Corps
(Wing & A Prayer)
**CHICAGO BUS STOP /SALSOUL RAINBOW/YOU'RE JUST
THE RIGHT SIZE** – Salsoul Orchestra (Salsoul)
EVERY BEAT OF MY HEART – Crown Heights Affair (De-Lite)
I AM SOMEBODY – Jimmy James & the Vagabonds (Pye)
I COULD HAVE DANCED All NIGHT/JUMP FOR JOY –
Biddu Orchestra (Epic)
I LOVE MUSIC/LIVING FOR THE WEEKEND – O'Jays
(Phila. Intl.)
LADY BUMP/THE LADY BUMPS ON – Penny McLean (Atco)
MY WAY – Bobby Azeff Orchestra (Aquarius Import)
NEVER GONNA LET YOU GO – Vicki Sue Robinson (RCA)
THAT OLD BLACK MAGIC – Softones (Avco)

DISCO 2001, LOS ANGELES
DJ: Wayne Thorberg

CAN'T TAKE MY EYES OFF YOU – Gerri Granger
(20th Century)
I FEEL A GROOVE COMIN' ON – Bobby Womack (UA)
I LOVE MUSIC – O'Jays (Phila. Intl.)
INSIDE AMERICA – Juggy Murray Jones (Jupiter)
KEEP HOLDING ON – Temptations (Gordy)
LET'S GROOVE – Archie Bell & the Drells (TSOP)
LOVE TO LOVE YOU BABY – Donna Summer (Oasis)
SING A SONG – Earth, Wind & Fire (Columbia)
SUNNY – Yambu (Montuno Gringo)
WALK AWAY FROM LOVE – David Ruffin (Motown)

NEW YORK EXPERIENCE, LOS ANGELES
DJ: Debbie Backus

BABY FACE – Wing & A Prayer Fife & Drum Corps
(Wing & A Prayer)
**CHICAGO BUS STOP/TANGERINE/YOU'RE JUST THE
RIGHT SIZE** – Salsoul Orchestra (Salsoul)
I LOVE MUSIC – O'Jays (Phila. Intl.)
LADY BUMP – Penny McLean (Atco)
LET'S DO THE LATIN HUSTLE – Eddie Drennon & BBS
Unltd. (Friends & Co.)
LITTLE DRUMMER BOY –Clifton Ridgewood (Era)
LOVE TO LOVE YOU BABY –Donna Summer (Oasis)
SING A SONG – Earth, Wind & Fire (Columbia)
SOUL DRACULA – Hot Blood (Era)
SUNNY – Yambu/Bobby Hebb (Montuno Gringo/Laurie)

READE STREET, NEW YORK
DJ: Larry Levan

AFRICAN SYMPHONY – Henry Mancini (RCA)
CHANGE (MAKES YOU WANT TO HUSTLE)
– Donald Byrd (Blue Note)
**CHICAGO BUS STOP/SALSOUL RAINBOW/YOU'RE JUST
THE RIGHT SIZE** – Salsoul Orchestra (Salsoul)
DANCE YOUR TROUBLES AWAY/LET'S GROOVE
– Archie Bell & the Drells (TSOP)
ELUSIVE – Babe Ruth (Capitol)
GIMME SOME MO – Red Holt Unlimited (Paula)
I LOVE MUSIC – O'Jays (Phila. Intl.)
INSIDE AMERICA – Juggy Murray Jones (Jupiter)
LADY BUMP – Penny McLean (Atco)
MIGHTY HIGH/EVERYTHING IS LOVE – Mighty Clouds
of Joy (ABC)

**❝News of a west
coast blossoming of the
Record Pool idea. The
Southern California
Disco DJs Association
has a little over 100
members❞**

new disco/mood music... And speaking of beautiful
mood music, I've neglected to mention the **Earth,
Wind & Fire** version of their **Ramsey Lewis**
collaboration, "Sun Goddess," which appears on their
two-record, mostly live set, "Gratitude" (Columbia). For
anyone who liked the original, this live rendition is not
to be missed, especially for the new horn parts.

BEST NEW SINGLE: **Jay & the Techniques** return after a
long absence with a **Jerry Ross** production called "You're
Number One-derful" (Event) that grabs you immediately.
The disco version runs 5:38 and is one of the most "
small-hole 45s into some New York clubs right now
with release plans for Christmas week. Listen for it.

OTHER RECOMMENDED SINGLES: **Ben E. King's**
latest, "We Got Love" (Atlantic), a **Norman Harris**
production (need I say more?) with a fine version of
Ashford/Simpson's "I Had a Love" on the other side;
Barry White's new one, "Let the Music Play" (20th
Century), which finds our hero in just about the same
place he was in the last episode, but it's hard not to fall
for him all over again (disco length: 4:30); a fine, if
decidedly left field, instrumental by a group called **Osiris**,
titled "Wallstreet" (Big Tree) and produced by **Silver
Convention's** man, **Michael Kunze**; "Wipe Your Feet
and Dance" by **Wee Willie and the Winners** (Mercury),
a hard, Afro-funk instrumental with chanting that sounds
better every time I put it on; **Van McCoy's** excellent
production for Bill Harris, "Am I Hot, Am I Cold" (RCA),
with a long version on one side of the single that runs
just over five minutes; **Poison's** "Get Up and Move Your
Body" (Roulette), which is a little too relentless and fast
but should appeal to **Kool & the Gang/ Ohio Players**
fans; and, finally, **Joe Simon's** very nice "I Need You, You Need
Me" (Spring), which I like better than his other recent
successful singles and is more consistently danceable, too.
Now out on 45s: **Henry Mancini's** "African Symphony,"
incorporating the additions made on the disco version
but cut to 3:10 (RCA), and **Revelation's** great "Just Too
Many People" (RSO). ◒

DECEMBER 27, 1975

Whew. It's been quite a year. If the concept of "disco music" was born for the masses in 1974, it grew up with astonishing precocity and virtually took over in 1975 if only because it was the only trend in sight. The music business stopped regarding Disco as some sort of freakish, tainted offspring of r&b and pop and took Disco out of the underground to see what sort of tricks it could turn at the top of the charts. Industry people are still wary of Disco – it refuses to be entirely respectable or definable, it still attracts a wonderfully raunchy crowd – but with **Frankie Valli**, **Barbra Streisand**, **Henry Mancini**, the **Bee Gees**, **Percy Faith** and **Al Martino** hurling themselves in the direction of the year's major musical move, it's enjoyed a grudging acceptance on most fronts. Radio, especially on the coasts, has welcomed Disco with growing enthusiasm, setting up disco hours, disco evenings, entire disco formats with the same sort of endless song blends they have in the clubs (and the resultant claims from club DJs that radio jocks were stopping by just to pick up new mixes for their next show). But the fears of some disco people that radio would co-opt the music, overdose the public and keep people out of the clubs have so far proven to be unfounded; radio play does tend to shorten the life of a record in the discos, but clubs still have a lead of two to four weeks on the average radio station and, so far at least, there's no such thing as a tight discotheque playlist.

kept Disco jumping was the surge of little label interest in the field. Because the disco market is wide open, small labels recognized it as an ideal breakout point and a prime jumping-off spot to radio. One of the year's great success stories was Wing & A Prayer's "Ease on Down the Road" by **Consumer Rapport** which had already reached monster proportions (without airplay) before Atlantic picked it up. Other labels had a more modest success – Monuno's "Sunny," Boogie Man's "Lady Lady Lady," Moving Up's "Somebody's Gotta Go," Black Magic's "Nowhere," Jupiter's "Inside America," among others – but in each case, discotheques provided the necessary spark to get things off the ground. And a glance at the lists of the year's essential albums and singles shows that Disco has also given a lively outlet for more established or newly-established independent labels: Midland International's **Silver Convention**, Salsoul's **Salsoul Orchestra** and Oasis/Casablanca's **Donna Summer** hold down the top three album spots.

The growing popularity of 12-inch "disco discs" for promotional purposes is another sign that Disco has had its effect on the record business. The DJs' demand for high quality, longer cuts has prompted companies to make special pressings just for this purpose – marked "for disco DJs only" – that allow discotheques a unique source of music all their own and often act as showcases for some very special studio artistry. (A list of 25

> ** In 1975 the music business stopped regarding Disco as some sort of freakish, tainted offspring of r&b and pop and took Disco out of the underground to see what sort of tricks it could turn at the top of the charts **

In spite of the fact that Disco's success as a commercial style had led to an increasing number of awful readymade "disco" records (the most imitated this year: DCA's terrific hard-edged productions for **Gloria Gaynor**), the music remains unpredictable and vital. The success of **Silver Convention's** ecstatic "Fly, Robin, Fly" could not have come a year or two ago – before the pre-conditioning of **Barry White**, **George McCrae**, **MFSB** and **Bohannon** – and more than any other song this year, it's an indication that the style and spirit of Disco have taken hold and begun changing popular taste significantly. Discotheque DJs have adventurous, avant garde tastes and their voracious appetite for import records has clearly had its influence: the eclectic European style of **Silver Convention**, **Barrabas**, **Crystal Grass**, **El Bimbo** and **Donna Summer** has more than offset American formula records and kept the disco sound from becoming stagnant. The other thing that

important disco pressings is included as a supplement to the essential album and single lists because these records were a significant part of 1975's disco playlist.)

Among the other developments of the year in Disco: The new disco circuit of clubs open to live entertainment in between recorded sets so stars like **Gloria Gaynor**, the **Trammps**, **Crown Heights Affair** and others have their own string of showcases across the country... The creation of the New York Record Pool and other disco DJ-operated distribution centers around the country to smooth out and firm up relations between the disco spinners and the record companies... The dance crazes – especially the Hustle and the Walk – which have prompted more attention and analysis than the music itself... And the resulting resurgence of dance contests and dance events which should continue to sweep the country next year.

RHINOCEROS, BOSTON
DJ: John Luongo

ELUSIVE – Babe Ruth (Capitol)
GET DOWN WITH THE PHILLY SOUND – MFSB (Phila. Intl.)
I AM SOMEBODY – Jimmy James & the Vagabonds (Pye)
I LOVE MUSIC – O'Jays (Phila. Intl.)
LADY BUMP – Penny McLean (Atlantic disco version)
LET'S GROOVE/DANCE YOUR TROUBLES AWAY – Archie Bell & the Drells (TSOP)
SALSOUL RAINBOW/CHICAGO BUS STOP/YOU'RE JUST THE RIGHT SIZE – Salsoul Orchestra (Salsoul)
SUNNY –Yambu (Montuno Gringo)
THAT OLD BLACK MAGIC – Softones (Avco)
UNION MAN – Cate Brothers (Asylum)

12 WEST, NEW YORK
DJ: Tom Savarese

BABY FACE – Wing & A Prayer Fife & Drum Corps (Wing & A Prayer)
BOOGIE FEVER – Sylvers (Capitol)
DANCE WITH ME – Ritchie Family (20th Century)
DRIVE MY CAR – Gary Toms Empire (PIP)
EXTRA EXTRA (READ ALL ABOUT IT) – Ralph Carter (Mercury)
I COULD HAVE DANCED All NIGHT/JUMP FOR JOY – Biddu Orchestra (Epic)
IF IT WASN'T FOR THE MONEY – Nanette Workman (Atco)
MIGHTY HIGH/EVERYTHING IS LOVE – Mighty Clouds of Joy (ABC)
THAT OLD BLACK MAGIC – Softones (Avco)
UNION MAN/I JUST WANNA SING – Cate Brothers (Asylum)

INFINITY, NEW YORK
DJ: Bobby Guttadaro

DON'T YOU HAVE ANY LOVE IN YOUR HEART – Margo Thunder (Capitol)
FIND MY WAY – Cameo (Chocolate City)
I COULD HAVE DANCED All NIGHT/JUMP FOR JOY – Biddu Orchestra (Epic)
I LOVE MUSIC – O'Jays (Phila. Intl.)
JOYCE – Papa John Creach (Buddah)
LET'S GROOVE – Archie Bell & the Drells (TSOP)
MIGHTY HIGH – Mighty Clouds of Joy (ABC)
SHARE MY LOVE – Dee Dee Sharp (TSOP)
DON'T LEAVE ME THIS WAY – Harold Melvin & the Bluenotes (Phila. Intl.)
THAT OLD BLACK MAGIC – Softones (Avco)

GALAXY 21, NEW YORK
DJ: Walter Gibbons

ELUSIVE – Babe Ruth (Capitol)
I COULD HAVE DANCED All NIGHT/JUMP FOR JOY – Biddu Orchestra (Epic)
THE JAM/IT'S ALRIGHT – Graham Central Station (Warner Bros.)
LET'S GROOVE – Archie Bell & the Drells (TSOP)
MIGHTY HIGH/EVERYTHING IS LOVE – Mighty Clouds of Joy (ABC)
SLOW BURN – LaBelle (Epic)
S.O.S. – Today's People (Gamma import)
TELL THE WORLD HOW I FEEL ABOUT 'CHA BABY – Harold Melvin & the Bluenotes (Phila. Intl. lp cut)
THAT OLD BLACK MAGIC – Softones (Avco)
WOW – Andre Gagnon (London import)

Quickly, some last-minute recommendations before taking a two-week leave to Get Away From It All. First a great single called "Merry Go-Round" by **Monday After** (Buddah), which starts with a **Spinners** feel and just gets better and better, peaking with a fine break toward the end; Buddah will be releasing a 5:35 version as their second special 12-inch disc. Also recommended: **Bobby Moore's** follow-up to "Call Me Your Anything Man," "Try to Hold On" (Scepter) with a disco version of just over five minutes and some obvious influences. The new **Fatback Band** album – "Raising Hell" on Event – is, as advance word had it, their best so far, sparked by a steamy "Spanish Hustle" (5:16) and a knockout "Party Time" (6:40) whose refrain is, "Party time is anytime/and anytime is party time" – but there's a lot of richness and variety here and every cut should be checked out (the change-of-pace: "Groovy Kind Of Day," very laid back). Two pleasant surprises: **Carl Carlton's** "I Wanna Be With You" (ABC), which far surpasses his last album, primarily because of the superb production of **Bunny Sigler** at Sigma Sound who managed to bring out Carlton's best early-**Stevie Wonder** qualities. Best cut for dancing: "Willing And Able" (7:30), but, again, the whole album is excellent. Surprise number two is the **Atlanta Disco Band** lp, "Bad Luck" (Ariola America), containing that instrumental and a very strong "Do What You Feel," written, produced and arranged by the **Trammps' Earl Young** and running right into another good track, "My Soul Is Satisfied;" also try "It's Love," Bobby Guttadaro's pick. Finally: De-Lite has issued the "new disco version" of "Every Beat Of My Heart" (5:20) on their first 12-inch pressing, and quite a handsome one.

NOTE: The lists of essential disco albums and singles have not been based in any systematic – much less scientific – way on the Disco File charts during the past year. Needless to say, the charts, compiled as they are from the top 10 lists submitted by different disco DJs each week, could provide only so much information and I wanted to go beyond the tight Top 20 for an end-of-the-year wrap-up. I also wanted to avoid a strict statistical tally and get down to a personal evaluation of 1975's disco releases. The combined lists are meant to form a basic disco library of records released this past year with as little overlap as possible. That is, a single is not listed if it was included on an album in the Essential Album list unless the 45 preceded the album (like "Get Down Tonight" or "Dreaming A Dream") or had a success quite independent of the album (as did "The Hustle"). Similarly, other singles were not listed because longer album cuts were available and being played instead (e.g., "Bad Luck," "Swearin' to God," "Forever Came Today") or if special disco pressings were preferable (e.g., "Baby Face," "Undecided Love," "Hollywood Hot"). The supplementary list of disco specials includes 12-inch single pressings and other variations. on the form designed especially for disco promotion – none available commercially, but important to any disco DJ's own collection. ✱

DISCO FILE ESSENTIALS 1975

THE ESSENTIAL DISCO ALBUMS OF 1975

1. **SAVE ME** – Silver Convention (Midland Intl.)
2. **THE SALSOUL ORCHESTRA** (Salsoul Records)
3. **LOVE TO LOVE YOU BABY**– Donna Summer (Oasis)
4. **TO BE TRUE** – Harold Melvin & the Bluenotes (Phila. Intl.)
5. **NEVER CAN SAY GOODBYE & EXPERIENCE** – Gloria Gaynor (MGM)
6. **BRAZIL** – The Ritchie Family (20th Century)
7. **NON-STOP** – B.T. Express (Scepter/Roadshow)
8. **TRAMMPS** (Golden Fleece)
9. **FAMILY REUNION** – O'Jays (Phila. Intl.)
10. **HEART OF THE CITY** – Barrabas (Atco)
11. **MOVING VIOLATION** – Jackson 5 (Motown)
12. **DANCE YOUR TROUBLES AWAY** – Archie Bell & the Drells (TSOP)
13. **INSIDE OUT** – Bohannon (Dakar)
14. **DISCO BABY & THE DISCO KID** – Van McCoy (Avco)
15. **DREAMING A DREAM** – Crown Heights Affair (De-Lite)
16. **KICKIN'** – Mighty Clouds of Joy (ABC)
17. **THE HEAT IS ON** – Isley Brothers (T-Neck)
18. **THAT'S THE WAY OF THE WORLD** – Earth, Wind & Fire (Columbia)
19. **SUN GODDESS** – Ramsey Lewis (Columbia)
20. **FIRST CUCKOO** – Deodato (MCA)
21. **FAITH, HOPE & CHARITY** (RCA)
22. **A SONG FOR YOU** – Temptations (Gordy)
23. **I'LL BE YOUR SUNSHINE** – Vernon Burch (UA)
24. **WAKE UP EVERYBODY** – Harold Melvin & the Bluenotes (Phila. Intl.)
25. **KOKOMO** (Columbia)
26. **SOUTH SHORE COMMISSION** (Wand)
27. **CLOSE-UP** – Frankie Valli (Private Stock)
28. **FOREVER, MICHAEL** – Michael Jackson (Motown)
29. **HAPPY 'BOUT THE WHOLE THING** – Dee Dee Sharp (TSOP)
30. **BUTT OF COURSE** – Jimmy Castor Bunch (Atlantic)
31. **ESTHER PHILLIPS W/ BECK** (Kudu)
32. **SPIRIT OF THE BOOGIE** – Kool & the Gang (De-Lite)
33. **YOU DON'T STAND A CHANCE IF YOU CAN'T DANCE** – Jimmy James & the Vagabonds (Pye)
34. **UNIVERSAL LOVE** – MFSB (Phila. Intl.)
35. **REVELATION** (RSO)
36. **THIRTEEN BLUE MAGIC LANE** – Blue Magic (Atco)
37. **SAFETY ZONE** – Bobby Womack (UA)
38. **CITY LIFE** – Blackbyrds (Fantasy)
39. **KC & THE SUNSHINE BAND** (TK)
40. **CITY OF ANGELS** – Miracles (Tamla)
41. **DISCO GOLD VOLUMES 1 & 2** – (Scepter)
42. **SURVIVAL** – O'Jays (Phila. Intl.)
43. **PLACES AND SPACES** – Donald Byrd (Blue Note)
44. **7-6-5-4-3-2-1 (BLOW YOUR WHISTLE)** – Gary Toms Empire (PIP)
45. **THE CHICAGO THEME** – Hubert Laws (CTI)
46. **FACE THE MUSIC** – Dynamic Superiors (Motown)
47. **CALIFORNIA SUNSET** – Originals (Motown)
48. **THE CAROL DOUGLAS ALBUM** – Carol Douglas (Midland Intl.)
49. **CIRCLE OF LOVE** – Sister Sledge (Atco)
50. **JUST ANOTHER WAY TO SAY I LOVE YOU** – Barry White (20th Century)
51. **RELEASE** – Barrabas (Atco)
52. **THE ARMADA ORCHESTRA** (Scepter)
53. **BOHANNON** (Dakar)
54. **ROCKIN' HORSE** (RCA)
55. **GEORGE McCRAE** (TK)
56. **STEALIN' HOME** – Babe Ruth (Capitol)
57. **THE HIT MAN** – Eddie Kendricks (Tamla)
58. **AIN'T NO 'BOUT-A-DOUBT IT** – Graham Central Station (Warner Bros.)
59. **WHEN LOVE IS NEW** – Billy Paul (Phila. Intl.)
60. **ANYTHING GOES** – Ron Carter (Kudu)

THE ESSENTIAL SPECIAL DISCO PRESSINGS OF 1975

1. **BABY FACE** – Wing & A Prayer Fife & Drum Corps (Wing & A Prayer)
2. **IT ONLY TAKES A MINUTE** – Tavares (Capitol)
3. **LADY BUMP** – Penny McLean (Atco)
4. **UNDECIDED LOVE** – Chequers (Scepter)
5. **CHINESE KUNG FU** – Banzai (Scepter)
6. **AFRICAN SYMPHONY** – Henry Mancini (RCA)
7. **DANCE WITH ME** – Ritchie Family (20th Century)
8. **HOOKED FOR LIFE** – Trammps (Atlantic)
9. **I'M IN HEAVEN** – Touch of Class (Midland Intl.)
10. **EVERY BEAT OF MY HEART** – Crown Heights Affair (De-Lite)
11. **SOUL TRAIN '75** – Soul Train Gang (Soul Train)
12. **CALL ME YOUR ANYTHING MAN** – Bobby Moore (Scepter)
13. **JOYCE** – Papa John Creach (Buddah)
14. **I WANNA KNOW** – Sunny Gale (Disco Soul/RCA)
15. **DANCE DANCE DANCE** – Calhoon (Warner Spector)
16. **DRIVE MY CAR** – Gary Toms Empire (PIP)
17. **HOLLYWOOD HOT** – Eleventh Hour (20th Century)
18. **FULL OF FIRE** – Al Green (Hi)
19. **SWEARIN' TO GOD** – Frankie Valli (Private Stock)
20. **MAGIC OF THE BLUE/WE'RE ON THE RIGHT TRACK** – Blue Magic (Atco)
21. **TORNADO** – "The Wiz" Original Cast (Atlantic)
22. **OOH WHAT A NIGHT** – Linda Thompson (Midland 'Intl.)
23. **LOVE OR LEAVE** – Spinners (Atlantic)
24. **YOU'D BE GOOD FOR ME** – Ronnie Spector (Tom Cat)
25. **NEVER GONNA LEAVE YOU** – Vicki Sue Robinson (RCA)

THE ESSENTIAL DISCO SINGLES OF 1975

1. **FREE MAN** – South Shore Commission (Wand)
2. **DREAMING A DREAM** – Crown Heights Affair (De-Lite)
3. **BRAZIL** – Ritchie Family (20th Century)
4. **EASE ON DOWN THE ROAD** – Consumer Rapport (Wing & A Prayer)
5. **I LOVE MUSIC** – O'Jays (Phila. Intl.)
6. **WHERE IS THE LOVE** – Betty Wright (Alston)
7. **HIJACK** – Herbie Mann (Atlantic)
8. **GET DOWN TONIGHT** – KC & the Sunshine Band (TK)
9. **LADY MARMALADE** – LaBelle (Epic)
10. **THE HUSTLE** – Van McCoy (Avco)
11. **SHAME, SHAME, SHAME** – Shirley & Company (Vibration)
12. **DO IT ANY WAY YOU WANNA** – People's Choice (TSOP)
13. **SUNNY** – Yambu (Montuno Gringo)
14. **IT ONLY TAKES A MINUTE** – Tavares (Capitol)
15. **LADY BUMP/THE LADY BUMPS ON** – Penny McLean (Atco)
16. **WHAT A DIFF'RENCE A DAY MAKES** – Esther Phillips (Kudu)
17. **CRYSTAL WORLD** – Crystal Grass (Polydor)
18. **INSIDE AMERICA** – Juggy Murray Jones (Jupiter)
19. **THREE STEPS FROM TRUE LOVE** – Reflections (Capitol)
20. **SAVE ME/SAVE ME AGAIN** – Silver Convention (Midland Intl.)
21. **SOMEBODY'S GOTTA GO** – Mike & Bill (Arista)
22. **FIRE/YOU SET MY HEART ON FIRE** – Tina Charles (Columbia)
23. **LADY LADY LADY** – Boogie Man Orchestra (Boogie Man)
24. **WHEN YOU'RE YOUNG AND IN LOVE** – Ralph Carter (Mercury)
25. **7-6-5-4-3-2-1 (BLOW YOUR WHISTLE)** – Gary Toms Empire (PIP)
26. **HELPLESSLY** – Moment of Truth (Roulette)
27. **HAPPY PEOPLE** – Temptations (Gordy)
28. **EL BIMBO** – Bimbo Jet (Scepter)
29. **EL CHICANO** – Black Blood (Mainstream)
30. **GIMME SOME** – Jimmy "Bo" Horne (Alston)
31. **MESSIN' WITH MY MIND** – LaBelle (Epic)
32. **SUPERSTAR REVUE** – Ventures (UA)
33. **SUMMER OF '42** – Biddu Orchestra (Epic)
34. **LA BOTELLA (THE BOTTLE)** – Joe Bataan (Salsoul/Epic)
35. **DYNOMITE** – Bazuka (A&M)
36. **DANCE DANCE DANCE** – Calhoon (Warner Spector)
37. **ONCE YOU: GET STARTED** – Rufus (ABC)
38. **TAKE IT FROM ME** – Dionne Warwick (Warner Bros.)
39. **TO EACH HIS OWN** – Faith, Hope & Charity (RCA)
40. **PEACE & LOVE** – Ron Butler & the Ramblers (Playboy)
41. **ONE DAY OF PEACE** – Love Committee (TSOP)
42. **LOVE IS EVERYWHERE** – City Limits (TSOP)
43. **JIVE TALKING** – Bee Gees (RSO)
44. **ARE YOU READY FOR THIS** – The Brothers (RCA)
45. **OUR DAY WILL COME** – Frankie Valli (Private Stock)
46. **I JUST CAN'T SAY GOODBYE** – Philly Devotions (Columbia)
47. **NOWHERE** – Hokis Poki (Black Magic/Shield)
48. **THAT OLD' BLACK MAGIC** – Softones (Avco)
49. **YUM YUM (GIMME SOME)** – Fatback Band (Event)
50. **SUPERNATURAL THING** – Ben E. King (Atlantic)
51. **(NOBODY LOVES ME) LIKE YOU DO DO** – Jeanne Burton (Cotton)
52. **LOVE INFLATION** – Joneses (Mercury)
53. **SALSOUL/SALSOUL HUSTLE** – Salsoul Orchestra (Salsoul)
54. **FIRE** – Ohio Players (Mercury)
55. **CHI-TOWN THEME** – Cleveland Eaton (Black Jazz)
56. **MAGIC'S IN THE AIR** – Ronnie Walker (Event)
57. **ONE WAY STREET** – Becket Brown (RCA)
58. **I'M IN HEAVEN** – Touch of Class (Midland Intl.)
59. **IF IT WASN'T FOR THE MONEY** – Nanette Workman (Atco)
60. **DO IT WITH FEELING** – Michael Zager & the Moon Band (Bang)
61. **FIND MY WAY** – Cameo (Chocolate City)
62. **LOVE POWER** – Willie Hutch (Motown)
63. **THERE'LL COME A TIME, THERE'LL COME A DAY** – Basic Black & Pearl (Polydor)
64. **HIGHWAY DRIVER** – Randy Pie (Polydor)
65. **HONEY BABY (BE MINE)** – Innervision (Private Stock)
66. **LOVE ROLLERCOASTER** – Ohio Players (Mercury)
67. **CAN'T GIVE YOU ANYTHING** – Stylistics (Avco)
68. **IT'S IN HIS KISS** – Linda Lewis (Arista)
69. **SENDING OUT AN S.O.S.** – Retta Young (All Platinum)
70. **DO THE BUS STOP** – Fatback Band (Event)
71. **NEW YORK CITY BUMP** – Black Rock (Black Rock Records)
72. **DISCO SAX** – Houston Perton (Westbound)
73. **TONIGHT'S THE NIGHT** – S.S.O. (Shadybrook)
74. **TRYING TO GET BACK TO YOU GIRL** – Jackey Beavers (Dade)
75. **DO THE CHOO CHOO** – Jack Ashford & the Sound of New Detroit (Blaze)

1976

Dancing at Infinity © **Toby Old**

JANUARY 17, 1976

CATCHING UP: First, a quartet of instrumental albums that were released while I was away. Tony Smith from the Barefoot Boy in New York already has the two best cuts on his new top 10 list: **Dennis Coffey's** "Some Like it Hot" and "Disco Connection" by the **Isaac Hayes Movement**. The Coffey cut is just over five minutes long, crackling, funky and unsweetened by strings; it's from an album titled "Finger Lickin' Good" (Westbound) which has one of the most outrageously suggestive covers in recent years and a number of other cuts worth checking into including the title track, an instrumental version of **David Bowie's** "Fame" and a song with the wonderful title, "If You Can't Dance To This You Got No Business Havin' Feet." Hayes' "Disco Connection" – from the **Hot Buttered Soul** album of the same name – is his best work in a long time: unmistakably **Isaac Hayes** – with the flash and punch of "Shaft" or "Theme From 'The Men'" but far from a mere retread of old vehicles. On the album's other side, there's a cut called "Choppers" that sounds like the more familiar Hayes soundtrack work and is also very danceable. Both "Some Like It Hot" and "Disco Connection" should be considered essential cuts right now.

cuts here – "Dance" (9:36), "Movin'" (8:39) and "Changin'" (8:12) – are all smokers sparked by powerful drumming, stinging horn work, heavy vocals and a sweet counterpoint of violins that only heightens the funk. The New York sound at its best and just the thing to make them scream on darkened dance floors all over.

Atlantic has released an excellent repackage of dance records unfortunately titled "Disco-Trek" but containing a number of hard-to-get songs from the past few years remixed and repolished especially for the collection, the knockout cut: "This World" by the **Sweet Inspirations**, is expanded from its original 2:45 single length to a fine 5:45 with the addition of a long break; it should pick up play from people who never heard it first time around. Also impressive: the original **Valentinos** version of **Bobby Womack's** "I Can Understand It" – 5:01 here and worth getting into again. **Jackie Moore's** "Time" (expanded to 4:21), "Got To Get You Back" by **Sons of Robin Stone**, "You Call Me Back" by **Clyde Brown**, "Look Me Up" by **Blue Magic** and **Sister Sledge's** "Mama Never Told Me" (not included on their album) are also in the package.

> **❝ The cut is just over five minutes long, crackling, funky and unsweetened by strings, from an album titled "Finger Lickin' Good," which has one of the most outrageously suggestive covers in recent years ❞**

To complete the quartet, there's the new album by tenor saxophonist **Joe Thomas**, "Masada" (Groove Merchant), whose title cut is a lush, long (5:42) instrumental that strikes a perfect balance between the flood of strings and the cutting edge of horns (the entire track is available on a 45 as well). "Masada" is followed on the album by a reworking of the standard "Poinciana" very much in the style of the **Ritchie Family** or **MFSB** but without any female vocals and a little on the raw side which gives it an interesting texture. Finally, the new **Love Unlimited Orchestra** release, "Music Maestro Please" (20th Century), with you-know-who leering from the front cover in a peach-colored suit with lapels wide enough to re-cover a sofa or two. **White's** instrumentals this time around are essentially more of the same – with "Bring It On Up," "It's Only What I Feel" and "I Wanna Stay" standing out – which makes for an overwhelming sense of deja vu but is pleasant enough for those odd romantic moments.

The first great album of 1976 is the debut of **Brass Construction** on United Artists, a nine-man New York group produced by **Jeff Lane** with the same energy and fervor that sent **B.T. Express** sky-high. The three longest

RATED X: The latest 12-inch record from Buddah is called "More More More" by something named the **Andrea True Connection** which sounds kind of like a second-string **Silver Convention** with cooing, sexy vocals that ask the important question, "How do you like your love?" It's a song with little depth or real character but one that has grown on me (and nearly everyone else I spoke to this week) with every new listening. In fact, it's so terrifically cute and catchy I found myself singing it on the street after hearing it only twice and long before I decided I liked it – this has the making of a big hit or a minor irritant or both. And since it turns out that Andrea True is a starlet in pornographic films ("Illusions Of A Lady"), this may inaugurate a whole new sub-genre: Porno Disco. But **Donna Summer** was there first.

RECOMMENDED SINGLES: **Morningside Drive's** update of the **Shirelles'** "Will You Love Me Tomorrow" (Copperfield) done under the influence of the **DCA** team so it has a **Gloria Gaynor** production sound but fairly undistinguished male vocals – however, the 6:48 "disco mix" is so good it's made the record an instant hit if the

BAREFOOT BOY, NEW YORK
DJ: Tony Smith

BOHANNON'S BEAT/THE BOHANNON WALK – Bohannan (Dakar)
DISCO CONNECTION – Isaac Hayes Movement (Hot Buttered Soul/ABC)
DO THE BUS STOP/SPANISH HUSTLE – Fatback Band (Event)
JUMP FOR JOY /I COULD HAVE DANCED ALL NIGHT – Biddu Orchestra (Epic)
LET'S GROOVE – Archie Bell & the Drells (TSOP)
MIGHTY HIGH/EVERYTHING IS LOVE – Mighty Clouds of Joy (ABC)
SOME LIKE IT HOT – Dennis Coffey (Westbound)
TELL THE WORLD HOW I FEEL ABOUT 'CHA BABY – Harold Melvin & the Bluenotes (Phila. Intl.)
THAT OLD BLACK MAGIC – Softones (Avco)
WOW – Andre Gagnon (London import)

BUTTERFIELD I, QUEENS, N.Y.
DJ: Richie Conte

DANCE WITH ME – Ritchie Family (20th Century)
ELUSIVE – Babe Ruth (Capitol)
FAMILY SIZE – Barrabas (Atco)
I AM SOMEBODY – Jimmy James & the Vagabonds (Pye)
I LOVE MUSIC – O'Jays (Phila. Intl.)
IF IT WASN'T FOR THE MONEY – Nanette Workman (Atco)
LET'S GROOVE – Archie Bell & the Drells (TSOP)
MIGHTY HIGH – Mighty Clouds of Joy (ABC)
SALSOUL RAINBOW/TANGERINE/YOU'RE JUST THE RIGHT SIZE – Salsoul Orchestra (Salsoul)
SHAKE ME, WAKE ME – Barbra Streisand (Columbia)

STUDIO ONE, LOS ANGELES
DJ: Jim Walters

BABY FACE – Wing & A Prayer Fife & Drum Corps (Wing & A Prayer)
BOHANNON'S BEAT – Bohannan (Dakar)
THE BREAKDOWN – Smokey Joe Grough (Wand)
EXTRA EXTRA (READ ALL ABOUT IT) – Ralph Carter (Mercury)
DO WHAT YOU FEEL – Atlanta Disco Band (Ariola America)
LADY BUMP/THE LADY BUMPS ON – Penny McLean (Atco)
MIGHTY HIGH – Mighty Clouds of Joy (ABC)
SHAKE ME, WAKE ME – Barbra Streisand (Columbia)
SING A SONG – Earth, Wind & Fire (Columbia)
THANK YOU BABY FOR LOVING ME – Quickest Way Out (Warner Bros.)

FLAMINGO, NEW YORK
DJ: Luis Romero

EXTRA EXTRA (READ ALL ABOUT IT) – Ralph Carter (Mercury)
LADY BUMP/THE LADY BUMPS ON – Penny McLean (Atco)
MIGHTY HIGH – Mighty Clouds of Joy (ABC)
OH NO NOT MY BABY – De Blanc (Arista)
ONE FINE DAY – Julie (Tom Cat)
S.O.S. – Today's People (Gamma import)
THAT OLD BLACK MAGIC – Softones (Avco)
THIS EMPTY PLACE – Stephanie Mills (Motown)
UNDECIDED LOVE – Chequers (Scepter & Creole import)
WILL YOU LOVE ME TOMORROW – Morningside Drive (Copperfield)

DISCO FILE TOP 20

1. **MIGHTY HIGH** – Mighty Clouds of Joy (ABC)
2. **I LOVE MUSIC** – O'Jays (Phila. Intl.)
3. **THAT OLD BLACK MAGIC** – Softones (Avco)
4. **LADY BUMP/THE LADY BUMPS ON** – Penny McLean (Atco)
5. **LET'S GROOVE** – Archie Bell & the Drells (TSOP)
6. **SALSOUL RAINBOW/YOU'RE JUST THE RIGHT SIZE/CHICAGO BUS STOP** – Salsoul Orchestra (Salsoul)
7. **JUMP FOR JOY/I COULD HAVE DANCED ALL NIGHT** – Biddu Orchestra (Epic)
8. **BABY FACE** – Wing & A Prayer Fife & Drum Corps (Wing & A Prayer)
9. **TANGERINE** – Salsoul Orchestra (Salsoul)
10. **EVERYTHING IS LOVE** – Mighty Clouds of Joy (ABC)
11. **TELL THE WORLD HOW I FEEL ABOUT 'CHA BABY** – Harold Melvin & the Bluenotes (Phila. Intl.)
12. **EXTRA, EXTRA (READ ALL ABOUT IT)** – Ralph Carter (Mercury)
13. **DANCE YOUR TROUBLES AWAY** – Archie Bell & the Drells (TSOP)
14. **I AM SOMEBODY** – Jimmy James & the Vagabonds (Pye
15. **ELUSIVE** – Babe Ruth (Capitol)
16. **LOVE TO LOVE YOU BABY** – Donna Summer (Oasis)
17. **SUNNY** –Yambu (Montuno Gringo)
18. **INSIDE AMERICA** – Juggy Murray Jones (Jupiter)
19. **SING A SONG** – Earth, Wind & Fire (Columbia)
20. **EVERY BEAT OF MY HEART** – Crown Heights Affair (De-Lite)

reactions at Flamingo and 12 West this past weekend are any indication; **Brown Sugar's** two-sided 45, "The Game Is Over" and "I'm Going Through Changes Now" (Capitol) with delicate spun-sugar production by **Vince Montana** who's fast becoming my favorite disco producer; **Blanche Carter's** "Rain" (RCA), produced by **Jacques Morali** (who brought you the **Ritchie Family**) and wonderfully overwrought (it's the B-side of a version of "My Man"); "The Devil Is Doing His Work" by the **Chi-Lites** (Brunswick), an unusual, strong record with all kinds of unexpected touches; "Feel the Spirit (In '76)," Bicentennial disco by **LeRoy Hutson and the Free Spirit Symphony** (Curtom) and if the other inevitable Bicentennial entries are this good it may not be such a bad year (long version: 5:54); and "Heaven Only Knows," a great mid-tempo song by the **Love Committee** (Ariola America) that I find irresistible. Finally, what has got to be the strangest disco record of the past year (it arrived just before I left): "Disco Lucy" by the **New York Rubber Rock Band** (Henry Street Records, a small New York label) which is, believe it or not, a disco version of the theme from "I Love Lucy" combined, it says on the label, with "Desi's Samba Medley." It's more amusing than danceable, but this is surely a novelty record for our time. What next? ✏

❝1976 is starting out to be a very good year for disco instrumentals, with the flood of new cuts from Dennis Coffey, the Isaac Hayes Movement, the Atlanta Disco Band, Joe Thomas and the Love Unlimited Orchestra❞

1976 is starting out to be a very good year for disco instrumentals: first the flood of new cuts from **Dennis Coffey**, the **Isaac Hayes Movement**, the **Atlanta Disco Band**, **Joe Thomas** and the **Love Unlimited Orchestra**, and now two fine new singles. 1) I've been hearing about an import called "Wow" by **Andre Gagnon** for weeks now and it had already turned up on three top 10 titles (Walter Gibbons' from Galaxy 21, Tony Smith's from Barefoot Boy and, this week, John Colon's from Friends Again) before I got a chance to hear it yesterday and finally understood what all the excitement was about. It brings together elements of "Lady, Lady, Lady" (that powerful use of strings) and "2 Pigs & a Hog" (the precise, invigorating Latin drumming) to create a kind of orchestrated jungle feeling I have a particular weakness for. Wow, indeed. The import from London in Canada has now been picked up by London in the States and is scheduled for release here this week. A must. 2) **Louie Ramirez** has a gorgeous Latin/disco instrumental in "Salsa" (Cotique) which has been released in two lengths back-to-back, 4:46 and 6:39. Disco has opened up a major avenue for Latin crossovers (**Yambu**, **Eddie**

FRIENDS AGAIN, NEW YORK
DJ: John Colon

BOHANNON'S BEAT – Bohannon (Dakar)
LEMME SEE YA GITCHYER THING OFF, BABY/FIO
MARAVILHA-TAJ MAHAL – Crystal Grass (Philips import)
MIDNIGHT SPIRIT – Beeghon'n (BLSW import)
MIGHTY HIGH – Mighty Clouds of Joy (ABC)
MOVIN' – Brass Construction (UA)
SOME LIKE IT HOT – Dennis Coffey (Westbound)
SPANISH HUSTLE/DO THE BUS STOP – Fatback Band (Event)
TELL THE WORLD HOW I FEEL ABOUT 'CHA BABY – Harold Melvin & the Bluenotes (Phila. Intl.)
THAT OLD BLACK MAGIC – Softones (Avco)
WOW – Andre Gagnon (London import)

LEVITICUS, NEW YORK
DJ: Michael Nias

BAD LUCK/BUCKHEAD/DO WHAT YOU FEEL – Atlanta Disco Band (Ariola)
BOHANNON'S BEAT – Bohannon (Dakar)
CHICAGO BUS STOP/SALSOUL RAINBOW/YOU'RE JUST THE RIGHT SIZE – Salsoul Orchestra (Salsoul)
DO THE BUS STOP – Fatback Band (Event)
I LOVE MUSIC – O'Jays (Phila. Intl.)
INSIDE AMERICA – Juggy Murray Jones (Jupiter)
LET'S GROOVE/DANCE YOUR TROUBLES AWAY – Archie Bell & the Drells (TSOP)
MASACA/POINCIANA – Joe Thomas Groove (Merchant)
MOVIN'/CHANGIN'/DANCE – Brass Construction (UA)
SING A SONG – Earth, Wind & Fire (Columbia)

CATCH ON, /LOS ANGELES
DJ: Randy Thomas

BABY FACE – Wing & A Prayer Fife & Drum Corps (Wing & A Prayer)
CASANOVA BROWN/DO IT YOURSELF – Gloria Gaynor (MGM)
CHANGE (MAKES YOU WANT TO HUSTLE) – Donald Byrd (Blue Note)
CHICAGO BUS STOP/YOU'RE JUST THE RIGHT SIZE – Salsoul Orchestra (Salsoul)
HAPPY MUSIC/ROCK CREEK PARK – Blackbyrds (Fantasy)
I LOVE MUSIC – O'Jays (Phila. Intl.)
INSIDE AMERICA – Juggy Murray Jones (Jupiter)
LOVE TO LOVE YOU BABY – Donna Summer (Oasis)
MIGHTY HIGH – Mighty Clouds of Joy (ABC)
SING A SONG – Earth, Wind & Fire (Columbia)

RUMBOTTOMS, HOLLYWOOD, FLORIDA
DJ: Bob Lombardi

DISCO CONNECTION – Isaac Hayes Movement (Hot Buttered Soul)
FIND MY WAY – Cameo (Chocolate City)
INSIDE AMERICA – Juggy Murray Jones (Jupiter)
JUMP FOR JOY – Biddu Orchestra (Epic)
LET'S GROOVE – Achie Bell & the Dells (TSOP)
MIGHTY HIGH – Mighty Clouds of Joy (ABC)
SMILE – Simon Said (Atco)
TELL THE WORLD HOW I FEEL ABOUT 'CHA BABY – Harold Melvin & the Bluenotes (Phila. Intl.)
THANK YOU BABY FOR LOVING ME – Quickest Way Out (Warner Bros.)
THAT OLD BLACK MAGIC – Softones (Avco)

Drennon, **Salsoul Orchestra**) and Ramirez should have no trouble following this path with "Salsa." Another instrumental deserving of attention is "Buckhead" from the **Atlanta Disco Band** album (Ariola America) – a cut that I passed up the first time around and only discovered this past weekend when it seemed to be the major new track at David Mancuso's Saturday night party at 99 Prince Street. "Buckhead" is another **MFSB**-style number characterized by a particularly handsome use of strings and it immediately jumped into the top 10 in my livingroom this week.

RECOMMENDED ALBUMS: "Collage," the debut album from **Eddie Drennon & BBS Unlimited** (Friends & Co.), marvelously seductive and sweet, although perhaps too relentlessly Latin-hustle oriented includes "Let's Do The Latin Hustle" and a reprise called "Let's Do It Again" plus six other cuts I find hard to choose from: try "Do It Nice And Easy," "Please Stay – Please Stay," "Prelude In Fugue" and "A Theme In Search;" the new **Eddie Kendricks** album (Tamla) has been produced by **Norman Harris** and contains a number of very good cuts –"He's A Friend," the title track, "All of My Love," "On My Way Home" and "Chains" – but the only one seems truly worthy of this merger of two super talents is "It's Not What You Got" ("it's how you use it") which starts out deceptively simple and turns into something special; Motown has also put out their third DiscoTech collection, containing, most importantly, Willie Hutch's "Love Power" expanded by one minute (which should lengthen the life of an already long-lasting song) and a new mix of the Jackson 5's "Forever Came Today" (also here: "Where Do I Go From Here" by the **Supremes**, "Glasshouse," "Keep on Truckin' " and "Don't Knock My Love" by **D. Ross & M. Gaye**, that ever-attractive duo).

READING ROOM: Pick up on **Fran Lebowitz's** latest "I Cover the Waterfront" column in the January issue of Andy Warhol's Interview where her views on That Dance are collected under the heading, "Dancing in Line: A Crime Against Nature, An Affront to Man." So there... And check out **Andrew Kopkind's** recent cover article in Boston's Real Paper (January 7) called "The Gay Hustle," an outsider's look at that city's gay disco scene centering on the new 15 Lansdowne Street – not because I agree with it (it's actually a pretty infuriating piece), but because it raises some interesting questions about exploitation – as does the issue's cover photo.

ALSO RECOMMENDED: The longer single version of **Retta Young's** "You Beat Me To The Punch" which runs to 5:41 (All Platinum); a disco 12-inch by **Hudson County** called "Heaven's Here On Earth" (RCA) which is whopping 7:05 and has a number of sharp breaks in a rather familiar but still moving style; and **Jeff Evans'** disco remake of "I'll Be Seeing You" (Grandstand) which has its moments and its non-moments but is bound to delight nostalgia freaks who haven't already ODed on revivals. ✍

Two excellent remakes I was prepared to hate:

1) "Autumn Leaves" by the **Jon Wite Group** (Cenpro) which turns out to be surprisingly attractive and quite well-made – a swirl of violins with a great, where-have-I-heard-that-before? drum break on the longer (4:22) version; a terrific winter song to balance that pile of hot summer records.

2) **Bette Midler's** incredibly fresh rendition of "Strangers in the Night," the kick-off cut from her "Song for the New Depression" album (Atlantic), which DJ Joe Palminteri rightly points out succeeds most of all because it's Midler – her rep carries the song as much as her voice (the inevitable comparison: **Streisand's** "Shake Me, Wake Me"). Producer **Arif Mardin** is working on a longer version which should take it past four minutes, for release in Atlantic's Disco Disc series – but it's already one of the most talked-about (and played) new album cuts.

And a third that grew on me (rapidly): **Hank Crawford's** gorgeous "I Hear A Symphony," the **Holland-Dozier-Holland** song (do you believe it was 10 years ago?) with opening and closing vocals by a multi-tracked **Patti Austin**. "Symphony" (4:45) is the title track of Crawford's new Kudu album, produced by **Creed Taylor** and also featuring "Madison (Spirit, the Power)" which has a slight **Marvin Gaye** feeling about the vocals and a little **Isaac Hayes** in the music; and, of all things, a disco version of the **David Rose** sleaze classic, "The Stripper," which is merely amusing. "Symphony" and "Madison" are already on David Todd's top 10 list from New York's Adams Apple this week.

"What About Love" by **Marboo** is just out as a Midland 12-inch disc and already on Joe Palminteri's top 10 at the new Chameleon club in New York. Palminteri says

he's been playing a shorter import (from Germany) for months now and is delighted to have this longer version (4:52) which has been disco-mixed by one of New York's favorite DJs, **Tony Gioe** of Hollywood, who doubled the length of the original.

The HOT new album: The A side of **Vicki Sue Robinson's** debut, "Never Gonna Let You Go" (RCA), advanced to disco DJs in New York this past week and due for general release the first week in February. Opening up is a searing jump cut called "Turn the Beat Around" with an extraordinary, driven vocal by VSR that makes use of her voice as another instrument. "Common Thief," rawer and nearly as energetic, follows (and, like the first cut, is over five-and-a half minutes long) with the side closed out by the title song, "Never Gonna Let You Go," which sounds even better in context with the others. Production is by **Warren Schatz**, who makes his real break-through here. Runner-up cut from Side B: "We Can Do Almost Anything."

Other recommended album cuts: "Into My Thing" from the new **Gene Page** album ("Lovelock" on Atlantic), an insinuating instrumental with occasional choruses of girls singing, "Get into my thing" and an introduction that makes quite clear what they mean – another good sex song, though the changes may not be the smoothest for dancing; and two cuts from the "Tymes Up" album by the **Tymes**: "Only Your Love" (5:01), which begins like the **Joneses** and sweeps you away, and a tough song called "To The Max(imum)" – the best album from the Tymes to date.

Left field: "Love For Hire" by the **Richard Hewson Orchestra** (Splash, available through Private Stock), in which the bizarre arrangement is at once the most off-putting and most interesting thing about the record. ◕

> **" The bizarre arrangement is at once the most off-putting and most interesting thing about the record "**

THE MIRAGE, BOSTON
DJ: Joe Carvello

CHICAGO BUS STOP /SALSOUL RAINBOW / YOU'RE JUST THE RIGHT SIZE – Salsoul Orchestra (Salsoul)
I LOVE MUSIC – O'Jays (Phila. Intl.)
JUMP FOR JOY– Biddu Orchestra (Epic)
LEMME SEE YA GITCHYER THING OFF, BABY – Crystal Grass (Philips import)
LET'S GROOVE/DANCE YOUR TROUBLES AWAY – Archie Bell & the Drells (TSOP)
MIGHTY HIGH – Mighty Clouds of Joy (ABC)
SING A SONG – Earth, Wind & Fire (Columbia)
SPANISH HUSTLE/PARTY TIME – Fatback Band (Event)
TELL THE WORLD HOW I FEEL ABOUT 'CHA BABY – Harold Melvin & the Bluenotes (Phila. Intl.)
UNION MAN – Cate Brothers (Asylum)

CHAMELEON, NEW YORK
DJ: Joe Palminteri

DON'T YOU HAVE ANY LOVE IN YOUR HEART – Margo Thunder (Capitol/Haven)
HEAVEN'S HERE ON EARTH – Hudson County (RCA)
I LOVE MUSIC – O'Jays (Phila. Intl.)
INSIDE AMERICA – Juggy Murray Jones (Jupiter)
IT'S NOT WHAT YOU GOT – Eddie Kendricks (Tamla)
LET'S GROOVE – Archie Bell & the Drells (TSOP)
MIGHTY HIGH – Mighty Clouds of Joy (ABC)
MORE, MORE, MORE – Andrea True Connection (Buddah)
THAT OLD BLACK MAGIC – Softones (Avco)
WHAT ABOUT LOVE – Marboo (Midland Intl.)

ADAMS APPLE, NEW YORK
DJ: David Todd

AFRICAN SYMPHONY – Henry Mancini (RCA)
CHANGIN'/MOVIN' – Brass Construction (UA)
CHICAGO BUS STOP/SALSOUL RAINBOW – Salsoul Orchestra (Salsoul)
DO THE BUS STOP– Fatback Band (Event)
EVERYTHING IS LOVE – Mighty Clouds of Joy (ABC)
GIMME SOME MO – Redd Holt Unlimited (Paula)
I HEAR A SYMPHONY/MADISON (SPIRIT, THE POWER) – Hank Crawford (Kudu)
IT'S NOT WHAT YOU GOT – Eddie Kendricks (Tamla)
SING A SONG – Earth, Wind & Fire (Columbia)
THAT OLD BLACK MAGIC – Softones (Avco)

DEN 1, CHICAGO
DJ: Artie Feldman

DO IT WITH FEELING – Michael Zager & the Moon Band (Bang)
I AM SOMEBODY – Jimmy James & the Vagabonds (Pye)
I LOVE MUSIC – O'Jays (Phila. Intl.)
INSIDE AMERICA – Juggy Murray Jones (Jupiter)
JUMP FOR JOY – Biddu Orchestra (Epic)
KEEP YOUR EYE ON THE SPARROW – Merry Clayton (Ode)
LADY BUMP – Penny Mclean (Atco)
LET'S GROOVE – Archie Bell & the Drells (TSOP)
THAT OLD BLACK MAGIC – Softones (Avco)
YOU'RE JUST THE RIGHT SIZE/CHICAGO BUS STOP – Salsoul Orchestra (Salsoul)

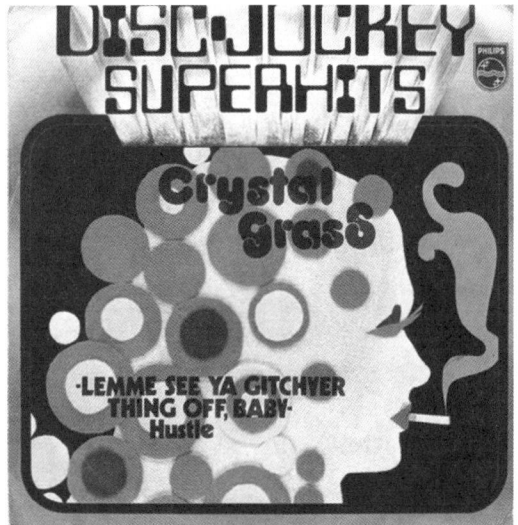

FEBRUARY 14, 1976

" Disco music is being run into the ground and there are fewer records each week I really feel excited about "

I had hoped that the notice of my absence from these pages last week would read simply, "Vince Aletti is too sick to listen to disco music this week," because that was exactly how I felt. The only problem is that while I feel back to normal, or as normal as I care to be, I'm still not sure I'm well enough to listen to disco music. I wouldn't go so far as to say that the thrill is gone, but it's certainly fading fast. Too many of the things that drew me to disco music in the first place – its crazy, explosive vitality; its willingness to take recording studio soul to its limits; its unpredictability; its weirdness – have been eased out in favour of easily duplicated formulas that can be stamped onto any available piece of material. Because disco remakes are beginning to sound alike – how awful when the dumbest critical remark, "it all sounds the same,!" becomes true – they've become the lowest, most laughable form of pop music: the muzak of the seventies, not so far removed from the stuff you hear in elevators. Sometimes I think that if I hear another record punctuated by a girl chorus who just scream "Wooo!" every once in a while, I'll be forced over the edge: Crazed Writer Nabbed in E. Village Incident; Cops, Passers-By Injured by Hurled "Disco" Discs.

Fortunately, or unfortunately, depending on how generous one feels at the moment, many of the most aggravating of disco records turn out to be naggingly irresistible after two or three exposures. After the initial groans of – "Not a disco version' of ——!" – one is, however reluctantly, won over; one finds oneself, as I did this morning, singing the damn song in all those barely conscious moments just after waking, "Wooos" and all. One feels slightly debased but that's life. Or a reasonable facsimile. What I'm trying to say is, disco music is being run into the ground (many critics feel it's been there for months) and there are fewer and fewer records each week that I really feel excited and

enthusiastic about. For every "Inside America" – an idiosyncratic, non-formula disco record if ever there was one – there are ten readymade disco records – eight of them remakes of standards – released, and the ratio is especially depressing when weeks go by without that special departure from formula. This week I asked everyone if they could suggest something to cheer me up, and here are some of the responses. Both Kurt Borusiewicz of the DCA Club in Philadelphia and Tom Savarese from 12 West in New York offered one of the more attractive disco remakes (the very one I woke up singing this morning), "I'll See You In My Dreams" by **The Pearls** (Private Stock) which Savarese went so far as to put on his top 10 this week. the best word for this one is "cute," but some of the instrumentation is quite tasty and Private Stock has made it available on a special 7-inch pressing at 4:15. Borusiewicz and Savarese alsio agreed on the latest **Bob Crewe** production spectacular, "Street Talk" by **B.C.G.** (20th Century), which they both top-tenned immediately. This also happens to be one of my current favorites, a lush but hard-punching instrumental that even at its longest (9:22) is constantly involving. "Street Talk"'s 12-inch pressing has the nine-minute version on one side with two shorter versions on the reverse, one 4:22, the other 6:08; take your pick.

Tom Savarese also recommends: **Terry Weiss'** "Superfine Sexy Lady" (Platinum) although he's not at all pleased with its mix – still, it has a hard-edged **Gary Toms Empire** sound; **Parliament's** five-minute "Supergroovalisticprosifunkstication," one of that group's typically off-the-wall bits of funk from the recent "Mothership Connection" album (Casablanca); and the re-mixed track of "This World" by the **Sweet Inspirations** on the "Disco Trek" album Atlantic released last month.

12 WEST, NEW YORK
DJ: Tom Savarese

BOHANNON'S BEAT – Bohannon (Dakar)
I HEAR A SYMPHONY – Hank Crawford (Kudu)
I SEE YOU IN MY DREAMS – The Pearls (Private Stock)
**I'M GOING THROUGH CHANGES NOW/THE GAME IS
OVER** – Brown Sugar (Capitol)
LOS CONQUISTADORES CHOCOLATES – Johnny
Hammond (Milestone)
MORE, MORE, MORE – Andrea True Connection (Buddah)
MOVIN'/CHANGIN'/DANCE – Brass Construction (UA)
NUMBER ONEDERFUL – Jay & the Techniques (Event)
STREET TALK – B.C.G. (20th Century)
THAT'S WHERE THE HAPPY PEOPLE GO – Trammps
(Atlantic import)

BOOMBAMAKAOO, NEW YORK
DJ: Jorge Wheeler

FOOLS RUSH IN /UNFORGETTABLE – Esther Phillips
(Kudu)
I HEAR A SYMPHONY – Hank Crawford (Kudu)
MORE, MORE, MORE – Andrea True Connection
(Buddah)
MOVIN'/CHANGIN' – Brass Construction (UA)
NUMBER ONEDERFUL – Jay & the Techniques (Event)
SALSA – Louie Ramirez (Cotique)
SPANISH HUSTLE – Fatback Band (Event)
WHY?... AND WE REPEAT – Taj Mahal (Columbia)
WHY DID YOU HAVE TO DESERT ME? – Taj Mahal (Columbia)
WOW – Andrea Gagnon (London import)

DCA CLUB, PHILADELPHIA
DJ: Kurt Borusiewicz

AUTUMN LEAVES – Jon White Group (Cenpro)
DISCO CONNECTION – Isaac Hayes Movement
(Hot Buttered Soul)
I HEAR A SYMPHONY – Hank Crawford (Kudu)
I'M GONE AND I'M GLAD/POINCIANA/MASADA – Joe
Thomas (Groove Merchant)
MORE, MORE, MORE – Andrea True Connection
(Buddah)
RAIN – Blanche Carter (RCA)
ROCK ON BROTHER – Chequers (Creole import)
SOME LIKE IT HOT – Dennis Coffey (Westbound)
STREET TALK – B.C.G. (20th Century)
UNION MAN – Cate Brothers (Asylum)

THE ABBEY, SAN JUAN, PUERTO RICO
DJ: Oscar Rodriguez

DON'T YOU HAVE ANY LOVE IN YOUR HEART – Margo
Thunder (Haven/Capitol)
I AM SOMEBODY – Jimmy James & the Vagabonds (Pye)
I'M IN HEAVEN – Touch of Class (Midland Intl.)
LADY BUMP/THE LADY BUMPS ON – Penny McLean (Atco)
MIGHTY HIGH – Mighty Clouds of Joy (ABC)
MORE, MORE, MORE – Andrea True Connection
(Buddah)
MY WAY – Bobby Azeff Orchestra (Aquarius import)
SAMBA – Andre Gagnon (London import)
TAJ MAHAL–FIO MARAVILHA – Crystal Grass
(Philips import)
THAT OLD BLACK MAGIC – Softones (Avco)

Oscar Rodriguez, one of the DJs at San Juan's The Abbey
whom we spoke with in Puerto Rico this week, said
these records – an unusual batch – were coming up at
his club right now: "Street Talk;" ""Disco Connection;"
"Disco Hop," by the **Third World Band**; Poison's
"Get Up And Move Your Body" and "Masada" by **Joe
Thomas**. He also lists the other side of **Andre Gagnon's**
"Wow" which is called "Ta Samba" and which has its
moments but most of them don't seem particularly
danceable. The record is now available in the States
on London and I'd like to underline my previous
recommendation of "Wow." Other recommendations
that beat underlining right now: "Poinciana" by **Joe
Thomas** (Groove Merchant); **Eddie Kendricks'** "It's Not
What You Got" (Tamla); "Heaven's Here On Earth," by
Hudson County (RCA); "I'm Going Through Changes
Now" and "The Game Is Over" by **Brown Sugar** (back
to back on Capitol); "Autumn Leaves" by the **Jon
White Group** (Cenpro) and **Johnny Hammond's**
"Los Conquistadores Chocolates" (Milestone) a number
of which were also listed or recommended by DJs this
week. Moving Up Fast: "More, More, More" by the
Andrea True Connection (Buddha) and "I Hear A
Symphony" by **Hank Crawford** (Kudu) – both of which
broke into the Disco File Top 20 this week in very high
positions – and the **Brass Connection** album.Jorge
Wheeler from New York's Boombamakaoo lists two
Taj Mahal cuts in his top 10 this week – "Why?...And
We Repeat Why?... And We Repeat!" the instrumental
from his latest album, "Music Keeps Me Together"
(Columbia), along with a vocal version of the same cut
called "Why Did You Have To Desert Me?" which was
included in Taj's 1974 "Mo Roots" album. Wheeler says
the earlier version is picking up in his club after the
instrumental was already established and suggests it
could spread. Definitely worth checking out.

RECOMMENDED: The **Biddu Orchestra** album (Epic),
finally available here after being one of the must-have
imports of1975 and including "Summer of '42,"
"Aranjuez Mon Amour," "Exodus," "I Could Have
Danced All Night," and "Jump For Joy" which they
actually were thinking of leaving off until it hit so
big – in all, two cuts more than the English import.
And these singles: "Night and Day," the old Cole Porter
song redone by **John Davis and the Monster Orchestra**
(Sam) and recommended this week in spite of all I said
at the beginning – the 5:06 disco version of this one
works in spite of its silly vocals; **Bobby Franklin's** oddly
absorbing "Mutha's Love" (Columbia), a possible cult
item; the new **Touch of Class** record, "Don't Want No
Other Love" (Midland Intl.), more up than their last
if not as perfect – in a 12-inch pressing at 5:27; a very
tough "Born To Get Down (Born To Mess Around)"
by the **Muscle Shoals Horns** with a great psychedelic
funk break in the 4:21 disco version (Bang); and its title
aside, "I Found Love On A Disco Floor" by the **Temprees**
(Epic), who sound very much like the O'Jays here which
can hardly be bad and the long version (6:34) fills in
with a fine break. ✪

FEBRUARY 21, 1976

❝ After last week's tirade about the scarcity of off-beat, unique disco records, two more surfaced this week to bring me up from the depths of pessimism ❞

Two new records that should cheer everybody up are celebrations of discotheques – according to the **Trammps**, "That's Where The Happy People Go," and the **3rd World Band** extends a sweet invitation to the "Disco Hop": "Come with me/I'm gonna set you free/We're going to the disco hop/where we never stop." Propaganda maybe, but highly effective stuff. The Trammps single has been around New York since last December when copies were leaked out in anticipation of a year-end release. Everyone who heard it agreed it was one of the great Trammps records; the perfect embodiment of its message: up, driving, happy, and very tightly crafted by the brilliant team of **Ronald Baker**, **Norman Harris** and **Earl Young**. But Atlantic plugged up the leak and held the single back while they waited for Buddah's successful release of an earlier Trammps cut, "Hold Back The Night," to level off in its move up the charts. Meanwhile, "Happy People" became one of the most in demand records in New York and the most frequently asked question in disco circles became, "So when is that Trammps record coming out?" followed by, "Can I tape your copy?" Finally, Atlantic released the record in England two weeks ago and flew a batch of singles back here to help stem the immediate demand, with promises of special 12-inch discs within the next week and a commercial release before the end of the month. The record is worth all the furor and anticipation; it should be one of the year's most successful disco singles.

The **3rd World Band's** "Disco Hop" (Abraxas) appeared last week with no advance word except Oscar Rodriguez' listing from The Abbey in San Juan and the absence of hype or hysteria made it all the more delightful. The record has a Latin hustle feel with bright horn lines and soft-edged vocals from what sounds like a very young male group which may explain some of its particular attraction. A personal favorite in spite of its title.

After last week's tirade about the scarcity of off-beat, unique disco records, two more surfaced this week to bring me up from the depths of pessimism. First, there's "It's You That I Need" by the **Duncan Sisters** (Hi), a

loud, shouting song by two girls who sound like **Sisters Love** or a hopped-up **Sweet Inspirations**. They just tear the song apart from beginning to end, aided by a swirling synthesizer and continuing in a more outrageous Part 2 which builds with a frenzy to a chant of "You're the one" quoted from the **Little Sister** record. The second part runs 4:17 and the two sides mixed together reach a little over seven minutes. The writer-producer is a man named **Gerald Floyd** from Memphis who bears watching after this one. The second record is considerably more off the wall: a bizarre, heavily orchestrated disco version (how I cringe at that phrase now) of the oldie "Ballin' the Jack" by a group that calls itself **Camp Galore** (which should give you an idea of their approach). In case you had no idea what this song was really about, this version should leave no doubt, girls. The label: D&M, in New York.

Other Recommended Singles: A more than usually robust and solid **Kool & the Gang** offering, "Love And Understanding (Come Together)" (De-Lite), one of their sharpest commercial records in some time; **South Side Coalition's** tough, funky "(Don't Cha Wanna) Get Down Get Down" (Brown Dog) – answer: yes yes; "Queen of Clubs" and "Do It Good," back to back **KC & the Sunshine Band** (TK) never released as a single in this country but a big hit in England more than a year ago and just the right double punch to follow up the group's string of successes here.

Left Field: **Kokomo's** "Rise And Shine" (Columbia), a terrific, building anthem which may take some getting into because of its somewhat off beginning but is worth checking out (from the group's next album, due out early March); a relentless instrumental by **Jo Bisso** called "Disco Amour" (Editions Makossa) that doesn't really pick up until the end but then gets quite interesting (length: 4:55), and another odd instrumental, "Living In Ecstacy" by **Ecstacy** (no, this does not represent a split from Passion & Pain) (on Disco Records) which speeds up almost out of control toward the end.

LEVITICUS, NEW YORK
DJ: Thomas Pearson

AMERICA (WE NEED THE LIGHT) – Billy Paul (Phila. Intl.)

BOHANNON'S BEAT – Bohannon (Dakar)

HONEY-BUTT – Mandrill (UA)

I AM SOMEBODY – Jimmy James & the Vagabonds (Pye)

I LOVE MUSIC – O'Jays (Phila. Intl.)

IT DIDN'T HAVE TO BE THIS WAY – Hidden Strength (UA)

MIGHTY HIGH – Mighty Clouds of Joy (ABC)

MORE, MORE, MORE – Andrea True Connection (Buddah)

MOVIN' – Brass Construction (UA)

THANK YOU BABY FOR LOVING ME – Quickest Way Out (Warner Bros.)

SPEAKEASY, LONG ISLAND, N.Y.
DJ: John Fraumeni

BOHANNON'S BEAT – Bohannon (Dakar)

ELUSIVE – Babe Ruth (Capitol)

FIND MY WAY – Cameo (Chocolate City)

I AM SOMEBODY – Jimmy James & the Vagabonds (Pye)

JOYCE – Papa John Creach (Buddah)

LET'S GROOVE – Archie Bell & the Drells (TSOP)

MOVIN'/CHANGIN' – Brass Construction (UA)

SALSOUL RAINBOW – Salsoul Orchestra (Salsoul)

SPANISH HUSTLE – Fatback Band (Event)

WOW – Andre Gagnon (London)

YESTERDAY, BOSTON
DJ: Cosmo Wyatt

CHAINS/ALL OF MY LOVE/ IT'S NOT WHAT YOU GOT – Eddie Kendricks (Tamla lp cuts)

CHANGIN'/MOVIN'/DANCE – Brass Construction (UA)

CHICAGO BUS STOP/TANGERINE/ YOU'RE JUST THE RIGHT SIZE – Salsoul Orchestra (Salsoul)

FINGER LICKIN' GOOD/SOME LIKE IT HOT – Dennis Coffey (Westbound)

HAPPY MUSIC/ROCK CREEK PARK – Blackbyrds (Fantasy)

LEMME SEE YA GITCHYER THING OFF, BABY/TAJ MAHAL – Crystal Grass (Philips import)

LET'S GROOVE/DANCE YOUR TROUBLES AWAY – Archie Bell & the Drells (TSOP)

MIGHTY HIGH/STANDING ON THE REAL SIDE – Mighty Clouds of Joy (ABC)

UNION MAN – Cate Brothers (Asylum)

WOW/TA SAMBA – Andre Gagnon (London)

C'EST LA VIE, NEW YORK
DJ: Jeff Baugh

AUTUMN LEAVES – Jon Wite Group (Cenpro)

DISCO CONNECTION – Isaac Hayes Movement (Hot Buttered Soul)

EXTRA, EXTRA (READ ALL ABOUT IT) – Ralph Carter (Mercury)

HEAVEN'S HERE ON EARTH – Hudson County (RCA)

I HEAR A SYMPHONY – Hank Crawford (Kudu)

LOS CONQUISTADORES CHOCOLATES – Johnny Hammond (Milestone)

MOVIN'/CHANGIN' – Brass Construction (UA)

SALSA – Louie Ramirez (Cotique)

SMOKE GETS IN YOUR EYES/BIG BAD BOY/DEVIL EYES – Penny Mclean (Columbia import)

STRANGERS IN THE NIGHT – Bette Midler (Atlantic)

And some previously recommended album cuts are now available as singles: **Johnny Hammond's** "Los Conquistadores Chocolates" (Milestone), edited down to a smart 3:20; **Bette Midler's** "Strangers in the Night" (Atlantic), cut only a few seconds; the **Isaac Hayes Movement's** "Disco Connection" (Hot Buttered Soul/ABC) cut from 6:14 to 3:33 and still terrific, and "Brasilia Carnaval," not by the original group but a fine facsimile by **Peter Popper's Soundkapelle** (Mainstream).

Recommended Album Cuts: **Esther Phillips'** "Caravan," which seems to be the cut generating the most excitement from the new album, "For All We Know" (Kudu) – a complex vocal version of the **Duke Ellington** song **Deodato** used to introduce his "Watusi Strut;" "Caravan" is also included in an instrumental version on the new **Rhythm Heritage** album (ABC), along with the successful "Theme from S.W.A.T.," a long treatment of "Baretta's Theme" ("Keep Your Eye On the Sparrow") and a tasty dance number called "Disco-fied" which opens and closes the album; and "Can You Get Down" (5:45), a chant and instrumental (nice drums, strings) cut from "**Universe City**" by the group of the same name (Midland International), NOTE: Sire Records has reissued **Martha Velez'** "Matinee Weepers" from some time back and including the complete "Aggravation" (5:17). ◐

DISCO FILE TOP 20

1. **MOVIN'** – Brass Construction (UA)
2. **MIGHTY HIGH** – Mighty Clouds of Joy (ABC)
3. **LET'S GROOVE** – Archie Bell & the Drells (TSOP)
4. **MORE, MORE, MORE** – Andrea True Connection (Buddah)
5. **CHANGIN'** – Brass Construction (UA)
6. **I LOVE MUSIC** – O'Jays (Phila. Intl.)
7. **THAT OLD BLACK MAGIC** – Softones (Avco)
8. **SPANISH HUSTLE** – Fatback Band (Event)
9. **I HEAR A SYMPHONY** – Hank Crawford (Kudu)
10. **WOW** – Andre Gagnon (London)
11. **BOHANNON'S BEAT** – Bohannon (Dakar)
12. **SING A SONG** – Earth, Wind & Fire (Columbia)
13. **INSIDE AMERICA** – Juggy Murray Jones (Jupiter)
14. **CHICAGO BUS STOP/SALSOUL RAINBOW/ YOU'RE JUST THE RIGHT SIZE** – Salsoul Orchestra (Salsoul)
15. **DO THE BUS STOP** – Fatback Band (Event)
16. **DISCO CONNECTION** – Isaac Hayes Movement (Hot Buttered Soul)
17. **SOME LIKE IT HOT** – Dennis Coffey (Westbound)
18. **TELL THE WORLD HOW I FEEL ABOUT 'CHA BABY** – Harold Melvin & the Bluenotes (Phila. Intl.)
19. **JUMP FOR JOY/I COULD HAVE DANCED ALL NIGHT** – Biddu Orchestra (Epic)
20. **I AM SOMEBODY** – Jimmy James & the Vagabonds (Pye)

FEBRUARY 28, 1976

Instant Hit: **Diana Ross'** spectacular eight-minute cut, "Love Hangover" (from her just-out Motown album, "Diana Ross"), the sort of record that goes top 10 after its first weekend in a club – as it did with all the New York discos surveyed this week – and stays there for some time. Produced by **Hal Davis**, "Love Hangover" is structured in two parts, the first slow and sexy, introduced by one of Ross' classic breathy sighs but gradually drawn out of its cushiony softness by a quickening beat. The beat shifts and breaks into a steady chug for the song's second part, embroidered with a tight guitar line, occasional rushes from the string section and wonderful exclamations from Diana, who seems to be almost panting from another track in the background during one segment: an incredible bridge of sighs. The form is like that of the **Jackson 5's** "I Am Love" but the overall pace and feeling of the cut is more consistent here and the break more perfectly executed. Ross sounds more spirited and alive than she has in years and that alone is exciting; after a long, long absence from the dance floor, it's fitting that she should return in top form. Almost all the DJs we spoke to this week agreed "Love Hangover" was their major record after only one or two nights' play and many reported the same process of breaking it: playing the upbeat second part several times during the night, then introducing the entire cut very late and watching the crowd go wild when the break hits them. This is Motown's most satisfying and successful disco cut since "Forever Came Today" and proves that Motown is still capable of fine peaks of studio craft. Welcome back, Diana.

Also coming on strong: **Vicki Sue Robinson's** powerful "Turn The Beat Around" (RCA) which also made all the New York top 10s this week and will probably be battling "Love Hangover" for position as number one disco record in a week or two.

FEEDBACK: The most talked-about import this week (and last week, too) is "Moving Like A Superstar" by a girl named **Jackie Robinson** on Ariola Eurodisc from Germany. Walter Gibbons put it on his top 10 and nearly everyone else we spoke to was raving about it, with Cosmo from Yesterday in Boston saying it was one of his fastest moving records. Ariola America has taken notice and plans to bring the single out within the next two weeks... Also on the Galaxy 21 top 10: "Eleanor Rigby," the cut that seems to be getting the most attention from the new **Wing & A Prayer Fife & Drum Corps** album (Wing & A Prayer) and a disco disc 12-inch by **T.T. Sotto** called "Chorus Line" (Stirling Gold Records) which is a zippy line-dance extravaganza (5:18 long) that Gibbons reports is one of the biggest records in his club right now. Other Walter Gibbons favorites: "Zone" by the **Rhythm Makers** (Vigor), an over five-minute instrumental that we've been hearing about for months now (originally released as the B side of the single "Prime Cut") and finally got a hold of this week – highly recommended; **Carl Carlton's** excellent "Willing And Able" (from his ABC album) which deserves more attention; "Consideration" by **Gail** (SMI), another 12-inch that has been picking up play in New York; **Cy Coleman's** "Speak Low," a cut from his RCA lp, "The Party's on Me," with a European instrumental feel; and a spunky instrumental called "Wet Weekend" by the **Rock Gazers** (Pilgrim) which has caught on very quickly with the "Erucu" /"2 Pigs & A Hog" /"Wow" crowd.

The new record on Bacho Mangual's list from Revelation II in Brooklyn is "More," the familiar theme from "Mondo Cane" revamped by star producer **Vince Montana** for singer **Carol Williams** on Salsoul Records and featuring, needless to say, the Salsoul Orchestra. Advance copies of the record were given to a number of New York DJs nearly a week ago and in spite of a backlash against disco remakes, this one has gotten over quite successfully, primarily because the vocals are sure and sharp, the breaks creamy smooth and the end, with its "quote" from "Bad Luck," a perfect clincher. The long disco version, to be available on 12-inch pressings, this week, is over seven minutes; the commercial release disco version runs 4:50. On Paul Dougan's top 10 from LA's Studio One are two singles that are apparently very big there which may yet catch on in New York. One is "Sing A Happy, Funky Song" by **Miz Davis** (Now), aptly described in its title, a party record with a full bottom and some particularly nice steel drum flourishes that comes out of a small LA label and has not yet reached this coast in any quantity. The other is **Banbarra's** "Shack Up" (UA), another hard r&b song, this one featuring a tough, aggressive drum line and shouting vocals. "Shack Up" is being played in New York, though

GALAXY 21, NEW YORK
DJ: Walter Gibbons

CAN YOU GET DOWN/SERIOUS – Universe City (Midland)

CHORUS LINE – T.T. Sotto (Stirling Gold Records)

ELEANOR RIGBY – Wing & A Prayer Fife & Drum Corps (Wing & A Prayer)

GIMME SOME MO – Redd Holt Unlimited (Paula)

HAPPY MUSIC – Blackbyrds (Fantasy)

LOVE HANGOVER – Diana Ross (Motown)

MOVIN'/CHANGIN' – Brass Construction (UA)

MOVING LIKE A SUPERSTAR – Jackie Robinson (Ariola)

NIGHT AND DAY – John David & Monster Orchestra (Sam)

TURN THE BEAT AROUND/COMMON THIEF – Vicki Sue Robinson (RCA)

HOLLYWOOD, NEW YORK
DJ: Tony Gioe

BUCKHEAD/IT'S LOVE/DO WHAT YOU FEEL – Atlanta Disco Band (Ariola America)

DISCO CONNECTION – Isaac Hayes Movement (Hot Buttered Soul)

DON'T WANT NO OTHER LOVER – Touch of Class (Midland Intl.)

HE'S A FRIEND/IT'S NOT WHAT YOU GOT/CHAINS – Eddie Kendricks (Tamla)

LOS CONQUISTADORES CHOCOLATES – Johnny Hammond (Milestone)

LOVE HANGOVER – Diana Ross (Motown)

MORE, MORE, MORE – Andrea True Connection (Buddah)

MOVIN'/CHANGIN' – Brass Construction (UA)

STREET TALK – B. C. G. (20th Century)

TURN THE BEAT AROUND – Vicki Sue Robinson (RCA)

REVELATION II, BROOKLYN, N.Y.
DJ: Bacho Mangual

CHAINS/ALL OF MY LOVE/IT'S NOT WHAT YOU GOT – Eddie Kendricks (Tamla)

DISCO CONNECTION – Isaac Hayes Movement (Hot Buttered Soul)

I HEAR A SYMPHONY – Hank Crawford (Kudu)

I'LL BE SEEING YOU – Jeff Evans (Grandstand)

LOVE HANGOVER – Diana Ross (Motown)

MORE – Carol Williams (Salsoul)

MORE, MORE, MORE – Andrea True Connection (Buddah)

MOVIN'/CHANGIN' – Brass Construction (UA)

THAT'S WHERE THE HAPPY PEOPLE GO – Trammps (Atlantic import)

TURN THE BEAT AROUND/COMMON THIEF – Vicki Sue Robinson (RCA)

STUDIO ONE, LOS ANGELES
DJ: Paul Dougan

EXTRA, EXTRA (READ ALL ABOUT IT) – Ralph Carter (Mercury)

HAPPY MUSIC – Blackbyrds (Fantasy)

MIGHTY HIGH – Mighty Clouds of Joy (ABC)

MORE, MORE, MORE – Andrea True Connection (Buddah)

SALSA – Louie Ramirez (Cotique)

SHACK UP – Banbarra (UA)

SING A HAPPY FUNKY SONG – Miz Davis (Now)

STRANGERS IN THE NIGHT – Bette Midler (Atlantic)

STREET TALK – B.C.G. (20th Century)

WOW – Andre Gagnon (London)

not as extensively as it is in LA, and most of the people we spoke to said they liked it because it was a change from the dominant disco sound. As Tony Gioe said, it has "that blackness that's been missing." The New York preference seems to be for "Shack Up Part II" which cuts the vocals down to some shouting of the title and heightens the pulse of the record.

Must Reading: The February 16 New Yorker's Talk of the Town piece on the recent Disco Forum which centers on two young disco entrepreneurs and includes such chilling quotes as, "Personally, I think ground control using discotheques – instead of parking lots, for instance – is a brilliant economic concept." Frightening.

RECOMMENDED: "Zone" by the **Rhythm Makers** (Vigor), "Wet Weekend" by **Rock Gazers** (Pilgrim), "More" by **Carol Williams** (Salsoul), "Shack Up Part II" by **Banbarra** (UA), "Sing A Happy, Funky Song" by **Miz Davis** (Now) – all mentioned above – and **Leone Thomas'** pumping, invigorating "Thank You Baby" (Don) which sounds like **Jerry Butler**, still one of my favorites; a 12-inch running close to six minutes should be generally available for DJs this week and a two-part single is already in release. Album cuts: Don't miss "Stop And Think It Over" from **Anthony White's** debut album, "Could It Be Magic" (Philadelphia International), a classic, upbeat Philadelphia Sound, happy and irresistible; **LeRoy Hutson's** "Feel The Spirit" album which features that cut (5:54) and one called "It's The Music" which begins with a great drum and chant segment (Curtom); and from the Attitudes album (Dark Horse), a drum-based instrumental called "Squank" (4:23) which has a core section that might appeal to all the DJs who love to blend beats together. Turn the beat around. ✪

> **"Many reported the same process of breaking the record: play the upbeat second part several times during the night, then introduce the entire cut very late and watch the crowd go wild when the break hits them "**

MARCH 6, 1976

A number of the strongest records out right now – and the fastest movers – are by women: **Vicki Sue Robinson's** "Turn The Beat Around" which shot from 15 to 4 on the DISCO FILE Top 20 this week where it was joined by another VSR cut, "Common Thief," **Diana Ross'** "Love Hangover" and **Andrea True's** "More, More, More." Make way for another – **Donna Summer's** latest sensual extravaganza, "Try Me/ I Know/We Can Make It" from her new Oasis album, "Love Trilogy," due out this week. The cut, again the entire side one of the album, running just under 18 minutes, is structured as three separate songs "Try Me," "I Know" and "We Can Make It" – blended together with a series of diamond-hard, brilliant breaks and merging at the end into one song. The effect is not unlike that of "Love to Love You Baby" with its orgasmic rise and fall, but the pace has been changed here, picked up and sent soaring, while Summer's voice has taken on more edge and depth. As before, the lyrics are minimal and determinedly sexy, but their chant-like repetition is even more hypnotic, soothing and exhilarating at the same time. And the **Pete Bellotte** production, with arrangements by **Giorgio Moroder**, is even more sublimely smooth than on "Love To Love" – another classic of disco styling with an especially distinctive use of strings.

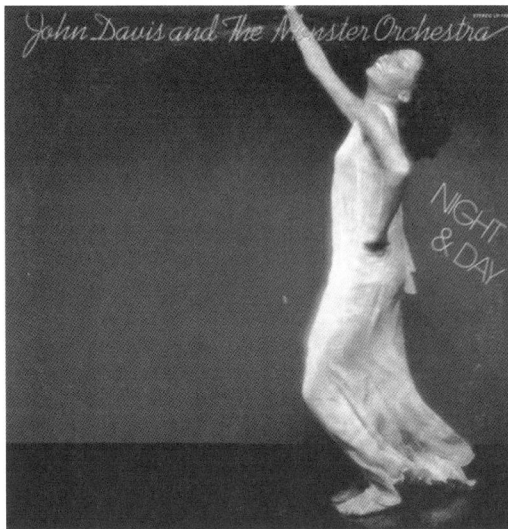

Aside from the upbeat of side one, the prime difference between this and the previous Donna Summer album is that it has a real side two, sparked by a punched-up version of **Barry Manilow's** successful ballad, "Could It Be Magic." Summer throws herself into the song and gives the first real glimpse of her power once she's let loose; sounds like a natural single. The other two cuts, "Waster" (5:10) and "Come With Me" (4:20), are also disco styled with more emphasis on vocals and another group of fine breaks to insure

screams on the dance floor. **Hal Davis** obviously drew "Love To Love You Baby" for his pace and production of Diana Ross, "Love Hangover" – Summer, in town last week for a series of shows at Radio City, said she took the song as "a compliment" – and the continued strong, unique style of "Love Trilogy" should influence even more of the music we'll be hearing this year. Certainly "Try Me I Know We Can Make It" will be a disco catch-phrase for some time to come. Another Summer smash.

Speaking of women singers, it's great to have **Ecstasy, Passion, & Pain's Barbara Roy** back with their first quality release in too long – that is, up to the high standard they set in their debut album, now more than a year and a half old. The group is back with producer **Bobby Martin** who continues their signature sound in "Touch And Go" with Roy up front and strong as ever. The 12-inch pressing Roulette has made available to DJs is just over five minutes. And this week should see the release of a new album from another group we've been missing, the **First Choice**, off the scene while **Stan Watson's** Philly Groove moved to Warners. **Silver Convention** also returns this week with their first release since "Fly, Robin, Fly," a nice variation on their established sound called "Get Up And Boogie" (Midland International). The title encompasses virtually all the lyrics except for some shouts of "That's right!" here and there by the male members of the band, supplementing the familiar females. The feeling is quite laid back in spite of the title – is it the new tribal beat? – and it grows on you. Midland has issued a 12-inch of nearly eight minutes and the single just released is 4:05.

Two brothers, **Michael** and **Basil Nias**, DJs from Leviticus in New York and the Palace in New Rochelle, respectively, alerted me to the opening cut on the new **Imaginations** album, a knockout production called "I Found My Dancing Girl." It's about dancing all over the world and I could do without the carnival barker touches but the drums and changes in the song's second half more than make up for the flaws. At six minutes, this could be a sleeper hit. The album, "Good Stuff" (20th Century), also features an update called "Love Jones '75" and a wonderfully raunchy, funny cover.

Event's release of its new disco version of "Spanish Hustle," the **Fatback Band's** huge success, is perfectly timed to strengthen or revive interest at the disco level just as the cut is being issued as a commercial single. The new break, beautifully executed, brings the track up to 5:54 and is highly recommended. Also, a note should be made of the re-release of the "Mahogany" soundtrack album with longer versions of "Erucu" (expanded from a mere 1 :23 to 3:31) and "She's the Ideal Girl" (from 2:43 to 3:24). The new album, on Motown, places "Erucu" as the first cut on side two so it can be distinguished from the original release.

FIFTEEN LANSDOWNE STREET, BOSTON
DJ: Danae Jacovidis

DANCE THE BUMP – The Bumpers (Vogue import)
LEMME SEE YA GITCHYER THING OFF, BABY/TAJ MAHAL
– Crystal Grass (Philips import)
LOS CONQUISTADORES CHOCOLATES – Johnny
Hammond (Milestone)
LOVE HANGOVER – Diana Ross (Motown)
MOVIN'/CHANGIN' – Brass Construction (UA)
NUMBER ONEDERFUL – Jay & the Techniques (Event)
SPANISH HUSTLE – Fatback Band (Event)
STREET TALK – B. C. G. (20th Century)
THAT'S WHERE THE HAPPY PEOPLE GO – Trammps
(Atlantic import)
TURN THE BEAT AROUND/COMMON THIEF – Vicki Sue
Robinson (RCA)

CORK & BOTTLE, NEW YORK
DJ: Eddie Rivera

ELEANOR RIGBY – Wing & A Prayer Fife & Drum Corps
(Wing & A Prayer)
FIND MY WAY – Cameo (Chocolate City)
HURT SO BAD – Philly Devotions (Columbia)
LET ME BE – Jackie Robinson (Pye import)
LOVE HANGOVER – Diana Ross (Motown)
MOVIN' – Brass Construction (UA)
NIGHT & DAY – John Davis & the Monster Orchestra (Sam)
SUPER QUEEN – Wall of Steel (Smile import)
THAT'S WHERE THE HAPPY PEOPLE GO – Trammps
(Atlantic)
TURN THE BEAT AROUND – Vicki Sue Robinson (RCA)

FLAMINGO, NEW YORK
DJ: Luis Romero

CHAINS/ IT'S NOT WHAT YOU GOT/HE'S A FRIEND –
Eddie Kendricks (Tamla)
IT'S HARD TO STOP WHEN I START LOVING YOU – Living
Inn (Epic)
JUMP FOR JOY– Biddu Orchestra (Epic)
LA VITA – Fussy Cussy (Aquarius import)
MORE, MORE, MORE – Andrea True Connection (Buddah)
ONE FINE DAY – Julie (Tom Cat)
RAIN – Blanche Carter (RCA)
SHARE MY LOVE/HAPPY 'BOUT THE WHOLE THING –
Dee Dee Sharp (TSOP)
THIS EMPTY PLACE – Stephanie Mills (Motown)
TURN THE BEAT AROUND – Vicki Sue Robinson (RCA)

PIER 9, WASHINGTON, DC
DJ: Don Blanton

BORN TO GET DOWN – Muscle Shoals Horns (Bang)
DISCO CONNECTION – Isaac Hayes Movement
(Hot Buttered Soul)
EXTRA, EXTRA (READ ALL ABOUT IT) – Ralph Carter
(Mercury)
I FOUND LOVE ON A DISCO FLOOR – Temprees (Epic)
JUMP FOR JOY– Biddu Orchestra (Epic)
LADY BUMP – Penny McLean (Atco disco version)
LOVE FOR HIRE – Richard Hewson Orchestra (Splash)
MORE, MORE, MORE – Andrea True Connection (Budda)
TURN THE BEAT AROUND – Vicki Sue Robinson (RCA)
WOW – Andre Gagnon (London)

RECOMMENDED: The new **Charles Earland** album,
"Odyssey" (Mercury), mainly because of a light, bouncy
instrumental called "From My Heart To Yours" that is
soft-core disco and quite pleasant. Other possibilities:
"We All Live In The Jungle," "Phire" (with an **Earth,
Wind & Fire** feel), "Sons of the Gods" and "Cosmic
Fever." And listen to two non-disco albums by performers
who've been inactive for a while, the **Stairsteps'**
"2nd Resurrection" (Dark Horse) and **Johnny Taylor's**
"Eargasm" (Columbia), the first an excellently produced
(by **Billy Preston**, **Robert Margouleff** and the group)
collection of new-style soul, the second a more
traditional sound that continues Taylor's r&b
"philosophy" with a '70s studio polish. Both very good
albums for those days when you've ODed on disco. ◐

DISCO FILE TOP 20

1. **MOVIN'** – Brass Construction (UA)
2. **MORE, MORE, MORE** – Andrea True Connection
   (Buddah)
3. **CHANGIN'** – Brass Construction (UA)
4. **TURN THE BEAT AROUND** – Vicki Sue Robinson
   (RCA)
5. **WOW** – Andre Gagnon (London)
6. **LOVE HANGOVER** – Diana Ross (Motown)
7. **DISCO CONNECTION** – Isaac Hayes Movement
   (Hot Buttered Soul)
8. **STREET TALK** – B. C. G. (20th Century)
9. **I HEAR A SYMPHONY** – Hank Crawford (Kudu)
10. **IT'S NOT WHAT YOU GOT/CHAINS** – Eddie
    Kendricks (Tamla)
11. **LOS CONQUISTADORES CHOCOLATES** – Johnny
    Hammond (Milestone)
12. **THAT'S WHERE THE HAPPY PEOPLE GO**
    – Trammps (Atlantic import)
13. **MIGHTY HIGH** – Mighty Clouds of Joy (ABC)
14. **SPANISH HUSTLE** – Fatback Band (Event)
15. **COMMON THIEF** – Vicki Sue Robinson (RCA)
16. **BOHANNON'S BEAT** – Bohannon (Dakar)
17. **LEMME SEE YA GITCHYER THING OFF, BABY/
    TAJ MAHAL** – Crystal Grass (Philips import)
18. **HAPPY MUSIC** – Blackbyrds (Fantasy)
19. **SALSA** – Louie Ramirez (Cotique)
20. **LET'S GROOVE** – Archie Bell & the Drells (TSOP)

MARCH 13, 1976

Again this week, the most important and exciting new releases are are by women. Heading the list: **First Choice**, back with their first album in a year and a half – "So Let Us Entertain You" on Warner Brothers – and more than ready to reclaim their position as the top disco girl group. White-cover advance copies of the lp were distributed through the New York Record Pool last week (with commercial release scheduled for this week) and already the album's blend-together opening cuts, "First Choice Theme" ("Let Us Entertain You") and "Ain't He Bad," have popped up on two new top 10 lists – Tony Smith's from Barefoot Boy and Louis Alers' from Charles Gallery, both in New York. The "Theme" is a light, frothy introduction that ends with a police siren and a radio bulletin voice warning of "three fantastic young ladies known as the First Choice" in a "quote" from "Armed And Extremely Dangerous." This segues immediately into "Ain't He Bad," another of the group's instant classic songs about an irresistible man ("Do you think we could meet him?" "I don't know, but I sure would like to try" – the exchanges between the girls remind me of the **Shangri-Las** in "Leader Of The Pack"). The song runs more than seven minutes, with a long instrumental build at the end and another fabulous disco cross-reference – this time to "Who Is He and What Is He To You." Other cuts to watch: "Gotta Get Away (From You Baby)" which begins and ends with a chugging train (5:27), "I Got A Feeling" (5:27) and "Are You Ready For Me?" with enough spunk to live up to its audacious title (4:05). **Rochelle Fleming's** lead voice is so tough and sharp and rich it deserves comparison with great girl group leads like **Martha Reeves**, and **Ursula Herring** and **Annette Guest** outdo the Vandellas. Production is by **Stan Watson** "with the assistance of" **Norman Harris** and, as usual, it's top notch. A delight. **Penny Mclean's** "Lady Bump" album is out now on Atco and these cuts have already been getting play from the import copies: "Devil Eyes," "Smoke Gets in Your Eyes," "Baby Doll" and "Big Bad Boy." None are quite as snappy as "Lady Bump," included here in its remixed disco version (5:26), but they have that smoothly pleasant **Silver Convention** feel, thanks to producer **Michael Kunze** and arranger **Silvester Levay**. Left field choice: "The Wizard of Bump," a cut that features some strange "witch-doctor" chanting and an attractive break. **Melba Moore's** next album, produced by **Van McCoy**, isn't due out until the end of the month, but Buddah is issuing one cut on a 12-inch pressing this week and the advance taste promises a banquet to come. "This Is It," the disco pressing, is as joyous and high-spirited as anything McCoy has done and, while unmistakeably Van McCoy, the sound always manages to seem fresh and brand new. Louis Alers included "This Is It" with two other Melba Moore cuts, "Free" and "Make Me Believe In You," on his top 10 this week because he's one of the few people who have an advance of the whole album and he's been raving about it.

MOVING UP: "Hurt So Bad" by the **Philly Devotions** (Columbia), "Night And Day" by **John Davis & the Monster Orchestra** (Sam), "More" by **Carol Williams** (Salsoul) and "Eleanor Rigby" from the **Wing & A Prayer Fife & Drum Corps** album (Wing & A Prayer) – all remakes that have proven to be the pick of the current crop.

RECOMMENDED: **Phyllis Hyman's** latest, "Reaching Out For Happiness" (SMI), with an idiosyncratic (and rather erratic) production by **Will Crittendon** (who did Gail's "Consideration") and a lot of surprises in just over seven minutes; **Oliver Sain's** "Party Hearty" (Abet) and **Family Plann's** two-part "Come On Dance with Me" (Drive) – both southern-style funk cuts with a lot of party spirit; and the B side of the new **Tina Charles** single, "Disco Fever" (it's been going around), a pounding Biddu production that goes a little soft in the center but picks up again at the end (4:12 and on Columbia; the A side: "I Love To Love (But My Baby Loves To Dance)"). ◐

> **❝ Again this week, the most important and exciting new releases are by women. Heading the list is First Choice, back and more than ready to claim their position as the top disco girl group ❞**

THE NEW YORK EXPERIENCE, L.A.
DJ: Debbie Backus

CHAINS/HE'S A FRIEND – Eddie Kendricks (Tamla)
DON'T YOU HAVE ANY LOVE IN YOUR HEART – Margo Thunder (Capitol)
ELEANOR RIGBY – Wing & A Prayer Fife & Drum Corps (Wing & A Prayer)
EVERYBODY'S GOTTA DO SOMETHING – Originals (Motown)
I AM SOMEBODY – Jimmy James & the Vagabonds (Pye)
LOVE HANGOVER – Diana Ross (Motown)
MISCHIEF MAKER – Roberta Kelly (Casablanca)
MOVIN'/CHANGIN' – Brass Construction (UA)
NIGHT & DAY – John Davis & the Monster Orchestra (Sam)
TURN THE BEAT AROUND – Vicki Sue Robinson (RCA)

BAREFOOT BOY, NEW YORK
DJ: Tony Smith

CAN YOU GET DOWN/SERIOUS – Universe City (Midland Intl.)
FIRST CHOICE THEME/AIN'T HE BAD – First Choice (Warner Bros.)
HURT SO BAD – Philly Devotions (Columbia)
I HEAR A SYMPHONY/SUGAR FREE – Hank Crawford (Kudu)
LOVE HANGOVER – Diana Ross (Motown)
MORE, MORE, MORE – Andrea True Connection (Buddah)
NIGHT & DAY – John Davis & the Monster Orchestra (Sam)
THAT'S WHERE THE HAPPY PEOPLE GO – Trammps (Atlantic)
TOUCH AND GO – Ecstasy, Passion & Pain (Roulette)
TURN THE BEAT AROUND – Vicki Sue Robinson (RCA)

CONTINENTAL BATHS, NEW YORK
DJ: Jorge Lanzo

ERUCU – "Mahogany" Soundtrack (Motown)
HEART BE STILL – Carl Graves (A&M)
HURT SO BAD – Philly Devotions (Columbia)
LEMME SEE YA GITCHYER THING OFF, BABY/ TAJ MAHAL – Crystal Grass (Philips import)
LOS CONQUISTADORES CHOCOLATES – Johnny Hammond (Milestone)
LOVE HANGOVER – Diana Ross (Motown)
MOVIN'/CHANGIN'/LOVE – Brass Construction (UA)
ROCK CREEK PARK– Blackbyrds (Fantasy)
TOUCH AND GO – Ecstasy, Passion & Pain (Roulette)
TURN THE BEAT AROUND/COMMON THIEF – Vicki Sue Robinson (RCA)

CHARLES GALLERY, NEW YORK
DJ: Louis "Angelo" Alers

FIRST CHOICE THEME – First Choice (Warner Bros.)
FREE/THIS IS IT/MAKE ME BELIEVE IN YOU – Melba Moore (Buddah)
GET UP AND BOOGIE – Silver Convention (Midland Intl.)
LOVE HANGOVER – Diana Ross (Motown)
MORE – Carol Williams (Salsoul)
MOVIN'/CHANGIN' – Brass Construction (UA)
DO THE BUS STOP – Fatback Band (Event)
THAT'S WHERE THE HAPPY PEOPLE GO – Trammps (Atlantic import)
TOUCH AND GO – Ecstasy, Passion & Pain (Roulette)
TURN THE BEAT AROUND – Vicki Sue Robinson (RCA)

We wish to share with you a celebration
in the time of
THE GALLERY
Nicky Siano's
21st Birthday

Saturday. March 20th '76 Midnight

THE GALLERY
172 Mercer Street, N.Y. N.Y. 10012
(212) 229-9667

Just as we expected, **Vicki Sue Robinson** and **Diana Ross** hit the top of the DISCO FILE chart together and both look like they're in for a comfortable stay up there. They lead the resurgence of great new disco product from women. **Jackie Robinson's** "Movin' Like A Superstar" was mentioned here three weeks back as the hot new import record. Now it's out on Ariola America, as a special 12-inch pressing and a regular 45, and proves to be well worth all the advance talk. Robinson sounds like a cross between **Tina Charles** and **Penny McLean**, and the record – like so many of the strongest disco imports, made in Germany – has a clean, razor sharp production with especially effective use of strings. The break on the American release was lengthened, bringing the record to 4:25. **Melba Moore's** new album is titled after its lead track and first single, "This Is It," reviewed and recommended here last week. But if that cut was startling and fresh, the rest of the album more than matches it for spirit and style. Producer **Van McCoy** provides Moore with a varied set, including one song in French ("Play Boy Scout"), one shouting gospel number ("Brand New," featuring **Benny Diggs' New York Community Choir**), a blistering new version of **Curtis Mayfield's** "Make Me Believe In You" (at just over seven minutes, the lp's longest track) and two more disco songs of varying tempo, "Free" and "One Less Morning," both with a typical Van McCoy spiritual uplift. At the end of the album, Moore is shouting, "I feel brand new," and she sounds brand new. This is one of McCoy's best outside production make-overs and should be Melba Moore's most successful album to date (the lucky label: Buddah).

Polly Brown's "You're My Number One" has also been released as a 12-inch and 7-inch 45 on Ariola America this week, after an initial release in England, Brown sounds even more like **Diana Ross** than she did on "Up in a Puff of Smoke" but that's hardly a drawback, and the **Paul Swern-Gerry Shury** production is a superb mix of old Motown and new disco. Happy music. Finally, there's **Candi Staton's** "Young Hearts Run Free" (Warner Brothers), another joyous sound – with an especially great chorus – with a production by **Dave Crawford** (**Mighty Clouds**, **Jackie Moore**). "Young Hearts" is Staton's first move to disco in some time and it works beautifully. Thanks to Cosmo Wyatt in Boston for alerting me to this one.

FEEDBACK: John Colon from Friends Again in New York lists two imports in his top 10 that might appeal to other DJs with a specialized taste for off-the-wall, drum-heavy instrumentals. One, "Yellow Train" by **Resonance** (Celebration, from Canada), is a steady, muffled drum track overlaid with various atmospheric train noises which should go over big with fans of "Erucu" and "2 Pigs & A Hog" – great for mixing. The other single, "Scuttlin'," by **Muscles** (Big Ben), is less attractive on one listening at least – it's a blend of rock guitar and Latin percussion – but Colon says it's grown on his crowd. Also on the Friends Again list, three cuts

❝ It may not be easy to find, but it's worth looking for ❞

INFINITY, NEW YORK
DJ: Bobby Guttadaro

COULD IT BE MAGIC/WASTED – Donna Summer (Oasis)
GOTTA GET AWAY – First Choice (Warner Bros.)
LOVE HANGOVER – Diana Ross (Motown)
MORE, MORE, MORE – Andrea True Connection (Buddah)
NIGHT & DAY – John Davis & the Monster Orchestra (Sam)
SPANISH HUSTLE – Fatback Band (Event)
STREET TALK – B. C. G. (20th Century)
THAT'S WHERE THE HAPPY PEOPLE GO – Trammps (Atlantic)
TOUCH AND GO – Ecstasy, Passion & Pain (Roulette)
TURN THE BEAT AROUND – Vicki Sue Robinson (RCA)

SALSA, BROOKLYN, NEW YORK
DJ: Joey Madonia

HURT SO BAD – Philly Devotions (Columbia)
LOS CONQUISTADORES CHOCOLATES – Johnny Hammond (Milestone)
LOVE HANGOVER – Diana Ross (Motown)
MORE, MORE, MORE – Andrea True Connection (Buddah)
NIGHT & DAY – John Davis & the Monster Orchestra (Sam)
SALSA – Louie Ramirez (Cotique)
SPANISH HUSTLE – Fatback Band (Event)
THAT'S WHERE THE HAPPY PEOPLE GO – Trammps (Atlantic)
TURN THE BEAT AROUND – Vicki Sue Robinson (RCA)
WOW – Andre Gagnon (London)

RHINOCEROS, BOSTON
DJ: John Luongo

DO IT (LIKE YOU AIN'T GOT NO BACKBONE) – Force of Nature (Phila. Intl.)
GET UP AND BOOGIE – Silver Convention (Midland Intl.)
GIVE UP THE FUNK (TEAR THE ROOF OFF THE SUCKER) – Parliament (Casablanca)
LET'S GROOVE – Archie Bell & The Drells (TSOP)
LOS CONQUISTADORES CHOCOLATES – Johnny Hammond (Milestone)
LOVE HANGOVER – Diana Ross (Motown)
LOVE ME RIGHT – Gary Toms Empire (PIP)
MOVIN'/CHANGIN' – Brass Construction (UA)
SPANISH HUSTLE/PARTY TIME – Fatback Band (Event)
TURN THE BEAT AROUND – Vicki Sue Robinson (RCA)

FRIENDS AGAIN, NEW YORK
DJ: John Colon

EVOLUTION – Roy Ayers Ubiquity (Polydor)
FIRST CHOICE THEME/AIN'T HE BAD/ GOTTA GET AWAY – First Choice (Warner Bros.)
LOVE HANGOVER – Diana Ross (Motown)
NIGHT & DAY – John Davis & the Monster Orchestra (Sam)
SCUTTLIN' – Muscles (Big Bear import)
TOUCH AND GO – Ecstasy, Passion & Pain (Roulette)
TRY ME, I KNOW WE CAN MAKE IT – Donna Summer (Oasis)
TURN THE BEAT AROUND – Vicki Sue Robinson (RCA)
YELLOW TRAIN – Resonance (Celebration import)
ZANZIBAR/CARAVAN/A CANCAO DO NOSSO AMOR – El Coco (AVI)

from the second **El Coco** album ("Brazil" on AVI): "Zanzibar," which **Earth, Wind & Fire** previously made; "Caravan," the **Duke Ellington** song again; and "A Cancao Do Nosso Amor," a Brazilian song. All are instrumentals with a European flavor though they were done in Los Angeles by two men, **Michael Lewis** and **Laurin Rinder**, who played all instruments and produced as well. Bobby Guttadaro adds "Delicado" to that list – a bizarre cut with a great drum break and jungle spirit which is also my favorite from the album. It may not be easy to find, but it's worth looking for... John Luongo from Rhinoceros in Boston leans toward the funky side of things, with two of the new cuts in his top 10 falling into this style: **Parliament's** "Give Up The Funk (Tear The Roof Off The Sucker)" (Casablanca album cut) and **Force of Nature's** "Do It (Like You Ain't Got No Backbone)" (Philadelphia International). Bobby Guttadaro says "Give Up The Funk" is doing well at Infinity in New York, too, and here's a few other Luongo favorites in this vein to check out: "Never Ever Do Without You" from the new **Chocolate Milk** album (RCA), produced by **Allen Toussaint** and **Marshall Sehorn**; "Get The Funk Out Ma Face" on the excellent, **Quincy Jones** – produced debut album by the **Brothers Johnson** ("Look Out For #1" on A&M); and "Psychoticbumpschool" by **Bootsy's Rubber Band**, an offshoot of the **Parliament/Funkadelic** thing headed by Funkadelic member **Bootsy Collins** and featuring **Fred Wesley** and **Maceo Parker** from the **James Brown** band.

RECOMMENDED: "Bye Love" by **5000 Volts** (Philips) and **Firefly's** "If You Ever Stopped Callin' Me Baby" (A&M), two singles I passed up the first time around that have since grown on me in spite of their flaws (Firefly's long version is the best one to have – it's 5:31); and "Everybody Party (Get Down)" by a New York group called the **Firebolts**, a rough-edged hustle instrumental but with enough grit to stand up to the other strong "get down" singles out now – "Born to etc." and "(Don't Cha Wanna) etc., etc." – the first release on a young New Jersey label, Greenback Records. Also, do yourself a favor and pick up **Third World** on Island, the most accessible reggae album I can think of, possibly because it's closer to the cool, smooth style of American black music than the usual rough and aggressive Jamaican sound, yet it's not without the distinctive reggae spice and spirit. All of side one is extremely listenable, especially "Sette Messgana" with its jungle intro and "Brand New Beggar." Not for reggae purists, perhaps, but certainly right for the rest of us.

HIGHLY RECOMMENDED: The new Atlantic disco disc version of **Gene Page's** "Wild Cherry," remixed by **Anita Wexler** and Atlantic staff engineer **Jimmy Douglass** from the original 3:52 to six minutes, They've taken all the unused potential of the original track and made the very best of it, bolstering the beginning and introducing a long, rich break at the end that completely transforms the song. One of the most successful and creative disco remixes since the concept began. ◑

MARCH 27, 1976

This week has brought a sudden rush of instrumental releases, the very best of which is the new album by **The Brothers**, "Don't Stop Now" (RCA). Advance word put this one on the level of the **Salsoul Orchestra** album which made me all the more sceptical – after all, The Brothers had had a substantial disco hit with "Are You Ready For This," but their first album was mostly a rehash of disco standards and hardly a preparation for creative giant step of the current album. "Don't Stop Now" deserves the comparison to the enormously successful Salsoul Orchestra lp primarily because both are richly textured instrumental albums without a single waste cut, but The Brothers are even more impressive for the variety of their tracks, each of which has a different flavor and mood. There are touches here from a number of other disco big bands as well as from classic **Isaac Hayes** productions, but the material has gone through an exciting synthesis and come out spanking new. The synthesizer here is producer **Warren Schatz**, who also did the **Vicki Sue Robinson** album; both releases establish him as the young producer to watch – one with something different to say in the disco idiom. Prime cuts: "Under The Skin," which got the kind of frenzied response usually reserved for old favorites on its first play at David Mancuso's Loft this past weekend; "Brothers Theme;" "Were You Ready For That;" "Last Chance To Dance;" "Make Love;" and a personal favorite, "Voce Abousou," a Brazilian song turned into a sweeping hustle that should turn even more people on to the beauties of the Brazilian sound, a style that could surface very big this year.

One of the best instrumental singles to come out so far this year is called "Get Off Your Aahh! And Dance" by **Foxy** (Dash), on one of the many TK labels but definitely not the usual Miami Sound. There's a little bit of everything here, set off by especially terrific conga breaks and flute riffs, and the record's A and B sides (Parts 1 & 2) together run over six minutes. Excellent. **Van McCoy** also has a new instrumental single out in the vein of his "Love Is The Answer" and "African Symphony": heavily orchestrated, just slightly overripe – a refinement of the movie soundtrack style with some of the genre's schlock still clinging around the edges. This one's called "Night Walk" (H&L, formerly Avco), and as usual, McCoy knows just the right combination of the sentimental and the severe to make things move on the dance floor.

Other notable instrumental albums: "Night Journey" by **Doc Severinsen**, the bandleader on the "Tonight Show," who turns out a totally unexpected set of jazz cuts with a number of disco possibilities including the title cut, "I Wanna Be With You," "You Put the Shine On Me" and "Spanish Dreams" (on Epic); "A Different Shade Of Black," **Louie Ramirez'** debut album featuring "Salsa" (at 6:55), a Latinized "Do It Any Way You Wanna," the familiar theme song, "Laura" (the only cut produced by – surprise – **Frankie Crocker**), and one other possible disco cut in the title track) also a nice Latin number called "Barrio Nuevo" – all on Cotique); and **Maynard Ferguson's** "Primal Scream" album (Columbia), which features a disco-style "Pagliacci" (?!) that seems to be picking up a lot of admirers though it has yet to win over this listener. Note: the "original television soundtrack recording" of music from the sci-fi series "Space: 1999" (RCA) includes an enticing, if quite short, synthesizer and percussion cut called "Black Sun" that should be checked out.

Just verging on the instrumental, there's the new **Silver Convention** album (Midland International), opening up, appropriately, with "Get Up And Boogie" (6:22), which has been steadily picking up in popularity (jumped 10 spots on the DISCO FILE Top 20 this week) and should help propel the album even if it isn't as strong and fully-packed as the group's first release. The most attractive cuts: "San Francisco Hustle," "You've Got What It Takes (To Please Your Woman)," "No No Joe" and "Old Wine In New Bottles," all featuring the kind of sexy vocals that distinguished the earlier lp and that wonderfully clean, cutting German production by **Michael Kunze**. Should get a lot of exposure in the next few weeks and, I suspect, grow on us the way "Get Up And Boogie" has.

Carl Graves' "Heart Be Still" (A&M), released last November, has been steadily picking up club play in the last month or two and now the song's co-writer, **Lee Garrett**, has come out with his own version, a fine one, on his impressive debut album just out on Chrysalis. On several cuts Garrett puts across the kind of unexpected, fresh slap in the face **Vernon Burch** delivered last year: the sound is rough and ready and hardly run-of-the-mill, especially on the exceptionally strong "How Can I Be Your Man" (7:20), a happy "You're My Everything" (the simultaneous single

> ❝ Prime cut "Under the Skin" got the kind of frenzied response usually reserved for old favorites on its first play at David Mancuso's Loft this past weekend ❞

PIPS INTERNATIONAL, LOS ANGELES
DJ: Don Tegler

COULD IT BE MAGIC – Donna Summer (Oasis)
DISCO LADY – Johnnie Taylor (Columbia)
GET UP AND BOOGIE – Silver Convention (Midland Intl.)
HAPPY MUSIC – Blackbyrds (Fantasy)
LIVIN' FOR THE WEEKEND – O'Jays (Phila. Intl.)
LOVE HANGOVER – Diana Ross (Motown)
MOVIN' – Brass Construction (UA)
MOVE ME – Jim Gilstrap (Chelsea)
STREET TALK – B.C.G. (20th Century)
WET WEEKEND – Rock Gazers (Pilgrim)

HOLLYWOOD, NEW YORK
DJ: Joe Palminteri

AMERICA (WE NEED THE LIGHT) – Billy Paul (Phila. Intl.)
FIRST CHOICE THEME/AIN'T HE BAD – First Choice (Warner Bros.)
GET UP AND BOOGIE – Silver Convention (Midland Intl.)
LOVE HANGOVER – Diana Ross (Motown)
REACHING OUT FOR HAPPINESS – Fay Hauser (SMI)
SPANISH HUSTLE – Fatback Band (Event)
STREET TALK – B.C.G. (20th Century)
THAT'S WHERE THE HAPPY PEOPLE GO – Trammps (Atlantic)
TRY ME I KNOW WE CAN MAKE IT – Donna Summer (Oasis)
TURN THE BEAT AROUND –Vicki Sue Robinson (RCA)

BROADWAY, BROOKLYN, N.Y.
DJ: Gary Antoniou

DISCO FEVER – Tina Charles (Columbia)
GET UP AND BOOGIE – Silver Convention (Midland Intl.)
I'M GOING THROUGH CHANGES NOW – Brown Sugar (Capitol)
LOVE HANGOVER – Diana Ross (Motown)
SMOKE GETS IN YOUR EYES – Penny Mclean (Atco)
SPANISH HUSTLE – Fatback Band (Event)
THAT'S WHERE THE HAPPY PEOPLE GO – Trammps (Atlantic)
TOUCH AND GO – Ecstasy, Passion & Pain (Roulette)
TRY ME I KNOW WE CAN MAKE IT – Donna Summer (Oasis)
TURN THE BEAT AROUND – Vicki Sue Robinson (RCA)

DEN 1, CHICAGO
DJ: Artie Feldman

HURT SO BAD – Philly Devotions (Columbia)
INSIDE AMERICA – Juggy Murray Jones (Jupiter)
LOVE HANGOVER – Diana Ross (Motown)
MORE, MORE, MORE – Andrea True Connection (Buddah)
MOVIN' – Brass Construction (UA)
SING A HAPPY FUNKY SONG – Miz Davis (Now)
TOUCH AND GO – Ecstasy, Passion & Pain (Roulette)
TURN THE BEAT AROUND –Vicki Sue Robinson (RCA)
WOW – Andre Gagnon (London)
YOU BEAT ME TO THE PUNCH – Retta Young (All Platinum)

release), "Love Enough For Two" and "Don't Let It Get You Down." Not to be missed. My favorite version of "Heart Be Still," however, remains Jackie Moore's – on her "Make Me Feel Like A Woman" album (Kayvette), released October 1975 and recently reserviced to give the cut another chance.

Also recommended: **Rare Earth's** "Do It Right," produced by **Norman Whitfield**, who did their whole new album, "Midnight Lady" (Rare Earth), and has given them a nice taste of his old **Temptations** sound – hard, funky, beautifully produced. "Do It Right" is 6:20 and gets better as it goes on; there's also a very interesting long (11 :30) instrumental called "Wine, Women And Song" that closes the album.

Recommended singles: "Disco Man" by **Three Ounces of Love** (where did they get that name?) on IX Chains, a tribute worthy of joining **Johnnie Taylor's** "Disco Lady" and considerably more disco-styled than that hit; and a gorgeous slow cut called "Goddess Of Love" by **Lonnie Liston Smith** (Flying Dutchman). ◉

DISCO FILE TOP 20

1. TURN THE BEAT AROUND –Vicki Sue Robinson (RCA)
2. LOVE HANGOVER – Diana Ross (Motown)
3. THAT'S WHERE THE HAPPY PEOPLE GO – Trammps (Atlantic)
4. MOVIN' – Brass Construction (UA)
5. SPANISH HUSTLE – Fatback Band (Event)
6. TOUCH AND GO – Ecstasy, Passion & Pain (Roulette)
7. MORE, MORE, MORE – Andrea True Connection (Buddah)
8. NIGHT & DAY – John Davis & the Monster Orchestra (Sam)
9. GET UP AND BOOGIE – Silver Convention (Midland Intl.)
10. HURT SO BAD – Philly Devotions (Columbia)
11. CHANGIN' – Brass Construction (UA)
12. STREET TALK – B.C.G. (20th Century)
13. FIRST CHOICE THEME/AIN'T HE BAD – First Choice (Warner Bros.)
14. LOS CONQUISTADORES CHOCOLATES – Johnny Hammond (Milestone)
15. WOW – Andre Gagnon (London)
16. TRY ME I KNOW WE CAN MAKE IT – Donna Summer (Oasis)
17. COMMON THIEF – Vicki Sue Robinson (RCA)
18. IT'S NOT WHAT YOU GOT/CHAINS – Eddie Kendricks (Tamla)
19. ELEANOR RIGBY – Wing & A Prayer Fife & Drum Corps (Wing & A Prayer)
20. LEMME SEE YA GITCHYER THING OFF, BABY/ TAJ MAHAL – Crystal Grass (Philips import)

APRIL 3, 1976

A mixed bag this week, highlighted by these records:

1) "Rocky Road," the first album from **The New Ventures** (UA) and a wonderfully solid one. No filler here, but side one has the choicest cuts: "Temptation, Temptation" which soars on a cool spray of strings and airy female vocals; an instrumental version of **Bobby Womack's** party-people anthem, "Daylight," that's almost as attractive as the original; and the opener, an interpretation of the standard "Moonlight Serenade," that manages to survive its formula styling (those awful "Wooo!" ·sounds) and turn into something quite nice ("Moonlight," in a somewhat abbreviated form, is the new single). Side two opens with "Superstar Revue," which still sounds great, and includes "The Stroke," a medium-tempo cut with some dramatic vocal touches, and "Step Out," closer to a hustle. All the cuts but "Step Out" run over four minutes, several over five, and most of them were co-written by **Vernon Burch**, **Denny Diante** and **Spencer Proffer** produced.

2) **Sweet Music's** reworking of **George McCrae's** "I Get Lifted" (Wand) which injects a driving energy into the ecstatically laid-back original. The new lead vocal is by a husky-voiced woman who shouts with the kind of fervor we've been missing lately and gives the song a whole new life. Too powerful to end just short of three minutes, this is one record that deserves a longer "disco version."

3) **Victoria Medlin's** "No Chain Reaction" (London) sounds like one of those odd, gutsy girl group records that develop cult followings (like "Dirty Feet" by **Jenny's Daughters** or "Now Is The Time" by **Sisters Love**) but is altogether too strange for the average taste. This one was produced by **Allen Toussaint** in a totally uncharacteristic style – a melting pot of New South funk and obscure '50s r&b. Who is Victoria Medlin and what is she saying? Probably for girl group freaks only, but definitely worth a listen.

4) **Fire & Rain's** "Make Love To Me" (20th Century) is another breathy, moaning sexsong that should feel very comfortable up there with "More, More, More," "Love Hangover" and "Try Me I Know We Can Make It" – the new pillow talk explosion. "Make Love To Me," as its title indicates, is not particularly into lyric subtlety, but the production is superb, especially on the 4:25 long version. Ooooh. Ahhhhh. Etc. Due out this week.

FEEDBACK: Tom Savarese alerted me to a fine cut on the latest **Boz Scaggs**, album "Silk Degrees" (Columbia). The track is called "Lowdown," it runs 5:15 and it's hardly standard disco, which is what makes it so satisfying. Scaggs has a distinctive, jazzy voice and his lyrics have intelligence and wit (two quantities disco lyrics are sadly lacking in; with few exceptions, disco tends to throw lyric verses aside in favor of repetitive lines or chants which do heighten the tribal mood but don't often communicate on any but the most basic level). "Lowdown"'s pace and delicacy may not work for many crowds, but Savarese makes it work at 12 West and it should be checked out, if only as an introduction to a strong performer who deserves more attention... Savarese and Ray Sasso from The Archdiocese in Queens both listed a long (eight minutes plus) "Medley" cut from the recently imported "Rhythmo Tropical" album by the **Chocolats** (also known as the **Chocolate Boys**) on Avalanche Records. The cut is a blend of six or seven songs with a Latin/Brazilian feel and a **Bimbo Jet** synthesizer sound. It's frivolously high-spirited, like a very funny party, and such an infectious mood is hard to resist. Disco-on-the-Run's Jeff Baugh, currently at C'est La Vie in New York, first mentioned this track to me a week or two back and advises that the album's title cut is also worth noting... Other tips from Tom Savarese: an import from France by the **Champ's Boys Orchestra** which is a danceable

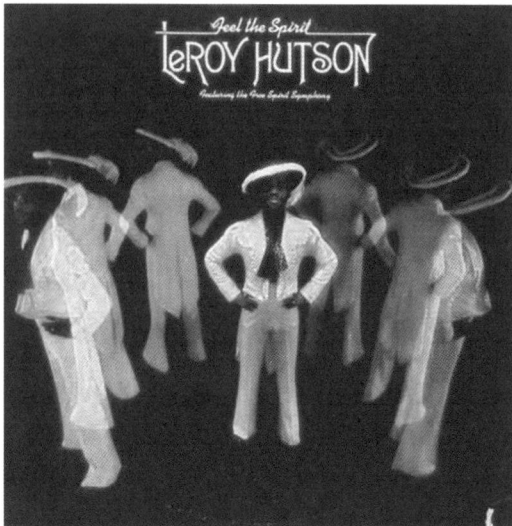

12 WEST, NEW YORK
DJ: Tom Savarese

GOTTA GET AWAY – First Choice (Warner Bros.)
LOVE HANGOVER – Diana Ross (Motown)
MEDLEY – Chocolats (Avalanche import)
NO, NO, JOE/SAN FRANCISCO HUSTLE – Silver Convention (Midland Intl.)
STREET TALK – B.C.G. (20th Century)
THAT'S WHERE THE HAPPY PEOPLE GO – Trammps (Atlantic)
THIS IS IT/PLAY BOY SCOUT/BRAND NEW – Melba Moore (Buddah)
TOUCH AND GO – Ecstasy, Passion & Pain (Roulette)
TRY ME I KNOW WE CAN MAKE IT/ WASTED/COULD IT BE MAGIC/COME WITH ME – Donna Summer (Oasis)
TURN THE BEAT AROUND/COMMON THIEF –Vicki Sue Robinson (RCA)

THE ARCHDIOCESE, QUEENS, N.Y.
DJ: Ray Sasso

GET UP AND BOOGIE – Silver Convention (Midland Intl.)
LET'S GROOVE – Archie Bell & the Drells (TSOP)
LOVE HANGOVER – Diana Ross (Motown)
MEDLEY – Chocolats (Avalanche import)
MIGHTY HIGH – Mighty Clouds of Joy (ABC)
MORE, MORE, MORE – Andrea True Connection (Buddah)
STREET TALK – B.C.G. (20th Century)
THAT'S WHERE THE HAPPY PEOPLE GO – Trammps (Atlantic)
THIS IS IT – Melba Moore (Buddah)
TURN THE BEAT AROUND –Vicki Sue Robinson (RCA)

15 LANSDOWNE STREET, BOSTON
DJ: Danae Jocovidis

FIRST CHOICE THEME/AIN'T HE BAD – First Choice (Warner Bros.)
GET UP AND BOOGIE/NO, NO JOE – Silver Convention (Midland Intl.)
LOVE HANGOVER – Diana Ross (Motown)
MOVIN' LIKE A SUPERSTAR – Jackie Robinson (Ariola)
THAT'S WHERE THE HAPPY PEOPLE GO – Trammps (Atlantic)
THIS IS IT – Melba Moore (Buddah)
TOUCH AND GO – Ecstasy, Passion & Pain (Roulette)
TRY ME I KNOW WE CAN MAKE IT/ WASTED/COULD IT BE MAGIC/COME WITH ME – Donna Summer (Oasis)
TURN THE BEAT AROUND/COMMON THIEF – Vicki Sue Robinson (RCA)
YOUNG HEARTS RUN FREE – Candi Staton (Warner Bros.)

THURSDAY'S, NEW YORK
DJ: Jules Franco

AMERICA (WE NEED THE LIGHT) – Billy Paul (Phila. Intl.)
FEEL THE SPIRIT – LeRoy Hutson (Curtom)
LET'S GROOVE – Archie Bell & the Drells (TSOP)
LOVE HANGOVER – Diana Ross (Motown)
MOVIN'/CHANGIN' – Brass Construction (UA)
NIGHT AND DAY – John Davis & Monster Orchestra (SAM)
THANK YOU BABY – Leone Thomas (Don)
THAT'S WHERE THE HAPPY PEOPLE GO – Trammps (Atlantic disco version)
TOUCH AND GO – Ecstasy, Passion & Pain (Roulette)
TURN THE BEAT AROUND –Vicki Sue Robinson (RCA)

version of "Tubular Bells" (Vogue); "Dancing Free" by **Hot Ice**, now with a label called Raggs, though not yet available all over; and "The Kool Gent," a kool instrumental from the new **Olympic Runners** album ("Don't Let Up" on London)... Danae Jacovidis at 15 Lansdowne Street in Boston picks the "Save Me" cut from **Nanette Workman's** debut album (Big Tree) – the one song everyone's zeroed in on. It's not as sharp as Workman's "If It Wasn't For The Money" – this one comes Closer to **Penny McLean** – but it's got a certain flash.

ALSO RECOMMENDED: The new **Choice 4** album on RCA, produced by **Van McCoy** (does that man ever sleep?) and featuring "Hey What's That Dance You're Doing," a real get-down song and a change of pace for McCoy; "A Beautiful Glow;" "Mysterious Lady" and "Come Down to Earth," another change of pace which is almost in the **Norman Whitfield** mold... "Ebb Tide," the instrumental lp from **Love Sounds** (Pye) which falls into a pleasant **Love Unlimited Orchestra** groove and includes a good remake of "I've Got You Under My Skin," "Tornado" from "The Whiz," two originals called "Sounds Of love" and "Return To The Stars," plus the title cut, already a minor disco hit. Good mood music... And these singles: "Don't Stop Now" by **Hot Chocolate** (Big Tree), definitely for anyone who liked "You Sexy Thing" – this new one sounds like an impassioned version of that song – and likely to pick up even more fans for the group; "Love Hangover" as done by the **Fifth Dimension** (ABC), not up to Miss Ross' original but respectable enough in its long version (5:46) to use as a variation every once in a while; and two cuts from the **Eddie Drennon & BBS Unlimited** album now out on a 45 back-to-back, "Do It Nice And Easy" and "Let's Do It Again" (Friends Be Co.). ◒

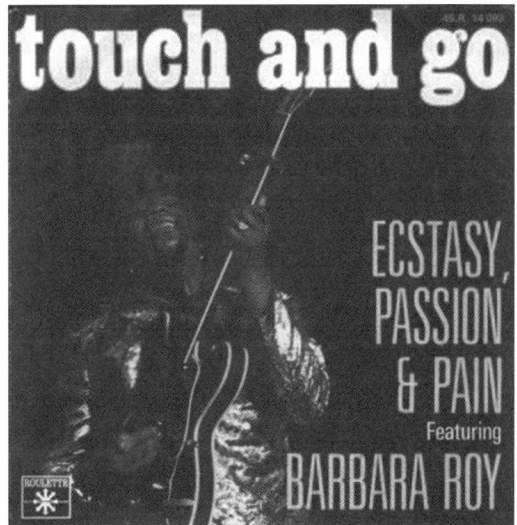

"On Walter Gibbons' top 10 this week there's a new record called "Ten Percent" by Double Exposure that Gibbons has had a near exclusive on after being called in by Salsoul's Ken Cayre to supervise the song's edit"

Though the flood of made-for-disco records shows no signs of letting up – the most common complaint I heard this week was about the difficulty of finding time to listen to them all – fewer records are receiving the kind of consensus that moves them into the Top 20 list in recent weeks. Not only is the list dominated by women – who occupy seven of the top 10 spots and 13 positions altogether – but more than ever before, it's dominated by a few albums whose widespread popularity has overshadowed and, for the moment, shut out all other contenders. Every cut on **Donna Summer's** "Love Trilogy" album is on the Top 20 this week, led off by the strongest track, "Try Me I Know We Can Make It," at number 5. Then there are three cuts each from the new albums by **Silver Convention** and **First Choice**, and two, including the number one spot, from **Vicki Sue Robinson's** debut lp. Two other albums with four or more cuts getting heavy play right now – **Melba Moore's** "This Is It" and "Don't Stop Now" by **The Brothers** – have a toe-hold on the Top 20 with one track each this week and are almost sure to be trailing in other tracks in the next week or two.

FEEDBACK: On Walter Gibbons' top 10 this week from Galaxy 21 in New York, there's a new record called "Ten Percent" by **Double Exposure** (Salsoul) that Gibbons has had a near exclusive on for the past two weeks after being called in by Salsoul's Ken Cayre to

help supervise the song's edit. The record, a **Baker, Harris & Young** production that sounds like the very best of their work with the **Trammps**, is due out late this week on a special 12-inch pressing featuring the Gibbons edit (9:45) on one side and a shorter (7:07) edit by Cayre himself on the reverse. Either one you choose, the record is superhot, with a classic Philadelphia male group sound – a mix of Trammps and **O'Jays** – among the most attractive I've heard in the past year. And in the background: the **Salsoul Orchestra**. The optimistic message for our times: "Ten percent of something beats 100 percent of nothing at all." A record to watch... Also on the Galaxy 21 list: the new **Biddu Orchestra** single from England, "Rain Forest" (Epic), which, if it follows the pattern of Biddu's past imports, should be cropping up on a number of other lists very soon; and **Ashford & Simpson's** "One More Try" which appears on Thomas Pearson's list from Leviticus (New York) as well, joined by another cut from the A&S "Come As You Are" album (Warner Bros.), "Sell The House." Gibbons also suggests: "Let It Shine," a fine danceable cut from the new **Santana** album ("Amigos" on Columbia) which he reports has been getting very good reaction.

Thomas Pearson is enthusiastic about the new **Kokomo** album, "Rise and Shine!" (Columbia), listing three cuts on the Leviticus top 10 – "Use Your Imagination," "Feelin' Good" and "Little Girl." My favorite is "Imagination" – I'm kicking myself for letting it get by on the first listening – so consider it recommended. Pearson also had praise for the new **Temptations** album, "Wings Of Love" (Gordy), from which he's playing two cuts, "China Doll" and "Sweetness in the Dark" (you might also try "Up The Creek (Without A Paddle)" which sounds like a follow-up to "Shakey Ground")... "Tee" Scott from Better Days in New York has some more Motown tips: "When You Came" by **Smokey Robinson** from Smokey's new Tamla album, "Smokey's Family Robinson," and doing well enough for Scott to pop up on his top 10 this week. Scott is also having some success with a second cut on the **Diana Ross** album – after "Love Hangover" that is – called "One Love In My Lifetime," a medium-paced cut that reminds me of the sort of material Ross did a year or two before she left the Supremes. Speaking of "Love Hangover," Scott also reports unexpected good reaction to the **Fifth Dimension's** version of that song and similar positive feedback has come from a number of other DJs, who usually blend with the two versions together.

Look out for **Millie Jackson's** next album, due out this week and titled "Free And In Love" (Spring). The tough, hard-talking queen of the sexual concept album has two disco cuts included here for the first time in quite a while and one, "House For Sale," is quite strong. The album traces Millie's breakaway from a marriage and a gradual drift into a new relationship with a lot of fooling around in between to give plenty of room for the sort of raunchy sexsongs she's famous for. "House

GALAXY 21, NEW YORK
DJ: Walter Gibbons

BORN TO GET DOWN – Muscle Shoals Horns (Bang)
EVOLUTION – Roy Ayers Ubiquity (Polydor)
ONE MORE TRY – Ashford & Simpson (Warner Bros.)
RAIN FOREST – Biddu Orchestra (Epic import)
SING A HAPPY FUNKY SONG – Miz Davis (Now)
TEN PERCENT – Double Exposure (Salsoul)
THIS IS IT – Melba Moore (Buddah)
TOUCH AND GO – Ecstasy, Passion & Pain (Roulette)
TRY ME I KNOW WE CAN MAKE IT/COULD IT BE MAGIC/COME WITH ME – Donna Summer (Oasis)
UNDER THE SKIN/MAKE LOVE/BROTHERS THEME – The Brothers (RCA)

LEVITICUS, NEW YORK
DJ: Thomas Pearson

ELEANOR RIGBY – Wing & A Prayer Fife & Drum Corps (Wing & A Prayer)
FEELIN' GOOD/USE YOUR IMAGINATION/ LITTLE GIRL – Kokomo (Columbia)
FIRST CHOICE THEME/AIN'T HE BAD – First Choice (Warner Bros.)
HEY, WHAT'S THAT DANCE YOU'RE DOING – Choice Four (RCA)
INSTANT LOVE – Main Ingredient (RCA)
LOVE HANGOVER – Diana Ross (Motown
MY SOUL IS SATISFIED/BUCKHEAD – Atlanta Disco Band (Ariola America)
SELL THE HOUSE/ONE MORE TRY – Ashford & Simpson (Warner Bros.)
TURN THE BEAT AROUND –Vicki Sue Robinson (RCA)
WHAT CAN I SAY /LOWDOWN – Boz Scaggs (Columbia)

DCA CLUB, PHILADELPHIA
DJ: Kurt Borusiewicz

BROTHERS THEME/VOCE ABOUSOU/ MAKE LOVE – Brothers (RCA)
GET OFF YOUR AAHH! AND JAM – Foxy (Dash)
GET UP AND BOOGIE/SAN FRANCISCO HUSTLE/YOU'VE GOT WHAT IT TAKES – Silver Convention (Midland Intl.)
I LOVE TO LOVE – Tina Charles/Al Downing (Columbia/Polydor)
LOVE HANGOVER – Diana Ross (Motown)
MY LOVE SUPREME – Milton Hamilton Crystalized (TR)
REACHING OUT FOR HAPPINESS – Fay Hauser (SMI)
THAT'S WHERE THE HAPPY PEOPLE GO – Trammps (Atlantic)
TURN THE BEAT AROUND –Vicki Sue Robinson (RCA)

BETTER DAYS, NEW YORK
DJ: "Tee" Scott

BROTHERS THEME/VOCE ABOUSOU/UNDER THE SKIN – Brothers (RCA)
FIRST CHOICE THEME/AIN'T HE BAD/ARE YOU READY FOR ME? – First Choice (Warner Bros.)
GET UP AND BOOGIE/SAN FRANCISCO HUSTLE/NO, NO JOE – Silver Convention (Midland Intl.)
LOVE HANGOVER – Diana Ross (Motown)
TAKE IT – Vast Majority (D&M Sound)
THAT'S WHERE THE HAPPY PEOPLE GO – Trammps (Atlantic)
TOUCH AND GO – Ecstasy, Passion & Pain (Roulette)
TRY ME I KNOW WE CAN MAKE IT – Donna Summer (Oasis)
TURN THE BEAT AROUND/COMMON THIEF – Vicki Sue Robinson (RCA)

For Sale" is the breakaway song and opens the set with a fine punch. The other disco possibility is "Bad Risk" – sample lyric: "You're a bad risk/I can't afford to take a chance on you/Just one kiss and there I'll be/ refinancing you." Jackson fits right in there with the other women on the disco charts these days but she's the only one who's actually producing her own material – with **Brad Shapiro** so she deserves a little extra attention.

RECOMMENDED: "Ma-Mo-Ah" by the **Tony Valor Sounds Orchestra** (Brunswick), a great, full-of-changes instrumental that sounds like a European import; "Tubular Bells," reported here last week as an import but now available on Janus by the **Champ's Boys Orchestra** who have taken the **Mike Oldfield** composition and made it sound like "Love To Love You Baby" and a number of other things all blended into one – fascinating (long version: 4:10); Neil Sedaka's "Love In The Shadows" (Rocket), which might be a little left field for some tastes but has a nice feel and terrific production; and, for those patriotic moments, **Paul Jabara's** new single, a disco version of, would you believe, "Yankee Doodle Dandy" (A&M) that is cute, fun and surprisingly attractive. ◉

DISCO FILE TOP 20

1. **TURN THE BEAT AROUND** –Vicki Sue Robinson (RCA)
2. **LOVE HANGOVER** – Diana Ross (Motown)
3. **THAT'S WHERE THE HAPPY PEOPLE GO** – Trammps (Atlantic)
4. **TOUCH AND GO** – Ecstasy, Passion & Pain (Roulette)
5. **TRY ME I KNOW WE CAN MAKE IT** – Donna Summer (Oasis)
6. **GET UP AND BOOGIE** – Silver Convention (Midland Intl.)
7. **FIRST CHOICE THEME/AIN'T HE BAD** – First Choice (Warner Bros.)
8. **SPANISH HUSTLE** – Fatback Band (Event)
9. **STREET TALK** – B.C.G. (20th Century)
10. **COULD IT BE MAGIC/WASTED** – Donna Summer (Oasis)
11. **THIS IS IT** – Melba Moore (Buddah)
12. **MOVIN'** – Brass Construction (UA)
13. **MORE, MORE, MORE** – Andrea True Connection (Buddah)
14. **NIGHT & DAY** – John Davis & the Monster Orchestra (Sam)
15. **BROTHERS THEME** – Brothers (RCA)
16. **NO, NO JOE/SAN FRANCISCO HUSTLE** – Silver Convention (Midland Intl.)
17. **COMMON THIEF** – Vicki Sue Robinson (RCA)
18. **GOTTA GET AWAY** – First Choice (Warner Bros.)
19. **HURT SO BAD** – Philly Devotions (Columbia)
20. **COME WITH ME** – Donna Summer (Oasis)

APRIL 17, 1976

An unusually large number of new 12-inch disco pressings have come out in the past two weeks, the most interesting of which are two eccentric small label productions, "Dancing Free" by **Hot Ice** (Rage) and "Making Love" by **Sammy Gordon & the Hip Huggers** (Greg). "Dancing Free," first reported by 12 West's Tom Savarese two issues back (when we incorrectly listed the label as Raggs) and now on Rene Hewitt's top 10 from Chase in New York, is essentially an instrumental with some rather shrill and not totally comprehensible singing by a girl group. That is to say, it's not the vocals but their setting that gives the record its flavor – a strange rawness, especially on the organ and horns, which gives the record a ragged, aggressive edge. Clearly, this will not be for all tastes but there is something very compelling about "Dancing Free" and Hewitt reports that it gets the same kind of response in his club as "Love Hangover," while John Hedges at The City in San Francisco says it's also doing very well with his crowd. The record is available on a 12-inch disc at just over 9 minutes and on a regular single at 6:10 or 3:10.

"Making Love" is another record that leaves something to be desired technically – there's a very muddy quality about some parts of the mix – but, again, it's an attractive eccentricity that sets this record off from the glossy, predictable productions we're used to (not that I'm recommending muddy mixes, but there's a certain crude energy here that often gets ironed out in the slick mixes). The record is overlaid with a dense layer of synthesizer effects – electronic squiggles and snaps – that give it a space trip atmosphere that makes an odd contrast to its sexy lyrics – "Feels so good when you're makin' love to me/I'm in ecstasy when you're makin' love to me" – especially when the girls settle into a chorus of moans and sighs toward the end. This one is also available in a large disc (7:02) and a 45 (5:00 on one side, 3:15 on the other), both on the Greg label, apparently named after the record's co-producer/co-writer, **Greg Carmichael**.

Other 12-inch pressings worth note: "Tears, Tears, Tears" by **Black Satin** (Buddah), longer than the album version and featuring a nice, string-swept break but still not a sharp as it should be; "Get The Funk Out Ma Face" by **The Brothers Johnson** (A&M), more than twice the length of the lp version (6:01) and even more of a delight for fans of sprightly jazz funk, with the additional material making it more plausible as a disco cut; and two remakes in the pop disco style, "Sweet Georgia Brown" by **Moonlion** (PIP) and "Music, Music, Music" by **Teresa Brewer** (Signature), both too cloyingly cute for my tastes and neither a model of disco originality, but perfect for some crowds (one DJ in Queens called up last week to say Teresa Brewer was number one in his

> **❝ An unusually large number of new 12-inch disco pressings have come out in the past two weeks, the most interesting of which are eccentric small label productions ❞**

BUTTERMILK BOTTOM, NEW YORK
DJ: Rafael Charres

COMMON THIEF –Vicki Sue Robinson (RCA)
LOVE HANGOVER – Diana Ross (Motown)
MOVIN' LIKE A SUPERSTAR – Jackie Robinson (Ariola)
ONE MORE TRY – Ashford & Simpson (Warner Bros.)
TEMPTATION, TEMPTATION – The New Ventures (UA)
TEN PERCENT – Double Exposure (Salsoul)
TOUCH AND GO – Ecstasy, Passion & Pain (Roulette)
USE YOUR IMAGINATION – Kokomo (Columbia)
WERE YOU READY FOR THAT/UNDER THE SKIN – Brothers (RCA)
YOUNG HEARTS RUN FREE – Candi Staton (Warner Bros.)

RUMBOTTOMS, HOLLYWOOD, FLORIDA
DJ: Bob Lombardi

BROTHERS THEME/UNDER THE SKIN/VOCE ABOUSOU – Brothers (RCA)
GET OFF YOUR AAHH! AND DANCE – Foxy (Dash)
GOTTA GET AWAY/I GOT A FEELING – First Choice (Warner Bros.)
LOVE HANGOVER – Diana Ross/Fifth Dimension (Motown/ABC)
LOVE ME RIGHT – Gary Toms Empire (PIP)
MOVIN'/CHANGIN' – Brass Construction (UA)
SOUL MAN – Calhoon (Warner Spector)
TURN THE BEAT AROUND –Vicki Sue Robinson (RCA)
YOU'VE GOT WHAT IT TAKES – Silver Convention (Midland Intl.)

THE CITY, SAN FRANCISCO
DJ: John Hedges

GET UP AND BOOGIE/NO, NO JOE – Silver Convention (Midland Intl.)
GOTTA GET AWAY/AR YOU READY FOR ME? – First Choice (Warner Bros.)
LOVE HANGOVER – Diana Ross (Motown)
MORE, MORE, MORE – Andrea True Connection (Buddah)
MOVIN' LIKE A SUPERSTAR – Jackie Robinson (Ariola America)
NIGHT AND DAY – John Davis & Monster Orchestra (SAM)
THAT'S WHERE THE HAPPY PEOPLE GO – Trammps (Atlantic)
TRY ME I KNOW WE CAN MAKE IT – Donna Summer (Oasis)
TURN THE BEAT AROUND –Vicki Sue Robinson (RCA)
WOW – Andre Gagnon (London)

CHASE, NEW YORK
DJ: Rene Hewitt

DANCING FREE – Hot Ice (Rage disco version)
HOW CAN I BE A MAN – Lee Garrett (Chrysalis)
LOS CONQUISTADORES CHOCOLATES – Johnny Hammond (Milestone)
LOVE HANGOVER – Diana Ross/Fifth Dimension (Motown/ABC)
MA-MO-AH – Tony Valor Sounds Orchestra (Brunswick)
ONE MORE TRY – Ashford & Simpson (Warner Bros.)
TEN PERCENT – Double Exposure (Salsoul)
THAT'S WHERE THE HAPPY PEOPLE GO – Trammps (Atlantic)
TIME MOVES ON – Strutt (Brunswick)
TURN THE BEAT AROUND –Vicki Sue Robinson (RCA)

club after only two nights). Finally, Motown has issued a 12-inch of **Diana Ross'** "Love Hangover" on which the same track is repeated four times, twice to a side. Are they trying to tell us something?

FEEDBACK: Rafael Charres at Buttermilk Bottom in New York reports that **Charles Earland's** "From My Heart To Yours," a loose, sparkling instrumental from his recent Mercury album, "Odyssey," is nearly a top 10 record at his club and that "Intergalactic Love Song" from the same album is also doing well... Rene Hewitt lists **Strutt's** "Time Moves On" in his top 10 this week and other DJs report playing "Front Row Romeo," especially the instrumental version which most justifies the group's comparison to **B.T. Express**, and "Funky Baby Feet" from the Brunswick album. Nothing stunning here, but a fine drive and intensity prevail on the best cuts... Moving up steadily: **Ashford & Simpson's** "One More Try," from the "Come As You Are" album (Warner Brothers); **Jackie Robinson's** "Movin' Like A Superstar" (Ariola America); "Ten Percent" by **Double Exposure** (Salsoul) – all new entries on the DISCO FILE Top 20 – and **Candi Staton's** "Young Hearts Run Free" (Warner Brothers).

RECOMMENDED SINGLES: The **Biddu Orchestra's** beautiful, lush "Rain Forest," to be issued on Epic this week – an atmospheric instrumental that sounds almost like a western theme done in a highly sophisticated style – fabulous; **Jimmy James & the Vagabonds'** wonderful "I'll Go Where Your Music Takes Me" (Pye), written and produced by **Biddu** and one of the nicest good-time songs in months; **Jesse Green's** "Nice & Slow" (Scepter), primarily because the instrumental side, disco-mixed to 4:40 by Scepter's **Mel Cheren**, is so bright and breezy, whipped to a perfect choppy beat; "Baby Face (Latin Feel)" by **Baby Face**, a former import now out on Pye and just what it says – a pleasant, quite workable variation; "Cafe-Cafe" by the **Nice People** (Shadybrook), another imported-from-Europe instrumental, this one with a Latin-Brazilian carnival feeling that is very appealing; "Sugar Boogie" by **Bobby Thomas & the Hotline** (MCA) which, according to the label, is "A **Michael Bennett** Production" – Bennett's the director and choreographer of "A Chorus Line" – though additional production and arrangement credits go to **Harold Wheeler** (of "Ease On Down The Road" fame) and **Bobby Thomas** (who also worked on "A Chorus Line" as music coordinator, whatever that means) – all this aside, the record is a perky, jumping instrumental that clearly means to pick up where "Ease On Down" left off (the key line of tile scattered vocals is "Boogie on down the highway") and sounds like it has a good start. ✪

This week's major release is the first Atlantic album by the **Trammps**, still the premier male disco group and in fine form here. In addition to the previously released title cut, "That's Where The Happy People Go" (extended to 7:50 and preceded by an unexpectedly graceful and moody slow introduction), and last year's "Hooked For Life," the album has five other tracks, two of which stand out as Trammps classics already. The favorites: "Soul Searchin' Time," one of the most powerful disco-style message songs to come along since "Bad Luck," and "Can We Come Together," a love song with a smoother finish and a terrific, soaring break. "Soul Searchin'" is very much in the "Love Epidemic" mold, though the message here is tougher and particularly timely: "People, it's about time to put your soul to a test/Cause somewhere down the line, man has put the world into a mess/Causing every man to turn on his brother/Crisis and tragedy, I've seen one after another." Toward the end, the line "Check out your mind" is repeated over and over, then echoed electronically to great effect. A knockout.

The third cut most likely to get heavy play is a new version of **Wilson Pickett's** soul standard "Ninety-Nine and a Half," just over five minutes in length here and appropriately rough and raucous. (It's interesting that producers **Ronald Baker**, **Norman Harris** and **Earl Young** should revive this song just when their production of **Double Exposure's** "Ten Percent" with the opposite message – compromising, making do with part of something – is spreading fast.) The album's longest cut, "Disco Party" (8:11), is not especially inventive but it does have a certain irresistible high-spirited mood that should get it some play. Finally, there's a change-of-pace closing instrumental called "Love Is A Funky Thing" that is spare and elegant and a little mysterious. Production credits go to Baker, Harris & Young of course, the disco production team, ready to steal top position from **Gamble & Huff**.

Leading the list of other notable albums is **James Gilstrap's** "Love Talk" (Roxbury) with the title track a 13:13 opus taking up the lp's entire first side. Clearly the idea was to make a male "Love To Love You Baby" and the results, avoiding direct imitation of the **Summer** style, are quite good. Producer **Wes Farrell** and arranger **Gene Page** provide enough changes to sustain the mood and Gilstrap's vibrant vocals are reminiscent here and there of **Marvin Gaye**, the master of sexy soul. Side two of the album features only three cuts, two of them extensions of "Love Talk"'s mood in different paces – a slower "Move Me" (7:41) and a more upbeat "Never Stop Loving Me" (6:10) – both worth checking into. And the album's all-nude cover is this week's conversation piece.

ALBUMS CONTINUED: Pick up on the following: "That's What Friends Are For," a spicy, Afro-Brazilian flavored cut from the new **Madeline Bell** album, "This Is One Girl" (Pye); "Searching For Love," great Philly upbeat material from "**The Manhattans**," the group's latest on Columbia (**Bobby Martin** co-produced); "It's The Music" (vocal and instrumental versions), "Nothing Beats A Failure (But a Try)," "I Think I Found That Girl" and "Night Chaser" from the **Natural Four** album just out on Curtom – all sharp, jumpy songs, most of them produced by **LeRoy Hutson**; and two cuts from an album called "Disco Magic" by **Inner City Symphony** (Midland International), a sweetened "Theme from 'S.W.A.T.'" and "Inner City Suite" which features **The Brothers'** "Are You Ready For This" (there's also an instrumental "Fly, Robin, Fly" which is not bad) – oddly, there's no producer listed here, but since the group's personnel is almost identical to that of The Brothers, it's not hard to guess who the man is.

FEEDBACK: Among the new records showing up on top 10 lists this week is "Pretty Maid" by the **Pretty Maid Company**, picked by both Bobby Guttadaro at Infinity and Jim Walters at Bahama Mama's. The song is another German production with touches of **Penny McLean** and **Jackie Robinson** and a strong string section so that even if the vocals are a little too cute, there's still something very attractive here (the flip side, "Hey Hey Big John," which Walters also lists, is equally good). Ariola released the record as a disco disc in Germany and Ariola America is picking it up for an American release due sometime this week... Rich Pampinella reports that **Yvonne Fair's** steamy version of "It Should Have Been Me" (Motown) is just outside of his top 10 and has been picking up requests at the Hippopotamus each time it's played. The song is definitely off-beat for disco play but such a heavy impact record that it goes over at a number of clubs. Pampinella said dancers often sing along with the song and one girl told him she comes to the Hippo just to hear Yvonne Fair. Check it out... The most talked-about import in New York right now is a knockout from Canada called "I Got Your Love" by **Stratavarious featuring Lady** which is bowling them over wherever it's played. (I heard it first at 12 West where Tom Savarese says they're screaming along.) The record, running over seven minutes, is quick-paced with vocals from a girl chorus and just the right changes to keep you excited and involved, ending with an incredible a cappella fade-out. Polydor in Canada pressed "I Got Your Love" on a 12-inch disc and Part 1/Part 2 singles are also

> **" "I Got Your Love," is bowling them over wherever it's played (I first heard it at 12 West where Tom Savarese says they're screaming along) "**

YESTERDAY, BOSTON
DJ: Cosmo Wyatt

DO IT (LIKE YOU AIN'T GOT NO BACKBONE) – Force of Nature (Phila. Intl.)
GET THE FUNK OUT MA FACE – Brothers Johnson (A&M)
I'LL GO WHERE YOUR MUSIC TAKES ME – Jimmy James & the Vagabonds (Pye)
LOVE HANGOVER – Diana Ross (Motown)
MORE – Carol Williams (Salsoul)
SHACK UP – Banbarra (UA)
THAT'S WHERE THE HAPPY PEOPLE GO – Trammps (Atlantic)
TRY ME I KNOW WE CAN MAKE IT/WASTED/COULD IT BE MAGIC – Donna Summer (Oasis)
TURN THE BEAT AROUND/COMMON THIEF – Vicki Sue Robinson (RCA)
YOUNG HEARTS RUN FREE – Candi Staton (Warner Bros.)

HIPPOPOTAMUS, NEW YORK
DJ: Rich Pampinella

DISCO FEVER – Tina Charles (Columbia)
GET OFF YOUR AAHH! AND DANCE – Foxy (Dash)
I'LL GO WHERE YOUR MUSIC TAKES ME – Jimmy James & the Vagabonds (Pye)
LOVE HANGOVER – Diana Ross (Motown)
MA-MO-AH – Tony Valor Sounds Orchestra (Brunswick)
THAT'S WHERE THE HAPPY PEOPLE GO – Trammps (Atlantic)
TOUCH AND GO – Ecstasy, Passion & Pain (Roulette)
TRY ME I KNOW WE CAN MAKE IT/COME WITH ME/COULD IT BE MAGIC – Donna Summer (Oasis)
TURN THE BEAT AROUND –Vicki Sue Robinson (RCA)
WILD CHERRY – Gene Page (Atlantic)

INFINITY, NEW YORK
DJ: Bobby Guttadaro

BROTHERS THEME – The Brothers (RCA)
CAN WE COME TOGETHER/NINETY-NINE AND A HALF/SOUL SEARCHIN' TIME – Trammps (Atlantic)
I'LL GO WHERE YOUR MUSIC TAKES ME – Jimmy James & the Vagabonds (Pye)
MOVIN' LIKE A SUPERSTAR – Jackie Robinson (Ariola)
PRETTY MAID – Pretty Maid Company (Ariola import)
RAINFOREST – Biddu Orchestra (Epic)
TEN PERCENT – Double Exposure (Salsoul)
THIS IS IT – Melba Moore (Buddah)
TOUCH AND GO – Ecstasy, Passion & Pain (Roulette)
TRY ME I KNOW WE CAN MAKE IT/COULD IT BE MAGIC/WASTED/COME WITH ME – Donna Summer (Oasis)

BAHAMA MAMA'S, LOS ANGELES
DJ: Jim Walters

BORN TO GET DOWN – Muscle Shoals Horns (Bang)
GET THE FUNK OUT MA FACE – Brothers Johnson (A&M)
GET UP AND BOOGIE – Silver Convention (Midland Intl.)
HAPPY MUSIC – Blackbyrds (Fantasy)
I AM SOMEBODY – Jimmy James & the Vagabonds (Pye)
LOVE HANGOVER – Diana Ross (Motown) **LOVE REALLY HURTS WITHOUT YOU** – Billy Ocean (Ariola America)
PRETTY MAID/HEY, HEY BIG JOHN – Pretty Maid Company (Ariola import)
TRY ME I KNOW WE CAN MAKE IT – Donna Summer (Oasis)
TURN THE BEAT AROUND –Vicki Sue Robinson (RCA)

available though not easy to find. Polydor in the States hasn't decided whether to release it or not (if you'll remember, they also passed up the last **Crystal Grass** single), but this one is too good to miss out on; check with your local importer.

RECOMMENDED SINGLES: **Joy Fleming's** sweet hustle, "Are You Ready For Love" (Private Stock) with a **Donna Summer/Penny McLean** feel, especially about the strings, probably because this, too, was made in Germany; **Will Collins & Willpower's** happy, fresh "Don't Fight The Feeling" (Mercury), which has a southern flavor in its vocals mixed with a northern use of strings; **Mike & Bill's** long-awaited, long-delayed "Things Won't Be This Bad Always" (Arista), an optimistic message that I like best in its mostly instrumental version (3:35) (there's a vocal "disco version" on the other side, running 3:30); and **Calhoon's** latest, a driving interpretation of **Sam & Dave's** Stax classic, "Soul Man" (Warner Spector) beautifully produced and also available on a 5 :48 12-inch pressing much preferable to the two-part single. ◗

DISCO FILE TOP 20

1. **LOVE HANGOVER** – Diana Ross (Motown)
2. **TURN THE BEAT AROUND** – Vicki Sue Robinson (RCA)
3. **TRY ME I KNOW WE CAN MAKE IT** – Donna Summer (Oasis)
4. **THAT'S WHERE THE HAPPY PEOPLE GO** – Trammps (Atlantic)
5. **TOUCH AND GO** – Ecstasy, Passion & Pain (Roulette)
6. **COULD IT BE MAGIC** – Donna Summer (Oasis)
7. **GET UP AND BOOGIE** – Silver Convention (Midland Intl.)
8. **BROTHERS THEME/UNDER THE SKIN/VOCE ABOUSOU** – The Brothers (RCA)
9. **COME WITH ME/WASTED** – Donna Summer (Oasis)
10. **THIS IS IT** – Melba Moore (Buddah)
11. **COMMON THIEF** – Vicki Sue Robinson (RCA)
12. **MOVIN' LIKE A SUPERSTAR** – Jackie Robinson (Ariola)
13. **TEN PERCENT** – Double Exposure (Salsoul)
14. **YOUNG HEARTS RUN FREE** – Candi Staton (Warner Bros.)
15. **ONE MORE TRY** – Ashford & Simpson (Warner Bros.)
16. **NO, NO, JOE/SAN FRANCISCO HUSTLE** – Silver Convention (Midland Intl.)
17. **I'LL GO WHERE YOUR MUSIC TAKES ME** – Jimmy James & the Vagabonds (Pye)
18. **FIRST CHOICE THEME/AIN'T HE BAD** – First Choice (Warner Bros.)
19. **GET OFF YOUR AAHH! AND DANCE** – Foxy (Dash)
20. **STREET TALK** – B.C.G. (20th Century)

> **❝ Produced by Vince Montana and never released commercially, it's a fascinating, unusual record that's almost turned into a cult item because of its very unavailability ❞**

A checklist of essential new albums: **The Supremes'** "High Energy" (Motown) is their glossiest and most satisfying album in some time. Like the **Temptations**, the Supremes are usually referred to as an "institution," a euphemism for a group that has gone through multiple personnel changes. But the myth, the spirit and **Mary Wilson** remain and all feel a lot fresher under the direction of **Brian Holland**, who produced, and **Eddie Holland**, executive producer; it's almost like old times again. The prime cut, already on two top 10 lists this week (Tony Smith's from Barefoot Boy and Richie Kaczor's from the new Top Floor), is "I'm Gonna Let My Heart Do The Walkin," a sassy, exhilarating song that sounds like a natural single. The title cut, with its shimmering, slow instrumental build-up, is the album's show piece production number, a beautiful job, and three other upbeat cuts – "You're What's Missing In My Life," "Only You (Can Love Me Like You Love Me)," "You Keep Me Moving On" – should be tested out too.

Ralph Carter's first album is called, appropriately, "Young And In Love" (Mercury), establishing its theme, tone and limitations. Carter's may not be one of the great voices of modern times, but bolstered by fine, sturdy productions (credit **Reid Whitelaw** and **Norman Bergen**), it serves the material quite well. "When You're Young and in love" and "Extra Extra (Read All About It)" are already familiar and they set the overall sound: bouncy, bright, cute. My favorite of the new cuts is "A Song In My Heart" (5:00), an irrepressibly happy song, but there's a solid list of other possibilities: "Headin' Back To Love Again," "Love Doesn't Grow On Trees" (originally made by another child singer, **Darren Green**, and a perfect choice here), "Love Is Like An Itching In My Heart"

(Holland-Dozier-Holland's song for the **Supremes** and one of the all-time great titles) and "As Long As There's Love (We're Gonna Make It)" which was written by near – legendary New York disco DJ **Alfie Davidson** (notice how more and more DJs are crossing over into the production and writing end of the music business).

"Disco Express Volume 1" is RCA's equivalent of the Atlantic "Disco Trek" and Scepter/Wand "Disco Gold" packages, collecting some of the more obscure and hard-to-get of the label's disco releases on one disc. This collection, produced and "edited for disco" by **Carl Maultsby** and **David Todd** (another New York DJ who's moved strongly into the record business), would be snapped up if only because it contained **Sunny Gale's** impossible-to-get "I Wanna Know," produced by **Vince Montana**, issued nearly a year ago on the promotion-only label Disco-Soul and never released commercially. It's a fascinating, unusual record that's almost turned into a cult item because of its very unavailability. Because the producers were clearly interested in searching beyond the obvious cuts by RCA performers, some of the selections aren't as strong as one would wish, but the inclusion of **Satyr's** "Free and Easy," "How Have You Been" by **Blood Hollins**, "Pressure Cookin'," by **LaBelle**, the **Choice Four's** "Hook It Up" and **Becket Brown's** "One Way Street" (but why no vocal-instrumental mix?) should be enough to satisfy most disco fans.

Other recommendations: **Groove Holmes** has an unexpectedly "disco" album out under the production of **Bob Thiele** that includes a pleasant version of "I'm In The Mood For Love" (the title cut), a splashy original called "I've Got Love For You" and yet another version of **Duke Ellington's** "Caravan," this one off-beat and atmospheric enough to deserve attention all over again, though the pace may be too down for most crowds (Flying Dutchman)... **Carol Townes and Fifth Avenue's** debut album (on Sixth Avenue, through RCA) includes a great "ain't nothin' but a party" cut in "Bring Your Body" (6:14), written and produced by **Lou Courtney**... and Tony Smith alerted me to a stirring, drum-based jungle-rhythm cut called "Uhuru" on the new **Osibisa** album (Island).

FEEDBACK: "Disco Party," the long cut on the new **Trammps** album that I pretty much dismissed in my review last week, has been shaping up as the album's surprise blockbuster according to reports this week. Nearly everyone we spoke to said that the cut caused a sensation the first time it was played and packed the floor consistently after that. This is one of those steamed-up, sweaty, turn-it-out cuts – sorry for underestimating it first time around... **Richie Kaczor** recommends "Super Disco" from the **Rimshots** album (Stang), a light-weight but delightful instrumental which he says has been getting good response from the crowd at the Top Floor, another new membership club in New York... Tony Smith calls attention to the new

BAREFOOT BOY, NEW YORK
DJ: Tony Smith
CATHEDRALS – D.C. LaRue (Pyramid)
FOXY LADY – Crown Heights Affair (De-Lite)
HIGH ENERGY/I'M GONNA LET MY HEART DO THE WALKING – Supremes (Motown)
LOWDOWN – Boz Scaggs (Columbia)
NICE & SLOW – Jesse Green (Scepter)
SOUL SEARCHIN' TIME/CAN WE COME TOGETHER/ DISCO PARTY – Trammps (Atlantic)
TEN PERCENT – Double Exposure (Salsoul)
TOUCH AND GO – Ecstasy, Passion & Pain (Roulette)
TRY ME I KNOW WE CAN MAKE IT/WASTED – Donna Summer (Oasis)
USE YOUR IMAGINATION – Kokomo (Columbia)

1270, BOSTON
DJ: Jim Stuard
DANCING FREE – Hot Ice (Rage)
FIRST CHOICE THEME/AIN'T HE BAD/GOTTA GET AWAY – First Choice (Warner Bros.)
I GET LIFTED – Sweet Music (Wand)
LOVE HANGOVER – Diana Ross (Motown)
NICE & SLOW – Jesse Green (Scepter)
RAINFOREST – Biddu Orchestra (Epic)
THAT'S WHERE THE HAPPY PEOPLE GO/ DISCO PARTY/SOUL SEARCHIN' TIME – Trammps (Atlantic)
TOUCH AND GO – Ecstasy, Passion & Pain (Roulette)
TRY ME I KNOW WE CAN MAKE IT/COULD IT BE MAGIC/ COME WITH ME/WASTED – Donna Summer (Oasis)
TURN THE BEAT AROUND/COMMON THIEF – Vicki Sue Robinson (RCA)

PARADISE BALLROOM, LOS ANGELES
DJ: A.J. Miller
COULD IT BE MAGIC/TRY ME I KNOW WE CAN MAKE IT – Donna Summer (Oasis)
FIRST CHOICE THEME/AIN'T HE BAD/GOTTA GET AWAY – First Choice (Warner Bros.)
GET UP AND BOOGIE/SAN FRANCISCO HUSTLE/NO, NO JOE – Silver Convention (Midland Intl.)
LOVE HANGOVER – Diana Ross (Motown)
MOVIN' LIKE A SUPERSTAR – Jackie Robinson (Ariola)
SOCK IT TO ME/IT'S YOUR THING/ BUMPER TO BUMPER – Eleventh Hour (20th Century)
THAT'S WHERE THE HAPPY PEOPLE GO/ SOUL SEARCHIN' TIME/NINETY-NINE AND A HALF – Trammps (Atlantic)
THIS IS IT – Melba Moore (Buddah)
TUBULAR BELLS – Champ's Boys Orchestra (Janus)
TURN THE BEAT AROUND/COMMON THIEF – Vicki Sue Robinson (RCA)

THE TOP FLOOR, NEW YORK
DJ: Richie Kaczor
BROTHERS THEME/UNDER THE SKIN – Brothers (RCA)
I'M GONNA LET ME DO THAT WALKING – Supremes (Motown)
IT'S GOOD FOR THE SOUL – Luther (Cotillion)
LOVE HANGOVER – Diana Ross (Motown)
MOVIN'/CHANGIN' – Brass Construction (UA)
TEN PERCENT – Double Exposure (Salsoul)
THAT'S WHERE THE HAPPY PEOPLE GO/CAN WE COME TOGETHER – Trammps (Atlantic)
TOUCH AND GO – Ecstasy, Passion & Pain (Roulette)
TRY ME I KNOW WE CAN MAKE IT/COULD IT BE MAGIC – Donna Summer (Oasis)
TURN THE BEAT AROUND/COMMON THIEF – Vicki Sue Robinson (RCA)

single release by **Crown Heights Affair**, an edited version of their album track, "Foxy Lady" (De-Lite), that is top 10 for him this week and quite an improvement of the original. Another Smith pick: **Heywood Cash's** debut on Epic, a funky, driving "Give It Up" whose 12-inch disco pressing (7:09) is rich and varied if a bit difficult to play all the way through… The newest item on Kaczor's top 10 is also the first release on the revived Cotillion label, "It's Good For The Soul" by **Luther** (Vandross, who also wrote and produced). The message: "If it feels good, do it… If it's good for the body, it's good for the soul" This definitely feels good, especially when extended to just over seven minutes on a 12-inch record full of powerful vocals and tough breaks. Strongly recommended… Also picking up very fast: **Jesse Green's** "Nice & Slow," and the **Biddu Orchestra's** "Rainforest."

RECOMMENDED SINGLES: **Jackie Carter's** hard, cutting "Treat Me Like a Woman" (Big Tree), yet another German-made record but with even more drive than most of the recent releases in this category; "Disco Babies" by **Love Machine** (Arista), a pulsing production with faintly nasty female vocals that mixes **Van McCoy** and **Bob Crewe** styles (disco version: 6:00); "Strokin'" by **Leon Haywood** (20th Century), another long production (5:25), this one by Haywood himself, with a funk disco style and some touches reminiscent of "Love Rollercoaster;" **Marlena Shaw's** "It's Better Than Walkin' Out" (Blue Note), produced by **Tony Silvester** and **Bert deCoteaux**, and a wonderful shout number; the instrumental "Black Sun" by **Barry Gray** (RCA), already suggested as the disco cut from the "Space:1999" album; and the first release from Damon Harris' group, **Impact**, called "Happy Man" (Atco), produced in an impossibly bouncy upbeat style by **Bobby Eli** – the long version is 6:10 and is a tantalizing taste of an album from the group due out in May. ❡

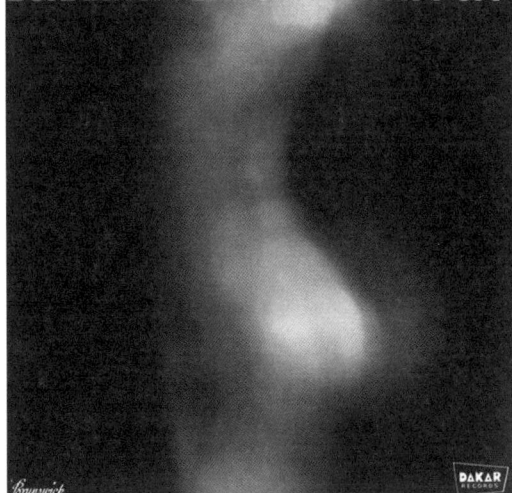

Two new albums from old favorites this week, both covering familiar ground but stylishly. **Bohannon's** is called "Dance Your Ass Off" (Dakar) and includes the note on its liner that, should anyone be offended, the title "is not used in the sense of profanity." How reassuring. The title cut, which opens up side one for nearly eight minutes, is my favorite, mainly because of its bold, sweeping use of strings which adds a new texture to the usual Bohannon instrumental mix; cut two, "Spread The Groove Around," continues "Dance Your Ass Off" after only a second's break and takes it 5:39 longer – almost a part two. "Bohannon's Theme," which closes side one, is yet another continuation, taking the instrumental portion of "Dance Your Ass Off" and letting it stand on its own, which it does quite well at just under four minutes. Aside from this major theme, there are four other cuts, all Bohannon upbeat, all long; the best: "The Groove I Feel." Missing and very much missed are Bo's delicious slow and moody instrumentals – the side two material on his last two albums that became everyone's favorite early morning and late night music.

Van McCoy's latest is "The Real McCoy" (H&L) and contains eight cuts, all over four minutes, most instrumentals, the rest instrumentals with vocal touches. Included is a new version of "African Symphony," an instrumental version of "To Each His Own" retitled "That's My Philosophy" and, a sparky, agile interpretation of "Theme from Star Trek." Of the new material, "Party" – which is just that – "Jet Setting" and "Sweet, Sweet Rhythm" stand out, with a longer (5:07) version of "Night Walk" included as well. At this point, McCoy's production work with other performers – notably **David Ruffin** and **Melba Moore** – has been so good that it overshadows his own output, but fans of McCoy's particular brand of hi-gloss pop disco won't be disappointed with this package.

The title cut from **D.C. LaRue's** debut album, "Cathedrals" (Pyramid), is picking up a lot of play in New York where advance copies have been circulating for a week or two. The song, over seven minutes, has LaRue singing about past lovers, the inevitable progress "from love to lust and back to love" – "Where are they now?" he wonders; "they could fill cathedrals." The mood is wistful, sounding more like **Dory Previn** than anyone else, but the production is lush and warm which is one of the reasons it's been catching on so quickly. The album's back cover shows LaRue standing casually in front of the carefully 'unmarked doors to three of New York's hottest private discos – Flamingo,

❝ Our favorite promotional device: Salsoul's ten-inch metal ruler imprinted "You're Just the Right Size." A bedroom accessory... ❞

FLAMINGO, NEW YORK
DJ: Roy Thode

DON'T FIGHT THE FEELIN' – Will Collins & Willpower (Mercury)
I'LL GO WHERE YOUR MUSIC TAKES ME – Jimmy James & the Vagabonds (Pye)
MOVIN' LIKE A SUPERSTAR – Jackie Robinson (Ariola)
NICE & SLOW – Jesse Green (Scepter)
SOUL SEARCHIN' TIME/CAN WE COME TOGETHER/DISCO PARTY/ THAT'S WHERE THE HAPPY PEOPLE GO – Trammps (Atlantic)
TEN PERCENT – Double Exposure (Salsoul)
TOUCH AND GO – Ecstasy, Passion & Pain (Roulette)
TRY ME I KNOW WE CAN MAKE IT/COULD IT BE MAGIC/WASTED/COME WITH ME – Donna Summer (Oasis)
TURN THE BEAT AROUND/COMMON THIEF – Vicki Sue Robinson (RCA)
YOUNG HEARTS RUN FREE/I KNOW – Candi Staton (Warner Bros.)

RHINOCEROS, BOSTON
DJ: John Luongo

DANCE YOUR ASS OFF/SPREAD THE GROOVE AROUND/ BOHANNON'S THEME – Bohannon (Dakar)
DANCING FREE – Hot Ice (Rage)
DISCO PARTY/NINETY-NINE AND A HALF/THAT'S WHERE THE HAPPY PEOPLE GO – Trammps (Atlantic)
HOW'S YOUR LOVE LIFE (PART 2) – Lee Eldred (Mercury)
LOVE HANGOVER – Diana Ross (Motown)
NICE & SLOW – Jesse Green (Scepter)
TEN PERCENT – Double Exposure (Salsoul)
TRY ME I KNOW WE CAN MAKE IT/COULD IT BE MAGIC/WASTED/COME WITH ME – Donna Summer (Oasis)
TURN THE BEAT AROUND –Vicki Sue Robinson (RCA)

UP, LOS ANGELES
DJ: Mitch Schatsky

I'LL GO WHERE YOUR MUSIC TAKES ME – Jimmy James & the Vagabonds (Pye)
IT SHOULD HAVE BEEN ME – Yvonne Fair (Motown)
LA LA LA – El Chicle (unreleased master, no label)
MOVIN' LIKE A SUPERSTAR – Jackie Robinson (Ariola)
MUSIC, MUSIC, MUSIC – Teresa Brewer (Signature)
NICE & SLOW – Jesse Green (Scepter)
PRETTY MAID/HEY, HEY BIG JOHN – Pretty Maid Company (Ariola import)
RAINFOREST – Biddu Orchestra (Epic)
TEN PERCENT – Double Exposure (Salsoul)
THAT'S WHERE THE HAPPY PEOPLE GO/DISCO PARTY/CAN WE COME TOGETHER/SOUL SEARCHIN' TIME – Trammps (Atlantic)

THE PALACE, NEW ROCHELLE, N.Y.
DJ: Basil Nias

DISCO PARTY/CAN WE COME TOGETHER/SOUL SEARCHIN' TIME – Trammps (Atlantic)
FIRST CHOICE THEME/AIN'T HE BAD – First Choice (Warner Bros.)
I FOUND MY DANCING GIRL – Imaginations (20th Century)
I'LL BE GOOD TO YOU/ GET THE FUNK OUT MA FACE – Brothers Johnson (A&M)
LOVE HANGOVER – Diana Ross/Fifth Dimension (Motown/ABC)
MOVIN'/CHANGIN'/LOVE – Brass Construction (UA)
PARTY/JET SETTING/NIGHT WALK – Van McCoy (H&L)
TURN THE BEAT AROUND –Vicki Sue Robinson (RCA)
UNDER THE SKIN/LAST CHANCE TO DANCE – Brothers (RCA)
USE YOUR IMAGINATION/THAT'S ENOUGH – Kokomo (Columbia)

12 West and Infinity – for an in-crowd appeal. Also out this week: the first album from **Carl Graves**, including his excellent "Heart Be Still" and another track by "Heart"'s author **Lee Garrett**, "How Can I Be a Man," in a racier (in more ways than one) version than the one included on Garrett's own album (which I would also like to re-recommend, if only for this cut). Carl Graves is on A&M; Lee Garrett is on Chrysalis.

Our favorite promotional device: Salsoul's ten-inch metal ruler imprinted "You're Just The Right Size." A bedroom accessory... and in a slightly more off-the-wall gesture, Ariola America's Mark Kreiner shipped the New York Record Pool – there is still only one and it's approaching its first-year birthday in fine health, thank you several dozen Mickey Mouse hats for distribution to the first DJs who want them.

RECOMMENDED SINGLES: A sexy, sleek "Love Chant" by **Eli's Second Coming** – MFSB musician **Bobby Eli**, that is who produced this sexsong complete with whispery females singing, "Ooo spend the night, let me hold you," and a closing climax; Part II is 6:06, Part I is the shorter version at 3:20 (on Silver Blue)... **Michel Polnareff's** full-bodied instrumental, "Lipstick" (Atlantic), very up with a steady drum pulse – also in two parts, 3:33 and 3:30... **Gamble & Huff's** superb production on "You'll Never Find Another Love Like Mine," **Lou Rawls'** first release with Philadelphia International which starts at a bright hustle pace and builds gradually with soaring choruses; a little slow for some tastes, perhaps, but a great record that I only wish were twice as long as its 3:38 length here... "Ooo Sweet Love" by **Marilyn Grimes** (Abraxas) whose mood is neatly summed up in its title – a pleasant, beautifully sung love song produced by the **Marier** brothers ("Lady, Lady, Lady") and including an instrumental version on the flip... **The Moments'** rousing, thoroughly enjoyable "Nine Times" (Stang), a song about telephone busy-signal frustration... **Hokis Pokis'** follow-up to "Nowhere" with a very similar "Swing" (Shield) and an attractive B-side, "Get Cha Girl"... "Take It," a string-laden instrumental by the **Vast Majority** (D&M Sound) that runs just over five minutes... and **Lou Courtney/Buffalo Smoke's** "Call The Police" (RCA) whose complaint is: "She's takin' my love and ain't givin' up none" – this is also available on a 12-inch pressing with a "911" instrumental on the reverse side.

NOW AVAILABLE: **Crystal Grass'** "Taj Mahal"/Lemme See Ya Gitcher Thing Off, Baby" has finally been released in this country by Private Stock and anyone who didn't pick up an import copy should consider this an essential addition to your collection. These previously recommended album cuts are now available as 45s: "Eleanor Rigby" by **Wing & A Prayer Fife and Drum Corps** (5:18 on Wing & A Prayer), "Smoke Gets in Your Eyes" by **Penny Mclean** (3:24 on Atco) and **Joe Thomas'** version of "Poinciana" (4:12 on Groove Merchant). ◉

MAY 15, 1976

❝ In a move that could have tremendous impact on the disco market, Salsoul Records plans to put its 12-inch disco pressings, previously "For Disco DJs Only," into regular commercial production ❞

In a move that could have tremendous impact on the disco market and disco marketing, Salsoul Records has announced plans to put its 12-inch disco pressings, previously available in limited numbers "For Disco DJs Only," into regular commercial production, beginning this week with **Double Exposure's** extraordinary "Ten Percent," currently for sale only in a shortened version on a standard single. The large discs, packaged in new Salsoul Disco sleeves punched out in the center (like Atlantic's Disco Disc covers) so as to expose label copy and shrink-wrapped like regular lps, include the two separate disco mixes (9:15 and 7:07) already released on promotional copies to disco DJs, one track to a side to allow for a higher quality, hotter pressing. This giant 45 will bear a suggested list price of $2.98 (discounted, that could come to less than the price of two regular 45s) and it should be pointed out that there's already a hot market, underground and under-the-counter, for disco 12-inchers which, because of their limited availability, have been selling for anything from $3 to $7. At those prices, the buyers were probably dedicated disco freaks, but at Salsoul's price, the disco pressings should appeal to people who want to be able to buy exactly what they've heard in the clubs – the people who aren't satisfied with Part 1 /Part 2 singles or the low sound quality that results from attempting to squeeze more than five minutes onto a 7-inch single.

A considerable percentage of the disco equipment being sold now is ending up in private homes with people who enjoy playing DJ for themselves and their friends, and these living room spinners can be expected to snap up special 12-inch pressings – whether for quality, novelty or status – especially if the material is commercially unavailable in any other form. "Ten Percent" is the perfect choice for this breakthrough move: it's a strong record already receiving saturation disco play only weeks after its release; it has great radiocrossover potential; and much of its success is due to its length – the sort of non-stop drive that could never be duplicated on a standard 45. Other companies already active in the promotional disco disc field will surely be watching Salsoul's experimental move very closely. If it works, this could be the start of something big.

This could also be start of a much-needed standardization of disco pressings, promotional or commercial. Of the 12 special 12-inch discs I received

this past week, six were pressed at 45 rpm, six at 33 – a neat split down the middle with two of those records unmarked as to speed. As any DJ can tell you, this situation can be pretty aggravating in a dimly-lit booth when there are only seconds left before the blend-in and you're still poring over tiny label copy trying to figure out what speed this one's at. The Salsoul Disco records are at 45 rpm, the preferred speed according to most DJs. If other companies follow Salsoul's marketing move, a standard disco-disc speed will have to be set for the consumer. Why can't one be established now for DJs?

Two of the new promotional 12-inch pressings that might make excellent commercial entries are "Heaven Must Be Missing An Angel" by **Tavares** (Capitol) and Scepter/Wand's back-to-back remixes of "Nice & Slow" by **Jesse Green** and "I Get Lifted" by **Sweet Music**. The Tavares record is their first away from **Lambert & Potter** and their producer here, **Freddie Perren**, a Motown veteran whose most recent success has been with the **Miracles'** "City Of Angels" album, makes the very best of the group, easily recapturing the peak they reached with "It Only Takes A Minute." The sound is exceptionally sharp, bright and happy from the very beginning and, at 6:32, it just gets better and better. Standard singles will be out in a two-part format but Capitol has pressed its first 12-inch records for DJs with the full length mono on one side, stereo on the other. Both "Nice & Slow" and "I Get Lifted" have been previously released as singles with vocal/instrumental formats and their re-mixes emphasize the instrumental elements, framing the vocals and highlighting them but making more of the breaks than the words. Both new versions are terrific –"Nice & Slow" is now 5:45, "I Get Lifted," 6:10 – but it's "Lifted" that is most improved and so transformed that it should enjoy a whole new life after this release (due out this week).

Other 12-inch DJ pressings of more than passing interest: "Black Sun 1999" by **Barry Gray** mixed up to 5:34 (RCA); **Michel Polnareff's** "Lipstick" instrumental at 4:58 (Atlantic); the **Pretty Maid Company's** "Pretty Maid" and "Hey Hey Big John" back-to-back on "An Ariola America Disco Production;" the **Biddu Orchestra's** "Rainforest" in its full 4:40 version (Epic); the **First Choice's** "Theme"/"Ain't He Bad" and "Are You Ready For Me?" the same lengths as on the album but in a wide-groove pressing now (Warner Bros.); and **Patrice**

GALAXY, NEW YORK
DJ: Walter Gibbons

CAN WE COME TOGETHER/DISCO PARTY/SOUL SEARCHIN' TIME – Trammps (Atlantic)
CATHEDRALS – D.C. LaRue (Pyramid)
GET OFF YOUR AAHH! AND DANCE – Foxy (Dash)
I'M GONNA LET MY HEART DO THE WALKING/HIGH ENERGY – Supremes (Motown)
LOVE CHANT (PART II) – Eli's Second Coming (Silver Blue)
MAKING LOVE – Sammy Gordon & the Hip Huggers (Greg)
NEW YORK CITY – Miroslav Vitous (Warner Bros.)
NO WAY BACK (PART 2) – Dells (Mercury)
TEN PERCENT – Double Exposure (Salsoul)
WHAT'S THE STORY – Patrice Rushen (Prestige)

ON STAGE, FREEPORT, LONG ISLAND
DJ: Dewane Dixon

BRING YOUR BODY – Carol Townes & Fifth Avenue (Sixth Avenue)
CAN WE COME TOGETHER/DISCO PARTY/SOUL SEARCHIN' TIME – Trammps (Atlantic)
GET OFF YOUR AAHH! AND DANCE – Foxy (Dash)
GIVE IT UP – Heywood Cash (Epic)
HIGH ENERGY/I'M GONNA LET MY HEART DO THE WALKING – Supremes (Motown)
LOVE HANGOVER – Diana Ross (Motown)
MAKING LOVE – Sammy Gordon & the Hip Huggers (Greg)
TEN PERCENT – Double Exposure (Salsoul)
TRY ME I KNOW WE CAN MAKE IT/COULD IT BE MAGIC/COME WITH ME– Donna Summer (Oasis)
YELLOW TRAIN – Resonance (Celebration import)

LOST AND FOUND, WASHINGTON, D.C.
DJ: Bill Owens

FIRST CHOICE THEME/AIN'T HE BAD – First Choice (Warner Bros.)
GET UP AND BOOGIE – Silver Convention (Midland Intl.)
I'M GONNA LET MY HEART DO THE WALKING/HIGH ENERGY – Supremes (Motown)
LOVE HANGOVER – Diana Ross (Motown)
MOVIN' LIKE A SUPERSTAR – Jackie Robinson (Ariola)
TEN PERCENT – Double Exposure (Salsoul)
THAT'S WHERE THE HAPPY PEOPLE GO/DISCO PARTY/NINETY-NINE AND A HALF – Trammps (Atlantic)
THIS IS IT – Melba Moore (Buddah)
TRY ME I KNOW WE CAN MAKE IT/COULD IT BE MAGIC/WASTED/COME WITH ME– Donna Summer (Oasis)
TURN THE BEAT AROUND –Vicki Sue Robinson (RCA)

REVELATION III, BROOKLYN, NEW YORK
DJ: Bacho Mangual

CATHEDRALS – D.C. LaRue (Pyramid)
DANCING FREE – Hot Ice (Rage)
I'M GONNA LET MY HEART DO THE WALKING/ONLY YOU – Supremes (Motown)
LOVE CHANT (PART II) – Eli's Second Coming (Silver Blue)
NEW YORK CITY – Miroslav Vitous (Warner Bros.)
PARTY – Van McCoy (H&L)
SOUL SEARCHIN' TIME/DISCO PARTY/CAN WE COME TOGETHER/THAT'S WHERE THE HAPPY PEOPLE GO – Trammps (Atlantic)
TEN PERCENT – Double Exposure (Salsoul)
TRY ME I KNOW WE CAN MAKE IT/COULD IT BE MAGIC/COME WITH ME– Donna Summer (Oasis)
WHAT YOU DON'T KNOW/I'VE BEEN WORKIN' – Charles Drain (RCA)

Rushen's "Kickin' Back" (7:32) and "What's The Story" (5:15) (Prestige), the latter a **Rufus** sound-alike chosen this week by Walter Gibbons for his top 10 at Galaxy 21.

FEEDBACK: Gibbons also listed – as did Bacho Mangual from Brooklyn's Revelation II – a wonderfully atmospheric, wild cut called "New York City" from the recent **Miroslav Vitous** album on Warner Brothers, "Magical Shepherd." "NYC" is an almost 10 minute synthesizer symphony full of eerie effects and chanted vocals; featured musicians: **Herbie Hancock**, **Airto Moreira**, **James Gadson**. Weird and fascinating and highly recommended for freaks… Shaping up as a favorite cut on the new **Bohannon** album: "Party People."

ALBUMS (LEFT FIELD DEPT.): When your crowd is ready for anything, try the album version of **Wings'** "Silly Love Songs" (untimed on the label, but about 5:30) which reminds me how much I once liked **Paul McCartney** and proves he still has his moments. Especially attractive: the beautiful overlapping chant passage near the end and the sly message, "Some people want to fill the world with silly love songs/And what's wrong with that?"… And in an entirely different vein, there's a hilarious new album called "Blow Fly Disco" (Weird World, a TK label) from the notorious masked comic, **Blow Fly**, who does indescribably dirty versions of a number of disco favorites including "Bad Luck" (it's not hard to imagine the change this title undergoes), "What A Diff'rence A Day Makes," "Swearin' to God" and a medley of "Get Down Tonight" (changed to "Freak Out Tonight") and "That's The Way I Like It." The songs are all reasonably sung and produced in faithful imitation of the originals and the new lyrics are so low-down nasty you can't ignore them. A novelty item. ◗

❝ Disco music is being pumped into the stadium and locker rooms for all Yankee home games ❞

If it holds few surprises, the new **B.T. Express** album, "Energy To Burn" (the group's first on Columbia), is solid, sweaty and hard punching: a stylish heavyweight whose moves might be familiar to the fans but who's still capable of delivering knockout after knockout. Producer **Jeff Lane**, who already has a top 10 disco album this year with his work for **Brass Construction**, continues to build powerful flexible structures of horns and strings to contain the spontaneous combustion of the vocals. Lane gives B.T. a piercingly direct sound that gets across best in the searing title cut, "Energy To Burn," "Can't Stop Groovin' Now, Wanna Do It Some More" (the album's first single release), and "Energy Level," Other possibilities: a to-the-point message song called "Depend On Yourself" (the longest cut at 7:03) and a smooth instrumental, "Time Tunnel." B.T. Express has a sound and stance that says a lot about black music and black style in the mid-seventies, but beyond their interest as a sociological footnote, the group continues to smoke and spark. Highly inflammable.

The **Isley Brothers'** "Harvest For The World" album (T-Neck) also covers familiar ground, but who's to argue with smashing success? A personal favorite: the title cut, one of the group's strongest message songs, asking "When will there be a harvest for the world?" This meshes seamlessly with the next cut, a more ambiguous "People of Today," which sounds brightly optimistic until you listen closely. Then of course there's the already-released single, "Who Loves You Better," included here in a full 5:31 version and typically zesty work for the Isleys.

Lou Rawls and **Natalie Cole** both have sleek, sophisticated, terrifically produced new albums out. Rawls' is "All Things In Time" (Philadelphia International), produced by **Gamble & Huff** with contributions from others in the Sigma Sound stable and containing a longer version (4:28) of one of my own current top 10 records, "You'll Never Find Another Love Like Mine" – though still not long enough to satisfy me. The album's other gem is a similar song called "This Song Will Last Forever" that's all about music and its place in our lives – delightfully sentimental (and a little self-congratulatory), it lists standards like

"Tangerine" and "My Way" with "Wake Up Everybody" and "I Love Music." A beauty. Natalie Cole's second album is titled simply "Natalie" (Capitol) and goes even further to establish her as one of the sharpest, most exciting and versatile singers around right now. The opening cut, a sprightly "Mr. Melody," is the most likely to pick up disco play with its zippy scat singing, but don't overlook the absolutely stunning interpretation of "Good Morning Heartache" if you're into deep, slow songs. Produced by **Chuck Jackson** and **Marvin Yancy**.

John Davis' Monster Orchestra album is due out this week on Sam Records featuring six **Cole Porter** remakes (the best: "In the Still Of The Night," "I Get A Kick" and, of course, "Night And Day") and two quite substantial originals that are the album's prime cuts, "Tell Me How You Like It" (5:16) and "I Can't Stop" (5:06). Frankly, I've had it with remakes, Cole Porter or not, but I know club audiences are still ready for sugary versions of standards and this should please them immensely. Buddah-distributed Pi Kappa has another disco instrumental album but in a different style – more New York eclectic than Philadelphia glossy. It's called "**The Super Disco Band**" by a group of the same name and while many of the cuts go on for some time to no apparent purpose, several are strangely attractive, notably a luscious "Clear Water" (6:31, the longest track), "Fire And Passion" and "A Song For You," which has some **Love Unlimited** overtones. Ariola America has issued a substantial package called, hopefully, "Big Dance Records in the Big Apple" and featuring the New York skyline on the back as well as these tracks: **Jackie Robinson's** "Movin' Like A Superstar" (the 4:24 disco version); **Polly Brown's** "Up In A Puff of Smoke" and "You're My # 1;" "Do What You Feel," "Buckhead" and "Bad Luck" by the **Atlanta Disco Band**; "Sexy Lady" by **Jumbo 76** and "Pretty Maid" by the **Pretty Maid Company**.

FEEDBACK: Dick Acraman of Le Club in New York informs us that, at the request of Yankee Stadium and the New York Yankees, disco music supplied by Acraman and Le Club is being pumped into the Stadium and the locker rooms for all Yankee home games for use in all warm-up and break periods. George Steinbrenner of the

DCA CLUB, PHILADELPHIA
DJ: Kurt Borusiewicz

ALWAYS THERE – Side Effect (Fantasy)
CATHEDRALS/I DON'T WANT TO LOSE YOU – D.C. LaRue (Pyramid)
DANCE YOUR ASS OFF/THE GROOVE I FEEL – Bohannon (Dakar)
DANCING FREE – Hot Ice (Rage)
DISCO PARTY/CAN WE COME TOGETHER/ SOUL SEARCHIN' TIME/NINETY-NINE AND A HALF – Trammps (Atlantic)
I'M GONNA LET MY HEART DO THE WALKING/HIGH ENERGY – Supremes (Motown)
MY LOVE SUPREME – Milton Hamilton Crystalized (TR)
NIGHT JOURNEY – Doc Severinsen (Epic)
TEN PERCENT – Double Exposure (Salsoul)
TIME MOVES ON – Strutt (Brunswick)

BOOMBAMAKAO, NEW YORK
DJ: Jorge R. Wheeler

DESPERATELY/BROADWAY STAR – Barrabas (Atco)
HEAVEN MUST BE MISSING AN ANGEL – Tavares (Capitol)
LIPSTICK – Michel Polnareff (Atlantic)
LOVE HANGOVER – Diana Ross (Motown)
NEW YORK CITY – Miroslav Vitous (Warner Bros.)
NICE AND SLOW – Jesse Green (Scepter)
TEN PERCENT – Double Exposure (Salsoul)
THAT'S WHERE THE HAPPY PEOPLE GO/SOUL SEARCHIN' TIME/DISCO PARTY CAN WE COME TOGETHER – Trammps (Atlantic)
TRY ME I KNOW WE CAN MAKE IT/COULD IT BE MAGIC/ WASTED/COME WITH ME – Donna Summer (Oasis)
USE YOUR IMAGINATION – Kokomo (Columbia)

15 LANSDOWNE STREET, BOSTON
DJ: Danae Jacovidis

CATHEDRALS – D.C. LaRue (Pyramid)
DISCO PARTY/THAT'S WHERE THE HAPPY PEOPLE GO/SOUL SEARCHIN' TIME/ CAN WE COME TOGETHER – Trammps (Atlantic)
HEAVEN MUST BE MISSING AN ANGEL – Tavares (Capitol)
I GET LIFTED – Sweet Music (Wand)
I'LL GO WHERE YOUR MUSIC TAKES ME – Jimmy James & the Vagabonds (Pye)
I'M GONNA LET MY HEART DO THE WALKING – Supremes (Motown)
JET SETTING/LOVE AT FIRST SIGHT/ PARTY – Van McCoy (H&L)
LOVE HANGOVER – Diana Ross (Motown)
NICE AND SLOW – Jesse Green (Scepter)
TEN PERCENT – Double Exposure (Salsoul)

LE CLUB, NEW YORK
DJ: Dick Acramon

GET UP AND BOOGIE – Silver Convention (Midland Intl.)
I LOVE TO LOVE – Al Downing (Polydor)
LA BALANGA – Bimbo Jet (EMI import)
LOVE HANGOVER/SMILE – Diana Ross (Motown)
NICE AND SLOW – Jesse Green (Scepter)
TEN PERCENT – Double Exposure (Salsoul)
THAT'S WHERE THE HAPPY PEOPLE GO/ SOUL SEARCHIN' TIME – Trammps (Atlantic)
TRY ME I KNOW WE CAN MAKE IT/WASTED/COULD IT BE MAGIC – Donna Summer (Oasis lp cuts)
TURN THE BEAT AROUND –Vicki Sue Robinson (RCA)
YOUNG HEARTS RUN FREE – Candi Staton (Warner Bros.)

Yankees reportedly wanted to do something new and boost players' morale and he felt top quality disco would work. Key track on Acraman's tape, which he'll be re-servicing every six weeks: **Paul Jabara's** "Yankee Doodle Dandy"... Warner Brothers has issued 12-inch pressings of **Miroslav Vitous'** excellent "New York City" and (on Chrysalis) **Lee Garrett's** incredibly strong "How Can I Be A Man." Both musts.

RECOMMENDED SINGLES: The batch this week includes a lot of new groups and a lot of obscure labels: like "Madison '76" by a Brooklyn group called **Venus** for whom Jeff Lane has whipped up a fine production with the clear intention of making the definitive record for the line dance (Columbia)... the **State Department** has my favorite group name this week and a song called "I'm Counting On You" (Sixth Avenue) that's real nice, even if the vocals don't entirely live up to the ornate, sparkling production **Van McCoy** has supported them with (long version: 6:33)... "APB's Theme (Chase The Pusher)" by the **All Points Bulletin** (on Little City Records, a D.C. label) is a perky, synthesized, very strange instrumental for specialized tastes as is an appropriately titled "Flashfever" by **Metropolis** (Nicetown, in Philadelphia) which is left field between Latin disco (or something like that)... back to normal with the **Chi-lites'** elegantly smooth, top-form "You Don't Have To Go" (Brunswick) at 4:46 one of their best in some time... and "Hungry" ("for your love") sung like she means it by **Sandy**, one assumes, of Sandy's Gang (Sunrise Records), written by **Patrick Adams** and **Fay Hauser**, co-produced by Adams and based on exactly the same music as "Making Love" which Adams also wrote and arranged for **Sammy Gordon & the Hip Huggers**; if you like one, you'll probably like the other, and "Hungry" has an instrumental version on its flip side of 4:33. ✪

**" The dance-halls
the Soho Weekly is so
outraged about are
three private discos
in the Soho section
of New York – Nicky
Siano's Gallery,
David Mancuso's
99 Prince St, and the
recently reopened
Frankenstein "**

One of the most fascinating allurements of city life to many a young girl is the dance-hall, which is truly the ante-room to hell itself. Here indeed is the beginning of the white slave traffic in many instances. A girl may in her country home have danced a little but here, 'mid the blazing lights, gaiety and so-called happiness, she enters. She is told she is awkward and will become more graceful, no harm in it. You know the rest.

(These dance-halls) have brought to this neighborhood the truly evil people who work New York. Their operators prey on the innocence of people in the community as well as on our society. There is nothing wrong with dancing and there is nothing wrong with music – but these places have nothing to do with either.

The first of the two righteous statements printed above comes from a book called Fighting the Traffic in Young Girls or War on the White Slave Trade (The Greater Crime in the World's History) which was issued in 1910. The second is taken from an editorial in a New York paper called the Soho Weekly News and dated May 13, 1976. The rhetoric of those people who set themselves up to tell the public about the endless, imagined evils of the world hasn't changed at all. The dance-halls the Soho Weekly is so outraged about are three private

discos in the Soho section of New York – Nicky Siano's Gallery, David Mancuso's 99 Prince (home of the New York Record Pool) and the recently reopened Frankenstein. A clue to why these discos are being treated like leper colonies is this quote from a recent New York Post article titled, unfortunately. "Soho Artists Saying No-Go to Go-Go Sounds of Disco": "The discos reportedly attract substantial numbers of blacks, Hispanics and homosexuals. Critics believe drug-taking occurs, but admit they have no evidence to back this up." If there is a disco community, and I believe there is, "black, Hispanics and homosexuals" are at its core. Maybe it's time for the Party People to get serious about their rights and assert their community against the barely-disguised bigotry, sexism and hypocrisy of "communities" like Soho around the country.

Stunner of the Week: "Trouble Maker," the title cut from **Roberta Kelly's** debut album on Oasis, produced by the team who transformed **Donna Summer**, **Giorgio Moroder** and Pete Bellotte. Like Summer (who contributes backgrounds here), Kelly is an American living in Germany who's had a substantial European success prior to her first American release, and if "Trouble Maker," at 8:48, isn't quite the tour de force "Love To Love You Baby" was, it more than makes up for what it lacks in minutes and seconds with an incredible, smoothly soaring drive and grace. The song combines the spirit of '60s girl group nastiness ("Trouble maker, stop spreadin' all those bad lies/ Trouble maker, 'cause you ain't gettin' my guy" – lines that could have come from "Keep Your Hands Off My Baby") with the delicious, violin-laced production that has become the trademark of German-made disco music. The singing is vibrant, the break is superb and full of pounding drums and the overall affect is overwhelming in the best sense. "Flawless" is an overused word on the New York disco scene, but it's the right word here. There are four other cuts on the Kelly album, three of them over six minutes, two of them excellent disco material: "Love Power" and "The Family."

This week's other essential album is "More, More, More" by the **Andrea True Connection** (Buddah), elegantly produced by **Greg Diamond** and containing four more cuts besides the familiar title track. All the new material is in a similar mold – long, pretty instrumentals awash with strings and featuring ethereal vocals electronically enhanced for infinite depth – but "Call Me," with the most minimal of vocals, is the standout here, followed by something called "Keep It Up Longer" which is the closest in style to "More, More, More." But the other two cuts –"Fill Me Up (Heart to Heart)," (10:03) and "Party Line" (6:50) – are sure to get disco play, too. A surprisingly substantial and attractive album.

Selected Album Cuts: "Sometimes" from **Lesley Gore's Quincy Jones** – produced comeback album ("Love Me By Name" on A&M) – a happy, jumping track featuring the **Brothers Johnson** and a lot of bright handclapping; key lines: "Sometimes... I don't know where I end and you

MR. LAFFS, NEW YORK
DJ: Freddie Mendoza

DANCE YOUR ASS OFF/PARTY PEOPLE – Bohannon (Dakar)
DISCO PARTY/SOUL SEARCHIN' TIME/ THAT'S WHERE THE HAPPY PEOPLE GO – Trammps (Atlantic)
HOW'S YOUR LOVE LIFE? (PART 2) – Lee Eldred (Mercury)
LIPSTICK – Michel Polnareff (Atlantic)
MOUZON MOVES ON – Alphonse Mouzon (Blue Note)
PICK IT UP – The Knack (Atco)
PRETTY MAID/HEY HEY BIG JOHN – Pretty Maid Company (Ariola America)
SUGAR BOOGIE – Bobby Thomas & the Hotline (MCA)
TELL ME HOW YOU LIKE IT/I CAN'T STOP/I GET A KICK/IN THE STILL OF THE NIGHT – John Davis & the Monster Orchestra (Sam)
TEN PERCENT – Double Exposure (Salsoul)

MANNEQUIN, NEW YORK
DJ: Phil Gill

CATHEDRALS – D.C. LaRue (Pyramid)
DISCO PARTY/CAN WE COME TOGETHER – Trammps (Atlantic)
HEAVEN MUST BE MISSING AN ANGEL – Tavares (Capitol)
HIGH ENERGY/I'M GONNA LET MY HEART DO THE WALKING – Supremes (Motown)
LET'S DANCE/IT'S MAD/GHETTOS OF THE MIND – Pleasure (Fantasy)
LOVE TALK – James Gilstrap (Roxbury)
LOWDOWN – Boz Scaggs (Columbia)
ROCK ME WITH YOUR LOVE – Biddu Orchestra (Epic import)
TELL ME HOW YOU LIKE IT/I CAN'T STOP/IN THE STILL OF THE NIGHT/I GET A KICK – John Davis & the Monster Orchestra (Sam)
TEN PERCENT – Double Exposure (Salsoul)

THE CITY, SAN FRANCISCO
DJ: John Hedges

DANCE YOUR ASS OFF – Bohannon (Dakar)
GET THE FUNK OUT MA FACE – Brothers Johnson (A&M)
HOLD ON – Sons of Champlin (Ariola America)
I'M GONNA LET MY HEART DO THE WALKING – Supremes (Motown)
NICE AND SLOW – Jesse Green (Scepter)
TEMPTATION, TEMPTATION – New Ventures (UA)
TEN PERCENT – Double Exposure (Salsoul)
THAT'S WHERE THE HAPPY PEOPLE GO/ DISCO PARTY/SOUL SEARCHIN' TIME – Trammps (Atlantic)
TRY ME I KNOW WE CAN MAKE IT/COULD IT BE MAGIC/WASTED – Donna Summer (Oasis)
TURN THE BEAT AROUND –Vicki Sue Robinson (RCA)

THE ARCHDIOCESE, QUEENS, NEW YORK
DJ: Frank Strivelli

BLACK SOUL MUSIC – Black Soul (Import Disque)
CATHEDRALS – D.C. LaRue (Pyramid)
ENERGY TO BURN/CAN'T STOP GROOVIN' – B.T. Express (Columbia)
I'M GONNA LET MY HEART DO THE WALKING – Supremes (Motown)
LOVE HANGOVER – Diana Ross (Motown)
NEW YORK CITY – Miroslav Vitous (Warner Bros.)
TEN PERCENT – Double Exposure (Salsoul)
THAT'S WHERE THE HAPPY PEOPLE GO/ DISCO PARTY/SOUL SEARCHIN' TIME/ CAN WE COME TOGETHER – Trammps (Atlantic)
TOUCH AND GO – Ecstasy, Passion & Pain (Roulette)
TRY ME I KNOW WE CAN MAKE IT/WASTED/COME WITH ME – Donna Summer (Oasis)

begin"… "Ready, Willing And Able," my first-impression favorite from the new **David Ruffin** album, "Everything's Coming Up Love" (Motown), again produced by **Van McCoy** and also containing a long (8:45) version of "First Round Knockout," previously made by the **New Censation**… and a number of perky, Latin-hustle influenced dance cuts from the **Tommy Stewart** album on Abraxas, the best of which are "Practice What You Preach," "Fulton County Line," "Riding High" and "Bump and Hustle Music" – all instrumentals with some girl chorus vocals and all very pleasant.

RECOMMENDED SINGLES: The only new 45 worth mentioning this week is already a smash judging on the reaction to advance copies in Boston and New York. It's "Take a Little" by **Liquid Pleasure** (sounds like the name of a porn novel) on Midland International, issued as a small-hole, European-style 45, running 5:41. The lead male vocal is strong but the production is even stronger, especially the persistent Latin percussion which opens the track. Also now available as singles: "I'm Gonna Let My Heart Do The Walking" by the **Supremes** (Motown), "Super Disco" by the **Rimshots** (Stang) and "Gotta Get Away" by **First Choice** (Warner Bros.). ✏

DISCO FILE TOP 20

1. **DISCO PARTY/SOUL SEARCHIN' TIME/ THAT'S WHERE THE HAPPY PEOPLE GO/CAN WE COME TOGETHER** – Trammps (Atlantic)
2. **TEN PERCENT** – Double Exposure (Salsoul)
3. **I'M GONNA LET MY HEART DO THE WALKING** – Supremes (Motown)
4. **TRY ME I KNOW WE CAN MAKE IT/COULD IT BE MAGIC/WASTED/COME WITH ME** – Donna Summer (Oasis)
5. **LOVE HANGOVER** – Diana Ross (Motown)
6. **NICE AND SLOW** – Jesse Green (Scepter)
7. **CATHEDRALS** – D.C. LaRue (Pyramid)
8. **TURN THE BEAT AROUND** – Vicki Sue Robinson (RCA)
9. **HIGH ENERGY** – Supremes (Motown)
10. **NINETY-NINE AND A HALF** – Trammps (Atlantic)
11. **DANCE YOUR ASS OFF** – Bohannon (Dakar)
12. **DANCING FREE** – Hot Ice (Rage)
13. **NEW YORK CITY** – Miroslav Vitous (Warner Bros.)
14. **MOVIN' LIKE A SUPERSTAR** – Jackie Robinson (Ariola)
15. **GET THE FUNK OUT MA FACE** – Brothers Johnson (A&M)
16. **PARTY** – Van McCoy (H&L)
17. **FIRST CHOICE THEME/AIN'T HE BAD** – First Choice (Warner Bros.)
18. **I'LL GO WHERE YOUR MUSIC TAKES ME** – Jimmy James & the Vagabonds (Pye)
19. **GET OFF YOUR AAHH! AND DANCE** – Foxy (Dash)
20. **YOUNG HEARTS RUN FREE** – Candi Staton (Warner Bros.)

JUNE 5, 1976

A spate of new releases from male vocal groups this week, a few top choice. Taking them one by one: "Watch Out" (on Atco) is the latest from everyone's favorite Spanish group, **Barrabas**, and, while not quite up to the high standards they set for themselves in their last album, "Heart Of The City," this one's satisfyingly solid. Lead cut: "Desperately," richly-textured and hard-edged, already the consensus cut according to the DJs surveyed this week. My own next favorite is "High Light," mainly because of the terrific Latin percussion lead-in and the on-edge vocals. Runners-up: "Broadway Star" and "Fire Girl," both unmistakably Barrabas, who continue to put out one of the most unique and eclectic sounds in the disco field.

"We Got the Rhythm" by **People's Choice** (Philadelphia International) was produced by **Gamble & Huff** and is a 100 percent improvement, a turn-it-out turnaround, on their debut album last year. This follow-up fulfils the promise of the group's "Do It Any Way You Wanna" with a tasty selection of Philly funk, the smooth, ultra-sheen variety, at its best here. Two standouts: "Here We Go Again" (4:55), in which the title is repeated as a chant, over a rollicking, rolling, repetitive theme (this, in a shorter version, is also the group's new single and could hit as big as "Do It Any Way") and a slower but equally involving "Movin' In All Directions" (6:38) with gorgeous string touches. Left field: "Cold Blooded & Down-Right-Funky," which is aptly named. All selections were written by **Leon Huff**, often in collaboration with members of the group, and even the mellow cuts are superb – especially "Opus-De-Funk," an atmospheric, warm-up instrumental.

Impact is ex-Temptation **Damon Harris'** new group and their debut album (on Atco) was produced by **Bobby Eli** from **MFSB** for WMOT Productions, the guys behind **Blue Magic**. With this heavy accumulation of credits, the album is, predictably, an attractive, carefully-crafted one, not unlike the recent **Norman Harris** production for **Eddie Kendricks** (the voice Harris replaced in the Temptations). Prime disco cut: "Give a Broken Heart A Break" (5:57) whose chugging pace is underlined by the repeated chorus. In addition to "Happy Man," already released as a single, there's another likely dance number: "Love Attack," which features another vocalist in the group. **Freddie Perren**, riding high with his **Sylvers** hit, has produced the new Tavares album, "Sky-High!" (Capitol) in his especially light, bright, highly-polished style. "Heaven Must Be Missing An Angel" is included and it alone is worth the price of the album, but another long cut, "Don't Take Away The Music" (6:18), is similarly high-spirited and strong. Runner-up here: "The Mighty Power Of Love." The most obvious dance cut on the new **Stylistics** lp, "Fabulous" (on H&L), is a **Van McCoy** song called "Starvin' For Love" that sounds very much like every other Van McCoy song recorded by the Stylistics. But my favorite is an off-beat, left-field cut called "It's So Good" which runs just over four minutes and is mostly instrumental except for the repeated title and one quick verse of singing. An excellent, pulsing production and an interesting change-of-pace.

That closes the male vocal group category, but there's another fine new album this week that would be difficult to categorize. It's a smooth blend of synthesizer-based jazz on the debut album by **Dexter**

12 WEST, NEW YORK
DJ: Tom Savarese

CAN WE COME TOGETHER/NINETY-NINE AND A HALF/SOUL SEARCHIN' TIME – Trammps (Atlantic)
DESPERATELY – Barrabas (Atco)
GIVE A BROKEN HEART A BREAK – Impact (Atco)
I GET LIFTED – Sweet Music (Wand)
I GOT YOUR LOVE – Stratavarious (Polydor import)
I'LL GO WHERE YOUR MUSIC TAKES ME – Jimmy James & the Vagabonds (Pye)
LOWDOWN – Boz Scaggs (Columbia)
NICE AND SLOW – Jesse Green (Scepter)
TAKE A LITTLE – Liquid Pleasure (Midland Intl.)
YOUNG HEARTS RUN FREE – Candi Staton (Warner Bros.)

LIQUID SMOKE, NEW YORK
DJ: Murray Brooks

BEDSIDE MANNERS – Super Disco Band (Pi Kappa)
CAN WE COME TOGETHER/DISCO PARTY/SOUL SEARCHIN' TIME – Trammps (Atlantic)
CATHEDRALS – D.C. LaRue (Pyramid)
HEAVEN MUST BE MISSING AN ANGEL – Tavares (Capitol)
LOVE CHANT – Eli's Second Coming (Silver Blue)
LOWDOWN – Boz Scaggs (Columbia)
SEXY LADY/DESPERATELY – Barrabas (Atco)
TEN PERCENT – Double Exposure (Salsoul)
TRY ME I KNOW WE CAN MAKE IT/COULD IT BE MAGIC/WASTED/COME WITH ME – Donna Summer (Oasis)
USE YOUR IMAGINATION – Kokomo (Columbia)

IPANEMA, NEW YORK
DJ: David Chrysostomas

BLACK SOUL MUSIC – Black Soul (Import Disque)
BROTHERS THEME/LAST CHANCE TO DANCE – Brothers (RCA)
CATHEDRALS – D.C. LaRue (Pyramid)
GET OFF YOUR AAHH! AND DANCE – Foxy (Dash)
LAURA – Biddu Orchestra (Epic import)
LIPSTICK – Michel Polnareff (Atlantic)
NICE AND SLOW – Jesse Green (Scepter)
SOUL SEARCHIN' TIME – Trammps (Atlantic)
TEN PERCENT – Double Exposure (Salsoul)
THINGS WON'T BE THIS BAD ALWAYS – Mike & Bill (Arista)

ADAMS APPLE, NEW YORK
DJ: Doug Carver

BEYOND THE SEA – Soul Price Orchestra (Philips import)
CAN WE COME TOGETHER/SOUL SEARCHIN' TIME/NINETY-NINE AND A HALF/DISCO PARTY – Trammps (Atlantic)
HAPPY MAN/GIVE A BROKEN HEART A BREAK – Impact (Atco)
HOLD ON – Righteous Brothers (Haven)
ONE MORE TRY – Ashford & Simpson (Warner Bros.)
PLAY BOYSCOUT/ONE LESS MORNING/ FREE/BRAND NEW – Melba Moore (Buddah)
SOUL MAN – Calhoon (Warner-Spector)
TELL ME HOW YOU LIKE IT/IN THE STILL OF THE NIGHT– I GET A KICK/NIGHT AND DAY – John Davis & the Monster Orchestra (Sam)
TEN PERCENT – Double Exposure (Salsoul)
YOU AND ME – Simon Said (Atco)

Wansel, "Life on Mars" (Philadelphia International), one of the best albums of this sort to come our way in some time. Nothing super disco here, but "You Can Be What You Wanna Be" (5:04) is certainly danceable and lusciously produced (by Wansel himself) and the title cut has a certain irresistible mystery. Not to be missed.

FEEDBACK: **Tom Savarese** reports a great floor reaction to **Passport's** 10-minute instrumental, "Ju-Ju-Man," from the group's new "Infinity Machine" album (Atco). He says the complex, free-form electronic track "worked from the first time I played it" at 12 West. "I Got Your Love," the **Stratavarious** cut Savarese lists and which we raved about some time back, is being released in the States by Roulette within the next two weeks, with 12-inch pressings for DJs. Watch for it... Once again, the new **Biddu Orchestra** album, "Rainforest," is one of the hottest imports in the discos. **David Chrysostomas** lists "Laura" in his Ipanema top 10 this week; **Phil Gill** chose "Rock Me With Your Love" last week; and several other cuts are being played as well. It's on Epic in England and Epic America is scheduling it, for release at the end of June with some modifications: "Jump For Joy" and "I Could Have Danced All Night," both included on the last Biddu U.S. release, will be dropped from "Rainforest" and replaced with newer cuts, one Biddu's current British single, "Bionic Boogie."

Doug Carver from Adams Apple in New York paints out that we missed mentioning the **Righteous Brothers'** recent **Lambert & Potter** single, "Hold On (To What You Got)" (Haven), which he's listed in his top 10 this week. Consider it mentioned and recommended, primarily because of its 4:20 disco version. ◐

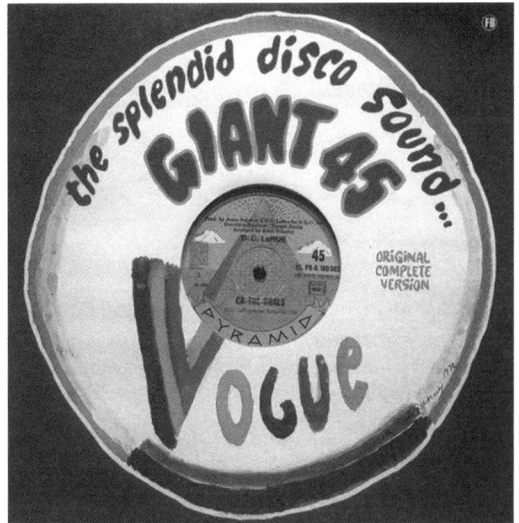

JUNE 12, 1976

"Arabian Nights," the new album from the **Ritchie Family** and their first on TK's Marlin label, is due out within the coming week but its pre-release leak to a select few DJs in New York has already started a buzz of high excitement. Produced by **Jacques Morali** and **Ritchie Rome**, one side of the album is a more than 14 minute medley on the "Arabian Nights" theme, including disco interpretations of three standards with Middle Eastern flavor – "Istanbul," "Lawrence of Arabia" and "In A Persian Market." The last cut, subtitled "Show Me How You Dance" and running just over six minutes, brings the medley to an exhilarating peak with the clipped punctuation of shouts – "Hey! hey! hey!" – that succeed in spite of an unfortunate echoing of Hitlerian rallies (music sociologists should have fun with this one). Even more attractive is the track Larry Sanders, DJ at the Sandpiper in Fire Island Pines as well as at Barefoot Boy and Pep McGuire's, lists in his top 10 this week: "The Best Disco in Town" (6:39), a celebration of discos and disco music that masterfully blends in key phrases from some of the hottest records of the past few years, including "Bad Luck," "Fly, Robin, Fly," "Love To Love You Baby," "Express," "Lady Marmalade" and, of course, the Family's own "Brazil." Brilliant. "Arabian Nights" seems to anticipate the mood of the summer and should be one of the season's major records.

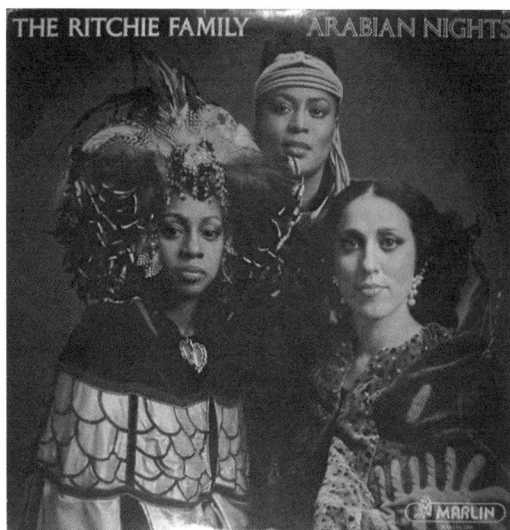

THE RITCHIE FAMILY · ARABIAN NIGHTS

In quite a different vein, there's the ominous undertow of **Lalo Schifrin's** vibrant jazz interpretation of the theme from "Jaws," just released by CTI on a 12-inch disco disc of exceptional quality. **Creed Taylor** produced, Schifrin arranged, and together they take the theme to a length of 8:15 and a depth the original movie score never dreamed of. Feels like the whole dance floor is suddenly underwater, fathoms down. "Jaws" will be available commercially in a slightly shorter version later this week when Schifrin's album, "Black Widow," is released.

NEWS & NOTES: Seeking some Official Statement on the endlessly-forthcoming **Stevie Wonder** album, "Songs In The Key of Life," we called Bob Jones, Motown's head of publicity in Los Angeles. "Motown's in the process of getting bits and pieces of it now," Jones said, but he knew better than to let himself be pinned down to a release date, saying only, "We hope sometime this month." We hope, too... **LaBelle** is switching producers for their next album, "Chameleon," due from Epic at the beginning of August. They're in the studio in San Francisco now with **David Rubinson**, the producer behind the **Pointer Sisters** and the new **Santana** and **Miroslav Vitous** albums... Now that the **Jackson 5**, minus **Jermaine**, are free to record for Epic Records, rumor has it that the group's next producers will be **Kenny Gamble** & **Leon Huff**. Sounds like disco heaven... Scepter is impressed enough by the initial reaction to Salsoul's commercial 12-inch disco pressings to enter the market themselves this week. Their first entry is an excellent back-to-back combination, **Jesse Green's** "Nice & Slow" and "I Get Lifted" by **Sweet Music**, which has the added attraction of giving the consumer two successful, long disco records for the price of one disco disc – just pennies more than two regular singles. But again there's the problem of standardization: the Scepter/Wand disc is at 33, while Salsoul's is a 45... Essential reading: **Nik Cohn's** "Tribal Rites Of The New Saturday Night" in the June 7 issue of New York magazine, an outsider's look inside a particular segment of the disco crowd, accompanied by illuminating paintings by **James McMullan**.

RECOMMENDED ALBUMS: "Just A Matter Of Time," **Marlena Shaw's** latest (on Blue Note), produced by **Bert deCoteaux** and **Tony Silvester** and highlighted by a stunning version of the **Spinners'** "Love Has Gone Away" (4:58) – an essential cut – plus the long version of the single, "It's Better Than Walkin' Out"... "Born to Get Down," the title cut from the new **Muscle Shoals Horns** lp (Bang), is still the best thing on the album (which has a half-open zipper on its cover), but two more cuts deserve attention: "Break Down," an instrumental which Walter Gibbons from Galaxy 21 paints out is a direct but irresistible steal from "Black Skin Blue Eyed Boys," and "Open Up Your Heart"... Lawrence Jacobson, who recently came to New York to take over as DJ at Vamps, called to say he'd gotten great reaction to the opening cut on the "Crazy Dancin'" album by **Bottom Line** (Greedy Records) called "That's The Way To Go," a light, spirited instrumental with vocal touches that sound something like the **Isley Brothers**; the title cut is also interesting.

RECOMMENDED SINGLES: "Can't Say No" by **S.S.O.** (Shadybrook), a witty, idiosyncratic production with **Barry White** overtones that runs 4:48 in its longer version... **Deodato's** version of the "Theme From Star Trek" (MCA), full of sharp electronic effects, the best treatment of this much-covered instrumental so far... **Paul Jabara's** bright, hilarious, raving "Dance" (A&M), which is brimming with sly references ("Take a sniff, a wicked whiff")... "Come On

STUDIO ONE, LOS ANGELES
DJ: Paul Dougan

CATHEDRALS – D.C. LaRue (Pyramid)
HEAVEN MUST BE MISSING AN ANGEL – Tavares (Capitol)
I'M GONNA LET MY HEART DO THE WALKING – Supremes (Motown)
LIPSTICK – Michel Polnareff (Atlantic)
NICE & SLOW – Jesse Green (Scepter)
PARTY – Van McCoy (H&L)
PARTY LINE/CALL ME – Andrea True Connection (Buddah)
SOUL SEARCHIN' TIME/THAT'S WHERE THE HAPPY PEOPLE GO-DISCO PARTY/NINETY-NINE AND A HALF – Trammps (Atlantic)
TEN PERCENT – Double Exposure (Salsoul)
TROUBLE-MAKER – Roberta Kelly (Oasis)

SANDPIPER, FIRE ISLAND PINES, N.Y.
DJ: Larry Sanders

THE BEST DISCO IN TOWN – Ritchie Family (Marlin)
CAN WE COME TOGETHER – Trammps (Atlantic)
DEEP, DARK, DELICIOUS NIGHT – D.C. LaRue (Pyramid)
GIVE A BROKEN HEART A BREAK – Impact (Atco)
HEAVEN MUST BE MISSING AN ANGEL – Tavares (Capitol)
LOVE CHANT – Eli's Second Coming (Silver Blue)
TEARS, TEARS, TEARS – Black Satin (Buddah)
TROUBLE-MAKER – Roberta Kelly (Oasis)
YOU'LL NEVER FIND ANOTHER LOVE LIKE MINE – Lou Rawls (Phila. Intl.)
YOUNG HEARTS RUN FREE – Candi Staton (Warner Bros.)

GALAXY 21, NEW YORK
DJ: Walter Gibbons

ALWAYS THERE – Side Effect (Fantasy)
FOR THE LOVE OF MONEY – Disco Dubs (Island import)
GIVE UP THE FUNK (TEAR THE ROOF OFF THE SUCKER) – Parliament (Casablanca)
HERE WE GO AGAIN – People's Choice (TSOP)
LIPSTICK – Michel Polnareff (Atlantic)
ONE MORE TRY/IT CAME TO ME – Ashford & Simpson (Warner Bros.)
PARTY – Van McCoy (H&L)
SUGAR BOOGIE – Bobby Thomas & the Hotline (MCA)
TAKE A LITTLE – Liquid Pleasure (Midland Intl.)
TROUBLE-MAKER – Roberta Kelly (Oasis)

LEVITICUS, NEW YORK
DJ: Thomas Pearson

BRING YOUR BODY – Carol Townes & Fifth Avenue (Sixth Avenue)
CAN WE COME TOGETHER/DISCO PARTY/THAT'S WHERE THE HAPPY PEOPLE GO – Trammps (Atlantic)
DANCE YOUR ASS OFF/THE GROOVE I FEEL – Bohannon (Dakar)
DISCO BABY – Nasty City (Hit-Bound Intl.)
FIRST CHOICE THEME/AIN'T HE BAD/ GOTTA GET AWAY – First Choice (Warner Bros.)
GOTTA BAD FEELING/YOU NEEDN'T WORRY NOW – Smoke (Chocolate City)
HEAVEN MUST BE MISSING AN ANGEL/THE MIGHTY POWER OF LOVE – Tavares (Capitol)
KEEP THAT SAME OLD FEELING – Crusaders (ABC Blue Thumb)
TAMBOURINE – John Tropea (Marlin)

And Ride" by **Enchantment** (Buddah), a chugging combination of the high spirits of "Express" and "Love Train" with a little "Free Man" riff thrown in – derivative but from all the best sources... **Fajardo's** "C'mon Baby, Do The Latin Hustle" which is Coco Records' first step into the disco field and a fine one even if it does follow very closely in the style established by **Eddie Drennon and BBS Unlimited** (disco version: 5:19). The following cuts are now available as singles: "Party" by Van McCoy (H&L), "Sometimes" by **Lesley Gore** featuring the **Brothers Johnson** (A&M), "Laura" by **Louie Ramirez** (Cotique) and an interesting 4:14 edit of **Donna Summer's** "Try Me, I Know We Can Make It" (Oasis).

This month's novelty record honors go to a bizarre disco backlash item called "Disco Tech" by **Homemade Theatre** (A&M), the story of "what happened when a group of young people listened to too much disco music and it fried their little brains and made them crazy," as narrated by a dead-pan Sergeant Saturday. A high school is taken over (re-named Disco Tech), teachers forced to dance against their will, a principal named Robin dragged to the electrical shop amid cries of "Fry, Robin, Fry." The students have OD-ed: Over Discoed; an atomic bomb is dropped (talk about overreaction) and the record ends with the sounds of a broken, skipping disc, stuck on the first bars of "That's The Way I Like It." A little frightening for disco lovers but very funny. ◗

JUNE 19, 1976

I thought there was supposed to be a summer slump in around here sometime, but the new releases keep arriving in surprising quantity. These are the best of the lot:

Candi Staton's new album, "Young Hearts Run Free" (Warner Brothers), is full of the sort of expansive high spirits that sent the title cut soaring (and kept it on the DISCO FILE Top 20 for nine weeks now). **Dave Crawford** produced and wrote nearly all the tracks and if the most danceable ones – "Run To Me," "Destiny" and "I Know," which was on the single's B side – follow closely in the formula established for "Young Hearts," it's just more of a very good thing. Also included: a wonderfully intense version of **Al Green's** "Living For You" and a perfect slow summer love song called "Summer Time With You."

Lalo Schifrin's "Black Widow" is due out this week and it again confirms CTI's position as the label with the most consistent, highest quality output of jazz-based disco music. Schifrin's fascinating version of "Jaws," the disco re-make of the moment, is here in a 5:47 edit with a note that **Hubert Laws** contributed the flute solo. There are so many other good tracks that it's hard to choose a favorite, but these stand out immediately: a long (5:36) blend of the standards "Moonglow" and "Theme From Picnic," a cool "Flamingo," and the three Schifrin originals, "Black Widow," "Dragonfly" and "Turning Point," though this last may be a little too zippy for dancing.

One of the nicest new male group albums comes from a Chicago trio called the Individuals whose debut lp, "Together (We Can Make Something Happen)" (PIP), is an impressive, varied collection. The group's sound is reminiscent of the **Dynamic Superiors** and their up-tempo cuts are immensely appealing, especially, "Never Too Late" ("for making love"), "Why Can't We Be Together" and "Gotta Make A Move." All the vocals are excellent, but this one's recommended mainly for people with a weakness for a stunning falsetto.

MFSB, the group behind the whole disco orchestra phenomenon, has come out with a breezy concept album called "Summertime" (Philadelphia International) that takes summer as its theme and a gorgeous

rendition of the **George Gershwin** tune as its title track. Unfortunately, the album as a whole is not up to the high standards the orchestra set for itself on the countless tracks it's recorded at Sigma Sound over the years, but there are several attractive cuts, the best being the opening tracks on each side, "Picnic In The Park" and "Summertime And I'm Feelin' Mellow," both in a light summery mood, and a spunky number called "We Got The Time" which closes the album. Refreshing.

Other notable albums: **Juggy Murray Jones**, whose "Inside America" remains one of the most interesting disco singles of the past year, has an album out now featuring that song as its title cut (again in two separate parts) plus a five-minute track of his disco success of a few years back, "Built For Speed" (which doesn't stand up quite as well today), and a 6:15 "Disco Extraordinaire" that has its moments; altogether, no match for the brilliance of the single, but a disco collector's item (on Jupiter)... "**Joe Simon** Today" (Spring) is full of upbeat material in the disco funk mold, including his recent single, "I Need You, You Need Me,'" a spicy "Come Get To This" (the best production here), and two surprising, almost unrecognizable re-makes, one of the **Stones'** "Let's Spend The Night Together," the other of **Sam Cooke's** "What A Wonderful World."

FEEDBACK: John Luongo, Boston club and radio DJ, called to report on the Boston Record Pool which is based in the offices of Luongo's successful Nightfall magazine (85 State Street, Boston 02109). Applications from Boston area disco DJs are being accepted and the membership, now at a little over 50, is expected to level off between 75 and 100 with service promised from a number of major companies including Columbia, United Artists, TK and Motown. Luongo hopes to publish a disco tipsheet starting in July directed to radio stations

> **❝ Lalo Schifrin's fascinating version of "Jaws," confirms CTI as the label with the highest quality output of jazz-based disco music ❞**

NOT FOR SALE

LALO SCHIFRIN

CTI RECORDS
A DIVISION OF
CREED TAYLOR, INC.
1 ROCKEFELLER PLAZA
NEW YORK, N.Y.
10020

CTI 6791
CTI 6791 A
Produced by
Creed Taylor

JAWS (theme from the Universal picture "Jaws") 8:15
(J. Williams)
Duchess Music Corp./BMI
ARRANGED BY LALO SCHIFRIN
® 1976, Creed Taylor, Inc.

BAREFOOT BOY, NEW YORK
DJ: Tony Smith

BROADWAY STAR/DESPERATELY/SEXY LADY – Barrabas (Atco)

CAN WE COME TOGETHER/SOUL SEARCHIN' TIME/DISCO PARTY – Trammps (Atlantic

FOR THE LOVE OF MONEY – Disco Dubs (Movers import)

HERE WE GO AGAIN/JAM, JAM, JAM – People's Choice (TSOP)

MADISON '76 – Venus (Columbia)

ONE MORE TRY – Ashford & Simpson (Warner Bros.)

THEME FROM "M.A.S.H." – New Marketts (Seminole)

SUGAR BOOGIE – Bobby Thomas & the Hotline (MCA)

TAKE A LITTLE – Liquid Pleasure (Midland Intl.)

TROUBLE-MAKER/LOVE POWER – Roberta Kelly (Oasis)

CIRCUS MAXIMUS, LOS ANGELES
DJ: Mitch Schatsky

CATHEDRALS – D.C. LaRue (Pyramid)

DESPERATELY/BROADWAY STAR – Barrabas (Atco)

GIVE A BROKEN HEART A BREAK/HAPPY MAN – Impact (Atec)

HEAVEN MUST BE MISSING AN ANGEL – Tavares (Capitol)

I'M GONNA LET MY HEART DO THE WALKING/HIGH ENERGY – Supremes (Motown)

LIPSTICK – Michel Polnareff (Atlantic)

LOWDOWN – Boz Scaggs (Columbia)

NICE & SLOW – Jesse Green (Scepter)

RAINFOREST/LAURA/ROCK ME WITH YOUR LOVE – Biddu Orchestra (Epic)

TROUBLE-MAKER/THE FAMILY – Roberta Kelly (Oasis)

ON STAGE, FREEPORT, NEW YORK
DJ: Dewane Dixon

BROADWAY STAR/IT/DESPERATELY – Barrabas (Atco)

CAN WE COME TOGETHER/DISCO PARTY /SOUL SEARCHIN' TIME/ NINETY-NINE AND A HALF – Trammps (Atlantic)

HERE WE GO AGAIN – People's Choice (TSOP)

LIPSTICK – Michel Polnareff (Atlantic)

MEAN MACHINE – Jimmy McGriff (Groove Merchant)

NICE & SLOW – Jesse Green (Scepter)

ONE FOR THE MONEY – Whispers (Soul Train)

RUNNING TO MEET THE MAN – ZBW Explosion (Dried Grape)

TAKE A LITTLE – Liquid Pleasure (Midland Intl.)

TROUBLE-MAKER – Roberta Kelly (Oasis)

RHINOCEROS, BOSTON
DJ: John Luongo

CATHEDRALS – D.C. LaRue (Pyramid)

DESPERATELY /HIGH LIGHT/IT/SEXY LADY – Barrabas (Atco)

DISCO PARTY/SOUL SEARCH IN' TIME/ CAN WE COME TOGETHER/THAT'S WHERE THE HAPPY PEOPLE GO – Trammps (Atlantic)

HEAVEN MUST BE MISSING AN ANGEL/ DON'T TAKE AWAY THE MUSIC – Tavares (Capitol)

I'M GONNA LET MY HEART DO THE WALKING – Supremes (Motown)

NICE & SLOW – Jesse Green (Scepter)

TAKE A LITTLE – Liquid Pleasure (Midland Intl.)

TEN PERCENT – Double Exposure (Salsoul)

TROUBLE-MAKER – Roberta Kelly (Oasis)

YOUNG HEARTS RUN FREE/I KNOW/RUN TO ME – Candi Staton (Warner Bros.)

in the New England area and advising them on the most likely disco crossover records. Contact the Boston Record Pool at (617) 723-3768. As for records, Luongo says that the seven-minute "Entrow" cut on the new **Graham Central Station** album, "Mirror" (Warner Brothers), is one of the top records in his club; it starts out with a crazy march riff and turns into one of those GCS self-promotional songs like "The Jam" on their last album... On Tony Smith's top 10 from Barefoot Boy this week, he's listed a luxurious, long (5:10) instrumental of the "Theme From M*A*S*H" by the **New Marketts** (Seminole) which sounds like an instant cult item with a great potential for crossing over to a larger audience. Also on his list, a terrific instrumental version of the **O'Jays'** "For The Love Of Money," an import on the Movers label by the **Disco Dubs**. Walter Gibbons also top-tenned this record last week (when the label was incorrectly identified as Island; Island is the distributor) and Dewane Dixon reports equally enthusiastic response at his club on Long Island... One of the more obscure items on Dixon's own list this week is a song from the Broadway show "Raisin" called "Runnin' To Meet The Man" by the **ZBW Explosion** (Dried Grape), an exhilarating, very upbeat instrumental that sounds nothing like a show tune. The new release by **The Whispers**, "One For The Money," a knockout **Norman Harris** production on a 12-inch pressing from Soul Train Records, is also on Dixon's top 10 and mentioned as a hot item by several of the DJs we spoke with this week.

RECOMMENDED SINGLES: "Them From M*A*S*H" by the **New Marketts** (Seminole) and "One for the Money" by **The Whispers**, both mentioned above... **Urszula Dudziak's** delightful, insane version of the standard "Tico Tico" (Arista) – an extraordinary vocal extrava-ganza (disco version: 3:53)... "Black Soul Music" by **Black Soul** (Beam Junction), the import a lot of DJs have been talking about, now in official American release (earlier 12-inch pressings were unauthorized) and sounding like **Bimbo Jet** meets **Manu Dibango**; this copy has long (4:31) and short (3:02) versions back-to-back... one of the better girl groups, the **Emotions**, returns with a beautiful slow song called "Flowers" (Columbia), produced by **Maurice White** and **Charles Stepney** of **Earth, Wind & Fire**... the record that everyone's been saying is **James Brown's** best in a long time, "Get Up Offa That Thing" (4:11 on Polydor) which proves once again that JB never really loses his touch... "Shake It Down," a tough, loud, hard-rock disco record by a group from England called **Mud** {Private Stock) – it's 3:36 with a neat false ending... "Mama Can You Meet the 6:15" by **Sondra Simon & Simon Said** (Atco), a fabulously sappy, sentimental girl group song with some great breaks in its long version (6:29), produced by the DCA group... a striking, original instrumental called "Porcupine" by **Nature Zone** (London), which the label promises in an even longer disco disc soon... and another German production with powerful, aggressive vocals: **Su Kramer's** strong "You've Got the Power" in two parts on London. ◙

JUNE 26, 1976

Best new album cut this week "The Word" from **L.T.D.'s** latest release, "Love To The World" (A&M), a major jump forward for this group, primarily because they've hooked up here with **Larry** and **Fonce Mizell** (producers of **Bobbi Humphrey, Donald Byrd, Johnny Hammond** and others) and the combination is superb. "The Word" (5:30) is in the Mizells' usual energetic, sweeping style, only here they're dealing with a lead vocal as well as their trademark breezy chanting choruses so the interplay of vocals and instrumental breaks is even more striking. The subject is gossip and infidelity; the key line: "The word is out on you" – another "I heard it through the grapevine." The album's title cut, opening up the record and setting its tone, is another pumping, spirited Mizell composition running just over five minutes, and one more track, "Get Your It Together," is danceable in the jazzy funk style L.T.D. established on their earlier lps.

The debut album of **Mark Radice**, a singer with a rough, self-consciously "soulful" style, is notable mainly because it was produced by **Jeff Lane** and features **Brass Construction**, who are enough to spark any record. So the singing is okay, but the production is terrific and in disco, production is all. The album's called "Ain't Nothin' But A Party" (United Artists) and the standout track is "If You Can't Beat 'Em Join 'Em" (7:01), which is hard and chugging with a long instrumental segment. Two other cuts –"Monkey See Monkey Do" and "Here I Go Fallin' In Love Again," both over six minutes – are similarly structured and close runners up in the dance, dance, dance department.

Jimmy James & the Vagabonds' second album is out now, titled "I'll Go Where Your Music Takes Me" (Pye) and featuring that cut plus a number of other **Biddu** productions. Among them: a strong version of "Disco Fever," the **Tina Charles** song; "Your Love Keeps Haunting Me," which sounds very **Four Tops**; and a short, cute cut called "Whatever Happened To The Love We Knew." "Now Is The Time," the album's longest track at 6:08, is an attempt to deliver a danceable message song à la the group's "I Am Somebody," but this one's too preachy and downbeat, only working in moments but with an interesting enough build in the production to be a possible left field hit.

Even more left field: an eight-minute instrumental cut called "Sweet Sixteen" from the debut album of the **Diga Rhythm Band** ("Diga" on Round Records, through United Artists) which Kiki Cuffee at the New York Record Pool alerted me to. The group is a rich mix of Latin and Indian percussion, a drum freak's dream, and "Sweet Sixteen" is one of the most lively cuts, not entirely danceable (except for a great break in the middle) but really inspiring. Perfect for early in the evening to start people's temperatures rising.

FEEDBACK: The new cut on Cosmo Wyatt's top 10 from Yesterday in Boston is a tight, pulsing jazz instrumental called "All The Time" from **Ronnie Laws'** "Fever" album on Blue Note. Wyatt and Infinity's Bobby Guttadaro (just beginning the summer season at Fire Island's Ice Palace) both recommend "Down To Love Town" on the new **Originals** album ("Communique" on Soul, also featuring "Everybody's Got To Do Something"), a very nice production by **Frank Wilson** and someone named **Michael B. Sutton**, who co-wrote the song. Guttadaro also reports fabulous reaction to the lengthy, lush, romantic "Midnight Rhapsody" (10:50) from the all-instrumental "Motown Magic Disco Machine Volume III" (Motown), which is a very effective blend of styles (**Barry White**, the **Ritchie Family, Salsoul Orchestra**, etc.). And he says he's playing the B side of the new **Deodato** single, a version of "I Shot The Sheriff" with a fine drum break (MCA)... John Colon at Friends Again says **Betty Wright's** rough-and-tumble version of the old **Darrell Banks** record, "Open The Door To Your Heart" (in her "Explosion!" album on Alston), is doing so well, he's putting it on his top 10 this week. And Alfie Davidson, alternating at Hippopotamus with Rich Pampinella, is crazy about **Natalie Cole's** perfect, overlooked "Mr. Melody" (Capitol)... "Tribal Rites Of The New Saturday Night," **Nik Cohn's** jagged profile of a group of discogoers that we recommended on its appearance in New York magazine a few issues back, has been purchased by the **Robert Stigwood** Organisation for conversion into a film with Cohn scripting.

Roulette's got the two hottest new 12-inch records in "I Got Your Love" by **Stratavarious Featuring Lady** (8:05), already highly recommended – I think it's one of this year's great records – and finally available; and "My Baby's Got E.S.P." by **Four Below Zero**, an amazingly up, driving **Patrick Adams** production with powerful male vocals that runs 5:24 with an incredible break. Atlantic is also issuing two new Disco Discs, one **Barrabas** back-to-back-"Desperately" and "Broadway Star" – the other with two cuts from the **Impact** album, "Give A Broken Heart A Break" and "Happy Man;" save for "Happy Man," all these cuts are already active, strong entries on the DISCO FILE Top 20.

RECOMMENDED SINGLES: "The Unexplained," a mysterious, sci-fi instrumental with great electronic effects by a group called **Ataraxia** (RCA)... "Jack In The Box," a **Blue Magic** kind of song by **David Morhis, Jr.** (Buddah) and produced in part by **Bobby Eli** who's been very busy lately – this one's a gem of Philadelphia styling (long version: 5:07)... and the return of **Lloyd Price** with an excellent mid-tempo record in an unexpectedly dreamy and seductive rendition: "What Did You Do With My Love" (JPG). ✪

INFINITY, NEW YORK
DJ: Bobby Guttadaro

BEST DISCO IN TOWN – Ritchie Family (Marlin)
DISCO PARTY/NINETY-NINE AND A HALF
– Trammps (Atlantic)
GIVE A BROKEN HEART A BREAK – Impact (Atco)
HEAVEN MUST BE MISSING AN ANGEL/ DON'T TAKE
AWAY THE MUSIC – Tavares (Capitol)
LOVE CHANT (PART II) – Eli's Second Coming (Silver Blue)
ONE MORE TRY – Ashford & Simpson (Warner Bros.)
RUN TO ME – Candi Staton (Warner Bros.)
TEN PERCENT – Double Exposure (Salsoul)
TROUBLE-MAKER – Roberta Kelly (Oasis)
TRY ME I KNOW WE CAN MAKE IT – Donna Summer (Oasis)

HIPPOPOTAMUS, NEW YORK
DJ: Alfie Davidson

CALL ME – Andrea True Connection (Buddah)
CATHEDRALS – D.C. LaRue (Pyramid)
DESPERATELY – Barrabas (Atco)
DISCO PARTY/NINETY-NINE AND A HALF/CAN WE COME
TOGETHER/SOUL SEARCHIN' TIME – Trammps (Atlantic)
I'M GONNA LET MY HEART DO THE WALKING – Supremes
(Motown)
LAURA – Biddu Orchestra (Epic import)
NICE & SLOW – Jesse Green (Scepter)
TEN PERCENT – Double Exposure (Salsoul)
TROUBLE-MAKER – Roberta Kelly (Oasis)
TRY ME I KNOW WE CAN MAKE IT – Donna Summer (Oasis)

YESTERDAY, BOSTON
DJ: Cosmo Wyatt

ALL THE TIME – Ronnie Laws (Blue Note)
DISCO PARTY – Trammps (Atlantic)
HEAVEN MUST BE MISSING AN ANGEL/DON'T TAKE
AWAY THE MUSIC/THE MIGHTY POWER OF LOVE –
Tavares (Capitol)
I'M GONNA LET MY HEART DO THE WALKING –
Supremes (Motown)
NICE & SLOW – Jesse Green (Scepter)
ONE FOR THE MONEY – Whispers (Soul Train)
RUN TO ME/YOUNG HEARTS RUN FREE – Candi Staton
(Warner Bros.)
TAKE A LITTLE – Liquid Pleasure (Midland Intl.)
TEN PERCENT – Double Exposure (Salsoul)
TROUBLE-MAKER – Roberta Kelly (Oasis)

FRIENDS AGAIN, NEW YORK
DJ: John Colon

ALWAYS THERE – Side Effect (Fantasy)
DESPERATELY/BROADWAY STAR/HIGH LIGHT
– Barrabas (Atco)
FOR THE LOVE OF MONEY – Disco Dubs (Movers import)
HERE WE GO AGAIN – People's Choice (TSOP)
JU JU MAN – Passport (Atco)
LIFE ON MARS/YOU CAN BE WHAT YOU WANNA BE –
Dexter Wansel (Phila. Intl.)
NEW YORK CITY – Miroslav Vitous (Warner Bros.)
ONE FOR THE MONEY – Whispers (Soul Train)
OPEN THE DOOR TO YOUR HEART – Betty Wright (Alston)
TAKE A LITTLE – Liquid Pleasure (Midland Intl.)

DISCO FILE TOP 20

1. **SOUL SEARCHIN' TIME/DISCO PARTY/CAN WE COME TOGETHER** – Trammps (Atlantic)
2. **TROUBLE-MAKER** – Roberta Kelly (Oasis)
3. **TEN PERCENT** – Double Exposure (Salsoul)
4. **NICE & SLOW** – Jesse Green (Scepter)
5. **HEAVEN MUST BE MISSING AN ANGEL** – Tavares (Capitol)
6. **DESPERATELY** – Barrabas (Atco)
7. **TAKE A LITTLE** – Liquid Pleasure (Midland Intl.)
8. **NINETY-NINE AND A HALF** – Trammps (Atlantic)
9. **LIPSTICK** – Michel Polnareff (Atlantic)
10. **CATHEDRALS** – D.C. LaRue (Pyramid)
11. **GIVE A BROKEN HEART A BREAK** – Impact (Atco)
12. **I'M GONNA LET MY HEART DO THE WALKING** – Supremes (Motown)
13. **HERE WE GO AGAIN** – People's Choice (TSOP)
14. **BROADWAY STAR/SEXY LADY** – Barrabas (Atco)
15. **LOWDOWN** – Boz Scaggs (Columbia)
16. **THAT'S WHERE THE HAPPY PEOPLE GO** – Trammps (Atlantic)
17. **ONE MORE TRY** – Ashford & Simpson (Warner Bros.)
18. **YOUNG HEARTS RUN FREE/RUN TO ME** – Candi Staton (Warner Bros.)
19. **TRY ME I KNOW WE CAN MAKE IT** – Donna Summer (Oasis)
20. **LOVE CHANT (PART II)** – Eli's Second Coming (Silver Blue)

❝Mark Radice's debut album features Brass Construction, who are enough to spark any record. The singing is okay, but the production is terrific, and in disco, production is all❞

Getting back to New York after two weeks of what travel agents like to call Real Relaxation in Florida is difficult in itself (the question keeps popping up: "Why am I here?"), but trying to contend with a knee-high pile-up of new records in a quick two-day catch-up session is enough to send me back to LaGuardia – "Destination Anywhere" as the Marvelettes sang – on the first Checker cab. In an attempt to preserve what little Real Relaxation I managed to smuggle back with me, this column is a cream-off-the-top survey of the most immediately interesting items in the flood of new releases that washed up in my post office box while I was away. A more in-depth investigation will follow next week.

Top of the list is the **Bee Gees'** instant hit, "You Should Be Dancing" (RSO) which should be even more of a success on the disco level than "Jive Talkin.'" The sound is tough and brittle, dense with percussion that makes an especially effective contrast to the shrill, cutting quality of the vocals. A promotional 12-inch disc is available at 4:47 and, as Rich Pampinella – who put the record on his top 10 from Hippopotamus this week – points out, the record is perfect for longer turntable blends and double plays. Irresistible.

Salsoul Records' second commercial "Giant 45" – their breakthrough in disco disc marketing – is **Moment of Truth's** "So Much For Love," a completely captivating I've-had-it-with-love song that manages to capture that particular feeling of elation edged with bitterness that comes at the end of an affair. The production, by **Reid Whitelaw and Norman Bergen** who also wrote the song, is smooth and bright with a nagging girl chorus providing just the right note of nastiness to balance the persevering male lead. Promotional copies of the 12- inch include a 6:36 vocal backed by a 5:45 instrumental version; commercial copies feature the vocal "So Much For Love" backed with the group's previous hit, "Helplessly" – an excellent package.

"Sun... Sun... Sun," the song producer/composer **Johnnymelfi** has been promising us for so long, is out now on a 12-inch from Pyramid that runs 9:15. This is surely one of the most idiosyncratic productions in some time – full of breaks and shifts in mood and possessed of an almost ritual chant quality in parts. The group of singers here is called **Jakki**, but it's Melfi's production that grabs the attention – it's very New York, with touches of **Crown Heights Affair** and the Latin hustle sound, but quite unique and, in flashes, bizarre.

Speaking of bizarre, be sure to check out "Smoke Your Troubles Away" by **The Glass Family** (a J. D. Salinger allusion?), an incredible pro-marijuana song done sort of **B.T. Express** style in which the girl singers actually characterize themselves as female hemp plants. "Don't burn me like a worthless vine," they sing, "I'll be good to you, I'll treat you kind... All I wanna be is free/If you're on my side, you can come with me." Part 1 is 4:14 and Part 2, which consists mainly of a chant of the song's title, runs 2:16. Could be a major underground hit. An indication of

❝ Rich Pampinella points out that the record is perfect for longer turntable blends and double plays. Irresistible ❞

PIER 9, WASHINGTON, D.C.
DJ: Curt Strack

BEST DISCO IN TOWN – Ritchie Family (Marlin)
CAN'T STOP GROOVIN' NOW, WANNA DO IT SOME MORE – B.T. Express (Columbia)
HEAVEN MUST BE MISSING AN ANGEL/ DON'T TAKE AWAY THE MUSIC/ MIGHTY POWER OF LOVE – Tavares (Capitol)
I'M GONNA LET MY HEART DO THE WALKING – Supremes (Motown)
LIPSTICK – Michel Polnareff (Atlantic)
MAKES YOU BLIND – Glitter Band (Bell import)
ONE FOR THE MONEY – Whispers (Soul Train)
RUN TO ME/YOUNG HEARTS RUN FREE/ DESTINY – Candi Staton (Warner Bros.)
TEN PERCENT – Double Exposure (Salsoul)
TROUBLE-MAKER/THE FAMILY – Roberta Kelly (Oasis)

SUNDAY'S, CHICAGO
DJ: Artie Feldman

DESPERATELY – Barrabas (Atco)
DISCO PARTY – Trammps (Atlantic)
HEAVEN MUST BE MISSING AN ANGEL – Tavares (Capitol)
I'M GONNA LET MY HEART DO THE WALKING – Supremes (Motown)
SOUR AND SWEET – Dr. Buzzard's Original Savannah Band (RCA)
TAKE A LITTLE – Liquid Pleasure (Midland Intl.)
TEN PERCENT – Double Exposure (Salsoul)
TROUBLE-MAKER/LOVE POWER – Roberta Kelly (Oasis)
TRY ME I KNOW WE CAN MAKE IT – Donna Summer (Oasis)
YOUNG HEARTS RUN FREE – Candi Staton (Warner Bros.)

HIPPOPOTAMUS, NEW YORK
DJ: Rich Pampinella

ALWAYS THERE – Side Effect (Fantasy)
CAN WE COME TOGETHER/DISCO PARTY/SOUL SEARCHIN' TIME – Trammps (Atlantic)
HEAVEN MUST BE MISSING AN ANGEL/DON'T TAKE AWAY THE MUSIC – Tavares (Capitol)
LIPSTICK – Michel Polnareff (Atlantic)
MAMA, CAN YOU MEET THE 6:15 – Sandra Simon & Simon Said (Atco)
TEN PERCENT – Double Exposure (Salsoul)
TROUBLE-MAKER – Roberta Kelly (Oasis)
YELLOW TRAIN – Resonance (Bradley's import)
YOU SHOULD BE DANCING – Bee Gees (RSO)
YOU'LL NEVER FIND ANOTHER LOVE LIKE MINE – Lou Rawls (Phila. Intl.)

LE DOMME, MIAMI
DJ: Aristides Jacobs

CALL ME/KEEP IT UP LONGER – Andrea True Connection (Buddah)
DANCING FREE – Hot Ice (Rage)
DESPERATELY /BROADWAY STAR – Barrabas (Atco)
GETAWAY – Earth, Wind & Fire (Columbia)
LIPSTICK – Michel Polnareff (Atlantic)
NEW YORK CITY – Miroslav Vitous (Warner Bros.)
S.O.S. – Today's People (Gamma import)
TROUBLE-MAKER – Roberta Kelly (Oasis)
YOU'LL NEVER FIND ANOTHER LOVE LIKE MINE – Lou Rawls (Phila. Intl.)
YOUNG HEARTS RUN FREE/RUN TO ME – Candi Staton (Warner Bros.)

how far the drug scene has come out into the open – from paranoia to coy references to all-out advocacy – this one's on Earhole Records (Record Company Name of the Month Award Winner) in Los Angeles.

Then there are three immensely attractive new albums, beginning with a stylish debut on RCA by a group called **Dr. Buzzard's Original Savannah Band**, five young New Yorkers whose material has a nostalgic flavor without any of **Manhattan Transfer's** elaborate posing. "This is mulatto music – it's a blend of everything," one group member says. "We're from Hollywood, simple and stupid like the '40s." Really, though, they're witty, quick and fun and their whole album is, in movie terms, great entertainment. Best cuts: "Sour And Sweet; Lemon In The Honey" (6:03), the standout – already on Artie Feldman's list from Sunday's in Chicago; "Cherchez La Femme" (5:54) and "I'll Play The Fool." Cool and refreshing. **Maurice White** and **Charles Stepney** of Earth, Wind & Fire produced the comeback album for the **Emotions** ("Flowers" on Columbia) and they've worked wonders with the standard girl group sound. EW&F make up the core of musicians here, supporting truly inspired vocals, the most danceable being "I Don't Wanna Lose Your Love." The third album is the U.S. release of the **Biddu Orchestra's** "Rain Forest" album (Epic), already quite successful as an import and featuring two tracks not included on the English release. Biddu's instrumentals are among the best in the disco field – at once sweeping and concise, with a nice pop gloss – and this is a fine collection with a lot of variety. Recommended, aside from the title cut which was advanced as a single: "Trippin' on A Soul Cloud," "Laura," "Rock Me With Your Love" and the new zippy cut, "Bionic Boogie."

RECOMMENDED SINGLES: "It's Not The World That's Messed Up" ("it's the people in it"), a hot **Norman Harris** production for **Tapestry** (Capitol) that reminds me of the **Baker, Harris & Young** Whispers album with some **Trammps** touches. **Earth, Wind & Fire's** "Getaway" (Columbia): though its changes are a little difficult for dancing, this is one of the group's best "Have Love Will Travel," the B side of the new **Sister Sledge** single (Cotillion) produced by **Bobby Eli** with a superb **Supremes** sound... **Bobby Caldwell's** "The House Is Rockin'" (PBR International), a macho pick-up song with a nice drive and energy... a two-part (4:57/4:34) song called "Nashville Soul," an out-of-the-ordinary instrumental by **The Syndicate** (who bill themselves as "Nashville's Disco Band") which has its moments... "Shelter Me" by **Fingertips** (MCA), a hard-edged girl group sound from England – something like a combination of **Cilla Black** and **Penny McLean**... **Roy Buchanan's** rock-hard "Keep What You Got" (Atlantic), an **Arif Mardin** production that Tom Savarese from 12 West had alerted us to some weeks back – now out on a 45 ... and **Phyllis Hyman's** "Baby (I'm Gonna Love You)" (Desert Moon), one of the very sweetest slow love songs I've heard in months by one of disco's rising stars. ✪

JULY 17, 1976

The new **Whispers** album, "The Whispers" on Soul Train Records, is mostly gorgeous slow ballads – some of the best around – but producer Norman Harris hasn't disappointed the disco crowd because the album also includes this week's best new cut. It's a very up message song called "Put Me In The News" (4:15) which sounds like "Bingo" crossed with "Bad Luck" and takes the soul searching philosophy of Philadelphia – where the strongest musical/political statements are coming from these days – a little deeper. Sample verse: "Heaven help me if I break the law/But the privileged they can break them all/And go free/But not you and me." The demand: "Put me in the news/Let me give my views." Powerful. Also included is the group's current single, "One For The Money" (in its short version, 3:05, meaning DJs with the 5:13 disco disc have an exclusive on the longer version), and a perky "I've Got A Feeling."

My favorite cuts from the **Maryann Farra & Satin Soul** debut lp ("Never Gonna Leave You" on Brunswick) are three handsome remakes of old **Chi-lites** songs: "You Got To Be The One," "Stoned Out Of My Mind" and "Living In The Footsteps Of Another Girl" run one after the other in lush, fluid **Tony Valor** productions. The first two songs both just over five minutes, are the most successful and it should be noted that **Eugene Record** of the Chi-lites participated in the up-dated re-arrangement of all his material. The rest of the album is also unexpectedly attractive, featuring a 5:35 version of the title track, a pleasant version of "Forget That Girl" and something called "Do Those Little Things" which is cute and sweet.

Other notable album cuts: "Queen Of My Soul," a six-minute song dedicated to the beauty and power of music from the new **Average White Band** album, "Soul Searching" (Atlantic) – an uplifting, very spiritual sound not unlike **Earth, Wind & Fire**; produced by **Arif Mardin**... "Prophecy" (5:19), written and produced by **Lamont Dozier** for the **Margie Joseph** album, "Hear The Words, Feel The Feeling" (Cotillion), and sung by Joseph with verve and drive... "Thank You Love" (4:45) by **Isaac Hayes** (from his new "Juicy Fruit" album on ABC/Hot Buttered Soul), featuring one of his distinctive dense, nervously electronic productions.

Watch out for a new album on Casablanca's Oasis label, due out in the next few weeks, featuring a long (nearly 15 minutes), **Donna Summer** – style interpretation of **Moody Blues'** "Nights in White Satin." The record, which is being tested with a select number of DJs around the country who've been given advance pressings of one side of the album, is the closest thing to a male version of "Love To Love You Baby" primarily because the singer, **Giorgio**, is **Giorgio Moroder** who, with **Pete Bellotte**, produced the recent work of both Summer and **Roberta Kelly**. So the production here is, again, compellingly grandiose, somehow larger than life.

MORE THAN 7 INCHES: Among the new 12-inch promotional releases, there's one from **Revelation**, one of last year's strongest new male groups, now being produced by **Freddie Perren** (for RSO). The song's a mid-tempo ballad called "You To Me Are Everything" that runs 6:20 and is quite pleasant. (Note: the record is available as a two-part single by Revelation and in two other single versions – the original English hit by **The Real Thing** on UA and a **Tony Silvester** production by **Broadway** on Granite.) Other essential disco discs: a longer mix of **Marlena Shaw's** dynamite "Love Has Gone Away" (5:06) backed with "It's Better Than Walking Out," also lengthened (to 5:30) – on Blue Note; a three-track disc from RCA featuring new, longer versions of instrumentals by **The Brothers** – "Brothers Theme" now 7:28, "Make Love" now 5:49, and "Under The Skin" at the original length but hotter – all worth reviving; and London's first entry into the field, "Porcupine" by **Nature Zone**, same length as the 45 (3:40) but deserving some attention.

NOTABLE SINGLES: Just last week I was wondering what ever happened to **Honey Cone** (maybe because ,their classic "Want Ads" popped up on the radio), and here, suddenly, happily, is a new single from the group on the re-activated Hot Wax label (through CBS). It's called "Somebody Is Always Messing Up A Good Thing" and the title should give you an idea of its style: emotional and screaming, a timeless girl group record. Both **Eddie** and **Brian Holland** were involved in writing and/or producing so the group is back in style... I thought **RW** singles reviewer/assistant editor/etc. Barry Taylor was kidding when he handed me a novelty record called

REVELATION II, BROOKLYN, NEW YORK
DJ: Joe Saltalamocchia

BEST DISCO IN TOWN/BABY I'M ON FIRE/IN A PERSIAN MARKET – Ritchie Family (Marlin)
CAN WE COME TOGETHER/DISCO PARTY/THAT'S WHERE THE HAPPY PEOPLE GO/NINETY-NINE AND A HALF – Trammps (Atlantic lp cuts)
HEAVEN MUST BE MISSING AN ANGEL/DON'T TAKE AWAY THE MUSIC – Tavares (Capitol)
MAKES YOU BLIND – Glitter Band (Bell import)
RUN TO ME – Candi Staton (Warner Bros.)
SOUR AND SWEET/CHERCHEZ LA FEMME – Savannah Band (RCA)
SUN... SUN... SUN – Jakki (Fyramid)
TAKE A LITTLE – Liquid Pleasure (Midland Intl.)
TROUBLE-MAKER/THINK I'M GONNA BREAK SOMEONE'S HEART TONIGHT – Roberta Kelly (Oasis)
YOU SHOULD BE DANCING – Bee Gees (RSO)

OLD PLANTATION, HOUSTON, TEXAS
DJ: Ram Rocha

HEAVEN MUST BE MISSING AN ANGEL – Tavares (Capitol)
LIPSTICK – Michel Polnareff (Atlantic)
NICE & SLOW – Jesse Green (Scepter)
PARTY – Van McCoy (H&L)
PARTY LINE/FILL ME UP – Andrea True Connection (Buddah)
SAN FRANCISCO HUSTLE/NO, NO, JOE – Silver Convention (Midland Intl.)
SUPER DISCO – Rimshots (Stang)
TEN PERCENT – Double Exposure (Salsoul)
THAT'S WHERE THE HAPPY PEOPLE GO – Trammps (Atlantic)
TRY ME I KNOW WE CAN MAKE IT / COULD IT BE MAGIC – Donna Summer (Oasis)

15 LANSDOWNE STREET, BOSTON
DJ: Conrad Cardenas

BEST DISCO IN TOWN' – Ritchie Family (Marlin)
DISCO PARTY/SOUL SEARCHIN' TIME/ THAT'S WHERE THE HAPPY PEOPLE GO – Trammps (Atlantic)
HEAVEN MUST BE MISSING AN ANGEL/ DON'T TAKE AWAY THE MUSIC – Tavares (Capitol)
LOVE HANGOVER – Diana Ross (Motown)
NICE & SLOW – Jesse Green (Scepter)
SO MUCH FOR LOVE – Moment of Truth (Salsoul)
TEN PERCENT – Double Exposure (Salsoul)
TRY ME I KNOW WE CAN MAKE IT – Donna Summer (Oasis)
TURN THE BEAT AROUND – Vicki Sue Robinson (RCA)
YOU'LL NEVER FIND ANOTHER LOVE LIKE MINE – Lou Rawls (Phila. Intl.)

CORK & BOTTLE, NEW YORK
DJ: Freddie Mendoza

BEST DISCO IN TOWN/BABY I'M ON FIRE/IN A PERSIAN MARKET – Ritchie Family (Marlin)
C'MON BABY, DO THE LATIN HUSTLE – Fajardo (Coco)
CAN WE COME TOGETHER/DISCO PARTY /SOUL SEARCHIN' TIME – Trammps (Atlantic)
GET DOWN BOY (INSTRUMENTAL) – Paper Dolls (Tyson)
IF YOU CAN'T BEAT 'EM, JOIN 'EM – Mark Radice (UA)
ONE FOR THE MONEY – Whispers (Soul Train)
SOY – Charanga '76 (TR)
TEN PERCENT – Double Exposure (Salsoul)
YOU SHOULD BE DANCING – Bee Gees (RSO)
YOU'LL NEVER FIND ANOTHER LOVE LIKE MINE – Lou Rawls (Phila, Intl.)

"Phillies Fever" (Grand Prix), a song boosting the Philadelphia ball team by five Phillies members (whose pitcures are on the sleeve, front and rear views) (?), and told me it was "Disco!" Actually, he probably was kidding, but – and I don't really believe this either – the record's B side, "Dancin' with the Phillies," an instrumental, is really kinda cute – not especially inventive as disco records go but serviceable and fun. The B side is credited to something called **QVRS**, apparently the studio band at Queen Village Recording Studio in Philly where the record was made... "Get Down Boy" is one of those freaky, electronic instrumentals that sounds like an immediate cult record. As sung by an eerie chorus of girls, the **Paper Dolls**, the song is about just what its title implies, with one side vocal and the other instrumental, though no credit is given to a performer or orchestra on the instrumental side. It's on Tyson, a small label in the Bronx, and I got my copy at the New York Record Pool... There are three good new records from established disco groups: **Undisputed Truth's** "You + Me = Love" (the first single release on **Norman Whitfield's** Whitfield Records, through Warner Brothers), "(Shake, Shake, Shake) Shake Your Booty" by **KC & the Sunshine Band** (TK) and "Dancin' Kid" by **Disco Tex & the Sex-O-Lettes** (Chelsea). No surprises here as far as style is concerned – there are no major shifts in any group's signature sound – but all the acts are in fine form, with the Disco Tex record being the first from the group to match the catchiness and punch of their debut "Get Dancin.'"

OTHER RECOMMENDED SINGLES: **The Meters'** "Disco Is the Thing Today" (Reprise, 4:16), the group's departure from New Orleans funk into smooth disco styling – a successful move under the direction of **Allen Toussaint**... "The Real Thing" by **Brotherhood** featuring **Salome Bey** (Buddah), which has a very sharp **Jackson 5** sound... **Etta James'** beyond-raunchy "Jump Into Love" (Chess), featuring a husky male chorus saying things like "Take a lunge, take a plunge" – but that's nothing compared to what Etta says... and, in left field, **Rogers & Hart's** standard "Lover" fitted into a rather bizarre erotic disco framework and sung by **Lily Fields** and a great chorus – uneven but it ends with a bang (Spectrum). ✇

" Philadelphia is where the strongest political statements come from these days: "Heaven help me if I break the law/But the privileged they can break them all." Powerful "

The **Fatback Band** seems to get stronger with each new album and the group's latest, "Night Fever," due out this week on Spring, is one of their best collections to date. Strongest cuts are the title track, a fast Latin hustle sound with some **Barrabas** overtones; "A Little Funky Dance," an excellent funk number with a driving chant and a feeling closer to the **Gary Toms Empire** or the **Ohio Players**; "The Joint (You And Me)" which continues in a similar vein but adds some fabulous tempo changes and an even more cutting edge on the horns; and "Disco Crazy" whose high-pitched chant is, "Everybody's goin' disco crazy" – very quick-paced with some fine breaks, unexpected flights of strings and steamy keyboard work. There's also an upbeat version of the recent **Four Seasons** hit, "December 1963 (Oh, What A Night)," which improves on the original for danceability. All the cuts mentioned are five minutes or over except for "Disco Crazy," which runs 4:15; production – all of it clean and sharp – is by the band itself, now eight members with some additions and subtractions from the group as they last appeared on record.

Among the other album releases, there's something called **Frankie Crocker's Heart and Soul Orchestra**, a group put together and produced by radio's top black DJ, the man who transformed WBLS in New York. Crocker doesn't exactly transform disco here – the album, titled "The Disco Suite Symphony No.1 In Rhythm And Excellence" (Casablanca), is four sides of elaborate disco orchestrations of standard tunes done in a style somewhere between the Monster and Love Unlimited Orchestras – but several of the tracks are attractive and perky, notably "Poinciana," "Moonlight In Vermont," "The Very Thought Of You" and "Friendly Persuasion." Except for "Poinciana," which is just over nine minutes, all the cuts are six minutes or more so there are just two instrumentals to a side and everything feels rather endless. Also, this is surely the first album ever dedicated to the memory of an Afghan hound. Horn and string arrangements are by **Gene Page**... Jazzman **Gene Harris** has a fine new album out – "In A Special Way" on Blue Note – with a very pretty, string-laden instrumental on it called "It's Your Love" that might go over as a luscious hustle. Among the performers on the album's impressive and wide-ranging list of session credits are **Verdine White**, **Merry Clayton**, **Lee Ritenour**,

D.J. Rogers, **Chuck Rainey** and **Azar Lawrence**. The best of the new 12-inch promotional discs: a great long (11:10) version of the **Undisputed Truth's** "You + Me = Love" (Whitfield Records), a disco mix (6:19) of the **Meters'** "Disco Is the Thing Today" (Reprise) and **James Brown's** first "special disco version" – a 9:16 "Get Up Offa That Thing/Release the Pressure" (Polydor), which is definitely a collector's item. All these records have been previously recommended here in their single versions and the Undisputed Truth's is the most improved of the batch.

FEEDBACK, NEWS & NOTES: Fastest moving new records: "You Should Be Dancing" by **The Bee Gees**, "Best Disco In Town" by the **Ritchie Family**, "Sun... Sun... Sun" by **Jakki** and **Dr. Buzzard's Original Savannah Band** album (especially "Sour And Sweet" and "Cherchez La Femme") which has hardly been off my turntable since it arrived... When a record pops up out of nowhere and appears on three different top 10 lists in its first week, it definitely bears watching and searching for. The record is "Disco Magic" by a group called the **T-Connection** and it's a gorgeous, full-of-changes instrumental running over seven minutes on a disco disc pressed in Miami for the Media label. Copies were dropped off with key DJs in New York this past week' and both Tom Savarese at 12 West and Barefoot Boy's Tony Smith put it on their lists immediately. Dean Ferguson, who also listed the record this week, plays at a Miami club called Stonewall Too and says the track is already a major success in his area. Should be picked up by a larger label very quickly... Also on Tom Savarese's top 10: "Oooh Baby" from British rocker **Alan White's** "Ramshackled" album (Atlantic), an interesting if not totally riveting cut in the soulful rock vein (5:30)... Richie Kaczor, who reports from the Top Floor in New York this week, says he'll be opening up a new club in Washington, D.C., beginning in August; it's called Ziegfeld's.

RECOMMENDED SINGLES: "Do It With Style" by **Webster Lewis** (Epic), a terrific song that builds and builds with some **Earth**, **Wind & Fire** flavor and a nice message: "Do however, whenever, whatever you feel/Do it with style" (long version: 5:13)... "Love Bite" by the **Richard Hewson Orchestra** (Splash), a cute, happy

> **ff A group put together and produced by radio's top black DJ, Frankie Crocker, the man who transformed WBLS in New York. And this is surely the first album ever dedicated to the memory of an Afghan hound JJ**

12 WEST, NEW YORK
DJ: Tom Savarese

BEST DISCO IN TOWN – Ritchie Family (Marlin)
CHERCHEZ LA FEMME/SOUR AND SWEET/I'LL PLAY THE FOOL – Savannah Band (RCA)
C'MON BABY, DO THE LATIN HUSTLE – Fajardo (Coco)
DISCO MAGIC – T-Connection (Media)
HEAVEN MUST BE MISSING AN ANGEL/ DON'T TAKE AWAY THE MUSIC – Tavares (Capitol)
OOOH BABY – Alan White (Atlantic)
RUN TO ME/YOUNG HEARTS RUN FREE – Candi Staton (Warner Bros.)
SUN... SUN... SUN – Jakki (Pyramid)
YOU SHOULD BE DANCING – Bee Gees (RSO)
YOU'LL NEVER FIND ANOTHER LOVE LIKE MINE – Lou Rawls (Phila, Intl.)

TOP FLOOR, NEW YORK
DJ: Richie Kaczor

BEST DISCO IN TOWN – Ritchie Family (Marlin)
CAN WE COME TOGETHER/DISCO PARTY/THAT'S WHERE THE HAPPY PEOPLE GO/SOUL SEARCHIN' TIME – Trammps (Atlantic)
DON'T TAKE AWAY THE MUSIC/ HEAVEN MUST BE MISSING AN ANGEL – Tavares (Capitol)
I DON'T WANNA LOSE YOUR LOVE – Emotions (Columbia)
I'M GONNA LET MY HEART DO THE WALKING – Supremes (Motown)
ONE FOR THE MONEY – Whispers (Soul Train)
TAKE A LITTLE – Liquid Pleasure (Midland Intl.)
YOU SHOULD BE DANCING – Bee Gees (RSO)
YOU'LL NEVER FIND ANOTHER LOVE LIKE MINE – Lou Rawls (Phila, Intl.)

STONEWALL TOO, MIAMI
DJ: Dean Ferguson

DISCO MAGIC – T-Connection (Media)
HEAVEN MUST BE MISSING AN ANGEL – Tavares (Capitol)
HERE WE GO AGAIN – People's Choice (TSOP)
THE HOUSE IS ROCKIN' – Bobby Caldwell (PBR)
NI'CE & SLOW – Jesse Green (Scepter)
RUN TO ME/YOUNG HEARTS RUN FREE – Candi Staton (Warner Bros.)
SOUL MAN – Calhoon (Warner Spector)
TROUBLE-MAKER/LOVE POWER/THE FAMILY – Roberta Kelly (Oasis)
YOU'LL NEVER FIND ANOTHER LOVE LIKE MINE – Lou Rawls (Phila. Intl.)
YOU'VE GOT EXTRA ADDED POWER IN YOUR LOVE – Chairmen of the Board (Invictus)

BAREFOOT BOY, NEW YORK
DJ: Tony Smith

BEST DISCO IN TOWN/BABY I'M ON FIRE/ARABIAN NIGHTS – Ritchie Family (Marlin)
BETWEEN DUSK AND DAWN – Whirlwind (Roulette)
DISCO MAGIC – T-Connection (Media)
DON'T TAKE AWAY THE MUSIC/HEAVEN MUST BE MISSING AN ANGEL – Tavares (Capitol)
HERE WE GO AGAIN/MOVING IN ALL DIRECTIONS – People's Choice (TSOP)
MAKES YOU BLIND – Glitter Band (Bell import)
ONE FOR THE MONEY/PUT ME IN THE NEWS – Whispers (Soul Train)
SUMMERTIME AND I'M FEELIN' MELLOW/ WE GOT THE TIME – MFSB (Phila. Intl.)
SUN... SUN... SUN – Jakki (Pyramid)
YOU SHOULD BE DANCING – Bee Gees (RSO)

instrumental with some pretty girl vocals (4:43)... "Gonna Have A Good Time," a hard party song by **Crystal Image** (IX Chains) which has an even better instrumental version on the flip side... the return of the **Sons of Robin Stone** with a very **Spinners**-style production by **Bobby Eli** called "Let's Do It Now" (Epic) which soars sweetly.

NOTE: Tony Smith pointed out that the **Emotions'** "I Don't Wanna Lose Your Love," the cut I raved about a few issues' back, is, also on the B side of the group's single, "Flowers," and at the same length. Listen to it. ⊘

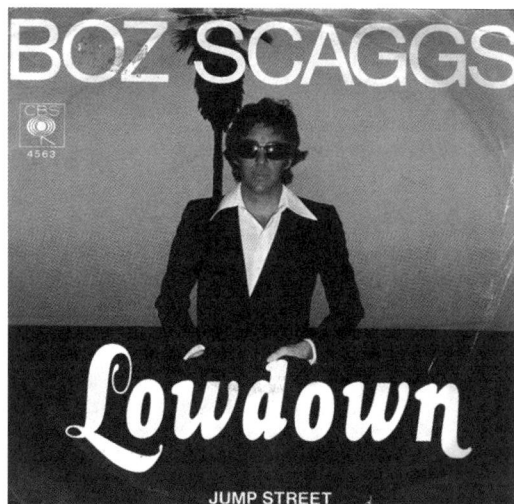

BOZ SCAGGS
CBS
4563

Lowdown

JUMP STREET

Two essential albums and one runner-up out this week, all in established, durable disco styles that are beginning to sound more comfortable than adventurous but remain, at their best, quite irresistible. The front-runners are **Gloria Gaynor's** "I've Got You" (Polydor), produced by the **DCA** group, **Monardo, Bongiovi & Ellis,** and "Knights In White Satin" by **Giorgio** (Moroder), who is one half of the **Donna Summer/Roberta Kelly** production team, so you know what to expect here (on Oasis). Gaynor's innovative side-one run-through is not as compelling as it once was – the cuts don't build and blend together as forcefully as they did on previous albums – but, individually, the three tracks stand up nicely and two are among her best work. "I've Got You Under My Skin" (8:14) is classic Gloria Gaynor: hard-driving, loud, dense with strings and a pounding bass, powerful and terrific to dance to. Gaynor sounds like she could sing over a hurricane with ease; that she can dominate these incredible full productions is perhaps her greatest talent. "Be Mine," the other knockout cut, follows "I've Got You" with an equally irrepressible sound that picks up pieces from several other DCA productions for a bright, steamy-hot effect. "Advance Disco Copies" of the Gaynor side one mix were made available to DJs last week and the entire album is out now.

In a similar promotional move, several advances of Giorgio's extended "Knights In White Satin" – the nearly 15-minute side one of the album – were given to a number of DJs on both coasts a few weeks back and reviewed here briefly at that time. "Knights," always a mysteriously involving song, has been broken into three segments, two vocal parts framing an instrumental break called "In The Middle Of The Night," and the full effect, with blurry, gruff vocals surrounded by muffled steady drums and those gorgeous Munich Machine strings, is rather amazing. **The Moody Blues** would surely approve. And side two here is far from

disappointing. Surely its most popular cut will be something called "I Wanna Funk With You Tonite" which is very upbeat and quite willing to slur the key word in its constantly repeated title so there's little doubt about what the singer (or the girl chorus) have in mind here. What could be more explicit? The remaining two tracks, both over five minutes, are also interesting, especially "Oh, L'Amour" which adds a touch of **B.T. Express** sound to the usual **Donna Summer** style.

The runner-up is the debut album from **Double Exposure** on Salsoul, titled "Ten Percent" after the record which is certainly one of the year's top five songs, but, as a whole collection, not up to the fantastic energy and impact of that song. **Baker, Harris & Young** produced with Philadelphia perfection but the album's other two extended cuts, "Everyman" (7:27) and "My Love Is Free" (7:00), while attractive and invigorating, are not the inspired explosions we've come to expect from this team. Still, any Baker, Harris & Young number is several giant steps above most other stuff on the disco market today and this one may grow on me yet. Note: The version of "Ten Percent" included here is 6:51, shorter than either of the mixes on the disco disc version now in the stores, so buyers of the first Giant 45 have something unavailable in any other form.

FEEDBACK: Walter Gibbons, the New York DJ famous for his disco mix on "Ten Percent," recommends a track from the new **Spinners** album, "Happiness Is Being With The Spinners" on Atlantic. The song, a **Thom Bell** production written by Bell and **Linda Creed,** is a 7:22 cut called "The Rubberband Man" which sounds like an early **Jackson 5** record – cute, bouncy and fun – but without that J5 spunk... John Hedges from The City in San Francisco suggests **Jeannie Reynolds'** "Hit And Run" (from her "Cherries, Bananas & Other Fine Things" album on Casablanca) which he rightly points out has a **Candi Staton** feel and a nice **Don Davis** production. Also doing well at The City: "Love Chant" by **Eli's Second Coming,** "Smoke Your Troubles Away" by the **Glass Family** and "Getaway" by **Earth, Wind & Fire**... My favorite single this week is an import Disco-On-The-Run's Jeff Baugh says he picked up at Downstairs Records in New York and which he described as "sounding like 'Yellow Train' but with the sounds of a clock instead of a train." The record is called "Tick Tack" by **Alarm Clock** (on Celebration, a Canadian label) and over an electronic tick tack that sounds like that coffee perking commercial there's a breathy kind of sustained shout and builds to an all-out scream at the end. It's completely weird and exciting in a driven, insane way. Definitely not for all tastes but if you liked "Yellow Train," "Wow" and "Erucu," you'll probably love this.

RECOMMENDED SINGLES: "The Magic Touch," a very **George McCrae**-sounding production by and for **Tony Sylvester and the New Ingredient** in case you'd forgotten that the producer whose name has been

CIRCUS MAXIMUS, LOS ANGELES
DJ: Mitch Schatsky

BEST DISCO IN TOWN/ARABIAN NIGHTS/BABY I'M ON FIRE – Ritchie Family (Marlin)
ENTROD – Graham Central Station (Warner Bros.)
HEAVEN MUST BE MISSING AN ANGEL/ DON'T TAKE AWAY THE MUSIC – Tavares (Capitol)
KNIGHTS IN WHITE SATIN/I WANNA FUNK WITH YOU TONITE – Giorgio (Oasis)
SO MUCH FOR LOVE – Moment of Truth (Salsoul)
SMOKE YOUR TROUBLES AWAY – Glass Family (Earhole)
SUN... SUN... SUN... – Jakki (Pyramid)
TAKE A LETTER – Liquid Pleasure (Midland Intl.)
TROUBLE-MAKER – Roberta Kelly (Oasis)
YOU SHOULD BE DANCING – Bee Gees (RSO)

THE CITY, SAN FRANCISCO
DJ: John Hedges

BEST DISCO IN TOWN/ARABIAN NIGHTS – Ritchie Family (Marlin)
DANCIN' KID – Disco Tex & the Sex-O-Lettes (Chelsea)
HERE WE GO AGAIN – People's Choice (TSOP)
I'VE GOT YOU UNDER MY SKIN/BE MINE – Gloria Gaynor (Polydor)
PICNIC IN THE PARK – MFSB (Phila. Intl.)
SHAKE YOUR BOOTY – KC & the Sunshine Band (TK)
SO MUCH FOR LOVE – Moment of Truth (Salsoul)
TAKE A LITTLE – Liquid Pleasure (Midland Intl.)
TEN PERCENT – Double Exposure (Salsoul)
YOU SHOULD BE DANCING – Bee Gees (RSO)

BETTER DAYS, NEW YORK
DJ: Walter Gibbons

ALWAYS THERE – Side Effect (Fantasy)
CHERCHEZ LA FEMME/SOUR AND SWEET/I'LL PLAY THE FOOL – Dr Buzzard's Original Savannah Band (RCA)
EVERYMAN/MY LOVE IS FREE – Double Exposure (Salsoul)
FIRST ROUND KNOCKOUT – David Ruffin (Motown)
GIVE A BROKEN HEART A BREAK – Impact (Atco)
JUMP/HOOKED ON YOUR LOVE – Aretha Franklin (Atlantic)
ONE FOR THE MONEY – Whispers (Soul Train)
PROPHECY – Margie Joseph (Cotillion)
SUN... SUN... SUN – Jakki (Pyramid)
YOU SHOULD BE DANCING – Bee Gees (RSO)

LA BOUCHERIE, NEW ORLEANS
DJ: David C. Wolf

ALWAYS THERE – Side Effect (Fantasy)
BEST DISCO IN TOWN – Ritchie Family (Marlin)
GET THE FUNK OUT MA FACE – Brothers Johnson (A&M)
GETAWAY – Earth, Wind & Fire (Columbia instrumental)
HEAVEN MUST BE MISSING AN ANGEL – Tavares (Capitol)
LOWDOWN/WHAT CAN I SAY – Boz Scaggs (Columbia)
PLAY THAT FUNKY MUSIC – Wild Cherry (Epic/Sweet City)
SHAKE YOUR BOOTY – KC & the Sunshine Band (TK)
TURN THE BEAT AROUND – Vicki Sue Robinson (RCA)
YOU SHOULD BE DANCING – Bee Gees (RSO)

cropping up all over started out as a member of the **Main Ingredient**; the song was written by **Fay Hauser** and **Patrick Adams** and runs 4:37 in its long, orgasmic version (Mercury)... "Baia" by the **Alice Street Gang** (on Amazon, yet another TK label), a **Ritchie Family**-like version of the standard that begins with a taste of the theme from "2001"... "Kill That Roach," a fine, funky drug song by Miami (Drive)... "Everybody Join Hands" by **Consumer Rapport** (remember them?), only because the song's second half (of its 4:51 length) is so powerful and spirited. ◗

Walter Gibbons © **Kenny Carpenter**

❝ Walter Gibbons, the New York DJ famous for his disco mix on "Ten percent," recommends a track from the new Spinners album ❞

The Disco Files 1973-78 **211**

AUGUST 7, 1976

FEEDBACK: Everybody's favorite album is **Dr. Buzzard's Original Savannah Band** on RCA which has become this summer's major surprise hit not only because three cuts are eminently danceable ("Sour And Sweet," "Cherchez La Femme" and "I'll Play The Fool" – all in the seventh slot on the DISCO FILE Top 20 this week), but because the group's fabulously eclectic sound – drawing on several decades of American pop music from Big Band jazz to doo-wop soul to sophisticated disco, full of sly musical quotes – is so fresh and appealing. Since I wrote my sick-of-disco column in February – when I said that disco remakes had become "the lowest, most laughable form of pop music: the Muzak of the seventies" – the trend to formula "disco versions" has been eclipsed by a wave of new releases full of the vitality and punch that attracted us to disco in the first place. **Vicki Sue Robinson, Double Exposure, Tavares**, the **Trammps, Diana Ross, Donna Summer**, the **Bee Gees**, the **Brothers, Roberta Kelly, Stratavarious, Lou Rawls, Jesse Green**, the **Ritchie Family, Candi Staton** – all these performers and more have come up with great reasons why you should be dancing during the past five months but the Savannah Band is one of the most persuasive reasons this year to believe that disco music, far from being at a dead end, is taking off in new and exciting directions.

FEEDBACK (CONTINUED): "C'mon Baby, Do The Latin Hustle," the deliciously smooth, full-bodied single by **Fajardo** (Coco) and probably the only Latin record with a "Tom Moulton Mix," is picking up play in New York after more than two months in release. It goes on the DISCO FILE Top 20 this week at number 18, pushed by its recent reports as a fine summer record. Also coming up: **Giorgio's** "I Wanna Funk With You Tonite" (Oasis); "So Much For Love," especially the instrumental side, by **Moment of Truth** (Salsoul disco disc) and **Gloria Gaynor's** new medley, "Let's Make A Deal/I've Got You Under My Skin/Be Mine" (Polydor)... Among the new records appearing on top 10 lists this week: "Let's Get Started" by the **Commodores** (from their "Hot on the Tracks" album on Motown), a sharp, lively party song listed by Robert Gordon from Southampton's new Bluecloud discotheque; **Jerry Butler's** version of **Syreeta's** spunky "I'm Goin' Left" on his first Motown album, "Love's On The Menu," chosen by Larry Sanders who plays at the Sandpiper, the disco where all the social energy of Fire Island Pines is concentrated on weekend nights; and **Luther's** "Funky Music (Is A Part Of Me)" (5:29), the stirring opening cut from the group's debut album on Cotillion and very much like their earlier release, "It's Good For The Soul" (also included on the lp) – reported by Bill Vos from Scarlett's in Westhampton Beach, who rounds out our mini-survey of the Hamptons/Fire Island weekend disco scene (more to come). All recommended album cuts.

The new **Faith, Hope & Charity** album, "Life Goes On" (RCA), is a typically pleasant, frothy **Van McCoy** production with a number of high-spirited disco cuts in the group's familiar perky, bright, optimistic style. The mood of the album is summed up nicely in the titles of its best cuts: "Positive Thinking" (4:59); "You're My Peace Of Mind" (6:53); "A Time for Celebration," a bicentennial salute that's a little too patriotic for my tastes; and the title track, "Life Goes On" (6:28), which is divided into a slow "overture" and an upbeat main section. Also included: a surprisingly fun medley of two pop classics, "Cherish" and "Monday, Monday," blended together and sounding better than ever. Lightweight but very pretty.

ALSO RECOMMENDED: "Full Time Thing (Between Dusk And Dawn)" by **Whirlwind**, a 12-inch disc from Roulette which asks the question, "If your love is true, why do I only see you between dusk and dawn?"-produced by **Aram Schefrin** who co-produced the **D.C. LaRue** album, this one runs 5:36... "Grasshopper," an instrumental by **Spin** (Ariola America) that sounds like a freakier **Average White Band**... "Listen To The Rhythm Band" by **MD-20-20** (Magic Show, a small Nashville-distributed label), a very off-beat production with a deep funk base and lots of odd changes (the B side is marked "disco" and runs 4:58)... "Love's Come At Last" by **Hosea** (A&M), a really pleasant, mid-tempo song for mellow moments. ◐

❝ Since I wrote my sick-of-disco column in February, the trend to formula "disco versions" has been eclipsed by a wave of new releases full of vitality and punch ❞

BLUECLOUD, SOUTHAMPTON, NEW YORK
DJ: Robert Gordon

BEST DISCO IN TOWN – Ritchie Family (Marlin)
CHERCHEZ LA FEMME/I'LL PLAY THE FOOL/SOUR AND SWEET – Savannah Band (RCA)
C'MON BABY, DO THE LATIN HUSTLE – Fajardo (Coco)
I WANNA FUNK WITH YOU TONITE/KNIGHTS IN WHITE SATIN – Giorgio (Oasis)
LET'S GET STARTED – Commodores (Motown)
LET'S MAKE A DEAL/I'VE GOT YOU UNDER MY SKIN/BE MINE – Gloria Gaynor (Polydor)
PROPHECY – Margie Joseph (Cotillion)
RUBBER BAND MAN – Spinners (Atlantic)
TROUBLE-MAKER – Roberta Kelly (Oasis)
YOU SHOULD BE DANCING – Bee Gees (RSO)

SCARLETT'S, WESTHAMPTON BEACH, N.Y.
DJ: Bill Vos

BEST DISCO IN TOWN – Ritchie Family (Marlin)
FUNKY MUSIC – Luther (Cotillion)
IF YOU CAN'T BEAT 'EM, JOIN 'EM – Mark Radice (UA)
I'LL PLAY THE FOOL/CHERCHEZ LA FEMME/SUNSHOWER – Savannah Band (RCA)
JUST A LITTLE TIMING/DO THOSE LITTLE THINGS – Maryann Farra & Satin Soul (Brunswick)
LUCK BE A LADY – Broadway Brass (20th Century)
SO MUCH FOR LOVE – Moment of Truth (Salsoul)
SUMMERTIME AND I'M FEELIN' MELLOW / PICNIC IN THE PARK – MFSB (Phila. Intl.)
SUN... SUN... SUN – Jakki (Pyramid)
YOU SHOULD BE DANCING – Bee Gees (RSO)

BOOMBAMAKAOO, NEW YORK
DJ: Jorge Wheeler

BEST DISCO IN TOWN – Ritchie Family (Marlin)
LOVE BITE – Richard Hewson Orchestra (Splash)
NO WAY BACK (PART 2) – The Dells (Mercury)
PITA CAMON – Charanga '76 (TR)
SUN... SUN... SUN – Jakki (Pyramid)
TO BE WITH YOU – Jimmy Sabater (Salsa)
YELLOW TRAIN – Resonance (Celebration)
YOU SHOULD BE DANCING – Bee Gees (RSO)
YOU TO ME ARE EVERYTHING – Revelation (RSO)
YOU'LL NEVER FIND ANOTHER LOVE LIKE MINE/THIS SONG WILL LAST FOREVER – Lou Rawls (Phila. Intl. lp cuts)

THE SANDPIPER, FIRE ISLAND PINES, N.Y.
DJ: Larry Sanders

BEST DISCO IN TOWN/ARABIAN NIGHTS/BABY, I'M ON FIRE – Ritchie Family (Marlin)
CHERCHEZ LA FEMME/SOUR AND SWEET/I'LL PLAY THE FOOL – Savannah Band (RCA)
DON'T TAKE AWAY THE MUSIC/HEAVEN MUST BE MISSING AN ANGEL – Tavares (Capitol)
I NEED YOU, YOU NEED ME – Joe Simon (Spring)
I'M GOIN' LEFT – Jerry Butler (Motown)
LET'S MAKE A DEAL/I'VE GOT YOU UNDER MY SKIN/BE MINE – Gloria Gaynor (Polydor)
ONE FOR THE MONEY – Whispers (Soul Train)
YOU SHOULD BE DANCING – Bee Gees (RSO)
YOU'LL NEVER FIND ANOTHER LOVE LIKE MINE – Lou Rawls (Phila. Intl.)
YOUNG HEARTS RUN FREE/RUN TO ME – Candi Staton (Warner Bros.)

DISCO FILE TOP 20

1. BEST DISCO IN TOWN – Ritchie Family (Marlin)
2. YOU SHOULD BE DANCING – Bee Gees (RSO)
3. HEAVEN MUST BE MISSING AN ANGEL – Tavares (Capitol)
4. YOU'LL NEVER FIND ANOTHER LOVE LIKE MINE – Lou Rawls (Phila. Intl. lp cuts)
5. DON'T TAKE AWAY THE MUSIC – Tavares (Capitol)
6. SUN... SUN... SUN – Jakki (Pyramid)
7. SOUR AND SWEET/CHERCHEZ LA FEMME/I'LL PLAY THE FOOL – Savannah Band (RCA)
8. ARABIAN NIGHTS/BABY, I'M ON FIRE – Ritchie Family (Marlin)
9. TEN PERCENT – Double Exposure (Salsoul)
10. ONE FOR THE MONEY – Whispers (Soul Train)
11. DISCO PARTY/SOUL SEARCHIN' TIME/CAN WE COME TOGETHER/THAT'S WHERE THE HAPPY PEOPLE GO – Trammps (Atlantic)
12. YOUNG HEARTS RUN FREE/RUN TO ME – Candi Staton (Warner Bros.)
13. TROUBLE-MAKER – Roberta Kelly (Oasis)
14. SO MUCH FOR LOVE – Moment of Truth (Salsoul)
15. TAKE A LITTLE – Liquid Pleasure (Midland Intl.)
16. NICE & SLOW – Jesse Green (Scepter)
17. LET'S MAKE A DEAL/I'VE GOT YOU UNDER MY SKIN/BE MINE – Gloria Gaynor (Polydor)
18. C'MON BABY, DO THE LATIN HUSTLE – Fajardo (Coco)
19. HERE WE GO AGAIN – People's Choice (TSOP)
20. LIPSTICK – Michel Polnareff (Atlantic)

AUGUST 14, 1976

The releases this week have been so dull and unappealing that, were it not for the few titles collected below, I'd be tempted to pack up my typewriter right now and forget the whole thing. This is the summer slump I was almost looking forward to several weeks back when the records were still flooding in, but now that they've been reduced to a thin trickle, I'm suddenly consumed by thirst for something new and terrific. It's a good time to go back and pick up on things that were passed over too quickly before – like the **MFSB** "Summertime" album which has turned into one of my favorite records of the season, or **Faith, Hope & Charity's** "Life Goes On" lp, also underestimated in my review here last week: it's a delight. But on to the new releases. These are this week's saving graces, starting with a group of 12-inch pressings:

The most interesting of these disco discs is also the most highly anticipated of the batch-the new **Salsoul Orchestra** release, "Nice 'n Naasty" (Salsoul), which sticks very close to the style **Vince Montana** established for the group with their debut album last year. The female chorus vocals, playfully chiding someone for his "nasty" thoughts, are cute but unnecessarily obtrusive; the instrumentation, full of those melancholy Philadelphia strings and featuring a fluid sax solo toward the end, is sublime but not as irresistibly danceable as most of the group's previous material. The other side of the commercial disco disc, a fascinating, complex version of "2001," is more successful as a production. It begins with an eerie jet engine whoosh that fades into bird calls and Latin percussion before dipping into the familiar opening notes of "2001" and continuing with zest for nearly seven minutes. "Like Her" by **The Gentlemen and Their Lady** (Roulette) is another unpredictable **Johnnymelfi** production from the man who made "Find My Way" and "Sun... Sun... Sun" and who prefers to spell his name in a run-on fashion. Best parts of this new record, which is 7:15 in length, are the opening with a girl saying "C'mon, talk about it" in a husky voice and the central instrumental section with all its breaks. The vocals are enthusiastic but not up to the production itself. Highly idiosyncratic and a welcome relief from formula disco.

A group called **Camouflage** has come out with a cover of **Su Kramer's** "You've Got The Power" that the **DCA** group produced on Roulette. Like the Kramer original, which was released in June on a London two-part single, this one's got a shouting girl group sound and if the vocals are not as feverish as Kramer's, the overall production, including a long break and running nearly eight minutes, is more forceful. Should bring some deserved attention to this overlooked song. **Family Tree's** "Family Tree" (Anada) is another idiosyncratic production, setting harsh horns against an airy flute for an effective textural contrast. The lyrics are rather enigmatic ("Trees grow tall in the woods/Bears'd make honey if they could") but the woman who sings the lead is strong and manages to carry it all off, both sense

PIPPIN'S, NEW YORK
DJ: Reggie T. Experience

ARABIAN NIGHTS – Ritchie Family (Marlin)
CAN WE COME TOGETHER – Trammps (Atlantic)
CATHEDRALS – D.C. LaRue (Pyramid)
FIRST ROUND KNOCKOUT – David Ruffin (Motown)
I DON'T WANNA LOSE YOUR LOVE – The Emotions (Columbia)
IF YOU CAN'T BEAT 'EM, JOIN 'EM – Mark Radice (UA)
LOWDOWN – Boz Scaggs (Columbia)
PICNIC IN THE PARK/SUMMERTIME AND I'M FEELIN' MELLOW MFSB (Phila. Intl.)
SUN... SUN... SUN – Jakki (Pyramid)
YOU SHOULD BE DANCING – Bee Gees (RSO)

LOST & FOUND, WASHINGTON, D.C.
DJ: Bill Owens

BE MINE – Gloria Gaynor (Polydor)
BEST DISCO IN TOWN – Ritchie Family (Marlin)
KNIGHTS IN WHITE SATIN/I WANNA FUNK WITH YOU TONITE – Giorgio (Oasis)
LIKE HER – The Gentlemen and Their Lady (Roulette)
MAKES YOU BLIND – Glitter Band (Bell import)
ONE FOR THE MONEY – Whispers (Soul Train)
SOUR AND SWEET/CHERCHEZ LA FEMME – Savannah Band (RCA)
THAT'S WHERE THE HAPPY PEOPLE GO/ DISCO PARTY/ CAN WE COME TOGETHER/SOUL SEARCHIN' TIME – Trammps (Atlantic)
YOU + ME = LOVE – Undisputed Truth (Whitfield)
YOU SHOULD BE DANCING – Bee Gees (RSO)

CRICKET CLUB, MIAMI
DJ: Aristides Jacobs

BAD GIRL – Manhattan Express (Friends & Co.)
BEST DISCO IN TOWN – Ritchie Family (Marlin)
DISCO MAGIC – T-Connection (Media)
I DON'T WANNA LOSE YOUR LOVE – The Emotions (Columbia)
I GOT YOUR LOVE – Stratavarious (Roulette)
I'LL PLAY THE FOOL – Savannah Band (RCA)
LE CHAT – Devil's Sauce (Carrere import)
ONE FOR THE MONEY – Whispers (Soul Train)
YOU SHOULD BE DANCING – Bee Gees (RSO)
YOU'LL NEVER FIND ANOTHER LOVE LIKE MINE – Lou Rawls (Phila. Intl.)

JAWS, SOUTHAMPTON, N.Y.
DJ: Jeff Baugh

BABY, I'M ON FIRE – Ritchie Family (Marlin)
DISCO MAGIC – T-Connection (Media)
IF YOU CAN'T BEAT 'EM, JOIN 'EM – Mark Radice (UA)
KNIGHTS IN WHITE SATIN – Giorgio (Oasis)
LET'S MAKE A DEAL/I'VE GOT YOU UNDER MY SKIN/BE MINE – Gloria Gaynor (Polydor)
MY LOVE IS FREE/EVERYMAN/BABY I NEED YOUR LOVING – Double Exposure (Salsoul)
SMOKE YOUR TROUBLES AWAY – Glass Family (Earhole)
SOUR AND SWEET/CHERCHEZ LA FEMME – Savannah Band (RCA)
YOU + ME = LOVE – Undisputed Truth (Whitfield)
YOU SHOULD BE DANCING – Bee Gees (RSO)

> ## " The most highly anticipated of the batch is the new Salsoul Orchestra release, "Nice 'n Naasty" "

and nonsense. The disco disc length of 4:41 is also available on a standard 45 from this small Los Angeles label. The latest **LTG Exchange** record, "Huddle" (Big Tree), supposedly named after a new dance, has definite **Van McCoy** overtones (it starts out sounding like "Party") but is a **Jerry Ross** production that's already getting some favorable feedback. The vocals are minimal, the sound bright and jumpy but somewhat monotonous on the long (5:25) disco disc version. The single, at 3:30, is more succinct and attractive. **Gary Toms**, formerly **Gary Toms Empire**, has delivered another knockout disco funk record in "Stand Up And Shout" (PIP) which, if it holds few surprises, is consistently danceable and fun. The singers and the production are enthusiastic and lively though it's hard to sustain this pitch for over seven minutes. Same holds true for the flip side, a nine-minute piece called "Party Hardy." This is PIP's first entry into the commercial disco disc market. Also now available on a 12-inch pressing: "Entrow" by **Graham Central Station**, already picking up play from their Warner Brothers album.

Only one RECOMMENDED SINGLE this week: **The Ebonys'** "Making Love Ain't No Fun" (Buddah), a **Norman Harris** production that seems to run counter to all prevailing attitudes (what would **Donna Summer** and **Andrea True** say?) until you get to the parenthetical subtitle, "(Without The One You Love)." This is one of Harris' more lightweight productions but it has his unmistakable touch and verve, including an instrumental "Part 2."

Disco aside, this week's best, most satisfying release is a collection of beautiful Brazilian songs by **Jorge Ben** on Island, called "Samba Nova." Ben's import albums have long been favorites of the musical avant garde and this album is a fine introduction to his work. Not to be missed – it puts you in another world, someplace cool, tropical and softly sensual. ◑

AUGUST 21, 1976

Another uneventful week here in the Land of 1000 Dances. The records that follow are, it seems to me, the only bright spots.

DISCO DISCS: **Power Play's** "Do It All The Night," a loud, rocking sexsong with a spoken male lead over a dense and driving female chorus that hypnotically repeats the song's title and makes demands, "Rock it to me, rock it to me," in a most irresistible fashion. The record was made in Germany so there's a characteristic underpinning of strings throughout. Pye's 12-inch version is a hefty 7:57 and packaged in a fine new "Piece of the Pye" disco sleeve... **El Coco**, the Los Angeles studio group that sounds like a European disco orchestra, has a "Giant 45" on AVI Records whose best side, "Let's Get It Together" (6:35), is their tastiest disco instrumental so far. The formula is simple: a girl chorus repeats the title over and over with an insistence made bearable only because the instrumentation is perky and fresh and the changes keep coming. The other side, "Fait Le Chat" (7:36), is more laid back and includes some sighs, groans and "Ooo la las" in addition to the title repetition. A nicely balanced package... Rocket Records has released its first 12-inch promotional disc in **Brian & Brenda Russell's** "Gonna Do My Best To Love You," lengthened to six minutes from a track on their recent album. The song is great – one of those rare happy love songs – the vocals clear and robust, and the new mix makes it all more plausible for the dance floor... Finally, Columbia has issued a disco disc of **Earth, Wind & Fire's** "Getaway" that runs just over five minutes and combines the vocal and instrumental sides of the recent single.

SINGLES: **Cloud One's** "Atmosphere Strutt" (P&P) is one of those terrific quirky instrumentals that producer **Patrick Adams** has been perfecting recently. The feeling here is similar to **Sammy Gordon & the Hiphuggers'** "Making Love" which Adams arranged but, as the title and artist suggest, more airy and romantic; very summery... **Carol Douglas'** "Midnight Love Affair" (Midland International) is a quick taste (3:55) of her new album of the same name which is due out this week. In a clever variation on **Gloria Gaynor** and **Donna Summer**, producer **Ed O'Loughlin** and arranger **John Davis** have whipped up an 18-minute run-through side for Douglas that carries the "Midnight Love Affair" concept through three songs and connecting interludes both lush and lusty. The key question: "Midnight love affair, how can I make you stay?" or, will you still love me tomorrow? Disco sex with a touch of heartache... Producer **Rick Hall** turns **Dobie Gray** disco in Muscle Shoals? Unlikely but true with Gray's new Capricorn release, "Find 'Em, Fool 'Em & Forget 'Em," which is hard-edged southern funk with some disco sweetening. Advice for the broken hearted on how to run your love life – the only drawback: it's a mere 2:43 in length. ... **Tata Vega's** "Full Speed Ahead" (Tamla) is, as the title indicates, a zesty, driving record about looking for a love by a singer who sounds like a combination of **Linda Lewis** and **Chaka Khan** (and even Sly Stone)... **The Soul Crusaders** have one of the most upbeat sad songs in a while with "Those Memories" (LuTall); "I'd like to forget about those memories/The ones you placed inside my mind," they sing mournfully, but the song's spirited arrangement contradicts them neatly and clinches the

HIPPOPOTAMUS, NEW YORK
DJ: Rich Pampinella

BEST DISCO IN TOWN/ARABIAN NIGHTS – Ritchie Family (Marlin)
CHERCHEZ LA FEMME/SOUR AND SWEET / I'LL PLAY THE FOOL – Savannah Band (RCA)
GONNA HAVE A GOOD TIME – Crystal Image (IX Chains)
JUMP – Aretha Franklin (Atlantic)
MAKES YOU BLIND – Glitter Band (Bell import)
ONE FOR THE MONEY – Whispers (Soul Train)
SUN... SUN... SUN – Jakki (Pyramid)
YOU + ME = LOVE – Undisputed Truth (Whitfield)
YOU SHOULD BE DANCING – Bee Gees (RSO)
YOU'LL NEVER FIND ANOTHER LOVE LIKE MINE – Lou Rawls (Phila. Intl.)

OIL CAN HARRY'S, LOS ANGELES
DJ: Lou Lacoste

BEST DISCO IN TOWN/ARABIAN NIGHTS – Ritchie Family (Marlin)
CATHEDRALS – D.C. LaRue (Pyramid)
DISCO MAGIC – T-Connection (Media)
HEAVEN MUST BE MISSING AN ANGEL – Tavares (Capitol)
IF YOU CAN'T BEAT 'EM, JOIN 'EM – Mark Radice (UA)
I'M GONNA LET MY HEART DO THE WALKING – Supremes (Motown)
SMOKE YOUR TROUBLES AWAY – Glass Family (Earhole)
TAKE A LITTLE – Liquid Pleasure (Midland Intl.)
YOU + ME = LOVE – Undisputed Truth (Whitfield)
YOU SHOULD BE DANCING – Bee Gees (RSO)

12 WEST, NEW YORK
DJ: Jimmy Stuard

BEST DISCO IN TOWN/ARABIAN NIGHTS/ BABY, I'M ON FIRE – Ritchie Family (Marlin)
CHERCHEZ LA FEMME/SOUR AND SWEET/I'LL PLAY THE FOOL – Savannah Band (RCA)
DON'T TAKE AWAY THE MUSIC/HEAVEN MUST BE MISSING AN ANGEL – Tavares (Capitol)
I DON'T WANNA LOSE YOUR LOVE – Emotions (Columbia)
THE JOINT/NIGHT FEVER/DECEMBER 1963 – Fatback Band (Spring)
LET'S MAKE A DEAL/I'VE GOT YOU UNDER MY SKIN/BE MINE – Gloria Gaynor (Polydor)
MY LOVE IS FREE/TEN PERCENT – Double Exposure (Salsoul)
RUBBERBAND MAN – Spinners (Atlantic)
SUN... SUN... SUN – Jakki (Pyramid)
YOU SHOULD BE DANCING – Bee Gees (RSO)

THE PALACE, NEW ROCHELLE, N. Y.
DJ: Basil Nias

BEST DISCO IN TOWN – Ritchie Family (Marlin)
BRING YOUR BODY – Carol Townes & Fifth Avenue (Sixth Avenue)
DISCO PARTY/SOUL SEARCHIN' TIME – Trammps (Atlantic)
GET THE FUNK OUT MA FACE – Brothers Johnson (A&M)
LOVE TALK – James Gilstrap (Chelsea)
TEN PERCENT – Double Exposure (Salsoul)
TO BE WITH YOU – Jimmy Sabater (Salsa)
TROUBLE-MAKER – Roberta Kelly (Oasis)
YOU SHOULD BE DANCING – Bee Gees (RSO)
YOU'VE GOT THE POWER – Camouflage (Roulette)

song, which runs 5:45... Two of the DJs I spoke with this week – Rich Pampinella from Hippopotamus and John Luongo currently in between jobs in Boston but playing on WTBS-FM – praised the re-mix on the new single release of **The Originals'** "Down To Love Town" (Soul) which has, in Pampinella's words, "all the bottom that's missing on the lp cut," even if it's been cut in length to 3:59; it's rerecommended... And the **Average White Band**, who have come out from behind their initials again, have released the best cut from their latest album as a 45: "Queen of My Soul" (Atlantic) in the original album length (6:05) and highly recommended all over again.

ALBUMS: **Peabo Bryson** sounds like a blend of **Stevie Wonder**, **Donny Hathaway** and **Carl Carlton** on his debut album ("Peabo" on Bullet), one of the nicest male vocalist lps in some time. Bryson wrote and produced, **Gene Page** arranged and a host of excellent studio musicians and singers participated, so this is a debut with style. The dance cuts aren't knockout and wild but they grow on you – try "Do You Believe in Love," "Smile," "Let the Music Play" and "Underground Music"... **Street People**, a five-man group on Vigor, has a debut album out now too, and sound more solid and impressive than their singles would lead us to expect. "Never Get Enough of Your Love" and "You're My One Weakness Girl" are, of course, included, along with their new single, "Wanna Spend My Whole Life With You, Baby;" other cuts to check out are "Gotta Get Back With You" and "Re-Run (From An Old-Time Movie)." ◗

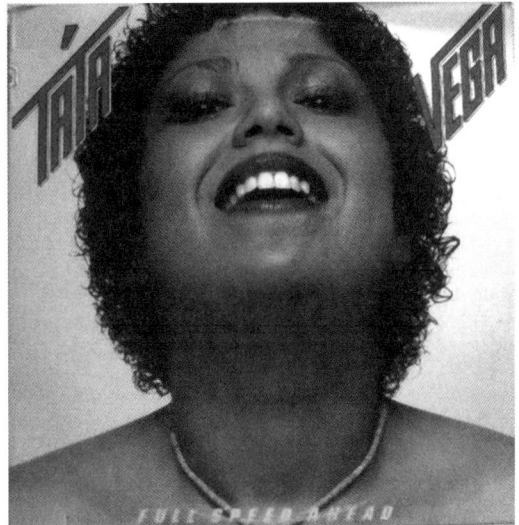

AUGUST 28, 1976

FEEDBACK: The fastest-moving records right now are **The Emotions'** "I Don't Wanna Lose Your Love" (Columbia), which jumped from 16 to 5 on the DISCO FILE Top 20; **Salsoul Orchestra's** "Nice 'N' Naasty" (Salsoul); "You're My Peace Of Mind" by **Faith, Hope & Charity** (RCA); "Full Time Thing (Between Dusk and Dawn)" by **Whirlwind** (Roulette) and **Gary Toms'** "Party Hardy," which is shaping up as the more popular side of that group's recent disco disc for PIP. Yet none of these cuts poses a serious threat at the moment to the top three records on that list. The **Bee Gees**, the currently **Ritchie Family** and **Dr. Buzzard's Original Savannah Band**, having been listed by virtually every DJ surveyed in the past few weeks, continue to be the strongest performers around with a lead over the runners-up that won't soon be narrowed... According to the latest survey sheet from the Canadian Record Pool, Canada's number one disco record is "Don't Stop The Music" by, of all people, the **Bay City Rollers** (Arista), and now, apparently, the single's broken out as an import in Boston. Mentioned last week by Boston DJs John Luongo and Jimmy Stuard (who's been dividing his week between Boston's 1270 and New York's 12 West recently), "Don't Stop" is listed this week on Conrad Cardenas' top 10 from 15 Lansdowne Street. Although an under-three-minute track called "Don't Stop The Music" – very catchy bubblegum disco with whiney vocals – was included on the Rollers last American album release, "Rock N' Roll Love Letter," the Canadian single is more than six minutes with, one assumes, an instrumental break that makes up for any weakness in the singing. The longer mix was reportedly prepared by the Canadian Record Pool for Arista in Canada but there are no plans for an American release... Warner Brothers has issued a 12-inch disc with a long remix of **Candi Staton's** great "Run To Me," adding another two minutes to the song, bringing it to 6:41. This should give the record another boost on the disco level – it's already on Louis Alers' top 10 from Charles Gallery this week... Our west coast correspondent reports that the new **Disco Tex & the Sex-O-Lettes** album, "Manhattan Millionaire" (Chelsea), is already out in Los Angeles where advances have gone to disco DJs. **Kenny Nolan** produced and included a version of "Hey There Little Firefly," a longer "Hot Lava" and "Dancin' Kid" with Disco Tex decidedly in the background here; should be out nationally this week... The **T-Connection's** "Disco Magic," already doing very well in the discos on the basis of a very limited disco disc pressing, has been picked up by TK Records for its Drive label. Single and 12-inch pressings are scheduled for release sometime next week.

Two records to lift the spirits this week: **Jermaine Jackson's** first release since the break-up of the Jackson 5, "Let's Be Young Tonight" (Motown), and jazz percussionist **Ralph MacDonald's** "Sound Of A Drum" album on Marlin which sounds like the most

"SOUND OF A DRUM"
(R. MacDonald-W. Salter)
Ralph MacDonald

" The other record to pull us out of this serious summer slump is Ralph MacDonald's Latin-spiced jazz set, "Sound of a Drum." The percussion throughout is terrific "

STUDIO ONE, LOS ANGELES
DJ: Paul Dougen

BEST DISCO IN TOWN/ARABIAN NIGHTS – Ritchie Family (Marlin)
DISCO MAGIC – T-Connection (Media)
I DON'T WANNA LOSE YOUR LOVE – Emotions (Columbia)
IF YOU CAN'T BEAT 'EM JOIN 'EM – Mark Radice (UA)
GONNA DO MY BEST TO LOVE YOU – Brian & Brenda (Rocket)
LET'S MAKE A DEAL/I'VE GOT YOU UNDER MY SKIN/ BE MINE – Gloria Gaynor (Polydor)
MIDNIGHT LOVE AFFAIR – Carol Douglas (Midland Intl.)
SUN... SUN... SUN – Jakki (Pyramid)
YOU + ME = LOVE – Undisputed Truth (Whitfield)

15 LANSDOWNE STREET, BOSTON
DJ: Conrad Cardenas

CHERCHEZ LA FEMME – Savannah Band (RCA)
DON'T STOP THE MUSIC – Bay City Rollers (Arista import)
I DON'T WANNA LOSE YOUR LOVE – Emotions (Columbia)
I WANNA FUNK WITH YOU TONITE – Giorgio (Oasis)
I'VE GOT YOU UNDER MY SKIN – Gloria Gaynor (Polydor)
NICE 'N' NAASTY – Salsoul Orchestra (Salsoul)
PICNIC IN THE PARK – MFSB (Phila. Intl.)
TEN PERCENT – Double Exposure (Salsoul)
YOU + ME = LOVE – Undisputed Truth (Whitfield)
YOU SHOULD BE DANCING – Bee Gees (RSO)

YESTERDAY'S, BOSTON
DJ: Cosmo Wyatt

BEST DISCO IN TOWN – Ritchie Family (Marlin)
CHERCHEZ LA FEMME/SOUR AND SWEET – Savannah Band (RCA)
DON'T TAKE AWAY THE MUSIC – Tavares (Capitol)
GET UP OFFA THAT THING – James Brown (Polydor)
HERE WE GO AGAIN/MOVING IN ALL DIRECTIONS – People's Choice (TSOP)
I DON'T WANNA LOSE YOUR LOVE – Emotions (Columbia)
LET'S GET STARTED – Commodores (Motown)
NICE 'N' NAASTY – Salsoul Orchestra (Salsoul)
WHO AM I – Quickest Way Out (Warner Bros.)
YOU SHOULD BE DANCING – Bee Gees (RSO)

CHARLES GALLERY, NEW YORK
DJ: Louis "Angelo" Alers

ARABIAN NIGHTS/BEST DISCO IN TOWN/ BABY, I'M ON FIRE – Ritchie Family (Marlin)
CHERCHEZ LA FEMME/SOUR AND SWEET/ I'LL PLAY THE FOOL – Savannah Band (RCA)
DISCO CRAZY/NIGHT FEVER – Fatback Band (Spring)
KNIGHTS IN WHITE SATIN/I WANNA FUNK WITH YOU TONITE/OH L'AMOUR – Giorgio (Oasis)
LET'S GET IT TOGETHER/FAIT LE CHAT – El Coco (AVI)
LIKE HER – Gentlemen and Their lady (Roulette)
NICE 'N' NAASTY – Salsoul Orchestra (Salsoul)
RUN TO ME – Candi Staton (Warner Bros.)
YELLOW TRAIN – Resonance (Celebration import)
YOU SHOULD BE DANCING – Bee Gees (RSO)

likely pop jazz album to follow **George Benson's** "Breezin'" to the top. Jermaine's "Let's Be Young Tonight" ("Let's go dancing in the party lights") comes at a time when the top two disco records – "Best Disco In Town" and "You Should Be Dancing," the latter already one of the hottest pop chart records, too – are as much **about** dancing as for dancing. So another song about disco partying, especially one so irresistibly bright and entertaining, could click with a similar success. Jermaine's singing is just a little uneven, but once the song gets going, dipping into a series of fine breaks, highlighted by some fast hand-clapping, I've got no complaints. The other record to pull us out of this serious summer slump is quite different: Ralph MacDonald's Latin-spiced jazz set, "Sound of a Drum," featuring six long tracks, one with vocals (**Patti Austin** in the lead), all of them rich and engaging. Clearly, this wasn't cut as a "disco" album and many of the best tracks are too complex to be easily danceable, but the percussion throughout is so terrific that several cuts are bound to catch on with the more sophisticated crowds. The best: "Calypso Breakdown" (7:50), the album's most involving and finely-crafted cut; "The Only Time You Say You Love Me (Is When We're Making Love)," "Jam On The Groove" and the single vocal, a six-minute version of "Where Is The Love" which MacDonald and his co-producer here, **William Salter**, wrote for **Roberta Flack** and **Donny Hathaway**. This one should be very big.

Other recommended records: **The Fania All Stars'** first album release through Columbia, in which such Latin greats as **Ray Barretto**, **Johnny Pacheco**, **Roberto Roena**, **Nicky Marrero** and others (including "special guest star" **Stevie Winwood**) are all but overpowered by a **Gene Page** production and come out sounding – surprise! – like the **Love Unlimited Orchestra** – all except for a fine, smooth version of **Tito Puente's** "Picadillo" which, at 5:33, is the lp's longest track; other cuts in the Latin hustle vein: "Desafio," "I'll See You Again"... A disco disc called "Too Hot To Stop" by **Five Easy Pieces** (Claridge) that a chorus is nearly as good as its title would indicate, if a little too relentless; really picks up from about the halfway point, with chanting, "Do it baby, do the do." Total length: 6:33... Although the new **O'Jays** single, "Message In Our Music" (Philadelphia International), is good, it doesn't seem fair to judge it on the basis of its single length (3:22) when there's a 6:24 album cut coming in September. What we have here sounds like standard O'Jays – about as high quality as you can get – but it cuts out just about the point you – and the group – are really getting into it. The message, at least, is intact, and it's a statement of Gamble & Huff's whole approach: "We wanna talk about the situation of our nation/Try and make you see: things aren't like they're supposed to be... We've got a message in our music/So understand while you dance." *Listen* to it. ◗

SEPTEMBER 4, 1976

No complaints this week – finally there are some records to get enthusiastic about. Now that it's in release, the **Ralph MacDonald** album, "Sound Of A Drum" on Marlin, is proving to be the most essential new lp, with the long "Calypso Breakdown" instrumental picking up the most response – three top 10 listings in its first week; already on the DISCO FILE Top 20 at number 14. The other new record that's going over very big is the **Love Unlimited Orchestra's** "My Sweet Summer Suite" (20th Century), just out on a long (7:17) 12-inch pressing after an earlier release as a rather truncated single of 2:48. This new version extends the record's Afro-Latin percussion intro almost to the point of boredom but the effect of this long, relentless pattern is to heighten the impact of the song's main section, so that when the strings finally burst in, as they inevitably do, it feels like a tornado touching down. This stunning moment is worth the whole record and it's the first great thing **Barry White** – who produced, arranged and conducted here – has done for disco since the opening notes of "Love's Theme."

Other recommended disco disc pressings: A commercial "Super Single" 12-inch 45 from H&L Records with completely reworked mixes of **Van McCoy's** "Love Is The Answer" (8:08) and the **Softtones'** "That Old Black Magic" (7:00) back to back. "Love Is The Answer" sounds like it's merely been doubled up with a drum break as a neat transition, but "Black Magic" has whole tracks of new vocals and a series of new changes that should inspire a revival of the song in the clubs... **Jimmy Sabater's** fine disco version of his pop Latin standard, "To Be With You" (Salsa), has been cropping up on recent top 10 lists and finally won me over this week. The vocals are smooth, almost nightclubby, but the production is spicey and bright with exhilarating instrumental breaks. The best Latin disco cut since **Fajardo's** "C'Mon Baby Do the Latin Hustle"... **The Willow Band's** "Willow Man" (Epic) starts off sounding like one of those rocking disco European imports with Spanish vocals – almost like early **Barrabas** – then the vocals turn into English (but remain cryptic) and you notice that the producer and writer is **Jesus Alvarez**, who's done some interesting things with All Platinum. This is his most interesting... Philadelphia International has made the full 6:24 version of the **O'Jays'** "Message In Our Music" available on a disco 12-inch which is, as we suspected, much more compelling in its entirety than the single version reviewed here last week. The long break in the end goes from sharp handclapping to a quieter, almost contemplative segment before breaking back to a final rush of vocals. But, again, as in all Gamble-Huff songs, it's the message of "Message"

that counts... Also strongly re-recommended: the flip side of the commercial disco disc of the **Salsoul Orchestra's** "Nice 'n' Naasty" – the version of "2001" that has been re-titled "Salsoul 3001." This has got to be one of the year's most extraordinary productions and although it may be too overwhelming and bizarre for some clubs, others, like New York's Loft, turn to pandemonium when the record comes on. Experiment with it if you haven't already... Motown has released a full version of the re-mixed "Down To Love Town" by **The Originals** on a 12-inch running 5:55. **Tata Vega's** Full Speed Ahead" (5:04) is on the flip side.

RECOMMENDED SINGLES. The single I want to go overboard about this week is "The More I Get To Know You," an absolutely ecstatic production by **Jimmy Roach** for a Detroit group called **Five Special** who with this one song have become my favorite new male group. This is a two-part falling-in-love song (Part I – 3:29; Part II – 2:30) with great vocals from all the voices in the group but especially from the tenor lead and lyrics like this: "I hear you say 'Hello' and my hands start to perspire/ It don't take much at all to put me all on fire." And it's the winner of the Record Company Name of the Week – probably the month – award for a label called TEAI (Tellin' Everybody About It) Records, through Mercury now, on that label soon... Also "Catfish," a real fine **Four Tops** smoothie (on ABC) about a "disco queen" whose dancing excites the singer – the record's strong build and ending clinch it after a listening or two; sounds like a radio hit, too.

RECOMMENDED ALBUMS: **The Jimmy Castor Bunch's** latest, "E-Man Groovin'" (Atlantic), with a good selection of his typically insane, left-field stuff, the best being the 5:02 title cut with the chant, "You've got to feel it in your gut/Get up and move your butt" and explosions of Castor's trademark drumming and "I Love A Mellow Groove," difficult for dancing because of its tempo changes (that's what the song's all about), but fun. Also listen to Castor's hilarious interpretation of the vampire myth, a two-part "Dracula" that is the lp's comedy centerpiece... Two cuts from the new **Hot Chocolate** lp, "Man To Man" (Big Tree), both uneven but hot: a terrifically nasty, pumping "Heaven's In The Backseat Of My Cadillac" (5:15), a slick seduction song that could work if the crowd will stick through its changes, and a driving, almost fierce "Sugar Daddy" (5:25) with a powerful guitar line. Also included: the previously released single, "Don't Stop It Now"... The **Walter Murphy Band's** "A Fifth Of Beethoven" album (Private Stock) contains several other witty disco-flavored versions

> ❝ When the strings finally burst in, it feels like a tornado touching down. This stunning moment is worth the whole record ❞

BAREFOOT BOY, NEW YORK
DJ: Tony Smith

CALYPSO BREAKDOWN/JAM ON THE GROOVE/WHERE
IS THE LOVE – Ralph MacDonald (Marlin)
CHERCHEZ LA FEMME/SOUR AND SWEET/I'LL PLAY THE
FOOL – Savannah Band (RCA)
EVERYMAN/MY LOVE IS FREE – Double Exposure (Salsoul)
I DON'T WANNA LOSE YOUR LOVE – Emotions (Columbia)
MY SWEET SUMMER SUITE – Love Unlimited Orchestra
(20th Century)
NICE 'N' NAASTY/SALSOUL: 3001 – Salsoul Orchestra
(Salsoul)
NIGHT FEVER/THE JOINT/DISCO CRAZY – Fatback Band
(Spring)
PROPHECY – Margie Joseph (Cotillion)
RIGHT ON – East Harlem Bus Stop (D&M)
YOU'VE GOT THE POWER – Camouflage (Roulette)

ENCHANTED GARDEN, DOUGLASTON, N.Y.
DJ: Paul Casella

ATMOSPHERE STRUT – Cloud One (P&P)
CALYPSO BREAKDOWN/WHERE IS THE LOVE – Ralph
MacDonald (Marlin)
FULL TIME THING – Whirlwind (Roulette)
HAVE YOU EVER SEEN THEM SHAKE – Ronnie McNeill
(Motown)
I DON'T WANNA LOSE YOUR LOVE – Emotions (Columbia)
IF YOU CAN'T BEAT 'EM, JOIN 'EM – Mark Radice (UA)
IT'S IMPORTANT TO ME – Deniece Williams (Columbia)
LOVE TO THE WORLD/THE WORD – L.T.D. (A&M)
YOU + ME = LOVE – Undisputed Truth (Whitfield)
YOU'RE WELCOME, STOP ON BY – Fantacy Hill (Prodigal)

THE SANDPIPER, FIRE ISLAND PINES, N.Y.
DJ: Tom Savarese

CALYPSO BREAKDOWN/THE ONLY TIME YOU SAY YOU
LOVE ME – Ralph MacDonald (Marlin)
CHERCHEZ LA FEMME/SOUR AND SWEET/I'LL PLAY THE
FOOL – Savannah Band (RCA)
DISCO MAGIC – T-Connection (Media)
DON'T STOP THE MUSIC – Bay City Rollers (Arista import)
DON'T TAKE AWAY THE MUSIC – Tavares (Capitol)
I DON'T WANNA LOSE YOUR LOVE/ FLOWERS –
Emotions (Columbia)
I NEED YOU, YOU NEED ME – Joe Simon (Polydor)
RUN TO ME – Candi Staton (Warner Bros.)
YOU SHOULD BE DANCING – Bee Gees (RSO)
YOU'RE MY PIECE OF MIND – Faith, Hope & Charity (RCA)

PENROD'S, EAST MEADOW, N.Y.
DJ: Jackie McCloy

CHERCHEZ LA FEMME/SOUR AND SWEET – Savannah
Band (RCA)
COMME UN OISEAU QUI S'ENVOLE – Maximilien
(CBS import)
DON'T STOP THE MUSIC – Bay City Rollers (Arista import)
HEAVEN MUST BE MISSING AN ANGEL – Tavares (Capitol)
MY SWEET SUMMER SUITE – Love Unlimited Orchestra
(20th Century)
PIANO CONCERTO – The Philharmonics (Polydor import)
TO BE WITH YOU – Jimmy Sabater (Salsa)
TOO HOT TO STOP – Five Easy Pieces (Claridge)
YOU SHOULD BE DANCING – Bee Gees (RSO)
YOU'LL NEVER FIND ANOTHER LOVE LIKE MINE – Lou
Rawls (Phila. Intl.)

of classical pieces, the best being "Flight '76" based on
Rimsky-Korsakov's "Flight Of The Bumble Bee," but
the most interesting disco track is an original called
"Midnight Express" (3:05) with an Isaac Hayes movie
theme flavor and a nice light chop to the beat. Other
possibilities are "California Strut," on "Beethoven's" B
side, and a slightly snappy "Get A little Lovin'" with an
AWB influence... Jermaine Jackson's "Let's Be Young
Tonight" – a strange song for a 21-year-old – is still the
best thing on his just-out Motown album, "My Name Is
Jermaine." At least here the song's been lengthened some,
to 5:05, which gives the central break more of a boost,
but the other material isn't up to even this level.

FEEDBACK: Among the new cuts on Paul Casella's list
this week from The Enchanted Garden on Long Island,
there are three we haven't mentioned here before:
"You're Welcome, Stop On By," a not entirely successful
revamping of the Bobby Womack song by a group called
Fantacy Hill (Prodigal) that's uneven and too short at
2:55; Ronnie McNeir's "Have You Ever Seen Them Shake"
(from his "Love's Comin' Down" lp, Motown), a spunky,
sexy song with Stevie Wonder overtones that just gets
goin when it's over abruptly; and "It's Important to Me"
from Deniece Williams' Columbia album. ◗

DISCO FILE TOP 20

1. YOU SHOULD BE DANCING – Bee Gees (RSO)
2. SOUR AND SWEET/CHERCHEZ LA FEMME/
   I'LL PLAY THE FOOL – Savannah Band (RCA)
3. BEST DISCO IN TOWN – Ritchie Family (Marlin)
4. I DON'T WANNA LOSE YOUR LOVE – Emotions
   (Columbia)
5. YOU + ME = LOVE – Undisputed Truth (Whitfield)
6. ARABIAN NIGHTS – Ritchie Family (Marlin)
7. IF YOU CAN'T BEAT 'EM, JOIN 'EM – Mark Radice
   (UA)
8. DISCO MAGIC – T-Connection (Media)
9. YOU'LL NEVER FIND ANOTHER LOVE LIKE MINE
   – Lou Rawls (Phila. Intl. lp cuts)
10. LET'S MAKE A DEAL/I'VE GOT YOU UNDER MY
    SKIN/BE MINE – Gloria Gaynor (Polydor)
11. NICE 'N' NAASTY – Salsoul Orchestra (Salsoul)
12. KNIGHTS IN WHITE SATIN/I WANNA FUNK
    WITH YOU – Giorgio (Oasis)
13. SUN... SUN... SUN – Jakki (Pyramid)
14. CALYPSO BREAKDOWN – Ralph MacDonald
    (Marlin)
15. HEAVEN MUST BE MISSING AN ANGEL/
    DON'T TAKE AWAY THE MUSIC – Tavares (Capitol)
16. ONE FOR THE MONEY – Whispers (Soul Train)
17. MY LOVE IS FREE/TEN PERCENT
    – Double Exposure (Salsoul)
18. BABY I'M ON FIRE – Ritchie Family (Marlin)
19. RUN TO ME – Candi Staton (Warner Bros.)
20. PICNIC IN THE PARK – MFSB (Phila. Intl.)

SEPTEMBER 11, 1976

Slim pickings again this week with very few exceptions. The exceptions follow. Producer **Norman Whitfield**, who has one of the holiest disco records out now in **Undisputed Truth's** "You + Me = Love," may give himself some competition with his first film score, a two-record set from the movie "Car Wash" (RCA) that has several interesting cuts. The two strongest are the opening title track (5:06) which begins with sharp hand-clapping and a bubbling guitar, then sweeps into a dense production with pleasant vocals from a group called **Rose Royce**; and "Daddy Rich," which has a more metallic sound and a tight, swirling track reminiscent of Whitfield's best work with the **Temptations**. Also worth checking out: "Keep On Keepin' On" (6:39) in a more thoughtful mood (compare "Runaway Child," "Papa Was A Rolling Stone"), a small beauty called "Water" that's a perfect celebration of the element, and a long (10:48) atmospheric instrumental called "Sunrise" that might make a great warm-up record.

Other recommended album cuts: "Dancing Feet" (6:52), a sprightly, varied instrumental with some female vocals and fine tenor sax send-off by **Houston Person** – from his recent "Pure Pleasure" album on Mercury... These tracks from the new **Persuaders** album "It's All About Love" on Calla – produced by **Robert Curington** and **Norman Harris**: a smoothly polished upbeat number called "Count The Ways" with a classic intro (5:03); "Two Women," about the hazards of infidelity; and a very fast "Quickest Way Out," included in both instrumental and vocal versions – these plus a number of excellent slow songs make this a most welcome return for the group who originally won us over with "Thin Line Between Love And Hate"... "Phoenix," "I'll Always Love You 'T'" and "Guitar Talk," all pleasant if oddly uneven songs in a kind of funk moderne style with vocals by a group called **Aquarian Dream**, an eight-member combination produced by **Norman Connors** (on Buddah).

❛❛ "We Will Make Love" sounds like a Phil Spector girl group perverted hilariously into a sigh and moan extravaganza with a tacky Spanish flavor (did someone cry "Ole!" during the orgasm?) ❜❜

CIRCUS MAXIMUS, LOS ANGELES
DJ: Mitch Schatsky

BLOWFLY DISCO – Blowfly (Weird World)
DISCO MAGIC – T-Connection (Media)
FULL SPEED AHEAD/LOVE IS ALL YOU NEED – Tata Vega (Tamla)
FULL TIME THING – Whirlwind (Roulette)
I DON'T WANNA LOSE YOUR LOVE – Emotions (Columbia)
LET'S GET IT TOGETHER – El Coco (AVI)
MY SWEET SUMMER SUITE – Love Unlimited Orchestra (20th Century)
NICE 'N' NAASTY/SALSOUL 3001 – Salsoul Orchestra (Salsoul)
PLEASE LOVE ME AGAIN – V.I.P. Connection (Morningstar)
YOU + ME = LOVE – Undisputed Truth (Whitfield)

EXECUTIVE LOUNGE, DOVER, DELAWARE
DJ: Tom Webb

BEST DISCO IN TOWN – Ritchie Family (Marlin)
CHERCHEZ LA FEMME/SOUR AND SWEET – Savannah Band (RCA)
FULL TIME THING – Whirlwind (Roulette)
I WANNA FUNK WITH YOU TONITE – Giorgio (Oasis)
I'VE GOT YOU UNDER MY SKIN/BE MINE – Gloria Gaynor (Polydor)
MAKES YOU BLIND – Glitter Band (Bell import)
NICE 'N' NAASTY – Salsoul Orchestra (Salsoul)
RUN TO ME – Candi Staton (Warner Bros.)
YOU + ME = LOVE – Undisputed Truth (Whitfield)
YOU SHOULD BE DANCING – Bee Gees (RSO)

LEVITICUS, NEW YORK
DJ: Michael Nias

CHERCHEZ LA FEMME/I'LL PLAY THE FOOL – Savannah Band (RCA)
FULL TIME THING – Whirlwind (Roulette)
FUNKY MUSIC – Luther (Cotillion)
LOVE TO THE WORLD/THE WORD/GET IT TOGETHER – LTD (A&M)
MESSAGE IN OUR MUSIC – O'Jays (Phila. Intl.)
NICE 'N' NAASTY – Salsoul Orchestra (Salsoul)
ONE FOR THE MONEY/PUT ME IN THE NEWS – Whispers (Soul Train)
TEN PERCENT/MY LOVE IS FREE/ EVERYMAN – Double Exposure (Salsoul)
YOU + ME = LOVE – Undisputed Truth (Whitfield)
YOU SHOULD BE DANCING – Bee Gees (RSO)

MAGGIE'S DISCO, PHOENIX, ARIZONA
DJ: Tom Ellsworth & Jack Witherby

FAMILY TREE – Family Tree (Anado)
I GOT YOUR LOVE – Stratavarious (Roulette)
KNIGHTS IN WHITE SATIN/OH, L'AMOUR/I WANNA FUNK WITH YOU TONITE – Giorgio (Oasis)
LET'S GET IT TOGETHER/FAIT DE CHAT – El Coco (AVI)
LET'S MAKE A DEAL/I'VE GOT YOU UNDER MY SKIN/BE MINE/ TALK, TALK, TALK – Gloria Gaynor (Polydor)
LOVE BITE – Richard Hewson Orchestra (Splash)
MY SWEET SUMMER SUITE – Love Unlimited Orchestra (20th Century)
NICE 'N' NAASTY/SALSOUL 3001 – Salsoul Orchestra (Salsoul)
SUN... SUN... SUN – Jakki (Pyramid disco disc)
YOU + ME = LOVE – Undisputed Truth (Whitfield)

Of the new records in 12-inch disco disc format, two deserve notice. One, **Laurie Marshall's** "(All Day and All Night) We Will Make Love" (Amherst) sounds like a '60s girl group production à la **Phil Spector** that's been perverted hilariously into a **Donna Summer**-ish sigh and moan extravaganza with an outrageously tacky Spanish flavor (did I hear someone cry "Ole!" during the orgasm?); an additional logo on the label says Hard Core Records and it runs 6:10. The second is more traditional – **Ace Spectrum's** "Live And Learn" (Atlantic) with a fitfully interesting production and cutting, aggressive vocals that seem to be struggling uncomfortably with the instrumental track and just barely winning.

RECOMMENDED SINGLES: **Gato Barbieri's** rich jazz instrumental interpretation of **Leon Ware's** song for **Marvin Gaye**, "I Want You" (A&M) – the long version is marked "Part II" and is 6:10 – gorgeous for a moody slow dance that increases in intensity as it goes on; produced by **Herb Alpert**... The Controllers' beautiful, almost laid-back song about music (compare "I Love Music," "Queen Of My Soul," "Don't Take Away The Music"), "The People Want Music" (Juana)... **The Four Tops'** "Catfish" (ABC), recommended here last week, has been remixed, dropping its most explicit verse and adding a longer instrumental break – it's hard to say whether this is an improvement or not (it may be simply an attempt to play up the record's disco side), but we like both versions. NOTE: Arista is, finally, convinced that the **Glitter Band's** rousing "Makes You Blind" is making a strong enough showing in the discos to merit an American release. The record's been on the verge of breaking into the DISCO FILE chart for several months now because of its steady popularity as an import single (on Bell in England) and Arista is planning to release it here around the middle of the month. ◐

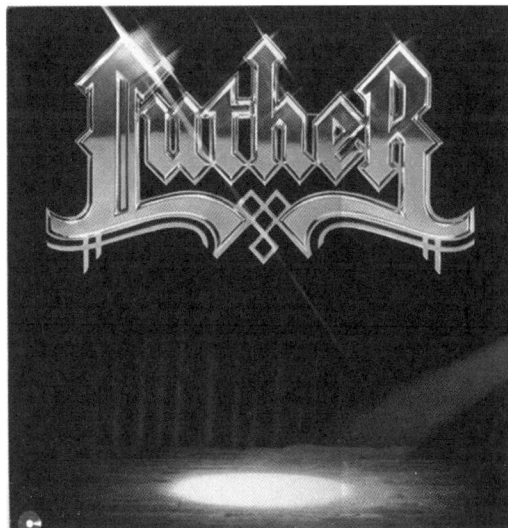

SEPTEMBER 18, 1976

The first major disco album of the fall season is producer **Vince Montana's** second **Salsoul Orchestra** collection, "Nice 'N' Naasty" Salsoul), due out this week... Even more varied than the group's first release, this lp ranges from the previously released stunner, "Salsoul 3001" – shortened slightly from its disco disc version to eliminate the jet exhaust fade-out but still one of the year's most exciting production numbers – to an MOR medley of the pop standards "We've Only Just Begun" and "Feelings" In between, the early favorites seem to be "Don't Beat Around the Bush" (3:30) with its steamy, pounding jungle drums, sweet string accents and nasty girls chanting "Don't beat around my bush;" "It's Good for the Soul" (4:20), which is alternately lush and sparse, blending stinging guitar and drum work with swooning violins; and "Standing And Waiting On Love" (3:31), which is closest in spirit to the first album's material, including a quick flash from Montana himself on vibes. The remainder of the album's cuts are also recommended for changing moods: "It Don't Have To Be Funky (To Be A Groove)," whose contents are adequate proof of its title; a Latin-flavored "Ritzy Mambo" (5:29); a wonderful, evocative slow number called "Night Crawler" that sounds like one of the best mellow mood records of the year; and, of course, "Nice 'N' Naasty." Vince Montana wrote nearly all the songs and his production here confirms his position as one of the most versatile and inventive disco producers. The Salsoul Orchestra's debut lp was among the most important disco releases of 1975 and this follow-up has an even broader appeal, making it the essential new dance album with great pop potential.

Other recommended albums: "Night People," the latest from the **Fantastic Four** (on Westbound) with a knockout first side consisting of a nearly eleven-minute medley, "Night People/Lies Divided by Jive," in which the second part seems to be making a cutting comment on the values of the first (though we find the background "party" noises in "Night People" unnecessarily distracting to the point of irritation) and another long (6:05) cut with fine lyrics called "If I Lose My Job" which is the record's sharpest track – the long intro clinches it. Also attractive: "Hideaway" (5:30)... **Deodato's** new album, "Very Together" (MCA), unfortunately contains nothing as explosive as "Caravan/Watusi Strut" but there are some bright spots, especially a fast "Spanish Boogie" which sounds heavily influenced by **Crystal Grass'** "Fio Maravilha/Taj Mahal," and three quirky versions of familiar songs: a surprising "Peter Gunn" theme, "I Shot The Sheriff" and "Theme From Star Trek." "Juanita" is a left-field bounce... The debut album by **Calender**, "It's A Monster" (Pi Kappa/ Buddah), contains their previous single, "Hypertension," a strange **B.T. Express** variation with a nice drive running nearly six minutes here, plus two other cuts in a similar vein, "Good Old Funky Music" (4:15), which has a terrific spunky beat and "Comin' on Strong" (3:55). For B.T. Express and Fatback Band fans... **Skip Mahoaney and the Casuals'** "Land Of Love" (Abet) has one very up cut, "Running Away From Love," and another that slips into a strong **Stylistics** mold, a nearly

six-minute "And It's Love" that would have to be considered left field only because of the tempo changes in the first half – the second half soars.

The week's other essential new release is a disco disc called "Love Bug" by **Bumblebee Unlimited** that DJ Tony Smith called to rave about the other day. "They're going crazy over it!" he said – and so am I. (It's also, you'll notice, on Cosmo Wyatt's top 10 list from Yesterday's in Boston this week.) Written and arranged by one of our favorites, **Patrick Adams**, produced by **Greg Carmichael** (the same team that put together "Making Love" earlier this year), this is off-the-wall disco at its best: "insect" vocals just the bearable side of "chipmunk" noises repeat that phrase "I'm a love bug, I'll sting you with my love" over a dense track most reminiscent of "Love Hangover." This goes on for more than seven minutes, complete with swirling electronics, Latin drum breaks and enough changes to satisfy any dance maniac. It's on Red Greg, Carmichael's own New York label, and available as a single and a 12-inch but, according to Smith, quite hard to find. Rare or not, it's the Pick of the Week.

FEEDBACK: These records are now beginning to break big: "Down To Love Town," the new mix of the **Originals** cut on a Motown disco disc; the other side of that same disc, **Tata Vega's** "Full Speed Ahead;" and **Carol Douglas'** medley side, "Midnight Love Affair" (Midland International)... Desi DJ from Swings in New York insists that his crowds love the **Manhattan Transfer's** sparkling jump version of that rock classic, "Don't Let Go," which he says he often repeats immediately from the break,

STARWOOD, LOS ANGELES
DJ: AJ Miller

BEST DISCO IN TOWN – Ritchie Family (Marlin)
CHERCHEZ LA FEMME/SOUR AND SWEET – Savannah Band (RCA)
DOWN TO LOVE TOWN – Originals (Motown)
I DON'T WANNA LOSE YOUR LOVE – Emotions (Columbia)
MIDNIGHT LOVE AFFAIR – Carol Douglas (Midnight Intl.)
MUSIC, MUSIC, MUSIC – California (Warner Bros.)
MY SWEET SUMMER SUITE – Love Unlimited Orchestra (20th Century)
NICE 'N' NAASTY – Salsoul Orchestra (Salsoul)
RUBBERBAND MAN – Spinners (Atlantic)
YOU + ME = LOVE – Undisputed Truth (Whitfield)

SWING'S, NEW YORK
DJ: Desi DJ

CHERCHEZ LA FEMME/SOUR AND SWEET/I'LL PLAY THE FOOL – Savannah Band (RCA)
DON'T LET GO/THE THOUGHT OF LOVING YOU – Manhattan Transfer (Atlantic)
I DON'T WANNA LOSE YOUR LOVE – Emotions (Columbia)
KILL THAT ROACH – Miami (Drive)
MIDNIGHT LOVE AFFAIR/CRIME DON'T PAY – Carol Douglas (Midland Intl.)
MY SWEET SUMMER SUITE – Love Unlimited Orchestra (20th Century)
STREET DANCE – Mexicanos (Klik import)
YOU + ME = LOVE – Undisputed Truth (Whitfield)
YOU NEED ME, I NEED YOU – Joe Simon (Spring)
YOU'RE MY PEACE OF MIND – Faith, Hope & Charity (RCA)

SANDPIPER, FIRE ISLAND PINES, N.Y.
DJ: Larry Sanders

BE MINE – Gloria Gaynor (Polydor)
CALYPSO BREAKDOWN – Ralph MacDonald (Marlin)
CHERCHEZ LA FEMME/I'LL PLAY THE FOOL/SOUR AND SWEET – Savannah Band (RCA)
FULL TIME THING – Whirlwind (Roulette)
IT'S GOOD FOR THE SOUL/DON'T BEAT AROUND THE BUSH/NICE 'N' NAASTY – Salsoul Orchestra (Salsoul)
LET'S GET IT TOGETHER – El Coco (AVI)
MIDNIGHT LOVE AFFAIR – Carol Douglas (Midland Intl.)
MY SWEET SUMMER SUITE – Love Unlimited Orchestra (20th Century)
YOU SHOULD BE DANCING – Bee Gees (RSO)
YOU'RE MY PEACE OF MIND – Faith, Hope & Charity (RCA)

YESTERDAY'S, BOSTON
DJ: Cosmo Wyatt

CAR WASH – Rose Royce (MCA)
DOWN TO LOVE TOWN – Originals (Motown)
HERE WE GO AGAIN – People's Choice (TSOP)
I DON'T WANNA LOSE YOUR LOVE – Emotions (Columbia)
LOVE BUG – Bumblebee Unlimited (Red Greg)
MAKES YOU BLIND – Glitter Band (Bell import)
PICNIC IN THE PARK – MFSB (Phila. Intl.)
SOUR AND SWEET /CHERCHEZ LA FEMME – Savannah Band (RCA)
YOU + ME = LOVE – Undisputed Truth (Whitfield)

usually after something by the **Savannah Band** since the spirit is similar. Not for all tastes, certainly, but interesting. The other cut listed in Desi's top 10 from the Manhattan Transfer lp ("Coming Out" on Atlantic) is a more accessible "The Thought Of Loving You": ritzy romance that also would work well with Savannah Band material... A reliable source reports that **Laurie Marshall**, whose orgasmic epic "(All Day And All Night) We Will Make Love" was reviewed here last issue, is not, as we reasonably assumed, a woman but a member of the opposite sex. DISCO FILE would appreciate an 8 x 10 glossy for verification... We hear that **Stevie Wonder's** people have made up a number of t-shirts for friends that read WE'RE ALMOST FINISHED. And San Francisco's newest disco is to be called Cathedral after **D.C. LaRue's** song, still going strong on the coast.

RECOMMENDED SINGLES: **Leon Haywood's** pounding, powerful "The Streets Will Love You To Death" (Columbia), a song about how the grass is never really greener on the other side of the fence and Haywood's best in some time... an appropriately titled "Philly Jump," produced by **Bunny Sigler** for a group called **Instant Funk** (on TSOP) – very gritty disco funk... the **New York Disco Orchestra's** formula disco version of "The Way We Were" in two parts (total time in nearly six minutes) on Artemis and really quite good... and **Delegation's** "The Promise Of Love" (State), a sweet record from England that Delaware DJ Tom Webb first alerted me to; he calls it a "little sad love song" – the sort we both apparently have a weakness for – and it grows on you. ✺

❝A reliable source reports that Laurie Marshall, whose orgasmic epic was reviewed here last issue, is not a woman but a member of the opposite sex. DISCO FILE would appreciate an 8x10 glossy for verification❞

With the release this week of three more interesting, essential albums to join the immediately successful **Ralph MacDonald** and **Salsoul Orchestra** lps, the season is off to an excellent, encouraging start. The **O'Jays'** "Message In The Music" (Philadelphia International), with its striking, brilliant cover, is fascinating, as always, not just as another step in the invigorating growth of the O'Jays as a group but as another chapter (in verses) of **Gamble & Huff's** philosophy, which is now almost exclusively God-directed, which can be oppressive or inspiring depending on your attitude toward preaching. "Make A Joyful Noise" is the most explicitly religious, uplifting, instructive song as well as one of the best dance cuts. The message in the music: "We got something to shout about/We got something to talk about/We got something to live about/We got to praise Him." Confirms the notion that discos are the new churches (or "cathedrals"). The longest cut is a slow track called "A Prayer" (6:30) which is, beautifully, just that. "Paradise," essentially a great love song, contains lyrics that extend Its area of concern far beyond a man and a woman: "Heaven is just a condition/Hell is a condition too/Whether we live in heaven or hell – It's up to me and it's up to you." Like the dancing drummers on the album cover, the O'jays are sending out the word.

Of the other cuts, the best are "Darlin', Darlin' Baby" whose spirit is perfectly captured in its parenthetical subtitle, "Sweet, Tender Love" – a creamy smooth, extremely pretty love song with a hustle beat – and "Let Life Flow" (the one cut written and produced by **Whitehead, McFadden and Carstarphen**) is deliciously laid-back and comfortable with a positive but decidedly secular and unrevolutionary (counter-revolutionary?) message: "Roll with the punches."

Eddie Kendricks' second album with **Norman Harris** – "Goin' Up In Smoke" (Tamla), even better than their previous collaboration which was very well received – is also very religious, underlining the point of the last album's "He's A Friend." The opening cut is the title song, which has a frightenly pessimistic viewpoint – "We're going up in smoke/We ain't got no hope" – that Kendricks preaches with a sweet, driven fervor. (But two songs later he's singing about "tight blue jeans" and girl watching in a cute, enjoyable "Sweet Tenderoni.") There's even a song called "Born Again" which is all about finding God ("I got a new lease on life/ I've got a

clean slate now") and very disco at the same time. Will it become a Carter campaign favorite? Is this a political statement? Immediately following is a similar cut called "Don't You Want Light," obviously referring to a spiritual, revelatory kind of vision or understanding. Sounds like the new scripture. Is there some sort of revival going on down in Philadelphia?

But there's more of interest on Kendricks' album. In fact my own favorite is a straight romantic track called "Thanks For The Memories" which has a knockout, consistently building production with a **Blue Magic** flavor. Then there's "Music Man," a kind of autobiographical statement with an intricate, up arrangement that carries an otherwise uninvolving lyric along; and "To You From Me," a perfect little love song that could have been made by the early **Temptations**. A really satisfying collection.

Taking the **Faith, Hope & Charity** album and now his own lp, "Rhythms of the World" (H&L), as evidence, **Van McCoy** is in fine form these days. The album is completely instrumental with only one or two songs featuring more than bare minimum chant vocals (as usual, by F,H&C and McCoy himself), the mood being set by the extremely long title cut (10:12) which blends the various rhythms that are developed in the other cuts, giving it an overture quality. Three of the distinctive (or stereotyped) rhythms are expanded in "Soul Cha Cha" (that features **Zulema** shouting encouragement in Spanish), "Indian Warpath" (crossing pounding "Indian" drums with sliding strings) and, the best, "Swahili Boogie" (highly sweetened African percussion). Also recommended: "That's The joint," with a hard-to-resist trademark McCoy bounce and a good sharp edge; and "The Shuffle," which is as light and fun as "The Hustle." Nearly all the cuts are over four minutes, making for a fully-packed album.

A wide-ranging, generally high-quality batch of disco discs this week, my favorite being a hot two-sided record by a young black bombshell who's recently become one of the most-photographed international models. Her name's **Grace Jones** and she sounds like a combination of **Gloria Gaynor** and **Donna Summer** with a trace of **Nico** to blur the edges. Both songs – "Sorry" (6:42) and "That's the Trouble" (7:02) – are at once very '60s, down to talk segments on one, and

❝ Grace Jones is a young black bombshell who's recently become one of the most-photographed international models. She sounds like a combination of Gloria Gaynor and Donna Summer with a trace of Nico to blur the edges ❞

INFINITY, NEW YORK
DJ: Vincent Carleo

CALYPSO BREAKDOWN – Ralph MacDonald (Marlin)
CAR WASH – Rose Royce (MCA)
CHERCHEZ LA FEMME/SOUR AND SWEET/I'LL PLAY THE FOOL – Savannah Band – RCA)
FULL TIME THING – Whirlwind (Roulette)
IF YOU CAN'T BEAT 'EM, JOIN 'EM – Mark Radice (UA)
KNIGHTS IN WHITE SATIN/I WANNA FUNK WITH YOU TONITE – Giorgio (Oasis)
LET'S GET IT TOGETHER – El Coco (AVI)
LET'S MAKE A DEAL/I'VE GOT YOU UNDER MY SKIN/BE MINE – Gloria Gaynor (Polydor)
LIKE HER! – Gentlemen and Their Lady (Roulette)
MY SWEET SUMMER SUITE – Love Unlimited Orchestra (20th Century)

REVELATION II, BROOKLYN, NEW YORK
DJ: Bacho Mangual

CALYPSO BREAKDOWN – Ralph McDonald (Marlin)
DAYLIGHT – Vicki Sue Robinson (RCA)
HEAVEN'S IN THE BACK SEAT OF MY CADILLAC – Hot Chocolate (Big Tree)
I DON'T WANNA LOSE YOUR LOVE – Emotions (Columbia)
IT'S GOOD FOR THE SOUL/DON'T BEAT AROUND THE BUSH/SALSOUL 3001/ STANDING AND WAITING FOR LOVE – Salsoul Orchestra (Salsoul)
I'VE GOT YOU UNDER MY SKIN/BE MINE – Gloria Gaynor (Polydor)
MY SWEET SUMMER SUITE – Love Unlimited Orchestra (20th Century)
PARTY HARDY – Gary Toms (PIP)
PHOENIX/EAST 6TH STREET/I'LL ALWAYS LOVE YOU "T" – Aquarian Dream (Buddah)
WITH ALL OUR LOVE – Chocolate Milk (RCA)

ZANZIBAR, WASHINGTON, D,C,
DJ: Mike Holland

CALYPSO BREAKDOWN/WHERE IS THE LOVE – Ralph MacDonald (Marlin)
DON'T BEAT AROUND THE BUSH/ SALSOUL 3001/IT'S GOOD FOR THE SOUL – Salsoul Orchestra (Salsoul)
DON'T STOP THE MUSIC – Bay City Rollers (Arista import)
DOWN TO LOVE TOWN – Originals (Motown)
FULL TIME THING – Whirlwind (Roulette disco disc)
LIKE HER! – Gentlemen and Their Lady (Roulette)
MY SWEET SUMMER SUITE – Love Unlimited Orchestra (20th Century)
PARTY HARDY – Gary Toms (PIP)
SMOKE YOUR TROUBLES AWAY – Glass Family (Earhole)
YOU + ME = LOVE – Undisputed Truth (Whitfield)

BOOMBAMAKAOO, NEW YORK
DJ: Jorge Wheeler

DISCO MAGIC – T-Connection (Media)
DON'T STOP THE MUSIC – Bay City Rollers (Arista import)
EL BODEQUERO – Chino y Su Cojunto Melao (TR)
I'VE GOT YOU UNDER MY SKIN'/BE MINE – Gloria Gaynor (Polydor)
MAKES YOU BLIND – Glitter Band (Bell import)
MIDNIGHT LOVE AFFAIR – Carol Douglas (Midland Intl.)
MY SWEET SUMMER SUITE – Love Unlimited Orchestra (20th Century)
NICE 'N' NAASTY /DON'T BEAT AROUND THE BUSH/STANDING AND WAITING ON LOVE – Salsoul Orchestra (Salsoul)
WHAT YOU NEED IS MY LOVE – Cindy Rodriguez (TR)
YA NO LLORES/BORINQUEN – Tito Rodriguez Jr. (TR)

super '70s with frothy but superb disco productions and dealing with much more liberated attitudes than the girl group records they echo at times. "That's The Trouble," where Jones complains about men wanting to tie her down, is the stronger of the two, with a particularly powerful instrumental break, but both are wonderful. The label: Beam junction, 360 East 72nd Street, New York 10021.

Vicki Sue Robinson's much-anticipated version of **Bobby Womack's** "Daylight" (7:28 on RCA) sounds more like **Bette Midler** meets **Bonnie Bramlett**. It's not a good sign that so far my favorite parts are the choruses and the breaks. This is not VSR at her height – we know how terrific that can be – but the middle ground has its attractions. Entertaining but not electrifying... I kept wondering what it was about a group called **California's** version of **Teresa Brewer's** "Music, Music, Music" (4:05 on Warner Brothers) that pushed it up California disco charts (besides a possible state-name chauvinism) but I finally got a copy of the disco disc length this week and now I know. The song, hardly a personal favorite, has been turned happily on its ear with a delightfully eccentric and effective production, especially the percussion bursts... Henry Street Records (which is actually located at 124 Montague Street in Brooklyn Heights 11201), the company that put out one of last year's great disco oddities, "Disco Lucy" (the "I Love Lucy" theme updated), has come up with one of this year's best disco disc gimmicks. It's a clear vinyl record with a nice blue label – very eye-catching and sure to be a collector's item. And the New York Rubber Rock Band's disco treatment of **Barbara Lewis'** "Hello Stranger" (4:45) is nice too... Also recommended: "Just Can't Be That Way" by the **Weapons of Peace** (Playboy), a rock-funky song that builds into something quite interesting – approaching **Norman Whitfield** strength; and "Ride the Tide" by the **Young Senators** (Epic), a solid, steady pumping message song – it's the tide of life they're singing about (compare the O'Jays "Let Life Flow") – that also becomes more involving as it goes on (6:25 on the 12-inch, also available as a 3:22 single).

Atlantic has picked up and is rush releasing a German top-of-the-charts record called "Daddy Cool" by a one-man, three-woman group named **Boney M.** (now on Hansa in Germany) who have a hard-edged European sound that crosses **Roberta Kelly** and **Hot Chocolate**. A freaky, solidly disco production with some slightly jarring commercial pop touches, the single's original German pressing came in a sleeve which shows the three female singers sprawled over each other in lacy underwear while the guy looks on. After **Donna Summer**, **Silver Convention** and **Giorgio**, all fetish items, one begins to wonder exactly what is going on in Germany anyway? ✪

OCTOBER 2, 1976

❝ Stevie Wonder himself introduced the record, descending a staircase into a crush of cameramen, wearing a cream-colored cowboy suit and hat, complete with a special gun belt whose holsters held copies of his album cover ❞

Two trips this past week for sneak previews of two major fall releases. The first flight was to Los Angeles, where the new **Donna Summer** album was officially unveiled at a dinner party to celebrate Donna's return from Germany and the completion of her third album with producers **Giorgio Moroder** and **Pete Bellotte**. I heard the record first as background to a deliciously endless Chinese meal; then in an improvised after-dinner discotheque; then, the following day, in Neil Bogart's car and Neil Bogart's office, where Bogart, Casablanca Record's energetic president, impressed me with his real enthusiasm for disco, and his inside-out, no-nonsense understanding of the medium and the market; and finally, I heard the record at four different discotheques Saturday night when ace promotion man Marc Paul Simon took me and an acetate on a whirlwind tour. By the time I left LA the record had become so imprinted in my brain that I hardly needed my own copy, yet that was the first thing I put on the turntable once I got back home, and it's been there almost without interruption ever since.

The album's called "Four Seasons of Love" and it contains just four cuts, two to a side, with a short reprise at the end. The concept, as the title indicates, is the seasonal blossoming and dying of a love affair, giving each track its own mood: "Spring Affair" (8:32), the exhilarating opening, full of the bright, high excitement of falling in love; "Summer Fever" (8:08), celebrating the more intense passion of love at its peak, steamy and throbbing, with some terrific screams from Donna to send the temperature even higher; "Autumn Changes" (5:30), when the sound is ominous and the love fading and unsure, captured in the syncopation of a reggae steel drum beat; "Winter Melody," opening with an icy rush of wind and settling into a contemplative, lost-love song with vocals reminiscent of **Dusty Springfield** in her "Memphis" days. The final reprise cut brings the cycle back to Spring again and the flowering of a new affair. The Moroder-Bellotte production is, as usual, disco perfection: sharp, crisp, clear and full of brilliant changes; the transitions between the cuts are particularly fine and fluid, making the entire album not only a great disco concept, but one of the best executed concept lps since the theme format began. And wait 'til you see the cover! Release date is set for the first week in October and it's destined to be a record for all seasons.

The second trip was an excursion to a place called Long View Farm, a comfortable recording studio in a farmhouse outside of Worcester, Massachussetts, where a plane load of press people were given a first listen to **Stevie Wonder's** already-legendary "Songs In The Key Of Life" album. Stevie himself introduced the record, descending a staircase into a crush of photographers and cameramen, wearing a cream-colored cowboy suit and hat, complete with a special gun belt whose holsters held copies of his album cover and across whose back was printed "#1 WITH A BULLET." He also wore dark glasses with orange-bronze frames, short leather gloves, boots and a kerchief tied around his neck; in his hands he carried four boxes of tapes. But before they were played, he offered "a little background," to the album, his first in more than two years. Much of what he said sounded unusually self-conscious and stilted and he rambled nervously through serious platitudes and measured acknowledgements of help on the album before saying, "I hope that you all enjoy it but really doesn't matter so much because I know that I gave my all and all at this time to do the best that I can do."

Fortunately, his music spoke more forcefully, more fluidly. There are 17 songs on four sides of the album, plus four additional cuts that will be pressed on a seven-inch EP and included with the package. I won't venture to say whether or not the entire collection lived up to the great expectations that have built up over the long period of anticipation and constant rumor preceding its completion. One listening would hardly be enough, especially with the varied, complex group of tracks that Wonder has come up with. But, happily, I can report that there are at least two dance cuts so Stevie hasn't let

12 WEST, NEW YORK
DJ: Jimmy Stuard

CALYPSO BREAKDOWN/WHERE IS THE LOVE – Ralph McDonald (Marlin)
CHERCHEZ LA FEMME/SOUR AND SWEET/I'LL PLAY THE FOOL – Savannah Band (RCA)
DON'T BEAT AROUND THE BUSH/NICE 'N' NAASTY/STANDING AND WAITING ON LOVE/IT'S GOOD FOR THE SOUL – Salsoul Orchestra (Salsoul)
GOIN' UP IN SMOKE/THANKS FOR THE MEMORIES/BORN AGAIN – Eddie Kendricks (Tamla)
I DON'T WANNA LOSE YOUR LOVE – Emotions (Columbia)
LET'S MAKE A DEAL/I'VE GOT YOU UNDER MY SKIN/BE MINE – Gloria Gaynor (Polydor)
MIDNIGHT LOVE AFFAIR – Carol Douglas (Midland Intl.)
MY LOVE IS FREE – Double Exposure (Salsoul)
YOU SHOULD BE DANCING – Bee Gees (RSO)
YOU'RE MY PEACE OF MIND – Faith, Hope & Charity (RCA)

LOST AND FOUND, WASHINGTON, D.C.
DJ: Bill Owens

CALYPSO BREAKDOWN – Ralph McDonald (Marlin)
CHERCHEZ LA FEMME – Savannah Band (RCA)
DOWN TO LOVE TOWN – Originals (Motown)
FULL TIME THING – Whirlwind (Roulette)
I DON'T WANNA LOSE YOUR LOVE – Emotions (Columbia)
LIKE HER! – Gentlemen and Their Lady (Roulette)
MIDNIGHT LOVE AFFAIR – Carol Douglas (Midland Intl.)
MY SWEET SUMMER SUITE – Love Unlimited Orchestra (20th Century)
NICE 'N' NAASTY/SALSOUL 3000/DON'T BEAT AROUND THE BUSH – Salsoul Orchestra (Salsoul)
YOU + ME = LOVE – Unlimited Truth (Whitfield)

CORK & BOTTLE, NEW YORK
DJ: Freddie Mendoza

DAYLIGHT – Vicki Sue Robinson (RCA)
DOING THE FEELING – Alvin Cash (Dakar)
FULL TIME THING – Whirlwind (Roulette)
FREAK-N-STEIN – Blue Magic (Atco)
I WANNA FUNK WITH YOU TONIGHT – Giorgio (Oasis)
IT'S GOOD FOR THE SOUL/DON'T BEAT AROUND THE BUSH/IT DON'T HAVE TO BE FUNKY – Salsoul Orchestra (Salsoul)
LET'S GET IT TOGETHER – El Coco (AVI)
LOVE IS WHAT WE NEED – Bimbo Jet (Roulette)
MIDNIGHT LOVE AFFAIR – Carol Douglas (Midland Intl.)
WHAT YOU NEED IS MY LOVE – Cindy Rodriguez (Disco Mania)

LA BOUCHERIE, NEW ORLEANS
DJ: David Wolf

BEST DISCO IN TOWN/BABY I'M ON FIRE – Ritchie Family (Marlin)
FIFTH OF BEETHOVEN/CALIFORNIA STRUT – Walter Murphy (Private Stock)
MY SWEET SUMMER SUITE – Love Unlimited Orchestra (20th Century)
PLAY THAT FUNKY MUSIC – Wild Cherry (Epic/Sweet City)
RUN TO ME/YOUNG HEARTS RUN FREE – Candi Staton (Warner Bros)
SHAKE YOUR BOOTY – KC & the Sunshine Band (TK)
SUMMERTIME – MFSB (Phila. Intl.)
THAT OLD BLACK MAGIC/LOVE IS THE ANSWER – Softones/Van McCoy (H&L)
YOU SHOULD BE DANCING – Bee Gees (RSO)
YOU + ME = LOVE – Unlimited Truth (Whitfield)

the disco audience down. One is a long track called "Black Man" that is essentially a history lesson set to a percolating, popping rhythm and introducing various historical figures of different races who've made up the American melting pot. The chorus that unites these short sketches is one of Wonder's most powerful and direct and the song comes to a head with a break full of jumpy, snappy synthesizer. The end of the song turns into an aggressive question-and-answer quiz that is a strong rhetorical device but becomes undanceable. The second stunning cut is "Another Star," a love song with a big disco-style beginning that changes into a pounding Brazilian/Latin quick beat and a hard, heavy production fuller than most of the other material on the album. It's clinched by a long, instrumental break toward the end which jumps off with intense Latin drumming and includes a pretty lacing of flute and girls singing "la, la, la." Both are powerful and long. Two other disco possibilities are an engaging song called "As" and the second part of "Ordinary Pain," which features **Shirley Brewer** from **Wonderlove** on tough, gritty lead vocals. Offical release date: September 30; shipping, needless to say, as a gold album. ◉

DISCO FILE TOP 20

1. **MY SWEET SUMMER SUITE** – Love Unlimited Orchestra (20th Century)
2. **YOU + ME = LOVE** – Undisputed Truth (Whitfield)
3. **SOUR AND SWEET/CHERCHEZ LA FEMME** – Savannah Band (RCA)
4. **NICE 'N' NAASTY** – Salsoul Orchestra (Salsoul)
5. **I DON'T WANNA LOSE YOUR LOVE** – Emotions (Columbia)
6. **FULL TIME THING** – Whirlwind (Roulette)
7. **CALYPSO BREAKDOWN** – Ralph MacDonald (Marlin)
8. **I'VE GOT YOU UNDER MY SKIN/BE MINE** – Gloria Gaynor (Polydor)
9. **MIDNIGHT LOVE AFFAIR** – Carol Douglas (Midland Intl.)
10. **DON'T BEAT AROUND THE BUSH** – Salsoul Orchestra (Salsoul)
11. **I'LL PLAY THE FOOL** – Savannah Band (RCA)
12. **SALSOUL 3001/IT'S GOOD FOR THE SOUL** – Salsoul Orchestra (Salsoul)
13. **YOU SHOULD BE DANCING** – Bee Gees (RSO)
14. **LET'S GET IT TOGETHER** – El Coco (AVI)
15. **DOWN TO LOVE TOWN** – Originals (Motown)
16. **I WANNA FUNK WITH YOU** – Giorgio (Oasis)
17. **MAKES YOU BLIND** – Glitter Band (Bell import)
18. **LIKE HER!** – Gentlemen and Their Lady (Roulette)
19. **BEST DISCO IN TOWN** – Ritchie Family (Marlin)
20. **YOU'RE MY PEACE OF MIND** – Faith, Hope & Charity (RCA)

OCTOBER 9, 1976

Swamped by new releases this week, I'd like to begin a quick rundown of the cream of the crop with a group of outstanding new disco discs. Top of the list is an energetic, rave-up version of **Marvin Gaye's** 1962 hit, "Stubborn Kind of Fella," by **Buffalo Smoke, Lou Courtney's** group. Though most of us were not sorry to see the disco remake trend fizzle and fade earlier this year, anyone would be happy with the revival of a record as fine as this, especially with the inspired transformation Courtney – as singer, producer and arranger – puts it through here. RCA's 12-inch pressing is 7:11 in length and a total knockout. On the same high energy level are the back-to-back remixes of two recent **Fatback Band** cuts, "The Joint" and "Disco Crazy," which Spring Records is issuing as its first entry into the commercial disco disc market. Both tracks are completely reworked and opened up – "The Joint" is expanded from 5:50 to 8:20, "Disco Crazy" from 4:15 to 6:21 – with sizzling hot results. In quite a different vein, there's the **Rock Gazers'** follow-up to "Wet Weekend," a less freaky but equally attractive "I Believe In Love" (Sixth Avenue/ RCA) with pert vocals and a nice, pick-me-up pace. Produced by **Warren Schatz** and running 4:43, this one already has a lot of early admirers.

and three of those were unmarked as to speed – meaning nowhere on the label was there an indication of what rpm to set the turntable at. How long will it take before 12-inch pressings are cut at a standardized speed and labeled with some regard to the people using them?

RECOMMENDED ALBUMS: **Earth, Wind & Fire's** new "Spirit" (Columbia) with a high-spirited instrumental called "BIYO" that I wish were a lot longer than 3:38, especially when the kalimba slips in, and, unaccountably, only the short version of "Getaway" so the long disco disc promotional length is unique... **Touch of Class'** pleasant, satisfying debut, titled "I'm In Heaven" (Midland International) and containing the full version of that record and several other solid **John Davis** productions including an interesting version of "Just Can't Say Goodbye." My favorites: "I Love You Pretty Baby" and "Anything"... The **Love Unlimited Orchestra** album on 20th Century is not quite as much of a departure from the already classic **Barry White, Gene Page** style as one would have expected from the title tune, "My Sweet Summer Suite" (opening up here in a five-minute version). "Brazilian Love Song" is the most innovative structurally and the closest to

> **" Nowhere on the label was there an indication of what rpm to set the turntable at. How long will it take before 12-inch pressings are cut at a standardized speed and labeled with some regard to the people using them? "**

The **Sylvers'** latest, "Hot Line" (Capitol), may be a little too fast and relentless for real disco popularity but I love it anyway if only for its bright, clever lyrics and snappy handclaps. It isn't really fair to keep comparing the Sylvers to the **Jackson 5** because they've certainly developed their own personality and style, but this one reminds me of the J5's vigorous "ABC" in spirit if not in substance. Available on disco discs of 5:35 or shorter 45 pressings, "Hot Line" sounds like another **Freddie Perren** hit. Other disco discs of interest: For the growing number of Brazilian music fans, there's a two-sided "Disco Samba" release on Brasilia Records that will attempt to capture some of the American disco market with "Nega Do Obaluae" and a version of the standard "Bahia" by a singer named **Wando**... **Dobie Gray's** "Find 'Em, Fool 'Em And Forget 'Em" (Capricorn), already recommended as a fine, spunky single, has been expanded to 4:48 just as we'd hoped it would be, and **Gato Barbieri's** luxurious, richly-textured version of **Marvin Gaye's** "I Want You" (A&M) has been put on a 12-inch 45 nearly six minutes in length with a great, splashy cover graphic... NOTE: Of the 15 disco discs I've received in the past two weeks, nine were 45 rpm, six were 33-1/3 rpm

"Summer Suite" in style but it races along at an almost dizzying clip for over six minutes; "You I Adore," "Blues Concerto" and "I'm Falling In Love With You" are more familiar and White's been dormant long enough for the sound to feel fresh again... **Tony Silvester and the New Ingredient**, produced by Silvester, have a lush, sexy sound in the debut "Magic Touch" album (Mercury) with the whole first side quite nice, especially an orgasmic "Pazuzu" (4:42) and a gorgeous Barry White homage, "Very White" (5:06), both written by **Patrick Adams**. Another favorite: "Cosmic Lady" (5:35)... Although it is not the follow-up album that "Turn The Beat Around" had led us to hope for and expect, **Vicki Sue Robinson's** second release on RCA has one excellent dance cut in a medley called "Should I Stay/I Won't Let You Go" (5:03) that begins a little like "Turn The Beat" but goes off into something quite different. Robinson's gutsy vocals are counterpointed with the gospel fervor of the New York Community Choir and the percussion breaks are flawless; the song's second half clinches it. There are other possibilities "How About Me" and "Something Like A Dream" – and VSR's vocals are more impressive throughout but the dance crowd will be disappointed.

MIND SHAFT, SAN FRANCISCO
DJ: Wes Bradley

CALYPSO BREAKDOWN/WHERE IS THE LOVE – Ralph MacDonald (Marlin)
DAYLIGHT – Vicki Sue Robinson (RCA)
DOWN TO LOVE TOWN – Originals (Motown)
FOUR SEASONS OF LOVE – Donna Summer (Oasis)
I DON'T WANNA LOSE YOUR LOVE – Emotions (Columbia)
IT'S IMPORTANT TO ME – Deniece Williams (Columbia)
LOVE BUG – Bumblebee Unlimited (Red Greg)
MY SWEET SUMMER SUITE – Love Unlimited Orchestra (20th Century)
THAT OLD BLACK MAGIC – Softones (H&L)
YOU + ME = LOVE – Undisputed Truth (Whitfield)

BETTER DAYS, NEW YORK
DJ: Walter Gibbons

CALYPSO BREAKDOWN/JAM ON THE GROOVE – Ralph MacDonald (Marlin)
DOWN TO LOVE TOWN – Originals (Motown)
FULL TIME THING – Whirlwind (Roulette)
GOIN' UP IN SMOKE – Eddie Kendricks (Tamla)
HARVEST FOR THE WORLD (INST.) – Isley Brothers (T-Neck)
IT'S GOOD FOR THE SOUL/DON'T BEAT AROUND THE BUSH/SALSOUL 3001 – Salsoul Orchestra (Salsoul)
LOVE BUG – Bumblebee Unlimited (Red Greg)
MAKES YOU BLIND – Glitter Band (Bell import)
MESSAGE IN OUR MUSIC/MAKE A JOYFUL NOISE – O'Jays (Phila. Intl.)
OH L'AMOUR – Giorgio (Oasis)

LA MARIPOSA, NEW YORK
DJ: John Benitez

CALYPSO BREAKDOWN/JAM ON THE GROOVE – Ralph MacDonald (Marlin)
DON'T BEAT AROUND THE BUSH/IT'S GOOD FOR THE SOUL/SALSOUL 3001 – Salsoul Orchestra (Salsoul)
DON'T LET GO – Manhattan Transfer (Atlantic)
HEY UH-WHAT YOU SAY COME ON – Roy Ayers (Polydor)
LOVE IS LONELINESS – Cherry Pie (Cherry Pie)
MIDNIGHT LOVE AFFAIR – Carol Douglas (Midland Intl.)
MY SWEET SUMMER SUITE – Love Unlimited Orchestra (20th Century)
RHYTHMS OF THE WORLD/SWAHILI BOOGIE – Van McCoy (H&L)
THANKS FOR THE MEMORIES/GOIN' UP IN SMOKE/MUSIC MAN – Eddie Kendricks (Tamla)
WHAT YOU NEED IS MY LOVE – Cindy Rodriguez (Disco Mania/TR)

SOUND STAGE, ANNANDALE, VIRGINIA
DJ: Rick Fowler

BEST DISCO IN TOWN – Ritchie Family (Marlin)
CHERCHEZ LA FEMME/SOUR AND SWEET – Savannah Band (RCA)
DOWN TO LOVE TOWN – Originals (Motown)
DON'T TAKE AWAY THE MUSIC – Tavares (Capitol)
LOWDOWN – Boz Scaggs (Columbia)
MIDNIGHT LOVE AFFAIR – Carol Douglas (Midland Intl.)
NICE 'N' NAASTY/SALSOUL 3001 – Salsoul Orchestra (Salsoul)
RHYTHMS OF THE WORLD/SOUL CHA CHA/THAT'S THE JOINT – Van McCoy (H&L lp cuts)
YOU + ME = LOVE – Undisputed Truth (Whitfield)

FEEDBACK: The record a lot of DJs are talking about – it was on Freddie Mendoza's top 10 last week – is another song I wish were longer: "Do The Feeling," an off-the-wall funk delight by **Alvin Cash** (a name from the past on Dakar) that – indescribable and completely insinuating – could become another "Do It Any Way You Wanna." It was produced by Cash (without the Crawlers this time out) and **Willie** ("Dance Master") **Henderson** and the "Ali Shuffle" on the other side is kind of fun, too... John Benitez says that **Cherry Pie's** "Love Is Loneliness," an intriguing if uneven song with a good production, is getting a surprisingly warm response at his club, La Mariposa in New York, pulling dancers on its first plays each night. It's on a 7-inch, 33-1/3 record with a small center hole on the Cherry Pie label (in New York) which features a picture of a cut-open pie... I'd like to underline here some previous recommendations of records I've come to like even more: **Van McCoy's** "Rhythms of the World" album (H&L), especially the title cut, "Swahili Boogie" and "Indian Warpath;" **Houston Pearson's** "Dancing Feet" album cut (Mercury); **Grace Jones'** "That's The Trouble"/"Sorry" disco disc (Beam Junction); and **Deodato's** "Very Together" lp (Paul Dougan and Tom Savarese are raving about "Peter Gunn," Walter Gibbons and John Colon about "Black Widow").

RECOMMENDED SINGLES: If you keep in mind that one of my critical mottoes is "The Weirder the Better" (this does not apply to my private life), you might understand why "Did You Mean Maybe," a real oddity by ETAP (Warner Brothers), is suddenly one of my favorite singles. It was produced by **Johnny Pate** (spell his last name backwards for the group's) and has possibly the most bizarre central break of all time. And if you like that you might also get into "Seven Days" by **The Treasures** (Mercury) which has an incredible driving bass beat and wild vocals and is altogether eerie... "Disconcerto" by **Philharmonic 2000** (Mercury) gets into an almost gutsy turnaround of **Tchaikovsky** that should have its fans, especially in the wake of "A Fifth Of Beethoven." It's competing with a Canadian import version of the same material on Polydor called just "Piano Concerto" by **The Philharmonics** that is longer and lusher but more lightweight... The Song I Want to Go Overboard About This Week (this could become a regular department) is my new favorite ballad, **Brenda and the Tabulations'** "Home To Myself" (the group's first with Chocolate City), produced by **Bobby Eli** and written by **Melissa Manchester** and **Carol Bayer Sager**. It's a smoothly classic song about inner strength and selfsufficiency for those moments when you need to reassure yourself. The key lines: "It's not so bad all alone/Coming home to myself again." A great, moving song. There's also a revival of the Brenda and the Tabulations classic, "A Little Bit Of Love," by **Gentle Persuasion** (remember "Dynamite Explodes"?), produced by **Bobby Martin** and **Jerry Ross** (Capitol). NOW AVAILABLE: **The Glitter Band's** terrific "Makes You Blind" finally on Arista. ✪

OCTOBER 16, 1976

Two albums that had their previews two weeks ago are now beginning to make their first impact. **Stevie Wonder's** ambitious, overwhelming "Songs In The Key Of Life" is officially out and after hearing "Another Star" on a heavy duty disco sound system for the first time, I'd like to underline my initial rave about this beautiful song it's a spectacular, excellently produced cut. And Donna Summer's new opus, "Four Seasons of Love," should be in the stores this week but special advance pressings have already hit a number of clubs on both coasts and, not surprisingly, it's on three out of four top 10 lists this week, with the most attention going to the "Spring Affair/Summer Fever" side – another instant hit.

Speaking of instant success, there's at least one track on the new **Crown Heights Affair** album ("Do It, Do It Your Way!" on De-Lite) that's headed for saturation disco play this fall. Already on two New York top 10 lists – John Colon's from Friends Again and Joey Madonia's from the Barefoot Boy – the cut's called "Dancin'" (6:13) and it's one of those tough, driving numbers, almost in a **Brass Construction** mold, much more aggressive and hard than the group's previous material. Powerful and immediately appealing. Two more tracks – "Searching For Love" (5:51) and "Music Is The World" (3:15) – are strong enough to make the album this week's most essential new release. Other recommended album cuts: "Hold On" from the debut album Enchantment (UA), a comfortable groove with cute chorus embellishments and a terrific build (6:29)... "City Of The Angels," a warm, gentle and typically intelligent **Bill Withers** song running nearly eleven minutes, two thirds in a nice, pulsing beat, the last part eased down to a restful glide – it's kind of a tribute to Los Angeles, part of Withers' "Naked & Warm" album just out on Columbia... **KC & the Sunshine Band's** "Part 3" (TK) is full of the group's trademark simplistic but terribly catchy music, including "Shake Your Booty" and several others in a similar vein,

notably "Wrap Your Arms Around Me" and KC's bow to the disco medley, "I'm Your Boogie Man" and "Keep It Comin' Love" which run together with a minimally inspired drum break. Arista is releasing a three-cut disco record for DJs, one side of which is a sixteen-and-a-half-minute live version of "The Bottle" by **Gil Scott Heron** which is more of a showpiece production (it's from a forthcoming two-record live set) than a typical disco track, since halfway through it turns into an extended Latin percussion tour de force that would discourage all but the most dedicated or insane dancers. But it should be heard. The other side features the **Glitter Band's** "Makes You Blind" which has, unfortunately not been lengthened (in fact, it's a few seconds shorter than the single version), and **General Johnson's** "Don't Walk Away," a song that's suddenly become a strong favorite of mine: over steady, muffled drumming Johnson begs his woman not to leave with the most convincing line: "Kick me, cuss me, slap me but please don't say we're through." The B side of the single version of "Don't Walk Away" is an involving instrumental called "Temperature Rising Part II" that makes you curious to hear Part 1 – obviously being saved for the General's first Arista lp.

RECOMMENDED SINGLES: "You're My Driving Wheel," a tough, nice and nasty **Brian Holland** production for **The Supremes**, very sharp-edged and bristling with crisp guitar (Motown)... "Oh Cha" by the **Soul Train Gang** (Soul Train), produced by super hot **Norman Harris** with an odd blend of styles that seems to combine the sugariness of Love Unlimited and the tightness of a First Choice production for a fine, smoothly attractive effect... and a lightweight, frothy instrumental originally from Canada called "Quebec" by **Sweet Blindness** that approaches easy listening music but is cute (on Celebration, through Buddah).

FLASH FORWARD: After a recent preview performance, one of the most anticipated albums of the new season should be **Norman Harris'** astonishingly strong production for **Loleatta Holloway**, an utterly compelling singer who sounds like she's got one of the year's strongest female vocal albums. Watch for it sometime this fall on Salsoul. ❷

MOTOWN

"SPECIAL DISCO VERSION" — NOT FOR SALE

THE ORIGINALS

33

33⅓ STEREO
63778

"DOWN TO LOVE TOWN" 5:55
(D. Daniels-M. B. Sutton-K. Wakefield)
Jobete Music Co., Inc. (ASCAP)
Stone Diamond Music Co., Inc. (BMI)
Produced by Frank Wilson & Michael Sutton
Available in the Album
"COMMUNIQUE" 56-746 S1
℗ 1976 Motown Record Corporation
A PRODUCT OF
MOTOWN RECORD CORP.

DCA CLUB, PHILADELPHIA
DJ: Kurt Borusiewicz

DISCO MAGIC – T-Connection (Dash (TK)
DON'T BEAT AROUND THE BUSH/IT'S GOOD FOR THE SOUL/SALSOUL 3001 – Salsoul Orchestra (Salsoul)
DON'T STOP THE MUSIC – Bay City Rollers (Arista import)
DOWN TO LOVE TOWN – Originals (Motown)
FOUR SEASONS OF LOVE – Donna Summer (Oasis)
LOVE BITE – Richard Hewson Orchestra (Splash)
LOVE BUG – Bumblebee Unlimited (Red Greg)
MAKES YOU BLIND – Glitter Band (Arista)
MIDNIGHT LOVE AFFAIR – Carol Douglas (Midland Intl.)
SOUL CHA CHA – Van McCoy (H&L)

BAREFOOT BOY, NEW YORK
DJ: Joey Madonia

CAR WASH – Rose Royce (MCA)
DANCIN' – Crown Heights Affair (De-Lite)
DOWN TO LOVE TOWN – Originals (Motown)
GOIN' UP IN SMOKE/THANKS FOR THE MEMORIES – Eddie Kendricks (Tamla)
LET'S GET IT TOGETHER – El Coco (AVI)
LOVE BUG – Bumblebee Unlimited (Red Greg)
MAKES YOU BLIND – Glitter Band (Arista)
NICE 'N' NAASTY/IT'S GOOD FOR THE SOUL/DON'T BEAT AROUND THE BUSH – Salsoul Orchestra (Salsoul)
SOUL CHA CHA – Van McCoy (H&L)
SPRING AFFAIR/SUMMER FEVER – Donna Summer (Oasis)

FRIENDS AGAIN, NEW YORK
DJ: John Colon

ANOTHER STAR/BLACK MAN – Stevie Wonder (Motown)
DANCIN' – Crown Heights Affair (De-Lite)
DOING THE FEELING – Alvin Cash (Dakar)
DOWN TO LOVE TOWN – Originals (Motown)
GOIN' UP IN SMOKE/BORN AGAIN/ MUSIC MAN/THANKS FOR THE MEMORIES – Eddie Kendricks (Tamla)
LOVE BUG – Bumblebee Unlimited (Red Greg)
SATURDAY NITE/BIYO – Earth, Wind & Fire (Columbia)
SHOULD I STAY /I WON'T LET YOU GO/ DAYLIGHT – Vicki Sue Robinson (RCA)
SPRING AFFAIR/SUMMER FEVER – Donna Summer (Oasis)
SWAHILI BOOGIE – Van McCoy (H&L)

SUNDAYS, CHICAGO
DJ: Artie Feldman

CAR WASH – Rose Royce (MCA)
CHERCHEZ LA FEMME/SOUR AND SWEET / I'LL PLAY THE FOOL – Savannah Band (RCA)
DON'T BEAT AROUND THE BUSH – Salsoul Orchestra (Salsoul)
FULL TIME THING – Whirlwind (Roulette)
HOW'S YOUR LOVE LIFE – Lee Eldred (Mercury)
I DON'T WANNA LOSE YOUR LOVE – Emotions (Columbia)
MAKES YOU BLIND – Glitter Band (Arista)
MY SWEET SUMMER SUITE – Love Unlimited Orchestra (20th Century)
SOMEBODY'S ALWAYS MESSIN' UP A GOOD THING – Honey Cone (Hot Wax)
YOU + ME = LOVE – Undisputed Truth (Whitfield)

GENERAL JOHNSON

" Over steady, muffled drumming Johnson begs his woman not to leave with the most convincing line: "Kick me, cuss me, slap me but please don't say we're through" "

No Big Names this week, but there are a number of pleasant surprises from new groups and a few old favorites. Perhaps the best – certainly the one that'll catch on fastest – is the debut album of a group called **Mass Production** – "Welcome To Our World" on Cotillion. Though this is a nine-man, one-woman congregation from Norfolk, Virginia, they've got an aggressive, dense, cutting New York sound – it's not just their name that suggests a heavy influence from **Brass Construction**, but if the style is derivative (cf. **Kool & the Gang**, **Crown Heights Affair**, too) the group is strong enough to be impressive in its own right. The album's title track, "Welcome To Our World (Of Merry Music)," is a long (7:32), chugging introduction to the group's brassy, gutsy sound, breaking and building and changing again and again without losing its terriffic momentum. "I Like To Dance" (5:07) is another celebration of dance/music in an equally feverish vein, featuring some powerful drumming and a chorus chanting the title and "Dance, dance, dance-boogie" quite hypnotically. The third standout cut, "Fun In The Sun" (6:00), is in a more open, looser style with a bouncy, bright opening vocal segment and a sensational second half that turns into a lively scat chant, irresistible for anyone who likes to sing along. Strongly recommended.

Another fine debut album comes from a seven-man group named **Karma** whose aptly titled "Celebration" is on Horizon/A&M. As their name might suggest, Karma is into a spiritual, jazz-based style reminiscent of **Earth**, **Wind & Fire** and the material on their record ranges from quietly serious to downright joyous. The most danceable cut is a sprightly number called "Funk De Mambo" (4:30) with an infectious synthesizer line and vocals by **Syreeta Wright** and **Deniece Williams**, a great combination of voices. Music for all moods. The old favorites are **Black Ivory**, that perpetually adolescent New York trio, whose latest album – simply "Black Ivory" on Buddah – is about their best; if they still look like teenagers, they no longer sound like kids and this record, produced by the group itself, should move their reputation up a few big steps. Hottest cut is an over eight-minute song called "Walking Downtown (Saturday Night)" that pumps insistently through an overblown but totally knockout production: party hardy. "Dance" (4:56) is a very similar sound in a tighter format and an even more driving orchestration – strings for days, coming on like a flashflood. And there are three more possibilities: "White Wind" (5:10), a disarmingly danceable song warning about the dangers of dope; "Making Love In My Mind," a very fast hustle; and "Longer Ride." Both of these albums deserve immediate attention.

Other interesting album cuts: "What Are We Gonna Do?" (5:30), a light, airy hustle with gorgeous flute work from **Hubert Laws'** first album for Columbia ("Romeo & Juliet"), produced by **Bob James** and containing mostly beautiful mood music.... "Sooner Or Later" (5:20), one of

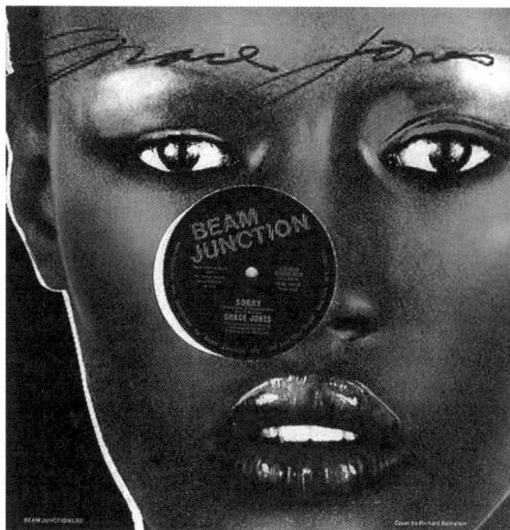

WAREHOUSE VIII, MIAMI
DJ: Bill Kelly

CALYPSO BREAKDOWN – Ralph MacDonald (Marlin)
CHERCHEZ LA FEMME/SOUR AND, SWEET/I'LL PLAY
THE FOOL – Savannah Band (RCA)
DAYLIGHT – Vicki Sue Robinson (RCA)
DOWN TO LOVE TOWN – Originals (Motown)
GOIN' UP IN SMOKE/SWEET TENDERONI/ THANKS FOR
THE MEMORIES/DON'T YOU WANT LIGHT – Eddie
Kendricks (Tamla)
I DON'T WANNA LOSE YOUR LOVE – Emotions (Columbia)
MIDNIGHT LOVE AFFAIR – Carol Douglas (Midland Intl.)
MY SWEET SUMMER SUITE – Love Unlimited Orchestra
(20th Century)
NICE 'N' NAASTY/IT'S GOOD FOR THE SOUL/STANDING
AND WAITING ON LOVE/SALSOUL 3001 – Salsoul
Orchestra (Salsoul)
SORRY/THAT'S THE TROUBLE – Grace Jones
(Beam Junction)

BACKSTREET, ATLANTA
DJ: Rick Wagner

DOWN TO LOVE TOWN – Originals (Motown)
I DON'T WANNA LOSE YOUR LOVE – Emotions (Columbia)
LET'S GET IT TOGETHER – El Coco (AVI)
MIDNIGHT LOVE AFFAIR – Carol Douglas (Midland Intl.)
MY SWEET SUMMER SUITE – Love Unlimited Orchestra
(20th Century)
SHOULD I STAY/I WON'T LET YOU GO – Vicki Sue
Robinson (RCA)
SOUL CHA CHA – Van McCoy (H&L)
CHERCHEZ LA FEMME – Savannah Band (RCA)
THAT OLD BLACK MAGIC – Softones (H&L)
YOU + ME = LOVE – Undisputed Truth (Whitfleld)

BJ'S DISCO, WORCESTER, MASS.
DJ: Nick "Baby Love" Salerno

ALI SHUFFLE/DOING THE FEELING – Alvin Cash (Dakar)
DO IT ALL THE NIGHT – Power Play (Pye)
DOWN TO LOVE TOWN – Originals (Motown)
FULL SPEED AHEAD/LOVE IS ALL YOU NEED/TRY LOVE
FROM THE INSIDE – Tata Vega (Motown)
FULL TIME THING – Whirlwind (Roulette)
I DON'T WANNA LOSE YOUR LOVE – Emotions (Columbia)
IT DON'T HAVE TO BE FUNKY/DON'T BEAT AROUND THE
BUSH/STANDING AND WAITING ON LOVE/IT'S GOOD
FOR THE SOUL – Salsoul Orchestra (Salsoul)
LIKE HER! – Gentlemen and Their Lady (Roulette)
I WANNA FUNK WITH YOU TONITE – Giorgio (Oasis)
SUNSHINE LOVE – Metal Weeds (RCA import)

BUTTERMILK BOTTOM, NEW YORK
DJ: Rafael Charres

THE BOTTLE – Gil Scott-Heron (Arista)
CAR WASH/SUNRISE – Rose Royce (MCA)
DOWN TO LOVE TOWN – Originals (Motown)
GOIN' UP IN SMOKE/MUSIC MAN/THANKS FOR THE
MEMORIES – Eddie Kendricks (Tamla)
PETER GUNN/BLACK WIDOW – Deodato
PHOENIX/I'LL ALWAYS LOVE YOU "T" – Aquarian Dream
(Buddah)
SHOULD I STAY/I WON'T LET YOU GO/ HOW ABOUT ME –
Vicki Sue Robinson (RCA)
SIR DUKE/ORDINARY PAIN/ANOTHER STAR/BLACK MAN
– Stevie Wonder (Tamla)
SORRY – Grace Jones (Beam Junction)
SPRING AFFAIR/SUMMER FEVER – Donna Summer (Oasis)

DISCO FILE TOP 20

1. **DOWN TO LOVE TOWN** – Originals (Motown)
2. **DON'T BEAT AROUND THE BUSH/IT'S GOOD FOR THE SOUL** – Salsoul Orchestra (Salsoul)
3. **MIDNIGHT LOVE AFFAIR** – Carol Douglas (Midland Intl.)
4. **MY SWEET SUMMER SUITE** – Love Unlimited Orchestra (20th Century)
5. **SOUR AND SWEET/CHERCHEZ LA FEMME** – Savannah Band (RCA)
6. **I DON'T WANNA LOSE YOUR LOVE** – Emotions (Columbia)
7. **CALYPSO BREAKDOWN** – Ralph MacDonald (Marlin)
8. **GOIN' UP IN SMOKE/THANKS FOR THE MEMORIES/ MUSIC MAN** – Eddie Kendricks (Tamla)
9. **NICE 'N' NAASTY/SALSOUL 3001** – Salsoul Orchestra (Salsoul)
10. **YOU + ME = LOVE** – Undisputed Truth (Whitfield)
11. **MAKES YOU BLIND** – Glitter Band (Bell import)
12. **FULL TIME THING** – Whirlwind (Roulette)
13. **SPRING AFFAIR/SUMMER FEVER** – Donna Summer (Casablanca)
14. **LOVE BUG** – Bumblebee Unlimited (Red Greg)
15. **DAYLIGHT** – Vicki Sue Robinson (RCA)
16. **I'LL PLAY THE FOOL** – Savannah Band (RCA)
17. **SOUL CHA CHA** – Van McCoy (H&L)
18. **LET'S GET IT TOGETHER** – El Coco (AVI)
19. **CAR WASH** – Rose Royce (MCA)
20. **LIKE HER!** – Gentlemen and Their Lady (Roulette)

those cuts saved from limbo by a very effective break and instrumental second half, still a little uneven – it's on the new **Ace Spectrum** lp, "just Like In The Movies" (Atlantic), which also contains two lengths of "Live And Learn" (5:50 and 3:28), a song that is only now beginning to grow on me... and a cut I neglected to mention last week when I wrote about the excellent new **Crown Heights Affair** album (De-Lite): a funny, sly and sexy number called "French Way," all about what the sex manuals call oral love – it's mainly a repetitious riff interrupted by suggestive variations on lines in well-known TV commercials (ct. **New Birth's** "Got To Get A Knutt") that could go over as a novelty record.

Calla Records has designed a handsome 12-inch disco disc sleeve covered with outrageously flashy dancing feet to wrap around their first two disco pressings: "Count The Ways" and "Two Women" back-to-back by the **Persuaders** and both vocal and instrumental versions of "Disco Queen" by **Rudy Love and the Love Family**, all tracks the same length as the previously available album cuts. ✪

OCTOBER 30, 1976

FEEDBACK: **Stevie Wonder's** "Another Star" and "Black Man" enter the DISCO FILE Top 20 this week accompanied by another cut from his "Songs In The Key Of Life" album that has been getting favorable response in the discos, "Sir Duke," Wonder's affectionate tribute to Ellington, the Big Bands and the power of music. Although its unusual tempo changes make "Sir Duke" a left field choice for disco dancing, a number of DJs picked up on it immediately because it blended so well with the **Savannah Band's** material. Other Wonder songs being played include "I Wish," a nostalgic look backward at childhood delights which features a strong brass section, and "As," at just over seven minutes one of the lp's longer tracks and one of Wonder's finest love songs: "I'll be loving you," he sings, "until the day is night and night becomes the day"... The **Glitter Band's** knockout instrumental, "Makes You Blind," after a successful summer as an import, is enjoying a resurgence now that it's become available as a single on Arista. DJs who are just now getting the record are reporting instant reaction – Pete Struve from San Francisco's Dance Your Ass Off says it's the first record in some time to get such immediate, fill-the-floor response – and several others have commented that its staying power is partly due to the fact that it mixes in so smoothly with so many other popular records... Other records on the move: **Deodato's** update of "Peter Gunn," and two two-song medleys – **Vicki Sue Robinson's** "Should I Stay/I Won't Let You Go," which is already getting a much more enthusiastic reception than "Daylight," and **KC & the Sunshine Band's** "I'm Your Boogie Man/ Keep It Comin' Love." And everybody's favorite new album is **Mass Production** (Cotillion), especially "Welcome To Our World (Of Merry Music)" which Joe Palminteri at the revamped Cork & Bottle in New York rushed right into his top 10 this week.

Two import records that have been picking up admirers recently are "Sunshine Love," a pulsating, string-laced, six-minute instrumental with a European feel by a group called **Metal Weeds** (available as a 12-inch promotional disc from RCA Canada), and a sharp medley of two old **Supremes** hits, "You Keep Me Hanging On" and "Stop! In The Name Of Love," by a girl named **Roni Hill** who doesn't exactly have the depth of **Diana Ross** but comes across with some punch anyway, aided by a snappy production. This last record was made in Germany, though it has none of the full

orchestral sound we've come to expect from that country, and released there on the Hotfoot label; Roulette is picking it up for American release, due within the next two weeks. **Tamiko Jones'** "Let It Flow" has also been getting play as an import in the past month and now it's available here as one of the first Contempo label releases through TK. Both sides of the single are shorter than the original (both run 2:55 while the vocal side of the import was 4:26) but the song remains a fascinating one, with sexy vocals and a terrific instrumental side that doesn't let up. One of this week's best single releases.

In fact, it's been a pretty ho-hum week and practically the only records worth getting excited about are a few singles. Top of the list is the new **Kool & the Gang**, "Open Sesame" (De-Lite), one of the group's best records ever: a hard-bumping, highly energetic number with some "Middle Eastern" touches and deep-voiced shouts from a jive "genie." Part 1 is 3:48 and Part 2, subtitled "Get Down With The Genie," is even stronger at 4:28. Very hot. Then there's "At The Top Of The Stairs" by **Wild Honey** (Drive) a record that might sound naggingly familiar because there was another version out some years ago, but this one's produced by Philadelphia's **Ron Kersey** with driving girl group vocals on one side and a longer instrumental Part 2 on the other. The song's almost impossibly upbeat – this one's for the wildest dancers – but it has a powerful **Ecstasy, Passion & Pain** quality at times and the second part is solid Philly push, complete with a false ending and surprise return. "The Hustle & The Bus Stop" by **The Destinations** (Master 5) is not a new release but it's been getting a steady build-up of positive feedback for several weeks now, with nearly everyone mentioning that it sounds a lot like the

CABARET, LOS ANGELES
DJ, Mitch Schatsky

ANOTHER STAR/BLACK MAN/SIR DUKE
– Stevie Wonder (Tamla)
CAR WASH/ PUT YOUR MONEY WHERE YOUR MOUTH IS
– Rose Royce (MCA)
DON'T BEAT AROUND THE BUSH/IT'S GOOD FOR THE SOUL/NICE 'N' NAASTY – Salsoul Orchestra (Salsoul)
FOUR SEASONS OF LOVE – Donna Summer (Casablanca)
FULL TIME THING – Whirlwind (Roulette)
I'M YOUR BOOGIE MAN/KEEP IT COMIN' LOVE/WRAP YOUR ARMS AROUND ME – KC & the Sunshine Band (TK)
IT'S IMPORTANT TO ME – Deniece Williams (Columbia)
LOVE BUG – Bumblebee Unlimited (Red Greg)
LOVE IS STILL BLUE – Paul Mauriat (Free Spirit)
PETER GUNN – Deodato (MCA)

ON STAGE, FREEPORT, LONG ISLAND
DJ: Dewane Dixon

BLACK MAN/ANOTHER STAR/I WISH/SIR DUKE
– Stevie Wonder (Tamla)
CAR WASH/I'M GOING DOWN/PUT YOUR MONEY WHERE YOUR MOUTH IS – Rose Royce (MCA)
CHERCHEZ LA FEMME/SOUR AND SWEET/I'LL PLAY THE FOOL – Savannah Band (RCA)
DOING THE FEELING – Alvin Cash (Dakar)
DOWN TO LOVE TOWN – Originals (Motown)
DANCIN/SEARCHING FOR LOVE – Crown Heights Affair (De-Lite)
GOIN' UP IN SMOKE/THANKS FOR THE MEMORIES – Eddie Kendricks (Tamla)
IT'S GOOD FOR THE SOUL/DON'T BEAT AROUND THE BUSH/SALSOUL 3001 – Salsoul Orchestra (Salsoul)
MIDNIGHT LOVE AFFAIR – Carol Douglas (Midland Intl.)
SPRING AFFAIR/SUMMER FEVER/AUTUMN CHANGES – Donna Summer (Casablanca)

CORK & BOTTLE, NEW YORK
DJ: Joe Palminteri

CALYPSO BREAKDOWN – Ralph MacDonald (Marlin)
DON'T STOP THE MUSIC – Bay City Rollers (Arista import)
ENJOY YOURSELF – The Jacksons (Epic)
FULL TIME THING – Whirlwind (Roulette)
MAKES YOU BLIND – Glitter Band (Arista)
MIDNIGHT LOVE AFFAIR – Carol Douglas (Midland Intl.)
SHOULD I STAY/I WON'T LET YOU GO – Vicki Sue Robinson (RCA)
SPRING AFFAIR/SUMMER FEVER – Donna Summer (Casablanca)
THAT'S THE TROUBLE – Grace Jones (Beam Junction)
WELCOME TO OUR WORLD – Mass Production (Cotillion)

DANCE YOUR ASS OFF, SAN FRANCISCO
DJ: Pete Struve

CALYPSO BREAKDOWN – Ralph MacDonald (Marlin)
CAR WASH – Rose Royce (MCA)
CHERCHEZ LA FEMME – Savannah Band (RCA)
DAYLIGHT/SHOULD I STAY/I WON'T LET YOU GO – Vicki Sue Robinson (RCA)
DOWN TO LOVE TOWN – Originals (Motown)
FULL TIME THING – Whirlwind (Roulette)
I'M YOUR BOOGIE MAN/KEEP IT COMIN' LOVE – KC and the Sunshine Band (TK)
MAKES YOU BLIND – Glitter Band (Arista)
MIDNIGHT LOVE AFFAIR – Carol Douglas (Midland Intl.)
SPRING AFFAIR – Donna Summer (Casablanca)

Trammps' version of "Zing Went The Strings Of My Heart." And while not as polished as "Zing," the record is attractive and tight; it's the instrumental version of "I've Got To Dance To Keep From Crying" (not the old **Miracles** song) which is on its flip side and which Joe Palminteri says he likes for its classic '50s qualities – it does sound a lot like the **Exciters**. **Paul Mauriat** has made a disco version of his MOR hit "Love Is Blue" called "Love Is Still Blue" that Mitch Schatsky at Cabaret in L.A. liked enough to put on his top 10 this week. As he commented, it's the central break that makes this record – it's percussive and somehow mysterious in the middle of what remains a slickly sentimental instrumental framework. A disco disc version for DJs only will be released this week or next on Free Spirit through Salsoul and it will be included on Mauriat's forthcoming album for that label.

Of the new albums, there are more disappointments than delights, but several are worth checking into. "Soul On Your Side" by the **Rhythm Makers** (Vigor) contains two heavy-duty instrumentals: "Zone," which had some success as a single last year and runs over five minutes here, and "Monterey," which is even more vibrant, with an intriguing horn line to tie it up neatly. **Webster Lewis**, whose fine "Do It With Style" went almost unnoticed a few months back, is here now with an album full of material and a group with the tongue-tying name of **The Post-pop Space-Rock Be-Bop Gospel Tabernacle Orchestra and Chorus** (Epic) which once had the questionable distinction of playing at **Sly Stone's** wedding party. Anyway, here they're into sophisticated disco orchestra material, some of it very nice in a low-key Latin hustle style: "Saturday Night Steppin' Out," "On The Town," "Love Is The Way" and "Do It With Style" – all between four and six minutes long. If you don't like it for dancing, you'll surely enjoy it for atmosphere/mood easy listening. The **Salsoul Orchestra** has released a disco-style Christmas album that includes, among other things, a 12-minute medley including snatches of "Joy To The World," "Jingle Bells," "White Christmas," "Winter Wonderland," "Rudolph the Red-Nose Reindeer," "O Come All Ye Faithful" and seven others. There's also a New Year's medley and a respectable version of last year's most-covered disco Christmas song, "Little Drummer Boy." The album's called "Christmas Jollies" (Salsoul) and I suppose it's an idea whose time has come but I can't listen to it seriously until after Thanksgiving. ◉

Practically all the interesting records this week are on disco discs and the very best of the batch is **Arthur Prysock's** version of "When Love Is New," the **Gamble & Huff** title tune from **Billy Paul's** last album, stylishly revamped by **John Davis** and featuring his **Monster Orchestra**. The obvious comparison here is to **Lou Rawls**: Prysock's is another of those classy, deep and rich voices and Davis has given him a comfortable love song with a smooth hustle beat – the perfect follow-up to Rawls' "You'll Never Find Another Love Like Mine." The song is over seven minutes with a wonderful break toward the end that begins with congas and layers on guitars, strings, voices and a steamy sax before joining Prysock's lead again. Watch this one. The label: Old Town Records in Long Island City, New York, and it's their first commercial disco disc.

Other recommended 12-inch pressings: **Esther Williams'** "You Gotta Let Me Show You" (Friends & Co.) produced by **Eddie Drennon** in his trademark sweet Latin style with light flute accents but made more substantial than Drennon's previous productions by Williams' strong vocals and a clever lyric. Also available on Williams' debut album, "Let Me Show You," just out... "Que Pasa" by the **Final Approach** (Gold Plate) has another kind of Latin sound, more spunky and brittle with sharp chorus vocals asking over and over, "Que pasa muchacha/ What's happenin' girl/What it is" – production was done in part by **Tommy Stewart** whose album on Abraxas several months back won him something of a following (length 6:16)... and yet another Latin-influenced record: "The Blue Danube Hustle" as done by the **Rice and Beans Orchestra** (TK) is "The Blue Danube Waltz" given a shot or two of speed – this one would almost certainly need slowing down for most crowds, but it's already getting action in Florida (where the single's been in release for some time) and in Puerto Rico (Pablo Flores, DJ at a San Juan club called Bachelor writes that it's the number one record in his club). This is one of the more bizarre ideas for a disco remake, but it's immensely entertaining. TK has issued it as one of their first 12-inch discs in a superbly designed tropical paradise "T.K. DISCO"sleeve, but the label itself is untimed and gives no indication of what speed the record is cut at... **Barry White's** "Don't Make Me Wait Too long" (20th Century) is an impossibly racy hustle with fervent vocals that is not much of a change from the Barry White material of the past but should satisfy those who can never get enough of his lushly ornate style (the lushness here runs

4:42)... **The Earls**, a group that goes way back, are on vinyl again with a tight rave-up song called "Get On Up And Dance" (a commercial disco disc from Woodbury Records, P.O. Box 402, Woodbury, New York); designed as a continental/walk dance record, this one gets a little mechanical after a time but manages to keep up a nice vocal spirit for just over seven minutes.

NOTE: Of the twelve disco discs received in the past week, including the ones reviewed above, all, for the first time, were at 45 rpm speed, but five of them – a larger percentage than before were unmarked as to speed. At a time when record companies are asking for more "professionalism" from disco DJs, one would expect them to demonstrate a little more professionalism and common sense of their own. The disco market is not a throwaway, second-class market; it's probably one of the most serious and technically sophisticated group of record buyers and players there is, and it deserves to be treated as such.

The new **Silver Convention** album is apparently the result of an attempt by the group's producers, **Michael Kunze** and **Silvester Levay**, to restructure the group's style and take them in a different direction. What they've come up with on "Madhouse" (Midland International) is certainly interesting but rarely inspired; its departure from the group's established ecstatic sound isn't strong enough to take the listener along on what seems to be an unsteady new course, so the tendency is to fall back on the few cuts that cling to the old style without any of the new pretensions to deeper meaning. The best of these is "Dancing In The Aisles" ("of a 747") which takes the fine image of its title and gives it life with a spirited production. "Everybody's Talking 'Bout love," once a truly inane vocal introduction is dispensed with, is also pleasant, as is "Midnight Lady." But even if this is something of a disappointment for the disco crowd, "Madhouse" grows on you as an at-home listening album – Levay and Kunze still have a delicate, highly polished production style and their concept is technically sharp – and deserves attention on that level.

Speaking of mood records, pick up on "Hotmosphere" by **Dom Um Romao** (Pablo, through RCA), an exciting, varied collection of cuts by this Brazilian percussionist that is one of the more vibrant Brazilian jazz records to come out this year. ◗

"Practically all the interesting records this week are on disco discs"

BOOMBAMAKAOO, NEW YORK
DJ: Jorge Wheeler

ANOTHER STAR – Stevie Wonder (Tamla)
DON'T WALK AWAY – General Johnson (Arista)
DOWN TO LOVE TOWN – Originals (Motown)
GOIN' UP IN SMOKE/THANKS FOR THE MEMORIES/MUSIC MAN – Eddie Kendricks (Tamla)
I BELIEVE IN LOVE – Rock Gazers (Sixth Avenue)
LIKE HER! – Gentlemen & Their Lady (Roulette)
MESSAGE IN OUR MUSIC – O'Jays (Phila. Intl.)
SPRING AFFAIR/SUMMER FEVER – Donna Summer (Casablanca)
WHEN LOVE IS NEW – Arthur Prysock (Old Town)
YOU'RE MY DRIVING WHEEL – Supremes (Motown)

PIPPINS, NEW YORK
DJ: The Reggie T Experience

ANOTHER STAR/I WISH – Stevie Wonder (Tamla)
BIYO – Earth, Wind & Fire (Columbia)
CAR WASH – Rose Royce (MCA)
DANCIN'/MUSIC IS THE WORLD – Crown Heights Affair (De-Lite)
GOIN' UP IN SMOKE/MUSIC MAN – Eddie Kendricks (Tamla)
I DON'T WANNA LOSE YOUR LOVE – Emotions (Columbia)
SPRING AFFAIR/SUMMER FEVER – Donna Summer (Casablanca)
WELCOME TO OUR WORLD/I LIKE TO DANCE – Mass Production (Cotillion)
WHITE WIND – Black Ivory (Buddah)
YOU'LL NEVER FIND ANOTHER LOVE LIKE MINE – Stanley Turrentine (Fantasy)

TRAMP'S, WASHINGTON, D.C.
DJ: Linda Schaefer

CAR WASH – Rose Royce (MCA)
CHERCHEZ LA FEMME/SOUR AND SWEET – Savannah Band (RCA)
DAYLIGHT/SHOULD I STAY/I WON'T LET YOU GO – Vicki Sue Robinson (RCA)
DOWN TO LOVE TOWN – Originals (Motown)
I DON'T WANNA LOSE YOUR LOVE – Emotions (Columbia)
IT'S GOOD FOR THE SOUL/DON'T BEAT AROUND THE BUSH/RITZY MAMBO – Salsoul Orchestra (Salsoul)
MIDNIGHT NIGHT AFFAIR – Carol Douglas (Midland Intl.)
MY SWEET SUMMER SUITE – Love Unlimited Orchestra (20th Century)
SPRING AFFAIR/SUMMER FEVER – Donna Summer (Casablanca)
YOU + ME= LOVE – Undisputed Truth (Whitfield)

END UP, SAN FRANCISCO
DJ: Tom Junell

CHERCHEZ LA FEMME/SOUR AND SWEET/ I'LL PLAY THE FOOL – Savannah Band (RCA)
DOWN TO LOVE TOWN – Originals (Motown)
FULL TIME THING – Whirlwind (Roulette)
GOIN' UP IN SMOKE – Eddie Kendricks (Tamla)
I WISH – Stevie Wonder (Tamla)
MAKES YOU BLIND – Glitter Band (Arista)
MIDNIGHT LOVE AFFAIR – Carol Douglas (Midland Intl.)
SHOULD I STAY/I WON'T LET YOU GO – Vicki Sue Robinson (RCA)
SPRING AFFAIR – Donna Summer (Casablanca)
YOU + ME = LOVE – Undisputed Truth (Whitfield)

OT-12450
12-450-1
STEREO

SIDE 1
Time: 7:13
45 RPM

WHEN LOVE IS NEW
(K. Gamble, L. Huff)
ARTHUR PRYSOCK
MUSIC: JOHN DAVIS & MONSTER ORCHESTRA
Publisher: Mighty Three Music BMI
EXECUTIVE PRODUCER: SAM WEISS
ARRANGED, PRODUCED AND CONDUCTED BY
JOHN DAVIS (COURTESY SAM RECORDS)
℗ 1976 OLD TOWN RECORD CORP.
MFG. BY OLD TOWN RECORD CORP., N.Y.C., N.Y.

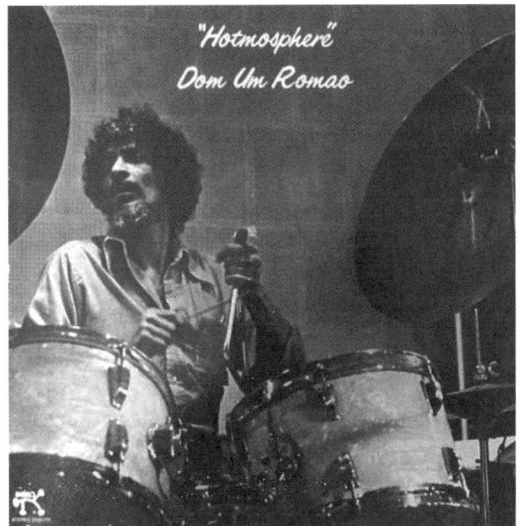

"Hotmosphere"
Dom Um Romao

A flash flood of new releases this week. Beginning with the albums, here's a quick rundown of the very best. **El Coco's** latest, titled "Let's Get It Together" (AVI), is the group's most diverse collection so far. The title cut, already a major success as a disco disc, remains the most compelling track on the album, its one flawless, memorable instrumental. "Fait Le Chat," its companion cut on the disco disc, has a similar European feel, but the other tracks are in a wide range of styles, from the hard-edged vocal drive of the message song "Under Construction" to the Memphis-meets-Neuva York pump of an instrumental called "Put On Your Jeans." Also notable: the zippy electronic backbone of "Love Vaccine" and two instrumental remakes, a haunting, lost-in-the-jungle "Quiet Village' and a nice twist on **Mancini's** "Mr. Lucky"... **The Blackbyrds** are back exactly a year after "City Life" with one of their strongest albums – not one ho-hum cut – in "Unfinished Business" (Fantasy). There are four powerful numbers: the title cut, a tight instrumental with "Gut Level" overtones; "Time Is Movin'," a song reminiscent of the **Mizells'** work, one that manages to jump and glide at the same time; an even smoother knockout, "Enter In;" and a lively, brassy change-of-pace with a female lead vocal and flashy funk styling, "Party Land." All are four or five minutes plus; Donald Byrd produced... One of the hottest new cuts this week is from the first **Thelma Houston** album in several years, "Any Way You Like It" (Tamla), and it's a version of the **Gamble-Huff** song for **Harold Melvin & the Bluenotes**, "Don't Leave Me This Way." The song is given a more upbeat treatment here, with a bass and drum underpinning right out of "Love Hangover" (Hal Davis produced both songs) and Houston's healthy vocals; it runs over five minutes. "Don't Leave Me" is framed by two other tracks that deserve attention: "Any Way You Like It" (6:13), unevenly paced but involving, and an update of **Stevie Wonder's** "Don't Know Why I Love You" (5:04) which also has a "Love Hangover" feel to it here. Already receiving strongly favorable feedback, "Don't Leave Me This Way" is on Carl Uruski's top 10 this week from the Rubaiyat in Ann Arbor.

MORE, MORE, MORE: **Boney M.** is the most bizarre German import in some time, possibly because they take the familiar elements of the Teutonic disco sound – the bass thump; crystal-clear, crisp production; clean sweeps of strings; ethereal vocal choruses – and recombine them in a fresh way. Not that there aren't moments when one is reminded – sometimes hit over the head – with flashes of **Donna Summer** or **Silver Convention** or **Penny Mclean**, but the overall feeling is something new and interesting. To build interest in the record, this one was made available to a number of people as an import on the Hansa label and several cuts are already catching on: a tough version of "Fever," a four-minute "Sunny" that goes Yambu one better, and "Take The Heat Off Me" in addition to the single, "Daddy Cool." But on the just-out Atco pressing, there's a track not included on the import lp and it's the one most likely to catch on big. It's called "Help, Help," runs six minutes, and is essentially an instrumental with girls singing the title over and over as the one guy in the group talks a few verses in a rumbling, cartoon sexy voice. The high point: a fine break. The German cover, featuring the three girls in a heap of long limbs and lingerie, has been retained for the American release and could be a key selling point... Producer **Jeff Lane** is apparently trying something new with the second **Brass Construction** album, "Brass Construction II" on UA, and the results are not as consistent or thrilling as the debut lp. Lane's combination of strings and brass is still unbeatable, especially on "Screwed," an early favorite, "Now Is Tomorrow" and "Get To The Point." "Ha Cha Cha," which opens up the set, is also hot, particularly the vocal segments, but I don't know what to make of the abrupt break in the center; I suspect it'll grow on me. All cuts listed are in three-four-to-five minute range and should be enough to make this a heavyweight contender in spite of our first-impression reservations... One of the mose eagerly awaited projects of the year, the **Gamble & Huff** production of **The Jacksons** (Epic/Philadelphia Internationai), is a fine, well-balanced album and Michael has never sounded better, but it's without a major disco cut. Of course there's "Enjoy Yourself," already released as a single and getting some disco play (Wes Bradley has it on his top 10 from the Mind Shaft in San Francisco this week), and there are two quite respectable new cuts: "Think Happy" which is fun but flimsy (especially considering the messages G&H are capable of elsewhere) and "Keep On Dancing," a song that changes pace about halfway through (like "I Am Love" or "Love Hangover") and is

> **❝ Boney M. is the most bizarre German import in some time; they take the Teutonic disco sound – the bass thump; crystal-clear, crisp production; clean sweeps of strings; ethereal vocal choruses – and recombine them in a fresh way ❞**

12 WEST, NEW YORK
DJ: Jimmy Stuard

ANOTHER STAR/AS/I WISH – Stevie Wonder (Tamla)
CALYPSO BREAKDOWN – Ralph MacDonald (Marlin)
I DON'T WANNA LOSE YOUR LOVE – Emotions (Columbia)
IT'S GOOD FOR THE SOUL/STANDING AND WAITING ON LOVE/RITZY MAMBO/NICE 'N' NAASTY – Salsoul Orchestra (Salsoul
LOVE I NEVER KNEW YOU COULD FEEL SO GOOD/LET YOURSELF GO/YOU'RE MY DRIVING WHEEL – Supremes (Motown)
MIDNIGHT LOVE AFFAIR – Carol Douglas (Midland Intl.)
MY LOVE IS FREE – Double Exposure (Salsoul)
SOUL CHA CHA/RHYTHMS OF THE WORLD/INDIAN WARPATH – Van McCoy (H&L)
SPRING AFFAIR/SUMMER FEVER/ AUTUMN CHANGES – Donna Summer (Casablanca)
YOU + ME = LOVE – Undisputed Truth (Whitfield)

RUBAIYAT, ANN ARBOR, MICHIGAN
DJ: Carl Uruski

ANOTHER STAR/SIR DUKE – Stevie Wonder (Tamla)
CALYPSO BREAKDOWN – Ralph MacDonald (Marlin)
DANCIN'/SEARCHING FOR LOVE – Crown Heights Affair (De-Lite)
DON'T LEAVE ME THIS WAY – Thelma Houston (Motown)
DOWN TO LOVE TOWN – Originals (Motown)
DREAMIN' – Loleatta Holloway (Gold Mind)
FREEDOM TO EXPRESS YOURSELF – Denise LaSalle (ABC)
HA CHA CHA – Brass Construction (UA)
SPRING AFFAIR/SUMMER FEVER – Donna Summer (Casablanca)
YOU + ME = LOVE – Undisputed Truth (Whitfield)

MIND SHAFT, SAN FRANCISCO
DJ: Wes Bradley

ANOTHER STAR/I WISH/SIR DUKE – Stevie Wonder (Tamla)
ENJOY YOURSELF – The Jacksons (Epic/Phila. Intl.)
MAKES YOU BLIND – Glitter Band (Arista)
NIGHT PEOPLE/LIVES DIVIDED BY JIVE – Fantastic Four (Westbound)
SHOULD I STAY/I WON'T LET YOU GO/ DAYLIGHT/HOW ABOUT ME – Vicki Sue Robinson (RCA)
TAKE THE HEAT OFF ME/HELP, HELP – Boney M. (Atco)
THAT'S THE TROUBLE – Grace Jones (Beam Junction)
WELCOME TO OUR WORLD – Mass Production (Cotillion)
WHEN LOVE IS NEW – Arthur Prysock (Old Town)
YOU GOTTA LET ME SHOW YOU – Esther Williams (Friends & Co.)

1270, BOSTON
DJ: Danae Jacovidis

ANOTHER STAR/BLACK MAN – Stevie Wonder (Tamla)
CALYPSO BREAKDOWN – Ralph MacDonald (Marlin)
I DON'T WANNA LOSE YOUR LOVE – Emotions (Columbia)
LET'S GET IT TOGETHER – El Coco (AVI)
MIDNIGHT LOVE AFFAIR – Carol Douglas (Midland Intl.)
MY SWEET SUMMER SUITE – Love Unlimited Orchestra (20th Century)
MY LOVE IS FREE – Double Exposure (Salsoul)
SOUL CHA CHA/SWAHILI BOOGIE – Van McCoy (H&L)
SPRING AFFAIR/SUMMER FEVER – Donna Summer (Casablanca)
YOU + ME = LOVE – Undisputed Truth (Whitfield)

perfect get-on-up material but far from the inspiration one would expect from this collaboration of talents. A saving grace: the end of "Strength Of One Man," one of the best cuts here, and brilliant slow cuts like "Good Times" and "Dreamer"... **Bunny Sigler** produced the album of a trio called **Instant Funk** ("Get Down With The Philly Jump" on TSOP) so this one's more idiosyncratic and enjoyable than a lot of Philadelphia soul, but also harder to get a comfortable grip on. I'm a big fan of "Philly Jump," the pulsing, involving single that is included here in a 5:10 version, and several other cuts have a similar attraction: "It Ain't Reggae (But It's Funky)," appropriately titled; "I Know Where You're Coming From," "Funky Africa" and "Hup Two, Hup Two (Get In Line, Say Get In Line)," a militaristic but delightful line dance song. All are in a sharp jazz/funk style, more instrumental than vocal. This is a personal favorite right now.

RECOMMENDED DISCO DISCS: Roxbury is bringing out the original English version of "Dream Express" by the **Honeybees** this week, joining competition with a version by a group called **Lady Rose** on Strawberry Records (1271 Sixth Avenue, New York), which has been out several weeks now. The Honeybees original (5:42) is the better of the two – stronger vocals, more punch, more unusual breaks – but Lady Rose (4:40) has its moments, too, although its smooth style approaches the homogenized... An excellent import 12-inch comes from RCA Canada this week – "Fighting On The Side of Love" by **T.H.P. Orchestra** is a solid message song (could have been done by the **Trammps**) with a full, driving production that sounds especially hot on the instrumental side (both are 6:34). Both sides are very strong and the lead vocals have a **Boz Scaggs** edge. Worth searching for... Left Field: a strange, drum-based instrumental called "Sessomatto" by **Sesso Matto**, the first disco pressing from West End, the label Mel Cheren (ex Scepter/Wand) recently formed. The song, from the soundtrack of the Italian farce, "How Funny Can Sex Be?" is available in 7:23 and 10:00 versions, both of which seem entirely too long, disco-mixed by Jimmy Stuard (who reports from 12 West this week). Although there is a strong debt here to "Soul Makossa," other parts of the song have a light **Nino Rota** touch; an odd combination, made slightly more credible as disco by the Latin percussion breaks, but better for early evening atmosphere.

ONE TERRIFIC SINGLE: The B side of **Loleatta Holloway's** first single for **Norman Harris** Gold Mind label is a fabulous **Baker, Harris & Young** production on a song called "Dreamin'." Holloway has a voice that could topple buildings and the production has the classic sound of **Ecstasy, Passion & Pain** or **First Choice**. Even at just over three minutes – which is, I believe, half the length of the album version – this is overwhelming (and the 45's A side, a steamy torchy version of "Worn Out Broken Heart," is a great ballad). Pick of the week. ✪

NOVEMBER 27, 1976

Everyone's talking this week about the difficulties of dealing with the influx of so many great new records, but no one's really complaining. Here's another batch of quality releases, beginning with several excellent disco discs. **Odia Coates and Paul Anka's** duet, "Make It Up To Me In Love" (Epic), has one of the most attractive, instantly irresistible opening instrumental passages of the year, a fitting introduction to a fine, beautifully sung Anka composition with a production that already sounds like a classic; at 5:35, it manages to feel fuller and deeper than most records twice that long. A sure hit, **The Tony Valor Sounds Orchestra** has a two-sided disc on Brunswick, the first 12-inch I've seen from that label. The essential side is "Gotta Get It," a long (7:36), hard-thumping instrumental with a terrific use of strings and standout guitar and flute riffs; flip side is an equally strong but much prettier song called "Girl" (5:01). Both are extended versions of cuts on Valor's new album, "Gotta Get It," which also contains his previous hit, "MA-MO-AH." **Greg Carmichael** and **Patrick Adams**, who've produced and written some of the most intriguing records of the past year, have come up with what sounds like their most commercial release in "Dance And Shake Your Tambourine" by the **Universal Robot Band** (where do they get these names?) on Carmichael's Red Greg label (3211 Paulding Avenue, Bronx 10469). Like their other records ('Love Bug," "Making Love"), this one is full of their trademark electronic squeals, the synthesizer darting playfully in and out of the rest of the instruments, teasing the singers while they chant the title or "Paaarty! Paaarty!" One side of this disco pressing is 6:26, the other 4:17, the latter length also available on a standard single. Within the coming week Salsoul will be bringing out a Double Exposure 12-inch featuring an exciting new mix of their best lp cut, "My Love Is Free," expanded from seven minutes to 9:36, lengthening the introduction and the break and making the song twice as powerful. The very few people who have advance copies are putting it on their top 10 lists already so look for this cut to make a big comeback. Scheduled for the other side of the Double Exposure disc: their version, of "Baby I Need Your Loving." I suppose we should note that, with the exception of the Universal Robot Band's, all the above records are Tom Moulton Mixes.

Other notable disco discs: **Blood Hollins'** instrumental version of his composition, "Don't Give It Up" (Strange Fruit, 101 Marrietta St., Atlanta 30303) which, at 9:28, has plenty of time to build into something quite interesting and absorbing after an awfully busy beginning. Try the vocal side, too, though the voices aren't as good as the lyrics: Hollins also produced... "Elevator" (5:27) by **Joanne Spain** (Casino, through GRT in Nashville) is one of those frothy, nasty girl vocals with minimal lyrics repeated over and over (the refrain: "Get it up, get it up/Higher, higher"), but it's really kind of pert and cute. Cosmo Wyatt from Yesterdays in Boston likes it so much he put it on his top 10 this week... **Stratavarious & Lady's** "Let Me Be Your Lady Tonight" doesn't have the incredible drive of "I Got Your Love," but it does have enough of that record's striking originality and unexpected moments (here it's a lovely harp solo) to get a lot of attention and play. Produced by **Johnny Usry**, the record's both compelling and off-beat; the instrumental B side is called "Love Me" and runs an identical 9:33. Right now it's an import from Polydor in Canada, sold in one of those colorful new disco sleeves, and Roulette hasn't yet set a date for its American release.

Now available in 12-inch discs: "Welcome to Our World" and "Wine-Flow Disco" by **Mass Production** back-to-back on Atlantic; **Bumblebee Unlimited's** "Love Bug" on Mercury; "Calypso Breakdown" and a longer (6:41) version of "Where Is The Love" by **Ralph MacDonald** (TK Disco); **Eddie Kendricks'** "Goin' Up In Smoke" (Tamla); a longer mix (5:13) of **Johnny Bristol's** "Do It To My Mind" (Atlantic) done by Ronald Coles; **Herbie Hancock's** "Doin' It" and **Wah Wah Watson's** bursting-with-energy "Together (Whatever)" – both hot jazz cuts – on one Columbia 12-inch.

RECOMMENDED ALBUMS: **D. C. LaRue's** "Tea Dance" (Pyramid) deserves a lot more space than we can give to it here – if it doesn't have a track as spectacular as "Cathedrals," it's a more complex, ambitious and satisfying album than his first, the kind of intelligent, dense album that merits more thorough examination than a quick listing of its disco cuts, but here goes: "Overture" (5:05), the most immediate turn-on, basically a fine chugging instrumental; "Indiscreet" (the longest cut at just over seven minutes), which asks, "Do you get what you pray for? /Or do you get what you pay for?"; "Don't Keep It in the Shadows" (5:41), with alternating falsetto and natural vocals and some

> ❝ I suppose we should note that, with the exception of the Universal Robot Band's, all the above records are Tom Moulton Mixes ❞

DCA CLUB, PHILADELPHIA
DJ: Kurt Borusiewicz

DANCIN' – Crown Heights Affair (De-Lite)
DOWN TO LOVE TOWN – Originals (Motown)
I'M YOUR BOOGIE MAN/KEEP IT COMIN' LOVE – KC & the Sunshine Band (TK)
NO, NO, NO MY FRIEND – Devoshun (SMI)
SHOULD I STAY/I WON'T LET YOU GO – Vicki Sue Robinson (RCA)
SPRING AFFAIR/SUMMER FEVER/AUTUMN CHANGES – Donna Summer (Casablanca)
STUBBORN KIND OF FELLA – Buffalo Smoke (RCA)
THAT'S THE TROUBLE – Grace Jones (Beam Junction)
WHEN LOVE IS NEW – Arthur Prysock (Old Town)
YOU KEEP ME HANGIN' ON/STOP! IN THE NAME OF LOVE – Roni Hill (Hot Foot import)

JOUISSANCE, NEW YORK
DJ: David Todd

CALYPSO BREAKDOWN – Ralph MacDonald (Marlin)
CAR WASH – Rose Royce (MCA)
DOWN TO LOVE TOWN – Originals (Motown)
I DON'T WANNA LOSE YOUR LOVE – Emotions (Columbia)
MY LOVE IS FREE – Double Exposure (Salsoul)
OPEN SESAME (PARTS 1 & 2) – Kool & The Gang (De-Lite)
SOUL CHA CHA/SWAHILI BOOGIE – Van McCoy (H&L)
SPIDER'S WEBB – Spiders Webb (Fantasy)
SPRING AFFAIR/SUMMER FEVER – Donna Summer (Casablanca)
STUBBORN KIND OF FELLOW – Buffalo Smoke (RCA)

BAREFOOT BOY, NEW YORK
DJ: Tony Smith

ANOTHER STAR/SIR DUKE – Stevie Wonder (Tamla)
FASCINATION/CENTER CITY/MUSIC MAKER – Fat Larry's Band (WMOT)
FEVER/HELP, HELP – Boney M. (Atco)
IT AIN'T REGGAE (BUT IT'S FUNKY) – Instant Funk (TSOP)
LET YOURSELF GO/COME INTO MY LIFE/ YOU'RE MY DRIVING WHEEL – Supremes (Motown)
OVERTURE/ INDISCREET O BA BA – D. C. LaRue (Pyramid)
PAZUZU – Tony Silvester and the New Ingredient (Mercury)
TRIED, TESTED AND FOUND TRUE – Ashford & Simpson (Warner Bros.)
24 HOURS A DAY – Barbara Pennington (UA import)
WELCOME TO OUR WORLD – Mass Production (Cotillion)

YESTERDAYS, BOSTON
DJ: Cosmo Wyatt

ELEVATOR – Joanne Spain (Casino)
GIFT WRAP MY LOVE – Reflections (Capitol)
GOIN' UP IN SMOKE/THANKS FOR THE MEMORIES – Eddie Kendricks (Tamla)
MAKES YOU BLIND – Glitter Band (Arista)
MIDNIGHT LOVE AFFAIR – Carol Douglas (Midland Intl.)
OPEN SESAME (PARTS 1 & 2) – Kool & the Gang (De-Lite)
SHOULD I STAY/I WON'T LET YOU GO/ HOW ABOUT ME – Vicki Sue Robinson (RCA)
SPRING AFFAIR – Donna Summer (Casablanca)
WELCOME TO OUR WORLD/WINE-FLOW – Mass Production (Cotillion)
YOU KEEP ME HANGING ON/MY GIRL – David Matthews (Kudu)

of the lp's best lyrics; and a delightful, exuberant "O Ba Ba" (5:06) inspired by a Brazilian carnival chant and just as infectious. "Tea Dance" itself is a six-minute mini-opera with outrageously effective production gimmicks (like an orchestrated "skip" in the record). Credit **Aram Schefrin** and D.C. himself for the production… The off-the-wall cut of the season is "Anambra" by a group called **OZO** (DJM Records, through Amherst in Buffalo), a mysterious song that starts with temple/church bells and turns into what sounds like a Gregorian chant over a steady, heavy drumbeat sparked by Latin percussion. It has an utterly hypnotic, almost religious quality (Tom Savarese called it a Christmas record and it does feel like a joyful hymn and runs 6:17 without losing you. "Anambra" is from an album OZO recorded in London called "Listen To The Buddha" – do listen… **Melba Moore's** second album with **Van McCoy** as writer-producer ("Melba" on Buddah) is as full of danceable cuts as the last one but the one that should get the strongest response is a longtrack (7:32) called· "Good Love Makes Everything Alright," a real beauty in the best McCoy high-spirited style. "The Way You Make Me Feel" sounds very much like "Free," a personal favorite from the last lp; "The Greatest Feeling," "I Need Someone" and "Ain't No Love Lost" are also good. A solid album if a bit too safe.

RECOMMENDED SINGLES: "Cream Of The Crop," **Sister Sledge's** latest on Cotillion, is a real change of pace for the group, produced by **Bobby Eli** in a style that sounds a lot like top form **Three Degrees** – I'd like to hear more of the same… **Ronnie LaShannon's** "Where Has Our Love Gone" (Brunswick) is really **Tony Valor's** "Girl" (see above) with okay male vocals but the production (4:35 here) is worth hearing again… "Easy To Love" (3:35 on Spring) ties one of **Joe Simon's** richer vocals into a sharp, building production that should get a lot of attention after his recent success with "I Need You, You Need Me." **The Reflections'** "Gift Wrap My Love" (Capitol) is their first in a while but they've sprung back very strong, sounding like a gospel group (Cosmo Wyatt, who also put this one on his top 10 this week, compared them to the **Mighty Clouds of Joy**) and carrying on… "Classically Elise" by **Dina Solera and the Munich Machine** and produced by **Giorgio Moroder** (the Giorgio) in his unmistakable style, is a disco interpretation of a familiar **Beethoven** composition that sounds like it was made for **Donna Summer** to ooze over. It's in two parts (3:33 and 2:51) and the label, Hidden Sign, part of Audiofidelity Enterprises in New York, reportedly has a deal with Moroder's Say Yes Productions for additional productions. ◐

DECEMBER 4, 1976

In an effort to catch up with the pre-Christmas surge of album releases, here's a quick list of recent lps that, for the most part, have already been well-received in the discos though only a few have seriously won this particular listener over. Starting with the strongest, they are: "Where Will You Go When The Party's Over" (an ominous question in the disco business) is the title of the new **Archie Bell & the Drells**, album (on Philadelphia International) and, while it doesn't quite have the immediate impact of the group's previous lp, Bell does have irresistibly spirited moments –"Everybody Have A Good Time" is the longest (6:15), best production (by **Bunny Sigler**); "Nothing Comes Easy," the single, sounds better here; and both "Dancin' Man" and the title track are fine …"You Name It" (Motown) presents the **Dynamic Superiors** in their established frantic falsetto style on a number of long tracks – check out "Stay Away" (5:39), a **Hal Davis** production, in particular, and "I Can't Stay Away" and "Looking Away" (do you detect an odd pattern here?)... **Side Effect's** "Always There" was one of the year's best songs primarily because of the gutsy vocals of the group's female lead singer, a combination of **Mavis Staples** and **Gladys Knight** – how disappointing, then, that their latest album, opening up with "Always There," contains nothing else as strong in that particular vein. "What You Need" (Fantasy) does have an interesting cut in a mellower mood, though: "Keep That Same Old Feeling"... **Spiders Webb** was produced by **Jeff Lane** (**B. T. Express, Brass Construction, Mark Radice**) so the tracks sound great but the vocals and lyrics on "I Don't Know What's On Your Mind" (Fantasy) leave something to be desired; "I've Learned From My Burns" is getting the most play, followed by the title cut and "Spider's Webb," which is mostly instrumental... **Fat Larry's Band** ("Feel It" on WMOT was produced by **Vince Montana** but he, too, can only go so far with lackluster lyrics and vocals from this group which usually backs up **Blue Magic**; "Center City" is the best here but the lyrics drag it down – try "Music Maker" or their version of "Fascination" (aka "Funky Music Is A Part Of Me"), the **Luther/David Bowie** song … **Jumbo** is a German group and its first American release, "Turn On To Love" (Pye), has a 17-minute cut (the title song) that is, not surprisingly, in the **Donna Summer/Giorgio** vein: sexy vocals (male), many breaks, frequent moaning and sighing (female). Altogether it's not bad, with some fine moments in the production. "Sexy Lady," also included here, had some success as a single last year... **Esther Phillips'** "Capricorn Princess"(Kudu) is a varied collection produced by **Creed Taylor** whose best cut, "Boy, I Really Tied One On," a bitter, biting morning-after song, is already getting top 10 listings; much of the rest is typically uneven: a version of **Ronnie Walker's** "Magic's In The Air" that cuts the pace of the original, leaving it limp; **Johnny Mercer's** "Dream" goes to the other extreme, speeding up impossibly; "Higher & Higher" is the same old song with no new inspiration. The ballads are the best... **Norman Harris** produced the new **Soul Train Gang** album (Soul Train), so it's far superior to their original effort but, again, many of the best cuts are slow. That leaves two good versions of the "Soul Train Theme" (which combine to nearly ten minutes) and "Ooh Cha," the sweet single, also available on a 12-inch pressing.

FEEDBACK: Both Ron Soares from Ipanema in New York and Mitch Schatsky from Circus Maximus in Los Angeles listed "No Tears Tomorrow" from **Lonnie Smith's** "Keep on Lovin'" lp (Groove Merchant) in their top 10 lists this week. The song is a breezy instrumental with a nice kick that reminds me of upbeat **George Benson** and could catch on big... Strongest cut this week: **Thelma Houston's** "Don't Leave Me This Way," which made every top 10 list. Also strong: the albums from **Boney M.** (Atco), **The Supremes** (Motown) and **D. C. LaRue**. ◐

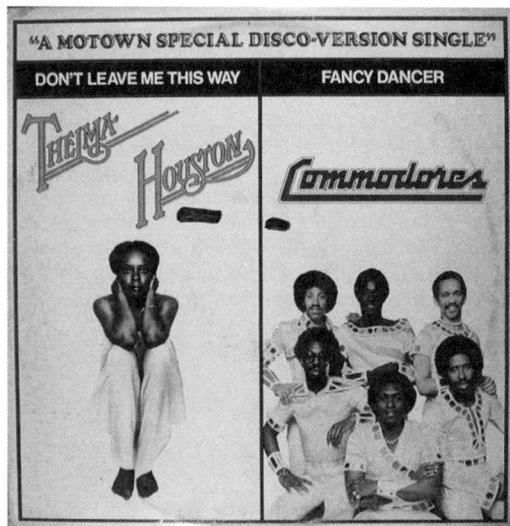

ZIEGFELD'S, WASHINGTON, D.C.
DJ: Richie Kaczor

ANOTHER STAR – Stevie Wonder (Tamla)
CALYPSO BREAKDOWN – Ralph MacDonald (Marlin)
CAR WASH – Rose Royce (MCA)
DANCIN'/SEARCHING FOR LOVE – Crown Heights Affair (De-Lite)
DON'T LEAVE ME THIS WAY – Thelma Houston (Tamla)
DOWN TO LOVE TOWN – Originals (Motown)
FOUR SEASONS OF LOVE – Donna Summer (Casablanca)
GOTTA GET IT – Tony Valor Sounds Orchestra (Brunswick)
WELCOME TO OUR WORLD – Mass Production (Cotillion)
YOU + ME = LOVE – Undisputed Truth (Whitfield)

IPANEMA, NEW YORK
DJ: Ronnie Soares

BAHIA/NEGA DO OBALUAE – Wando (Brasilia)
BOY, I REALLY TIED ONE ON/DREAM – Esther Phillips (Kudu)
DON'T LEAVE ME THIS WAY – Thelma Houston (Tamla)
DOWN TO LOVE TOWN – Originals (Motown)
MIDNIGHT LOVE AFFAIR – Carol Douglas (Midland Intl.)
NO TEARS TOMORROW – Lonnie Smith (Groove Merchant)
O BA BA/INDISCREET/DON'T KEEP IT IN THE SHADOWS – D.C. LaRue (Pyramid)
SPRING AFFAIR/SUMMER FEVER/AUTUMN CHANGES – Donna Summer (Casablanca)
TAKE THE HEAT OFF ME/SUNNY /FEVER – Boney M. (Atco)
YOU KEEP ME HANGING ON/STOP! IN THE NAME OF LOVE – Roni Hill (Hot Foot import)

CIRCUS MAXIMUS, LOS ANGELES
DJ: Mitch Schatsky

ANOTHER STAR/I WISH/SIR DUKE – Stevie Wonder (Tamla)
DADDY COOL/HELP, HELP/TAKE THE HEAT OFF ME – Boney M. (Atco)
DANCIN' /SEARCHING FOR LOVE – Crown Heights Affair (De-Lite)
DON'T LEAVE ME THIS WAY – Thelma Houston (Tamla)
LOVE BUG – Bumblebee Unlimited (Mercury)
LOVE IS STILL BLUE – Paul Mauriat (Free Spirit)
MAKES YOU BLIND – Glitter Band (Arista)
NO TEARS TOMORROW – Lonnie Smith (Groove Merchant)
WELCOME TO OUR WORLD/WINE-FLOW DISCO – Mass Production (Cotillion)
WHEN LOVE IS NEW – Arthur Prysock (Old Town)

CASBAH , ATLANTA
DJ: Jim Burgess

ANOTHER STAR/I WISH – Stevie Wonder (Tamla)
DON'T LEAVE ME THIS WAY – Thelma Houston (Tamla)
DOWN TO LOVE TOWN – Originals (Motown)
DREAMIN' – Loleatta Holloway (Gold Mind)
HELP, HELP/SUNNY /FEVER – Boney M. (Atco)
LET YOURSELF GO/YOU'RE DRIVING MY WHEEL/LOVE I NEVER KNEW YOU COULD FEEL SO GOOD – Supremes (Motown)
SPRING AFFAIR/SUMMER FEVER/AUTUMN CHANGES – Donna Summer (Casablanca)
THAT'S THE TROUBLE/SORRY – Grace Jones (Beam Junction)
WELCOME TO OUR WORLD – Mass Production (Cotillion)
WHEN LOVE IS NEW – Arthur Prysock- (Old Town)

DISCO FILE TOP 20

1. **SPRING AFFAIR/SUMMER FEVER** – Donna Summer (Casablanca)
2. **ANOTHER STAR** – Stevie Wonder (Tamla)
3. **WELCOME TO OUR WORLD** – Mass Production (Cotillion)
4. **DOWN TO LOVE TOWN** – Originals (Motown)
5. **DANCIN'/SEARCHING FOR LOVE** – Crown Heights Affair (De-Lite)
6. **WHEN LOVE IS NEW** – Arthur Prysock (Old Town)
7. **CALYPSO BREAKDOWN** – Ralph MacDonald (Marlin)
8. **SIR DUKE/I WISH** – Stevie Wonder (Tamla)
9. **YOU + ME = LOVE** – Undisputed Truth (Whitfield)
10. **DON'T LEAVE ME THIS WAY** – Thelma Houston (Tamla)
11. **MAKES YOU BLIND** – Glitter Band (Bell import)
12. **MIDNIGHT LOVE AFFAIR** – Carol Douglas (Midland Intl.)
13. **THAT'S THE TROUBLE/SORRY** – Grace Jones (Beam Junction)
14. **TAKE THE HEAT OFF ME/HELP,HELP/FEVER/ SUNNY** – Boney M. (Atco)
15. **SHOULD I STAY/I WON'T LET YOU GO** – Vicki Sue Robinson (RCA)
16. **LET YOURSELF GO/YOU'RE DRIVING MY WHEEL** – Supremes (Motown)
17. **GOIN' UP IN SMOKE/THANKS FOR THE MEMORIES** – Eddie Kendricks (Tamla)
18. **CAR WASH** – Rose Royce (MCA)
19. **I DON'T WANNA LOSE YOUR LOVE** – Emotions (Columbia)
20. **STUBBORN KIND OF FELLA** – Buffalo Smoke (RCA)

❝ The title song is,a 17-minute cut, not surprisingly in the Donna Summer vein: sexy vocals (male), many breaks, frequent moaning and sighing (female)❞

DECEMBER 11, 1976

" Nearly all the new 12-inch releases are remixes or longer versions of previously available singles or album cuts and now they all deserve a second listen "

Now that the great tidal wave of pre-Christmas releases has broken, we're easing into the December lull, a period of calm before the storm of new releases that begins building up again in January. A good time to go back and pick up on some records that were lost in the shuffle during the last few months (suggestions: "Catfish" by the **Four Tops**, **Devoshun's** "No, No, No, My Friend," "Saturday Night Stepping Out" by **Webster Lewis**, "Que Pasa" by the **Final Approach**, "Anything" by **Touch of Class** and **Instant Funk's** "It Ain't Reggae [But It's Funky]") and a number of the best disco discs out this week should put everyone in the proper spirit for a re-examination of the recent past. That's because nearly all the new 12-inch releases are remixes or longer versions of previously available singles or album cuts and now they all deserve a second listen. **John Davis** and the **Monster Orchestra** have lengthened the best cut on their last album, "I Can't Stop," until it runs just over seven minutes and sounds suddenly ten times better. Another two minutes have been added to the group's fine version of **Cole Porter's** "I Get A Kick" (now 5 :25) and this too should fare better than it did the first time out when we were all too tired of disco remakes to appreciate a good one. "I Can't Stop" and "I Get A Kick" are back-to-back on a 12-inch from Sam Records. De-Lite and **Kool & the Gang** have come out with a "Special Disco Version" of their knockout, "Open Sesame," combining parts 1 and 2 of the single to a length of 8:48 that is steaming hot and not available on the album; on the flip side: the full 7:53 length of "Love & Understanding" from the group's previous album. We've already raved about the new mix of **Double Exposure's** "My Love Is Free," which brings this cut shooting close to the heights reached by "Ten Percent," but now that it's out, we discover Salsoul has changed its mind about the disco disc's B side. Instead of another Double Exposure cut, they've given us a new version of the **Salsoul Orchestra's** "It Don't Have To Be

RED GREG
RECORDS

RG - 210 DISCO
Sug - Sug Music
(ASCAP)
P. A. P.
(ASCAP)
TIME: 6:26
45 RPM

SIDE 2
STEREO
℗1976
Master No:
RG - 210
Arranged by:
P. Adams

DANCE AND SHAKE YOUR TAMBOURINE
Universal Robot Band

Produced by: P. Adams and G. Carmichael
Red Greg Enterprises Inc.
3211 Paulding Ave.
Bronx, N.Y. 10469.

BANG
RECORDS

B-727 DISCO
(W-10386-S12)
SILVER CLOUD
MUSIC/TROLLEY
MUSIC (ASCAP)
TIME: 5:35

12" 45 RPM

FROM BRICK'S LP
"GOOD HIGH"

DAZZ
(R. Ransom, R. Hargis, E. Irons)
BRICK

PRODUCERS:
JIM HEALY, JOHNNY DUNCAN, ROBERT E. LEE,
AND BRICK FOR BRICKHOUSE PRODUCTIONS

℗1976 Bang Records

Div of Web IV Music Inc., 2107 Faulkner Rd., N.E., Atlanta, Ga.

BETTER DAYS, NEW YORK
DJ: Toraino "Tee" Scott

ANOTHER STAR/I WISH/AS – Stevie Wonder (Tamla)
CAR WASH – Rose Royce (MCA)
DANCE AND SHAKE YOUR TAMBOURINE – Universal Robot Band (Red Greg)
DON'T LEAVE ME THIS WAY/DON'T KNOW WHY I LOVE YOU – Thelma Houston (Tamla)
I'VE LEARNED FROM MY BURNS – Spiders Webb (Fantasy)
OPEN SESAME – Kool & the Gang (De-Lite disco disc)
OVERTURE – D.C. LaRue (Pyramid)
STUBBORN KIND OF FELLA – Buffalo Smoke (RCA)
UNDER CONSTRUCTION – El Coco (AVI)
YOU'RE MY DRIVING WHEEL/LET YOURSELF GO – Supremes (Motown)

THE FOX TRAPPE, WASHINGTON, D.C.
DJ: Frank Edwards

CALYPSO BREAKDOWN – Ralph MacDonald (Marlin)
CAR WASH – Rose Royce (MCA)
DAZZ – Brick (Bang)
DON'T LEAVE ME THIS WAY – Thelma Houston (Tamla)
DOWN TO LOVE TOWN – Originals (Motown)
FOUR SEASONS OF LOVE – Donna Summer (Casablanca)
GOTTA GET IT – Tony Valor Sounds Orchestra (Brunswick)
I WISH – Stevie Wonder (Tamla)
UNFINISHED BUSINESS – Blackbyrds (Fantasy)
WELCOME TO OUR WORLD – Mass Production (Cotillion)

DANCE YOUR ASS OFF, SAN FRANCISCO
DJ: Pete Struve

CAR WASH – Rose Royce (MCA lp cut)
CATFISH – Four Tops (ABC lp cut)
DANCIN' – Crown Heights Affair (De-Lite lp cut)
DON'T LEAVE ME THIS WAY – Thelma Houston (Tamla)
DOWN TO LOVE TOWN – Originals (Motown)
FOUR SEASONS OF LOVE – Donna Summer (Casablanca)
I WISH/ANOTHER STAR – Stevie Wonder (Tamla)
MAKES YOU BLIND – Glitter Band (Arista)
WELCOME TO OUR WORLD – Mass Production (Cotillion)
YOU'RE MY DRIVING WHEEL/LET YOURSELF GO – Supremes (Motown)

BOOMBAMAKOO, NEW YORK
DJ: Jorge Wheeler

BRAZILIAN LOVE SONG – Love Unlimited Orchestra (20th Century)
CENTER CITY/FASCINATION – Fat Larry's Band (WMOT)
DON'T LEAVE ME THIS WAY – Thelma Houston (Tamla)
GOTTA GET IT/MA-MO-AH – Tony Valor Sounds Orchestra (Brunswick)
I CAN'T STAY AWAY – Dynamic Superiors (Motown)
LOVE I NEVER KNEW YOU COULD FEEL SO GOOD/WE SHOULD BE CLOSER TOGETHER-Supremes (Motown)
OYE ME SON/SE COMIENZA POR EL UNO – Tito Rodriguez (TR)
TAKE THE HEAT OFF ME/HELP, HELP/ LOVIN' OR LEARNIN' – Boney M. (Atco)
TURN ON TO LOVE – Jumbo (Pye)
WHEN LOVE IS NEW – Arthur Prysock (Old Town)

Funky (To Be A Groove)," expanded from 3:36 to 7:20 and given a new fullness and thrust that's very likely to spark the kind of enthusiastic interest the album cut never enjoyed. **The Reflections'** "Gift Wrap My Love" (Capitol) has been picking up a groundswell of positive feedback since its release a few weeks back – we noted its gospel fervor and **Spinners/Mighty Clouds of Joy** feel – and now it, too, is available in a longer version at 4:31 with a nice saxophone-laced break. TK has added two more titles to its disco series, both deserving of more attention than they've received as singles: **Tamiko Jones'** excellent, surging "Let It Flow" in long vocal and instrumental versions back-to-back, and **Wild Honey's** driving "At The Top Of The Stairs" which combines the two-part single version into one long (7:18) piece with a superb break (though the 12-inch is labeled Part I and Part II, both sides are the identical full length).

"Dazz" by **Brick** (Bang) is one of those out-of-nowhere records that surprised everyone by becoming a major radio crossover record and, inevitably, it's been cropping up here and there on disco playlists (Frank Edwards, who reports from a club in Washington, D.C., called the Fox Trappe, put it in his top 10 this week), but we chose to pass on it as a disco recommendation until a 12-inch pressing arrived this week. The disco disc adds two minutes to the album and single version of "Dazz" (which stands, I understand, for disco/jazz, a fairly accurate description of the record's stylistic blend) and gives the record the extra shot of an instrumental segment that could widen its popularity as a dance record, bringing it into clubs that had ignored the single. Beam Junction, the New York label that has had a great success with the sensational **Grace Jones** disco disc, has brought out another 12-inch by **Black Soul** called "Black Brother." The song has a raw, Afro-European sound (like a combination of early **Barrabas** with **Osibisa**) that's effectively highlighted by a swirling synthesizer and strong chanting. A number of varied breaks keep this one exciting for its entire 7:21 length. There's nothing else quite like this around these days and it's a sound ripe for revival. Contempo Records in England has issued a series of "Giant 45s" at least one of which will eventually be distributed here through TK's disco series. That one, now available as an import, is the new **Ultrafunk** record, "Gotham City Boogie," a chugging locomotive of an instrumental with a terrific propulsive beat and sweet string and flute accents; like **MFSB** with a funky edge. The other side is equally good it's a slightly stronger, snappier version of "Sunrise," the long atmospheric instrumental from the "Car Wash" album, an excellent choice for a remake. Other titles in the Contempo series include **Tamiko Jones'** "Let It Flow" (vocal version) backed with "Woman Of The Ghetto" by **Doris Duke**, and **Banzai's** "Chinese Kung Fu" backed with **Ernie Bush's** "Breakaway," both in their U.S.-produced re-mixed versions. Because these four tracks are already available (and some already out-of-print) in the States, they will probably remain imports only, but Ultrafunk should be out on a TK Disco pressing before the end of the year. ❧

DECEMBER 18, 1976

SOCIAL NOTES & COMMENT: I went to the opening of one of those starkly moderne private discotheques in New York last week – gray industrial carpeting, walls of mirrors, isolated tubs of flowers each lit by a single spotlight, etc. The DJ was playing a nice mix of very new records and recent standards, including a number of cuts I'd never heard outside of my apartment before (**Instant Funk's** "I Know Where You're Coming From" sounded especially stunning), and the dance floor was packed and sweating. But halfway through the evening, I began to hear people muttering about the music and one overweight man near me yelled, "Play some music, already!" Clearly, music was being played, but what this man wanted was familiar music, music he already knew. Why, I wondered, wasn't he home listening to his radio? This isn't the first time I've encountered this attitude: One night, hanging out in the booth of an after-hours club downtown, a guy came up and asked me to tell the DJ to please "play some music." Again, music was certainly being played – a heady blend of atmospheric, jungle-beat records that was building to a peak – and even as we were talking I could hear the dance floor erupt in whoops and screams. And here was this man asking for music. "Like what?" I said, and he named a record that had been popular for about two months and had been played only half an hour earlier in the night. I told him this was a discotheque, not an AM radio station, and he went back to the dance floor.

One of the most exciting things about discos, one of the keys to their vitality and power, has always been the fact that DJs were aggressively seeking out and playing new music. And the hip disco crowd went dancing where they could hear not just the records they screamed to last week and the week before, but entirely new records that they wouldn't hear anywhere else. The demand to "play some music" is basically a regressive way of saying, "play the hits," and I'm sure there are clubs that do just that, over and over, but I don't have any desire to go to them. Discos, it seems to me, should be about adventurous discovery in music, expanding and challenging the tastes of the dancers as well as playing "the hits." After all, discos are an alternative to radio – a whole new thing – not an imitation.

FASHION: Record Mirror, an English rock paper with excellent disco coverage and charts, has an article in a recent issue called "The Year of the Poly teen" with the first reports and photos we've seen of a new British style in disco dance clothes. The basic ingredient of this style is polyvinylchloride (PVC) – that thin, sturdy plastic used for garbage bags – and garbage bags are exactly what these kids are wearing: garbage bags, skirts, pants, dresses, blouses. There's one photo of a pretty girl in a knee-length black garbage bag belted at the waist, accessorized by a simple strand of pearls, black gloves and black tights: a classic look. A 17-year-old named Kathy is reported as

" That's all they can afford there now. It's not a style – it's an economy measure "

REGINES, NEW YORK
DJ: Jonata Garavaglia

BLACK BROTHER – Black Soul (Beam Junction)
CAMPESINO – Jorge Ben (CBS import)
CAR WASH – Rose Royce (MCA lp cut)
DON'T LEAVE ME THIS WAY – Thelma Houston (Tamla)
HA CHA CHA – Brass Construction (UA)
I WISH/ISN'T SHE LOVELY/AS – Stevie Wonder (Tamla)
JUST TO BE CLOSE TO YOU – Commodores (Motown)
LOVE BUG – Bumblebee Unltd. (Mercury)
RUBBERBAND MAN – Spinners (Atlantic)
WHEN LOVE IS NEW – Arthur Prysock (Old Town)

WHEREHOUSE VII, MIAMI
DJ: Bill Kelly

ANOTHER STAR/ISN'T SHE LOVELY – Stevie Wonder (Tamla)
DANCIN' – Crown Heights Affair (De-Lite)
DON'T LEAVE ME THIS WAY/ANY WAY YOU LIKE IT – Thelma Houston (Tamla lp cuts)
DOWN TO LOVE TOWN – Originals (Motown)
LET YOURSELF GO/I DON'T WANT TO BE TIED DOWN/YOU'RE MY DRIVING WHEEL – Supremes (Motown)
LOVE BUG – Bumblebee Unltd. (Mercury)
MAKES YOU BLIND – Glitter Band (Arista)
SPRING AFFAIR/SUMMER FEVER – Donna Summer (Casablanca)
THAT'S THE TROUBLE/SORRY – Grace Jones (Beam Junction)
WHEN LOVE IS NEW – Arthur Prysock (Old Town)

LES MOUCHES, NEW YORK
DJ: Robert Gordon

DON'T LEAVE ME THIS WAY – Thelma Houston (Tamla)
GIFT WRAP MY LOVE – Reflections (Capitol)
GOOD LOVE MAKES EVERYTHING ALRIGHT/THE GREATEST FEELING/ THE WAY YOU MAKE ME FEEL – Melba Moore (Buddah)
I KNOW WHERE YOU'RE COMING FROM – Instant Funk (TSOP)
LET YOURSELF GO – Supremes (Motown)
SPRING RAIN – Silvetti (Salsoul)
TAKE THE HEAT OFF ME – Boney M. (Atco)
THAT'S THE TROUBLE – Grace Jones (Beam Junction)
24 HOURS A DAY – Barbara Pennington (UA import)

TRAMPS, WASHINGTON, D.C.
DJ: Linda Schaefer

ANOTHER STAR – Stevie Wonder (Tamla)
CAR WASH – Rose Royce (MCA)
DOWN TO LOVE TOWN – Originals (Motown)
MY SWEET SUMMER SUITE – Love Unlimited Orchestra (20th Century)
NO, NO, NO, MY FRIEND – Devoshun (SMI)
RHYTHMS OF THE WORLD/SOUL CHA CHA – Van McCoy (H&L)
SPRING AFFAIR/SUMMER FEVER – Donna Summer (Casablanca)
STUBBORN KIND OF FELLA – Buffalo Smoke (RCA)
WELCOME TO OUR WORLD/WINE FLOW DISCO – Mass Production (Cotillion)
YOU + ME = LOVE – Undisputed Truth (Whitfield)

saying, "I've been wearing plastic for two months now. I've got two dresses, one short and the other long. My friend wears a Marks & Spencer carrier bag. But there's one drawback when wearing plastic bags – they tear when you take them off!" The boys, all with short, short hair, wear store-bought PVC pants and leather-like jackets or bulky mohair sweaters. Is this the Next Big Thing? **Fran Lebowitz**, who covers the waterfront every month in Interview, scoffs at the idea. Pointing out the state of the British economy, she says, "That's all they can afford there now. It's not a style – it's an economy measure."

RECORDS: The only thing to write about this week is – I can't believe this – another disco version of the theme from "I Love Lucy" called "Disco Lucy" by the **Wilton Place Street Band**, which Island Records has released as their first commercial disco disc. The record is essentially the same concept as the "Disco Lucy" by the **New York Rubber Rock Band** that Henry Street Records released just about this time last year, only here the production has more verve and drive and the overall effect is kind of delightful (though we could have done without the girls chirping, "Dance, dance, Disco Lucy!"). One of the best things about the record is its smart packaging .... Another nostalgia/novelty item that should be noted: the hilarious new version of "In the Mood" by the **Henhouse Five Plus Too** (Warner Brothers), featuring a harmonizing chorus of "hens" clucking away over a classy swing arrangement. The inevitable, and utterly insane, result of "Disco Duck's" success and even more fun. ◗

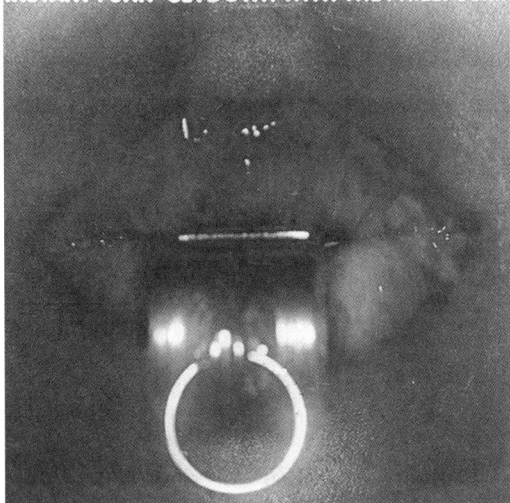

DECEMBER 25, 1976

The end of the year came up so suddenly that there's no time for a considered reflective remembrance of things past so we'll do a fast hustle through the highlights of 1976 in the Land of 1000 Dances. Remember, it wasn't until 1974, with the success of "Love's Theme," "Rock Your Baby" and "Rock The Boat," that the music business began to acknowledge the existence of disco music as a style and a force. The popular question then – "Disco is just a fad, isn't it?" – has been replaced with the slightly more enlightened, "How much longer do you think this thing will last?" If this year is any indication, disco, having outlived the stigma of a "fad" phenomenon, is here to stay – if only because the stakes are so high: as one shrewd producer pointed out, with the number of discotheques in the country nearly doubling within the past year, disco can't afford to die. But the fact that disco music has developed its own prosperous, self-sustaining market wouldn't matter much if the music itself hadn't grown and prospered artistically as well. And disco music did more than survive its own success in 1976, it had one of its most creative years.

By "surviving its own success," I mean that disco has gotten past stagnating formulas and its own baddish popularity – it's usually the kiss of death when a word becomes as overused as "disco" was this past year, especially after it's been attached to two number one singles, "Disco Lady" and "Disco Duck" – to take stock of itself and move on with fresh confidence. Disco remakes were still around this year (there were disco versions of "Poinciana," "Smoke Gets In Your Eyes," "Eleanor Rigby," "Tubular Bells,'" "Pagliacci," "Sweet Georgia Brown" and the theme from the "I Love Lucy" show), but formula-ridden revampings of old tunes have practically disappeared, eclipsed by the vitality and variety of the new disco music. **Dr. Buzzard's Original "Savannah" Band** is still the prime example of the unexpected, complex, irresistibly involving music that drew us to disco in the first place and, resurfacing so stylishly here, gives us hope for its continuing growth. But the Savannah Band on its own couldn't have turned the beat around this year. A number of performers working in different, but always danceable, styles made the dance floor the best place to hear exciting, aggressively new music this year: music by **Donna Summer**, **The Ritchie Family**, **Brass Construction**, **Vicki Sue Robinson**, **The Trammps**, **Double Exposure**, **Salsoul Orchestra**, **Stratavarious**, **Ralph MacDonald**, **Fatback Band**, **Undisputed Truth** – the list is, happily, endless. Disco has also brought out a whole new bunch of producers whose individual styles are brilliantly diverse: Giorgio Moroder & Pete Bellotte; Baker, Harris & Young (with Norman Harris the most prolific member of that team); John Davis; Patrick Adams and Greg Carmichael; Warren Schatz; Jacques Morali; Jeff Lane; Vince Montana – these are the men to watch right now.

Looking back over 1976, I realized something that I hadn't been aware of week-to-week: disco has become primarily an album market. Last year in the year-end issue we listed 75 "essential" disco singles; this year the list contains only 30 records and it was stretched with some personal favorites. But clearly, this is a case of singles being squeezed from two sides – shut out by better, fuller albums on the one hand and by the new and ever-expanding market of disco disc pressings on the other. Salsoul Records was the first to bring disco discs into the record store with **Double Exposure's** "Ten Percent" early last spring and since their move nearly all the independent labels involved seriously with disco product have released special 12-inch pressings for the consumer. The impact on the marketplace hasn't been sufficiently assessed, but disco discs, being the first new record format in years, are being packaged and sold with more creativity and verve than singles and, at least in big disco cities like New York, Boston and San Francisco, are demanding and getting the kind of open display space singles rarely have. The year-end list of "essential" disco discs doubles this year to 50, but only about half the list was available commercially – the rest were pressed in a limited edition for disco DJs only. Disco discs came into their own in 1976 and as an indication of the impact of the disco market, they should be watched closely in '77.

> **❝ The popular question back in 1974 – "Disco is just a fad, isn't it?" – has been replaced with the slightly more enlightened, "How much longer do you think this thing will last?" ❞**

THE LOFT, NEW YORK
DJ: David Mancuso

ANAMBRA – Ozo (DJM)
DON'T LEAVE ME THIS WAY – Thelma Houston (Tamla)
GOTTA GET IT – Tony Valor Sounds Orchestra (Brunswick)
IT AIN'T REGGAE (BUT IT'S FUNKY) – Instant Funk (TSOP)
IT DON'T HAVE TO BE FUNKY – Salsoul Orchestra (Salsoul)
I'VE LEARNED FROM MY BURNS – Spiders Webb (Fantasy)
KEEP ON DANCING—Jacksons (Epic)
LOVE IN C MINOR – Cerrone (Malligator import)
OPEN SESAME – Kool & the Gang (De-Lite)
SUNRISE – Ultrafunk (Contempo import)

THE ANVIL, NEW YORK
DJ: Richie Rivera

BLACK BROTHERS – Black Soul (Beam Junction)
CAR WASH – Rose Royce (MCA)
DANCIN' – Crown Heights Affair (De-Lite)
DON'T LEAVE ME THIS WAY – Thelma Houston (Tamla)
GOIN' UP IN SMOKE – Eddie Kendricks (Tamla)
JUNGLE PEOPLE – Soulful Dynamics (Epic import)
LITTLE DRUMMER BOY – Salsoul Orchestra (Salsoul)
SPRING AFFAIR – Donna Summer (Casablanca)
SWAN SONG – Philharmonic 2000 (Mercury)
WELCOME TO OUR WORLD – Mass Production (Cotillion)

THE SECOND STOREY, PHILADELPHIA
DJ: Walter Gibbons

DON'T LEAVE ME THIS WAY/ANY WAY YOU LIKE IT/DON'T KNOW WHY I LOVE YOU – Thelma Houston (Tamla)
EVERYBODY HAVE A GOOD TIME – Archie Bell & the Drells (Phila. Intl.)
FREEDOM TO EXPRESS YOURSELF – Denise LaSalle (ABC)
IT AIN'T REGGAE (BUT IT'S FUNKY) – Instant Funk (TSOP)
IT DON'T HAVE TO BE FUNKY – Salsoul Orchestra (Salsoul)
LET YOURSELF GO/YOU'RE MY DRIVING WHEEL – Supremes (Motown)
NO, NO, NO, MY FRIEND – Devoshun (SMI)
OVERTURE/INDISCREET/DON'T KEEP IT IN THE SHADOWS – D.C. LaRue- (Pyramid)
THAT'S THE TROUBLE – Grace Jones (Beam Junction)
TRIED, TESTED AND FOUND TRUE – Ashford & Simpson (Warner Bros.)

CIRCUS MAXIMUS, LOS ANGELES
DJ: Mike Lewis

CAR WASH – Rose Royce (MCA)
DAZZ – Brick (Bang)
DISCO LUCY – Wilton Place Street Band (Island)
DISCO TRAIN – Jerry Rix (GM import)
DON'T LEAVE ME THIS WAY – Thelma Houston (Tamla)
DREAM EXPRESS – Honeybees (Roxbury)
GET UP AND DANCE THE CONTINENTAL – The Earls (Woodbury)
OVERTURE/O BA BA/INDISCREET/DON'T KEEP IT IN THE SHADOWS – D.C. LaRue (Pyramid)
SPRING AFFAIR/SUMMER FEVER – Donna Summer (Casablanca)
TAKE THE HEAT OFF ME/HELP, HELP/DADDY COOL – Boney M. (Atco)

A quick list of disco discs to pick up on right now: **Karma's** "Funk De Mambo," a bright, snap, crackle and pop jazz number with fine synthesizer percussion and delightful vocals from **Syreeta Wright** and **Deniece Williams** – this version is nearly two minutes longer than the album cut we already raved about and A&M is making it its first commercial disco disc (on its Horizon label), though distribution will be exclusive to New York City for the moment at least... **Silvetti's** "Spring Rain" (Salsoul), a luscious, frothy instrumental in the **Barry White** vein that turns on a nice percussion break and is already getting heavily favorable feedback from the clubs... "Center City" by **Fat Larry's Band** (Atlantic), a **Vince Montana** production that really comes across in this new long mix (extended from 3:38 to 7:47); "Fascination," also in a different mix, is on the B side, and Atlantic has asked that we note the fact that none of their disco discs are available commercially – they're pressed for promotional use to disco DJs only... **Charles Earland's** "Drifting" (Mercury), whose title really captures its mood: floating on a cloud, nudged by a deep bass beat – this is a better mix of the lp cut already available, identically timed at 6:23... **Undisputed Truth's** "Let's Go Down To The Disco" (Whitfield/Warner Brothers), previously available only as a single, now a churning 9:10 and closer in style to producer **Norman Whitfield's** "Car Wash" material than "You + Me = Love" (which has been put on the reverse side of this promotional disc) – really picks up in the second segment which begins with "Car Wash"-like hand-clapping... "Let Me Be Your Lady Tonight" by **Stratavarious & Lady** has grown on me since I first reviewed it here – like "I Got Your Love," this is a terrific, out-of-the-ordinary production, running more than nine minutes, with a unique use of voices – unfortunately, Roulette didn't include the import version's mostly instrumental flip side on its promotional pressings... **Melba Moore's** joyous "Good Love Makes Everything All Right" (1:32), the knockout cut from her latest album with Van McCoy, now available as a 12-inch disc from Buddah... **Caress'** "Fill Me Up (Heart To Heart)" (Roulette), a nice but not substantially different version of the song from the **Andrea True** album, running 6:12... **Black Soul's** "Mangous Ye," a neo-African chant propelled by excellent drumming which has been expanded to six minutes from a cut on the group's earlier import album and put on the B side of commercial copies of "Black Brothers" on Beam Junction Records "Black Brothers" is suddenly one of the strongest disco discs out now and its flip side is also beginning to pick up play... **Ultrafunk's** "Gotham City Boogie," the great, swirling instrumental we already reviewed as an import, is out now on TK, but its B Side has been changed for the American release from "Sunrise" (the "Car Wash" number) to a pleasant, **MFSB**-styled instrumental called "Indigo Country." ◑

DISCO FILE ESSENTIALS 1976

THE ESSENTIAL DISCO ALBUMS OF 1976

1. **DR BUZZARD'S ORIGINAL "SAVANNAH" BAND** (RCA)
2. **WHERE THE HAPPY PEOPLE GO** – Trammps (Atlantic)
3. **FOUR SEASONS OF LOVE & A LOVE TRILOGY** – Donna Summer (Casablanca/Oasis)
4. **NEVER GONNA LET YOU GO & VICKI SUE ROBINSON** – Vicki Sue Robinson (RCA)
5. **DIANA ROSS** (Motown)
6. **ARABIAN NIGHTS** – The Ritchie Family (Marlin)
7. **NICE 'N' NAASTY** – Salsoul Orchestra (Salsoul)
8. **BRASS CONSTRUCTION & BRASS CONSTRUCTION II** (UA)
9. **SKY HIGH!** – Tavares (Capitol)
10. **TROUBLE MAKER** – Roberta Kelly (Oasis)
11. **CATHEDRALS & THE TEA DANCE** – D.C. LaRue (Pyramid)
12. **SONGS IN THE KEY OF LIFE** – Stevie Wonder (Tamla)
13. **SOUND OF A DRUM** – Ralph MacDonald (Marlin)
14. **YOUNG HEARTS RUN FREE** – Candi Staton (Warner Bros.)
15. **FLOWERS** – The Emotions (Columbia)
16. **MIDNIGHT LOVE AFFAIR** – Carol Douglas (Midland Intl.)
17. **HIGH ENERGY & MARY, SCHERRIE & SUSAYE** – The Supremes (Motown)
18. **HE'S A FRIEND & GOING UP IN SMOKE** – Eddie Kendricks (Tamla)
19. **I'VE GOT YOU** – Gloria Gaynor (Polydor)
20. **RAISING HELL & NIGHT FEVER** – Fatback Band (Event/Spring)
21. **SO LET US ENTERTAIN YOU** – First Choice (Warner Bros.)
22. **DON'T STOP NOW** – The Brothers (RCA)
23. **ANY WAY YOU LIKE IT** – Thelma Houston (Tamla)
24. **THIS IS IT & MELBA** – Melba Moore (Buddah)
25. **KNIGHTS IN WHITE SATIN** – Giorgio (Oasis)
26. **MORE, MORE, MORE** – Andrea True Connection (Buddah)
27. **TEN PERCENT** – Double Exposure (Salsoul)
28. **SILVER CONVENTION & MADHOUSE** – Silver Convention (Midland Intl.)
29. **WATCH OUT** – Barrabas (Atco)
30. **DO IT YOUR WAY** – Crown Heights Affair (De-Lite)
31. **RHYTHMS OF THE WORLD & THE REAL MCCOY** – Van McCoy (H&L)
32. **UNFINISHED BUSINESS** – Blackbyrds (Fantasy)
33. **LIFE GOES ON** – Faith, Hope & Charity (RCA)
34. **WELCOME TO OUR WORLD** – Mass Production (Cotillion)
35. **CAR WASH** – Rose Royce (MCA)
36. **MESSAGE IN THE MUSIC** – O'Jays (Phila. Intl.)
37. **SILK DEGREES** – Boz Scaggs (Columbia)
38. **MY SWEET SUMMER SUITE** – Love Unlimited Orchestra (20th Century)
39. **SUMMERTIME** – MFSB (Phila. Intl.)
40. **WE GOT THE RHYTHM** – People's Choice (Phila. Intl.)
41. **GEARS** – Johnny Hammond (Milestone)
42. **NIGHT AND DAY** – John Davis & the Monster Orchestra (Sam)
43. **ENERGY TO BURN** – B.T. Express (Columbia)
44. **PART III** – KC & the Sunshine Band (TK)
45. **TAKE THE HEAT OFF ME** – Boney M. (Atco)
46. **VERY TOGETHER** – Deodato (MCA)
47. **ALL THINGS IN TIME** – Lou Rawls (Phila. Intl.)
48. **I HEAR A SYMPHONY** – Hank Crawford (Kudu)
49. **RAINFOREST** – Biddu Orchestra (Epic)
50. **LET'S GET IT TOGETHER & BRAZIL** – El Coco (AVI)
51. **COME AS YOU ARE** – Ashford & Simpson (Warner Bros.)
52. **JOE SIMON TODAY** (Soul Train)
53. **LOVE TO THE WORLD** – LTD (A&M)
54. **GET DOWN WITH THE PHILLY JUMP** – Instant Funk (TSOP)
55. **I'M IN HEAVEN** – Touch of Class (Midland Intl.)
56. **BAD LUCK** – Atlanta Disco Band (Ariola America)
57. **AIN'T NOTHING BUT A PARTY** – Mark Radice (UA)
58. **LOVE TALK** – James Gilstrap (Roxbury)
59. **DANCE YOUR ASS OFF** – Bohannon (Dakar)
    [Only 59 albums in the original]

THE ESSENTIAL DISCO RECORDS OF 1976

1. **DR BUZZARD'S ORIGINAL "SAVANNAH" BAND** (RCA lp)
2. **TEN PERCENT** – Double Exposure (Salsoul disco disc)
3. **WHERE THE HAPPY PEOPLE GO** – Trammps (Atlantic lp)
4. **FOUR SEASONS OF LOVE & A LOVE TRILOGY** – Donna Summer (Casablanca/Oasis lps)
5. **TURN THE BEAT AROUND** – Vicki Sue Robinson (RCA lp cut)
6. **LOVE HANGOVER** – Diana Ross (Motown lp cut)
7. **ARABIAN NIGHTS** – The Ritchie Family (Marlin lp)
8. **NICE 'N' NAASTY** – Salsoul Orchestra (Salsoul lp)
9. **BRASS CONSTRUCTION** (UA lp)
10. **YOU'LL NEVER FIND ANOTHER LOVE LIKE MINE** – Lou Rawls (Phila. Intl.)
11. **YOU + ME = LOVE** – Undisputed Truth (Whitfield disco disc)
12. **HEAVEN MUST BE MISSING AN ANGEL/DON'T TAKE AWAY THE MUSIC** – Tavares (Capitol lp cuts)
13. **DOWN TO LOVE TOWN** – Originals (Motown disco disc)
14. **TROUBLE MAKER** – Roberta Kelly (Oasis lp cut)
15. **I DON'T WANT TO LOSE YOUR LOVE** – The Emotions (Columbia lp cut)
16. **CATHEDRALS** – D.C. LaRue (Pyramid lp cut)
17. **YOU SHOULD BE DANCING** – Bee Gees (RSO disco disc)
18. **ANOTHER STAR/I WISH/SIR DUKE** – Stevie Wonder (Tamla lp cuts)
19. **CALYPSO BREAKDOWN** – Ralph MacDonald (Marlin lp cut)
20. **YOUNG HEARTS RUN FREE** – Candi Staton (Warner Bros. lp cuts)
21. **MIDNIGHT LOVE AFFAIR** – Carol Douglas (Midland Intl. lp medley)
22. **LET'S GET IT TOGETHER** – El Coco (AVI disco disc)
23. **DON'T LEAVE ME THIS WAY** – Thelma Houston (Tamla lp cut)
24. **MY SWEET SUMMER SUITE** – Love Unlimited Orchestra (20th Century disco disc)
25. **MORE, MORE, MORE** – Andrea True Connection (Buddah disco disc)

THE ESSENTIAL DISCO SINGLES OF 1976

1. **YOU'LL NEVER FIND ANOTHER LOVE LIKE MINE** – Lou Rawls (Phila. Intl.)
2. **YOUNG HEARTS RUN FREE** – Candi Staton (Warner Bros.)
3. **MAKES YOU BLIND** – Glitter Band (Arista)
4. **WOW** – Andre Gagnon (London)
5. **LOVE CHANT** – Eli's Second Coming (Silver Blue)
6. **TAKE A LITTLE** – Liquid Pleasure (Midland Intl.)
7. **TAJ MAHAL/LET ME SEE YA GITCHER THING OFF, BABY** – Crystal Grass (Private Stock)
8. **I'LL GO WHERE YOUR MUSIC TAKES ME** – Jimmy James & the Vagabonds (Pye)
9. **GET OFF YOUR AAHH! AND DANCE** – Foxy (Dash)
10. **SHAKE YOUR BOOTY** – KC & the Sunshine Band (TK)
11. **SMOKE YOUR TROUBLES AWAY** – Glass Family (Ear Hole)
12. **WET WEEKEND** – Rock Gazers (Pilgrim)
13. **STRANGERS IN THE NIGHT** – Bette Midler (Atlantic)
14. **HOW'S YOUR LOVE LIFE** – Lee Eldred (Mercury)
15. **MA-MO-AH** – Tony Valor Sounds Orchestra (Brunswick)
16. **DANCIN' KID** – Disco Tex & the Sex-O-Lettes (Chelsea)
17. **ATMOSPHERE STRUTT** – Cloud One (P&P)
18. **GIFT WRAP MY LOVE** – Reflections (Capitol)
19. **C'MON BABY, DO THE LATIN HUSTLE** – Fajardo (Coco)
20. **BORN TO GET DOWN** – Muscle Shoal Horns (Bang)
21. **DAZZ** – Brick (Bang)
22. **KILL THAT ROACH** – Miami (Drive)
23. **FOXY** – Crown Heights Affair
24. **THE GAME IS OVER/I'M GOING THROUGH CHANGES NOW** – Brown Sugar (Capitol)
25. **FEEL THE SPIRIT IN '76** – LeRoy Hutson (Curtom)
26. **DREAMIN'** – Loleatta Holloway (Gold Mine)
27. **THE MORE I GET TO KNOW YOU** – Five Special (Mercury)
28. **ZONE** – Rhythm Makers (Vigor)
29. **GET UP OFFA THAT THING** – James Brown (Polydor)
30. **AUTUMN LEAVES** – Jon White Group (Cenpro)

1977

New Orleans Dancefloor © **Toby Old**

JANUARY 8, 1977

It should come as no surprise that the record everyone is talking about this week is "Disco Inferno," the new album by **The Trammps** which Atlantic serviced in advance to disco DJs across the country in special white sleeves stamped, "Spend New Year's Eve With The Trammps." (Official release date: January 4). The Trammps are the definitive Philadelphia disco group with one of the best lead vocalists in the business – the gritty, hard-shouting **Jimmy Ellis** – and the most consistently sharp production team around – **Ron Baker**, **Norman Harris** and **Earl Young**. Their last two albums have been major records with immediate and long-lasting impact and growing critical recognition is edging them toward the position of top black male vocal group. So the release of "Disco Inferno," whose title is heavy with unintentional literary reference (can we expect a "Disco Paradisio" and "Disco Purgatorio" to follow?), is being treated as an Event – the first Major Disco Album of 1977 – with all the inevitable hoopla and controversy that surrounds the premiere of a Major Motion Picture or the publication of a Major New Novel.

On the most immediate level, "Disco Inferno" is a stunning yet entirely predictable dance album. It contains six cuts, three to a side, with the title track the group's longest on record (10:54) and all the others save one running in the six-to-seven-minute range. Every cut is supremely danceable, feverishly uptempo but, as several other people commented, "nothing new" – The Trammps have been over this ground before and the results were richer, more inspired the first time. It's not entirely true, as one DJ remarked, that "it all sounds alike," but, initially at least, it all *feels* alike: cut after cut ends with a long instrumental build, Ellis shouting and riffing vocally, and an extended series of repeated choruses –

❝ The release of "Disco Inferno," is being treated as an Event, with all the inevitable hoopla and controversy that surrounds the premiere of a Major Motion Picture or the publication of a Major New Novel ❞

individually, they may sparkle but one on top of the other, they tend to dull. But in spite of these reservations, the album is powerful and effective – if it doesn't take the group a giant step forward, it certainly establishes them as the very best at what they do: "Inferno" seethes with scorching hot dance music and searing vocals.

The typical response from DJs has been "I love it," and even when the love was tempered with pointed criticism, most people agreed that the crowd really loves it and this should propel "Disco Inferno" quickly to the top. The two cuts that drew the most reaction first time out were "Disco Inferno," though there was disappointment in its lack of truly innovative breaks, and "Body Contact Contract," which cleverly parodies the language of a business contract when the real business at hand is let's-make-a-deal sex. Coming in strong seconds right now are "Don't Burn No Bridges" and "Starvin'" – both driving, perfectly balanced songs, both personal favorites. And "I Feel Like I've Been Livin' (On The Dark Side Of The Moon)," which races along as the album's fastest cut, delightfully frantic, is the track nearly everyone we spoke to said was his own favorite. Expect to see all five zooming up the charts together. "You Touch My Hot Line," the shortest cut at 4:23 (if nothing else, this is a fully-packed album, more than 20 minutes to a side), is the only slight track here – bright but not brilliant– but it, too, has its fans. As usual with The Trammps, everyone's having some initial trouble adjusting great expectations with first impressions, and since "Disco Inferno" demands some intense involvement, tune in next week for some more leisurely second thoughts.

Among the other albums already showing up on top 10 lists this week, the most favorably received is another Philadelphia album (executive producers: **Gamble & Huff**) in quite a different vein by a wonderful singer named **Jean Carn**. Carn's album on Philadelphia International (titled simply "Jean Carn") is from the sweeter side of the Philly sound and, like **Dee Dee Sharp** did the year before, Carn seems to inspire the array of producers working with her to marvellously sublime heights. Her voice ranges from tough **Dionne Warwick** to sultry **Barbara Roy** (from Ecstasy, Passion & Pain), but on her best songs – "If You Wanna Go Back," "Time Waits For No One," "Free Love," "You Got A Problem" and "I'm In Love Once Again" – she defies comparison. Listen to this one. **George McCrae's** new album was produced by **Gregg Diamond** (best known for his success with **Andrea True**) and it's titled "Diamond Touch" (TK) so this is very much a producer-first effort. Diamond's style is strong, often flashy, but he keeps McCrae out front most of the time and the album rises and falls with McCrae's uneven vocals. The best cuts are the ones Tony Smith selected for his top 10 – "Love In Motion" (5:00), with a nice, swirling break, and "Givin' Back The Feeling" (5:31), more syncopated and brittle with a fine bass line. Runners up: "Dance In A Circle" and "Cut The Rug." And the album grows on you little by little. **Arthur Prysock's** "All My Life"

HARRAH, NEW YORK
DJ: Tom Savarese

DON'T LEAVE ME THIS WAY – Thelma Houston (Tamla)
FREE LOVE/IF YOU WANNA GO BACK/TIME WAITS FOR NO ONE – Jean Carn (Phila. Intl.)
GOOD LOVE MAKES EVERYTHING ALRIGHT/THE WAY YOU MAKE ME FEEL/(I NEED) SOMEONE – Melba Moore (Buddah)
I WANTCHA BABY/WHEN LOVE IS NEW/ALL MY LIFE/I LOVE MAKIN' LOVE TO YOU – Arthur Prysock (Old Town)
KEEP ON DANCING – Jacksons (Epic)
LOVE ME – Stratavarious (Polydor import)
ON THE TOWN/SATURDAY NIGHT/STEPPING OUT – Webster Lewis (Epic)
OPEN SESAME – Kool & the Gang (De-Lite)
OVERTURE – D.C. LaRue (Pyramid)
TATTOO MAN – Denise McCann (Polydor import)

IT'S A WAY OF LIFE, CHICAGO
DJ: Laurence Jacobson

ANAMBRA – Ozo (DJM)
DANCE AND SHAKE YOUR TAMBOURINE – Universal Robot Band (Red Greg)
DISCO INFERNO/I FEEL LIKE I'VE BEEN LIVIN' ON THE DARK SIDE OF THE MOON – Trammps (Atlantic)
DON'T LEAVE ME THIS WAY – Thelma Houston (Tamla)
EVERYBODY HAVE A GOOD TIME – Archie Bell & the Drells (Phila. Intl.)
MY LOVE IS FREE – Double Exposure (Salsoul)
ROCKY'S THEME – Motion Picture Soundtrack (UA)
SPRING RAIN – Silvetti (Salsoul)
STAY AWAY/I CAN'T STAY AWAY – Dynamic Superiors (Motown)

HIPPOPOTAMUS, NEW YORK
DJ: Rich Pampinella

A CHACUN SON ENFANCE – Recreation (Union import)
ANAMBRA – Ozo (DJM)
DON'T LEAVE ME THIS WAY/I DON'T KNOW WHY I LOVE YOU – Thelma Houston (Tamla)
GIFT WRAP MY LOVE – Reflections (Capitol)
ISN'T SHE LOVELY/ANOTHER STAR/SIR DUKE/I WISH – Stevie Wonder (Tamla)
LET YOURSELF GO/LOVE I NEVER KNEW YOU COULD FEEL SO GOOD – Supremes (Motown)
LOVE IN C MINOR – Cerrone (Malligator import)
MAKE IT UP TO ME IN LOVE – Odia Coates & Paul Anka (Epic)
MANGOUS YE – Black Soul (Beam Junction)
SPRING AFFAIR – Donna Summer (Casablanca)

BAREFOOT BOY, NEW YORK
DJ: Tony Smith

DANCE AND SHAKE YOUR TAMBOURINE – Universal Robot Band (Red Greg)
DON'T LEAVE ME THIS WAY – Thelma Houston (Tamla)
HERE FOR THE PARTY/LET'S GET ON DOWN – Bottom & Co (Gordy)
I WANTCHA BABY – Arthur Prysock (Old Town)
INDISCREET/OVERTURE – D.C. LaRue (Pyramid)
LOVE IN MOTION/GIVIN' BACK THE FEELING – George McCrae (TK)
MAKE IT UP TO ME IN LOVE – Odia Coates & Paul Anka (Epic)
SPRING RAIN – Silvetti (Salsoul)
DISCO INFERNO/I FEEL LIKE I'VE BEEN LIVIN' ON THE DARK SIDE OF THE MOON – Trammps (Atlantic)
UNDER CONSTRUCTION – El Coco (AVI)

album on Old Town, produced by **John Davis** and featuring the **Monster Orchestra** along with some of Philadelphia's best session musicians and singers, has also popped up on top 10 lists this week, riding on the success of "When Love Is New," which is included here in a 7:13 version. The choice cut so far is "I Wantcha Baby," also featured on **Billy Paul's** "When Love Is New" album, written by **Gamble & Huff** and redone in a style similar to "When Love Is New"; very smooth, sexy and hustle-perfect. Also recommended: "All My Life" and "All I Need Is You Tonight." Now out: the new **Undisputed Truth** album, "Method To The Madness" on Whitfield Records, containing the full 11:10 version of their spectacular "You + Me = Love," previously unavailable to the average consumer, and the long version of "Let's Go Down To The Disco."

United Artists has brought out a single version of **Barbara Pennington's** "24 Hours a Day," the English import we've been getting a number of top 10 reports on. It's sassy, has insinuating, lively vocals and a vibrant production that the 3:20 single can give us only a taste of right now – UA is scheduling a commercial release of the 12-inch disco disc. ◐

Along with the **Trammps'** "Disco Inferno" – three cuts of which entered the DISCO FILE Top 20 at the number three spot, the highest new entry since the chart began – the most exciting new record around is an import album from France called "Love In C Minor" by a man named **Cerrone** on Malligator Records. In style and impact "Love In C Minor" can only be compared to **Donna Summer's** "Love to Love You Baby": both are unexpected utterly thrilling extravaganzas, pulsing sexual symphonies with lush neoclassic productions that sweep you away. And there is a clear debt here to Summer and her production team, **Giorgio Moroder** and **Pete Bellotte**; they established the expansive, invigorating format, the deliciously orgasmic rise and fall of the music, that Cerrone makes use of throughout. But Cerrone pumps it up and makes it fresh, giving it a kind of lusty bite all his own.

"Love In C Minor" is the title of an approximately 16-minute track on the album's first side which begins with three girls talking, no music. One imagines them at an intimate bar or cafe, finishing off their champagne, cruising the men. One of them hits on a fantasy: "Maybe we could share one," she suggests, and the others jump at the idea, narrowing down the field to a man who apparently has money. When he turns toward them, one of the girls comments, "Money ain't all he's got– look at the front of him. That ain't no banana!" He approaches their table, one of them says, "You're on for tonight," and a throbbing drum beat starts, signalling the beginning of the music and a very steamy ménage à quatre. Most of the words from then on are muffled by the electric blanket of the music, but soon the record erupts in a trio of moans, erotic screams and cries of "Don't stop!" or "Right there! Right there!" It's Donna Summer times three, a Playgirl/Playboy dream come true, set to a brilliant, energetic track that never lets up. The album's second side is divided between two songs, a fine remake of "Black Is Black" (5:22) and an original called "Midnight Lady" (7:28) which is similar in style to the title cut and equally forceful, especially in its use of strings. All were produced, and the original songs co-written, by Cerrone, a young French musician who reclines on the album's cover wearing only a robe and a knowing look which is considerably more than the three girls are pictured in.

I first heard "Love In C Minor" at David Mancuso's Loft in New York where it caused an immediate sensation and has become the hottest record in the club (Mancuso listed it in his top 10 three weeks back). After a frantic search to find more copies of the record, I discovered that Richie Pampinella at Hippopotamus had also been given a copy and he listed it as a top 10 record last week. Import copies are still extremely rare – most importers are unfamiliar with both the label and the artist – but Cotillion Records, alerted by contacts in France, has already picked up the album for American release, scheduled February 2 if not sooner, and advances are leaking out. This is the hot one right now, just what we need to heat up these cold winter nights.

OTHER IMPORTS: The **Stratavarious** album is out now in Canada on Polydor (Roulette plans to release it here by the first week in February), and it contains "I Got Your Love," which sounds as great as it did the very first time; "Let Me Be Your Lady Tonight" and that cut's instrumental version, "Love Me," both over nine minutes; and three other cuts, all featuring the unique, harp-accented sound producer **John Usry, Jr.** developed for the group. Of the new tracks, "Nightfall" (8:30), a lovely, mid-tempo cut reminiscent of the **Mizell** brothers work with **Bobbi Humphrey** or **Donald Byrd**, and a sexy-slow song called "Touching" (6:49) are most appealing. Superbly produced... **Tina Charles**, the English singer who set our heart on fire with her sultry voice, has a second album on the CBS label in England that's been picking up interest here for some months now. The album's title track, "Dance Little Lady Dance," is a typical **Biddu** number – perky, highly polished, cute – and it's already been released on an American single (Columbia). But a couple of other tracks are even better, particularly "It's Time For A Change of Heart," a terrific, bittersweet let's-call-it-quits love song (5:05), and "Boogiethon" (4:45), an excellent instrumental that recalls **Carl Douglas'** "Blue Eyed Soul." Other possibilities: "Dr. Love" and a nice version of "Halfway To Paradise"... **Denise McCann's** "Tattoo Man," a disco disc from Polydor in Canada, was on Tom Savarese's top 10 last week from Harrah, suddenly one of New York's chicest, most talked-about clubs, and the record deserves some mention here. Its sound is reminiscent of **Babe Ruth's**, brittle, guitar and drum based, coming from the rock side of the disco spectrum. McCann, who also wrote the song about obsessive love, has a sharp almost bluesy voice and she carries the song perfectly. Worth looking for.

RECOMMENDED ALBUMS: **The Rice & Beans Orchestra** had a disco disc and single out last year on Dash called "The Blue Danube Hustle," a Latinization of the waltz standard that was pleasant, no more than that. But the group's album, recorded mostly in Puerto Rico and quite a success there, is much better than the initial single would lead us to expect. The sound takes off from the Latin disco styling already established here by **Eddie Drennon** and **Fajardo** – sweet, lush with flute and violins, oriented to a Latin hustle and very lively – and the best cuts really sparkle. Try "Rice & Beans Theme,"

"I first heard "Love In C Minor" at David Mancuso's Loft in New York where it caused an immediate sensation "

PIPPINS, NEW YORK
DJ: Reggie T Experience

DISCO INFERNO/I FEEL LIKE I'VE BEEN LIVIN' – Trammps (Atlantic)
DON'T LEAVE ME THIS WAY – Thelma Houston (Tamla)
EVERYBODY HAVE A GOOD TIME – Archie Bell & the Drells (Phila. Intl.)
FOLEY SQUARE – Con Funk Shun (Mercury)
FOUR SEASONS OF LOVE – Donna Summer (Casablanca)
FREE – Deniece Williams (Columbia)
FUNK DE MAMBO – Karma (A&M/ Horizon)
HA CHA CHA – Brass Construction (UA)
I WANTCHA BABY – Arthur Prysock (Old Town)
OPEN SESAME – Kool & the Gang (De-Lite)

CHARLES GALLERY, NEW YORK
DJ: Louis "Angelo" Alers

ALL MY LIFE/I LOVE MAKIN' LOVE TO YOU – Arthur Prysock (Old Town)
BODY HEAT – James Brown (Polydor)
DANCE, DANCE, DANCE – Martha Acuna (Scorp Gemi)
DISCO INFERNO/BODY CONTACT CONTRACT/I FEEL LIKE I'VE BEEN LIVIN'/DON'T BURN NO BRIDGES/ STARVIN' – Trammps (Atlantic)
DON'T LEAVE ME THIS WAY – Thelma Houston (Tamla)
EVERYBODY HAVE A GOOD TIME – Archie Bell & the Drells (Phila. Intl.)
GIFT WRAP MY LOVE – Reflections (Capitol)
MAGIC'S IN THE AIR/BOY, I REALLY TIED ONE ON – Esther Phillips (Kudu)
OVERTURE – D. C La Rue (Pyramid)
SPRING RAIN – Silvetti (Salsoul)

RUBAIYAT, ANN ARBOR, MICHIGAN
DJ: Karl Uraski & Fred Uhl

AT THE TOP OF THE STAIRS – Wild Honey (TK)
DISCO INFERNO/BODY CONTACT CONTRACT – Trammps (Atlantic)
DON'T LEAVE ME THIS WAY – Thelma Houston (Tamla)
DREAMIN'/HIT AND RUN – Loleatta Holloway (Salsoul)
GET ON UP AND DANCE – The Earls (Woodbury)
LET YOURSELF GO/LOVE I NEVER KNEW YOU COULD FEEL SO GOOD – Supremes (Motown)
LOVE IN MOTION/CUT THE RUG – George McCrae (TK)
MAGIC'S IN THE AIR/BOY, I REALLY TIED ONE ON – Esther Phillips (Kudu)
OPEN SESAME – Kool & the Gang (De-Lite)
TRIED, TESTED AND FOUND TRUE – Ashford & Simpson (Warner Bros.)

INFINITY, NEW YORK
DJ: Vincent Carleo

ANOTHER STAR/I WISH/SIR DUKE – Stevie Wonder (Tamla)
CAR WASH – Rose Royce (MCA)
DON'T LEAVE ME THIS WAY – Thelma Houston (Tamla)
DOWN TO LOVE TOWN – Originals (Motown)
ENJOY YOURSELF/THINK HAPPY – Jacksons (Epic)
GOIN' UP IN SMOKE/THANKS FOR THE MEMORIES – Eddie Kendricks (Tamla)
LOVE IN MOTION – George McCrae (TK)
SPRING AFFAIR – Donna Summer (Casablanca)
STUBBORN KIND OF FELLA – Buffalo Smoke (RCA)
THAT'S THE TROUBLE – Grace Jones (Beam Junction)

"Cantano Ferry," "Disco Dancing," and "Our Love Concerto." The album's on Dash, through TK... **Mystique** is a four-man group whose lead singer is a former lead with the **Impressions**, **Ralph Johnson**; another former Impression, **Curtis Mayfield**, is the executive producer on the group's debut album for Curtom; and **Jerry Butler**, **Bunny Sigler**, **Rich Tufa**, **Gene McDaniels** and others produced individual tracks. This impressive array of talent isn't wasted – the album is a fine example of the male group sound and two cuts are quite danceable: "If You're In Need," very smoothly up-tempo with a percolating beat and strong, building vocals; and "What Would The World Be Without Music," a long (6:37), jumping song that has a touch of **Mighty Clouds of Joy** fervor. Definitely check this one out.

RECOMMENDED SINGLE: Speaking of the Mighty Clouds of Joy, that group is back with a single produced by **Frank Wilson** (**The Supremes**, **Eddie Kendricks**) and **Larry Brown** and titled, "There's Love In The World (Tell The Lonely People)" (ABC). As usual, the Cloud's gospel roots are very much in evidence and the song is even more of a rave-up than we're used to, bursting with energy and featuring a bass line that here and there falls into a "Love Hangover"/"Don't Leave Me This Way" groove. The long version on the 45 is 5:11 – enjoy yourself. ◐

DISCO FILE TOP 20

1. **DON'T LEAVE ME THIS WAY** – Thelma Houston (Tamla)
2. **SPRING AFFAIR/SUMMER FEVER** – Donna Summer (Casablanca)
3. **DISCO INFERNO/BODY CONTACT CONTRACT/ I FEEL LIKE I'VE BEEN LIVIN'** – Trammps (Atlantic)
4. **CAR WASH** – Rose Royce (MCA)
5. **LET YOURSELF GO/YOU'RE MY DRIVING WHEEL** – Supremes (Motown)
6. **OVERTURE** – D. C La Rue (Pyramid)
7. **OPEN SESAME** – Kool & the Gang (De-Lite)
8. **ANOTHER STAR/I WISH** – Stevie Wonder (Tamla)
9. **THAT'S THE TROUBLE/SORRY** – Grace Jones (Beam Junction)
10. **SPRING RAIN** – Silvetti (Salsoul)
11. **EVERYBODY HAVE A GOOD TIME** – Archie Bell & the Drells (Phila. Intl.)
12. **DOWN TO LOVE TOWN** – Originals (Motown)
13. **WHEN LOVE IS NEW** – Arthur Prysock (Old Town)
14. **INDISCREET/DON'T KEEP IT IN THE SHADOWS** – D. C La Rue (Pyramid)
15. **WELCOME TO OUR WORLD** – Mass Production (Cotillion)
16. **DANCIN'** – Crown Heights Affair (De-Lite)
17. **LOVE IN MOTION** – George McCrae (TK)
18. **DANCE AND SHAKE YOUR TAMBOURINE** – Universal Robot Band (Red Greg)
19. **NO, NO, NO, MY FRIEND** – Devoshun (SMI)
20. **LOVE BUG** – Bumble Bee Unltd. (Mercury)

JANUARY 22, 1977

Happy New Year! Here we are only three weeks into 1977, and already we have three albums that are sure to be among the best the year has to offer: The **Trammps'** "Disco Inferno," which gets better with each new listening; **Cerrone's** "Love In C Minor" (though its American release is still two weeks off); and now **Loleatta Holloway's** knockout, "Loleatta": this week's most talked-about, most swooned-over record. The first album on **Norman Harris'** Gold Mind label (distributed by Salsoul), "Loleatta" sounds like an instant classic, the kind of record cult figures are based upon. A great deal of the album's impact lies in the perfect balance producer Harris strikes between the flawless, highly-polished, Philadelphia-style productions and Holloway's powerhouse, rough-edged vocals – Loleatta rides on the silken sweep of violins singing and shouting like the last of the southern gospel queens, utterly triumphant. The **Salsoul Orchestra** provides the most elegant foil for Holloway and the creamy cooing of background vocalists **Barbara Ingram**, **Evette Benton** and **Carla Benson** seem to inspire her to tougher heights, just as she inspires them to all-out gospel brilliance at the end of "Dreamin'": already successful as a single, is expanded to 6:17 here and ends up sounding like a combination of the **Soul Sisters'** "I Can't Stand It" and **Gloria Spencer's** "I Got It" – hardly the usual Philly disco fare and all the more welcome for that reason. "Hit And Run" (5: 52) opens up the album with a hint of the **First Choice** in theme and styling: "Now that you've had your fun, you wanna run," Loleatta sings to a faithless man – perhaps the same guy who was always leaving the girls in First Choice stranded – then halfway through soars into a classic break and never comes down, swooping off with some words into a delicately echoed heaven somewhere.

"Hit And Run" and "Dreamin'" are the two strongest cuts, but "We're Getting Stronger (The Longer We Stay Together)" (4:34), a chugging love song that ends with a soulful talking break and an irresistible build, and "Ripped Off" (4:39), another song in the First Choice mold, are also favorites. All these were produced by Harris, but other tracks, mostly fine ballads, were handled by **Floyd Smith** or **Ron Kersey** working in both Chicago and Philadelphia studios. Yet, for once, it is the singer not the production team that shines most brightly here. Loleatta Holloway has one of those BIG voices you don't hear too often these days – make room for her. Overwhelming.

Two other cream-of-the-crop releases this week: **Andre Gagnon's** "Surprise," an ecstatic, extended instrumental with a Latin feel, a pumping beat, gorgeous strings and fabulous breaks – very full and dense; London has released it as a commercial disco disc at 5:53 with Gagnon's previous hit, "Wow," on the flip side – an excellent package – or as a 4:36 standard 45 on the Phase 4 Stereo label... and **Tasha Thomas'** "Stay With Me" on Buddah, which is, it says here, "From the motion picture 'The Next Man'" and reminds me of

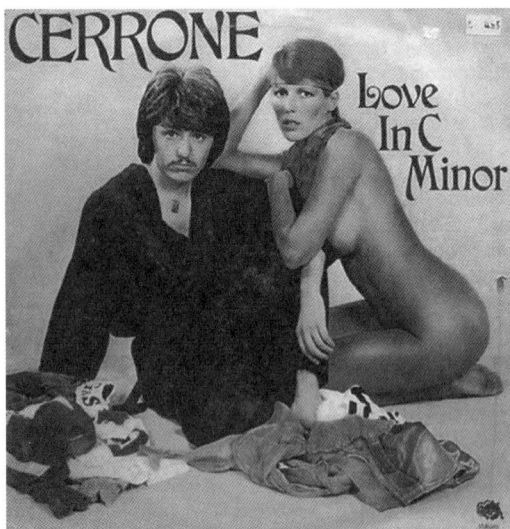

Tamiko Jones' "Let It Flow" with slightly softer edges, nice horn solos in the breaks, and great lead vocals reminiscent of **Merry Clayton** at times; I fell in love with it the first time I put it on, but don't ask me what condition I was in. Buddah has "Stay With Me" out on a single with a 6:20 disco version on one side and a 3:40 version on the other, but it deserves a 12-inch pressing.

Other notable album releases: **Kalyan** on MCA, a band from Trinidad which was produced by **Tony Silvester** and has an infectious, drum-sparked sound called "Soca" (soul/calypso) – very Afro-Latin and exciting, like **Brass Construction** meets **Osibisa**, especially on the opening cut, "Disco Reggae" (6:27). Also try "La La Jam Back" and a very upbeat version of **Jesse Green's** "Nice 'N' Slow;" a natural for crowds that are getting off on **Black Soul's** "Black Brother"... "Vibrations" by the **Roy Ayers Ubiquity** (Polydor), the group's most attractive, varied collection so far, with a fine cut in "Moving, Grooving," a driving, nervous jazz number with vocals (it's on Bill Kelly's top 10 from Warehouse VIII in Miami this week); other possibilities: "Do Melo (Give It To Me)," a bright romp, and "Come Out And Play," a free-your-mind song that ends with the group urging everyone to "Come out the closet and play"... Although **Herbie Mann** did nothing but badmouth disco after he had a hit with **Barrabas'** "Hijack," he's come back to the genre with "Bird In A Silver Cage" (Atlantic), produced in Germany by **Silver Convention's Michael Kunze** and **Sylvester Levay**, and the results are predictable but really nice. Mann's flute fits perfectly into the Silver Convention style, especially on "The Piper" and "Years Of Love," the two most likely dance cuts, though the zippy "Birdwalk" might catch on too; altogether very pleasant and extremely listenable. ◙

IPANEMA, NEW YORK
DJ: Ron Soares

DISCO DANCING/OUR LOVE CONCERTO/ RICE & BEANS THEME – Rice & Beans Orchestra (Dash)
DISCO INFERNO/DON'T BURN NO BRIDGES/BODY CONTACT CONTRACT – Trammps (Atlantic)
DISCO LUCY – Wilton Place Street Band (Island)
DON'T LEAVE ME THIS WAY – Thelma Houston (Tamla)
DON'T PUT THE BLAME ON ME BABY – Roger Troy (RCA)
I WANTCHA BABY/ALL MY LIFE – Arthur Prysock (Old Town)
IT AIN'T REGGAE (BUT IT'S FUNKY – Instant Funk (TSOP)
NO TEARS TOMORROW – Lonnie Smith (Groove Merchant)
SURPRISE – Andre Gagnon (London)
THOSE MEMORIES – Soul Crusaders (Lu-Tall)

WAREHOUSE VIII, MIAMI
DJ: Bill Kelly

DANCIN' – Crown Heights Affair (De-Lite)
DON'T LEAVE ME THIS WAY/ANY WAY YOU LIKE IT – Thelma Houston (Tamla)
DREAMIN' – Loleatta Holloway (Salsoul)
GOOD LOVE MAKES EVERYTHING ALRIGHT – Melba Moore (Buddah)
LET YOURSELF GO/I DON'T WANT TO BE TIED DOWN – Supremes (Motown)
LOVE BUG – Bumblebee Unlimited (Mercury)
MAGIC'S IN THE AIR/BOY I REALLY TIED ONE ON – Esther Phillips (Kudu)
MOVING, GROOVING – Roy Ayers Ubiquity (Polydor)
OOH OOH OOH I LIKE IT – Milton Wright (TK)
SPRING AFFAIR – Donna Summer (Casablanca)

WHIMSEY'S, BOSTON
DJ: John Luongo

DANCIN' – Crown Heights Affair (De-Lite)
DON'T LEAVE ME THIS WAY – Thelma Houston (Tamla)
DREAMIN'/HIT AND RUN – Loleatta Holloway (Gold Mind)
I FEEL LIKE I'VE BEEN LIVIN'/BODY CONTACT CONTRACT/STARVIN' – Trammps (Atlantic)
I'VE LEARNED FROM MY BURNS – Spiders Webb (Fantasy)
MY LOVE IS FREE – Double Exposure- (Salsoul)
OVERTURE/O BA BA – D. C. La Rue- (Pyramid)
SPRING RAIN – Silvetti (Salsoul)
WELCOME TO OUR WORLD – Mass Production (Cotillion)

L'ESPRIT, DETROIT
DJ: Rod Linnum

ALL MY LIFE/WHEN LOVE IS NEW – Arthur Prysock (Old Town)
CAR WASH – Rose Royce (MCA)
DARLIN', DARLIN' BABY – O'Jays (Phila. Intl.)
DAZZ – Brick (Bang)
DISCO INFERNO/BODY CONTACT – Trammps (Atlantic)
DON'T LEAVE ME THIS WAY – Thelma Houston (Tamla)
I DON'T WANNA LOSE YOUR LOVE/ FLOWER – Emotions (Columbia)
OPEN SESAME – Kool & the Gang (De-Lite)
WELCOME TO OUR WORLD/WINE-FLOW DISCO – Mass Production (Cotillion)
YOU + ME = LOVE/LET'S GO DOWN TO THE DISCO – Undisputed Truth (Whitfield)

> **Although Herbie Mann did nothing but badmouth disco after he had a hit with Barrabas' "Hijack," he's come back to the genre with "Bird In A Silver Cage," and the results are predictable but really nice**

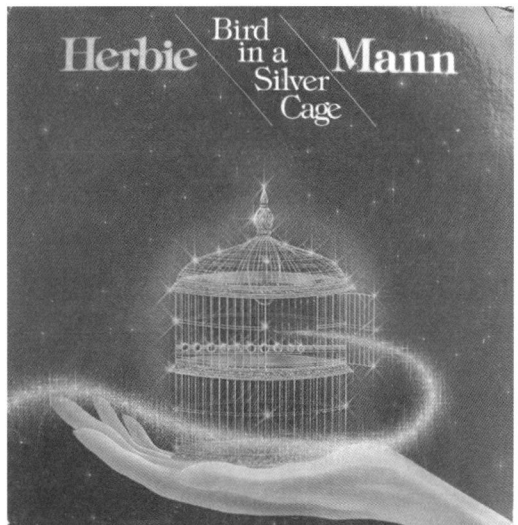

JANUARY 29, 1977

In a surprising and rather audacious move, Casablanca Records' **Heart and Soul Orchestra** (formerly known as **Frankie Crocker's Heart and Soul Orchestra**) is rushing out a disco disc cover version of **Cerrone's** sexsong of the moment, "Love In C Minor." Due in the stores this week as Casablanca's first commercial disco disc, the record was hand delivered to discos on both coasts last week by this version's co-producer, Provocative Promotion man Mark Paul Simon (F. Crocker is also given production credit), launching the first serious disco cover battle in some time. The Heart and Soul version is significantly different from Cerrone's in that the song's most suggestive elements – the moans, groans, orgasmic screams and the entire opening dialogue segment – have been dropped out, leaving the musical framework to stand on its own with only occasional singing from a somewhat muffled, bland girl chorus. The pace has been cut down slightly at the beginning so that it builds gradually which, as one DJ pointed out, "makes good dancing sense," and the length has been trimmed by about four minutes to something over twelve minutes. But perhaps the most obvious change is in the quality of the American recording, which is simply no match for the incredible brightness and clarity of the European original; the brilliant cutting edges of the Cerrone record – particularly the ecstatic zig zag of strings about halfway through – are softened here, blurred into a fuller, more cushy sound. Yet it remains an exciting, compelling record with some nice moments of its own, certainly nothing to be dismissed out of hand as an American knock-off of a French original. Needless to say, Casablanca is preparing a major push for the disco disc (which will be released with a blank, waffle-printed B side) and Cotillion is meeting the challenge with a flood of advance copies and a rush-release production schedule for the Cerrone album version (though rumors persist that it, too, may be somewhat bowdlerized by the removal of the three girls' opening dialogue). Cerrone has the edge on quality and sex but the Heart and Soul Orchestra looks like it might beat him into the marketplace.

The flood of way-above-average releases continues this week with the following albums: **Jerry Butler's** "Suite For The Single Girl" (Motown), a beautifully executed and cohesive concept album dealing with the problems and pleasures of a woman alone, highlighted by "Chalk It Up" (6:06), a complex production full of unexpected changes in pace and shifts in style – including a brief talk segment toward the end that fits in obliquely but perfectly –all of them handled with surprising ease and wit. It's a song of affectionate advice to the modern Cosmopolitan Girl on dealing with the end of an affair: "Chalk it up to experience/Call it education." Also attractive: a thumping "Let's Go Get Out Of Town" and a sly, subtle "Ms. Fine." Butler sounds like he's back at the top of his form – as good as you can get – and this one of his best albums ever... Just in time for an apparent revival of interest in the Afro-rock sound, **Osibisa** has come out with their strongest album in years, "Ojah Awake" (Island), an extremely varied collection sparked by their outstanding, explosive percussion. Best tracks: a terrific version of "The Warrior," a high-spirited song from the currently controversial South African musical "Ipi Tombi" that was something of an underground disco hit several years back (one complaint: at 3:43 the song is too short; it just starts getting hot – as the group chants "O-si-bi-sa"– when it ends abruptly); "Ojah Awake," "Keep On Trying" and "Sakabo" – all more deeply tribal in feeling. Also, "Flying Bird" is a fine atmospheric, early-evening cut. Highly invigorating... **The Ritchie Family's** "Life Is Music" (Marlin) seems to be taking the group in a decidedly more commercial pop direction, emphasizing the girls' voices and a brassy, high-gloss production style, frequently at the expense of musical depth or subtlety. The album features six tracks in the group's unmistakable brash, gushy style and the most appealing are those that best resist the overall tendency to rush off into a frantic French music hall can-can: "Super Lover" (5:45), which has the irresistible charm and exuberance of the group's best material, and the zippy title song, a celebration of the delights of music itself whose sheer joy should make it the album's first hit. Also destined for disco play: "Lady Luck," with its dense, swirling production, and "Disco Blues," which has the sound of an early rock & roll dance number. Production is by **Jacques Morali** and **Ritchie Rome**... **The Originals'** latest lp on the Soul label is titled, not surprisingly, "Down To Love Town" after their tremendously successful disco disc of the same name and that version of the song (re-mixed from the version that appeared on the group's last lp) is a key style-setter track here, with

"Ojah Awake" is deeply tribal, sparked by their outstanding, explosive percussion "

TATTOO LAGOON, SAN FRANCISCO
DJ: Wes Bradley

DISCO INFERNO/BODY CONTACT CONTRACT/STARVIN'/ DON'T BURN NO BRIDGES – Trammps (Atlantic)
DON'T LEAVE ME THIS WAY/ANY WAY YOU LIKE IT – Thelma Houston (Tamla)
FREE LOVE/YOU GOT A PROBLEM/IF YOU WANNA GO BACK – Jean Carn (Phila. Intl.)
FUNK DE MAMBO – Karma (Horizon)
HIT AND RUN/DREAMIN' – Loleatta Holloway (Gold Mind)
LOVE IN C MINOR – Cerrone (Malligator import)
LOVE IN MOTION/GIVIN' BACK THE FEELING – George McCrae (TK)
SPY FOR THE BROTHERHOOD – Miracles (Columbia)
TATTOO MAN – Denise McCann (Polydor import)
WHEN LOVE IS NEW/I WANTCHA BABY/ALL MY LOVE/ ALL I NEED IS YOU TONIGHT – Arthur Prysock (Old Town)

ON STAGE, FREEPORT, NEW YORK
DJ: Dewane Dixon

DISCO INFERNO/DON'T BURN NO BRIDGES/YOU TOUCH MY HOT LINE/ BODY CONTACT CONTRACT – Trammps (Atlantic)
FOR ELISE – Masters in Philadelphia (Capricorn)
FREE LOVE/IF YOU WANNA GO BACK – Jean Carn (Phila. Intl.)
FREEDOM TO EXPRESS YOURSELF – Denise LaSalle (ABC)
FUNK DE MAMBO – Karma (Horizon)
HIT AND RUN/DREAMIN'/RIPPED OFF – Loleatta Holloway (Gold Mind)
LOVE IN C MINOR – Cerrone (Malligator import)
LOVE IS YOU/COME BACK/MY TIME OF NEED/RATTLESNAKE – Carol Williams (Salsoul)
ON THE TOWN/SATURDAY NIGHT STEPPIN' OUT – Webster Lewis (Epic)
WE GOT AWAY/YOU GOTTA BE WILLIN' TO LOSE – Seawind (CTI)

PLAYGROUND, NEW YORK
DJ: Tony Carrasco

BODY CONTACT CONTRACT/DISCO INFERNO/I FEEL LIKE I'VE BEEN LIVIN'/ DON'T BURN NO BRIDGES – Trammps (Atlantic)
DON'T LEAVE ME THIS WAY – Thelma Houston (Tamla)
EVERYBODY HAVE A GOOD TIME – Archie Bell & the Drells (Phila. Intl.)
FREE LOVE/IF YOU WANNA GO BACK – Jean Carn (Phila. Intl.)
HIT AND RUN/DREAMIN' – Loleatta Holloway (Gold Mind)
HURRY UP AND WAIT/YOU ARE A BLESSING TO ME/SIX-MILLION DOLLAR MAN/BEEN DECIDED – Originals (Soul)
I WANTCHA BABY/ALL MY LIFE/ALL I NEED IS YOU TONIGHT – Arthur Prysock (Old Town)
LOVE IN MOTION/GIVIN' BACK THE FEELING – George McCrae (TK)
LOVE IS YOU/MY TIME OF NEED/COME BACK – Carol Williams (Salsoul)
THIS WILL MAKE YOU DANCE/LET'S RUNAWAY TOGETHER – G. C. Cameron (Motown)

several other cuts nearly matching it in intensity. The best: "Six-Million Dollar Man" (5:52), a smoothly upbeat and cleverly written number promising bionic pleasures; "Hurry Up And Wait" (5:22), which turns a tale of frustrations into a delightfully danceable song; "You Are A Blessing To Me" (6:02), sweeter, fuller and more expansive but slightly cut-up when it comes to a consistent dance beat; and "Been Decided" (5:22), the most laid-back of the up-tempo tracks, also very sweet (all four are on Tony Carrasco's Top 10 from Playground in New York this week). Altogether, a solid and satisfying album.

More recommended albums: The debut of a 9-man group called **Lakeside**, produced by **Frank Wilson** (on ABC), and containing two very good long tracks: "Taboo" (6:24), featuring a break bristling with jagged synthesizer and guitars, rumbling bass and jiving talk segments in a light metal framework, and "Diamond Girl (Tell Me Why You're Crying)" (6:07), which is brighter, lighter, kind of breezy and nice... "Reaching For The World" (ABC) is the appropriately titled first album from the newly structured, non-Philadelphia International **Harold Melvin & the Bluenotes** and while lead singer **David Ebo** is no real match for the grace and force of **Theodore Pendergrass** and H. Melvin himself is not about to challenge his former producers **Gamble & Huff**, still this new direction has its moments. Two prime instances: "Hostage Part 1 & 2" (6:30), driving and very upbeat, propelled by tough, aggressive vocals and a stirring string section – and "Reaching For The World" (4:24), already released as a single and the most Philadelphia-styled track (overtones of "When Love Is New") with a sharp, gripping commercial sound. ●

FEBRUARY 5, 1977

The two most irresistible and interesting new cuts this week are **George Benson's** nearly ten-minute version of **War's** "This World Is A Ghetto" and **Smokey Robinson's** charming, clever "Vitamin U." Benson's "Ghetto," from "In Flight" (Warner Brothers), his just-out follow-up to the tremendously successful "Breezin'," is structured in two parts, the first an airy, energetic instrumental featuring Benson's fluid, lightly stinging guitar, the second a vocal that is, again, a **Stevie Wonder** sound-alike. This one may not have been pre-cut for disco play – its complex construction, with several sharp, full-stop breaks, is not designed for a breezy dance-through because the pace is constantly being cut and then quickened again until the very upbeat final section – but that makes it all the more exciting and fresh. David Todd, who reports this week from Jouissance (the old Le Jardin) in New York, called to rave about the Benson cut, which he was playing from an advance sampler of new Warners jazz product. On the basis of the initial reaction at his club, he's listed it in his otherwise con- servative top 10 this week and I suspect it'll be cropping

up on a lot more lists once the album gets around. "Nature Boy" (5:58), also on Todd's list, is an equally gorgeous cut, a vocal version of an almost mystical, very beautiful **Nat "King" Cole** song which is done here as a laid-back hustle. Featured on the album as Benson's sidemen: **Ralph MacDonald**, **Phil Upchurch**, **Ronnie Foster**, **Harvey Mason**; **Tommy LiPuma** produced.

The **Smokey Robinson** track, "Vitamin U," opens up his latest solo album, "Deep In My Soul" (Tamla), on a delightful note. It starts out slow, then picks up to a gently chugging pace which seems a little unsure at times until it falls into a nice groove somewhere between "Tears Of A Clown" and "Love Hangover." Though the song wasn't written by Smokey himself, it has the wit and ease of one of his **Miracles** classics: "Since you went away from me," he sings, "I've got a love deficiency." He runs through the alphabet of vitamins and concludes he needs only "vitamin U, girl, to see me through." Robinson is, as usual, achingly sweet and never more so than when he runs through the alphabet near the end; I've always felt he could sing anything and make it touching – here he proves it again. The whole album, produced and written by a number of Motown's up-and coming staff talent – **Michael Sutton**, **Jeffrey Bowen**, **Larry Brown** – along with **Hal Davis**, feels like Smokey's own work (especially "There Will Come A Day," the current single, which picks up its opening notes from "You Really Got A Hold On Me") and seems to have been conceived as a tribute to his fine style.

Other recommended albums: **Brian Holland** produced the new **G.C. Cameron** album, "You're What's Missing In My Life" (Motown), for his Holland-Dozier-Holland Productions, so a few fine dance cuts should come as no surprise here and each side opens up with a long one. "This Will Make You Dance" (5:25) is the hotter of the two, full of punch and strong vocals; "Let's Run Away Together" (5:40) is more a choppy hustle. The rest of the album is superb, too, mostly slow and soulful; and check out the cover here... The magic cut on **Taj Mahal's** first Warner Brothers album, "Music Fuh Ya' (Musica Para Tu)," is "Curry" (6:43), a mysterious, lovely instrumental that seems to bloom like a field of flowers, highlighted by what sounds like the perfect steel drum and featuring hushed male voices whispering the title on the beat throughout. Very sensuous and the perfect atmospheric opening number for a night of music... **Vince Montana's** production work on the debut **Carol Williams** album, "'Lectric Lady" (Salsoul), featuring the **Salsoul Orchestra**, is not as inspired or deep as his work with the Orchestra but the best songs have a certain glossy attractiveness and are already cropping up on a number of club top 10 lists. "Come Back" and "Love Is You" are my two favorites and "My Time Of Need," with its unexplained chorus repetition of the McDonald's commercial formula ("Two all-beef patties etc.") is notable for its oddity. "Rattlesnake," which leaked out as a single last year and received some club play before being recalled from the release

CASBAH, ATLANTA
DJ: Jim Burgess

BODY CONTACT CONTRACT/DISCO INFERNO/STARVIN'/ I FEEL LIKE I'VE BEEN LIVIN' – Trammps (Atlantic)
COME BACK/LOVE IS YOU/RATTLESNAKE – Carol Williams (Salsoul)
DON'T LEAVE ME THIS WAY/I DON'T KNOW WHY I LOVE YOU – Thelma Houston (Tamla)
FREE LOVE/IF YOU WANNA GO BACK – Jean Carn (Phila. Intl.)
HIT AND RUN/DREAMIN'/RIPPED OFF – Loleatta Holloway (Gold Mind)
LIFE IS MUSIC/LADY LUCK/SUPERLOVER – Ritchie Family (Marlin)
LOVE IN MOTION/GIVIN' BACK THE FEELING – George McCrae (TK)
SPRING RAIN – Silvetti (Salsoul)
THEME FROM KING KONG – Love Unlimited Orchestra (20th Century)

BOOMBAMAKAOO, NEW YORK
DJ: Jorge Wheeler

DISCO INFERNO/BODY CONTACT CONTRACT – Trammps (Atlantic)
ESTOY EN ALGO/PORQUE NO ME DICE – Linda Lidia (TR)
FOLEY PARK – Con-Funk-Shun (Mercury)
FREE LOVE – Jean Carn (Phila. Intl.)
JUGETE DE TU CARINO – Ray Hernandez (TR)
O BA BA – D.C. La Rue (Pyramid)
OPEN SESAME – Kool & the Gang (De-Lite)
NO, NO, NO, MY FRIEND – Devoshun (SMI)
SPRING RAIN – Silvetti (Salsoul)
WHAT HAPPENED/SUNDAY KIND OF LOVE – Bobby Rodriguez & La Compania (Vaya)

JOUISSANCE, NEW YORK
DJ: David Todd

CALYPSO BREAKDOWN – Ralph MacDonald (Marlin)
DANCIN' – Crown Heights Affair (De-Lite)
DARLIN', DARLIN' BABY – O'Jays (Phila. Intl.)
DISCO INFERNO/BODY CONTACT CONTRACT – Trammps (Atlantic)
DON'T LEAVE ME THIS WAY – Thelma Houston (Tamla)
MY LOVE IS FREE – Double Exposure (Salsoul)
RITZY MAMBO/IT'S GOOD FOR THE SOUL – Salsoul Orchestra (Salsoul)
THIS SONG WILL LAST FOREVER – Lou Rawls (Phila. Intl.)
THE WORLD IS A GHETTO/NATURE BOY – George Benson (Warner Bros.)
YOU + ME = LOVE – Undisputed Truth (Whitfield)

CHERCHEZ LA FEMME, NEW YORK
DJ: Doug Riddick

ANOTHER STAR – Laso (MCA)
BENIHANA – Marilyn Chambers (Roulette)
DANCE IF YOU WANT TO – Randy Pie (Polydor import)
EVERYBODY HAVE A GOOD TIME – Archie Bell & the Drells (Phila. Intl.)
GIVE IT UP – Isis (UA lp)
LOVE IN C MINOR – Cerrone (Malligator import)
REACHING FOR THE WORLD – Harold Melvin & the Bluenotes (ABC)
SIX MILLION DOLLAR MAN – Originals (Soul)
SPACED OUT/CHARLESTON HOPSCOTCH – Cloud 9 (P&P)
TATTOO MAN – Denise McCann (Polydor import)

schedule, is okay, and "More," Williams' earlier success, is included here in a 4:54 version... "Truth Is The Power" (ABC) is the first **Mighty Clouds of Joy** album produced by **Frank Wilson** and, while it's not up to the group's first two crossover-to-pop lps under the direction of **Dave Crawford**, it has its moments. The best cut, "There's Love In The World (Tell The Lonely People)," has already been released as a single, but listen to "Like A Child" which combines gospel-style organ and clipped Latin percussion with a synthesizer underlining – best part is the final segment when a wooden stick beat dominates and the group gets carried away.

For fans of Brazilian music, both **Jorge Ben** and **Milton Nascimento** have new albums available on American labels now. Ben's, titled "Tropical" (Island), is more upbeat and danceable than his last collection for that label. This one opens up with his "Taj Mahal" (4:18), the song **Crystal Grass** covered last year; and check out "Os Alquimistas Estao Chegando As Alquimistas" and "Chove Chuva," both sparkling. The **Nascimento** album, on A&M, is oriented more to the English-speaking market and was recorded in Los Angeles with side men like **Herbie Hancock**, **Wayne Shorter** and **Airto Moreira**. It's a balanced, classy set alternating Portuguese and English vocals of great delicacy.

Recommended singles: "Mucho Macho" is a two-part sexsong by a group called **Macho** on Event that consists of some terrific horns, a steamy, dense arrangement, and girls repeating the title with near-orgasmic enthusiasm. When they start oozing, "So strong, so big," one is not entirely sure of just what they're talking about but one can guess: X-rated and fine, produced by some guys from **Fatback Band**... Speaking of Fatback, that group's own new single, "Double Dutch" (Spring), is not as driving or creative as most of their recent work, but it's an entertaining, serviceable dance song, complete with directions to the title step in case you want to follow along... It's been just about a year since the great **Brown Sugar** single, "The Game Is Over"/"I'm Going Through Changes Now," and their new release is with a new producer and in a different mold: called "Don't Tie Me Down" (Capitol), it's brittle and funky with a **Jones Girls** feel and some great lead vocals – for gritty girl group fans. ✆

❝ He runs through the alphabet and concludes he needs "vitamin U, girl, to see me through" ❞

FEBRUARY 12, 1977

I've accumulated a tremendous backlog of 12-inch pressings in the past few weeks, so, in an effort to catch up, here's a quick rundown of the best and/or most noteworthy of the lot: The **Love Unlimited Orchestra's** "Theme From King Kong" (20th Century) becomes rather overlong toward the end of its eight minutes but its structure – an ominous, percussive opening section followed by a pretty symphonic section – echoes "My Sweet Summer Suite" so it's catching on fast. The pounding first part is like entering a dark and teeming jungle; **Barry White** produced … **Barbara Pennington's** "Twenty-four Hours A Day" (UA) was already reviewed here as a single but now that it's available as a disco disc (promotional copies only), it deserves another mention. This 9:22 version highlights the plaintive sweep of strings and cushions Pennington's vocals between thick slabs of instrumentation; already successful as an import, this longer length should do very well... The **Black Light Orchestra's** "Touch Me, Take Me," an import disc from RCA in Canada, starts out sounding suspiciously like "Love In C Minor" but after a nearly identical opening, the song shifts and moves in a slightly different direction – a few choruses of light-weight female vocals, a very good percussion break and a dense instrumental reprise followed by another neat break, running 6:55 altogether. One suspects "C Minor" was the take-off point for "Touch Me, Take Me" – and they would certainly make an easy mix – but the end result is something else again and should stand on its own quite well. Made in Montreal, this one's worth searching for... **Silver Blue's** "We Got Love On Our Side" (TK) is a bright, Philadelphia-style instrumental with an effusive female chorus repeating the song's title throughout and some particularly nice flute, drum and horn solos – delightful and breezy, especially in its 6:25 length (also available on the "disco version" side of the Marlin single)... "Uptown Festival" by **Shalamar** (Soul Train) is a fabulous medley of Motown classics kicking off, appropriately, with "Going To A Go Go" and running through old favorites like "Uptight," "This Old Heart Of Mine," "Stop! In The Name Of Love" and a number of others all strung on a tight, throbbing drumbeat continuum and sung by a variety of voices. Very zippy, great fun and certain to be a crowd-pleaser in a lot of clubs (also contains one fine instrumental break that you wish was longer). Also recommended: "Classically Elise" by **Dino Solera**

and the **Munich Machine** (Hidden Sign), the **Donna Summer** treatment of **Beethoven** produced by **Giorgio Moroder**, now on a 12-inch disc 6:20 on one side, 5:34 on the other ("For Elise," another disc-style version of the same piece by **The Philarmonics**, a British studio group whole lp, "The Masters In Philadelphia," was previously mentioned as an import, is out now as a 4:37 single or album cut (same length) on Capricorn (yes, Capricorn)... **The Softones'** "Call It Love" (H&L) sounds a little like "Hollywood Hot" with an **Eddie Kendricks** style falsetto in the lead and has an especially strong final segment when the violins cut through like bolts of lightning; the message: "Call it love/(When you get down)/Any other name just don't sound right."... Collector's item: a French version of "Disco Duck" by **Paul Vincent** which Beam Junction has released on a 12-inch backed with an exuberant instrumental version, "Disco Duck Symphony" (5:44), that's an incongruous mixture of quacks and strings. Hilarious, and packaged in a Richard Bernstein-designed Donald Duck sleeve that should appeal to Disney fetishists... Also now available on disco discs: **The Destinations'** "I've Got To Dance To Keep From Cryin'," which AVI has lengthened to 5:34, blending in "The Hustle And The Bus Stop" from the single's B side – both songs are included as separate cuts on the Giant 45's flip side; "Philly Armada" and "For The Love Of Money" by the **Armada Orchestra** back-to-back on TK; and, finally, **Crown Heights Affair's** great "Dancin'" and "Love Me" tracks, both same lengths as on the album, on one De-Lite disc.

Recommended album cuts: Two fiery Brazilian instrumentals in the carnival rhythm known as batucada, one called "Batucada" (4:42) from the new **Airto** album, "Promises Of The Sun" (Arista), the other titled "Ritmo Number One" (8:26) from an album called "Agora" by another Brazilian percussionist, **Paulinho da Costa** (on Pablo, through RCA). Both are incredible percussive explosions, Airto's the more intense, da Costa's the more sustained. Anyone who got off on the Brazilian-flavored opening of "My Sweet Summer Suite" will be in ecstasy with these tracks – the ultimate drum solos, but featuring a whole spectrum of unusual percussion instruments (da Costa lists solos by pandeiro, cuica, a-go-go, reco-reco, whistle, spoons, frying pan, congas) for a particularly spicy effect. Sensational.

❝ I've accumulated a tremendous backlog of 12-inch pressings in the past few weeks ❞

MOON'S TRUCK, PHOENIX
DJ: Jack Witherby

DANCIN' /LOVE ME – Crown Heights Affair (De-Lite)
DISCO INFERNO/BODY CONTACT CONTRACT/I FEEL LIKE I'VE BEEN LIVIN' STARVIN' – Trammps (Atlantic)
DON'T LEAVE ME THIS WAY /ANY WAY YOU LIKE IT/I DON'T KNOW WHY I LOVE YOU – Thelma Houston (Tamla)
FUNK DE MAMBO – Karma (Horizon)
GOTHAM CITY BOOGIE/INDIGO COUNTRY – Ultrafunk (TK)
HIT AND RUN/RIPPED OFF/DREAMIN' – Loleatta Holloway (Gold Mind)
LOVE IN C MINOR – Heart & Soul Orchestra (Casablanca)
LOVE IN MOTION/GIVIN' BACK THE FEELING/DANCE IN A CIRCLE – George McCrae (TK)
O BA BA/OVERTURE/INDISCREET /DON'T KEEP IT IN THE SHADOWS – D.C. LaRue (Pyramid)
THEME FROM 'KING KONG' – Love Unlimited Orchestra (20th Century)

REGINES, NEW YORK
DJ: Jonata Garavaglia

DISCO INFERNO – Trammps (Atlantic)
DISCO REGGAE – Kalyan (MCA)
DOUBLE DUTCH – Fatback Band (Spring)
HIT AND RUN – Loleatta Holloway (Gold Mind)
LIFE IS MUSIC – Ritchie Family (Marlin)
LOVE IN C MINOR – Cerrone (Malligator import)
REACHING FOR THE WORLD – Harold Melvin & the Bluenotes (ABC)
SIX-MILLION DOLLAR MAN – Originals (Soul)
THAT'S THE TROUBLE – Grace Jones (Beam Junction)
THEME FROM 'KING KONG' – Love Unlimited Orchestra (20th Century)

LE JOCK, NEWARK, NEW JERSEY
DJ: Rafael Charres

BODY CONTACT CONTRACT/DISCO INFERNO/DON'T BURN NO BRIDGES – Trammps (Atlantic)
FREE LOVE/IF YOU WANNA GO BACK/TIME WAITS FOR NO ONE/YOU GOT A PROBLEM – Jean Carn (Phila. Intl.)
HIT AND RUN/RIPPED OFF/DREAMIN' – Loleatta Holloway (Gold Mind)
HURRY UP AND WAIT /SIX-MILLION DOLLAR MAN/YOU ARE A BLESSING TO ME – Originals (Soul)
I'VE LEARNED FROM MY BURNS – Spiders Webb (Fantasy)
LADY LUCK/SUPER LOVE – Ritchie Family (Marlin)
LET'S GO DOWN TO THE DISCO/LOOSE – Undisputed Truth (Whitfield)
LOVE IN C MINOR/BLACK IS BLACK/ MIDNIGHT LADY – Cerrone (Malligator import)
LOVE IN MOTION/GIVIN' BACK THE FEELING – George McCrae (TK)
LOVE IS YOU/YOU'RE SO MUCH A PART OF ME/MY TIME OF NEED – Carol Williams (Salsoul)

CIRCUS MAXIMUS, LOS ANGELES
DJ: Mitch Schatsky

BENIHANA – Marilyn Chambers (Roulette)
BON BON – S.D.V. & Friends (Deram import)
DISCO INFERNO/DON'T BURN NO BRIDGES/STARVIN' – Trammps (Atlantic)
DON'T LEAVE ME THIS WAY – Thelma Houston (Tamla)
FOR ELISE – Philarmonics (Capricorn)
LOVE IN C MINOR – Heart & Soul Orchestra (Casablanca)
LOVE IN MOTION/GIVIN' BACK THE FEELING – George McCrae (TK)
SIX-MILLION DOLLAR MAN/HURRY UP AND WAIT/YOU ARE A BLESSING TO ME – Originals (Soul)
THIS WILL MAKE YOU DANCE – G.C. Cameron (Motown)
UPTOWN FESTIVAL – Shalamar (Soul Train)

The records people are talking about this week: **Kalyan's** infectious "Disco Reggae" (MCA); the whole **Originals** album, especially "Six Million Dollar Man" (Soul); **G.C. Cameron's** "This Will Make You Dance" (Motown); "O Ba Ba," the strong second-wind cut from **D.C. LaRue's** "Tea Dance" lp (Pyramid) and, still, "Love In C Minor," both in its original **Cerrone** version and the **Heart and Soul Orchestra** interpretation. The latter, on Casablanca's first commercial disco disc, hit the stores nearly a week before Cotillion's album, but Cerrone's already on our Top 20 as an import so far now he has the edge. A number of DJs, like David Mancuso at the Loft, are playing both versions, getting into each one's unique qualities. ❂

DISCO FILE TOP 20

1. **DISCO INFERNO/BODY CONTACT CONTRACT** – Trammps (Atlantic)
2. **DON'T LEAVE ME THIS WAY** – Thelma Houston (Tamla)
3. **DREAMIN'/HIT AND RUN** – Loleatta Holloway (Gold Mind)
4. **LOVE IN MOTION/GIVIN' BACK THE FEELING** – George McCrae (TK)
5. **DON'T BURN NO BRIDGES/I FEEL LIKE I'VE BEEN LIVIN'/STARVIN'** – Trammps (Atlantic)
6. **FREE LOVE/IF YOU WANNA GO BACK** – Jean Carn (Phila. Intl.)
7. **LOVE IN C MINOR** – Cerrone (Malligator import)
8. **SIX-MILLION DOLLAR MAN** – Originals (Soul)
9. **O BA BA/OVERTURE** – D. C. La Rue (Pyramid)
10. **DANCIN'** – Crown Heights Affair (De-Lite)
11. **RIPPED OFF** – Loleatta Holloway (Gold Mind)
12. **LOVE IS YOU/COME BACK/MY TIME OF NEED** – Carol Williams (Salsoul)
13. **SPRING RAIN** – Silvetti (Salsoul)
14. **HURRY UP AND WAIT/YOU ARE A BLESSING TO ME** – Originals (Soul)
15. **I WANTCHA BABY/ALL MY LIFE** – Arthur Prysock (Old Town)
16. **WELCOME TO OUR WORLD** – Mass Production (Cotillion)
17. **OPEN SESAME** – Kool & the Gang (De-Lite)
18. **EVERYBODY HAVE A GOOD TIME** – Archie Bell & the Drells (Phila. Intl.)
19. **LET YOURSELF GO** – Supremes (Motown)
20. **SPRING AFFAIR/SUMMER FEVER** – Donna Summer (Casablanca)

FEBRUARY 19, 1977

An unusually good batch of unexpected, interesting, even exciting records this week. Beginning with the disco discs, these are the cream of the crop: "Do What You Wanna Do," the **T-Connection's** first release since "Disco Magic" early last summer, is the record all the New York DJs seem to be talking about this week. It's very different from its predecessor, more hard-edged and vocal as well as instrumental, sparked by several terrific breaks, the first one a lively Latin percussion segment that's timed separately on the label at 2:15 (in an overall 7:15 track). The message (cf. "Do It Any Way You Wanna," "Do What You Feel," etc.) is already a popular one and the production is definitely crowd-pleasing, supple yet driving. (On a TK disco disc, this one's also available as a Dash single at 3:30)... "Am I Losing You?" (Cotton) is a sensational duet between **Dooley Silverspoon** and **Jeanne Burton** about their love relationship, which deepens considerably in the course of this 6:10 disc – Burton erupts in convincingly orgasmic moans and shouts at one point as the orchestra seethes along behind her, followed by a return to the duet with doubled fervor. In addition to being an excellent pairing of voices, this is the most commercial and compelling production we've heard from New York producer **Sonny Cassella**, who styles himself in the label credits as S.D.N.N.Y. (The Sound of New New York). Very strong... I've raved about **Black Ivory's** "Walking Downtown" (Buddah) before – it's the most powerful and involving cut on their last album, released several months back – but the quality of the original pressing had kept it off most turntables in spite of the fact that it's one of the best hard-partying cuts around. Now it's been re-mixed and issued on a 12-inch pressing and is too hot to ignore: more than eight minutes of super energetic music that deserves comparison with **Brass Construction** or **Mass Production.** Two other fine cuts from the same album – "Dance" and "White Wind" – are on the flip side... Also on Buddah, more, more, more of the **Andre True Connection** with "N.Y., You Got Me Dancing," featuring a typically aggressive, busy **Gregg Diamond** production and repetitive lyrics arranged around some drive-'em-up-the walls breaks. This one's already been getting a solid response in its shorter single version, but now that the six-minute disc is finally available, it could really take off. Not exactly subtle, but rousing and fun, and a passing tribute to some New York disco hot spots (Barefoot Boy, 12 West) rhymes "come in your jeans" with "Regine's." **Marilyn Chambers**, another porno star (and ex-Ivory Soap mother), has entered the X-rated disco field in True's wake with a thumping number called "Benihana" on Roulette (4:21). Her prolonged mock orgasm at the song's climax is only slightly more believable than her singing, but the production is kinda cute and commercial and it's already being touted as, you'll pardon the expression, a comer by a number of DJs. Is Harry Reems next?... **John Davis & the Monster Orchestra's** latest, "Up Jumped The Devil" (Sam), is tough and invigorating, full of pumping bass, bristling percussion (especially in the opening and several breaks) and more vocals than before. It runs 5:42 and doesn't let up; the second side of this disco disc is a six-minute track called "You Got To Give It Up" whose overall pace is

LES MOUCHES, NEW YORK
DJ, Roy Thode

DISCO INFERNO/BODY CONTACT CONTRACT – Trammps (Atlantic)
DON'T LEAVE ME THIS WAY – Thelma Houston (Tamla)
DOWN TO LOVE TOWN – Originals (Motown)
FLIP – Jesse Green (Red Bus Tempo import)
LADY LUCK/LIFE IS MUSIC – Ritchie Family (Marlin)
LOVE IN C MINOR/BLACK IS BLACK – Cerrone (Cotillion)
LOVE IN MOTION – George McCrae (TK)
MY LOVE IS FREE – Double Exposure (Salsoul)
SPRING RAIN – Silvetti (Salsoul)
THAT'S THE TROUBLE – Grace Jones (Beam Junction)

DCA CLUB, PHILADELPHIA
DJ: Kurt Borusiewicz

DISCO BLUES/LIFE IS MUSIC/LADY LUCK – Ritchie Family (Marlin)
DISCO INFERNO/BODY CONTACT CONTRACT – Trammps (Atlantic)
DISCO REGGAE/NICE AND SLOW – Kalyan (MCA)
DON'T LEAVE ME THIS WAY – Thelma Houston (Tamla)
DREAMIN'/HIT AND RUN/RIPPED OFF – Loleatta Holloway (Gold Mind)
FREE LOVE – Jean Carn (Phila. Intl.)
LOVE IN C MINOR/BLACK IS BLACK/ MIDNIGHT LADY – Cerrone (Cotillion)
MUCHO MACHO – Macho (Event)
MY TIME OF NEED/COME BACK – Carol Williams (Salsoul)
SPRING RAIN – Silvetti (Salsoul)

OLD PLANTATION, DALLAS
DJ: Howard Metz

BOY, I REALLY TIED ONE ON – Esther Phillips (Kudu)
DISCO INFERNO – Trammps (Atlantic)
DON'T LEAVE ME THIS WAY – Thelma Houston (Tamla)
I'VE GOT TO DANCE (TO KEEP FROM CRYIN') – Destinations (AVI)
LADY LUCK – Ritchie Family (Marlin)
LOVE IN C MINOR – Heart & Soul Orchestra (Casablanca)
LOVE IN MOTION – George McCrae (TK)
SPRING RAIN – Silvetti (Salsoul)
THEME FROM KING KONG – Love Unlimited Orchestra (20th Century)
UPTOWN FESTIVAL – Shalamar (Soul Train)

HARRAH, NEW YORK
DJ: Wayne Scott

DANCIN' – Crown Heights Affair (De-Lite)
DISCO INFERNO – Trammps (Atlantic)
DON'T LEAVE ME THIS WAY – Thelma Houston (Tamla)
FREEDOM TO EXPRESS YOURSELF – Denise LaSalle (ABC)
HIT AND RUN/DREAMIN' – Lolleatta Holloway (Gold Mind)
LADY LUCK – Ritchie Family (Marlin)
LET YOURSELF GO – Supremes (Motown)
LOVE IN C MINOR – Cerrone (Cotillion)
LOVE IN MOTION – George McCrae (TK)
TATTOO MAN – Denise McCann (Polydor import)

somewhat more laid back but worth checking out... Now available on a 12-inch pressing: **George McCrae's** "Love In Motion" and "Givin' Back The Feeling" back-to-back on TK.

RECOMMENDED ALBUMS: **Eloise Laws** joins the ranks of the strong, idiosyncratic women singers – **Thelma Houston**, **Loleatta Holloway**, **Jean Carn** – currently so successful on the disco floor, with an album called "Ain't It Good Feeling Good" (Invictus) and produced by **Brian Holland** (executive producer: **Eddie Holland**). The best tracks – "You Got Me Loving You Again," "Love Goes Deeper Than That," "Put a Little Love Into It (When You Do It)" and "Make It Last Forever" feel like a combination of **Laura Lee** and Thelma Houston: no-nonsense singing with full-bodied productions and just the right raw, sultry edge to both. All the cuts cited run between four and five minutes and should be checked out without delay... **The Players' Association** is a jazz/disco group whose first album on Vanguard contains six long tracks, four of which are excellent, cooking instrumentals. Two are versions of disco hits – "Love Hangover" (6:08) and "Let's Groove" (7:16) – that sound startlingly fresh (key ingredient: sax and flute solos by CTI's **Joe Farrell**); the other pair – "Hustlin'" (4:22) and "I Like It" (5:22) – are lively, high-spirited numbers with the kind of zest that you pick up on immediately. David Todd from New York's Jouissance brought this album to my attention and says it's his pick of the week, especially "Love Hangover." I'll second that.

RECOMMENDED SINGLES: **Timmy Thomas'** "Stone To The Bone" (Glades), a real Miami off-the-wall instrumental leaning to the style of **Foxy's** "Get Off Your Aahh!" and featuring delightful floating vocals riffing with the title over and over; a high point: the rising scream near the middle. Haunting... **Garland Green's** "Don't Let Love Walk Out On Us" (RCA), a gorgeous song in the mold of "You'll Never Find Another Love Like Mine" that just builds and builds. Green sounds like a combination of **Lou Rawls** and **Arthur Prysock** and the production, by **Leon Haywood**, who co-arranged with **Gene Page**, is superb... **Elvin Bishop's** "Keep It Cool" (Capricorn) has a thump-thump bass line and ecstatic, high-pitched vocals advising, "Keep it cool, keep it loose" – almost anthemic and quite attractive; could be a big left-field hit for some clubs (thanks to RW's Barry Taylor for alerting us to this one)... Noted: a guy with a falsetto voice named **Danny White** has done a version of **Tina Charles'** "Dance Little Lady Dance" on TK's Rocky Coast label.

Excellent response recently to: **The Ritchie Family's** "Lady Luck," the favorite disco cut on the group's new album, followed by the title cut, "Life Is Music" (Marlin); **Karma's** "Funk De Mambo" (the disco-disc length of 6:20 has just been issued on a standard 45 on A&M's Horizon label); and **Denise McCann's** "Tattoo Man," the import disco disc from Polydor Canada. ◐

Three excellent new albums this week whose stylistic diversity reflects the wide-ranging tastes of the disco crowd, from the cool, spacey synthesizer symphonies of **Cloud One's** "Atmosphere Strut" (P&P), to the earthy, neo-African chants of **Black Soul** (Beam Junction) to classic, classy **Gamble & Huff** Philadelphia soul on the first solo album from **Teddy Pendergrass** (Philadelphia International). Cloud One is essentially producer **Patrick Adams**, one of the most interesting young talents around, who is also the writer, arranger, vocalist and one-man band here (he played everything but the drums). The title instrumental, quite successful last year as a single and a disco disc, sets the tone: airy, electronic, shimmering with bright highlights and shot through with piercing, playful synthesizer wails, the signature of most Adams productions. Of the six cuts on the album, all but one are danceable, with "Spaced Out" and "Disco Juice" strong favorites right now. Only one complaint: though all the tracks are long, no time is indicated on the cover or label. (Note: Patrick Adams is also the producer, arranger and writer for the debut album by a fine young flute-player named **Art Webb** – "Mr. Flute" on Atlantic – which contains some nice atmospheric, early or late evening cuts and two that might work any time: "Come And Get Some Of This" and "Smile.")... **Black Soul's** music is a strong, rich Afro-rock blend; like **Manu Dibango's** group, the core musicians here came to France from Africa and

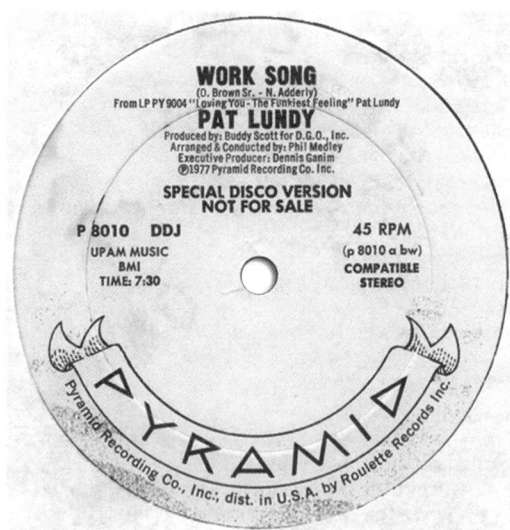

> **" Cloud One is essentially producer Patrick Adams, one of the most interesting young talents around, who is also the writer, arranger, vocalist and one-man band here (he played everything but the drums) "**

the resultant mix of influences is similar. In addition to the previously available "Black Brothers," "Mangous Ye" and a somewhat remixed "Black Soul Music," there are three other cuts in this sinuous, heavily percussive style, all of them excellent: "Africa Africa," "People" and "Dakar Sound"... **Teddy Pendergrass**, formerly the riveting lead voice with **Harold Melvin & the Bluenotes**, stayed with Gamble & Huff when the group broke up and his loyalty to that team paid off handsomely on this new album. The sound is hardly a departure for G&H, but two cuts rate with their best work and Teddy's, too: "The More I Get, The More I Want" (4:27), an energetic, aggressive love song with a series of great breaks at the end; and "You Can't Hide From Yourself" (4:06), one of Gamble & Huff's more potent message songs with an especially tough bottom. Pendergrass sounds as powerful as ever; one of the great soul voices soaring on his own (listen also to his performance on "Somebody Told Me," another effective message song).

EXPERIMENT, NEW YORK
DJ: John Benitez

BODY CONTACT CONTRACT/DISCO INFERNO
– Trammps (Atlantic)
DISCO FANTASY – Coke Escovado (Mercury)
DISCO REGGAE – Kalyan (MCA)
DO WHAT YOU WANNA DO – T-Connection (TK)
DREAMIN'/HIT AND RUN – Loleatta Holloway (Salsoul)
FLIP – Jesse Green (Red Bus Tempo import)
I LIKE IT/LOVE HANGOVER/LET'S GROOVE
– Player's Association (Vanguard)
LOVE IN C MINOR – Cerrone (Cotillion)
SIX MILLION DOLLAR MAN/ HURRY UP AND WAIT
– Originals (Soul)
UP JUMPED THE DEVIL – John Davis & Monster Orch. (Sam)

EAGLE IN EXILE, WASHINGTON, D.C.
DJ: Jon Carter Davis

DISCO INFERNO – Trammps (Atlantic)
DON'T LEAVE ME THIS WAY – Thelma Houston (Tamla)
DREAMIN' /HIT AND RUN/ WE'RE GETTING STRONGER
– Loleatta Holloway (Salsoul)
IF YOU WANNA GO BACK/FREE LOVE – Jean Carn (Phila. Intl.)
LOVE IN C MINOR – Heart & Soul Orchestra (Casablanca)
MANGOUS YE/ BLACK BROTHER/BLACK SOUL MUSIC –
Black Soul (Beam Junction)
OJAH AWAKE/THE WARRIOR – Osibisa (Island)
REACHING FOR THE WORLD – Harold Melvin & the
Bluenotes (ABC)
SIX MILLION DOLLAR MAN/HURRY UP AND WAIT
– Originals (Soul)
THERE'S LOVE IN THE WORLD/LISTEN PEOPLE
– Mighty Clouds of Joy (ABC)

TATTOO LAGOON, SAN FRANCISCO
DJ: Wes Bradley

BLACK IS BLACK/MIDNIGHT LADY – Cerrone (Malligator)
DO WHAT YOU WANNA DO – T-Connection (TK)
HELLO AFRICA/ NICE AND SLOW – Kalyan (MCA)
LOVE IN C MINOR – Heart & Soul Orchestra (Casablanca)
N.Y. YOU GOT ME DANCING – Andrea True Connection
(Buddah)
**SIX MILLION DOLLAR MAN/HURRY UP AND WAIT/YOU
ARE A BLESSING TO ME** – Originals (Soul)
TATTOO MAN – Denise McCann (Polydor import)
THERE'S LOVE IN THE WORLD – Mighty Clouds of Joy (ABC)
TWENTY-FOUR HOURS A DAY – Barbara Pennington (UA)
THE WORK SONG – Pat Lundy (Pyramid)

TRINITY'S, NEW ORLEANS
DJ: Stu Neal

DISCO INFERNO – Trammps (Atlantic)
DISCO LUCY – Wilton Place Street Band (Island)
DON'T LEAVE ME THIS WAY – Thelma Houston (Tamla)
FUNK DE MAMBO – Karma (Horizon)
LIFE IS MUSIC/LADY LUCK – Ritchie Family (Marlin)
MAGIC'S IN THE AIR/BOY I REALLY TIED ONE ON
– Esther Phillips (Kudu disco disc)
N.Y., YOU GOT ME DANCING – Andrea True Connection
(Buddah)
SORRY – Grace Jones (Beam Junction)
THEME FROM KING KONG – Love Unlimited Orchestra
(20th Century)
UP JUMPED THE DEVIL – John Davis & Monster Orch. (Sam)

Other recommended album cuts: "Pictures And Memories" (4:33) by **Marlena Shaw**, who's been teamed with producer **Bert deCoteaux** again (he did "It's Better Than Walking Out" and "Love Has Gone Away" for her) on her first Columbia album, "Sweet Beginnings." He's given this opening cut thumping, loping beat that carries Shaw's sharp, sexy vocals along with appealing ease… A number of people have been after me for ignoring a very hot cut from the recent **Brainstorm** album ("Stormin'" on Tabu, through RCA) called "Lovin' Is Really My Game" and featuring a terrific, full-bodied female lead and a vigorously building production. Accept my apologies and check it out… Also showing up on playlists these days: "People With Feeling," a typically robust, though awfully show-biz, track from the recent **Three Degrees** album ("Standing Up For Love" on Epic).

Another aspect of the broadening and diversifying of taste on the disco scene is the recent success of a number of hard-core funk records, most notably **Denise LaSalle's** "Freedom To Express Yourself" (ABC), which continues to crop up on playlists from all over. Now single, a funk delight called "Ain't Gonna Bump No More (With No Big Fat Woman)" (Epic), which has a pumping southern soul sound with some **KC & the Sunshine Band** overtones. Wayne Scott, who reported from Harrah in New York last week, said the Tex record was going over nicely and mentioned that he's also playing a gritty number called "Lowdown, Dirty, Good Lover," the B side of the new Arista single by **Shirley Brown** (remember "Woman To Woman"?). Lowdown, dirty and good is a pretty accurate description of the record's style and it should go over well with Denise LaSalle and **Loleatta Holloway** fans. **Oliver Sain's** "B-OO-G-IE" (Abet) is funk in a disco instrumental format with some tasty guitar work over an insistent pulse beat and a girl chorus chanting "Do it, do it, do it;" this one's available as a disco disc running 6:43. Finally, there's "Funk Machine" by **Funk Machine** on a TK 12-inch pressing (8:00 on one side, 5:45 on the other), which is also summed up in its title: funky maybe, but very mechanical.

Now available and re-recommended on disco disc: **George Benson's** beautiful "The World Is A Ghetto" (Warner Brothers); longer versions of **The Philarmonics'** "For Elise" and "Piano Concerto" on one disc (Capricorn); **Mystique's** excellent "What Would The World Be Like Without Music," "If You're In Need" and "Keep On Playing The Music," also on one record (Curtom); a terrific re-mix and lengthening of **Skip Mahoaney & the Casuals'** "Running Away From Love" (Abet) and **The Players' Association** version of "Love Hangover" that everyone's wild about, on Vanguard – this is the hottest record on the grapevine this week. ⊘

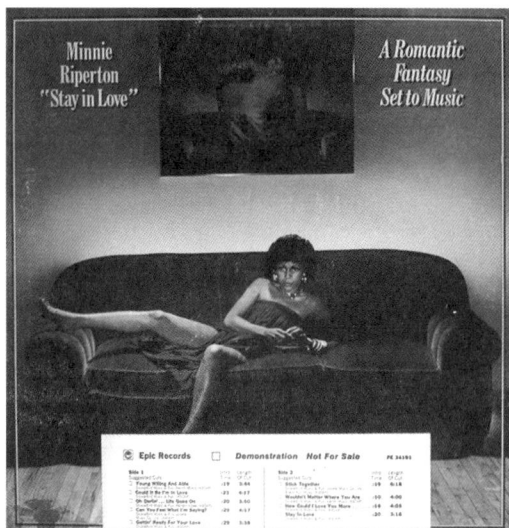

A mixed bag of new material by women this week, headed by new albums from **Gloria Gaynor** and **Minnie Riperton**. Gaynor's, titled simply "Glorious" (Polydor), is her first lp without the DCA production team, **Monardo, Bongio, Ellis**, and the first to depart from the format that had set the GG/DCA albums apart from the beginning: the heavily percussive three-song medley that always filled side one has been dispensed with. The result is a more balanced album but one whose impact is considerably more diffused. Producers **Gregg Diamond** (hot right now with **George McCrae** and **Andrea True**) and **Joe Beck** (the guitarist featured on all of **Esther Phillps'** recent albums) haven't totally dispensed with Gloria Gaynor tradition – there is a remake-of-a-standard, in this case "As Time Goes By," sung in a rather sluggish drone and the least successful cut here –but for once the singer isn't forced to scream over an impossibly overblown instrumental track and the effect is at once less compelling and more bearable in the long run. All but one of the tracks are upbeat, with "We Can Start Over Again," "Why Should I Pay" and "Life Ain't Worth Living" standing out as the most spunky, but the most interesting thing on the album is also the most unexpected and uncharacteristic. This is a long (9:15) track called "Most of All," which is largely instrumental, gorgeously string-laced, and sounds nothing like anything either Gaynor or Diamond have done before. "Most of all," GG sings, in a hushed voice that sounds like a combination of **Carol Douglas** in "Midnight Love Affair" and **Donna Summer** in "Winter Melody," "I wanna love you like you've never been loved before." But the prime lyric dispenses with all others: "We don't need no words – let the music speak for itself." And it speaks quite beautifully – a little slow for some crowds, perhaps, but the sound is so rich and creamy I find it hard to resist.

Minnie Riperton's "Stay In Love" (subtitled "A Romantic Fantasy Set To Music," on Epic), is also a change-of-pace for her under the direction of producer **Freddie Perren**. As usual, Minnie is sexy and sensuous, but Perren takes the precious edge off her music and makes it more propulsive and sharp. The standout cut is the longest: "Stick Together" (6:18), written in part by **Stevie Wonder** and Riperton, set to a comfortably pulsing beat and accented by some of Minnie's familiar vocal acrobatics. Bobby DJ, back at Infinity in New York, put the two-part single version on his top 10 this week but now it's available on the album and on a promotional 12-inch pressing as well. Also worth checking out: "How Could I Love You More." Note: among the impressive cast of musicians and back-up vocalists assembled here, there's one name we're more accustomed to seeing on movie marquees: **Pam Grier**, who makes an appearance on "Stick Together."

Other notable releases by women: **Natalie Cole's** new album, "Unpredictable" (Capitol), features a terrific, snappy number called "Party Lights" – not the **Claudine Clark** classic but a new song with a similar theme that has Natalie singing "C'mon party with me children;" her enthusiasm is catching... **Yvonne Elliman's** latest, "Love Me" (RSO), was produced by **Freddie Perren** and includes, in a generally high-level assortment, a nice re-make of "Uphill Peace Of Mind," the **Gospel Truth** single that had some scattered success last year, and a sweet mid-tempo tune called "(I Don't Know Why) I Keep Hangin' On;" Elliman's versions of **Barbara Lewis'** "Hello Stranger" and the **Bee Gees'** "Love Me" are also fine... **Valerie Carter's** debut on Columbia lists everyone from **Linda Ronstadt** to **Deniece Williams**, from **Jackson Browne** to **Verdine White**, on the back-cover credits and the one cut with disco possibilities, "City Lights," was co-produced by **Earth, Wind & Fire's Maurice White**, so Carter's in very good company. "City Lights" is in the EW&F mold with a good pumping beat, great rushes of horns and kind of whispy but effective vocals; should go over with fans of **The Emotions'** "I Don't Wanna Lose Your Love" though it lacks that song's sting... On the disco disc front, there's "I Gotta Keep Dancin'" by **Carrie Lucas** (Soul Train) whose theme is the now familiar dance-to-keep-from-crying, but it's treated with a light, pleasant touch and the production is full and substantial enough to sustain it at a good level for just over five minutes... **Pat Lundy's** disco disc on Pyramid is a version of the **Oscar Brown** chain-gang

LOST AND FOUND, WASHINGTON, D.C.
DJ: Bill Owens

BODY CONTACT CONTRACT/DISCO INFERNO/DON'T BURN NO BRIDGES/STARVIN' – Trammps (Atlantic)

DO WHAT YOU WANNA DO – T-Connection (TK disco disc)

DON'T LEAVE ME THIS WAY –Thelma Houston (Tamla)

HIT AND RUN/RIPPED OFF/DREAMIN' – Loleatta Holloway (Gold Mind)

IF YOU WANNA GO BACK/FREE LOVE/ TIME WAITS FOR NO ONE – Jean Carn (Phila. Intl.)

LET YOURSELF GO/I DON'T WANT TO BE TIED DOWN – Supremes (Motown)

LOVE IN C MINOR/MIDNIGHT LADY – Cerrone (Cotillion)

LOVE IN C MINOR – Heart & Soul Orchestra (Casablanca)

UPTOWN FESTIVAL – Shalamar (Soul Train)

YOU GOT ME LOVING YOU AGAIN – Eloise Laws (Invictus)

PIPPINS, NEW YORK
DJ: Reggie T Experience

DANCE BAND – Donald Byrd (Blue Note)

DISCO INFERNO/BODY CONTACT CONTRACT/DON'T BURN NO BRIDGES – Trammps (Atlantic)

DO WHAT YOU WANNA DO – T-Connection (TK)

DREAMIN'/HIT AND RUN – Loleatta Holloway (Gold Mind)

I BELIEVE IN LOVE – Barbra Streisand ("A Star Is Born" Soundtrack Columbia)

LOVE HANGOVER/LET'S GROOVE – Players' Association (Vanguard)

LOVE IN C MINOR/BLACK IS BLACK – Cerrone (Cotillion)

STANDING UP FOR LOVE – Three Degrees (Epic)

THE WORLD IS A GHETTO – George Benson (Warner Bros.)

YOU TAKE MY HEART AWAY – Laura Green (Epic)

INFINITY, NEW YORK
DJ: Bobby Guttadaro

ARE YOU IN THERE? – Andy Williams (Columbia)

DISCO INFERNO/BODY CONTACT CONTRACT – Trammps (Atlantic)

DO WHAT YOU WANNA DO – T-Connection (TK)

DREAMIN'/HIT AND RUN – Loleatta Holloway (Gold Mind)

FALLIN' IN LOVE WITH YOU – Jimmy Ruffin (Epic)

LOVE IN C MINOR – Cerrone (Cotillion)

LOVE IN C MINOR – Heart & Soul Orchestra (Casablanca)

PARTY LIGHTS – Natalie Cole (Capital)

STICK TOGETHER – Minnie Riperton (Epic)

UPTOWN FESTIVAL – Shalamar (Soul Train)

CORK & BOTTLE, NEW YORK
DJ: Freddie Mendoza

BODY CONTACT CONTRACT/DISCO INFERNO/STARVIN' – Trammps (Atlantic)

DOWN TO LOVE TOWN/SIX MILLION DOLLAR MAN/YOU ARE A BLESSING TO ME – Originals (Soul)

HIT AND RUN/DREAMIN' – Loleatta Holloway (Gold Mind)

LADY LUCK/LIFE IS MUSIC – Ritchie Family (Marlin)

LOVE IN C MINOR/MIDNIGHT LADY – Cerrone (Cotillion)

OPEN SESAME – Kool & the Gang (De-Lite)

THE PIPER – Herbie Mann (Atlantic)

SIR DUKE/I WISH/ISN'T SHE LOVELY – Stevie Wonder (Tamla)

TWENTY-FOUR HOURS A DAY – Barbara Pennington (UA)

UP JUMPED THE DEVIL – John Davis & Monster Orch. (Sam)

MARCH 12, 1977

Many of the best disco discs this week are revised, usually lengthened and remixed, versions of previously released material. Like **Timmy Thomas'** infectious "Stone To The Bone," a current favorite of mine, which TK has expanded to 4:45 for the 12-inch pressing or the **Ritchie Family's** "Lady Luck" (also on TK), opened up from just under four to just over seven and a half minutes and sure to inspire a new surge of interest in the already charted cut ("Life Is Music" is featured on the flipside). "Let's Do The Latin Hustle" by **Eddie Drennon and B.B.S. Unlimited** has been remixed up to 6:07 and put into commercial release on a nicely-packaged Friends & Co. disco disc with **Manhattan Express'** "Bad Girl (Mala Femmena)," a slight, **Bimbo Jet**-style instrumental, on the flipside. "You Gotta Let Me Show You," the **Esther Williams** cut on Friends & Co., has also been brightened and filled out – to 7:02 – with a six-minute version of another William track, "Every Dog Has His Day," on the reverse side. "Theme From M*A*S*H," an invigorating, involving instrumental by the **New Marketts** originally released on the Seminole label last June, is now out as a disco disc on Farr, 5:10 on one side, 3:10 on the other. **Cameo's** "Rigor Mortis," which sounds almost like a parody of a funky party record with "Dazz" overtones, is much improved with the addition of a long instrumental section, bringing it up to 6:14 on this Chocolate City/Casablanca disco pressing (also included: the group's first hit, "Find My Way," pressed on the same side of this unaccountably one-sided disc). The most ambitious revisions of this whole group of revised works are those David Todd, RCA's DJ-in-residence, did on four **Faith, Hope & Charity** cuts: "You're My Peace Of Mind" (now 10:36), "Positive Thinking" (7:54), "Life Goes On" (6:06) and "Gradually" (7:46). Some of these new versions are, to my taste, excessively long and one wonders why they weren't attempted six months ago when the material was still fresh, but much of Todd's mixing is creative and sharp – his new slant on "Gradually" is particularly interesting – so this is a valuable addition to the Faith, Hope & Charity collection (unfortunately not in commercial release).

Other notable disco discs: I was enthusiastic about **Oliver Sain's** "B-OO-G-IE" two issues back but since then, encouraged by my friend Judy who won't stop talking about it, I've gotten seriously into the other side of the record, "Feel Like Dancin'" (Abet). This one's in a laid-back funk groove, featuring a loping guitar line, some stinging sax solos and minimal vocals; makes this disc a fine back-to-back package... **Jimmy Ruffin's** "Fallin' In Love With You" (Epic) is a lively production by Ruffin and **Richard Rome**, whose guitar work is reminiscent of "Tell Me What You Want " though the overall pace has a lot more punch... **Silver, Platinum & Gold's** "Just Friends " (4:52 on Farr) is one of those taut, tough girl group vocals from this **Dee Ervin**-produced group, remixed from a three-minute track on their recent debut lp and strengthened considerably – could grow on you... "Caribbean Disco" by **Bobby Sax** (Abet) is a snappy instrumental with a very slight calypso/reggae flavor that runs 7:10 and manages to be entertaining all the way through.

A trio of excellent import singles: The instrumental version of **K.K. Kong's** "Monster Walk" (on the Pink Elephant label from Belgium) is a hard, brilliantly, uniquely European record that has to be one of the strongest instrumentals (off-the-wall division) we've come across in some time. It begins with a muffled, pounding beat and layers on guitar, then razor-sharp strings for a rich urban jungle sound. At four minutes, it's hot enough to make you want to hear four minutes more; produced by **Jan Olofsson** and **Keith Bonsoir**, this one is for fans of the off-beat... The **Gibson Brothers'** "Come To America" is an anthemic, happy, arm-waving kind of song that is reportedly one of the biggest disco hits in France, where it was cut, and is currently the number one import on the Canadian Record Pool chart. **D.C. LaRue** picked up a copy for me on his recent visit to Montreal (now he's off on a European tour) and Richie Rivera from the Anvil in New York lists it in his top 10 this week, so the word-of-mouth on this record is already

> **❝ Many of the best disco discs this week are revised, usually lengthened and remixed, versions of previously released material. Like Timmy Thomas' infectious "Stone To The Bone," a current favorite of mine ❞**

THE ANVIL, NEW YORK
DJ: Richie Rivera

BODY CONTACT CONTRACT/DISCO INFERNO – Trammps (Atlantic)
COME TO AMERICA – Gibson Brothers (Zagora import inst.)
DANCE IF YOU WANT IT – Randy Pie (Polydor import)
DO WHAT YOU WANNA DO – T-Connection (TK)
LOVE CONNECTION – Casanovas (Polydor import)
LOVE IN C MINOR/BLACK IS BLACK/ MIDNIGHT LADY – Cerrone (Cotillion)
LOVE IN MOTION – George McCrae (TK lp cut)
SUPERMAN – Celi Bee & the Buzzy Bunch (TK disco disc)
TWENTY-FOUR HOURS A DAY – Barbara Pennington (UA)
UPTOWN FESTIVAL – Shalamar (Soul Train disco disc)

FOX TRAPPE, WASHINGTON, D.C.
DJ: Frank Edwards

BEEN DECIDED/SIX MILLION DOLLAR MAN/YOU ARE A BLESSING TO ME – Originals (Soul)
BODY CONTACT CONTRACT/DISCO INFERNO/STARVIN' – Trammps (Atlantic)
BODY HEAT – James Brown (Polydor)
FUNK MACHINE – Funk Machin (TK)
GIFT WRAP MY LOVE – Reflections (Capitol)
I DON'T LOVE YOU ANYMORE/THE MORE I GET, THE MORE I WANT/ YOU CAN'T HIDE FROM YOURSELF – Teddy Pendergrass (Phila. Intl.)
LOVE GOES DEEPER THAN THAT/PUT A LITTLE LOVE INTO IT – Eloise Laws (Invictus)
THERE'S LOVE IN THE WORLD – Mighty Clouds of Joy (ABC)
THIS WILL MAKE YOU DANCE – G. C. Cameron (Motown)
TWENTY-FOUR HOURS A DAY – Barbara Pennington (UA)

CIRCUS MAXIMUS, LOS ANGELES
DJ: Mike Lewis

BAD GIRL – Manhattan Express (Friends & Co.)
DISCO INFERNO/BODY CONTACT CONTRACT – Trammps (Atlantic)
DO WHAT YOU WANNA DO – T-Connection (TK)
DON'T LEAVE ME THIS WAY – Thelma Houston (Tamla)
LOVE IN C MINOR/MIDNIGHT LADY– Cerrone (Cotillion)
LOVE IN C MINOR – Heart & Soul Orchestra (Casablanca)
SLOW DOWN – John Miles (London)
THIS WILL MAKE YOU DANCE – G. C. Cameron (Motown)
TWENTY-FOUR HOURS A DAY – Barbara Pennington (UA)
UPTOWN FESTIVAL – Shalamar (Soul Train)

BOOMBAMAKAOO, NEW YORK
DJ: Hector Saez

ISLA DEL ENCANTO – Orquestra Broadway (Coco lp cut)
I WANTCHA BABY – Arthur Prysock (Old Town)
LOVE HANGOVER – Players Association (Vanguard)
LOVE IN C MINOR/BLACK IS BLACK/ MIDNIGHT LADY – Cerrone (Cotillion lp cuts)
MAKE IT UP TO ME IN LOVE – Odia Coates & Paul Anka (Epic)
PABLO PUEBLO – Willie Colon & Ruben Blades (Fania)
SIX MILLION DOLLAR MAN – Originals (Soul)
TATTOO MAN – Denise McCann (Polydor)
TOUCH ME, TAKE ME – Black Light Orchestra (RCA import)
VITAMIN U – Smokey Robinson (Tamla)

pretty strong. The single is on Zagora, vocal on one side, instrumental on the other – I prefer the latter but both versions have a lot of energy... **Boule Noir's** "Loin D'lci " is another instrumental in the European style, though this one was cut in Montreal for the Magique label and has a somewhat more romantic spirit than the other two. The beat is choppy and appealing and there are a number of attractive changes in the 3:20 length; again, there's a vocal version on the other side, sung in French here, also highly recommended in this case. As far as I know, none of these records have hit America in any great quantity and none are currently scheduled for. U.S. release, but all are worth looking for.

The fastest-moving records right now: "Do What You Wanna Do" by **T-Connection** (TK), "Twenty-Four Hours A Day" by **Barbara Pennington** (UA), "Uptown Festival" by **Shalamar** (Soul Train), "Up Jumped The Devil" by **John Davis & the Monster Orchestra** (Sam), and "Love Hangover" by the **Players Association** (Vanguard) – all disco discs. Also moving up: albums by **Teddy Pendergrass, Eloise Laws, G.C. Cameron.** ✺

DISCO FILE TOP 20

1. **DISCO INFERNO/BODY CONTACT CONTRACT** – Trammps (Atlantic)
2. **LOVE IN C MINOR** – Cerrone (Malligator import)
3. **DREAMIN'/HIT AND RUN** – Loleatta Holloway (Gold Mind)
4. **DON'T LEAVE ME THIS WAY** – Thelma Houston (Tamla)
5. **LOVE IN C MINOR/BLACK IS BLACK/ MIDNIGHT LADY** – Cerrone (Cotillion)
6. **DO WHAT YOU WANNA DO** – T-Connection (TK)
7. **LOVE IN C MINOR** – Heart & Soul Orchestra (Casablanca)
8. **SIX-MILLION DOLLAR MAN** – Originals (Soul)
9. **LADY LUCK/LIFE IS MUSIC** – Ritchie Family (Marlin)
10. **UPTOWN FESTIVAL** – Shalamar (Soul Train)
11. **TWENTY-FOUR HOURS A DAY** – Barbara Pennington (UA)
12. **LOVE IN MOTION** – George McCrae (TK lp cut)
13. **DON'T BURN NO BRIDGES/STARVIN'** – Trammps (Atlantic)
14. **YOU ARE A BLESSING TO ME/HURRY UP AND WAIT** – Originals (Soul)
15. **FREE LOVE/IF YOU WANNA GO BACK** – Jean Carn (Phila. Intl.)
16. **THIS WILL MAKE YOU DANCE** – G. C. Cameron (Motown)
17. **LOVE HANGOVER** – Players' Association (Vanguard)
18. **TATTOO MAN** – Denise McCann (Polydor)
19. **DISCO REGGAE** – Kalyan (MCA)
20. **RIPPED OFF** – Loleatta Holloway (Gold Mind)

MARCH 19, 1977

This was one of those weeks when I felt I'd rather be unloading large appliances at Korvettes than writing about the new releases, but a few spunky records changed my mind. Howard Merritt, DJ at Flamingo, the chic New York club that has been very on-again/off-again this year, got me to go back into my singles pile and listen to the **Hues Corporation's** "I Caught Your Act" (Warner Brothers) a second time and this time it really clicked. While this new 45 sounds nothing like "Rock The Boat," it has a similar snap and spirit perfectly captured in a bright, churning pop arrangement. The song's story line is love comical – a guy follows his girl into a movie house and watches broken-hearted while she makes out with another man – but the treatment is upbeat and cute with emphasis on the interplay of male and female voices in the group. Nothing especially brilliant here, yet "I Caught Your Act" was one of the few records that really made me happy this week. Another was **Jimmy "Bo" Horne's** "Get Happy" (a TK disco disc and single) which both Tom Savarese and Tony Smith put on their top 10 lists this week. A **Casey-Finch** production with that no-nonsense, no-frills Miami sound to underline the irresistible command of the lyric ("Get happy, get happy, etc."), the song is TK formula at its best – fresh, brassy good-time music that reeks of fun-in-the-sun. The clincher here is a section near the end of just robust handclapping and a snappy cowbell.

TK, as a number of people mentioned this week, is certainly the hot label right now: not only is the **T-Connection's** "Do What You Wanna Do" one of the strongest records on the disco charts – it is virtually tied for top place on our Top 20 with the **Trammps** and **Cerrone's** "Love In C Minor" – but so many of the label's other recent releases are getting heavy play that it's hard to ignore their combined impact. While the **Ritchie Family** and **George McCrae** are still holding on, **Timmy Thomas'** "Stone To The Bone" is coming on strong and "Funk Machine" by **Funk Machine** is showing up very high on the charts of clubs between the two coasts. And every week brings a few new entries: Howard Merritt points out the attraction of the title tune from Timmy Thomas' album, "The Magician" (Glades), which has a somewhat George McCrae feel; one cut on **King Sporty's** "Deep Reggae Roots" album (Konduko), called "Hold Down To The Funk," is a jagged, juicy number that's half southern funk and half off-the-wall Miami rock with some bluegrass-flavored guitar work and rough vocals; and **Facts of Life**, the **Millie Jackson**-produced trio whose ballad "Sometimes" is a big r&b hit, has come out with an album ("Sometimes" on Kayvette) containing two good funk dance cuts –"Hundred Pounds Of Pain" and "Givin' Me Your Love" – and their original version of "Uphill Peace Of Mind" (the group was formerly known as **Gospel Truth**).

> **❝ This was one of those weeks when I felt I'd rather be unloading large appliances at Korvettes than writing about the new releases, but a few spunky records changed my mind ❞**

BAREFOOT BOY, NEW YORK
DJ: Tony Smith

DO WHAT YOU WANNA DO – T-Connection (TK)
GET HAPPY – Jimmy "Bo" Horne (TK)
HOW CAN I KEEP IN TOUCH WITH YOU – Hamilton Affair (Moment)
THE MORE I GET, THE MORE I WANT/ YOU CAN'T HIDE FROM YOURSELF/I DON'T LOVE YOU ANYMORE – Teddy Pendergrass (Phila. Intl.)
N.Y. YOU GOT ME DANCING – Andrea True Connection (Buddah)
SIX MILLION DOLLAR MAN/YOU ARE A BLESSING TO ME/BEEN DECIDED – Originals (Soul)
SLOW DOWN – John Miles (London)
STICK TOGETHER – Minnie Riperton (Epic)
SUPERMAN – Celi Bee & the Buzzy Bunch (TK)
THIS WILL MAKE YOU DANCE – G.C. Cameron (Motown)

FLAMINGO, NEW YORK
DJ: Howard Merritt

DO WHAT YOU WANNA DO – Connection (TK)
I'VE GOT TO DANCE – Destinations (AVI)
LADY LUCK/LIFE IS MUSIC – Ritchie Family (TK)
LOVE IN C MINOR/BLACK IS BLACK/ MIDNIGHT LADY – Cerrone (Cotillion)
LOVE IN MOTION/GIVIN' BACK THE FEELING – George McCrae (TK)
STONE TO THE BONE/THE MAGICIAN – Timmy Thomas (Glades)
SUPERMAN – Celi Bee & the Buzzy Bunch (TK)
TATTOO MAN – Denise McCann (Polydor import)
TURN ON TO LOVE – Jumbo (Pye/Prelude)
UPTOWN FESTIVAL – Shalamar (Soul Train)

BONES, SAN FRANCISCO
DJ: Michael Lee

DO WHAT YOU WANNA DO – T-Connection (TK)
FALLIN' IN LOVE WITH YOU – Jimmy Ruffin (Epic)
IT'S TOO LATE/COME IN HEAVEN EARTH IS CALLING – Tata Vega (Tamla)
LOVE GOES DEEPER THAN THAT/YOU GOT ME LOVING YOU AGAIN – Eloise Laws (Invictus)
LOVE HANGOVER – Players' Association (Vanguard)
LOVE IN C MINOR – Heart & Soul Orchestra (Casablanca)
SIX MILLION DOLLAR MAN/HURRY UP AND WAIT/BEEN DECIDED – Originals (Soul)
SLOW DOWN – John Miles (London)
UP JUMPED THE DEVIL – John Davis & the Monster Orchestra (Sam)
WORK SONG – Pat Lundy (Pyramid)

HARRAH, NEW YORK
DJ: Tom Savarese

BODY CONTACT CONTRACT – Trammps (Atlantic)
DISCO JUICE/CHARLESTON HOPSCOTCH – Cloud One (P&P)
GET HAPPY – Jimmy "Bo" Horne (TK)
I GOTTA KEEP DANCIN' – Carrie Lucas (Soul Train)
I LIKE IT – Players' Association (Vanguard)
LOVE IN C MINOR/MIDNIGHT LADY – Cerrone (Cotillion)
PUT A LITTLE LOVE INTO IT/LOVE GOES DEEPER THAN THAT/MAKE IT LAST FOREVER – Eloise Laws (Invictus)
STONE TO THE BONE – Timmy Thomas (TK)
UPHILL PEACE OF MIND/I KEEP HANGIN' ON – Yvonne Elliman (RSO)
THE WORLD IS A GHETTO – George Benson (Warner Bros.)

ADDITIONAL FEEDBACK: Tom Savarese recommends **Eddie Russ'** "Stop It Now" (on a disco and lp from Monument), a delightfully lowdown instrumental that teases a young lady with lascivious guitar solos, sexy saxophones and a long synthesizer grope. The girl says little more than "stop it now" throughout but long before the end of this 5:30 cut, it's clear she means just the opposite. Very jazzy foreplay... Tony Smith lists another Monument record, also available on a disco disc and album, called "How Can I Keep In Touch With You" by the **Hamilton Affair**. This one's awfully long (7:51) and a little too adolescent for me – it's sung by a boy in his early teens who happens to be **Roy Hamilton's** son – but there's something insistent about the beat, especially toward the end, that gets to you after a while... Scattered reports are coming in from the hinterlands that indicate Buddah's recent reissue of the **Glenn Miller Orchestra's** classic "In The Mood" on a single is picking up some disco playas a novelty change of-pace. Nostalgia strikes again... Also picking up at a number of places: "At Midnight," the **Rufus** single and lp cut (ABC) with an unusual structure that sounded at first too off-beat for dancing but has since won us over, too. ◉

MARCH 26, 1977

RECOMMENDED ALBUMS: **Marvin Gaye's** latest, a two-record set titled "Live At The London Palladium" (Tamla), arrived with a yellow sticker on its cover that says, "Includes full-length (11:48) version of the smash disco hit 'Got To Give It Up.'" Naturally we were a little skeptical about a "smash disco hit" we'd never heard of before, but after a number of listenings, the skepticism has been replaced by admiration, if not total enthusiasm. "Got To Give It Up," a studio track that takes up one whole side of this otherwise live set, is a down-to-basics groove using a tight rhythm section rather than a full orchestra. Gaye begins by singing, in his highest, float-away voice, "I used to go out to parties/and stand around/Cause I was too nervous/to really get down," and the rest of the song is about the conversion of a wallflower into a heavy dancer. The feeling is laid-back and loose, with a constant background of encouraging party noise and a relentless, nearly unchanging beat broken by several fine horn solos; at first it sounded monotonous but now it's downright hypnotic. And it gets better with each new listening. Definitely Gaye's strongest dances cut in years – watch out for another Motown blockbuster...

❝Naturally we were a little skeptical about a "smash disco hit" we'd never heard of before❞

Norman Connors, who introduced both **Jean Carn** and **Michael Henderson** to wider audiences on his previous albums, is showcasing some new singers on his just-released Buddah lp, "Romantic Journey." **Phillip Mitchell**, who sounds disarmingly like Marvin Gaye, is featured on the most danceable cut, a song Mitchell also wrote, called "Once I've Been There." Despite the song's rather remarkable macho egotism – "Once I've been there," the singer brags, "I can always go back again/No matter how long I've been gone/I can always get back in" it has a sweet, ingratiating quality beautifully supported by a solid production. The instrumental intro is particularly good here.

Also of interest: a 6:43 version of **Gato Barbieri's** "Last Tango In Paris" theme... **Phyllis Hyman**, another Norman Connors alumnus, has a debut album out on Buddah that deserves comparison with Jean Cam's recent lp. Not as much disco material here, perhaps, but the voice is flexible and fine, especially on **Thom Bell's** "Loving You/ Losing You" (7:41 and also scheduled for a disco disc pressing), which is reminiscent of Bell's early **Johnny Mathis** material (Mathis includes the song on his latest Thom Bell-produced album, too) and would make a gorgeous slow dance number. There's also an excellent version of **Evie Sands'** sharply clever "One Thing On My Mind" (5:30)... **Vitamin E** also has a

Norman Connors connection – he produced their first album, "Sharing," also on Buddah. This trio, blending male and female vocals, has two attractive cuts for dancing here, both of them saved from a slow start by a snappy production move before the end. "Kiss Away" (4:57) is the stronger of the two, with a nice build to the vocals, but a remake of "Laughter In The Rain" is also given a pleasant twist... The debut of **Lifestyle**, a five-man singing group from Rochester, is even more impressive. Their MCA album, produced by **Billy Jackson**, opens with three thoroughly enjoyable songs: "I Just Wanna Be With You," which sounds like it was based on the **Isley Brothers'** "This Old Heart Of Mine" but has a flair all its own; "This Feeling," with a cute nursery rhyme opening verse and an irresistible build-a personal favorite; and "Trying To Make It Up To You," very snappy and bright. The voices are outstanding, at times up to **Spinners** quality, and this one should not be overlooked in the dizzying pile-up of new releases... **Lalo Schifrin's** "Towering Toccata" (CTI), a collection dominated by themes from movies and TV shows, is already getting strongly favorable feedback, with most of the attention going to a lively, heavily synthesized track called "Roller Coaster" (4:48) – already on Tony Carrasco's top 10 from Playground in New York this week. Also worth checking out: "Most Wanted Theme," "Towering Toccata" (based on a Bach piece), "Macumba" and "Theme From King Kong." **Creed Taylor** produced and the musician credits include **Ralph MacDonald**, **John Tropea**, **Eric Gale**, **Steve Gadd**, **Joe Farrell** and **Jeremy Steig**.

OTHER RECOMMENDED ALBUMS: **Slave** (on Cotillion), which continues in the line of development that runs from **B.T. Express** to **Brass Construction** to **Mass Production** – a tough, excellently-produced, nine man group with a rich funk edge. Best cuts: "You And Me" (6:41), "Slide" (6:47) and "Son Of Slide (5:29). Nice and nasty... **S.S.O.**, a Belgian group with that European eclectic sound (close to **El Coco**), has a substantial set in "Shine Your Light" (Shadybrook). "Right Here, Right Now," "Give A Damn," "Bring It Up Front" and "What It Be "Foxy Baby" stand out... It's been a long time since **Cleveland Eaton's** "Chi-town Theme," but he's back with a solid jazz/funk album called "Instant Hip" (Ovation), containing two tasty disco-style tracks, "The Funky Cello" and "Bama Boogie Woogie," both of them energetic and fun... **Tata Vega's** second album, "Totally Tata" (Tamla), is better than its title and has been generally well-received, largely due to the charm and spark of her vocals. "It's Too Late" is the only cut that really holds me, but the second half of "Come In Heaven Earth Is Calling" and "Jesus Takes Me Higher" – both too blatantly religious for my taste – are also getting some club play. NOTE: Roulette has finally released the **Stratavarious** album in the States, including the ever-fabulous "I Got Your Love" and the vocal and instrumental versions of "Let Me Be Your Lady Tonight" – plus some great slow cuts on the second side.

LEVITICUS, NEW YORK
DJ: Tom Pearson

AT MIDNIGHT/HOLLYWOOD/ EVERLASTING LOVE/BETTER DAYS – Rufus (ABC)
BODY CONTACT CONTRACT/STARVIN'/ DISCO INFERNO – Trammps (Atlantic)
IF YOU'RE IN NEED – Mystique (Curtom)
THE MORE I GET, THE MORE I WANT / YOU CAN'T HIDE FROM YOURSELF – Teddy Pendergrass (Phila. Intl.)
NATURE BOY/THE WORLD IS A GHETTO – George Benson (Warner Bros.)
SATURDAY NIGHT STEPPIN' OUT/DO IT WITH STYLE/LOVE IS THE WAY /SINCE I'VE BEEN GONE – Webster Lewis (Epic)
TIME/SOLID/BE MY GIRL – Michael Henderson (Buddah)
UPTOWN FESTIVAL – Shalamar (Soul Train)
WAKE UP AND BE SOMEBODY/THIS MUST BE HEAVEN – Brainstorm (Tabu)

PARADISE BALLROOM, LOS ANGELES
DJ: Denny McGowan

DANCIN' – Crown Heights Affair (De-Lite)
DISCO INFERNO/BODY CONTACT CONTRACT – Trammps (Atlantic)
DON'T LEAVE ME THIS WAY – Thelma Houston (Tamla)
DREAMIN' – Loleatta Holloway (Gold Mind)
I'VE GOT TO DANCE – Destinations (AVI)
LOVE IN C MINOR – Cerrone (Cotillion)
MAKES YOU BLIND – Glitter Band (Arista)
N.Y. YOU GOT ME DANCING – Andrea True Connection (Buddah)
TWENTY-FOUR HOURS A DAY – Barbara Pennington (UA)
UPTOWN FESTIVAL – Shalamar (Soul Train)

BACHELOR, SAN JUAN, PUERTO RICO
DJ: Pablo Flores

BODY CONTACT CONTRACT – Trammps (Atlantic)
COME TO AMERICA – Gibson Brothers (Zagora import)
DANCING QUEEN – Carol Douglas (Midsong Intl.)
DON'T LEAVE ME THIS WAY – Thelma Houston (Tamla)
DREAMIN'/HIT AND RUN – Loleatta Holloway (Gold Mind)
JUNGLE PEOPLE – Soulful Dynamics (Epic import)
LOVE GOES DEEPER THAN THAT – Eloise Laws (Invictus)
LOVE IN C MINOR – Cerrone (Cotillion)
SUPERMAN/ONE LOVE – Celi Bee & the Buzzy Bunch (Orange import)
UP JUMPED THE DEVIL – John Davis & the Monster Orchestra (Sam)

PLAYGROUND, NEW YORK
DJ: Tony Carrasco

BRING IT UP FRONT/RIGHT HERE, RIGHT NOW – S.S.O. (Shadybrook)
DO WHAT YOU WANNA DO – T-Connection (TK)
MARY HARTMAN, MARY HARTMAN – Sounds of Inner City (West End)
PARTY LIGHTS – Natalie Cole (Capitol)
ROLLERCOASTER – Lalo Schifrin (CTI)
SLOW DOWN – John Miles (London)
STICK TOGETHER – Minnie Riperton (Epic)
STONE TO THE BONE – Timmy Thomas (TK)
UPTOWN FESTIVAL – Shalamar (Soul Train)
YOU CAN'T HIDE FROM YOURSELF/THE MORE I GET, THE MORE I WANT/I DON'T LOVE YOU ANYMORE – Teddy Pendergrass (Phila. Intl.)

RECOMMENDED DISCO DISCS: The feeling of **Ted Taylor's** "Ghetto Disco" (TK) is aptly summed up in its title – more funky southern disco that gets off to a somewhat uneven start but gradually grabs you. The 12-inch is seven minutes long and a 3:20 single version is also available on the Alarm label. (Note that TK has changed their disco disc speed here from 45 to 33 – a move sure to add to the confusion in an already confusingly unstandardized market.)... **Crown Heights Affair** is always coming back with remixed, revitalized versions of their records – this time it's "Dancin'" that undergoes the transformation (on De-Lite). The track's been lengthened to 7:50 and totally revamped and the result is terrific. On the reverse side of this commercial disc is something called "Dreaming A Dream (Goes Dancin')" which combines the classic cut with "Dancin'" in a not particularly deft disco blend (7:17). (There's no speed indicated on the label here – more confusion – but it's a 45.) Now available on commercial disco discs: David Todd's excellent remixes of **Faith, Hope & Charity's** "You're My Peace Of Mind" and "Life Goes On" (RCA), "Spaced Out" by **Cloud One** (P&P) and the **Rice & Beans Orchestra's** "Disco Dancing" backed with "Our Love Concerto" (TK). Promotional items: **The Hues Corporation's** "I Caught Your Act," which sounds even better at 4:31 than it did on the single (Warner Bros.); **Gloria Gaynor's** "Most Of All," just beginning to catch on after the initial surprise, backed with "As Time Goes By" (Polydor) and four cuts from the **Kalyan** lp – "Disco Reggae," "Hello Africa," "Sweet Music" and "Nice And Slow" – all their original lengths (MCA).

RECOMMENDED SINGLES: **Jesse Green's** "Flip," the follow-up to "Nice And Slow" that has already been cropping up on disco playlists as an import, now out on United Artists and spunky enough to reach an even wider audience... "The Party Song" by **Lavender Hill Mob**, a Montreal group, is another successful disco import (in the top 10 on the most recent Canadian Record Pool chart) that UA has released here – it's good-time rock flavored almost a blend of early **Beatles** and **Bay City Rollers** gone disco... **Garnett Mimms'** "What It Is" (Arista) was produced and written by Jeff Lane and Randy Muller so this is a voice from the past in a whole new format.

OFF THE WALL: A new single called "Demolition Disco" by **Spike Jones, Jr.**, who is apparently following in the footsteps of his father, king of bizarre novelty records, with this insane mix of auto sound effects (beeping horns, skidding tires), unusual instruments and an ultra-bright girl chorus. The lyrics begin with an animated cartoon image – "All the Chryslers, Fords and Chevys are dancin'" – and end shortly thereafter with this verse: "In Demolition Disco, start your engines/ And plow your front-end into someone's rear!" "Demolition Disco" is in two parts, the second the longer (4:07) and more instrumental of the two, and was disco-mixed in part by L.A. DJ Mitch Shatsky. The label: Florence Greenberg's new company, Chinchilla Records, in Beverly Hills. ◉

APRIL 2, 1977

One of the hottest items on the disco grapevine in recent weeks has been an import record from Puerto Rico called "Superman" by **Celi Bee & the Buzzy Bunch** which began popping up on top 10 lists from New York clubs almost as soon as it appeared in the city and, as a result, edged into the bottom of the DISCO FILE Top 20 before its official release as a TK disco disc this week. Pablo Flores, who reported from the Bachelor in San Juan last week, said "Superman" was the strongest record in his club and especially popular among American tourists. According to Flores, Celi Bee is the popular singer known as **Celines** and is married to the record's producer, Pe**pe Luis Soto**, who co-produced the **Rice & Beans Orchestra** album. "Superman," which also features the Rice & Beans musicians, combines vacuous vocals (à la **Andrea True**) in breathless praise of her "superman"'s lovemaking with a vigorous track awash with strings and propelled by an insistent, bouncy bass line. It's a captivatingly commercial pop sound with just the right kind of disco flair in the breaks to give it instant pick-up on the dance floor. The TK 12-inch version runs 5:09 and is backed by a long (8:08) cut called "One Love" which is even more impressive structurally (great organ sweeps and conga breaks) but perhaps too quickly-paced for most crowds. Both tracks are included on the group's debut album, due out on TK's APA label within the week, and featuring at least one other song of interest to the disco-goer: "Closer, Closer" (4:15), whose pace is more sensuous and laid-back (compare **Gloria Gaynor's** "Most of All") with a delicately textured instrumentation shimmering with flute and strings – the album's technical high-point. All together, an extremely attractive, glossily-wrapped package that should be lwell-received.

Among the other imports that have been getting a lot of attention these days is **Claudja Barry's** aptly titled "Sweet Dynamite," recorded in Germany for the Lollipop label and making a big impression here as an import disco disc from London in Canada. "Listen to the music: sweet dynamite!" Barry and a girl chorus scream, as if one's attention needed to be drawn to the full, pulsing track behind them. This one's sharp and powerful, especially in the 5:09 12-inch, version (a minute longer than the original lp cut) which Artie Feldman from Chicago's Sundays lists in his top 10 this week and San Francisco retailer Ernie Lazar says is one of his hottest disco pressings right now. Salsoul has picked the record up in the U.S. and is rushing a re-mixed disco disc and single sometime this week with the album to follow... My faithful west coast correspondent sent me a copy of another popular import recently – "Jungle People" by the **Soulful Dynamics** which alert readers will have noted on scattered playlists over the past few months .. Though I'm not sure exactly where it was originally made, "Jungle People" comes here on an Epic single from England and bursts with a warm, raw energy, evoking early Barrabas (especially "Wild Safari"), Exuma, Black Soul. The production is simple, unencumbered and utterly invigorating, building on a chant-like chorus of male voices. Sounds like a classic... Finally, there's "The Final Thing" by **Steve Bender**, a German import on the Telefunken label which was produced by **Pete Bellotte**, half of the **Donna Summer** production team. The sound is pure Summer but Bender's vocals, reminiscent of Hot Chocolate, give it a whole new flavor. Not surprisingly, the "final thing" is s-e-x so a lot of the intensity is quite orgasmic, with a minimum of moaning but a constant chorus of girls exulting, "Now we've done the final thing," over and over. Appropriately, this is spread over two parts totalling over six minutes but hopefully someone will pick it up and release it in one piece on a 12-inch – it's excellent. Sharon White, the sassy DJ at Sahara in New York, added it to her top 10 this week-she got her copy from the New York Record Pool.

NEWS & NOTES: Atlantic Records will be distributing Westbound Records, meaning that one of the most talked-about unreleased albums, **C.C. & Company's** "Devil's Gun," will actually come out sometime in early May (with the group's name changed – don't ask me why – to C.J. & Company). Also coming on Atlantic/Westbound: the **Detroit Emeralds'** "Feel The Need" album, featuring what is rumored to be a sensational new version of that classic, and a new **Dennis Coffey** lp... Mercury is releasing a new **Dells** album with a stunning Trammps-style production by Norman Harris late this week. Also in production on Mercury: **Bohannon's** first album for that label, said to be very different from his previous work – off in a deeper, more European-influenced vein... just shipping: the new **Heart & Soul Orchestra** album featuring their version of "Love In C Minor" plus "Midnight Lady" and

> **❝ One of the hottest items on the disco grapevine is an import record from Puerto Rico. Pablo Flores, who reported from the Bachelor in San Juan, said "Superman" was the strongest record in his club ❞**

THE CASBAH, ATLANTA
DJ: Jim Burgess

DO WHAT YOU WANNA DO – T-Connection (TK)
I GOTTA KEEP DANCIN' – Carrie Lucas (Soul Train)
LIFE GOES ON/PEACE OF MIND/GRADUALLY – Faith, Hope & Charity (RCA)
LIFE IS MUSIC/LADY LUCK – Ritchie Family (TK)
LOVE IN C MINOR – Heart & Soul Orchestra (Casablanca)
N.Y. YOU GOT ME DANCING – Andrea True Connection (Buddah)
STONE TO THE BONE – Timmy Thomas (TK)
UPTOWN FESTIVAL – Shalamar (Soul Train)
WE CAN START ALL OVER AGAIN – Gloria Gaynor (Polydor)
YOU CAN'T HIDE FROM YOURSELF/THE MORE I GET, THE MORE I WANT/I DON'T LOVE YOU ANYMORE – Teddy Pendergrass (Phila. Intl.)

SAHARA, NEW YORK
DJ: Sharon White

DO WHAT YOU WANNA DO – T-Connection (TK)
DREAMIN' – Loleatta Holloway (Gold Mind)
THE FINAL THING – Steve Bender (Telefunken import)
FREE LOVE – Jean Carn (Phila. Inti.)
I GOTTA KEEP DANCIN' – Carrie Lucas (Soul Train)
LOVE IN C MINOR/MIDNIGHT LADY – Cerrone (Cotillion)
STICK TOGETHER – Minnie Riperton (Epic)
STONE TO THE BONE – Timmy Thomas (TK)
UPTOWN FESTIVAL – Shalamar (Soul Train)
THE WORLD IS A GHETTO – George Benson (Warner Bros.)

12 WEST, NEW YORK
DJ: Jimmy Stuard

BODY CONTACT CONTRACT/DISCO INFERNO/STARVIN' – Trammps (Atlantic)
DO WHAT YOU WANNA DO – T-Connection (TK)
FREEDOM TO EXPRESS YOURSELF – Denise LaSalle (ABC)
HIT AND RUN/DREAMIN' – Loleatta Holloway (Gold Mind)
I DON'T LOVE YOU ANYMORE/THE MORE I GET, THE MORE I WANT/YOU CAN'T HIDE FROM YOURSELF – Teddy Pendergrass (Phila. Inti.)
I GOTTA KEEP DANCIN' – Carrie Lucas (Soul Train)
LOVE IN C MINOR/BLACK IS BLACK/MIDNIGHT LADY – Cerrone (Cotillion)
LOVE IN C MINOR – Heart & Soul Orchestra (Casablanca)
TWENTY-FOUR HOURS A DAY – Barbara Pennington (UA)
UPTOWN FESTIVAL – Shalamar (Soul Train)

SUNDAYS, CHICAGO
DJ: Artie Feldman

DISCO INFERNO/BODY CONTACT CONTRACT – Trammps (Atlantic)
DO WHAT YOU WANNA DO – T-Connection (TK)
DON'T LEAVE ME THIS WAY – Thelma Houston (Tamla)
DREAMIN'/HIT AND RUN/WE'RE GETTING STRONGER – Loleatta Holloway (Gold Mind)
FREEDOM TO EXPRESS YOURSELF – Denise LaSalle (ABC)
N.Y. YOU GOT ME DANCING – Andrea True Connection (Buddah)
SIX MILLION DOLLAR MAN/YOU ARE A BLESSING TO ME – Originals (Soul)
SWEET DYNAMITE – Claudja Barry (London import)
UPTOWN FESTIVAL – Shalamar (Soul Train)
YOU CAN'T HIDE FROM YOURSELF – Teddy Pendergrass (Phila. Intl.)

a number of originals – on Casablanca... Now available: **Denise McCann's** "Tattoo Man" on an American disco disc (Polydor); the disco disc of **John Miles'** "Slowdown" (London), which has been slowed down from the incredibly racey lp cut for this version; singles of **Instant Funk's** "It Ain't Reggae (But It's Funky)" (TSOP) and **The Jacksons'** "Show You The Way To Go" (Epic) – all terrific records, with the John Miles doing especially well.

DON'T MISS: **Morning, Noon & Night** (Roadshow/UA). ◐

DISCO FILE TOP 20

1. **DO WHAT YOU WANNA DO** – T-Connection (TK)
2. **UPTOWN FESTIVAL** – Shalamar (Soul Train)
3. **LOVE IN C MINOR** – Cerrone (Malligator import)
4. **THE MORE I GET, THE MORE I WANT/YOU CAN'T HIDE FROM YOURSELF/I DON'T LOVE YOU ANYMORE/** – Teddy Pendergrass (Phila. Intl.)
5. **DISCO INFERNO/BODY CONTACT CONTRACT** – Trammps (Atlantic)
6. **GONNA KEEP DANCIN'** – Carrie Lucas (Soul Train)
7. **DREAMIN'/HIT AND RUN** – Loleatta Holloway (Gold Mind)
8. **N.Y. YOU GOT ME DANCING** – Andrea True Connection (Buddah)
9. **STONE TO THE BONE** – Timmy Thomas (TK)
10. **SIX-MILLION DOLLAR MAN** – Originals (Soul)
11. **LOVE IN C MINOR** – Heart & Soul Orchestra (Casablanca)
12. **DON'T LEAVE ME THIS WAY** – Thelma Houston (Tamla)
13. **SLOW DOWN** – John Miles (London)
14. **MIDNIGHT LADY/BLACK IS BLACK** – Cerrone (Cotillion)
15. **SUPERMAN** – Celi Bee & the Buzzy Bunch (APA)
16. **TWENTY-FOUR HOURS A DAY** – Barbara Pennington (UA)
17. **STICK TOGETHER** – Minnie Riperton (Epic)
18. **STARVIN'** – Trammps (Atlantic)
19. **LOVE GOES DEEPER THAN THAT** – Eloise Laws (Invictus)
20. **THIS WILL MAKE YOU DANCE** – G. C. Cameron (Motown)

APRIL 9, 1977

The new **Dells** album, "They Said It Couldn't Be Done, But We Did It" (Mercury), sounds like it could be the Next Big Album. Producer **Norman Harris** has packed it with five top quality dance cuts and three excellent ballads, providing the best showcase in years for the Dells' wonderfully rich and expressive vocals. As he demonstrated with the **Loleatta Holloway** album, Harris is particularly adept at producing for powerful, unrestrained black voices, and he gives the great, rough-hewn voice of the Dells' lead just the right kind of space and support, making this the strongest collection of male vocals since the **Trammps** lp. And the production style here can only be compared to the Trammps – it's tight, beautifully balanced, sparked by dynamic, sharply-crafted breaks which are never allowed to overwhelm the thrust of the vocals. Prime cuts, in order of preference: "They Said It Couldn't Be Done" (8:22), "Our Love" (5:04), "Rich Man, Poor Man" (5:42), "Get On Down" (4:13) and "Teaser" (3:16). "Rich Man" is the message song here – Philadelphia producers remain concerned with "peace and love" and, apparently, obsessed by the abortion issue made palatable in this case by an especially fine instrumental break full of playful phasing effects. All together, an exciting and essential album, a high point for both the Dells and Norman Harris.

The list of other recommended albums is topped this week by a pair of terrific debuts: **Morning, Noon & Night** (Roadshow/UA) and **Formula V** (20th Century). Morning, Noon & Night's is the most impressive because it draws from so many diverse sources and presents an unexpectedly varied batch of tracks – from the straight-ahead, hard-edged funk of "Bite Your Granny" (which,

at 3:46, is only half as long as we'd wish it to be) to the jazzy, open style of "Time," an instrumental that has a light **Eddie Drennon** feel, especially when it comes to the flute line. In between, there's a broad range of material, with "Le Joint" (4:39) and "Feelin' Strong" (5:46), both with something of a **Brass Construction** sound, standing out right now. It's also an extremely listenable album – not a single wasted cut; production is by **Michael Stokes**, who's already hit big with the **Enchantment** lp. **Formula V's** album, "Phase 1," is also pleasantly varied, highlighted by two very different cuts – "I Wanna Give You My Love" (4:07), a relaxed, thumping arrangement that really picks up after a break when the female lead begins to take off; and "Dance All Night" (6:17), a more elemental jungle-beat funk sound with a great, energetic production and minimal lyrics. There's also a high-powered cut called "Disco Funkinstein" about a "friendly disco freak" which is a high-spirited blend of **Ohio Players** and **Parliament** styles. Both albums are too good to be overlooked.

OTHER RECOMMENDED ALBUMS: **Gladys Knight & the Pips'** "Still Together" (Buddah) is the group's most interesting and vital album in some time and one of the rare cases in which several different producers complement rather than clash with each other on one project. The most unusual cut is the ten-and-a-half-minute opener, "Love Is Always On Your Mind," which Buddah has issued as a promotional 12-inch – it's very laid-back and doesn't exactly go anywhere – no real peaks here – but, like **Marvin Gaye's** "Got To Give It Up," there's something very attractive and hypnotic about it; a cooled-out tour-de force. **Jerry Peters**, suddenly very hot with his other production credits these days (**Carrie Lucas'** tremendously successful "I Gotta Keep Dancin'," the **Brainstorm** lp and cuts on the **Phyllis Hyman** album), also produced "Love Is Always On Your Mind." **Van McCoy** and **Charles Kipps** contributed a few cuts here, too, including a classy, deep version of McCoy's classic "Little Bit Of Love;" a bright reading of "Baby Don't Change Your Mind," formerly made by the **Stylistics**; and a new McCoy song called "Home Is Where The Heart Is" that presents Gladys in top vocal form – which is about as good as you can get. A delight... Although the second side of the new **Lou Rawls** album, "Unmistakably Lou" (Philadelphia International), is distressingly mushy, there is at least one track on side one that compares with "You'll Never Find Another Love Like Mine" for danceability: "See You When I Git There" (4:43), a warm, mellow **Gamble & Huff** number that opens with a short spoken intro and sweeps into a gently pulsing production that gets more irresistible with each new listening. Another possibility: "Some Folks Never Learn"... **Ruby Andrews**, whose last big hit was the wonderful "Casanova," is back with an album called "Genuine Ruby" (ABC) that kicks off with an almost baroque cut called "Queen Of The Disco," which sounds like one of those melodramatic girl group songs of the sixties – quite overdone but with a nice punch to the vocals. The final cut of the lp is even better if equally light-weight – "I Wanna Be Near You" (4:18) with a perfect little break.

THE GALLERY, NEW YORK
DJ: Nicky Siano

CHARLESTON HOPSCOTCH – Cloud One (P&P)
I CAUGHT YOUR ACT – Hues Corporation (Warner Bros.)
JUST FRIENDS – Silver, Platinum & Gold (Farr)
MY LOVE IS ON HIS WAY – Retta Young (All Platinum)
ONE TO ONE/I DON'T KNOW/TIKI TIKI DONGA
– Syreeta (Tamla)
PARTY LIGHTS – Natalie Cole (Capitol)
ROLLERCOASTER/THEME FROM KING KONG
– Lalo Schifrin (CTI)
SLOW DOWN – John Miles (London)
SUPERMAN/CLOSER, CLOSER – Celi Bee & the Buzzy
Bunch (APA)
WE'RE SO HOT – Sun (Capitol)

CRICKET CLUB, MIAMI
DJ: Aristides Jacobs

DO WHAT YOU WANNA DO – T-Connection (TK)
DO YOU WANNA GET FUNKY WITH ME – Peter Brown (TK)
DON'T TURN AWAY – Midnight Flite (SRI)
LIFE IS MUSIC/LADY LUCK – Ritchie Family (TK)
LOVE IN C MINOR – Cerrone (Cotillion)
**THE MORE I GET, THE MORE I WANT/YOU CAN'T HIDE
FROM YOURSELF** – Teddy Pendergrass (Phila. Intl.)
ONE LOVE/CLOSER, CLOSER/HURT ME, HURT ME z
– Celi Bee & the Buzzy Bunch (APA)
TOUCH ME/TAKE ME – Black Light Orchestra
(RCA import)
UPTOWN FESTIVAL – Shalamar (Soul Train)
YOU TAKE ME HEART AWAY – Laura Green (Epic)

SECOND STORY, PHILADELPHIA
DJ: Wayne Geftman

BODY CONTACT CONTRACT/DISCO INFERNO –
Trammps (Atlantic)
DO WHAT YOU WANNA DO –T-Connection (TK)
HOW CAN I KEEP IN TOUCH WITH YOU
– Hamilton Affair (Monument)
I CAUGHT YOUR ACT – Hues Corporation (Warner Bros.)
**I DON'T LOVE YOU ANYMORE/YOU CAN'T HIDE FROM
YOURSELF/THE MORE I GET, THE MORE I WANT**
– Teddy Pendergrass (Phila. Intl.)
I GOTTA KEEP DANCIN' – Carrie Lucas (Soul Train)
LOVE IN C MINOR – Heart & Soul Orchestra (Casablanca)
N.Y. YOU GOT ME DANCING – Andrea True Connection
(Buddah)
**SIX MILLION DOLLAR MAN/HURRY UP AND WAIT/YOU
ARE A BLESSING TO ME** – Originals (Soul)
UPTOWN FESTIVAL – Shalamar (Soul Train)

DOUBLES, NEW YORK
DJ: Ted Currier

BODY CONTACT CONTRACT – Trammps (Atlantic)
DISCO REGGAE – Kalyan (MCA)
DO WHAT YOU WANNA DO – T-Connection (TK)
DON'T LEAVE ME THIS WAY – Thelma Houston (Tamla)
DOWN TO LOVE TOWN – Originals (Soul)
I GO TO RIO – Peter Allen (A&M)
I GOTTA KEEP DANCIN' – Carrie Lucas (Soul Train)
SWEET DYNAMITE – Claudja Barry (London import)
TOUCH ME, TAKE ME – Black Light Orchestra (RCA import)
UPTOWN FESTIVAL – Shalamar (Soul Train)

Quickly, three essential new disco discs: "Boogie Nights"
by **Heatwave** (Epic), an English record already in the top
five on the British charts that is thin on vocals but very
strong in the instrumental department – loose and
sinuous, understated but right to the point: not, in the
end, the usual disco sound but with more and more
records in innovative styles gaining acceptance these
days, this one could be a major hit... **Lamont Dozier's**
"Going Back To My Roots" (Warner Brothers) is really
stunning both as a vocal – Dozier's raw, unpolished voice
has rarely sounded as compelling or appropriate to the
material – and as a production which combines African
chant-style segments with a pounding disco beat.
Warners has pressed a 9:45 version and a 6:00 version
back to back on their promotional 12-inch and the longer
track includes a fabulous tribal chant break at the end
that is one of the most unusual and riveting things we've
heard in a while. A must... **Grace Jones'** latest from Beam
Junction is "I Need A Man," a full-bodied, extremely
dense new version of the record that brought Grace her
first success in Paris last year. The vocals are more assured
and aggressive than on her previous U.S. releases and the
production, an odd blend of European romanticism and
New York get-down, is just off-the-wall enough to catch
on. Due out within the week as a commercial release with
a 7:30 vocal on one side and 4:53 instrumental on the
other... Also due within the week, **Steve Bender's**
excellent "The Final Thing," praised here last issue and
already scooped up by London for American release as a
disco disc, vocal on one side, instrumental on the other.
NOTE: **Barbara Pennington's** "Twenty-Four Hours A Day"
has been so successful on a disco level that United Artists
is now releasing the disco disc version commercially – it
should be available in the stores now. ◉

Cory Wade, the young Miami-based producer responsible for the **T-Connection's** "Do What You Wanna Do" (now in its third week as number one on the DISCO FILE Top 20), is back this week with what may be the most outrageous, adventuresome and off-the-wall productions of the year: a disco called "Do You Wanna Get Funky" by **Peter Brown** on TK. Brown and Wade have concocted an 8-minute masterpiece of funk disco with a series of vocal and instrumental segments, each more intense and explosive than the one before. Beginning with a loose, insinuating intro, the record unfolds rather unexpectedly, like a pot of water gradually heating up and boiling over, Brown's rough-edged, shouting vocals – after setting the scene for his seduction by a fire-eyed devil-woman who catches him with the no-nonsense line, "Do you wanna get funky with me?" – are followed by a steamy sax break over muffled sighs and moans. A deeply echoed percussion effect signals the next break and a chorus enters chanting, "I wanna set you on fire/'cause it's hot!" and gradually grows louder, as if they're being wheeled into the room. This, too, changes, cutting into a synthesizer and percussion section that is eventually joined by the chorus again, singing "It's so hot!, I'm burning up!" in a sizzling staccato which is then doubled-tracked and echoed in upon itself – a favorite disco DJ technique that sounds terrific here. When the chorus reaches a peak, it's overwhelmed by a sudden rising synthesizer siren that cuts off at an impossible height and turns back with a jolt to Brown, shouting at the top of his voice and ready to resume his vocals. Whew.

The flip side of "Do You Wanna Get Funky" is a 5:26 cut called "Burning Love Breakdown," which is essentially the same composition reduced to its instrumental basics with the two girl chorus segments retained. More, more, more of the same with variations. Both sides seem to demand the loudest volume settings and I've been straining my system to luxuriate in the music's jagged percussion waterfalls as they crash through the living room. Obviously I'm crazy about this record, if only because it's so unlike anything else out right now and so incredibly unpredictable. Yet these very factors might keep it off a lot of turntables. Like **Marvin Gaye's** "Got to Give It Up," which is going over quite well, surprising everyone who was initially skeptical, "Do You Wanna Get Funky" is an unusual record whose course should be interesting to watch for anyone interested in the viability of new directions for the disco sound.

Also out this week is a special limited edition of a new disco by **D. C. LaRue:** entirely re-mixed versions of "Indiscreet" (4:53) and "Face Of Love" (5:51) back-to-back on a 12-inch that D.C. himself designed and executed, "I wanted to do something spectacular; I wanted a first," he said, so each disc is being stamped with a number – 1 to 2000 – by LaRue, who is determined to attend to every detail himself. Like a run of lithograph prints or a limited edition book, the first 15 copies of the disc have been signed as well as numbered and a master list is being kept of the recipient of each record, Though the discs are packaged in Pyramid's familiar disco sleeves, the company's logo doesn't appear on the record itself, being replaced here by a photo of D.C. full-face on "Face Of Love" but purposely slipping off the side on "Indiscreet" – like he's sliding into the shadow. The new mixes are fine and they are definitely Not For Sale in the stores – a real disco collector's item for DJs only, sure to be one of the most sought-after discs on the circuit this month.

Other recommended disco discs: **Joe Bataan's** new group, **LaSo** (Latin Soul?), debuts with a 6:53 instrumental version of **Stevie Wonder's** "Another Star" (MCA) that is paced for a fast hustle and features a prominent horn section as well as a smooth underpinning of strings. Strong Latin-flavored jazz, similar in concept to the **Players' Association** and just as attractive... "What It Is," the **Garnett Mimms** song we recommended here as a single several issues back, is available in a 6:20 disco version now and the smoking **Jeff Lane/Randy Muller** production sounds considerably more impressive at this length – full of great **Brass Construction** moves, angular and jumpy – on Arista... **Tony Valor's** new production for a group named **Touch**, "Me and You" (Brunswick), has a bright, bouncing feels with vocals reminiscent of the **Stylistics** and a long, involving break (total time: 5:19). The feedback on this one is already very favorable – Bill Owens listed it in his top 10 this week from Lost & Found in Washington – and the disc's other side, "Energizer" (6:02), with more of a funk edge, should be checked out as well. Now available on disco discs: **Paulinho da Costa's** excellent Brazilian percussion breakdown, "Ritmo Number One" (8:26) that lists solos on a number of Brazilian instruments plus "whistle, spoons, frying pan, congas" (Pablo/RCA); and **S.S.O.'s** "Give a Damn" and "Right Here, Right Now" back-to-back on Shadybrook, same lengths as on the lp.

> ❝ Obviously I'm crazy about this record, if only because it's so unlike anything else out right now and so incredibly unpredictable. Yet these very factors might keep it off a lot of turntables ❞

STUDIO ONE, LOS ANGELES
DJ: Paul Dougan

DO WHAT YOU WANNA DO – T-Connection (TK)
GOT TO GIVE IT UP – Marvin Gaye (Tamla)
I CAUGHT YOUR ACT – Hues Corporation (Warner Bros.)
I GOTTA KEEP DANCIN' – Carrie Lucas (Soul Train)
I NEED A MAN – Grace Jones (Beam Junction)
JUNGLE PEOPLE – Soulful Dynamics (Epic import)
STONE TO THE BONE – Timmy Thomas (TK)
SUPERMAN/HURT ME HURT ME/CLOSER, CLOSER
– Celi Bee & the Buzzy Bunch (APA)
SWEET DYNAMITE – Claudja Barry (London import)
TOUCH ME, TAKE ME – Black Light Orchestra (RCA import)

FLAMINGO, NEW YORK
DJ: Howard Merritt

DO WHAT YOU WANNA DO – T-Connection (TK)
HOW CAN I KEEP IN TOUCH WITH YOU – Hamilton Affair
(Monument)
I DON'T LOVE YOU ANYMORE/THE MORE I GET, THE
MORE I WANT/BE SURE/YOU CAN'T HIDE FROM
YOURSELF – Teddy Pendergrass (Phila. Intl.)
LIFE IS MUSIC/LADY LUCK – Ritchie Family (TK)
LOVE IN C MINOR/MIDNIGHT LADY/BLACK IS BLACK –
Cerrone (Cotillion)
MOST OF ALL – Gloria Gaynor (Polydor)
SLOW DOWN – John Miles (London)
STUBBORN KIND OF FELLA – Buffalo Smoke (RCA)
SUPERMAN/CLOSER, CLOSER/ONE LOVE/ SMILE
– Celi Bee & the Buzzy Bunch (APA)
UP JUMPED THE DEVIL/YOU GOT TO GIVE IT UP
– John Davis & the Monster Orchestra (Sam)

LOST AND FOUND, WASHINGTON D.C.
DJ: Bill Owens

COME TO AMERICA – Gibson Brothers (Zagora import)
DO WHAT YOU WANNA DO – T-Connection (TK)
GOT TO GIVE IT UP – Marvin Gaye (Tamla)
I CAUGHT YOUR ACT – Hues Corporation (Warner Bros.)
I DON'T LOVE YOU ANYMORE/YOU CAN'T HIDE FROM
YOURSELF/THE MORE I GET, THE MORE I WANT – Teddy
Pendergrass (Phila. Intl.)
I GOTTA KEEP DANCIN' – Carrie Lucas (Soul Train)
KING OF CLUBS – Chocolat's (Able import)
ME AND YOU – Touch (Brunswick)
SLOW DOWN – John Miles (London)
SUPERMAN/CLOSER, CLOSER/HURT ME, HURT ME
– Celi Bee & the Buzzy Bunch (APA)

EXPERIMENT, NEW YORK
DJ: John Benitez

I GOT IT – New York Port Authority (Invictus)
I WANNA BE NEAR YOU – Ruby Andrews (ABC)
JUNGLE PEOPLE – Soulful Dynamics (Epic import)
MARY HARTMAN, MARY HARTMAN
– Sound of Inner City (West End)
ONCE I'VE BEEN THERE – Norman Connors (Buddah)
SEE YOU WHEN I GET THERE – Lou Rawls (Phila. Intl.)
SLOW DOWN – John Miles (London)
SUPERMAN/CLOSER, CLOSER/ONE LOVE
– Celi Bee & the Buzzy Bunch (APA)
WE'RE SO HOT – Sun (Capitol)
YOU CAN'T HIDE FROM YOURSELF/THE MORE I GET, THE
MORE I WANT – Teddy Pendergrass (Phila. Intl.)

COMING ON STRONG: Marvin Gaye's "Got To Give It Up" (Tamla), the Hues Corporation's "I Caught Your Act" (WB), the Celi Bee & the Buzzy Bunch album – especially "Superman" and "Closer, Closer" (TK), Lamont Dozier's "Going Back To My Roots" (WB), Grace Jones' "I Need A Man" (Beam Junction) and the Lifestyle album (MCA).

NOTE: Thelma Houston's "Don't Leave Me This Way" entered the DISCO FILE Top 20 at number 10 in the December 4, 1976 issue and has been on the list ever since – 20 weeks so far, a good many of them in the number one spot. Just a tip of the hat to a lady with great staying power. ✪

T.K. DISCO
45 RPM
℗ⓒ 1977, T.K. Productions, Inc.
™ Drive Records
Distributed by T.K. Productions, Inc., 495 S.E. 10th Court, Hialeah, Florida 33010
Sherlyn Publishing Co., Inc. (BMI)/ Decibel (BMI)
Recorded at Studio Center Sound Studios, Miami, Fla..
Sound Engineer: Gary Vandy
35 STEREO
(TKD-35-A)
Time: 8:30
Drum break: 4:25
Intro: :10
Produced & Mixed by Cory Wade for TransAmerica Productions, Inc.
Arranged by: Peter Brown & Cory Wade
Background vocals: Featuring-Wildflower
"DO YA WANNA GET FUNKY WITH ME"
(Peter Brown-Robert Rans)
Peter Brown
℗ 1976 T.K. PRODUCTIONS, INC.

CHOICE CUTS: **Neal Fox's** pounding "In The Jungle," from his debut album, "A Painting" (RCA), could be the next hot rock disco record to follow **John Miles'** fast-moving "Slow Down" up the chart. The sound is something between **Barrabas** and **Randy Pie**, opening with a short bit of jungle atmosphere (bird calls, animal cries) which most DJs will choose to skip in order to jump in on the first beat set by a guitar, underlined by drums. The jungle wells up again at the end, this time in the form of an excellent, wildly tribal percussion break that is itself overwhelmed by a swelling organ chord that then fades to finish the song. The subject, surprisingly, is ecology, questionable progress and the eclipse of wilderness by "civilization" – a little heavy-handed, but perfectly danceable nevertheless. Watch this one... For the more adventurous, there's "Trans-Europe Express" (Capitol), the new album of cerebral, conceptual, totally-synthesized music from the avant garde German group **Kraftwerk**. The cut that Tom Savarese lists in his top 10 from Harrah this week is "Europe Endless," a 9:35 track that starts out slowly – almost like stately classical music – and gradually gets very interesting. The flatly sung vocals are slightly off-putting but quite minimal and as the piercing, insinuating instrumental intensifies, it draws you in like quicksand. Coldly spacey, but fascinating. David Rodriguez, long-time New York disco DJ now performing behind the singles counter at Downstairs Records, one of the city's key disco outlets, considers another Kraftwerk cut "to die": "Trans-Europe Express"/"Metal on Metal," two tracks that run together to form one spectacular 13:32 composition much more metallic and menacing in feeling than "Europe Endless." It's a stylized version of the sound of a train speeding along a track like **Resonance's** "Yellow Train" fed through a computer, broken down and put together again – very relentless. Not exactly light entertainment, but quite incredible, especially on a powerful system. Highly recommended for freaky crowds, otherwise a little too off-the-wall...

Talk about off-the-wall, listen to "Dirty Love," a hilarious, vaguely obscene **Frank Zappa** composition from the **Mandre** album just out on Motown. The song sounds like a combination of **Sly Stone**, the **Ohio Players** and **Funkadelic** – bizarre and funky. The album itself seems to be a new incarnation of the **Maxayn** group, the terrific avant garde funk outfit that produced several now out-of-print albums and then disbanded several years ago. **Andre Lewis**, that group's producer/songwriter, is back in the same role here and Maxayn herself is listed prominently in the credits. Outside of "Dirty Love,"

many of the album's other material is space funk like "Solar Flight (Opus I)," a 7:57 instrumental with a pulsing beat that would make nice early-evening/late-night mood music – especially with its gorgeous use of synthesizer. Could be a big cult album.

RECOMMENDED DISCO DISCS: The two best dance cuts from the new **Brecker Brothers** album have been pressed on a promotional 12-inch from Arista: "Don't Stop The Music" (6:33), a driving, sharp edged instrumental with girls repeating the title over and over, building in intensity; and "Finger Lickin' Good" (3:58), which is more light-hearted and loose. Both really nice. **Ralph MacDonald**, **Lenny White** and **Steve Gadd** are among the guest stars. Also available, same lengths, on the lp, "Don't Stop The Music"... The **Detroit Emeralds'** new long (7:04) version of their classic "Feel The Need" is the first record coming out of the new Atlantic-Westbound deal and, while it doesn't really take the song in any new direction, it should serve to revive interest in this fine song. Basically, it's the same or the same-sounding vocals in a more expansive setting but the setting lacks drama and punch. Wonderful nostalgia, nevertheless. Now available on (promotional) disco discs: **Herbie Mann's** excellent "The Piper" backed with "Bird In A Silver Cage," his records with the **Silver Convention** group given a sharper new mix (Atlantic), and **Norman Connors'** "Once I've Been There" with great vocals by **Phillip Mitchell** (Buddah).

OTHER RECOMMENDED ALBUMS: The **Moment of Truth's** debut album on Salsoul, written and produced by **Reid Whitelaw** and **Norman Bergen**, took some time to sink in and if it still doesn't have the depth or fire we would have hoped for, it sounds stronger with each new listening. "Helplessly" and "So Much For Love" are of course included, though only in their short versions (3:40 and 3:37 respectively), and there's also a short version of the group's latest disco disc, "Loving You Is Killing Me" (4:21 on the lp, 7:04 on the 12-inch, which flips to a 6:53 instrumental version). But the early feedback is centering on another of the album's new tracks, "Chained To Your Love" (5:04), which, as Tony Smith pointed out, has a quote from the horn line of **Sam & Dave's** "Hold On I'm Coming" and one of the best breaks on the lp. The other cut to check out is "You Got Me Hummin'" (4:11), a joyous, high-spirited song with an infectious beat... **Dexter Wansel**, whose name has been cropping up in the credits on more and more Philadelphia International product lately, has a second album of his own out now, "What The World Is Coming To" (Philadelphia

" Nicky Siano is one of New York's most eccentric and sensational DJs; his club, The Gallery, packs in loyal crowds every weekend "

MY PLACE, LOS ANGELES
DJ: Elton Ahi

COME TO AMERICA – Gibson Brothers
(Phonogram import inst.)
I CAUGHT YOUR ACT – Hues Corporation
(Warner Bros.)
I GOTTA KEEP DANCIN' – Carrie Lucas (Soul Train)
LOVE HANGOVER – Players' Association (Vanguard)
RICE & BEANS THEME/DISCO DANCING – Rice & Beans
Orchestra (Dash)
SURPRISE – Andre Gagnon (London)
TATTOO MAN – Denise McCann (Polydor)
TWENTY-FOUR HOURS A DAY – Barbara Pennington (VA)
UPTOWN FESTIVAL/BEAUTIFUL NIGHT/INKY DINKY –
Shalamar (Soul Train)

EL MOROCCO, NEW YORK
DJ: Jeff Baugh

BITE YOUR GRANNY/LE JOINT /TIME – Morning, Noon &
Night (Roadshow/UA)
GOT TO GIVE IT UP – Marvin Gaye (Tamla)
**I DON'T LOVE YOU ANYMORE/YOU CAN'T HIDE FROM
YOURSELF/THE MORE I GET, THE MORE I WANT**
– Teddy Pendergrass (Phila. Intl.)
I GOTTA KEEP DANCIN' – Carrie Lucas (Soul Train)
I NEED A MAN – Grace Jones (Beam Junction)
MAGIC FLY – Space (Vogue import)
SEE YOU WHEN I GIT THERE – Lou Rawls (Phila. Intl.)
SLOW DOWN – John Miles (London)
SUPERMAN/ONE LOVE – Celi Bee & the Buzzy Bunch (TK)
THIS WILL BE A NIGHT TO REMEMBER – Eddie Holman
(Salsoul)

HARRAH, NEW YORK
DJ: Tom Savarese

EUROPE ENDLESS – Kraftwerk (Capitol)
THE FINAL THING – Steve Bender (London)
GOING BACK TO MY ROOTS – Lamont Dozier
(Warner Bros.)
GOT TO GIVE IT UP – Marvin Gaye (Tamla)
I GONNA KEEP DANCIN' – Carrie Lucas (Soul Train)
I NEED A MAN – Grace Jones (Beam Junction)
LOVING YOU, LOSING YOU – Phyllis Hyman
(Buddah)
SLOW DOWN – John Miles (London)
SUPERMAN/ONE LOVE/CLOSER, CLOSER
– Celi Bee & the Buzzy Bunch (APA)
YOU'RE MY PEACE OF MIND – Faith, Hope & Charity (RCA)

GIRAFFE, PITTSBURGH
DJ: Gary Larkin

DANCIN' – Crown Heights Affair (De-Lite)
DO WHAT YOU WANNA DO – T-Connection (TK)
I GOTTA KEEP DANCIN – Carrie Lucas (Soul Train)
LOVE IN C MINOR – Cerrone (Cotillion lp cut)
SLOW DOWN – John Miles (London)
SON OF SLIDE – Slave (Cotillion)
THIS FEELING/KATRINA – Lifestyle (MCA)
TWENTY-FOUR HOURS A DAY – Barbara Pennington (VA)
UP JUMPED THE DEVIL – John Davis & the Monster
Orchestra (Sam)
UPTOWN FESTIVAL – Shalamar (Soul Train)

International). Best dance track: "Disco Lights" (4:09), a
bright, perky instrumental. "Dance With Me Tonight"
(5:38) is another possibility, though it's somewhat uneven
rhythm structure could prove difficult. **Jean Carn**
provides wonderful vocals on one of the slower cuts,
"Dreams Of Tomorrow." All together, then, a stylish, well-
made album, one that should serve to turn people on to
Wansel's first, even better lp... Nicky Siano, one of New
York's most eccentric and sensational DJs whose private
club, The Gallery, packs in loyal crowds every weekend,
alerted us to "We're So Hot" by **Sun** when he listed it in
his top 10 two weeks ago. The instrumental, from Sun's
new album, "Sun Power" (Capitol), is aggressive, brassy
and hard, combining rock and funk styles for maximum
impact. And, for your Visual enjoyment, the record's
pressed on clear, golden yellow vinyl... For something
different, try the **20th Century Steel Band's** steel-drum
renditions of "Love's Theme" and "Theme From Shaft"
on their new "Warm Heart Cold Steel" album (Island). ✦

DISCO FILE TOP 20

1. **DO WHAT YOU WANNA DO** – T-Connection (TK)
2. **GONNA KEEP DANCIN'** – Carrie Lucas
   (Soul Train)
3. **UPTOWN FESTIVAL** – Shalamar (Soul Train)
4. **YOU CAN'T HIDE FROM YOURSELF/THE MORE
   I GET, THE MORE I WANT/I DON'T LOVE YOU
   ANYMORE/** – Teddy Pendergrass (Phila. Intl.)
5. **SLOW DOWN** – John Miles (London)
6. **SUPERMAN/CLOSER, CLOSER** – Celi Bee & the
   Buzzy Bunch (APA)
7. **LOVE IN C MINOR** – Cerrone (Malligator import)
8. **DISCO INFERNO/BODY CONTACT CONTRACT**
   – Trammps (Atlantic)
9. **I CAUGHT YOUR ACT** – Hues Corporation
   (Warner Bros.)
10. **GOT TO GIVE IT UP** – Marvin Gaye (Tamla)
11. **ONE LOVE/HURT ME, HURT ME** – Celi Bee & the
    Buzzy Bunch (APA)
12. **DREAMIN'/HIT AND RUN** – Loleatta Holloway
    (Gold Mind)
13. **TWENTY-FOUR HOURS A DAY** – Barbara
    Pennington (UA)
14. **MIDNIGHT LADY/BLACK IS BLACK** – Cerrone
    (Cotillion)
15. **N.Y. YOU GOT ME DANCING** – Andrea True
    Connection (Buddah)
16. **STONE TO THE BONE** – Timmy Thomas (TK)
17. **LOVE IN C MINOR** – Heart & Soul Orchestra
    (Casablanca)
18. **TOUCH ME, TAKE ME** – Black Light Orchestra
    (RCA import)
19. **DON'T LEAVE ME THIS WAY** – Thelma Houston
    (Tamla)
20. **SIX-MILLION DOLLAR MAN** – Originals (Soul)

The essential new disco discs, an especially fine lot this week, are topped by the long-awaited, much-discussed **C.J. & Company** record, "Devil's Gun" (Atlantic/Westbound), which more than lives up to the advance praise. Like **Peter Brown's** "Do You Wanna Get Funky With Me," another song about devilish doings, "Devil's Gun" is a powerful, hard funk production, but here the energy is even more concentrated and intense so that at times the music seems to be welling up from fiery depths and its pounding, like the message of the song, is ominous. "Fe fi fo fum," a deep bass voice chants, "You're looking down the barrel of the devil's gun." The vocals, both male and female, are tough, but the production, by **Dennis Coffey** and **Mike Theodore**, is tougher: big, bold and explosive. At just over seven minutes, this should be one of the major disco pressings of the next few months; the non-commercial disc is due for release to DJs within the week, followed shortly by the group's debut album. Hot as hell...

In quite a different vein, there's **Eddie Holman's** wonderful double-punch, "This Will Be A Night to Remember" backed with "Time Will Tell" on Salsoul. Holman, remembered for "Hey There Lonely Girl," still has one of the most terrific tenor/falsetto voices around and **Ron Baker's** production on "Night To Remember" (5:50) is as rousing and irresistible as anything that's come out of Philadelphia so far this year. By the way, according to Salsoul, the rumor that the zippy piano playing here was contributed by **Elton John** is interesting but untrue. No matter, this is a near-perfect track and it's made even more attractive by the inclusion of another excellent record on the flip side. "Time Will Tell" (4:34), also a Ron Baker production, cuts the pace down considerably but the vocals are so superb and the whole spirit so loose and comfortable that you can't help falling right into it. Not to be missed – and watch for a Holman lp early in May... The **Soul Train Gang** have their best record yet in their version of **Stevie Wonder's** "My Cherie Armour" (Soul Train), produced by **Don Cornelius**, arranged by **Jerry Peters** and running an invigorating 6:49. The bouncy, percussive opening seems perfectly designed to blend with "Uptown Festival"'s intro and break and if the group's vocals are a little thin, the sparkling production more than makes up for them. Another record whose breaks are effective enough to clinch its success, "My

Cherie Amour," looks like it's set to follow the other Soul Train hits, "Uptown Festival" and "I Gotta Keep Dancin'," on their chart zoom... **Eli's Second Coming** has a gorgeous new instrumental called "Foxfire" (3:18 on both the disco disc and the single) written and produced by **Bobby Eli** and the group's first release since their success with "Love Chant" last year. "Foxfire" is in a very different mood: mysterious, sensuous, richly evocative but with a nice drive to its loping beat. A personal favorite this week. The other side, "Hopscotch" (planned as the A side), might be bearable to those of you who don't share my particular aversion to bagpipes.

OTHER RECOMMENDED DISCO DISCS: Four of the best this week are new or extended versions of records we've recommended here before – **Steve Bender's** "The Final Thing," now out as a London disco disc, combines the two sides of the import single on a 6:15 vocal side and adds a previously unavailable instrumental (4:51) whose freaky synthesizer twists should push this record even further; **Brainstorm's** jumping "Lovin' Is Really My Game" (Tabu/RCA) has been remixed from 4:59 to a fabulous 7:39 and if you haven't picked up on this yet, don't ignore this excellent second chance; two of the best cuts from **Carol Williams'** album, "Love Is You" and "Come Back," have been expanded, the former from 4:52 to 5:08, the latter from 3:40 to 7:15 (!) and including a great **Vince Montana** vibes break (on Salsoul); and **Ralph MacDonald's** heightened the impact on his "Jam On The Groove" track with some mix changes and a few additional seconds (now 6:10) for TK ("Sound Of A Drum" is on the other side)... The first record by a studio group called **IRT** is a fairly standard but generally well-executed disco treatment of the camp nostalgia tune, "Lullaby Of Broadway" (5:22 on UA), which is blatantly commercial but bright and cute enough to go over with many crowds. The flip side makes it a collector's item: the original soundtrack version of the song, as recorded by **Winifred Shaw**, from the movie "Gold Diggers Of 1935" where it accompanied one of the most elaborate and unusual Busby Berkeley dance sequences ever filmed. It runs 6:03 here and includes what sounds like the sound of one hundred tapping feet ... Left field except for lovers of Brazilian music (whom it should delight): "Onda" by **Cassiano**, a song reportedly a major hit in Brazil, done

" The rumor that the zippy piano playing here was contributed by Elton John is not true "

THE ANVIL, NEW YORK
DJ: Richie Rivera

DO WHAT YOU WANNA DO – T-Connection (TK)
DON'T STOP THE MUSIC – Brecker Brothers (Arista)
THE FINAL THING – Steve Bender (London)
GOING BACK TO MY ROOTS – Lamont Dozier (Warner Bros)
HOW CAN I KEEP IN TOUCH WITH YOU – Hamilton Affair (Monument)
I CAUGHT YOUR ACT – Hues Corporation (Warner Bros.)
I GOTTA KEEP DANCIN' – Carrie Lucas (Soul Train)
I NEED A MAN – Grace Jones (Beam Junction)
TRANS-EUROPE EXPRESS/METAL ON METAL – Kraftwerk (Capitol)
TURN THIS MOTHER OUT – Idris Muhammad (Kudu)

BAREFOOT BOY, NEW YORK
DJ: Tony Smith

CHAINED TO YOUR LOVE/LOVIN' YOU IS KILLING ME – Moment of Truth (Salsoul)
DISCO MANIA (PART II) – The Lovers (Marlin)
DON'T STOP THE MUSIC – Brecker Brothers (Arista)
EVERYBODY DANCE – Bumblebee Unlimited (Direction import)
GIVE A DAMN/RIGHT HERE RIGHT NOW – S.S.O. (Shadybrook)
I GOTTA KEEP DANCIN' – Carrie Lucas (Soul Train)
I NEED A MAN – Grace Jones (Beam Junction)
JUST WANT TO BE WITH YOU/KATRINA – Lifestyle (MCA)
MY CHERIE AMOUR – Soul Train Gang (Soul Train)
TEASER/THEY SAID IT COULDN'T BE DONE/RICH MAN, POOR MAN – Dells (Mercury)

BROADWAY LIMITED, CHICAGO
DJ: Jim Thompson

DISCO LIGHTS – Dexter Wansel (Phila. Intl.)
DO WHAT YOU WANNA DO – T-Connection (TK)
I DON'T LOVE YOU ANYMORE/YOU CAN'T HIDE FROM YOURSELF/THE MORE I GET, THE MORE I WANT – Teddy Pendergrass (Phila. Intl.)
I GOTTA KEEP DANCIN' – Carrie Lucas (Soul Train)
I NEED A MAN – Grace Jones (Beam Junction)
N.Y. YOU GOT ME DANCING – Andrea True Connection (Buddah)
SLOW DOWN – John Miles (London)
STICK TOGETHER – Minnie Riperton (Epic)
SUPERMAN – Celi Bee & the Buzzy Bunch (APA)
SWEET DYNAMITE – Claudja Barry (London import)

YESTERDAYS, BOSTON
DJ: Cosmo Wyatt

BRICK HOUSE – Commodores (Motown)
DO WHAT YOU WANNA DO – T-Connection (TK)
I CAUGHT YOUR ACT – Hues Corporation (Warner Bros.)
I DON'T LOVE YOU ANYMORE/YOU CAN'T HIDE FROM YOURSELF/THE MORE I GET, THE MORE I WANT – Teddy Pendergrass (Phila. Intl.)
I GOTTA KEEP DANCIN' – Carrie Lucas (Soul Train)
LOCKED IN THIS POSITION/LOVE SONG – Barbara Mason & Bunny Sigler (Curtom)
ONCE I'VE BEEN THERE – Norman Connors (Buddah)
SUPERMAN – Celi Bee & the Buzzy Bunch (APA)
TRYING TO MAKE IT UP TO YOU/ KATRINA/ JUST WANT TO BE WITH YOU – Lifestyle (MCA)
UPTOWN FESTIVAL – Shalamar (Soul Train)

in a beat that resembles a slow but totally entrancing hustle. Very pretty, featuring hushed, wonderful vocals (in Portuguese), and nearly eight minutes long. It's an import from Polydor-Brazil pressed for International Book & Record Distributors in Long Island City, New York... **Bobby Byrd's** new record on Strawberry is a version of Bottom & Co.'s "Here For The Party" that doesn't really live up to the original – but the instrumental version, titled "Byrd's In Flight" (3:10), is tasty.

RECOMMENDED SINGLES: "Discomania" by **The Lovers** is a **Jacques Morali** production that picks up where the **Ritchie Family's** "Best Disco In Town" left off. It's another highly commercial medley – this time including "Don't Leave Me This Way," "That's Where The Happy People Go," "Life Is Music," "Shake Your Booty" and two more big hits – set into a glossy disco propaganda framework. The framework is weak in parts but the transitions and the imitations are so perfect that you get into it in spite of yourself. The B side is an entirely different version that takes off in some interesting and amusing directions both vocally and instrumentally – this is the side that should please the progressive DJs. But both are sure to be crowd pleasers (on Marlin, with no disco disc version planned)... One of our favorite groups, **Brenda and the Tabulations**, is back with a driving 5:09 cut called "(I'm a) Superstar" (Chocolate City), which puts the group in a bright but sometimes over-busy arrangement that goes through a lot of good changes, especially toward the end (when that "Love Hangover" bassline slips in). Not as sustained as it could be, but strong as a whole and worth spending some time with... **Bumblebee Unlimited's** new record, "Everybody Dance," has instant cachet simply because it came out on Direction, a new, hip Canadian label, before its American release on Mercury (due later this week) and is appearing in disco stores as an import. Tony Smith, who put it in his top 10 this week, said he bought two copies of the single so he could play Part I (2:56) and Part II (2:40) together, but Mercury is planning to issue a 12-inch (for promotional use only). "Everybody Dance" doesn't grab you as strongly as "Love Bug" did, though they are very similar (**Patrick Adams** composed, **Greg Carmichael** produced) and a lot of fun. Adams and Carmichael certainly have a way of making their music infectious in spite of all those "bee" voices buzzing in your ear... **Jennifer's** "Do It For Me" is supposed to be a major hit in France where it originated and Motown has rushed it out with a sexy, wet-T-shirt sleeve here. It has a brittle, almost mechanical feel but the beat is perfect, the vocals have a strange edge I love and the subject is, naturally, sex. A combination of **Andrea True** and **Grace Jones** with a European stamp of approval – could hit big... Speaking of Europe, **Boney M.'s** new single release, "Sunny" (Atco), has been released with a B side not previously available on either the German or American version of their album. It's called "New York City" and is a tribute in few words to the Big Town. It has a nice pace, a crackling guitar and snappy breaks-definitely up to the level of their previous material. ✪

MAY 7, 1977

❝ Kudu's preview disc of the Idris Muhammad album is already one of the hottest advance pressings around ❞

A quick run-down of the most interesting new albums: The showpiece track of the **Shalamar** debut lp is, of course, the group's sensational Motown medley, "Uptown Festival" (8:52), which gives the album its title. One of the best-selling disco discs so far, "Festival" is included here in its entirety and it sets the tone of the album: bright, slick, crisply produced. "Festival"'s producer, **Simon Soussan**, handled side one here, beginning with' "Inky Dinky Wang Dang Doo" (4:04), the cut that comes closest in spirit to "Festival" itself – light entertainment with a snappy break – and ending with "Festival." In between there's a bouncy instrumental called "Beautiful Night" (5:20) which has an **Eddie Drennon** feel with a sparkling use of synthesizer to achieve many of its best effects. Side two is the work of **Don Cornelius** and **Dick Griffey**, executive producers on the lp, and includes a version of "Forever Came Today" (5:55) that falls somewhere between the **Supremes** and the **Jackson 5** versions: a very pretty "Ooh Baby, Baby;" and a slow falling-out-of-love song called "You Know," that contains my favorite drop-dead line of the week, "You know what you can do with your love." Altogether, a solid and pleasant album – on Soul Train... The **Idris Muhammad** album won't be out for a week or two, but CTI/Kudu has issued a special preview disc that is already one of the hottest advance pressings around these days. All three advance tracks were written by **David Matthews** (who also produced and arranged) and **Tony Sarafino**, everyone's disco connection at CTI – together they've captured a fine, progressive, jazzy disco spirit. My favorite is the longest cut, an expansive, lovely song called "Could Heaven Ever Be Like This" (8:37), yet another record to make use of the familiar "Love Hangover" bass riff, though the borrowed motif is quickly woven into a far more original texture as the song builds. Very pretty male vocals, excellent breaks – a sure hit. The two other cuts included here, "Tasty Cakes" (4:23) and "Turn This Mutha Out" (6:50), are a little more predictable but equally, exciting instrumentally, especially the latter which has a strong, relentless feel. All three are beginning to turn up on New York top 10 lists (see David Mancuso's and Reggie T's this week), so expect quick action when the album appears... Sharon White from Sahara convinced me to give a second listen to "A Disco Symphony" by **Camouflage** (Honeybee) after she listed it in her top 10 and said it was going over in a big

THE LOFT, NEW YORK
DJ: David Mancuso

BATUKA #3 – Es Cola de Samba (Philips import)
COULD HEAVEN EVER BE LIKE THIS
– Idris Muhammad (Kudu)
DO WHAT YOU WANNA DO – T Connectlon (TK)
DO YOU WANNA GET FUNKY WITH ME – Peter Brown (TK)
DREAMIN' – Loleatta Holloway (Gold Mind)
FACE OF LOVE – D.C. LaRue (Pyramid)
GOING BACK TO MY ROOTS – Lamont Dozier (Warner Bros)
**I DON'T LOVE YOU ANYMORE/YOU CAN'T HIDE FROM
YOURSELF/THE MORE I GET, THE MORE I WANT** – Teddy
Pendergrass (Phila. Intl.)
IN THE JUNGLE – Neal Fox (RCA)
ONCE I'VE BEEN THERE – Norman Connors (Buddah)

SAHARA, NEW YORK
DJ: Sharon White

DISCO LIGHTS – Dexter Wansel (Phila, Intl.)
A DISCO SYMPHONY/MACARTHUR PARK/BEE STING
– Camouflage (Honeybee)
DO WHAT YOU WANNA DO – T Connectlon (TK)
I CAUGHT YOUR ACT – Hues Corporation (Warner Bros.)
**I DON'T LOVE YOU ANYMORE/YOU CAN'T HIDE FROM
YOURSELF/THE MORE I GET, THE MORE I WANT**
– Teddy Pendergrass (Phila. Intl.)
I GOTTA KEEP DANCING – Carrie Lucas (Soul Train)
I NEED A MAN – Grace Jones (Beam Junction)
LOVING YOU, LOSING YOU – Phyllis Hyman (Buddah)
SLOW DOWN – John Miles (London)
TRANS EUROPE EXPRESS/METAL ON METAL
– Kraftwerk (Capitol)

PIPPINS/NEW YORK
DJ: Reggie T. Experience

DEVIL'S GUN – C.J. & Company (Atlantic/Westbound)
**DO YOU WANNA GET FUNKY WITH ME/ BURNING LOVE
BREAKDOWN** – Peter Brown (TK)
DISCO LIGHTS/DANCE WITH ME TONIGHT
– Dexter Wansel (Phila. Intl.)
GOT TO GIVE IT UP – Marvin Gaye (Tamla)
**I DON'T LOVE YOU ANYMORE/YOU CAN'T HIDE FROM
YOURSELF/THE MORE I GET, THE MORE I WANT** – Teddy
Pendergrass (Phila. Intl.)
LOVIN' IS REALLY MY GAME – Brainstorm (Tabu)
**TEASER/OUR LOVE/RICH MAN, POOR MAN/THEY SAID
IT COULDN'T BE DONE** – Dells (Mercury)
THIS WILL BE A NIGHT TO REMEMBER/ TIME WILL TELL
– Eddie Holman (Salsoul)
TURN THIS MUTHA OUT/TASTY CAKES
– Idris Muhammad (Kudu)
WHAT IT IS – Garnett Mimms & Truckin' Company (Arista)

BARBARY COAST, HOUSTON
DJ: Sam Meyer

DO WHAT YOU WANNA DO – T Connectlon (TK)
FUNK MACHINE – Funk Machine (TK)
I CAUGHT YOUR ACT – Hues Corporation (Warner Bros.)
**I DON'T LOVE YOU ANYMORE/YOU CAN'T HIDE FROM
YOURSELF** – Teddy Pendergrass (Phila. Intl.)
I GOTTA KEEP DANCING – Carrie Lucas (Soul Train)
LOVE IN C MINOR – Cerrone (Cotillion)
RIGHT HERE, RIGHT NOW – S.S.O. (Shadybrook)
TOUCH ME, TAKE ME – Black Light Orchestra (RCA import)
TWENTY-FOUR HOURS A DAY – Barbara Pennington (UA)
UPTOWN FESTIVAL – Shalamar (Soul Train)

way at her club. Part of my resistance to the cut, which runs 14:45 and takes up the entire first side of the group's debut lp, was the fact that it builds into **Jimmy Webb's** "MacArthur Park," a song I've always found impossibly heavy-handed and melodramatic. But I've gotta admit there's something very winning here. The "symphony," presented as a dream of the ultimate disco, collects light- and semi-classical bits and pieces along with quick quotes from other sources ("I Hear A Symphony" wafts in, at one point) in a sleekly danceable framework. At times – in the end, for instance – the production (by **Meco Monardo**, **Tony Bongiovi**, **Harold Wheeler** & **Jay Ellis**) is marvellously pretentious, but many of the touches are quite clever and witty and the transition to "MacArthur Park" is superb. Perhaps too pop-styled for many tastes, it does, however, deserve several listenings. "Bee Sting" (7:10), on the album's flip side, should go over with a greater number of people – it's sexy, string-laden and sharp, A surprising debut.

"Function At The Junction" (Columbia), **B.T. Express'** latest, doesn't hold many surprises – just their usual high level of New York disco funk; no knockouts, no disappointments, "Funky Music," "Expose Yourself" and "Scratch My Itch" are all good, hard-edged cuts; "We Got It Together" is a little more laid-back; and "Eyes" is a particularly hypnotic instrumental that attracts me more than anything else' here. All are about four minutes long and are produced by **Jeff Lane**... The title cut on the new **Brenda and the Tabulations** album, "I Keep Coming Back For More" (Chocolate City), was produced by **Bobby Eli** and **Gilda Woods** in a style that blends the smoother sides of First Choice and Ecstasy, Passion & Pain. It's a song about one of those on-again, off-again romances and Brenda sings It wonderfully, backed up by the Sigma Sound Studio crew at their best. At 3:30, this one should be twice as long, but it's this week's personal pick nevertheless, Also included here: "Superstar," released last week as a single, and a tough, Philly raunch song called "Let's Go All The Way (Down)."

CHOICE CUTS: **Peaches & Herb** are back, more or less (same Herb, new Peaches), and **Van McCoy** and **Charles Kipps** produced their new album (MCA) in their smoothly refined style. You know what it sounds like and it works best here on "That's The Way I Love You," "I'm Counting On You," "We're Still Together" and "We've Got A Lot To Be Thankful For": all happy, uplifting songs with perfect vocals. **Faith, Hope & Charity**, **Zulema** and **McCoy** himself contributed to the background vocals... **Touch**, a six-man group produced by **Tony Valor**, has an album titled "Energizer" out on Brunswick which contains the previously recommended "Me And You" and something called "Love Hangover (Breaking Down)" which is just that – a jazzy instrumental version of the most-imitated song of the past year and one people never seem to tire of. ⊘

MAY 14, 1977

Salsoul has just released **Claudja Barry's** "Sweet Dynamite" album and it turns out to be an entirely different and beautifully improved version of the German lp. Five cuts from the original album have been dropped and the remaining tracks polished, frequently speeded up and expanded by several minutes; the result is a completely new and more stunning piece of work. "Sweet Dynamite" runs 7:22 here, cushioned by billowing instrumental segments; "Love For The Sake Of Love" is transformed into a 7:53 number with a measured, dreamy tempo comparable to **Gloria Gaynor's** "Most Of All" and even more luxurious; the delightfully syncopated "Why Must A Girl Like Me" is now 7:21 with the addition of an excellent instrumental second half. Barry's voice is unremarkable (so much so that one cut here, "Live A Little Bit," is improved simply by dropping the voice track off the original recording), but the production is clean and straightforward (closest to the **Boney M** sound) and the remix (by **Tom Moulton**) erases all the original flaws. Very satisfying. Also available now: the **Idris Muhammad** album, "Turn This Mutha Out" (Kudu), containing the three tracks recommended here last week on the basis of an advance disco promotional pressing: "Could Heaven Ever Be Like This," "Tasty Cakes," and the album's title cut. Since writing the column last week, "Could Heaven Ever Be Like This," has become my favorite every-minute-of-the-day record – one of the most inventive and irresistible records around right now – so consider all previous praise underlined, boldfaced and followed by a string of exclamation points

FEEDBACK: Both John Luongo (Whimsey's in Boston) and Kathy Duca (Tramps in Washington) were enthusiastic this week about **21st Creation's** "Tailgate" (Gordy), Luongo going so far as to say the speedy, invigorating single could turn into another "Love Town" were it expanded on a 12-inch. It does have a strong **Originals/O'Jays** feel (very "Backstabbers") and Motown is reported planning a disco disc version, longer, I assume, that the mere 2:46 here so this should be an interesting record to watch... Karl Uruski from Rubaiyat in Ann Arbor joined Duca and Luongo in praising a cut I neglected to mention from the new **Hodges, James & Smith** lp on London – a really marvellous, expansive (6:47) version of the standard "Since I Fell for You," that is nearly, as the DJs say, "flawless!" The first section has some uneven moments but the second half is gorgeous – like a whole different song... The other cut I'm ashamed to admit I passed up on the first few listens is **Brenda & the Tabulations'** "Everybody's Fool" (6:05) which has a classic early Philadelphia sound and wonderful, breathless vocals. Brenda's complaint: "Falling In love comes much too easy/Throw me a line and I'll believe it/Why am I always everybody's fool?" **John Davis** and **Gilda Woods** provided a varied, fresh production. Bobby Guttadaro (Mr. DJ) put "Fool" on his Infinity top' 10 this week and this cut added to "I'll Keep Coming Back For More" and "Superstar" makes Brenda's Chocolate City lp one of the essential albums of the moment... Guttadaro also likes a cute single called "Engine Of Love" by **Earl and the Steam Team** (MCA), which was written and produced in England by **Andrew Lloyd Webber** (half of the "Jesus Christ Superstar" team) as the theme for an animated cartoon, so it has simplistic pop/bubblegum overtones with a few sharp disco touches (and an intro that picks up on "Express"). Left-field fun,

RECOMMENDED DISCO HITS: "Doctor Love," the **First Choice's** debut disco for **Norman Harris'** Gold Mind Records, is entirely predictable and hard to resist for First Choice fans. That is, it doesn't take the group's familiar sound in any new direction, just carries it on in grand style – not as nasty as we like it, but smooth and glossy. The long version is 7:35 and Harris produced... **Jakki's** "You Are the Sun" (West End) isn't as spectacular as "Sun Sun Sun" (**Johnnymelfi** is no longer producing), but it's cool and attractive with a very laid-back, "Nice And Slow" style. Comfortable and very summery, so it should have a long life on the dance floor... **Marta Acuna's** "Dance, Dance, Dance" (P&P) is similar in feel to "You Are the Sun" but it goes through more changes and finally takes quite a different turn. The style here is Latin, disco fused with Patrick Adams' distinctive, quirky instrumentation; Adams produced and New York disco DJ Louis "Angelo" Alers worked on the disco mix: Acuna's sensuous, half-Spanish vocals are especially appealing... The whole of the **Sweet Inspirations** new record, "Black Sunday" (the movie theme, on Caribou Records), isn't up to the level of individual parts, but when the song breaks free of its morbid subject matter, it soars in fine form, reminiscent of the **Three Degrees** at times. Produced by Richie Rome and "Featuring the Richie Rome Orchestra," this is somewhat of a left field choice but worth experimenting with... **The Salsoul Orchestra's** latest) "Magic Bird of Fire" (5:25 on Salsoul), is similarly uneven, completely captivating at one moment – particularly in the beginning – and almost off-putting the next. **Vince Montana** has produced, arranged, conducted and written what sounds like a movie theme of shifting moods; it's dramatic, overdone and exciting at the same time, like a clash of "Salsoul 3001" and "My Sweet Summer Suite." Mystifying yet oddly haunting. The flip side is a forceful, brassy instrumental version of the Earth, Wind & Fire song, "Getaway" (4:37), which is very jazz-styled... "When Did You Stop" by **The J's**. (Dante Records, Glen Mills, Pennsylvania 19342) is a personal favorite this 'week because it has a young and ambitious fee1 to it and a sound that falls somewhere between **Morningside Drive**, **Calhoon** and **Crown Heights Affair**. As with many of the records reviewed this week, this one's slightly uneven, but it's cumulative effect in the 6:18 version is terrific. The whole long version is also available on a regular single... Now out on disco disc pressings: **Bumblebee Unlimited's** "Everybody Dance" (8:31 on Mercury – promotional only and with no speed marked); "Discomania by **The Lovers** (TK changed its mind and issued a 12-inch with the medley side at 5:40 and the flip 6:27); and **Vitamin E's** "Kiss Away" and "Laughter In The Rain'; back-to-back and same length as the lp cuts (Buddah).

INFINITY, NEW YORK
DJ: Bobby Guttadaro

DEVIL'S GUN – C.J. & Co. (Westbound/Atlantic)
DOCTOR LOVE – First Choice (Gold Mind)
DO WHAT YOU WANNA DO – T Connectlon (TK)
DO YOU WANNA GET FUNKY WITH ME – Peter Brown (TK)
I NEED A MAN – Grace Jones (Beam Junction)
I'M IN WONDERLAND – Carol Woods (RCA import)
SLOWDOWN – John Mills (London)
SUPERSTAR/EVERYBODY'S FOOL – Brenda & the Tabulations (Chocolate City)
TURN ON THE LIGHTS – Kellee Pallerson (Shadybrook)
WHEN DID YOU STOP – The J's (Dante)

TRAMP'S, WASHINGTON, D.C.
DJ: Kathy Duca

DEVIL'S GUN/WE GOT OUR OWN THING – C.J. & Co. (Westbound/Atlantic)
DISCOMANIA – The Lovers (TK)
GOT TO GIVE IT UP – Marvin Gaye (Tamla)
I NEED A MAN – Grace Jones (Beam Junction)
LOVING YOU IS KILLING ME/CHAINED TO YOUR LOVE – Moment of Truth (Salsoul)
SINCE I FELL FOR YOU – Hodges, James & Smith (London)
SLOWDOWN – John Miles (London)
SUPERSTAR – Brenda & the Tabulations (Chocolate City)
SWEET DYNAMITE – Claudja Barry (London import)
TASTY CAKES/TURN THIS MUTHA OUT/COULD HEAVEN EVER BE LIKE THIS – Idris Muhammad (Kudu)

WHIMSEY'S, BOSTON
DJ: John Luongo

COULD HEAVEN EVER BE LIKE THIS – Idris Muhammad (Kudu)
DEVIL'S GUN – C.J. & Co. (Westbound/ Atlantic)
GOT TO GIVE IT UP – Marvin Gaye (Tamla)
I CAUGHT YOUR ACT – Hues Corporation (Warner Bros.)
I DON'T LOVE YOU ANYMORE/YOU CAN'T HIDE FROM YOURSELF – Teddy Pendergrass (Phila. Intl.)
I NEED A MAN – Grace Jones (Beam Junction)
JUST WANT TO BE WITH YOU/KATRINA – Lifestyle (MCA)
ONE LOVE/SUPERMAN/IT'S SAD – Celi Bee & the Buzzy Bunch (APA)
SLOWDOWN – John Miles (London)
UPTOWN FESTIVAL/INKY DINKY – Shalamar (Soul Train)

RUBAIYAT, ANN ARBOR
DJ: Karl Uruski

CHAINED TO YOUR LOVE – Moment of Truth (Salsoul)
DEVIL'S GUN – C.J. & Co. (Westbound/Atlantic)
DO YOU WANNA GET FUNKY WITH ME – Peter Brown (TK)
THE FINAL THING (INST.) – Steve Bender (London)
GOING BACK TO MY ROOTS – Lamont Dozier (Warner Bros.)
GOT TO GIVE IT UP – Marvin Gaye (Tamla)
I NEED A MAN – Grace Jones (Beam Junction)
I WANNA BE NEAR YOU – Ruby Andrew (ABC)
LOVIN' IS REALLY MY GAME – Brainstorm (Tabu)
LOVING YOU, LOSING YOU – Phyllis Hyman (Buddah)

RECOMMENDED SINGLES: **Kellee Patterson's** ultrasexy "Turn On The Lights" (Shadybrook) is creamy raunch – like a blend of **Sylvia**, **Tamiko Jones** and **Diana Ross** ("Love Hangover") again). Key lines: "Turn on the lights/I wanna see/See what you're doing to me." The song's "Phase II" is one of the best things we've heard this week and a mix of both parts is due out on a disco disc within the week. Sensational... **The Emotions** are back with a bubbly, energetic song called "Best Of My Love" which continues the sound of their last album with a happy, chugging arrangement that reaches out and pulls you right in... English rock legend **Cliff Richard's** new record, "Don't Turn The Light Out" (Rocket), sounds like off-center Bee Gees, basically disco rock threaded with heavy Kraftwerk synthesizer and studded by a sharp disco percussion break – an odd combination of ingredients, but interesting'... **Innervision's** "Gotta Find A Way To Get Back Home" (Ariola America) is a zippy pick-me-up of a record featuring especially strong male vocals (remember the group's excellent "Honey Baby Be Mine"?); check it out. ✏

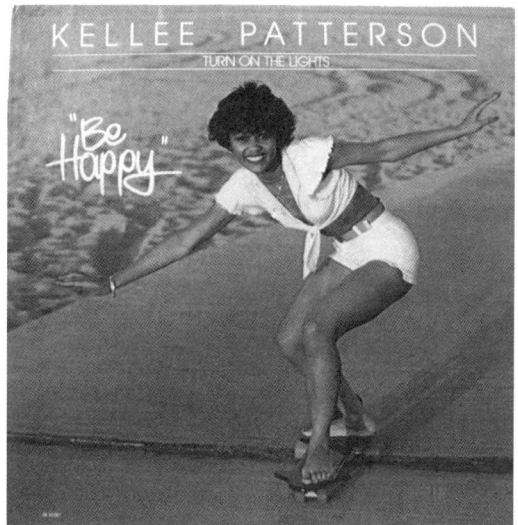

"Kellee Patterson's ultrasexy "Turn On The Lights" is creamy raunch. Key lines: "Turn on the lights/I wanna see/See what you're doing to me""

The new **Donna Summer** album, "I Remember Yesterday" (Casablanca), is hardly what we've come to expect from disco's steamy "First Lady of Love." This is the inevitable change of pace album: a smooth but sudden shift away from the audacious, orgasmic concepts of Summer's previous three releases toward something more varied, more conventionally structured and more commercial. The trademark side-one medley hasn't been totally dispensed with here, but it is no longer as submissive to the demands of the dance floor. Opening with "I Remember Yesterday," a zesty, high-gloss nostalgia number with Big Band and **Savannah Band** touches, the medley then swings into a **Phil Spector**-style cut called "Love's Unkind" with a tough, pounding sound that's a perfect, witty parody of the **Crystals** and the **Ronnettes** (Bobby DJ's first reaction: "I didn't know **Darlene Love** made a disco record!"). The track that follows, a fine Motown-styled song that has Donna sounding very much like **Diana Ross** in her "Baby Love" period, is delightful but not particularly danceable by today's standards, and a reprise of "I Remember Yesterday" doesn't exactly salvage the side for disco goers. But by any other criteria, the medley is immensely successful; the parodies are clever, the production (**Giorgio Moroder** and **Pete Bellotte** again) crisp and sharp, and Summer's vocals richer and more substantial than ever before.

If the disco contingent feels slighted on the medley side, however, no one's complaining because side two, which contains four separate songs, closes with the most startling, high-energy Donna Summer track so far. Already listed on three of our four top 10 lists this week, "I Feel Love" (5:55) is a brilliant combination of whipped-up synthesizer (compare **Kraftwerk's** "Metal on Metal") and Summer's dreamy, driven, ecstatic vocals. The pace is fierce and utterly gripping with the synthesizer effects particularly aggressive and emotionally charged. Again, this is unlike anything Summer or Moroder and Bellotte have done before and the move is nearly as innovative as their "Love to Love You Baby" concept, so "I Feel Love" should easily equal if not surpass that record's success on a disco level. As if that weren't enough, there's still another cut on the album to check out: "Take Me" (5:03), which reaches back to the familiar Summer sound – very "Summer Fever" – and could be a sleeper track, the one people will pick up on a month or two from now when it will seem like a change-of-pace all over again.

Also just out: The **C.J. & Company** album, "Devil's Gun" (Westbound/ Atlantic), whose title song is surely one of the year's most outstanding and powerful productions. It remains the strongest cut on the album, but the rest of the material is quite excellent, with two standouts: "We Got Our Own Thing," which runs 9:30 and falls into a comfortable groove with a wonderful, lively synthesizer threaded through its central break and rough vocals on either end; and "Get A Groove In Order To Move" (5:11), a fine, equally relaxed song with a message as pointed as "Devil's Gun." Produced by **Dennis Coffey** and **Mike Theodore**, this should be one of the summer's biggest albums. ◙

❛❛ "I Feel Love" is a brilliant combination of whipped-up synthesizer and Summer's dreamy, driven, ecstatic vocals. It should easily equal if not surpass the success of "Love to Love You Baby" on a disco level ❜❜

FANTASIA, NEW YORK
D.J: Walter Gibbons

BEST OF MY LOVE – Emotions (Columbia)
BURNING LOVE BREAKDOWN – Peter Brown (TK)
DEVIL'S GUN – C.J. & Co. (Westbound/Atlantic)
DOCTOR'S LOVE – First Choice (Gold Mind)
HIT AND RUN/WE'RE GETTING STRONGER – Loleatta Holloway (Gold Mind)
I FEEL LOVE – Donna Summer (Casablanca)
LET'S GO ALL THE WAY (DOWN) – Brenda & the Tabulations (Chocolate City)
TAILGATE – 21st Creation (Gordy)
THE MORE I GET, THE MORE I WANT/ YOU CAN'T HIDE FROM YOURSELF – Teddy Pendergrass (Phila. Intl.)
TURN ON THE LIGHTS – Kellee Patterson (Shadybrook)

BONES, SAN FRANCISCO
DJ: Michael Lee

BULL CITY PARTY – N.C.C.U. (UA)
COULD HEAVEN EVER BE LIKE THIS/ TASTY CAKES/ TURN THIS MUTHA OUT – Idris Muhammad (Kudu)
DEVIL'S GUN – C.J. & Co. (Westbound/Atlantic)
DO YOU WANNA GET FUNKY WITH ME – Peter Brown (TK)
THE FINAL THING – Steve Bender (London)
I FEEL LOVE/REMEMBER/LOVE'S UNKIND – Donna Summer (Casablanca)
I NEED A MAN – Grace Jones (Beam Junction)
LOVIN' IS REALLY MY GAME – Brainstorm (Tabu)
MISS BROADWAY – Belle Epoque (EMI import)
THIS WILL BE A NIGHT TO REMEMBER – Eddie Holman (Salsoul)

THE POOP DECK, FORT LAUDERDALE
DJ: Bob Viteritti

DEVIL'S GUN – C.J. & Co. (Westbound/Atlantic)
DO WHAT YOU WANNA DO – Connection (TK)
DISCOMANIA – The Lovers (TK)
GOT TO GIVE IT UP – Marvin Gaye (Tamla)
I CAUGHT YOUR ACT – Hues Corporation (Warner Bros.)
I DON'T LOVE YOU' ANYMORE/ YOU CAN'T HIDE FROM YOURSELF – Teddy Pendergrass (Phila. Intl.)
I GOTTA KEEP DANCIN' – Carrie Lucas (Soul Train)
I NEED A MAN – Grace Jones (Beam Junction)
LIFE GOES ON/YOU'RE MY PEACE OF MIND – Faith, Hope & Charity (RCA)
SLOW DOWN – John Miles (London)

DCA CLUB, PHILADELPHIA
DJ: Kurt Borusiewicz

DEVIL'S GUN' – C.J. & Co. (Westbound/Atlantic)
DISCOMANIA –The Lovers (TK)
GOT TO GIVE IT UP – Marvin Gaye (Tamla)
I DON'T LOVE YOU ANYMORE/YOU CAN'T HIDE FROM YOURSELF/ THE MORE I GET, THE MORE I WANT –Teddy Pendergrass (Phila. Intl.)
I FEEL LOVE – Donna Summer (Casablanca)
I GOTTA KEEP DANCIN' – Carrie Lucas (Soul Train)
I NEED A MAN – Grace Jones (Beam Junction)
MAGIC BIRD OF FIRE – Salsoul Orchestra (Salsoul)
SWEET DYNAMITE/WHY MUST A GIRL LIKE ME – Claudja Barry (Salsoul)
TOUCH ME, TAKE ME – Black Light Orchestra (RCA import)

DISCO FILE TOP 20

1. **I NEED A MAN** – Grace Jones (Beam Junction)
2. **DEVIL'S GUN** – C.J. & Co. (Westbound/Atlantic)
3. **DO WHAT YOU WANNA DO** – T-Connection (TK)
4. **YOU CAN'T HIDE FROM YOURSELF/THE MORE I GET, THE MORE I WANT/I DON'T LOVE YOU ANYMORE/** – Teddy Pendergrass (Phila. Intl.)
5. **I GOTTA KEEP DANCIN'** – Carrie Lucas (Soul Train)
6. **GOT TO GIVE IT UP** – Marvin Gaye (Tamla)
7. **DO YOU WANNA GET FUNKY WITH ME** – Peter Brown (TK)
8. **SLOW DOWN** – John Miles (London)
9. **I CAUGHT YOUR ACT** – Hues Corporation (Warner Bros.)
10. **COULD HEAVEN EVER BE LIKE THIS/TASTY CAKES/TURN THIS MUTHA OUT** – Idris Muhammad (Kudu)
11. **DISCOMANIA** – The Lovers (TK)
12. **SUPERMAN** – Celi Bee & the Buzzy Bunch (APA)
13. **SWEET DYNAMITE** – Claudja Barry (Salsoul)
14. **UPTOWN FESTIVAL** – Shalamar (Soul Train)
15. **GOING BACK TO MY ROOTS** – Lamont Dozier (Warner Bros)
16. **KATRINA/JUST WANT TO BE WITH YOU** – Lifestyle (MCA)
17. **THE FINAL THING** – Steve Bender (London)
18. **DISCO LIGHTS/DANCE WITH ME TONIGHT** – Dexter Wansel (Phila. Intl.)
19. **ONCE I'VE BEEN THERE** – Norman Connors (Buddah)
20. **LOVE IN C MINOR** – Cerrone (Cotillion)

JUNE 4, 1977

Although import records have always been a vital part of the disco scene, this year has brought a new intensity of interest in import releases at discos all over the country. New York, Boston and Washington, D.C. are no longer the only cities where imports are considered necessary ingredients for a well-rounded playlist; Los Angeles, San Francisco, Phoenix, Fort Lauderdale – nearly every city reached by the disco boom is now experiencing an import boom. As **Claudja Barry**, **Barbara Pennington**, the **Black Light Orchestra**, **Cerrone**, **Denise McCann** and others have demonstrated, recent imports are not just chic status items played to demonstrate how hip and esoteric the DJ is – they're major request records that have been able to move on to substantial success as American releases (the exception here is Black Light Orchestra, which was, oddly, never picked up by a label in the States). Right now the two most talked-about albums around are from France: **Cerrone's** follow-up to "Love In C Minor," "Cerrone's Paradise" (Malligator), and the debut of a group called **Love and Kisses** (Rei-vera). Since "Love And Kisses" was composed and produced by **Alec R. Costandinos**, who co-wrote "Love In C Minor" and "Midnight Lady," and includes among its credits a number of singers and musicians who also perform on the Cerrone albums, there is a definite similarity between the two records. Both contain extended disco compositions that take up entire sides of the lps ("Love And Kisses" features only two cuts, one on each side); both were recorded at London's Trident Studios and have the crisp, clean sound we've come to expect from European recordings; both are about sex.

"Cerrone's Paradise" (16:30) is the track that fills up side one of Cerrone's album and, like "Love In C Minor," it begins with a short segment of dialogue among several girls about to enter a club to see Cerrone "perform." Though it isn't as clear here as it was on the previous record what this one's "about," aside from Cerrone's fantasy of female adoration and submission, there are the inevitable orgasmic accents, even more explicit than before, and a fuller set of lyrics about the ecstasies of the disco experience and the sexual experience. So the vocals are more prominent (and wonderfully sharp), but the production is still the thing and here again it's stunning in its precision, clarity and consistency. It never lets up, never becomes tedious and maintains a kind of sensual serenity at the same time it propels you along with its steady bass/drum line. "Paradise" is

already on three out of the four top 10 lists reported this week, coupled with the album's other outstanding cut, "Take Me" (6:07), not the same song **Donna Summer** includes on her new album, but a mostly vocal track that kicks along at a fast clip and brings in something of a **Barrabas** feeling. A particularly beautiful slow cut called "Time For Love" (6:15) and a 'reprise of "Cerrone's Paradise" (3:31) fill out the album.

> ❝ New York, Boston and Washington, D.C. are no longer the only cities where imports are considered necessary for a well-rounded playlist ❞

While using many of the same stylistic elements as Cerrone, Love and Kisses seems to take more risks and is consequently both more uneven and more exciting. "I've Found Love (Now That I've Found You)" (16:14) runs through so many different changes and recovers from all of them with such unexpected grace that the dancer is always in a state of delighted surprise and anticipation. There are sections of male and female vocals, excellent drum breaks, a false ending and one knockout segment of prancing violins that gradually veer into an eccentric skip which is one of the most unusual and striking instrumental changes I've heard this year. "Accidental Lover" (17:20), on the other side, is closer in spirit to "Love In C Minor" and concerns a girl who at first makes insulting remarks to a guy who's apparently trying to pick her up, gradually relents ("Did you know your hand is on my knee?" She asks; he grunts yes), changes her "don't want to love you" to "I wanna love you" as the composition dips into a swirling central section of passion and fantasy, and then turns against him in the end after he's ditched her. The vocals are strong and rough-edged, the strings as bright and cutting as diamonds slashed across vinyl, and the pace is fast and furious. Because it's less readily available than the Cerrone lp, the Love and Kisses album is reportedly selling for $15 at New York disco import stores and even at that price they're being snatched up like candy bars. (My copies of both albums came from **Record World's** excellent French correspondent, Gilles Petard.) "Cerrone's Paradise" is due out on Cotillion at the end of June but "Love and Kisses" has not been scheduled for American release as yet. No matter – they both are assured of heavy disco play in the next few months as the hottest imports available.

UNCLE CHARLY'S, MILL VALLEY, CAL.
DJ: Wes Bradley

CERRONE'S PARADISE/TAKE ME – Cerrone
(Malligator import)
COULD HEAVEN EVER BE LIKE THIS – Idris Muhammad
(Kudu)
DEVIL'S GUN – C. J. & Co. (Westbound/Atlantic)
DO YOU WANT TO GET FUNKY WITH ME – Peter Brown (TK)
GET ON THE FUNK TRAIN/MEDLEY – Munich Machine
(Casablanca)
**I FEEL LOVE/I REMEMBER YESTERDAY / LOVE'S UNKIND/
BACK IN LOVE AGAIN** – Donna Summer (Casablanca)
I NEED A MAN – Grace Jones (Beam Junction)
MAGIC BIRD OF FIRE – Salsoul Orchestra (Salsoul)
MISS BROADWAY/BLACK IS BLACK – Belle Epoque
(EMI import)
TERROR ON THE DANCE FLOOR – Hot Blood (RCA import)

PLAYGROUND, NEW YORK
DJ: Tony Carrasco

BEST OF MY LOVE – Emotions (Columbia)
BROTHER MAN/RIGHT ON TIME – Brothers Johnson (A&M)
CERRONE'S PARADISE/TAKE ME – Cerrone
(Malligator import)
DEVIL'S GUN – C. J. & Co. (Westbound/Atlantic)
DO YOU WANT TO GET FUNKY WITH ME – Peter Brown (TK)
I FEEL LOVE/TAKE ME – Donna Summer (Casablanca)
I NEED A MAN – Grace Jones (Beam Junction)
SUPERSTAR/LET'S GO ALL THE WAY (DOWN) – Brenda
& the Tabulations (Chocolate City)
TAILGATE – 21st Creation (Motown)
**TRAVELIN' AT THE SPEED OF THOUGHT/THOSE LIES/
I'M SO GLAD I GOT YOU, GIRL** – O'Jays (Phila. Intl.)

EXPERIMENT, NEW YORK
DJ: John Benitez

BEST OF MY LOVE – Emotions (Columbia)
CERRONE'S PARADISE/TAKE ME – Cerrone
(Malligator import)
**COULD HEAVEN EVER BE LIKE THIS/ TURN THIS MUTHA
OUT** – Idris Muhammad (Kudu)
DO YOU WANT TO GET FUNKY WITH ME – Peter Brown (TK)
FUNKY TROPICAL/BOOGIETHON – Biddu Orchestra (Epic)
I FEEL LOVE – Donna Summer (Casablanca)
I NEED A MAN – Grace Jones (Beam Junction)
LET'S GO ALL THE WAY (DOWN)/ SUPERSTAR
– Brenda & the Tabulations (Chocolate City)
TAILGATE – 21st Creation (Motown)
**TRAVELIN' AT THE SPEED OF THOUGHT/ STAND UP/
THOSE LIES** – O'Jays (Phila. Intl.)

LOST AND FOUND, WASHINGTON, D.C.
DJ: Bill Owens

DEVIL'S GUN – C. J. & Co. (Westbound/Atlantic)
DOCTOR LOVE – First Choice (Gold Mind)
I NEED A MAN – Grace Jones (Beam Junction)
JOURNEY INTO LOVE – Kebekelektrik (RCA import)
MAGIC BIRD OF FIRE – Salsoul Orchestra (Salsoul)
SLOW DOWN – John Miles (London)
SUPERMAN/HURT ME, HURT ME – Celi Bee & the Buzzy
Bunch (APA)
SWEET DYNAMITE – Claudja Barry (Salsoul)
THIS WILL BE A NIGHT TO REMEMBER – Eddie Holman
(Salsoul)
YOU ARE THE SUN – Jakki (West End)

Quickly, a check list of highly recommended new albums
and disco discs to be reviewed more fully next week:
"But What Is A Dream," "Andrea" and "Bohannon's
Disco Symphony" from the **Bohannon**-with-strings
album, "Phase II" (Mercury); the extraordinary Walter
Gibbons remixes of **Loleatta Holloway's** "Hit And Run"
and "We're Getting Stronger" back-to-back on a Gold
Mind disco disc; the **People's Choice** disco disc version
of "If You're Gonna Do It (Put Your Mind To It)" (TSOP);
Brian Holland's great new version of "Nowhere To Run"
as sung by the **Dynamic Superiors** on their new "Give
And Take" album (Motown); and the whole **Munich
Machine** album on Casablanca, especially the "Get On
The Funk Train" side. ◐

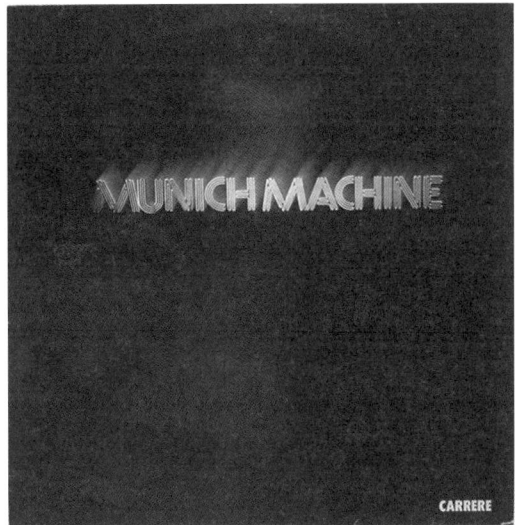

Overwhelmed by new and recent releases, I'm going to try to zip through as many as possible this week, skimming off the cream of the albums first. **Bohannon's** "Phase II," his first release on Mercury, is his best album in some time, making as it does the inevitable bridge between Bo's familiar steady-groove disco productions and those moody, mellow compositions that often filled out the second sides of his albums. "Bohannon's Disco Symphony" (6:39) is the transition cut, with strings coming in elegantly, like rolling waves, but falling back quickly, leaving one of those trademark monogroove numbers, the sort that kick you along almost involuntarily. "Andrea" (6:15) and "But What Is A Dream" (5:16), the latter my favorite here, are more representative of the new style-both are supple, beautifully spacious instrumentals, the kind you float through effortlessly. Note: "Andrea" and "Disco Symphony" are also available on a promotional 12-inch pressing; Atlanta DJ Jim Burgess worked on the disco remix... **Dennis Coffey's** "Back Home" album (Westbound) has an especially strong instrumental track in "Wings Of Fire"

Brian Holland has taken the **Holland-Dozier-Holland Martha & the Vandellas** song, "Nowhere To Run," and totally transformed it for the **Dynamic Superiors**. It takes up just over nine minutes of the group's new Motown album, "Give & Take," and is proof again that classic Motown never dies: Holland and the Superiors translate the vitality and drive of the original with such boldness and verve that they completely sidestep the conventional "disco remake" problems. This is not a remake, it's a revival, like "Forever Came Today," and already it's cropping up on top 10 lists from all over. Not to be missed... Another first-rate import: the **Space** album on the Vogue label from France whose title cut, "Magic Fly" (4:18), a light-hearted but decidedly eerie synthesizer gem, has been appearing on top 10 lists here and there. But the rest of the album is even better: "Fasten Seat Belt" (5:58), "Tango In Space" (4:28), "Flying Nightmare" (3:31) and especially "Carry On, Turn Me On" (8:18) – all in a futuristic, electronic style that ties in neatly with **Donna Summer's** immensely successful "I Feel Love" and

> ## ❝ To people outside the disco milieu, the idea that someone spinning records is thought of as performing "his music" — creating his own particular sound out of other people's music — may seem rather presumptuous ❞

(7:39), which is brassy and loose, given a rich texture with some synthesizer effects and a hot percussion break. "Free Spirit" (5:46) and "Boogie Magic" (5:47) are also pleasant and well worth checking out... I'm not too crazy about **John Davis'** vocals on "The Magic Is You," the 14:15, three-part medley that fills up side 2 of the new **John Davis and the Monster Orchestra** album ("Up Jumped The Devil" on Sam), but his production is certainly attractive, particularly in the central section ("You're the One") and the largely instrumental final part ("Recapitulation"), which sums it up perfectly. This one grows on you. Also included: the still-exciting title cut, "You Gotta Give It Up" (also on the disco disc), and a sweet song called "Once Upon A Time" (6:11)... The new **Salsoul Orchestra** album, "Magic Journey" (Salsoul), is their most varied collection so far though it's less explicitly disco-oriented than their previous work. Happily, however, the disco cuts are excellent, starting with "Magic Bird Of Fire," which is quickly turning into one of the monster records of the moment. But the real delight here is "Runaway," a very comfortable, pretty production featuring vocals by **Loleatta Holloway** and a wonderful vibes break by producer **Vince Montana**. For Loleatta Halloway freaks – and I'm definitely one – this cut is worth the whole album; if only it were longer than 4:44. "Journey To Phoebus" and "Alpha Centuri" are dense instrumentals that might appeal to more adventurous crowds; "It's A New Day" is bright and spunky; and "Getaway" is also included.

Kraftwerk. "Carry On" is particularly powerful as the only vocal – sexy, vibrant, driven – and deserves comparison with and play alongside Summer, **Claudja Barry**, **Love & Kisses** and **Cerrone**. "Fasten Seat Belt" ends with an abrupt crash, but the album soars; United Artists is scheduling it for release the first week in July for the American market... The Gospel According to **Gamble & Huff** continues on the new **O'Jays** album, "Travelin' At The Speed of Thought" (Philadelphia International), more pedantic than ever but, as always, quite danceable. The cuts already getting the most favorable feedback are "Travelin' ," the unusually-structured title cut; "Work On Me" and "Stand Up," a live-sounding, gospel-style rave-up that is a personal favorite.

RECOMMENDED DISCO DISCS: Walter Gibbons, the New York DJ who disco-mixed "Ten Percent," has completely revamped two **Loleatta Holloway** cuts for a special Gold Mind 12-inch: "Hit And Run," at 11:07, is bolstered with a new, more gradual introduction and a long, long series of breaks at the end that feature some entirely new vocal flourishes from Holloway – if you thought it was stunning before, wait 'til you hear this! "We're Getting Stronger," a cut that was sadly overlooked on the lp, has been expanded to 7:23 and pumped up a little so it's now a full-fledged knockout. A collector's item, flawlessly done... Producer **Warren Schatz** (**Vicki Sue Robinson**, **The Brothers**) has brought out an uncommonly exciting gospel album in "**The New**

FOX TRAPPE, WASHINGTON, D.C.
DJ: Frank Edwards

BEST OF MY LOVE – Emotions (Columbia)
COULD HEAVEN EVER BE LIKE THIS/ TURN THIS MUTHA OUT – Idris Muhammad (Kudu)
DEVIL'S GUN – C. J. & Co. (Westbound)
DO YOU WANNA GET FUNKY WITH ME – Peter Brown (TK)
EXPRESS YOURSELF – New York Community Choir (RCA)
FACE THE FACTS/HEARTACHE IN DISGUISE – Anacostia (MCA)
HIT AND RUN – Loleatta Halloway (Gold Mind)
I FEEL LOVE – Donna Summer (Casablanca)
NOWHERE TO RUN – Dynamic Superiors (Motown)
SWEET DYNAMITE – Claudja Barry (Salsoul)

BAREFOOT BOY, NEW YORK
DJ: Tony Smith

DEVIL'S GUN/WE GOT OUR OWN THING/SURE CAN'T GO TO THE MOON – C. J. & Co. (Westbound)
DOCTOR LOVE – First Choice (Gold Mind)
I FEEL LOVE – Donna Summer (Casablanca)
I'VE FOUND LOVE – Love and Kisses (Rei-Vera import)
LET'S GO ALL THE WAY DOWN/ SUPERSTAR – Brenda & the Tabulations (Chocolate City)
NOWHERE TO RUN – Dynamic Superiors (Motown)
MAGIC BIRD OF FIRE/RUNAWAY – Salsoul Orchestra (Salsoul)
THE MAGIC IS YOU/ONCE UPON A TIME – John Davis & the Monster Orchestra (Sam)
TOUCH ME UP – Aretha Franklin (Atlantic)
WINGS OF FIRE/FREE SPIRIT – Dennis Coffey (Westbound)

HARRAH, NEW YORK
DJ: Tom Savarese

CARRY ON, TURN ME ON/ TANGO IN SPACE/FASTEN SEAT BELTS – Space (Vogue import)
CERRONE'S PARADISE – Cerrone (Malligator import)
COULD HEAVEN EVER BE LIKE THIS – Idris Muhammad (Kudu)
I FEEL LOVE/LOVE'S UNKIND – Donna Summer (Casablanca)
I'VE FOUND LOVE – Love and Kisses (Rei-Vera import)
MAGIC BIRD OF FIRE – Salsoul Orchestra (Salsoul)
THE MAGIC IS YOU – John Davis & the Monster Orchestra (Sam)
SINCE I FELL FOR YOU – Hodges, James & Smith (London)
TRAVELIN' AT THE SPEED OF THOUGHT/ STAND UP/WORK ON ME – O'Jays (Phila. Intl.)
WINGS OF FIRE – Dennis Coffey (Westbound)

THE COPA, FORT LAUDERDALE
DJ: Jerry Bossa

DEVIL'S GUN – C. J. & Co. (Westbound)
DISCO LIGHTS – Dexter Wansel (Phila. Intl.)
DOCTOR LOVE – First Choice (Gold Mind)
FUNKY TROPICAL – Biddu & the Orchestra (Epic)
GOT TO GIVE IT UP – Marvin Gaye (Tamla)
I FEEL LOVE – Donna Summer (Casablanca)
I NEED A MAN – Grace Jones (Beam Junction)
JOURNEY INTO LOVE – Kebekelektrek (Direction import)
LOVE TO LOVE YOU BABY/ETC.IMEDLEY – Munich Machine (Casablanca)
MAGIC BIRD OF FIRE – Salsoul Orchestra (Salsoul)

York Community Choir" (RCA) and David Todd, RCA's DJ-in-residence, has joined with him to remix two cuts for an even more unusual effect on a disco disc. "Express Yourself," lengthened from 4:22 to 11:45, is difficult but rather amazing in its austerity – especially the handclaps-and-drums sparseness of much of the final section; this is a trip that demands an intense, adventurous and probably very high crowd. The other side is also unexpected: "Have A Good Time" (9:20), which sounds like gospel taken back to African roots with chants and drums. Todd is also responsible for the recent creative remixes of **Faith, Hope & Charity**, so this disc should be given special attention... Two other revised records that are much improved on their disco disc versions: **Ashford & Simpson's** "Over And Over," now 5:18 (Warner Bros.); and **Morning, Noon & Night's** terrific "Bite Your Granny," nearly doubled in length to 7:18 and not to be ignored, with a longer (5:45) "Feelin' Strong" on the flip side (Roadshow/UA)... The "Tailgate" record by **21st Creation** has also been filled out for a disco disc – it's also 5:45; Motown's released it back-to-back with a remix of **Eddie Kendricks'** "Born Again"... The **People's Choice** record, "If You're Gonna Do It (Put Your Mind To It)," was also previously released as a single, in a Part I/Part II format, but had none of the impact that comes across on the full disco disc version (6:36) which has all the punch of the group's classic "Do It Any Way You Wanna": an utterly irresistible groove.

NOTE: The **Emotions'** breathtaking "Best Of My Love" is the first record to appear on the DISCO FILE Top 20 as a standard single since "Makes You Blind" which went off the list after January 8, 1977. Six months: that's quite a tribute to the power of the disco disc.

SOCIAL NOTE: There was an after-concert party at New York's poshly comfortable New York, New York club for **Joan Baez** last week and we are happy but somewhat taken aback to report that, from the moment she was introduced to the gathered crowd, Joanie was a nonstop dancer. Though she was usually surrounded by flashing cameras, Baez tore up the dance floor with wonderful, anything-goes abandon for several hours. Among her partners: **Melvin Van Peebles**, **Sarah Dash** and **Nona Hendryx** (Nona has already finished a solo album for Epic, the first work to come out since the LaBelle split-up; it's due early this summer). Baez made one request from DJ Bobby Guttadaro: "Something Latin."

To people outside the disco milieu, the idea that someone spinning records is thought of as performing "his music" – creating his own particular sound out of other people's music – may seem rather presumptuous. But there's no question that a real DJ can shape a night of music with his personality, style and spirit, magically turning a string of records into a spontaneous symphony. **Jimmy Stuard**, the 1270-to-12 West DJ who died in a fire at New York's Everard Baths last week, was one of the best of these new dance masters and his music will be greatly missed. ●

JUNE 18, 1977

RECOMMENDED ALBUMS: The record I spent the weekend with was the **Trammps'** "Disco Champs" collection, Philadelphia International's welcome repackage/remix of the group's early hits for the Golden Fleece label, which includes three previously unreleased tracks, two of which I must have heard a hundred times in the past few days. Included here are excellent if unspectacular new mixes of Trammps favorites like "Stop and Think," "Love Epidemic," "Trusting Heart," "Where Do We Go From Here," "Save A Place" and "Trammps Disco Theme" – most of the tracks lengthened by a minute or two and cleaned up nicely; nothing fancy but that's just fine – the originals are too perfect to tamper with beyond a certain point. The new material was apparently recorded around the same period as the other songs (1974-75) and fits into the same smoothly crafted, wonderfully comfortable groove. Both "Promise Me" and "Just Say The Word" feature Jimmy Ellis' elegantly gritty vocals against the warm, rich back-up of other male voices and tightly contained productions that are compact versions of the sort of energetic extravaganzas the group has gotten into recently. The third new/old cut is a churning little instrumental called "Oh Waa Hey" that makes pleasant filler. "Disco Champs" was released with no fanfare several weeks ago and, as part of CBS' budget-priced line, it wasn't slated for any big promo push, but this is a major collector's item for Trammps fans and with the high quality of the remix and new selections, It should have more than a merely nostalgic appeal... The famed **Munich Machine**, Germany's answer to **MFSB** and the MusicLand Studios house band that backs **Donna Summer**, **Roberta Kelly** and **Giorgio**, has its first album out now on Casablanca. One side is a fairly predictable but quite winning medley of the Munich Machine's Greatest Hits: "Love To Love You Baby," "Trouble Maker," "Try Me, I Know We Can Make It," "I Wanna Funk With You Tonite," "Spring Affair" – all speeded up and blended together with just a touch of vocals. The transitions are brilliant and the whole things runs about 16 minutes without a boring second. Even more interesting, however, is "Get On The Funk Train" (15:45) which has a terrifically idiosyncratic production that's both witty and riveting. It took me some time to get into "Funk Train" as a whole – I'm still not sure about the whiney, prancing violins in the romantic central section – but the cumulative effect is so involving (especially in the final part with the horn flourishes) that now I find it hard to resist. Production is, of course, by **Giorgio Moroder** and **Pete Bellotte** and it's as sharp and glorious as ever.

❝ "Soul Dracula" has a gory cover by fashion photographer Chris Von Wangenheim ❞

"Heaven is a disco/The Lord is a DJ/The angels are the waiters/ and there's nothin' to pay" – that bizarre utopian vision is from the big, brassy, all-out production number opening of **Paul Jabara's** debut album, "Shut Out" (Casablanca). "Shut Out/Heaven Is a Disco" (9:30) is the fantasy of a boy turned away from a club on a Saturday night who turns to his Donna Summer records only to have Donna appear Peter Pan-like, swooning "Oooo Paul" and beckoning him away with her to the ultimate disco: "Open up those golden gates/Here we come on roller skates." The style is very pop disco with Broadway show overtones (compare **D.C. LaRue's** "Tea Dance") and one can almost see the cast-of-thousands movie musical version. Summer's guest appearance is a highlight, especially when she goes into a **Tina Turner** spoof, and the production swirls and soars non-stop, Jabara swooping above it all, delightfully manic. The medley blends right into "Dance," a remixed version of an earlier Jabara single that sounds even more rousing and fun here, and the whole side winds down beautifully with another transition into "Slow Dancing" (5:00), a compelling ballad. The other side includes Jabara's nutsy version of "Yankee Doodle Dandy" and several other non-dance cuts. Jabara and promo wiz **Marc Paul Simon** are listed as executive producers with **Art Wright**, **Ron Dante** and **Stan Vincent** contributing individual cuts. One of the most entertaining albums of the season, it's also pressed on cherry-red vinyl. Disco people will be deeply disappointed to learn that a current favorite, "Best Of My Love," is no longer on the **Emotions'** just-out album than it is on the single (3:40), but "Rejoice" (Columbia), one of the most eagerly anticipated albums of the past few months, is otherwise too dazzling to complain. If there is nothing to compare to "I Don't Wanna Lose Your Love," the vocals are so breathtakingly good that you won't want to miss this one. **Maurice White** produced in his unique style and the Emotions are clearly so in tune with him that the whole

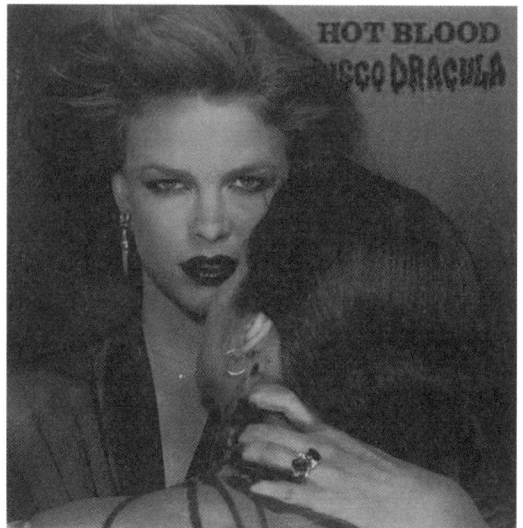

IPANEMA, NEW YORK
DJ: Ray Velazquez

A CHACUN SON ENFANCE – Recreation (Option import)
DISCOMANIA – The Lovers (TK)
FLICK THE BICK – Rick Dees (RSO)
GET ON THE FUNK TRAIN – Munich Machine (Casablanca)
I'VE FOUND LOVE – Love & Kisses (Rei-Vera import)
ISABELLE AND THE RAIN – Jo Boyer (JOB)
THE MAGIC IS YOU – John Davis & the Monster Orchestra (Sam)
RITMO NUMBER 1 – Paulinho da Costa (Pablo)
TRANS-EUROPE EXPRESS/METAL ON METAL – Kraftwerk (Capitol)
WINGS OF FIRE – Dennis Coffey (Westbound)

TRINITYS, NEW ORLEANS
DJ: Stu Neal

BABY LOVE, SWEET SWEET LOVE/GONNA HAVE A PARTY – Wilton Place Street Band (Island)
COULD HEAVEN EVER BE LIKE THIS/TASTY CAKES – Idris Muhammad (Kudu)
DEVIL'S GUN – C. J. & Co. (Westbound)
EXPRESS YOURSELF – New York Community Chair (RCA)
GET ON THE FUNK TRAIN/LOVE TO LOVE YOU BABY – Munich Machine (Casablanca)
I FEEL LOVE/LOVE'S UNKIND – Donna Summer (Casablanca)
LASO SQUARE/ANOTHER STAR – LaSo (MCA)
MAGIC BIRD OF FIRE – Salsoul Orchestra (Salsoul)
NA NA HEY HEY KISS HIM GOODBYE – Garrett Scott (West End)
SWEET DYNAMITE/DANCE, DANCE, DANCE – Claudja Barry (Salsoul)

BOATHOUSE, REHOBOTH BEACH, DE
DJ: Tom Webb

CERRONE'S PARADISE/TAKE ME – Cerrone (Malligator import)
DEVIL'S GUN – C. J. & Co. (Westbound)
DOCTOR LOVE – First Choice (Gold Mind)
EXPRESS YOURSELF – New York Community Choir (RCA)
I FEEL LOVE – Donna Summer (Casablanca)
I NEED A MAN – Grace Jones (Beam Junction)
I'VE FOUND LOVE – Love & Kisses (Rei-Vera import)
THE MAGIC IS YOU – John Davis & the Monster Orchestra (Sam)
NOWHERE TO RUN – Dynamic Superiors (Motown)
TERROR ON THE DANCE FLOOR – Hot Blood (Dynamo)

SIGLO 21, BRONX, NEW YORK
DJ: Jorge Wheeler

ANOTHER STAR – LaSo (MCA)
CERRONE'S PARADISE – Cerrone (Malligator import)
DEVIL'S GUN – C. J. & Co. (Westbound)
HIT AND RUN – Loleotta Holloway (Gold Mind)
I FEEL LOVE – Donna Summer (Casablanca)
SALSA DISCO PARTY – Various Artists (TR)
SUPERSTAR/I KEEP COMING BACK FOR MORE – Brenda & the Tabulations (Chocolate City)
SWEET DYNAMITE – Claudja Barry (Salsoul)
TRANS-EUROPE EXPRESS/METAL ON METAL – Kraftwerk (Capitol)
WINGS OF FIRE/BOOGIE MUSIC – Dennis Coffey (Westbound)

album seems to glow with a vibrant spirituality. Standouts: "How'd I Know That Love Would Slip Away" (which was included on **Deniece Williams'** album as "Slip Away") "Rejoice" and "Blessed." A real beauty.

CHOICE CUTS: "Running Away:' a sprightly jumping cut from the new **Roy Ayers Ubiquity** album, "Lifeline" (Polydor), that has marvelous, multi-level vocals in a complex arrangement... "Terror On The Dance Floor" a strong strings-and-synthesizer European instrumental by **Hot Blood** (recorded in Munich and featuring the Munich Philharmonic) with a lot of very commercial hooks and horrified-crowd sound effects that sound like they came from some low-budget Japanese monster movie. "Terror" has already been appearing on a number of top 10 lists and reportedly was a major hit in Japan (that figures) but the album, "Soul Dracula" (Dynamo), has little else of interest but a chicly gory cover by fashion photographer Chris Von Wangenheim of one stylishly demonic woman ' with red, red lips grasping that bloody neck of another woman, like a cat bringing in its prey. "Terror on the Dance Floor" (5:44) is also available on a disco disc... "Glider" (4:38) by the Dutch group **Focus:** a left field instrumental with synthesizer, guitars, eerie voices, driving piano and a great deal of spirit, from the "Ship of Memories" album on Sire. . A lot of DJs have been calling my attention to the **"Keith Barrow"** album on Columbia (produced by **Bobby Eli**), especially a song called "A World Of Lonely People" (6:30). Barrow has a unique, high, gospel-tinged voice that he makes superb use of in "World" an invigorating message song in the **Baker, Harris & Young** tradition. The rest of the album is also impressive – great vocals! – and this is a fine debut.

RECOMMENDED DISCO DICSC: I raved about the **Hodges, James & Smith** version of "Since I Fell For You" several weeks back but now producer **William Mickey Stevenson** has expanded the song to 10:30 and London has brought the whole thing out as an incredible 12-inch pressing. The remix adds emotional, jazzy sax breaks; a wonderful wash of strings; and ecstatic vocal sweeps that double the record's impact and make it an essential disc right now... One of the more popular import disco discs of recent weeks has been **Kebekelektrik's** "Journey Into Love" on Direction, a new Canadian label already making a strong impression with its excellent selection of material and its striking graphic design. "Journey Into Love," which was disco-mixed by George Cucuzzela and Dominic Zgarka of the Canadian Record Pool ("Created for the Canadian Record Pool" it says right on the label), sounds like it was inspired by **Space's** "Magic Fly" (much the way the **Black Light Orchestra's** "Touch Me Take Me" was obviously inspired by "Love In C Minor") and, like that record, this is a sprawling synthesizer composition with a gripping pulse beat. The main thing that sets "Journey" apart from "Magic Fly" is a short, bare percussion intro which is repeated as a break in slightly longer form toward the end. Derivitive but exciting. ◗

JUNE 25, 1977

RECOMMENDED DISCO DISCS: My favorite new record this week is the latest **Cory Wade** production, his first with the Miami group **Foxy**, "The Way You Do the Things You Do" (TK). Wade, who has had stunning success this year with **T-Connection** and **Peter Brown** has whipped up a wonderfully idiosyncratic sound that is at once angular and lush: bristling with playful, off-the-wall effects and away with violins. If the lyrics – sung by a guy who's been stood up, again by his girl – are loose to the point of being aimless, the vocals are spirited and nicely rough-edged. But it's the production that gives the vocals the necessary drive and the instrumentation here is particularly witty and fresh, highlighted by the most elegant and invigorating use of strings this side of the Atlantic. The disco disc has a vocal side (8:20) and an instrumental side (7:45) with the instrumental standing on its own quite well (especially since there are terrific back-and-forward conversational effects among the instruments), but the vocal coming on stronger right now. Watch this one... "Nuthin' 'Bout Nuthin'" is a funky, chunky instrumental with some vocal touches from **Ronnie Laws'** recent "Friends And Strangers" album (Blue Note) that's now available on a promotional 12-inch, sounding sharper and running a few seconds longer (to 5:17). Laws' sax propels a straightforward chugging jazz ensemble and **Eloise Laws** contributes to the chorus. Uncomplicated and utterly enjoyable... **Noel Pointer's** violin-based interpretation of **Stevie Wonder's** "Living For The City" (featured on "Phantazia" album) has been released on another Blue Note disco disc. Like the lp version, this one runs 6:36 and is shot through with startling electric violin flights as Pointer darts, hummingbird-like through a rhythm section that includes **Ralph MacDonald**, **Earl Klugh**, **Steve Gadd** and **Francisco Centeno**... **Jo Boyer's** "Isabelle And The Rain" is a light-weight, frothy instrumental with an insinuating synthesizer line and a pleasantly laid-back feel. It sounds vaguely European and vaguely like theme music for a TV game show. Boyer wrote, arranged and produced; I suspect he also pressed up the limited number of 12-inch pressings now surfacing in New York on the JOB label while he's shopping around for a big-label deal. Wish him luck: "Isabelle" is real cute... I've never been particularly taken with the song "Na Na Hey Hey Kiss Him Goodbye," originally released in 1969, but **Garrett Scott**, reportedly one of the singers on the earlier hit, has come up with an infectious disco version for West End Records that runs five minutes and has several strong breaks that make the record work all over again. Very pop still, but once the production starts building, it brings out very disco screams... **Sassy's** "Theme from Disco 77" (TK), the television disco variety show, was produced in Miami by **Ray Martinez**, former Foxy producer, and is a bright and zippy disco propaganda instrumental. The drum intro and percussion breaks are fine and the overall sound crisply commercial. "Let's go to the disco," the girls sing, "Disco 77"... Now available on disco discs: **Formula V's** excellent "Dance All Night" (6:17) on 20th Century and **Cleveland Eaton's** delightful "The Funky Cello" and "Bama Boogie Woogie" back-to-back on Ovation.

RECOMMENDED ALBUMS: The "Original Motion Picture Soundtrack" to "The Deep" (Casablanca) was composed, conducted and produced by **John Barry** and includes a vocal version of the "Theme From The Deep (Down, Deep Inside)" by none other than **Donna Summer**. Summer sings somewhat listlessly and the theme itself is hardly inspired compared to her usual material, but it does have a certain quirky charm. We like the break, with its ominous deep-sea quality and popping percussion, and as always we like Donna moaning, but this is not about to rival "I Feel Love." The "Theme" is repeated in a very nice instrumental version and again as "A Love Song" with Summer's vocals but considerably slowed down (sounds like they just shifted speeds on the track). What all this has to do with searching for sunken treasure off Bermuda, I don't know, but any excuse for a new Donna Summer cut is all right by me... **Carol Douglas'** "Full Bloom" album (Midsong International) is sumptuous and sensuous, with all of side one danceable though not a continuous concept run-through like "Midnight Love Affair." The opener, "I Want To Stay With You" (at 5:18 the album's longest cut), has a sweet "Midnight Love Affair" mood which links up with **Rupert Holmes'** clever "Who, What, When, Where, Why" through a quick, graceful transition, "Full Bloom Suite #1." After a full stop, another "Full Bloom Suite" (#2) introduces the surprise closing track, a sharp, string-laced version of **The Doors'** "Light My Fire" that producer **Ed O'Loughlin** has transformed marvelously for Douglas. The instrumental breaks throughout are perfect and Douglas sounds in top form. Also included: "Dancing Queen"... With the **New York Community Choir's** astonishing

"It sounds vaguely European and vaguely like theme music for a TV game show"

LES MOUCHES, NEW YORK
DJ: Joel Jacobs

CERRONE'S PARADISE – Cerrone (Malligator import)
DEVIL'S GUN – C. J. & Co. (Westbound)
GET ON THE FUNK TRAIN – Munich Machine (Casablanca)
I CAUGHT YOUR ACT – Hues Corporation (Warner Bros.)
I FEEL LOVE – Donna Summer (Casablanca)
I NEED A MAN – Grace Jones (Beam Junction)
I'VE FOUND LOVE – Love and Kisses (Rei-Vera import)
JOURNEY INTO LOVE – Kebekelektrik (Direction)
MAGIC BIRD OF FIRE – Salsoul Orchestra (Salsoul)
NA NA HEY HEY KISS HIM GOODBYE – Garrett Scott
(West End)

STUDIO ONE, LOS ANGELES
DJ: Paul Dougan

BOHANNON'S DISCO SYMPHONY/ANDREA
– Bohannon (Mercury)
DO YOU WANNA GET FUNKY WITH ME – Peter Brown (TK)
DEVIL'S GUN/WE GOT OUR OWN THING – C. J. & Co.
(Westbound)
EXPRESS YOURSELF/HAVE A GOOD TIME
– New York Community Choir (RCA)
**I FEEL LOVE/I REMEMBER YESTERDAY/ LOVE'S
UNKIND/TAKE ME** – Donna Summer (Casablanca)
I NEED A MAN – Grace Jones (Beam Junction)
I'VE FOUND LOVE – Love and Kisses (Rei-vera import)
LOVIN' IS REALLY MY GAME – Brainstorm (Tabu)
NOWHERE TO RUN – Dynamic Superiors (Motown)
SPANDISCO – Love Childs Afro-Cuban Blues Band
(Midsong Intl.)

SUNDAY'S, CHICAGO
DJ: Carmen Adduci

BEST OF MY LOVE – Emotions (Columbia)
CERRONE'S PARADISE – Cerrone (Malligator import)
**DEVIL'S GUN/WE GOT OUR OWN THING/ SURE CAN'T
GO TO THE MOON** – C. J. & Co. (Westbound)
DOCTOR LOVE – First Choice (Gold Mind)
**GET ON THE FUNK TRAIN/LOVE TO LOVE YOU BABY,
ETC. (MEDLEY)** – Munich Machine (Casablanca)
I FEEL LOVE/LOVE'S UNKIND/TAKE ME – Donna Summer
(Casablanca)
I'VE FOUND LOVE – Love and Kisses (Rei-Vera import)
SINCE I FELL FOR YOU – Hodges, James & Smith (London)
SWEET DYNAMITE – Claudja Barry (Salsoul)
THE WAY YOU DO THE THINGS YOU DO – Foxy (TK)

INFINITY, NEW YORK
DJ: Bobby Guttadaro

EXPRESS YOURSELF – New York Community Choir (RCA)
HIGHER AND HIGHER – Dolly Parton (RCA)
I'VE FOUND LOVE – Love and Kisses (Rei-Vera import)
LISTEN TO THE MUSIC/NIGHTS ON BROADWAY
– Candi Staton (Warner Bros.)
NOWHERE TO RUN/ALL YOU CAN DO WITH LOVE –
Dynamic Superiors (Motown)
RUNAWAY – Salsoul Orchestra (Salsoul)
SINCE I FELL FOR YOU/DON'T TAKE AWAY YOUR LOVE –
Hodges, James & Smith (London)
SPANDISCO/QUE RICO VACILON – Love Childs Afro -
Cuban Blues Band (Midsong Intl.)
THEME FROM THE DEEP – Donna Summer (Casablanca)
THE WAY YOU DO THE THINGS YOU DO – Foxy (TK)

"Express Yourself" one of the hottest records around right now, special attention should be paid to the new album by gospel queen **Shirley Caesar**, "First Lady" (Roadshow /UA). Standout track on the album is a rousing number called "Jesus Is Coming" which producer **Michael Stokes** has powered with a rich, pumping arrangement. ✪

DISCO FILE TOP 20

1. **I FEEL LOVE** – Donna Summer (Casablanca)
2. **DEVIL'S GUN** – CJ. & Co. (Westbound/Atlantic)
3. **I'VE FOUND LOVE** – Love and Kisses
(Rei-Vera import)
4. **CERRONE'S PARADISE/TAKE ME CERRONE**
– Cerrone (Malligator import)
5. **I NEED A MAN** – Grace Jones (Beam Junction)
6. **MAGIC BIRD OF FIRE** – Salsoul Orchestra
(Salsoul)
7. **DOCTOR LOVE** – First Choice (Gold Mind)
8. **SWEET DYNAMITE** – Claudja Barry (Salsoul)
9. **DO YOU WANNA GET FUNKY WITH ME**
– Peter Brown (TK)
10. **COULD HEAVEN EVER BE LIKE THIS**
– Idris Muhammad (Kudu)
11. **EXPRESS YOURSELF/HAVE A GOOD TIME**
– New York Community Choir (RCA)
12. **GET ON THE FUNK TRAIN/LOVE TO LOVE YOU
BABY, ETC. (MEDLEY)** – Munich Machine
(Casablanca)
13. **NOWHERE TO RUN** – Dynamic Superiors
(Motown)
14. **LOVE'S UNKIND** – Donna Summer (Casablanca)
15. **BEST OF MY LOVE** – Emotions (Columbia)
16. **WINGS OF FIRE** – Dennis Coffey (Westbound)
17. **SUPERSTAR/LET'S GO ALL THE WAY DOWN**
– Brenda & the Tabulations (Chocolate City)
18. **THE MAGIC IS YOU** – John Davis & the Monster
Orchestra (Sam)
19. **SINCE I FELL FOR YOU** – Hodges, James & Smith
(London)
20. **WE GOT OUR OWN THING** – C.J. & CO.
(Westbound)

STATUS REPORT: Casablanca, which snatched up the American rights to the hottest disco import album around, "**Love And Kisses**," had their pressings at the record pools and in the stores this past week – barely three weeks after the signing announcement. The album went through a quick technical clean-up mix for the American release, but retains the same torn t-shirt cover as the French original with a new fire engine red border... Cotillion's release of "**Cerrone's** Paradise" is, however, still about two weeks away in spite of their rush-release schedule. It's been delayed, just as "Love In C Minor" was, for a time-consuming cover change (seems the nude draped over the refrigerator was a bit much); meanwhile, the Malligator import album has flooded the market in New York at discount prices. Also scheduled for early July on Cotillion: the new **Mass Production**... Anther French import, the "Magic Fly" album by **Space** (on Vogue) is slated for American release on United Artists the first week in July, after the single release of "Carry On, Turn Me On"/"Tango in Space"... **The Ritchie Family's** "African Queens," which promises to be their most successful album to date – it's also their best and most ambitious work so far – will be out on Marlin in time for the big July 4th weekend after a series of disco sneak previews around the country... Beam Junction says **Grace Jones'** first album, "Portfolio," won't be ready for at least three weeks but Grace sang a cut from the lp at a recent knockout performance at New York's Les Mouches – an astonishing interpretation of the French cabaret classic "La Vie En Rose" that must be heard to be believed... And finally, rumors are flying about the new **Savannah Band** album, to be titled "Dr. Buzzard's Original Savannah Band Meets King Pe-nutt," but anyone claiming to have or have heard a test pressing is apparently pulling your leg since the record is still in the final mixing stages. RCA expects it in about three weeks and with band members describing the new material as "music from God, voices from the angels," anticipation is high. Titles include: "Nocturnal Interludes," "Mr. Love," "Transistor Madness," "Auf Wiedersehen," "The Gigolo And I," "The Organ Grinder's Tale." The Savannians, who are anxious to get back to New York from Los Angeles where the album was recorded – "Californians need to come to New York to get some energy," they say-promise to be "giving sunshine back to living." We're ready.

The records to pick up on right now: "I Robot," the intriguing synthesizer instrumental opening cut on the new **Alan Parsons Project** album of the same name (on Arista) – at just over six minutes, this track has time to ease up on you gradually and then envelope you in electronic surges. The effect is at once shimmering, sinister, spiritual and spacey: compare **Kraftwerk, Ozo's** "Anambra," **Space**. Also check out the cut that follows, "I Wouldn't Want To Be Like You," which has some fine rock vocals, and the surprising instrumental core of "The Voice"... The **T.H.P. Orchestra's** cleverly titled "Two Hot For Love," an import disco disc from RCA in Canada that's very much in the orgasmic Love and Kisses/Cerrone vein – a richly textured instrumental studded with all kinds of breaks, waves of sparkling strings, popping electronics and sexy girl chorus work (singing and sighing). Sensational summer music... Also perfect for the summer: **D.D. Sound's** "Burning Love" (another RCA Canada disco disc), a dense, driving instrumental with some vocals that was originally released in Italy and is already picking up fast on the New York disco market. At 9:32, the 12-inch version becomes a bit monotonous, but once you fall into this particular groove, it's hard to resist... In a similar style, **Amanda Lear's** delightfully lurid "Blood & Honey" was made in Germany and has been imported here from Polydor in Italy and Direction in Canada as a standard 45. Lear, who is England's answer to Candy Darling and Potassa, sings in her sexually ambiguous voice about a female vampire stalking the streets "looking for a bite to eat." Perfectly decadent. "Blood & Honey" (4:45) is the vocal, with an instrumental version called "She's Got the Devil In Her Eyes" (3:05) on the flip side... At the opposite end of the disco spectrum, there's former Beach Boys **Bruce Johnston's** entirely unexpected disco version of "Pipeline" (Columbia) which fans of the **Chantays** original would never recognize in this elaborate disguise. Producer **Gary Usher** has thrown in a number of disco cliches (spare percussion breaks, zinging strings, scatting voices) for the special disco disc version (6:30) but the effect is, finally, inspired and fun – a little **Bohannon**, a little **T-Connection**, even touches reminiscent of "Good Vibrations" and other good-time Beach Boys music.

The great new single is Philadelphia International's **All Stars** record, "Let's Clean Up The Ghetto" featuring **Lou Rawls, Billy Paul, Archie Bell, Teddy Pendergrass, O'Jays** and **Dee Dee Sharp Gamble** – an incredible collection of voices! It's one of the hardest-hitting message songs out of **Gamble & Huff** city since "Bad Luck," propelled by a track nearly equal to that song in drive and grace. The opening rap is by Rawls, with the others contributing, individually and collectively, to the choruses that follow. The message is clear in the title

❝ Grace Jones sang an astonishing interpretation of the French cabaret classic "La Vie En Rose" that must be heard to be believed ❞

SANDPIPER, FIRE ISLAND PINES, N.Y.
DJ: Richie Rivera

CARRY ON, TURN ME ON/MAGIC FLY – Space (Vogue import)
DEVIL'S GUN/WE GOT OUR OWN THING – C.J. & Co. (Westbound)
GET ON THE FUNK TRAIN – Munich Machine (Casablanca)
I FEEL LOVE – Donna Summer (Casablanca)
I'VE FOUND LOVE – Love & Kisses (Casablanca)
LET'S CLEAN UP THE GHETTO – Phila. Intl. All Stars/MFSB (Phila. Intl.)
MAGIC BIRD OF FIRE – Salsoul Orchestra (Salsoul)
THE MAGIC IS YOU – John Davis & the Monster Orchestra (Sam)
YOU ARE THE MUSIC WITHIN ME – Barbara Pennington (UA import)
ZODIACS/LOVE-SIGN/FUNKY STARDUST – Roberta Kelly (Durium import)

COCKRING, NEW YORK
DJ: Howard Merritt

CERRONE'S PARADISE – Cerrone (Malligator import)
DEVIL'S GUN/WE GOT OUR OWN THING – C. J. & Co. (Westbound)
EROTIC SOUL – Larry Page Ork (Penny Farthing import)
I CAUGHT YOUR ACT – Hues Corporation (Warner Bros.)
I FEEL LOVE – Donna Summer (Casablanca)
I'VE FOUND LOVE – Love & Kisses (Casablanca)
JOURNEY INTO LOVE – Kebekelektrik (Direction import)
MAGIC BIRD OF FIRE – Salsoul Orchestra (Salsoul)
THE MAGIC IS YOU – John Davis & the Monster Orchestra (Sam)
WINGS OF FIRE – Dennis Coffey (Westbound)

CELEBRATION, BOSTON
DJ: Joe Carvello

DEVIL'S GUN/WE GOT OUR OWN THING – C J. & Co. (Westbound)
DON'T TURN AWAY – Midnite Flite (TK)
I FEEL LOVE – Donna Summer (Casablanca)
I'VE FOUND LOVE – Love & Kisses (Casablanca)
MAGIC BIRD OF FIRE/RUNAWAY – Salsoul Orchestra (Salsoul)
THE MAGIC IS YOU – John Davis & the Monster Orchestra (Sam)
MAKE IT WITH YOU – Whispers (Soul Train)
NA, NA, KISS HIM GOODBYE – Garrett Scott (West End)
THEME FROM DISCO 77 – Sassy (TK)
THE WAY YOU DO THE THINGS YOU DO – Foxy (TK)

CLUB SWAMP, EASTHAMPTON, N.Y.
DJ: Jeff Baugh

BLOOD & HONEY – Amanda Lear (Polydor import)
CARRY ON, TURN ME ON – Space (Vogue import)
HAVE A GOOD TIME – New York Community Choir (RCA)
I NEED A MAN – Grace Jones (Beam Junction)
LOCKED IN THIS POSITION – Barbara Mason & Bunny Sigler (Curtom)
MAGIC BIRD OF FIRE – Salsoul Orchestra (Salsoul)
NOWHERE TO RUN – Dynamic Superiors (Motown)
SINCE I FELL FOR YOU/DON'T TAKE AWAY YOUR LOVE – Hodges, James & Smith (London)
TOUCH ME UP – Aretha Franklin (Atlantic)
THE WAY YOU DO THE THINGS YOU DO – Foxy (TK)

but the lyrics make the details explicit: "Let's get rid of everything we don't need/The pushers, the dealers, the pocketbook-snatchers and thieves." Could be politically controversial, but it will certainly be Philadelphia's biggest single in some time. The flip side is **MFSB's** instrumental version of the song, so everyone's going out and buying two copies for turntable blends. The other hot record from Philadelphia International is a 9:41 remixed version of the **Intruders'** classic "I'll Always Love My Mama" just out as a disco disc (a two-part single has been out for several weeks already). ◐

JULY 9, 1977

The **Ritchie Family's** new album, "African Queens" (Marlin), their strongest and most satisfying release to date, represents several shifts in direction for the group: It's their first album without co-producer **Richard Rome**; the first to be recorded away from Philadelphia (the new Sigma Sound Studios in New York were used instead); and the frothy pop sound of the "Life Is Music" album has been replaced, for the most part, with a more audacious, powerhouse disco styling which pushes the group's vocals out front more effectively than ever before. On his own here, **Jacques Morali** proves to be an assured and, frequently, inspired producer, urging the music beyond the merely entertaining into something more gutsy and fierce. "African Queens," a five-part, 12:45 track that takes up the record's entire first side, is a relentless, pounding jungle celebration in tribute to Nefertiti, Cleopatra and the Queen of Sheba (which is quite a mouthful of names for a repeated chant chorus). The song encourages a "back to the roots" approach to the "three black queens," each of whom is given a separate "theme" to develop. The lyrics may leave some-thing to be desired (or am I the only one who feels that saying Cleopatra has "a lifestyle of her own" only reduces her to the level of That Cosmopolitan Girl?), but the vocals are rich and the music irresistibly grabbing. A favorite highlight: the male chanting in the Queen of Sheba theme.

Side two contains three cuts, all over five minutes long, beginning with "Summer Dance" which is very much in the group's trademark style: bouncy, cute, jubilant and lighter-than-air. The following two tracks – an atmospheric, involving interpretation of "Quiet Village" and an original cut called "Voodoo" – are blended together to form one continuous song in a steamy jungle mood. The drumming stands out particularly here and among the seven percussionists listed on the album are **Olatunji** and **Ralph MacDonald**. Clearly designated to match the hot, hedonistic mood of summer-in-the-city, "African Queens" should be one of the season's dominant albums. The week's other most-likely-to-succeed record is **Vicki Sue Robinson's** new disco disc, "Hold Tight" (RCA). Producer **Warren Schatz** prepared us for this one with the **New York Community Choir's** "Express Yourself": "Hold Tight" has a similar innovative, jagged construction, heavy on the handclaps and stark percussion, as if the drum break has expanded to take over the whole song. So the result is really more about production than singing: though VSR really belts out what few lyrics she has here, she's only present for about a third of the record's 11:33 run. Still, this is Vicki Sue's best since "Turn The Beat Around" (which backs the 12-inch in a new, technically-sharpened mix, same length as the original) and, with "Express Yourself" paving the way, a sure chart item.

OTHER RECOMMENDED ALBUMS: **Silver Convention's** "Golden Girls" (Midsong International), whose best songs are the ones that make a link between their familiar **Michael Kunze-Silvester Levay** sound and that of the more recent spate of European producers. Like the run of three songs on the album's second side: "Wolfchild" (4:20)' the group's sketchy treatment of the "Runaway Child" theme – feral youth "living in the asphalt jungle" – which carries an interesting tension, underlined by screeching police sirens; "Hotshot" (5:57), notable for its eerie use of strings; and "Voodoo Woman" (4:00). "Save Me 77," on the other side, is a brief update and reminder of past heights. All these cuts are tighter and more constrained than the music we've come to expect from Europe, but a longer disco disc version of "Hollywood Movie" (expanded from 5:06 to 7:41) helps to open things up some, though the result still doesn't feel as spacious as one would hope... **Frank Wilson** produced the new album by **Lenny Williams**, former lead singer for **Tower of Power** (the group's

> ❝ The lyrics leave something to be desired (or am I the only one who feels that saying Cleopatra has "a lifestyle of her own" only reduces her to the level of That Cosmopolitan Girl?) ❞

ICE PALACE, CHERRY GROVE, N.Y.
DJ: Roy Thode

AFRICAN QUEENS/QUIET VILLAGE – Ritchie Family (Marlin)
AMOUR – Rod McKuen (Discus)
BURNING LOVE – D.D. Sound (Baby import)
CARRY ON, TURN ME ON/TANGO IN SPACE – Space (UA)
FIRE ISLAND – Village People (Casablanca)
HOLD TIGHT – Vicki Sue Robinson (RCA disco disc)
I'VE FOUND LOVE/ACCIDENTAL LOVER – Love & Kisses (Casablanca)
MAGIC BIRD OF FIRE – Salsoul Orchestra (Salsoul)
SPIRIT OF SUNSHINE – Chuck Davis Orchestra (West End)
THEME FROM THE DEEP – Donna Summer (Casablanca)

CRICKET CLUB, MIAMI
DJ: Richard McVay

CERRONE'S PARADISE – Cerrone (Malligator import)
DEVIL'S GUN – C. J. & Co. (Westbound)
DOCTOR LOVE – First Choice (Gold Mind)
GET ON THE FUNK TRAIN – Munich Machine (Casablanca)
GOT TO GIVE IT UP – Marvin Gaye (Tamla)
I FEEL LOVE – Donna Summer (Casablanca)
I NEED A MAN – Grace Jones (Beam Junction)
I'VE FOUND LOVE – Love & Kisses (Casablanca)
MAGIC BIRD OF FIRE – Salsoul Orchestra (Salsoul)
THE WAY YOU DO THE THINGS YOU DO – Foxy (TK)

HIS COMPANY, PHOENIX
DJ: Jack Witherby

AFRICAN QUEENS/QUIET VILLAGE/ VOODOO – Ritchie Family (Marlin)
CARRY ON, TURN ME ON/TANGO IN SPACE – Space (UA)
CERRONE'S PARADISE/TAKE ME – Cerrone (Malligator import)
GET ON THE FUNK TRAIN/LOVE TO LOVE YOU BABY – Munich Machine (Casablanca)
I FEEL LOVE/I REMEMBER YESTERDAY/TAKE ME – Donna Summer (Casablanca)
I'VE FOUND LOVE – Love & Kisses (Casablanca)
NA NA HEY HEY KISS HIM GOODBYE – Garrett Scott (West End)
SUPER ELTON (INST.) – Paul Vincent (Salsoul)
SWEET LUCY – Raul de Souza (Capitol)
THE WAY YOU DO THE THINGS YOU DO – Foxy (TK)

CASABLANCA II, NEW YORK
DJ: Hector Saez

CERRONE'S PARADISE – Cerrone (Malligator import)
COULD HEAVEN EVER BE LIKE THIS – Idris Muhammad (Kudu)
DEVIL'S GUN/WE GOT OUR OWN THING – C.J. & Co. (Westbound)
DISCO LIGHTS – Dexter Wansel (Phila. Intl.)
ESA PRIETA – Johnny Pacheco (Fania)
FREE SPIRIT/WINGS OF FIRE – Dennis Coffey (Westbound)
I FEEL LOVE – Donna Summer (Casablanca)
I'VE FOUND LOVE – Love & Kisses (Casablanca)
JUAN PACHANGA – Fania All Stars (Columbia)
MAKE IT WITH YOU – Whispers (Soul Train)

horn section guests here), on ABC and the results are rather tasty. Check out the very beautiful "Look Up With Your Mind" which is light-hearted and joyous in keeping with its message ("When you look up with your mind, you see higher") and two long, building cuts, "Choosing You" (the lp's title song, 6:13 in length) and "Please Don't Tempt Me" (7:52). Wonderful singing, fine music... **Belle Epoque's** "Miss Broadway" has already had some exposure here as an import, primarily in San Francisco, and Shadybrook has just issued the album in America. The sound is European hard-edge with rough, sometimes abrasive vocals from a girl trio. The tile cut, about a prostitute out looking for her "money man," is particularly lowdown and a long (14:15), four-part opus based on "Black Is Black" which fills the second side is appropriately raunchy and off-beat in the new strings & synthesizer tradition. Nothing especially new, but fun... **The Controllers'** "In Control" album (Juana, through TK) is worth getting if only for the longer version (5:01) of "People Want Music," a delicate but forceful cut that a lot of people fell in love with on its previous release as a single. The perfect start-the-night-off-right song.

RECOMMENDED DISCO DISCS: "Spirit Of Sunshine" by the **Chuck Davis Orchestra** (West End) is a crackling European composition with a superb full sound that sounds like it could be one of the biggest instrumentals of the summer: mellow but sturdily built, vibrating with a strong bass pulse and excellent strings (long version: 6:52)... "Sweet Lucy," a fast-bumping, high-spirited jazz-funk cut by **Raul de Souza** (Capitol) that Jack Witherby in Phoenix alerted me to... and the previously recommended "Carry On, Turn Me On" and "Tango In Space" by **Space**, now out back-to-back on a United Artists promotional 12-inch. ●

Producer **Jacques Morali**, whose latest **Ritchie Family** album has proven to be an instant hit in its first week of official release, already has another album project in the sneak-preview stage at select clubs on both coasts. Titled "**Village People**," it's a four-cut concept album that celebrates the gay male lifestyles in San Francisco, Hollywood and Fire Island and closes with a tough, rousing liberation song. An upfront gay album is clearly an idea whose time has come, especially for the disco market, and "Village People's" title cut (5:11), in spite of its simplistic lyrics, is bold and forceful enough to become an anthem for the strong new thrust of the gay movement. But the album as a whole sidesteps politics and chooses fun, fun, fun as the rough-edged male lead and mucho macho chorus take us on a quick tour, name-dropping key hot spots along the way (Folsom Street, Polk Street, Studio One, Ice Palace, Sandpiper). Morali's production here is similar to the more aggressive and pounding parts of "African Queens" though there are occasional lapses into high-gloss pop. "San Francisco/Hollywood," a pairing that runs 10:16, is at its best in the first part, a high-powered, driving cut, but "Hollywood," which contains clever, detailed instructions on putting up an LA front, is marred for me by some Broadway show touches and the cliche that "everybody is a star in Hollywood." "Fire Island" (5:19) recovers the punch of "San Francisco" and feels like the final section of "Arabian Nights," but how are we supposed to take the repeated chorus, "Don't go near the bushes/Somethin' might grab ya"? In spite of its flaws, this is bound to be a big summer record, kicking off at the three places named, and Casablanca, which already has more records on the Top 20 chart than any other label, is shipping advances to disco DJs this week with copies due in the stores on the 18th. Watch this one – it's breaking new ground and could start a trend.

CHOICE CUTS: Not only is **Smokey Robinson** the producer, composer and singer of the original-score music for a new movie called "Big Time," he's also the film's executive producer and scoring his own project apparently brought out the best in him. The "Theme" from the resultant Tamla album runs nine and a half minutes and is Robinson's sharpest, most disco-styled production in years, bubbling with an irrepressible energy that should send it shooting up the charts, ready to pick up where **Marvin Gaye** left off. The Marvin Gaye connection is not a merely passing one –"Theme From Big Time" has a loping pace and tight but wide-open rhythmic structure that links it inevitably with "Got To Give It Up" – but Smokey's song is both more concise and more texturally varied than Gaye's, pulling elements of European disco styling into a heady Motown mix. Though there is a vocal framework to the "Theme," it's essentially an instrumental piece, like "Got To Give It Up" mated with "Vitamin U" and threaded deftly with spirited synthesizer and brilliant percussion passages. David Mancuso, who, along with Tony Gioe, put "Big Time" into his top 10 the first week out, says he also feels some of **War's** "City, Country, City" in here. All together, it's an unexpected piece of music from Smokey and this week's most essential lp cut... Also on the Mancuso and Gioe top 10s this week is a great **Stevie Wonder** composition from the new **Sergio Mendes and the New Brasil '77** album, "The Real Thing'" (Elektra). Featuring vibrant female vocals and a sprightly, Brazilian-beat arrangement, "The Real Thing" is utterly captivating in a distinctly wonderful way. Also attractive here: "Mozambique," which takes the "Express Yourself"/ "Hold Tight" percussive style in a Brazilian carnival direction... The best of the many variations on the "Star Wars" theme is **Meco's** full-side run-through from the Millennium album, "Star Wars And Other Galactic Funk." Actually a 15:47 medley of disco-ized versions of various pieces of music from the movie, "Star Wars" is a pastiche of moods – at times dramatically "futuristic," both symphonic and electronic (delightful "conversations" between synthesizers here and there); at other times, whimsical, big band jazzy, then grandiose, almost pompous toward the end. The result is fun, occasionally compelling dance music but the soft, slow spots might keep it from being played straight through. Still, there's enougb here to keep the dancers zipping through space. The pilot producers on this particular journey: **Meco Monardo**, **Harold Wheeler**, **Tony Bongiovi**, all key

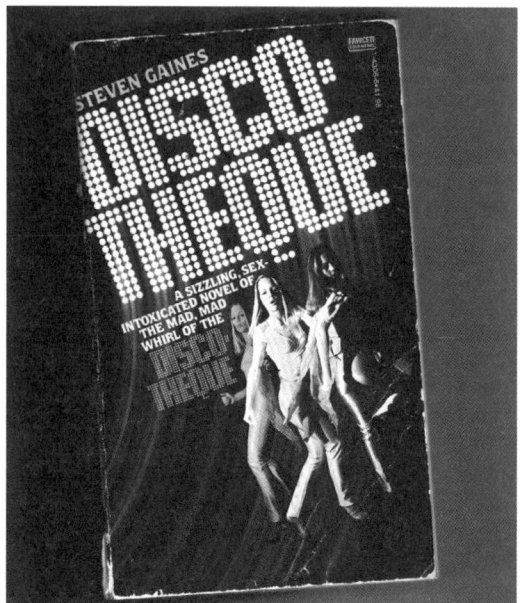

66 The fun–trash novel everyone in the business will be talking about 99

THE LOFT, NEW YORK
DJ: David Mancuso

EXPRESS YOURSELF – New York Community Choir (RCA)
LET'S HAVE A PARTY/DISCO PARTY CONTINUED
– Chaplin Band (EMI import)
MAGIC FLY – Space (Vogue import)
QUIET VILLAGE/VOODOO/ AFRICAN QUEENS
– Ritchie Family (Marlin)
THE REAL THING – Sergio Mendes (Elektra)
RUNAWAY – Salsoul Orchestra (Salsoul)
RUNNING AWAY – Roy Ayers Ubiquity (Polydor)
THEME FROM BIG TIME – Smokey Robinson (Tamla)
WE GOT OUR OWN THING – C.J. & Co. (Westbound)
WORK ON ME/TRAVELLING AT THE SPEED OF THOUGHT
– O'Jays (Phila. Intl.)

BONES, SAN FRANCISCO
DJ: Michael Lee

AFRICAN QUEENS/QUIET VILLAGE/VOODOO
– Ritchie Family (Marlin)
CARRY ON, TURN, ME ON/TANGO IN SPACE – Space (UA)
DON'T TAKE AWAY YOUR LOVE/SINCE I FELL FOR YOU
– Hodges, James & Smith (London)
EXPRESS YOURSELF/HAVE A GOOD TIME – New York
Community Choir (RCA)
HOLD TIGHT – Vicki Sue Robinson (RCA)
I'VE FOUND LOVE/ACCIDENTAL LOVER – Love & Kisses
(Casablanca)
MACUMBA – Marboo (Columbia import)
SAN FRANCISCO/HOLLYWOOD/FIRE ISLAND – Village
People (Casablanca)
SWEET LUCY – Raul De Souza (Capitol)
WINGS OF FIRE/FREE SPIRIT – Dennis Coffey (Westbound)

SAHARA, NEW YORK
DJ: Sharon White

AFRICAN QUEENS/QUIET VILLAGE/VOODOO
– Ritchie Family (Marlin)
CARRY ON, TURN ME ON/MAGIC FLY/ TANGO IN SPACE
– Space (Vogue import)
HOLD TIGHT – Vickie Sue Robinson (RCA)
I FEEL LOVE – Donna Summer (Casablanca)
I'VE FOUND LOVE/ACCIDENTAL LOVER – Love & Kisses
(Casablanca)
JOURNEY INTO LOVE – Kebekelektrik (Direction import)
JUDAS ISCARIOT /SIMON PETER – Sphinx (RAAL import)
SOLAR FLIGHT/DIRTY LOVE – Mandre (Motown)
THEME FROM THE DEEP – Donna Summer (Casablanca)
THE WAY YOU DO THE THINGS YOU DO – Foxy (TK)

COPACABANA, NEW YORK
DJ: Tony Gioe

CHOOSING YOU/PLEASE DON'T TEMPT ME
– Lenny Williams (ABC)
**I WANT TO STAY WITH YOU/WHO, WHAT, WHEN, WHERE,
WHY/LIGHT MY FIRE** – Carol Douglas (Midsong Intl.)
LET'S CLEAN UP THE GHETTO – Philadelphia
International All Stars (Phila. Intl.)
QUIET VILLAGE/VOODOO – Ritchie Family (Marlin)
THE REAL THING – Sergio Mendes (Elektra)
RUNAWAY – Salsoul Orchestra (Salsoul)
SPANDISCO/OYE COMO VA – Love Child's Afro-Cuban
Blues Band (Midsong Intl.)
STAR WARS – Meco (Millennium)
THEME FROM BIG TIME – Smokey Robinson (Tamla)
WINGS OF FIRE/FREE SPIRIT – Dennis Coffey (Westbound)

members of the original **Gloria Gaynor** team... And from left field: "Exodus," the 7:38 title cut from the new **Bob Marley & the Wailers** album (on Island) which sounds like old get-down **Bohannon** given a reggae twist and a Rastafarian message, is rich enough to get some attention at adventurous clubs.

RECOMMENDED DISCO DISCS: My favorite import this week is the **Larry Page Ork's** "Erotic Soul" (on the Penny Farthing label from Canada, distributed by A&M/Canada), one of the most graceful, exuberant and sustained instrumentals out right now. A pumping drumbeat pins down flights of strings and gusts of brass: variations on that theme for just over seven minutes. Already a bestselling import in San Francisco and New York and getting DJ raves from all over... **Renee Harris** begins "Doctor Music" (Epic) squealing "Turn it out, y'all" in this nasty little voice — the perfect crazy introduction to an entirely atypical **Michael Kunze-Silvester Levay** production. There are few flashes of **Silver Convention** here — instead, the style is Miami/Southern funk with a great, kicking beat. Basically, it's Harris' gritty voice that keeps the record funky as she sings about seeking solace from a broken heart with "Doctor Music"; "Think I'm Goin' out Tonight," the chorus chants. My west coast correspondent turned me on to this one when it was a single (3:30) but now it's out on a 12-inch at 6:30 and it's even more impressive... "Don't Turn Away" (4:25) by **Midnite Flite** (TK) is an instrumental with a certain eerie charm and some terrific breaks that is, believe it or not, based on the NBC Sports theme, It's been out in Miami for several months and quite a success there before TK picked it up and brought it out nationally.

OTHER MEDIA: "Discotheque," a paperback original by New York Daily News pop columnist Steve Gaines, is the fun-trash novel everyone in the business will be talking about. Just out on Fawcett and bearing cover lines that describe it as "a sizzling, sex-intoxicated novel of the mad, mad whirl of the discotheque" and a "big, reverberating novel of love, lust and violence in the blinding world of the etc.," the book takes place over the three-day Fourth of July weekend in New York's biggest disco, Elysium, and centers around characters like Bobby DJ (full name: Bobby Benedetto), top spinner in the city but also a coke addict with a wife and a kid; Maurice Cameron, flashy owner of the club who might be seen as a thinly disguised John Addison (the man behind Le Jardin, 15 Lansdowne Street, etc.); and a disco promotion man named Willy Buckels. Other members of the cast include an aging movie queen, a Jewish secretary, a coke dealer, a sex pervert, a Lesbian go-between for the Mob, other shadowy Mob-music biz figures and a DJ named Bob Tavarase. They're all thrown together in a spoof of disaster film "novelizations" with a hilarious made-for-tv-movie finale worth wading through a lot of nonsense for. This is hardly "big, reverberating" stuff, but I raced through it in one day over, appropriately, the Fourth of July weekend and have been telling people about it ever since. Take it to the beach. ◐

JULY 23, 1977

It's probably more a coincidence than a substantial trend, but the majority of new releases we've gotten into this week could be loosely classified as funk. The styles range over a wide spectrum, from southern raunch to New York jungle stomp, linked by a common hard-edged passion and fierceness in the music and the vocals. The best of the batch is, not surprisingly, the **Mass Production** disco disc on Atlantic, containing two cuts from the group's forthcoming Cotillion album, "Believe." Both "I Believe in Music" (6:54) and "People Get Up" (5:43) continue Mass Production's chunky, pounding, shake-the-foundations sound but with even more intensity and originality than they displayed on their debut last year. The horns are as rambunctious as ever, but the synthesizer is more out front, especially on "People Get Up," and the vocals are tougher than before, so they've gone beyond the **B.T. Express/Brass Construction** basics and stepped closer to the **T-Connection/Peter Brown** approach. "I Believe In Music" is clinched by a long, driving chant segment at the end during which the voices are electronically altered, but "People Get Up" has got me hooked, too. Both end abruptly, "People" rather awkwardly, as if the production ran into a brick wall and crumbled; and when they're over, you feel as if an enormous, chugging assembly line (mass production?) has been brought to a sudden stop. Extremely powerful.

group chants as if hypnotized (or lobotomized). "Every day the same: we groovin'" just about sums up the mood here; it's lyrically dead but musically kind of absorbing, though not necessarily for the full 11:52 length. All together, however, this is an excellent, balanced collection, perfect summer listening.

Other assorted funk: **Tyrone Davis'** "All You Got" (6:06) should appeal to fans of **Joe Simon's** "I Need You, You Need Me" since it's got a similar frothy funk feeling and equally mellow vocals. It starts out a little slow, but the violin parts just carry you off after a while and the final break is superb. New York DJ **Wayne Scott** turned me on to this track this past weekend when he played it at the Boatel in Fire Island Pines (a weekend in the Pines is like a crash course in up-to-the-minute disco, among other things) – it's from Davis' first Columbia album, "Let's Be Closer Together"... **Sylvester**, whose stunning performances with the outrageous Cockettes in San Francisco brought him his first fame and notoriety, has always been one of the more extraordinary performers on the fringes of disco and his new album – just "Sylvester," his first for Fantasy – is the most satisfying so far. The disco highlight is a funkified version of **Ashford & Simpson's** great song, "Over and Over" which Sylvester runs for more than seven, minutes,

" The majority of new releases this week could be loosely classified as funk – from southern raunch to New York jungle stomp "

Eddie Henderson and **War** each take the funk in a lighter, jazzier direction. "Say You Will" (4:28), the opening track on Henderson's new Capitol album, "Comin' Through" (due out this week), is an instrumental that sounds like a **Mizell** brothers production (especially their **Johnny Hammond** number, "Los Conquistadores Chocolates") crossed with some Mass Production spunk. "The Funk Surgeon" (4:59) has a similarly big, bold style minus the underlying sweetness of "Say You Will" which makes it a little more obvious in its appeal. **Skip Drinkwater** produced in fine style and Henderson's horn work is brilliant throughout. War's "Platinum Jazz" album (Blue Note) is a two-record set that collects some of the group's best jazz-styled material (including the classic "City, Country, City" as well as "Four Cornered Room," "Deliver The Word" and "Smile Happy") and matches it with two sides of new music. Best of the new stuff is "War Is Coming! War Is Coming!" (7:12) their most convincing disco cut in a long time. It's a throbbing message song with outstanding vocals and terrific flute and steel drum/percussion passages that's infectiously high-spirited in spite of its essentially pessimistic slant. The longest cut here, "L.A. Sunshine," is appropriately laid-back funk: "We get high off the sunshine," the

culminating in a pumping rave-up. Another long cut, "Down, Down, Down" (5:18), has a churning rock-style arrangement that hasn't yet won me over, but both songs are reportedly going over strong in Sylvester's home base San Francisco and Fantasy is reportedly planning a better mix of both for a disco disc... **O.V. Wright's** "Into Something (Can't Shake Loose)" (Hi) is a single of lowdown southern r&b with a disco edge and all the rawness of old-time **James Brown/Johnnie Taylor** funk; **Willie Mitchell** produced... And for a continuation of the same theme ("hooked on love") in a slightly different vein, there's **New Birth's** neo-funky "Deeper" with a nice 'n' nasty male lead. This is a major change in style for the group, produced by **Frank Wilson** (whose **Lenny Williams** album on ABC is growing on a lot of people; the single I have is exciting at a little over three minutes – can't wait to get the disco disc version with vocal and instrumental sides each over six minutes... The **Chaplin Band's** "Let's Have a Party," an English import single on EMI, is a classic, timeless party-hearty song with a no-nonsense production and shouting male vocals. The vocal side is sharp but the instrumental version on the flip, "Disco Party Continued" (5:22), is even better – reminds me of "Makes You Blind" but at a

THE SANDPIPER, FIRE ISLAND PINES, N.Y.
DJ: Larry Sanders

DEVIL'S GUN/WE GOT OUR OWN THING – CJ & Co (Westbound)
DOCTOR LOVE – First Choice (Gold Mind)
HOLD TIGHT – Vicki Sue Robinson (RCA)
I FEEL LOVE – Donna Summer (Casablanca)
I'VE FOUND LOVE – Love & Kisses (Casablanca)
MAGIC BIRD OF FIRE – Salsoul Orchestra (Salsoul)
THE MAGIC IS YOU – John Davis & The Monster Orchestra (Sam)
VILLAGE/AFRICAN QUEENS – Ritchie Family (Marlin)
SCHEHERAZADE – Fenati & the Munich Machine (Ariston import)
SINCE I FELL FOR YOU – Hodges, James & Smith (London)

FOX TRAPPE, WASHINGTON, DC
DJ: Frank Edwards

BITE YOUR GRANNY – Morning, Noon & Night (UA)
BURNING LOVE – D.D. Sound (Baby import)
CARRY ON, TURN ME ON – Space (UA)
CHOOSING YOU – Lenny Williams (ABC)
I FEEL LOVE – Donna Summer (Casablanca)
MAKE IT WITH YOU – Whispers (Soul Train)
MAGIC BIRD OF FIRE – Salsoul Orchestra (Salsoul)
PIPELINE – Bruce Johnston (Columbia)
THEME FROM BIG TIME – Smokey Robinson (Tamla)
WINGS OF FIRE/FREE SPIRIT – Dennis Coffey (Westbound)

DINGBAT'S, CHICAGO
DJ: Rick Gianatos

BEST OF MY LOVE – Emotions (Columbia)
DEVIL'S GUN/ SURE CAN'T GO TO THE MOON – CJ & Co (Westbound)
DO YOU WANNA GET FUNKY WITH ME – Peter Brown (TK)
HAVE A GOOD TIME – New York Community Choir (RCA)
HOLD TIGHT – Vicki Sue Robinson (RCA)
I FEEL LOVE/ I REMEMBER YESTERDAY – Donna Summer (Casablanca)
I'VE FOUND LOVE – Love & Kisses (Casablanca)
MY FIRST MISTAKE – Chi-lites (Mercury)
RUNAWAY – Salsoul Orchestra (Salsoul)
SINCE I FELL FOR YOU – Hodges, James & Smith (London)

SIGLO 21, BRONX, NEW YORK
DJ: Louis "Angelo" Alers

AFRICAN QUEENS/QUIET VILLAGE/ VOODOO – Ritchie Family (Marlin)
CARRY ON, TURN ME ON/TANGO IN SPACE – Space (UA)
HOLD TIGHT – Vicki Sue Robinson (RCA)
THE MAGIC IS YOU – John Davis & The Monster Orchestra (Sam)
NOWHERE TO RUN – Dynamic Superiors (Motown)
THE REAL THING – Sergio Mendes & Brazil '77 (Elektra)
RUNAWAY/MAGIC BIRD OF FIRE – Salsoul Orchestra (Salsoul)
STAR WARS – Meco (Millennium)
WINGS OF FIRE/FREE SPIRIT – Dennis Coffey (Westbound)
ZODIACS/LOVE SIGN/FUNKY STARDUST/I'M SAGITTARIUS – Roberta Kelly (Durium import)

more relaxed pace. **David Mancuso** listed this one on his top 10 last week from the Loft in New York and I'm crazy about it, too. (Thanks to **David Rodriguez** from Downstairs' Records for supplying my copy)... Finally, another single: **Bert de Coteaux** has sculpted a big, full-bodied production for **Linda Hopkins** called "It's In Your Blood" (Columbia), a very heavy-duty, gospel-inspired cut with knockout vocals.

NOTES: **Cerrone's** "Paradise" is out now on Cotillion with its newly sanitized cover... It looks like London has picked up rights to the **Larry Page Ork's** excellent "Erotic Soul"... Capitol is releasing its first commercial disco disc on **Raul de Souza's** "Sweet Lucy" with "Time Is On My Side" by **Maze** on the other side and a fabulous new sleeve... Due out this week: a new **Giorgio** album titled "From Here To Eternity" (Casablanca) that everyone who's heard it is screaming about. ◐

DISCO FILE TOP 20

1. **I FEEL LOVE** – Donna Summer (Casablanca)
2. **AFRICAN QUEENS/QUIET VILLAGE/VOODOO** – Ritchie Family (Marlin)
3. **I'VE FOUND LOVE** – Love and Kisses (Casablanca)
4. **CARRY ON, TURN ME ON/TANGO IN SPACE** – Space (UA)
5. **HOLD TIGHT** – Vicki Sue Robinson (RCA)
6. **MAGIC BIRD OF FIRE** – Salsoul Orchestra (Salsoul)
7. **DEVIL'S GUN/WE GOT OUR OWN THING** – CJ. & Co. (Westbound/Atlantic)
8. **WINGS OF FIRE/FREE SPIRIT** – Dennis Coffey (Westbound)
9. **CERRONE'S PARADISE** – Cerrone (Cotillion)
10. **GET ON THE FUNK TRAIN** – Munich Machine (Casablanca)
11. **NOWHERE TO RUN** – Dynamic Superiors (Motown)
12. **THEME FROM BIG TIME** – Smokey Robinson (Tamla)
13. **CHOOSING YOU** – Lenny Williams (ABC)
14. **THE MAGIC IS YOU** – John Davis & the Monster Orchestra (Sam)
15. **THE WAY YOU DO THE THINGS YOU DO** – Foxy (TK)
16. **SINCE I FELL FOR YOU/DON'T TAKE AWAY YOUR LOVE** – Hodges, James & Smith (London)
17. **EXPRESS YOURSELF/HAVE A GOOD TIME** – New York Community Choir (RCA)
18. **JOURNEY INTO LOVE (MAGIC FLY)** – Kebekelektric (Direction import)
19. **DOCTOR LOVE** – First Choice (Gold Mind)
20. **I NEED A MAN** – Grace Jones (Beam Junction)

JULY 30, 1977

With essential American releases slacking off for the moment, we can catch up on some recent successful imports, like the pair of European concept albums that have been turning up on disco playlists here and there in the past month: "Judas Iscariot/Simon Peter" by **Sphinx** and **Roberta Kelly's** "Zodiac Lady." The Sphinx album, on the Raal label, was produced in England by **Alec R. Costandinos** with most of the same singers, musicians and technicians he used on the **Love & Kisses** album, so the sound and the format – each side contains one long composition – should be quite familiar. But the concept is decidedly different, focusing as it does on two prominent Christian guilt figures, Judas Iscariot, who betrayed Christ, and Simon Peter, the disciple who denied Christ; instead of orgasmic release, Sphinx gives us religious soul-searching a go-go: Jesus Christ Superstar at the Disco. In the style of "Love In C Minor" and "Accidental Lover," each side here is staged as a mini-drama: "Judas Iscariot" (19:16) opens with a prostitute accosting Judas in the rain and pestering him until he confesses his name, whereupon the music starts (towards the end, he commits suicide in front of her and her scream rips through the violins); "Simon Peter" (17:06) starts right off with one of Peter's denials, adds on two more and throws in some muffled readings from the Bible for good measure. Though these dramatic spoken parts are brief and scattered, they're rather at odds with the otherwise exultant mood of the music and the characters' British accents give the whole thing the unfortunate feeling of an educational TV soundtrack. Luckily, the music itself is so strong that it overwhelms the subject and sweeps the listener along almost involuntarily: form swamps content and the agonies of Judas and Peter are swallowed up in the ecstacies of the production. Costandinos has created exquisite, sustained pieces full of kaleidoscopic changes, mixing in brilliant bits of music in other accents (Middle-Eastern, Turkish, Oriental) to heighten the textural richness. As on "I've Found Love," the arrangement (by **Don Ray**) is extraordinarily complex and effective – no false moves,

" Instead of orgasmic release, Sphinx gives us religious soul-searching a go-go: Jesus Christ Superstar at the Disco "

no lagging moments. Again the violins are incredible and the percussive pulse wonderfully relentless. The effect may not be as invigorating as "I've Found Love," but both sides are powerful and contain some of the very best music for dancing out at the moment. Casablanca, which already has quite a number of European productions, including Costandinos' **Love & Kisses**, is picking up American rights to Sphinx with the release scheduled for the middle of August. Polydor has already released the albumin Canada. Though certainly not as progressive or deep as Sphinx, **Roberta Kelly's** "Zodiac Lady" is going over bigger right now primarily because it's a lot more accessible and a lot less pretentious. Basically, this is an entertaining album that even those of us who feel astrology is totally foolish can't help falling for. I put the album aside weeks ago after hearing Kelly prattling on about sun signs, lunar moons and astral hearts, but after hearing "Zodiac Lady"'s side-one medley ("Zodiacs," "Love-Sign" and "Funky Stardust" – 15:12 total) everywhere I went on my recent Fire Island weekend, I found myself wandering around singing, "Capricorns, Leos, Sagittarians/Scorpios, Virgos, Aquarians." The words are just plain silly but here again the music makes up for it all and producers **Giorgio Moroder** and **Pete Bellotte** have provided Kelly with a terrifically catchy, zesty and irresistible track. "Zodiacs" and "Love-Sign" are the prime cuts and they're great fun to dance to, nothing more, nothing less. The album's second side remains for me quite resistible, but the opening cut, "I'm Sagittarius," is getting some play. My copy of "Zodiac Lady" is on L'Oasis from France but most of the import copies that have flooded the market in the States are on Durium in Italy; since Casablanca has passed on this lp – they've already scheduled another Roberta Kelly album for early fall – there may be no American release.

Another import I heard all over Fire Island is a vigorous party-party record called "Music" by **Montreal Sound**, a disco disc on the Smash Disco label from Canada. The side that was getting all the reaction (and some looks of stunned disbelief) is designated "Very Special Disco Mix by PAJ" and contains so many outrageous mixing effects (right up to the final tape-reversal cut-off) that the result is at once dazzling, dizzying and numbing (especially at nearly 9 minutes in length). The vocals are few but the key line is, "Hey, would you like to sing along," and after a while, it's hard not to. There are lots of whistles, some playful send-ups of "Frère Jacques," party noises, and more breaks than necessary. But even if the editing is sometimes abrupt and intrusive, the record is so brash it's fun. For crazed crowds only.

Amanda Lear's deliciously vicious "Blood And Honey," already recommended here as a single, is now out on a 12-inch from Direction in Canada that runs 8:58. It's been lengthened with some hypnotic if rather laconic conga drumming in the introduction and a break, the latter beautifully meshed back into the velvety violins of the main section; "Disco Mix by the Canadian Record Pool" it says on the label – congratulations to them again (this

12 WEST, NEW YORK
DJ: Jonathan Fearing

AFRICAN QUEENS/QUIET VILLAGE/VOODOO
– Ritchie Family (Marlin)
CARRY ON, TURN ME ON/TANGO IN SPACE – Space (UA)
CERRONE'S PARADISE – Cerrone (Cotillion)
DEVIL'S GUN/WE'VE GOT OUR OWN THING – C.J. & Co.
(Westbound)
I FEEL LOVE/LOVE'S UNKIND – Donna Summer
(Casablanca)
JOURNEY INTO LOVE (MAGIC FLY) – Kebekelektric
(Direction import)
LOCKED IN THIS POSITION – Barbara Mason & Bunny Sigler
(Curtom)
MAGIC BIRD OF FIRE – Salsoul Orchestra (Salsoul)
NOWHERE TO RUN – Dynamic Superiors (Motown)
WATCH OUT FOR THE BOOGIE MAN – Trax (Polydor import)

YESTERDAY'S, BOSTON
DJ: Cosmo Wyatt

BACK IN LOVE AGAIN – LTD (A&M)
CHOOSING YOU – Lenny Williams (ABC)
**DEVIL'S GUN/WE'VE GOT OUR OWN THING/SURE CAN'T
GO TO THE MOON** – C.J. & Co. (Westbound)
GET ON THE FUNK TRAIN – Munich Machine (Casablanca)
HOLD TIGHT – Vicki Sue Robinson (RCA)
NOWHERE TO RUN – Dynamic Superiors (Motown)
PIPELINE – Bruce Johnston (Columbia)
SAN FRANCISCO/HOLLYWOOD/FIRE ISLAND – Village
People (Casablanca)
VOODOO – Ritchie Family (Marlin)
WINGS OF FIRE – Dennis Coffey (Westbound)

WAREHOUSE, MIAMI
DJ: Bill Kelly

AFRICAN QUEENS/QUIET VILLAGE – Ritchie Family (Marlin)
CARRY ON, TURN ME ON/TANGO IN SPACE – Space (UA)
CERRONE'S PARADISE – Cerrone (Cotillion)
GET ON THE FUNK TRAIN – Munich Machine (Casablanca)
HOLD TIGHT – Vicki Sue Robinson (RCA)
I FEEL LOVE – Donna Summer (Casablanca)
I'VE FOUND LOVE – Love & Kisses (Casablanca)
**MAKE IT WITH YOU/I FELL IN LOVE LAST NIGHT AT THE
DISCO)** – Whispers (Soul Train)
RUNAWAY/MAGIC BIRD OF FIRE – Salsoul Orchestra
(Salsoul)
WINGS OF FIRE/FREE SPIRIT – Dennis Coffey (Westbound)

EXPERIMENT, NEW YORK
DJ: John Benitez

AFRICAN QUEENS/VOODO – Ritchie Family (Marlin)
CARRY ON, TURN ME ON/TANGO IN SPACE/MAGIC FLY
– Space (UA/Vogue)
CHOOSING YOU/PLEASE DON'T TEMPT ME
– Lenny Williams (ABC)
DISCO PARTY CONTINUED – Chaplin Band (EMI import)
FIRE ISLAND/SAN FRANCISCO/ HOLLYWOOD
– Village People (Casablanca)
HOLD TIGHT – Vicki Sue Robinson (RCA)
PIPELINE – Bruce Johnston (Columbia)
RUNNING AWAY – Roy Ayers Ubiquity (Polydor)
SPIRIT OF SUNSHINE – Chuck Davis Orchestra (West End)
THEME FROM BIG TIME – Smokey Robinson (Tamla)

ambitious Montreal-based pool has had more success and recognition than any of its American equivalents). This longer version should give the record the extra edge it needed to get over... The "Magic Fly" album by **Space**, including the super-hot "Carry On, Turn Me On" and "Tango In Space," is now available from United Artists... And **Kebekelektrik's** "Journey Into Love," long successful as an import from Direction, is out now on a TK disco disc but re-titled, as are the Canadian pressings, "Magic Fly." The name change was apparently unacceptable to the song's publishers and the record, a cover of the Space track, has reverted to its original title. ✪

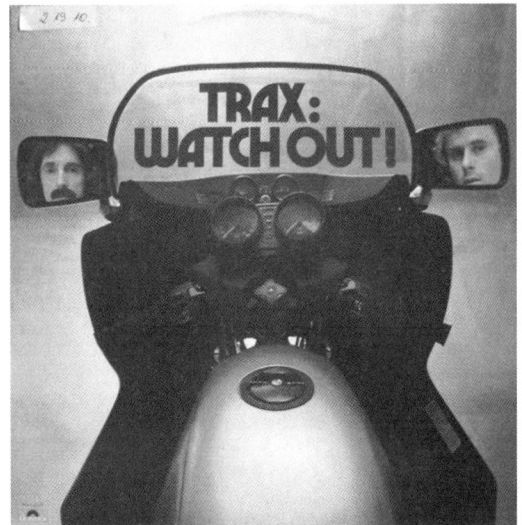

AUGUST 6, 1977

RECOMMENDED DISCO DISCS: The top two this week are **Arthur Prysock's** "You Can Do It" (Old Town) and **Michael Henderson's** "I Can't Help It" (Buddah), both pleasantly off-beat records. Prysock's is the sort of record DJs call "sleaze" – in this case a very sexy midtempo number that falls into a gorgeous, pumping groove you just never want to get out of. "You Can Do It" is an **Evie Sands** song (she also wrote "One Thing On My Mind") that got a little attention when it was included on the Hot album earlier this year, but Prysock's versiorο, produced by **John Davis** and backed by the **Monster Orchestra**, is tighter and much more insinuating. Prysock's voice is as creamy and mellow as always so Davis' comfy arrangement matches it perfectly, filling things out with three fine breaks, each featuring a separate lead instrument – sax, organ guitar – the sax section (played by Davis himself) being everyone's favorite right now. Already on two top 10 lists in its first week out, "You Can Do It" runs just over eight minules. Michael Henderson's "I Can't Help It" (4:16) has a certain sleazy edge as well but here the feeling is more intensely jazzy and vibrant. Henderson's vocals remind me of **Marvin Gaye** – they have a similar sharp, high, cutting edge – and the setting is full of echoes of **Quincy Jones** (especially "If I Ever Lose This Heaven") and **Norman Conners**. But the end product is unique and engrossing with a bubbling synthesizer track that takes you away. "I Can't Help It" is included on Henderson's new album, "Goin' Places," which begins with a very similar cut called "Whip It" (same background voices singing "Get down, get on down") that might work on its own.

A number of the best disco discs out now are remixed versions of album cuts: **Donna Summer's** "I Feel Love" (Casablanca) has been expanded to 8:15 and followed by a fuller, faster version of her "Theme From The Deep (Down Deep Inside)" (6:06) that sounds much better than the soundtrack cut and should help put this cut over in clubs that have previously passed on it. Both mixes were done by Bobby DJ Guttadaro and Marc Paul Simon though there's no credit on the label... **Sylvester's** "Over And Over" was brought up from 7:02 to 9:27 for a Fantasy promotional 12-inch which has a lot more clarity and punch than the lp track (though the bass at the end seems boosted way out of proportion); "Down, Down, Down," on the flip side is also longer and minus some vocals. "Over And Over" deserves a lot more attention than it's been getting up 'til now and this new mix, by San Francisco DJ Wes Bradley, might do the trick... **Barbara Mason** and **Bunny Sigler** teamed up on an album recently called "Locked In This Position" whose title track had some scattered disco success – nothing compared to what it could get with the stunning new version just out on Curtom. All the soft spots in the original cut have been firmed up and now it chugs along for just over ten minutes and emphasizes Barbara's rather than Bunny's riffing vocals at the end. Very spiffy funk, remixed and mastered by New York DJ Jimmy Simpson (Valerie's brother) who did a terrific transformation job... **Paul Kelly's** "To the Bone, Get It On" (Warner Brothers)

> **❝ This is the sort of record DJs call "sleaze" – in this case a very sexy midtempo number that falls into a gorgeous, pumping groove you just never want to get out of ❞**

is just slightly longer than the lp version (5:06) but the quality of the pressing seems better and the song jumps. This is a variation of the "Locked In This Position" theme (what position do you think?), with girls crying "All night long" over and over and a typically Paul Kelly funk beat (Kelly produced along with **Gene Page**).

CHOICE CUTS: "Cocomotion," the 10:30 title cut from the new **El Coco** album (AVI), is a synthesizer-and-strings instrumental with occasional vocals that, while missing the spark that gave "Let's Get It Together" its special charm, has a certain light, attractive quality that grows on you. As with many El Coco songs, the music tends to be trivialized by the flimsy vocals, but once the girls singing, "C'mon, let's do the Cocomotion," fade away, producers **Michael Lewis** and **Laurin Rinder** stretch out quite gracefully. Basically this is glossy hustle music but percussion breaks and passages of crisp handclapping cut against the sugary strings and vocals, balancing the sound nicely. The synthesizer segments are also excellent, like tingles up the spine of the song. Uneven but kinda fascinating; should be an interesting track to watch in the next few weeks. Tony Carrasco, the New York DJ who listed "Cocomotion" in his top 10 this week, also includes two shorter cuts we might recommend as well: "Love To The World" (4:25) and "I'm Mad As Hell" (4:17), the latter the more involving of the two (nice horns, quick pace) but again we could do without the vocals... Much of the new **Demis Roussos** album ("The Demis Roussos Magic" on Mercury) is heavy-handed, sentimental and slow, but two tracks – "Let It Happen" (4:04) and "I Dig You" (4:07) – are real

CLUB FEVER, DETROIT
DJ: Michael Melkonian

EROTIC SOUL – Larry Page Ork (Penny Farthing import)
EXPRESS YOURSELF – New York Community Choir (RCA)
HOLD TIGHT – Vicki Sue Robinson (RCA)
QUIET VILLAGE/AFRICAN QUEENS – Ritchie Family (Marlin)
RUNAWAY – Salsoul Orchestra (Salsoul)
SURE CAN'T GO TO THE MOON/WE GOT OUR OWN THING – C.J. & Co. (Westbound)
TWO HOT FOR LOVE – THP Orchestra (RCA import)
WHAT AM I TO DO? – Ralph Graham (RCA)
WOULD YOU DANCE TO MY MUSIC – Eddie Drennon & the B.B.S. Unltd. (Casablanca)
YOU CAN DO IT – Arthur Prysock (Old Town)

PLAYGROUND, NEW YORK
DJ: Tony Carrasco

BUST IT – Craig Snyder & Lix (Midsong Intl.)
CHOOSING YOU/ PLEASE DON'T TEMPT ME – Lenny Williams (ABC)
COCOMOTION/LOVE TO THE WORLD/I'M AS MAD AS HELL – El Coco (AVI)
DEEPER – New Birth (Warner Bros.)
IF YOU GIVE A DOGGONE ABOUT IT – James Brown (Polydor)
PEOPLE GET UP – Mass Production (Cotillion)
PIPELINE – Bruce Johnston (Columbia)
SAN FRANCISCO/ HOLLYWOOD/FIRE ISLAND – Village People (Casablanca)
THEME FROM BIG TIME – Smokey Robinson (Tamla)
YOU CAN DO IT – Arthur Prysock (Old Town)

BACK DOOR, PHILADELPHIA
DJ: Williard Ludrick

CARRY ON, TURN ME ON – Space (UA)
CERRONE'S PARADISE – Cerrone (Cotillion)
COULD HEAVEN EVER BE LIKE THIS – Idris Muhammad (Kudu)
DEVIL'S GUN – C.J. & Co. (Westbound)
DOCTOR LOVE – First Choice (Gold Mind)
GET ON THE FUNK TRAIN – Munich Machine (Casablanca)
HOLD TIGHT – Vicki Sue Robinson (RCA)
I'VE FOUND LOVE – Love & Kisses (Casablanca)
MAGIC BIRD OF FIRE/RUNAWAY – Salsoul Orchestra (Salsoul)
NOWHERE TO RUN – Dynamic Superiors (Motown)

THE POOP DECK, FORT LAUDERDALE, FLA.
DJ: Bob Viteritti

CARRY ON, TURN ME ON/TANGO IN SPACE – Space (UA)
DEVIL'S GUN – C.J. & Co. (Westbound)
DOCTOR LOVE – First Choice (Gold Mind)
I FEEL LOVE – Donna Summer (Casablanca)
I'VE FOUND LOVE/ACCIDENTAL LOVER – Love & Kisses (Casablanca)
MAGIC BIRD OF FIRE/RUNAWAY – Salsoul Orchestra (Salsoul)
THE MAGIC IS YOU – John Davis & The Monster Orchestra (Sam)
QUIET VILLAGE/AFRICAN QUEENS – Ritchie Family (Marlin)
SAN FRANCISCO/ HOLLYWOOD/FIRE ISLAND – Village People (Casablanca)
THE WAY YOU DO THE THINGS YOU DO – Foxy (TK)

departures, dipping as they do into the particularly European, lushly electronic sound dominating the disco charts right now. Roussos' version is closer to **Randy Pie** and **Barrabas** than **Love & Kisses** and **Donna Summer**, but there are touches of both styles, and plenty of synthesizers, in these two cuts. Left field, perhaps, but worth checking into... The **Philadelphia International All Stars** album, "Let's Clean Up The Ghetto," contains an 8:42 version of the title track that combines the vocals and instrumental portions of the single and bridges the two with some beautiful horn work. Again, this is a highly recommended cut not just for the way it sounds but for what it says. Unfortunately, the remainder of the album doesn't carry through the All-Stars concept: rather than have **Lou Rawls**, **Teddy Pendergrass**, **The O'Jays**, **Billy Paul**, **Archie Bell**, **Dee Dee Sharp Gamble**, etc. sing together as they do on "Ghetto," each singer or group is given a separate track. All the message songs here are inter-related but none are as strong as "Ghetto" or many previous **Gamble-Huff** songs and only one, "Now Is The Time To Do It" by Pendergrass, is likely to get any disco attention – and that one only because of Teddy's always marvelous voice.

The up-and-coming cuts right now: the entire **Village People** album but especially "San Francisco/Hollywood" and "Fire Island" (Casablanca); **Lenny Williams'** "Choosing You" and "Please Don't Tempt Me" (ABC); **Bruce Johnston's** "Pipeline" (Columbia); and "Erotic Soul" by the **Larry Page Ork** (Canadian import on Penny Farthing). Also looking good: "Spirit of Sunshine" by the **Chuck Davis Orchestra** (West End); "I, Robot" by the **Alan Parsons Project** (Arista); "Running Away" from the **Roy Ayers Ubiquity** album (Polydor); and "Make It With You" by the **Whispers** (Soul Train). ◐

AUGUST 13, 1977

Perhaps the most significant development in disco sound this year is the success of totally synthesized music. **Kraftwerk's** "Trans-Europe Express" was the breakthrough record – not a smash hit, though it did meet with an astonishing degree of acceptance at a number of clubs in New York, but an important introduction to the group's cool and hypnotic way with electronic keyboards. Kraftwerk's impact was almost immediately underlined by **Donna Summer's** "I Feel Love" which took the synthesizer rhythm and compressed and intensified it so it was both more physically exciting – like stepping into a tangle of high-voltage wires – and more commercial. **Space**, the French group that consists of three synthesizer keyboards and

> ❝ The most significant development in disco sound this year is the success of totally synthesized music. "Trans-Europe Express" was the break-through record — an important introduction to the group's hypnotic way with electronic keyboards ❞

drums, came along about the same time with its own spirited, quirky variation on sci-fi disco and its American release has put "Carry On, Turn Me On"/"Tango In Space" on the charts close behind Summer. Now **Giorgio (Moroder)**, half of Donna Summer's production team, has tied all these moves together and come up with the ultimate disco synthesizer album, "From Here To Eternity" (Casablanca), and, judging from the initial reaction, it's going to be one of the year's biggest hits.

The first side of "From Here To Eternity" begins with the title track and contains four other interconnected cuts, the last a short reprise, for a total of 14:27. The first cut is the only one with traditional lyrics or vocals, though even here the voice is often transformed electronically into a robot drone and the female backing vocals are kept to a minimally emotional level. So the real emotional content of the record is in the pulsing, squirming,

bubbling synthesizer as it ebbs and flows, a wash of sound at once dispassionate and stimulating. Parts of the record recall the crisp, chugging train sounds of "Trans-Europe Express;" others are more like "I Feel Love"'s surging, crackling quality. In the "Utopia – Me Giorgio" section the feeling is dreamy and ecstatic, sustained by shimmering female voices floating in the background. The cumulative effect is an icy brilliance, a heady trip through star-dusted space. The album's second side features three separate cuts, "First Hand Experience In Second Hand Love," "I'm Left, You're Right, She's Gone" and "Too Hot To Handle," all primarily vocals (both electronic and non) over vibrant synthesizer tracks, all quite danceable. Of the three, my favorite is "Too Hot To Handle," the most upbeat, but all three should be getting disco play. All together a strikingly original and satisfying album, "From Here To Eternity" could become one of 1977's most influential records.

"Je T'Aime," a French/American co-production by a group called **Saint Tropez**, will be one of the most talked-about records of the summer if only because of its ultra-glossy, classy European packaging: a neon-pink, see-through vinyl disc with a pale pink label inside an album whose cover features a picture of three attractive, ambiguously posed women; open the cover, however, and the pose becomes explicit – two of the women are about to kiss as the third, dressed in a man's hat and coat, looks off with studied indifference. The album doesn't entirely sustain the Sapphic overtones of the cover, but the longest cut, "Violation" (8:13), is like a scene from Emanuelle set to music: a spoken French monologue over a fluid, luxuriously slow track (**Barry White** on downs) that gradually becomes a dialogue of sighs and whispers between two women: an extremely sensuous seduction set against a backdrop of velvety richness.

The album's title cut is, of course, the **Serge Gainsborg-Jane Birkin** record that was the first major European song to reach orgasm (the landmark year: 1969). The Saint Tropez version (6:36) is more elaborately produced, breaking into two parts, the first very slow, the second punched up Donna Summer-style and quite danceble. Here the dialogue is between a man and woman in the throes of rather talky love but sex always sounds somehow more chic in a foreign language (though the orgasmic repetition of "Je T'aime" does become comic) and this is definitely high-fashion passion.

With these two cuts on the side marked "Amour," the album's flip contains three tracks designed for dancing. Though their instrumental version of **Van McCoy's** durable "African Symphony" could be a little more passionate – only rarely does it catch fire – the treatment of "Coeur A Coeur" (**Andrea True's** "Fill Me Up (Heart to Heart)") is just right: delicately spicy, highlighted by strings and female vocals that both have the feel of quick jets of sweet syrup. The third cut is also a remake, but a less familiar one; originally made by the French-Canadian group **Toulouse**, "On A Rien Perdre" (loosely

PEP MCGUIRES, QUEENS, N.Y.
DJ: Walter Gibbons

AFRICAN QUEENS/SUMMER DANCE – Ritchie Family
(Marlin)
HEY YOU SHOULD BE DANCING – Gene Farrow (Magnet)
LOVIN' IS REALLY MY GAME – Brainstorm (Tabu)
MY LOVE IS ON HIS WAY – Retta Young (All Platinum)
RUNAWAY – Salsoul Orchestra (Salsoul)
RUN TO ME – Elaine Overholt (RCA import)
THEME FROM BIG TIME – Smokey Robinson (Tamla)
WATCH OUT FOR THE BOOGIE MAN – Trax (Polydor import)
**WE GOT OUR OWN THING/GET A GROOVE IN ORDER TO
MOVE** – C.J. & Co. (Westbound)
YOU ARE THE MUSIC WITHIN ME – Barbara Pennington (UA)

12 WEST, NEW YORK
DJ: Jim Burgess

ACCIDENTAL LOVER/I'VE FOUND LOVE – Love & Kisses
(Casablanca)
AFRICAN QUEENS/SUMMER DANCE/ QUIET VILLAGE
– Ritchie Family (Marlin)
**FROM HERE TO ETERNITY/ FIRST HAND EXPERIENCE/
TOO HOT TO HANDLE** – Giorgio (Casablanca)
HOLD TIGHT – Vicki Sue Robinson (RCA)
I FEEL LOVE – Donna Summer (Casablanca)
THE MAGIC IS YOU – John Davis & The Monster
Orchestra (Sam)
SAN FRANCISCO/FIRE ISLAND/VILLAGE PEOPLE
– Village People (Casablanca)
SIMON PETER – Sphinx (Raal import)
THEME FROM BIG TIME – Smokey Robinson (Tamla)
TWO HOT FOR LOVE – THP Orchestra (RCA import)

THE BROADWAY, DENVER
DJ: Bob Parsons

AFRICAN QUEENS/QUIET VILLAGE/ VOODOO
– Ritchie Family (Marlin)
CARRY ON, TURN ME ON/TANGO IN SPACE – Space (UA)
GOTTA GET A HOLD ON ME – Margie Alexander (Chi-sound)
HOLD TIGHT – Vicki Sue Robinson (RCA)
HYMN FOR AFRICA – Daniel Jackson Explosion (Blu import)
I'VE FOUND LOVE/ACCIDENTAL LOVER – Love & Kisses
(Casablanca)
LOCKED IN THIS POSITION – Barbara Mason & Bunny
Sigler (Curtom)
MUSIC – Montreal Sound (Smash Disco import)
OVER AND OVER/DOWN, DOWN, DOWN – Sylvester
(Fantasy)
SAN FRANCISCO/HOLLYWOOD/FIRE ISLAND – Village
People (Casablanca)

PIPPINS, NEW YORK
DJ: Reggie T Experience

AFRICAN QUEENS/QUIET VILLAGE/ VOODOO
– Ritchie Family (Marlin)
**CHOOSING YOU/ PLEASE DON'T TEMPT ME/ SHOO DOO
FU FU OOH!** – Lenny Williams (ABC)
COCOMOTION/LOVE TO THE WORLD – El Coco (AVI)
FROM HERE TO ETERNITY – Giorgio (Casablanca)
HOLD TIGHT – Vicki Sue Robinson (RCA)
IT'S ECSTASY WHEN YOU LAY DOWN NEXT TO ME –
Barry White (20th Century)
LOCKED IN THIS POSITION – Barbara Mason & Bunny
Sigler (Curtom)
PEOPLE GET UP – Mass Production (Cotillion)
PIPELINE – Bruce Johnston (Columbia)
THEME FROM BIG TIME/HIP TRIP – Smokey Robinson
(Tamla)

translated, "You've Got Nothing To Lose") is a jumpy, string-laced French song that's kinda repetitive but really attractively produced. Production, by the way, is credited to **Michael Lewis** and **Laurin Rinder**, the **El Coco** team, and "Je T'Aime" is certainly a giant step forward for them, though it remains more stunning graphically and conceptually than musically. The album's total effect (right down to the fact that all the credits are in French) would lead one to believe it's an import, but this is an American pressing, recorded in France and Los Angeles, and the first release on a new L.A. label named Butterfly. An excellent first impression for a new company. (Note: the shocking-pink vinyl is for a limited pressing, mainly for promotional purposes and first store shipments; later pressings will be on black vinyl)

After these two records, the new **Mass Production** album, "Believe" (Cotillion), sounds almost traditional, but it's far from that. The group has perfected their progressive funk style and jumped to the head of their class with their second lp. The previously released disco disc cuts, "I Believe In Music" and "People Get Up," have already been reviewed and recommended but there are two more strong tracks here, the best being a loose, wonderfully jazzy instrumental called "Cosmic Lust" (5:53) that reminds me of **Donald Byrd** and **War**. "Free And Happy" (5:20) is more in the group's aggressive, brassy, hard-edged style with great, rapid-fire vocals. Solid and serious.

ALSO RECOMMENDED: **Margie Alexander's** "Gotta Get A Hold On Me" (6:02), a disco disc on Chi-sound (through UA) that's one of those hard, down and dirty woman's songs – the best we've heard in some time. Alexander, who sings with a **Patti LaBelle/Tina Turner** fierceness, has some tough words for her no-good old man and the track is appropriately raunchy; a throw-back sound but a welcome change of pace for just that reason... "Easy Come, Easy Go" (7:01), a delightful, laid-back, West Indian-flavored number sparked by steel drums' and regal, full lead vocals from a woman who sounds like a supple combination of **Odetta** and **Cory Daye** – it's the best cut from the debut album of a trio called Odyssey (RCA). Another possibility from the same lp: "Native New Yorker" whose lyrics sound like a TV theme song but whose music and singing have just enough vitality to carry things off... "Bust It" (6:02) by **Craig Snyder** & **Lix** (Midsong International), a tight, muscular instrumental pumped up by Snyder's taut guitar playing and produced by Snyder and **John Davis**. Walter Gibbons says he prefers the other side of this disco disc pressing, a more fast-hustle, Philly-style song called "Hold Me" with a sweet female chorus and some **Benson**-like guitar. ◑

Two albums to get excited about this week: "In Full Bloom," the official debut of **Rose Royce** (Whitfield) and an import called "Watch Out!" by **Trax** (Polydor France). The Rose Royce lp proves that their phenomenal out-of-the-blue success with the "Car Wash" soundtrack was no fluke; they've inspired producer **Norman Whitfield's** best album work since his peak years with the **Temptations**. The super dance cut here is "Do Your Dance," a nine-minute piece that begins with crisp clapping reminiscent of "Car Wash" and carries the spirit of that song through its dense, vocal first half. But the second half takes off in an entirely new direction: after a section of relaxed vocal riffing, the synthesizer that could be heard threading through the arrangement earlier on comes more into the foreground, swooping like a diving bird through a spare combination of vibes and handclapping that gradually becomes fuller and more intense. The movement of the synthesizer through the piece is so unexpected and exhilarating that it clinches the production almost singlehandedly, but the variety and shift of the vocals is also impressive. The other standout cut is "It Makes You Feel Like Dancin'" (8:45), a pumping number with some **People's Choice** and **Parliament** overtones ("Feel the funk, feel the funk" they chant). This one's more "black" and boisterous than "Do Your Dance," but the sharp handclapping remains (compare "Hold Tight," "Express Yourself," "Theme from Big Time") and the vocals are again superb. Two other shorter, upbeat possibilities: "You Can't Please Everybody" and "Love, More Love." Should be an instant hit, with "Do Your Dance" doing even better on a disco level than "Car Wash."

The Trax album was recorded in Germany by **Pete Bellotte**, the other half of **Donna Summer's** production team, and makes an interesting contrast with **Giorgio's** recent work on his own. Bellotte's approach is more aggressive and hard-edged than Moroder's and while the synthesizer and other electronic devices play a key role, the effects are integrated into a more conventional instrumental context that is not as insistently spacey as Giorgio's "From Here to Eternity." Still, Bellotte and his collaborator here, **Keith Forsey**, have planted themselves very firmly in the European disco avant garde with Trax, one of the most high-energy albums produced on the continent so far this year. The strongest cut here, "Watch Out For The Boogie Man"

(14:26), fills up all of side one and features a shouting male lead vocal plus a female chorus. The vocals have a metallic quality that's emphasized as the song develops by various electronic distortion techniques without reducing it to robot level. The production is very fast-paced and bold, with the synthesizer effects especially stunning in this heavy-metal setting. "Watch Out" is finally more driving and, well, funky than most of the other extended-format European records that have come out in 1977 with the possible exception of "Get On The Funk Train," but it's missing the rich eccentricity of **Love & Kisses**. Two of the three cuts on the album's second side are also excellent: "Breathless" (5:08) and "Any Way You Want It" (5:24). Already one of the most successful imports on the disco front at the moment, Trax is being picked up by Polydor in the States for release by the end of this month.

NEWS & NOTES: **Grace Jones** has moved to Island Records where her first album, "Portfolio," a Beam Junction production, will be released the second week in September... "Erotic Soul," the fine **Larry Page Ork** instrumental, is now an American release on a London disco disc-available commercially... Philadelphia International has put out a disco disc of "Let's Clean Up the Ghetto" featuring the album cut vocal on one side and a longer (8:42) **MFSB** instrumental version on the other... **Patti LaBelle's** first solo album is due out this week on Epic... and don't expect that new **Dr. Buzzard's Original Savannah Band** lp until sometime in late September. ❂

> **" "Watch Out" is more driving and, well, funky than most of the other extended-format European records, with the possible exception of "Get on the Funk Train""**

BAREFOOT BOY, NEW YORK
DJ: Tony Smith

AFRICAN QUEENS/QUIET VILLAGE/ VOODOO – Ritchie Family (Marlin)
COCOMOTION/I'M MAD AS HELL – El Coco (AVI)
COSMIC LUST/I BELIEVE IN MUSIC – Mass Production (Cotillion)
DO YOUR DANCE – Rose Royce (Warner Bros.)
FIRST HAND EXPERIENCE/TOO HOT TO HANDLE/FROM HERE TO ETERNITY – Giorgio (Casablanca)
HOLD TIGHT –Vicki Sue Robinson (RCA)
PIPELINE – Bruce Johnston (Columbia)
PLEASE DON'T TEMPT ME – Lenny Williams (ABC)
SAN FRANCISCO/HOLLYWOOD/FIRE ISLAND – Village People (Casablanca)
YOU ARE THE MUSIC WITHIN ME – Barbara Pennington (UA)

IPANEMA, NEW YORK
DJ: Ronnie Soares

AFRICAN QUEENS/SUMMER DANCE – Ritchie Family (Marlin)
THE CHASE – MBT Soul (Polydor import)
CHOOSING YOU – Lenny Williams (ABC)
DISCO BLOOD – The Vamps (Building import)
EROTIC SOUL – Larry Page Ork (London)
FROM HERE TO ETERNITY/FIRST HAND EXPERIENCE – Giorgio (Casablanca)
HEY YOU SHOULD BE DANCING – Gene Farrow (Magnet)
PIPELINE – Bruce Johnston (Columbia)
RITMO NUMBER ONE – Paulinho do Costa (Pablo/RCA)
RUN TO ME – Kelly Marie (Pye import)

THE CLUBHOUSE, WASHINGTON, D.C.
DJ: Bryce Tarry

CARRY ON, TURN ME ON/TANGO IN SPACE – Space (UA)
DOCTOR LOVE – First Choice (Gold Mind)
EXPRESS YOURSELF – New York Community Choir (RCA)
HOLD TIGHT – Vicki Sue Robinson (RCA)
I'VE FOUND LOVE – Love & Kisses (Casablanca)
MAGIC BIRD OF FIRE – Salsoul Orchestra (Salsoul)
MISS BROADWAY – Belle Epoque (Shadybrook)
RUNNING AWAY – Roy Ayers Ubiquity (Polydor)
SWEET LUCY – Raul de Souza (Capitol)
WINGS OF FIRE – Dennis Coffey (Westbound)

CLUB SWAMP, EAST HAMPTON, N.Y.
DJ: Jeff Baugh

AFRICAN QUEENS/QUIET VILLAGE – Ritchie Family (Marlin)
CHOOSING YOU – Lenny Williams (ABC)
COCOMOTION – El Coco (AVI)
FROM HERE TO ETERNITY/TOO HOT TO HANDLE – Giorgio (Casablanca)
HOLD TIGHT – Vicki Sue Robinson (RCA)
I FEEL LOVE – Donna Summer (Casablanca)
LAND OF MAKE BELIEVE – Champs Boys Orchestra (Vogue import)
LET'S CLEAN UP THE GHETTO – Phila. Intl. All Stars (Phila. Intl.)
RUNAWAY – Salsoul Orchestra (Salsoul)
SAN FRANCISCO/HOLLYWOOD/FIRE ISLAND/ VILLAGE PEOPLE – Village People (Casablanca)

DISCO FILE TOP 20

1. **AFRICAN QUEENS/QUIET VILLAGE/VOODOO** – Ritchie Family (Marlin)
2. **HOLD TIGHT** –Vicki Sue Robinson (RCA)
3. **SAN FRANCISCO/HOLLYWOOD/FIRE ISLAND** – Village People (Casablanca)
4. **I FEEL LOVE** – Donna Summer (Casablanca)
5. **CARRY ON, TURN ME ON/TANGO IN SPACE** – Space (UA)
6. **I'VE FOUND LOVE** – Love & Kisses (Casablanca)
7. **RUNAWAY/MAGIC BIRD OF FIRE** – Salsoul Orchestra (Salsoul)
8. **CHOOSING YOU/PLEASE DON'T TEMPT ME** – Lenny Williams (ABC)
9. **PIPELINE** – Bruce Johnston (Columbia)
10. **FROM HERE TO ETERNITY/FIRST HAND EXPERIENCE/TOO HOT TO HANDLE** – Giorgio (Casablanca)
11. **THEME FROM BIG TIME** – Smokey Robinson (Tamla)
12. **DEVIL'S GUN/WE GOT OUR OWN THING** – CJ. & Co. (Westbound/Atlantic)
13. **THE MAGIC IS YOU** – John Davis & the Monster Orchestra (Sam)
14. **COCOMOTION** – El Coco (AVI)
15. **WINGS OF FIRE** – Dennis Coffey (Westbound)
16. **DOCTOR LOVE** – First Choice (Gold Mind)
17. **NOWHERE TO RUN** – Dynamic Superiors (Motown)
18. **CERRONE'S PARADISE** – Cerrone (Cotillion)
19. **GET ON THE FUNK TRAIN** – Munich Machine (Casablanca)
20. **ACCIDENTAL LOVER** – Love and Kisses (Casablanca)

FEEDBACK: John Colon, DJ at the Make-Believe Ballroom in New York, suggests flipping over the latest release from **Kaleidoscope**, "Thank You" (TSOP), and getting into the B side, "I'm a Changed Person," a pleasant, spirited number with a **Baker, Harris & Young** production similar to their work a while back with the **Whispers**. Colon is also one of a number of New York DJs who report playing "Breakaway," the instrumental side of a British Contempo import by **Ernie Bush**. According to the charts in the excellent English magazine, Blues & Soul, "Breakaway" is one of the most popular disco records in England right now, and the only British product on the magazine's Disco Dozen list. But a Blues & Soul article reveals that though the record is an English release, it was made in the States by a native of Bridgeport, Connecticut, more than a year ago and never put out. The vocal is interesting– a warning about the powers of black magic – but the instrumental is even better and worth searching out. (For the curious, Blues & Soul's most recent Disco Dozen also includes a few other songs doing much better over there than they are here: "Action Speaks Louder Than Words" by **Chocolate Milk**, "London Express" by **Oliver Sain**, **Bobby Moore's** "Call Me Your Anything Man" and "Monaurail" by **Fred & the New JBs**; number one was "Crystal World" and "Breakaway" was in second place.

Joe Palminteri, who's playing at The Monster on Fire Island (the Grove) for the summer, is enthusiastic about **Ace Spectrum's** "Keep Holding On" from their "Low Rent Rendezvous" album (Atlantic) and recently issued on the label's 12-inch disco series, same length (8:41) but effectively remixed. Reminiscent of the **Trammps'** more driving, optimistic material, "Keep Holding On" was produced by **Ed Zant**, a member of the group, and **Tony Silvester**. My only complaint: the long instrumental second half doesn't hold up to the powerful vocal half and interest falls off rapidly. Also on Palminteri's playlist: "Tell The People" and "Drive My Car," an interesting re-make of **The Beatles** song, from the new **Gary Toms Empire** album, "7-6-5-4-3-2-1 Blow Your Whistle" (PIP). We also like "Do Your Thing" from the same album, the cut Tom Savarese plays at 12 West... AJ Miller from the Paradise Ballroom in Los Angeles (which had been renamed Our Side until the Other Side disco across the street burned down recently) reports playing **Ray Charles'** version of **Stevie Wonder's** "Living For The City" (from his "Renaissance" album, on Crossover) but points out that he speeds it up and cuts out the rap; in any case, a very left field choice.

RECOMMENDED SINGLES: **Tina Charles'** "You Set My Heart On Fire" (Columbia), a **Biddu** composition and production with a classic girl group sound (down to the "bomp-shu-bomp-shu-bomps") which is already being played as an import around New York and should go even further with its instrumental B side, "Fire" (3:15); "Hustling" by the **Hustlers** (People), a **James Brown** number that, typically, has nothing to do with the Hustle as a dance, but who cares when it's this spunky?

SMOKEY ROBINSON

PR-29
STEREO

64192-D
33 1/3 RPM

"THEME FROM BIG TIME" 8:29
(W. Robinson)
Bertam Music Company (ASCAP)
PRODUCED BY WILLIAM "SMOKEY" ROBINSON
From The Album, T6-355S1 and Motion Picture "BIG TIME"
FOR DISCO USE ONLY
NOT FOR SALE
℗1977 Motown Record Corp./
Trademark Motown Record Corporation

LOST AND FOUND, WASHINGTON, D.C.
DJ: Bill Owens

EROTIC SOUL – Larry Page Ork (London)
FROM HERE TO ETERNITY/FIRST HAND EXPERIENCE – Giorgio (Casablanca)
HOLD TIGHT – Vicki Sue Robinson (RCA)
JE T'AIME/ON A RIEN A PERDRE/ COEUR A COEUR – Saint Tropez (Butterfly)
NATIVE NEW YORKER/EASY COME, EASY GO – Odyssey (RCA)
QUIET VILLAGE/AFRICAN QUEENS/SUMMER DANCE – Ritchie Family (Marlin)
RUNAWAY/ MAGIC BIRD OF FIRE – Salsoul Orchestra (Salsoul)
RUN TO ME – Kelly Marie (Pye import)
SAN FRANCISCO/HOLLYWOOD/FIRE ISLAND – Village People (Casablanca)
THEME FROM BIG TIME – Smokey Robinson (Tamla)

CASABLANCA II, NEW YORK
DJ: Jorge Wheeler

THE CHASE – MBT Soul (Polydor import)
FIRE ISLAND – Village People (Casablanca)
FROM HERE TO ETERNITY/FIRST HAND EXPERIENCE – Giorgio (Casablanca)
I'VE FOUND LOVE – Love & Kisses (Casablanca)
MAGIC FLY – Kebekelektrik (TK)
NOWHERE TO RUN – Dynamic Superiors (Motown)
QUIET VILLAGE/ VOODOO/SUMMER DANCE – Ritchie Family (Marlin)
THEME FROM BIG TIME – Smokey Robinson (Tamla)
THEME FROM DISCO 77 – Sassy (TK)
WE GOT OUR OWN THING – C.J. & Co. (Westbound)

LES MOUCHES, NEW YORK
DJ: Joel Jacobs

AFRICAN QUEENS/QUIET VILLAGE – Ritchie Family (Marlin)
THE CHASE – MBT Soul (Polydor import)
FROM HERE TO ETERNITY – Giorgio (Casablanca)
HOLD TIGHT –Vicki Sue Robinson (RCA)
I FEEL LOVE – Donna Summer (Casablanca)
I'VE FOUND LOVE/ACCIDENTAL LOVER – Love & Kisses (Casablanca)
MA BAKER – Boney M (Atlantic)
SAN FRANCISCO/HOLLYWOOD/FIRE ISLAND/VILLAGE PEOPLE – Village People (Casablanca)
SPIRIT OF SUNSHINE – Chuck Davis Orchestra (West End)
WATCH OUT FOR THE BOOGIE MAN – Trax (Polydor import)

FACES, CHICAGO
DJ: Carmen Adduci

AFRICAN QUEENS/QUIET VILLAGE/ VOODOO – Ritchie Family (Marlin)
CARRY ON, TURN ME ON/TANGO IN SPACE – Space (UA)
FIRE ISLAND/SAN FRANCISCO/HOLLYWOOD – Village People (Casablanca)
FROM HERE TO ETERNITY – Giorgio (Casablanca)
I'VE FOUND LOVE – Love & Kisses (Casablanca)
LIVING FOR TODAY – Jimmy Briscoe & the Little Beavers (TK)
SUPERDANCE – Bus Connection (CBS import)
TWO HOT FOR LOVE – THP Orchestra (RCA import)
WATCH OUT FOR THE BOOGIE MAN – Trax (Polydor import)
YOU ARE THE MUSIC WITHIN ME – Barbara Pennington (UA)

– a steal from **Van McCoy's** "Disco Baby" cut, but wonderfully funked-up; "Oh Baby" by **Wayne Miranda and Rush Release** (Roulette), with a 4:25 long version and an easy, smooth hustle sound much like **Bobby Moore's**; "All I Need" by **Anacostia** (Columbia), another fine **Baker, Harris & Young** production with a nice upbeat; **Jeanne Burton's** "(Nobody Loves Me) Like You Do" (Cotton), "arranged, produced and conducted under the influence of S.O.N.N.Y. (Sound of New New York)" – **Sonny Casella**, that is – and, in two parts that together run nearly five and a half minutes, an elaborate and rather impressive job try the mostly instrumental Part 2 first; "Samson" by **Ebony, Ivory & Jade** (Columbia), a cautionary tale with a loud, over-gimmicky but finally quite terrific production by the DCA group, **Tony Bongiovi, Meco Monardo** & **Jay Ellis**; the **Ghetto Children's** "Don't Take Your Sweet Lovin' Away" (Roulette), with a tight Philly production by **Bobby Martin** and a co-producer; and, for those of your not already tired of **AWB**-style instrumentals, "Gimme The Key" by session man **Bobby Keys** (Ring O), released to discos in a special 4:06 version. Now available: "Summer of '42" by the **Biddu Orchestra** (Epic) and the **Sunshine Band's** fine instrumental, "Shotgun Shuffle" (TK), which had never been officially released and promoted before. ⊘

❝ AJ Miller from the Paradise Ballroom in Los Angeles reports playing Ray Charles' version of Stevie Wonder's "Living For The City" but points out that he speeds it up and cuts out the rap; in any case, a very left field choice ❞

SEPTEMBER 3, 1977

NEWS & NOTES: TK has announced that sales of **Peter Brown's** disco disc of "Do You Wanna Get Funky With Me" have reached the million dollar mark, according to the company, making it the first disco disc to achieve gold record status since the format was introduced commercially a little more than a year ago. We're excited about this not just because "Do You Wanna Get Funky" is one of our favorite records of the year so far, but because it establishes a precedent, a goal for others to strive toward. The disco disc field has endured more than its share of skepticism and resistance from both record companies and retailers; and the fact that nearly everyone in the business has approached the disco disc as a fad rather than a true commercial phenomenon has certainly kept the format from realizing its full potential. But now that the field has its first gold record, maybe some attitudes will change. Disco discs deserve to be taken seriously, both commercially and artistically – the consumer already knows it and the success of Peter Brown proves it... For the second week in a row, producer **Jacques Morali** not only holds down the top two spots on the DISCO FILE Top 20 – "African Queens" and "Quiet Village" by the **Ritchie Family** followed by "San Francisco/ Hollywood" and "Fire Island" by **Village People** – but with the addition of the "Village People" cut to the chart this week, right below the Ritchie Family's "Voodoo" and "Summer Dance," both Morali-produced albums are now represented on the top half of the list in their entirety. An unprecedented sweep. **Donna Summer's** production team isn't doing so bad either, with **Giorgio Moroder's** "From Here To Eternity," probably the hottest record on the chart right now, pushing up strong from the number three spot; **Pete Bellotte** (who, along with **Keith Forsey**, is **Trax**) at 14 with "Watch Out For The Boogie Man" and their production for Summer, "I Feel Love," still riding high at number six, buoyed by the recent release of the longer disco disc version... Most tantalizing rumor this week: Casablanca, already the disco label of the moment, is planning to release another Donna Summer disco disc within the week. The song: "Je T'Aime," recently remade by **Saint Tropez**, but certainly an inevitable choice for Summer. Donna had, in fact, recorded her own version of "Je T'Aime" with Giorgio at the end of last year and there was talk for a while about putting it out as a special valentine package, but it was shelved. Now, reportedly, the song's been redone for the Casablanca/ Motown disco film

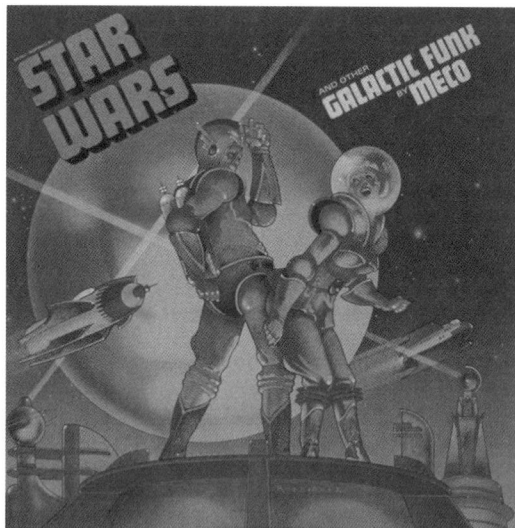

currently in production in Los Angeles, "Thank God It's Friday," and it's this new Moroder-Bellotte version that's slated for release. Should be very steamy...

COMING ON STRONG: **Meco's** "Star Wars" (Millennium) which is finally beginning to grow on me – it's already top five on a lot of club playlists we've been seeing recently; "Music" by **Montreal Sound**, one of the summer's wildest records, now available on a TK disco disc; and both "Native New Yorker" and "Easy Come, Easy Go" by **Odyssey** which RCA has released back-to-back on a disco disc. Also coming up from left field: **Margie Alexander's** "Gotta Get A Hold On Me" (Chi-sound/UA).

ALBUM OF THE MOMENT: "Cosmic Wind" by the **Mike Theodore Orchestra** (Westbound), test pressings of which have spread coast to coast in the past week, building up quite a pitch of excitement prior to its official release date September 6. The album, already represented by various cuts on three out of four top 10 lists this week, is one of the best disco orchestra collections this year and was produced, arranged and written by Mike Theodore, **Dennis Coffey's** partner on the production side of the **C.J. & Co.** album. Though there are flashes of the C.J. & Co. sound here, the music

> **❝Sales of "Do You Wanna Get Funky With Me" have reached the million dollar mark, making it the first disco disc to achieve gold record status since the format was introduced commercially❞**

THE COCKRING, NEW YORK
DJ: Howard Merritt

AFRICAN QUEENS/QUIET VILLAGE – Ritchie Family (Marlin)
DOCTOR LOVE –First Choice (Gold Mind)
EROTIC SOUL – Larry Page Ork (London)
FROM HERE TO ETERNITY – Giorgio (Casablanca)
I FEEL LOVE – Donna Summer (Casablanca)
IT'S ECSTASY WHEN YOU LAY DOWN NEXT TO ME – Barry White (20th Century)
I'VE FOUND LOVE – Love & Kisses (Casablanca)
LOVIN' IS REALLY MY GAME – Brainstorm (Tabu)
PLEASE DON'T LET ME BE MISUNDERSTOOD – Santa Esmerelda (Philips import)
SAN FRANCISCO/HOLLYWOOD/FIRE ISLAND/VILLAGE PEOPLE – Village People (Casablanca)

HARRISON SQUARE, MIAMI
DJ: Aristides Jacobs

AGE OF THE SHOWDOWN/BACK IN LOVE AGAIN/YOU COME FIRST AT LAST – L.T.D. (A&M)
CHOOSING YOU – Lenny Williams (ABC)
COSMIC WIND/BRAZILIAN LULLABY/I LOVE THE WAY YOU MOVE – Mike Theodore Orchestra (Westbound)
DO YOUR DANCE – Rose Royce (Warner Bros.)
FROM HERE TO ETERNITY – Giorgio (Casablanca)
HEY YOU SHOULD BE DANCING – Gene Farrow (UA import)
NATIVE NEW YORKER – Odyssey (RCA)
ON A RIEN A PERDRE/COUER A COEUR – Saint Tropez (Butterfly)
SPACE DISCO/SUNSHINE – Universal Robot Band (Red Greg)
STAR WARS – Meco (Millennium)

WHIMSEY'S, BOSTON
DJ: John Luongo

COSMIC WIND/THE BULL – Mike Theodore Orchestra (Westbound)
IT MAKES YOU FEEL LIKE DANCIN'/DO YOUR DANCE – Rose Royce (Warner Bros.)
I'VE FOUND LOVE – Love & Kisses (Casablanca)
LASO SQUARE – LaSo (MCA)
MUSIC – Montreal Sound (TK)
NATIVE NEW YORKER/EASY COME, EASY GO – Odyssey (RCA)
ON A RIEN A PERDRE/LA SYMPHONIE AFRICAINE – Saint Tropez (Butterfly)
OVER AND OVER – Sylvester (Fantasy)
SAN FRANCISCO/FIRE ISLAND/VILLAGE PEOPLE – Village People (Casablanca)
STAR WARS – Meco (Millennium)

RUBAIYAT, ANN ARBOR, MICHIGAN
DJ: Karl Uruski

COSMIC WIND/THE BULL – Mike Theodore Orchestra (Westbound)
DOCTOR LOVE/CHANCES GO AROUND – First Choice (Gold Mind)
FIRE ISLAND/SAN FRANCISCO – Village People (Casablanca)
FROM HERE TO ETERNITY – Giorgio (Casablanca)
GOTTA GET A HOLD ON ME – Margie Alexander (Chi-sound)
HOLD TIGHT – Vicki Sue Robinson (RCA)
MOVE YOUR BODY – Denise LaSalle (ABC)
MUSIC – Montreal Sound (TK)
QUIET VILLAGE/VOODOO/ AFRICAN QUEENS – Ritchie Family (Marlin)
SUNSHINE – Universal Robot Band (Red Greg)

DISCO FILE TOP 20

1. **AFRICAN QUEENS/QUIET VILLAGE** – Ritchie Family (Marlin)
2. **SAN FRANCISCO/HOLLYWOOD/FIRE ISLAND** – Village People (Casablanca)
3. **FROM HERE TO ETERNITY/FIRST HAND EXPERIENCE** – Giorgio (Casablanca)
4. **HOLD TIGHT** –Vicki Sue Robinson (RCA)
5. **I'VE FOUND LOVE** – Love & Kisses (Casablanca)
6. **I FEEL LOVE** – Donna Summer (Casablanca)
7. **THEME FROM BIG TIME** – Smokey Robinson (Tamla)
8. **VOODOO/SUMMER DANCE** – Ritchie Family (Marlin)
9. **VILLAGE PEOPLE** – Village People (Casablanca)
10. **CHOOSING YOU/PLEASE DON'T TEMPT ME** – Lenny Williams (ABC)
11. **EROTIC SOUL** – Larry Page Ork (London)
12. **PIPELINE** – Bruce Johnston (Columbia)
13. **CARRY ON, TURN ME ON/TANGO IN SPACE** – Space (UA)
14. **WATCH OUT FOR THE BOOGIE MAN** – Trax (Polydor import)
15. **COCOMOTION** – El Coco (AVI)
16. **RUNAWAY/MAGIC BIRD OF FIRE** – Salsoul Orchestra (Salsoul)
17. **DOCTOR LOVE** – First Choice (Gold Mind)
18. **ACCIDENTAL LOVER** – Love and Kisses (Casablanca)
19. **WE GOT OUR OWN THING** – C.J. & Co. (Westbound)
20. **THE MAGIC IS YOU** – John Davis & the Monster Orchestra (Sam)

eludes categories or established styles, making occasional bows to the influences of the **Salsoul Orchestra** or the **Ritchie Family** (particularly in "Brazilian Lullaby," "I Love The Way You Move" and "Ain't Nothing To It"), but maintaining an utterly original approach. The most successful tracks are "The Bull" (6:33), which has a terrific Latin percussion intro and is outstanding for the wonderful textural contrast created by the horns and the strings sweeping against and echoing one another, wave on wave (it also brings back fond memories of "The Mexican" by **Babe Ruth**) and "Cosmic Wind" (6:58), a spectacularly varied and involving production that envelops you in a dream-like environment – a mysterious space trip you don't want to end. "Belly Boogie" is also attractive but it invites the comparison to **Silver Convention's** "Get Up And Boogie" a little too obviously; happily, however, it overcomes the comparison with some sharp breaks. All together, this is an album without a single waste track and if the initial response is any indication, it's going to be a major chart contender in the next few months. ✺

New disco releases have been coming hot and heavy in the past two weeks, anticipating the back-to-serious-business fall season, and in an attempt to catch up an this vinyl avalanche, we're skimming the cream off the top in a capsule run-down of the essential records to pick up an right now.

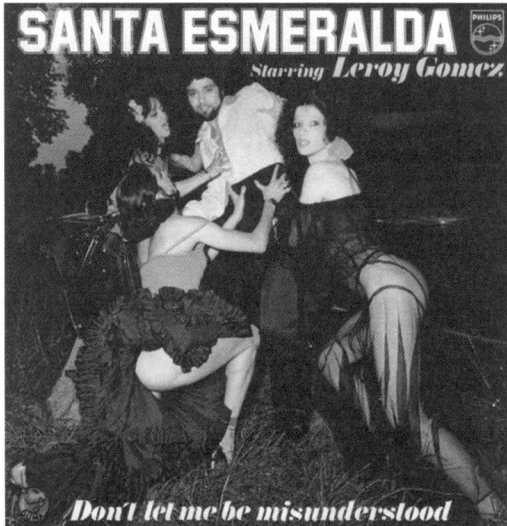

SANTA ESMERALDA *Starring Leroy Gomez*

Don't let me be misunderstood

RECOMMENDED ALBUMS: Our favorite new import is **Santa Esmeralda's** "Don't Let Me Be Misunderstood" on Philips whose title track is a 16-minute version of the **Animals** hit done in a vibrant flamenco disco style. Lead singer **Leroy Gomez**, pictured on the album cover enjoying the cat-like advances of three gypsy women, has more vocal presence than **Cerrone** or **Alec Costandinos** (on "I've Found Love") though the production here is very much in the style those performer/producers have developed and, with **Giorgio Moroder** and **Pete Bellotte**, brought to a position of virtual dominance of the disco sound this year. The touches that give "Misunderstood" its particular attraction are the flamenco guitar, sizzling Spanish-style horns and a fine hand-clapping intro, but it's the vocals and the familiarity of the original material that could turn this record into one of the biggest crossover-to-pop disco releases of the year. The album's side two contains a version of another rock classic, "Gloria," and a song called "Black Pot" that has a **Barrabas** feel to it – nothing to really divert your attention from the first side. The French import is doing extremely well already – popping up an top 10 lists wherever it's played – so it should come as no surprise that Casablanca, prime purveyor of the European disco sound, has picked this one up far American release; should be available by the end of the month... Producer **Simon Soussan** (who hit big first time out with **Shalamar's** "Uptown Festival") has came up with a fine American interpretation of the Euro-disco style far the debut of singer **Pattie Brooks** ("Love Shook" an Casablanca). Brooks, reportedly one of **Donna Summer's**

back-up singers, has a supple, light voice and Soussan's arrangements give her the backbone she needs. Of the four cuts here, two are outstanding – "Let's Make Love To The Music" (8:45) and "Girl Dan't Make Me Wait" (10:50) – and the remaining two are nearly as strong: the bouncy title tune and a "Pop Collage Medley" of "Popcorn," "Black Is Black" and "Na Na Hey Hey Kiss Him Goodbye" that is a minor "Uptown Festival" and might be more interesting if much of the material hadn't already been covered repeatedly for disco. The **Simon Orchestra**, also debuting here, includes a number of hot west coast studio musicians plus **El Coco** producers **Michael Lewis** and **Lauren Rinder**; and the executive producers, aside from Soussan and wife, are three Las Angeles disco DJs, Paul Dougan, Elton Ahi and Tony Miller. So expect this one to pick up in LA first and spread fast... **Barry White's** "It's Ecstasy When You Lay Down Next To Me" is shaping up as his strongest disco record as a performer in years and it's the seven-minute centerpiece of his latest album, "Barry White Sings for Someone You Love" (20th Century). Unfortunately, the whole album doesn't share in the revitalized style of "It's Ecstasy," but even the trademark lush-and-dreamy Barry White sound feels fresher this time around and at least one other track – "You're So Good, You're Bad" – has that irresistible sweetly raunchy quality that always got White over in the past... Two pleasant disco-style mood music albums: "Erotic Soul" by the **Larry Page Orchestra** (London, due out this week), featuring the long version of the title cut and several other sturdy, danceable instrumentals (try "Chasing," "Tokyo Melody" and "Touch," the last very Barry White) – an improvement over the original Canadian lp release which contained two filler remakes; and "The Sensuous Sounds Of **Silvetti**" performing "Spring Rain" (Salsoul), a much stronger album than his first American release because

HIS COMPANY, PHOENIX
DJ, Jack Witherby
COCOMOTION – El Coco (AVI)
COSMIC WIND/THE BULL/BELLYBOOGIE – Mike Theodore Orchestra (Westbound)
DANCE, DANCE, DANCE – Chic (Buddah)
FIRE ISLAND/SAN FRANCISCO/ HOLLYWOOD – Village People (Casablanca)
FROM HERE TO ETERNITY/TOO HOT TO HANDLE – Giorgio (Casablanca)
HEY, YOU SHOULD BE DANCING – Gene Farrow (UA import)
JE T'AIME/VIOLATION/ON A RIEN A PERDRE – Saint Tropez (Butterfly)
MUSIC – Montreal Sound (TK)
NATIVE NEW YORKER/EASY COME, EASY GO – Odyssey (RCA)
SPEAK WELL – Philly USA (West End)

ROBERT'S, SAN JOSE, CALIFORNIA
DJ: Jose Martinez
AFRICAN QUEENS/QUIET VILLAGE – Ritchie Family (Marlin)
EROTIC SOUL – Larry Page Ork (London)
FROM HERE TO ETERNITY/FIRST HAND EXPERIENCE – Giorgio (Casablanca)
JE T'AIME/ON A RIEN A PERDRE – Saint Tropez (Butterfly)
MAKE IT SOON/LET THE MUSIC PLAY – Dorothy Moore (Malaca)
MUSIC – Montreal Sound (TK)
OVER AND OVER – Sylvester (Fantasy)
SAN FRANCISCO/HOLLYWOOD/FIRE ISLAND – Village People (Casablanca)
THEME FROM BIG TIME – Smokey Robinson (Tamla)
WATCH OUT FOR THE BOOGIE MAN – Trax (Polydor import)

REGINES, NEW YORK
DJ: Jonata Garavaglia
CHOOSING YOU – Lenny Williams (ABC)
COCOMOTION – El Coco (AVI)
FROM HERE TO ETERNITY – Giorgio (Casablanca)
I GOT TO HAVE YOUR LOVE – Fantastic Four (Westbound/Atlantic)
IT'S ECSTASY WHEN YOU LAY DOWN NEXT TO ME – Barry White (20th Century)
LA VIE EN ROSE – Grace Jones (Island)
MUSIC – Montreal Sound (TK)
NATIVE NEW YORKER/EASY COME, EASY GO – Odyssey (RCA)
PLEASE DON'T LET ME BE MISUNDERSTOOD – Santa Esmeralda (Philips import)
WHAT AM I TO DO – Ralph Graham (RCA)

SAHARA, NEW YORK
DJ: Ellen Bogen
FIRE ISLAND/SAN FRANCISCO/ HOLLYWOOD/ VILLAGE PEOPLE – Village People (Casablanca)
FROM HERE TO ETERNITY/FIRST HAND EXPERIENCE – Giorgio (Casablanca)
HOLD TIGHT – Vicki Sue Robinson (RCA)
I FEEL LOVE – Donna Summer (Casablanca)
IT'S ECSTASY WHEN YOU LAY DOWN NEXT TO ME – Barry White (20th Century)
JE T'AIME/COEUR A COEUR/ VIOLATION – Saint Tropez (Butterfly)
NATIVE NEW YORKER/EASY COME, EASY GO – Odyssey (RCA disco disc)
PLEASE DON'T LET ME BE MISUNDERSTOOD – Santa Esmeralda (Philips import)
QUIET VILLAGE – Ritchie Family (Marlin)
SPEAK WELL – Philly USA (West End)

this time the title cut, included in its 5:52 version, sets the mood very effectively; best of the new material: "Primitive Man," which is excellent, "Voyage Of No Return" and "Contigo."

RECOMMENDED DISCO DISCS: **Donna Summer's** version of "Je T'Aime" is available now on Casablanca, rushed out to compete with the already successful **Saint Tropez** version of the French pillow talk classic, and the First Lady of (Explicit) Love has protected her turf in exquisite style. Like the Saint Tropez interpretation, Donna's is constructed in two sections, the second more upbeat and insistent than the first, but Summer's Moroder-Bellatte production is more consistently up and more richly textured – at 15:50 it's also more than twice as long. The sound is very "Spring Affair/Summer Fever": sinuous horns, luscious strings, breathy vocals. The transition between the first and second parts ofthe song is particularly good: an electronic kind of morse code that swirls into a brittle, stacatto stick percussion and gradually becomes enveloped in the full arrangement again. Watch this one soar... Far all the people who've been looking for more strong male vocal records, there's the new **Fantastic Four** disc, "I Got To Have Your Love" (Westbound/Atlantic), produced in part by **Dennis Coffey** and just bursting with energy. The sound is classic tight r&b – aggressive, tough vocals with a beat to match – given a fine contemporary polish and a terrific "breakdown": the kind of record we've been missing... Another power-packed record is **Joe Simon's** "One Step At A Time" (Spring), driven by Simon's distinctive big voice and a stunning **Teddy Randazzo** production full of pounding drum rolls and crashing strings. Simon rides the music with a mighty vocal – anyone else would have been swamped – clinching his most satisfying disco entry so far. Spring pressed up a batch of promotional copies of the disc on golden yellow vinyl, 5:33 on one side, 3:39 (same length as the single) on the other... **Anthony White** is back with a version of **Otis Redding's** knockout "I Can't Turn You Loose" (Salsoul) which producer **Earl Young** has interpreted in a chunky hard-disco style. The vocal is ok in a rough-and-Redding way but it's the instrumental version an the other side, titled "Black Party" and credited to **Baker, Harris and Young**, that seems to be getting most of the attention right now. At 5:46, "Block Party" is an energetic number that comes across like a **Trammps** instrumental – extremely well-crafted, with a disco mix by **Walter Gibbons**, but I'm not sure about the percussion break toward the end which is abrupt and slightly off-putting – very much like that controversial break in "Theme From Big Time": if the crowd is up enough, they'll push right through it, otherwise, it could prove difficult. In any case, both sides grow on you and both are picking up last. NOTE: **Smokey Robinson's** "Theme From Big Time" has been remixed to eliminate that difficult break and the new 8:29 version released for promotional use by Motown; and **Roy Ayers'** "Running Away," a favorite of ours, is now available in a much longer version (6:57) from Polydor – both highly recommended disco discs. ✺

RECOMMENDED DISCO DISCS: By far the best new 12-inch pressing this week is **Chic's** "Dance, Dance, Dance (Yowsah, Yowsah, Yowsah)" (Buddah), one of the most perfect, elegantly functional dance records this year. The production is precise, polished, uncomplicated yet surprisingly thrilling: surging with violins, pulsing to a tight, intertwined guitar/drum line. The vocals are simple but glowing with occasional exclamations of "Yowsah, yowsah, yowsah" that recall the yells of encouragement at dance marathons. The overall feeling is somehow relaxed and invigorating at the same time – the ideal combination for a dance record you'll never get tired of – and the disco mix was done by **Tom Savarese**, who ended the track with a spare vocal/hand-clap/drum-thump segment that gradually breaks down the pace and is designed to mix into or over just about anything the DJ wants to play next. Advance copies of the record are doing extremely well (Christine Matuchek from Buzzby's in San Francisco listed hers in the club's top 10 this week) and Buddah promises promotional copies will be available to DJs this week with a commercial disco disc to follow. Executive producer here is disco promo man Marc Kreiner – looks like he's got a hot one... One of the records that has grown on me in the past few weeks is "Speak Well" by **Philly USA** (West End), which has become something of a DJ favorite and should get even more popular now that mixmaster Tom Moulton has revamped the original disc. The new version runs 7:33, a bit longer than necessary here, but it gives the song just the kick it needed to put the cute but rather lazy girl vocals across. The vocal side contains a rather fabulous extended put-down of a man who put the singer's business "out in the street" (in the course of which she advises, "It's not the size of your pencil, but how well you write with it (that counts)") and the new version flips to an instrumental side, "Instrumentally Speaking" (5:45) that's quite strong. This new mix will presumably replace the earlier pressing (which had long and short versions back to back) and should be commercially available soon... The **Johnny King Band's** "Show Me What You're Made Of" (RCA) is a cover of a British single released earlier this year by a group named **Mista Charge** and the main thing it has going for it is a catchy, insistent horn/vocal phrase that opens the record and hooks you right off. At just over 12 minutes, this cute hook is very nearly run into the ground before the song is half over (does everything have to be long these days?), but the band throws in enough variations along the way to keep our interest for the bulk of the record... Sam Records had **John Davis** remix an Italian record by the **Daniel Jackson Explosion** – a two-sided disc containing "Cinderella (Queen Of The Dance)" and "Hymn For Africa" – and this new version of the record that has already attracted some interest as an import (primarily because of its sexy cover, which has been retained) is now available here. Davis' new mix is doubtless an improvement on the original but neither version is especially inventive or inspired; it's pleasant and pretty musically – "Cinderella" has a good repeated horn motif and nice swirling horns – but the vocals are without spark. Both sides do, however, have their moments – "Africa" gets into some good riffing toward the end – and are well worth checking into... **Ann C. Sheridan's** "Sing It Low" (RCA) was recorded in France and has a haunting, laid-back quality that's hard to resist after a few playings. The vocals are repetitive, chant-like and breathy, the music mellow, breezy: a sweet cream-puff of a record, with a vocal side (5:45)

❝ The disco mix was done by Tom Savarese, who ended the track with a spare vocal/hand-clap/drum-thump segment that breaks down the pace and is designed to mix into or over just about anything the DJ wants to play next ❞

HIPPOPOTAMUS, NEW YORK
DJ: Rich Pampinella

COSMIC WIND/THE BULL/I LOVE THE WAY YOU MOVE
– Mike Theodore Orchestra (Westbound)
HEY, YOU SHOULD BE DANCING – Gene Farrow (Magnet)
I GOT TO HAVE YOUR LOVE – Fantastic Four
(Westbound/Atlantic)
MUSIC – Montreal Sound (TK)
NATIVE NEW YORKER – Odyssey (RCA)
ON A RIEN A PERDRE/COEUR A COEUR – Saint Tropez
(Butterfly)
POP COLLAGE/GIRL DON'T MAKE ME WAIT – Pattie
Brooks (Casablanca)
SAN FRANCISCO/HOLLYWOOD/FIRE ISLAND – Village
People (Casablanca)
STONE FOX CHASE – Charlie McCoy (Monument import)
WHAT'S YOUR NAME, WHAT'S YOUR NUMBER – Andrea
True Connection (Buddah)

RESURRECTION, NEW YORK
DJ: Toraino "Tee" Scott

CHOOSING YOU/PLEASE DON'T TEMPT ME
– Lenny Williams (ABC)
DAN SWIT ME/FUNKY MUSIC – Patti LaBelle (Epic)
DO YOUR DANCE – Rose Royce (Warner Bros.)
I GOT TO HAVE YOUR LOVE – Fantastic Four
(Westbound/Atlantic)
IT'S ECSTASY WHEN YOU LAY DOWN NEXT TO ME –
Barry White (20th Century)
LET'S GO ALL THE WAY (DOWN)
– Brenda & the Tabulations (Chocolate City)
MUSIC – Montreal Sound (TK)
MY FIRST MISTAKE – Chi-lites (Mercury)
RUNNING AWAY – Roy Ayers (Ubiquity Polydor)
SAN FRANCISCO – Village People (Casablanca)

BUZZBY'S, SAN FRANCISCO
DJ: Christine Matuchek

BLOCK PARTY/I CAN'T TURN YOU LOOSE
– Anthony White (Salsoul)
COSMIC WIND/THE BULL/ BELLY BOOGIE
– Mike Theodore Orchestra (Westbound)
DANCE, DANCE, DANCE – Chic (Buddah)
DON'T LET ME BE MISUNDERSTOOD – Santa Esmeralda
(Philips import)
GIRL DON'T MAKE ME WAIT/LOVE SHOOK/POP COLLAGE
– Pattie Brooks (Casablanca)
HEY, YOU SHOULD BE DANCING – Gene Farrow (UA import)
I GOT TO HAVE YOUR LOVE – Fantastic Four (Westbound)
IT'S ECSTASY WHEN YOU LAY DOWN NEXT TO ME –
Barry White (20th Century)
MAMBO #5 – Samba Soul (RCA)
MUSIC – Montreal Sound (TK)

CIRCUS MAXIMUS, LOS ANGELES
DJ: Mike Lewis

AFRICAN QUEENS – Ritchie Family (Marlin)
BLOCK PARTY – Anthony White (Salsoul)
COCOMOTION – El Coco (AVI)
DON'T LET ME BE MISUNDERSTOOD – Santa Esmeralda
(Philips import)
EROTIC SOUL – Larry Page Orchestra (London disco disc)
HEY, YOU SHOULD BE DANCING – Gene Farrow (UA)
JE T'AIME/SYMPHONY AFRICAINE – Saint Tropez
(Butterfly)
MUSIC – Montreal Sound (TK)
PIPELINE – Bruce Johnson (Columbia)
SAN FRANCISCO/HOLLYWOOD/FIRE ISLAND – Village
People (Casablanca)

and an instrumental side (5:30), though there's very little difference between the two.

RECOMMENDED SINGLES: **Gene Farrow's** "Hey, You Should Be Dancing," whose Magnet import version was appearing on top 10 lists here and there all summer, is out now on UA as a 45 with a disco disc to follow soon. The record, which went on the DISCO FILE Top 20 this week at number 11, is a hard-party song with a relentless drive and a very simple, at times, monotonous, structure: pop disco at its most unpretentious. The instrumental side of the single is studded with percussion effects that keep the basic pattern from becoming too tedious and the concentration of energy here (at 3:14) is terrific. **Hot Butter** has recorded a cover version of the record now out on a Dynamo disco disc that is not as sharp and cutting as Farrow's but, at 5:13, is certainly a lot more monotonous; the B side is marked "track without lead vocal" and doesn't add anything new to make up for what was subtracted. Stick to the original... The 45 edit of **Giorgio's** magnificent "From Here to Eternity" (Casablanca) is out now and begins differently from the lp version, with that synthesized "voice" over only a zigzagging electronic pulse that runs from speaker to speaker and might be blended into the album cut for a change of pace.

RECOMMENDED ALBUM: If you're as mesmerized by the total-synthesizer sound as so many people are right now, get a hold of **Jean Michel Jarre's** "Oxygene," a six-part electronic symphony recorded in Paris and just released here by Polydor. It's already been a major success in France and the haunting, mysterious Part II (8:10) might catch on here with crowds who were into "I Robot" and "Anambra."

Coming on strong on playlists this week: "I Got To Have Your Love" by the **Fantastic Four** (Westbound/ Atlantic-with an album due the first week in October); **Anthony White's** "Block Party" (Salsoul); **Gene Farrow's** "Hey, You Should Be Dancing" (UA); "Cosmic Wind" and "The Bull" by the **Mike Theodore Orchestra** (Westbound); "It's Ecstasy When You Lay Down Next to Me" by **Barry White** (20th Century); and the entire **Pattie Brooks** album on Casablanca (especially "Girl Don't Make Me Wait" and "Pop Collage"). ✪

OCTOBER 1, 1977

RECORDS OF THE WEEK: It's been rumored for some time now that the next **Diana Ross** album was going to be, depending on who told you, "all disco" or "very disco" – a bow to the audience that made "Love Hangover" such a smash. But "Baby It's Me," just out on Motown, is hardly that; instead it's an elegant, highly polished pop record under the direction of the elegant, highly polished pop producer **Richard Perry** (whose previous credits include **Carly Simon**, **Barbra Streisand**, **Ringo Starr** and **Harry Nilsson**). However, if there's no new "Love Hangover" here, the album is not without its attractions for the disco crowd. Prime cut: "You're Love Is So Good for Me," at 4:14 the longest track on the record and the hottest; Diana soars, effortlessly over a tight, chugging track punched along by horns and occasional synthesizer accents – completely irresistible and one of the few records around that actually deserves to be twice as long as it is. "Top Of The World" (3:06) is equally joyous but in a slightly lower key (the short break or prancing violins is especially nice) and "Getting' Ready For Love" (2:45) is cute pop fluff, very bouncy and reminiscent of the early **Supremes** B sides. Ross doesn't break any new ground here but she gets over just the same; "You're Love Is So Good For Me" could happen big in the next few weeks... **Thelma Houston's** new single, "I'm Here Again," the first taste of her forthcoming Tamla album, "The Devil In Me" (due sometime in October), is an obvious but thoroughly enjoyable copy of "Don't Leave Me This Way," right down to the shouted "baby!" that signals the break, only in this case the producers are **Brenda** and **Michael B. Sutton** instead of **Hal Davis**. Such a close follow-up deprives us of the excitement of something genuinely new, but the record is so good it's impossible to complain for long. Houston, of course, sounds superb, especially in the final section over a tight guitar, piano and sheets of strings. At just under four minutes, the single goes through two shifts in pace, each time speeding up a notch until it fairly races in the end. While we're all waiting for the album version, this could be one of the most essential disco singles of the year... Another strong single is "Dance Craze" by **New Image** (on Cat, one of the many TK labels), a dense, churning pop funk record that **Cory Wade** has remixed. The message: "Get out of your seat, move your feet, generate some body heat," delivered in feverish male vocals. It's just 3:35 but it's power-packed... The **Love Committee** has a new Gold Mind disco disc, the best side of which is already on two New York top 10s this week: both Tony Smith and Tony Carrasco picked "Where Will It End" (7:40), a message song produced by **Baker, Harris & Young** that sounds like a combination of the **Temptations** (the group has a great **Eddie Kendricks**-style falsetto) and the **Trammps**. The lyrics are more sharply pointed than many other recent this-whole-world-is-so-messed-up songs and the pessimism is underlined by ticking time-bomb and explosion at the end, but as always the feeling is up and invigorating – a happy song about an unhappy situation. The production is classic Philadelphia, one of the best examples of the genre this year, with a great intro and break; plus, this is "A Walter Gibbons Mix."

FEEDBACK: Two albums that are getting a lot of favorable comment from DJs right now are **Syreeta & G.C. Cameron's** "Rich Love, Poor Love" (Motown) and "Smooth Talk" by' **Evelyn "Champagne" King** (RCA). The title song from Syreeta and G.C.'s album, the one that's picking up the most reaction, reminds me of those great uplifting love duets **Ashford & Simpson** wrote for **Marvin Gaye** and **Tammi Terrell** but **Michael Smith's** production is rather inflated at just over six minutes and it kind of drags in the end. Conversely, "Let's Make A Deal" (5:09) is better in the second half when it picks up the fine introductory guitar, vocal, half. In both cases, however, the singing is terrific – one of Motown's better combinations. Evelyn King is only 16 but she has a vigorous, supple voice that shines through beautifully on her debut album. The production is competent, even classy at times, but it never quite gets past being merely stylish. With these reservations, there are still some cuts to recommend: "Shame," "Smooth Talk" (the two that seem to be getting the most attention), and "Dancin', Dancin', Dancin'."

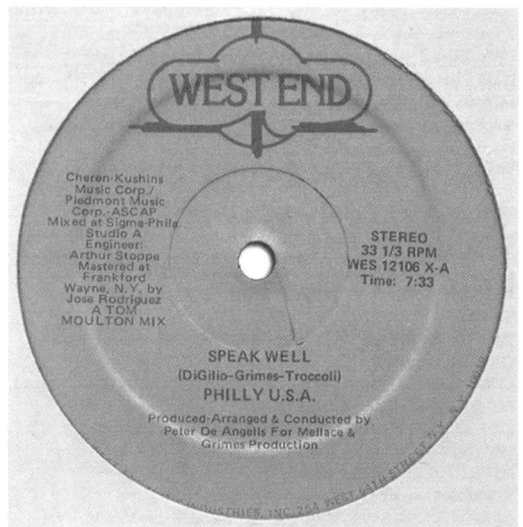

BAREFOOT BOY, NEW YORK
DJ: Tony Smith
BLOCK PARTY – Anthony White (Salsoul)
COSMIC WIND/THE BULL/ BELLY BOOGIE – Mike Theodore Orchestra (Westbound)
DANCE, DANCE, DANCE – Chic (Buddah)
DON'T LET ME BE MISUNDERSTOOD – Santa Esmeralda (Philips import)
I GOT TO HAVE YOUR LOVE – Fantastic Four (Westbound)
IT'S ECSTASY WHEN YOU LAY DOWN, NEXT TO ME – Barry White (20th Century)
LOVE SHOOK/LET'S MAKE LOVE TO THE MUSIC/GIRL DON'T MAKE ME WAIT – Pattie Brooks (Casablanca)
SPEAK WELL – Philly USA (West End)
WHERE WILL IT END – Love Committee (Gold Mind)
YOU'VE GOT MAGIC/COCONUT GROVE – Rice & Beans Orchestra (Orange import)

12 WEST, NEW YORK
DJ: Jim Burgess
DON'T LET ME BE MISUNDERSTOOD – Santa Esmeralda (Philips)
FROM HERE TO ETERNITY/FIRST HAND EXPERIENCE/ I'M LEFT, YOU'RE RIGHT, SHE'S GONE – Giorgio (Casablanca)
HOLD TIGHT – Vicki Sue Robinson (RCA)
I GOT TO HAVE YOUR LOVE – Fantastic Four (Westbound)
IT'S ECSTASY WHEN YOU LAY DOWN NEXT TO ME – Barry White (20th Century)
LA VIE EN ROSE/SEND IN THE CLOWNS/ WHAT I DID FOR LOVE – Grace Jones (Island)
MUSIC – Montreal Sound (TK)
NATIVE NEW YORKER/EASY COME, EASY GO – Odyssey (RCA)
SAN FRANCISCO/HOLLYWOOD/FIRE ISLAND/VILLAGE PEOPLE – Village People (Casablanca)
SPEAK WELL – Philly USA (West End)

DOC RICKETT'S LAB, MONTEREY, CA.
DJ: Wes Bradley
THE BULL/COSMIC WIND – Mike Theodore Orch. (Westbound)
DANCE, DANCE, DANCE – Chic (Buddah)
DON'T LET ME BE MISUNDERSTOOD – Santa Esmeralda (Philips import)
FROM HERE TO ETERNITY/I'M LEFT, YOU'RE RIGHT, SHE'S GONE – Giorgio (Casablanca)
GIRL DON'T MAKE ME WAIT/POP COLLAGE/LOVE SHOOK – Pattie Brooks (Casablanca)
IT MAKES YOU FEEL LIKE DANCIN' – Rose Royce (Whitfield)
IT'S ECSTASY WHEN YOU LAY DOWN NEXT TO ME – Barry White (20th Century)
MUSIC – Montreal Sound (TK)
SAN FRANCISCO/HOLLYWOOD/FIRE ISLAND – Village People (Casablanca)
WATCH OUT FOR THE BOOGIE MAN – Trax (Polydor)

PLAYGROUNDS, NEW YORK
DJ: Tony Carrasco
BLOCK PARTY – Anthony White (Salsoul)
COSMIC WIND/THE BULL/BRAZILIAN LULLABY – Mike Theodore Orchestra (Westbound)
DON'T LET ME BE MISUNDERSTOOD – Santa Esmeralda (Philips import)
IT'S ECSTASY WHEN YOU LAY DOWN NEXT TO ME – Barry White (20th Century)
LET'S MAKE LOVE TO THE MUSIC/GIRL DON'T MAKE ME WAIT/POP COLLAGE – Pattie Brooks (Casablanca)
MUSIC HAS THE POWER/ MI SABRINA 'TEQUANA/ THAT'S ALL – Ingram (H&L)
SPEAK WELL – Philly USA (West End)
TROPICAL NIGHTS/BALI HAI – Liza Minnelli (Columbia)
WHERE WILL IT END – Love Committee (Gold Mind)
YOU ARE THE MUSIC WITHIN ME – Barbara Pennington (UA)

NOTES: Both London and TK are preparing four-sided collections of the labels' biggest disco records pre-blended for at-home partying (Tom Savarese is doing the honors on the TK package); and the "Disco Boogie" set Walter Gibbons blended for Salsoul, available for months as a TV mail-order item, should be in the stores too before long... After some delay, Polydor has released "Watch Out!," the Trax album, in the States – if you haven't already gotten it, don't miss the "Watch Out For The Boogie Man" cut – it's among the best records this year... Due out within the week: **Grace Jones'** splendid "Portfolio" (Island); **Santa Esmeralda's** "Don't Let Me Be Misunderstood," already one of the strongest records in the country prior to its Casablanca release; and, next week, **Mandrill's** "We Are One" (Arista), produced by **Jeff Lane**... According to RCA, the new album by **Dr. Buzzard's Original Savannah Band** is finished but until things are smoothed out between the group and its management, the actual release date can only be guessed at. Right now they're saying by the end of October.... **Chic's** excellent "Dance, Dance, Dance (Yowsah, Yowsah, Yowsah)," reviewed here last week, is in limbo at the moment. Buddah, currently between distribution deals (leaving RCA for Arista), has put the record on hold and the producers have put it back on the market. Don't be surprised to see it on TK instead... **Gene Farrow's** "Hey, You Should Be Dancing" is out now on a UA domestic disco disc, 4:42 on one side, 7:54 (the instrumental version) on the other, both highly recommended though the instrumental is more than I can take. The original Magnet single from England remains a unique collector's record, by the way, because the "version" side was finished in a special groove that looped back endlessly and kept the last beats of the song going on and on and on and on... ◉

> ❝ The original Magnet single from England remains a unique collector's record, because the "version" side was finished in a special groove that looped back endlessly and kept the last beats of the song going on and on and on and on ❞

OCTOBER 8, 1977

The most important new release this week is **Grace Jones'** much anticipated "Portfolio" (Island), a superbly crafted album that should bring one of the biggest disco sensations of the year to an even larger audience. In addition to Grace's three previous releases – "That's The Trouble," "Sorry" and "I Need A Man," all in condensed, under-four-minute versions – the album contains a magnificent compelling modern interpretation of **Edith Piaf's** cabaret classic, "La Vie En Rose," and a medley of three recent show tune standards – "Send In The Clowns," "What I Did For Love" and "Tomorrow – done Philadelphia disco style. Of the new material, "La Vie En Rose" (7:27) is the most arresting and exciting, building to an emotional peak from a minimal, delicate, seductively languorous arrangement of piano, guitar and percussion. Grace, singing in both French and English, uses the simplicity of the production as the perfect foil, strutting across it, purring, growling, shouting and whispering like an actress working her lines for all they're worth. Grace doesn't dominate the Broadway medley as easily or as dramatically – at times she seems to strain uncomfortably – but both "Send In The Clowns" and "What I Did For Love" succeed beautifully as pop disco and producer **Tom Moulton** demonstrates a deft handling of Philly soul styling, particularly the orchestration of the creamy backing vocals of **Barbara Ingram**, **Carla Benson** and **Evette Benton** – just the right balance for Grace's robust lead. Only "Tomorrow," the song from "Annie," is a disappointment, primarily because it's no match for the **Stephen Sondheim** and **Marvin Hamlisch** tunes that precede it, but also because the song leaves no room for subtlety or real charm. In the end, however, this is an impressive and unexpectedly intelligent album, complete with a splashy package designed by artist Richard Bernstein. It's bound to be an instant hit with the disco crowd, but it's sure to have an even broader appeal.

Two other albums to pick up on right now: **Ashford & Simpson's** "Send It" (Warner Brothers), their most satisfying, immediately involving lp in years with the prime cut being a departure for them – an instrumental called "Bourgie Bourgie" (6:07) that features Valerie herself on piano, **Eric Gale** on guitar and **Ralph MacDonald** on percussion and congas. "Bourgie Bourgie" is sophisticated and snappy, building to fine guitar-strutting peaks, then ebbing back to lush waves of strings. This one's a personal favorite at the moment and DJ Larry Levan says the first-time-out response from his crowd was so good that he's already put it on his top 10 from the still-under-construction 84 King Street club in New York. **Ripple** is back after a rather long absence with an album called "Sons Of The Gods"

on Salsoul, highlighted by a happy funk cut titled "The Beat Goes On And On" (4:29). "Beat" is one of those smooth, sprightly songs with cool, repeated vocals that feels so up and optimistic it's hard to resist.

RECOMMENDED DISCO DISCS: **Samba Soul's** "Chove Chuva/Mas Que Nada" (RCA) is a bright, jazzy Brazilian instrumental (written by **Jorge Ben**) that perks along delightfully for most of its 7:47 length, only losing me toward the end when almost everything is stripped from the song but the drum beat. Producer **Warren Schatz** disco-mixed this one from an original Brazilian production – his previous two records – "Express Yourself" and "Hold Tight" – proved he has a sure enough sense of the disco market to put across progressive and potentially "difficult" arrangements and it looks like he's scored with this one, too: both Tom Webb and Michael Melkonian have included it on heir top 10s this week. The flip side, "Mambo No.5," takes off from a familiar-sounding **Perez Prado** composition for nearly nine minutes; the first five minutes struck me as one of the best Latin dance records in some time, but after that, I was ready to throw something at the turntable. Too long for my taste... **Alfie Davidson**, a New York DJ from way back with a loyal following among a number of younger spinners, has come out with a disco record of a song he wrote, called "Who Is Gonna Love Me" (RCA), making him, I believe, the first DJ to turn big-label recording artist– the ultimate professional crossover. The record is a sweet hustle and has the distinction of being released in two separate versions back-to-back on one disc; the battle of the disco mixes. Both sides are something over six minutes, one mixed by Tom Moulton, the other by **David Todd**, both in their characteristic styles (Moulton's lush, Todd's more brittle and percussion-obsessed)... "Keep It Up" by **Nightfall** (RCA), available in back-to-back vocal/instrumental versions (both 5:25), is a wonderfully sleezy record that outdoes "More, More, More" in the porno disco category with a sweet sex fantasy of a girl vocal praising the man who can "keep it up, whip it up, stand it up, etc." Very cute and featuring a fine piano break; produced by a young New York DJ named **Cory Robbins** with **Eric Matthew**.

NEWS & NOTES: **Donna Summer's** version of "Je T'Aime," has never been officially released by Casablanca though a test run of 500 copies was distributed to disco DJs a month ago, and now, it seems, the disco disc pressing might go back on the shelf. Initially, a company source said, the record was being held to avoid immediate competition with the **Saint Tropez** album cut, but the

> **❝ DJ Larry Levan says the response was so good he's already put it on his top 10 from the still-under-construction 84 King Street club ❞**

84 KING STREET, NEW YORK
DJ: Larry Levan

BLOOD AND HONEY – Amanda Lear (Direction import)
BOURGIE BOURGIE – Ashford & Simpson (Warner Bros.)
DEEPER – New Birth (Warner Bros.)
I GOT TO HAVE YOUR LOVE – Fantastic Four (Westbound)
I'M HERE AGAIN – Thelma Houston (Tamla)
LOCKED IN THIS POSITION – Barbara Mason & Bunny Sigler (Curtom)
SAY YOU WILL – Eddie Henderson (Capitol)
SPEAK WELL – Philly USA (West End)
YOUR LOVE IS SO GOOD FOR ME – Diana Ross (Motown)
[only 9 entries in the original]

MY FAIR LADY, DETROIT
DJ: Michael Melkonian

THE BULL/BRAZILIAN LULLABY/COSMIC WIND – Mike Theodore Orchestra (Westbound)
CHOVE CHUVA/MAS QUE NADA – Samba Soul (RCA)
FROM NOW ON – Linda Clifford (Curtom)
I GOT TO HAVE YOUR LOVE – Fantastic Four (Westbound)
KEEP IT UP – Nightfall (RCA)
LOVE SHOOK/GIRL DON'T MAKE ME WAIT – Pattie Brooks (Casablanca)
MY DAYS ARE NUMBERED – John Wells (Polydor import)
NATIVE NEW YORKER – Odyssey (RCA)
WHEN YOU'VE DROPPED YOUR GUARD (LOVE KNOCKS YOU DOWN) – The Knights (Little Star)
YOU AND I – Disco Drive (London import)

THE BOATHOUSE, REHOBOTH BEACH, DE
DJ: Tom Webb

BLOCK PARTY – Anthony White (Salsoul)
CHOVE CHUVA/MAS QUE NADA – Samba Soul (RCA)
COME DOWN TO EARTH – Choice Four (RCA)
COSMIC WIND/THE BULL – Mike Theodore Orchestra (Westbound)
DAN SWIT ME/FUNKY MUSIC – Patti LaBelle (Epic)
DON'T LET ME BE MISUNDERSTOOD – Santa Esmeralda (Philips import)
GIRL DON'T MAKE ME WAIT/LOVE SHOOK – Pattie Brooks (Casablanca)
I GOT TO HAVE YOUR LOVE – Fantastic Four (Westbound/Atlantic)
IT'S ECSTASY WHEN YOU LAY DOWN NEXT TO ME – Barry White (20th Century)
NATIVE NEW YORKER/EASY COME, EASY GO – Odyssey (RCA)

TOWNHOUSE 48, NEW YORK
DJ: John Benitez

BLOCK PARTY – Anthony White (Salsoul)
DO YOUR DANCE – Rose Royce (Whitfield)
DON'T LET ME BE MISUNDERSTOOD – Santa Esmeralda (Philips import)
FROM HERE TO ETERNITY – Giorgio (Casablanca)
GIRL DON'T MAKE ME WAIT/LET'S MAKE LOVE TO THE MUSIC – Pattie Brooks (Casablanca)
I GOT TO HAVE YOUR LOVE – Fantastic Four (Westbound)
IT'S ECSTASY WHEN YOU LAY DOWN NEXT TO ME – Barry White (20th Century)
MOON BOOTS – Orlando Riva Sound (Salsoul/Tom & Jerry)
SPEAK WELL/INSTRUMENTALLY SPEAKING – Philly USA (West End)
WHERE WILL IT END – Love Committee (Gold Mind)

lack of any real enthusiasm for the advance copies and the abundance of Summer material already on the market has made the label rethink plans for a commercial release. An additional 500 copies of "Je T'Aime" may be tested on the club level in the next week or two, but if the response is still disappointing, this could turn into one of the year's hottest limited edition collector's items… The continuing saga of **Chic's** "Dance, Dance, Dance (Yowsah, Yowsah, Yowsah)" got very complicated this week. Buddah, its distribution deal with Arista now in action, announced that it was rush-releasing both a disco disc and a standard single. But simultaneously, Atlantic reported that not only had it purchased "Dance, Dance, Dance," but it was planning to issue the record, also on a rush-release schedule, as its first commercial disco disc – a major move for the company, that pioneered the format but 'has previously held back from marketing it. At press time it looks like both companies are releasing the record at the same time. It's showdown time at the disco. ✄

DISCO FILE TOP 20

1. **COSMIC WIND/THE BULL** – Mike Theodore Orchestra (Westbound)
2. **I GOT TO HAVE YOUR LOVE** – Fantastic Four (Westbound)
3. **IT'S ECSTASY WHEN YOU LAY DOWN NEXT TO ME** – Barry White (20th Century)
4. **DON'T LET ME BE MISUNDERSTOOD** – Santa Esmeralda (Philips import)
5. **SAN FRANCISCO/HOLLYWOOD/FIRE ISLAND** – Village People (Casablanca)
6. **MUSIC** – Montreal Sound (TK)
7. **NATIVE NEW YORKER/EASY COME, EASY GO** – Odyssey (RCA)
8. **FROM HERE TO ETERNITY/FIRST HAND EXPERIENCE** – Giorgio (Casablanca)
9. **GIRL DON'T MAKE ME WAIT/LOVE SHOOK** – Pattie Brooks (Casablanca)
10. **SPEAK WELL** – Philly USA (West End)
11. **BLOCK PARTY** – Anthony White (Salsoul)
12. **HEY, YOU SHOULD BE DANCING** – Gene Farrow (UA import)
13. **JE T'AIME/ON A RIEN A PERDRE/COEUR A COEUR** – Saint Tropez (Butterfly)
14. **POP COLLAGE/LET'S MAKE LOVE TO THE MUSIC** – Pattie Brooks (Casablanca)
15. **AFRICAN QUEENS/QUIET VILLAGE** – Ritchie Family (Marlin)
16. **I FEEL LOVE** – Donna Summer (Casablanca)
17. **EROTIC SOUL** – Larry Page Ork (London)
18. **COCOMOTION** – El Coco (AVI)
19. **WATCH OUT FOR THE BOOGIE MAN** – Trax (Polydor import)
20. **HOLD TIGHT** – Vicki Sue Robinson (RCA)

My favorite new record this week is a ten-and-a-half-minute disco disc instrumental-with-vocals called "Le Spank" by **Le Pamplemousse** (AVI) – a surprising choice, perhaps in light of all my recent kvetching about overlong cuts, but this one is so well-paced that, instead of dragging you along, it picks you up almost effortlessly and takes you on a rocket ride. Produced by **Michael Lewis**, half of the **El Coco/Saint Tropez** production team, "Le Spank" has some of the light bounce of "Cocomotion" but the overall sound is smoother, cooler and more elegant, down to the high, breathy female vocals. The girls are singing about what is allegedly a new dance though it sounds more like light-weight S&M to me ("There's nothing else I want to do but spank it with you") – either way, if it's accompanied by music this sparkling and comfortable, I'm ready for it. Highlights: the first break which combines thumping drums and a long, rising air-raid siren wail – a brilliant flash of both "I Feel Love" and "Do You Wanna Get Funky With Me" – and the long, sinuous sax solo at the end.

Also highly recommended: The new **Rice & Beans Orchestra** disco disc, "You've Got Magic," which has already been appearing on some top 1 0 lists (like Michael Lee's from Bones in San Francisco this week) as an import on the Orange label from Puerto Rico but is due out this week on TK. "Magic" (7:15), produced by **Pepe Luis Soto**, who also did **Celi Bee & the Buzzy Bunch**, takes this particular Latin disco sound one step further, cutting the cuteness with a strong bass/synthesizer line that pulses through a wash of strings and sweet, chanting vocals. The appeal is similar to that of "Le Spank": uncomplicated, fresh, but even more elemental; the best thing from this producer so far. "Coconut Grove," on the B side of the 12-inch, is a little more sugary but no less attractive and should be given equal time. The Rice & Beans album, with shorter versions of both these tracks, is also available currently as an import but domestic copies should be out within a week or two on TK's APA label – watch for it... After a long absence, **Andrea True's** latest is a snappy disco pickup song titled "What's Your Name, What's Your Number" (Buddah) with a crackling production by **Michael Zager** and vocals that may be rawer than usual (True has always had very cosmetic production jobs, the equivalent of air-brushing on photos) but just right, just raunchy enough, for this record. This doesn't mean True has suddenly developed a fine voice, only that for once it's used with a degree of spunk and personality – she even does some aggressive scatting – and it turns out to be a lot of fun. The flip side is her original version of "Fill Me Up (Heart To Heart)," (at its full 10:03 length) – the song recently recorded by Saint Tropez as "Coeur A Coeur."

Two disco discs that have been getting a lot of favorable comment from DJs recently are **Doris Jones'** "No Way Out" (UA) and the new mix of "Come Down To Earth" by the **Choice 4** (RCA). Jones has a voice that one would have to compare to Andrea True's except it's even more pinched and shrill, but the production, done in England, does have an undeniable kick and spirit, with swirling strings and lots of background vocals for support. "Come Down To Earth" is a **Van McCoy** production from the last Choice 4 lp, which **David Todd** has set in one of his typically spare, chugging disco mixes. Parts of the record are involving and sharp – particularly the vocals and one or two changes that follow – but, at 10:24, this is awfully long for something that is basically looping back upon itself over and over with variations too subtle and sly for their own good. But if I find "Come Down" ultimately tedious, I seem to be in the minority at the moment – it's going over big at the club level. ✿

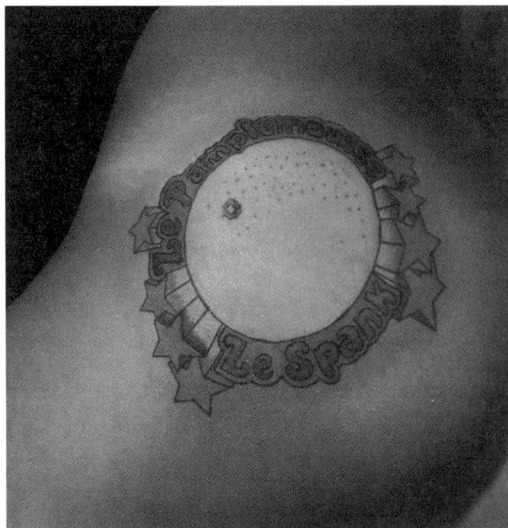

> **❝ The girls are singing about what is allegedly a new dance, though it sounds more like light-weight S&M to me ❞**

STARSHIP DISCOVERY 1, NEW YORK
DJ: Joe Palminteri

BLOCK PARTY – Anthony White (Salsoul)
CHOOSING YOU – Lenny Williams (ABC)
COSMIC WIND – Mike Theodore Orchestra (Westbound)
DANCE, DANCE, DANCE – Chic (Buddah/Atlantic)
DON'T LET ME BE MISUNDERSTOOD – Santa Esmeralda (Philips import)
FIRE ISLAND/SAN FRANCISCO – Village People (Casablanca)
GIRL DON'T MAKE ME WAIT/ POP COLLAGE – Pattie Brooks (Casablanca)
INVITATION TO THE WORLD – Jimmy Briscoe & the Little Beavers (TK)
SPEAK WELL – Philly USA (West End)
VOYAGE OF NO RETURN – Silvetti (Salsoul)

LOST & FOUND, WASHINGTON, D.C.
DJ: Bill Owens

BLOCK PARTY/I CAN'T TURN YOU LOOSE – Anthony White (Salsoul)
COME DOWN TO EARTH – Choice 4 (RCA)
DANCE, DANCE, DANCE – Chic (Buddah/Atlantic)
DAN SWIT ME – Patti LaBelle (Epic)
GIRL DON'T MAKE ME WAIT/ LOVE SHOOK/LET'S MAKE LOVE TO THE MUSIC – Pattie Brooks (Casablanca)
IT'S ECSTASY WHEN YOU LAY DOWN NEXT TO ME – Barry White (20th Century)
MOON-BOOTS – Orlando Riva Sound (Salsoul/Tom & Jerry)
NATIVE NEW YORKER – Odyssey (RCA)
SAN FRANCISCO/HOLLYWOOD – Village People (Casablanca)
SPEAK WELL – Philly USA (West End)

BONES, SAN FRANCISCO
DJ: Michael Lee

BLOCK PARTY/I CAN'T TURN YOU LOOSE – Anthony White (Salsoul)
DANCE, DANCE, DANCE – Chic (Buddah/Atlantic)
DON'T LET ME BE MISUNDERSTOOD – Santa Esmeralda (Philips import)
I GOT TO HAVE YOUR LOVE – Fantastic Four (Atlantic)
LA VIE EN ROSE – Grace Jones (Island)
LOVE SHOOK/GIRL DON'T MAKE ME WAIT – Pattie Brooks (Casablanca)
NATIVE NEW YORKER – Odyssey (RCA)
SPEAK WELL/INSTRUMENTALLY SPEAKING – Philly USA (West End)
WATCH OUT FOR THE BOOGIE MAN/ ANY WAY YOU WANT IT – Trax (Polydor)
YOU'VE GOT MAGIC/COCONUT GROVE – Rice & Beans Orchestra (Orange import)

PIPPINS, NEW YORK
DJ: Reggie T. Experience

BOURGIE, BOURGIE/SEND IT – Ashford & Simpson (Warner Bros.)
DANCE, DANCE, DANCE – Chic (Buddah/Atlantic)
DO YOUR DANCE/IT MAKES YOU FEEL LIKE DANCIN'/WISHING ON A STAR – Rose Royce (Whitfield)
DON'T LET ME BE MISUNDERSTOOD – Santa Esmeralda (Philips import)
LA VIE EN ROSE/SEND IN THE CLOWNS/ WHAT I DID FOR LOVE – Grace Jones (Island)
LOVE SHOOK/POP COLLAGE/GIRL DON'T MAKE ME WAIT – Pattie Brooks (Casablanca)
MUSIC HAS THE POWER/MI SABRINA TEQUANA/THAT'S ALL – Ingram (H&L)
NATIVE NEW YORKER – Odyssey (RCA)
NO WAY OUT – Doris Jones (UA)
YOUR LOVE IS SO GOOD FOR ME – Diana Ross (Motown)

RECOMMENDED ALBUMS: Topping the list this week are two excellent European albums whose prime distinction lies not so much in the original productions but in the way those productions have been transformed through that increasingly crucial process that is known as the "disco mix." Both "Kings Of Clubs" by the **Chocolat's** (Salsoul) and "Magic Love" by **Michele** (West End) are **Tom Moulton** mixes and, from all indications, are utterly different from the versions originally released in Belgium and France, respectively. Not only has Moulton expanded all the material – "Kings Of Clubs," for instance, was originally a 3:55 single; here it runs 14:30 – he's also added percussion (tambourine, cowbells, and entire conga breaks by Philadelphia's **Larry Washington**) and, on the Michele album, new background vocal tracks. Not surprisingly, Moulton receives co-producer credit on "Magic Love" in addition to his disco mix

third listening it feels like an old favorite. Echoes here of both **Celi Bee** and **Andrea True**, especially on the "Can't You Feel It" and "Disco Dance" cuts, but the fusion of styles is unique. Since there are only four tracks on the album, there are occasional moments of tedium – "Can't You Feel It" at 9:42, doesn't really go anywhere after the first six minutes – but the best cuts – "Magic Love" and "Disco Dance" – are perfectly involving and invigorating, striking just the right balance between vocals and instrumental breaks. The **Chocolat's** lp is already out (with "Kings Of Clubs' on two top 10 lists in its first week) and Michele's, the first album on the West End label, is scheduled for release this week and if early response is any indication, we should be hearing a lot about both of them in the next few months.

> ❝ **Moulton also added percussion (tambourine, cowbells, and entire conga breaks) and new background vocal tracks. Not surprisingly, he receives co-producer credit.** ❞

credit but his work on the Chocolat's album – the first to bear Moulton's own label imprint, Tom n' Jerry Records, released through Salsoul – is the more successful and impressive of the two. Though the Chocolat's have had some success with their import albums, this is the group's first American release and it consists of both current and previously available material remixed specially for this album. The group's style is uniquely European but leans closer to the earlier disco sound from the continent – **Titanic**, **Bimbo Jet**, **Barrabas** – than to **Cerrone** or **Costandinos**, though there are definitely overtones of the latter on "Kings Of Clubs," the strongest track here. Actually, "Kings" sounds like **T. Rex** (several passages are taken from "Get It On") meets **Claudja Barry**, with negligible vocals but a marvelously crisp and appealing production – a bit long, perhaps, but sustained nicely with a series of breaks and changes that get better as the song progresses. "El Caravanero" (10:37), previously available on the group's "Brazilia Carnaval" lp, was also lengthened and spiced up; primarily sultry organ and Afro-Latin drumming, this one already has the sound of a European classic and Moulton's additional synthesizer accents and breaks give it a fresh feel. A version of "Orfeu Negro," the song from "Black Orpheus," completes the album.

The **Michele** album fits right in with the **Pattie Brooks'** sound though the vocals may not be as accomplished or the production as polished. Still, it's one of those records that sounds immediately familiar (sure I haven't heard this before?) and so easy to fall into that by the

RECOMMENDED ALBUMS (CONTINUED): The **Fantastic Four's** new "Got To Have Your Love" album (Westbound), produced by the group and **Dennis Coffey**, is their best in some time even if nothing quite equals the impact of the title cut. "Fire Down Below" (6:23) comes closest as a progressive kind of soul/disco sound, taking a **Trammps** type vocal arrangement and mixing in some unexpected **Ritchie Family**-style girl chorus work; it chugs along irresistibly. Also of interest: "Disco Pool Blues," a lament any disco DJ could relate to ("I DJ each night and my show's outasight/But I got no new records to play") if the vocal portions drag, the intro and break are hot; and "Cash Money" which is nice and hard-edged but also plods in some parts again the break rescues it... "Crossover," the **Rice & Beans Orchestra** album now available on TK's Dash label (not APA as we'd previously stated), is a giant step ahead of the group's first lp with the bulk of the music being more sophisticated, polished and European-styled. The spirit is still very "up" and bright in an almost naive way but the technique is far from that and the results are immensely attractive. In addition to shorter versions of "You've Got Magic" and "Coconut Grove," already recommended here in their disco disc versions, these cuts are essential: "Music In The Air," "Midnight Gossip" and "Dancing Vibrations"... The debut album by **Brooklyn Dreams** on Millennium contains a cut called "Music, Harmony And Rhythm" that could be one of those gorgeous, emotional cuts that, like **Odyssey's** "Native New Yorker," people don't simply like – they love. The singing, by a trio of New York white boys (the inevitable comparison: the **Rascals** when they were still Young – plus **Hall and**

FLAMINGO, NEW YORK
DJ: Richie Rivera

BLOCK PARTY – Anthony White (Salsoul)
DANCE, DANCE, DANCE – Chic (Buddah/Atlantic)
DISCO POOL BLUES/I GOT TO HAVE YOUR LOVE/FIRE DOWN BELOW – Fantastic Four (Westbound)
GIRL DON'T MAKE ME WAIT/POP COLLAGE/LOVE SHOOK – Pattie Brooks (Casablanca)
KEEP IT UP – Olympic Runners (London)
KINGS OF CLUBS – Chocolat's (Salsoul)
LE SPANK – Le Pamplemousse (AVI)
NATIVE NEW YORKER – Odyssey (RCA)
RUNNING AWAY – Roy Ayers Ubiquity (Polydor)
YOUR LOVE IS SO GOOD FOR ME – Diana Ross (Motown)

THE POOP DECK, FORT LAUDERDALE
DJ: Bob Viteritti

THE BULL/COSMIC WIND/BRAZILIAN LULLABY – Mike Theodore Orchestra (Westbound)
DANCE, DANCE, DANCE – Chic (Buddah/Atlantic)
DON'T LET ME BE MISUNDERSTOOD – Santa Esmeralda (Philips import)
GIRL DON'T MAKE ME WAIT/POP COLLAGE – Pattie Brooks (Casablanca)
I GOT TO HAVE YOUR LOVE – Fantastic Four (Atlantic)
IT'S ECSTASY WHEN YOU LAY DOWN NEXT TO ME – Barry White (20th Century)
LA VIE EN ROSE/SEND IN THE CLOWNS/ TOMORROW – Grace Jones (Island)
NATIVE NEW YORKER – Odyssey (RCA)
SAN FRANCISCO/HOLLYWOOD – Village People (Casablanca)
SPEAK WELL – Philly USA (West End)

FACES, CHICAGO
DJ: Carmen Adduci

THE BULL/COSMIC WIND/BRAZILIAN LULLABY – Mike Theodore Orchestra (Westbound)
DANCE, DANCE, DANCE – Chic (Buddah/Atlantic)
DON'T LET ME BE MI'SUNDERSTOOD – Santa Esmeralda (Philips import)
GIRL DON'T MAKE ME WAIT/LET'S MAKE LOVE TO THE MUSIC/POP COLLAGE/LOVE SHOOK – Pattie Brooks (Casablanca)
I GOT TO HAVE YOUR LOVE/FIRE DOWN BELOW/CASH MONEY – Fantastic Four (Westbound)
JOHNNY, JOHNNY/DANCING FEVER – Claudja Barry (London import)
KINGS OF CLUBS – Chocolat's (Salsoul)
LE SPANK – Le Pamplemousse (AVI)
LIVING FOR TODAY/INVITATION TO THE WORLD – Jimmy Brisco & the Beavers (TK)
MY FIRST MISTAKE – Chi-Lites (Mercury)

IPANEMA, NEW YORK
DJ: Ray Velazquez

CHILDHOOD FOREVER (A CHACUN SON SON ENFANCE) – Recreation (Dynamo)
CHOVE CHUVA/MAS QUE NADA – Samba Soul (RCA)
COSMIC WIND/THE BULL – Mike Theodore Orchestra (Westbound)
DANCE, DANCE, DANCE – Chic (Buddah/Atlantic)
DON'T LET ME BE MISUNDERSTOOD – Santa Esmeralda (Philips import)
GIRL DON'T MAKE ME WAIT/POP COLLAGE/LOVE SHOOK/LET'S MAKE LOVE TO THE MUSIC – Pattie Brooks (Casablanca)
HEY YOU SHOULD BE DANCING – Gene Farrow (UA)
RUNNING AWAY – Roy Ayers Ubiquity (Polydor)
SAN FRANCISCO/HOLLYWOOD/FIRE ISLAND – Village People (Casablanca)
SOMETHING'S UP – Wayne St. John (RCA import)

Oates and the Bee Gees), is rich and full of feeling and the lyrics, in celebration of "the magical mystery of music, harmony and rhythm," are worthy of the voices. This is one cut you wouldn't mind hearing at much greater length, but the succinct four minutes here is just fine, thanks. Could become a big favorite, trailing another cut from the album, "Street Dance," in its wake.

NEWS & NOTES: Polydor has re-released the classic and long out-of-print "Sex Machine" album by **James Brown** – a two-record live set featuring a 16:06 version of "Get Up I Feel Like Being A Sex Machine" that collectors have been paying upwards of $20 for. Pick it up – it's a brilliant piece of history and a reminder of just how far we've come since then... Both **Roberta Kelly's** "Zodiac Lady" and **Santa Esmeralda's** "Don't Let Me Be Misunderstood" are out now on the Casablanca label... Two cuts from the **Pattie Brooks** album (also on Casablanca) went to number one on the DISCO FILE Top 20 this week with the remaining two tracks not far behind at number 8. Clearly, this album deserved more attention than we were able to give it in our initial review – **Simon Soussan's** production, perhaps the best American assimilation of the Eurodisco style, gets better with each listening – and we're glad to see the record getting its due in the clubs... Another record finally coming into its own is "Running Away" by the **Roy Ayers Ubiquity**, recommended here as an album cut in June but just now catching on as a result of the recent release of a longer disco disc version. Its appearance on the Top 20 chart this week (at 14) is a measure of this new surge in popularity... Also picking up; both sides of the **Samba Soul** disc on RCA, but especially "Chove Chuva/Mas Que Nada;" **Grace Jones'** "La Vie En Rose" (Island); "Your Love Is So Good for Me" by **Diana Ross** (Motown) and **Silvetti's** "Voyage Of No Return" and "Primitive Man" (Salsoul)... Some recent disco disc pressings of note: **Archie Bell & the Drells'** "Glad You Could Make It" (Philadelphia International) and **L.T.D.'s** "Back In Love Again" (A&M), the best dance cuts from the group's recent lps, are available now in expanded 12-inch versions-Bell's running 5:36, L.T.D.'s 8:37-and "Back in Love" is already reported to be going over well with crowds that had previously passed on the album version: TK has released the longer version of **Dorothy Moore's** tasty "Let The Music Play" (5:23); and these album tracks are also being pressed, in most cases for promotional purposes only, on disco discs: **Patti LaBelle's** "Dan Swit Me" (Epic), "Magic Fly" and "Fasten Your Seat Belt" by **Space** (UA), "The Bull" by the **Mike Theodore Orchestra**, "As" by **Sister Sledge** and "We Got Our Own Thing" by **C.J. & Co.** (all Atlantic). ✪

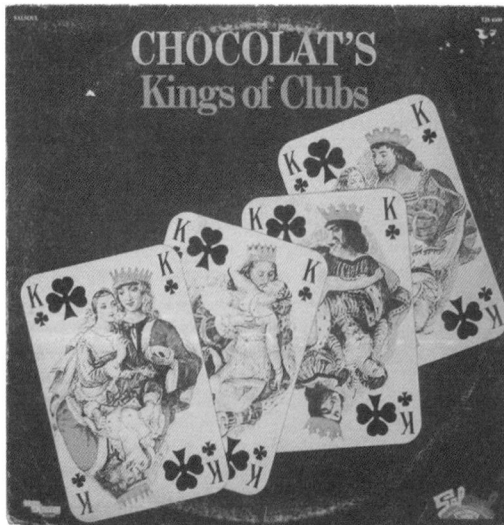

RECOMMENDED DISCO DISCS: Producer **Cory Wade** has come up with one of the more off-beat records of the month in "Harlem Nocturne" (TK), an unusually stylized, highly atmospheric version of the pop jazz standard sung by a Miami girl group named **Wildflower**. Running through a number of moods – from the vibrant street-scene intro to the bouncy vocal segments to the bluesy horn riff toward the end – the production is an odd pastiche of tempos and styles that takes some getting into. The vocals remain somewhat unsatisfying – often shrill and thin – but the instrumental version on the flip side sounds uncomfortably empty without them (both sides run an even five minutes). Clearly, this is not an easy record, but it's an adventurous, intriguing one, the sort of thing that suddenly clicks in on the fifth or sixth hearing and from then on sounds better and better. Left field pick of the week... For all those people who got hooked on "Catfish," there's a new **Four Tops** song in an equally high-spirited style that's even more irresistible for fans of the Tops'

ff Some say the sound is better on 45, but the majority of DJs seem to have no preference. But everyone thinks it's time the format was standardized JJ

classy soul sound. The song is "The Show Must Go On," title track of the group's latest ABC album now available as a disco disc (promotional only; same length in both formats: 7:04), and it's a great behind-the-scenes show biz number, full of incident, wit and emotion. The repeated chorus clinches it nicely: "The whole world is a stage/get up on it/All you got to do is get up and dance/and do your thing." As usual, wonderful vocals and a clean no-nonsense production (by **Lawrence Payton**) prove the Tops' show goes on in fine form... **Kelly Marie's** "Run To Me" has been one of the more popular imports on the disco grapevine in the past few weeks and now the English record, also very big in Canada, is out on a disco pressing from Vanguard. The vocalist sounds like a combination of **Tina Charles** and **Vicki Sue Robinson** on their off days but the production, running 5:15 on the longer side, is cute and spunky if not particularly original. All these things aside, however, "Run To Me" is great fun to dance to and that, I suppose, is the bottom line here... The **Inner City Jam Band's** version of "What I Did For Love" (Bareback) may not be as sultry or sophisticated as **Grace Jones'**, but it definitely has an appeal all its own. Here again the vocals are occasionally strained and rough, but the arrangement has a certain spark, especially at the

Arranged by Brainstorm
Produced by Jerry Peters
for Music Mecca West
Productions/Executive
Producer: Clarence Avant
Engineered by F. Bryon
Clark

STEREO
QD-10963
QD-10963-A
Interior Music, BMI
33 1/3 rpm

Brainstorm
Lovin' Is Really My Game 7:39
(from the "Stormin'" album, BQL1-2048)
(Belita Woods-Tranita Womack)
Manufactured & Distributed by RCA Records,
New York, N.Y. • Printed in U.S.A.
℗1977 Tabu Records, Inc.

CHOCOLAT'S
Kings of Clubs

THE LOFT, NEW YORK
DJ: David Mancuso

BLOCK PARTY – Anthony White (Salsoul)
BOURGIE, BOURGIE – Ashford & Simpson (Warner Bros.)
CHOOSING YOU/PLEASE DON'T TEMPT ME/LOOK UP WITH YOUR MIND – Lenny Williams (ABC)
COCOMOTION – El Coco (AVI)
DEEPER – New Birth (Warner Bros.)
DISCO DANCE – Michele (West End)
FUNKY MONKEY – Mandrill (Arista)
LE SPANK – Le Pamplemousse (AVI)
RUNNING AWAY – Roy Ayers Ubiquity (Polydor)
WHAT'S YOUR NAME, WHAT'S YOUR NUMBER – Andrea True Connection (Buddah)

SUNDANCE SOCIAL PUB, CHICAGO
DJ: Jim Thompson

DON'T LET ME BE MISUNDERSTOOD – Santa Esmeralda (Casablanca)
ELLA FUE (SHE WAS THE ONE) – Fania All Stars (Columbia)
GIRL DON'T MAKE ME WAIT/LOVE SHOOK/POP COLLAGE – Pattie Brooks (Casablanca)
HARLEM NOCTURNE – Wildflower (TK disco disc)
KINGS OF CLUBS – Chocolat's (Salsoul)
LA VIE EN ROSE – Grace Jones (Island)
LE SPANK – Le Pamplemousse (AVI)
LOVIN' IS REALLY MY GAME – Brainstorm (Tabu)
SUNSHINE OF YOUR LOVE – Rosetta Stone (Private Stock)
THERE'S FIRE DOWN BELOW/CASH MONEY /I GOT TO HAVE YOUR LOVE – Fantastic Four (Westbound)

WINDJAMMER, SADDLE BROOK, N.J.
DJ: Jerry Lembo

BLOCK PARTY/I CAN'T TURN YOU LOOSE – Anthony White (Salsoul)
COSMIC WIND/THE BULL – Mike Theodore Orchestra (Westbound)
DANCE, DANCE, DANCE – Chic (Buddah/Atlantic)
DON'T LET ME BE MISUNDERSTOOD – Santa Esmeralda (Casablanca)
I GOT TO HAVE YOUR LOVE – Fantastic Four (Atlantic)
LA VIE EN ROSE/WHAT I DID FOR LOVE – Grace Jones (Island)
LE SPANK – Le Pamplemousse (AVI)
NATIVE NEW YORKER – Odyssey (RCA)
YOUR LOVE IS SO GOOD FOR ME – Diana Ross (Motown)
YOU'VE GOT MAGIC – Rice & Beans Orchestra (TK)

TRINITY, NEW ORLEANS
DJ: Stu Neal

COCOMOTION/I'M MAD AS HELL – El Coco (AVI)
DANCE, DANCE, DANCE – Chic (Buddah/Atlantic)
FUNKY STARDUST/I'M SAGITTARIUS – Roberta Kelly (Casablanca)
HEY YOU SHOULD BE DANCING – Gene Farrow (UA)
LOVE IS ALL YOU NEED – High Energy (Gordy)
RUNNING AWAY – Roy Ayers Ubiquity (Polydor)
SHAME/DANCIN', DANCIN', DANCIN' – Evelyn "Champagne" King (RCA)
TELEGRAM OF LOVE – Hues Corporation (Warner Bros.)
WATCH OUT FOR THE BOOGIE MAN/ DANCE – Trax (Polydor)
WHAT I DID FOR LOVE/TOMORROW – Grace Jones (Island)

beginning and in the central break. At a little more than six minutes, the record has plenty of time to recover from the early soft spots and wraps things up neatly in the stronger, punched-up second half.

NOTE: It's been a while since we did a speed check survey of disco discs, so we checked out the most recent arrivals – about ten days' worth – this week and were surprised to discover that the results are virtually unchanged in all these months. The field is still split – in this case exactly in half – between standard single and standard lp speeds: of the 24 American releases received, 12 were at 45 rpm and 12 at 331/3 rpm. The same stand-off remains between companies that prefer to regard the disco disc as a bigger single – the "Giant 45" – and those who insist a 12-inch format compatible with album speed will allow the consumer to stack both discs and lps for easier at-home partying .. Although a number of people we've spoken to say the sound quality is better – hotter – on 45, the majority of DJs seem to have no preference. But everyone thinks it's about time the format was standardized one way or the other – I volunteer to flip a coin if necessary – and, short of that sensible move, is it too much. to ask that the speed be indicated prominently and in large type before we have to add magnifying glasses to the list of essential disco equipment?

RECOMMENDED ALBUMS: **Mandrill's** "We Are One" (Arista) is undoubtedly their best album in years, getting back to the strong, Afro-Latin neofunk sound that was the group's signature style early on. They've recaptured that spirit and energy with the help of producer **Jeff Lane** whose approach meshes with and supports Mandrill's perfectly; particularly on "Funky Monkey," a theme song of-sorts that adds a unique West Indies accent to Lane's hard-edged, dense New York sound. The result, running just over seven minutes, is perhaps the hottest funk cut of the season; as the group chants, "Let the monkey funk you down."

ALSO EXCELLENT: "Can You Get It" (6:30), a jumping cut with delightful; enthusiastic vocals and a terrifically chunky arrangement. Another song, "Happy Beat," might work well early in the evening. Should put Mandrill back at the top with other progressive soul groups... The debut album by **Eli's Second Coming** (Silver Blue, through TK) is one of those records that crept up on me little by little, cut by cut, until it turned into one of the most frequent records on my turntable. Producer **Bobby Eli** has whipped up a superb, slick Philadelphia package that deserves comparison with the **Salsoul Orchestra** or **MFSB**: creamy, sharp female vocals blended with crisp, bright instrumentals with the emphasis on the lush and sexy. "Love Chant," the group's first single, still sounds great here but two new cuts –"Heavenly" and "Why Don'cha" – come off even better. Also included: an interesting version of **Laura Nyro's** "Eli's Coming" which opens up the album; a mostly instrumental treatment of "Love Won't Let Me Wait;" and a fascinating instrumental called "Foxfire." ◗

NOVEMBER 5, 1977

" This will be the first Salsoul disco disc pressed at 33 rpm — which is sure to add to the overall confusion on disco 12-inch speed "

Although they aren't due for release until sometime later this week or next – depending on the priorities of the already overworked pressing plants – three of the strongest new disco discs around right now are making so much noise in their advance-pressing stage that they demand immediate attention. One record –"Moon-Boots" by **Orlando Riva Sound** (Salsoul/Tom n' Jerry) – appears on three out of our four top 10 lists this week which, combined with a couple of earlier listings, just nudges the disc into the Top 20 at number 19 – an unusual and auspicious move for a test pressing. The other two are big-name releases – the new **T-Connection**, "On Fire, Getting Higher," and the new **George McCrae**, "Kiss Me," both on TK – that have had a much more limited advance-copy distribution but are also shaping up as instant hits based on the early word-of-mouth. "Moon-Boots," an Italian production disco-mixed and co-produced by **Tom Moulton** (it's also the first 12-inch single release on his Tom n' Jerry label), seems to be everyone's favorite new all-electronic number – an instrumental with a bright yet richly sensuous sound that's closer in spirit to **Space** than **Kraftwerk**. Chanting female vocals, repeating the title – crooning "moon" until the word floats off, balloon-like, then popping it

playfully with a sharp "boots!" – add warmth to the percolating synthesizers (supplemented occasionally by drums) and a deep bass gives the spacey effects a solid base. At 9:30, "Moon-Boots" is rather long, but a series of breaks keeps it fresh and invigorating right to the end. NOTES: 1) For the final pressings, the group's name has been shortened to initials – **ORS**; 2) The flip side of the disco disc features two shorter versions of "Moon-Boots," one a 2:59 single version, the other a percussion variation running 3:54; 3) This will be the first Salsoul disco disc pressed at 33 rpm – which does not represent, at this point, a major policy shift for the label but is sure to add to the overall confusion on disco 12-inch speed anyway.

George McCrae's "Kiss Me" is a wonderful flashback: it's that old George McCrae formula – the one that sent him to number one with "Rock Your Baby" – but it feels great all over again, especially with all the new touches that refine the original sound, making it cleaner and sweeter, adding tight percussion breaks. It's McCrae streamlined but sexy as ever, his voice honed to a delightfully sharp cutting edge. "Kiss Me" is in two parts, the first 5:47, the second, beginning with a break, 3:42 – both brilliant and a welcome return to basics. Since the **T-Connection's** "Do What You Wanna Do" was one of the most successful disco discs of the year, their follow-up has been eagerly awaited and "On Fire, Getting Higher" won't disappoint anyone. The sound is still hard and aggressive, firmly rooted in funk but this time around drawing much closer to rock than ever before. Both the quality of the vocals – prominent throughout – and the prominence of the lead guitar make this the perfect rock/disco crossover, a record that could easily elude all labels and win everyone over. **Cory Wade** and **Alex Sadkin** produced so you know the breaks are hot and there are plenty of off-the-wall touches to keep you happy (an almost classical piano out of nowhere and, later, zippy synthesizer accents). "On Fire" (7:20) should have them screaming in no time; it flips to T-Connection's first hit, "Disco Magic" (7:15) which sounds as good as ever – cleaner even, so this may be an improved mix. Both records are likely to be monsters-spearheads in TK's winter assault on the disco charts.

STUDIO ONE, LOS ANGELES
DJ: Manny Slali

BLOCK PARTY/I CAN'T TURN YOU LOOSE
– Anthony White (Salsoul)

DANCE, DANCE, DANCE – Chic (Atlantic)

DISCO DANCE/CAN'T YOU FEEL IT/MAGIC LOVE
– Michele (West End)

DON'T LET ME BE MISUNDERSTOOD
– Santa Esmeralda (Casablanca)

GIRL DON'T MAKE ME WAIT/LOVE SHOOK/POP
COLLAGE – Pattie Brooks (Casablanca)

LE SPANK – Le Pamplemousse (AVI)

MOON-BOOTS – Orlando Riva Sound (Salsoul)

NATIVE NEW YORKER – Odyssey (RCA)

ON FIRE, GETTING HIGHER – T-Connection (TK)

THERE'S FIRE, DOWN BELOW/I GOT TO HAVE YOUR
LOVE/DISCO POOL BLUES – Fantastic Four (Westbound)

BEDROCK, BROOKLYN, N.Y.
DJ: Bacho Mangual

CHOOSING YOU – Lenny Williams (ABC)

DANCE, DANCE, DANCE – Chic (Atlantic)

DANCE A LITTLE BIT CLOSE – Charo (Salsoul)

DON'T LET ME BE MISUNDERSTOOD
– Santa Esmeralda (Casablanca)

I'M HERE AGAIN – Thelma Houston (Tamla)

LOVE SHOOK/GIRL DON'T MAKE ME WAIT
– Pattie Brooks (Casablanca)

MAGIC LOVE/ DISCO DANCE – Michele (West End)

MOON-BOOTS – Orlando Riva Sound (Salsoul)

SPEAK WELL – Philly USA (West End)

YOUR LOVE IS SO GOOD FOR ME – Diana Ross (Motown)

HARRAH, NEW YORK
DJ: Wayne Scott

DANCE, DANCE, DANCE – Chic (Atlantic)

I GOT TO HAVE YOUR LOVE – Fantastic Four (Westbound)

IT'S ECSTASY WHEN YOU LAY DOWN NEXT TO ME –
Barry White (20th Century)

KISS ME – George McCrae (TK)

LE SPANK – Le Pamplemousse (AVI)

LOVE SHOOK/GIRL DON'T MAKE ME WAIT
– Pattie Brooks (Casablanca)

MAGIC LOVE/CAN'T YOU FEEL IT – Michele (West End)

NATIVE NEW YORKER – Odyssey (RCA)

YOUR LOVE IS SO GOOD FOR ME – Diana Ross (Motown)

YOU'VE GOT MAGIC – Rice & Beans (TK)

THE EXILE, WASHINGTON, DC
DJ: Vince Michaels

BLOCK PARTY – Anthony White (Salsoul)

DANCE, DANCE, DANCE – Chic (Atlantic)

DISCO DANCE/MAGIC LOVE/CAN'T YOU FEEL IT/HOLD
ME, SQUEEZE ME – Michele (West End)

I GOT TO HAVE YOUR LOVE/THERE'S FIRE DOWN
BELOW – Fantastic Four (Westbound)

LE SPANK – Le Pamplemousse (AVI)

LET THE MUSIC PLAY – Dorothy Moore (TK)

MOON-BOOTS – Orlando Riva Sound (Salsoul)

RUNNING AWAY – Roy Ayers Ubiquity (Polydor)

YOUR LOVE IS SO GOOD TO ME – Diana Ross (Motown)

YOU'VE GOT MAGIC – Rice & Beans (TK)

DISCO FILE TOP 20

1. DANCE, DANCE, DANCE – Chic (Atlantic)
2. GIRL DON'T MAKE ME WAIT/LOVE SHOOK
   – Pattie Brooks (Casablanca)
3. DON'T LET ME BE MISUNDERSTOOD
   – Santa Esmeralda (Casablanca)
4. I GOT TO HAVE YOUR LOVE – Fantastic Four
   (Westbound)
5. NATIVE NEW YORKER – Odyssey (RCA)
6. BLOCK PARTY – Anthony White (Salsoul)
7. LE SPANK – Le Pamplemousse (AVI)
8. POP COLLAGE/LET'S MAKE LOVE TO THE MUSIC
   – Pattie Brooks (Casablanca)
9. YOUR LOVE IS SO GOOD FOR ME – Diana Ross
   (Motown)
10. RUNNING AWAY – Roy Ayers Ubiquity (Polydor)
11. SPEAK WELL – Philly USA (West End)
12. COSMIC WIND/THE BULL – Mike Theodore
    Orchestra (Westbound)
13. SAN FRANCISCO/HOLLYWOOD/FIRE ISLAND
    – Village People (Casablanca)
14. LA VIE EN ROSE – Grace Jones (Island)
15. THERE'S FIRE, DOWN BELOW – Fantastic Four
    (Westbound)
16. YOU'VE GOT MAGIC – Rice & Beans (TK)
17. DISCO DANCE/CAN'T YOU FEEL IT/MAGIC LOVE
    – Michele (West End)
18. IT'S ECSTASY WHEN YOU LAY DOWN NEXT TO ME
    – Barry White (20th Century)
19. MOON-BOOTS – Orlando Riva Sound (Salsoul)
20. WATCH OUT FOR THE BOOGIE MAN – Trax
    (Polydor import)

Thelma Houston's new album, "The Devil In Me" (Tamla), contains the expected longer version (6:31) of "I'm Here Again" and if the additional few minutes don't entirely redeem this "Don't Leave Me This Way" retread, they definitely do give it the added punch at the end that it needed. Whether a few superb piano runs and string accents can dispel the general disinterest that has greeted the single in the clubs remains to be seen, but "I'm Here" deserves another listening in this expanded form. Unfortunately, the rest of Houston's album seems to lack a coherent spirit in the product and many of the cuts fall far short of what they could be, but, for the dancers, "It's Just Me Feeling Good" has a certain appealing bounce. Much more satisfying as an album is **Freda Payne's** latest, "Stares And Whispers" (Capitol), which should put her right back up there at the top of the female vocal field again. Producer **Frank Wilson**, who has done so much fine work this year, suits Payne as handsomely as **Holland Dozier-Holland** did once, particularly on "Love Magnet" (6:23), with its darting synthesizer touches, and "Master Of Love." ✍

A new **Donna Summer** album is always an event, but "Once Upon A Time... " (Casablanca), which made a swift and sudden appearance at a number of key discos across the country this past weekend and should be hitting the stores just about the time we hit the newsstands, is deserving of even more attention and celebration than usual. Summer's first two-record set, "Once Upon A Time" is a modern interpretation of the Cinderella story, a disco fairy tale in four acts apparently designed to work as both a concept album and a musical score for future film or play. As such, it's not only the most ambitious project Summer and producers **Giorgio Moroder** and **Pete Bellotte** have undertaken but it's also the most commercially accessible record of their combined careers to date; "flawless" may be too absolute a word to apply to something so broad and varied, but the album approaches that level of technical brilliance. Like all four-sided albums, this one takes some getting into, only here the nearly seamless design – three of the four sides (Acts 1, 2 and 4) are unbroken song medleys – and the clarity and consistency of the story line make it easier to grasp: everything falls into place smoothly and precisely. With all this space and time to work with, Moroder and Bellotte are able to experiment with a variety of styles and moods, making one whole side (Act 2) into a crackling synthesizer tour de force (the logical extension of the "I Feel Love" sound) and elsewhere drawing upon elements of light classical, pop and Broadway show music. Like "I Remember Yesterday," "One Upon A Time ..." was clearly intended as a vehicle to satisfy both disco and pop audiences and it succeeds primarily because the production team has synthesized rather than polarized the two styles. Their songs are more memorable, more hook-filled than ever before; they are also more focused on lyrics and vocals than the early Donna Summer material. Now that everyone else is doing long aural landscape tracks with minimal, hypnotically repeated vocals, Summer, Moroder & Bellotte have moved on to elaborate song cycles that give Donna a wider, more exciting role as a singer without cramping the musical adventurousness of her producers. If nothing else, this album should put an end to the idea that Donna Summer can't sing; here she sings and sings and sings, using as many different voices as the producers have styles, matching her mood to theirs, and proving utterly involving throughout.

As far as disco material is concerned, the three medley sides are all excellent and probably will be played both whole and in part. Act 2's synthesizer-laced cuts – "Now I Need You," "Working The Midnight Shift" and "Queen For A Day," running a total time of seventeen minutes – make it the most compelling and intense run through side – not as complex or forbidding as **Giorgio's** "From Here To Eternity," but wonderfully dense and sharp. Act 4, the happy ending side, is very up and pretty, with the second cut, "I Love You," standing out as a big favorite already; the mood here is broken after the third cut for a reprise of the album's opening title theme with an over-dramatic reading by Summer (who sounds surprisingly like **Diana Ross**) which sums up the Cinderella story. Most of Act 1,

> **❝ Now that everyone else is doing long aural landscape tracks with minimal, hypnotically repeated vocals, Summer, Moroder & Bellotte have moved on to elaborate song cycles ❞**

12 WEST, NEW YORK
DJ: Jim Burgess

ACT 1/ ACT 2/ ACT 4 – Donna Summer
(Casablanca)
DANCE, DANCE, DANCE – Chic (Atlantic)
KISS ME – George McCrae (TK)
LE SPANK – Le Pamplemousse (AVI)
LOVE BUG – Tina Charles (CBS import)
MOON-BOOTS – ORS (Salsoul)
NATIVE NEW YORKER/EASY COME, EASY GO
– Odyssey (RCA)
**THERE'S FIRE DOWN BELOW/I GOT TO HAVE YOUR
LOVE** – Fantastic Four (Westbound)
TWO HOT FOR LOVE – THP Orchestra (Butterfly)

YESTERDAY'S, BOSTON
DJ: Cosmo Wyatt

BLOCK PARTY/I CAN'T TURN YOU LOOSE – Anthony
White (Salsoul)
DANCE, DANCE, DANCE – Chic (Atlantic)
DISCO CONGO – King Errisson (Westbound)
FROM NOW ON – Linda Clifford (Warner Bros.)
MUSIC'S TAKING OVER/JUMP FOR JOY – Jacksons (Epic)
NATIVE NEW YORKER – Odyssey (RCA)
ON FIRE, GETTING HIGHER – T-Connection (TK)
RUNNING AWAY – Roy Ayers Ubiquity (Polydor)
TOMORROW/LA VIE EN ROSE – Grace Jones (Island)
YOUR LOVE IS SO GOOD FOR ME – Diana Ross
(Motown)

THE FOX TRAPPE, WASHINGTON, D.C.
DJ: Frank Edwards

THE BEAT GOES ON AND ON – Ripple (Salsoul)
BOURGIE, BOURGIE – Ashford & Simpson
(Warner Bros.)
COME GO WITH ME – Pockets (Columbia)
DANCE, DANCE, DANCE – Chic (Atlantic)
DISCO DANCE – Michele (West End)
DON'T LET ME BE MISUNDERSTOOD
– Santa Esmeralda (Casablanca)
MUSIC'S TAKING OVER – Jacksons (Epic)
OU SONT LES FEMMES – Patrick Juvet
(Barclay import)
WHO LOVES YOU – The Joneses (Epic)
YOUR LOVE IS SO GOOD FOR ME – Diana Ross
(Motown)

CASABLANCA 2, NEW YORK
DJ: Hector Saez

THE BULL/COSMIC WIND – Mike Theodore Orchestra
(Westbound)
CAN'T YOU FEEL IT – Michele (West End)
CHOVE CHUVA/MAS QUE NADA – Samba Soul (RCA)
DANCE, DANCE, DANCE – Chic (Atlantic)
DON'T LET ME BE MISUNDERSTOOD
– Santa Esmeralda (Casablanca)
THE MAD RUSSIAN/DANCING IN THE DARK
– Enoch Light & the Light Brigade (Project)
NATIVE NEW YORKER – Odyssey (RCA)
USTED ABUSO – Celia Cruz & Willie Colon (Vaya)
YOU'VE GOT MAGIC – Rice & Beans Orchestra (TK)

save for the final cut, is equally upbeat, the strongest cuts being "Faster And Faster To Nowhere," a nightmare vision of big city life, and "Fairy Tale High," the compensating fantasy that follows. People are also playing "If You Got It, Flaunt It," the opening track on side/Act 3, but this medium-tempo song strikes me as being rather too strident and theatrical – it is fun, however, and that's probably what's putting it over right now. Actually, the whole album is great fun – it's Donna's loosest, most entertaining work so far. Enjoy.

The other essential album this week is **Isaac Hayes'** "New Horizon," his first for Polydor and a major comeback move for the man who was one of the early influences on the modern disco style. Hayes pushed soul album cuts to new lengths and his movie themes established the stylistic landscape that many disco producers still build upon, but it's obvious he's been influenced in turn by the Eurodisco avant garde on this, his first album in two and a half years. The result is a knockout cut called "Moonlight Lovin' (Ménage A Trois)," that sounds like Isaac Hayes meets **Cerrone**. It's a long (10:02), three-way seduction record that combines Hayes' most insinuating, sensuous vocals with female back-up singers cooing, "Voulez-vous couchez avec nous." There are trademark Isaac Hayes touches (the crooning horns, stinging hi-hats) and some electronic squiggles that recall **Gloria Gaynor's** "Casanova Brown," but the structure and the changes are very continental. "Moonlight Lovin'" is like nothing we've heard from Hayes before, and his interpretation of the European sound is so fresh, we're anxious to hear more in the same vein. The album's other notable track is a complex, awfully speedy version of "Stranger In Paradise" (10:07) that begins with a fine, richly atmospheric instrumental section but eventually turns into just another fast-hustle-styled remake – nice but no breakthroughs here. Polydor has made both cuts available on a promotional disco disc.

"Goin' Places," the new **Jacksons** album (Epic/ Philadelphia International) doesn't really go any places they haven't been before, but at least two cuts are attractive enough to begin picking up some disco play (see this week's top 10s from Cosmo Wyatt in Boston and Frank Edwards in D.C.). "Music's Takin' Over" and "Jump For Joy" are both lively, energetic songs with wonderful vocals from **Michael Jackson** but they're the kind of light-weight pop that the group should have outgrown years ago – all surface, no depth. Cute. Period.

NOTES: A number of people have called to reprimand me for ignoring another great cut (besides "Bourgie Bourgie") on the recent **Ashford & Simpson** album ("Send It" on Warner Brothers), titled "Don't Cost You Nothin'." Yes, it's terrific – absolutely beautiful vocals, a glowing production. I hang my head in shame... Both **Thelma Houston's** "I'm Here Again" (Tamla) and **Freda Payne's** "Love Magnet" (Capitol) are now available on promotional disco discs, same lengths as the lp cuts and Payne's is backed with the vibrant "Sky Islands" cut from **Caldera's** latest album. ◐

NOVEMBER 19, 1977

THE ESSENTIAL ALBUMS: The new **Trammps** lp, "The Trammps III" (Atlantic), was preceded this week by the promotional disco disc release of its premier cut, "The Night The Lights Went Out," a highly romanticized vision of last summer's New York City blackout that proves the group is still at the top of its form. Clearly, **Baker, Harris & Young** have become the sharpest, most consistently interesting producers working in the Philadelphia style and even if, like past masters **Gamble & Huff**, they seem unwilling or unable to revamp or redirect their formula approach, the results are so perfect, so utterly enjoyable that one can hardly complain. And of course having an instantly recognizable sound doesn't hurt when it comes to breaking a new record: "The Night The Lights Went Out" is so unmistakably the Trammps that it goes over like an old favorite the first time out. All the ingredients are here: **Jimmy Ellis'** gritty, razor-edged lead vocals; **Earl Young's** relentless, irresistible drumming; the vivacious strings and stinging guitars. But what gives this "Night" its particular excitement is the blackout break, when everything but the drums and the voices cuts out, introducing what is perhaps the best spoken interlude out of Philadelphia since "I'll Always Love My Mama;" when the power is restored and the strings come flowing back, the song reaches its peak and you're hooked (for life). The album's other outstanding track is a nine-minute rave-up titled "People Of The World" that is basically "Disco Party" Part II – an intense peak cut. In between the two, there's a nice, chunky song called "Love Per Hour" that gets over on its chugging breaks and inventive vocal effects. In a departure from earlier albums, the second side contains a number of shorter cuts, inducing three wonderful mid-tempo smooth numbers – "I'm So Glad You Came Along," "Living The Life" and "Life Ain't Been Easy," the first my personal pick – and one lovely ballad, "Season For Girls" (7:56) that could turn into a big slow favorite. Though we'd appreciate a little more innovation here, the Trammps remain the unchallenged dance kings and it's always a delight to have them back on the turntables; already serviced in advanced to most discos, the lp should be in the stores sometime this week... Butterfly Records' first big disco release since **Saint Tropez** is also the first American lp from Canada's **THP Orchestra** and features an amazing 16-minute version of its title song, "Two Hot for Love." Though the import disco disc version of "Two Hot" was already enthusiastically reviewed here last June, this edition, reworked in Los Angeles, is a whole new thing. Not only has the record been expanded to more than twice its original length and broken down into banded, subtitled sections –"Four-play," "Excitement Part 1 & 2," "Climax" and "Resolution" – but a lead female vocal and a number of synthesizer and drums tracks have been added to beef up the track. Though the rough texture of the new lead voice seems occasionally out of keeping with the overall feel of the record, it definitely helps give the cut continuity and spark, and the other changes are undoubtedly improvements, turning a minor but appealing import item into a major knockout. Side two contains four cuts that originally appeared on the group's "Early Riser" import album, all remixed as well; check out "Early Riser" and their version of the "Theme From Black Orpheus," here titled "Carnival." Again, Butterfly has made the first run of the album a collector's edition, pressed on opaque white vinyl.

RECOMMENDED DISCO DISCS: **Linda Clifford's** vivacious version of "From Now On" has been taken off her recent Warner Brothers album and expanded to seven minutes for a 12-inch pressing that is fast becoming my favorite new female vocal. A nice, pumping production supports her snappy delivery beautifully. The flip side is Clifford's interpretation of "You Can Do It," the song **Arthur Prysock** did a few months back, also running seven minutes... The **Olympic Runners'** "Keep It Up" (London), a hard-edged disco cut with rock overtones, is rousing but awfully mechanical and, because its structure is an unchanging loop, too long at 6:40. In spite of this, early word-of-mouth is favorable, it's already showing up on scattered top 10 lists, and it looks like the record could be the Runners' first disco success in quite some time... "You're So Right For Me" by the **Eastside Connection** (Rampart) has been around for a while already without causing much stir, maybe because it's in the Latin hustle style now passing out of fashion, but there's something so attractive here that it's hard to resist even if it does seem an anachronism. The sound is very Young & Latin, sweetly innocent and fresh, with **Eddie Drennon**-ish strings and flute ornamentation and cuts, ingratiating vocals from a mixed group of singers. Added attraction: the record, which has a vocal and an instrumental side, both about six minutes long, is pressed on multi-colored vinyl so it's more fun to watch on the turntable.

> **❝ First played as an unnamed tape at David Mancuso's Loft more than a month ago, "Come Into My Heart" was slow to get on the disco grapevine, but once TK picked up the record, word spread fast ❞**

INFERNO, NEW YORK
DJ: Walter Gibbons

ACT 1/ACT 2/ACT 4/IF YOU GOT IT FLAUNT IT – Donna Summer (Casablanca)

BLOCK PARTY – Anthony White (Salsoul)

BOURGIE BOURGIE/DON'T COST YOU NOTHIN' – Ashford & Simpson (Warner Bros.)

DAN SWIT ME – Patti LaBelle (Epic)

DANCE, DANCE, DANCE – Chic (Atlantic)

I'M HERE AGAIN – Thelma Houston (Motown)

KISS ME – George McCrae (TK)

LE SPANK – Le Pamplemousse (AVI)

TOP OF THE WORLD/YOUR LOVE IS SO GOOD FOR ME – Diana Ross (Motown)

WHAT'S YOUR NAME, WHAT'S YOUR NUMBER – Andrea True Connection (Buddah)

FLAMINGO, NEW YORK
DJ: Howard Merritt

ACT 1/ ACT 2/ ACT 4 – Donna Summer (Casablanca)

BLOCK PARTY – Anthony White (Salsoul)

DANCE, DANCE, DANCE – Chic (Atlantic)

DON'T LET ME BE MISUNDERSTOOD – Santa Esmeralda (Casablanca)

GIRL DON'T MAKE ME WAIT – Pattie Brooks (Casablanca)

I GOT TO HAVE YOUR LOVE – Fantastic Four (Westbound)

IT'S ECSTASY WHEN YOU LAY DOWN NEXT TO ME – Barry White (20th Century)

KISS ME – George McCrae (TK)

LE SPANK – Le Pamplemousse (AVI)

NATIVE NEW YORKER – Odyssey (RCA)

IPANEMA, NEW YORK
DJ: Ronnie Soares

ACT 1/ACT 2/ACT 4 – Donna Summer (Casablanca)

CHILDHOOD FOREVER – Recreation (Dynamo)

CHOVE CHUVA/MAS QUE NADA – Samba Soul (RCA)

DANCE, DANCE, DANCE – Chic (Atlantic)

DISCO BLOOD – The Vamps (Building import)

KISS ME – George McCrae (TK)

LOVE BUG – Tina Charles (CBS import)

MAGIC LOVE/DISCO DANCE – Michele (West End)

THE NIGHT THE LIGHTS WENT OUT – Trammps (Atlantic)

STANDING IN THE RAIN – John Paul Young (Midsong)

BUZZBY'S, SAN FRANCISCO
DJ: Christine Matuchek

ACT 1/ACT 2/RUMOR HAS IT – Donna Summer (Casablanca)

BACK IN LOVE AGAIN – L.T.D. (A&M)

DISCO CONGO/L.A. BOUND/SALSOUL SISTER – King Errisson (Westbound)

DISCO DANCE/MAGIC LOVE/CAN'T YOU FEEL IT – Michele (West End)

JOHNNY, JOHNNY PLEASE COME HOME – Claudja Barry (Salsoul)

KEEP IT UP – Olympic Runners (London)

MOON-BOOTS – ORS (Salsoul)

ON FIRE, GETTING HIGHER – T-Connection (TK)

TWO HOT FOR LOVE – THP Orchestra (Butterfly)

WHAT'S YOUR NAME, WHAT'S YOUR NUMBER – Andrea True Connection (Buddah)

NEWS & NOTES: The hottest unreleased record on the New York circuit is an incredible side called "Come Into My Heart/Good Loving" that is one of the most striking and exciting pieces of music I've heard this year. First played as an unnamed tape at David Mancuso's Loft more than a month ago, the song was slow to get on the disco grapevine, but once TK picked up the record, word spread fast and sneak previews have been held in a number of other dubs. Now it's getting the kind of intense word-of-mouth that greeted "Love In C Minor" and **Love & Kisses** and it seems destined to be among 1977's most important debuts. But it'll get in just under the wire: the album which contains "Come Into My Heart" as one full side isn't scheduled for release until mid-December. The group, a studio aggregation, is called **USA/European Connection** because, though it was produced in Philadelphia, the track sounds very European – a brilliant fusion. And those people already swooning over "Come Into My Heart" won't be disappointed by the album's flip side, another innovative long cut called "Love's Coming/Baby Love"... **Jacques Morali**, who promises that the next **Village People** album will be even more bold than the first (after the group returns from their current disco promo tour, they're going back into the studio), alerted us to some other interesting European/USA connections this past week: **Nicholas Skorsky**, co-producer of **Santa Esmeralda** is also the composer of "Crystal World" by **Crystal Grass**; **Don Ray**, star arranger for Santa Esmeralda, **Cerrone**, **Love & Kisses** and **Sphinx**, can also be found in the "Crystal World" credits – only there he was using his real name: Raymond Donnez; and, finally, **Leroy Gomez**, lead singer for Santa Esmeralda, is yet another American performer who was discovered in Europe – like **Donna Summer**, he's from Boston, but he'd been doing session work in Paris for years before the international success of "Don't Let Me Be Misunderstood." Morali says "Misunderstood" is still riding high in Paris discos but **Grace Jones** is soaring even higher with "La Vie En Rose," a sentimental favorite for the French... Not surprisingly, **Donna Summer's** "Once Upon A Time..." album appears on every top 10 list this week and hits the DISCO FILE Top 20 at number 10, but with three sides being listed in their entirety – Acts 1, 2 and 4 – it's still too early to single out one or two cuts as most-likely-to-succeed on their own. We've been asking everyone for favorites anyway and, though most people end up rattling off practically every track on the album, these do stand out now: "Rumor Has It," "Now I Need You," "I Love You," "Faster And Faster To Nowhere" and "If You Got It Flaunt It." Other records that are looking good: **Freda Payne's** "Love Magnet" (Capitol), **George McCrae's** "Kiss Me" (TK), "What's Your Name, What's Your Number" by the **Andrea True Connection** (Buddah), "Bourgie Bourgie" and "Don't Cost You Nothin'" by **Ashford & Simpson** (Warner Brothers) and the entire **Michele album** (West End). ◉

NOVEMBER 26, 1977

There are so many important new albums this week that the reviews will have to be brief. Too bad, 'cause **Cerrone's** new "Supernature" (Cotillion) is just the sort of album I'd love to spend several paragraphs on. "Love In C Minor" is surely one of the key albums of the year – it signaled the emergence of a new European disco style and opened the way for a rush of new performers and producers from the continent as well as firmly establishing the one side/one song format pioneered by **Summer**, **Moroder** and **Bellotte** – but "Supernature" is even more satisfying as a whole. The title side adds a little **Giorgio** synthesizer to the usual pulsing Cerrone production and comes up with something appropriately ominous-sounding for this song of ecological perversion – animals poisoned by pollution taking their "sweet revenge" on mankind. The final verse is a little too preachy but the music is so superb – a fascinating mix of sci-fi doom and sensuality, pounding drums and wooshing synthesizers – that nothing else really matters. A fabulous percussion segment ("Sweet Drums," 2:43) caps the ten-minute "Supernature" and then dips into a moody, almost classical instrumental called "In the Smoke" (5:32) which closes side one on a meditative, dreamy note. Side two, three interlocking cuts, "Give Me Love"/"Love Is the Answer" (total time: 16:30), is in an entirely different mood: optimistic, cheery, very up. The female vocals are sharper and more prominent than on previous Cerrone numbers; the orchestration is bright and sweeping with the strings, as always, finely etched and dramatic. Two peak records back-to-back make this one an especially essential album right now.

We've been hearing rumors about and sneak previews from a collection of Philadelphia International hits disco-mixed by **Tom Moulton** for months. But now that the two-record set, titled "Philadelphia Classics," has finally been released, it's even more impressive than we'd expected. Included are entirely remixed versions of "Love Is The Message," "Don't Leave Me This Way," "Dirty Ol' Man," "I Love Music," "Bad Luck," "I'll Always Love My Mama," "Love Train" and "TSOP" – two to a side and all substantially longer and hotter sounding than in their original form. The two most stunning tracks are "Love Is The Message" (11:27), featuring vocals by the **Three Degrees** at their finest, and the original **Harold Melvin & the Bluenotes** version of "Don't Leave Me This Way" (11:00), with **Teddy Pendergrass** in the lead and marvelous echo effects in the long vamp ending. But all the songs represent the Philadelphia Sound at its height and the new versions are exciting enough to spark revivals of many of them, especially the **MFSB** which never went out of date anyway. A most respectable and rewarding way to re-release old material, the "Philadelphia Classics" package sets a new high standard for "oldies" collections. But where's the disco-mix credit on the cover?

Also coming on very strong in its first week out is the **Chic** debut album on Atlantic with the instant pick-up cut being "Everybody Dance" (6:40), which has the same sort of easy elegance and quick energy that sent "Dance,

Dance, Dance" to the top. The pace here isn't quite as driven as "DDD," but everything's so smoothly polished and comfortable that you just slip into it irresistibly on first listening. Two other cuts, "You Can Get By" and "Est-ce Que C'est Chic," are lighter-weight but attractive, especially the instrumental build on the former. Excellent pop disco, so tastefully, carefully done that it could turn into one of the year's major crossover albums, too.

FUNK IT UP – An accumulation of quality funk records in several formats: **Jeff Lane** puts **Brass Construction** through its paces again on "Brass Construction III" (UA) – as usual, very classy, elegantly turned progressive funk. If their sound is a little overfamiliar by now, and "III" represents no great advance on their first lp, Brass Construction remains a reliable stand-by at many clubs and we'll go along with the selection of cuts Graylin Riley chose for his top 10 from Brooklyn's jazz club/disco, the Guest House, this week: "We," "Get It Together," "Top Of The World" and "Celebrate"... It's just **Fatback** now according to the cover of the new Fatback Band album, "Man With The Band" (Spring), and maybe trimming the name was just what they needed because this is a nice bounce back after the group's last lp. No major shifts in style here either, but they're in top form on "Master Booty," the ecstatic, jazzy "Mile High," and the bizarre "Midnight Freak" – also check out "Funk Backin'." One side is titled VINTAGE/House Party, the other TASTY/Disco Party but they both cook... The **Players Association** is back with their second album, "Born To Dance" (Vanguard), and more pleasant excursions into the jazz/funk/disco field. Among the star names in the credits this time: **David Sanborn**, **Michael Brecker**, **Nicky Marrero**, **Jon Faddis** and leader **Chris Hills**, who wrote nearly all the material. Outstanding cuts: a wonderfully different interpretation of "Disco Inferno" (great horns!), "Goin' To The Disco" and "How Do You Like It;" "We Were Born To Dance" has a rather uneven tempo but gets quite zesty, too... The new **B.T. Express** disco disc, "Shout It Out" (Roadshow/Columbia), is their first work away from producer **Jeff Lane** and the move, while not that radical, does seem to have perked them up some. The song is an encouragement to go off by yourself and shout out your frustrations (is this a plug

STUDIO 54, NEW YORK
DJ: Richie Kaczor

BLOCK PARTY – Anthony White (Salsoul)
DANCE, DANCE, DANCE/YOU CAN GET BY – Chic (Atlantic)
DANCE A LITTLE BIT CLOSER/YOU'RE JUST THE RIGHT SIZE – Charo (Salsoul)
DON'T LET ME BE MISUNDERSTOOD – Santa Esmeralda (Casablanca)
I DON'T KOW WHAT I'D DO – Sweet Cream (Bareback)
KEEP IT UP – Olympic Runners (London)
LE SPANK – Le Pamplemousse (AVI)
NATIVE NEW YORKER/EASY COME, EASY GO – Odyssey (RCA)
THE NIGHT THE LIGHTS WENT OUT/PEOPLE OF THE WORLD/LOVE PER HOUR – Trammps (Atlantic)
ON FIRE – T-Connection (TK)

PENROD'S, EAST MEADOW, NEW YORK
DJ: Jackie McCloy

ACT I – Donna Summer (Casablanca)
DANCE, DANCE, DANCE – Chic (Atlantic)
DISCO DANCE – Michele (West End)
DON'T LET ME BE MISUNDERSTOOD – Santa Esmeralda (Casablanca)
I GOT TO HAVE YOUR LOVE – Fantastic Four (Westbound)
MAKE YOUR MOVE – Tommy Smiley (RCA)
NATIVE NEW YORKER – Odyssey (RCA)
THE NIGHT THE LIGHTS WENT OUT – Trammps (Atlantic)
SUPERNATURE/GIVE ME LOVE – Cerrone (Cotillion)
WHAT'S YOUR NAME, WHAT'S YOUR NUMBER – Andrea True Connection (Buddah)

OIL CAN HARRY'S, SAN FRANCISCO
DJ: John Hedges

ACT 2/ACT 4 – Donna Summer (Casablanca)
BACK IN LOVE AGAIN – L.T.D. (A&M)
CAN'T YOU FEEL IT/MAGIC LOVE/ DISCO DANCE – Michele (West End)
DANCE, DANCE, DANCE – Chic (Atlantic)
KISS ME – George McCrae (TK)
MOON-BOOTS – ORS (Salsoul)
THE NIGHT THE LIGHTS WENT OUT/PEOPLE OF THE WORLD – Trammps (Atlantic)
ON FIRE – T-Connection (TK)
SALSOUL SISTER/MANHATTAN LOVE SONG/WELL, HAVE A NICE DAY – King Errisson (Westbound)
SUPERNATURE/SWEET DRUMS/GIVE ME LOVE – Cerrone (Cotillion)

THE GUEST HOUSE, BROOKLYN, N.Y.
DJ: Graylin Riley

BOP GUN – Parliament (Casablanca)
DISCO INFERNO/GOING TO THE DISCO – Players Association (Vanguard)
IF YOU FEEL LIKE DANCIN' – Al Hudson & the Soul Partners (ABC)
MOONLIGHT LOVIN' (MENAGE A TROIS) – Isaac Hayes (Polydor)
MOON-BOOTS – ORS (Salsoul)
THE NIGHT THE LIGHTS WENT OUT – Trammps (Atlantic)
NOW I NEED YOU/WORKING THE MIDNIGHT SHIFT – Donna Summer (Casablanca lp cuts)
POP COLLAGE/GIRL DON'T MAKE ME WAIT/LOVE SHOOK – Pattie Brooks (Casablanca)
RUNNING AWAY – Roy Ayers Ubiquity (Polydor)
TOP OF THE WORLD/CELEBRATE/WE/GET IT TOGETHER – Brass Construction (UA)

for primal scream therapy?) and, though the message may prove antithetical to the feelings of most disco-goers, who much prefer to do their shouting in crowds, the chunky rhythmic structure is engaging. The pace bogs down slightly here and there but the group has preserved the incantory, almost Middle-Eastern quality of their horn work and that carries the whole thing off... **Al Hudson and the Soul Partners** also have a hot disco disc out right now, an expanded version (6:08) of their recent single, "If You Feel Like Dancin'" (ABC), that starts out like any other funk-based disco cut but turns into a terrific instrumental jam. Very "get on down" with percussion, horns, chanting voices, plenty of breaks – not to be overlooked... And finally, two singles that deserve attention: **Parliament's** pumping, delightfully spacey "Bop Gun" (Casablanca), their strongest disco entry in years, running a substantial 4:20 on the 45; and **Stargard's** "Theme Song from 'Which Way Is Up" (MCA), written by **Norman Whitfield** for the new Richard Pryor movie and very much in the jagged, jumping mold of "Car Wash," right down to the relentless handclaps. ◐

DISCO FILE TOP 20

1. **DANCE, DANCE, DANCE** – Chic (Atlantic)
2. **DON'T LET ME BE MISUNDERSTOOD** – Santa Esmeralda (Casablanca)
3. **NATIVE NEW YORKER** – Odyssey (RCA)
4. **LE SPANK** – Le Pamplemousse (AVI)
5. **DISCO DANCE/CAN'T YOU FEEL IT/MAGIC LOVE** – Michele (West End)
6. **I GOT TO HAVE YOUR LOVE** – Fantastic Four (Westbound)
7. **ACT 1/ACT 2/ACT 4** – Donna Summer (Casablanca)
8. **GIRL DON'T MAKE ME WAIT/LOVE SHOOK** – Pattie Brooks (Casablanca)
9. **MOON-BOOTS** – ORS (Salsoul)
10. **BLOCK PARTY** – Anthony White (Salsoul)
11. **KISS ME** – George McCrae (TK)
12. **YOUR LOVE IS SO GOOD FOR ME** – Diana Ross (Motown)
13. **THE NIGHT THE LIGHTS WENT OUT** – Trammps (Atlantic)
14. **ON FIRE** – T-Connection (TK)
15. **RUNNING AWAY** – Roy Ayers Ubiquity (Polydor)
16. **THERE'S FIRE DOWN BELOW** – Fantastic Four (Westbound)
17. **YOU'VE GOT MAGIC** – Rice & Beans (TK)
18. **LA VIE EN ROSE** – Grace Jones (Island)
19. **POP COLLAGE/LET'S MAKE LOVE TO THE MUSIC** – Pattie Brooks (Casablanca)
20. **THE BULL/COSMIC WIND** – Mike Theodore Orchestra (Westbound)

DECEMBER 3, 1977

I was feeling pretty down about this week's batch of disco releases until a few records proved sharp enough to cut through the prevailing mush. Among the best: The new disco disc mix of **Evelyn "Champagne" King's** "Shame" (RCA) lengthens and utterly revitalizes that cut from her recent album so that it snaps and sparkles like it never did before. Disco mixers **David Todd** and **Al Garrison** have given the song the clarity and drive that the original version lacked, bringing up handclaps, guitar and other elements that had been buried so that the new track grabs you from the very beginning and doesn't let go. King's vocals also benefit from the restorative mix and now she dominates the song brilliantly, newly impressive. Flip side of the disc is "Dancin', Dancin', Dancin'" in pretty much its original form but the quality of the pressing makes it, too, sound brighter... Most of "Galaxy" is classic, down-to-basics **War** – that trademark steady percussion, Afro-jazz tinged, with heavy, chanted vocals – but the theme's outer space: "goin' one on one with a meteorite." And surrounding, sometimes even zipping through, this central funk core is some very spacey instrumental – part "Star Wars," part tribal rite, part jazz jam, part house party, but all terrific if a bit far out for many crowds. The cut's just over eight minutes on War's new album ("Galaxy" on MCA) or it's available in two parts on a 45 – 4:18/3:29, with all the crazy stuff on Part II. This is War at its best: freaky and fun... "Saturday Night Fever," the sound track from the forthcoming John Travolta disco movie, is a two-record set on RSO starring the **Bee Gees** – who are represented by four new songs plus "Jive Talkin'" and "You Should Be Dancing" – and featuring an excellent selection of material by the **Trammps** ("Disco Inferno"), **Ralph MacDonald** ("Calypso Breakdown"), **Kool & the Gang** ("Open Sesame"), **MFSB** ("K-Jee") and others. Two of the new Bee Gees songs, "Stayin' Alive" and "Night Fever," are crisp and pumping in the "Jive Talkin'" vein and the group's piercing little voices keep you on edge throughout. But **David Shire's** three original instrumentals, all done in an elegant, pseudo-Philadelphia style, have the often unbalanced sound of a live dance band rather than the ultra sleek disco orchestra sound we're used to. Still, this is a fine collection, a nice combination of new and familiar material, and it certainly whets our appetite to finally see the film. (It should be noted that disco music also forms the bulk of the material on Columbia's "Looking For Mr. Goodbar" sound track album, too. Among the selections are the original, if much shortened, versions of "Try Me I Know We Can Make It," "Don't Leave Me This Way," "Love Hangover," "Lowdown" and "Backstabbers."... The disco disc version of **Leo Sayer's** "Thunder In My Heart" (6:30 on Warner Brothers) emphasizes the pounding rock/disco potential only hinted at on the single and lp cut versions. The break, intertwining Latin percussion and swirling strings and then blending back to the powerhouse vocals, gives the record just the edge it needed.

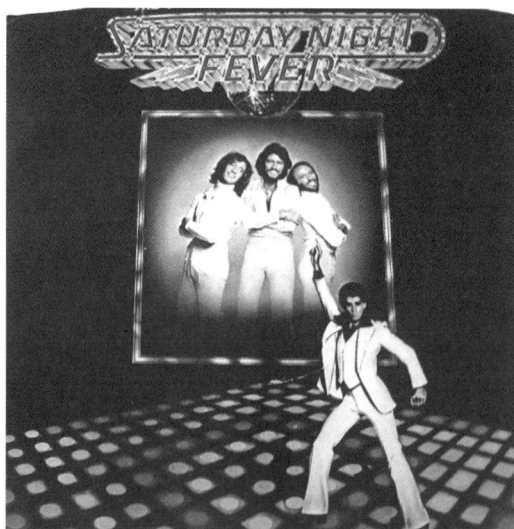

❝ It certainly whets our appetite to finally see the film ❞

Other notable albums: **King Errisson's** "L.A. Bound" (Westbound) has been showing up on top 10 listings for several weeks now with nearly everyone of its five cuts getting reports. Produced by **Dennis Coffey** and **Mike Theodore**, masters of the modern Detroit sound, the album is technically exciting but, for me at least, it falls short of the kind of involvement and depth previous Westbound records have always delivered in abundance. With those reservations, "Manhattan Love Song" (10:21) is still a fascinatingly moody composition (compare "Harlem Nocturne" for style) that has a number of fine passages and "Disco Congo" is certainly a percussive tour de force. Also getting a lot of play: "Sal Soul Sister," which echoes "Fire Down Below" at first, and "Well, Have A Nice Day"... The title cut from **Billy Paul's** new album, "Only The Strong Survive" (Philadelphia International) is a revival of the **Gamble & Huff** song originally recorded by Jerry Butler, but here it's given a modern, upbeat slant and an energetic, long ending with some of Paul's better riffing vocals that puts it over...I'm not really won over by the lead vocals on **Lonnie Smith's** "Funk Reaction" (the title cut of his new Lester Radio Corp. album, available through TK), but the disco break is so effective, the female vocals so slickly sweet 'n' sexy, and the final instrumental section so chugging-hot that it began to really get to me after a few listens. Nice funked-up jazz; see what you think. ◎

CIRCUS DISCO, LOS ANGELES
DJ: Mike Lewis

ACT 1/ ACT 2/ ACT 4 – Donna Summer (Casablanca)
DANCE A LITTLE BIT CLOSER – Charo (Salsoul)
IT'S IN YOUR BLOOD – Linda Hopkins (Columbia)
LE SPANK – Le Pamplemousse (AVI)
MOON-BOOTS – ORS (Salsoul)
ON FIRE – T-Connection (TK)
RUN TO ME – Kelly Marie (Vanguard)
TWO HOT FOR LOVE – THP Orchestra (Butterfy)
WHAT'S YOUR NAME, WHAT'S YOUR NUMBER
– Andrea True Connection (Buddah)
YOUR LOVE IS SO GOOD FOR ME – Diana Ross (Motown)

PLAYGROUND, NEW YORK
DJ: Tony Carrasco

ACT 1/ACT 2/ACT 4 – Donna Summer (Casablanca)
DANCE, DANCE, DANCE/EVERYBODY DANCE
– Chic (Atlantic)
I'M HERE AGAIN – Thelma Houston (Tamla)
MASTER BOOTY/MIDNIGHT FREAK/MILE HIGH
– Fatback (Spring)
MOONLIGHT LOVIN'/STRANGER IN PARADISE
– Isaac Hayes (Polydor)
**PEOPLE OF THE WORLD, RISE/THE NIGHT THE LIGHTS
WENT OUT** – Trammps (Atlantic)
SUPERNATURE/GIVE ME LOVE – Cerrone (Cotillion)
THUNDER IN MY HEART – Leo Sayer (Warner Bros)
TWO HOT FOR LOVE – THP Orchestra (Butterfly)
WELL, HAVE A NICE DAY/MANHATTAN LOVE SONG
– King Errisson (Westbound)

REGINES, NEW YORK
DJ: Janota Garavaglia

ACT 1/ACT 2 – Donna Summer (Casablanca)
CITATIONS (ININTERROMPUES BEATLES MEDLEY)
– Cafe Creme (Bimbo import)
DANCE, DANCE, DANCE/EVERYBODY DANCE
– Chic (Atlantic)
GALAXY – War (MCA)
KEEP IT UP – Olympic Runners (London disco disc)
**MANHATTAN LOVE SONG/WELL, HAVE A NICE DAY/
SAL SOUL SISTER** – King Errisson (Westbound)
THE NIGHT THE LIGHTS WENT OUT – Trammps (Atlantic)
ON FIRE – T-Connection (TK)
ONE LIFE TO LIVE – Lou Rawls (Phila. Intl.)
SUPERNATURE – Cerrone (Cotillion)

SESAME, NEW YORK
DJ: John Benitez

ACT I/ACT 2/ACT 4 – Donna Summer (Casablanca)
DANCE, DANCE, DANCE/EVERYBODY DANCE – Chic
(Atlantic)
**I KNOW THAT HE KNOWS/THE OTHER SIDE OF
MIDNIGHT/HEARTACHE** – Marsha Hunt (Aves import)
KISS ME – George McCrae (TK)
ON FIRE – T-Connection (TK)
SUPERNATURE/SWEET DRUMS/GIVE ME LOVE –
Cerrone (Cotillion)
**THE NIGHT THE LIGHTS WENT OUT/ PEOPLE OF THE
WORLD RISE** – Trammps (Atlantic)
TRINIDAD – John Gibbs & the U.S, Steel Orchestra
(Solid Steel)
TWO HOT FOR LOVE – THP Orchestra (Butterfly)
WHAT'S YOUR NAME, WHAT'S YOUR NUMBER – Andrea
True Connection (Buddah)

DECEMBER 10, 1977

IMPORT REPORT: The most talked-about import on the disco front right now is a fascinating album called "Golden Tears" by **Sumeria** (Raal, from France) which was produced and written by **Alec R. Costandinos**, the creative force behind **Love & Kisses** and **Sphinx**. Although the dramatic narrative form used here picks up from "Accidental Lover" and "Simon Peter," "Golden Tears" is a departure from Costandinos' previous work in that the story/concept fills both sides of the album and the music is not entirely disco. Instead, the story – a woman named Eva, on the rebound from a relationship that crumbles during the opening minutes, meets a man who calls himself Nezet, a "cosmic traveller" sent to Earth to experience two things that do not exist on his planet: love and death – is told in a series of spoken interludes and in separate cuts of widely varying styles. The danceable cuts are brilliant, however, exquisite examples of the dense, thrilling Costandinos style, throbbing with life, lush with violins that somehow manage to be simultaneously euphoric and melancholy. "Dance And Leave It All Behind You" (4:40), which opens the album, is very reminiscent of the vocal portions of "I've Found Love"; "Cosmic Traveller" (3:00) is all instrumental, quite fast, sparkling with synthesizer; and "Why Must There Be An End"/"Golden Tears," a 12:32 blend of two tracks with some singing and some spoken parts, is the most experimental, ambitious and impressive (in spite of the fact that the transit between the songs is awkward and the voices a little intrusive). The title track closes the album with a spectacular mix of instrumental textures, a glowing sunburst of synthesizer, percussion, strings and electronic effects that breaks for Nezet's death and then sweeps into a Sphinx-like orchestral uplift. These cuts alone make "Golden Tears" the most interesting and exciting disco concept album since **Donna Summer's** "Once Upon a Time" and **Cerrone's** "Supernature," but add another two-cut blend, "Love Me Now"/"The Man From The Stars" (5:03), a lovely, moving slow piece that would make gorgeous early-evening or late-night music, and you've got a record that I suspect will become everyone's favorite at-home listening, too. Difficult, adventurous, highly stylized – "Golden Tears" isn't the sort of album you absorb on one or two listenings and it may prove too weird and talky for many crowds, but it deserves to be heard. Another album that's getting a lot of attention now is **Marsha Hunt's** "Marsha" (Aves, from Germany), a solid collection of vocals produced by **Pete Bellotte**. Hunt, who you may remember as the singer of the extremely bizarre "Oh No Not the Beast Day" several years back, sounds like a mix of **Tina Charles** and **Dee Dee Sharp** and Bellotte has packed the album with upbeat songs that emphasize her driving vocals–no long breaks here. As was obvious on **Trax**, Bellotte's approach is more hard-edged, more rock-oriented and less spacious or spacey than his partner **Giorgio Moroder's**, and the result here is more conventional than anything either of them have yet produced but extremely satisfying. My favorite cuts are the three DJ John Benitez chose for his top 10 from New York's Sesame last week: "The Other Side Of Midnight" (the best), "I Know That He Knows" and "Heartache" – but the two tracks Ellen Bogen from Sahara added to that list for her top 10 this week, "Body Language" and "Your love Is a Rollercoaster," are also worth checking out. Back to the more freaky end of the disco spectrum, there's an intriguing album from France called "Come And Dance" by **Computer** (AB Productions), one side of which is a witty, pulsing track about a computer in love called "Nobody Loves A Computer Because A Computer Doesn't Dance" (untimed here, but running about 15 minutes). The production isn't particularly inspired and its sameness becomes tiring after a time, but the beat is hard to resist and the mechanical computer "voice" (slightly accented) with its perplexed repetition of "I L.O.V.E. Y.O.U. WHY?" is fun for a while. Shimmering female voices give it a sweet edge and busy electronics keep the texture vibrant, but its length defeats it in the end and long before the computer self-destructs in a terrific flurry of sounds, one has probably lost interest. Still, Computer is clever enough to go over in part if not as a whole and should be checked into.

RECOMMENDED IMPORT DISCO DISCS: **G.M.T. Sound's** "Malaguena" (Barclay, from France) sounds just like **Santa Esmeralda** without **Leroy Gomez** – two seven-minute sides of opulent flamenco disco, a little too bombastic at times and not quite as gracefully crafted as "Don't Let Me Be Misunderstood," but rousing nevertheless. Ellen Bogen, who included this, too, on her Sahara list this week, noted that it works best slowed down... **Wayne St. John's** "Something's Up" (RCA Canada) has been out for several months now but it's due for American release on Salsoul soon and deserves an advance push. Produced by **Ian Guenther** and **Willi Morrison** (original producers of **THP Orchestral**, the record crackles with energy, soars on sharply-cut strings; in a vocal/instrumental format, both running just under seven minutes, we prefer the instrumental which retains enough female chorus material and some of the male lead to give it substance... "Space Rock" by **Rockets** (Decca, from France) is a "Magic Fly"-styled instrumental that's synthesizer-based but notable primarily for its wonderful waves of strings upon strings, anchored by a steady, deep pulse beat. Electronic voices thread through occasionally, adding a kind of computerized doo-wop. At exactly nine minutes, this is somewhat long but there are enough changes to sustain it... "Love Bug" "Sweets For My Sweet"

" Eva meets a man who calls himself Nezet, a "cosmic traveller" sent to Earth "

PARADISE GARAGE, NEW YORK
DJ: Larry Levan

THE BEAT GOES ON AND ON – Ripple (Salsoul)
COSMIC LUST – Mass Production (Cotillion)
DEEPER – New Birth (Warner Bros.)
EVERYBODY DANCE/YOU CAN GET BY/DANCE, DANCE, DANCE – Chic (Atlantic)
GIVE ME LOVE/SUPERNATURE/SWEET DRUMS – Cerrone (Cotillion)
I'M HERE AGAIN/IT'S JUST ME/FEELIN' GOOD – Thelma Houston (Tamla)
LET'S GET TOGETHER/MAKING LOVE – Pam Todd & Love Exchange (Shryden lp cuts)
LOCKED IN THIS POSITION – Barbara Mason & Bunny Sigler (Curtom)
THE NIGHT THE LIGHTS WENT OUT / LOVE PER HOUR/ PEOPLE OF THE WORLD, RISE – Trammps (Atlantic)
WHICH WAY IS UP? – Starguard (MCA)

1270, BOSTON
DJ: Danae Jacovidis

ACT I/ACT 2/ACT 4 – Donna Summer (Casablanca)
EVERYBODY DANCE – Chic (Atlantic)
KISS ME – George McCrae (TK)
LE SPANK – Le Pamplemousse (AVI)
MOON-BOOTS – ORS (Salsoul)
THE NIGHT THE LIGHTS WENT OUT/LOVE PER HOUR/ PEOPLE OF THE WORLD, RISE/LIVING THE LIFE – Trammps (Atlantic)
ON FIRE – T-Connection (TK)
SOONER OR LATER/ONLY THE STRONG SURVIVE – Billy Paul (Phila. Intl.)
SUPERNATURE/GIVE ME LOVE – Cerrone (Cotillion)
THUNDER IN MY HEART – Leo Sayer (Warner Bros.)

STUDIO ONE, LOS ANGELES
DJ: Manny Slali

ACT 1/ACT 2/ACT 4 – Donna Summer (Casablanca)
GIVE ME LOVE/SUPERNATURE/SWEET DRUMS – Cerrone (Cotillion)
IT'S IN YOUR BLOOD – Linda Hopkins (Columbia)
LOVE PER HOUR/PEOPLE OF THE WORLD, RISE/THE NIGHT THE LIGHTS WENT OUT/I'M SO GLAD YOU CAME ALONG – Trammps (Atlantic)
MOON-BOOTS – ORS (Salsoul)
ON FIRE – T-Connection (TK)
PHILADELPHIA CLASSICS – Various Artists (Phila.Intl.)
SPANK YOUR BLANK BLANK – Morris Jefferson (Parachute)
TWO HOT FOR LOVE – THP Orchestra (Butterfly)
WHAT'S YOUR NAME, WHAT'S YOUR NUMBER – Andrea True Connection (Buddah)

SAHARA, NEW YORK
DJ: Ellen Bogen

ACT 1/ACT 2/ACT 4 – Donna Summer (Casablanca)
DANCE, DANCE, DANCE – Chic (Atlantic)
DANCING FEVER/JOHNNY, JOHNNY PLEASE COME HOME – Claudja Barry (London import)
I KNOW THAT HE KNOWS/THE OTHER SIDE OF MIDNIGHT/ BODY LANGUAGE/ YOUR LOVE IS A ROLLERCOASTER/ HEARTACHE – Marsha Hunt (Aves import)
LE SPANK – Le Pamplemousse (AVI)
LOVE BUG/SWEETS FOR MY SWEET/I'LL GO WHERE MUSIC TAKES ME – Tina Charles (CBS import)
MALAGUENA – G.M. T. Sound (Barclay import)
MOON-BOOTS – ORS (Salsoul)
SUPERNATURE/GIVE ME LOVE – Cerrone (Cotillion)
WHAT'S YOUR NAME, WHAT'S YOUR NUMBER – Andrea True Connection (Buddah)

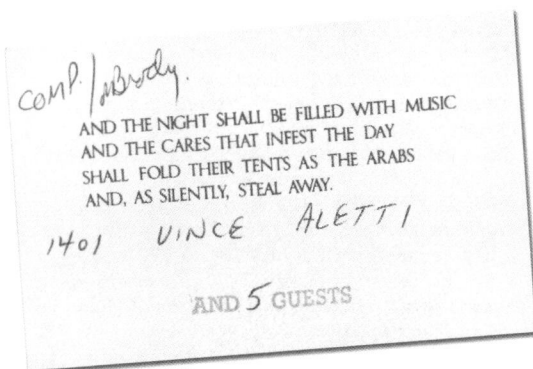

COMP./Brody.

AND THE NIGHT SHALL BE FILLED WITH MUSIC
AND THE CARES THAT INFEST THE DAY
SHALL FOLD THEIR TENTS AS THE ARABS
AND, AS SILENTLY, STEAL AWAY.

1401   VINCE ALETTI

AND 5 GUESTS

(Columbia, Canada) is **Tina Charles** at her most delightful – sweet, lightly-whipped pop disco with nice vocals and a cute Biddu production. The medley is clever, a good mix of new and old material, but it doesn't stray past the limits of "nice" and "cute" to make the deeper impression Charles is surely capable of... "Disco Blood" by the **Vamps** (Building) is interesting mainly as an example of disco music from Brazil, though it sounds like it could have been made almost anywhere else. The vampire theme is familiar and a bit tired but there's a fine Latin hustle feeling here and plenty of pumping drums, strings, horns, etc. to keep things hot. NOTE: Thanks to everyone who made these imports available to DISCO FILE – Scott, Joe and Jonathan at Record Haven; Robert Ouimet from Montreal's Limelight club; the Canadian Record Pool and Ronnie Soares from Ipanema. ◐

DECEMBER 17, 1977

Topping the list of recommended albums this week are **Bionic Boogie's** debut on Polydor and **Claudja Barry's** second American lp, "Claudja," scheduled for immediate release on Salsoul. Both are solid no-waste records that present the sort of problem no one would really complain about: there are so many good cuts, it's hard to choose a favorite. Bionic Boogie is a New York studio outfit put together by producer/writer **Gregg Diamond** (best known for his work with **Andrea True** and **George McCrae**, who also plays keyboards here. Their sound is extremely commercial, tightened-up disco music – not unlike **Chic's** "Dance, Dance, Dance" style but with a lot more funk depth. The songs themselves are a quirky melange of styles with oddly strung-together catch-word lyrics that focus on dancing and other pleasures: "Fresh and hot/We'll show you what we've got," the girl chorus sings in "Risky Changes;" elsewhere, they urge "If it feels good, do it" ("Stop The Music") and insist "We are children of the night/We will carry on until the daylight" ("Boogie Boo"). Nothing serious, nothing revolutionary, perhaps, but the album's bright infectious high-spirits are quite irresistible after a few listenings and instead of worrying about the lack of subtlety or nuance, one simply loosens up and parties right through both sides. Diamond has taken advantage of the open studio-group format to try a variety of approaches – including both male and female lead vocals, female group numbers and two instrumentals – within the overall New York jazz-funk-disco sound (compare the **Players Association**). Again, nearly every cut is top choice but our favorite is "Risky Changes" (very "fresh and hot") with strongest runner-ups being "Boogie Boo," "Don't Lose That Number (Mumbo Jumbo)," "We Must Believe In Magic" and "Dance Little Dreamer." You can't go wrong with this one.

As was the case with her "Sweet Dynamite" album, Claudja Barry's newest collection is substantially different from the import version currently in the stores under the title "The Girl Most Likely." **Tom Moulton's** disco mix opens up much of the material, adds more extensive background vocals (the **Sweethearts of Sigma**, of course) and generally sharpens up the second considerably, filling in all the empty spaces so that the original (done in Munich, Germany, by **Jurgen Korduletsch**) sounds stripped-down and tentative by comparison (listen to Barry's version of "Take Me In Your Arms," the only track to retain its original form,

for a stark comparison). Barry also benefits immensely from the remix's more luxurious support because it cushions her weak spots and shows her off in the most flattering light possible. The sound here picks up from her previous work and shares some elements of style with recent material by **Michele**, **Donna Summer** and **Marsha Hunt**: the European basics with some fine Philadelphia polish. Vocals predominate and the tracks are somewhat shorter than on her previous release which means we've got a lot more variety and a lot less production-for-the-sake-of-production. Standout cut right now is "Johnny, Johnny Please Come Home" (7:09), which is both wonderfully '60s (the theme and girl-group format recall the days of "It's My Party" and "My Boyfriend's Back") and strictly '70s (the production is streamlined, sleek, precise yet luscious). Other strong tracks include "Open The Door," "Love Machine" (both sounding **Giorgio**-influenced), "Take It Easy" and "Dancin' Fever." Even the slow songs are great – an essential lp for all moods.

CHOICE CUTS: "Let's Get Together" by **Pam Todd & Love Exchange** is the title cut from their **Greg Carmichael**-produced debut album on Shyrlden Records and it's been picking up fans among DJs in New York recently (Larry Levan, who listed it in his top 10 from Paradise Garage last week, is the one who convinced me to give it a second listen and Larry Sanders at Infinity also includes the record in his top 10 this week). The song is straightforward, pumping disco and very attractive with its chanting vocals ("Let's get together/Make some love, make some love") and sexy, swelling synthesizer work. Also on the album: a good new version of "Making Love," the song originally made by **Sammy Gordon & the Hip Huggers** a while back... Two cuts are getting a lot of attention off the new **Harold Melvin & the Bluenotes** album ("Now Is the Time" on ABC) – "Baby, You Got My Nose Open" (5:05), an attempt at recapturing the spirit of "Bad Luck" that, while falling far short, still manages to get over; and "Power Of love" (7:29), a rousing track with hefty lead vocals that remind me of **Otis Redding** toward the end... For **Parliament** freaks it should be noted that "Bop Gun (Endangered Species)," their recently-recom- mended single, has been lengthened to 8:32 and opens up their latest Outrageous album, "Funkentelechy vs. The Placebo Syndrome" on Casablanca.

> **"Tom Moulton's disco mix opens up much of the material, adds more extensive background vocals and generally sharpens it up considerably."**

BONES, SAN FRANCISCO
DJ: Michael Lee

ACT 1/ACT 2/ACT 4 – Donna Summer (Casablanca)
I WOULDN'T GIVE YOU UP – Goldie Alexander (Amour)
MOONLIGHT LOVIN' – Isaac Hayes (Polydor)
ON FIRE – T-Connection (TK)
THE OTHER SIDE OF MIDNIGHT/I KNOW THAT HE KNOWS/HEARTACHE – Marsha Hunt (Aves import)
THE NIGHT THE LIGHTS WENT OUT / LOVE PER HOUR/ PEOPLE OF THE WORLD, RISE – Trammps (Atlantic)
STAYIN' ALIVE/NIGHT FEVER – Bee Gees "Saturday Night Fever Soundtrack" (RSO)
SUPERNATURE/SWEET DRUMS/GIVE ME LOVE – Cerrone (Cotillion)
THUNDER IN MY HEART – Leo Sayer (Warner Bros.)
TWO HOT FOR LOVE – THP Orchestra (Butterfly)

HONEY FOR THE BEES, STATEN ISLAND
DJ: Mike Pace

THE BULL – Mike Theodore Orchestra (Westbound)
DON'T LET ME BE MISUNDERSTOOD – Santa Esmeralda (Casablanca)
I GOT TO HAVE YOUR LOVE/THERE'S FIRE DOWN BELOW – Fantastic Four (Westbound)
MANHATTAN LOVE SONG – King Errisson (Westbound)
NATIVE NEW YORKER – Odyssey (RCA)
RUMOR HAS IT – Donna Summer (Casablanca)
SAN FRANCISCO – Village People (Casablanca)
TRINIDAD – U.S. Steel Orchestra (Solid Steel)
TWO HOT FOR LOVE – THP Orchestra (Butterfly)
VOYAGE OF NO RETURN – Silvetti (Salsoul)

INFINITY, NEW YORK
DJ: Larry Sanders

DANCE, DANCE, DANCE – Chic (Atlantic)
DANCE A LITTLE BIT CLOSER – Charo (Salsoul)
GIRL DON'T MAKE ME WAIT /LOVE SHOOK – Pattie Brooks (Casablanca)
LET'S GET TOGETHER – Pam Todd & the Love Exchange (Shyrlden)
PEOPLE OF THE WORLD, RISE/LOVE PER HOUR/LIVING THE LIFE – Trammps (Atlantic)
RISKY CHANGES/DANCE LITTLE DREAMER – Bionic Boogie (Polydor)
RUMOR HAS IT/I LOVE YOU/WORKING THE MIDNIGHT SHIFT – Donna Summer (Casablanca)
SUPERNATURE/GIVE ME LOVE – Cerrone (Cotillion)
WHAT'S YOUR NAME, WHAT'S YOUR NUMBER – Andrea True Connection (Buddah)
YOUR LOVE IS SO GOOD FOR ME/TOP OF THE WORLD/ THE SAME LOVE THAT MADE ME LAUGH – Diana Ross (Motown)

FACES, CHICAGO
DJ: Carmen Adduci

DANCE, DANCE, DANCE/EVERYBODY DANCE – Chic (Atlantic)
DISCO DANCE/CAN'T YOU FEEL IT/ MAGIC LOVE – Michele (West End)
GIVE ME LOVE/SUPERNATURE – Cerrone (Cotillion)
HARLEM NOCTURNE – Wildflower (TK)
I KNOW THAT HE KNOWS/THE OTHER SIDE OF MIDNIGHT/HEARTACHE – Marsha Hunt (Aves import)
I LOVE YOU/RUMOR HAS IT/ACT 1 – Donna Summer (Casablanca)
KISS ME – George McCrae (TK)
MOONLIGHT LOVIN'/STRANGER IN PARADISE – Isaac Hayes (Polydor)
PEOPLE OF THE WORLD, RISE/THE NIGHT THE LIGHTS WENT OUT/LOVE PER HOUR – Trammps (Atlantic)
WE MUST BELIEVE IN MAGIC – Bionic Boogie (Polydor)

FEEDBACK & NEWS: Several DJs we've spoken to recently admitted they didn't care much for the lyrics or the vocals on **John Paul Young's** "Standing In The Rain" (from the Australian rock singer's new album on Midsong) but they liked the cut anyway and their crowds were even more enthusiastic. Both Larry Sanders and Michael Lee reported the record was going over particularly well (Lee said it worked nicely after "Disco Congo") and one listen is enough to see why: the percussion opening, mechanical and bare as it is, has a fine, elemental, chugging quality that carries through the song and is almost good enough to overwhelm the somewhat weak singing. Almost but not quite. Your move... Casablanca says it will release **Sumeria's** "Golden Tears," the **Alec R. Costandinos** import we were so enthusiastic about last week, sometime in January... Now that **Silvester Levay** and **Michael Kunze** have gone their separate ways, Kunze has teamed up with producer **John Davis** for the next **Silver Convention** album, now in the works in Philadelphia for February release... Chrysalis is bringing out **Amanda Lear's** "I Am A Photograph" album, currently available as an import, sometime this week along with the long version of her still-exciting "Blood And Honey" which will be the label's first commercial disco disc. ◗

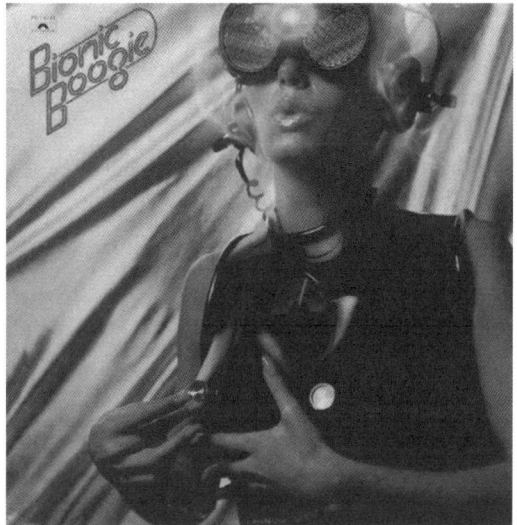

DECEMBER 24, 1977

SOUTHROAD CONNECTION

MAHOGANY

M 1277-1B   33 1/3 RPM
                 Time: 7:53

YOU LIKE IT, WE LOVE IT
(L. Job-D. Gillman)
Harrindur Pub. Co. (B.M.I.)/Ensign Music Corp. (B.M.I.)
Produced by Lionel Job
Arranged by L. Job and D. Gillman
Strings Arranged by L. Job
Disco Mixed by Rafael Charres
for S.E.P. Inc.
℗1977 Mahogany Records

MANUFACTURED & DISTRIBUTED BY MAHOGANY RECORDS 1697 BROADWAY, N.Y. N.Y. 10019

❝ Tony Smith, DJ from New York's Barefoot Boy, called to rave about a sensational off-the-wall funk piece called "You Like It, We Love It" by Southroad Connection ❞

With new releases dwindling down to a precious few in these final days of the record biz countdown to Christmas, this is a great time to go back and give a second chance to some records that might have gotten lost in the frantic shuffle of the past few months (some suggestions: **Freda Payne's** "Love Magnet," the disco disc remix of "Shame" by **Evelyn "Champagne" King**, **Leo Sayer's** disco disc version of "Thunder In My Heart," "If You Feel Like Dancin'" by **Al Hudson & the Soul Partners** and two cuts from the Eli's Second Coming album: "Heavenly" and "Why Don'cha". But we're not entirely without some last-minute surprises this week and these three records should boost your holiday spirits: **Peter Brown's** "Fantasy Love Affair" album (Drive) is not at all what one would expect after the serious funk of "Do You Wanna Get Funky With Me?" but it's all the more exciting for the way it overturns our expectations and then satisfies them in a completely different style. What Brown and producer **Cory Wade** have come up with is a near-perfect blend of

pop sounds, drawing upon some of the richest rock influences of the last decade (including the **Beatles** and **Crosby, Stills & Nash**) and revitalizing them with a fresh funk approach: progressive rock meets progressive soul in a brilliant synthesis. After several days of almost constant playing, I've fallen for every cut here – each one has its own special feel and the overall range is marvelous two stand out immediately for dancing. The best is "Dance With Me" (5:18), a percolating, easy groove with vibrant vocals first from Brown, then from Brown and **Betty Wright**, a delightful, inspired combination of voices that turns the song into a TK classic – and a sure disco-to-pop crossover. "You Should Do It" has a similar feeling and an irresistible bounce but the skipping synthesizer and the light-hearted approach to the vocals (with Betty Wright and **Wildflower** providing an especially fine interlude here, too recall **Stevie Wonder** at his most playful. Another possibility: the throbbing, utterly haunting "For Your Love," for slower moments. Brown, who wrote and arranged all the cuts, also plays the bulk of the instruments throughout – synthesizers, electric and acoustic piano, drums, timbales and other percussion as well as singing all lead vocals; on several cuts he is the only musician. Surely it's too soon to make any other Stevie Wonder comparisons, but it's been a long time since I've come across a performer so obviously, prodigiously talented – Peter Brown is definitely the man to watch right now. By the way, the phenomenal "Do You Wanna Get Funky With Me?" is, of course, included here in a compressed 9:13 version that joins it with the "Burning Love Breakdown."

The two other favorites this week are disco discs – first, the record Tony Smith, DJ from New York's Barefoot Boy, called to rave about this week (it immediately went on his top 10 list, too): a sensational off-the-wall funk piece called "You Like It, We Love It" by **Southroad Connection** (Mahogany Records, 1697 Broadway, New York). This one sounds like **B.T. Express** in the old days: hard-pounding bass, chanted vocals from a mixed group, hot breaks, stunning strings and synthesizer; but so much more unpredictable than B.T. or the other funk outfits that it trips you out. The flip side, "Just Laying It Down," is equally good – an instrumental with "Star Wars" accents and an "Inside America" feel that is one of the best wild party cuts to come out this year; a freak masterpiece that deserves comparison with the insanity of "Music" by **Montreal Sound**. Should help steam up the dance floors this winter. Both sides approach eight minutes in length and were produced, co-written and co-arranged by **Lionel Job**, another new name to pick up on. D.J Rafael Charres did the disco mix. The final essential 12-inch this week is the long version (7:00) of **Stargard's** "Theme Song From 'Which Way Is Up'"(MCA), the song everyone is touting as the new "Car Wash." Though there are places where the new track could have been tightened up some, it certainly satisfies the need for more of this spirited record than was available on the single: more drive, more vocals (including some fine chants), more complexity, more jivey synthesizer, more fun. Don't ignore this one. ◐

THE LIGHT CO., HOUSTON
DJ: Ken Smith

DANCE, DANCE, DANCE – Chic (Atlantic)
KEEP IT UP – Olympic Runners (London)
KISS ME – George McCrae (TK)
LE SPANK – Le Pamplemousse (AVI)
MANHATTAN LOVE SONG – King Errisson (Westbound)
NATIVE NEW YORKER – Odyssey (RCA)
ONCE UPON A TIME/FASTER AND FASTER TO NOWHERE/NOW I NEED YOU/ WORKING THE MIDNIGHT SHIFT – Donna Summer (Casablanca)
SUPERNATURE/GIVE ME LOVE – Cerrone (Cotillion)
TWO HOT FOR LOVE – THP Orchestra (Butterfly)
WHAT'S YOUR NAME, WHAT'S YOUR NUMBER – Andrea True Connection (Buddah)

SHEPARD'S, NEW YORK
DJ: Jeff Baugh

ACT 4/IF YOU GOT IT FLAUNT IT – Donna Summer (Casablanca)
DANCE, DANCE, DANCE/EVERYBODY DANCE – Chic (Atlantic)
DANCE AND LEAVE IT ALL BEHIND YOU/ COSMIC TRAVELLER – Sumeria (Raal import)
I KNOW THAT HE KNOWS/HEARTACHE/ THE OTHER SIDE OF MIDNIGHT – Marsha Hunt (Aves import)
JOHNNY, JOHNNY PLEASE COME HOME – Claudja Barry (Salsoul)
LOVE BUG/SWEETS FOR MY SWEET – Tina Charles (CBS)
MIDNIGHT FLIGHT TO YOUR LOVE/SINCE I FOUND LOVE – The Pips (Casablanca)
RISKY CHANGES/DANCE LITTLE DREAMER – Bionic Boogie (Polydor)
SHAME – Evelyn "Champagne" King (RCA)
WHICH WAY IS UP? – Stargard (MCA)

BAREFOOT BOY, NEW YORK
DJ: Tony Smith

ACT 1/ACT 2/ACT 4 – Donna Summer (Casablanca)
DANCE WITH ME/YOU SHOULD DO IT – Peter Brown (Drive)
GIVE ME LOVE/SUPERNATURE – Cerrone (Cotillion)
GOD HELP THOSE (WHO HELP THEMSELVES)/LOVE CONNECTION – The Dells (Mercury)
I'M HERE AGAIN – Thelma Houston (Tamla)
JOHNNY, JOHNNY PLEASE COME HOME/ LOVE MACHINE/TAKE IT EASY – Claudja Barry (Salsoul)
PHILADELPHIA CLASSICS – Various Artists (Phila.Intl.)
RISKY CHANGES/DON'T LOSE THAT NUMBER/DANCE LITTLE DREAMER – Bionic Boogie (Polydor)
TWO HOT FOR LOVE – THP Orchestra (Butterfly)
YOU LIKE IT, WE LOVE IT/JUST LAYING IT OWN – Southroad Connection (Mahogany)

WHIMSEY'S, BOSTON
DJ: John Luongo

ACT 1/ ACT 2/ ACT 4 – Donna Summer (Casablanca)
CAN'T YOU FEEL IT – Michele (West End)
COME GO WITH ME – Pockets (Columbia)
EVERYBODY DANCE/DANCE, DANCE, DANCE – Chic (Atlantic)
GALAXY – War (MCA) **GIVE. ME LOVE/SUPERNATURE** – Cerrone (Cotillion)
LOVE PER HOUR/THE NIGHT THE LIGHTS WENT OUT/ PEOPLE OF THE WORLD, RISE – Trammps (Atlantic)
MANHATTAN LOVE SONG/SAL SOUL SISTER – King Errisson (Westbound)
ON FIRE – TK Connection (TK)
TWO HOT FOR LOVE – THP Orchestra (Butterfly)

DISCO FILE TOP 20

1. **ACT 1/ACT 2/ACT 4** – Donna Summer (Casablanca)
2. **SUPERNATURE/GIVE ME LOVE** – Cerrone (Cotillion)
3. **DANCE, DANCE, DANCE/EVERYBODY DANCE** – Chic (Atlantic)
4. **THE NIGHT THE LIGHTS WENT OUT/PEOPLE OF THE WORLD, RISE/LOVE PER HOUR** – Trammps (Atlantic)
5. **TWO HOT FOR LOVE** – THP Orchestra (Butterfly)
6. **ON FIRE** – T-Connection (TK)
7. **WHAT'S YOUR NAME, WHAT'S YOUR NUMBER** – Andrea True Connection (Buddah)
8. **MOON-BOOTS** – ORS (Salsoul)
9. **KISS ME** – George McCrae (TK)
10. **LE SPANK** – Le Pamplemousse (AVI)
11. **MANHATTAN LOVE SONG** – King Errisson (Westbound)
12. **NATIVE NEW YORKER** – Odyssey (RCA)
13. **DISCO DANCE/CAN'T YOU FEEL IT/MAGIC LOVE** – Michele (West End)
14. **DON'T LET ME BE MISUNDERSTOOD** – Santa Esmeralda (Casablanca)
15. **MOONLIGHT LOVIN'** – Isaac Hayes (Polydor)
16. **THE OTHER SIDE OF MIDNIGHT/I KNOW THAT HE KNOWS/HEARTACHE** – Marsha Hunt (Aves import)
17. **JOHNNY, JOHNNY PLEASE COME HOME** – Claudja Barry (Salsoul)
18. **RISKY CHANGES/DANCE LITTLE DREAMER** – Bionic Boogie (Polydor)
19. **I GOT TO HAVE YOUR LOVE/THERE'S FIRE DOWN BELOW** – Fantastic Four (Westbound)
20. **YOUR LOVE IS SO GOOD FOR ME** – Diana Ross (Motown)

For those of us who've always taken disco seriously, 1977 was a very good year. Comfortably past that awkward fad stage when it was always on the defensive, disco was more confident, more relaxed and more creatively expansive than ever. The rise of new wave rock has helped ease the antagonism of the rock audience and its critical establishment toward disco; the resulting mood of peaceful coexistence (approaching mutual appreciation) has tended to open up the pop charts to a wider range of genuine disco records. Disco now makes fewer compromises and so comes on much stronger.

Surely the most influential disco music this year has come from Europe where French producer/performers like **Cerrone** and **Alec Coslandinos** took the **Giorgio Moroder/Pete Bellotte** sound one step further with sustained, dramatically structured, intriguingly avant-garde compositions that filled the entire side of the record. Albums with two tracks, one to each side, became commonplace and import music had its hottest year, with nearly every major European record being snatched up for American release almost as soon as it broke. Of course, Moroder and Bellotte were not about to be outdone and their work with **Donna Summer** (particularly "I Feel Love" and the "Once Upon A Time" double album) as well as their individual work (Giorgio's "From Here To Eternity," Bellotte's

production with **Trax** and **Marsha Hunt**) prove that both are lively, consistent and vital talents quick to absorb new influences (**Kraftwerk** was a key one this year) and certain to remain at the head of their class. The Eurodisco sound found many American proponents – some innovators, others mere imitators – but, more importantly, it opened up the entire field to longer, wilder, and more complex material; more risks were taken on the creative side and the results were, more often than not, rich and exciting. The commercial disco disc field continued to expand, involving nearly every major label including Columbia (though their program seems tentative and directionless) and Atlantic (whose very first commercial release, **Chic's** "Dance, Dance, Dance," has become a major hit and might encourage further expansion in this area). Although the actual viability of the disco disc market is still open to debate, as far as discos are concerned, the 12-inch disc has pushed the standard single nearly to extinction. Our first year-end list of "essential" disco singles ran to 75 entries; last year there were only 30. This year, we've eliminated the list completely because very few singles had any impact in the clubs since virtually everything was pressed up on disco discs. In fact, the only standard 45 to make the DISCO FILE Top 20 list all year was the **Emotions'** wonderful "Best Of My Love" (which was later included on their "Rejoice" lp, number 35 on the Essential Album chart). At the moment, practically the only singles in the current disco DJ's repertoire are imports – is this the shape of things to come?

A few final notes: In addition to the producers mentioned above – Cerrone, Costandinos, Moroder, Bellotte – these are the men who made an impact on disco music this past year and the names to look for in 1978: **Cory Wade**, **Jacques Morali**, **Dennis Coffey** & **Mike Theodore**, **Simon Soussan**, **Michael Lewis** & **Laurin Rinder** and **Tom Moulton**. Two stand-bys: **Norman Harris** and **Vince Montana** – always dependable... Collectors items: the unreleased "Je T'Aime" disc by **Donna Summer**; D.C. **LaRue's** signed and numbered limited edition disco disc of "Indiscreet" and "Face Of Love"; the pink vinyl first pressing of **Saint Tropez'** "Je T'Aime" album and the opaque white vinyl edition of the **THP Orchestra's** "Two Hot For Love" lp; the import versions of Cerrone's "Love In C Minor" (remember the dialogue they slipped off for the American release?) and "Paradise" (with the nude- draped refrigerator and the suspicious white powder on the cover) any other suggestions? ◐

" 1977 was a very good year for disco. Comfortably past that awkward fad stage, disco was more confident, more relaxed and more creatively expansive than ever "

FLAMINGO, NEW YORK
DJ: Richie Rivera

ACT 1/ACT 2/ACT 4 – Donna Summer (Casablanca)
AFRICANISM/GIMME SOME LOVING/DR. DOO-DAH
– Kongas (Crocos import)
BOOGIE BOO/DANCE LITTLE DREAMER/ DON'T LOSE THAT NUMBER/RISKY CHANGES – Bionic Boogie (Polydor)
DON'T STOP ME I LIKE IT – David Christie (Polydor import)
ELEANOR RIGBY/HELP – Average Disco Band (H&L)
GIVE ME LOVE/SUPERNATURE – Cerrone (Cotillion)
HAWAII CALLS ME HOME – D.D. Sound (Baby import)
LOSING YOU – Hearts of Stone (Disco I import)
LOVE EXPRESS/LET'S ALL CHANT – Michael Zager Band (Private Stock)
WHICH WAY IS UP? – Stargard (MCA)

POOP DECK, FORT LAUDERDALE, FLA.
DJ: Bob Viteritti

DANCE, DANCE, DANCE – Chic (Atlantic)
I LOVE YOU/RUMOR HAS IT/NOW I NEED YOU/FAIRY TALE HIGH – Donna Summer (Casablanca)
JOHNNY, JOHNNY PLEASE COME HOME/DANCING FEVER – Claudja Barry (Salsoul)
MAGIC LOVE/CAN'T YOU FEEL IT/ DISCO DANCE/HOLD ME, SQUEEZE ME – Michele (West End)
MANHATTAN LOVE SONG/WELL, HAVE A NICE DAY/ SAL SOUL SISTER/DISCO CONGO – King Errisson (Westbound)
MOON-BOOTS – ORS (Salsoul)
THE NIGHT THE LIGHTS WENT OUT – Trammps (Atlantic)
SINGING IN THE RAIN – Sheila B. Devotion (Carrere import)
SUPERNATURE/GIVE ME LOVE – Cerrone (Cotillion)
TWO HOT FOR LOVE – THP Orchestra (Butterfly)

THE BISTRO, CHICAGO
DJ: Rick Gianatos

BORRIQUITO/DANCE A LITTLE BIT CLOSER
– Charo (Salsoul)
DANCE LITTLE DREAMER/RISKY CHANGES/ BOOGIE BOO – Bionic Boogie (Polydor)
DISCO INFERNO/GOIN' TO THE DISCO
– Players Association (Vanguard)
GIVE ME LOVE/SUPERNATURE – Cerrone (Cotillion)
LOVE MAGNET – Freda Payne (Capitol)
MANHATTAN LOVE SONG/L.A. BOUND – King Errisson (Westbound)
ON FIRE – T-Connection (TK)
STANDING RIGHT HERE – Melba Moore (Buddah)
TWO HOT FOR LOVE – THP Orchestro (Butterfly)
WHY DON'CHA/HEAVENLY – Eli's Second Coming (Silver Blue)

HIPPOPOTAMUS, NEW YORK
DJ: Rich Pampinella

CLOSE ENCOUNTERS OF THE THIRD KIND – Gene Page (Arista)
DANCE DOWN – Katheline del Casino (Trolley import)
GIVE ME LOVE/SUPERNATURE – Cerrone (Cotillion)
IT'S GOT TO BE LOVE – Darcus (RCA)
KISS ME – George McCrae (TK)
LOVE EXPRESS/LET'S ALL CHANTS – Michael Zager Band (Private Stock)
PEOPLE OF THE WORLD/DANCE GROOVE/C'MON LET'S DO IT SOME MORE – Juggy Murray (Jupiter)
PHILADELPHIA CLASSICS – Various Artists (Phila. Intl.)
RISKY CHANGES/DANCE LITTLE DREAMER – Bionic Boogie (Polydor)
TWO HOT FOR LOVE – THP Orchestra (Butterfly)

DISCO FILE ESSENTIALS 1977

THE ESSENTIAL DISCO ALBUMS OF 1977

1. **LOVE IN C MINOR/CERRONE'S PARADISE/ SUPERNATURE** – Cerrone (Cotillion)
2. **LOVE & KISSES** (Casablanca)
3. **ONCE UPON A TIME/I REMEMBER YESTERDAY** – Donna Summer (Casablanca)
4. **DEVIL'S GUN** – C.J. & Co. (Westbound)
5. **VILLAGE PEOPLE** (Casablanca)
6. **DISCO INFERNO/TRAMMPS III** – Trammps (Atlantic)
7. **DON'T LET ME BE MISUNDERSTOOD** – Santa Esmeralda (Casablanca)
8. **AFRICAN QUEENS** – Ritchie Family (Marlin)
9. **LOLEATTA** – Loleatta Holloway (Gold Mind)
10. **TEDDY PENDERGRASS** (Phila. Intl.)
11. **LOVE SHOOK** – Pattie Brooks (Casablanca)
12. **PORTFOLIO** – Grace Jones (Island)
13. **COCOMOTION** – El Coco (AVI)
14. **LIVE AT THE LONDON PALLADIUM** – Marvin Gaye (Tamla)
15. **FROM HERE TO ETERNITY** – Giorgio (Casablanca)
16. **MAGIC JOURNEY** – Salsoul Orchestra (Salsoul)
17. **COSMIC WIND** – Mike Theodore Orchestra (Westbound)
18. **BACK HOME** – Dennis Coffey (Westbound)
19. **MAGIC LOVE** – Michele (West End)
20. **MUNICH MACHINE** (Casablanca)
21. **SWEET DYNAMITE/CLAUDJA** – Claudja Barry (Salsoul)
22. **TWO HOT FOR LOVE** – THP Orchestra (Butterfly)
23. **WATCH OUT** – Trax (Polydor)
24. **STAR WARS AND OTHER GALACTIC FUNK** – Meco (Millennium)
25. **CHIC** (Atlantic)
26. **PHILADELPHIA CLASSICS** – Various Artists (Phila. Intl.)
27. **MAGIC FLY** – Space (UA)
28. **KINGS OF CLUBS** – Chocolats (Salsoul)
29. **DELUSIONS** – First Choice (Gold Mind)
30. **GOT TO HAVE YOUR LOVE** – Fantastic Four (Westbound)
31. **CHOOSING, YOU** – Lenny Williams (ABC)
32. **TURN THIS MUTHA OUT** – Idris Muhammed (Kudu)
33. **JEAN CARN** (Phila. Intl.)
34. **JE T'AIME** – St. Tropez (Butterfly)
35. **REJOICE** – Emotions (Columbia)
36. **UP JUMPED THE DEVIL** – John Davis & the Monster Orchestra (Sam)
37. **TRANS-EUROPE EXPRESS** – Kraftwerk (Capitol)
38. **LIFE IS MUSIC** – Ritchie Family (Marlin)
39. **DOWN TO LOVE TOWN** – Originals (Motown)
40. **GIVE AND TAKE** – Dynamic Superiors (Motown)
41. **NEW HORIZON** – Isaac Hayes (Polydor)
42. **BIONIC BOOGIE** (Polydor)
43. **BIG TIME SOUNDTRACK** – Smokey Robinson (Tamla)
44. **IN FULL BLOOM** – Rose Royce (Whitfield)
45. **BABY IT'S ME** – Diana Ross (Motown)
46. **I KEEP COMING BACK FOR MORE** – Brenda & the Tabulations (Chocolate City)
47. **SEND IT** – Ashford & Simpson (Warner Bros.)
48. **THE DEVIL IN ME** – Thelma Houston (Tamla)
49. **L.A. BOUND** – King Errisson (Westbound)
50. **DIAMOND TOUCH** – George McCrae (TK)
51. **WHAT'S ON YOUR MIND** – Hodges, James & Smith (London)
52. **AIN'T IT GOOD FEELING GOOD** – Eloise Laws (Invictus)
53. **THE PLAYERS' ASSOCIATION/BORN TO DANCE** – Players' Association (Vanguard)
54. **CROSSOVER** – Rice & Beans Orchestra (Dash)
55. **CELI BEE & THE BUZZY BUNCH** (APA)
56. **DISCO CHAMPS** – Trammps (Phila. Intl.)
57. **GLORIOUS** – Gloria Gaynor (Polydor)
58. **ELI'S SECOND COMING** (Silver Blue)
59. **SONS OF THE GODS** – Ripple (Salsoul)
60. **ZODIAC LADY** – Roberta Kelly (Casablanca)

THE ESSENTIAL DISCO RECORDS OF 1977

1. **LOVE IN C MINOR/CERRONE'S PARADISE/ SUPERNATURE** – Cerrone (Cotillion lp)
2. **LOVE & KISSES** (Casablanca lp)
3. **ONCE UPON A TIME/I REMEMBER YESTERDAY** – Donna Summer (Casablanca lps)
4. **DEVIL'S GUN** – C.J. & Co. (Westbound lp)
5. **VILLAGE PEOPLE** (Casablanca lp)
6. **I NEED A MAN/PORTFOLIO** – Grace Jones (Beam Junction/Island disco disc/lp)
7. **DISCO INFERNO/TRAMMPS III** (Atlantic lps)
8. **DON'T LET ME BE MISUNDERSTOOD** – Santa Esmeralda (Casablanca lp cut)
9. **AFRICAN QUEENS** – Ritchie Family (Marlin lp)
10. **DO YOU WANNA GET FUNKY WITH ME** – Peter Brown (TK disco disc)
11. **DO WHAT YOU WANNA DO** – T-Connection (TK disco disc)
12. **LOLEATTA** – Loleatta Holloway (Gold Mind lp)
13. **DANCE, DANCE, DANCE** – Chic (Atlantic disco disc)
14. **NATIVE NEW YORKER** – Odyssey (RCA disco disc)
15. **TEDDY PENDERGRASS** (Phila. Intl. lp)
16. **LOVE SHOOK** – Pattie Brooks (Casablanca lp)
17. **MAGIC BIRD OF FIRE** – Salsoul Orchestra (Salsoul disco disc)
18. **LE SPANK** – Le Pamplemousse (AVI disco disc)
19. **HOLD TIGHT** – Vicki Sue Robinson (RCA disco disc)
20. **COCOMOTION** – El Coco (AVI lp cut)
21. **DR. LOVE** – First Choice (Gold Mind disco disc)
22. **GOT TO GIVE IT UP** – Marvin Gaye (Tamla lp cut)
23. **UPTOWN FESTIVAL** – Shalamar (Soul Train disco disc)
24. **I CAUGHT YOUR ACT** – Hues Corporation (Warner Bros. disco disc)
25. **FROM HERE TO ETERNITY** – Giorgio (Casablanca lp)

THE ESSENTIAL DISCO DISCS OF 1977

1. **DEVIL'S GUN** – C.J. & Co. (Atlantic)
2. **I NEED A MAN** – Grace Jones (Beam Junction)
3. **DO YOU WANNA GET FUNKY WITH ME** – Peter Brown (TK)
4. **DO WHAT YOU WANNA DO** – T-Connection (TK)
5. **DANCE, DANCE, DANCE** – Chic (Atlantic)
6. **NATIVE NEW YORKER/EASY COME, EASY GO** – Odyssey (RCA)
7. **MAGIC BIRD OF FIRE** – Salsoul Orchestra (Salsoul)
8. **LE SPANK** – Le Pamplemousse (AVI)
9. **HOLD TIGHT** – Vicki Sue Robinson (RCA)
10. **DR. LOVE** – First Choice (Gold Mind)
11. **UPTOWN FESTIVAL** – Shalamar (Soul Train)
12. **I CAUGHT YOUR ACT** – Hues Corporation (Warner Bros.)
13. **BLOCK PARTY/I CAN'T TURN YOU LOOSE** – Anthony White (Salsoul)
14. **HIT AND, RUN/WE'RE GETTING STRONGER** – Loleatta Holloway (Gold Mind)
15. **UP JUMPED THE DEVIL** – John Davis & the Monster Orchestra (Sam)
16. **I GOT TO HAVE YOUR LOVE** – Fantastic Four (Atlantic)
17. **MUSIC** – Montreal Sound (TK)
18. **RUNNING AWAY** – Roy Ayers Ubiquity (Polydor)
19. **PIPELINE** – Bruce Johnston (Columbia)
20. **SLOW DOWN** – John Miles (London)
21. **IT'S ECSTASY WHEN YOU LAY DOWN NEXT TO ME** – Barry White (20th Century)
22. **I FEEL LOVE/THEME FROM "THE DEEP"** – Donna Summer (Casablanca)
23. **I GOTTA KEEP DANCIN'** – Carrie Lucas (Soul Train)
24. **LOVIN' IS REALLY MY GAME** – Brainstorm (Tabu)
25. **MOON-BOOTS** – ORS (Salsoul)
26. **SPRING RAIN** – Silvetti (Salsoul)
27. **MAGIC FLY (JOURNEY INTO LOVE)** – Kebekelektrik (TK)
28. **EROTIC SOUL** – Larry Page Orchestra (London)
29. **WHAT'S YOUR NAME, WHAT'S YOUR NUMBER** – Andrea True Connection (Buddah)
30. **STONE TO THE BONE** – Timmy Thomas (TK)
31. **ON FIRE** – T-Connection (TK)
32. **EXPRESS YOURSELF** – New York Community Choir (RCA)
33. **DANCIN'** – Crown Heights Affair (De-Lite)
34. **KISS ME** – George McCrae (TK)
35. **SHAME** – Evelyn "Champagne" King (RCA)
36. **SUPERMAN** – Celi Bee & the Buzzy Bunch (TK)
37. **YOU'VE GOT MAGIC** – Rice & Beans Orchestra (TK)
38. **SINCE I FELL FOR YOU** – Hodges, James & Smith (London)
39. **GOING BACK TO MY ROOTS** – Lamont Dozier (Warner Bros.)
40. **LOCKED IN THIS POSITION** – Barbara Mason & Bunny Sigler (Curtom)
41. **TATTOO MAN** – Denise McCann (Polydor)
42. **24 HOURS A DAY** – Barbara Pennington (UA)
43. **TOUCH ME, TAKE ME** – Black Light Orchestra (RCA)
44. **DEEPER** – New Birth (Warner Bros.)
45. **BACK IN LOVE AGAIN** – L.T.D. (A&M)
46. **HEY YOU SHOULD BE DANCING** – Gene Farrow (UA)
47. **I'VE GOT TO DANCE' TO KEEP FROM CRYING** – Destinations (AVI)
48. **SPEAK WELL** – Philly USA (West End)
49. **DISCOMANIA** – The Lovers (TK)
50. **BLOOD AND HONEY** – Amanda Lear (Chrysalis/Direction)
51. **NEW YORK, YOU GOT ME DANCING** – Andrea True Connection (Buddah)
52. **GET HAPPY** – Jimmy "Bo" Horne (TK)
53. **THE WAY YOU DO THE THINGS YOU DO** – Foxy (TK)
54. **OVER AND OVER/DOWN, DOWN, DOWN** – Sylvester (Fantasy)
55. **SPIRIT OF SUNSHINE** – Chuck Davis Orchestra (West End)
56. **THE FINAL THING** – Steve Bender (London)
57. **TURN ON THE LIGHTS** – Kellee Patterson (Shadybrook)
58. **LOVE IN C MINOR** – Heart and Soul Orchestra (Casablanca)
59. **MARY HARTMAN, MARY HARTMAN** – Sounds of Inner City (West End)
60. **DISCO LUCY** – Wilton Place Street Band (Island)

DISCO 'ESSENTIALIZED': Again this year, I feel I should point out that the year-end lists of "top disco records" and "essential" albums and disco discs are personal, rather than statistical, compilations; they are an attempt to organize and rank the most important, influential and interesting disco releases of 1977 from a critical perspective, so while general popularity has, of course, been taken into account, weekly chart positions have not. In the top 25 records for the year, albums, album cuts and disco discs are listed as equals but, inevitably, albums have more weight and groups of records – representing one performer's output for the year, like the Cerrone trio at the top – count as one and naturally have the most impact of all. The "essential" lists are meant to be basic library collections – the 120 records most necessary for survival on the dance floors of America (no imports) this year. In an effort to have as little overlap as possible between the two lists, disco discs were listed only if they preceded or varied from the album versions and albums were listed only if they contained considerably more than their popular disco-disc cut. A number of disco discs (like my number one choice, "Devil's Gun") were pressed in limited quantities for promotional use only and are listed as necessities in any DJ's own collection. ❂

1978

Refreshments at New York, NY © **Toby Old**

JANUARY 7, 1978

Happy New Year! Though the tide of record releases is at its lowest ebb this time of year, here are a few things to carry you through until the next wave breaks. Top of the list: "Africanism," the new **Kongas** album produced by **Cerrone** and currently an import on the Crocos label from France. Key cut here is a full side devoted to a vibrantly percussive disco version of the **Spencer Davis Group's** hard rock classic, "Gimme Some Loving," clearly designed to follow in the footsteps of **Santa Esmeralda's** "Don't Let Me Be Misunderstood." The song, with its chunky changes and insistent, pounding beat, is a natural candidate for disco treatment and Cerrone plays up the junglestomp drums with a short introductory conga/chant segment called "Africanism" whose spirit underlies the rest of the approximately 14-minute track. The vocals, in a raw rock and roll style very close to the original (major change: the background vocals are by Cerrone's familiar female chorus), are prominent throughout so the breaks are tighter, less spacious than usual and the best one – where the lead singer starts shouting "Feels good!" – comes quite late in the track. These factors might make the record more commercial but slightly less durable than "Misunderstood;" the excitement is there but the momentum doesn't hold. So, while the side is hot – surely the strongest new import we know of – and it's certain to hit big in the clubs, it could peak and plummet unless it's programmed creatively. But that's not all – there's another long cut on the other side of the Kongas lp called "Dr. Doo-Dah" (9:30) that's even more interesting. A combination of the dense, rhythmic Afro-Latin of **War** and **Barrabas** with Cerrone's trademark creamy strings, "Dr. Doo-Dah" is raucous, throbbing and utterly unlike anything we've heard from Cerrone before. There are moments that recall the intense vocals of "Give Me Love," but the feeling here is wilder – approaching **Doctor John's** crazy voodoo passion (including an inspired drum break) but tempered with some European cool. All together, a fascinating package – looks like Polydor will be releasing it in the States soon. (Note: The first Kongas album, originally released on Barclay in 1974, is back on the import market again in its original cover featuring the alligator that later became the Malligator logo on the front and Cerrone in a group shot on the back. Plus, **Alec Costandinos** confesses that "R. Rupen," credited as a writer on several cuts, is one of his many noms de plume. As I remember, the cut that made the album a cult item on its first release was "Anikana-O," an unusual mix of African chant and English lyrics that retains much of its power, but there's also an early version of "Sweet Drums," the "Supernature" cut, and a Barrabas-like track called "Jungle." Primarily of interest to disco historians and fanatics.)

Strongest new disco disc: The **Michael Zager Band's** two-sided 12-inch for Private Stock, "Let's All Chant" /"Love Express," both seven-minute cuts that began showing up on DJ top 10 lists as soon as the record became available. Both sides are in the same glossy pop-disco style that makes **Bionic Boogie** so attractive, but both break out of this mold frequently enough to give them a special appeal. "Love Express" is, of course, chugging and kinda cute but its breaks are sharper than expected and they make the side brighter, more memorable than this sort of thing usually is. Similarly, "Let's All Chant," basically a formula concept incorporating just about every known disco chant in rather overpolished interpretations, comes off surprisingly well because of a really off-the-wall, quite beautiful neo-chamber music break. And "Your body/my body/everybody/ work your body," though not as tough-sounding as it is in real life, clinches the record.

THEY ARE NOT ALONE: **Gene Page's** version of the **John Williams** "Theme from 'Close Encounters of the Third Kind'" (6:00 on an Arista disco disc) starts out quite promising with a thumping, hard-edged, ominous/anticipatory take-off on the "five tones," then turns into a soft, violin-based disco thing (typical Gene Page stuff) but resolves and redeems itself in a glowing, electronically bubbling last section that manages to capture some of the awe and delight of the movie. **Meco**, in his version, "inspired by the soundtrack of 'Close Encounters'" (4:21 on his just-released lp, "Encounters Of Every Kind," on Millennium, and on a single that is timed just slightly longer), is more whimsical, more manic, definitely more freaky, but perhaps a little too overworked for his own good. The beginning is playful and perplexing but once the five tones break comes in, the song begins to pick up style and pace and the overall feeling is triumphant. Could be addictive. The early reaction is more favorable to Page though neither version seems likely to make the "Star Wars" zoom in the discos. However, several people have pointed out another interesting cut on Meco's lp that goes over like that "Cantina Band" segment of "Star Wars: "Topsy," a bizarre revamp of the old **Cozy Cole** hit with a very similar electric honky-tonk band sound and quite a good drum break (after which the song self-destructs very quickly). Strange. Also listen to the album's opening cuts – "In the Beginning"/"Roman Nights," the first a pounding, grandiose, movie-thematic evocation of the terrors and wonders of prehistory that segues right into the lighter-weight next cut.

OTHER NOTABLE RECORDS: **Charo** is, inevitably, as much of a camp joke on record as she is on the talk show circuit, but her song "Dance A Little Bit Closer," recently made available in an extended version (6:18 on a Salsoul disco disc), has had an unexpected staying power in many clubs and can no longer be ignored. Of course the record's success is not so much a tribute to Charo's talents as to the talents of **Vince Montana's Salsoul Orchestra**, which provides an elegant, spunsugar backdrop to the frequently silly (often spoken) singing. Other plusses: Montana's sparkling vibes segment; the exquisite backing vocals of **Barbara Ingram**, **Evette Benton** and **Carla Benson**; a sense of humor. And a sense of humor is clearly what one needs to truly appreciate Charo as a singer – my amazed congratulations to Montana and crew for making her not just fun but close to irresistible on "Dance A Little Bit Closer" ("Cuchi-Cuchi," now 6:55 on the flip side, is pushing it, however)... "Let Me Party With

STUDIO 54, NEW YORK
DJ: Richie Kaczor

ACT 1/ACT 4 – Donna Summer (Casablanca)
AFRICANISM/GIMME SOME LOVING – Kongas (Crocos)
DANCE A LITTLE BIT CLOSER – Charo (Salsoul)
I DON'T KNOW WHAT I'D DO – Sweet Cream (Bareback)
KEEP IT UP – Olympic Runners (London)
ON FIRE – T-Connection (TK)
RISKY CHANGES – Bionic Boogie (Polydor)
STAYIN' ALIVE/NIGHT FEVER – Bee Gees "Saturday Night Fever" Soundtrack (RSO)
SUPERNATURE/GIVE ME LOVE – Cerrone (Cotillion)
WHICH WAY IS UP? – Stargard (MCA)

DANCE YOUR ASS OFF, SAN FRANCISCO
DJ: Michael Lee

I FEEL GOOD – Al Green (Hi)
IF YOU FEEL LIKE DANCIN' – Al Hudson & the Soul Partners (ABC)
KEEP IT UP – Olympic Runners (London)
LET ME PARTY WITH YOU/YOUR LOVE IS SO GOOD – Bunny Sigler (Gold Mind)
MANHATTAN LOVE SONG/SAL SOUL SISTER/WELL, HAVE A NICE DAY – King Errisson (Westbound)
THE OTHER SIDE OF MIDNIGHT/I KNOW THAT HE KNOWS/HEARTACHE – Marsha Hunt (Aves import)
RISKY CHANGES/DON'T LOSE THAT NUMBER – Bionic Boogie (Polydor)
SUPERNATURE/GIVE ME LOVE – Cerrone (Cotillion)
TWO HOT FOR LOVE – THP Orchestra (Butterfly)
WHICH WAY IS UP? – Stargard (MCA)

LOST AND FOUND, WASHINGTON, D.C.
DJ: Bill Owens

CAN'T YOU FEEL IT – Michele (West End)
DANCE A LITTLE BIT CLOSER – Charo (Salsoul)
DON'T STOP ME (I LIKE IT) – David Christie (Polydor)
EVERYBODY DANCE/EST-CE QUE C'EST CHIC – Chic (Atlantic)
FAIRY TALE HIGH/WORKING THE MIDNIGHT SHIFT/I LOVE YOU – Donna Summer (Casablanca)
ON FIRE – T-Connection (TK)
RISKY CHANGES/DANCE LITTLE DREAMER/DON'T LOSE THAT NUMBER – Bionic Boogie (Polydor)
SUPERNATURE/GIVE ME LOVE – Cerrone (Cotillion)
THERE'S FIRE DOWN BELOW – Fantastic Four (Westbound)
TWO HOT FOR LOVE – THP Orchestra (Butterfly)

PIPPINS, NEW YORK
DJ: Reggie T. Experience

DANCE LITTLE DREAMER/RISKY CHANGES/BOOGIE BOO – Bionic Boogie (Polydor)
GALAXY – War (MCA)
GIVE ME LOVE/SUPERNATURE/SWEET DRUMS – Cerrone (Cotillion)
GOD HELPS THOSE (WHO HELP THEMSELVES)/LOVE CONNECTION – The Dells (Mercury)
LET'S GET TOGETHER/MAKING LOVE – Pam Todd & Love Exchange (Sherlyn)
LOVE EXPRESS/LET'S ALL CHANT – Michael Zager Band (Private Stock)
SHAME – Evelyn "Champagne" King (RCA)
TWO HOT FOR LOVE – THP Orchestra (Butterfly)
WHICH WAY IS UP? – Stargard (MCA)
WHY MUST THERE BE AN END/GOLDEN TEARS/COSMIC TRAVELLER/DANCE AND LEAVE IT ALL BEHIND YOU – Sumeria (Raal import)

You (Party, Party, Party)," the title cut from **Bunny Sigler's** first Gold Mind (Salsoul) album, is obviously Sigler's "Got To Give It Up" – it runs over 12 minutes in the same sort of groove (just whipped up some) Gaye established, which may be regulation length for this kind of thing but seems too long (especially when it feels like the second time around). Happily though, the Bunny has a wonderful brightness and charm that saves the cut and makes it truly enjoyable. And the whole album is full of good material this time – it's the most consistent record

❝ Sweet Cream's "I Don't Know What I'd Do" has been a number one record at Studio 54 for weeks now ❞

Sigler has put out so far; try "Your Love Is So Good" and "I'm A Fool" and maybe even "It's Time To Twist"... **Sweet Cream's** "I Don't Know What I'd Do" (7:02 on a Bareback disco disc) is an excellent, classically-styled girl group song (recalls **Martha & the Vandellas**, **Sisters Love**) with fine, robust lead vocals (listen to her riff at the end) that Richie Kaczor says has been a number one record at Studio 54 for weeks now. Check it out... The new **Dells** album, "Love Connection" on Mercury, is a product of "The Harris Machine" – **Norman Harris** & Co. – so it has the same spunky Philly production sound that sparked the last Dells release but fewer driving cuts and perceptibly less energy. "God Helps Those (Who Help Themselves)" and the title track are the two songs that have already been included on top 10 lists and both have a nice **Trammps** feel. Unfortunately, like so much disco stuff out of Philadelphia these days, it sounds like it could have been made three or four years ago... London has released its two-record disco hits collection, "Star Discs," including "Erotic Soul," "Slow Down," "Since I Fell For You," "Wow," "The Final Thing" and five other cuts in their extended versions. Some of the secondary cuts – like **Bloodstone's** "Stand Up, Let's Party" and "Put the Music Where Your Mouth Is" by the **Olympic Runners** – are questionable entries but it's nice to have **Hodges, James & Smith's** "One More Love Song" and "Porcupine" by **Nature Zone**, both somewhat overlooked originally. Billy Smith gets part credit for having "conceived, compiled and coordinated" the package and there's a thanks to New York DJ Wayne Scott who apparently advised on the order of tracks, so we're especially puzzled by the fact that the material hasn't been disco-blended. Only once – going from "Wow" to "Slow Down" – is the change from one cut to another a danceable one; more often the mix is just a fade-down and a fade-up or just an abrupt back-to-back jump. A decent collection but not the party record we were expecting. ◉

JANUARY 14, 1978

A real ho-hum week here in the Land of 1,000 Dances – the first weeks of January are always serious withdrawal periods for vinyl junkies, only it seems worse than usual this year. But take heart: a flood of new releases is scheduled in the next few weeks – many of them postponed by the pressing-plant overloads in December – and the records below should help fill in the gap.

RECOMMENDED DISCO DISCS: **Timmy Thomas'** "Africano" (TK), the 4:45 cut from his recent "Touch To Touch" album now available on a 12-inch pressing, is a Miami-style Afro-funk instrumental-with-chant that sounds like it was recorded in a garage during a combined bar-band rehearsal and voodoo ceremony. Very weird, rather uneven but brilliantly off-the-wall, "Africano" is a **King Sporty** production that begins with an echo of "Law Of The Land," throws in a little **Barrabas**, a pinch of **Osibisa**, a lot of crackling guitar, drums and moaning chants. This drug-dream version of a Ramar-of-the-Jungle native ritual may be nothing more than a fascinating oddity but it's perfect for one of those crazed, charged atmospheric sets and we like it, we love it. "Touch To Touch," the flip side of the disc, and the song to accompany an alleged new dance of the same name, is not too convincing (at least with "Le Spank," whether you believed there was such a dance or not, the music made you want to do it) but is has a nice chunky TK sound and more of that brittle guitar work... "Trinidad" by **John Gibbs & the U.S. Steel Orchestra** (Solid Steel Records in Philadelphia) is another strange record – a frothy instrumental with a **Salsoul Orchestra** feel and a Latin slant that begins with, and occasionally breaks into, tight timbales-and-congas rhythms. Pretty, lightly spiced but broken into needlessly by breathy female vocals repeating, "Trinidad – where I'm going/Trinidad – island of love." If this is a tourist pitch, unleashed on the unsuspecting disco market in a "Special Limited Edition," it's an attractive one but we prefer the summery music without commercial interruption. Thanks to John Luongo from the Boston Record Pool for sending a copy to DISCO FILE... **Linda Hopkins'** "It's In Your Blood" (Columbia) is hardly a new record – initially reviewed (and raved over) in this space on its single release last June, the record became available as a disco disc sometime in the fall and, typically, we didn't receive a copy until about a month ago – but it's still turning up on top 10 lists (Walter Gibbons' from Inferno this week) and it deserves another plug. Produced by **Bert de Coteaux**, "It's In Your Blood" is a rousing gospel-raunch number with robust, shouting vocals (cf. **Loleatta Holloway**) and, in this longer version (5:58), a great percussion-into-strings break. Steamy, funked-up music with vocals to match... **Ashford & Simpson's** "Don't Cost You Nothing" (Warner Brothers) has been remixed from the version on the "Send It" album and now runs nearly seven minutes. There are no radical changes in the new version, which was done by Valerie's brother, **Jimmy Simpson**, but the vocals are extended in the chorus section at the end; a new, sharp percussion-and-handclap break has been added; and the final vamping vocals are hotter, more spontaneous-sounding. All this makes an already fine track even finer, surely worth a revival of interest... **True Example's** debut disc contains two classic Philadelphia-style songs back-to-back, "Love Is Finally Coming My Way" (5:36) and "As Long As You Love Me" (6:04), both very familiar-sounding to fans of **Baker-Harris-Young** productions (they were produced by **T.G. Conway**, Philly keyboard man, for B-H-Y Productions) but saved from the same-old-thing category by truly wonderful vocals (a superb male lead, beautiful female counterpart and chorus), first-rate lyrics and perfect breaks. Both are smooth, comfortable songs, elegantly polished (mixed by **Walter Gibbons**) but neither pushes over the edge into the area of the unexpected and exciting. Perfectly-crafted but predictable... **Ralph Graham's** "Changing Up My Life" (RCA) is a new mix (by New York DJ Raphael Charres) of the cut from his recent "Extensions" album released appropriately at this time of resolutions for the new year the time everyone's promising to "change up" their life. Graham's is a good hurt song, moving on from a failed relationship and facing it all in high spirits-spirits reflected in the drive and pulse-beat of the music. The new mix is uneven – fine breaks but often muddy, with the vocals blurred and levels shifting – but Graham overcomes it all in the end and takes you soaring happily. ✪

> **❝ The first weeks of January are always serious withdrawal periods for vinyl junkies. But take heart: a flood of new releases is scheduled in the next few weeks – many of them postponed by the pressing-plant overloads in December ❞**

CLUB FEVER, DETROIT
DJ: Claude Dunn

DANCE A LITTLE BIT CLOSER – Charo (Salsoul)
DANCE WITH ME – Peter Brown (Drive)
FUNK REACTION – Lonnie Smith (LRC)
GIVE ME LOVE/LOVE IS THE ANSWER – Cerrone (Cotillion)
MOON-BOOTS – ORS (Salsoul)
THE NIGHT THE LIGHTS WENT OUT/LOVE PER HOUR – Trammps (Atlantic)
RISKY CHANGES/DANCE LITTLE DREAMER/DON'T LOSE THAT NUMBER/ WE MUST BELIEVE IN MAGIC/STOP THE MUSIC/FEEL LIKE DANCING – Bionic Boogie (Polydor)
SHAME – Evelyn "Champagne" King (RCA)
SOMETHING'S UP – Wayne St. John (Salsoul)
TATTOO WOMAN/DR. DOO-DAH – Kongas (Crocos import)

INFERNO, NEW YORK
DJ: Walter Gibbons

AT LAST MY SEARCH IS OVER/ MIDNIGHT FLIGHT TO YOUR LOVE – The Pips (Casablanca)
IT'S IN YOUR BLOOD – Linda Hopkins (Columbia)
KEEP ON DANCING/LOOKING FOR SOMEBODY – TC James & the Fist-o-Funk Orchestra (Fist-o-Funk)
LET YOURSELF GO – T-Connection (Dash)
LET'S ALL CHANT/LOVE EXPRESS – Michael Zager Band (Private Stock)
LOVE CONNECTION/HOW CAN ONE MAN BE SO LUCKY – Dells (Mercury)
MISTER LOVE – Savannah Band (RCA)
PLAY WITH ME/YOU ARE MY LOVE – Sandy Mercer (H&L)
VOLGA BOATMAN – Tuxedo Junction (Butterfly)
WHICH WAY IS UP? – Stargard (MCA)

BAREFOOT BOY, NEW YORK
DJ: Jerry Bossa

DR. DOO-DAH – Kongas (Crocos import)
GIVE ME LOVE/SUPERNATURE – Cerrone (Cotillion)
I LOVE YOU/NOW I NEED YOU/ HAPPILY EVER AFTER/ ONCE UPON A TIME – Donna Summer (Casablanca)
LOVE EXPRESS/LET'S ALL CHANT – Michael Zager Band (Private Stock)
LOVE MAGNET – Freda Payne (Capitol)
THE OTHER SIDE Of MIDNIGHT/I KNOW THAT HE KNOWS – Marsha Hunt (Aves import)
PEOPLE OF THE WORLD, RISE/THE NIGHT THE LIGHTS WENT OUT – Trammps (Atlantic)
RISKY CHANGES/DON'T LOSE THAT NUMBER/DANCE LITTLE DREAMER – Bionic Boogie (Polydor)
SHAME – Evelyn "Champagne" King (RCA)
TAKE IT EASY/JOHNNY, JOHNNY PLEASE COME HOME/DANCING FEVER – Claudja Barry (Salsoul)

EIGHTBALL'S LOUNGE, ALBANY, N.Y.
DJ: Douglas Forrester

ACT 1/ACT 4 – Donna Summer (Casablanca)
CHANGING UP MY LIFE – Ralph Graham (RCA)
CLOSE ENCOUNTERS OF THE THIRD KIND – Gene Page (Arista)
DANCE, DANCE, DANCE – Chic (Atlantic)
DANCE A LITTLE BIT CLOSER – Charo (Salsoul)
I WOULDN'T GIVE YOU UP – Goldie Alexander/Chatelaine (Amour import)
MEDLEY DISCOLAT'S – Chocolats (Ibach import)
RISKY CHANGES/DANCE LITTLE DREAMER/DON'T LOSE THAT NUMBER – Bionic Boogie (Polydor)
SUPERNATURE/GIVE ME LOVE – Cerrone (Cotillion)
TWO HOT FOR LOVE – THP Orchestra (Butterfly)

DISCO FILE TOP 20

1. GIVE ME LOVE/SUPERNATURE – Cerrone (Cotillion)
2. TWO HOT FOR LOVE – THP Orchestra (Butterfly)
3. RISKY CHANGES/DANCE LITTLE DREAMER/DON'T LOSE THAT NUMBER – Bionic Boogie (Polydor)
4. ACT 1/ACT 2/ACT 4 – Donna Summer (Casablanca)
5. DANCE, DANCE, DANCE/EVERYBODY DANCE – Chic (Atlantic)
6. THE NIGHT THE LIGHTS WENT OUT/PEOPLE OF THE WORLD, RISE/LOVE PER HOUR – Trammps (Atlantic)
7. MANHATTAN LOVE SONG – King Errisson (Westbound)
8. DANCE A LITTLE CLOSER – Charo (Salsoul)
9. WHICH WAY IS UP? – Stargard (MCA)
10. LET'S ALL CHANT/LOVE EXPRESS – Michael Zager Band (Private Stock)
11. ON FIRE – T-Connection (TK)
12. THE OTHER SIDE OF MIDNIGHT/I KNOW THAT HE KNOWS/HEARTACHE – Marsha Hunt (Aves import)
13. JOHNNY, JOHNNY PLEASE COME HOME – Claudja Barry (Salsoul)
14. SHAME – Evelyn "Champagne" King (RCA)
15. MOON-BOOTS – Orlando Riva Sound (Salsoul)
16. CAN'T YOU FEEL IT/DISCO DANCE/MAGIC LOVE – Michele (West End)
17. WHAT'S YOUR NAME, WHAT'S YOUR NUMBER – Andrea True Connection (Buddah)
18. KISS ME – George McCrae (TK)
19. LE SPANK – Le Pamplemousse (AVI)
20. NATIVE NEW YORKER – Odyssey (RCA)

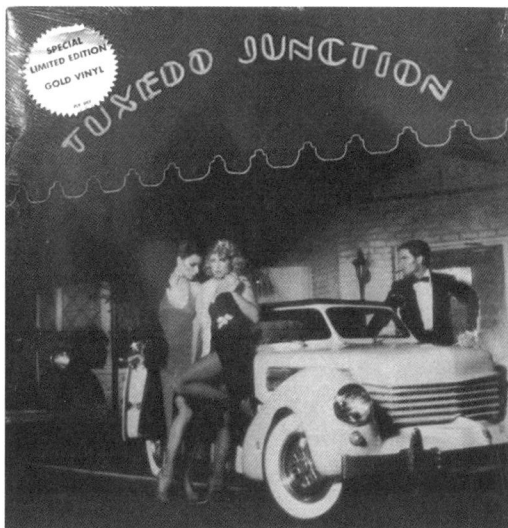

JANUARY 21, 1978

The second **Savannah Band** album, titled "Dr. Buzzard's Original Savannah Band Meets King Penett" (only with the "e"'s printed backwards in that last word), will be officially released by RCA within the week – a year and a half since the group's debut and nearly a year since the group went to Los Angeles to begin recording this follow-up. After all the anticipation (it was promised nearly every month since last June), wild rumour, management shifts, false reports of advance leaks and a final intense flurry of disco sneak previews in the past two weeks, the album itself seems, at first, an anticlimax. On first impression, "King Penett," from the title on down, is willfully obscure – purposely more allusive, esoteric and difficult to get into, as if the Savannians decided to take one step further through the avant garde looking glass. It's an intriguing, utterly eccentric but vaguely forbidding place they're leading us to – how many will follow?

It's not so much that the sound here is different – the music (by **Stony Browder, Jr.**, who is also the producer this time around) is, again, a brilliant pastiche of periods, evoking the romance and swank of the '40s with just the right '70s razor-edged irony – but it is rather less varied then on the previous album and it replaces much of the softness and affection that lit up the debut with a jittery nervousness, a bittersweet bounce. **Cory Dayne**, the lead vocalist who swept everyone away first time around, sounds intentionally "off" throughout the new record, giving all the material an odd, on-edge quality that may not be comfortable but can become invigorating. Also, **August Darnell's** lyrics are knottier, tougher and more personal than before, so, though there are a number of wonderful images ("scarlet smears across the bathroom tile") and verses ("When Crosby starts to croon/The jitterbuggies cruise the

room/Their fingers poke the air/Man-o-man-o-man-o-man, they look just like that Fred Astaire!"), there are few passages of sustained clarity to compare with the memorable "Cherchez La Femme" (or "I'll Play The Fool" or "Sour And Sweet"). Taking all this into account, "King Penett" is still an extraordinarily rich and rewarding album – not the disco extravaganza we'd hoped for, perhaps, but something quite special and original. It takes time, but eventually all the songs click into place in your head (reading the lyrics helps because otherwise much of the nuance and delightful word play is lost in the delivery) and the album takes hold. For the disco audience, the highlights are "Mister Love" (4:33), a jumping big-band number sliced with raucous horns that revives the mood of a '40s dance hall and sounds like a hopped-up "Sour And Sweet" and "The Gigolo And I" (4:36), which leans more toward the feel of "Cherchez La Femme," contains a number of French verses (in which the singer explains why she pays for a companion), and ends up a crazy rumba tribute to Manhattan. Neither are as persuasive as dance records as the Band's earlier material, but both grow on the listener rather irresistibly. Clearly however, an album of such complexity, wit and intelligence cannot stand or fall on the effectiveness of its disco cuts. Even if "King Penett" won't light up the dance floors with the brilliance of its predecessor, the album deserves (and demands) time, patience and an adventurous spirit before any judgment is made. Tune in next week for second thoughts.

A much glossier vision of the '40s is available on **Tuxedo Junction**, the new **Michael Lewis** and **Laurin Rinder** production for Butterfly Records. Though I have never been a big fan of pop vocals from that period or disco remakes of same, this collection – including classics like "Chatanooga Choo Choo," "Moonlight

THE CITY, SAN FRANCISCO
DJ: John Randazzo

ACT 1/ACT 4 – Donna Summer (Casablanca)
CHATANOOGA CHOO CHOO – Tuxedo Junction (Butterfly)
GALAXY – War (MCA)
GIVE ME LOVE – Cerrone (Cotillion)
I FEEL GOOD – Al Green (Hi)
LOVE MACHINE/TAKE IT EASY – Claudja Barry (Salsoul)
LET'S ALL CHANT/LOVE EXPRESS– Michael Zager Band (Private Stock)
THE OTHER SIDE OF MIDNIGHT – Marsha Hunt (Aves import)
RISKY CHANGES – Bionic Boogie (Polydor)
TWO HOT FOR LOVE – THP Orchestra (Butterfly)

ICE PALACE 57, NEW YORK
DJ: Roy Thode

ACT 1/ACT 2/ACT 4/IF YOU'VE GOT IT, FLAUNT IT – Donna Summer (Casablanca)
DANCE A LITTLE BIT CLOSER – Charo (Salsoul)
DANCE WITH ME – Peter Brown (Drive)
GIVE ME LOVE/SUPERNATURE – Cerrone (Cotillion)
I DON'T KNOW WHAT I'D DO – Sweet Cream (Bareback)
LET'S ALL CHANT/LOVE EXPRESS– Michael Zager Band (Private Stock)
LET'S GET TOGETHER – Pam Todd & Love Exchange (Sherlyn)
RISKY CHANGES/DANCE LITTLE DREAMER – Bionic Boogie (Polydor)
STAYIN' ALIVE – Bee Gees "Saturday Night Fever" Soundtrack (RSO)
TWO HOT FOR LOVE – THP Orchestra (Butterfly)

FOX TRAPPE, WASHINGTON, DC
DJ: Frank Edwards

AT LAST MY SEARCH IS OVER/MIDNIGHT FLIGHT TO YOUR LOVE – The Pips (Casablanca)
DANCE WITH ME – Peter Brown (Drive)
GETTING READY FOR YOU – Flakes (Magic Disc)
GIVE ME LOVE/SUPERNATURE – Cerrone (Cotillion)
LOVE EXPRESS– Michael Zager Band (Private Stock)
LOVE IS FINALLY COMING MY WAY – True Example (Salsoul)
MISTER LOVE/THE GIGOLO AND I – Savannah Band (RCA)
RISKY CHANGES – Bionic Boogie (Polydor)
TWO HOT FOR LOVE – THP Orchestra (Butterfly)
WHICH WAY IS UP? – Stargard (MCA)

DCA CLUB, PHILADELPHIA
DJ: Kurt Borusiewicz

ACT 1/ ACT 4 – Donna Summer (Casablanca)
AFRICANISM/GIMME SOME LOVING – Kongas (Crocos)
AFRICANO/TOUCH TO TOUCH –Timmy Thomas (TK)
EVERYBODY DANCE/DANCE, DANCE, DANCE – Chic (Atlantic)
GIVE ME LOVE/SUPERNATURE – Cerrone (Cotillion)
LET'S ALL CHANT – Michael Zager Band (Private Stock)
MR. RHYTHM – King Sporty (Konduko)
THE NIGHT THE LIGHTS WENT OUT / PEOPLE OF THE WORLD, RISE/LOVE PER HOUR – Trammps (Atlantic)
RISKY CHANGES/DANCE LITTLE DREAMER/BOOGIE BOO – Bionic Boogie (Polydor)
STANDING IN THE RAIN – John Paul Young (Midsong)

Serenade" and "Tuxedo Junction" – succeeds admirably, not really transcending the genre except for passages, but certainly enlivening and illuminating it. All the cuts save one are vocals featuring a close-harmony female trio that sounds terribly authentic if a little too homogenized and reddi-whipped for my taste. The feeling here is slick, brassy, innocently carefree and the pace is bright and snappy. "Chatanooga Choo Choo" (7:15) is perhaps the most fun; "Moonlight Serenade" (5:45) the most attractive; and "Volga Boatman" (6:07), the only instrumental, the most inventive and different. All the tracks have fine, often unexpected breaks that give them a fresh slant, like the tight percussion change in "Moonlight Serenade" and the instrumental segment that follows (high quality horns here and throughout). Personal pick: "Volga Boatman." But all the tracks work nicely (aside from those already mentioned, try "Foxtrot") and Lewis & Rinder's interpretations prove this is still highly delectable pop music. As usual, Butterfly's packaging is something special and Tuxedo Junction is pressed on clear, golden yellow vinyl.

Two excellent disco disc remixes are now available: **Ripple's** "The Beat Goes On And On" (Salsoul), one of the season's hottest, happiest party records, expanded to seven minutes on "A Jim Burgess Mix" (the first such credit for the former 12 West DJ) that gives us more, more, more of the breaks and sharpens up the sound; and **War's** "Galaxy" (MCA), actually shorter than the lp version at 7:28 but minus the change-of-pace movement that made that track difficult to play in the clubs – this new mix (by Los Angeles DJ Manny Slali) smooths things out and adds a crackling drum break, making one of our favorite funk songs (those lyrics!) even more accessible. Both highly recommended, though only the former is available commercially. ⏻

❝August Darnell's lyrics are knottier, tougher and more personal than before❞

JANUARY 28, 1978

Three essential new releases this week, signalling the end of the great post-holiday record slump and the beginning of what promises to be an unusually rich and stimulating year in disco: "Romeo & Juliet" (Casablanca), the latest disco drama by **Alec R. Costandinos**, producer of **Love & Kisses**, **Sphinx** and **Sumeria**; "Half And Half," **Vicki Sue Robinson's** first album in nearly a year and a half – also her best so far (on RCA); and **Montana's** "A Dance Fantasy," a musical collage by producer **Vince Montana** based on the film "Close Encounters Of The Third Kind" (due out within the week as Atlantic's second commercial disco disc). Taking them one at a time, as fine examples of the Eurodisco, Neo-New York and Neophiladelphia sounds, they encourage our conviction that disco's prime strength is in its growing diversity and depth.

"Romeo & Juliet," credited to Alec Costandinos and the **Syncophonic Orchestra**, is this producer-composer's first American release since Love & Kisses and in many ways his most accomplished and fully-satisfying work, combining the urgency and fire of "I've Found Love" with the delicacy and drama of "Golden Tears" in one splendid, seamless piece. With a plot so familiar, the lyric structure can be sketchy, dispensing with the sometimes awkward spoken segments that intrude on other Costandinos productions and allowing for a dense, uninterrupted flow of music. In a rather audacious move, two "songs" from Shakespeare's play – the prologues to Acts I and II – are included here along with the new lyric passages and the combination works brilliantly. The singers, both male and female, usually in full chorus, are strong, and stirring, emotional even when narrating events but at a peak when assuming the lovers' roles and soaring with them. In spite of my enthusiasm for the European disco sound, even I must admit that its stylistic vocabulary is being overworked and threatening to wear thin, but the best producers – and certainly Costandinos is among the finest – have been pushing the form ahead record by record, experimenting with the narrative structure, intensifying the movement and thematic flow of the music. So, while there may be nothing startlingly different about the style of "Romeo & Juliet," Costandinos has brought that style to a certain perfection here and retained its freshness with countless musical surprises. Side two recalls the thrilling changes of "I've Found Love" – rushes of violins and voices, ominously blaring horns

jittering to a nervous beat – and the music throughout is always grand but never pompous; warm but never calculating. To get down to disco details, both sides are strong enough to dance straight through with Acts I and II on side 1 (16:08) and Acts III, IV and V filling out side 2 (17:25). **Don Ray**, whose name appears on all the best European product, arranged here as well. A moving, important album and the first major American disco lp of 1978. **Vicki Sue Robinson's** "Half And Half" is sharp, sassy New York disco – funk with flair – plus some wonderful ballads that together make for the singer's most effective and well-balanced album. Robinson sounds more at ease, looser than before so the rough, grainy quality of her voice achieves just the right cutting edge here – tough yet tender. "Turn the Beat Around" remains unmatched, but "Hold Tight" is included here in a somewhat abbreviated version (5:27) and several other cuts have a comparable punch. The stand-outs: "Don't Try To Win Me Back Again," which is very similar to "Hold Tight" (an almost identical intro) with robust vocals underlined by hand-clapping and an angular kind of structure; "Trust In Me," slightly uneven but the most enjoyable, driving track with a great chorus and tight breaks (plus some Motown echoes); and "Feels So Good It Must Be Wrong," which is clinched by a nice drum break and the following chorus/ instrumental build. On the slow side, listen to "Freeway Song," a lovely number Robinson wrote, and "Jealousy." No outrageous peaks, maybe, and the hot cuts could all stand some lengthening, but this is still the best showcase Vicki Sue's enjoyed to date – credit producer **Warren Schatz**.

"A Dance Fantasy," nearly 19 minutes of music drawn from and inspired by "Close Encounters of the Third Kind," is **Vince Montana's** most ambitious and fascinating production. Arranged in seven "movements" that trace the development of the film, this is a dramatic mood collage similar to **Meco's** "Star Wars" medley but with the grace and poetry of a Costandinos side. Some sections may be too down-paced for a continuous dance-through but the force of the whole piece should keep dancers absorbed and if not, it's a marvellous record to just listen to. Montana conjures up the mystery and splendor of the movie with some great **Salsoul Orchestra**-like sections but he retains much of the film's wit as well (with a light "Comin' 'Round The Mountain" passage and the final singing of "When You Wish Upon A Star," the song Spielberg had originally tagged "Close Encounters"

> **" This is the most imaginative and beautiful of the "Close Encounters" records – right down to the female voices ooo-ing the "five tones" at the end "**

LES MOUCHES, NEW YORK
DJ: Joel Jacobs

ACT 1/ACT 2/ACT 4 – Donna Summer (Casablanca)
FROM EAST TO WEST – Voyage(Polydor/Sirocco import)
JOHNNY, JOHNNY PLEASE COME HOME/LOVE MACHINE – Claudja Barry (Salsoul)
LET'S ALL CHANT/LOVE EXPRESS– Michael Zager Band (Private Stock)
THE OTHER SIDE OF MIDNIGHT/I KNOW THAT HE KNOWS – Marsha Hunt (Aves import)
RISKY CHANGES/DANCE LITTLE DREAMER – Bionic Boogie (Polydor)
STAYIN' ALIVE/NIGHT FEVER – Bee Gees "Saturday Night Fever" Soundtrack (RSO)
SUPERNATURE/GIVE ME LOVE – Cerrone (Cotillion)
TWO HOT FOR LOVE – THP Orchestra (Butterfly)
YOU LIKE IT, WE LOVE IT – Southroad Connection (Mahogany)

GIRAFFE, PITTSBURGH
DJ: Gary Larkin

CHATANOOGA CHOO CHOO – Tuxedo Junction (Butterfly)
DANCE WITH ME – Peter Brown (Drive)
DON'T COST YOU NOTHING – Ashford & Simpson (Warner Bros.)
GIVE ME LOVE/SUPERNATURE – Cerrone (Cotillion)
HOUSE OF THE RISING SUN – Revelacion (Crocos import)
LET'S ALL CHANT – Michael Zager Band (Private Stock)
LOVE BUG/SWEETS FOR MY SWEET – Tina Charles (CBS)
STAYIN' ALIVE/NIGHT FEVER – Bee Gees "Saturday Night Fever" Soundtrack (RSO)
SWAY – Peter Nicholas (RSO)
TWO HOT FOR LOVE – THP Orchestra (Butterfly)

BUZZBY'S, SAN FRANCISCO
DJ: Christine Matuchek

CHATANOOGA CHOO CHOO/RAINY NIGHT IN RIO – Tuxedo Junction (Butterfly)
GALAXY – War (MCA)
GIMME SOME LOVING/DR. DOO-DAH/ TATTOO WOMAN – Kongas (Crocos import)
I FEEL GOOD – Al Green (Hi)
LET ME PARTY WITH YOU/YOUR LOVE IS SO GOOD – Bunny Sigler (Gold Mind)
LET'S ALL CHANT/LOVE EXPRESS – Michael Zager Band (Private Stock)
THE OTHER SIDE OF MIDNIGHT/I KNOW THAT HE KNOWS/HEARTACHE – Marsha Hunt (Aves import)
RISKY CHANGES/BOOGIE BOO/DANCE LITTLE DREAMER – Bionic Boogie (Polydor)
STAYIN' ALIVE/NIGHT FEVER – Bee Gees "Saturday Night Fever" Soundtrack (RSO)
TOUCH TO TOUCH/AFRICANO –Timmy Thomas (TK)

SIGLO 21, BRONX, NEW YORK
DJ: Louis "Angelo" Alers

CLOSE ENCOUNTERS/CRAZY RHYTHM/TOPSY – Meco (Millennium)
HOUSE OF THE RISING SUN – Revelacion (Crocos import)
LET'S ALL CHANT – Michael Zager Band (Private Stock)
MELODIES – Made in USA (De-Lite)
RISKY CHANGES/DON'T LOSE THAT NUMBER/BOOGIE BOO – Bionic Boogie (Polydor)
SHAME – Evelyn "Champagne" King (RCA)
STAYIN' ALIVE/NIGHT FEVER/MORE THAN A WOMAN – Bee Gees "Saturday Night Fever" Soundtrack (RSO)
SUPERNATURE/SWEET DRUMS/GIVE ME LOVE – Cerrone (Cotillion)
TAKE IT EASY/JOHNNY, JOHNNY PLEASE COME HOME/DANCING FEVER – Claudja Barry (Salsoul)
TWO HOT FOR LOVE – THP Orchestra (Butterfly)

with). This is the most imaginative and beautiful of the "Close Encounters" records – right down to the female voices ooo-ing the "five tones" at the end – and should be experimented with.

FEEDBACK: Christine Matuchek is the third San Francisco DJ to add Al Green's "I Feel Good" to her top 10 list (Michael Lee and John Randazzo preceded her) – enough to indicate a solid regional breakout for this glowing modern gospel cut from "The Belle Album" (Hi). When asked why Green is doing it in San Francisco, Christine said, "This city really likes its funk and Al Green has always been a favorite. People know his voice and this one was so instant I couldn't believe it." No wonder – Green sounds infectiously joyful and the music churns along at a fine clip; this one deserves to spread across the country (though a sharper mix might help). Check it out. ⊘

DISCO FILE TOP 20

1. **SUPERNATURE/GIVE ME LOVE** – Cerrone (Cotillion)
2. **RISKY CHANGES/DANCE LITTLE DREAMER/DON'T LOSE THAT NUMBER** – Bionic Boogie (Polydor)
3. **TWO HOT FOR LOVE** – THP Orchestra (Butterfly)
4. **LET'S ALL CHANT/LOVE EXPRESS** – Michael Zager Band (Private Stock)
5. **ACT 1/ACT 2/ACT 4** – Donna Summer (Casablanca)
6. **THE OTHER SIDE OF MIDNIGHT/I KNOW THAT HE KNOWS/HEARTACHE** – Marsha Hunt (Aves import)
7. **STAYIN' ALIVE/NIGHT FEVER** – Bee Gees "Saturday Night Fever" Soundtrack (RSO)
8. **JOHNNY, JOHNNY PLEASE COME HOME** – Claudja Barry (Salsoul)
9. **WHICH WAY IS UP?** – Stargard (MCA)
10. **SHAME** – Evelyn "Champagne" King (RCA)
11. **DANCE A LITTLE CLOSER** – Charo (Salsoul)
12. **DANCE WITH ME** – Peter Brown (Drive)
13. **DANCE, DANCE, DANCE/EVERYBODY DANCE** – Chic (Atlantic)
14. **THE NIGHT THE LIGHTS WENT OUT/PEOPLE OF THE WORLD, RISE/LOVE PER HOUR** – Trammps (Atlantic)
15. **AFRICANISM/GIMME SOME LOVING** – Kongas (Crocos)
16. **BOOGIE BOO** – Bionic Boogie (Polydor)
17. **ON FIRE** – T-Connection (TK)
18. **MANHATTAN LOVE SONG** – King Errisson (Westbound)
19. **MOON-BOOTS** – ORS (Salsoul)
20. **CAN'T YOU FEEL IT** – Michele (West End)

FEBRUARY 4, 1978

Funny, it was just about this time last year that **Cerrone** and Casablanca Records (represented by the **Heart and Soul Orchestra**) were engaged in the battle of "Love In C Minor" – in retrospect, not much of a contest though the initial action was hot and heavy and Casablanca's cover version made quite a respectable showing. Now, however, both contenders are back for what promises to be an even more exciting round two, centering on two very similar versions of **The Animals'** rock hit, "House Of The Rising Sun." One, already available as an import and jumping into a number of disco top 10 lists, is a Cerrone production for a group called **Revelacion** on the Crocos label. The other, due out this week from Casablanca, is by **Santa Esmeralda**, the follow-up to their immensely successful "Don't Let Me Be Misunderstood." There seems to be some controversy about who had the idea first – Santa Esmeralda claims to have wrapped up its recording before Revelacion went into the studio (November and December 1977 according to the liner notes), but Cerrone beat the competition into the marketplace and audaciously stamped his record "Original Version." No matter – both versions are essentially slavish copies of the crisp flamenco disco style producers **Nicolas Skorsky** and **Jean-Manuel de Scarano** established with "Don't Let Me Be Misunderstood," and even after a week of listening, it's hard to find enough substantial differences between the two to settle a definite preference.

It's easy to be critical about both "Houses" especially when the original material, an aimless, self-pitying blues rip-off, was never a big personal favorite. Neither vocalist here achieves the rock/soul balance **Leroy Gomez** (back on his own) struck on "Misunderstood," though the unidentified man on Santa Esmeralda has the edge if only because he sings less and because Revelacion's "L. Rich" is perhaps too authentically British '60s for general disco taste. Then, because this is the second time around for this particular concept (third

" The original material, an aimless, self-pitying blues rip-off, was never a big personal favorite "

if you count **Kongas'** "Gimme Some Loving" which takes a somewhat different approach) and because both sides are, of course, quite long (Santa Esmeralda about 15 minutes, Revelacion 16:10), you begin to feel you've gotten stuck in the gypsy camp scene of some low-budget bullfighting movie. Not that both productions aren't elaborately staged, but the Spanish cliches – the flamenco guitar, blaring horns, castanets, maracas and all that handclapping – do tend to get heavy. Both records have a similar structure – vocal/break/vocal/break & finale – but the central break in Revelacion is somewhat longer, cutting down on the finale and Santa Esmeralda cuts its intro handclaps very short and to the point while Cerrone runs them on. To get down to more important distinctions, the Cerrone production feels like it has more verve – its flourishes are brighter, fuller; the instrumentation, aside from the requisite flamenco guitar, etc., is more varied and inspired. There's even a definite "Supernature" overtone (plus a lot more bottom) in Revelacion's first big break and this gives it a slightly different flavor. But then Revelacion almost blows it at other points by duplicating too closely the breaks from "Misunderstood" while Santa Esmeralda has tried to avoid imitating itself and, at times, succeeds by injecting some fresh enthusiasm into the breaks. Santa Esmeralda's guitar work is more original and moving and the changes remain lively but without arranger **Don Ray**, who chose to join Cerrone rather than Skorsky and de Scarano this time, the sound doesn't mesh with the same sort of density and spark the group displayed first time out. In the end, it's a toss-up, but a crucial one. Santa Esmeralda is coming off a very successful album and single and it has the force of Casablanca behind it, but Cerrone is riding high right now with his own "Supernature" lp and Kongas and, even if Revelacion is still without an American label, the import has the jump on the club level. Contributing to each album's eventual success could be the B side material: on Santa Esmeralda, three cuts, only one of which might have any disco impact –"Dance You Down Tonight" (7:07), a rock-styled piece with an oddly uneven pace but a nice feel; and on Revelacion, a two-part song called "Crocos Dance" (8:30) which has a similar pace to "Dr. Doo-Dah" and is bizarre as only Cerrone can be – a male lead vocal with chanting female chorus and a weird mix of breaks, jumbled and fascinating. Whichever side you're on, these are the records to watch in the next few weeks – both essential releases.

OTHER RECOMMENDED ALBUMS: Here's a batch of funk-based instrumentals to check out right now: all the cuts on the **Sine** album, "Happy Is The Only Way" (Prelude), produced by **Patrick Adams** and shimmering with his particular brand of freaky synthesizer (remember "Love Bug" and "Dance And Shake Your Tambourine") – all the first side is terrific, especially "Chimi" and a vocal/chant, "Just Let Me Do My Thing"; "Keep It Coming," nearly 12 minutes on the other side is also fine... **Bohannon** also gets very freaky on the long showpiece cut from his latest album ("On My Way,"

STUDIO ONE, LOS ANGELES
DJ: Manny Slali

AFRICANISM/GIMME SOME LOVING/ DR. DOO-DAH – Kongas (Crocos import)
THE BEAT GOES ON AND ON – Ripple (Salsoul)
DANCE WITH ME – Peter Brown (Drive)
DANCING FEVER/JOHNNY PLEASE COME HOME/TAKE IT EASY – Claudja Barry (Salsoul)
GALAXY – War (MCA)
GIVE ME LOVE/SUPERNATURE – Cerrone (Cotillion)
I CAN'T STAND THE RAIN – Eruption (Ariola)
LET'S ALL CHANT/LOVE EXPRESS– Michael Zager Band (Private Stock)
THE OTHER SIDE OF MIDNIGHT/HEARTACHE/I KNOW THAT HE KNOWS – Marsha Hunt (Aves import)
RISKY CHANGES/DANCE LITTLE DREAMER/BOOGIE BOO – Bionic Boogie (Polydor)

SESAME STREET, NEW YORK
DJ: John Benitez

AFRICANISM/GIMME SOME LOVING – Kongas (Crocos)
GOTTA KEEP ON TRYING – Tenderness (RCA)
I DON'T KNOW WHAT I'D DO – Sweet Cream (Bareback)
IT'S SERIOUS – Cameo (Chocolate City)
LET'S ALL CHANT – Michael Zager Band (Private Stock)
MISTER LOVE/THE GIGOLO AND I – Savannah Band (RCA)
PLAY WITH ME/ YOU ARE MY LOVE – Sandy Mercer (H&L)
ROMEO & JULIET – Alec R. Costandinos (Casablanca)
STAYIN' ALIVE/NIGHT FEVER – Bee Gees "Saturday Night Fever" Soundtrack (RSO)
VOYAGE – Voyage (Polydor/Sirocco import)

INFINITY, NEW YORK
DJ: Jim Burgess

ACT 1/ACT 2/ACT 4 – Donna Summer (Casablanca)
AFRICANISM/GIMME SOME LOVING/DR. DOO-DAH – Kongas (Crocos import)
THE BEAT GOES ON AND ON – Ripple (Salsoul)
DANCE WITH ME – Peter Brown (TK)
GALAXY – War (MCA)
HOUSE OF THE RISING SUN – Revelacion (Crocos import)
NIGHT FEVER/STAYIN' ALIVE – Bee Gees "Saturday Night Fever" Soundtrack (RSO)
RISKY CHANGES – Bionic Boogie (Polydor)
ROMEO & JULIET – Alec R. Costandinos (Casablanca)
SUPERNATURE/GIVE ME LOVE – Cerrone (Cotillion)

PLAYGROUNDS, NEW YORK
DJ: Tony Carrasco

A DANCE FANTASY – Montana (Atlantic)
COSMIC TRAVELLER/MAN FROM THE STARS/WHY MUST THERE BE AN END/ GOLDEN TEARS/DANCE AND LEAVE IT ALL BEHIND YOU – Sumeria (Casablanca)
GOTTA KEEP ON TRYING – Tenderness (RCA disco disc)
I JUST WANT TO TURN YOU ON – Muscle Shoals Horns (Ariola)
I WAS BORN THIS WAY – Carl Bean (Motown)
LET ME PARTY WITH YOU – Bunny Sigler (Gold Mind)
LET'S ALL CHANT/LOVE EXPRESS– Michael Zager Band (Private Stock)
MISTER LOVE/SORAYA/MARCH OF THE NIGNIES – Savannah Band (RCA)
ROMEO & JULIET – Alec R. Costandinos (Casablanca)
VOYAGE – Voyage (Polydor/Sirocco import)

his first for Mercury) – "Maybe You Can Dance" (12:42) keeps that trademark chug-beat but throws in all kinds of off-the-wall elements (skittish jazz horns, nervous percussion, floaty strings) for a piece that could bring Bo back in a big way... "It's Serious" (7:58) is the appropriately-titled instrumental track on the new **Cameo** album, "We All Know Who We Are" (Chocolate City), an alternately light and driving number with a definite New York feel (echoes of early **B.T. Express**); choppy but hot... And "Space Disco" (6:34) stands out on the "Kilowatt" album by the **Kay Gees** (De-Lite) – a rousing, synthesizer-laced track that's very fast-paced and dense with effects; great horns and guitar work – it sizzles. Also check out "Kilowatt" and "Kilowatt/Invasion," two Parliament-like cuts, and "Tango Hustle."

NOTE: We were misinformed about the length of **Montana's** "A Dance Fantasy" – the Atlantic disco disc is nearly four minutes shorter than reported last week, but still a hefty 15:47. And the commercial version, just out, is backed by a long (7:40) instrumental called "Warp Factor II," vibrant atmospheric music with a warm pulse beat and one of producer **Vince Montana's** trademark vibes breaks. Very different from his **Salsoul Orchestra** work, probably because it's the first time he's been able to stretch out so comfortably. By the way, the angelic vocals at the end of "Dance Fantasy," the girls singing "When You Wish Upon a Star," are **Sister Sledge** – their section is lengthened some for the B side of the standard single version of the record (the A side is an interesting 3:27 edit)

RECOMMENDED SINGLES: The new single release of **Retta Young's** "My Love Is On His Way" (All Platinum) bears this note: "Thanks to John Monaco, Larry Levan and Nicki (sic) Siano" – apparently because it was due to the persistence and enthusiasm of these three New York DJs that this track from an album more than nine months old is being rescued from oblivion. Unfortunately, it isn't the entire lp cut (at 3:20, the single's about a minute shorter), but it's appeal is clear; the vocals are innocently sweet, the spirit brightly romantic. A classic '60s sentiment in an updated format. A longer 12-inch version is rumored (or is that wishful thinking?)... In "Trust Your Heart" (Columbia) **Bobby Womack** has come up with one of those sleazy, slow-pumping numbers he does so well – a little uneven at times for disco, but that great play of voices before the fade – Womack set off by a fine female chorus – serves it in the end. Top level Womack, and at just 3:34, I hope we can anticipate a longer version on his forthcoming album, "Pieces"... "Hollywood," the one cut from **Boz Scaggs'** recent (excellent) Columbia album "Down Two Then Left" that was getting some disco play, is now out on a 45, same length as the lp track (3:08). The beat is somewhat jerky but Scaggs is enjoying himself, the music is lively enough, and many will find it hard not to join him on this bouncy ride. ✪

Heading the run-down of recommended disco discs this week are three favourites – all strong female vocals – that seem most likely to succeed:

1) "Melodies" by **Made in USA** (De-Lite) was composed, arranged and produced by **Freida Nerangis** and **Britt Britton** and recalls this team's best, most lively work with **Crown Heights Affair**. Having only heard a previously-released single version of "Melodies," I was unprepared for the energy and playful complexity of this expanded track, now running close to eight minutes (timing on the label is incorrect). The music dips and soars, nearly turns somersaults, and the lead singer, whose voice is high and wonderfully flexible, is equally adventurous, riffing right along on the breaks, never letting go. The song has more changes than many songs twice its length, the most inventive coming toward the end when everything but vocals (chanting "Don't stop") and handclaps drops from the track and a voice comes in, asking, "Come on, where's the rest of the tape now?" This is followed by the squeaky rush of a tape winding backward which breaks quickly into a strong rippling piano and back into the song again – a brilliant touch. It's hard to tell which of the many technical flourishes were the producers' inspiration and which the work of the "remix engineer," **Rafael Charres**, but the result is a joy – witty, surprising and totally enjoyable. Comparisons to "Dreaming A Dream" are inevitable – this one is much more elaborate but shares a similar spirit – and "Melodies" could be just as big a hit.

2} "You Are My Love" by **Sandy Mercer** (H&L) is a simpler, more conventionally structured record but its total effect is no less gripping. Mercer, who sounds a little like **Jackie Moore** (with some **Betty Wright** thrown in), starts out kinda slow and careful like the steady pumping arrangement but eases into the song, singing, "You take me higher than I've ever been baby/Take it easy cause you're drivin' me crazy." Neither the singer or the song reach for outrageous peaks, but the production is rocking and comfortable and after a few listenings, the groove has a solid hold on you. The breaks are nice, if unexceptional, and they keep things going for over seven minutes but in the end it's Mercer's vocals and what she's saying that put the record across. Already popping up on some New York top 10 lists on the basis of advance pressings, "You Are My Love" looks like a hot item. The flip side, "Play With Me" (7:39), has a freaky nostalgia sound – slabs of big-band horns laid into an otherwise very modern framework – that is also attractive. The pace here is odd but this, too, grows on you. Both sides were disco-mixed by New York DJs Steve D'Acquisto and Walter Gibbons.

3) "I Can't Stand The Rain" by **Eruption** (Ariola) gives a slightly European twist to the r&b original with a lead vocalist as tough and invigorating in her own way as **Ann Peebles** was the first time around. The pace has been kicked up, of course, and the percolating electronics that suggest raindrops are highlighted to maximum effect (with some crashing "thunder" added), but here again it's the singing that carries the track and makes the breaks even more delicious. Backed by a mixed chorus but more often going solo, the lead sounds like a combination of Peebles and **Loleatta Holloway**, rough edged and soulful, anguished but still powerful. A must for fans of the original record but recommended to all.

NOTES: The import boom continues to have a strong effect on everyone's essential playlist and, with **Marsha Hunt**, **Kongas** and **Revelacion** already on the DISCO FILE chart, the most enthusiastically received new album from Europe is **Voyage**. Recorded, like all the **Cerrone** and **Costandinos** records, at London's Trident Studios and composed, performed and produced by some of the same studio musicians who appear on these tracks, Voyage takes the dancer on a musical trip around the world in two non-stop medleys. All instrumental save for the opening and closing cuts, this French import should be the next big hit from abroad (more details and a real review next issue). Also hot on the import circuit: new albums by the **Chocolat's**, **Space**, **D.D. Sound** and **Kebekelektrik**... Another hot import: **Amanda Leer**, who was in New York last week promoting the release of her "I Am A Photograph" album and "Blood and Honey" 12-inch on Chrysalis after the enormous success of both records in Europe. Although her publicity photos show her either girl-next-door wholesome or quite nude (behind a recording studio baffle and wearing headphones), Lear was neither when we met her. Instead, she's spicy, sharp, very funny and has one of the best smiles in the world. Among the things she told us: her favorite movie star is Peter Berlin; her group is called the Lear Jets; **David Bowie** encouraged her to tell everyone she was a transsexual but it was just a joke for publicity; her next album, already recorded in Germany, includes a medley of songs on one side based on "Faust" with Lear playing all roles (the devil is a woman); and for her third lp, she hopes to work with **Eno**, an old friend from the days when she posed for Roxy Music covers... Alec Costandinos' man-who-fell-to-earth fantasy, "Golden Tears" by **Sumeria**, is out on Casablanca now and, though it may not be the total-disco piece so many people seem to demand these days, the album contains some of the most beautiful, moving music to come out of the European disco explosion. Give it some time...

> **Bowie encouraged her to tell everyone she was a transsexual but it was just a joke for publicity**

FACES, CHICAGO
DJ: Carmen Adduci

AFRICANISM/GIMME SOME LOVING/DR. DOO-DAH/ TATTOO WOMAN– Kongas (Crocos)
THE BEAT GOES ON AND ON – Ripple (Salsoul)
DANCE WITH ME – Peter Brown (TK)
I WAS BORN THIS WAY – Carl Bean (Motown)
LET'S ALL CHANT/LOVE EXPRESS – Michael Zager Band (Private Stock)
MELODIES – Made in USA (De-Lite)
RISKY CHANGES/WE MUST BELIEVE IN MAGIC/DANCE LITTLE DREAMER/ DON'T LOSE THAT NUMBER – Bionic Boogie (Polydor)
ROMEO & JULIET (ACTS I & II) – Alec R. Costandinos (Casablanca)
TAKE IT EASY /LOVE MACHINE/OPEN THE DOOR/ JOHNNY, JOHNNY, PLEASE COME HOME/DANCING FEVER – Claudja Barry (Salsoul)
YOU LIKE IT, WE LOVE IT – Southroad Connection (Mahogany disco disc)

SHOWCASE, EAST ORANGE, N.J.
DJ: John Matarazzo

AFRICANISM/GIMME SOME LOVING – Kongas (Crocos)
THE BEAT GOES ON AND ON – Ripple (Salsoul)
GIVE ME LOVE – Cerrone (Cotillion)
I KNOW THAT HE KNOWS – Marsha Hunt (Aves import)
MISTER LOVE/AUF WIEDERSEHEN, DARRIO – Savannah Band (RCA)
MOONLIGHT SERENADE/FOX TROT – Tuxedo Junction (Butterfly)
RISKY CHANGES – Bionic Boogie (Polydor)
ROMEO & JULIET ACT V – Alec R. Costandinos (Casablanca)
STAYIN' ALIVE – Bee Gees "Saturday Night Fever" Soundtrack (RSO)
TAKE IT EASY/DANCING FEVER – Claudja Barry (Salsoul)

SAHARA, NEW YORK
DJ: Ellen Bogen

A DANCE FANTASY – Montana (Atlantic)
THE BEAT GOES ON AND ON – Ripple (Salsoul)
DANCE WITH ME – Peter Brown (Drive)
DESPERATELY – Love Machine (London import)
LET'S ALL CHANT – Michael Zager Band (Private Stock)
MELODIES – Made in USA (De-Lite)
ROMEO & JULIET – Alec R. Costandinos (Casablanca)
RISKY CHANGES/DANCE LITTLE DREAMER – Bionic Boogie (Polydor)
SUPERNATURE/GIVE ME LOVE – Cerrone (Cotillion)
YOU ARE MY LOVE – Sandy Mercer (H&L)

KIX, BOSTON
DJ: Cosmo Wyatt

BABY, YOU GOT MY NOSE OPEN – Harold Melvin & the Bluenotes (ABC)
THE BEAT GOES ON AND ON – Ripple (Salsoul)
DANCE WITH ME – Peter Brown (TK)
DON'T COST YOU NOTHING – Ashford & Simpson (Warner Bros.)
IT'S SERIOUS – Cameo (Chocolate City)
LOVE EXPRESS/LET'S ALL CHANT – Michael Zager Band (Private Stock)
RISKY CHANGES/DANCE LITTLE DREAMER/BOOGIE BOO – Bionic Boogie (Polydor)
SHAME – Evelyn "Champagne" King (RCA)
TWO HOT FOR LOVE – THP Orchestra (Butterfly)
WHICH WAY IS UP? – Stargard (MCA)

OTHER RECOMMENDED DISCO DISCS: First, several extended versions of already successful records, beginning with **Bionic Boogie's** "Risky Changes," number one on our chart this week and now available in a 7:18 version ("Mixing Consultant: Jim Burgess") on a special Polydor promotional pressing which includes "Dance Little Dreamer" and "Boogie Boo" on the reverse side in their original versions. This new track gives us more intro, a revamped break, more bottom and added sharpness throughout – icing on an already irresistible cake. RSO has also come out with a disc-full of remixes – four of the new songs from "Saturday Night Fever" ("Stayin' Alive," "Night Fever," "More Than A Woman" – all by the Bee Gees – and Yvonne Elliman's "If I Can't Have You") plus "You Should Be Dancing" all in extended lengths. "Stayin' Alive," now 6:55 (up from 4:43), is the most substantial revamp though no major breaks have been added – only some new horn riffs and several repeats of the chorus section. The same is true of the remaining cuts: no creative changes, just more of the same which should still give a boost to these already smoking songs. Also available now: a hotter, longer (by about two minutes) version of the **Players Association** cut, "Going To The Disco," backed with "Disco Inferno" on Vanguard; **Fatback Band's** "Midnight Freak" (6:18, was 5:12) and "Mile High" (same as lp cut) on Spring; and the two best cuts from the recent **Harold Melvin & the Bluenotes** album, "Baby, You Got My Nose Open" and "Power Of Love," both identical to the album cuts but released anyway as ABC's first commercial disco disc... **Carol Douglas** may not be the perfect person to make the first of what is likely to be a gang of cover versions of the Bee Gee's "Night Fever." Her voice is a bit too thin and wispy to drive the song – the vibrant buzz-saw edge of the original is missing – but **Ed O'Loughlin's** production and **Michael Zager's** arrangement have a certain zip (worn rather thin at just over six minutes, however). Of course, the percussion break and the boost it gives to everything that follows could save this one and the phenomenal success of everything connected with "Saturday Night Fever" could carry Douglas as well (the record's on Midsong, now distributed through MCA)... At first I thought **Andre Gagnon's** "Donna" (6:03 on London), supposedly a tribute to **D. Summer**, was a cold and overblown instrumental, but the record has won me over little by little just as Gagnon's previous pieces, "Wow" and "Surprise," did. Much of it is furiously grandiose music, very full and stirring, which can get tiring when short patterns are repeated at this length, but the threading of synthesizer and strings, the unexpected country rock accents and the percussion breaks always perk up flagging interest and could turn this into a sleeper favorite. ✸

RECOMMENDED ALBUMS: Beginning with the import we touched on lightly last week – **Voyage**, recorded at London's Trident Studios, released in France on Polydor and now scheduled for American release on TK in three weeks or less. The producer, Roger Tokarz, is new to us, but a number of the musicians and singers credited here, including two members of the four-man core group of composer/arranger/performers, have been involved in **Alec Costandinos** and **Cerrone** productions in the past. While not really introducing anything new into the basic vocabulary of the Eurodisco Sound (French Division), Voyage hits on new combinations and variations that make it feel fresh all over again, reviving our faith in the fertility of this style. And the very concept of the album enlivens things: Voyage is a musical world tour, swinging continent-to-continent in two full-side medleys, each cut incorporating a different native music. The sensational send-off is a breezy, irresistible "From East To West," inviting the listener along for the trip and the dance. The following cut, "Point Zero," delivers us into the heart of the jungle with a rhythmic chant of male voices and a rich, dense layering of percussion that recalls **Manu Dibango**, **Osibisa** and **Titanic**. This blends into "Orient Express," an evocation of both Indian and Japanese styles reminiscent of parts of Sphinx. Only on the two short tracks that open up side two does the theme tend to grate: "Scotch Machine" (bagpipes, but mercifully little of them) and "Bayou Village" (a square-dance at 1:50). But things pick up again with "Latin Odyssey," a spicy cut that manages to avoid nearly all the cliches already covered by Santa Esmeralda, and the closing song,

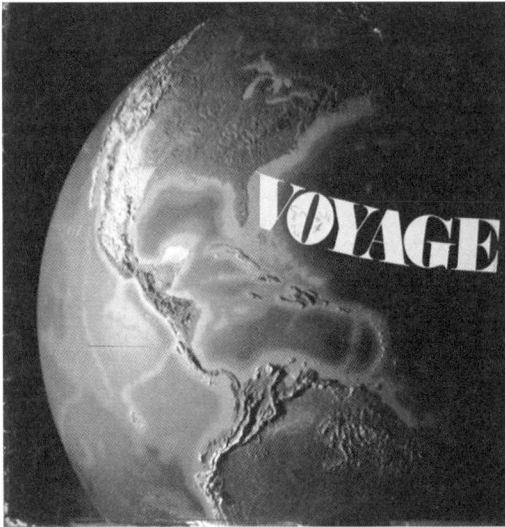

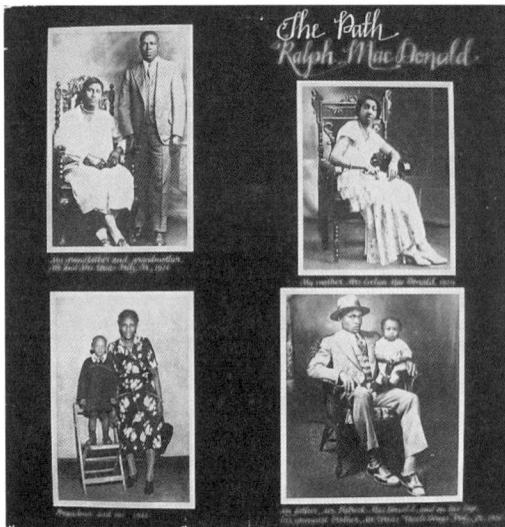

> **" The atmosphere it creates should appeal to the more adventurous crowds; the rest of this epic piece is the finest jazz-disco fusion we've heard in some time "**

LEVITICUS, NEW YORK
DJ: Porter Wynn

DANCE WITH ME – Peter Brown (TK)

DR. DOO-DAH – Kongas (Crocos)

FROM EAST TO WEST/POINT ZERO/ LATIN ODYSSEY
– Voyage (Polydor import)

GIVE ME LOVE – Cerrone (Cotillion)

IT'S YOU GIRL – Universal Love (TK)

LOVE EXPRESS– Michael Zager Band (Private Stock)

THE OTHER SIDE OF MIDNIGHT – Marsha Hunt (Aves)

PLAY WITH ME/YOU ARE MY LOVE – Sandy Mercer (H&L)

ROMEO & JULIET – Alec Costandinos (Casablanca)

STAYIN' ALIVE/NIGHT FEVER/MORE THAN A WOMAN –
Bee Gees "Saturday Night Fever" Soundtrack (RSO)

CIRCUS DISCO, LOS ANGELES
DJ: Mike Lewis

A DANCE FANTASY – Montana (Atlantic)

AFRICANISM/GIMME SOME LOVING – Kongas (Polydor)

THE BEAT GOES ON AND ON – Ripple (Salsoul)

CHATANOOGA CHOO CHOO – Tuxedo Junction (Butterfly)

COME INTO MY HEART/GOOD LOVING
– USA-European Connection (TK)

GALAXY – War (MCA)

I FEEL GOOD – Al Green (Hi)

LET'S ALL CHANT – Michael Zager Band (Private Stock)

RISKY CHANGES – Bionic Boogie (Polydor)

SHAME – Evelyn "Champagne" King (RCA)

HIS COMPANY, PHOENIX
DJ: Jack Witherby

THE BEAT GOES ON AND ON – Ripple (Salsoul)

**CHATTANOOGA CHOO CHOO/VOLGA BOATMAN/
MOONLIGHT SERENADE** – Tuxedo Junction (Butterfly)

COME INTO MY HEART/GOOD LOVING
– USA-European Connection (TK)

DANCE WITH ME – Peter Brown (TK)

HOUSE OF THE RISING SUN
– Santa Esmeralda (Casablanca)

I CAN'T STAND THE RAIN – Eruption (Ariola)

MELODIES – Made in USA (De-Lite)

MISTER LOVE/AUF WIEDERSEHEN, DARRIO
– Savannah Band (RCA)

ROMEO & JULIET – Alec Costandinos (Casablanca)

WHAT SHALL WE DO WHEN THE DISCO'S OVER –
Richard Hewson Orchestra (AVI)

REGINES, NEW YORK
DJ: Jonata Garavaglia

AFRICANISM/GIMME SOME LOVING – Kongas (Polydor)

CHANGING UP MY LIFE – Ralph Graham (RCA)

HOUSE OF THE RISING SUN
– Santa Esmeralda (Casablanca)

LET'S ALL CHANT – Michael Zager Band (Private Stock)

MACHO, A REAL, REAL ONE
– Celi Bee & the Buzzy Bunch (TK)

RISKY CHANGES – Bionic Boogie (Polydor)

STAYIN' ALIVE/JIVE TALKIN/NIGHT FEVER – Bee Gees
"Saturday Night Fever" Soundtrack (RSO)

SUPERNATURE/GIVE ME LOVE – Cerrone (Cotillion)

THEME FROM CLOSE ENCOUNTERS/CRAZY RHYTHM
– Meco (Millennium)

WHIP – Eddie Kendricks (Arista)

"Lady America," a tribute to the U.S.A. in rousing vocals (compare Village People) and a pounding production. All together, a brilliant, beautifully-paced album, worth playing straight through or focusing in on particular cuts; the standouts: "From East to West," "Point Zero," "Latin Odyssey" and "Lady America." Already one of the strongest items on the import market – it took New York by storm the first week it was available – Voyage promises to be one of the season's major disco releases.

Another essential album that takes the listener on a musical voyage is **Ralph MacDonald's** "The Path" (Marlin), whose 17-minute title track traces MacDonald's ancestral roots from Africa to the Caribbean to America in one vibrant, propulsive sweep of sound. Beginning with just the sound of a drum (or, more precisely, a syndrum, a percussive synthesizer that MacDonald introduces here), "The Path" includes hypnotic narration and chanting in an African tongue plus a glowing range of percussion in "Part One," a bamboo steel band that picks up the "Calypso Breakdown" sound in "Part Two," and a modern jazz fusion of the two in the third segment which then returns full circle to pick up the initial chant. MacDonald's genius with all sorts of percussion gives the journey both vitality and intensity, and he's assembled a supporting cast that includes some of the finest performers in jazz and pop. Among the musicians and singers credited on the album: **Idris Muhammad**, **Grover Washington**, **Eric Gale**, **Patti Austin**, **Bob James**, **Mike** and **Randy Brecker**, **David Sanborn**, **Hugh Maskela**, **Miriam Makeba**, **Valerie Simpson** and **Barry Rogers**. For disco dancing, "Part One" of "The Path" may prove too leisurely but the atmosphere it creates should appeal to the more adventurous crowds; the rest of this epic piece is the finest jazz-disco fusion we've heard in some time and will have no trouble finding an enthusiastic audience in the clubs. Also check out the final cut on the album's other side, a superb female vocal called "If I'm Still Around Tomorrow" with a wonderfully catchy percussion arrangement. And don't overlook the debut album of **21st Creation**, "Break Thru" on Gordy, which includes their previously-released "Tailgate" and an excellent, **Hal Davis**-produced version of **Marvin Gaye's** "After The Dance" (5:34) with a hot, punched-up arrangement. Another possibility: "Thanks For Saving Me" (5:33), which begins slowly but picks up beautifully; uneven but very interesting. And these kids can sing!

ONE HOT SINGLE: **Frank Wilson's** fast, sexy production for **Cheryl Barnes** called "Save And Spend" (Millennium). The message: "I've been saving it/Saving all my love for you/Now I'm gonna spend it/ Spend all my love with you," sung appropriately hot by a woman who sounds like a blend of **Martha Reeves** and **Freda Payne**. Serious, especially for fans of tough, emotive female vocals. ⦿

" "I Was Born This Way," the gay liberation song, has been remade by Carl Bean. The message is a relevant one for the disco community, though many of us are ready for something considerably more militant "

Kind of dull this week – a sudden slump in the middle of an otherwise prolific month – but these items should see you through: "What Shall We Do When The Disco's Over?" by the **Richard Hewson Orchestra** (8:07 on an AVI disco disc) begins with a tantalizing female chorus chanting, "Dance with me, dance with me, dance with me/Come on and catch me if you can" – an irresistible invitation when combined with a swirling arrangement of strings and horns that sweeps you right along. The voices, lushly echoed and layered, have an ecstatic but slightly desperate edge, just right for the song's central

theme: "What shall we do when the dancing beat is dead?" Even the final suggestion, "Shall we all go home to bed?" seems more a stall than a solution because the song's underlying question is apparently the same one the **Shirelles** asked – "Will you still love me tomorrow?" – Whatever the theme, this is an involving, exciting record and the orchestration – very sensuous and sleek – also has a certain tension that sustains the song through a number of changes. Sounds like a hit... **Roy Ayers'** new album, "Let's Do It" (Polydor), is one of his best, sparked by two recommended dance tracks in Ayers' distinctive funked-up jazz style. "Freaky Deaky," already getting some attention as a single but lengthened to 5:30 here, is playful, jivey and jumpin'. **Merry Clayton** shares vocals with Roy – a fine, gritty combination – and a synthesizer zips through a delightfully choppy arrangement – great funk fun. In a very different vein, there's the adventuresome, wonderfully sophisticated "Sweet Tears" (6:27), light as a cloud but whipped by a quick beat, darting strings, luscious vibes. Compare **Donald Byrd**, **Bobbi Humphrey**, **Earth Wind & Fire** but add something totally unique. With Ayers' quiet lead vocal and a sweet female (chorus, "Sweet Tears" is quite mellow, perhaps too much so for f some tastes, but incredibly appealing. Just listen... The first **Eddie Kendricks** album on Arista, "Vintage '78," was produced by **Jeff Lane**, who makes a definitive departure from his heavy, high-powered **B.T. Express/Brass Construction** sound, scaling things down, one assumes, to suit the more intimate requirements of Kendricks' famous falsetto. But the adjustment isn't an entirely comfortable one – both producer and singer seem somewhat strained – and even the two upbeat tracks that are already getting disco play feel flawed. Both "Ain't No Smoke Without Fire" (previously made by the **King Musker Band**) and "Whip" have a crackling energy, aggressive strings and Kendricks' unmistakable cutting vocals but both lack fullness and drive. Maybe "Whip" is merely too short at 4:00 to build its impact (it ends just as it seems to be gearing up) but "Smoke" (5:58) has a similar lack of intensity even with a lively break. Still, both cuts should be well received for the opportunity they give to hear Kendricks on the dance floor again; maybe they'll grow on us.

ALSO RECOMMENDED: **Eloise Laws'** bright, bouncy "Number One" (ABC), expanded to six minutes for a disco disc and just bursting with high spirits. Laws sounds solid and rich; **Linda Creed** produced... **Tenderness**, a female quartet from Washington, D.C., with a sharp gospel edge and a powerful vocal mix debuts with a song called "Gotta Keep On Trying" on an RCA disco disc – a hot girl group sound sustained by a churning, burning production... "I Was Born This Way," the **Valentino** gay liberation song from a few years ago, has been remade for a Motown disco disc by **Carl Bean** with a superb, driving Philly production by **Norman Harris**, **Ron Kersey** and **T.G. Conway** (executive producer is the song's composer and prime champion, **Bunny Jones**). The message is a relevant one for the disco community, though many of us are ready for something considerably more militant and

12 WEST, NEW YORK
DJ: Paul Poulos

COME INTO MY HEART/LOVE IS COMING
– USA-European Connection (TK)
DR. DOO-DAH/AFRICANISM/GIMME SOME LOVING
– Kongas (Polydor)
GIVE ME LOVE/SUPERNATURE – Cerrone (Cotillion)
LET'S ALL CHANT/LOVE EXPRESS– Michael Zager Band
(Private Stock)
RIO DE JANEIRO – Gary Criss (Salsoul)
RISKY CHANGES/DANCE LITTLE DREAMER
– Bionic Boogie (Polydor)
ROMEO & JULIET – Alec Costandinos (Casablanca)
STAYIN' ALIVE – Bee Gees (RSO)
VOYAGE – Voyage (Polydor import)
WHIP/AIN'T NO SMOKE WITHOUT FIRE
– Eddie Kendricks (Arista)

DOC RICKETT'S LAB, MONTEREY, CA.
DJ: Wes Bradley

ACT 1/ACT 4 – Donna Summer (Casablanca)
AFRICANISM/GIMME SOME LOVING – Kongas (Polydor)
DANCE WITH ME/YOU SHOULD DO IT – Peter Brown (Drive)
GALAXY – War (MCA)
I FEEL GOOD – Al Green (Hi)
LET ME PARTY WITH YOU/YOUR LOVE IS SO GOOD –
Bunny Sigler (Gold Mind)
LOVE IS COMING/COME INTO MY HEART
– USA-European Connection (TK)
PLAY WITH ME/YOU ARE MY LOVE – Sandy Mercer (H&L)
**RISKY CHANGES/DANCE LITTLE DREAMER/DON'T LOSE
THAT NUMBER/BOOGIE BOO** – Bionic Boogie (Polydor)
TRUST IN ME/DON'T TRY TO WIN ME BACK AGAIN
– Vicki Sue Robinson (RCA)

SUNDANCE SOCIAL PUB, CHICAGO
DJ: Jim Thompson

AFRICANISM/GIMME SOME LOVING – Kongas (Polydor)
THE BEAT GOES ON AND ON – Ripple (Salsoul)
DANCE WITH ME/YOU SHOULD DO IT – Peter Brown (Drive)
DONNA/HOLIDAY FEELING – Andre Gagnon (London)
LOVE IS COMING/COME INTO MY HEART
– USA-European Connection (TK)
**RISKY CHANGES/DANCE LITTLE DREAMER/WE MUST
BELIEVE IN MAGIC** – Bionic Boogie (Polydor)
SHAME – Evelyn "Champagne" King (RCA)
STAYIN' ALIVE/NIGHT FEVER/MORE THAN A WOMAN –
Bee Gees "Saturday Night Fever" Soundtrack (RSO)
VOYAGE – Voyage (Polydor import)
WHIP/AIN'T NO SMOKE WITHOUT FIRE
– Eddie Kendricks (Arista)

4141, NEW ORLEANS
DJ: Al Paez

AFRICANISM/GIMME SOME LOVING – Kongas (Polydor)
THE BEAT GOES ON AND ON – Ripple (Salsoul)
CHATANOOGA CHOO CHOO – Tuxedo Junction (Butterfly)
DANCE WITH ME – Peter Brown (Drive)
HOUSE OF THE RISING SUN
– Santa Esmeralda (Casablanca)
LET'S ALL CHANT/LOVE EXPRESS– Michael Zager Band
(Private Stock)
RISKY CHANGES – Bionic Boogie (Polydor)
**RUMOUR HAS IT/I LOVE YOU/FAIRY TALE HIGH/QUEEN
FOR A DAY** – Donna Summer (Casablanca)
SUPERNATURE/GIVE ME LOVE – Cerrone (Cotillion)
TWO HOT FOR LOVE – THP Orchestra (Butterfly)

aggressive, and the vocals are energetic if uneven.
However, most DJs seem to be bypassing the vocal side
and playing the instrumental (5:51), a very classy piece of
music indeed. (Note: neither the sleeve nor the label of
this Motown pressing indicate the record's speed, which
turns out to be 33.)

NOTES: The **Kongas** album, "Africanism," has just been
released in America on Polydor with the same cover as
the import... AVI has released G.M.T. **Sound's Santa
Esmeralda**-esque version of "Malaquena" in a
somewhat different mix for a "Giant 45" – still recommended if you haven't yet OD'd on the flamenco
disco sound. Also on AVI: **D.B.M's** "Discobeatlemania,"
perhaps the only bearable **Beatles** medley, disco style.
Originally released in France and running more than six
minutes, this is still for fans of the Fab Four only and
has been retitled "Beatlemania" for U.S. consumption...
Due out this coming week, but already on the DISCO
FILE Top 20 due to heavy advance promotional
pressings: TK's **USA-European Connection**. ◢

DISCO FILE TOP 20

1. **RISKY CHANGES/DANCE LITTLE DREAMER**
   – Bionic Boogie (Polydor)
2. **LET'S ALL CHANT/LOVE EXPRESS**
   – Michael Zager Band (Private Stock)
3. **AFRICANISM/GIMME SOME LOVING/
   DR. DOO-DAH** – Kongas (Crocos)
4. **DANCE WITH ME** – Peter Brown (Drive)
5. **SUPERNATURE/GIVE ME LOVE** – Cerrone
   (Cotillion)
6. **STAYIN' ALIVE/NIGHT FEVER** – Bee Gees
   "Saturday Night Fever" Soundtrack (RSO)
7. **THE BEAT GOES ON AND ON** – Ripple (Salsoul)
8. **ROMEO & JULIET** – Alec Costandinos
   (Casablanca)
9. **COME INTO MY HEART/LOVE IS COMING**
   – USA-European Connection (TK)
10. **VOYAGE** – Voyage (Polydor import)
11. **ACT 1/ACT 2/ACT 4** – Donna Summer (Casablanca)
12. **BOOGIE BOO/DON'T LOSE THAT NUMBER**
    – Bionic Boogie (Polydor)
13. **GALAXY** – War (MCA)
14. **JOHNNY, JOHNNY PLEASE COME HOME/TAKE IT
    EASY/DANCING FEVER** – Claudja Barry (Salsoul)
15. **TWO HOT FOR LOVE** – THP Orchestra (Butterfly)
16. **THE OTHER SIDE OF MIDNIGHT/I KNOW THAT HE
    KNOWS/HEARTACHE** – Marsha Hunt
    (Aves import)
17. **MISTER LOVE** – Savannah Band (RCA)
18. **CHATANOOGA CHOO CHOO** – Tuxedo Junction
    (Butterfly)
19. **MELODIES** – Made in USA (De-Lite)
20. **HOUSE OF THE RISING SUN** – Santa Esmeralda
    (Casablanca)

MARCH 11, 1978

> ❝ **Leon Spinks, the heavyweight champion of the world, was photographed at Studio 54 and told the Times, "I like the music. I jump rope, hit the bags, do my training to the music."** ❞

Though the **USA-European Connection** album was only released this past week on TK's Marlin label, months of anticipation and a barrage of advance copies to key DJs have already zoomed it into the number five spot on the DISCO FILE Top 20, making it one of the strongest new disco albums of the moment (also red-hot: "Romeo & Juliet" and "Voyage"). To a certain extent, this is another confirmation of the strength of the Eurodisco sound – the format and musical vocabulary developed by **Moroder**, **Bellotte**, **Cerrone** and **Costandinos** have been freely borrowed from here – but what makes USA-European so interesting is the fact that it originated in Philadelphia and represents the first totally new disco sound from that city since the **Gamble & Huff** phenomenon. Composed, arranged, conducted and co-produced by **Boris Midney**, an Eastern-European emigre who has established his own recording studio (ALPHA International) in Philly, USA-European Connection is more than just the best American interpretation of the Eurodisco style to date – it's also original enough to stand on its own as one of the most exciting disco albums of the year. Each side is one long composition sustained by occasional vocals (by an excellent female trio) and stunning, constant orchestral movement: a series of breaks and changes that rivals the rhythmic ebb and flow of such masterpieces of this form as "I've Found Love" and "Give Me Love." The key line in "Come Into My Heart/Good Loving," the album's title track, sets the mood perfectly: "High winds of feeling tear me apart." The listener is caught up in the surge of the music and each wave of strings or eruption of synthesizers hits you with a distinctly emotional force. The sound here is somewhat sparer and more precise than on many European records, perhaps because Midney is working with a smaller instrumental group, but the impact is incredible. Both sides are gloriously ecstatic, grand pieces of music that sweep you onto the dance floor and keep you there. Overwhelm-ingly good and well worth the wait. Boris Midney should also be added to everyone's list of producers to watch; he's already at work on the second USA-European album, set for release later in the year.

This week's other essential album is the second release by **Jacques Morali's Village People**, titled "Macho Man," on Casablanca. Basically a re-run of "San Francisco" and "Fire Island" from the group's enormously successful first record, "Macho Man" makes few innovations within the tough, hard-pounding style established for those tracks. The music and the singing are appropriately, if unrelievedly, macho, from the thumping, nearly brutal drumming to lead vocalist **Victor Willis'** wonderfully gritty shouting – all best captured on the title cut and "I Am What I Am," which together form an 11-minute medley that fills up the album's first side. I find the glorification of macho dubious at best (oppressive at worst, especially in a gay context, which this certainly is), but its treatment by the Village People is comic enough not to be taken seriously ("Body," the guys chant, "Wanna touch my body/Body-it's too much, my body") and driving enough to be irresistible dance material: Following this shamelessly narcissistic number, "I Am What I Am" extends the same sound to a rousing song, part plea, part demand for tolerance, taking "I Was Born This Way" the necessary one step further: Willis and the chorus are especially powerful and convincing here. Prime cut on side two is another stop on the Village People tour of gay hot spots: "Key West" (5:42), an enthusiastic tribute to fun, fun, fun in the sun with all the emotional and intellectual content of **Jan & Dean's** "Surf City." The remainder of the album is filled by the inordinately campy medley of "Just a Gigolo" and "I Ain't Got Nobody" and a song called "Sodom and Gomorrah" whose cheerful retelling of the Biblical story strikes an oddly discordant note in the midst of all this aggressive hedonism. Still, everything here is undeniably catchy and entertaining – instant top 10 material, especially welcome at a time when there are so few strong male vocal records around.

RECOMMENDED DISCO DISCS: "Rio De Janeiro" by **Gary Criss** (Salsoul) is a Philadelphia record – produced and written by **Billy Terrel**, arranged and conducted by John Davis – previously released only in Brazil and now available here with a "midnight mix" by New York DJ Richie Rivera that opens up the record beautifully. The

THE BROADWAY, DENVER
DJ: Bob Parsons
AFRICANISM/GIMME SOME LOVING/DR. DOO-DAH
– Kongas (Polydor)
THE BEAT GOES ON AND ON – Ripple (Salsoul)
COME INTO MY HEART/LOVE IS COMING
– USA-European Connection (TK)
FEELS SO GOOD IT MUST BE WRONG/TRUST IN ME/DON'T
TRY TO WIN ME BACK AGAIN – Vicki Sue Robinson (RCA)
FROM EAST TO WEST/POINT ZERO/LATIN
ODYSSEY/LADY AMERICA – Voyage (Polydor import)
HOUSE OF THE RISING SUN – Revelacion (Crocos import)
THE PATH (PARTS II & IIII) – Ralph MacDonald (Marlin)
RISKY CHANGES/BOOGIE BOO – Bionic Boogie (Polydor)
ROMEO & JULIET – Alec Costandinos (Casablanca)
YOU ARE MY LOVE – Sandy Mercer (H&L)

MR. DREAMS, QUEENS, N. Y.
DJ: Frank Strivelli
AFRICANISM/GIMME SOME LOVING/DR. DOO-DAH
– Kongas (Polydor)
COME INTO MY HEART/LOVE IS COMING
– USA-European Connection (Marlin)
FROM EAST TO WEST/POINT ZERO/ LATIN
ODYSSEY/LADY AMERICA – Voyage (Polydor import)
LET'S ALL CHANT/LOVE EXPRESS
– Michael Zager Band (Private Stock)
LET'S GET TOGETHER/TURN ON LADY
– Detroit Emeralds (Westbound)
MACHO MAN/I AM WHAT I AM/ KEY WEST – Village
People (Casablanca lp cuts)
PHONIC – Cristal (Crocos import)
RISKY CHANGES/DANCE LITTLE DREAMER/DON'T LOSE
THAT NUMBER – Bionic Boogie (Polydor)
ROMEO & JULIET – Alec Costandinos (Casablanca)
STAYIN' ALIVE/NIGHT FEVER – Bee Gees (RSO)

FLAMINGO, NEW YORK
DJ: Howard Merritt
COME INTO MY HEART/LOVE IS COMING
– USA-European Connection (Marlin)
DANCE WITH ME – Peter Brown (TK)
FROM EAST TO WEST/LATIN ODYSSEY – Voyage (Polydor)
I CAN'T STAND THE RAIN – Eruption (Ariola)
LET'S ALL CHANT/LOVE EXPRESS – Michael Zager Band
(Private Stock)
THE PATH (PARTS II & IIII) – Ralph MacDonald (Marlin)
RISKY CHANGES/DANCE LITTLE DREAMER – Bionic
Boogie (Polydor)
ROMEO & JULIET – Alec Costandinos (Casablanca)
STAYIN' ALIVE/NIGHT FEVER – Bee Gees (RSO)
YOU ARE MY LOVE/PLAY WITH ME – Sandy Mercer (H&L)

RUBAIYAT, ANN ARBOR, MICH.
DJ: Karl Uruski
AIN'T NO SMOKE WITHOUT FIRE – Eddie Kendricks
(Arista lp cut)
COME INTO MY HEART/LOVE IS COMING
– USA-European Connection (Marlin)
FROM EAST TO WEST/POINT ZERO – Voyage (Polydor)
GALAXY – War (MCA)
I AM WHAT I AM/KEY WEST/I AIN'T GOT NOBODY/
SODOM & GOMORRAH – Village People (Casablanca)
LET'S GET TOGETHER – Pam Todd & Love Exchange
(Shyriden)
NIGHT FEVER – Bee Gees "Saturday Night Fever"
Soundtrack (RSO)
ROMEO & JULIET – Alec Costandinos (Casablanca)
SAVE AND SPEND – Cheryl Barnes (Millennium)
YOU ARE MY LOVE – Sandy Mercer (H&L)

song's first half is a pulsing, mostly vocal tribute to the attractions of Rio that is quite lovely and involving, but it's the soaring, spirited second half – chock full of changes, the orchestration vivid and glistening – that clinches the track. Excellent... **Lucy Hawkins**, who, it seems, was discovered as a worker in the Sam Records warehouse, now has a two-sided disco disc out on that label, both sides terrific: "Lady Of The Night" (5:30), an **Evie Sands** song that catches a warm, comfortable groove much like her often-covered "One Thing On My Mind," also has lyrics as memorable as those in "Native New Yorker" and Hawkins' fine, vibrant vocals; "Gotta Get Out Of Here" (5:50) has a funkier, chunkier beat (cf. "Up Jumped The Devil"), heftier vocals (sounds closer to **Merry Clayton** here) and quite a good break leading to a hot, rave-up ending. **John Davis** produced... The **Larry Page Orchestra's** "Slinky Thighs" (London) follows in the instrumental mold established with "Erotic Soul" – a sensuous meshing of the electronic and the acoustic – in a varied, alternately heavy and light composition, full of deep drums, ominous synthesizer or bursting with high strutting strings. A must for drum freaks.

A number of songs already reviewed here as album cuts have recently been made available as disco discs, most in substantially different versions, and are heartily re-recommended: "Street Dance" and "Music, Harmony And Rhythm" by **Brooklyn Dreams** (Millennium), both lengthened, the latter by about three minutes at the end which totally transforms the song and should give it a whole new appeal – terribly neglected on their original release, both cuts deserve a new hearing, especially since they're perhaps the best re-mixes **Bobby Guttadaro** did during his tenure with Casablanca... **Al Green's** fine "I Feel Good" (Hi), now running a hefty 7:30 with no major structural changes but some added riffing and a vastly improved sound quality... **Peter Brown's** "Dance With Me" (TK), same length as the lp track that's already so successful, just spruced-up technically for a sharper edge... **Chic's** "Everybody Dance" (Atlantic), expanded to 8:25 in honor of its release as a single-minor revisions only... "My Man Is On His Way," the **Retta Young** record on All Platinum that became something of a cult favorite in New York, deserved better than merely being looped up to 6:45, but here it is... A 13:45 slice of **Alec Costandinos & the Syncophonic Orchestra's** "Romeo & Juliet" (Casablanca) isn't really satisfying – the jump-cut from material on side one to the beginning of side two is slightly jarring – but this music in any form is so exciting that this, too, is well worth having... **Lonnie Smith's** "Funk Reaction" (TK), same length as the album track and still sounding attractive.

DISCO FILE HERO OF THE MONTH: **Leon Spinks**, the heavyweight champion of the world, was photographed at Studio 54 recently and later told the Times, "I want to go out and see the people and talk to them and touch their hands. That's part of the reason I went to the discos." The other part? "I like the music. I jump rope, hit the bags, do my training to the music." Wonder what he listens to. ✪

MARCH 18, 1978

RECOMMENDED ALBUMS (A QUICK RUNDOWN): Two new **Vince Montana** productions this week, one for **Salsoul Orchestra** ("Up The Yellow Brick Road" on Salsoul) one for **Montana** ("A Dance Fantasy Inspired By Close Encounters Of The Third Kind" on Atlantic), both employing essentially the same Sigma Sound musicians (**MFSB** by any other name...) but each taking a distinctly different direction.

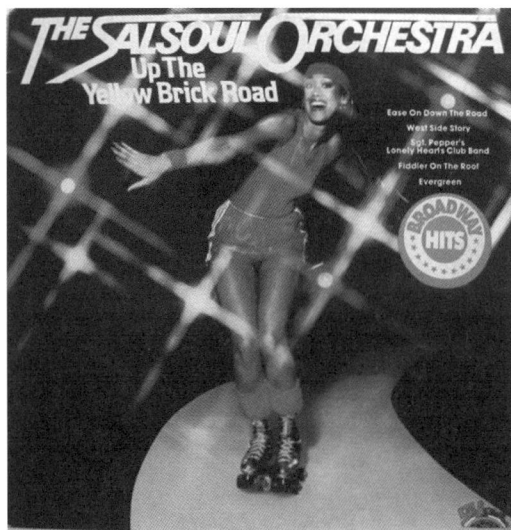

The Salsoul Orchestra has turned toward a highly commercial pop-disco sound reminiscent of the **Wing & A Prayer Fife & Drum Corps** albums, abandoning original material for disco interpretations of the music from "West Side Story" and "Fiddler on the Roof" (two separate 12-minute medleys take up the bulk of the record) and pedestrian versions of "Ease On Down The Road," "Sgt. Pepper's Lonely Hearts Club Band" and "Evergreen." The "West Side Story" medley comes across with the brightness and verve of the Salsoul Orchestra at its best, but doesn't seem to have the consistency to hold up on the dance floor from beginning to end. Happily, the strong core of the medley has been transferred to a separate disco disc, paring away vocals that tend to drag it down at the beginning, leaving nearly eight minutes of shimmering, cool-whipped instrumental with occasional lines of vocals (**Benton, Benson & Ingram**, of course) zinging in and out. The "Fiddler" medley also has its moments – one or two hot little breaks – but it would take more than that to generate interest in this particular collection of melodies (including "Havah Nagila" and "Theme From 'Exodus'"). The **Montana** album, though hardly all-out disco, is more sophisticated, more progressive and more appealing. Though the medley style of "A Dance Fantasy" – the 15:45 first side here, already released as a disco disc – is much the same as the "West Side Story" and "Fiddler" run-throughs, the "Fantasy" is so precisely crafted that it glows. Montana

spreads "Close Encounters" out before us in all its fascinating detail and instead of reducing the film to a few glossy cliches, the producer has recreated the experience in his own medium. The three instrumentals that open up the second side – one, "Warp Factor II," backed "A Dance Fantasy" on the 12-inch – are in the classic Salsoul Orchestra style: gently pulsing, very pretty, sleekly sensuous but perhaps a bit too short to make any impact on the dance floor. A version of "Fly Me To The Moon" sounds like it belongs on the Salsoul album except the vocalists here are **Sister Sledge**. Marginal disco, maybe, but great at home. Try "V.M. IV" for a luxurious, spacey mood.

Two class acts: the new albums from **Dexter Wansel** and **Jean Terrell** are also at the edge of disco, but both are so fine they deserve mention and attention. **Wansel's** "Voyager" is his third Philadelphia International album and perhaps his most accomplished, setting this writer/arranger/producer/ musician/singer outside the increasingly constricting confines of the Philadelphia Sound and establishing him as a sharp maverick with his own jazz/rock/soul fusion. The majority of material on this new album is sparkling jazz but two danceable vocals stand out: "All Night Long" (5:35) and "I Just Want To Love You" (4:17), both chunky, pumping numbers. **Jean Terrell's** album, "I Had To Fall In Love" on A&M, is another personal favorite right now, bringing back one of the richest female vocals around – surely the best lead singer the **Supremes** have had since the departure of **Diana Ross** – In a near-perfect showcase production by **Bobby Martin**. The style here is sophisticated soul, closer to the sort of tasteful yet emotionally touching material Terrel did with the Supremes under **Frank Wilson's** direction than to the Philadelphia get down stuff Martin was famous for. Terrell sounds as good if not better than ever, her creamy, aching vocals transforming every song and, for our purposes, especially fine on "That's The Way Love Grows," the only consistently upbeat song here and a real beauty. Neither album is heavy-duty disco but both are essential for anyone concerned with keeping up on the best new music in any area.

CHOICE CUTS: **Dusty Springfield's** great comeback album; "It Begins Again" (UA), includes a semi-hot version of "That's The Kind Of Love I've Got For You," the **Rita Jean Bodine** near-hit of a few years' back, running 4:58 here. Highlights: the intriguing electronic opening – so good it promises more than it can possibly deliver; the raucous jungle percussion break toward the end; and Dusty's ever-astonishing vocals. Interesting – even more so when you note **Pattie Brooks** and **Brenda Russell** are doing background vocals – but needs something. A new mix?... The new **Tyrone Davis** album, "I Can't Go On This Way" (Columbia); features a just-under-ten-minute version of "Get On Up (Disco)," his recent single release. Taken to this length, the song has a certain hypnotic attraction, slow-pumping and funky with steamy female vocals in the background and some strong instrumental interludes.

ICE PALACE, NEW YORK
DJ: Roy Thode

BLACKJACK – Baciotti (Yona import)
COME INTO MY HEART/LOVE'S COMING – USA-European Connection (Marlin)
DANCE WITH ME – Peter Brown (TK)
GALAXY – War (MCA)
LADY AMERICA/FROM EAST TO WEST/POINT ZERO – Voyage (Marlin)
LET'S ALL CHANT – Michael Zager Band (Private Stock)
RIO DE JANEIRO – Gary Criss (Salsoul)
RISKY CHANGES – Bionic Boogie (Polydor)
ROMEO & JULIET – Alec Costandinas (Casablanca)
STAYIN' ALIVE – Bee Gees (RSO)

SHEPHEARD'S, NEW YORK
DJ: Jeff Baugh

COME INTO MY HEART/LOVE'S COMING – USA-European Connection (Marlin)
DISCO DANCE (MEGA MIX) – Michele (West End)
FEVER/ROUGH DIAMOND/TOUCH MY HEART – Madleen Kone (CBS import)
GYPSY LADY/IF MY FRIENDS COULD SEE ME NOW – Linda Clifford (Curtom)
RISKY CHANGES/DANCE LITTLE DREAMER – Bionic Boogie (Polydor)
ROMEO & JULIET – Alec Costandinas (Casablanca)
STAYIN' ALIVE/NIGHT FEVER – Bee Gees "Saturday Night Fever" Soundtrack (RSO)
STREET DANCE – Brooklyn Dreams (Millennium)
VOYAGE – Voyage (Marlin)
YOU ARE MY LOVE – Sandy Mercer (H&L)

STUDIO ONE, LOS ANGELES
DJ: Manny Slali

AFRICANISM/GIMME SOME LOVING/DR. DOO-DAH – Kongas (Polydor)
COME INTO MY HEART/LOVE'S COMING – USA-European Connection (Marlin)
GALAXY – War (MCA)
I CAN'T STAND THE RAIN/PARTY PARTY – Eruption (Ariola)
I FEEL GOOD – Al Green (Hi)
PLAY WITH ME/YOU ARE MY LOVE – Sandy Mercer (H&L)
RIO DE JANEIRO – Gary Criss (Salsoul)
ROMEO & JULIET – Alec Costandinas (Casablanca)
VOYAGE – Voyage (Marlin)
WEST SIDE STORY – Salsoul Orchestra (Salsoul)

NEW YORK, N.Y. NEW YORK
DJ: François Kevorkian

COME INTO MY HEART/LOVE'S COMING – USA-European Connection (Marlin)
DANCE WITH ME – Peter Brown (TK)
I FEEL GOOD – Al Green (Hi)
I LOVE NEW YORK – Metropolis (Salsoul)
KEY WEST/MACHO MAN/I AM WHAT I AM/JUST A GIGOLO/I AIN'T GOT NOBODY – Village People (Casablanca)
MELODIES – Made in USA (De-Lite)
NIGHT FEVER – Carol Douglas (Midsong)
THAT'S THE KIND OF LOVE I'VE GOT FOR YOU – Dusty Springfield (UA)
WHY YOU WANNA SEE MY BAD SIDE – Smokey Robinson (Tamla)

Grows on you... Also in the funk vein, there's "Get Down" (4:20) from **Raydio's** debut album on Arista – a spunky instrumental with a heavy guitar line that sounds like **Sine** meets **Parliament**.

RECOMMENDED DISCO DISCS: My favorites this week are two excellent longer versions of records already praised here: '**Michele's**, "Disco Dance" (West End) and' "Save And Spend" by **Cheryl Barnes** (Millennium). The first, a 13:40 "Mega Mix" by San Francisco DJ **Patrick Cowley**, turns the song inside-out with an incredible electronic second half which seem to layer a crackling, whip-snapping synthesizer over the original song and sets the unusual precedent of re-mixing a "Tom Moulton Mix" (Moulton's name remains on the record but Cowley has chosen the relative anonymity of the "Mega Mix" credit). Hot enough to revive this song in a big way, the disc features the original cut (8:42) on the reverse. The **Cheryl Barnes** record has been expanded from the single version to nearly twice that length – six minutes of first-rate **Frank Wilson** hustle-beat with a snappy guitar-and-percussion break that send the track soaring... "I Love New York" (Salsoul), reportedly commissioned to attract tourists to the big city, was produced by **Thor Baldursson**, the keyboard and Moog man on nearly all the Munich Machine products (**Donna Summer**, **Roberta Kelly**, **Giorgio**, **Trax**, etc.) and, most recently, co-writer and arranger on the **Marsha Hunt** album; hardly a native New Yorker. Though the song is show-biz schmaltzy at heart (and the overall feeling is much more Philadelphia than New York or Munich), the tune is definitely catchy, stirringly optimistic (like the finale of a Broadway musical) and fun. Besides, as someone who loves New York, I'd feel disloyal if I didn't sway around the living room to this record once in a while. ✐

> ❝ It sets the unusual precedent of re-mixing a "Tom Moulton Mix" (Moulton's name remains on the record but Cowley has chosen the relative anonymity of the "Mega Mix" credit) ❞

MARCH 25, 1978

Laurin Rinder and **W. Michael Lewis**, the producer / arranger / composer team responsible for virtually all the music made by "groups" called **El Coco**, **Le Pamplemousse**, **St. Tropez** and **Tuxedo Junction**, have taken a giant step with their first album under their own names, "Seven Deadly Sins" on AVI. Freed of the restrictions of making music that fits the style of one of their imaginary acts, Rinder and Lewis sound looser, more assured, more innovative and certainly more exciting than ever. The over-glossy commercial veneer of some of the team's earlier work has been stripped, revealing a new intensity and drive. "Seven Deadly Sins" consists of seven instrumental tracks, several of which may not fit one's own notion of what the sins should sound like – "Sloth," for instance, is unexpectedly spirited, just jumping with musical activity – but most are lively, involving interpretations of the theme. The album opens with a swirling, electronic wind and mysterious cries – a brief introduction to the descent into the Inferno – then kicks off with the familiar Eurodisco thump, thump, thump drums that signal the beginning of "Lust" (7:30), a combination of **Cerrone's** "Supernature" austerity and cool with **Barry White's** stylized, let-it-flow sensuality and passion. Controlling both styles, and a strong feature throughout the album, is Rinder and Lewis's

second lp and another leap forward. Written and produced by **Curtis Mayfield** and Motown vet **Gil Askey**, this is one of the best female vocal collections of the season, highlighted by a number of strong dance cuts. My two favorites are "Runaway Love" (7:04), a comfortably pumping get-out-of-my-life song that recalls **Jackie Moore** and **Loleatta Holloway** right down to the spoken kiss-off at the end, and "Gypsy Lady" (5:42 on the lp, 9:58 on an expanded disco disc), a more punched-up, invigorating cut with a hot break, strong horns and jolting vocals (and in the background: **The Jones Girls**). Also interesting are "I Feel Like Falling In Love Again" (5:04), very up and positive, and "You Are, You Are" (5:16), a Curtis Mayfield composition (also his just-released single) with a quick pace, kicking drums and occasional synthesizer accents – perhaps a little too manic for some tastes, but superb at the right moment. The album's title song, "If My Friends Could See Me Now," has already been getting some club action on the basis of a long disco disc version released before the lp (10:12, remixed and mastered by **Jimmy Simpson**) but, though the vocals are powerful, the treatment of this standard tune is too fast and furious for my taste, especially when taken to this length; a great intro, some tough breaks, but generally for speed-freaks only.

❝ A seriously funky, typically insane chant number – currently the group's single and already a major record in many black clubs ❞

own sure sense of pace and flair; the feeling is clean, spacious, precise. "Sloth" (7:48), though oddly manic, is an irresistible, almost circus-like piece full of playful organ runs and Spanish interludes right out of **Santa Esmeralda**. "Gluttony" (7:15), truer to the spirit of the sin, begins with jittery synthesizer music (cf. **Space**, **Kraftwerk**) that suggests a swarm of insects which is gradually penetrated by a jazzy sax-wail pattern and other deeper, more flowing moog movements. And "Anger" (5:37) is perfect, being essentially a solo of furious, hot-brooded drumming punctuated by aggressive, nearly animal shouts and relieved by two segments of more decorative, horn-and-organ-laced material. The very beginning sounds like a boiling cauldron but later the feeling goes beyond menacing – it's like being caught in the middle of a heavyweight fight: a percussive tour de force. The remaining cuts are also fine, with "Pride" and "Covetousness" taking more of a vibrant jazz/disco bent. Altogether, then, a solid, no-filler album designed for listening and dancing, with the three longer cuts on side one –"Lust," "Sloth," "Gluttony" – the standouts and "Anger" a prime choice for percussion freaks. Not to be missed.

This week's other favorite album is **Linda Clifford's** "If My Friends Could See Me Now" (Curtom), the singer's

RECOMMENDED DISCO DISC: **Baciotti's** "Black Jack," listed enthusiastically by the Ice Palace's Roy Thode last week when it was still a French import, is out now as an RCA 12-inch running something over ten minutes. The record has elements of so many recent successful records –"Supernature" (ominous synthesizer), "Star Wars" (trippy synthesizer) and "Magic Fly" (deep-space, "singing" synthesizer) plus male vocals that are mostly in a classic falsetto-edged rock style (very **Zombies**) but edge into **Bee Gees**-modern – that it sounds like a tailor-made hit. The pace is brisk and sharp, sweeping you along and the vocals are prominent, perhaps too much so since they tilt the mood closer to rock than most current disco has gone. Still, very interesting and worth checking into.

EXPANSION: The following songs are now available in new, mostly longer, versions on 12-inch pressings: "Flash Light" (Casablanca), **Parliament's** seriously funky, typically insane chant number – currently the group's single and already a major record in many black clubs – run way into the ground at 10:31 (nearly twice the length of the original lp cut) but still crazy fun... "We're On Our Way Home," a 6:34 combination of two separate Part I/Part II sections of the same song from **Brainstorm's** first Tabu/Columbia album – nothing like

FLAMINGO, NEW YORK
DJ: Richie Rivera

COME INTO MY HEART/LOVE'S COMING
– USA-European Connection (Marlin)
**FEVER/TOUCH MY HEART/LET'S MAKE LOVE/ROUGH
DIAMOND** – Madleen Kane (CBS import)
**FROM EAST TO WEST/LADY AMERICA/SCOTCH
MACHINE/BAYOU VILLAGE** – Voyage (Marlin import)
KEY WEST/MACHO MAN/I AM WHAT I AM
– Village People (Casablanca)
LUST/SLOTH – Laurin Rinder & W. Michael Lewis (AVI)
NOBODY BUT YOU – Theo Vaness (CBS import)
RIO DE JANEIRO – Gary Criss (Salsoul)
ROMEO & JULIET – Alec Costandinos (Casablanca)
STARTING NOW/ROBOT DEATH/ROBOT DISCO DANCE
– Robot (Vogue import)
STEREO – Limits Up (AB import)

PARADISE GARAGE, NEW YORK
DJ: Larry Levan

**AFRICANISM/GIMME SOME LOVING/TATTOO
WOMAN/DR. DOO-DAH** – Kongas (Polydor)
CHAPTER THREE – African Dub All-Mighty
(Joe Gibbs Records import)
DISCO DANCE (MEGA MIX) – Michele (West End)
I THINK I'LL DO SOME STEPPIN' ON MY OWN
– Sandy Barber (Olde World)
THE MEXICAN – Bombers (Telson import)
RIO DE JANEIRO – Gary Criss (Salsoul)
SAVE AND SPEND – Cheryl Barnes (Millennium)
VOYAGE – Voyage (Marlin)
YOU ARE MY LOVE/PLAY WITH ME – Sandy Mercer (H&L)
**YOU ARE, YOU ARE/RUNAWAY LOVE/IF MY FRIENDS
COULD SEE ME NOW/I FEEL LIKE FALLING IN LOVE
AGAIN** – Linda Clifford (Curtom)

WAREHOUSE VIII, MIAMI
DJ: Bill Kelly

CHATANOOGA CHOO CHOO – Tuxedo Junction (Butterfly)
COME INTO MY HEART/LOVE'S COMING
– USA-European Connection (Marlin)
DANCE WITH ME – Peter Brown (TK)
DON'T COST YOU NOTHING – Ashford & Simpson
(Warner Bros.)
FROM EAST TO WEST/POINT ZERO – Voyage (Marlin)
GALAXY – War (MCA)
I CAN'T STAND THE RAIN – Eruption (Ariola)
ROMEO & JULIET – Alec Costandinos (Casablanca)
WHICH WAY IS UP? – Stargard (MCA)
YOU LIKE IT, WE LOVE IT – Southroad Connection
(Mahogany)

FACES, CHICAGO
DJ: Carmen Adduci

COME INTO MY HEART/LOVE'S COMING
– USA-European Connection (Marlin)
FEVER/ROUGH DIAMOND/LET'S MAKE LOVE
– Madleen Kane (CBS import)
FREAKY DEAKY/LET'S DO IT/SWEET TEARS
– Roy Ayers (Polydor)
I CAN'T STAND THE RAIN – Eruption (Ariola)
MILE HIGH – Fatback Band (Spring)
RIO DE JANEIRO – Gary Criss (Salsoul)
ROMEO & JULIET – Alec Costandinos (Casablanca)
TURN ON LADY – Detroit Emeralds (Westbound)
VOYAGE – Voyage (Marlin)
WE'RE ON OUR WAY HOME – Brainstorm (Tabu)

the drive of "Lovin' Is Really My Game," but fine vocals
and a nice spirited arrangement very much in the
Stevie Wonder style... "You Got Me Hummin'," the
Moment of Truth track originally released as an album
cut just about a year ago, now doubled to a neat eight
minutes (on Salsoul) with a stylish **Rafael Charres** mix
that adds a nice break, lots of echo and much-needed
depth – could rescue the song from oblivion... Two
other songs in need of rescue efforts are **Vicki Sue
Robinson's** "Trust In Me" and "Don't Try To Win Me
Back Again" (RCA), greatly enhanced by longer (7:03
and 6:06, respectively) and sharper versions than those
previously available on her "Half And Half" album...
Diana Ross' "Your Love Is So Good For Me" has been
stretched out to 6:32 (why?) for a Motown disco disc
backed by **Thelma Houston's** un-disco, un-expanded
"I Can't Go On Living Without Your Love"... **Cameo's**
"It's Serious" (Chocolate City), the **Brass Construction**-
esque instrumental-with-chant cut from their last
album, is a few seconds longer – now 8:06... and **Ralph
MacDonald's** "The Path" (TK) has been broken down to
its more accessible parts – II (5:07) and III (6:22), back-
to-back on a promotional pressing.

NOTES: The **Voyage** album is now available on a
domestic label – TK's Marlin – and currently number
three on the DISCO FILE Top 20... Another ex-import,
Alec R. Costandinos' Sphinx production "Simon
Peter"/"Judas Iscariot," has been given an Easter-season
release by Casablanca – give it another listen... We
neglected to mention last week that the performer of
Salsoul's "I Love New York' is a group called **Metropolis**. ⊘

SIDE 1

LAURIN RINDER
& W. MICHAEL LEWIS

AVI RECORDS

AVI-6035
(018-6035-A)
Engineer: David Ruffo

SEVEN DEADLY SINS
1. LUST(W.Michael Lewis-Laurin Rinder) 7:30
Equinox Music (BMI)
2. SLOTH (W.Michael Lewis-Laurin Rinder) 7:48
Equinox Music (BMI)
3. GLUTTONY (W.Michael Lewis-Laurin Rinder) 7:15
Equinox Music (BMI)
Producers: W. Michael Lewis & Laurin Rinder-
A RinLew Production
Executive Producers: Ray Harris & Ed Cobb
Arranged/Conducted by
W. Michael Lewis & Laurin Rinder
℗ © 1977 AVI Records Dist. Corp.
All Rights Reserved

The list of recommended albums this week includes three releases by women with European connections: **Madleen Kane**, **Roberta Kelly** and **Sheila & B. Devotion**. Kane, a Swedish model/singer whose debut on CBS France has been one of the most popular imports of the past few weeks, leads the pack with a highly flattering, glamour-girl production in the European style, She has a dreamy, occasionally flimsy voice that needs a lot of

> **❝A near-hysterical pace – but it's such perfect pop disco that it wore down even my resistence.❞**

support (underlining backing tracks plus a girl chorus that includes **Sue Glover** and **Sunny (Leslie)**, vocalists on nearly all the **Cerrone** and **Costandinos** productions) but is ideally suited to the breathy insinuation of "Fever," the **Peggy Lee** signature song teased into a delicious 12-minute production number here, and the rest of the album's material. The mood is warm, sexy, inviting (titles: "Let's Make Love," "Touch My Heart") with a solid, if standard, production that mixes elements of both the French and German styles (though the producers are new to us, key Munich Machinist **Thor Baldursson** is one of the arrangers and super-drummer **Keith Forsey** is credited as well). The production is not, however, merely cosmetic; Kane's vocals predominate, she doesn't get wiped out by long breaks or shoved into a corner by an overwhelming arrangement, so the songs have a fine balance missing in many other European records. The entire album is danceable (even the slow cut, a tantalizing version of "C'est Si Bon" would make a fabulous slow grind) and the four cuts that jumped into the DISCO FILE Top 20 this week are all excellent, beginning with the title cut, "Rough Diamond" (6:22), a female-submission fantasy ("I'm only a rough diamond," Kane sighs, "I need your love to shape me") studded with flamenco disco handclaps and castanets, "Touch My Heart" has a chunky beat and a nice, echoed fade-out break; "Let's Make Love" is bright and sunny (very **Claudja Barry**); and "Fever," combined with an original blend-in cut called "Make Me Like It," is beautifully kicked-up and irresistible. With Kane on the cover in black leather, diamonds and furs and stretched out cat-like in leopard skin for the center spread, this is a chic package, suggesting ecstasy, fashion and pain but delivering something considerably more substantial. An important debut. Warner Brothers has picked up the album for American release in about three weeks (significant note: "Rough Diamond" was **Jerry Wexler's** first signing for the label); a remixed disco disc of the title cut will precede the album.

Roberta Kelly, whose last album was obsessed with astrology, takes up religion on her latest release, a pop-gospel concept lp produced by **Giorgio Moroder** and **Bob Esty** called "Gettin' The Spirit" (Casablanca). Though the record as a whole is not totally convincing – the production's blend of Top 40 gospel ("Oh Happy Day," "My Sweet Lord"), German disco synthesizer (Moroder) and L.A. gloss is more calculated than inspired – Kelly has an undeniable energy and several of the cuts approach a rich gospel intensity. Side one blends "Oh Happy Day," another **Edwin Hawkins** song called "To My Father's House" and **George Harrison's** "My Sweet Lord" for an approximately 16-minute medley that is only partially effective. "Father's House" brings Kelly and a great chorus (including **Pattie Brooks**) to peaks of fervent singing (though they never seem to cross the line into truly spontaneous spiritual singing – this is not "I Got It") and stands out here, but "Happy Day" is not freshened sufficiently by the zippy synthesizer opening and "Lord" is cut with a bit of preaching that I for one would not welcome on the dance floor. "Gettin' The Spirit," which opens up the other side, succeeds primarily because its feeling is more secular and accessible; Kelly sounds very like **Melba Moore** here and the mood is appropriately invigorating. The closing cut "Speaking My Mind In His Ear," is also interesting, sparked by a mysterious synthesizer woosh that flows in with the choruses and the lovely repeated chant of "Yaweh-Adone-Jehovah-Allah." Recommended: "To My Father's House" and "Gettin' The Spirit;" the rest is for more specialized tastes.

Sheila & B. Devotion's "Singin' In The Rain" album, just released on Casablanca after some success as a French import a few months back, is almost unrelievedly up and bouncy in a style that draws heavily upon frothy French pop (Sheila was reportedly a major star in that genre before moving into disco last year) and synthesizer-based Eurodisco (something between **Claudja Barry** and **Michele** with a little **Celi Bee** thrown in), The title track, the movie-musical favorite done with a slight French accent, is set to a near-hysterical pace – the sort that either discourages dancers or sends them into a delighted, swirling frenzy – but it's such perfect pop disco that it wore down even my determined resistence after repeated listenings (at the urging of Alan Bell, Gaysweek editor/publisher and DJ, who insisted it was a big hit whenever he played it). Most of the remaining cuts reach for a similar spirit, and though none achieve quite the same effect, all are fun, particularly "Kiss Me Sweetie," which fans into a "Black Is Black" groove, "Love Me Baby" and "Shake Me." Predictable but surprisingly good.

CHOICE CUTS: Sometime New York DJ Steve D'Acquisto has brought a number of people's attention to an interesting cut on a recent album by a woman named **Sandy Barber** ("The Best Is Yet To Come" on Olde Town in New York). The song, "I Think I'll Do Some Steppin' On My Own" (7:59), is an unexpected, uneven but very hot number with roots deep in the r&b tradition of tough women's songs. Barber, who has a fun, strong

LOST AND FOUND, WASHINGTON, D.C.
DJ: Bill Owens

COME INTO MY HEART/LOVE'S COMING
– USA-European Connection (Marlin)
DANCE WITH ME – Peter Brown (TK)
I CAN'T STAND THE RAIN – Eruption (Ariola)
IF MY FRIENDS COULD SEE ME NOW/GYPSY
LADY/RUNAWAY LOVE – Linda Clifford (Curtom)
RISKY CHANGES – Bionic Boogie (Polydor)
ROMEO & JULIET – Alec Costandinos (Casablanca)
TRUST IN ME/DON'T TRY TO WIN ME BACK AGAIN
– Vicki Sue Robinson (RCA)
VOYAGE – Voyage (Marlin)
WEST SIDE STORY – Salsoul Orchestra (Salsoul)
YOU ARE MY LOVE – Sandy Mercer (H&L)

GUEST HOUSE, BROOKLYN, NEW YORK
DJ: Graylin Riley

COME INTO MY HEART/LOVE'S COMING
– USA-European Connection (Marlin)
DANCE, DANCE, DANCE/DON'T STOP THE MUSIC/
SUPER MAX – Bombers (Telson import)
DANCE WITH ME – Peter Brown (TK)
FLASH LIGHT – Parliament (Casablanca)
JAYWALKING – Leroy Gomez (Total import)
OH HAPPY DAY/TO MY FATHER'S HOUSE/MY SWEET
LORD – Roberta Kelly (Casablanca)
THE OTHER SIDE OF MIDNIGHT I HEARTACHE
– Marsha Hunt (Aves import)
RUNAWAY LOVE/IF MY FRIENDS COULD SEE ME
NOW/GYPSY LADY – Linda Clifford (Curtom)
VOYAGE – Voyage (Marlin)
WEST SIDE STORY – Salsoul Orchestra (Salsoul)

BAREFOOT BOY, NEW YORK
DJ: Tony Smith

COME INTO MY HEART/LOVE'S COMING
– USA-European Connection (Marlin)
I LOVE NEW YORK – Metropolis (Salsoul)
LADY AMERICA/FROM EAST TO WEST/SCOTCH
MACHINE/BAYOU VILLAGE – Voyage (Marlin)
LET'S GET TOGETHER – Detroit Emeralds (Westbound)
RIO DE JANEIRO – Gary Criss (Salsoul)
ROMEO & JULIET – Alec Costandinos (Casablanca)
RUNAWAY LOVE/GYPSY LADY/IF MY FRIENDS COULD
SEE ME NOW – Linda Clifford (Curtom)
SAVE AND SPEND – Cheryl Barnes (Millennium)
TOUCH MY HEART/LET'S MAKE LOVE/ROUGH DIAMOND
– Madleen Kane (CBS import)
YOU ARE MY LOVE – Sandy Mercer (H&L)

LIMELIGHT, HOLLYWOOD, FLORIDA
DJ: Bob Lombardi

CHATANOOGA CHOO CHOO – Tuxedo Junction (Butterfly)
COME INTO MY HEART/LOVE'S COMING
– USA-European Connection (Marlin)
DANCE WITH ME – Peter Brown (TK)
DON'T TRY TO WIN ME BACK AGAIN
– Vicki Sue Robinson (RCA)
FROM EAST TO WEST/POINT ZERO/LADY AMERICA
– Voyage (Marlin)
GIVE ME LOVE/SUPERNATURE – Cerrone (Cotillion)
HOUSE OF THE RISING SUN – Revelacion (Crocos import)
LET'S ALL CHANT/LOVE EXPRESS – Michael Zager Band
(Private Stock)
MACHO MAN/I AM WHAT I AM/ KEY WEST
– Village People (Casablanca)
MELODIES – Made in USA (De-Lite)

voice, talks mean to her man, first telling him, "before I'll be your stepping stone/I think I'll do some steppin' on my own," threatening to "bring you back some blues," then escalating the backtalk in the chorus sections, abetted by a gritty girl chorus, Tempo varies but it remains solidly funky throughout with some terrific peaks and changes. A sleeper – especially considering the album's been out over three months, Also checkout: "Can't You Just See Me" and "Don't Worry Baby" ... Two songs of prime interest on the new **Cory Wade**-produced **Foxy** album: "Get Off," a spunky, funky number with down-to-basics lyrics and a delivery to match – jivey synthesizer, a disco chant and additional vocals by **Wildflower** clinch it as a party song; and "Tena's Song," in an entirely different mold – syncopated, neo-Big Band stuff with **Savannah Band** overtones that is definitely off-beat but nutsy enough to go over big as a novelty, Another possibility: "You," eliminating the intro and getting into the Latin-beat purse of it, with **Peter Brown** on synthesized bass. A strong and varied album. ✪

DISCO FILE TOP 20

1. **COME INTO MY HEART/LOVE'S COMING** – USA-European Connection (Marlin)
2. **VOYAGE** – Voyage (Polydor import)
3. **ROMEO & JULIET** – Alec Costandinos (Casablanca)
4. **DANCE WITH ME** – Peter Brown (Drive)
5. **RISKY CHANGES/DANCE LITTLE DREAMER** – Bionic Boogie (Polydor)
6. **YOU ARE MY LOVE/PLAY WITH ME** – Sandy Mercer (H&L)
7. **AFRICANISM/GIMME SOME LOVING/DR. DOO-DAH** – Kongas (Crocos)
8. **LET'S ALL CHANT/LOVE EXPRESS** – Michael Zager Band (Private Stock)
9. **STAYIN' ALIVE/NIGHT FEVER** – Bee Gees "Saturday Night Fever" Soundtrack (RSO)
10. **RIO DE JANEIRO** – Gary Criss (Salsoul)
11. **I CAN'T STAND THE RAIN** – Eruption (Ariola)
12. **KEY WEST/MACHO MAN/I AM WHAT I AM** – Village People (Casablanca)
13. **GALAXY** – War (MCA)
14. **IF MY FRIENDS COULD SEE ME NOW/GYPSY LADY/RUNAWAY LOVE** – Linda Clifford (Curtom)
15. **ROUGH DIAMOND/TOUCH MY HEART/LET'S MAKE LOVE** – Madleen Kane (CBS import)
16. **WEST SIDE STORY** – Salsoul Orchestra (Salsoul)
17. **CHATANOOGA CHOO CHOO** – Tuxedo Junction (Butterfly)
18. **I FEEL GOOD** – Al Green (Hi)
19. **MELODIES** – Made in USA (De-Lite)
20. **THE BEAT GOES ON AND ON** – Ripple (Salsoul)

APRIL 8, 1978

The **Saturday Night Band's** "Come On Dance, Dance," the 13-minute title track from this studio group's debut album on Prelude, is such strong, on-target pop disco that it only takes a few listenings to convince you this is the natural successor to "Dance, Dance, Dance," "Risky Changes" and "Let's All Chant." Clean, slick, energy-packed and full of irresistible hooks – a terrific bass/piano line threaded by strings; a wailing synthesizer that swoops in playfully – "Come On Dance, Dance" picks up the **Chic** sound and runs with it. This is not what you'd expect from a couple of young, relatively

❝ If you are of the opinion that an evening without amyl nitrate is like a day without sunshine... ❞

unknown producers who work out of Muscle Shoals, Alabama, but **Jessie Boyce** and **Moses Dillard**, who also arranged, composed and performed most of the music here, have clearly studied the field carefully and come up with their own fresh variation of the New York studio group sound with nods here and there to **Laurin Rinder** and **Michael Lewis**. The song moves swiftly, surely through a series of tightly-structured segments, both vocal and instrumental, that mesh, change and repeat. As usual, the vocals are raceless and predominately female and sound as though they were spread on like so much canned icing, but they are used sparingly – just enough to give the song an identifying tag line and pull it together from both ends – and flow perfectly with the song's overall production feel. Happily, "Come On Dance, Dance" is given excellent support from the rest of the album: only two other cuts – "Don't (Take My Love Away)" (5:10) and "Touch Me On My Hot Spot" (13:36) – but both of them spirited and danceable, if not quite as knockout as the title song. Should be an instant hit.

OTHER RECOMMENDED ALBUMS: Producers **Willi Morrison** and **Ian Guenther** have followed up their sizzling "Two Hot for Love" album for the **THP Orchestra** with a new project in a cooler, more elegant style, called **Grand Tour**. The group's first album, "On Such A Winter's Day" (pressed on clear blue vinyl by Butterfly Records), is highlighted by several attractive, sophisticated cuts in the disco-orchestra mold that manages to be simultaneously delicate and deep. The best two open up each side of the record: "The Grand Tour" (6:03) features sweet creamy vocals and a production to match, sparked by an unexpectedly rich break; "Flight To Versailles" (6:20) weaves strings, horns and synthesizers for a wonderful texture and sets them to a quick-throbbing beat. Another track, the

instrumental "Late November," is quietly engrossing, a nice hustle; and there's a passable version of "California Dreamin'" that lends the album its title quote. A pretty, perhaps overly tasteful collection with just enough disco hard-edge to get over... Graylin Riley, DJ from the Guest House in Brooklyn called my attention to **Deodato's** "Whistle Bump:' a vibrant, rather mellow instrumental with a subtly percolating beat that features some Big Band interludes (when the horn section floats in like a fat, elegant cloud) around a core of jumping guitar, an inevitable whistle/conga break and Deodato's jazzy keyboards. Sunny and fresh, it's only 3:55 on the new "Love Island" album (Warner Brothers) but a longer 12-inch version is promised very soon... The **Michael Zager Band** album is, of course, called "Let's All Chant" (Private Stock), but it doesn't match the promise and verve of that highly commercial pop disco hit. Outside of a short version of "Chant" (3:07) and the disco disc version of "Love Express" (7:02), the album is uneven and overcalculated with only one cut approaching the sort of stylish and surprising blend that makes "Chant" click – "Music Fever" (6:37), which is stuffed with freaky synthesizer breaks similar to those in "Chant" and gets across primarily on the infectious enthusiasm of its singers and its comfortably chunky beat. A decent follow-up to "Chant" but hardly a creative leap forward. "Soul To Soul" (5:51) picks up interest during a long break but also remains uneven, caught between two styles.

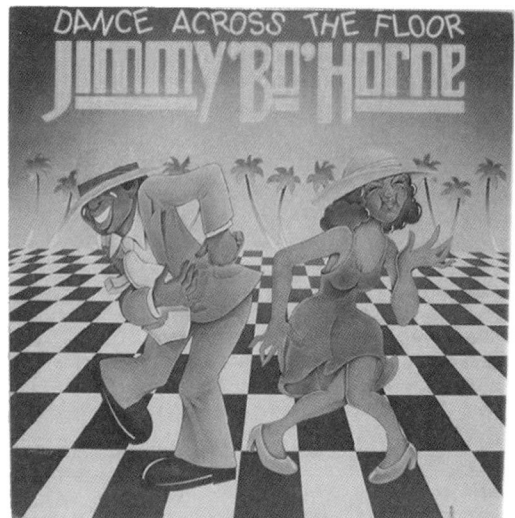

FUNK IT UP (A quick survey of the best new funk disco records): "Freak With Me" (Red Greg), the new **Universal Robot Band** disco disc written and produced by **Greg Carmichael** and **Patrick Adams**, insistent orgasmic cries that underline the bulk of the record, other more intimate things. The sound is very similar to that in "Dance And Shake Your Tambourine" – noisy, jumping party music with a driving bass line and wild synthesizer

LES MOUCHES, NEW YORK
DJ: Joel Jacobs

COME INTO MY HEART/LOVE'S COMING
– USA-European Connection (Marlin)
COME ON DANCE, DANCE – Saturday Night Band (Prelude)
BLACK JACK – Baciotti (RCA)
IF MY FRIENDS COULD SEE ME NOW/GYPSY LADY –
Linda Clifford (Curtom)
MACHO MAN/I AM WHAT I AM/ KEY WEST
– Village People (Casablanca)
RIO DE JANEIRO – Gary Criss (Salsoul)
RISKY CHANGES – Bionic Boogie (Polydor)
ROMEO & JULIET – Alec Costandinos (Casablanca)
TRUST IN ME – Vicki Sue Robinson (RCA)
VOYAGE – Voyage (Marlin)

BUZZBY'S, SAN FRANCISCO
DJ: Michael Lee

AIN'T NO SMOKE WITHOUT FIRE/WHIP
– Eddie Kendricks (Arista)
COME INTO MY HEART/LOVE'S COMING
– USA-European Connection (Marlin)
FLIGHT INTO VERSAILLES – Grand Tour (Butterfly)
**IF MY FRIENDS COULD SEE ME NOW/GYPSY
LADY/RUNAWAY LOVE** – Linda Clifford (Curtom)
**LET'S GET TOGETHER/TURN ON LADY/I CAN'T SEEM
TO FORGET** – Detroit Emeralds (Westbound)
NUMBER ONE – Eloise Laws (ABC)
OH HAPPY DAY/GETTIN' THE SPIRIT – Roberta Kelly
(Casablanca)
RIO DE JANEIRO – Gary Criss (Salsoul)
VOYAGE – Voyage (Marlin)
YOU ARE MY LOVE – Sandy Mercer (H&L)

1270, BOSTON
DJ: Danae Jacovidis

AT THE DISCOTHEQUE – Lipstique (Tom 'n' Jerry)
COME INTO MY HEART/LOVE'S COMING
– USA-European Connection (Marlin)
DISCO DANCE (MEGA MIX)/CAN'T YOU FEEL IT
– Michele (West End)
**THE GRAND TOUR/FLIGHT TO VERSAILLES/LATE
NOVEMBER** – Grand Tour (Butterfly)
I LOVE NEW YORK – Metropolis (Salsoul)
**IF MY FRIENDS COULD SEE ME NOW/GYPSY LADY/
RUNAWAY LOVE** – Linda Clifford (Curtom)
LADY AMERICA/FROM EAST TO WEST – Voyage (Marlin)
RIO DE JANEIRO – Gary Criss (Salsoul)
SEVEN DEADLY SINS – Michael Lewis & Laurin Rinder (AVI)
**WEST SIDE STORY (MEDLEY)/EASE ON DOWN THE ROAD/
FIDDLER ON THE ROOF** – Salsoul Orchestra (Salsoul)

THE GRAND BALLROOM, NEW YORK
DJ: John Benitez

COME INTO MY HEART/LOVE'S COMING
– USA-European Connection (Marlin)
**COME ON DANCE, DANCE/TOUCH ME ON MY HOT
SPOT/DON'T** – Saturday Night Band (Prelude)
DANCE WITH ME – Peter Brown (TK)
DOWN BY THE DOCKS – Sailor (Columbia)
GALAXY – War (MCA)
LET YOURSELF GO – T-Connection (TK)
MACHO MAN/I AM WHAT I AM/ KEY WEST
– Village People (Casablanca)
RIO DE JANEIRO – Gary Criss (Salsoul)
**RUNAWAY LOVE/GYPSY LADY/IF MY FRIENDS COULD
SEE ME NOW** – Linda Clifford (Curtom)
VOYAGE – Voyage (Marlin)

work, the group's signature touch. Lots of fun, but kind of over-long at 8:09 on the 12-inch pressing (which includes two cuts on the flip side by two different artists; "Groove On Down" by **Dunn Pearson, Jr.** is interesting); a 3:12 single version is also available… **T-Connection's** "Let Yourself Go," now out on a TK disco disc is, at 5:08, only eight seconds longer than the original album cut, but now it starts out with a long percussion/guitar intro that grabs you immediately and holds you tight. Another break adds punch to the center of the song and everything's been sharpened up considerably – should give this cut a whole new life… Also out of Miami – two new singles produced by **Casey & Finch**, the strongest being "Black Water Gold" (TK) by the **Sunshine Band** whose elemental/mechanical/archetypal Miami Sound is perfect for this remake of an obscure early disco instrumental – horns, a great bass and drums carry this nice n' nasty chug beat (in two parts, 3:11 and 1:42); **Jimmy "Bo" Horne's** "Dance Across The Floor" (Sunshine Sound) is a more predictable piece of KC-style funk but it's a good, raucous get-down and the 12-inch version should be worth checking out when it comes… "Welcome To The Party" by **Wood, Brass & Steel** (6:05 on a Turbo disco disc, through All Platinum) is fine, knife-edged neo-funk in the vein of **Kool & the Gang** and **Mass Production** but somewhat rawer – very strong, hard-party record that sounds like a live show… "Hotel Sheets" by **Jack Ashford** (remember his "Do the Choo Choo"?) is another loud party cut that's hard to resist; the gimmick here is the title instrument – that metal sheet that, when shaken, makes a bubbling, percolating sound – supported by an invigorating arrangement of horns and guitars (out on a Magic-Disc 12- inch running 5:29)… Finally, two excellent singles from Motown that have become surprise favorites this week: "You and I" by **Rick James** (Gordy), a powerful, heavy-pumping, rock-hard cut with a highly-charged lead vocal and riveting female chorus work ("As far as I'm concerned, they all can go to hell," they scream); and "Star Love" by **3 Ounces of Love** (Motown), a girl group that recalls the **Emotions** singing passionately to the "secret man of my future" – this one edges out of the funk vein but it's fiercely sung, with great, pounding choruses and a real knockout. Both songs deserve expanded disco disc versions.

MEDIA: Even though **Fran Lebowitz** did tell an incredulous Marc Balet in the latest Interview that, as far as she's concerned, disco is "over… it's lost a lot of its sparkle. It's come to lack visual appeal," we feel compelled to mention the appearance in print of Metropolitan life, a collection of her writing already recommended in RW by the guys at New York, NY. You can't dance to it, but it's brilliantly, bitingly funny and often instructive (see "Notes on Trick"). Included are her cutting "Disco Hints," one of which is "If you are of the opinion that an evening without amyl nitrate is like a day without sunshine, you should avail yourself of this substance in the privacy of your own truck and not in the middle of a crowded dance floor." ❂

An especially fine selection of new releases this week, all of them foreign-made (in France, Canada, Puerto Rico, South Africa), all essential additions to any disco playlist or collection right this moment. Top of the list is the **Don Ray** album, "Garden Of Love," on which the premier arranger of the Eurodisco sound (French Division) steps out front for the first time – co-writing and co-producing all the material with **Cerrone** as well as arranging and playing keyboards and synthesizer – with astoundingly good results. The supporting cast is familiar – guitarist **Slim Pezin** and percussionist **Marc Chantereau** from **Voyage**; **Madeline Bell**, **Sue Glover** and **Kay Garner** handling backing vocals – and the studio is, primarily, Trident in London (with mixing

including "Standing In The Rain" (6:34) with its "rain" effects, a combination of jetting synthesizer and percussion; "Body And Soul" (4:23), which comes closest to the lively jungle jump of "Dr. Doo-Dah;" and "Midnight Madness" (5:41), which falls into a rapid-pulsing rock beat with a frantic fun-house aura and intensity to the break. Even "My Desire," which starts out like a typical crooner record from the bossa nova period, turns hot with the female chorus and even hotter in the breaks. All in all, a sensational album and a welcome change of pace – currently an import on Cerrone's Malligator label, it's due out in the States on Polydor the first or second week in May.

" Dipping into the chant and percussion in ever-increasing waves of passion, this is the most compelling piece of African dance music we've heard in years. Very, very hot "

done at Munich's Musicland), but the sound is unexpected: tougher, wilder, tighter than many of the recent French imports to have hit these shores. Like Voyage, Ray takes the European sound off in a direction all his own, first by breaking down the extended-cut format (the longest track here is eight minutes, a perfect length, and there are three substantial songs to a side, a notable exception to the trend of shorter and shorter disco albums), then by introducing a rich undercurrent of funk and rock elements. Anyone looking for an indication of where the Eurodisco sound is heading can start right here.

The album's opening song, "Got To Have Loving" (8:15), is the kind of cut that, after only two listenings, had me calling up friends to rave extravagantly. Is it too much to call this an instant classic, perhaps one of the great disco songs, certainly one of the very best single cuts this year? Decide for yourself. I'll just say "Got To Have Loving" brings back the kind of first-impression excitement I felt with "Do You Wanna Get Funky With Me," "Devil's Gun," "Give Me Love," "Come Into My Heart" and a few other special records. The song begins with the kind of high-impact, hard-hitting intro that made "Devil's Gun" such a knockout from the very beginning – a steady synthesizer/bass/percussion build and blaring horn break: heavy metal disco – and gradually layers in vocals. First Bell, Glover and Garner singing "It's a shame to complain, but we gotta have a lot more loving," the song's key line, then a hard-rock-styled male lead who carries most of the lyrics. All of them are strong, cutting singers but, as usual, it's the production that stands out here: the synthesizer that rumbles in like vibrant thunderclaps, the supple guitar work, the swirl of electronics and percussion in the break, shattering horn sections. Whew. I could go on: three other tracks here are nearly as impressive,

The second album by **Love and Kisses**, the group that introduced French producer/composer **Alec R. Costandinos** to the disco world, is titled "How Much, How Much I Love You" (Casablanca) and has more in common with recent Costandinos works like "Romeo & Juliet" and "Golden Tears" than the group's earlier "I've Found Love." As the Costandinos vision and style become increasingly romantic (who else would follow Romeo and Juliet with a retelling of the fairy tale of Beauty and the Beast which takes up the bulk of side two here?), the fierce passion, tension and casual sexiness of the Love and Kisses debut have either faded away or been given a soft-focus treatment. The music remains thrilling, lovely, almost effortlessly brilliant with an instrumental grace and vigor that is never merely lush or pretty. But though the string passages in the 16-minute title cut are so full-bodied and stirringly sensuous they border on the palpably erotic, the song doesn't approach the electrifying cumulative impact of "I've Found Love." Still, "How Much, How Much I Love You" – especially the chorus repetition of that title phrase – is, like all of Costandinos' long pieces, irresistibly beautiful. Heavenly music – but we miss the earthy touches. Much the same could be said about "Beauty And The Beast" (14:30), though the style here is more elaborate and involving, piecing together the story, like Romeo and Juliet's, through chorus narrative and both spoken and sung dialogue. This opens up the song to a variety of moods and an opulent mix of instrumental textures; it becomes a glowing tapestry, bright with detail, but, again, the effect is more cerebral than emotional. Costandinos is never less than masterful here, but when you know someone can sweep you off your feet, it's hard to be satisfied with a tender two-step, no matter how delightful.

I BEAM, SAN FRANCISCO
DJ: Tim Rivers

BLACK WATER GOLD – Sunshine Band (TK)

COME ON DANCE, DANCE/DON'T TOUCH ME ON MY HOT SPOT – Saturday Night Band (Prelude)

GOT TO HAVE LOVING/STANDING IN THE RAIN – Don Ray (Malligator import)

LET'S GET TOGETHER – Detroit Emeralds (Westbound)

OH HAPPY DAY/TO MY FATHER'S HOUSE/GETTIN' THE SPIRIT – Roberta Kelly (Casablanca)

NUMBER ONE – Eloise Laws (ABC)

RUNAWAY LOVE/IF MY FRIENDS COULD SEE ME NOW/GYPSY LADY – Linda Clifford (Curtom)

SCOTCH MACHINE/BAYOU VILLAGE/ FROM EAST TO WEST/POINT ZERO – Voyage (Marlin)

TENA'S SONG/GET OFF – Foxy (Dash)

YOU ARE MY LOVE/PLAY WITH ME – Sandy Mercer (H&L)

LEVITICUS, NEW YORK
DJ: Porter Wynn

COME ON DANCE, DANCE – Saturday Night Band (Prelude)

DANCE WITH ME – Peter Brown (TK)

GOTTA GET OUT OF HERE – Lucy Hawkins (Sam)

MACHO MAN/KEY WEST – Village People (Casablanca)

MUSIC FEVER – Michael Zager Band (Private Stock)

RIO DE JANEIRO – Gary Criss (Salsoul)

RUNAWAY LOVE/GYPSY LADY – Linda Clifford (Curtom)

SHAME – Evelyn "Champagne" King (RCA)

THERE ARE SO MANY STOPS ALONG THE WAY – Joe Sample (ABC)

YOU USED TA BE MY GIRL – O'Jays (Phila. Intl.)

INFINITY, NEW YORK
DJ: Jim Burgess

COME INTO MY HEART/LOVE'S COMING – USA-European Connection (Marlin)

DANCE WITH ME – Peter Brown (TK)

FROM EAST TO WEST/POINT ZERO/LATIN ODYSSEY/LADY AMERICA – Voyage (Marlin)

GALAXY – War (MCA)

LET YOURSELF GO – T-Connection (TK)

LET'S GET TOGETHER/I CAN'T SEEM TO FORGET – Detroit Emeralds (Westbound)

MACHO MAN/I AM WHAT I AM/ KEY WEST – Village People (Casablanca)

RISKY CHANGES/DANCE LITTLE DREAMER – Bionic Boogie (Polydor)

ROMEO & JULIET – Alec Costandinos (Casablanca)

SIMON PETER – Sphinx (Casablanca)

LOCKER ROOM, ATLANTA
DJ: Kathy White

AFRICANISM/GIMME SOME LOVING – Kongas (Polydor)

THE BEAT GOES ON AND ON – Ripple (Salsoul)

COME INTO MY HEART/LOVE'S COMING – USA-European Connection (Marlin)

GALAXY – War (MCA)

LET YOURSELF GO – T-Connection (TK)

LET'S ALL CHANT – Michael Zager Band (Private Stock)

RISKY CHANGES – Bionic Boogie (Polydor)

RUMOUR HAS IT/I LOVE YOU – Donna Summer (Casablanca)

SUPERNATURE/GIVE ME LOVE – Cerrone (Cotillion)

VOYAGE – Voyage (Marlin)

Quickly now, the other highlights of the week: **The Bombers** album, previously a Telson import, now available on West End, is one of the strongest disco albums to come out of Canada in some time. The sound is heavy-duty disco, mostly instrumental, with a synthesizer undertow and an energetic, Afro-Latin feel. A nearly 12-minute version of "The Mexican," **Babe Ruth's** unusual early disco classic, sets the tone here: quietly intense, atmospheric, spacey around the edges, gripping. But while that cut only really hits its stride after the vocals, the three cuts on the album's first side – especially "Dance, Dance, Dance" and "Don't Stop The Music" (both originals in spite of familiar titles) – are entirely on target. Exceptional... **Celi Bee's** new "Alternating Currents" album (APA, through TK) is her best so far, produced by **Pepe Luis Soto** in Puerto Rico and New York and combining his usual sharply-etched, ecstatic Latin-hustle sound with something more hard-edged this time. "Macho (A Real, Real One)," already released on a disco disc, is lyrically offensive and impossibly fast, but it does have a sexy vitality that's hard to resist. Even more exciting, though, are "Hold Your Horses, Babe" and "Comin' Up Strong" which prove Celi Bee can outdo **Andrea True** on her turf: zippy, driving sexsongs. The album's title track, "Alternating Currents," is more comfortable and laid-back; its breathy, jazzy feel makes it perhaps the most attractive number here. A glossy, entertaining album, and a significant step forward for both the producer and performer... "African Warrior" by **Soweto** (Atlantic/Cotillion disco disc) was discovered by Cotillion Records president **Henry Allen** on a trip to Johannesburg last year before it was banned by South African radio. A terrific, surprising record now available here in two parts (8:40 and 7:16), "African Warrior" sounds like **Cerrone** or **Giorgio** meets **Osibisa**. The pounding of the drums is both Eurodisco pump and African frantic and the blend of both styles is utterly hypnotic. Part I's pace is almost hysterically fast – it whips you along – then it breaks from a tough vocal into an incredibly incantory chant section that is at first measured and restrained but powerful, then gradually builds, breaks and doubles back several times. The song runs through several levels of intensity but keeps the heat on throughout. But it's the second part that is the knockout here: beginning with a synthesizer beat out of "I Feel Love," then dipping into the chant and percussion in ever-increasing waves of passion, this is the most compelling piece of African dance music we've heard in years. Very, very hot. ⊘

The only truly essential album this week is **Idris Muhammad's** "Boogie To The Top" on Kudu with an eleven-minute title track that has the same kind of depth, ecstatically optimistic spirit and slightly hushed chorus vocals that made "Could Heaven Ever Be Like This" so appealing. In many ways, this is "Heaven, Part 2," an extension and a refinement of the earlier style written and produced by **David Matthews** and **Tony Sarafino**. The lyrics are a hodgepodge of current catch phrases that link sex, dancing, drugs and a vague spirituality in an attempt to capture the general (un)consciousness of the dance floor, but several lines stand out – the repeated title, the call to "Pass it on, and on and on" or "Look up, look up, up, up/Look high, high, high to the sky" – and the result is compelling, nearly anthemic. The music blends pop disco (a la Bionic Boogie) with Latin-flavored jazz, easing into a comfortable pump established by Muhammad's drums but full of movement and surprise (like **Jeremy Steig's** lovely flute solo and **Hugh McCracken's** totally unexpected harmonica flourish). Vocals tie it all together nicely, leaving room for a series of breaks, each one a gem, that never let your interest lag. The album's other highlight is "One With A Star" (7:54) which varies the approach with a slightly European feel and achieves a beautifully complex instrumental texture. Sizzling, quick percussion breaks slide into shimmering vibes or rippling keyboard work and the male vocals are again breathlessly attractive. The cut resolves itself with a rush of horns and a final cascade of harps that fades as if carried off on a breeze. "Stick It In Your Face" takes Muhammad and company off in quite a different direction, with both vocals and music taking on a hard funk edge that feels almost vulgar after "Star"'s radiance but might attract dancers nonetheless. The title cut remains the knockout and should send the album on its way to the top very quickly.

one of the better rock-to-disco remakes to come along this year. Also listen to the album's "Space Love," which plays with the same idea as **Computer's** "Nobody Loves A Computer," and a fairly traditionalist version of **Steppenwolf's** powerhouse "Born To Be Wild." Rock left field possibility: "Surprise"... **The Originals** "Another Time, Another Place" album, their first since leaving Motown for Fantasy, is produced by **Freddie Gorman** and the group (the same combination that produced "Hurry Up And Wait" on their last lp) and contains two top-notch cuts: "Take This Love" (3:50), with a solid drive and some hot percussion effects; and "Don't Put Me On" (5:20), which has a mellower, wonderfully ingratiating pace and generous breaks. The vocals here are typically polished but both cuts, especially the former, would benefit from longer new mixes... **Webster Lewis'** "Touch My Love," from his new Epic album of the same name, is very loose and exhilarating in a distinctly **Earth, Wind & Fire** style with a thrusting funk edge. Also great: "There's A Happy Feeling" which is immensely attractive but slightly uneven for dancing until it settles into its final groove... The new **Trax** album, produced by **Pete Bellotte** and starring Bellotte and Munich superdrummer **Keith Forsey**, is so disconcertingly different from their previous release that it's hard to get a handle on at first. Versions of "Dancing In The Street" and "Never Been To Spain" don't interest me, but "Crusader:' a nearly five-minute percussion tour-de-force with chanting vocals, is terriffic Afro-rock and highly recommended. Also try "Do You Wanna Be A Star"... "Sweet Thunder" (5:12), by a fine new WMOT vocal group named **Sweet Thunder** (Fantasy), is a hard-pumping, oddly raw and most welcome departure from the Philly style with a tight little break toward the end to snap it together. The album's

> ❝ **Pete Bellotte doesn't see a real future for totally synthesized music. "I love the mini-Moogs," he says, "but not so much the programmed stuff;" besides, he adds, "it can cause headaches"** ❞

Choice cuts from other albums of interest: "You Really Got Me" (8:06), a hot version of the **Kinks** klassic by a Canadian group named **Eclipse** (on their debut Casablanca lp, "Night And Day"), is built around two breaks – one a wild, anything – goes percussion/sound effect explosion, the other more seriously electronic: throbbing jets of synthesized sound overlaid with "handclaps" sharp as gun shots – strong enough to sell the song on their own. Add rippling synthesizer throughout and hard-rock vocals in the same sexy style as the original and you've got

longest track, "Baby I Need Your Love Today" (8:52), is a gorgeous slow song that could also become a favorite... Frank Edwards, DJ at Washington's Fox Trappe, called my attention to an unusual cut on the new **Johnnie Taylor** album ("Ever Ready" on Columbia) – "Hey Mister Melody Maker," a heavily produced (by **Don Davis**) number with the kind of impressive, building intro that draws you into the song irresistibly. The rest lives up to the promise of this beginning and is so richly sung (by Taylor and a vibrant female chorus) and elegantly crafted that it feels a good deal

FLAMINGO, NEW YORK
DJ: Richie Rivera

CHILD OF THE WIND – Caesar Frazier (Westbound)
COME INTO MY HEART/LOVE'S COMING – USA-European Connection (Marlin)
COME ON DANCE, DANCE/DON'T/TOUCH ME ON MY HOT SPOT – Saturday Night Band (Prelude)
FROM EAST TO WEST/ LADY AMERICA/SCOTCH MACHINE/BAYOU VILLAGE – Voyage (Marlin)
GOT TO HAVE LOVING/STANDING IN THE RAIN/MIDNIGHT MADNESS – Don Ray (Malligator import)
MACHO MAN/KEY WEST – Village People (Casablanca)
NOBODY BUT YOU – Theo Vaness (CBS import)
RIO DE JANEIRO – Gary Criss (Salsoul)
ROUGH DIAMOND – Madleen Kane (Warner Bros.)
RUNAWAY LOVE/IF MY FRIENDS COULD SEE ME NOW – Linda Clifford (Curtom)

FOX TRAPPE, WASHINGTON, D.C.
DJ: Frank Edwards

BEYOND THE CLOUDS – Quartz (Vogue import)
COME ON DANCE, DANCE – Saturday Night Band (Prelude)
FREAK WITH ME – Universal Robot Band (Red Greg)
FROM EAST TO WEST/POINT ZERO/LADY AMERICA – Voyage (Marlin)
HOOPS (INSTRUMENTAL) – Jimmy Miller (Capitol)
LET'S GET TOGETHER – Detroit Emeralds (Westbound)
MUSIC, HARMONY AND RHYTHM/ STREET DANCE – Brooklyn Dreams (Millennium)
RUNAWAY LOVE/GYPSY LADY – Linda Clifford (Curtom)
WEST SIDE STORY – Salsoul Orchestra (Salsoul)
WON'T YOU TRY – Udell (Tom 'n' Jerry)

THE HUNT & THE CHASE, INDIANAPOLIS
DJ: Mark Hultmark

COME INTO MY HEART/LOVE'S COMING – USA-European Connection (Marlin)
COME ON DANCE, DANCE/TOUCH ME ON MY HOT SPOT – Saturday Night Band (Prelude)
HAVE A CIGAR – Rosebud (Flarenasch import)
I CAN'T STAND THE RAIN – Eruption (Ariola)
LET'S GET TOGETHER/TURN ON LADY – Detroit Emeralds (Westbound)
OH HAPPY DAY/GETTIN' THE SPIRIT – Roberta Kelly (Casablanca)
RIO DE JANEIRO – Gary Criss (Salsoul)
ROMEO & JULIET – Alec Costandinos (Casablanca)
RUNAWAY LOVE/GYPSY LADY/IF MY FRIENDS COULD SEE ME NOW – Linda Clifford (Curtom)
VOYAGE – Voyage (Marlin)

TRUDE HELLER'S, NEW YORK
DJ: Danny Krivit

BOOGIE TO THE TOP/ONE WITH A STAR – Idris Muhammad (Kudu)
COME INTO MY HEART/LOVE'S COMING – USA-European Connection (Marlin)
COME ON DANCE, DANCE/DON'T/TOUCH ME ON MY HOT SPOT – Saturday Night Band (Prelude)
GOT TO HAVE LOVING/STANDING IN THE RAIN/BODY AND SOUL/MIDNIGHT MADNESS – Don Ray (Malligator)
RIO DE JANEIRO – Gary Criss (Salsoul)
RUNAWAY LOVE/IF MY FRIENDS COULD SEE ME NOW/GYPSY LADY – Linda Clifford (Curtom)
STAR LOVE – 3 Ounces of Love (Motown)
TAKE ME, SHAKE ME, WAKE ME/LOVE IN A SLEEPER/ SPEND THE NIGHT WITH ME – Silver Convention (Midsong)
TILL YOU TAKE MY LOVE/PACK UP YOUR BAGS – Harvey Mason (Arista)
WE'RE ON OUR WAY HOME – Brainstorm (Tabu)

more than 3:54. Also: "Ever Ready," a superstud song with a clever brand-name battery metaphor, has a funk beat with **Bobby Womack** overtones and a constant Latin chop percussion; and "Keep On Dancing," basic disco funk, is also basic Johnnie Taylor get-down.

NEWS & NOTES: Both **Alec Costandinos** and **Pete Bellotte** were in town last week – one for interviews in connection with the release of his fourth American release this year, the new **Love and Kisses** album; the other for meetings with prospective buyers of a just completed project and coincidental with the release of his second **Trax** lp – so DISCO FILE took the opportunity to grill them about present activities and future plans. Costandinos, who composed the title theme for the 2-record "Thank God It's Friday" soundtrack (due out April 21), has three completed albums scheduled for release over the next few months: "The Hunchback Of Notre Dame," a dramatic concept album with the **Syncophonic Orchestra** much in the style of "Golden Tears," the debut of a new group called, for the moment, the **Lauriston Connection**, with an extended medley of "You've Lost That Loving Feeling" and "Unchained Melody;" and a disco medley of songs Costandinos wrote for European superstar **Demis Roussos**, part of which is already in release in Europe as a disco disc by the **Demis Collection**. By the end of the year, he hopes to have begun two major projects: the construction of his own 48-track studio in Paris and the first record of a projected 12-album interpretation of the "Arabian Nights" that he plans to spread out over two years. As if this weren't enough work, Costandinos is also composing the music for the American ad campaign of France's Perrier water. Bellotte reports that he and **Giorgio Moroder** are just putting the finishing touches on the next **Munich Machine** album, "A Whiter Shade Of Pale," and after Giorgio completes revisions on his own lp, their next major project is a live double album for **Donna Summer**, three sides of which will be recorded during her June concert appearance in L.A. with the remaining side new studio material. Although he was delighted with the successful impact of synthesizers on "I Feel Love" – a touch that he says was actually a last-minute addition to the track – Bellotte doesn't see a real future for totally synthesized music. "I love the mini-Moogs," he says, "but not so much the programmed stuff;" besides, he adds, "it can cause headaches"... **Madleen Kane's** "Rough Diamond" album is now available on Warner Brothers – minus, unfortunately, the leopard-skin and leather center spread. A **Jim Burgess** re-mix of the title track should follow on a disco disc shortly... **Grace Jones** has been in the studio with **Tom Moulton** recently and a single, her first new work since the end of last summer, is tentatively scheduled for late May with an album on Island to follow in June. In between her massive touring schedule, Grace has found time to write some new songs, a couple of which are planned for the lp which **John Davis** is arranging. ✇

This week's major release is, without a doubt, Casablanca's blockbuster "Thank God It's Friday" soundtrack, a "boxed" three-record set including 18 cuts by 14 acts on four long sides plus a "special bonus" disco disc filled to overflowing with **Donna Summer's** sultry, if excessively dreamy, 16-minute version of "Je T'Aime" – the same 12-inch that was almost released last September and whose advance promo copies became instant collector's items. Bound to be one of the most heavily-hyped disco releases this year (the promotional budget for the album alone is over $1 million), "TGIF" precedes the film by about a month and is clearly aimed at the enormous new audience for disco music created by the "Saturday Night Fever" set. And "TGIF," though lacking the sort of quick-energy single tracks the **Bee Gees** seem to produce so effortlessly, is much more representative of disco music right this minute than the "Saturday Night Fever" collection of oldies. With only two exceptions – **The Commodores'** "Too Hot Ta Trot" and **Cameo's** "Find My Way" – the material here is brand new and the package is a fine feast of music from some of the most innovative and influential producers and performers in the field.

The highlights: **Pattie Brooks'** sensational "After Dark" (7:55), produced by **Simon Soussan** and very reminiscent of this team's earlier "Girl Don't Make Me Wait" (including those introductory la-la-la-las) with a little "Black Is Black" thrown, in, but finally so strong on its own that you forgive the obvious echoes. Brooks' vocals, though occasionally strained, are marvellously loose and involving, a perfect match for Soussan's

pulsing arrangement which is built around the best and longest break on the album – a multi-level percussion spectacular that should easily turn this into one of the season's peak cuts. After the break, Pattie returns for some more ecstatic riffing until the final fade... Donna Summer's "Last Dance" (7:10), written by **Paul Jabara**, produced by **Giorgio Moroder** and **Bob Esty**, is absolutely wonderful pop disco: up, invigorating, thoroughly enjoyable. Its structure – a slow intro and a slow break toward the end of an otherwise upbeat song – demands special treatment on the dance floor, but Summer's rich vocals and the swirling-string arrangement are so effective that what could be merely an interesting experiment with disco format is instead a stunning surprise likely to be everyone's finale number for months to come... "You're The Most Precious Thing In My life" (8:02) by **Love and Kisses** is **Alec R. Costandinos** in top form, similar to "Romeo & Juliet" and the recent "How Much, How Much I Love You," but pared down and sharpened up nicely. The vocals, often ragged and rushed on that mouthful of a title, are oddly flawed, yet, as usual, the production sweeps things along swiftly and surely with some unexpected touches – like that first break, stranger and more outlandish than what we're used to from Costandinos with its nutsy jumble of percussion and stray guitar cries over a mechanical thump beat that eventually rises and supplants them. The jittery, accumulating string pattern that follows this break and later reappears sticks in the memory and clinches the song neatly. The other Costandinos composition, the film's title theme, also by Love and Kisses, sounds like a movement from "Romeo & Juliet" but is again weakened by its vocals, an unbalanced combination of thin individual voices and creamy chorus work. The production is generally rousing enough to carry things off, however, and this too grows on you... **Santa Esmeralda's** "Sevilla Nights" (6:08) is all instrumental and, happily, avoids nearly all the Spanish cliches and predictable changes that bogged down their last album. The result is cleaner, subtler, more forcefully atmospheric, with the flamenco guitar and castanets saved for bright flourishes rather than squandered throughout. Perfect... "Take It To The Zoo" (8:00) by **Sunshine** was written by **Donna Summer** and two members of **Brooklyn Dreams** and features Donna's sister, **Mary Ellen Gaines** in the lead. Gaines has a direct, almost declamatory voice that at times seems too unadorned (an in the unnerving "gotta get down" repetition) but, with support; strikes just the right attitude for this sharp pop/funk number full of vocal and instrumental builds. Really heats up toward the end... **Marathon's** "I Wanna Dance" (6:00), written and produced by **Pete Bellotte**, is perhaps the strangest piece of music here – a zippy pastiche of styles from

" Whew. Casablanca is not fooling around: "TGIF" is sure to be a monster "

PARADISE GARAGE, NEW YORK
DJ: Larry Levan

AT THE DISCOTHEQUE – Lipstique (Tom 'n' Jerry)
COME ON DANCE, DANCE – Saturday Night Band (Prelude)
**GYPSY LADY/IF MY FRIENDS COULD SEE ME NOW/
RUNAWAY LOVE/LOVE ARE, YOU ARE** – Linda Clifford
(Curtom)
HOLD YOUR HORSES, BABE – Celi Bee (APA)
IT'S SERIOUS – Cameo (Chocolate City)
**LADY AMERICA/FROM EAST TO WEST/ POINT ZERO/
LATIN ODYSSEY/ORIENT EXPRESS** – Voyage (Marlin)
LET YOURSELF GO – T-Connection (TK)
LET'S GET TOGETHER – Detroit Emeralds (Westbound)
**SPEND THE NIGHT WITH ME/LOVE IN A SLEEPER/
MISSION TO VENUS** – Silver Convention (Midsong)
TENA'S SONG – Foxy (Dash)

DCA CLUB, PHILADELPHIA
DJ: Kurt Borusiewicz

**AFTER DARK/THANK GOD IT'S FRIDAY/LAST DANCE/
YOU'RE THE MOST PRECIOUS THING IN MY LIFE**
– "Thank God It's Friday" Soundtrack (Casablanca)
COME INTO MY HEART/LOVE'S COMING
– USA-European Connection (Marlin)
DESPERATELY– Love Machine (Buddah)
GETTIN' THE SPIRIT – Roberta Kelly (Casablanca)
I CAN'T STAND THE RAIN – Eruption (Ariola)
IF MY FRIENDS COULD SEE ME NOW/RUNAWAY LOVE
– Linda Clifford (Curtom)
MACHO MAN – Village People (Casablanca)
RIO DE JANEIRO – Gary Criss (Salsoul)
ROMEO & JULIET – Alec Costandinos (Casablanca)
YOU ARE MY LOVE/PLAY WITH ME – Sandy Mercer (H&L)

TROCADERO TRANSFER, SAN FRANCISCO
DJ: Gary Tighe

AFRICAN WARRIOR (PART 2) – Soweto (Atlantic/Cotillion)
AT THE DISCOTHEQUE – Lipstique (Tom 'n' Jerry)
BLACK JACK – Baciotti (RCA)
COME INTO MY HEART/LOVE'S COMING
– USA-European Connection (Marlin)
COMIN' UP STRONG/MACHO – Celi Bee (APA)
COPACABANA – Barry Manilow (Arista)
NOBODY BUT YOU – Theo Vaness (CBS import)
ROUGH DIAMOND/TOUCH MY HEART – Madleen Kane
(Warner Bros.)
**SEVILLA NIGHTS/TAKE IT TO THE ZOO/LAST DANCE/
YOU'RE THE MOST PRECIOUS THING IN MY LIFE**
– "Thank God It's Friday" Soundtrack (Casablanca)
YOU REALLY GOT ME – Eclipse (Casablanca)

IPANEMA, NEW YORK
DJ: Ray Velazquez

BEYOND THE CLOUDS/QUARTZ – Quartz (Vogue import)
BOOGIE TO THE TOP – Idris Muhammad (Kudu)
COME INTO MY HEART/LOVE'S COMING – USA-European
Connection (Marlin)
COME ON DANCE, DANCE – Saturday Night Band (Prelude)
GET OFF/TENA'S SONG – Foxy (Dash)
GOT TO HAVE LOVING/STANDING IN THE RAIN
– Don Ray (Malligator import)
MACHO MAN/KEY WEST – Village People (Casablanca)
NEVER BEEN TO SPAIN/CRUSADER – Trax (Polydor)
**OH HAPPY DAY/TO MY FATHER'S HOUSE/MY SWEET
LORD** – Roberta Kelly (Casablanca)
RUNAWAY LOVE/GYPSY LADY – Linda Clifford (Curtom)

Bimbo Jet to Trax with 'sudden rushes of strings
and quick, sizzling percussion breaks that make for
an unsettling but exciting combination.

But wait, there's even more. Also recommended:
Donna Summer's "With Your Love," Paul Jabara's
"Queen Of the Disco," Diana Ross' "Livin', Lovin',
Givin' " and D.C. LaRue's great, super-sexy slow grind;
"Do You Want The Real Thing." Nearly all these tracks –
ten selections in all – will be available to disco DJs for
promotion only on a special set of disco discs running
an average length of eight minutes each and due in a
week or so. Whew. Casablanca is not fooling around:
"TGIF" is sure to be a monster. ✪

DISCO FILE TOP 20

1. **COME INTO MY HEART/LOVE'S COMING**
   – USA-European Connection (Marlin)
2. **RUNAWAY LOVE/IF MY FRIENDS COULD SEE
   ME NOW/GYPSY LADY** – Linda Clifford (Curtom)
3. **VOYAGE** – Voyage (Polydor import)
4. **COME ON DANCE, DANCE** – Saturday Night Band
   (Prelude)
5. **RIO DE JANEIRO** – Gary Criss (Salsoul)
6. **KEY WEST/MACHO MAN/I AM WHAT I AM**
   – Village People (Casablanca)
7. **ROMEO & JULIET** – Alec Costandinos
   (Casablanca)
8. **LET'S GET TOGETHER** – Detroit Emeralds
   (Westbound)
9. **OH HAPPY DAY/GETTIN' THE SPIRIT**
   – Roberta Kelly (Casablanca)
10. **YOU ARE MY LOVE/PLAY WITH ME**
    – Sandy Mercer (H&L)
11. **DANCE WITH ME** – Peter Brown (Drive)
12. **TOUCH ME ON MY HOT SPOT/DON'T**
    – Saturday Night Band (Prelude)
13. **LET YOURSELF GO** – T-Connection (TK)
14. **I CAN'T STAND THE RAIN** – Eruption (Ariola)
15. **RISKY CHANGES/DANCE LITTLE DREAMER**
    – Bionic Boogie (Polydor)
16. **GOT TO HAVE LOVING/STANDING IN THE RAIN**
    – Don Ray (Malligator)
17. **TENA'S SONG** – Foxy (Dash)
18. **ROUGH DIAMOND/FEVER/TOUCH MY HEART/
    LET'S MAKE LOVE** – Madleen Kane (CBS import)
19. **GALAXY** – War (MCA)
20. **WEST SIDE STORY** – Salsoul Orchestra (Salsoul)

Catching up on the recent crop of disco dish, here's a checklist of the most essential ones right this moment: Two of the best are longer versions of records already praised in this space – **Deodato's** "Whistle Bump" (Warner Brothers) and **Rick James'** "You and I" (Gordy). Jimmy Simpson has remixed "Whistle Bump" to nearly twice its album length (it's now 7:42), bringing up and extending slightly the drum and tambourine intro; sprucing up the track so everything sounds brighter, fresher and filling in with new guitar, flute and whistle parts that are both lovely and lively. The result is a vibrant and witty piece of disco jazz that should be the perfect instrumental refreshment for the spring season. The Rick James song, now 8:04 and available as a track on his just-released "Come Get It!" album as well as a non-commercial 12-inch, already had knockout impact as a 45 but the full version is stunning: aggressive rock-based funk with the sort of pumping drive that shakes foundations. The first segment here remains virtually unchanged (though it would probably work better if the first ten seconds were dropped) but the new second half is quite a switch, falling into a **Parliament/Funkadelic** groove glittering with horns, guitars, chanted vocals. Real hot and a must for funk fans... Producers **Michael Lewis** and **Laurin Rinder** continue to surprise us with their diversity – latest example: their new project on AVI, "Come On Down, Boogie People" by a session musician they discovered named **David Williams**. Featuring tough, rough-textured vocals by **Dee Ervin**, "Boogie People" (7:37) is a new direction for Lewis and Rinder, starting off as uncomplicated disco funk – somewhere between **Marvin Gaye** and TK – but turning kind of jazzy, touching on some **Bobby Womack**-style scatting, rich veins of horns, an undertow of strings, fabulous guitar (by Williams, I believe) – all cut with a razor edge. Earthier than "Cocomotion" or "Le Spank" but retaining that same sure sense of what makes a dance record click, "Boogie People" gradually wraps you up and carries you off. Excellent... Judy Weinstein of New York's For the Record pool reports a lot of her member DJs have been raving about **A Taste of Honey's** "Boogie Oogie Oogie" (Capitol) and, while the charm of the single eluded me, a disco disc (5:37) is out now that has proven to be utterly irresistible. A female duo produced by pop-jazz masters **Fonce** and **Larry Mizell**, A Taste of Honey calls on everyone to "boogie 'till you can't boogie no more" in timelessly sexy voices over a cute, snappy arrangement based on guitars and crackling hand-claps. Nothing spectacular here, perhaps, but the record's very unpretentiousness is a delight in itself; sure to grow on you... Also entertaining is **Barry Manilow's** "Copacabana (At the Copa)" which Arista has issued in a longer disco disc format. A tragicomedy in three verses set in the famous Manhattan nightclub where "music and passion were always the fashion," the story of Lola, Tony and Rico sounds like a perfect plot for a glitzy '40s musical with a modern tag line. Manilo and Ron Dante have whipped up just the right arrangement, flirting with camp but easing out of it before it gets too sticky, gliding through on an ornate Latin-styled big band sound – a hustle with a swing flourish – that sweeps into a highly theatrical break and breaks down again with some tight percussion. Wonderfully balanced and fun... Detroit's **Mike Theodore** produced **Caesar Frazier's** "Child Of The Wind" (7:33; on Westbound) somewhat more expansively than most of his own work and the result is a little uneven but often exciting. I particularly like the contrast set up between the sweet, polished female chorus, sometimes speaking for the elusive "child" of the title, and Frazier's deep, aching, slightly husky lead vocals. The prime break comes late in the track – percolating with subtle synthesizer bleeps and swept by gusts of violins, it ends too soon – but the overall feel of the song is rich and rather involving. "Song Of The Wind," the 7:10 instrumental version on the other side, is also effective and the changes stand out in higher relief here, but without the vocals it feels somehow aimless. Left field, maybe, but very interesting... Eve more unusual is the **Simbora Orchestra's** two-sided Atlantic disc: "Brazuca" (7:46), oddly fragmented but fascinating, goes from chica-boom Latino to ooo-wa, ooo-wa disco chanting to flashy, at times cliched, Brazilian material with chunks of **Bimbo Jet** and **Samba Soul** thrown in – a wild percussion break makes it; and "Simbora" (5:05), which has a similar anything-goes construction but the changes aren't quite as outrageous here and the beat is even more frantic so one is neither as dazzled nor as indulgent with it. Try "Brazuka" when the crowd is crazed – they deserve it.

ADDENDA: Footnotes to last week's review of the "Thank God It's Friday" Soundtrack: I believe this album sets a precedent as the first lp release from a major label to indicate each cut's beats-per-minute (as in BPM 128) along with its credits, apparently as an aid

> **❝ I believe this album is the first lp release from a major label to indicate each cut's beats-per-minute along with its credits, as an aid to DJs making a compatible beat-pattern blend ❞**

SAHARA, NEW YORK
DJ Sharon White

COME ON DANCE, DANCE/TOUCH ME ON MY HOT SPOT
– Saturday Night Band (Prelude)
CRUSADER – Trax (Polydor)
GOT TO HAVE LOVING/STANDING IN THE RAIN/BODY AND SOUL/MIDNIGHT MADNESS – Don Ray (Malligator)
HOW MUCH, HOW MUCH I LOVE YOU/ BEAUTY AND THE BEAST – Love & Kisses (Casablanca)
IF MY FRIENDS COULD SEE ME NOW/RUNAWAY LOVE – Linda Clifford (Curtom)
LAST DANCE/AFTER DARK/SEVILLA NIGHTS – "Thank God It's Friday" Soundtrack (Casablanca)
LOVE IN A SLEEPER/SPEND THE NIGHT WITH ME/MISSION TO VENUS – Silver Convention (Midsong)
OH HAPPY DAY/MY SWEET LORD/GETTIN' THE SPIRIT – Roberta Kelly (Casablanca)
RIO DE JANEIRO – Gary Criss (Salsoul)
YOU REALLY GOT ME – Eclipse (Casablanca)

THE BROADWAY, DENVER
DJ: Rob Parson

AT THE DISCOTHEQUE – Lipstique (Tom 'n' Jerry)
COME ON DANCE, DANCE/TOUCH ME ON MY HOT SPOT – Saturday Night Band (Prelude)
COME INTO MY HEART/LOVE'S COMING – USA-European Connection (Marlin)
FROM EAST TO WEST/LADY AMERICA/POINT ZERO/LATIN ODYSSEY – Voyage (Marlin)
GOT TO HAVE LOVING/STANDING IN THE RAIN – Don Ray (Malligator import)
HOW MUCH, HOW MUCH I LOVE YOU/BEAUTY AND THE BEAST – Love & Kisses (Casablanca)
RUNAWAY LOVE/GYPSY LADY – Linda Clifford (Curtom)
TAKE IT TO THE ZOO/AFTER DARK/TGIF/WITH YOUR LOVE/ SEVILLA NIGHTS – "Thank God It's Friday" Soundtrack (Casablanca)
TENA'S SONG/GET OFF – Foxy (Dash)
YOU REALLY GOT ME – Eclipse (Casablanca)

STUDIO ONE, LOS ANGELES
DJ: Manny Slali

AT THE DISCOTHEQUE/MAH-NAH-MAH-NAH – Lipstique (Tom 'n' Jerry)
COME ON DANCE, DANCE/TOUCH ME ON MY HOT SPOT – Saturday Night Band (Prelude)
GOT TO HAVE LOVING/STANDING IN THE RAIN/BODY AND SOUL/MIDNIGHT MADNESS/GARDEN OF LOVE – Don Ray (Malligator import)
HOW MUCH, HOW MUCH I LOVE YOU/ BEAUTY AND THE BEAST – Love & Kisses (Casablanca)
LAST DANCE/TAKE IT TO THE ZOO/TGIF/ WITH YOUR LOVE – "Thank God It's Friday" Soundtrack (Casablanca)
OH HAPPY DAY/TO MY FATHER'S HOUSE/GETTIN' THE SPIRIT – Roberta Kelly (Casablanca)
RIO DE JANEIRO – Gary Criss (Salsoul)
RUNAWAY LOVE/IF MY FRIENDS COULD SEE ME NOW/ GYPSY LADY/YOU ARE, YOU ARE – Linda Clifford (Curtom)
VOYAGE – Voyage (Marlin)
YOU AND I – Rick James (Motown)

to DJs seeking to make a compatible beat-pattern blend. I know that Tom Lewis, an upstate New York DJ, has compiled – and continually supplements – an extensive "Disco Bible" of computer print-out beats-per-minute listings that makes a valuable reference work, but I've always wondered just how useful this information was to most DJs. I'd like to hear opinions pro and con on BPM notations from any DJ who wants to take the time to drop DISCO FILE a line... The list of songs from "TGIF" slated for disco disc treatment shortly: **Pattie Brooks'** "After Dark," "Last Dance" and "With Your Love" by **Donna Summer**, "TGIF" and "You're The Most Precious Thing In My Life" by **Love and Kisses**, **Sunshine's** "Take It To The Zoo," **Marathon's** "I Wanna Dance," **Cameo's** "Find My Way," **Paul Jabara's** "Disco Queen" and "Do You Want The Real Thing" by **D.C. LaRue** – all ten averaging about eight minutes each save for LaRue's which runs 12:15... Not surprisingly, seven tracks from the "TGIF" set entered the DISCO FILE chart at number ten this week... On other matters, these records are also looking good: **Idris Muhammad's** "Boogie to the Top," the **Bombers** album, **Baciotti's** "Black Jack," **Lewis & Rinder's** "Seven Deadly Sins," the **Michael Zager Band's** "Music Fever," "Gotta Get Out Of Here," by **Lucy Hawkins** and "You Really Got Me" by **Eclipse**. ✪

"confessions" of others and follows with the tender (but slightly mocking) assurance that "It's all right you know/my shoulder is always here/I just hope that you know/I am a sympathetic ear." "Anything, Anything," the back-up girls (including **Pattie Brooks**) whisper, inviting further indiscretions and D.C., in his little-boy-lost-voice, ends on an emotional note – part grasping, part resigned – begging, "Tell me everything before you go." "I Wake Up Screaming" picks up on that note and gets pretty overwrought on the subject of sleeping alone but with just enough concrete (and comic) details to ground it in real feeling and keep it from slipping into the pathetic (the song's spoken introduction falls over that particular edge, however; emotion has a dangerous tendency to turn into self-parody when taken too seriously but La Rue is smart enough to keep things ironic if not cool). The side, a continuous medley with a gradually building pace, finishes with "Let Them Dance," the most characteristic D.C. LaRue cut and the most abandoned, just-fun song here, commenting on people as they whirl past, scattering gossip and fragmented conversation on a nervous, energizing synthesizer track. This and "Dancing with Strangers" (6:00) which opens up the other side are the two most upbeat, consistently danceable cuts and both evoke the ambiance of the dancefloor as accurately and richly as short stories. "Dancing With Strangers," whose key line is a fine shock of recognition: "Well, it looks like I'm dancing with strangers/but it feels like I'm dancing with you babe," is a perfect series of images and emotions caught in a disco rush "in the heat and the dark night/through the smoke and the black light." **Bob Esty's** production throughout is invigorating and involving, wonderfully matched to LaRue's moods and full of gemlike breaks; he makes up for any hesitancy and weakness in the vocals by throwing everything into D.C.'s support and letting him ride the productions in an effortless zoom. Also recommended: "Pounding With Desire." All together, LaRue's best so far – his most charming and intelligent – and Esty's first real showcase on his own. Only one complaint: Why is there no lyric sheet?

Other recent albums of interest: **Silver Convention's** "Love In A Sleeper" (Midsong), their first album recorded largely outside of Germany, brought producer **Michael Kunze** (minus **Silvester Levay**) to Philadelphia's Sigma Sound Studios to work with arranger **John Davis** in an attempt to breathe new life into the group's increasingly moribund sound. The result may be their most attractive album in years, but the make-over's merely a quick face-lift, not the total transformation the group needs so badly. The album's whole first side – especially "Spend The Night With Me," "Mission To Venus" and the title track – is pleasant if unexceptional; the strings are still an unmistakable signature but the lead vocals sometimes turn hard and shrill around the edges and the combination is too sour and sweet for my taste. A promotional 12-inch is also available with "Spend The Night" running 9:27 and "Mission To Venus" 8:45 –

"Confessions," the new **D. C. LaRue** album (his first for Casablanca), is as gloriously melodramatic and relentlessly clever as **Donna Summer's** "Once Upon a Time... ," but instead of seeing life as a fairly tale come true, LaRue creates a modern love comic (the titles: "I'll Wake Up Screaming In The Middle Of The Night," "Pounding With Desire," "Dancing With Strangers") in which he is alternately the amused, detached observer and the passionate, anguished, neurotic central character. "Confessions" (6:53), the opening cut, sets the tone and pace: after a grandiose, dramatically overstated intro of thumping synthesizer, crashing percussion and elegantly-crafted strings – the sort of thing that might be appropriate for a wind-swept confrontation scene between two lovers in a Hollywood gothic movie – LaRue repeats the intimate (but hardly titillating)

BUZZBY'S, SAN FRANCISCO
DJ: Michael Lee

COME ON DANCE, DANCE/TOUCH ME ON MY HOT SPOT
– Saturday Night Band (Prelude)
GET OFF/TENA'S SONG – Foxy (Dash)
GOT TO HAVE LOVING/STANDING IN THE RAIN
– Don Ray (Malligator import)
I BELIEVE IT/UNTIL WE LEARN – Lois Snead (Spire)
**LAST DANCE/TAKE IT TO THE ZOO/AFTER DARK/
SEVILLA NIGHTS/WITH YOUR LOVE/TGIF**
– "TGIF" Soundtrack (Casablanca)
MISSION TO VENUS/SPEND THE NIGHT WITH ME
– Silver Convention (Midsong)
NOBODY BUT YOU – Theo Vaness (CBS import)
ROUGH DIAMOND/TOUCH MY HEART – Madleen Kane
(Warner Bros.)
WHISTLE BUMP – Deodato – (Warner Bros.)
YOU REALLY GOT ME – Eclipse (Casablanca)

NEW YORK, NEW YORK, NEW YORK
DJ: François Kevorkian

**AFTER DARK/LAST DANCE/TAKE IT TO THE ZOO/WITH
YOUR LOVE/TGIF/ SEVILLA NIGHTS/DISCO QUEEN**
– "TGIF" Soundtrack (Casablanca)
**COME ON DANCE, DANCE/TOUCH ME ON MY HOT
SPOT/DON'T** – Saturday Night Band (Prelude)
**DANCING WITH STRANGERS/CONFESSIONS/I WAKE UP
SCREAMING/LET THEM DANCE** – D.C. LaRue (Casablanca)
**GOT TO HAVE LOVING/STANDING IN THE RAIN/BODY AND
SOUL/GARDEN OF LOVE** – Don Ray (Malligator import)
**HOW MUCH, HOW MUCH I LOVE YOU/ BEAUTY AND THE
BEAST** – Love & Kisses (Casablanca)
LET YOURSELF GO – T-Connection (TK)
MUSIC FEVER/FREAK/LET'S ALL CHANT
– Michael Zager Band (Private Stock)
ROUGH DIAMOND/TOUCH MY HEART – Madleen Kane
(Warner Bros.)
**RUNAWAY LOVE/IF MY FRIENDS COULD SEE ME
NOW/GYPSY LADY**– Linda Clifford (Curtom)
TWO DOORS DOWN – Joe Thomas (TK)

1270, BOSTON
DJ: Danae Jacovidis

**AFTER DARK/LAST DANCE/LIVIN', LOVIN',
GIVIN'/SEVILLA NIGHTS** – "TGIF" Soundtrack
(Casablanca)
BACK TO MUSIC – Theo Vaness (CBS import)
BRING ON THE LOVE – Gloria Jones (Capitol)
COME INTO MY HEART/LOVE'S COMING
– USA-European Connection (Marlin)
COPACABANA – Barry Manilow (Arista)
GOT TO HAVE LOVING/STANDING IN THE RAIN
– Don Ray (Malligator import)
GRAND TOUR/FLIGHT TO VERSAILLES – Grand Tour
(Butterfly)
**IF MY FRIENDS COULD SEE ME NOW/ GYPSY
LADY/RUNAWAY LOVE** – Linda Clifford (Curtom)
LET'S MAKE LOVE/TOUCH MY HEART/ROUGH DIAMOND
– Madleen Kane (Warner Bros.)
RIO DE JANEIRO – Gary Criss (Salsoul)

nearly OD lengths, but some of the gimmicks added in the new mixes are worth it… **Gloria Gaynor** is another performer in search of a revitalizing style but she, too, stops just short of truly getting over on her "Park Avenue Sound" album on Polydor. Produced almost entirely by **Ron Tyson**, **Alan Felder** and **Norman Harris** (who call themselves TAN Productions) with a lot of the Sigma Sound standbys in full support (including luscious backups by the **Sweethearts of Sigma**), the record sounds bright, tight but somehow dated. At its best, it's extremely reminiscent of **First Choice** and certain mid-tempo **Trammps** stuff and if "This Love Affair" and "Kidnapped" sound like retreaded classics for this reason, that may be just what many people want. But it's not enough here and Gaynor never quite makes that leap into raw excitement we know she's capable of. Still, she has her moments, mostly toward the ends of several cuts and the two already mentioned plus a nice version of "You're All I Need To Get By" are recommended. A disco disc is available here, too, but, reportedly at Gaynor's request, the four cuts included

❝ That leap into raw excitement we know she's capable of ❞

were not expanded (three were, in fact, clipped by a few seconds), only sharpened up; "Kidnapped" is not among them… **Lipstique's** "At The Discotheque" (Tom n' Jerry) was produced by **Jurgen Korduletsch** and remixed for American consumption by **Tom Moulton** so it's no surprise that it has a lot in common with **Claudja Barry's** work. Without Barry to add zip, however, the productions occasionally go limp and the singers here are rarely forceful enough to get them up again. But much of the album's 17:20 title medley is sprightly and fun – particularly the instrumental breaks in the center and the final section, "I'm Still Dancing" – and if it doesn't work in its entirety, individual parts are well worth salvaging. "At The Discotheque" is already in its second week on our chart (#16) and the album's other three cuts are also getting sporadic mention, with the "Venus"/"Light My Fire" medley leading; also featured: a disco version of the Muppets song, "Mah-Nah-Mah-Nah"… "Dance Across The Floor," the new **Jimmy "Bo" Horne** album (Sunshine Sound), contains "Get Happy," a somewhat reworked "Gimme Some," and the promised longer version of the title song which turns out to be quite awkwardly pasted together – the track fades to an end just as the single does, then suddenly begins again from the beginning without any vocals and ends with a new chanted chorus. Weird, but if you're a fan of the hard-core Miami/KC sound, this is definitely it; **Casey & Finch** wrote and produced everything on the record. ◙

One of the most interesting recent disco discs is **Passport's** "Loco-Motive" (Atlantic), an expanded (to 6:33), substantially re-mixed (by **Issy Sanchez**) version of an instrumental on this progressive/electronic German group's latest album, "Sky Blue." "Loco-motive" is a stylized, comfortably streamlined train ride with much of the drive provided by synthesizers (most at the hands of producer/composer **Klaus Doldinger**), but this is a far cry from the chilly austerity of **Kraftwerk's** "Trans-Europe Express." Though both groups explore the exhilaration of travel, Passport's sound is denser, more vibrant and, since it includes a regular rhythm section, more jazzy, though hardly in a traditional manner; their approach is less intense, less machine-obsessed than Kraftwerk's and more lyrical. (In fact, their style here is closer to **Don Ray's** on "Standing In The Rain" or parts of "Supernature.") What gives the track its particular fascination is an intermittent punc-tuation of percussive pops and plaintive noises – something between morse-code signals and bird cries – from the electronic keyboard, both nearly buried in the original mix but pulled out front by Sanchez. A searing sax solo by Doldinger near the end also brightens things up considerably. Most of the group's album is on the jazzy side, but the title cut, "Sky Blue" (4:35), is also of interest to DJs with a progressive bent; though not as tightly-paced as "Loco-motive," the feeling here is ideal for a richly atmospheric set.

" Kraftwerk remains in the electronic avant-garde, with an irresistible, hypnotic feel, a deeply pulsing electronic coil of sound that lulls you and sucks you in almost against your will "

In the more strictly synthesized vein, there's the new album froM **Kraftwerk**, "The Man Machine" (Capitol), which is less severely minimal than their last release and somewhat more intentionally danceable. Several cuts have an irresistible, hypnotic feel, wrapping the listener in a deeply pulsing electronic coil of sound that lulls you and sucks you in almost against your will. The beat is steady, mechanical, haunting; but the embellishments here are more delicate and dreamy (especially on the lovely "Neon Lights," the longest cut at 9:03) than on much of "Trans-Europe" and it's this slight soft focus that makes the new material more appealing. Still, the effect is not quite as riveting as it was last time out, perhaps because we've been so thoroughly steeped in the synthesizer sound since that time, perhaps because the stark forward thrust of "Trans-Europe" is missing. No matter, Kraftwerk remains in the electronic avant-garde and these cuts are recommended: "Neon Lights," "Spacelab" and "Metropolis." The **McLane Explosion's** "Pulstar" album (Tom n' Jerry) is also totally synthesized with the exception of additional percussion added in the mix by **Tom Moulton** and the result sounds – much like a **Space** album. Included are four tracks: **Jean Michel Jarre's** "Oxygene" with the pace kicked up some; "Accidental Lover" from the first **Love & Kisses** album turned into an instrumental with minimal vocals from **Ingram**, **Benton & Benson**, the Sweethearts of Sigma (Sound); **Vangelis'** title track; and yet another version of "Magic Fly," certainly a redundant choice. With the possible exception of "Accidental Lover," which works more efficiently here than it did originally, little fresh insight is offered and no new ground broken. But "Accidental Lover" is worth it if only for the breaks and "Pulstar" is decent filler. Collectors' note: A limited edition on blue vinyl was pressed up by the Canadian manufacturer and may still be available as an import item; the American pressings are basic black.

RECOMMENDED DISCO DISCS: **Demis Roussos**, the international star who's attempting once again to break into the American market, should make a solid impression on the disco crowd with "L.O.V.E. Got A Hold On Me," a ten-minute version of the strongest cut from his first Mercury album. **Freddie Perren** produced, so the sound is sharp, pop-flavored disco with rousing vocals, sexy choruses and swirling breaks. A trifle over-long, perhaps, but it grows on you... "I'm Glad You're Mine," the first release by a young Chicago group on AVI, is another record that sounds better with every new listening. Their style is smooth but funky, close to **AWB's** with light vocals and several jumping breaks that neatly clinch the track. The disco mix is by former New York and Chicago DJ Rick Gianatos and runs a perfect eight minutes. Also check out the pretty ballad on the flip side, "Starchild"... "Mellow Lovin' " by **Judy Cheeks** (5:14 on Salsoul) was produced by **Anthony Monn** (Amanda Lear) in a high-spirited style that sounds like a frantic mix of **Donna Summer** and **Santa Esmeralda** – a little busy but full of punch and sparked by Cheeks' stirring vocals as she pleads with someone – anyone – for "some mellow lovin'."

LOST AND FOUND, WASHINGTON, D.C.
DJ: Bill Owens

AFTER DARK/SEVILLA NIGHTS/LAST DANCE/WITH YOUR LOVE – "TGIF" Soundtrack (Casablanca)
BOOGIE OOGIE OOGIE – A Taste of Honey (Capitol)
FLIGHT TO VERSAILLES – Grand Tour (Butterfly)
LET YOURSELF GO – T-Connection (TK)
NOBODY BUT YOU/BACK TO MUSIC – Theo Vaness (CBS)
OH HAPPY DAY/GETTIN' THE SPIRIT – Roberta Kelly (Casablanca)
ROUGH DIAMOND – Madleen Kane (Warner Bros.)
RUNAWAY LOVE/IF MY FRIENDS COULD SEE ME NOW/GYPSY LADY – Linda Clifford (Curtom)
STANDING IN THE RAIN/GOT TO HAVE LOVING – Don Ray (Malligator import)
WAR DANCE – Kebekelektrik (Tom n' Jerry)

59 FIFTH, NEW YORK
DJ: Tony Carrasco

AFTER DARK/TGIF/LAST DANCE/TAKE IT TO THE ZOO – "TGIF" Soundtrack (Casablanca)
BOOGIE DOWN AND MESS AROUND/ MOVE YOUR ASS GRINGO/I LOVE TO SEE YA DANCIN' – Blackwell (Butterfly)
BOOGIE TO THE TOP – Idris Muhammad (Kudu)
COME INTO MY HEART/LOVE'S COMING – USA-European Connection (Marlin)
COME ON DANCE, DANCE/DON'T TOUCH ME ON MY HOT SPOT – Saturday Night Band (Prelude)
COME ON DOWN BOOGIE PEOPLE – David Williams (AVI)
HOW MUCH, HOW MUCH I LOVE YOU/BEAUTY AND THE BEAST – Love & Kisses (Casablanca)
MUSIC FEVER/FREAK/LET'S ALL CHANT – Michael Zager Band (Private Stock)
ROUGH DIAMOND/TOUCH MY HEART – Madleen Kane (Warner Bros.)
YOU AND I – Rick James (Gordy)

HARRAH, NEW YORK
DJ: Wayne Scott

BOOGIE OOGIE OOGIE – A Taste of Honey (Capitol)
COME INTO MY HEART – USA-European Connection (Marlin)
COME ON DANCE, DANCE – Saturday Night Band (Prelude)
COME ON DOWN BOOGIE PEOPLE – David Williams (AVI)
GETTIN' THE SPIRIT – Roberta Kelly (Casablanca)
GOT TO HAVE LOVING/GARDEN OF LOVE – Don Ray (Malligator import)
HOLD YOUR HORSES BABE/COMING UP STRONG – Celi Bee (APA)
IF MY FRIENDS COULD SEE ME NOW/RUNAWAY LOVE/GYPSY LADY – Linda Clifford (Curtom)
LAST DANCE/AFTER DARK/TAKE IT TO THE ZOO – "TGIF" Soundtrack (Casablanca)
ROUGH DIAMOND/TOUCH MY HEART – Madleen Kane (Warner Bros.)

LIMELIGHT, HALLANDALE, FLORIDA
DJ: Bob Lombardi

COME INTO MY HEART/LOVE'S COMING – USA-European Connection (Marlin)
COME ON DANCE, DANCE – Saturday Night Band (Prelude)
COPACABANA – Barry Manilow (Arista)
DANCE WITH ME – Peter Brown (TK)
GARDEN OF LOVE – Don Ray (Malligator import)
HOW MUCH, HOW MUCH I LOVE YOU – Love & Kisses (Casablanca)
IF MY FRIENDS COULD SEE ME NOW/GYPSY LADY/RUNAWAY LOVE – Linda Clifford (Curtom)
MACHO MAN/I AM WHAT I AM/ KEY WEST – Village People (Casablanca)
ROUGH DIAMOND – Madleen Kane (Warner Bros.)
THIS LOVE AFFAIR – Gloria Gaynor (Polydor)

Here, too, the slower B side, "Darling, That's Me," is also excellent... **Deborah Washington's** debut on Ariola, "Ready Or Not" (4:42), sounds like it could be the new Diana Ross record – the voice, the nuances, and the style are nearly identical on large portions of the song and this similarity should pull an immediate reaction. Happily, there's a lot more going on here than imitation, and the sweetly snappy production, restrained at first but gradually breaking loose, ties things up nicely. Real cute and definitely deserving of a longer mix... I neglected to mention that the flip side of **A Taste of Honey's** delicious "Boogie Oogie Oogie," recently raved over in this space, is also attractive. As with a number of Capitol disco discs, this side is by another performer, **Gloria Jones,** whose "Bring On The Love (Why Can't We Be Friends Again)" (7:07) was recorded in England. The style is relaxed, naggingly familiar (what other record does this sound like?) but totally enjoyable; may be too slow for some tastes, but Danae Jacovidis from Boston's 1270 says his crowd can't get enough of it. See what you think.

NOW AVAILABLE ON DISCO DISCS: **Madleen Kane's** "Rough Diamond" (Warner Brothers) in a spruced-up, more aggressive new mix by **Jim Burgess** with an elegant, shimmering new break after the first verse and an extended, brilliantly clarified closing section crackling with castanets and handclaps and even more reminiscent of **Santa Esmeralda** than before; the new total length is 8:20, about two minutes longer than the album track, and the original version of "Touch My Heart" is on the reverse side... Both "Come Into My Heart/Good Loving" and "Love's Coming/Baby Love" by **USA-European Connection** which, in a reversal of standard operating procedure, TK has decided to make available in edited form (6:15 and 5:59, respectively) for those who are either overwhelmed or intimidated by the full lp versions... and **Raydio's** tasty "Get Down" backed by "Is This A Love Thing," both in their album versions (on Arista).

NEWS & NOTES: The **Don Ray** "Garden Of Love" album – already one of the best-received imports of the year and a personal favorite – is out now on Polydor after having been remastered in the U.S.... Two other recent import successes have been signed to American label and should be released before the end of the month: **Quartz** to TK and **Theo Vaness** to Prelude... On the **Grace Jones** front: a new single, "Do Or Die," is promised within two weeks, to be followed sometime in June by an album for Island titled "Fame" containing a French version of "Autumn Leaves" done in the style of "La Vie en Rose" (which has enjoyed phenomenal success in Europe) and a Jones original named, teasingly, "Below The Belt." ✪

MAY 27, 1978

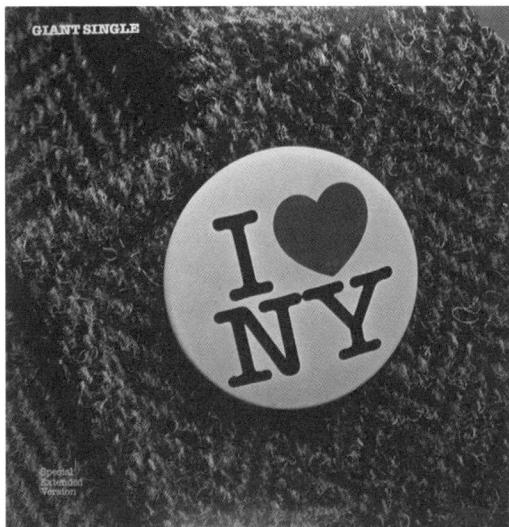

Am I just being cranky or are most of the new releases this week as depressing as the weather in New York? Returning from ten days in Fort Lauderdale to find Spring still on hold has put me in a decidedly unreceptive mood, but a few records have managed to break through and one, **Patrick Juvet's** "Got A Feeling" album, is worth raving about. Juvet, a young French pop star whose previous album – "Paris By Night" produced by **Jean-Michel Jarre** – had some success as an import last year, has teamed up with **Jacques Morali** for his first American release on Casablanca. The combination is perfect: Juvet's songs (all but one co-written with Morali and **Village People** lead **Victor Willis**) and his falsetto-edged tenor (which, when multi-tracked and echoed, bears a strong resemblance to the **Bee Gees**) have inspired Morali's most entertaining and delightful production in some time. The showpiece of the album is "I Love America" (at 13:55 the only track on side two), an affectionate tribute to this country's music from funk to country and western to rock & roll. There's a touching naivete to the song's view of America ("magic fills the air/there's music everywhere") that would not be quite as acceptable coming from a native (where it would read

as simple chauvinism), but in Juvet's very slight French accent it's quite charming. As the song ticks off various elements of America's musical melting pot, there are short interludes in each style, the snappiest being funk and salsa, and this clever, neatly-structured blend of diverse sounds brings to mind the **Voyage** album – there's a smoothness and spirit here that sets it far apart from earlier Morali song collages like "Best Disco In Town" and "Disco-mania" that lacked the genuinely anthemic qualities of "America." The repeated "I Love America" refrain that holds the song together is haunting, almost overwhelmingly sweet: swept with strings in the Philadelphia style, it's the perfect foil for Juvet's voice and the various breaks – even the "rock & roll" segment near the end (a hard guitar and drums riff that sounds "live") meshes beautifully into this lovely pattern. In the end, the entire piece may be a little long and certain changes lag a bit, but "I Love America" feels so good it should prove irresistible everywhere. "Got A Feeling," which opens up the album, has more of a bright pop feel with a kicked-up production pace and a driving optimism to the vocals as Juvet kisses off an old romance ("got a feeling I won't be needing you") and moves on to something better. Though it's only 3:30, this cut is getting nearly as good first-impression reaction from deejays as "America." Also very strong: "Where Is My Woman" (6:58), a revamped version of "Où Sont Les Femmes,"

> **There's a touching naivete to its view of America ("magic fills the air/there's music everywhere") that would not be quite as acceptable from a native**

INFINITY, NEW YORK
DJ: Jim Burgess

AFTER DARK/LAST DANCE/TGIF/TAKE IT TO THE ZOO – "TGIF" Soundtrack (Casablanca)
COME INTO MY HEART/LOVE'S COMING – USA-European Connection (Marlin)
COME ON DANCE, DANCE – Saturday Night Band (Prelude)
GOT TO HAVE LOVING/BODY AND SOUL/GARDEN OF LOVE – Don Ray (Polydor)
I LOVE AMERICA – Patrick Juvet (Casablanca)
LET YOURSELF GO – T-Connection (TK)
MACHO MAN – Village People (Casablanca)
ROUGH DIAMOND – Madleen Kane (Warner Bros.)
RUNAWAY LOVE/IF MY FRIENDS COULD SEE ME NOW – Linda Clifford (Curtom)
STAR LOVE/BET YOU'LL COME RUNNING – 3 Ounces of Love (Motown)

MARQUEE, NEW YORK
DJ: Tony Smith

AFTER DARK/LAST NIGHT/SEVILLA NIGHTS/TAKE IT TO THE ZOO – "TGIF" Soundtrack (Casablanca lp cuts)
BOOGIE OOGIE OOGIE – A Taste of Honey (Capitol)
LAW AND ORDER – Love Committee (Gold Mind)
L.O.V.E. GOT A HOLD OF ME – Demis Roussos (Mercury)
READY OR NOT – Deborah Washington (Ariola)
SPEND THE NIGHT WITH ME – Silver Convention (Midsong)
STANDING IN THE RAIN/GOT TO HAVE LOVING/MY DESIRE – Don Ray (Polydor)
TWO DOORS DOWN – Joe Thomas (TK)
WHISTLE BUMP – Deodato (Warner Bros.)
YOU AND I – Rick James (Gordy)

ALFIE'S, SAN FRANCISCO
DJ: Marty Blecman

AFTER DARK/LAST DANCE/SEVILLA NIGHTS – "TGIF" Soundtrack (Casablanca)
BIG CITY SIDEWALK/BIG CITY THEME – C.J. & Co. (Westbound)
COME ON DANCE, DANCE – Saturday Night Band (Prelude)
IF MY FRIENDS COULD SEE ME NOW – Linda Clifford (Curtom)
LET THE DANCE – D.C. LaRue (Casablanca)
MISSION TO VENUS/SPEND THE NIGHT WITH ME – Silver Convention (Midsong)
RIO DE JANEIRO – Gary Criss (Salsoul)
ROUGH DIAMOND – Madleen Kane (Warner Bros.)
VOYAGE – Voyage (Marlin)
YOU REALLY GOT ME – Eclipse (Casablanca)

POOP DECK, FORT LAUDERDALE
DJ: Bob Viteritti

COME INTO MY HEART/LOVE'S COMING – USA-European Connection (Marlin)
COME ON DANCE, DANCE – Saturday Night Band (Prelude)
HOW MUCH, HOW MUCH I LOVE YOU – Love & Kisses (Casablanca)
I LOVE NEW YORK – Metropolis (Salsoul)
I THINK I'LL DO SOME STEPPIN'ON MY OWN/WONDER WOMAN – Sandy Barber (Olde World)
LAST DANCE/AFTER DARK/TAKE IT TO THE ZOO/YOU'RE THE MOST PRECIOUS THING IN MY LIFE/SEVILLA NIGHTS – "TGIF" Soundtrack (Casablanca)
OH HAPPY DAY/TO MY FATHER'S HOUSE – Roberta Kelly (Casablanca)
RIO DE JANEIRO – Gary Criss (Salsoul)
ROMEO & JULIET – Alec Costandinos (Casablanca)
RUNAWAY LOVE/IF MY FRIENDS COULD SEE ME NOW/GYPSY LADY – Linda Clifford (Curtom)

the Juvet-Jarre composition from the last album, with new English lyrics and a tighter, fuller production. All together, then, an album well worth coming home for.

NEWS & NOTES: We neglected to name the group that made AVI's "I'm Glad Your Mine," a recommended disco disc from last week's column – they're **Davis Import** from Chicago... Due out this week or next: long-awaited new albums by **Teddy Pendergrass** and **Jean Carn**... Choice cuts: **Deodato's** "Whistle Bump," A Taste of Honey's "Boogie Oogie Oogie," "Come On Down Boogie People" by **David Williams**, D. C. LaRue's "Let Them Dance," **Rick James'** "You and I" – all getting strong feedback this week. Still strong: **Idris Muhammad's** "Boogie to the Top," the **Sunshine Band's** "Black Water Gold," **Celi Bee's** "Hold Your Horses Babe." ◐

DISCO FILE TOP 20

1. **AFTER DARK/LAST DANCE/TAKE IT TO THE ZOO/SEVILLA NIGHTS/TGIF/WITH YOUR LOVE** – "TGIF" SOUNDTRACK (Casablanca)
2. **RUNAWAY LOVE/IF MY FRIENDS COULD SEE ME NOW/GYPSY LADY** – Linda Clifford (Curtom)
3. **COME ON DANCE, DANCE** – Saturday Night Band (Prelude)
4. **GOT TO HAVE LOVING/STANDING IN THE RAIN** – Don Ray (Polydor)
5. **COME INTO MY HEART/LOVE'S COMING** – USA-European Connection (Marlin)
6. **ROUGH DIAMOND/TOUCH MY HEART** – Madleen Kane (CBS import)
7. **RIO DE JANEIRO** – Gary Criss (Salsoul)
8. **HOW MUCH, HOW MUCH I LOVE YOU/BEAUTY AND THE BEAST** – Love & Kisses (Casablanca)
9. **TOUCH ME ON MY HOT SPOT/DON'T** – Saturday Night Band (Prelude)
10. **OH HAPPY DAY/TO MY FATHER'S HOUSE/GETTIN' THE SPIRIT** – Roberta Kelly (Casablanca)
11. **KEY WEST/MACHO MAN/I AM WHAT I AM** – Village People (Casablanca)
12. **GARDEN OF LOVE/BODY AND SOUL** – Don Ray (Polydor)
13. **VOYAGE** – Voyage (Polydor import)
14. **SPEND THE NIGHT WITH ME/MISSION TO VENUS** – Silver Convention (Midsong)
15. **LET YOURSELF GO** – T-Connection (TK)
16. **MUSIC FEVER** – Michael Zager Band (Private Stock)
17. **TENA'S SONG** – Foxy (Dash)
18. **NOBODY BUT YOU/BACK TO MUSIC** – Theo Vaness (CBS import)
19. **AT THE DISCOTHEQUE** – Lipstique (Tom 'n' Jerry)
20. **ROMEO & JULIET** – Alec Costandinos (Casablanca)

JUNE 3, 1978

The two most interesting records this week are off-the-wall surprises: the **Rolling Stones'** disco disc version of their current single, "Miss You" (Rolling Stones Records/Atlantic), the group's most impressive foray into the disco field; and newcomer **Karen Young's** steamy "Hot Shot," a 12-inch on West End and a precedent-setting co-production by a disco DJ, Philadelphia's **Kurt Borusiewicz**. Unlike "Hot Stuff," the Stone's previous attempt at "disco," "Miss You" seems to come out of some genuine record. Set in that raunchy, near-bluesy mid-tempo DJs call "sleazy," "Miss You" is unmistakably the Stones – **Jagger's** manic mood swings and the group's razor-edged playing is in the classic mold – and the instrumentation is minimal by disco's often over-stuffed standards, but the rhythm, the subtly insistent bass/drum beat, and the structure ease it comfortably into disco territory. What's exciting about this move is that it involves neither the abandonment of traditional (if that word can ever apply to the Stones) rock & roll nor the slavish accommodation to one disco formula or another. Instead, the Stones have brought about a brilliant merger of the two forms – one that should delight devotees of both. The past year's disco adaptations of rock standards with hard rock vocals ("Don't Let Me Be Misunderstood," "Gimme Some Loving," "House Of The Rising Sun," "You Really Got Me") have done something to bridge the gap between the two genres, and the **Bee Gees** have certainly broken down a lot of barriers, but it might take a group of the Rolling Stones' stature to convince some people that disco is not an alien form and the discotheque is not enemy territory.

What clinches "Miss You" as a dance cut is the break on the 8:36 12-inch pressing, when the band swings into a quiet mood: a thumping drum meshes with light organ work and the tense underlining of guitar and bass. Jagger enters stealthily, like a thief or a madman, and tells us he's taken to walking in Central Park at night "scufflin' through the street," singing to himself: "People think I'm craaazy." Loneliness has brought him this low, and he breaks into the wordless song that sets the mood of the entire record – a melancholy yet oddly spirited sort of tune that sounds like a standoff of rage and sadness. This is far from the usual disco break – there is no sudden burst of percussion, no shimmering expanse of strings – but the song's intensity grips you here and Jagger displays the sort of eccentric electricity that can charge any song with drama. "Miss You" may not be a peak dance record – it's too freakish, somewhat too uneven in parts, and a little too long – but, judging by the first-impression reaction to it this past weekend at the Loft, it will go over big with crowds that are open to something out of the ordinary. Deserves special programming attention. NOTE: The disco disc version is currently for promotional use only, making it a prime collector's item since the single (3:31) and the forthcoming (early June) album cut (4:50) are entirely different tracks. If there is enough demand and interest, however, there may be a commercial release in the future.

Karen Young's "Hot Shot," perhaps the most talked-about new record in New York this past week, is also quite out of the ordinary. Kurt Borusiewicz, the DJ who co-wrote and co-produced (with **Andy Kahn**) the song in Philadelphia, has come up with one of the wildest female vocal tracks in some time and matches it with an equally unpredictable arrangement – something like **Vicki Sue Robinson** meets **Montreal Sound**. The production is far from polished and at times the simple repeated pattern under the vocals sounds listless, but its very rawness is appealing and the main break crackles with the sort of elemental energy that is too often smothered in glossier productions. But all this is nothing next to Young's singing: she tears through the song like a tornado, not always in the best of voice (the very beginning is rather tentative), but so wonderfully carried away that here again the lack of polish doesn't matter, the spirit is all. Her scatting is fierce and inspired, hot and sexy in a frankly aggressive way; when she screams, the crowd screams. This is one of those records that starts a DJ cult-pre-release word-of-mouth is already phenomenal – so watch for immediate strong response on "Hot Shot." ◐

> ❝ The Bee Gees have certainly broken down a lot of barriers, but it might take a group of the Rolling Stones' stature to convince some people that disco is not an alien form and the discotheque is not enemy territory ❞

SANDPIPER, FIRE ISLAND PINES, NY
DJ: Richie Rivera

COME ON DANCE, DANCE/TOUCH ME ON MY HOT SPOT
– Saturday Night Band (Prelude)
DISCO QUEEN/LAST DANCE/AFTER DARK
– "TGIF" Soundtrack (Casablanca)
**GOT TO HAVE LOVING/STANDING IN THE
RAIN/MIDNIGHT MADNESS** – Don Ray (Polydor)
HOT SHOT – Karen Young (West End)
**IF MY FRIENDS COULD SEE ME NOW/GYPSY LADY/
RUNAWAY LOVE** – Linda Clifford (Curtom)
MELLOW LOVIN' – Judy Cheeks (Salsoul)
NOBODY BUT YOU/BACK TO MUSIC – Theo Vaness (CBS)
**RIO DE JANEIRO/GIRL FROM IPANEMA/ BRAZILIAN
NIGHTS/AMAZON QUEEN** – Gary Criss (Salsoul)
WAR DANCE – Kebekelektrik (Salsoul)
WHISTLE BUMP – Deodato (Warner Bros.)

HIS COMPANY, PHOENIX
DJ: Jack Witherby

BOOGIE OOGIE OOGIE – A Taste of Honey (Capitol)
BOOGIE TO THE TOP/S-E-X – Idris Muhammad (Kudu)
**GOT TO HAVE LOVING/STANDING IN THE RAIN/GARDEN
OF LOVE** – Don Ray (Polydor)
I LOVE AMERICA/GOT A FEELING/WHERE IS MY WOMAN
– Patrick Juvet (Casablanca)
I'M GLAD YOU'RE MINE – Davis Import (AVI)
**LAST DANCE/AFTER DARK/SEVILLA NIGHTS/ TAKE IT
TO THE ZOO/TGIF/YOU'RE THE MOST PRECIOUS THING
IN MY LIFE** – "TGIF" Soundtrack (Casablanca)
**MISSION TO VENUS/SPEND THE NIGHT WITH ME/LOVE
IN A SLEEPER** – Silver Convention (Midsong)
READY OR NOT – Deborah Washington (Ariola)
ROBOTS/NEON LIGHTS – Kraftwerk (Capitol)
YOU AND I – Rick James (Gordy)

STUDIO 54, NEW YORK
DJ: Richie Kaczor

AFTER DARK/LAST DANCE – "TGIF" Soundtrack
(Casablanca)
BEYOND THE CLOUDS – Quartz (Vogue import)
BOOGIE OOGIE OOGIE – A Taste of Honey (Capitol)
GOT TO HAVE LOVING/STANDING IN THE RAIN
– Don Ray (Polydor)
HEAVEN – Gibson Brothers (Zagora import)
I LOVE AMERICA/GOT A FEELING – Patrick Juvet
(Casablanca)
**IF MY FRIENDS COULD SEE ME NOW/GYPSY
LADY/RUNAWAY LOVE** – Linda Clifford (Curtom)
READY OR NOT – Deborah Washington (Ariola)
TOUCH MY HEART/FEVER/ROUGH DIAMOND – Madleen
Kane (Warner Bros.)
VOYAGE – Voyage (Marlin)

SAHARA, NEW YORK
DJ: Ellen Bogen

BOOGIE OOGIE OOGIE – A Taste of Honey (Capitol)
COME INTO MY HEART/LOVE'S COMING
– USA-European Connection (Marlin)
COME ON DANCE, DANCE – Saturday Night Band (Prelude)
I LOVE AMERICA/WHERE IS MY WOMAN – Patrick Juvet
(Casablanca)
**LAST DANCE/AFTER DARK/ TGIF/YOU'RE THE MOST
PRECIOUS THING IN MY LIFE/ SEVILLA NIGHTS/TAKE IT
TO THE ZOO** – "TGIF" Soundtrack (Casablanca)
MELLOW LOVIN' – Judy Cheeks (Salsoul)
ROUGH DIAMOND – Madleen Kane (Warner Bros.)
**RUNAWAY LOVE/IF MY FRIENDS COULD SEE ME
NOW/GYPSY LADY/YOU ARE, YOU ARE** – Linda Clifford
(Curtom)
SPEND THE NIGHT WITH ME – Silver Convention (Midsong)
YOU AND I – Rick James (Gordy)

JUNE 10, 1978

RECOMMENDED ALBUMS: The most joyously upbeat new cut this week comes off of the second **Teddy Pendergrass** album, "Life Is A Song Worth Singing" (Philadelphia International). The song, "Only You" (5:05), is **Gamble & Huff** at their best: an uncomplicated, non-nonsense production (with arrangement by **Dexter Wansel**) so tight and perfectly polished that is knocks you out without upstaging the singer. Of course it would be hard to really overshadow Pendergrass – his vocals have a kind of rough warmth that takes over the material almost effortlessly; the combination of gritty sexual energy and romantic tenderness brings out the best in even the most mundane lyrics (unfortunately, however, there's not much he can do with something

two totally-synthesized instrumentals that are a little heavy-handed but quite forceful – "La Nuit Blanche" which incorporates the familiar "Also Sprach Zarathustra" ("2001") and "In Love With Love."

With a number of former import albums being heavily revised before their release on the American market, perhaps the most thorough transformation so far is the **Blackwell** album, a Canadian production by **David Baker** and **Larry Page** recently released by Butterfly in the States. The new album, titled "Boogie Down," credits "additional production and remix" to **Jim Taylor** (who helped redo the **THP Orchestra** lp), but this was no small editing job. Much of the material

> ❝ A number of former import albums have been heavily revised before their release on the American market. Much of the material bears little resemblance to tracks of the same name on the original album ❞

as trite as "Get Up, Get Down, Get Funky, Get Loose," a throwaway party song included here). "Only You" is one of those irresistible Philly pump records that gets under your skin immediately and with Pendergrass, the more you get, the more you want (like how about a longer disco disc version?). Also immensely appealing: the **Thorn Bell/Linda Creed** title song, previously recorded by **Johnny Mathis** and still a gorgeous laid-back groove cut with the added spark of Teddy's gripping vocals... Because the new **Munich Machine** album (on Casablanca) lacks a spectacular, extended production number like "Get On The Funk Train," it takes some getting used to. Producers **Giorgio Moroder** and **Pete Bellotte** have overturned our expectations with a collection of shorter cuts (three to a side), nearly all of them vocals by a not particularly exciting woman named **Chris Bennett** who sounds like a harsher version of **Penny McLean**; the result suggests what might have happened if Morodor and Bellotte had teamed up with the old **Silver Convention**. The title track, the inevitable disco version of **Procol Harum's** "A Whiter Shade Of Pale" (6:20), is given a sparkling synthesizer treatment but sinks under Bennett's vocals and the relentless over-articulation of the original nonsense lyrics. More successful are two less pretentious cuts called "It's For You" (5:13) and "Love Fever" (4:36) that strike a nice balance between bubbly synthesizer, terrific sheets of brass (and occasional striking solos) and the hard vocals. Both songs have a sharp cutting edge sweetened by strings that makes them highly effective dance numbers. Also of interest:

bears little resemblance to tracks of the same name on the original album (released in Canada on Penny Farthing): not only have entire new instrumental elements been added, giving much-needed fullness and punch to the tracks, but the grating male vocals on the early album have been replaced here with a hot female chorus. So Butterfly has essentially a whole new thing here, not especially innovative (**Rinder & Lewis** have worked this territory quite effectively already), but bright, spunky and, in the end, hard to ignore. The style is pop disco with tasty jazz/funk overtones, mixing swinging instrumentals like the **Junior Walker**-esque "Put The Funk Back" with its sizzling sax) and jumping vocals with simple, to-the-point lyrics and tight moves ("That's What It's All About" is my favorite, followed closely by "Boogie Down Mess Around," "I Love To See Ya Dancin'," "Give It All Ya Got" and "Move Your Ass Gringo" – just about the whole album). Very good, highly commercial disco pop, pressed on hot red vinyl.

Theo Vaness' "Back To Music" album, recorded in Paris and Munich and already enjoying considerable success as a CBS/ France import, is available now on Prelude with a sharp new American mix by **Jim Burgess**. Vaness has a rough, squealy, rather unappealing voice but the production on the two key cuts has a sweeping strength that more than makes up for his deficiencies as a singer. "Nobody But You" (8:40), the more highspirited and driving of the two, is lively enough to propel the practically non-stop vocals into several fine flights of

CELEBRATION, BOSTON
DJ: Joseph Iantosca

BOOGIE OOGIE OOGIE – A Taste of Honey (Capitol)
COME ON DANCE, DANCE/TOUCH ME ON MY HOT SPOT – Saturday Night Band (Prelude)
CONFESSIONS/I'LL WAKE UP SCREAMING/LET THEM DANCE – D.C. LaRue (Casablanca)
DO OR DIE – Grace Jones (Island)
I LOVE AMERICA/WHERE IS MY WOMAN – Patrick Juvet (Casablanca)
LAST DANCE/TGIF/SEVILLA NIGHTS/AFTER DARK – "TGIF" Soundtrack (Casablanca)
MISSION TO VENUS/SPEND THE NIGHT WITH ME – Silver Convention (Midsong)
ROUGH DIAMOND/TOUCH MY HEART – Madleen Kane (Warner Bros.)
VOYAGE – Voyage (Marlin)
WHISTLE BUMP – Deodato (Warner Bros.)

4141, NEW ORLEANS
DJ: Al Paez

AFTER DARK/TAKE IT TO THE ZOO/TGIF/WITH YOUR LOVE – "TGIF" Soundtrack (Casablanca)
AT THE DISCOTHEQUE/VENUS/LIGHT MY FIRE – Lipstique (Tom 'n' Jerry)
BOOGIE OOGIE OOGIE – A Taste of Honey (Capitol)
BOOGIE TO THE TOP – Idris Muhammad (Kudu)
COME ON DANCE, DANCE – Saturday Night Band (Prelude)
FLIGHT FROM VERSAILLES/THE GRAND TOUR – Grand Tour (Butterfly)
HOW MUCH, HOW MUCH I LOVE YOU – Love & Kisses (Casablanca)
LET THEM DANCE – D.C. LaRue (Casablanca)
MISSION TO VENUS/SPEND THE NIGHT WITH ME/LOVE IN A SLEEPER – Silver Convention (Midsong)
STANDING IN THE RAIN/GOT TO HAVE LOVING – Don Ray (Polydor)

I-BEAM, SAN FRANCISCO
DJ: Tim Rivers

BOOGIE OOGIE OOGIE – A Taste of Honey (Capitol)
BOOGIE TO THE TOP – Idris Muhammad (Kudu)
COME ON DANCE, DANCE/TOUCH ME ON MY HOT SPOT – Saturday Night Band (Prelude)
COME ON DOWN BOOGIE PEOPLE – David Williams (AVI)
GET OFF/TENA'S SONG – Foxy (Dash)
L.O.V.E. GOT A HOLD ON ME – Demis Roussos (Mercury)
MIDNIGHT MADNESS/GOT TO HAVE LOVING/STANDING IN THE RAIN – Don Ray (Polydor)
ROUGH DIAMOND/TOUCH MY HEART – Madleen Kane (Warner Bros.)
WAR DANCE – Kebekelektrik (Salsoul)
YOU AND I – Rick James (Gordy)

THE RAFTERS, SARATOGA SPRINGS, NY
DJ: Tom Lewis

BOOGIE OOGIE OOGIE – A Taste of Honey (Capitol)
COPACABANA – Barry Manilow (Arista)
DANCE ALL OVER THE WORLD/BUMPSIE'S WHIPPING CREAM – T.C. James & the Fist-O-Funk (Fist-O-Funk)
GOT TO HAVE LOVING/BODY AND SOUL/STANDING IN THE RAIN – Don Ray (Polydor)
HOT SHOT – Karen Young (West End)
I LOVE AMERICA/WHERE IS MY WOMAN – Patrick Juvet (Casablanca)
LAST DANCE/AFTER DARK/TAKE IT TO THE ZOO/TGIF/LIVIN', LOVIN', GIVIN'/WITH YOUR LOVE – "TGIF" Soundtrack (Casablanca)
LOCO-MOTIVE – Passport (Atlantic)
LOVE FEVER/IT'S FOR YOU/A WHITER SHADE OF PALE – Munich Machine (Casablanca)
MELLOW LOVIN' – Judy Cheeks (Salsoul)

riffing. And the title track, a ten-minute plus medley of songs supposedly recaptured in a time machine by a dying culture, is a bizarre pastiche (ranging from "I Who Have Nothing" to "Feelings," from "Tutti Frutti" to Brahms' "Third Symphony") that works only because the "Back To Music" refrain is so rich and the central instrumental section with its breaks is so hot (the bulk of this segment is new to this mix, apparently, covering the absence of some other **Beatles** material besides "Yesterday"); uneven but often invigorating stuff... The **Kebekelektrik** album is another import just making its American debut in revamped form – produced by Quebec's **Pat Deserio** and available for some time on the Direction label from Canada, it's out now as a "**Tom Moulton** Mix" on Salsoul. As usual, Moulton has added additional material to some of original tracks (primarily percussion by **Larry Washington**, **Keith Benson** and himself) and the result is one of the most attractive synthesizer instrumental albums so far this year. "War Dance" (8:57) is the standout – the original had an almost muted quality, but the new one's got a zippy, electronic sting like a shiver up the spine that never lets up; a weird thump break at the end of the early version is gone, but the overall energy is more than doubled. Much the same can be said for everything here – it all has a new charge and a more vibrant pace. The version of **Ravel's** "Bolero" no longer takes up an entire side-cut by nearly two minutes (to 14:00), it has more snap, picks up faster; "Mirage" (7:50) suddenly hums with life; and even "Magic Fly" (6:23) sounds fresh. "War Dance" is the important cut here, but everything works.

The following records have all been remixed to some degree and are now available as disco discs; without going into too much detail, each has made a significant improvement and are highly recommended: "The Mexican" and "Dance, Dance, Dance" by **Bombers** (A Paul Poulos mix for West End that considerably restructures and refines the original with only slight lengthening); "Get Off" and "Tena's Song" by **Foxy** (the latter with a great but unattached instrumental version included-on TK); **Linda Clifford's** still-magnificent "Runaway Love" (Curtom; brightened and lengthened from 7:04 to 9:44 with the addition of new vocal parts and breaks by Jim Burgess); "Lady America" and "Scotch Machine" by **Voyage** (TK); "Flight From Versailles" and "The Grand Tour" by **Grand Tour** (Butterfly; speedier) and **Sweet Cream's** "I Don't Know What I'd Do" (now on Shadybrook and sounding better than ever somehow – never noticed how much it resembled "Lovin' Is Really My Game" at the start; Richie Kaczor says it's a long-term favorite at Studio 54 and it deserves wider recognition). A number of the above records are already showing new club action as a result of their disco disc release... **Heatwave's** "The Groove Line" stands a good chance of expanding its currently limited disco audience with the pressing of a longer disco disc version by Epic – it's now 7:28 and wonderfully easy to slip into during a mellow part of the evening. ✇

The two records I'm most infatuated with right this moment are the **Constellation Orchestra's** "Perfect Love Affair" album (Prelude) and "Over and Over," the prime cut on **Charles Earland's** new "Perceptions" lp (Mercury). The Constellation Orchestra is essentially the **Saturday Night Band** under another name: producers **Moses Dillard** and **Jesse Boyce** (who also arranged, composed and play key instruments on all the tracks) repeat their performance here along with nearly all the musicians and singers from the earlier album. The second time around may not have turned up anything as immediately involving as "Come On Dance, Dance," which achieved an effortless kind of pop perfection just a notch below **Chic's** "Dance, Dance, Dance," but the four cuts here are solid disco numbers with a glossy pop polish. Each track displays a sure sense of pacing and movement with a series of sweet changes to keep things flowing. The title cut, "Perfect Love Affair" (7:20), has an underlying melody very similar to the **Brooklyn Dreams** song, "Street Dance," but the mood here is more sweepingly sensuous, highlighted by very pretty vocals, enforced by pulsing breaks. "Cosmic Melody" (7:07) follows, picking up on the same string-laced style and mood but meshing it with a bass pattern right out of "Come On Dance, Dance" and reducing the vocals to a minimum. "Dancing Angel" (6:24) is rather fast and "Funk Encounter" (6:40) takes on a space-funk mode not quite as slick as the rest of the stuff here, but both click effectively when the breaks come around. Like Saturday Night Band's album, this is a no-waste package; every cut is danceable, with "Perfect Love Affair" and "Cosmic Melody" the personal favorites right now.

❝ "What does it take to keep you satisfied?" he cries. ❞

The **Charles Earland** album takes this jazz performer further into disco than he's previously ventured, but this time he's taking direction from **Randy Muller** writer and arranger for **Brass Construction** who co-produced (with Earland himself), arranged and composed most of the material here. The knockout track is "Over And Over" (9:00), a heady fusion of Eurodisco and funk styles reminiscent of **Cerrone** and **Isaac Hayes** instrumentals (particularly "Theme From 'The Men'"). This makes for a rich, invigorating instrumental track, sliced with violins, pumped up with bass and percussion, rippling with Earland's keyboard wizardry. Earland also sings in a non-singing style close to both **Bill Withers** and **Barry White** and the song turns out to be a plea of impassioned frustration to a never-satiated lover: "What does it take to keep you satisfied?" he cries, and the female chorus chants, "Can't stop lovin' you/Over and over." The

structure is powerful, giving you a long intro before the vocals and an equally long instrumental section after, making this a predominately instrumental cut – and one that grows stronger with each listening. Also hot: "Let The Music Play" (6:50), a marvellously jumpy jazz/funk number that is a great party record; and the somewhat more relaxed "I Like It" (4:57) – both instrumentals.

THREE ESSENTIAL DISCO DISCS: "Do Or Die," her long-awaited new record on Island, is **Grace Jones'** most wildly uneven work to date. She sounds both better and worse than ever – hitting some sour notes right off but proving more durable and full-bodied in the long run – and, though the material is somewhat flimsy and foolish, the production (by **Tom Moulton**, with arrangement by **John Davis**) is tightly-structured and more compact than previous Jones records, so the punch is concentrated and connects immediately. From about the halfway point – after the first percussion etc. break where the title is breathlessly repeated – the record picks up enough steam to overwhelm even the most critical listener and the final chorus surge is a knockout. Perhaps only Grace Jones could get away with a record like this – only she has the sort of drop-dead style and disco star status to put it across – and it's instant success at most clubs is a measure of her strength as a personality, a cult figure. Happily, the reverse side of the 12-inch, a lovely French song called "Comme Un Oiseau Qui S'Envole" ("Like a Bird Who's Flown Away"), is evidence that Jones has grown considerably as a vocalist – though the style is still rather declamatory, it's more vibrant – and this could be the sleeper cut. Both definitely songs to watch... Another unusual singer/personality, San Francisco's **Sylvester**, is back with his hottest disco release so far: two records back-to-back on a Fantasy 12-inch, both in his unique, crazed, churchy style, as eccentric as ever. "You Make Me Feel (Mighty Real)" (6:39) is classic Sylvester and a stunner – set to a driving yet comfortable synthesizer pace, jumping with electronic effects but always emphasizing Sylvester's androgynous lead which builds to a nice gospel-tinged climax. "Dance (Disco Heat)" (5:54) is even more attractive: the sound here is more group-oriented (in fact it's hard to place Sylvester at times – is his the exaggerated bass voice or the wailing "chorus" or both?) and the structure delightfully jumpy and fun. Both are thoroughly enjoyable high-stepping cuts – expect them to hit big and fast in San Francisco and spread cross-country... **Bob Esty** produced the new **Brooklyn Dreams** disco disc, "Street Man" (7:55 on Millennium), giving the group its first clearly made-for-disco (also made-for-TV since this is a "Police Story" theme) record and a highly effective one at that. The feeling – matching its gritty street-life theme – is ominous, dark, jittery but ultimately bold and hopeful. Excellent group vocals, an insistent synthesizer blip line and a heavy bass/ percussion pattern drive the song deep and hard. Real hot.

HARRAH, NEW YORK
DJ: John Benitez

ACTION 78 (PART 2) – Erotic Drum Band (Champagne import)
BOOGIE OOGIE OOGIE – A Taste of Honey (Capitol)
GET UP, GET DOWN, GET FUNKY, GET LOOSE/LIFE IS A SONG WORTH SINGING/ ONLY YOU – Teddy Pendergrass (Phila. Intl.)
HOT SHOT – Karen Young (West End)
I LOVE AMERICA – Patrick Juvet (Casablanca)
LAST DANCE/AFTER DARK/TGIF/TAKE IT TO THE ZOO – "TGIF" Soundtrack (Casablanca)
MISS YOU – Rolling Stones (Rolling Stones)
SAVE THE LAST DANCE FOR ME – Patti LaBelle (Epic)
ROUGH DIAMOND – Madleen Kane (Warner Bros.)
WAR DANCE – Kebekelektrik (Salsoul)

BACKSTREET, ATLANTA
DJ: Angelo Solar

BOOGIE OOGIE OOGIE – A Taste of Honey (Capitol)
COME ON DANCE, DANCE – Saturday Night Band (Prelude)
HOT SHOT – Karen Young (West End)
IF MY FRIENDS COULD SEE ME NOW/RUNAWAY LOVE – Linda Clifford (Curtom)
LADY AMERICA – Voyage (TK)
LAST DANCE/AFTER DARK/TAKE IT TO THE ZOO – "TGIF" Soundtrack (Casablanca)
LET YOURSELF GO – T-Connection (TK)
RIO DE JANEIRO – Gary Criss (Salsoul)
ROUGH DIAMOND – Madleen Kane (Warner Bros.)
YOU AND I – Rick James (Gordy)

REGINES, NEW YORK
DJ: Jonata Garavaglia

BIG CITY SIDEWALK – C. J. & Co. (Westbound)
CHEEK TO CHEEK/TIC TAC TOE – Régine (CBS import)
DO OR DIE – Grace Jones (Island)
HOT SHOT – Karen Young (West End disco disc)
LAST DANCE/TGIF/AFTER DARK – "TGIF" Soundtrack (Casablanca)
LAW AND ORDER – Love Committee (Gold Mind)
LET'S START THE DANCE/ME AND THE GANG – Bohannon (Mercury)
RUNAWAY LOVE – Linda Clifford (Curtom)
WAR DANCE – Kebekelektrik (Salsoul)
WHISTLE BUMP – Deodato (Warner Bros.)

TROCADERO TRANSFER, SAN FRANCISCO
DJ: Paul Dougan

AFTER DARK/LAST DANCE/TGIF/YOU'RE THE MOST PRECIOUS THING IN MY LIFE – "TGIF" Soundtrack (Casablanca)
BOOGIE OOGIE OOGIE – A Taste of Honey (Capitol)
GET OFF – Foxy (TK)
GET ON UP – Tyrone Davis (Columbia)
HOT SHOT – Karen Young (West End)
I LOVE AMERICA – Patrick Juvet (Casablanca)
MELLOW LOVIN' – Judy Cheeks (Salsoul)
RUNAWAY LOVE – Linda Clifford (Curtom)
WAR DANCE – Kebekelektrik (Salsoul)
WHISTLE BUMP – Deodato (Warner Bros.)

FUNK IT UP: **Joe Thomas'** "Two Doors Down" (6:11 on a TK disco disc) is a bright, brash country funk record written by **Dolly Parton** and interpreted here as a light-hearted blend of Memphis and Miami with occasional dashes of jazz: an uncommon but surprisingly appealing combination. Picking up the "Party Lights" theme, a strong female chorus sings about missing a party "two doors down" as the noise of a raucous good time drifts in, sometimes on a breeze of Thomas' festive flute riffs. The pace is laid-back, loose but the song's already getting strong reaction from a number of clubs already for a little change of pace... In the harder funk vein; there's "Get On Up (Get On Down)" by **Roundtree** (a 6:47 disco disc on Omni, through Island Records), which features a deep-jabbing horn pattern right out of early **B.T. Express** and a sharp-edged girl chorus with serious partying in mind. Produced, arranged and co-written by **Kenny Lehman**, part of the **Chic** team, the cut has some small dips in pace but a terrifically chunky pump groove predominates and the whole is a fresh new take on the sort of New York funk style that's all but faded away in recent years. The formula here is simple, no-frills, but it works like a charm and it's one of this week's personal favorites... Though a far cry from the stunning force of "Devil's Gun," **C.J. & Co's** "Big City Sidewalk" (a Westbound disco disc) has a fine toughness. Producers **Dennis Coffey** and **Mike Theodore** have whipped up a hard-pounding combination of Detroit and Philadelphia styles – their own special mix – strung on a compelling horn line and sweetened by strings. The lyric is about trying to break away from the kind of place where "You learn to shoot before you can talk," but a sugary chorus segment and an impossible quick tempo cut its effectiveness and early club response favors the instrumental flip side, "Big City Theme" (both versions run around six minutes). Might work better on a slowed-down turntable.

ETC., ETC.: Allow me to underline the previous recommendations of the following records: **Karen Young's** "Hot Shot" (West End), which is definitely that (heavy reaction this week shot it into the Top 20 at number eight), **Deborah Washington's** "Ready Or Not" (Ariola, and now available on a longer (5:10) disco disc, speeded-up, gimmicked-up, with a somewhat longer break) and "I'm Glad You're Mine" by **Davis Import** on AVI... TK's "Disco Party," a two-record, 14-cut collection of the label's best dance music, is the finest disco repack-age so far. Not only is the material excellent ("Do What You Wanna Do," "Do You Wanna Get Funky With Me," "Where Is The Love," "Superman," "Gimme Some," "Calypso Breakdown," etc., etc. – a widely varying and uncompromising selection), but **Tom Savarese's** disco blending meshes it all together superbly so one can party right through each side. No remixes – a collection of TK classics handsomely recycled (complete with striking Studio 54 impressionist cover). ◐

JUNE 24, 1978

"TGIF" X 10: That ten-record set of remixed cuts from Casablanca's spectacularly successful "Thank God It's Friday" soundtrack is available now as a limited edition package to disco DJs. This non-commercial "Collectors Gift Series" includes ten one-sided 12-inch discs in identical sleeves – an excessive use of vinyl, perhaps, but one that allows for endless combinations of intermixing within the set itself. The very bulk of the project is impressive and all the cuts benefit from the enhanced sharpness and clarity of the new pressings, but several are so significantly revised and expanded that they deserve special, if brief, mention: **Paul Jabara's** "Queen Of The Disco," already shaping up as one of the sleeper cuts on the album, has been more than doubled to 8:10 here, giving Jabara's hilarious portrait of a mysterious, frantic dancer ("Where does she get her energy? What's she on?") the necessary movement and scope to become one of the soundtrack's key songs... **Donna Summer's** "With Your Love" (now 7:35) layers on new, more jittery and playful synthesizer elements, adds more zip to the already existing break

❝ A limited edition ten-record set of remixed cuts for disco DJs ❞

and, with the repetition of the final verse, inserts a few new breaks – notably a thump-percussion and synthesizer change toward the end that really heats it up... **D.C. LaRue's** "Do You Want The Real Thing" went through the greatest transformation – jumping from 4:42 on the album to 12:15 here – slipping in several ominous, intriguing electronic moans that glide from speaker to speaker during the intro and allowing the song to ooze on in a kind of sultry ecstacy, keeping to its dreamy grind tempo but building in intensity and passion (LaRue sounds like he's in heat); the pace picks up slightly along the way and the changes are totally seductive – hard core action... **Love and Kisses'** "Thank God It's Friday" theme (now 7:40), the only song that takes on any new resonance after seeing the movie, bristles with fresh moves, including some furious percussion breaks **Costandinos** says he improvised alone in the studio late one night – cushioned by this new instrumental material, the vocals, with their **Village People** overtones feel more comfortable. Also included in the series: "Last Dance" (8:10), "After Dark" (same length as before, 7:55), "Take It To The Zoo" (8:23), "You're The Most Precious Thing In My Life" (8:10), "I Wanna Dance" (7:31) and "Find My Way" (5:18). The omission of **Santa Esmeralda's** "Sevilla Nights," one of the album's most popular cuts, is puzzling but hardly heartbreaking in light of the riches already gathered together. A perfectly-timed promotional device, the set is also likely to be the year's most important disco collector's item.

RECOMMENDED DISCO DISCS: Three bright new female vocalists this week, starting with **Norma Jean**, the lead singer in the **Chic** team, whose debut on her own, "Saturday" (Bearsville/WB), was written and produced by other members of the group. So the sound here is highly professional, right-on-target disco pop but something of a departure from the zippy "Dance, Dance, Dance"/"Everybody Dance" style. Instead "Saturday" picks up the mood of "Boogie Oogie Oogie" (including a similar bass pattern) but quickens the tempo some, running the song through a down, anticipatory phase before hitting the upswing euphoria that captures the joy of Saturday-night partying. The message, a natural after "TGIF": "I just can't wait 'til Saturday." Norma Jean has a husky, soulful, already familiar voice and the production is flawless (loose but surprisingly compact-feeling at just over six minutes), so this one seems destined to be a major hit on the radio as well as in the clubs. A packaging plus: "Saturday" is pressed on clear red vinyl and slipped in a special "Norma Jean" sleeve... **Samona Cooke's** new version of "One Night Affair" (Mercury, 6:02), already a favorite in **Jerry Butler** and **Esther Phillips** versions; is so spicy and appealing it could revive this song all over again. Cooke's voice, underlined and counterpointed by a terrific female chorus, is emphatic and enticing, crying, "Kiss me! Thrill me!" but insisting on nothing more involving. Stinging guitar and knife-edged strings keep the track sharp and perky – really fine... **Carolyne**

CLUB SWAMP, EAST HAMPTON, N.Y.
DJ: Jeff Baugh

AMERICAN GENERATION/I FEEL GOOD/GOOD IN LOVE/MUSIC MAN – Ritchie Family (Marlin)
BOOGIE OOGIE OOGIE – A Taste of Honey (Capitol)
DO OR DIE – Grace Jones (Island)
HOT SHOT – Karen Young (West End)
I LOVE AMERICA – Patrick Juvet (Casablanca)
LOCO-MOTIVE – Passport (Atlantic)
PERFECT LOVE AFFAIR – Constellation Orchestra (Prelude)
ROUGH DIAMOND – Madleen Kane (Warner Bros.)
STREET MAN – Brooklyn Dreams (Millennium)
WITH YOUR LOVE/TGIF/AFTER DARK/ LAST DANCE – "TGIF" Soundtrack (Casablanca)

ROBICONTI'S, TAMPA
DJ: J. G. Knapp

AT THE DISCOTHEQUE/VENUE/LIGHT MY FIRE – Lipstique (Tom 'n' Jerry)
COPACABANA – Barry Manilow (Arista)
GET OFF – Foxy (TK)
HOLD ME, TOUCH ME – Carolyne Bernier (Private Stock)
HOW MUCH, HOW MUCH I LOVE YOU – Love & Kisses (Casablanca)
IF MY FRIENDS COULD SEE ME NOW/RUNAWAY LOVE – Linda Clifford (Curtom)
ROUGH DIAMOND – Madleen Kane (Warner Bros.)
SPEND THE NIGHT WITH ME/MISSION TO VENUS – Silver Convention (Midsong)

PARADISE GARAGE, NEW YORK
DJ: Larry Levan

BOOGIE OOGIE OOGIE – A Taste of Honey (Capitol)
GOT TO HAVE LOVING/STANDING IN THE RAIN/BODY AND SOUL/MY DESIRE/GARDEN OF LOVE – Don Ray (Polydor)
HOT SHOT – Karen Young (West End)
LADY AMERICA – Voyage (TK)
LET'S START THE DANCE/ME AND THE GANG – Bohannon (Mercury)
L.O.V.E. GOT A HOLD ON ME – Demis Roussos (Mercury)
MISS YOU – Rolling Stones (Rolling Stones)
MUSIC FEVER – Michael Zager Band (Private Stock)
WHISTLE BUMP – Deodato (Warner Bros.)
YOU AND I – Rick James (Gordy)

PARADE, NEW ORLEANS
DJ: Pete Van Waesberge Jr.

BACK TO MUSIC/NOBODY BUT YOU – Theo Vaness (Prelude)
BOOGIE OOGIE OOGIE – A Taste of Honey (Capitol)
COME ON DOWN BOOGIE PEOPLE – David Williams (AVI)
COPACABANA – Barry Manilow (Arista)
GOT TO HAVE LOVING – Don Ray (Polydor)
I LOVE AMERICA/WHERE IS MY WOMAN – Patrick Juvet (Casablanca)
LAST DANCE /WITH YOUR LOVE/AFTER DARK/SEVILLA NIGHTS/TGIF – "TGIF" Soundtrack (Casablanca)
TWO DOORS DOWN – Joe Thomas (TK)
WHISTLE BUMP – Deodato (Warner Bros.)
YOU AND I – Rick James (Gordy)

DISCO FILE TOP 20

1. **AFTER DARK/LAST DANCE/TAKE IT TO THE ZOO/ SEVILLA NIGHTS/TGIF/WITH YOUR LOVE** – "TGIF" SOUNDTRACK (Casablanca)
2. **BOOGIE OOGIE OOGIE** – A Taste of Honey (Capitol)
3. **ROUGH DIAMOND/TOUCH MY HEART** – Madleen Kane (CBS import)
4. **RUNAWAY LOVE/IF MY FRIENDS COULD SEE ME NOW/GYPSY LADY** – Linda Clifford (Curtom)
5. **GOT TO HAVE LOVING/STANDING IN THE RAIN** – Don Ray (Polydor)
6. **I LOVE AMERICA/WHERE IS MY WOMAN** – Patrick Juvet (Casablanca)
7. **HOT SHOT** – Karen Young (West End)
8. **COME ON DANCE, DANCE** – Saturday Night Band (Prelude)
9. **YOU AND I** – Rick James (Gordy)
10. **WHISTLE BUMP** – Deodato (Warner Bros.)
11. **SPEND THE NIGHT WITH ME/MISSION TO VENUS** – Silver Convention (Midsong)
12. **WAR DANCE** – Kebekelektrik (Salsoul)
13. **HOW MUCH, HOW MUCH I LOVE YOU/BEAUTY AND THE BEAST** – Love & Kisses (Casablanca)
14. **GARDEN OF LOVE/BODY AND SOUL** – Don Ray (Polydor)
15. **BOOGIE TO THE TOP** – Idris Muhammad (Kudu)
16. **COPACABANA** – Barry Manilow (Arista)
17. **COME INTO MY HEART/LOVE'S COMING** – USA-European Connection (Marlin)
18. **TOUCH ME ON MY HOT SPOT/DON'T** – Saturday Night Band (Prelude)
19. **LADY AMERICA** – Voyage (Polydor import)
20. **OH HAPPY DAY/TO MY FATHER'S HOUSE/ GETTIN' THE SPIRIT** – Roberta Kelly (Casablanca)

Bernier, on "Hold Me, Touch Me" (Private Stock), sounds like a French **Charo** – very cute, bubbly and kind of campy, at least on the vocal side here which begins with a sexy phone call and turns into something more intimate. The inviting lyrics alternate between French and English and the production (by Canada's **Tony Green**) is appropriately sunny and sweet – irresistibly bouncy. Flip is an instrumental version, running, as does the vocal, about 5:30.

NOTES: J.G. Knapp, who reports from Tampa this week, alerted us to the fact that **Barry Manilow's** "Copacabana," which eased onto the new Top 20 with this issue, is available in a Spanish version from Arista. A limited edition disco disc, "En El Copa," is being sold commercially only in selected markets at this point (New York, Miami and Los Angeles are the key areas), but may be more widely available depending on the demand... **The Rolling Stones'** "Miss You" is being imported from England on pink vinyl disco discs. ◗

JULY 1, 1978

A sudden rush of excellent new material this week, with the two most outstanding items being the latest albums by **Grace Jones** and **Lenny Williams**. Grace's "Fame," her second album on Island, is all the more remarkable considering the flaws it overcomes. Jones remains an erratic singer, subject to bizarre vocal fluctuations that turn nearly every song into a reckless, daring roller-coaster ride – both unsettling and exhilarating. Like Dietrich, her voice has more character than polish and the revelation of "Fame" is just how far Jones can go on sheer style and guts. While avoiding the sort of Broadway show tunes that filled much of her last album, the bulk of the material here is by a new songwriting team whose lyrics are sometimes frankly unsophisticated but often approach the direct, spare energy of the great romantic pop songs: a modern equivalent of the '60s girl group mentality – more knowing, more ironic, but still soppy around the edges. So the songs are frequently as brash, presumptuous, exaggerated and, ultimately, endearing as the singer. But neither would stand much chance of getting off the ground were it not for the stunningly stylish, carefully balanced production by **Tom Moulton** who, working with arranger **John Davis** and a number of Sigma Sound session regulars, has captured a timeless Philadelphia feel with rich settings reminiscent of the **Three Degrees** and lighter **Trammps** material. Though most of the songs are similarly structured – quick intro, two verses of vocals, luscious break, a third verse or reprise and out – each break is a gem, usually

because it's decorated by the beautiful vocal riffing of **Benson**, **Benton** and **Ingram**, the **Sweethearts of Sigma**, who lend Jones the most elegant and flattering support throughout.

The album's first side is a three-song medley beginning with "Do Or Die," followed by "Pride"(6:23), in which Grace admits to and then renounces this particular sin, insisting "It doesn't matter now who's wrong or right," and closing with "Fame" (5:37), which is also treated as something to be renounced – a trap to be rescued from. Both songs are addressed to absent lovers, sometimes with a touching desperation: "Can't you hear me singing for you, baby?" she wails in "Fame," "Come on back, I need you, won't you save me?" And, whipped by strings, both songs achieve a memorable, even haunting, intensity (a confession: they're the sort of songs I find myself blurting out at unexpected moments– on the street, pacing around the house just as I'm waking up in the morning; they've really got a hold on me). The strongest cut on the second side is "All On A Summer's Night" (4:17), the ultimate summer romance song about a beach party for two, which Jones sings with a coy, girlish excitement, tinged here and there with a shadow of sultry passion that comes out front in a sexy, tongue-in-cheek spoken segment, (compare the breathy telephone conversation in **Love Unlimited's** "Walking in the Rain"). "Am I Ever Gonna Fall In Love In New York City (5:28)" is also bright and attractive though the

Some Grace in your face:
Miss Jones & friend
© **Kenny Carpenter**

44 Grace Jones is an erratic singer. The revelation is just how far she can go on sheer guts 77

PIPPINS, NEW YORK
DJ: James Richardson

BOOGIE OOGIE OOGIE – A Taste of Honey (Capitol)
COME ON DANCE, DANCE – Saturday Night Band (Prelude)
GARDEN OF LOVE/GOT TO HAVE LOVING/ STANDING IN THE RAIN – Don Ray (Polydor)
GET UP, GET DOWN, GET FUNKY, GET LOOSE/ ONLY YOU – Teddy Pendergrass (Phila. Intl.)
HOT SHOT – Karen Young (West End)
IF MY FRIENDS COULD SEE ME NOW/ RUNAWAY LOVE/GYPSY LADY – Linda Clifford (Curtom)
PERFECT LOVE AFFAIR – Constellation Orchestra (Prelude)
ROUGH DIAMOND– Madleen Kane (Warner Bros.)
THANK GOD IT'S FRIDAY – "TGIF" Soundtrack (Casablanca)
YOU MAKE ME FEEL (MIGHTY REAL)/ DANCE (DISCO HEAT) – Sylvester (Fantasy)

N–TOUCH, SAN FRANCISCO
DJ: Carmen Adduci

HOT SHOT – Karen Young (West End)
I DON'T KNOW WHAT I'D DO – Sweet Cream (Shadybrook)
I LOVE AMERICA – Patrick Juvet (Casablanca)
IT'S FOR YOU/LOVE FEVER/IN LOVE WITH LOVE/ WHITER SHADE OF PALE – Munich Machine (Casablanca)
LADY AMERICA – Voyage (Marlin)
LOVE IS IN THE AIR – Martin Stevens (CBS import)
MELLOW LOVIN' – Judy Cheeks (Salsoul)
MISS YOU – Rolling Stones (Rolling Stones)
WAR DANCE – Kebekelektrik (Salsoul)
YOU MAKE ME FEEL (MIGHTY REAL) – Sylvester (Fantasy)

DILLON'S DOWNTOWN, LOS ANGELES
DJ: Jon Randauo

BOOGIE OOGIE OOGIE – A Taste of Honey (Capitol)
DO OR DIE – Grace Jones (Island)
LADY AMERICA – Voyage (Marlin)
LAST DANCE/AFTER DARK –"TGIF" Soundtrack (Casablanca)
LET YOURSELF GO – T-Connection (TK)
LET'S START THE DANCE – Bohannon (Mercury)
MISS YOU – Rolling Stones (Rolling Stones)
ROUGH DIAMOND/FEVER – Madleen Kane (Warner Bros.)
STUFF LIKE THAT – Quincy Jones (A&M)
YOU AND I – Rick James (Gordy)

12 WEST, NEW YORK
DJ: Alan Dodd

AFTER DARK/LAST DANCE/DISCO QUEEN/WITH YOUR LOVE –"TGIF" Soundtrack (Casablanca)
BOOGIE OOGIE OOGIE – A Taste of Honey (Capitol)
GARDEN OF LOVE – Don Ray (Polydor)
HOT SHOT – Karen Young (West End)
I LOVE AMERICA/GOT A FEELING – Patrick Juvet (Casablanca)
MELLOW LOVIN' – Judy Cheeks (Salsoul)
ROUGH DIAMOND/TOUCH MY HEART – Madleen Kane (Warner Bros.)
RUNAWAY LOVE/IF MY FRIENDS COULD SEE ME NOW/GYPSY LADY – Linda Clifford (Curtom)
SPEND THE NIGHT WITH ME – Sliver Convention (Midsong)
WHISTLE BUMP – Deodato (Warner Bros.)

lyrics have the corny insistence of an overstated show tune. And "Below The Belt" (4:55), written by Grace herself, if not as sure a dance cut, is the most tantalizing lyric here since it seems as much about fame as about the conflicts of love: "I trained hard for this fight," she sings, and many of her comments could be directed at her critics, particularly the warning, "No hitting below the belt," and the invitation to "please stick around, it's not over yet." If this album's any indication, it's only just begun. Also included: a seven minute French version of "Autumn Leaves" that is at times ludicrously overdone, with especially uneven singing, but might appeal to fans of "La Vie En Rose" who are willing to sacrifice subtlety for audacity. Not included here is the B side of the "Do Or Die" disco disc, "Comme Un Oiseau," so the 12-inch is still an essential part of the Grace Jones collection. Finally, "Fame" is a marvellous combination of chutzpah and charisma from which Grace emerges quite triumphant. An added attraction: Richard Bernstein's ultrafashionable cover.

Lenny Williams' "Spark Of Love (ABC) is everything that one could have hoped for as a follow-up to the "Choosing You" lp that shot him immediately into the ranks of disco's top male vocalists. Teamed again with star producer **Frank Wilson**, Williams is boundlessly energetic, superbly controlled, rough and ready. His voice is strong and gritty enough to belt out the upbeat numbers and make you feel he's right there in the room, yet warm enough to give an effortless glow and a whole other kind of intimacy to the ballads. Disco standouts here are "You Got Me Running" (7:45), with a theme similar to, but less ambiguous than, Jones' "Below The Belt" – both singers hope to "go the distance," but the metaphor here is track – and "I Still Reach Out" (5:37), which picks up and underlines the theme and style of "Choosing You" while going for a more low-down feel. "Running" is the looser of the two, with a loping, easy pace and a fine, violin-laced break section that builds to a shouting "Ooo baby" climax right out of "Choosing You." "I Still Reach Out" packs a more concentrated punch and includes a tough break full of nervous, noodling guitars and drums. On both songs, the seven-person background chorus (including Frank Wilson) is perfection. Also highly recommended: "Midnight Girl" (6:01), a mellower groove that gathers intensity as it goes on and would make a great transition record between slow and fast sets. "Changes" is another spirited song included here, but its pace is probably too zippy for most dance crowds.

A quick check-list of some new female vocal records not to miss out on: **Jean Carn's** "There's A Shortage Of Good Men" from her just-out "Happy To Be With You" album on Philadelphia International; **Candi Staton's** "Victim," a revival of her "Young Hearts Run Free" sound and a reunion with producer **Dave Crawford** from her new "House Of Love" lp (Warner Brothers) and **Cissy Houston's** knockout "Think It Over," a disco disc from Private Stock produced by **Michael Zager**. Details next week. ✪

JULY 8, 1978

Two new albums from producer **Jacques Morali** this week: The **Ritchie Family's** just-in-time-for-summer "American Generation" (Marlin) and **Phylicia Allen's** musical biography of Josephine Baker, "Josephine Superstar" (Casablanca). "American Generation," sung by an entirely new trio of girls (who remain uncredited on the lp although their hairdresser and make-up man are named), is essentially a disco anthem, a paean to partying in the fun, fun, fun spirit of the Beach Boys but with an extra dash of sex (and breathy vocals) to bring it up to date. The key side here begins with the title song, a frantic celebration of "disco in the street" that belongs alongside **Patrick Juvet's** "I Love American" – another Morali salute to American music – and closes with "I Feel Disco Good" (total time for the two-part medley: 11:05). Both songs are predominately vocals, the first looser, breezier, clinched by the joyous repetition of "Aaah-merican generation," sometimes in **Bee Gees**-falsetto, and a bubbly synthesizer; the second punching up the pace some but still alternating between oozy sensuous – woman sections and snappy, hyped-up chorus chants bristling with catch phrases ("can you dig it... let's do it!") and jagged energy. The relentless pace of "I Feel Disco Good" makes it one of Morali's most effective and exciting disco songs – just the sort of peak number that brings screams from the crowd. But Morali has a weakness for show-biz pop (with camp overtones) that is beyond my comprehension – witness "Just A Gigolo" on the **Village People** album, nearly all of "Josephine Superstar," and the inclusion here of "Big Spender" as the first song in another two-part medley. Passing over this in silence, we come to the medley's second half, "Good In Love," a sweet, sexy invitation to heavy action that picks up on the mood of the "Life Is Music" album; included are some of Morali's typically manic changes, like the one when the "Rock me 'til you get enough" chorus shifts abruptly into the high-gear title chant. The remaining song, "Music Man," is sung as both a tribute and a plea to a disco DJ acknowledging his power to change one's mood and begging him to keep things romantic and hot so the singer can catch herself a man. The feeling of "Music Man" is most similar to the Village People sound – a little less pumpy but bright with horns. The "American Generation"/"I Feel Disco Good" medley should establish the Ritchie Family once again as the sirens of summer even if the album as a whole doesn't have the depth and impact of "African Queens." **Phylicia Allen's** "Josephine Superstar,' conceived, composed and produced by Morali, is an obviously sincere and enthusiastic tribute to La Baker, following her sensational story-book career from poverty in St. Louis to stardom in Paris, but it often veers into the pathetic ("Don't Cry Mommy") and the ludicrous (from the title cut: "She's kept her body so together/Her spirit will live on forever"). Allen, who looks delicious on the cover, has a serviceable, occasionally diverting Broadway show voice and there are moments of genuine delight here, but the music sounds like Village People/Ritchie Family out-takes or retreads and, while it is considerably better than much Broadway-musical material, it rarely strikes the spark necessary to heat up the dance floor. That said, I should still report that a number of disco DJs are quite taken with "Josephine Superstar" – particularly the side one medley of "Saint Louis," "Broadway" and "Star Of Paris" – and it's already enjoying scattered club play in its first week of release. The inclusion of both Village People and the Ritchie Family as background singers here is an added attraction– see what you think.

Other recommended female vocal records: **Jean Carn's** "There's A Shortage Of Good Men,' the opening cut on her new Philadelphia International album, "Happy To Be With You,' is an insinuating, beautifully sung number delivered without bitterness but with a lot of feeling. Written and produced by **Gamble & Huff**, this one's in the Philadelphia laid-back style, but a loping beat and a tasty violin pattern that fills up the break make it a fine, off-beat dance cut. Carn sticks to ballads

> ## ❝ "Music Man" is a plea to a disco DJ, acknowledging his power to change one's mood ❞

THE LOFT, NEW YORK
DJ: David Mancuso

BOOGIE OOGIE OOGIE – A Taste of Honey (Capitol)
GET READY FOR THE FUTURE – Winners (Roadshow)
L.O.V.E. GOT A HOLD ON ME – Demis Roussos (Mercury)
MISS YOU – Rolling Stones (Rolling Stones)
ONLY YOU – Teddy Pendergrass (Phila. Intl.)
SKY BLUE/LOCO-MOTIVE – Passport (Atlantic lp cut)
STUFF LIKE THAT/I'M GONNA MISS YOU IN THE MORNING/LOVE, I NEVER HAD IT SO GOOD – Quincy Jones (A&M)
THIS TIME BABY – O'Jays (Phila. Intl.)
YOU AND I – Rick James (Gordy)
YOU MAKE ME FEEL (MIGHTY REAL) – Sylvester (Fantasy)

BUZZBY'S, SAN FRANCISCO
DJ: Michael Lee

AMERICAN GENERATION/I FEEL DISCO GOOD – Ritchie Family (Marlin)
BOOGIE OOGIE OOGIE – A Taste of Honey (Capitol)
COMME UN OISEAU/DO OR DIE/PRIDE/ALL ON A SUMMERS NIGHT/FAME – Grace Jones (Island)
FLY – Pegasus (Sunshine import)
HOT SHOT – Karen Young (West End)
I LOVE AMERICA/WHERE IS MY WOMAN – Patrick Juvet (Casablanca)
LET'S START THE DANCE/ME AND THE GANG – Bohannon (Mercury)
MISS YOU – Rolling Stones (Rolling Stones)
WAR DANCE – Kebekelektrik (Salsoul)
YOU MAKE ME FEEL (MIGHTY REAL)/DANCE DISCO HEAT – Sylvester (Fantasy)

LOST AND FOUND, WASHINGTON, DC
DJ: Bill Owens

BEYOND THE CLOUDS – Quartz (Vogue import)
BOOGIE OOGIE OOGIE – A Taste of Honey (Capitol)
DO OR DIE – Grace Jones (Island)
DOING THE BEST THAT I CAN – Bettye Lavette (West End)
GET ON UP (GET ON DOWN) – Roundtree (Omni disco)
HOT SHOT – Karen Young (West End)
I LOVE AMERICA/GOT A FEELING – Patrick Juvet (Casablanca)
LAST DANCE/AFTER DARK/TGIF – "TGIF" Soundtrack (Casablanca)
THINK IT OVER – Cissy Houston (Private Stock)
YOU MAKE ME FEEL (MIGHTY REAL) – Sylvester (Fantasy)

EIGHTBALL'S LOUNGE, ALBANY, NY
DJ: Douglas Forrester

AFTER DARK/TGIF/LAST DANCE/TAKE IT TO THE ZOO/WITH YOUR LOVE/YOU'RE THE MOST PRECIOUS THING IN MY LIFE/DISCO QUEEN – "TGIF" Soundtrack (Casablanca)
AMERICAN GENERATION – Ritchie Family (Marlin)
DANCE ALL OVER THE WORLD – T.C. James & Fist-O-Funk Orchestra (Quality import)
DO OR DIE – Grace Jones (Island)
HOT SHOT – Karen Young (West End)
I LOVE AMERICA/GOT A FEELING – Patrick Juvet (Casablanca)
MISS YOU – Rolling Stones (Rolling Stones)
PLUG ME TO DEATH – Erotic Drum Band (Champagne)
RUNAWAY LOVE/IF MY FRIENDS COULD SEE ME NOW/GYPSY LADY – Linda Clifford (Curtom)
YOU MAKE ME FEEL (MIGHTY REAL)/DANCE (DISCO HEAT) – Sylvester (Fantasy)

this time around, but another track here, "No, No, You Can't Come Back Now,' is worth trying… West End Records, which already has one of the fastest-rising new performers on the chart in **Karen Young's** "Hot Shot:' is following close on its heels with another female vocal that promises to be nearly as successful: **Betty LaVette's** "Doin' the Best That I Can" (7:43 on a disco disc that should be commercially available later this week). LaVette, who has been around the nightclub/theatre circuit for some time, with occasional r&b hits to her credit, belts out this zippy lost-love song in a style reminiscent of **Linda Clifford's** "If My Friends Could See Me Now" but without that song's often-frantic overreaching. But if LaVette's vocals are hot, the production here, by newcomers **Eric Matthew** and **Cory Robbins**, is even hotter, slipping in two unexpected breaks, the first with a prancing violin figure that comes out of nowhere, that double the song's impact. The mix is by Walter Gibbons – watch this one.

Cissy Houston, former lead singer with the **Sweet Inspirations**, seems to be heading in the right direction again with "Think It Over" (6:00 on a Private Stock 12-inch disc), a tight r&b song written by Houston, producer **Michael Zager** and another writer. A stern but patient warning to a wayward lover, "Think" is a welcome relief after years of inappropriate pop material and Zager's arrangement gives it a nice, smooth drive. Excellent vocals (plus a sharp female chorus), but Zager's breaks are all teasers, too short to get off on… **Carolyn Crawford's** lead vocals on the new **Bohannon** album ("Summertime Groove" on Mercury) are striking and dominant enough to merit inclusion in this female vocal round-up even if she is only one member of Bo's newest aggregation. Crawford's a knockout on the album's opening track, "Let's Start The Dance" (5:30; also available on a promo 12-inch), which is basic Bohannon – heavy on the bass groove, jittery guitars, full of striking funk changes – sent soaring by her rambunctious, rough, shouting vocals. Though I could do without the individual group-member intros on "Me And The Gang" ("My name is Ted but you can call me 'Nick"?!). Crawford also wraps this one up with her gritty riffing, giving some spice to an otherwise restrained funk groove. Both cuts are already showing up on a number of Top 10 lists – putting Bohannon back where he belongs… **Candi Staton** is also back where she belongs – with producer **Dave Crawford**, who worked with Staton on the superb "Young Hearts Run Free" album and now rejoins her for "House Of Love" (Warner Brothers). The spirit of "Young Hearts" is revived here in a somewhat subdued mood on the album's longest cut, "Victim" (8:26), where Candi confesses, "I'm a victim of the very songs I sing" (aren't we all?). The pace is exceedingly laid-back and there is not a single break, but "Victim" might be great early in the evening or real, real late. Disco mixer **Jimmy Simpson** reports that he may be reworking the track and speeding it up some, so watch for a disco disc version soon. ✪

JULY 15, 1978

RECOMMENDED DISCO DISCS: Although I'm a big fan of producers **Michael Lewis** and **Laurin Rinder**, it's always taken me some time to get into each **El Coco** record, but after weeks of great ambivalence nearly everyone has won me over: certainly "Let's Get It Together" and "Cocomotion" and now "Dancing In Paradise" (just out on AVI). Perhaps this is because the Lewis & Rinder formula for their El Coco work is so effortlessly appealing that it feels almost flimsy at first – hard to believe there's actually something substantial under that slick, calculated pop veneer – but the records usually prove to have a remarkable durability ("Cocomotion" came out last July and lasted far into the fall). El Coco records tend to thrive in the discos where one quickly forgives them their trite lyrics or overused hooks because the sturdy, elegant simplicity of each song takes hold and sweeps you off again and again. On first impression, "Dancing In Paradise" struck me as being unnecessarily derivitive of the group's earlier successes – that Latin/hustle, spun-sugar synthesizer style is beginning to sound a little dated – but, sure enough, three weeks later the song seems to be the perfect distillation of the El Coco sound. The vocals are sweeter, more seductive than ever (they end with an invitation to "Come with me to paradise/Come with me to sweet ecstasy"); the sound clean, cool, entrancing. Structurally, the track builds in layers of slowly increasing intensity, kicked up by breaks and several vocal chorus passages set deep into the record. One "handclap" break's been done better before (in "Cocomotion" where it was a peak moment of the song; here it's almost a throwaway), but others are fresh or diverting (like the chorus of jungle cries) and the cumulative effect is irresistible. Very pretty, very summery–"Dancing" may not hit as big as "Cocomotion" did at this time last year, but it should come close. AVI has high hopes: a numbered limited-edition first pressing of the disco disc was released on yellow gold vinyl in anticipation of an eventual "gold" record. (Note: the B side here is also of interest – a frothy, fast-paced cut called "Love In Your Life.")

Another elegantly-crafted record is **Tony Orlando's** "Don't Let Go" (Elektra), a nearly nine-minute, utterly engaging version of **Roy Hamilton's** 1958 hit that is Orlando's first serious move into the disco field (another convert, for the moment at least, from the pop side). Produced by **Jerry Wexler** and **Barry Beckett**, "Don't Let Go" starts out deceptively slow – a cushy, relaxed groove that gradually gathers steam, enveloping the listener in a warm, glowing arrangement. Orlando's vocals have a nice, laid-back "blue-eyed soul" quality; he doesn't push for emotional effect, but he holds you nevertheless. Only it's after the vocals that the cut really becomes intriguing, with a fine progression of changes that follows immediately upon the female chorus segment. Vibes, a thumping drum beat and striking horns signal the change as the cut is reduced to instrumental basics and rebuilds. A sinuous, subtly electrifying organ/synthesizer passage that had earlier wound its way underneath the chorus chant is brought out front here (by disco mixer **Jimmy Simpson**, one suspects) and provides a focus for the song's energies. A soft, lovely wash of strings follows, then a return to the vocal chorus for a wrap-up. Never expected to rave about a Tony Orlando record, but this one's really terrific and it's the cooled-down change-of-pace that makes it even hotter. My pick right now for a summer refresher... Also wonderfully refreshing: **Paul Horn's** "Undercurrents" (5:40), which Mushroom Records has recently issued on a deep blue 12-inch disc to call attention to this vibrant, airy cut from Horn's "Dream Machine" album, composed, arranged and conducted by **Lalo Schifrin**. Horn, long a favorite for his exquisite atmospheric flute albums (particularly the ones recorded inside the **Taj Mahal** and the **Great Pyramid**), is perfectly at home in this shimmering jazz setting and the song flows like a quiet, crystal clear mountain stream with Horn's flute darting and gliding just above its surface. The rest of the album is just as sensuous, but "Undercurrents" would make the best summer-night opening in a club or at home: not to be missed.

NOTES: The **Michael Zager Band's** "Music Fever" and "Freak:' both from the group's recent "Let's All Chant" album, have been released back-to-back on a disco disc by Private Stock: "Music Fever" is essentially the same, but "Freak" has been lengthened from 3:20 to 5:30, making room for all kinds of wild synthesizer moves

> **❝ I never expected to rave about a Tony Orlando record, but this one's really terrific and it's the cooled-down change-of-pace that makes it even hotter ❞**

VAMP'S, NEW ORLEANS
DJ: Tom Quinn

BEYOND THE CLOUDS/CHAOS – Quartz (Vogue import)
BOOGIE OOGIE OOGIE – A Taste of Honey (Capitol)
BOOGIE TO THE TOP – Idris Muhammad (Kudu)
DANCING IN PARADISE – El Coco (AVI)
DOIN' THE BEST THAT I CAN – Bettye Lavette (West End)
HOT SHOT – Karen Young (West End)
I LOVE AMERICA/WHERE IS MY WOMAN – Patrick Juvet (Casablanca)
LAST DANCE/TGIF/AFTER DARK/TAKE IT TO THE ZOO/YOU'RE THE MOST PRECIOUS THING IN MY LIFE – "TGIF" Soundtrack (Casablanca)
MELLOW LOVIN' – Judy Cheeks (Salsoul)
YOU MAKE ME FEEL (MIGHTY REAL) – Sylvester (Fantasy)

FUTURE, BOSTON
DJ: Joe Carvello

AMERICAN GENERATION/ I FEEL DISCO GOOD – Ritchie Family (Marlin)
BOOGIE OOGIE' OOGIE – A Taste of Honey (Capitol)
DANCING IN PARADISE – El Coco (AVI)
DO OR DIE/FAME – Grace Jones (Island)
HOT SHOT – Karen Young (West End)
I DON'T KNOW WHAT I'D DO – Sweet Cream (Shadybrook)
I LOVE AMERICA – Patrick Juvet (Casablanca)
PERFECT LOVE AFFAIR/COSMIC MELODY – Constellation Orchestra (Prelude)
TGIF/LAST DANCE/DISCO QUEEN – "TGIF" Soundtrack (Casablanca)
WHISTLE BUMP – Deodato (Warner Bros.)

ALFIE'S, SAN FRANCISCO
DJ: Marty Bleckman

AMERICAN GENERATION/I FEEL DISCO GOOD/MUSIC MAN – Ritchie Family (Marlin)
BEYOND THE CLOUDS/QUARTZ – Quartz (Vogue import)
BOOGIE OOGIE OGGIE – A Taste of Honey (Capitol)
DANCE DISCO HEAT/ YOU MAKE ME FEEL (MIGHTY REAL) – Sylvester (Fantasy)
HOT SHOT – Karen Young (West End)
I LOVE AMERICA/GOT A FEELING – Patrick Juvet (Casablanca)
IN THE BUSH – Musique (Prelude)
SANDSTORM – La Bionda (Baby import)
WAR DANCE – Kebekelektrik (Salsoul)
YOU AND I – Rick James (Gordy)

INFINITY, NEW YORK
DJ: Jim Burgess

AFTER DARK/LAST DANCE/THANK GOD IT'S FRIDAY/ DO YOU WANT THE REAL THING – "TGIF" Soundtrack (Casablanca)
AMERICAN GENERATION/I FEEL DISCO GOOD/ MUSIC MAN – Ritchie Family (Marlin)
BOOGIE OOGIE OOGIE – A Taste of Honey (Capitol)
DO OR DIE – Grace Jones(Island)
GOT TO HAVE LOVING/STANDING IN THE RAIN/GARDEN OF LOVE – Don Ray (Polydor)
HOT SHOT – Karen Young (West End)
IN THE BUSH/ SUMMERTIME LOVE – Musique (Prelude)
RUNAWAY LOVE/IF MY FRIENDS COULD SEE ME NOW – Linda Clifford (Curtom)
YOU AND I – Rick James (Gordy)
YOU MAKE ME FEEL MIGHTY REAL)/DANCE DISCO HEAT – Sylvester (Fantasy)

and greatly improving the track... Much longer versions of two key tracks from **Michael Lewis** and **Laurin Rinder's** "Seven Deadly Sins" album are now out on an AVI disc – "Lust" runs 7:30 here and "Envy (Animal Fire)" is 9:54... Though **Dusty Springfield's** "That's The Kind Of Love I've Got For You" faded some time ago, UA has released it on a **Tom Moulton**-mixed 12-inch running 7:06 and it sounds excellent – much cleaner and brighter than originally; worth another listen... Casablanca has pressed a collector's edition version of **Patrick Juvet's** "I Love America" – a Fourth of July package on clear blue vinyl with red stars on a white label and a special picture sleeve – same length as the lp cut (plus a shorter single version for radio play), but even more attractive.

RECOMMENDED ALBUMS: It's been more than four years since the last American release of a **Crystal Grass** album but now the studio group's original producer, **Lee Hallyday**, is back with a new concept album by CG called "The Love Train" (Mercury). Like **Voyage**, this is a travel theme album, but the itinerary is more limited (Greece, Spain, Italy, London) and much of the material borrowed ("Never On Sunday," "Arrivederci Roma"), so a good deal of the record gets bogged down in remakes. Still, the album's opening medley, "Overture To Love Train"/"Believe In Magic"/"Love Train Theme" (8:26), is so strong that it's worth the whole album. A pastiche of songs and styles, incorporating quick snatches of "A Foggy Day In London Town,' "Never On Sunday" and "Roma,' the medley sweeps through all the chic Eurodisco styles and yet somehow manages to sound fresh if not original. One change, with some sassy dialogue between a few women, is right off "Cerrone's Paradise" with some **Linda Clifford** inflection thrown in for good measure, but it all works together so neatly one can only marvel at the ease of the synthesis. Best part: the twangy synthesizer pattern in "Theme," a chugging line I can't get out of my head. Another possible cut: "Love Train To Greece,' the instrumental before a "Never On Sunday" vocal on the flip side, though it's only a little over two minutes. This album may not be the revelation "Crystal World" was, but it's great fun... The Quartz album, an import favorite for several months, is out now on TK's Marlin label – not remixed by Jim Burgess as first announced, but sounding perfectly good in its original form. Made in France by someone named **C. Quartz**, the album consists of four instrumentals, the two most powerful being "Beyond The Clouds" (5:06), a pounding interplay of drums, keyboards (knockout piano, some synthesizer) and horns more effective than many full-orchestra tracks we've been hearing recently; and "Quartz" (12:54-the entire first side), a stirring, original track with a haunting chant that sticks in the mind after one hearing. This second cut is a little long, perhaps, but it's one of the more exciting, off-the-wall European cuts this year; not for all tastes, but very interesting. Also of interest: "Chaos" (6:12), the album's closing cut which starts slow and zips up beautifully. ◗

JULY 22, 1978

I'm rushing off for a short but much-anticipated vacation (there will be no DISCO FILE column for the next two weeks), still frantic with last-minute arrangements, so what follows is a quick, nervous run-down of those new records exceptional enough to carry us all through until I return. Top of the list is **Boris Midney's** follow-up to **USA-European Connection**, **Beautiful Bend**, which should be out within the week on Marlin after nearly two months of sneak previews in and around New York (again, David Mancuso at the Loft had this one on tape first). Midney, who came out of nowhere with USA-European earlier this year and immediately established himself as one of the most important new disco producers of 1978, proves equally astonishing with this new release. Beautiful Bend's format is similar to that of the first Midney lp – one long, two-part track on each side, each running about 15 minutes – and the sound is still very much under the influence of Europe's current dance masters (particularly **Costandinos** and **Cerrone**) but the synthesis of various European approaches and elements of the New York and Philadelphia disco/funk sound (Midney's studio is in Philly; he's got another under construction in New York) is even more profound and captivating here. After only two or three listenings– long before I had a copy of the record – key phrases of the music and its haunting lyric were swirling in my head: a chorus of girls singing "Make that feeling come again" (in the song of the same name) underlined by lovely, sighing waves of "ahh"s – angelic siren calls; those same voices, alternately hushed and chirping, velvety and sparkling, begging, "Ah do it do it to me do it do it to me/I wanna feel it feel it" over a jittery, burbling synthesizer track until you feel like you're in the calm eye of a hurricane, the music and voices a hypnotic rush all around; and, in still another song, those heavenly voices exulting, "That's the meaning/ that's the feeling/that's the joy good loving brings," framed by a short, intricate pattern of violins skipping over a thump-thump-thump grid. The changes here – and all the songs are in constant movement, kaleidoscopes of sound – are so distinctive and inventive they recall the fresh surprise of "Love In C Minor" and "I've Found Love;" Midney is surer, freer and the confidence shows at every turn. If USA-European was an impressive debut, Beautiful Bend is ample confirmation of an exciting talent and, like the earlier album, should prove to be one of disco's most durable records. Look for both sides to show up on Top 10 lists almost immediately and last long into the fall. I, for one, am overwhelmed.

OTHER SUMMER ESSENTIALS: **Gary Criss'** wonderful, light-as-a-feather "Rio De Janeiro" album (Salsoul), a smoothly sophisticated Philadelphia production by **Billy Terrell** with arrangements by **John Davis** which includes the full-length title cut and several other songs of equal charm, notably the stylish medley, "The Girl From Ipanema/Brazilian Nights," and a swinging "Amazon Queen." An ideal summer cooler, with a **Richie Rivera** mix throughout... **Musique**, produced and arranged by **Patrick Adams**, and this veteran New York talent's most polished and appealing work so far – funk with a fine edge like "In the Bush" (8:20), the standout cut here, chunky, raunchy and full of crazy, catch-phrase female vocals; or softer fare like "Summer Love," included here in vocal (6:17) and instrumental or "theme" (8:00) versions, the latter my favorite. The album's title cut, "Keep On Jumpin'" (6:56), is also cute and the whole thing's on Prelude... The latest **John Davis & the Monster Orchestra** album, "Ain't That Enough For You" (Sam Records), steps back from the funk punch of "Up Jumped The Devil" but expands his tasty "Magic Is You" approach quite nicely; choice cuts: "A Bite Of The Apple," "Disco Fever" and the title track; even the "Kojak Theme," previously released on a 12-inch, sounds good here (and note the Beats Per Minute indications alongside each title)... Recorded in Munich and originally released in France, La Bionda is now out in the States on Polydor and presents yet another aspect of the Eurodisco sound – more straight songs here, with lead male and background female vocals and less expansive instrumental fill, no all-inclusive concept but a lot of atmosphere on individual cuts – particularly "Sandstorm" (10:15) with its Middle-Eastern styling that recalls **Sphinx** with some **Santa Esmeralda** thrown in: mysterious, enticing, often invigorating musically and the track that should sell the album. Runner-up: "One For You, One For Me" (5:56), which is bouncy and delightful... The new **C. J. & Co.** album, "Deadeye Dick" (Westbound) is a puzzling, hit-and-miss affair with only occasional stretches that approach the fierce passion of "Devil's Gun" but enough flashy moves to keep the dance floor churning. The vocals can be intrusive, especially on the title track, a frontier shoot-'em-up saga, but even that has its sharp moments and both "Burning Drums Of Fire" and "Hear Say" have grown on me.

❝ It should be out within the week after nearly two months of sneak previews in and around New York (again, David Mancuso at the Loft had this one on tape first) ❞

THE HUNT & THE CHASE, INDIANAPOLIS
DJ: Mark Hultmark

AFTER DARK/TIME/LAST DANCE/DISCO QUEEN/YOU'RE THE MOST PRECIOUS THING IN MY LIFE – "TGIF" Soundtrack (Casablanca)
AMERICAN GENERATION – Ritchie Family (Marlin)
BOOGIE OOGIE OOGIE – A Taste of Honey (Capitol)
DO OR DIE/COMME UN OISEAU/FAME/PRIDE/ALL ON A SUMMER'S NIGHT – Grace Jones (Island)
HOT SHOT – Karen Young (West End)
MISS YOU – Rolling Stones (Rolling Stones)
ROUGH DIAMOND/TOUCH MY HEART – Madleen Kane (Warner Bros.)
RUNAWAY LOVE/IF MY FRIENDS COULD SEE ME NOW/GYPSY LADY – Linda Clifford (Curtom)
YOU AND I – Rick James (Gordy)
YOU MAKE ME FEEL (MIGHTY REAL) – Sylvester (Fantasy)

IPANEMA, NEW YORK
DJ: Ray Velazquez

BEYOND THE CLOUDS/QUARTZ – Quartz (Marlin)
BOOGIE OOGIE OOGIE – A Taste of Honey (Capitol)
DO OR DIE/PRIDE/FAME – Grace Jones (Island)
DON'T LET GO – Tony Orlando (Elektra)
GET ON UP (GET ON DOWN) – Roundtree (Omni)
HOT SHOT – Karen Young (West End)
LOVE DISCO STYLE – Erotic Drum Band (Champagne import)
MIRAGE/WAR DANCE – Kebekelektrik (Salsoul)
MISS YOU – Rolling Stones (Rolling Stones)
TAKE IT TO THE ZOO/AFTER DARK/WITH YOUR LOVE/TGIF – "TGIF" Soundtrack (Casablanca)

RUBAIYAT, ANN ARBOR, MICHIGAN
DJ: Karl Uruski

BOOGIE OOGIE OOGIE – A Taste of Honey (Capitol)
DO OR DIE/PRIDE/FAME – Grace Jones (Island)
DOING THE BEST THAT I CAN – Bettye Lavette (West End)
HEARSAY – C.J. & Co. (Westbound)
HOT SHOT – Karen Young (West End)
I DON'T KNOW WHAT I'D DO – Sweet Cream (Shadybrook)
LET'S START THE DANCE – Bohannon (Mercury)
STAR LOVE – 3 Ounces of Love (Motown)
YOU GOT ME RUNNING/I STILL REACH OUT FOR YOU/MIDNIGHT GIRL – Lenny Williams (ABC)
YOU MAKE ME FEEL (MIGHTY REAL)/DANCE (DISCO HEAT) – Sylvester (Fantasy)

LES NUAGES, NEW YORK
DJ: Tony Carrasco

AIN'T THAT ENOUGH FOR YOU/DISCO FEVER – John Davis & the Monster Orch. (Sam)
AMERICAN GENERATION/I FEEL DISCO GOOD/MUSIC MAN – Ritchie Family (Marlin)
BEYOND THE CLOUDS/QUARTZ – Quartz (Marlin)
BOOGIE OOGIE OOGIE – A Taste of Honey (Capitol)
DANCING IN PARADISE – El Coco (AVI)
No. 1 DEEJAY – Goody Goody (Atlantic)
DO OR DIE/PRIDE/FAME/AUTUMN LEAVES – Grace Jones (Island)
HOT SHOT – Karen Young (West End)
I LOVE AMERICA – Patrick Juvet (Casablanca)
YOU MAKE ME FEEL (MIGHTY REAL)/DANCE (DISCO HEAT)/GRATEFUL – Sylvester (Fantasy)

DISCO DISC FUTURES: Three hot records to watch for in the next weeks: **Dan Hartman's** "Instant Replay" (Blue Sky) a shouting, highspirited song written, produced and sung by this usually rock-oriented studio star – beginning with a number countdown, this cut just takes off and won't stop, especially in the new **Tom Moulton** mix version running about eight minutes. Could be one of the summer's major disco-to-pop crossovers – a natural... "Plato's Retreat," the new **Joe Thomas** release on TK, a tribute to the New York sex palace which is sexy, pumped-up and utterly different from his "Two Doors Down" – wild breaks, the hottest being all weird scatting and percussion joined by sheets of strings... The **Gibson Brothers'** "Heaven," a French import picked up by TK that's another real knockout– heavy overtones of Voyage in the arrangement, so it already sounds familiar, and the vocals are fine and forceful. ✪

DISCO FILE TOP 20

1. **BOOGIE OOGIE OOGIE** – A Taste Of Honey (Capitol)
2. **HOT SHOT** – Karen Young (West End)
3. **YOU MAKE ME FEEL (MIGHTY REAL)/DANCE (DISCO HEAT)** – Sylvester (Fantasy)
4. **DO OR DIE** – Grace Jones (Island)
5. **AFTER DARK/LAST DANCE/TGIF/ TAKE ME TO THE ZOO/WITH YOUR LOVE/DISCO QUEEN** – "TGIF" Soundtrack (Casablanca)
6. **I LOVE AMERICA** – Patrick Juvet (Casablanca)
7. **YOU AND I** – Rick James (Gordy)
8. **MISS YOU** – Rolling Stones (Rolling Stones)
9. **AMERICAN GENERATION/I FEEL DISCO GOOD/MUSIC MAN** – Ritchie Family (Marlin)
10. **RUNAWAY LOVE/IF MY FRIENDS COULD SEE ME NOW** – Linda Clifford (Curtom)
11. **PRIDE/FAME** – Grace Jones (Island)
12. **ROUGH DIAMOND/TOUCH MY HEART** – Madleen Kane (Warner Bros.)
13. **BEYOND THE CLOUDS/QUARTZ** – Quartz (Marlin)
14. **GOT TO HAVE LOVING/STANDING IN THE RAIN/GARDEN OF LOVE/BODY AND SOUL** – Don Ray (Polydor)
15. **WAR DANCE** – Kebekelektrik (Salsoul)
16. **WHISTLE BUMP** – Deodato (Warner Bros.)
17. **LET'S START THE DANCE** – Bohannon (Mercury)
18. **MELLOW LOVIN'** – Judy Cheeks (Salsoul)
19. **DANCING IN PARADISE** – El Coco (AVI)
20. **COME ON DANCE, DANCE** – Saturday Night Band (Prelude)

AUGUST 12, 1978

RECOMMENDED DISCO DISCS: "Love Is In The Air," a hopelessly romantic song saved from potential mush by a soaring disco arrangement, is currently available in three different versions, two domestic releases, one an import. The choice: **John Paul Young's** original version, produced by the song's writers, **Harry Vanda** and **George Young**, is also the most persuasive pop interpretation of the song – the sound is crisp yet full with an invigorating thrust and clean, strong vocals. Already a considerable success as a chart single on the Scotti Brothers label (through Atlantic), the 5:16 disco mix would benefit by a break of some substance, but it still has the most concentrated punch of the three contenders. The Martin Stevens version (7:19), produced in Quebec by **Michel Daigle** and **Dominic Sciscente** and released on CBS Canada, is the most satisfying from a disco standpoint–its arrangement is involving and frequently ornate, opening into an expansive, intricate central break with strings whipped lip through-out like a fancy frosting. The break gives this one the edge even if the vocals aren't as powerful as they might be; Stevens also has the advantage of being the first version to attract the attention of disco DJs, a number of whom have had the import for several months now (a note of thanks

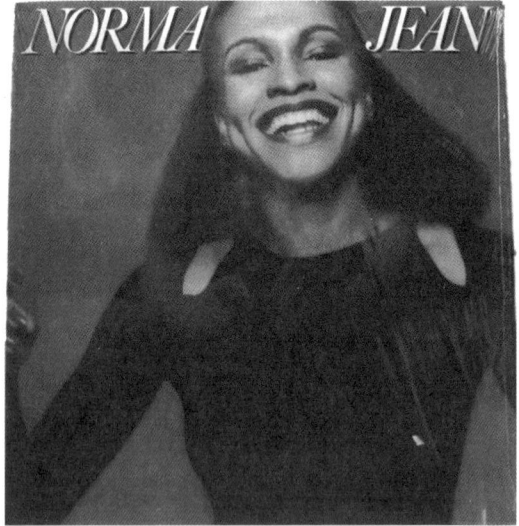

" Richie Rivera and I have put together a two-record greatest disco hits package "

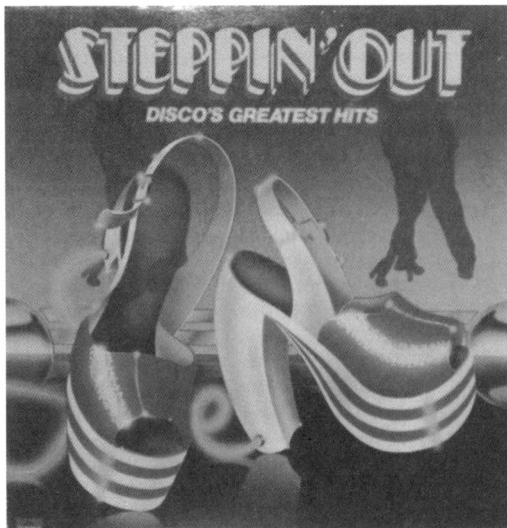

here to Boston DJ **Joseph Lantosca** who sent me a copy some time ago), Finally, there's **Jay Black**, formerly of Jay and the Americans, who returns from a long absence with a version on Millennium (6:45), Black sounds rather too '30s rock crooner-ish for my taste (something between **Elvis** and **Perry Como**), but **Joel Diamond's** production (with a **Leon Pendarvis** arrangement) has a certain flair and a nice female chorus adds some zip... With the trend to down-paced cuts (or at least a greater acceptance of slower, dance beats), **Ashford & Simpson** could enjoy one of their bigger disco hits with their latest, "It Seems To Hang On" (6:57 on Warner Brothers). A song about love's deep, mysterious entanglements, this is one of the team's most inspired lyrics (it grabs you even before you're sure what it's about) and most complex arrangements. The complexity and the frequent shifts in pace (like the short breaks where they just shout, "loose me!" over a tinkling triangle) might present difficulties to dancers at first, but the overall production has a mellow, haunting quality that pulls the listener in as surely as the unshakable love they're singing about. Definitely out of the ordinary, even for the idiosyncratic A&S, and excellent.

REMIXES, REVISED VERSIONS, ETC.: New and, in most cases, improved disco disc pressings are now available (for DJs only) on the following tracks: **Candi Staton's** "Victim" (Warner Brothers), currently a strong personal favorite, remains about the same length as the album cut (8:31) but **Jimmy Simpson** has speeded it up some and created a break near the end by dropping out the vocals and isolating some instrumental tracks for fleeting solos... **D.C. LaRue's** "Let Them Dance" (Casablanca) is already enjoying a big resurgence of interest as a result of the new 9:15 mix which tags the song with a long, predominately instrumental segment rippling with synthesizers .. . **Patti LaBelle's** witty, outrageously energetic and quite off-the-wall "Eyes In The Back of My Head" (Epic) is nearly three minutes

CLUB SWAMP, EAST HAMPTON, N.Y.
DJ: Jeff Baugh

BEAUTIFUL BEND – Beautiful Bend (Marlin)
BOOGIE FUND – Solar Flare (RCA)
BOOGIE OOGIE OOGIE – A Taste of Honey (Capitol)
DO OR DIE – Grace Jones (Island)
HOT SHOT – Karen Young (West End)
KEEP ON JUMPIN'/IN THE BUSH – Musique (Prelude)
LAST DANCE/AFTER DARK – "TGIF" Soundtrack (Casablanca)
PLEASURE ISLAND/LAST DANCE/DIDN'T THE TIME GO FAST – Paul Jabara (Casablanca)
THINK IT OVER – Cissy Houston (Private Stock)
YOU MAKE ME FEEL (MIGHTY REAL)/ DANCE DISCO HEAT – Sylvester (Fantasy)

FUTURE, BOSTON
DJ: Joe Calvallo

DO OR DIE/PRIDE/FAME – Grace Jones (Island)
HOT SHOT – Karen Young (West End)
IT DON'T MEAN, A THING/DISCO JAM – Eddie Drennon (Casablanca)
KEEP ON JUMPIN'/IN THE BUSH – Musique (Prelude)
LET'S START THE DANCE – Bohannon (Mercury)
LET THEM DANCE – D.C. LaRue (Casablanca)
MR, DJ YOU KNOW HOW TO MAKE ME DANCE – Glass Family (Joe)
STAND UP – Atlantic Starr (A&M)
THINK IT OVER – Cissy Houston (Private Stock)
YOU MAKE ME FEEL (MIGHTY REAL)/ DANCE (DISCO HEAT) – Sylvester (Fantasy)

STUDIO ONE, LOS ANGELES
DJ: Manny Slali

BEAUTIFUL BEND – Beautiful Bend (Marlin)
DO OR DIE/PRIDE/FAME – Grace Jones (Island)
DON'T LET GO – Tony Orlando (Elektra)
I LOVE AMERICA – Patrick Juvet (Casablanca)
KEEP ON JUMPIN' /IN THE BUSH/SUMMER LOVE/SUMMER LOVE THEME – Musique (Prelude)
SATURDAY/SORCERER – Norma Jean (Bearsville)
THINK IT OVER – Cissy Houston (Private Stock)
YOU MAKE ME FEEL (MIGHTY REAL)/ DANCE (DISCO HEAT) – Sylvester (Fantasy disco disc)

THE RANCH, CHICAGO
DJ: Jim Thompson

AUTUMN LEAVES/DO OR DIE/AM I EVER GONNA FALL IN LOVE IN NEW YORK CITY – Grace Jones (Island)
BEAUTIFUL BEND – Beautiful Bend (Marlin)
YOU MAKE ME FEEL (MIGHTY REAL)/ DANCE (DISCO HEAT) – Sylvester (Fantasy)
HOT SHOT – Karen Young (West End)
LOVE TO SEE YOU DANCE/YOU DANCE INTO MY LIFE/DANCIN' ON – Finished Touch (Motown)
KEEP ON JUMPIN'/IN THF BUSII/SUMMER LOVE THEME – Musique (Prelude)
MOTHER LOOK WHAT THEY'VE DONE TO ME – Amanda Lear (Chrysalis)
ONLY YOU/WHEN SOMEBODY LOVES YOU BACK – Teddy Pendergrass (Phila. Intl.)
SATURDAY/SORCERER/HAVING A PARTY – Norma Jean (Bearsville)
YOU GOT ME RUNNING – Lenny Williams (ABC)

longer than the lp version (now 8:02), giving more space to the intro and opening up the wild second half of the song so Patti can shout, soul gospel-style, to her heart's content; still uneven, quirky, but constantly amazing (on the flip side: a longer version of her syncopated, Jamaican-flavored "Save The Last Dance For Me," running 7:15)... **George McCrae's** "Let's Dance (People All Over The World)" (TK) has undergone a Richie Rivera mix that sharpens up the intro with percussion, strengthens the rhythmic backbone of the track and injects whole new bursts of Latin drumming and terrific vocal/violin counterpoint and is now 6:10... **Brooklyn Dreams'** unjustly slighted "Street Man" (Millennium) has been revised for a second 12-inch pressing marked "disco remix" that deletes much of the vocals in favor of churning synthesizer – laced instrumental segments that are good but tend to cut the punch of the original; and those nervous electronic bleeps that stud the production have now been altered so it sounds like the turntable is slowing down – think I'd prefer a less radical revision, but both versions deserve attention... A **Jim Burgess** remix of the **Ritchie Family's** "American Generation" (TK) is aimed primarily at sharpening up the sound qualities of the track, so there are not many major structural changes here, only a richer break at the end and an altogether richer sound; "I Feel Disco Good" is included as a separate cut on the reverse side... **Lenny Williams'** "You Got Me Running" (ABC) is also improved quality-wise now that it's on a disco disc, but no other changes have been made from the 7:45 original lp cut – still the 12-inch comes just in time to catch the growing enthusiasm for this song (too bad they didn't include "I Still Reach Out" on the other side).

FEEDBACK: In an effort to assure myself that I'd not fallen too far behind in my time off, I called a number of people this week to ask what were the strongest records of the past few weeks. The following were the most frequently mentioned releases: **Musique's** entire lp, especially "In the Bush" and "Keep on Jumpin'," **Cissy Houston's** "Think It Over;" **Beautiful Bend** (still available only on test pressings because of a pressing plant delay, due this week sometime); **Joe Thomas'** "Plato's Retreat," "You Got Me Running" by **Lenny Williams**; **Tony Orlando's** "Don't Let Go" and the **D.C. LaRue** "Let Them Dance" remix.

NOTED: Richie Rivera and I put together a two-record greatest disco hits package for Polydor entitled "Steppin' Out" and including previously non-commercial mixes ("Risky Changes" and "Running Away"), a somewhat longer version of "Dance Little Dreamer" (5:ll) and a number of classics-- "Jungle Fever," "Crystal World," "Never Can Say Goodbye:' "Casanova Brown" – as well as recent gems like "Got To Have loving," "Dr. Doo-Dah," "Moonlight Lovin'" and Joe Simon's hard-to-find '" Need You, You Need Me." Rivera mixed, I did the liner notes, and we both hope you'll enjoy. ◗

AUGUST 19, 1978

RECOMMENDED ALBUMS: like the group's previous release, "Smoke Your Troubles Away" (the 1976 single on Earhole Records, still one of the most interesting underground records of the past few years), the **Glass Family's** first album, "Mr. DJ You Know How to Make Me Dance," arrived out of the blue (JDC Records, 610 Venice Blvd. South, Marina del Rey, California, to be exact) recently and rapidly became a personal favorite. The sound here is eccentric, crisp, fairly sparse, with few references to mainstream disco styles but a certain affinity with the lighter side of **Musique** and the **Saturday Night Band**. The title cut, "Mr. DJ" (7:05), is the one that won me over for several reasons: the lyrics, written by ace disco promotion woman **Starr Arning**, address the DJ from an insider's viewpoint that's biting, often clever (sample: "All the promo men are rushin' tests directly to your door/The trades all have your number/Pools are beggin' your support"); vocalist **Taka Boom** (**Chaka Khan's** sister – no kidding) is at her best here – sharp, resilient, perfectly controlled even at her most abandoned; and the production (by **Jim Callon**) is supple, simple, unexpectedly engaging, with a deep stroking horn pattern that sticks in the mind after a couple of hearings. The album's two other compositions, particularly the 16-minute "Disco Concerto" that fills up side two, have a strange fascination – not driving like "Mr. DJ," but dreamy, moody, involving. Definitely out of left field, the Glass Family may be an acquired taste, but this album only whets my appetite for more. (Thanks to Judy Weinstein for turning me on to this one.)

Paul Jabara, star of disc and screen, is back with his strongest disco record to date – the "Pleasure Island" cut from the **Bob Esty**-produced "Keeping Time" album on Casablanca. A celebration of Fire Island high (and low) life that captures the spirit and spice of the place with more subtlety than the **Village People's** earlier tribute, "Pleasure Island" (10:40) begins as a breezy, seductive invitation to a "paradise" any tourist might appreciate, but once Jabara's breathy vocals end, it's apparent the song is concerned with something more serious than sun and surf. Jabara says he wanted to evoke the rising excitement of a walk, with detours, between the Grove and the Pines very late some summer night, and he does so vividly, forcefully. The mood here slipss superbly through several gears, a fever chart of changes that build in passion and intensity, pumped along by jagged horns, hot drums and reaching a sudden climax. Also included here: "Last Dance," Jabara's own composition now slowed-down, super-sensuous, irresistible: "Take Good Care Of My Baby," the standard, in a rather predictable and relentlessly bouncy arrangement, but anything that brings Jabara and **Pattie Brooks** together for a duet is a welcome treat (Brooks also contributes background vocals on most of the other cuts here) and an upbeat pop disco cut called "Dancin' (Lifts Your Spirits Higher)." But "Pleasure Island" is the set's summer stunner, the one that will put Jabara back in the discos where he belongs.

> **"All the promo men are rushin' tests directly to your door"**

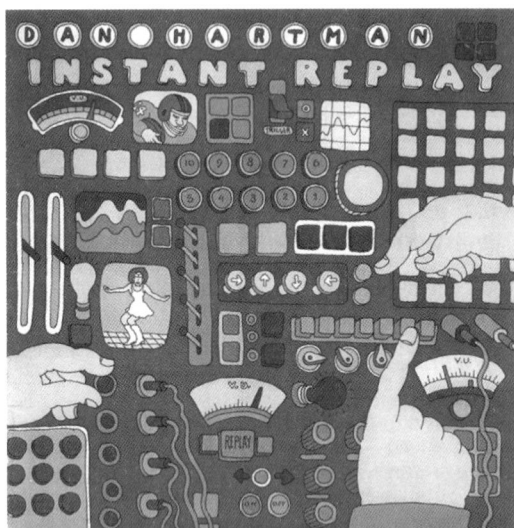

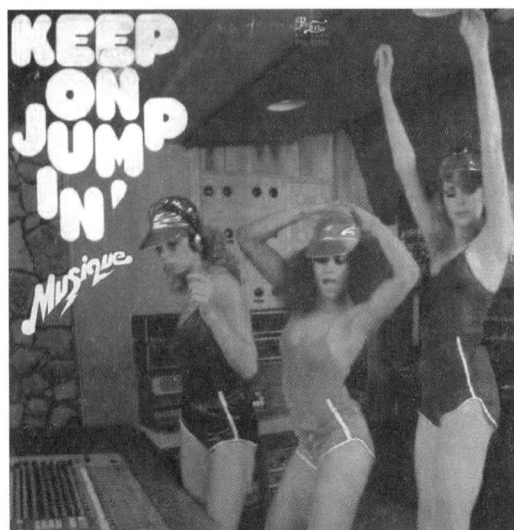

I-BEAM, SAN FRANCISCO
DJ: Michael Garrett

BEAUTIFUL BEND – Beautiful Bend (Marlin)
BURNING DRUMS OF FIRE – C.J. & Co. (Westbound)
DO OR DIE/FAME – Grace Jones (Island)
IN THE BUSH/KEEP ON JUMPIN' – Musique (Prelude)
IT DON'T MEAN A THING/DISCO JAM/ STOMP YOUR FEET – Eddie Drennon (Casablanca)
OVER AND OVER – Charles Earland (Mercury)
PLEASURE ISLAND – Paul Jabara (Casablanca)
SUPERSTAR – Bob McGilpin (Butterfly)
YOU COULD HAVE BEEN A DANCER – Sea Cruise (Celsius import)
YOU MAKE ME FEEL GUILTY (MIGHTY REAL)/ DANCE (DISCO HEAT) – Sylvester (Fantasy)

SANDPIPER, FIRE ISLAND PINES, N.Y,
DJ: Richie Rivera

CHANGIN' – Sharon Ridley (Tabu)
DO OR DIE – Grace Jones (Island)
I GOT DANCIN' IN MY FEET – Laura Taylor (TK)
INSTANT REPLAY – Dan Hartman (Blue Sky)
LET'S DANCE – George McCrae (TK)
SUMMER LOVE/SUMMER LOVE THEME/IN THE BUSH/KEEP ON JUMPIN' – Musique (Prelude)
THAT'S THE MEANING/BOOGIE MOTION – Beautiful Bend (Marlin)
THINK IT OVER – Cissy Houston (Private Stock)
VICTIM – Candi Staton (Warner Bros.)
YOU MAKE ME FEEL (MIGHTY REAL)/ DANCE (DISCO HEAT) – Sylvester (Fantasy)

DCA CLUB, PHILADELPHIA
DJ: Kurt Borusiewicz

BEAUTIFUL BEND – Beautiful Bend (Marlin)
HOT SHOT – Karen Young (West End)
IN THE BUSH – Musique (Prelude)
LET'S START THE DANCE/ME AND THE GANG – Bohannon (Mercury)
LET THEM DANCE – D.C. LaRue (Casablanca)
MISS YOU – Rolling Stones (Rolling Stones)
PLEASURE ISLAND – Paul Jabara (Casablanca)
TWO LOVES HAVE I/JOSEPHINE SUPERSTAR/ SAINT LOUIS/BROADWAY/STAR OF PARIS – Phylicia Allen (Casablanca)
YOU GOTTA DANCE – Pacific Blue (Prelude)
YOU MAKE ME FEEL (MIGHTY REAL)/ DANCE (DISCO HEAT) – Sylvester (Fantasy)

MR. PIPS/FORT LAUDERDALE
DJ: Tom Saccoman

DO OR DIE/FAME – Grace Jones (Island)
DOIN' THE BEST THAT I CAN' – Bettye Lavette (West End)
HOT SHOT – Karen Young (West End)
IN THE BUSH/KEEP ON JUMPINI' /SUMMER LOVE – Musique (Prelude)
INSTANT REPLAY – Dan Hartman (Blue Sky)
LET THEM DANCE – D.C. LaRue (Casablanca)
NO GOODBYES – Curtis Mayfield (Curtom)
PLATO'S RETREAT – Joe Thomas (TK)
THINK IT OVER – Cissy Houston (Private Stock)
YOU MAKE ME FEEL (MIGHTY REAL)/ DANCE (DISCO HEAT) – Sylvester (Fantasy)

OTHER RECOMMENDED ALBUMS: The title song from **War's** soundtrack for "Youngblood" (UA) may not be as catchy/cute and accessible as "Galaxy," but it has the depth and power of War at its best and it develops into one of those richly-textured, jazzy work-outs the group has always done so well. The album cut has its own elegant, almost ritualistic pace, as if a serious but high-spirited ceremony were about to take place following the vocals (I first heard the track in Paris at Le Palace, where it sounded mysterious, moving, very African). But a disco disc remix version becomes available this week that trims the cut some (from 10:42 to 9:07), adds a longer, more crackling intro and considerably tightens up the final instrumental segment by slipping in a neat little break and emphasizing the song's punch. The remix gets right to the point on the dance floor and also features a much more brilliant sound quality, so it should have the edge on the club level. "Keep On Doin'" (3:50) is basic funk with wild, chanting vocals and an insinuating horn winding sinuously through the dense rhythm; it, too, is included on the disco disc. Other possibilities: "Flying Machine (The Chase)" (7:39), a Latin-beat, loose jazz instrumental with strong flute and piano solos that might make a good early evening/late night cooler, and "This Funky Music Makes You Feel Good" (6:26) which gets so nice toward the end that its plodding beginning might be overlooked by some... **Norma Jean's** album on Bearsville is somewhat lacking in drive but, like her previously-released "Saturday" (included here), it has a pleasant, immensely attractive style and the best cuts are sweet, sophisticated pop/soul songs, beautifully sung. Already happening in the clubs: "Sorcerer" (4:58) and "Having A Party" (4:28), the **Sam Cooke** song given a truly delightful, frothy treatment here. Production is by **Nile Rogers** and **Bernard Edwards**, the Chic team... **Eddie Drennon's** "It Don't Mean a Thing" album on Casablanca has been picking up a lot of action in the past few weeks and may prove to be one of the summer's most interesting sleeper records. Drennon's Latinspiced funk fits in with the current surge of neo-funk cuts (especially **Bohannon**, **Rick James**) and he has never sounded more polished or on-target. The knockout: "Disco Jam" (5:57), with its chunky, vibrant arrangement of percussion, strings and live-wire guitar. But don't ignore "It Don't Mean A Thing," "Stomp Your Feet" and "Can You Dig It."

RECOMMENDED DISCO DISCS: As night fever spreads, there are more and more songs about partying, hard dancing and what two of the best call the nightlife. Pick up on the following right now (details will follow next week): "I Love the Nightlife (Disco Round)" by **Alicia Bridges**, an off-the-wall surprise that everyone's been talking about, available this week as a **Jim Burgess** remix (Polydor); **Blair's** "Nightlife" (Solar Sound); **Solar Flare's** "Boogie Fund" (RCA); "You Gotta Dance" by **Pacific Blue** (blue vinyl on Prelude); and **Stargard's** "What You Waitin' For" (MCA). All essentials. ✎

RECOMMENDED DISCO DISCS: While so many of the best dance records out at the moment celebrate disco itself, **Alicia Bridges** does it most remarkably in her "I Love The Nightlife" (Polydor), an eccentric, sharp-tongued, decidedly off-beat song that could turn out to be one of the summer's surprise sensations. Bridges, who sounds like an unsentimental **Phoebe Snow**, slings barbs at a tiresome boyfriend and tells him she'd rather go out "on the disco-round"– "I want some action! I wanna live!" – than stay in and Talk It Over. The pace is bright, looser than most current cuts and very attractive; production: spare, uncomplicated – a hot sax flourish, a crisp break (courtesy disco mixer **Jim Burgess**, who also expanded the intro, lengthening the track from 3:09 on the lp and single to 5:37 here). Bridges' unique, scratchy voice and the unusual production make "I Love The Nightlife" stand out on any "disco-round," but this may be an acquired taste. In any case, it's a personal pick this week... Another favorite: **Blair's** "Nightlife" (7:25 on Solar Sound Records in Buffalo, N.Y.), a gently pumping, vibrant jazz/neofunk cut that is also deceptively simple and effective. The male lead vocals (and the lyrics, which display an almost adolescent delight in merely up late and meeting girls) leave room for improvement, but they're more than made up for by the female chorus and the rich, mellow feel of the production. There's a long break with a tingling guitar solo followed by a synthesizer outing, but the basic arrangement hardly needs trimmings –it had me from the very beginning. Again, this may not be for all crowds, but it should be checked out – and watch for a **Jimmy Simpson** remix due later this week.

Briefly, these other disco discs continue the celebration of the party life: **Solar Flare's** "Boogie Fund" (RCA), written and produced by Sigma Studio stars **T. G. Conway** and **Allan Felder,** has a sound that recalls both the **Trammps** and **Double Exposure** – plenty of density and snap in a big production that retains its fine edge. The sound is Philadelphia at its most energetic and joyous, never falling into a rut because the shifts between the excellent male vocals and the instrumental breaks are frequent and consistently sharp. Time: 7:06... **Stargard's** "What You Waitin' For" (7:30 on MCA) is basically "Which Way Is Up" continued (or "Car Wash Part III"): same brassy funk sound; same tough, biting vocals. Not as fresh as it was the first time around (or the second), but it's irresistible on the dancefloor anyway – and that's precisely the point. One drawback:

the fade-to-nothing halfway through which leads into a sizzling instrumental section but is, in itself, hard to work with... Appearing on three out of four top 10 lists its first week out, the **Afro-Cuban Band's** "Rhythm Of life" (6:25 on Arista) looks like another hit for producer/arranger/composer **Michael Zager** (currently on our chart with **Cissy Houston's** "Think It Over"). Zager definitely has a flair for slickly-styled pop disco and "Rhythm" continues his MZ Band sound with a slightly lighter touch – nothing particularly new, but the song has a nice bouncy hook, chirpy female vocals. Pleasant, quite unpretentious, the only gimmicks are in the packaging: clear vinyl and a sleeve that glows in the dark once it's exposed to light... **Pacific Blue's** "You Gotta Dance" (Prelude) has a stinging, crunchy **Bee Gees** sound, relentlessly upbeat with the European power – pop disco drive (formerly an import 12-inch, it originated in France). The flip side, "Argentina Forever" (8:19), has a more expansive, more sumptuous production (swirling strings, crackling guitars, falsetto chants) but sustains the drive of "Dance." Although the message of "You Gotta Dance" is neatly summed up in its title, "Argentina" is a song of hope for peace in that repressive country and a bit of counter-revolutionary propaganda at the same time. The political thrust may be lost on the dancefloor, but the terrific sound of both songs will have its impact nevertheless. Pressed on bright blue vinyl... **Atlantic Starr's** "Stand Up" (6:24 on A&M) has a double-edged message – it's an invitation to "check out your mind" and/or start partying. But the message of the music is clear: this is hard funk for serious dancing, similar to **Stargard** but with punchier male vocals, a denser group sound. Production is by **Bobby Eli** and the group's debut album (featuring a shorter version of "Stand Up") is well worth picking up – listen to "Where There's Smoke There's Fire" and "Gimme Your Lovin'."

WELCOME BACK: It's been nearly two years since the original release of **Buffalo Smoke's** "Stubborn Kind Of Fella," a great, marvelously high-spirited version of the **Marvin Gaye** classic produced and arranged for disco by Lou Courtney, and in that time the record has reached the status of a cult item – copies of the non-commercial disco disc are reported to be going for $50 at New York disco stores. Now RCA has reissued the record in a special edition (both commercial and promo copies on milk-white vinyl in a black sleeve)

❝ The record has reached the status of a cult item — copies of the non-commercial disco disc are reported to be going for $50 at New York disco stores ❞

RISE CLUB, BOSTON
DJ: Cosmo Wyatt

GET ON UP (GET ON DOWN) – Roundtree (Omni)
IN THE BUSH/KEEP ON JUMPINI' – Musique (Prelude)
INSTANT REPLAY – Dan Hartman (Blue Sky)
JUST AS LONG AS WE'RE TOGETHER/SOFT AND WET – Prince (Warner Bros.)
LET'S START THE DANCE – Bohannan (Mercury)
NO GOODBYES/DO IT ALL NIGHT – Curtis Mayfield (Curtom)
RHYTHM OF LIFE – Afro-Cuban Band (Arista)
STAND UP/WHERE THERE'S SMOKE THERE'S FIRE – Atlantic Star (A&M)
YOU GOT ME RUNNING – Lenny Williams (ABC)
YOU MAKE ME FEEL (MIGHTY REAL) – Sylvester (Fantasy)

CIRCUS DISCO, LOS ANGELES
DJ: Mike Lewis

BEAUTIFUL BEND – Beautiful Bend (Marlin)
DANCE (DISCO HEAT)/YOU MAKE ME FEEL (MIGHTY REAL) – Sylvester (Fantasy)
DANCING IN PARADISE – El Coco (AVI)
GET READY FOR THE FUTURE – Winners (Roadshow/Ariola)
I CAN HEAR MUSIC – California (RSO)
LOVE WON'T BE DENIED – Len Boone (Chrysalis)
PLEASURE ISLAND – Paul Jabara (Casablanca)
RHYTHM OF LIFE – Afro-Cuban Band (Arista)
SUPERSTAR/GO FOR THE MONEY – Bob McGilpin (Butterfly)
THINK IT OVER – Cissy Houston (Private Stock)

TROCADERO TRANSFER, SAN FRANCISCO
DJ: Gary Tighe

BEAUTIFUL BEND – Beautiful Bend (Marlin)
I LOVE MY DISCO BABY – Squallor (Epic import)
INSTANT REPLAY – Dan Hartman (Blue Sky)
LOVE IS IN THE AIR – Martin Stevens (Columbia import)
LOVE WON'T BE DENIED – Len Boone (Chrysalis)
NO.1 DEEJAY – Goody Goody (Atlantic)
RHYTHM OF LIFE – Afro-Cuban Band (Arista)
SUPERSTAR – Bob McGilpin (Butterfly)
THINK IT OVER – Cissy Houston (Private Stock)
VICTIM – Candi Staton (Warner Bros.)

BAREFOOT BOY, NEW YORK
DJ: Tony Smith

BEAUTIFUL BEND – Beautiful Bend (Marlin)
HOT SHOT – Karen Young (West End)
IN THE BUSH/KEEP ON JUMPIN'/SUMMER LOVE – Musique (Prelude)
INSTANT REPLAY – Dan Hartman (Blue Sky)
LET'S START THE DANCE – Bohannon (Mercury)
PLATO'S RETREAT – Joe Thomas (K)
VICTIM – Candi Staton (Warner Bros.)
WARNING-DANGER/THINK IT OVER/ SOMEBODY SHOULD HAVE TOLD ME – Cissy Houston (Private Stock)
YOU GOT ME RUNNING/MIDNIGHT LADY/ I STILL REACH OUT – Lenny Williams (ABC)
YOU MAKE ME FEEL (MIGHTY REAL)/ DANCE (DISCO HEAT) – Sylvester (Fantasy)

featuring the original cut (7:10) on one side and a new mix by **David Todd** on the other (7:42). Both are exceptional but, back to back, they tend to high light each other's deficiencies. Sharp, explosive handclaps seem to be a Todd trademark and he uses them liberally here to give a nice kick to the track, but he also drops out several tracks, leaving things cleaner but sometimes empty, and pushes the female chorus back into the mix too far. Next to Todd's reworked version, however, the original sounds kinda jumbled and muddy at times and one misses the new intro and the sparkle of the new break. DJs will probably switch back and forth – either way, they've got one of the freshest productions of the past few years. Watch it show up on charts all over again.

FEEDBACK: **Len Boone's** "Love Won't Be Denied," a disco disc on Chrysalis, has been around for several months now without causing of a stir on the nation's dancefloors, but if this week's reports are any indication, it's a song whose time has come. Suddenly, not only is the record being talked about, it's being included on top 10 lists (see those from Gary Tighe in San Francisco and Mike Lewis in l.A.), so a quick (re)evaluation is in order. One side of "Love Won't Be Denied" is vocal (6:51), the other instrumental (8:04), both rather over-long but brightened by an optimistic, zippy arrangement bubbling with electronic effects. These effects tend to overpower the instrumental version (it begins to sound like a roomful of excited, highly amplified mosquitos), but the vocal is well-structured and features a sudden conga break at just the right moment. Cute and catchy... Another record which seems to have caught on with our west coast reporters is **Bob McGilpin's** "Superstar" (the disco disc version of the title track from McGilpin's debut on Butterfly). The approach here is neither disco nor rock, but an extremely comfortable and workable fusion; McGilpin sings (in a high but appealing voice – this is surely the year of the white falsetto) and plays guitar against an energetic arrangement of swift strings and pounding drums. The break is odd (an after-thought?) but the whole thing grows on you. Also recommended: the flip side, "Go For The Money," with an even stronger string arrangement, gutsy sound... Although advance copies of "# 1 Dee Jay" by **Goody Goody** were made available to disco DJs about two months ago, the record is only now going into official release and the earlier disco disc version has been replaced with a new Atlantic 12- inch revised by producer/arranger **Vincent Montana** himself. This "Montana Mix" gives the song the frame it originally lacked: a very tasty intro, a somewhat fuller break (wonderful vibes, sax), a smoother flow. It also gives DJs the option of playing an instrumental side should they find the vocals (and lyrics) too sugar-coated for their tastes; here Montana is as inventive and entertaining as ever, minus the strings, and the singer (Montana's daughter, in fact) is held to an occasional word or two. Both versions are about seven and a half minutes long.

ALBUM OF THE MOMENT: **"Gregg Diamond's Starcruiser"** on Marlin. Review next week. ◐

SEPTEMBER 2, 1978

Producer **Gregg Diamond**, whose **Bionic Boogie** album was one of the prime examples of disco, American pop style, released last year, continues in much the same bright, rich vein with his **Starcruiser** album, just out on Marlin. Using a number of the key studio musicians assembled for Bionic Boogie and repeating his own performance on piano, Fender Rhodes and other keyboards, Diamond preserves the brilliant, highly-polished feel of the earlier album while stepping out in a somewhat more sophisticated direction. Diamond displays a softer, subtler and surer touch than many of the other producers working the pop disco field and the best material on Starcruiser is wonderfully easy to get into – catchy and comfortable. "Fancy Dancer" (6:14) is open, airy, a fine summer tonic with its darting guitar work and sweet-flowing strings; a falsetto chorus (girls in the lead) swoons in the ecstasies of the dance and the fancy dancer that sweeps them through it "cheek to cheek": "Never get off/never get off my feet." "Starcruisin'" (6:14) is a more energetic trip with both vocals and instrumental flourishes sharp-edged, clipped, giving the song a springy, exhilarating feel with plenty of zip in the break. The third favorite, "This Side Of Midnight" (5:24), is a combination of the first two – the looseness and shimmering quality of "Fancy Dancer" plus the happy bounce of "Starcruisin'" – with particularly striking vocals and a pulsing, attention-grabbing break that plays off the strings and guitars. As with Bionic Boogie, many of the remaining tracks – notably "Island Boogie," "Bring Back Your Love" and the instrumental "Arista Vista" – are attractive, strong runners-up, making this another solid album from Diamond & Co. and one that should last well into the fall.

HEAVYWEIGHT BOUT (ROUND ONE): Anyone watching the trend of rock-to-disco remakes over the past year could have predicted the eventual emergence of a disco version of "I'm A Man," which, after "Gimme Some Lovin'," was the **Stevie Winwood/Spencer Davis Group** classic most likely to succeed on the dance floor. Now, however, we're faced with not one but two new versions, both in nearly simultaneous release at the disco level: one an Italian import on Prelude by a group named **Macho** which runs nearly 18 minutes on one side of an lp due for commercial release within the week; the other made in Canada by **Star City** and out already as an 8:44 disco disc on TK with an album to follow. Macho draws most creatively upon the precedents already set by **Santa Esmeralda**, **Kongas** and **Revelacion** toning down the flamenco touches (the Spanish flavor comes out in some of the horn passages here but is otherwise minimal) but

recalling the others in its rough, shouted vocals (though they're often so heavily accented one has only the faintest idea of what they're saying) and superb, expansive central break. Macho's break begins with an echoing trade-off of riffs between the horns and one of those deep, froggy synthesizers – much like the "five tones" exchange in "Close Encounters Of The Third Kind." It builds relentlessly over a crackling synthesizer pattern, layering on breathy chants, percussion, guitars, then breaking back into the swirling density of the basic track. Star City's approach is more tightly aggressive, cleaner and pop-oriented (the opening picks up from "Let's All Chant") but it holds few surprises. A mock-macho tone is established with the male chorus chanting the title or growling "Gimme, gimme" in unnaturally deep-chested voices, so a four-line female vocal segment toward the end is at first unsettling in the midst of all this masculine ego-strutting, but her throaty tribute to The Man adds a seductive, velvety underlining to the rest. The Latin percussion break is standard but steamy nonetheless – only it's no match for the instrumental tour de force of the Macho version. Star City, on the other hand, is the more concentrated knockout (thanks, one suspects, to its **Jim Burgess** mix) and the one with the most commercial edge. Macho's "Man" is overlong, perhaps, but its changes make it supremely satisfying as a disco workout and it has that European appeal which could prove to be a key deciding factor. Prelude has a temporary jump with "I'm A Man" test-pressings rushed into a number of clubs across the country (and already appearing on two 01 this week's top 10 lists) but TK is first in the marketplace and coming on strong. Should be an interesting battle.

RECOMMENDED ALBUMS: Briefly, a rundown of recent releases of interest by female vocalists: **Carol Douglas'** "Burnin'" (Midsong/ MCA), her first album in two years, picks up where she left off with "Midnight Love Affair" in the three-part, 17-minute medley on side one here. The medley's opener, "Fell In love For The First Time Today," closest in style to "Midnight," captures the exultant, "caught-up-in-a-dream" mood of a new love that gets more intense in "Burnin'," the crunchy central cut with its driving break and syndrum accents. "Let's Get Down To Doin' It Tonight" closes the side on' a nitty gritty note, taking the romance and passion to its logical conclusion with both the vocals and the production more hard-edged here. Side one production credit: **Ed O'Loughlin** and **John Davis**. Also included: the previously released Douglas version of "Night Fever"... **Cissy Houston's** "Think It Over" (Private Stock) provides at least one other

> ## **" Anyone watching the trend of rock-to-disco remakes over the past year could have predicted a disco version of "I'm A Man" "**

PARADISE GARAGE, NEW YORK
DJ: Larry Levan

BLACK WIDOW WOMAN – Afro-Cuban Band (Arista)
GET UP AND DO SOMETHING/IT SEEMS TO HANG ON – Ashford & Simpson (Warner Bros.)
IN THE BUSH/KEEP ON JUMPIN – Musique (Prelude)
LET'S START THE DANCE/ME AND THE GANG – Bohannon (Mercury)
LET THEM DANCE – D.C. LaRue (Casablanca)
MR, DJ YOU KNOW HOW TO MAKE ME DANCE – Glass Family (JDC)
ONLY YOU – Teddy Pendergrass (Phila. Intl.)
VICTIM – Candi Staton (Warner Bros.)
WARNING–DANGER/THINK IT OVER – Cissy Houston (Private Stock)
YOU MAKE ME FEEL (MIGHTY REAL)/DANCE (DISCO HEAT) – Sylvester (Fantasy)

SAHARA, NEW YORK
DJ: Sharon White

BEAUTIFUL BEND – Beautiful Bend (Marlin)
BEYOND THE CLOUDS – Quartz (Marlin)
DISCO JAM – Eddie Drennon (Casablanca)
I'M A MAN – Macho (Prelude)
IN THE BUSH/KEEP ON JUMPIN'/SUMMER LOVE/SUMMER LOVE THEME – Musique (Prelude)
INSTANT REPLAY – Dan Hartman (Blue Sky)
LAST DANCE/PLEASURE ISLAND – Paul Jabara (Casablanca)
MR, DJ YOU KNOW HOW TO MAKE ME DANCE – Glass Family (JDC)
VICTIM – Candi Staton (Warner Bros.)
YOU MAKE ME FEEL (MIGHTY REAL)/DANCE (DISCO HEAT) – Sylvester (Fantasy)

PARADE, NEW ORLEANS
DJ: Pete Van Waesberge, Jr.

BEAUTIFUL BEND – Beautiful Bend (Marlin)
DO, OR DIE – Grace Jones (Island)
DOIN' THE BEST THAT I CAN – Bettye Lavette (West End)
FANCY DANCER/STARCRUISIN'/THIS SIDE OF MIDNIGHT – Gregg Diamond's Starcruiser (Marlin)
HOT SHOT – Karen Young (West End)
I'M A MAN/BECAUSE THERE IS MUSIC IN THE AIR – Macho (Prelude)
#1 DEEJAY – Goody Goody (Atlantic)
PLEASURE ISLAND – Paul Jabara (Casablanca)
VICTIM – Candi Staton (WB)
YOU MAKE ME FEEL (MIGHTY REAL)/DANCE (DISCO HEAT) – Sylvester (Fantasy)

RAINBOW RANCH, E. LANSING, MI.
DJ: Larry Sanders

AIN'T THAT ENOUGH FOR YOU/DISCO FEVER – John Davis & the Monster Orch. (Sam)
GREGG DIAMOND'S STARCRUISER (Marlin)
INSTANT REPLAY – Dan Hartman (Blue Sky)
LET'S START THE DANCE – Bohannan (Mercury)
LITTERBUG – Gentle Persuasion (Warner Bros.)
LOVIN' FEVER/YOU CAPTURED MY HEART/ EVERYTIME I SEE YOU I GO WILD – High Energy (Gordy)
PLEASURE ISLAND/DIDN'T THE TIME GO FAST – Paul Jabara (Casablanca)
STUFF LIKE THAT/LOVE, I NEVER HAD IT SO GOOD – Quincy Jones (A&M)
THINK IT OVER/WARNING (DANGER)/LOVE DON'T HURT PEOPLE – Cissy Houston (Private Stock)
YOU GOT ME RUNNING – Lenny Williams (ABC)

track with the appeal of its title tune: "Warning – Danger" (5:56), a fine showcase for Houston's roughly-textured vocals' and producer **Michael Zager's** no-nonsense approach to disco – sleek, pumping with lots of zest in the break. Also recommended: "Somebody Should Have Told Me," whose energetic pace and great, aching vocals recall peak period **Dionne Warwick**... **Deborah Washington's** "Any Way You Want It" (Ariola) proves that her elegant, sexy "Ready Or Not" was no fluke – she recaptures the tantalizing earth-angel quality of early **Diana Ross** with her silky, whispery vocals that always have an edge of simmering sensuality. The knockout here: "Love Shadow/Standing In The Shadow Of Love" (6:11), a delicious interpretation of the **Four Tops** hit with "Love Hangover" overtones that should make it irresistible on the dance floor. Washington's versions of **Arthur Brown's** "Fire" and **Joe Cocker's** "The Letter" add little to the vocabulary of rock-into-disco interpretations, but "The Letter," at least, has a certain punch (it's included on a separate disco disc available to DJs with "Love Shadow/Standing In The Shadow" on the other side, same length as the lp cuts). Also check out, for audacity, "Baby Love" minus **The Supremes'** enchanting innocence but surprisingly good anyway... **Vivian Reed**, who's starred on the cabaret/Broadway show circuit for some time, has never sounded better on vinyl than she does on her new, **Jeff Lane**-produced album, "Another Side" (UA). Her vocals are grainy, strong, warm and intriguing– Lane matches her spirit with his supple productions, particularly on "It's Alright (This Feeling I'm Feeling)," the album's energy peak, and "Start Dancin'," a down-paced funky-beat number that succeeds in spite of its many gimmicks (the super-bassy male vocal accents seem especially unnecessary). "Sweet Harmony" is a very pretty slower track that also deserves attention – it and "It' Alright" are featured on a separate disco disc in slightly longer versions. ●

SEPTEMBER 9, 1978

Donna Summer's new two-record set is called "Live And More" (Casablanca) which means that, in addition to three sides of unaccountably speedy in-concert renditions of her greatest hits (from "Love To Love You Baby" to "Last Dance") plus a few variety-show throwaways ("The Way We Were," a bluesy medley that includes "The Man I Love" and "Some Of These Days"), Donna delivers one entirely new studio side, much as **Marvin Gaye** did with the "Live" album that featured his "Got To Give It Up." And it's this fourth side, a medley built upon **Jimmy Webb's** "MacArthur Park," that makes the set an absolutely essential one for the disco crowd. "MacArthur

> ## 66 More than anything I can remember, Dancer From The Dance captures the feeling and flow of the disco life of New York's Serious Dancers. 99

Park" might seem a peculiar choice for a song to base a 17- minute disco suite upon – not only is it unrelievedly maudlin and obsessively melancholic, but it requires the singer to repeat and presumably take seriously lines like "Someone left the cake out in the rain/I don't think that I can take it/Cause it took so long to bake it," etc. – but Summer, with riveting production by **Giorgio Moroder** and **Pete Bellotte**, transforms the song from the inside out, sweeping aside all preconceptions with the force of her own convictions. The lyrics remain, for the most part, ludicrous but Donna whips them around like brilliant banners – she knows now how to reach right through the words and seize the emotional core of a song – and the Morodor/Bellotte arrangement - swirling, dramatic, dense but brightly-etched with synthesizers, horns – is so rich that the song opens itself up and delivers more than ever before. But what really cinches the "MacArthur Park Suite" – what assures its place on disco playlists for some months to come – is a pair of original songs that flow out of and finally back into "Park." The first, "One of a Kind," pulsates with a new energy, highlighted by Summer's moving vocals – carried away on lines like, "Body and soul you took me out of control/You stole the best part of my heart" – and by Giorgio's softer approach to the synthesizer, letting it bubble up from under stunning sheets of horns, crackling handclaps; the feeling is closer to **Don Ray** than the usual Donna Summer record but the Summer sheen here is unmistakable and totally invigorating. "Heaven Knows," the shorter section that follows, varies the pace with a tender, moving duet between Donna and **Joe Esposito** of **Brooklyn Dream's**

that rises and falls passionately, dipping in the end back into "MacArthur Park's" peak reprise. This is Summer's first full-scale disco remake and if the choice of material is puzzling, it's interpretation is quite spectacular – magnificent and intense enough to overcome all doubts; strong enough to survive in segments, should DJs care to break it down to its several parts. Looks like an instant smash.

RECOMMENDED REMIXES: **Walter Gibbons'** major reworking of **Love Committee's** "Law and Order" (now 9:35 on Gold Mind) including a longer, stronger intro (minus the "gunshots" in the original) and an outrageous Philadelphia rave-up break that recalls **Blue Magic, Trammps, Double Exposure** – a classic. One cringes at the implications of the song's plea to "Lock up the criminals and throw away the keys," but if the messages from Philly are sounding pretty conservative these days, the music retains much of its old fervor... Another prime example of Philly fervor: **Teddy Pendergrass,** whose "Only You" has been opened up from 5:05 to 7:58 for a Philadelphia International disco disc – taking it from hot to hotter... **Musique's** already-knockout "In The Bush" (Prelude) in a substantially different version mixed by **François Kevorkian,** a New York DJ who's trimmed the song by about a minute to 7:35 but still managed to add a number of new things (even additional vocals) to give this version a character all its own! Flip side is "Keep On Jumpin," the lp version with slight technical changes... Philadelphia veteran producer/songwriter **Phil Hurtt's** "Giving It Back" (Fantasy), expanded from the version on his debut album so that it now runs six minutes with a luscious sax break and vastly improved sound quality; it's laid-back but quite tasty, reminiscent of **Marvin Gaye...** The **Winners'** "Get Ready For The Future," a strong funk disco cut that's already been getting a lot of playoff the group's impressive cut that's already been getting a lot of a playoff the group's impressive somewhat longer form (5:44) that emphasizes the song's heavy metal break and adds punch to the opening.

RECOMMENDED READING; Christopher Street has already called Andrew Holleran's **Dancer From The Dance,** just out in hardcover from Morrow, the "chic gay novel of the year," but, at the risk of trivializing it further, it might also be called the disco novel of the year. More than anything I can remember, Dancer captures the feeling and flow of the disco life of New York's Serious Dancers – men "bound together by a common love of a certain kind of music, physical beauty and style – all the things one shouldn't throwaway an ounce of energy pursuing, and sometimes throw away a life pursuing." There's a whole chapter of brilliant observation and overheard gossip from a night at the Tenth Floor (here elevated to the Twelfth Floor) that no one who danced at this trend-setting private club in the early Seventies will want to miss. Dancer is for anyone who remembers **Patti Jo's**

HIS COMPANY, PHOENIX
DJ: Jack Witherby

BEAUTIFUL BEND – Beautiful Bend (Marlin)
DANCING IN PARADISE/LOVE IN YOUR LIFE – El Coco (AVI)
I MAY NOT BE THERE WHEN YOU WANT ME
– Loleatta Holloway (Gold Mind)
I'M A MAN/BECAUSE THERE'S MUSIC IN THE AIR
– Macho (Prelude)
IN THE BUSH/KEEP ON JUMPIN' – Musique (Prelude)
LOVE SHADOW/STANDING IN THE SHADOW OF LOVE
– Deborah Washington (Ariola)
MR. DJ YOU KNOW HOW TO MAKE ME DANCE/DISCO
CONCERTO – Glass Family (JDC)
SATURDAY/SORCERER/HAVING A PARTY – Norma Jean
(Bearsville)
SUPERSTAR – Bob McGilpin (Butterfly)
YOU DANCE INTO MY LIFE/I LOVE TO SEE YOU DANCE
– Finished Touch (Motown)

XENON, NEW YORK
DJ: Jonathan Fearing

BEAUTIFUL BEND – Beautiful Bend (Marlin)
BOOGIE OOGIE OOGIE – A Taste of Honey (Capitol)
DANCING IN PARADISE – El Coco (AVI)
DO OR DIE – Grace Jones (Island)
HOT SHOT – Karen Young (West End)
INSTANT REPLAY – Dan Hartman (Blue Sky)
IN THE BUSH/KEEP ON JUMPIN' – Musique (Prelude)
MISS YOU – Rolling Stones (Rolling Stones)
VICTIM – Candi Staton (WB)
YOU MAKE ME FEEL (MIGHTY REAL)/
DANCE (DISCO HEAT) – Sylvester (Fantasy)

RASCALS, LOS ANGELES
DJ: Rusty Garner

BEAUTIFUL BEND – Beautiful Bend (Marlin)
DANCE (DISCO HEAT)/YOU MAKE ME FEEL
(MIGHTY REAL) – Sylvester (Fantasy)
INSTANT REPLAY – Dan Hartman (Blue Sky)
JUNGLE DJ – Kikrokos (Polydor import)
KEEP ON JUMPIN'/IN THE BUSH – Musique (Prelude)
RHYTHM OF LIFE/BLACK WIDOW WOMAN
– Afro-Cuban Band (Arista)
STARCRUSIN'/THIS SIDE OF MIDNIGHT/ FANCY DANCER
– Gregg Diamond's Starcruiser (Marlin)
THINK IT OVER/WARNING/DANGER
– Cissy Houston (Private Stock)
VICTIM – Candi Staton (WB)
YOU DANCE INTO MY LIFE – Finished Touch (Motown)

CLUB MARAKESH, WESTHAMPTON, NY
DJ: John Benitez

BEAUTIFUL BEND – Beautiful Bend (Marlin)
I LOVE THE NIGHTLIFE – Alicia Bridges (Polydor)
I'M A MAN – Macho (Prelude)
INSTANT REPLAY – Dan Hartman (Blue Sky)
IN THE BUSH/KEEP ON JUMPIN' – Musique (Prelude)
IT SEEMS TO HANG ON – Ashford & Simpson (WB)
LOVE SHADOW/STANDING IN THE SHADOW OF LOVE –
Deborah Washington (Ariola)
STARCRUSIN'/FANCY DANCER – Greg Diamond's
Starcruiser (Marlin)
VICTIM – Candi Staton (WB)
YOU MAKE ME FEEL (MIGHTY REAL)/
DANCE (DISCO HEAT) – Sylvester (Fantasy)

"Make Me Believe In You" and **Zulema's** "Giving Up" and anyone excited by a book that serves up one thrilling recognition after another.

NOTES: JDC Records has remastered the second pressing of their **Glass Family** album, "Mr. DJ You Know How To Make Me Dance," to give it some extra bottom and red vinyl copies of this new, improved version are available to DJs now. Both the title track and "Disco Concerto" deserve another listen... Jack Witherby, the DJ from His Company in Phoenix, called my attention to the fact that the disco disc version of **Deborah Washington's** "The Letter" (Ariola) has an unusual feature: the last groove of the song is looped back in such a way that it repeats the final second over and over, like an eerie electronic wave. The technique is the same as that used on the Magnet import 45 version of **Gene Farrow's** "Hey You Should Be Dancing" but the effect here is wilder. ◐

DISCO FILE TOP 20
1. **YOU MAKE ME FEEL (MIGHTY REAL)/DANCE (DISCO HEAT)** – Sylvester (Fantasy)
2. **IN THE BUSH/KEEP ON JUMPIN'** – Musique (Prelude)
3. **BEAUTIFUL BEND** – Beautiful Bend (Marlin)
4. **INSTANT REPLAY** – Dan Hartman (Blue Sky)
5. **THINK IT OVER** – Cissy Houston (Private Stock)
6. **HOT SHOT** – Karen Young (West End)
7. **VICTIM** – Candi Staton (WB)
8. **DO OR DIE/PRIDE/FAME** – Grace Jones (Island)
9. **LET'S START THE DANCE** – Bohannan (Mercury)
10. **PLEASURE ISLAND** – Paul Jabara (Casablanca)
11. **YOU GOT ME RUNNING** – Lenny Williams (ABC)
12. **BOOGIE OOGIE OOGIE** – A Taste of Honey (Capitol)
13. **I'M A MAN** – Macho (Prelude)
14. **MISS YOU** – Rolling Stones (Rolling Stones)
15. **RHYTHM OF LIFE** – Afro-Cuban Band (Arista)
16. **LET THEM DANCE** – D.C. LaRue (Casablanca)
17. **DANCING IN PARADISE** – El Coco (AVI)
18. **STARCRUSIN'/FANCY DANCER** – Greg Diamond's Starcruiser (Marlin)
19. **YOU AND I** – Rick James (Gordy)
20. **SATURDAY/SORCERER** – Norma Jean (Bearsville)

SEPTEMBER 16, 1978

RECOMMENDED ALBUMS: "Anikana-O," the "new" **Kongas** album on Salsoul, is actually based on material originally released four years ago on the very first Kongas album from Barclay Records in France. Though the original lp had a certain underground success – I still remember it as a highlight of early parties at **David Mancuso's** Loft – and it surfaced again as an import after the "Gimme Some Loving" album hit big. The

arranged and produced by **Norman Harris** in the style to which we've been accustomed – tight, driving Philly soul propelled by Holloway's spunky, witty always-on-target vocals-with a terrific sports metaphor twist to the lyrics, this one's as perfect and timeless as the **First Choice** classics or the best of Holloway's last album; and "I May Not Be There When You Want Me (But I'm Right On Time)" (7:35), the one already getting most of

> **❝ An article in Komsomolskaya Pravda, the newspaper of the Young Communist League, claims that "due to the powerful law of youth demand, discos are growing like mushrooms" in the Soviet Union ❞**

Salsoul release is so totally restructured that it deserves to be approached as a new piece of work. The album's original producer, **Jean Claudel**, is still credited here, but clearly it's mixer **Tom Moulton** who's responsible for this remarkable transformation. He's dropped all but five of the original 12 cuts, reworking and expanding them with additional drum work by Sigma Sound's **Larry Washington** and others until they explode with an energy and vitality only hinted at in the earlier versions. Of the original group, pictured on the back cover here, **Jean-Marc Cerrone** is the most prominent today and **Alec Costandinos**, whose credits on the first album read **R. Rupen**, co-wrote the two longest tracks, but Moulton takes their work and runs with it beautifully. The sound is Afro-European, much like early **Barrabas** – those gruff male leads, jungle percussion and haunting chants – with some echoes in the "Point Zero" segment of the **Voyage** album: back-to-the-roots disco, recalling a period when all the best music had a wild, joyous, tribal dance spirit. Every cut here is fine, but the title tune, "Anikana-O" (10:14) and "Jungle" (5:55) stand out for their tough vocals and intense chants. One of the most extensive remix jobs of the year, this is also a welcome revival for what might have been a lost record.

It's been more than a year and a half since **Loleatta Holloway's** last album – too long for those of us enamored with her wonderfully textured, big, gutsy voice (though her guest appearance on the **Salsoul Orchestra's** "Runaway" kept us satisfied for a time) – and if her new release, "Queen Of The Night" on Gold Mind, doesn't quite live up to the great expectations developed since then, well, we'll take what we can get – and make the best of it for now. The best of it in this case is a pair of tracks that lead off each side of the album: "Catch Me On The Rebound" (6:10), co-written,

the disco action, written and produced by **Bunny Sigler** in his usual full-speed-ahead, quirky style: a rough-and-ready, shouting rave-up with more energy than many whole albums, it jumps through a number of erratic changes, only drifting off somewhat toward the end when Loleatta and Bunny have a short spoken exchange. Another possibility: "Mama Don't, Papa Won't." While not up to the "Hit And Run" level, of the last album, "Queen Of The Night" is a necessary fix for Loleatta Holloway addicts but a **Walter Gibbons** mix should be much appreciated here.

RECOMMENDED DISCO DISCS: **Laura Taylor's** "Dancin' In My Feet" (6:02 on TK), the theme song from TV's "Disco Magic:" has a cute, fresh sound dominated by a sharp falsetto lead (multi-tracked) and a male falsetto chorus who are absent from the track only long enough to allow for a fast, tasty break; very slick, super-pop, but so ultrabright it's an immediate turn-on (mix by **Jim Burgess**... Gentle Persuasion's "Litterbug" (WB) is a classic sort of Girl Group record, complete with clever metaphor (the boyfriend is a litterbug – she warns him about "throwing his love around"), combining delicious cliche elements of the '60s and '70s in a creamy-smooth mix most reminiscent of the **Three Degrees**. Just slightly long at 6:35, but **Jerry Ross's** production and **Meco Monardo's** arrangement keep things interesting... **Lemon's** "Freak On" (4:33 on golden yellow transparent vinyl from Salsoul), "produced, arranged and conducted" by **Kenny Lehman** (originally with the **Chic** team; latest success: **Roundtree's** "Get On Up," whose writers reappear here), is off-the-wall, funk-tinged disco in the **Patrick Adams/Greg Carmichael** vein – alternately sleek and freak/gritty, the song puts itself through a lot of changes but pulls through them all quite nicely. Reportedly a hit

INFINITY, NEW YORK
DJ: Jim Burgess

BEAUTIFUL BEND – Beautiful Bend (Marlin)
HEAVEN – Gibson Brothers (TK)
I GOT DANCING IN MY FEET – Laura Taylor (TK)
I LOVE THE NIGHTLIFE – Alicia Bridges (Polydor)
INSTANT REPLAY – Dan Hartman (Blue Sky)
IN THE BUSH/KEEP ON JUMPIN'/SUMMER LOVE
– Musique (Prelude)
LET'S START THE DANCE – Bohannon (Mercury)
**STARCRUISIN'/FANCY DANCER/ARISTA VISTA/THIS SIDE
OF MIDNIGHT** – Gregg Diamond's Starcruiser (Marlin)
WARNING -DANGER/THINK IT OVER – Cissy Houston
(Private Stock)
**YOU MAKE ME FEEL (MIGHTY REAL)/
DANCE (DISCO HEAT)** – Sylvester (Fantasy)

INFERNO, NEW YORK
DJ: Rene Hewitt

ANIKANA-O – Kongas (Salsoul)
BURNIN' – Carol Douglas (Midsong)
HOT SHOT – Karen Young (West End)
I'M A MAN – Macho (Prelude)
IN THE BUSH/KEEP ON JUMPIN' – Musique (Prelude)
LAW AND ORDER – Love Committee (Gold Mind)
LET'S START THE DANCE – Bohannon (Mercury)
**LOVE SHADOW/STANDING IN THE SHADOW Of
LOVE/FIRE** – Deborah Washington (Ariola)
MACARTHUR PARK SUITE – Donna Summer (Casablanca)
**YOU MAKE ME FEEL (MIGHTY REAL)/
DANCE (DISCO HEAT)** – Sylvester (Fantasy)

CELEBRATION, BOSTON
DJ: Joe Iantosca

BEAUTIFUL BEND – Beautiful Bend (Marlin)
DANCING IN PARADISE – El Coco (AVI)
**FANCY DANCER/ARISTA VISTA/STARCRUSIN'/ THIS
SIDE OF MIDNIGHT** – Gregg Diamond's Starcruiser (Marlin)
HOT SHOT – Karen Young (West End)
I'M A MAN – Macho (Prelude)
INSTANT REPLAY – Dan Hartman (Blue Sky)
IN THE BUSH/KEEP ON JUMPIN' – Musique (Prelude)
PLATO'S RETREAT – Joe Thomas (TK)
VICTIM – Candi Staton (WB)
**YOU MAKE ME FEEL (MIGHTY REAL)/
DANCE (DISCO HEAT)** – Sylvester (Fantasy)

THE HUNT & THE CHASE, INDIANAPOLIS
DJ: Mark Hultmark

BEAUTIFUL BEND – Beautiful Bend (Marlin)
**CATCH ME ON THE ROUND/I MAY NOT BE THERE WHEN
YOU WANT ME** – Loleatta Holloway (Gold Mind)
DON'T KNOW WHAT I'D DO – Sweet Cream (Shadybrook)
INSTANT REPLAY – Dan Hartman (Blue Sky)
LET'S START THE DANCE – Bohannon (Mercury)
MACARTHUR PARK SUITE – Donna Summer (Casablanca)
MR. DJ YOU KNOW HOW TO MAKE ME DANCE
– Glass Family (JDC)
THINK IT OVER – Cissy Houston (Private Stock)
VICTIM – Candi Staton (WB)
**YOU MAKE ME FEEL (MIGHTY REAL)/
DANCE (DISCO HEAT)** – Sylvester (Fantasy)

in Paris (where its release preceded ours by a few weeks),
Lemon is this week's left field pick... "Never Let Go" by
Eastbound Expressway (9:55 on AVI) is very much like
Roy Ayers' "Running Away" – the bouncy bass line is
nearly identical and it goes for that same sort of cheery,
comfortable feel, particularly with the repeated, clipped
group vocals. But British producer **Ian Levine** has
fashioned an elaborate variation here, throwing in
innumerable breaks (some excess baggage) yet keeping
it perky, fun. Mix by **Rick Gianatos**; could be a sleeper...
"Tossing, Turning And Swinging" by **Shalamar** (5:47 on
Solar Records, through RCA) links the group for the first
time with **Leon Sylvers**, who co-produced (with **Dick
Griffey**), co-wrote and co-arranged – the result is
energetic, hi-gloss pop (cf, of course, **The Sylvers**, **The
Jacksons** and, for the jittery keyboard line, **Marvin
Gaye**), a bit bubblegum, but the snappy kind. Flip side,
"Take That To The Bank" (6:14) is given a lighter touch
but the approach is basically the same.

RADIO FREE DISCO?: Under the headline, "Russia
Running a Disco Fever:' the San Francisco Examiner last
week reported on an article in Moscow's Komsomolskaya
Pravda, the newspaper of the Young Communist League,
which claimed that "due to the powerful law of youth
demand, discos are growing like mushrooms" in the
Soviet Union. Over the four-month life-span of one
popular club in 1977, it attracted more than 40,000
young people. And in the Ukraine, where the club scene
is reported to be "especially hot," disco operators are
organizing to further the development of disco
technology in the face of what is likely to be a
permanent shortage of special equipment – basics like
turntables, speakers, lights. Another critical shortage:
disco records, which, like nearly all American records,
are strictly black market items. ❷

"Brash, ballsy, off-the-wall and full of crazy intensity. An aggressive, knockout package"

LIGHT & LIVELY: Two entertaining albums that work variations on the familiar Philadelphia sound are "The Greatest Show On Earth" by **Metropolis** (Salsoul) and the debut of **Vince Montana's Goody Goody** on Atlantic. The first, produced by Tom Moulton and Munich keyboard star **Thor Baldursson** (who wrote much of the material with Pete Bellotte), was recorded in part at Munich's Musicland Studios (with **Keith Forsey** at the drums and strings by the Munich Philharmonic) and in part at Sigma Sound (where vocals and Don Renaldo's horns were added), so the result is an interesting amalgam. If the Philly style dominates, it's probably because the album is in large part a showcase for **The Sweethearts** (of Sigma) – **Carla Benson**, **Evette Benton** and **Barbara Ingram** – and their vocals are inevitable reminders of their work with **MFSB**, the **Salsoul Orchestra**, and countless other classically Philadelphia sounding projects like the group's "I Love NY," included here in a 4:21 version, the bulk of the material is light, attractive, and smoothly polished with the occasional lapses of show-biz schmaltz usually made up for by the clarity and glow of the music itself. The two choice cuts open up each side: "New York Is My Kind Of Town" (7:14), the closest to "I Love NY" in style and spirit but even perkier, fresher with spunky, sweet, razor-edged vocals and a jumping string section – my personal favorite; and "The Greatest Show On Earth" (7:03), which has a bubbling synthesizer undertow and both spoken and sung vocals (theme: fake romance, appearance and reality) arranged around a bright central break–nice but a little heavy-handed lyrically. Also fine: "Go Get It" (3:57), a tight, pumping little instrumental with an MFSB sheen; and "Here's To You" (4:00), a really pretty slower hustle cut and a great love tribute song. All together, a winning combination of talents plus an especially welcome chance to hear three of disco's best voices truly out front for once.

The **Goody Goody** album, produced, arranged and largely written by **Vince Montana**, also jumps off from the Philly basics but strives for a simpler, almost jazzy sound on several cuts – the sort of clean, glossy style Montana achieves in "#1 Dee Jay," which leads off the album in a 6:58 version. The two tracks that come closest to this sound, "Super Jock" and "Bio-Rhythms," are essentially instrumentals making use of a vibrant rhythm section without strings or horns so they evoke a stripped-down Salsoul Orchestra – both a little loose, perhaps, for the dance floor, but rich, inventive pieces of music that would enliven the atmosphere of a club early in the evening. Two other cuts, "You Know How

Good It Is" and "It Looks Like Love," are more into what one has come to think of as the Vince Montana style – full orchestra, lots of strings, prominent percussion, dreamy but biting but "You Know How Good It Is," an instrumental, turns incongruously into a nightclub combo number and drifts off in this gentle haze at exactly eight minutes. So that leaves "It Looks like Love" as the standout cut – the best vocal outing for Goody Goody lead, **Denise Montana** (Vince's daughter), the most sparkling arrangement and punchiest break; unfortunately, the prominent guitar and drum pattern are lifted almost directly from **Chic's** "Dance, Dance, Dance."

WORK THAT BODY: In an entirely different vein, there's the **Erotic Drum Band** album just out on a new American label called Prism after months in various stages of release as a Canadian import. This current mix of the album was preceded by three separate disco discs on the Champagne label from Montreal – two versions of an insane, wonderfully rough cut called "Action '78," which is almost all hot percussion and handclaps, like a break that goes on for ten minutes; and "Plug Me To Death," another drum-and-percussion tour de force that is very derivitive of the "After Dark" break – and an earlier version of the lp that was made widely available in the test pressing stage and, as far as I know, never got any further. The Prism album takes the best of these previous releases and combines them, two cuts to a side, for an aggressive, knockout package. "Action '78" (5:10) and "Plug Me To Death" (7:19) remain the highlights – brash, ballsy, off-the-wall and full of that crazy intensity that made **Montreal Sound's** "Music" so exciting. The impact of both cuts may be diluted after months of exposure, here and there, to the import versions, but they deserve renewed attention here. The album's other favorite is "Love Disco Style" (10:13), remixed by DJ **Paul Poulos**, featuring a tough male vocal, horns, bizarre synthesizer segments, drums for days and one wild break after the other. "Jerky Rhythm" (9:12), combines stinging organ with the drums and gets a bit carried away with itself.

NOTED: THE FALL COLLECTIONS – Several compilation albums of interest to the disco buff: The Salsoul Orchestra's "Greatest Disco Hits" (Salsoul), subtitled "Music For Non-Stop Dancing," which means **Walter Gibbons** has imaginatively blended together eleven of the group's most successful dance records (including "Magic Bird Of Fire," "Nice 'N' Naasty," "Tangerine," "Salsoul Hustle," "Getaway") and sandwiched them between "Salsoul 3001;" the records

LIMELIGHT, HOLLYWOOD, FLORIDA
DJ: Bob Lombardi

BEAUTIFUL BEND – Beautiful Bend (Marlin)
DANCING IN PARADISE – El Coco (AVI)
I'M A MAN – Macho (Prelude)
IN THE BUSH/KEEP ON JUMPIN'/SUMMER
LOVE/SUMMER LOVE THEME – Musique (Prelude)
LOVE DISCO STYLE – Erotic Drum Band (Prism)
MACARTHUR PARK SUITE – Donna Summer
(Casablanca)
NO GOODBYES – Curtis Mayfield (Curtom)
PLEASURE ISLAND – Paul Jabara (Casablanca)
VICTIM – Candi Staton (WB)
YOU MAKE ME FEEL (MIGHTY REAL)/
DANCE (DISCO HEAT) – Sylvester (Fantasy)

220 DISCO, NEW YORK
DJ: Richie Mair

HOT SHOT – Karen Young (West End)
I'M A MAN – Macho (Prelude)
INSTANT REPLAY – Dan Hartman (Blue Sky)
LAW AND ORDER – Love Committee (Gold Mind)
MACARTHUR PARK SUITE – Donna Summer
(Casablanca)
NEWSY NEIGHBORS – Double Exposure (Salsoul)
#1 DEE JAY – Goody Goody (Atlantic)
RHYTHM OF LIFE – Afro-Cuban Band (Arista)
STUBBORN KIND OF FELLA – Buffalo Smoke (RCA)
YOU MAKE ME FEEL (MIGHTY REAL) – Sylvester (Fantasy)

SAHARA, NEW YORK
DJ: Ellen Bogen

AIN'T THAT ENOUGH FOR YOU – John Davis & the
Monster Orch. (Sam)
ANIKANA-O/JUNGLE – Kongas (Salsoul)
BEAUTIFUL BEND – Beautiful Bend (Marlin)
BURNIN' IN MY FEET – Laura Taylor (TK)
FANCY DANCER/STARCRUISIN'/ARISTA VISTA/THIS SIDE
OF MIDNIGHT – Gregg Diamond's Starcruiser (Marlin)
I LOVE THE NIGHTLIFE – Alicia Bridges (Polydor)
IN THE BUSH/KEEP ON JUMPIN' – Musique (Prelude)
LIVE AND MORE – Donna Summer (Casablanca)
SUBSTITUTE – Gloria Gaynor (Polydor)

VAMPS, NEW ORLEANS
DJ: Tom Quinn

BEAUTIFUL BEND – Beautiful Bend (Marlin)
DANCIN' IN MY FEET – Laura Taylor (TK)
I'M A MAN – Macho (Prelude)
INSTANT REPLAY – Dan Hartman (Blue Sky)
IN THE BUSH/KEEP ON JUMPIN' – Musique (Prelude)
#1 DEE JAY – Goody Goody (Atlantic)
PLEASURE ISLAND – Paul Jabara (Casablanca)
STARCRUISIN'/FANCY DANCER/ARISTA VISTA
– Gregg Diamond's Starcruiser (Marlin)
SUPERSTAR – Bob McGilpin (Butterfly)
YOUNGBLOOD (LIVIN' IN THE STREET) – War (UA)

are often shorter than the original cuts (and nothing is timed here) but the execution is perfect... Salsoul's "Saturday Night Disco Party," an unblended collection of the label's recent hits ("Dr. Love," "Hit And Run," "Dance A Little Bit Closer," "My Love Is Free," "The Beat Goes On And On") plus three entirely new Salsoul Orchestra interpretations of the **Bee Gees'** "Night Fever," "Stayin' Alive" and "You Should Be Dancing" – again, some of the cuts are dose-cropped, but most are substantial... De-Lite's "Saturday Night Disco," disco blended by **Raphael Charres** with each side jumping off with a long track – "Melodies" (the 12-inch version) and "Open Sesame" – and mixing into short versions of **Crown Heights Affair's** "Dancin'," "Dreaming A Dream," "Foxy Lady" and "Every Beat Of My Heart" and the **Kay-Gees'** "Tango Hustle"... "Hot Disco Night Vol. 1" (AVI), a wildly uneven selection of the label's catalogue material including "Let's Get Together" and "Mondo Disco" by **El Coco**, the **Destinations'** "I've Got To Dance (To Keep from Cryin')," and something new to me called "Hot Disco Night (Are You Ready?)" by **Sweet Potato Pie** which seems to be a **Rick Gianatos** reworking of the break from El Coco's "Delicado" – an essential item for drum freaks; not disco blended... And The **Trammps'** "Best Of" collection on Atlantic, also not blended for dancing but featuring long versions of "Disco Inferno" and "Disco Party" at the beginning of each side, then trailing off into very abbreviated versions of the group's other prime cuts with Atlantic, which means that the oldest cut here is "Hooked For Life."

NEW AND IMPROVED: Our favorite track from the recent **Crown Heights Affair** album was "Say a Prayer For Two," now available in a new 12-inch mix from De-Lite – it's not much longer than the original lp cut at 6:27, but the beginning is completely new, some weird electronics have been brought in to soup up the break, and the whole thing's been given more depth and punch. The song recalls **War** and **Earth, Wind & Fire**, both in message and spirit, and it's one of Crown Heights' sharpest cuts; the disc version should focus some new attention on it. Flip side: a medley of two other cuts from the "Dream World" album, "Galaxy Of Love" and "I'm Gonna Love You Forever" (9:45, and stretched pretty thin)... **John Davis** has seriously reworked his **Monster Orchestra** cut, "Ain't That Enough For You" (Sam), so that it now begins with congas and a long intro, opens into an expansive break, and lasts just over nine minutes – a superb new version (it's also commercially available with "A Bite Of The Apple," also given a booster mix, on the B side). ☻

SEPTEMBER 30, 1978

I'M A MAN: A small surge of records by male vocalists this week is topped by our favorite new album of the moment – **James Wells'** "My Claim To Fame" (AVI), producer **Ian Levine's** liveliest, most interesting work so far. Levine, whose previous credits include **Barbara Pennington**, **Doris Jones**, **Evelyn Thomas** and the current Eastbound Expressway 12-inch, "Never Let Go," has an expansive, highly decorative style that harks back to the more ornate examples of early American disco without losing its sure hold in the modern world of Eurodisco. Sometimes Levine's approach is overly busy, but on the Wells album he's struck just the right balance between the catchy and the quirky – the sort of thing that grabs you right off and keeps you involved through the most unexpected changes. Unfortunately, Levine is working at a disadvantage with vocalist Wells, whose singing is strained, mannered, often wobbly – hardly powerful enough to support the intricately orchestrated arrangements Levine has concocted for him, but if Wells sinks beneath its weight here and there, the production is strong enough to carry on in spite of him. The knockout here is the 16-minute "My Claim To Fame," which is full of movement and wonderful textural contrasts like the section about halfway through that jumps with quick juxtapositions of robust horns and glistening, knife-sharp strings (compare the jittery strings in "I've Found Love"). The female back-up singers carry much of the emotional weight of the song, and even though they're mostly restricted to repetitions of the phrase, "My claim to fame is your love for me," they get to shine at the end with a superb, if short, a cappella break. Both cuts on the album's side two are also notable, but it's "True Love Is My Destiny" (12:42) that has the immediate edge with its perky synthesizer pattern, swirling strings, and **Stevie Wonder** overtones. A real breakthrough album for Ian Levine (who has **Rick Gianatos'** assistance on the disco mix), "My Claim To Fame" is likely to be one of the next hot shot disco records.

David Christie's "Don't Stop Me, I Like It" has been around since the spring as one of the most popular import album cuts on the disco scene and now it's finally available in America on Salsoul's Tom n' Jerry label. Titled "Back Fire," the Christie album contains seven new tracks plus an expanded, **Tom Moulton**-mixed version of "Don't Stop Me" which remains the package's main attraction. Though "Don't Stop Me" loses some of its original urgency in the process of being lengthened from 4:45 to 7:19, and some of Moulton's new mix material seems merely noodling filler, the song remains a fine example of pop-rock disco (ct. the **Glitter Band**, **Bay City Rollers**, **Bee Gees**): piercing falsetto vocals, equally piercing synthesizer, crackling guitar and a quick-pulsing beat. The two cuts that flank "Don't Stop Me" here are also of interest: "Back Fire" (5:59), with a slower, funkier pace; and "Come And Get It" (6:17), which is ricky-ticky, zipped-up with a '50s **Buddy Holly** feel that's quite infectious.

Veterans **General Johnson** and **Barry White** are also back on the disco round this week with new disco disc releases. Johnson's is a full-bodied, hard-pumping record called "Can't Nobody Love Me Like You Do" (5:25 on Arista) that's already catching on very big. The General's aching, expressive voice with its distinctive catch-in-the-throat drives the production ahead full-force; flecked with hand claps and gutsy horns, featuring a "Love Hangover" bass line in the break, the song has the sort of compact energy that should put it over both in the clubs and on the radio. A personal pick. **Barry White** goes for a considerably more laid-back groove on "Your Sweetness Is My Weakness" (20th Century) and, as usual, succeeds in being totally seductive in spite of himself. White's vocals are especially lethargic and smug here – he sounds like he's lying down, either just waking up or just falling asleep, but maybe this is his idea of pillow talk – though he rouses himself somewhat toward the end and offsets his growling perfectly with the honeyed lusciousness of the Love Unlimited chorus. The music is bright, shimmering, often luminous, particularly at the beginning and in a brief break. Surprisingly, though it runs nearly ten minutes, it feels shorter, so "Sweetness" could prove as irresistible as "It's Ecstasy" even for Barry White skeptics. Also back after a long absence is **Double Exposure**, with a Norman Harris-produced revival of "Newsy Neighbors" (4:52 on Salsoul) that sounds like a combination of the **O'Jays** and the **Trammps** – real snappy, with not one false step-but still doesn't replace the **First Choice** original. This version stands up beautifully on its own, but one longs for an expanded break here to really gets things moving.

Finally, there's the **Gibson Brothers'** "Heaven" (TK), a 7:14 disco disc that was originally scheduled for release in August, shortly after it first surfaced as a French import on the Zagora label, but is out now in a **Jim Burgess** re-mixed version (though Burgess is not credited on the label itself). Burgess has cut the pace just slightly but the song remains one of the most rousing, invigorating records around: spirited vocals, several involving breaks that give the song a new spaciousness, and a great hook right out of Voyage's "From East To West." Excellent and essential.

" Tom Savarese has filed a $1 million suit against Prelude Records as well as an injunction against the further sale of Macho's "I'm A Man" album "

BETTER DAYS, NEW YORK
DJ: Toraino "Tee" Scott

FANCY DANCER/STARCRUISIN' – Gregg Diamond's Starcruiser (Marlin)
INSTANT REPLAY – Dan Hartman (Blue Sky)
IN THE BUSH/KEEP ON JUMPIN' – Musique (Prelude)
IT SEEMS TO HANG ON/GET UP AND DO SOMETHING – Ashford & Simpson (WB)
LOVE SHADOW/STANDING IN THE SHADOW OF LOVE – Deborah Washington (Ariola)
MACARTHUR PARK SUITE – Donna Surnmer (Casablanca)
ME AND THE GANG/LET'S START THE DANCE – Bohannon (Mercury)
MR. DJ YOU KNOW HOW TO MAKE ME DANCE – Glass Family (JDC)
NEVER LET GO – Eastbound Expressway (AVI)
SIX MILLION STEPS – Rahni Harris & F.L.O. (Inspirational Sounds)

STUDIO ONE, LOS ANGELES
DJ: Manny Slali

BEAUTIFUL BEND – Beautiful Bend (Marlin)
HOT SHOT – Karen Young (West End)
I LOVE THE NIGHTLIFE – Alicia Bridges (Polydor)
I MAY NOT BE THERE WHEN YOU WANT ME/ CATCH ME ON THE REBOUND/MAMA DON'T, PAPA WON'T/TWO SITES TO EVERY STORY – Loleatta Holloway (Gold Mind)
I'M A MAN – Macho (Prelude)
INSTANT REPLAY – Dan Hartman (Blue Sky)
IN THE BUSH/KEEP ON' JUMPIN – Musique (Prelude)
MACARTHUR PARK SUITE – Donna Summer (Casablanca)
VICTIM – Candi Staton (WB)
YOU MAKE ME FEEL (MIGHTY REAL)/DANCE (DISCO HEAT) – Sylvester (Fantasy)

I-BEAM, SAN FRANCISCO
DJ: Tim Rivers

DANCIN' IN, MY FEET – Laura Taylor (TK)
DON'T HOLD BACK/I CAN TELL – Chanson (Ariola)
FANCY DANCER/STARCRUISIN'/THIS SIDE OF MIDNIGHT – Gregg Diamond's Starcruiser (Marlin)
HI-TENSION – Hi-Tension (Island import)
I LOVE THE NIGHTLIFE – Alicia Bridges (Polydor)
MR. DJ YOU KNOW HOW TO MAKE ME DANCE – Glass Family (JDC)
MY CLAIM TO FAME/TRUE LOVE IS MY DESTINY – James Wells (AVI)
SUPERSTAR – Bob McGilpin (Butterfly)
YOU MAKE ME FEEL (MIGHTY REAL)/DANCE (DISCO HEAT) – Sylvester (Fantasy)
YOUNGBLOOD – War (UA)

12 WEST, NEW YORK
DJ: Rickey Ybarra

DANCIN' IN MY FEET – Laura Taylor (TK)
FANCY DANCER/THIS SIDE OF MIDNIGHT/STARCRUISIN' – Gregg Diamond's Starcruiser (Marlin)
THE GREATEST SHOW ON EARTH/NEW YORK IS MY KIND OF TOWN/HERE'S TO YOU – Metropolis (Salsoul)
I'M A MAN – Macho (Prelude)
INSTANT REPLAY – Dan Hartman (Blue Sky)
LOVE DISCO STYLE – Erotic Drum Band (Prism)
MACARTHUR PARK SUITE – Donna Summer (Casablanca)
NEVER LET GO – Eastbound Expressway (AVI)
ONE NIGHT AFFAIR – Samona Cooke (Mercury)
WORKIN' AND SLAVIN' – Midnight Rhythm (Atlantic)

NEWS & NOTES: **Tom Savarese** has filed a $1 million suit against Prelude Records seeking $500 thousand in actual damages and $500 thousand in punitive damages as well as an injunction against the further sale or distribution of **Macho's** "I'm A Man" album without credit on the album's label and cover for Savarese's disco mix. Prelude claims it was unaware of Savarese's contractual agreements with the record's producer, which specified not only the appearance of credits but the size type they were to be printed in, until the album was already being pressed, so the first run includes only a mix credit line on the back cover. The second pressing run, Prelude insists, credits Savarese on the record label as well. Meanwhile, the album's title cut is number 5 on the DISCO FILE Top 20... **Cerrone's** "Supernature" is in the top ten on the British singles charts and "Cerrone IV" is scheduled for simultaneous American and European release on October 13... Looking Good: **Alicia Bridges'** "I Love The Nightlife (Disco Round)" (Polydor), **Laura Taylor's** "Dancin' In My Feet" (TK), **Carol Douglas'** "Burnin'" (Midsong), **Loleatta Holloway's** "I May Not Be There When You Want Me" (Gold Mind), "Never Let Go" by **Eastbound Expressway** (AVI) and **John Davis & the Monster Orchestra's** remixed version of "Ain't That Enough For You" (Sam) are all enjoying significant new action this week. ◗

DISCO FILE TOP 20

1. **IN THE BUSH/KEEP ON JUMPIN'** – Musique (Prelude)
2. **INSTANT REPLAY** – Dan Hartman (Blue Sky)
3. **YOU MAKE ME FEEL (MIGHTY REAL)/DANCE (DISCO HEAT)** – Sylvester (Fantasy)
4. **BEAUTIFUL BEND** – Beautiful Bend (Marlin)
5. **I'M A MAN** – Macho (Prelude)
6. **STARCRUSIN'/FANCY DANCER/THIS SIDE OF MIDNIGHT** – Greg Diamond's Starcruiser (Marlin)
7. **MACARTHUR PARK SUITE** – Donna Surnmer (Casablanca)
8. **VICTIM** – Candi Staton (WB)
9. **HOT SHOT** – Karen Young (West End)
10. **THINK IT OVER/WARNING-DANGER** – Cissy Houston (Private Stock)
11. **LET'S START THE DANCE** – Bohannan (Mercury)
12. **MR. DJ YOU KNOW HOW TO MAKE ME DANCE** – Glass Family (JDC)
13. **I LOVE THE NIGHTLIFE** – Alicia Bridges (Polydor)
14. **DANCIN' IN MY FEET** – Laura Taylor (TK)
15. **DANCING IN PARADISE** – El Coco (AVI)
16. **PLEASURE ISLAND** – Paul Jabara (Casablanca)
17. **SUPERSTAR** – Bob McGilpin (Butterfly)
18. **BOOGIE OOGIE OOGIE** – A Taste of Honey (Capitol)
19. **DO OR DIE** – Grace Jones (Island)
20. **RHYTHM OF LIFE** – Afro-Cuban Band (Arista)

GIRL CRAZY: Overwhelmed this week by a flood of new releases by female vocalists, the following is a quick survey of the cream of the crop, beginning with ALBUMS: **Pattie Brooks** heads the list here with "Our Ms. Brooks," just out on Casablanca, a fine follow-up to last year's sensational debut. Brooks, who sounds as spectacular as she looks on the album's cover, whips through most of these new **Simon Soussan** productions like a dazzling tropical storm, risking occasional shrillness and moments of dramatic overreach to achieve an impassioned, on-edge frenzy in prime cuts "Heartbreak In Disguise" (6:58) and "This Is The House Where Love Died" (8:57), the latter an astonishing revival of an early **First Choice** cut. Soussan's production on both these cuts picks up the "After Dark" style (that song, full-length, opens up the album) and varies it slightly – looser here, tighter there – while retaining the distinctive multi-layered percussion, spun-sugar strings, and peak-time drum breaks that make

❝ Karen Young's "Hot Shot" is the kind of marvellously freakish song that depends upon a very delicate balance of the unsophisticated and the spontaneous ❞

his work so exciting on the dance floor. The real departures here are a medley of two songs Brooks wrote, "Come Fly With Me"/"Let's Do It Again" (6:50) that's softer, prettier, utterly entrancing and a lovely, perfect slow cut called "The Backup Singer," produced and arranged by **Bob Esty**, that contains the lament and question, "I'm always in the backup/always from afar/When will they discover that I could be a star?" Sounds like the Pattie Brooks story, but if there's any question after this album that she is a star, then someone's just not listening.

Melba Moore sounds brand-new, extra-spunky on her first album for Epic, titled "Melba," produced by the Philadelphia team of **Gene McFadden** and **John Whitehead**, and featuring a terrific version of the **Bee Gees'** "You Stepped Into My Life" (7:50, also available on a disco disc, both formats remixed by Boston DJ/promotion man **John Luongo**). Already

one of the hottest items on the DJ grapevine, "You Stepped" is a best-of-both-worlds blend of Bee Gees pop and Philly soul with just the right disco crunch touches (handclaps, congas, perky guitar figures). MM, avoiding her overused vocal flourishes and octave-jumps, sounds sweeter, more intimate and more at ease than ever and "You Stepped" could be her biggest disco success so far. Also delightful: "Pick Me Up, I'll Dance" and "I Promise To Love You," both lighter, frothier and about five minutes long... One suspected **Karen Young's** "Hot Shot" would be a difficult record to build an album around – it's the kind of marvellously freakish song that, for all its raucous, raw appeal, depended upon a very delicate balance of the unsophisticated and the spontaneous. You knew it was far from perfection, but it was the song's homemade, slightly "off" qualities that made it so real, so right, so irresistible. Both Young and the producers (**Andy Kahn** and Philadelphia DJ **Kurt Borusiewicz**) were able to push right past their own amateurishness to achieve a crazy brilliance most professionals would give their right arm for. But something as off-the-wall great as "Hot Shot" is not easy to fallow up and most of the material on Young's first lp ("Hot Shot" on West End) tends to be merely eccentric. There's still something loveably quirky in all the dance cuts here – Young does some more bizarre scatting, the producers (who also wrote and arranged) pull off several outrageous breaks – but nothing hammers it home with the force of the title track. In any case, the cuts to watch are "Bring On The Boys," which is campy, kinda raunchy (is Young the Mae West of disco?) and has a punchy break; and "Where Is He," though the pace and the message is rather downbeat. Note: "Hot Shot" is pressed, appropriately enough, on cherry red vinyl.

The new **Diana Ross** album ("Ross" on Motown) kicks off with an entirely new version of "Lovin', Livin' & Givin'," previously included on the "Thank God It's Friday" soundtrack in a shorter, considerably less elaborate form. Here, the song is totally restructured, strung along a nervous, bubbly synthesizer track that gives Diana's breathy vocals a vibrant support; the producer is **Hal Davis**, but the influence is **Giorgio**. The other key cut is "What You Gave Me," an **Ashford & Simpson** song originally recorded by **Marvin Gaye** and **Tammi Terrell**, which has all that early Motown charm with a tasty disco update courtesy Hal Davis... **Denise LaSalle** can always be depended on for at least one funky, hard party cut per album and her new release, "Under the Influence" (ABC), hits you with one right off: "P.A.R.T.Y. (Where It Is)," which is good-time southern funk, shot through with bright horns, biting guitars and LaSalle's rough, rich vocals. Another possibility here: "Under the Influence." Funk favorite of the week... **Teri DeSario's** debut, "Pleasure Train" (Casablanca), was preceded by a wonderful single called "Ain't Nothing Gonna Keep Me From You" that was produced by **Barry Gibb**, **Albhy Galuten** and **Carl Richardson** in their spirited, sure-fire

TRUDE HELLER'S, NEW YORK
DJ: Danny Krivit

DON'T HOLD BACK/ I CAN TELL – Chanson (Ariola)
I MAY NOT BE THERE WHENI YOU WANT ME/CATCH ME ON THE REBOUND – Loleatta Holloway (Gold Mind)
IN' THE BUSH/ KEEP ON JUMPIN' – Musique (Prelude)
LOVIN', LIVIN' & GIVIN'/WHAT YOU' GAVE ME/YOU WERE THE ONE – Diana Ross (Motown)
MR. DJ YOU KNOW HOW TO MAKE ME DANCE – Glass Family (JDC)
ONLY YOU – Teddy Pendergrass (Phila. Intl.)
SHOOT ME (WITH YOUR LOVE) – Tasha Thomas (Orbit)
VICTIM – Candi Staton (WB)
YOU MAKE ME FEEL (MIGHTY REAL)/ DANCE (DISCO HEAT) – Sylvester (Fantasy)
YOU STEPPED INTO MY LIFE – Melba Moore (Epic)

BOSTON, BOSTON, BOSTON
DJ; Jeff Tilton

EYES IN THE, BACK OF MY HEAD – Patti LaBelle (Epic)
I LOVE THE NIGHTLIFE – Alicia Bridges (Polydor)
I'M A MAN – Macho (Prelude)
INSTANT REPLAY – Dan Hartman (Blue Sky)
IN THE BUSH – Musique (Prelude)
LET'S START THE DANCE – Bohannon (Mercury)
LOVE NOW HURT LATER – Giorgio & Chris (Casablanca)
NO GOODBYES – Curtis Mayfield (Curtom)
VICTIM – Candi Staton (WB)
YOUR SWEETNESS IS MY WEAKNESS – Barry White (20th Century)

XENON, NEW YORK
DJ: Jonathan Fearing

AIN'T THAT ENOUGH FOR YOU – John Davis & the Monster Orch. (Sam)
BEAUTIFUL BEND – Beautiful Bend (Marlin)
I LOVE THE NIGHTLIFE – Alicia Bridges (Polydor)
I'M A MAN/BECAUSE THERE'S MUSIC IN THE AIR – Macho (Prelude)
INSTANT REPLAY – Dan Hartman (Blue Sky)
IN THE BUSH/KEEP ON JUMPIN' – Musique (Prelude)
MACARTHUR PARK SUITE – Donna Summer (Casablanca)
STARCRUISIN'/THIS SIDE OF MIDNIGHT/ FANCY DANCER – Gregg Diamond's Starcruiser (Marlin)
VICTIM – Candi Staton (WB)
YOU MAKE ME FEEL (MIGHTY REAL) – Sylvester(Fantasy)

ALFIE'S, SAN FRANCISCO
DJ: Marty Bleckman

BEAUTIFUL BEND – Beautiful Bend (Marlin)
BURNIN' – Carol Douglas (Midsong)
DANCIN' IN' MY FEET – Laura Taylor (TK)
I LOVE THE NIGHLIFE – Alicia Bridges (Polydor)
INSTANT REPLAY – Dan Hartman (Blue Sky)
MACARTHUR PARK SUITE – Donna Summer (Casablanca)
RHYTHM OF LIFE – Afro-Cuban Band (Arista)
STANDING IN THE SHADOW OF LOVE – Fever (Fantasy)
STUBBORN KIND OF FELLA – Buffalo Smoke (RCA)
YOU MAKE ME FEEL (MIGHTY REAL)/ DANCE (DISCO HEAT) – Sylvester (Fantasy)

trademark style, so that song is this album's big come-on cut even though it's the team's only contribution. Happily, the rest of the material more than lives up to the promise of "Ain't Nothing" – the whole album has a gorgeous glow and all the tracks are so stylishly produced and seductively sung that "Pleasure Train" promises to turn into a constant at-home favorite. For the dance floor, the most attractive cut is the title song, a pretty, lightly pulsing number reminiscent of **Evie Sands**. Runners-up: "The Stuff Dreams Are Made Of" and "Back In Your Arms Again."

DISCO DISCS: Up there with Melba Moore's "You Stepped Into My Life" as this week's hot new property is **Sarah Dash's** stunning "Sinner Man" (Kirshner), the first recording from the former **LaBelle** member since the group's parting of ways. As if to compensate for her absence, Sarah returns full-force here, kicking up a storm with a determination and ferocity that recalls LaBelle's most appealing work. Dash builds to a belting intensity over an arrangement of shifting styles (highlights: the opening, the sax break), lashing into a faithless "sinner man" while acknowledging the temptation he presents, so there's a sly, sexy underside to the rejection here. A foretaste of Dash's first solo album, "Sinner Man" is due out within the week as a 6:29 **Tom Moulton** Mix – don't miss it (available through Columbia)... **Chaka Khan's** first solo move is also of interest: "I'm Every Woman" (WB), produced by **Arif Mardin** and written by **Ashford & Simpson**, features Khan as a strutting superwoman, coming at us from several tracks with her special sort of gusty tenderness. The Mardin production is big and handsome but, at 4:22, it doesn't hit full disco stride or draw its energies together for a peak moment. Still, this is too stylish, too rich to ignore... The same might be said for **Cheryl Lynn's** "Got To Be Real" (Columbia), a superb debut that combines elements of **The Emotions** work (that loping, chunky beat; the handclap accents; the strong interplay of voices) with a **Jean Carn** – like soul sophistication, serenely comfortable but with all the "realness' the song insists upon. The 5:10 disco-disc length allows for a subtle break, but the song remains material for a slower set where, placed just right, it's likely to cause a sensation... **Tasha Thomas**, whom we haven't heard since "Stay With Me" some time back, returns with a left field, small label entry called "Shoot Me (With Your Love)" (Orbit Records, Box 334, Centerport, N.Y. 11721) that has a certain flair in spite of its decidedly unpolished production sound. The sexual metaphor is a neat one, the percussion/ horn break is snappy and Thomas flashes on some Merry Clayton fervor here and there – uneven, but it has its fine moments... The **Gloria Gaynor** version of **Clout's** British success, "Substitute" (Polydor) is cute, fitfully clever but so relentlessly pop that it becomes something of an OD at the 8:29 length it's carried to here. ◗

OCTOBER 14, 1978

No categories this week, just a prime collection of recent records from all points of the disco spectrum. Top of the list: "Workin' & Slavin'" by **Midnight Rhythm** (Atlantic), one of the most powerful disco discs so far this year – a high-impact combination of the mucho macho aggressiveness of **Village People** (via a tough male chorus which chants the song's title with the sweaty fervor of a chain gang) and the sweeping, ecstatic Eurodisco style of **Cerrone** or **Boris Midney** (especially evident in the sharp, lovely work of the female chorus when it sings, "I've got sooo, so much soul for you baby"). The song snatches you up immediately, plunging the listener into what sounds like a factory production line at full swing: bursts of steam, metallic klangs, heavy grunts from the workers – all strung together by an intertwined percussion/guitar line that's gradually joined by a liquid rush of strings. The whole effect is both hellish and intensely exciting and when the men finally break into the title chant, the moment is absolutely riveting. This peak is followed immediately by another, contrasting high as the female chorus enters, soothing and enticing, their demands for love mixing with the men's work chant until both fall back and make way for a long instrumental break. The energy continues unabated here, too, sparked by a series of synthesizer solos –the first sounding like a frantic mandolin –that merge with and climax in an extraordinary piano flourish. A peak record if there ever was one, "Workin' & Slavin'" runs just over nine minutes with an equally knockout instrumental version of the same length on the flip side. It's due out any day now on a commercial disco disc and should be considered one of the most essential records of the fall season.

Another essential release: The **Village People's** new "Cruisin'" album on Casablanca, the group's most assured and enjoyable lp so far, perfectly timed to catch them at the crest of their popularity and boost them further. Producer **Jacques Morali's** style here varies little from the group's previous two albums – he retains that distinctive thumping beat; the pop gloss; the shouting, hard-hitting vocal arrangements – but his use of synthesizers is more sophisticated and extensive than before and most of the songs have a new, elegant edge that makes an excellent foil for the gritty roughness of the vocals. Lead **Victor Willis**, who co-wrote all the songs with Morali and executive **Henri Belolo**, is also in top form here, whipping the group up to fever pitch; knocking out the words like his whole body was behind them, with the choruses given the impact of a prize fighter's combination punch; yet maintaining a sure sense of humor throughout. And a sense of humor is key here: from the opening track extolling the virtues of the "Y.M.C.A." for homeless, struggling young men (only once does the fatherly sincerity of the advice slip and suggest "you can hang out with all the boys"), to the hilarious (but appalling) confession of a pill-popper in the closing cut, "Ups And Downs" ("Sometimes I feel very strange/Sometimes I forget my name"), all the songs are very tongue-in-cheek, both rousing and hilarious. The highlights: "Hot Cop," with its chorus of "Party, boogie boogie, get on down" and a steamy break featuring wailing sirens; "The Women" and "I'm A Cruiser," a 12:57 medley whose first half recalls "African Queens" and seems intended to counter the group's gay image by sending them into

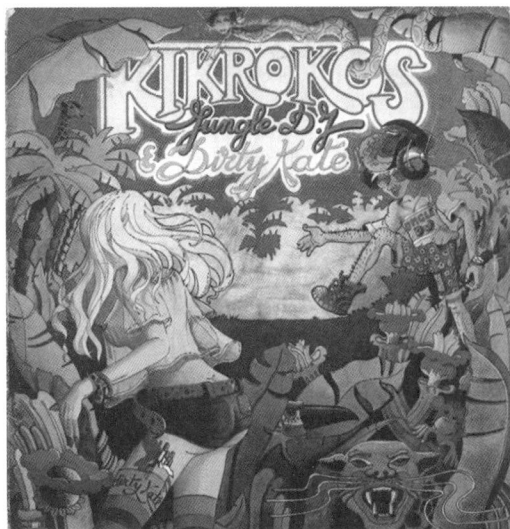

CIRCUS DISCO, LOS ANGELES
DJ: Mike Lewis

HOT SHOT/BRING ON THE BOYS/BABY YOU AIN'T NOTHING WITHOUT ME – Karen Young (West End)
I LOVE THE NIGHTLIFE – Alicia Bridges (Polydor)
I MAY NOT BE HERE WHEN YOU WANT ME/ CATCH ME ON THE REBOUND – Loleatta Holloway (Gold Mind)
INSTANT REPLAY – Dan Hartman (Blue Sky)
MACARTHUR PARK SUITE – Donna Summer (Casablanca)
MR. DJ YOU KNOW HOW TO MAKE ME DANCE – Glass Family (JDC)
#1 DJ/BIORHYTHMS/SUPER JOCK/IT LOOKS LIKE LOVE – Goody Goody (Atlantic)
STAND UP – Atlantic Starr (A&M)
STARCRUISIN'/FANCY DANCER/ARISTA VISTA – Gregg Diamond's Starcruiser (Marlin)
SUPERSTAR – Bob McGilpin (Butterfly)

IPANEMA, NEW YORK
DJ: Ray Velasquez

BEAUTIFUL BEND – Beautiful Bend (Marlin)
CAN'T NOBODY LOVE ME LIKE YOU – General Johnson (Arista)
LOVE DISCO STYLE – Erotic Drum Band (Prism)
FANCY DANCER/STARCRUISIN'/THIS SIDE OF MIDNIGHT/ARISTA VISTA – Gregg Diamond's Starcruiser (Marlin)
INSTANT REPLAY – Dan Hartman (Blue Sky)
IN THE BUSH/KEEP ON JUMPIN' – Musique (Prelude)
LAW AND ORDER– Love Committee (Salsoul)
STUBBORN KIND OF FELLA – Buffalo Smoke (RCA)
VICTIM – Candi Staton (WB)
YOU FOOLED ME – Grey and Hanks (RCA)

REFLECTIONS, NEW YORK
DJ: Billy Carroll

BOOGIE FUND – Solar Flare (RCA)
CAN'T NOBODY LOVE ME LIKE YOU – General Johnson (Arista)
I MAY NOT BE THERE WHEN YOU WANT ME/MAMA DON'T, PAPA WON'T – Loleatta Holloway (Gold Mind)
I'M A MAN – Macho (Prelude)
INSTANT REPLAY – Dan Hartman (Blue Sky)
IN THE BUSH – Musique (Prelude)
SHOOT ME WITH YOUR LOVE – Tasha Thomas (Orbit)
VICTIM – Candi Staton (WB)
YOU MAKE ME FEEL (MIGHTY REAL)/ DANCE (DISCO HEAT) – Sylvester (Fantasy)
YOU STEPPED INTO MY LIFE – Melba Moore (Epic)

EIGHT BALLS LOUNGE, ALBANY, N.Y.
DJ: Douglas Forrester

BEAUTIFUL BEND – Beautiful Bend (Marlin)
I'M A MAN – Macho (Prelude)
INSTANT REPLAY – Dan Hartman (Blue Sky)
IN THE BUSH/KEEP ON JUMPIN' – Musique (Prelude)
JUNGLE DJ – Kikrokos (Polydor import)
LOVE SHADOW/STANDING IN THE SHADOW OF LOVE – Deborah Washington (Ariola)
MACARTHUR PARK SUITE – Donna Summer (Casablanca)
THE WIZARD OF OZ – Meco (Millennium)
YMCA/HOT COP – Village People (Casablanca)
YOU MAKE ME FEEL (MIGHTY REAL)/ DANCE (DISCO HEAT) – Sylvester (Fantasy)

all-out tribute to "women who know they are women" only to have them end up shouting out the first names of nearly every gay cult figure around (my favorite combination: Jackie! ZaZa!) and the stirring "Y.M.CA." But every cut is danceable, every cut is fun, and with both earlier albums now gold records, "Cruisin'" seems destined for an even higher plateau of success.

Two radically different versions of the **O'Jays** "Now That We Found Love" appeared this week, both unexpected new takes on this especially satisfying, joyous and on-target **Gamble & Huff** message-in-the-music. One, a disco disc by the progressive reggae group **Third World** (Island), is propelled by rich, slightly accented male vocals and a wonderfully spirited arrangement of brilliant percussion and guitars. The sound is spare, vivid, spicy and as refreshing as the slap of a wave on a summer's day. This 7:37 track is an expanded version of the cut that appears on Third World's current album, "Journey To Addis," further evidence of the charm of the group's smoothly polished, highly accessible soul/reggae blend. The second new "Now That We Found Love" is on the **Thelma Jones** album just out on Columbia, produced and arranged by **Bert de Coteaux**. De Coteaux's approach is Philly sweet, lighter and not as cutting as Third World's, but Jones' throaty vocals carry it off, particularly in the final break when she begins riffing over an increasingly passionate chorus. The song reaches for a Philly gospel-style peak here but levels off at just under five minutes; a new mix could send it soaring. Another possibility on the Jones album: "How Long." ✪

OCTOBER 21, 1978

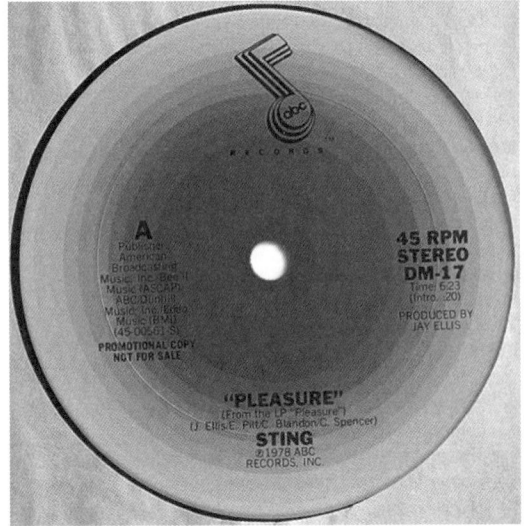

It's impossible to keep up with the rush of interesting disco discs in recent weeks, but here's a quick round-up of some that you should pick up on right away: **Gene Chandler**, off the scene for some time, makes a major comeback move with "Get Down" (Chi-Sound/20th Century), a bright, perky cut with a loose structure that opens up constantly for a variety of instrumental breaks. A jittery, chirping synthesizer pattern ties the song together and a stuttering chorus ("Get down, baby ba-ba-baby get down") strikes a playful note, but it's the frequent changes in **Carl Davis'** production (and **Rick Gianatos'** disco mix) that turn the track around and, at 8:14, there's never a dull moment... **Peaches & Herb** are also back (which reincarnation is this?) sounding quite unlike any of their former selves on "Shake Your Groove Thing" (Polydor), a **Freddie Perren** production that's already getting a lot of excited feedback. "Shake" is pop/funk with Perren's usual slick veneer but the balance here tilts slightly toward funk and the arrangement is lively enough to burn right through the gloss. Sounds like the early **Sylvers** chorus work at times – stinging, sweet – with a great intro, extra-snappy breaks and a percolating, bassy synthesizer line to keep things jogging at a cute pace. Right on target and ideally timed at 6:36... **Chic's** "Le Freak" (Atlantic), on the other hand, seems merely ultra-sheen pop-catchy as hell and, according to early reports, a crowd-pleaser, but not a whole lot more. The guitar line is a great hook as is the "Freak out!" chorus segment, but "Le Freak" has neither the inspiration nor the streamlined sophistication that made "Dance, Dance, Dance" click instantly. Yet this is likely to be the most commercially successful of the freak records released so far if only because the others (**Universal Robot Band's** "Freak With Me," still the best, and "Freak On" by **Lemon**) were too genuinely freaky.

After a few months as an import from A&M in Canada, "A Little Lovin' (Keeps The Doctor Away)" by **The Raes**, one of the season's sunniest records, is now available as a 12-inch from A&M in the States. And not a minute too soon – the song, which has been generating a lot of interest in the last few weeks, popped up on three out of four top 10s this week which helped nudge it into the Top 20 just before the U.S. version was issued. The feeling here is pure pop but the zing of the female vocals, especially the cutting lead; the soulful sax break; and the key percussion/high-hat break near the end raise it above the ordinary. **John Luongo** gets co-production credit for his disco mix, seven minutes in

❝ For truly off-the-wall tastes, there's Sting's raw, funky "Pleasure", a fascinating oddity ❞

RENDEZVOUS, WORCESTER, MASS.
DJ: Bill Stooke

A LITTLE LOVIN' – The Raes (A&M import)
AIN'T THAT ENOUGH FOR YOU – John Davis & the Monster Orch. (Sam)
DON'T HOLD BACK – Chanson (Ariola)
EYES IN THE BACK OF MY HEAD – Patti LaBelle (Epic)
INSTANT REPLAY – Dan Hartman (Blue Sky)
KEEP ON JUMPIN'/IN THE BUSH – Musique (Prelude)
LE FREAK – Chic (Atlantic)
MACARTHUR PARK SUITE – Donna Summer (Casablanca)
ONE NATION UNDER A GROOVE – Funkadelic (WB)
YOU MAKE ME FEEL (MIGHTY REAL)/
DANCE (DISCO HEAT) – Sylvester (Fantasy)

DECAMERON, LEVITTOWN, NY
DJ: Paul Casella

A LITTLE LOVIN' – The Raes (A&M import)
AIN'T THAT ENOUGH FOR YOU – John Davis & the Monster Orch. (Sam)
HOT COP – Village People (Casablanca)
I'M EVERY WOMAN – Chaka Khan (WB)
IN THE BUSH/KEEP ON JUMPIN' – Musique (Prelude)
IT'S ALL THE WAY LIVE – Lakeside (Solar)
IT'S TIME TO BE REAL – LTD (A&M)
TAKE THAT TO THE BANK/TOSSING, TURNING AND SWINGING – Shalamar (Solar)
WHAT YOU WAITIN' FOR – Stargard (MCA)
YOU STEPPED INTO MY LIFE – Melba Moore (Epic)

BACKSTREET, ATLANTA
DJ: Angelo Solar

AIN'T THAT ENOUGH FOR YOU – John Davis & the Monster Orch. (Sam)
BEAUTIFUL BEND – Beautiful Bend (Marlin)
DANCE DISCO (HEAT)/YOU MAKE ME FEEL (MIGHTY REAL) – Sylvester (Fantasy)
DANCIN' IN MY FEET – Laura Taylor (TK)
I LOVE THE NIGHTLIFE – Alicia Bridges (Polydor)
I'M A MAN – Macho (Prelude)
IN THE BUSH/KEEP ON JUMPIN' – Musique (Prelude)
INSTANT REPLAY – Dan Hartman (Blue Sky)
MACARTHUR PARK SUITE – Donna Summer (Casablanca)
SUBSTITUTE – Gloria Gaynor (Polydor)

ICE PALACE 57, NEW YORK
DJ: Roy Thode

A LITTLE LOVIN' – The Raes (A&M import)
BAISE MOI – Pam Todd & Gold Bullion Band (Channel)
C IS FOR COOKIE – Sesame Street Fever (Sesame Street)
I LOVE THE NIGHTLIFE – Alicia Bridges (Polydor)
I'M EVERY WOMAN – Chaka Khan (WB)
INSTANT REPLAY – Dan Hartman (Blue Sky)
IT'S A BETTER THAN GOOD TIME
– Gladys Knight & the Pips (Buddah)
MACARTHUR PARK SUITE – Donna Summer (Casablanca)
TRUE LOVE IS MY DESTINY/MY CLAIM TO FAME
– James Wells (AVI)
YOU STEPPED INTO MY LIFE – Melba Moore (Epic)

length... Another popular Canadian record now out on a domestic label is the **Wonderland Disco Band's** "Wonder Woman Disco," released by Roadshow (through UA) with an "American version" (6:57) on one side and a "European version" (about 12:30) on the other. Putting aside the essential triviality of the song's lyrics ("In my satin tights/I'm just fighting for your rights/ And the old red, white and blue" – what can you expect from a tv theme?), both versions are amazingly good, with the "European" one a fine example of how a creative, take-it-to-the-limit arrangement can transform otherwise flimsy material. The "European" side (both versions were recorded, by the way, in Los Angeles) slides through some very freaky changes, throwing in a little orgasmic heavy breathing; some amusing screams of "Shake my wonder-maker;" "Star Wars" synthesizer effects; delicious horn, vibes, synthesizer solos – all of it in unexpected juxtaposition so the listener/dancer is constantly involved. Happily, the "American" side, though more straightforward, is no less sparkling. A pleasant surprise no matter which way you flip it... **Tom Moulton** produced the new **Charo** record, "Ole, Ole" (in a limited edition of hot pink vinyl from Salsoul) in a flashy, energetic style that sounds like **Santa Esmeralda** Philly style. At times **John Davis'** dense arrangement of flamenco guitar, castanets, quick handclaps, horns, strings, synthesizers, etc., etc. whirls at such a frantic speed it becomes dizzying, but the song still suggests the tension and spectacle of a bullfight while Charo contributes real, steamy vocals (without the camped-up accent) and countless breathy repetitions of the title. This is a much more ambitious and serious effort than "Dance A Little Bit Closer," yet not entirely without that record's light appeal... **Pam Todd**, who had a cult success with "Let's Get Together" last year, is now on Channel Records with a cute, left field record called "Baise Moi (Kiss Me)," now in the advance (or, as they would have it, "press testing") stage but due for release very soon. Todd's vocals are the grabber here but the production provides plenty of interesting support, particularly in the central break with its crunchy New York feel and Philly overtones – a little busy at times, but tight enough to stand up on its own as an instrumental flip side. Could be a sleeper.

For truly off-the-wall tastes, there's **Sting's** raw, funky "Pleasure" (ABC), a fascinating oddity that sounds like it was made in the halls of some tough urban high school with the strings added later for a marvellously incongruous touch. Both the male and female lead voices are rough, expressive, strained at times, but so down-to-earth believable that the song takes on the feel of an authentic adolescent anthem: "Everything we do brings us pleasure – If it's nothing more than playing paddle-ball or kissing in the hall." The production sound is strange, with a bassy undertow, sheets of strings, light percussion – all together quite haunting, but it's those voices that make the song so special, so very out-of-the-ordinary. Definitely not for all tastes, but a classic. ✇

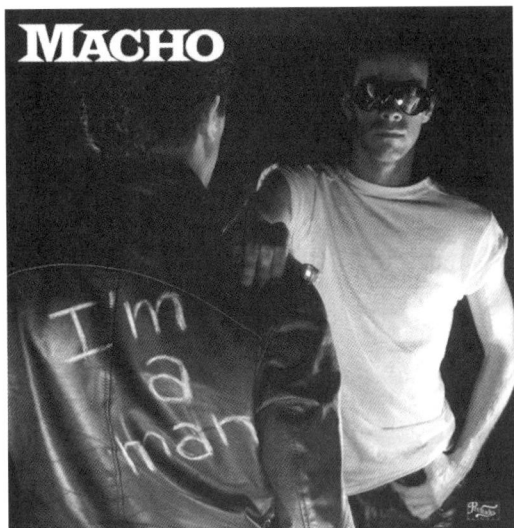

More than a little under the weather this week, I'm afraid all I have the energy far is a quick list of new releases that just can't wait – more detailed reviews of the key items will follow in the next issue. THE ESSENTIAL ALBUMS: "Cerrone IV: The Golden Touch" (Cotillian), the album **Cerrone** considers his most serious, includes four tracks in strikingly different styles and moods, all more densely vocal than mast of his previous work but all bearing the unmistakable Cerrone touch. No sustained, side-long production numbers here, but "Je Suis Music" ("I Am Music") and "Look for Love" are especially stirring and "Music Of Life" is Cerrone's lightest, loveliest, most seductive piece of music so far... **Kikrokos**, the group that came together for "Jungle D.J." (Polydor), includes ace Trident session musicians who were key members of **Kongas** and **Voyage**, so the sound here is supple Eurodisco with pop overtones. The title track, which appears as a three-part, 15-minute cut on side one as well as a sevenminute medley/reprise an side two, is bright, spunky, quite entertaining and stylishly produced with alternating male and female vocals and mucho changes. One of the most popular imparts an the disco round in the past few months, its American release has already popped it into the Top 20 this week, so watch this one... **Gregg Diamond's** latest **Bionic Boogie** collection, "Hot Butterfly" (Polydor) covers much the same ground as the group's first lp and the current Starcruiser album – sharp, invigorating pop disco with a fine funk edge and involving vocals. As usual, there's not a wasted track here, but the stand-outs immediately are "Chains" and "Cream (Always Rises To The Top)," though the latter suffers slightly from repetition; "Fess Up To The Boogie" and "When the Shit Hits The Fan" are strong runners-up. Rather more predictable than one would hope, but immensely attractive nonetheless... **El Coco's** "Dancing In Paradise" album (AVI) is similarly predictable –we know most of the **Michael Lewis** and **Laurin Rinder** moves by now – but they, too, have a kind of effortless pop assurance that gets under one's skin after only a few listenings. The title cut and "Love In Your Life," both previously released on a disco disc, are included here full-length and, of the new material, all three cuts an the second side are noteworthy: the atmospheric instrumental "Afrodesia" (8:24): "It's Your Last Chance" (5:58), a catchy dance-floor drama; and the sly, slick and wicked "Coca Kane" (5:06).

CHOICE CUTS: **Cheryl Lynn's** debut album on Columbia is terrific; she combines the vocal styles of **Dee Dee Sharp** and **Jean Carn** while coming up with something different and fresh of her own. Aside from the already recommended "Got To Be Real," which opens up the album (though in a shorter version than the disco disc currently available), there's a pulsing,

"My favorite after-disco cool-out record these days is Steve Reich's penetrating "Music For 18 Musicians." There are no identifiable words and the effect is both soothing and energizing, eerie and coolly elegant"

12 WEST, NEW YORK
DJ: Alan Dodd

A LITTLE LOVIN' – The Raes (A&M)
AIN'T THAT ENOUGH FOR YOU – John Davis & the Monster Orch. (Sam)
BEAUTIFUL BEND – Beautiful Bend (Marlin)
DANCIN' IN MY FEET – Laura Taylor (TK)
I LOVE THE' NIGHTLIFE – Alicia Bridges (Polydor)
I MAY NOT BE THERE WHEN YOU WANT ME – Loleatta Holloway (Gold Mind)
INSTANT REPLAY – Dan Hartman (Blue Sky)
MACARTHUR PARK SUITE – Donna Summer (Casablanca)
MY CLAIM TO FAME/TRUE LOVE IS MY DESTINIY/THAT'S THE WAY THE WIND BLOWS – James Wells (AVI)
WORKIN' & SLAVIN' – Midnight Rhythm (Atlantic)

L.A. CAFE, WASHINGTON, D. C.
DJ: Preston Powell

AIN'T THAT ENOUGH FOR YOU – John, Davis & the Monster Orch. (Sam)
CREAM (ALWAYS RISES TO THE TOP)/CHAINS – Bionic Boogie (Polydor)
DO A DANCE FOR LOVE – Sweet Cream (Shadybrook)
GOT TO BE REAL – Cheryl Lynn (Columbia)
IN THE BUSH – Musique (Prelude)
JE SUIS MUSIC/LOOK FOR LOVE – Cerrone (Cotillion)
LE FREAK – Chic (Atlantic)
MACARTHUR PARK SUITE – Donna Summer (Casablanca)
STARCRUISIN'/THIS SIDE OF MIDNIGHT – Gregg Diamond's Starcruiser (Marlin)
YOU STEPPED INTO MY LIFE – Melba Moore (Epic)

XENON, NEW YORK
DJ: Tony Smith

A LITTLE LOVIN' – The Raes (A&M)
AIN'T THAT ENOUGH FOR YOU – John Davis & the Monster Orch. (Sam)
FESS UP TO THE BOOGIE/CREAM ALWAYS RISES TO THE TOP)/CHAINS –Bionic Boogie (Polydor)
HEARTBREAK IN DISGUISE/COME FLY WITH ME/THIS IS THE HOUSE WHERE LOVE DIED – Pattie Brooks (Casablanca)
I'M A MAN – Macho (Prelude)
JUNGLE DJ – Kikrokos (Polydor)
MACARTHUR PARK SUITE – Donna Summer (Casablanca)
MY CLAIM TO FAME/TRUE LOVE IS MY DESTINY – James Wells (AVI)
SHOOT ME WITH YOUR LOVE – Tasha Thomas (Orbit)
SWEET CITY RHYTHM – Fantasia (Amazon)

TROCADERO TRANSFER, SAN FRANCISCO
DJ: Gary Tighe

AIN'T THAT ENOUGH FOR YOU – John Davis & the Monster Orch. (Sam)
DANCIN' IN MY FEET – Laura Taylor (TK)
GIVING UP, GIVING IN/FALLING IN LOVE WITH, LOVE/LOOKING FOR LOVE/RUNNER – Three Degrees (Ariola)
JE SUIS MUSIC/LOOK FOR LOVE/MUSIC OF LIFE – Cerrone (Cotillion)
JUNGLE DJ – Kikrokos (Polydor)
LOVE SHADOW/STANDING IN THE SHADOW OF LOVE – Deborah Washington (Ariola)
MY CLAIM TO FAME/TRUE LOVE IS MY DESTINY – James Wells (AVI)
SINNER MAN – Sarah Dash (Epic)
STARCRUISIN'/THIS SIDE OF MIDNIGHT/ ARISTAVISTA/ FANCY DANCER – Gregg Diamond's Starcruiser (Marlin)
SUITE FOR LOVERS – Marsius (Unidisc import)

exciting cut called "Star Love" (7:23) that is already causing a lot of comment and another up number titled "You Saved My Day" – both not to be missed... The new **Isaac Hayes** album, "For The Sake Of Love" (Polydor), contains a new version of his classic movie theme, "Shaft," now titled "Shaft II" and running nearly 10 minutes. **Jim Burgess** did the mix here and the result is interesting but some what reserved; not the total revamp the track needs to jump in a truly contemporary way, but perhaps Hayes didn't want to tamper with the original too radically. Still, worth attention for the nostalgic thrill of it all and the brilliant crackle of the production. Also check out "Zeke The Freak."

ETC.: My favorite after-disco cool-out record these days is **Steve Reich's** penetrating "Music For 18 Musicians" (ECM/Warner Brothers) which is shimmering acoustical music with voice accompaniment that has a distinctly electronic feel. The voices are used as instruments, so there are no identifiable words and the effect is both soothing and energizing, eerie and coolly elegant. ◓

DISCO FILE TOP 20

1. **MACARTHUR PARK SUITE** – Donna Surnmer (Casablanca)
2. **INSTANT REPLAY** – Dan Hartman (Blue Sky)
3. **IN THE BUSH/KEEP ON JUMPIN'** – Musique (Prelude)
4. **BEAUTIFUL BEND** – Beautiful Bend (Marlin)
5. **I LOVE THE NIGHTLIFE** – Alicia Bridges (Polydor)
6. **YOU MAKE ME FEEL (MIGHTY REAL)/DANCE (DISCO HEAT)** – Sylvester (Fantasy)
7. **STARCRUSIN'/FANCY DANCER/THIS SIDE OF MIDNIGHT/ARISTA VISTA** – Greg Diamond's Starcruiser (Marlin)
8. **AIN'T THAT ENOUGH FOR YOU** – John Davis & the Monster Orch. (Sam)
9. **I'M A MAN** – Macho (Prelude)
10. **VICTIM** – Candi Staton (WB)
11. **DANCIN' IN MY FEET** – Laura Taylor (TK)
12. **YOU STEPPED INTO MY LIFE** – Melba Moore (Epic)
13. **MY CLAIM TO FAME/TRUE LOVE IS MY DESTINIY** – James Wells (AVI)
14. **A LITTLE LOVIN'** – The Raes (A&M)
15. **I MAY NOT BE THERE WHEN YOU WANT ME/ CATCH ME ON THE REBOUND** – Loleatta Holloway (Gold Mind)
16. **JUNGLE DJ** – Kikrokos (Polydor import)
17. **MR. DJ YOU KNOW HOW TO MAKE ME DANCE** – Glass Family (JDC)
18. **SUPERSTAR** – Bob McGilpin (Butterfly)
19. **BURNIN'** – Carol Douglas (Midsong)
20. **LET'S START THE DANCE** – Bohannan (Mercury)

LES GIRLS: Heading this week's round-up of female vocal records are two releases from trios that were disco favorites even before the genre got its name – **First Choice** and, back after a long absence from the dancefloor, the **Three Degrees**. Both groups have taken a new direction this

sound is reminiscent of European disco/pop like **Boney M.** and **Abba**. The concept is interesting throughout but the execution is less than satisfying; both producer and performers are giving up, giving in, but it's Giorgio who wins this round.

❛❛ It's Gibbons at his most outrageous and progressive, an amazing pile-up of percussive changes that broad-jump from speaker to speaker and merge into a final thump thump thump. Hard-core disco ❜❜

time out, leaving the safe confines of the Philadelphia sound for extensive Eurodisco make-overs, First Choice hedging somewhat with a **Tom Moulton/Thor Baldursson** co-production that retains Philly roots, Three Degrees going more or less all the way with **Giorgio Moroder**, who showers them with synthesizers in his best production job outside of **Donna Summer** in some time. The only problem is that, in putting aside a production style they'd been identified with for so long, both groups sound suddenly unfamiliar, not like themselves, and the change can be disconcerting. This is especially true of the First Choice's record, a disco disc preview of their forthcoming album called "Hold Your Horses" (Gold Mind), which is only occasionally recognizable as the First Choice, primarily because vocals are at a minimum here. With only two verses before the break, lead **Rochelle Fleming** tends to get buried in the driving chorus work and only breaks loose at the end (when she sings, "You gotta know/I like it slow") and then too briefly. Still, "Horses" is hot and spunky with a brassy, fast-pumping beat and an effective, if overly simplified break; it's already getting enthusiastic response at a short, sweet 5:50 length but an expanded version could strengthen its punch. "New Dimensions," Giorgio's Three Degrees album on Ariola, was recorded in London and Los Angeles, which might account for its sometimes muddy density of sound and lack of clarity, usually a Giorgio trademark. Much of the synthesizer work retains that cutting edge but sometimes the productions tend to thicken up and get awfully bassy, losing the vocals in the electronic soup. The key cuts here are on side one, whose three songs trace an emotional passage out of love and back in again: "Giving Up, Giving In" (6:07, also available on a 12-inch) is the energy peak and continues with variations in "Looking For Love" (5:26) to form a two-part medley – in the midst of both songs' synthesizer swirls, the group sounds rougher, somewhat rawer than before and, though I miss the more delicate balance of the Philly vocals, the new style is more gutsy. The side ends with "Falling In Love With Love Again" (5:34) which is more in that familiar Philly style vocally and has an overly quick pace that is nonetheless irresistible. "The Runner" (6:18) is also of interest; again, the pace is fast and the

OTHER NOTABLE REMIXES: Though he's uncredited on the disco disc label, **Richie Rivera** has also remixed **Gentle Persuasion's** "Litterbug" (WB), restructuring the intro, plumping up the breaks, dropping a piano track here, bringing up the synthesizer there. The song remains a little stiff and uneven but it's cuter than ever (and runs 7:10 now)... **Jim Burgess** was called into to perk up two cuts from the Karen Young album – "Bring On The Boys" and "Baby You Ain't Nothin' Without Me" (back-to-back on West End) – and, though my original reservations about the records still hold, both new versions have hotter breaks and flashy moves that should bring them renewed attention from DJs... **Loleatta Holloway's** "I May Not Be There When You Want Me" (Gold Mind) has been reissued on a disco disc in a somewhat different version that adds little but takes away the talk break at the end and smooths things out nicely (I'd still love to hear a Walter Gibbons mix on this one); "Mama Don't, Papa Won't" is on the flip side. NOTES: **Denise LaSalle's** get-down "P.A.R.T.Y. (Where It Is)" is now available on a disco disc from ABC, same length (4:56) as the lp cut... Butterfly has issued a direct-to-disk 12-inch of **Denise McCann's** two previous hits, "Tattoo Man" and "I Don't Wanna Forget You," to coincide with the release of her first album for the label; next they might consider a serious reworking of "Midnight Madness" from the lp.

NEWS: Atlantic Records has picked up **Tasha Thomas'** smash "Shoot Me (With Your Love)" from Orbit and is planning a simultaneous American and European disco disc release immediately to be followed by a single version shortly.

OTHER RECOMMENDED ALBUMS: **Saturday Night Band** and **Constellation Orchestra** production team **Moses Dillard** and **Jesse Boyce** continue their winning streak with the new **Lorraine Johnson** album, "Learning To Dance All Over Again" (Prelude). Likely to be one of the best-received female solo albums in the discos this fall, Johnson's record contains two knockout eight-minute tracks – "I'm Learning To Dance All Over Again" and "Feed The Flame" –that combine the best of **Dillard & Boyce's** funk-tinged pop/disco styling with superb,

STUDIO ONE, LOS ANGELES
DJ: Manny Slali

CONTACT – Edwin Starr (20th Century)
CREAM (ALWAYS RISES TO THE TOP)/CHAINS
– Bionic Boogie (Polydor)
FEED THE FLAME/I'M LEARNING TO DANCE ALL OVER AGAIN – Lorraine Johnson (Prelude)
HOLD YOUR HORSES – First Choice (Gold Mind)
I MAY NOT BE THERE WHEN, YOU WANT ME/TWO SIDES TO EVERY STORY/CATCH ME ON THE REBOUND/MAMA DON'T PAPA WON'T – Loleatta Holloway (Gold Mind)
MACARTHUR PARK SUITE – Donna Summer (Casablanca)
MY CLAIM TO FAME – James Wells (AVI)
SHAKE YOUR GROOVE THING – Peaches & Herb (Polydor)
SHOOT ME (WITH YOUR LOVE) – Tasha Thomas (Orbit)
WORKIN' & SLAVIN' – Midnight Rhythm (Atlantic)

G.G. BARNUM ROOM, NEW YORK
DJ: Willie Guzman

A LITTLE LOVIN' – The Raes (A&M import)
AIN'T THAT ENOUGH FOR YOU – John Davis & the Monster Orch. (Sam)
CREAM ALWAYS RISES TO THE TOP – Bionic Boogie (Polydor)
HOLD YOUR HORSES – First Choice (Gold Mind)
THE HUNCHBACK OF NOTRE DAME – Alec Costandinos (Casablanca)
MACARTHUR PARK SUITE – Donna Summer (Casablanca)
MY CLAIM TO FAME – James Wells (AVI)
SHOOT ME (WITH YOUR LOVE) – Tasha Thomas (Orbit)
SING SING/BOOGIE WOMAN – Gaz (Salsoul)
WORKIN' & SLAVIN' – Midnight Rhytnm (Atlantic)

LES MOUCHES, NEW YORK
DJ: Vince Michael

AIN'T THAT ENOUGH FOR YOU – John Davis & the Monster Orchestra (Sam)
CAN'T NOBODY LOVE ME LIKE YOU DO – General Johnson (Arista)
GET DOWN – Gene Chandler (20th Century)
I LOVE THE NIGHTLIFE – Alicia Bridges (Polydor)
KEEPING MY HEAD ABOVE WATER – Ted Taylor (MCA)
MACARTHUR PARK SUITE – Donna Summer (Casablanca)
SHOOT ME (WITH YOUR LOVE) – Tasha Thomas (Orbit)
SING SING – Gaz (Salsoul)
YOU FOOLED ME – Grey & Hanks (RCA)
YOU STEPPED INTO MY LIFE – Melba Moore (Epic)

CLUB FEVER, DETROIT
DJ: Claude Dunne

BABY YOU AIN'T NOTHING WITHOUT ME/ BRING ON THE BOYS/WHERE IS HE – Karen Young (West End)
CREAM ALWAYS RISES TO THE TOP/ CHAINS/FESS UP TO THE BOOGIE – Bionic Boogie (Polydor)
HEARTBREAK IN DISGUISE/THIS IS THE HOUSE WHERE LOVE DIED/COME FLY WITH ME/LET'S DO IT AGAIN – Pattie Brooks (Casablanca)
I CAN TELL/DON'T HOLD BACK – Chanson (Ariola)
I MAY NOT BE THERE WHEN YOU WANT ME/TWO SIDES TO EVERY STORY/GOOD, GOOD FEELING/MAMA DON'T PAPA WON'T – Loleatta Holloway (Gold Mind)
I'M IN YOU/BLACK COCO/SOMETIMES WHEN WE TOUCH/ KEEP YOUR EYE ON THE SPARROW – Samba Soul (RCA)
LOVIN', LIVIN', GIVIN'/WHAT YOU GAVE ME/YOU WERE THE ONE/REACH OUT – Diana Ross (Motown)
MY CLAIM TO FAME/TRUE LOVE IS MY DESTINY – James Wells (AVI)
NEVER LET GO/CLOUDBURST – Eastbound Expressway (AVI disco disc)
WORKIN' & SLAVIN – Midnight Rhythm (Atlantic)

shouting vocals strong enough to stand up to the big, bright productions. Both these cuts are clean, razor-sharp, no-nonsense productions, excellent showcases for Johnson's singing which is often played off against male chorus work. Another possibility here: "Who Do You Think You're Fooling," which has a near-sleaze feel. All together, a high impact album, highly recommended... **Thelma Houston's** new release, "Ready To Roll" (Tamla) has a lot more disco material than any of her previous albums. My favorites are "Love Is Comin' On" (6:13), a high-spirited, happy number with good breaks and a solid building arrangement that probably needs slowing down some; "Strange" (4:36), which sounds like a **Diana Ross** number, but suffers from an odd thinness in the production; "Saturday Night, Sunday Morning," which seems to be the early favorite among DJs, too, though it's kind of off-beat and real short at 3:56; and "Midnight Mona" (4:22), about a girl with "heels five inches high and the devil in her eye."

REMIXES: One of my favorite "new" records this week is **Al Garrison's** total revamping of an overlooked cut on the **Evelyn "Champagne" King** album called "I Don't Know If It's Right" (RCA). Almost twice as long as the original cut at 8:15, this version brings the song to full bloom with the addition of new vocal and instrumental elements, some dropped or buried in the original mix, others, I suspect, newly recorded for this disco disc. Key touch-ups: King's vigorous moaning, shouting, give-it-to-me intro, picked up again for the song's vamp ending; precise, clipped handclaps to tighten things up and a sizzling sax break. The song, in the slightly slower lyric verses at least, recalls the emotion and adolescent candor of female vocal records of the '60s, but it's a classic feel updated beautifully. "I Don't Know" may not become the standard "Shame" has grown into, but it should hold us until the next album comes along... **Zulema**, who, save for her frequent background work with **Faith, Hope & Charity** and **Van McCoy**, has been absent from the disco scene for too long, returns with a rousing, urgent plea for "Change" (Le Joint/London). **Richie Rivera's** new mix, available on a non-commercial disco disc, also nearly doubles the original lp track with the addition of a much-needed break – featuring a perky synthesizer, skipping horns and a smooth flow of strings for lubrication – and gives Zulema's strong, husky-around-the-edges vocals extra presence. Already on a lot of disco playlists, this one looks like it might have staying power, especially with the radio boost it's getting as a single... **Walter Gibbons** has gone back and reworked his disco mix of Bettye Lavette's "Doin' The Best That I Can" for West End and the result is a radically different record so full of new instrumental shifts and breaks that cataloguing them all would take more adjective-spiked paragraphs than we have space for here. Suffice it to say that this new eleven-minute version is Gibbons at his most outrageous and progressive, ending with an amazing pile-up of percussive changes that broad-jump from speaker to speaker and merge into a final thump thump thump. Hard-core disco that's already getting strong club reaction; should bring LaVette back from vinyl limbo. ◙

NOVEMBER 18, 1978

The key releases this week come from concept groups – those elusive entities that producers create in the studio (e.g., **El Coco**, **USA-European Connection**, **Love & Kisses**, **Starcruiser**, **St. Tropez**, **Sumeria**, **Sphinx**, etc.): aggregations that perform on vinyl, not on stage. Though most of these records represent concept debuts by **Amant**, **Gaz** and **Fantasia** – perhaps the brightest entry is THP #2, the second album from the **THP Orchestra**, titled "Tender Is The Night" (Butterfly). But even this bears little resemblance to the first THP album that featured the steamy "Two Hot For Love" – the sound here is smoother, crisper, not as wild, with a creamy blend of two female lead vocals replacing the raw, scorching vocals of "Two Hot" is **Barbara Fry**. So producers **Willi Morrison** and **Ian Guenther** – also responsible for **Grand Tour** – have fashioned a new sound for THP that leans toward the Los Angeles high-gloss modern pop of **Rinder & Lewis** with a snap and sheen all its own. Of the album's four tracks, it's hard to pick a favorite, but the opener, "Weekend Two Step" (13:34), has a hold on me right now – it's super bouncy, super cute and chock full of changes, a few of which go off slightly, but most have not only flair but a fine sense of fun. The Charleston beat is recalled, but the clincher here is a thoroughly modern synthesized voice that scats an intro to most of the chorus breaks and changes and makes a great counterpoint to the sharp leads. Plus, the space is both sprightly and laid-back, just right for gliding through effortlessly –and often. Both "Half As Nice" (5:18) and "Music Is All You Need" (9:29) are quicker-paced, the first studded with a bomp, bomp, deep-plunging drum/horn pattern that adds drama in contrast to the happy la-la-las of the singers; the second more in the European mold but staying away from cliche and keeping the emphasis on the ecstatic vocals. "Tender Is The Night" (6:46) is the most conventionally romantic of the cuts but its complex vocal arrangement, lovely fast hustle beat and clean break make it as attractive as the other material here. Hardly the album one was expecting from THP, but Morrison and Guenther's revamp of the group is one of the season's most pleasant surprises. Note: DJ copies of THP #2 are pressed on milk-white vinyl.

Amant is making the biggest splash of the other new concept groups currently, probably because TK house producer **Ray Martinez** proves to be the perfect synthesizer of other people's music. Amant's "If There's Love," out now on a TK disco disc in advance of the album release, sounds like a medley of Eurodisco changes and hooks – a snatch from **Voyage** here, some **Santa Esmeralda** claps there, touches from **Cerrone**, **Costandinos**, **Midney**, **Don Ray**; clearly, Martinez has studied the modern masters and, to be nice, we can call the results an hommage rather than a rip-off. Because the track does work, does have a lot of drive and holds up beautifully in this 11:18 **Jim Burgess** mix, but there are few flashes of inspiration or originality. Indeed, practically the only different thing Martinez has done here is to use male instead of female voices for the lyric passages and even that is only fitfully successful, at best falling somewhere

between Costandinos and **Don Ray** in effect. The flip side, "Hazy Shades Of Love" (8:50), is essentially more of the same, somewhat fresher but not as sure-fire a combination of borrowed hooks. Still, both cuts are so shrewdly calculated they can't miss and the early feedback is already overwhelmingly favorable... **Gaz** is one of those international productions, recorded by **Jurgen Korduletsch** (**Claudja Barry's** producer) in Munich and Philadelphia and using session stars like **Keith Forsey**, **Thor Baldursson** (who also arranged here), **Don Renaldo**, **Zach Zachery** and the team of **Benson**, **Benton** & **Ingram** on vocals. Bring all these people together with a **Richie Rivera** mix and the results are varied and unpredictable, each cut taking a new direction with the overall emphasis on slick, pop-oriented dance music. The standout is "Sing Sing" (7:14), which has a tricky, involving synthesizer twist; a nice bass line; bouncy, sing-song vocals and a jazzy feel with nostalgic overtones. "Indian Gaz" reminds me of the **Salsoul Orchestra** or

" "Flamingo!" the chorus girls scream, Les Mouches, Infinity, Studio 54, Regines... "

Goody Goody and "Boogie Woman" takes these elements and adds a flash of Bionic Boogie. "Interstellar Love Affair" zooms off in a more interesting direction, introducing three female space freaks anxious to seduce the listener; their vocals and imitation sex and the Cerrone-style production here are hard to resist. Derivative, perhaps, but, like Amant, extremely well-made... **Billy Terrell**, the producer behind **Gary Criss**, also created **Fantasia** which debuts with a disco disc titled "Sweet Sweet City Rhythm" (TK), a frothy, pulsing, highly commercial record that, like Andrea True's "N.Y. You Got Me Dancing," pays tribute to a number of big name New York clubs ("Flamingo!" the chorus girls scream, and Les Mouches, Infinity, Studio 54, Regines and one or two others are name-dropped in passing). The vocals, too, are generally on the Andrea True level, but the production – especially the sweeping strings, much of the chorus work and the pick-me-up changes – is better than that and Terrell carries things off smartly in spite of the textural unevenness. This is a Richie Rivera "midnight mix" though, again, TK does not credit him (or Burgess on Amant) on the record label.

BRING ON THE BOYS: A new **Vernon Burch** album slipped by virtually unnoticed a few months back, but, happily one cut has been salvaged and thoroughly revised for disco play. At 5:52, the remix of "Brighter Days"

1270, BOSTON
DJ: Danae Jacovidis

A LITTLE LOVIN' – The Raes (A&M)
BRING ON THE BOYS/BABY YOU AIN'T NOTHIN' WITHOUT ME – Karen Young (West End)
CHAINS/CREAM ALWAYS RISES TO THE TOP – Bionic Boogie (Polydor)
DOIN' THE BEST THAT I CAN – Bettye Lavette (West End)
GIVING UP, GIVING IN/THE RUNNER – Three Degrees (Ariola)
HOLD YOUR HORSES – First Choice (Gold Mind)
I LOVE THE NIGHTLIFE – Alicia Bridges (Polydor)
IF THERE'S LOVE/HAZY SHADES OF LOVE – Amant (TK)
JE SUIS MUSIC/LOOK FOR LOVE – Cerrone (Cotillion)
MACARTHUR PARK SUITE – Donna Summer (Casablanca)
MY CLAIM TO FAME/TRUE LOVE IS MY DESTINY – James Wells (AVI)
SHOOT ME (WITH YOUR LOVE) – Tasha Thomas (Atlantic)
SINNER MAN – Sarah Dash (Kirshner)
VICTIM/HONEST I DO – Candi Staton (WB)
WONDER WOMAN DISCO – Wonderland Disco Band (RS)

ALFIE'S, CHICAGO
DJ: Michael Graber

AIN'T THAT ENOUGH FOR YOU – John Davis & the Monster Orch. (Sam)
BURNIN' – Carol Douglas (Midsong)
CREAM (ALWAYS RISES TO THE TOP)/ CHAINS – Bionic Boogie (Polydor)
HOLD YOUR HORSES – First Choice (Gold Mind)
I LOVE THE NIGHTLIFE – Alicia Bridges (Poydor)
I WILL SURVIVE – Gloria Gaynor (Polydor)
INSTANT REPLAY – Dan Hartman (Blue Sky)
KEEP ON JUMPIN'/IN THE BUSH – Musique (Prelude)
LE FREAK – Chic (Atlantic)
MACARTHUR PARK SUITE – Donna Summer (Casablanca)
SUPERSTAR – Bob McGilpin (Butterfly)
VICTIM – Candi Staton (WB)
WORKIN' & SLAVIN' – Midnight Rhythm (Atlantic)
YMCA – Village People (Casablanca)
YOU STEPPED INTO MY LIFE – Melba Moore (Epic)

SAHARA, NEW YORK
DJ: Sharon White

A LTTLE LOVIN' – The Raes (A&M)
CHAINS/CREAM (ALWAYS RISES TO THE TOP)/ HOT BUTTERFLY – Bionic Boogie (Polydor)
CHANGIN' – Sharon Ridley (Tabu)
FEED THE FLAME/I'M LEARNING TO DANCE ALL OVER AGAIN/NOBODY'S WRONG – Lorraine Johnson (Prelude)
HOLD YOUR HORSES – First Choice (Gold Mind)
IF THERE'S LOVE – Amant (TK)
I'M EVERY WOMAN – Chaka Khan (WB)
IT LOOKS LIKE LOVE – Goody Goody (Atlantic)
JE SUIS MUSIC/LOOK FOR LOVE/MUSIC OF LIFE – Cerrone (Cotillion)
MACARTHUR PARK SUITE – Donna Summer (Casablanca)
SINNER MAN – Sarah Dash (Kirshner)
SUPERSTAR – Bob McGilpin (Butterfly)
TRUE LOVE IS MY DESTINY/MY CLAIM TO FAME – James Wells (AVI)
WORKIN' & SLAVIN' – Midnight Rhythm (Atlantic)
YOU STEPPED INTO MY LIFE – Melba Moore (Epic)

(Chocolate City/Casablanca) is not substantially longer than the original track, but the reconstruction is extensive: a full intro, featuring an energetic string section that had been buried in the earlier mix, was added for instant pick-up; more instrumentation was inserted behind Burch's vocals, giving the central section extra fullness and punch; and the mostly instrumental second half of the cut was enlivened considerably with several lost tracks (again, the strings are striking) and more emphasis on a bright female chorus. Burch still bears a strong resemblance to **Stevie Wonder** and he's wonderfully optimistic here, so this is a particularly welcome remix... I've always had a weakness for Joe Simon's rich, achingly deep voice and it sounds especially good on his new release, a **Norman Harris** production called "Love Vibration" (5:05 on a Spring disco disc) that sets the vocals off against an insinuating, irresistible bass line. The result is one of Simon's more effective dance records – and a definite change of pace for Harris, who puts all the Philly conventions aside for this fine foray into more serious funk, New York style but with a Southern accent... **Keith Barrow**, who made one of the more promising debuts last year, is back with a new album, "Physical Attraction" on Columbia, that contains his most interesting disco entry so far. It's a track called "Turn Me Up" (7:35) with a lightly chugging arrangement and oddly casual, incongruously off-hand falsetto vocals; the whole thing comes together in the final break segment when the strings well up, the organ takes off and, just before the fade a percussion change sparks the mix. Though both the vocals and the production here wear thin in spots and could be greatly benefited by a disco-style remix, the feeling is intriguing, almost gospel with some **Sylvester** overtones, and if the intensity confined within the track were let loose, it might be rather powerful. Turn it up... **Edwin Starr's** "Contact" (20th Century) is a spicy, percolating record that jumps with percussion, handclaps and nervous synthesizer blips. Singing about the beginning of love, disco style-the "contact" is eye-to-eye: "I was looking at you/you were looking at me" – Starr sounds as rough and ready as ever and the mix by **Rick Gianatos** plays up the zippy percussion movement in the intro and breaks. Watch this one – it's out as a 12-inch and lp cut, both 7:21... **Damon Harris**, ex **Temptations**, ex **Impact**, still sounds just like **Eddie Kendricks** only now he seems to be getting better disco material than his former inspiration. Case in point: "It's Music" (a disco disc on Fantasy/WMOT running 8:40), a spirited song about the power of music that matches Harris' cutting, vibrant falsetto with a dense, shimmering track full of movement and surprise... **David Simmons**, on the other hand, sounds very like **Teddy Pendergrass**, though the comparison may be flattering him somewhat, and both sides of his debut disco disc (also on Fantasy/WMOT) are of interest: "Will They Miss Me" (6:07) tackles a potentially morbid, moody theme – "Will they miss me when I'm gone? /Will the memory linger on?" – with a delightful light-heartedness and verve: "Hard And Heavy" (7:31), is by comparison, the weightier cut (the message: "living is hard, loving is heavy") but it, too, pumps along nicely and picks up steam in the final chorus build and the break. Both worth checking into. ●

First, a discreet announcement: Alert readers may have noticed that, beginning in the last issue, the Discotheque Hit Parade lists below were increased from ten to fifteen titles, primarily because, in these times of disco plenty (glut even), the shorter list had proven to be too tight and restrictive. Adding five more titles not only makes a stronger, more well-balanced and satisfying list, it also gives us a lot more input for the Disco File chart, which jumps this week from a Top 20 to a Top 30 list. Oh happy day! By the way, the Disco File column enters its fifth year this month. Our motto: Disco Does Not Suck. Do you wanna dance?

first album and the overall feeling here is sophisticated MOR soul with some disco thrown in for spice. "Le Freak," in essentially the same version that appeared on the disco disc, remains the choicest cut – a brittle, brilliantly crafted, super-glossy pop tune that manages to be quite charming and quite heartless at the same time: there is nothing in the least bit freaky about "Le Freak," but its very safeness has been the key to its success. Everything else here is similarly safe, and the only track likely to make an impact in the clubs is the self-promotional "Chic Cheer" (4:42), a spare, light-weight instrumental with fine intertwined bass and guitar lines by producers **Nile Rodgers** and **Bernard**

❝ Disco File enters its fifth year. Our motto: Disco Does Not Suck. Do you wanna dance? ❞

The two albums most likely to succeed this week are both disco with decided pop leanings – **Dan Hartman's** "Instant Replay" lp (Blue Sky), which takes a Top 40 rock slant, and **Chic's** "C'est Chic" (Atlantic), which is largely MOR disco. Hartman's "Instant Replay," a shorter version of which is included here, was one of the year's zippiest, most appealing pop disco items – bright, clean, spunky, totally unpretentious, it has the quick-energy cutting edge of a great radio record plus the instrumental moves that make it work on the dance floor. Clearly the sensibility behind "Instant Replay" was more good-time rock & roll than disco, but Hartman's approach was fresh, fun and right on target – dazzling All-American at a time when Eurodisco was reaching the OD point. That same approach is carried through on the album, particularly on a fourteen-minute medley called "Countdown/This Is It" which picks up where "Replay" lets off and fills up nearly all of side one here. But "Countdown" is even more feverishly disco-driven than its predecessor and more complexly structured, capturing Hartman's mood of delighted anticipation "Counting every minute/counting every second/every beat of your heart" – in a rush of wonderful changes. Highlights: the **Edgar Winter** sax solo that whips the song up to its first peak; the crunching, crashing electronic punches in another break; the final rocket take-off: and all of Hartman's spirited vocals – he tumbles through the song like an athletic in peak form. Following that rocket launching, "This Is It" is a slight let-down in pace but it's a fine fit lyrically and soon achieves an elated mood nearly equal to the medley's first part. The four songs on the record's flip side are less satisfying as disco workouts, but both "Double-A-Love" and a tasty titbit called "Chocolate Box," in the funk rock vein, bear watching, and "Love Is A Natural" is very pretty. Hartman not only wrote, produced and engineered here, he also performed on keyboards, bass, rhythm guitar –all instruments, in fact, on "Instant Replay" except Winter's sax and **Larry Washington's** conga work; a veritable one-man band. **Gene Page** arranged and conducted; **Tom Moulton** mixed. Hot pop and sure to be a big seller. **Chic's** "C'est Chic" is even more pop-oriented than the group's

Edwards and a nice, tantalizing beat. The highschool cheer lyrics are less than enchanting but, yes, it's very cute. Actually, the best track here is a lovely mid-tempo song called "I Want Your Love" that has a loose hustle beat and the most shimmering, attractive production on the album – perfect for a slower set. Not matter how calculated, Chic has a definite flair for pop disco and one wishes they'd made more extensive use of it here.

CHERCHEZ LES FEMMES: Yet another round-up of work by women singers, beginning with two songs I've been meaning to include for some time now, **Gloria Gaynor's** sensational "I Will Survive" and **Sharon Ridley's** ultra sleazy "Changin'." It was my former west coast correspondent who first alerted me to the Gaynor cut, tucked away on the flip side of "Substitute" (Polydor), but in the weeks since then, it's been discovered with such enthusiasm by so many people that "Survive" jumps into the Top 30 this week at number 23. No wonder – this is Gaynor's very best work in years, a return to the sort of gutsy vitality that brought her to everyone's attention in the first place. Like **Linda Clifford's** "Runaway Love," "I Will Survive" is a final kiss-off song, a wonderfully brutal diatribe addressed to an errant boyfriend ("Go on, now go/Walk out the door/Just turn around now/Cause you're not welcome anymore") and delivered with such relish that one can't help but get caught up in the emotion. But there's little bitterness here, more a fierce pride at pulling through and a determination survive and love again, so the spirit is up, thoroughly exhilarating. The production matches the mood of the message, starting out with a sly, mock-melodramatic intro, and building steadily, but it is Gaynor who's the knockout here. Highly recommended. Ridley's "Changin'," from her "Full Moon" album on Tabu/Columbia, is another end-of-the-affair song, but the feeling here is more melancholy and tender – a strong but sensible let's-end-as-friends number. The lyrics are marvelous, **Jerry Peters'** production nicely understated, and Ridley's vocals – aching, soaring, eccentrically phrased – totally absorbing. Because "Changin'" falls into that measured sleaze pace

DCA CLUB, PHILADELPHIA
DJ: Kurt Borusiewicz

AIN'T THAT ENOUGH FOR YOU – John Davis & the Monster Orch. (Sam)

BRING ON THE BOYS/BABY YOU AIN'T NOTHING WITHOUT ME – Karen Young (West End)

CONTACT – Edwin Starr (20th Century)

DOIN' THE BEST THAT I CAN – Bettye Lavette (West End)

GET DOWN – Gene Chandler (20th Century)

HEARTBREAK IN DISGUISE/THIS IS THE HOUSE WHERE LOVE DIED – Pattie Brooks (Casablanca)

I WILL SURVIVE – Gloria Gaynor (Polydor)

IF THERE'S LOVE/HAZY SHADES OF LOVE – Amant (TK)

LE FREAK – Chic (Atlantic)

MY CLAIM TO FAME – James Wells (AVI)

SINNER MAN – Sarah Dash (Kirshner)

SHAKE YOUR GROOVE THING – Peaches & Herb (Polydor)

SHOOT ME (WITH YOUR LOVE) – Tasha Thomas (Atlantic)

YOU STEPPED INTO MY LIFE – Melba Moore (Epic)

YOUR SWEETNESS IS MY WEAKNESS – Barry White (20th Century)

RASCAL'S, LOS ANGELES
DJ: Rusty Garner

A LITTLE LOVIN' – The Raes (A&M)

AIN'T THAT ENOUGH FOR YOU – John Davis & the Monster Orch. (Sam)

CERRONE IV – Cerrone (Cotillion)

CHAINS/CREAM (ALWAYS RISES TO THE TOP) – Bionic Boogie (Polydor)

GET DOWN – Gene Chandler (20th Century)

GIVING UP, GIVING IN/THE RUNNER – Three Degrees (Ariola)

HOLD YOUR HORSES – First Choice (Gold Mind)

HUNCHBACK OF NOTRE DAME – Alec Costandinos (Casablanca)

I LOVE THE NIGHTLIFE – Alicia Bridges (Polydor)

LE FREAK – Chic (Atlantic)

MACARTHUR PARK SUITE – Donna Summer (Casablanca)

RASPUTIN – Boney M (Sire)

SHOOT ME (WITH YOUR LOVE) – Tasha Thomas (Atlantic)

WEEKEND TWO STEP /MUSIC IS ALL YOU NEED – THP (Butterfly)

WORKIN' & SLAVIN' – Midnight Rhythm (Atlantic)

ICE PALACE, NEW YORK
DJ: Roy Thode

BABY YOU AIN'T NOTHING WITHOUT ME – Karen Young (West End)

BAISE MOI – Pam Todd (Channel)

THE CHASE – Giorgio Moroder "Midnight Express" Soundtrack (Casablanca)

CONTACT/I'M SO INTO YOU – Edwin Starr (20th Century)

FEED THE FLAME – Lorraine Johnson (Prelude)

GET DOWN – Gene Chandler (20th Century)

I WAS MADE FOR DANCIN' – Leif Garrett (Atlantic)

I WILL SURVIVE – Gloria Gaynor (Polydor)

IF THERE'S LOVE – Amant (TK)

LOVE VIBRATION – Joe Simon (Spring)

SHAFT II – Isaac Hayes (Polydor)

SHAKE YOUR GROOVE THING – Peaches & Herb (Polydor)

SINNER MAN/TOUCH AND GO – Sarah Dash (Kirshner)

TRUE LOVE IS MY DESTINY – James Wells (AVI)

YOU STEPPED INTO MY LIFE – Melba Moore (Epic)

not all crowds appreciate, it's become something of a cult item (prime boosters: New York DJs Richie Rivera and Sharon White) but it deserves a wider audience as one of the year's classiest falling-out-of-love songs. Warner Brothers has revived a "lost" cut from the **Candi Staton** "House Of Love" album, "Honest I Do Love You," with a **Jimmy Simpson** remix that, at 6:31, may not be that much longer than the original lp cut but has it beat on every other count. Simpson's version cleans up the sound, adds more sparkle to the intro, deletes much of the chorus work so that what's left has maximum effect, and lets the song run into a whimsical riff ending threaded by country-style ◐

DISCO FILE TOP 30

1. **MACARTHUR PARK SUITE** – Donna Summer (Casablanca)
2. **AIN'T THAT ENOUGH FOR YOU** – John Davis & the Monster Orch. (Sam)
3. **MY CLAIM TO FAME/TRUE LOVE IS MY DESTINIY** – James Wells (AVI)
4. **WORKIN' & SLAVIN'** – Midnight Rhythm (Atlantic)
5. **YOU STEPPED INTO MY LIFE** – Melba Moore (Epic)
6. **LE FREAK** – Chic (Atlantic)
7. **CREAM (ALWAYS RISES TO THE TOP)/CHAINS** – Bionic Boogie (Polydor)
8. **I LOVE THE NIGHTLIFE** – Alicia Bridges (Polydor)
9. **SHAKE YOUR GROOVE THING** – Peaches & Herb (Polydor)
10. **A LITTLE LOVIN'** – The Raes (A&M)
11. **SHOOT ME (WITH YOUR LOVE)** – Tasha Thomas (Atlantic)
12. **HOLD YOUR HORSES** – First Choice (Gold Mind)
13. **SINNER MAN** – Sarah Dash (Kirshner)
14. **JE SUIS MUSIC** – Cerrone (Cotillion)
15. **CONTACT** – Edwin Starr (20th Century)
16. **GET DOWN** – Gene Chandler (20th Century)
17. **INSTANT REPLAY** – Dan Hartman (Blue Sky)
18. **BRING ON THE BOYS/BABY YOU AIN'T NOTHING WITHOUT ME** – Karen Young (West End)
19. **IF THERE'S LOVE** – Amant (TK)
20. **DOIN' THE BEST THAT I CAN** – Bettye Lavette (West End)
21. **IN THE BUSH/KEEP ON JUMPIN'** – Musique (Prelude)
22. **DANCIN' IN MY FEET** – Laura Taylor (TK)
23. **I WILL SURVIVE** – Gloria Gaynor (Polydor)
24. **YOUR SWEETNESS IS MY WEAKNESS** – Barry White (20th Century)
25. **YMCA** – Village People (Casablanca)
26. **I MAY NOT BE THERE WHEN YOU WANT ME/ CATCH ME ON THE REBOUND** – Loleatta Holloway (Gold Mind)
27. **BAISE MOI** – Pam Todd (Channel)
28. **HUNCHBACK OF NOTRE DAME** – Alec Costandinos (Casablanca)
29. **BEAUTIFUL BEND** – Beautiful Bend (Marlin)
30. **VICTIM** – Candi Staton (WB)

DECEMBER 2, 1978

No questions about it, this week's most essential release is the new **Voyage** album, "Fly Away" (Marlin), a handsome follow-up to the group's debut earlier this year and one that should prove to be equally durable. Again, the theme is travel and the songs form one continuous musical journey, but the stops along the way are not as identifiable this time around because, rather than drawing upon a

> **❝ The old dark disco, which did not know it was disco, which was simply a song played in a room where we gathered to dance... ❞**

specific national sound for each new track, the group has gone for more general songs about the romance of travel: "Let's flyaway for holidays," "Come join us/Don't hesitate/Just be yourself/Be free." The messages are enticing but the music, written, arranged, produced (with **Roger Tokarz**) and performed by Trident studio stars **Marc Chantereau**, **Slim Pezin** and **Pierre-Alain Dahan** is even more seductive, taking hold immediately with the album's opening cut, "Souvenirs," already an instant hit. Opening on a dark, slightly ominous note with electronic moans and a welter of zippy synthesizer effects, "Souvenirs" suddenly breaks free, – like a plane coming out of storm clouds into the brilliant sun above, and zooms off on a joyous, carefree flight. The music is bright, crystal-clear but dense and richly textured – flawless Eurodisco with lovely female vocals that sweep the listener along effortlessly. Just before the end, the song takes another turn, both vocals and production become more insistent, heavier, rushing toward a peak again with the invitation, "Let's find a place for celebration and dance/for souvenirs and romance/let's keep on moving." Then, with a delicious, jump-cut jolt, we're in the midst of a group of forcefully chanting men and hard-beaten drums – "Kechak Fantasy," softened somewhat by the introduction of sparkling guitar and keyboard work but this album's equivalent of the first record's "Point Zero." A short, Indian-flavored "Eastern Trip" and "Tahiti, Tahiti" with its happy, childish female chanting and Hawaiian guitar accents suggesting a kind of feverish country & western, fill up the rest of the itinerary on side one (total time: 16:36). Side two, though blended seamlessly, falls more naturally into three separate songs, the best of which is "Let's Fly Away," which has slight overtones of "Scotch Machine" in its percolating synthesizer but, like sweet, airy number with easy-listening leanings saved by its sharp instrumentation. "Golden Eldorado," a conquistador fantasy, and "Gone With The Music," a

spirited rock & soul cut, are both interesting but somewhat flat and a reprise of "Souvenirs" ties things up nicely. After a magnificent take-off, the voyage this time out is a little bumpy, especially toward the end, but I suspect that even these latter tracks will find favor much as several of the unlikely cuts on Voyage I did. Besides, "Souvenirs" is strong enough on its own to make this one of the major albums of the holiday season.

RECOMMENDED DISCO DISCS: "Disco Extravaganza" by **G. B. Experience** (Atlantic) is just what its title promises – a sensational production number that makes use of nearly every disco move in the book, an audacious rush of changes, flourishes, breaks and musical quotes (like the phrase from "Love In C Minor" copied here) collected by veteran Philadelphia producer **Stan Watson** and a newcomer named **George Bussey Jr.** who co-produced, arranged, conducted and composed this amazing melange. The style is essentially Philadelphia at its most streamlined and progressive with flashes of Eurodisco inspiration – a heady blend that captures the best of both worlds while remaining firmly dedicated to its TSOP roots. There are definite debts to MFSB and the **Salsoul Orchestra** here and the female vocals are pure Philly (**The Sweethearts**, I suspect, with lead vocals by **Angie Griffin**). The most memorable lines are bound to be "listen to the drums/Gonna make you come to the maximum". There's a bit of an energy lag toward the end and the vocal side's 13:35 length but it's no discouragement once you're into this one: if it is, there's an instrumental side that runs 11:45. Enjoy... **Dinosaur's** "Kiss Me Again" (Sire/WB) takes even more risks and ends up quite far out in left field, usually one of my favorite locations, but in this case kind of forbidding territory. Produced by **Arthur Russell** and DJ legend **Nicky Siano**, "Kiss Me Again" is a dark, intense avant garde oddity that sounds like it could become a New York cult item but might prove a bit too heavy, man, for wider audiences. "My visions are real," the singer insists and both she and the song have a certain fascination, though perhaps not enough to hold up for the 13-minute Jimmy Simpson mix or the nearly as long variation on the flip side. Your move. Added attraction: Dinosaur is pressed on bright red vinyl... "Shine On Silver Moon" by **Marilyn McCoo** & **Billy Davis Jr.** (Columbia) begins surprisingly like **Grace Jones'** "Below The Belt" but after a short time, no other comparisons can be made. The sound, whipped up by **Steve Cropper** (ex **Booker T** & the **MG's**) and Davis, is ultra-sophisticated and smooth but with just the right snap in the intro and breaks – which mix rapid, jittery percussion and waves of strings beautifully – to get over disco-style. McCoo and Davis sound more zesty than usual, especially in the final riffiing build, and their enthusiasm combined with the pump of the production should put this one on some playlists in no time.

Another of the key disco discs this week is the remix of **Village People's** "Y.M.CA." (Casablanca), which opens that number up to a rousing 6:47, bringing it on with a wholly new handclap, percussion and trippy synthesizer

VAMPS, NEW ORLEANS
DJ: Tom Quinn

AIN'T THAT ENOUGH FOR YOU – John Davis & the Monster Orch. (Sam)
CHANGE – Zulema (Le Joint)
FEED THE FLAME/I'M LEARNING TO DANCE ALL OVER AGAIN – Lorraine Johnson (Prelude)
GIVING UP, GIVING IN – Three Degrees (Ariola)
I LOVE THE NIGHTLIFE – Alicia Bridges (Polydor)
IF THERE'S LOVE/HAZY SHADES OF LOVE – Amant (TK)
LE FREAK – Chic (Atlantic)
SHAKE YOUR GROOVE THING – Peaches & Herb (Polydor)
SHOOT ME (WITH YOUR LOVE) – Tasha Thomas (Atlantic)
SINNER MAN – Sarah Dash (Kirshner)
SOUVENIRS – Voyage (Marlin)
STANDING IN THE SHADOWS Of LOVE – Fever (Fantasy)
SYMPHONY OF LOVE – Miguel Brown (Polydor)
WORKIN' & SLAVIN' – Midnight Rhythm (Atlantic)
YMCA/HOT COP – Village People (Casablanca)

LIMELIGHT, HOLLYWOOD, FLA.
DJ: Bob Lombardi

AIN'T THAT ENOUGH FOR YOU – John Davis & the Monster Orch. (Sam)
BAISE MOI – Pam Todd (Channel)
CONTACT – Edwin Starr (20th Century)
DANCING, IN THE FIRE – Delilah (Sunshine)
DOIN' THE BEST THAT I CAN – Bettye Lavette (West End)
FLY ME – Celi Bee (APA)
INSTANT REPLAY – Dan Hartman (Blue Sky)
IF THERE'S LOVE – Amant (TK)
JUNGLE DJ – Kikrokos (Polydor)
LE FREAK – Chic (Atlantic)
LOVE DISCO STYLE – Erotic Drum Band (Prism)
MACARTHUR PARK SUITE – Donna Summer (Casablanca)
MY CLAIM TO FAME/TRUE LOVE IS MY DESTINY – James Wells (AVI lp cuts)
SHAKE YOUR GROOVE THING – Peaches & Herb (Polydor disco disc)
TENDER IS THE NIGHT – THP Orchestra (Butterfly lp cut)

ALFIES, SAN FRANCISCO
DJ: Marty Blecman

A LITTLE LOVIN' – The Raes (A&M)
BRING ON THE BOYS – Karen Young (West End)
BRIGHTER DAYS – Vernon Burch (Casablanca)
DANCE/POINCIANA – Paradise Express (Fantasy)
FLY AWAY – Voyage (Marlin)
GIVING UP GIVING IN/THE RUNNER – Three Degrees (Ariola)
HOLD YOUR HORSES – First Choice (Gold Mind)
JE SUIS MUSIC/LOOK FOR LOVE – Cerrone (Cotillion)
SHOOT ME (WITH YOUR LOVE) – Tasha Thomas (Atlantic)
SINNER MAN – Sarah Dash (Kirshner)
SLY-HI – Philly Cream (Fantasy/WMOT)
STANDING IN THE SHADOWS Of LOVE – Fever (Fantasy)
WEEKEND TWO STEP/MUSIC IS ALL YOU NEED – THP Orchestra (Butterfly)
THIS SIDE OF MIDNIGHT/STARCRUISIN' – Gregg Diamond's Starcruiser (Marlin lp cuts)
YMCA – Village People (Casablanca)

intro that proves irresistible. The same elements repeated in an extra break should make this song acceptable in a number of clubs that had shunned it up until now. Mix is by **Michael Hutchinson**, one of the engineers at New York's Sigma Sound... **El Coco's** "Coco Kane" has also been reworked some for an AVI disco disc: nearly three minutes of new instrumental material have been added here – like the spacious, delicately spacey central break-filling the song out to 7:45. Flip side is "It's Your Last Chance," also from the much-overlooked "Dancing In Paradise" album... Though not actually remixed, the two prime **James Wells** cuts are out back-to-back on another AVI 12-inch (promotional only), trimming "My Claim To Fame" from an overstretched 16:10 to a neater 11:57 while leaving "True Love Is My Destiny" as is. Both more stunning than ever.

MEDIA: A trio of quotes from recent articles on disco: From Andrew Kopkind's intelligent, provocative piece in Boston's Real Paper (October 28), "The Disco Decade/Notes on the Tremor of the Times": "Disco is the revolt against the 'natural' Sixties, the seriousness, the confessions, the struggles, the sincerity, pretensions and pain of the last generation. Disco is the affirmation of the 'unreal' Seventies, the fantasies, fashions, gossip, frivolity and fun. The Sixties were braless, lumpy, heavy; disco is stylish, chic, sleek, light. Disco emphasizes surfaces over substance, mood over meaning. The Sixties were a mind trip (marijuana, acid); disco is a body trip (Quaaludes, cocaine). The Sixties were cheap; disco is expensive. On a Sixties trip you saw God; on a disco trip you see Jackie O at Studio 54"... From **Andrew Holleran's** "Dark Disco: A Lament" in the December Christopher Street, in which the author of Dancer From The Dance defines his terms: "... The old dark disco, which did not know it was disco, which was simply a song played in a room where we gathered to dance... songs you could dance to for a long time, because they concentrated energy rather than evaporated it; songs that went inside you, rather than lodging in your feet and joints the way light disco does, You hardly moved, but suddenly you were closer – ever so slightly – to the person dancing with you, and you became conscious of your limbs, which even, as I remember, became heavier. You lowered your eyes. You closed them finally. It was gripping, real dancing, and the atmosphere in the room was one of surrender. Dark disco was our fado, our flamenco, our blues; it spoke of things in a voice partly melancholic, partly bemused by life, and wholly sexual"... From a Russian journalist's report on American discos –as printed in Moscow's Literary Gazette and excerpted in a recent AP dispatch in The Times – which describes disco as a kind of "nirvana for lonely people who don't want to have contact with anyone and who couldn't anyway": "How many lonely people are there in America? Very many! In any case the numbers are sufficient that in two years' time the multibillion-dollar disco industry founded on loneliness has spread rapidly through the country... (Dancers) spend the whole night shaking with the lights and dreaming of fame, success and money." Who said no one takes disco seriously? ✺

RECOMMENDED ALBUMS: Two new releases from very different points on the disco spectrum: The latest **Patrick Adams** creation is **Phreek**, a studio group whose first album on Atlantic is dominated by Adams' trademark synthesizer work – much the same skittish, buzzing, darting electronics that characterized his earlier productions with **Cloud Nine**, **Sine** and the **Universal Robot Band**, but the touch here is finer, more sophisticated in general and has a wider appeal. There may be nothing as riveting as "In the Bush," the Adams production for **Musique** which turned out to be one of the year's disco classics, but the six cuts here offer a variety of phreeky delights. Prime cuts: "Weekend" (6:49), which recalls **Gregg Diamond's** creamy funk approach and the soft-focus feel of Musique's "Summer Love," only to turn spicy hot and gently sizzling with excellent female vocals (chanting "This time it's party time/It's party time tonight"); subdued synthesizer work; a bright, chiming percussion break and sparkling guitar – and "I'm a Big Freak (R.U.1.2.)" (10:19), which is loud, busy with synthesizers that well up on all sides, snapping and crackling like a space station gone beserk; and the height of Adams' freak-funk style complete with shouting vocals and imitation orgasm – wild as you can get. In between these two very different peaks, there's two more tracks of interest, "Much Too Much" and "Everybody Loves A Good Thing," both lighter, wonderfully textured and appealing. And don't miss **Donna McGhee's** vocals on the slower-paced "May My Love Be With You" which starts out with a spoken segment reminiscent of "Casanova Brown." Phreek out – in style. Note: as a great reminder of where Patrick Adams came from, there's a new Bumblebee Unlimited record out now, written and produced by Adams and frequent teammate **Greg Carmichael** in that same dizzy cut style that made "Love Bug" so much fun. This time around, on "Lady Bug" (9:52 on a Red Greg disco disc), the formula gets kind of grating – too much of those processed "insect" voices when a little of this novelty goes a long way – but the swirling synthesizers and insistent bass, though much rawer than on Adams' solo work, are involving.

"Hunchback Of Notre Dame," the latest disco adaptation of literary classic by **Alec Costandinos and the Syncophonic Orchestra** (Casablanca), consists of two continuous sides of music, singing and occasional dialogue or narration that traces in a rather elliptical, sometimes confusing, fashion the Victor Hugo story of passion and deceit. As usual with Costandinos' work, the music is thrilling, brilliantly crafted, precise yet emotionally rich but, from a dancer's standpoint, the flow of "Hunchback" is broken too often for dramatic exposition to allow for much sustained movement. Only here and there does the record achieve the soaring rush of "Romeo & Juliet" and in a tale more complex than "Golden Tears," few moods are held long enough to inspire more than a few turns around the dancefloor. The production, with arrangements by **Don Ray**, is both intelligent and exciting but, in the end, its intellectual qualities weigh it down and make it much heavier than the prevailing mood of the discos can accept. Happily, however, Casablanca has pressed up a condensed version for a disco disc that is being included in the album package as a special bonus. This 7:46 track of the most danceable sections of the album, primarily the gorgeous, moody "Pope Of' Fools," emphasizes the texture and clarity of the music with only a few bits of dialogue or singing, salvaging the spirit of the "Hunchback" while cutting loose its narrative freight. The album is a must for Costandinos fans and admirers of Eurodisco class; the disco disc (for which DJ Rusty Garner was the consultant) is the version now picking up in the clubs. Other key releases this week – to be reviewed in next week's issue – are albums by **Arpeggio** and **Miguel Brown** (both on Polydor) and **Wild Fantasy** (Midsong).

RECOMMENDED DISCO DISCS: Pick of the week – it should be hitting the stores about the time RW hits the stands – is "Keep On Dancin'" by **Gary's Gang** (Sam) which, like **Amant's** "If There's Love" and "Disco Extravaganza" by **G. B. Experience**, borrows freely from a number of key disco sources (in this case **Patrick Juvet**, **Chic**, **Costandinos**, **Peter Brown** and **Cerrone** are among the unwitting lenders), rearranges and recharges the various elements of style with an idiosyncratic new slant, and comes up with something quite special in its own right. At 7:15, there's time for such a wide variety of changes that the dancer is never let down and the handling of derivative snatches of material is refreshingly, irreverently fast and loose. The break with its gorgeous synthesizer passages folding in upon each other, and the "Dance, dance, dance" chorus of warm, hushed male voices clinch the song for me. The record's flip' side, "Do It At The Disco," is an entirely different but equally eclectic style; this time the parts don't hold together quite as effectively (one is especially unprepared for the Latin-esque section here) but it has a nutty, eccentric sound that's left field and fun. Producer **Eric Matthew**, on the charts now with Bettye Lavette... A group called **Paradise Express** has released a splashy new version of **Paul Jabara's** "Dance" (Fantasy) that runs 8:16, the best part in the second half after most of the vocals have dispensed with and the song takes on a **Sylvester** frenzy, throws in some Eurodisco sex and ends on a shouting gospel note.

❝ It's loud, busy with synthesizers, snapping and crackling like a space station gone beserk ❞

PARADISE GARAGE, NEW YORK
DJ: Larry Levan

CHAINS/CREAM (ALWAYS RISES TO THE TOP)
– Bionic Boogie (Polydor)
CONTACT – Edwin Starr (20th Century)
**FEED THE FLAME/I'M LEARNING TO DANCE ALL OVER
AGAIN/NOBODY'S WRONG** – Lorraine Johnson (Prelude)
HOLD YOUR HORSES – First Choice (Gold Mind)
I DON'T KNOW IF IT'S RIGHT – Evelyn "Champagne" King
(RCA)
I WILL SURVIVE – Gloria Gaynor (Polydor)
I'M EVERY WOMAN – Chaka Khan (WB)
JE SUI'S MUSIC/ROCKET IN THE POCKET – Cerrone
(Cotillion)
KISS ME – Dinosaur (Sire)
LADY BUG – Bumblebee Unltd. (Red Greg)
LE FREAK/I WANT YOUR LOVE – Chic (Atlantic)
MY CLAIM TO FAME/TRUE LOVE IS MY DESTINY
– James Wells (AVI)
SHOOT ME (WITH YOUR LOVE) – Tasha Thomas (Atlantic)
**SOUVENIRS/KECHAK FANTASY/EASTERN TRIP/TAHITI,
TAHITI** – Voyage (Marlin)
YOU STEPPED INTO MY LIFE – Melba Moore (Epic)

CENTER STAGE, CHICAGO
DJ: Peter Lewicki

BRING ON THE BOYS – Karen Young (West End)
THE CHASE – Giorgio ("Midnight Express" Soundtrack
(Casablanca)
CREAM (ALWAYS RISES TO THE TOP)/CHAIN'S
– Bionic Boogie (Polydor)
FLY AWAY – Voyage (Marlin)
HEARTBREAK IN DISGUISE – Pattie Brooks (Casablanca)
HOLD YOUR HORSES – First Choice (Gold Mind)
HUNCHBACK OF NOTRE DAME – Alec Costandinos
(Casablanca)
I WILL SURVIVE – Gloria Gaynor (Polydor)
LE FREAK – Chic (Atlantic)
MY CLAIM TO FAME – James Wells (AVI)
ONE NATION UNDER A GROOVE – Funkadelic (WB)
SHAKE YOUR GROOVE THING – Peaches & Herb (Polydor)
SHOOT ME (WITH YOUR LOVE) – Tasha Thomas (Atlantic)
SING SING – Gaz (Salsoul)
WORKIN' & SLAVIN' – Midnight Rhythm (Atlantic)

UNION STATION, BOSTON
DJ: Joe Iantosca

BAISE MOI – Pam Todd (Channel)
CHAINS – Bionic Boogie (Polydor)
COCO KANE – El Coco (AVI)
CONTACT – Edwin Starr (20th Century)
DOIN' THE BEST THAT I CAN – Bettye Lavette (West End)
GOT TO BE REAL – Cheryl Lynn (Columbia)
HOLD YOUR HORSES – First Choice (Gold Mind)
IF THERE'S LOVE – Amant (TK)
LE FREAK/CHIC CHEER – Chic (Atlantic)
LOVE DISCO STYLE/PLUG ME TO DEATH – Erotic Drum
Band (Prism)
SHAKE YOUR GROOVE THING/LOVE IT UP TONIGHT –
Peaches & Herb (Polydor lp cuts)
SINNER MAN – Sarah Dash (Kirshner disco disc)
WEEKEND TWO STEP/MUSIC IS ALL YOU NEED – THP
Orchestra (Butterfly)
YMCA – Village People (Casablanca)
YOUR SWEETNESS IS MY WEAKNESS – Barry White
(20th Century)

Jabara called to give it his enthusiastic stamp of
approval (and to leak the news that he's doing his next
album with Alec Costandinos in London) and the third
time around might be the lucky one for this, song.
Though we hardly need another disco version of
"Poinciana," the B side attempts one and, again, once
the primary vocals are over, it has its fine moments,
too. Another possible double-header... **Fever's** version
of "Standing In the Shadows Of Love" (Fantasy) is the
project of two San Francisco disco DJs, **John Hedges**
and **Marty Blecman**, who also disco mixed the 7:11
track. They've restored much of the original song's
gripping, ominous feeling which had been smoothed
out of the **Deborah Washington** version and they've
injected a crunchy electronic break that sends tremors
across the dance floor. The vocals are amateurish and
leaden but the production can't be held down – it
nudges into the Top 30 this week at 29... The inevitable
disco version of Exile's "Kiss You All Over" comes from
a group called Broadway (on Hilltak/ Atlantic) under the
production of Willie Henderson (the "Dance Master"?)
and, though it begins on a monotonous, predictable
note, halfway through its 8:30 length, the production
begins to take hypnotic hold. Against a dense backdrop
of electronics and strings, a breathy female chorus
chants "I wanna kiss you all over" and we are treated to
a revival of the extended disco orgasm which runs until
the song fades. Sigh, squeal, moan, etc.... There's more
of the same in **Brenda Harris'** "Making Love Will Keep
You Fit" (Hot City), a freaky romp that carries on for
nearly twelve minutes in and out of ecstasy. Harris'
vocals are as rough and raw as much of the production
here and the sound is occasionally pretty homemade,
but it gets better and better as it goes on – a funk
extravaganza with very down-to-basics instrumentation.
"Freakin' Freak", (8:35) on the B side is more of the
same only further off the wall. ◐

DECEMBER 16, 1978

RECOMMENDED ALBUMS: A quick check-list of prime contenders for this week's "essential" honors: **Simon Soussan's** first release and production for his new Harem/Polydor label is **Arpeggio**, a three-man, one-woman group whose debut album, "Let the Music Play... ", picks up where **Pattie Brooks** leaves off. The arrangements are vibrant, bright, and high-spirited but, at times, somewhat erratic and unfocused, drifting off on a tangent (like the "I Wanna Tango" part of the title track) that leaves the dancers puzzled. The bulk of "Let The Music Play" (12:40), however, is tightly produced and exciting even if it starts out sounding like a "Black Is Black" remake (a sound Soussan can't seem to shake) and even if the vocals are occasionally thin, shrill and slightly "off" – Soussan ties together oddly disparate elements with a kind of zany haphazard flair that's quite unexpectedly winning. "Love And Desire" is a bit more compact at 8:57 but it combines many of the same attractions and distractions (the jittery synthesizer line, the screachy-thin female vocals) and delivers them in an appealing, neat package complete with super syndrum break. Added attraction: "Spellbound"... The new **T-Connection** album ("T-Connection" on Dash/TK) is more evidence of producer **Cory Wade's** sure touch with r&b-based disco. Though he's de-emphasized for the moment the sort of long, riveting percussion break that became the group's trademark after "Do What You Wanna Do," Wade has chosen looser, more richly textural effects here and the feel is effortless, new-breed funk. The group's vocals are more prominent than on their previous disco releases and they sound better than ever, combining rock and soul inflections on the three key dance cuts here – "Saturday Night" (4:28), with its shouts of "All right!," quick "ooowa-ooowa" chant and strong build; "At Midnight" (5:06), the most rock-oriented, with driving lead vocals and a hot percussion break with bell and syndrum effects that has been expanded for a forthcoming disco disc; and "Midnight Train" .(4:32), the loosest track but just as insinuating as the others with its solid string break. All aboard. And for quiet moments off the dancefloor, check out "Love Supreme," a lovely song in the **Earth, Wind & Fire** mold.

Lemon, a studio group put together by producer **Kenny Lehman** whose debut album is out on Prelude, has one of the freshest, cleanest pop disco sounds around right now. An instrumental version of the group's previously released "Freak On" is included here, but most of the newer material is stronger, more assured, highlighted by the opening cuts on each side: "A-Freak-A" (6:14) and "Chance To Dance" (6:12), both recalling bits of **Chic**, **Bionic Boogie**, **Musique** (and the former pulling in a snatch of **Pam Todd's** "Let's Get Together"), but coming up with something extremely catchy of their own. Two other cuts worth dipping into: "Hot Bodies" and "Inside My Heart"... **Miquel Brown's** "Symphony Of Love" album (Polydor) was recorded at Trident in London with a number of singers and musicians who are familiar to Eurodisco fans and it preserves that studio's reputation for brilliance and clarity in production. But the sound here is not strict Eurodisco,

maybe because the vocals are unusually robust and out-front and there's a strong pop drive to the arrangements that puts the material across with a special punch. "Symphony Of Love" (also available on a disco disc with a **Jim Burgess** mix) and "Dancin' With The Lights Down Low" are the knockouts here, but the whole album is solid, varied and thoroughly listenable. Try "The Day That They Got Disco In Brazil" when the mood is especially lighthearted.

❝ After more than four years, this is my final dispatch from the Land of 1,000 Dances, my last Disco File ❞

RECOMMENDED DISCO DISCS: A new **Trammps** release is always a disco event and "Soul Bones" (7:27 on Atlantic) should be no exception. The sound is instantly recognizable, perhaps overly so, because the group is still firmly rooted in a Philly funk style that has changed little over the past five years; once innovators, they now sound like traditionalists. But if they don't really take us anyplace we haven't been before, the Trammps remain supremely entertaining and "Soul Bones" is a no-nonsense good time, a gritty, pumping party song driven by **Jimmy Ellis'** raspy, snappy vocals and sparked by a playful, darting, **Stevie Wonder**-style harmonica break that is the one unexpected touch here. The B side here, "Love Magnet," presents the familiar flip side of the Trammps sound – sweeter, more luscious and ecstatic, lubricated with strings, but not as gripping or sustained as "Soul Bones." Both cuts are in the classic mold and are likely to hit disco playlists immediately... "(Dance It) Freestyle Rhythm" by **Mantus** (SMI) is anything but traditional – producer **Will Crittendon** has come up with a busy, quirky, funked-up number that sounds like one long break collage with lazy, often monotonous vocals dropped In. Available in a 9:33 and an 11 :00 version, the back-to-back mixes done by **Crittendon** and **John Benitez**, New York DJ and disco critic, "Freestyle" is at best mysterious and atmospheric, accented by shimmering, fluttery electronics that skim over a strong synthesizer/percussion/handclap track. The longer version ends with a sharp percussion segment that jumps with energy but seems oddly tacked on following a false ending; perhaps it's an added option for DJs' use. There's already strong word-of-mouth on this one as a result of advance pressings distributed in New York and it's due out commercially any day now... **Leif Garrett's** "I Was Made For Dancin'" (Atlantic) is a super-pop record that's a

I-BEAM, SAN FRANCISCO
DJ: Tim Rivers

A NICE FEELING – Caroline Crawford (Mercury)
CHANGE – Zulema (Le Joint)
CREAM (ALWAYS RISES TO THE TOP)/CHAINS/FESS UP TO THE BOOGIE – Bionic Boogie (Polydor)
DANCE – Paradise Express (Fantasy)
DOIN' THE BEST THAT I CAN – Bettye Lavette (West End)
FEED THE FLAME/LEARNING TO DANCE ALL OVER AGAIN'/NOBODY'S WRONG – Lorraine Johnson (Prelude)
HEY LOVE – Marti (Euphoria)
HANG IT UP – Patrice Rushen (Elektra)
HOLD YOUR HORSES – First Choice (Gold Mind)
IT'S MUSIC – Damon Harris (Fantasy/WMOT)
JE SUIS MUSIC – Cerrone (Cotillion)
SHAKE YOUR GROOVE THING – Peaches & Herb (Polydor)
SHOOT ME (WITH YOUR LOVE) – Tasha Thomas (Atlantic)
SINNER MAN – Sarah Dash (Kirshner)
WEEKEND/MUCH TOO MUCH – Phreek (Atlantic)

PARADE, NEW ORLEANS
DJ: Pete Van Waesberge

A-FREAK-A/CHANCE TO DANCE – Lemon (Prelude)
A LITTLE LOVIN' – The Raes (A&M)
BAISE MOI – Pam Todd (Channel)
CONTACT – Edwin Starr (20th Century)
DISCO SANTA CLAUS – Raindolls (AVI)
EASE ON DOWN THE ROAD – Diana Ross & Michael Jackson (MCA)
FEED THE FLAME/LEARNING TO DANCE ALL OVER AGAIN – Lorraine Johnson (Prelude)
GET DOWN – Gene Chandler (20th Century)
I WILL SURVIVE – Gloria Gaynor (Polydor)
IF THERE'S LOVE – Amant (TK)
SHAFT II – Isaac Hayes (Polydor)
SHAKE YOUR GROOVE THING – Peaches & Herb (Polydor)
SLY-HI – Philly Cream (Fantasy)
STANDING IN THE SHADOWS OF LOVE – Fever (Fantasy)
YMCA/THE WOMAN/I'M A CRUISER – Village People (Casablanca)

XENON, NEW YORK
DJ: Tony Smith

CHAINS/CREAM (ALWAYS RISES TO THE TOP)/FESS UP TO THE BOOGIE – Bionic Boogie (Polydor)
CONTACT – Edwin Starr (20th Century)
COUNTDOWN/THIS IS IT – Dan Hartman (Blue Sky)
HOLD YOUR HORSES – First Choice (Gold Mind)
I WILL SURVIVE – Gloria Gaynor (Polydor)
IF THERE'S LOVE/HAZY SHADES OF LOVE – Amant (TK)
KEEP ON DANCIN' – Gary's Gang (Sam)
LE FREAK/I WANT YOUR LOVE – Chic (Atlantic)
LET THE MUSIC PLAY/LOVE AND DESIRE – Arpeggio (Polydor)
LOOK FOR LOVE/JE SUIS MUSIC – Cerrone (Cotillion)
MY CLAIM TO FAME/TRUE LOVE IS MY DESTINY – James Wells (AVI)
SHAKE YOUR GROOVE THING – Peaches & Herb (Polydor)
SHOOT ME (WITH YOUR LOVE) – Tasha Thomas (Atlantic)
SOUVENIRS/KECHAK FANTASY – Voyage (Marlin)
YMCA/HOT COP – Village People (Casablanca disco)

fairly convincing **Michael Lloyd** imitation/variation of the **Brothers Gibb** – lots of falsetto chorus chanting and a central lyric section that sounds very like "Grease" at a slight upbeat. In spite of (and partly because of) the formula elements here, the song gets over – it has zest, a nice break, a few obligatory European touches – all thrown into even higher relief on the 6:28 instrumental side. Besides, a teenage sex symbol deserves all the encouragement he can get.

I've been thinking about this column for several weeks now, wondering how corny I should get. After more than four years of reporting on "current and upcoming discotheque breakouts" for Record World, this is my final dispatch from the Land of 1,000 Dances, my last Disco File. An announcement elsewhere in the magazine should explain where I'm going and why and I'd like to keep this short and sweet. Since the beginning, on November 16, 1974, when the first record reviewed was the "Do It 'Til You're Satisfied" lp by **B.T. Express** (I called it "an essential album"), Disco File has been primarily a fan's notes. It's been very satisfying to watch disco grow and prosper, but it's been even more of a pleasure to describe, dissect and delight in the music bit by bit, because hardly a week went by without some fine surprise, some new excitement. Disco File would have been nothing without the inspiration of performers and producers like **Donna Summer**, **Giorgio Moroder** & **Pete Bellotte**, **Alec Costandinos**, **Cerrone**, **Jacques Morali**, **Norman Harris**, **Patrick Adams**, **Cory Wade**, **Vince Montana**, **Grace Jones**, **Loleatta Holloway**, the **Trammps**, the **Savannah Band**, **Gloria Gaynor**, **First Choice**, **Lauren Rinder** & **Michael Lewis**, **Boris Midney**, **Don Ray**, **Gregg Diamond**, **Peter Brown**, **D.C. LaRue** – oh, the list could go on for days. My other prime inspiration was the enthusiasm and encouragement of disco DJs across the country who continue to be the avant garde of the disco force, ready for every new twist and turn; it's to them that this column has always been dedicated.

Taking over the column, beginning next week, will be Brian Chin, currently writing about disco for Gaysweek in New York, who can be expected to inform and entertain you in the style to which you've been accustomed. I can think of no better replacement – enjoy. But can I let go so easily? I imagine being pulled from the typewriter, hands still flailing at the keys, yelling – if it's possible to yell such things – some last-minute tips: **Fantastic Four!** ("B.Y.O.F. Bring Your Own Funk)" from the album of the same name on Westbound and the disco disc version of "Sexy Lady" with an **Issy Sanchez** disco mix, The Originals! ("While The Cat's Away" on a Fantasy disco disc), **Beverly & Duane!** ("Glad I Gotcha Baby" on an Ariola 12-inch), **Dolly Parton!** (the longer disco disc version of "Baby I'm Burnin' " available on pink vinyl from RCA), **Gonzalez!** ("Haven't Stopped Dancing Yet" on a Capitol disco disc), **Wild Fantasy!** (especially "Jungle Drums" from their Midsong lp of the same name), **Grey & Hanks!** (lots of nice stuff on their new album, including "You Fooled Me" and a super "Dancin'"). ❷

❝ The way I sold it was, "Look, here's this music that nobody else is writing about, it's really happening" ❞

Vince Aletti Interviewed

By Frank Broughton & Bill Brewster, October 12, 1998

Where did you grow up?

I was born in Philadelphia in 1945, grew up outside Philadelphia and Fort Lauderdale. I studied literature. I went to college just to go to college. It was 1962. And as much as I was not exactly caught up in the hippie thing, I was undoubtedly affected by what was going on. But I was focusing on my career; I wanted to be a writer – in a sort of vaguest way.

In a 'Vegas' way?

In the *vaguest* way.

Had you already been a record collector?

I was a music fan. I remember being a record collector as a kid, but not again until I went to college, when I completely got into Motown, in the early early Motown years. I started writing about music for the college paper. I went to school in Ohio, which really had schizophrenic radio. There were a lot of country stations there, but there were also some really strong R&B stations. So I was constantly listening to R&B, and I started writing about R&B records I heard on the radio. And that's what got me my job, my friend was sort of associated with a New York underground paper called *The Rat*. It was an important paper for New York. I don't think I was getting paid.

What year was that?

'67 or '68.

Were you writing about R&B?

I was writing about everything at that point. I wrote about Crosby, Stills and Nash, Woodstock. I wrote about everything that was happening, because I was interested in everything that was happening. But I was much more interested in R&B personally.

Did you go to Woodstock?

I went to Woodstock. Well, I left after the first day. It was too crazy. Anyway, because of *Rat* I ended up getting a job at Columbia Records for a year, writing publicity material. I was very lucky to get a job with that much money because most of the papers that were publishing rock'n'roll criticism really didn't have much money. When I was at Columbia I started writing for *Fusion*, *Crawdaddy* and a few other places that were happening at that point in publishing rock criticism. I realised that it would help me to focus on an area that I like and that no-one else was writing about, which was black music. So that's what I did. I specialised. Rock'n'roll criticism was totally started by fans. But not very many of them really listened to black music. It helped me specialise, because every time they wanted a Jackson 5 record reviewed, I did it. Little by little, other people started broadening and writing about black music, but for a long time I was the specialist. I was really a Motown fanatic: Mary Wells and that period. So I got all the records from the record company. I was on all the lists. And I was this R&B expert. Until I went to the Loft.

I started hanging out with friends who were going out to clubs, and most of my friends had discovered the Loft. I would go their houses and they would have this collection of records that I'd never heard of before, I didn't know anything about them. It really threw me off, because I was supposed to be this expert and I really didn't understand how that could have happened. And I realised, most of them had this very similar collection because they were all going to the same club. This is like First Choice, Creative Source, really off the wall, but completely early disco collections. I was really excited because here were all these records that I really liked that were at small labels, or they were things that didn't get promoted. Or perhaps they were on records that I already had but had not really listened to. So disco was really exciting for me because it was stuff I was already kind of into, yet it was a revelation. Also, here was another area I realised I could specialise in because nobody else was listening to it at all. Certainly not my critic friends. I wrote a piece for *Rolling Stone* in 1973 that I think was the first piece ever written about disco.

Brian Chin said it was one of the articles that transformed his life.
(*Laughs*) I didn't realise that. The way I sold it was, "Look, here's this music that nobody else is writing about, it's really happening," and I had a hook because just that summer Soul Makossa became a big national record after breaking out of the clubs in New York.

Didn't Mancuso break that record?
He was one of many people, but he really couldn't take all the credit. But it was a perfect thing to write about, because you could really trace how quickly it broke in the clubs, how quickly it got to radio and how it became a national record.

Was it new at that stage?
It was new to us. Someone had discovered it in some reggae shop.

Nick at Downstairs says he gave it to David. But then someone else told me that Mancuso found it in a Jamaican store in Brooklyn.
That's what I heard too. I don't remember hearing, for sure, that David had the record first. But that's what interested me too: the New York grapevine was so intense. A record could break in a club one night and next day everybody who cared about it, would know about that record and would be running around town trying to find it, would try to find the store that had it. It was a small scene and everybody knew everybody.

Were DJs protective of their records?
Not really. It wasn't like a white label scene.

The impression we got from D'Acquisto, Mancuso and co. was that they would meet and swap ideas, and records and tips.

Right. That whole thing with putting white labels on things wouldn't come up until later when disc jockeys were trying to preserve things for themselves. At this point everybody was friendly and it didn't feel like a scene full of rivals. They really wanted to share the music with the people in the club and tell their friends about it.

What was it like going to the Loft first time?

I heard about it through this group of friends, some of whom were would-be disc jockeys. Very mixed-race, mostly gay, but not entirely. A group of friends who I had become very close once we started going out. But I wasn't used to staying up until 12 in order to go out to some place, so they had to really get me into it. But once they did it was like nothing I've ever done before. And again, it was exciting to go to a place where almost every record I heard was completely new and great. So all I wanted to do was write down all the titles. What *is* this? It was very exciting.

And also the atmosphere. What excited me socially about clubs was that it was like going to a party. Completely mixed, racially and sexually, where there wasn't any sense of someone being more important than anyone else. And it really felt like a lot of friends hanging out. David had a lot to do with creating that atmosphere. Everybody who worked there was very friendly. There were people putting up buffets and fruit and juice and popcorn and all kinds of stuff. It did feel like going to someone's party, yet you were completely welcome at it. It was very hot and very crowded.

Was there a lot of drug-taking?

It's hard for me to say because, I know I was smoking pot, but I was not particularly aware of what other people were doing. I didn't have the sense that there were a lot of people out of control on drugs, the way that some clubs became later, where people were falling over themselves. I remember people smoking, but I don't remember any obvious drug-taking happening.

So where did you go from there?

I had also gone to this other club that was also, I felt, significant in the period, that was more a gay prototype. The Tenth Floor. And there was a disc jockey there called Ray Yeates, who was one of the few black jocks who was really successful in the crossover clubs. And he really had great taste, played a number of unusual records and it seemed to me he was always discovering things.

"It was exciting to go to a place where almost every record I heard was totally new and great."

What kind of unusual records?

Singles, like, literally 45s at that time. Basic black material. Patti Jo. Did you ever read Dancer From The Dance? By Andrew Holleran. All of the records he describes in there and the club he writes about: that's Tenth Floor. And he mentions a number of records that are all Tenth Floor records. Sort of light R&B with female vocals.

Wasn't it a prototype hi-NRG club?
No. That's what I thought. It became a prototype for 12 West and Flamingo. Infinity was more of a straight money-making club. Tenth Floor was a very private club that became influential because of the people who went there. And because of the style. That whole look was completely what all the gay clubs ended up doing later: grey industrial carpeting, banquettes, juice bar, flower arrangements. It just had a look that everybody copied. Industrial, hi-tech, chic.

> **"What was important about the Loft was this whole cultural mix. You felt very brotherly toward other people"**

Who were the influential people who went there?
Fashion designers, but more like second-level: fashion designer assistants. I didn't go there that often, but it really became one of those places that was a legend, even if it didn't last, because of all the things that came out of there. But what was important to me about the Loft was this whole cultural mix that was going on there and it really felt like this sort of New York melting pot that totally worked. And David made it clear that everybody was there because he wanted them to be there and so you felt very brotherly toward other people.

Did you get to know him personally in that period?
I just knew him very casually. I was always bugging him with, "What is that record?" Then in '74 I did the *Voice* interview and became much more friendly. I always felt he was a difficult person to get friendly with. But then my schedule was not the same as his.

Are you referring to his nocturnal habits?
Mainly. He was a great DJ. He was a person who really discovered records and synthesised things. But there were certain people who worked with him who became so completely caught up in his myth that it was very destructive for them. And I just tried to stay away from that because it was too intense. Judy Weinstein, who was very close to him when the Record Pool happened, then pulled away to form her own record pool, but was very disillusioned by him.

Didn't you recommend Judy to him?
Yes I did. I was involved in the Record Pool at the very beginning.

How did that come about?
Out of necessity. I was at *Record World* at that point and part of my job was calling disc jockeys each week to get their top ten lists and to find out what they were playing. And a lot of what I heard was how difficult it was to get records. At this point, it was clear that disc jockeys were really breaking records, selling records that the companies thought they would never sell. So they were becoming more and more important, and the labels didn't

know what to do about them. Here were all these people knocking on their door saying we want a record and the labels didn't know how to verify where they were working, didn't know who they were. So it was obvious there had to be some kind of organisation to give the disc jockeys credibility and power in the business; and to verify who they were.

Had the record companies recognised this need?
To some extent. A lot of companies were giving out records, but as soon as they did, a lot of people were coming and saying give me one too. So the record companies needed help and the disc jockeys needed help. And so the disc jockeys got organised enough to say what can we do, how can we form a group that the record companies will recognise and the group will vouch for its members.

The independents understood anyway, didn't they, because they were the ones that saw their records broken in the clubs.
The independents were the people that helped it get going because they were so much more tied in. There were enough people who realised that they were getting really great returns from giving records out, but they still needed help getting it organised.

So who galvanised the whole thing?
I think David to a great extent, because he was still someone who people looked up to. Even though I think some people resented his being a figurehead, he was always very well meaning and always looking out for other people. He was the only person who could pull people together. And he had this space. He had 99 Prince to work out of and offered it as a place run to the Record Pool. He was the only person who owned his own club, that's the bottom line. Everyone else was working as an employee somewhere. David had a place that he could actually bring people to and use as a distribution point. If he didn't they would have tried to rent some place, but he certainly made it a lot easier. It was idealistic, but it was also a very workable and smart thing to do. And everybody else, once they saw that it worked, started imitating it around the country.

Who did that first?
People in the area. There became little splinter groups. I don't remember exactly when things broke off. This guy Eddie Rivera, he was the first person to form another big record pool. Most of his members were from outlying areas, they were not the key jocks, but they were all working in Brooklyn and Queens. He was Puerto Rican and had a loyalty from the Puerto Rican jocks who might not have already been a member of the Record Pool. Now that I think about it, I think he worked at the Record Pool for a while but didn't get along with David, they had a falling out and broke off and took some of them with him. It very quickly became a lot of splinters. Partly in New York, and then when Judy was there that was essentially the end of David's pool.

When did it actually start, because you were involved, weren't you?
I'm terrible at dates. Steve D'Acquisto would be able to tell you better than I can. He was one of the other people who wrote up the whole proposal that we did. I guess about '73 or '74.

When did For The Record start? 75?

Sounds right. But what was sad about that, sad about Eddie Rivera, sad about Judy having to pull away; was that it had started out as a very idealistic thing pulling everybody together. And more and more it became a big business and became more ego-driven and complicated. The more money was involved, the less people got along.

How tied into the hippie era do you think it was?

Not enough to make a difference to anybody. It was only David. You know, David and his idealism. It certainly didn't feel like any hippie outpost to anybody who went there.

How quick were the labels to jump on it and exploit it?

Because I was writing about the music during this whole period, I would say not quick at all until Rock The Boat, Rock Your Baby, Love's Theme, all became number one records.

Wasn't there a story about Billy Smith and the Barry White record?

Right. That was another great record business story. For a record that the label didn't even know they had, to become huge in the clubs. Six months after it became a number one club record it became a number one pop record. It took that long for it to really catch on.

> **❝ Instead of being creative and seeing what this new music's about, at first all they tried to do was imitate Barry White ❞**

That was the best thing about that period. The record companies were very happy to see these little things pick up and get sold. I'm sure Atlantic were very delighted with what happened to Soul Makossa, but that was a one-shot. It didn't turn into an album thing for them. Soul Makossa was such a fluke, but these other records. You don't have three flukes in a row and not have record companies paying attention.

So the first problem, instead of being creative and seeing what this new music's about, at first all they tried to do was imitate Barry White. Imitate George McRae. Imitate Gwen McCrae. There were all these records that were just exactly like those. They didn't happen. And this is what the record business still does to some extent. Something becomes big and they imitate it. And the imitations fail completely. And then they say, "Well, this is not a real thing." It's so easy to have something fall apart quickly because the commercial impulse that follows it, just kills it off by imitating it without any creativity. It took a while for the imitations to fall away and for people to start making creative records again. And that's when I think disco had a second wind of really good music.

I think the second wind was the Eurodisco stuff that started coming in. Especially the European records. They became imitated, but at least they had a longer life. Had it not been for Donna Summer's record, it gave it another punch. But during the time I was at *Record World* – basically 1974-79 – I was doing a weekly column. Each week I would call four different jocks and ask them what their top ten was. And there was a sort of cumulative list of what the top records where. I became close to a lot of disc jockeys because I loved that they were so completely dedicated to the music

It was what I loved about music writing when I first got into it – there were all these music enthusiasts. People who completely lived for music. Who spent all their money on music. I just loved their drive. It seemed to me that they lived for what they were doing and since I was just as excited about the records, a lot of our talking on the phone was about what records they had heard, and what records I had heard. It was the best period of music, for me, to feel completely tuned into it from the ground up. To hear things before they were pressed on a record. I felt very privileged. I felt like I was in the middle of the scene. Most of the records I was singing to myself hadn't even been released yet. I was lucky enough to get a tape or acetate. It was a really interesting and exciting period for me and, I think, for all the guys who were working in it.

Do you think part of its charm was that secret world?
Yeah. One of the things I loved about David, one of the records I remember him playing was this cut off a Bonnie Bramlett album, Crazy 'Bout My Baby. And no way were they aware how that track was being used. But there it was: a top ten Loft record. It was those sort of accidents that kept things creative. The things designed for discos were not always the best records. The things that people discovered and made work kept it going and they were usually what pushed it off into another direction, or pushed into more creative areas. And I think it's still the same. It's the records you just don't expect, that no one's ever made before, that are the ones that indicate where things are going.

What happened once a record took off?
Well, one of the things that discouraged me about disc jockeys was that once a record became a hit, they would usually stop playing it. Usually because they had already been playing it for three months and they were tired of it, but once it became a radio record, they just weren't interested in it any more. They were glad to claim it, and it gave them a lot more leverage with the record companies. But they also disowned it on a certain level. They just didn't want to know about it any more because they were already on to the next record. And that kind of hurt them in the long run with the record companies. But I do think a lot of disc jockeys were really proud to see their records happen, especially at the beginning. When Love's Theme became such a big record, they could really claim that as their own. It was strictly a club record.

What effect, if any, do you think Stonewall had on clubs?
I'd have to say only a residual effect. Before Stonewall it was illegal for men to dance in clubs together. But most of the clubs that were big early on were private so they didn't have to deal with that anyway. You wouldn't even have known the Tenth Floor was there.

Was that going on in the sixties?
I don't really know. I never went out to bars, so I don't really know that scene. Once I started going out to discos I remember hearing about those things, but I never went to them. I mean, I was definitely an aberration in terms of disco. I would go at 12, sometimes 11.30, hang out with David in the booth, because I loved hearing the music that started

out the night. And some of my favourite music was David's early records. He would play this sort of jazz, environmental things, very loose. He would make this whole atmosphere when people where coming in. Before people started dancing.

What kind of records?

I would have a hard time pinning down records at this point. But David could give you some examples, I'm sure. These oddball things that he would discover, that were mostly like jazz-fusion records, or international world music things. Things that didn't have any lyrics for the most part, but were just cool-out or warm-up records. And I loved that kind of stuff. It was great to see the mood getting set. Little by little they would get more rhythmic and more and more danceable and people would start dancing. I loved seeing the whole theatre get underway. It was like being in a play before the actors had started. And I did the same thing at the Loft and the Garage. I would go early and by the time a lot of my friends got there, at about 4 o'clock, I'd be leaving.

Were there different shifts of people?

Yeah. Some people would come early and wait for things to pick up. And then it would get to a certain peak at about 4 or 5 in the morning and would get so crowded that you couldn't dance

In the Loft or the Garage?

Both places. A lot of my friends in the business, because of course during this whole period my friends were disc jockeys, other clubgoers and promoters. Most of my promoter friends would arrive at the club at about 4 o'clock in the morning because they'd already been to a lot of other clubs. Well, it was the Garage at that point because the Loft was sort of pre-promotion to a great degree. But they'd come to the Garage because they'd already been to four or five places and dropped off records.

When the Garage opened with the construction parties did it eat into what the Loft was doing?

I wasn't going out quite as much for a while. I wasn't all that tuned into what was going on. But there were enough places that siphoned off typical Loft-goers, but David would have this hardcore crowd. He had a crowd that always went there. But he lost some of that to other places, which were newer, crazier.

One thing I wanted to mention: when disco promotion really took off, in '74, '75 I guess, it was the first time that a lot of gay people were working in the record business, which had always always been a very very traditional, straight business. I was working at CBS Records in '69, it was a period of what they called the 'House Hippie', where there'd be one or two people who would work at a label who could plug them into what kids were really listening to. So there'd be some long-haired guy working at the record label who would be their hippie. When disco came, they knew that all the traditional promotion guys – who were all, typically, these straight, older out-of-shape guys – were not going to work.

They weren't exactly going out dancing at Tenth Floor.

Actually, this is post-Tenth Floor, this is when Le Jardin happened, and Infinity and the other big clubs. They were in the press all the time, and they were getting attention; they realised that they had to deal with these clubs, and they had to deal with the disc jockeys. The men who were already at the companies were at a loss. Little by little, they realised they would have to bring someone in, and often they would hire somebody who was an ex-disc jockey, or someone who was working in a club.

The only older person on the scene was this guy named Juggy Gayles. I think he died. He was the only record biz character, and he loved disco. He was the only old-guard promotion person who attached himself to the scene and became everybody's father figure. But all the other guys who got hired were almost exclusively gay. And it really changed record companies. I mean, it was really interesting to me to watch this happen because I was already dealing with a lot of people when I was working at *Record World* and as they started hiring people and changing and having to deal with some fairly flamboyant characters. But they knew that these guys knew what they were doing; and they were getting the records played.

> **"The guys who got hired were almost exclusively gay. And it really changed record companies, dealing with some fairly flamboyant characters"**

The House Homos!

Well, "Homo Promo" was what they all called themselves! (*Laughter*) The person who became the symbol of all this was my eventual boss Ray Caviano, who was a true record business person, and happened to be gay. He really was a very savvy record guy who made disco his thing. A lot of the others were a little flakier and a little crazier.

I think a lot of people within the business resented it. When I worked with Ray at RFC/Warners, there was still a lot of tension, because Ray was very out and very gay, but very straight-acting in a way. They wouldn't have known what his preferences were, except he talked about them whenever he did an article. And he got lots of publicity when he got that deal and he always talked about being gay. I don't think the company was very comfortable with it, but they had to deal with it as long as he was successful. RFC happened at this very crucial turning point. We signed the deal in '79.

It was very late in disco wasn't it?

It was. It seemed like everything was happening, then suddenly it was all over. So halfway through our tenure there, disco was over and they changed the department's name to dance music. And they lost so much confidence in the whole thing that all these issues of sexuality became much more sticky and much more difficult for everybody to deal with. But through the period when it was happening, I think it was a really good thing for the business. It really opened the business in a way that I had never seen before. I was glad.

Where people able to hold on to their positions?

Only a few of them. They really disbanded the departments really quickly. There were a lot of records that were still happening, but nobody wanted to call them disco any more so a lot of those departments continued as dance music departments.

Was there a point where one record didn't happen, but the previous one had?

No, it wasn't quite like that.

How significant was the Comiskey Park anti-disco riot?

I happened to see, coming over on the plane, the Last Days of Disco which I hadn't seen before. There's footage from the Comiskey Park thing, and really that was just a sort of acting out of a feeling that had always been in the air.

Because Steve Dahl, who hosted it, was a rock DJ, wasn't he?

Right. And there was always that feeling and resentment.

Was it labelled as fag music around that time?

To some extent, I don't think people were that brazen, or obviously homophobic about it, but certainly that was the undercurrent. There was a definitely a level of resentment that this music had so much attention. Not just the music, but a real movement of people, and people really cared about it. It had just drawn in a lot of disparate elements, who all felt a common interest in this music. The fact that a lot of them were gay didn't make any difference to the people who were into the music, but from the outside it really became an issue, I think. I think it made it easier for people to put it down.

Was it distaste from the record-buying public, or distaste for this social movement?

A little bit of both. I think the record companies and radio just got tired of it. To some extent, the success of Saturday Night Fever was the end of it all, and also the influence of Eurodisco at a certain point. When something becomes so big and so successful that the business thinks it's got to move on, it milks it for all its worth. And then it's over. For a long time, it didn't seem like a fad, but it became so big that it had to be done with. I don't think the general public had anything to do with it.

My feeling was at that point it was very much radio. Radio was still very traditional. It was very straight, very rock'n'roll and most of the people there were just not interested. They didn't care about the music, they only played it because it was a hit. And they were only too glad to see it go. What was weird about us being at Warner Brothers at that point was Ray, as part of his deal with Warner Brothers was that he created a promotions department for all their dance music records, not just the label he set up. So just as disco was supposedly over, he made huge hits out of D'Ya Think I'm Sexy? and Rock Lobster. Neither of which could really be classified as disco records but were real dance records.

What about labels like Prelude and West End. A lot of their interesting records, like D Train, came after the fall of disco.

Well, a lot of the records that came out after that period I thought were really stronger. They didn't have to fit into a mould. They were less and less formulaic. It was what I like about disco in the first place. It had no formula. It was completely unexpected. There were all these things you just couldn't predict. What bothered me about the label "disco," especially as it became used by the business, was that it meant formula to a great extent. And so it wasn't open to the creativity that was there in the music. When the Eurodisco sound – like Donna Summer – became the definitive disco sound, everything else around it became less and less disco and more and more freaky, in a way. It was possible for all these other records to happen, but the Eurodisco thing was like over. Except, embarrassingly enough I think, in certain gay clubs, where the only thing that they played were these hi-NRG disco records.

> **❝ It became another creative period for the disc jockeys, the same way pre-disco was, because they had to go out and look for records ❞**

This was the period when I was most intensely involved with the music. Once RFC was disbanded it was the end of the period for me as well. Not so much disbanded, but once they left Warner Bros. I was let go, as the label fell apart. So it was a very definitive period for me in terms of involvement. Except I was still going to the Garage. Now I think about it, I do think that a lot of the records that came after that that were big Garage records, were more interesting than some of the records that came out at the height of disco.

Were there a lot of casualties?
Well, there already were casualties in the business because there was a huge drug-taking period. A lot of the people who didn't die later of AIDS, overdosed. A lot of the key, early disc jockeys, overdosed during the early Eighties.

Which DJs are you talking about here?
I can't actually remember any names.

What drugs are you talking about?
Combinations of downers and coke, usually.

What about the clubs post-disco?
It became another creative period for the disc jockeys, the same way pre-disco was, because they had to go out and look for records. They had to go out and find odd things. So there became more quirky records, more oddities. And that's what had drawn me to it in the first place. I mean, all along there had always been these weird fluky records. But after the whole disco thing fizzled, it went back to something more strange. And people made more unusual more unusual connections. It was easier to play the Clash *and* Loleatta Holloway.

Were you aware at that time of what was happening in the Bronx?
Not so much. One of my most embarrassing moments in the business was when I was at RFC Records I was doing A&R and getting all these tapes. And the Kurtis Blow record had

become a hit, a semi-hit, Christmas Rapping. So we started getting some very imitative rap records and I remember writing to somebody, "This is just a fad. It'll never happen." And of course regretting it six months later. But there were certainly a lot of bad rappers at that point. There was some crossover with the graffiti East Village art scene and the sense that this whole Bronx thing was very hip. With hip-hop and Keith Haring and the early people working in the East Village.

So tell us about Larry Levan and the Paradise Garage.

My experiences of the Garage are so much different from everybody else's because I went there as it was opening up. My whole connection to Larry was through Judy Weinstein.

She managed him the whole time didn't she?

Yeah. She was close to him. That's why I started going, because I was hanging out with her. We'd all hang out together.

The first time you saw him was at the Garage?

Yes. I never went out as much as most of my friends did. When I went to the Garage, I'd hang out in the booth which usually ended up being a number of Larry groupies and promotion people and other club employees. And seeing this scene of people coming to play my record, getting Larry to hear something, or leaving off an acetate. It was mainly because Larry had the ear of Frankie Crocker at WBLS. At that point it was *the* radio station and he was the big disc jockey. And he was the only one who was really clued into disco. And he would go to the Garage. He knew he could go and be comfortable and hear new things. So Larry became incredibly important. Beyond the fact that he was a good disc jockey and he had a great club, he had the ear of the most important radio disc jockey in the city. Promotion people could pretty much count on it, that if their record got played it would be heard by Frankie Crocker. And that was doubly important. All those factors made it the hot club. Everybody who had a record to push would get to perform there. One thing fed into another. It became important because of all of these factors. And it helped that Larry had a great ear, was a good mixer, and had an interesting crowd.

So how valid is the Larry legend?

The legend, as regards Larry, totally depended on him being up there in the booth. It was a theatrical place. The way it was set up with this booth overlooking the floor – it was also one of the largest booths in New York – you could get 30 people up there if you wanted. So it became a whole other scene. It became like the VIP room of VIP rooms. And yet it was not very much about celebrity. It was about Larry's friends. Some of the celebrities who came, never got up there at all. The Larry legend is like beyond any reason. It's just sort of feeds on itself to some extent.

And also the fact that he's dead.

I was talking mostly about what gave him power within the New York scene. He really became the ruling disc jockey and that was to do with the promoters giving him that power.

Did Studio 54 have a similar power? It was more publicly known.

Studio was still more of a pop place and the Garage was much blacker. The music they played, the people who went there, the crowd was probably 75% black, and it was important that Larry plugged into that. I really can't say that the Garage was underground for more than a year after it opened. It was still private, and still had its membership list, so not everybody could get in, but it was so known as the hot place to go.

Do you think it maintained its hotness right till the end?

Almost till the end. It helped that it was still inaccessible to a lot of people. In the same way that it helped Studio that it was inaccessible to a lot of people who wanted to go there, not everyone could get in to the Garage. So if you got in, it was a scene. It was definitely a scene. People from Europe and everywhere knew about it – I'm not sure how the word spread, but the way those things do. It was always interesting, because it always attracted the kind of music business and celebrity that was not like the Studio scene at all. It was hipper and younger, to some extent.

What marked him out as a DJ compared to the others?

That I'm not so sure about, because I often thought that he made very clumsy mixes. He was not the most elegant of mixers, but he did have a great ear. I loved the kinds of things that he would pick up and put together. It really just gets down to taste.

Was it him picking these odd records, or did he get them from someone else?

I think he had a lot of good advice from other people, the same way all good disc jockeys do – David Mancuso, from the very beginning, had people bringing him records – but in the end it was Larry who decided to play them. I'm sure he listened to everything that came his way and made a decision that this one would work and that one would work. He also made certain records his records, even though everybody else was playing them.

Such as?

Such as Love Is The Message. Not that he was the first to play it, by any means, it was out long before the club opened, but it became such a defining record for the Garage.

Was that the bootleg edited mix or the original?

The original, although he started doing his thing with it. I always think of that and Weekend by Phreeek, any Loleatta Holloway record, the Clash's Magnificent Dance, Lace. It makes a certain force of personality to make records that everybody else is playing your own. It wasn't always that he played them first, he played them... all the time! *(Laughs)* It felt like they belonged in that club.

It's to do with context isn't it?

Yeah, that's right, it's the context. And he was really good at making this night happen. For me it was the crowd he got. One of the things that excited me about disco was that it really did bring people together and it was a way of being out partying with people who you would never be with in another context, and with whom suddenly you became friendly with. I don't really like clubs that are one thing. I don't like clubs that are just gay. Or just black. So it was really important to him to have a real mixture all the time. If it was essentially a black club, that was also important because it was never tipped over in another direction. It was important to him that it was essentially a black club, but also very mixed. And also essentially a gay club, but a mixed one.

Nicky Siano was very critical of Studio 54 when we interviewed him. He said he thought the elements Rubell introduced to the party were the beginning of the end.

It totally got rid of the democracy of the party. It was the beginning of disco becoming a business of a whole other sort. And, I thought, really unattractive. The only time I was in Studio was when RFC Records had a kick-off party there when it first formed, and another party later. I would never go to a place where I had to worry about whether they would let me in or not. There was nothing else before Studio, though there were other clubs that led up to Studio. Before that there was Arthur and other pre-disco clubs. A lot of other clubs aspired to that status and were jealous when it happened for Studio. But I think it was destructive to have a velvet rope. It was completely against the idealism of disco and the community of disco, in the sense that everybody was together.

Did people at the Garage regard Studio as the anti-Christ?

To an extent. I certainly did. It was not what we thought this was all about. David's idealism was very widespread in terms of the way people felt. I think disco was, to some extent, a movement and a lot of people felt very strongly. And a lot of people got very caught up in what they felt it should and shouldn't be.

What was the reaction when Studio 54 took off?

There's a scene at the end of the Last Days Of Disco one of the characters has this very idealistic speech where he says disco was a whole movement. It was funny, but it was really true and people felt that. They felt disappointed that the idealistic quality of it was being trampled over, in favour of money and celebrity. As much as disco was glitzy and certainly loved celebrity culture, there was never a sense of it being driven by that. It was much more driven by an underground idea of unity.

If it was idealistic, what would you say was the manifesto?

Love Is The Message. The manifesto was the music. That's another thing I loved about Larry – and which I don't feel in clubs any more – he liked playing records because he liked what they were saying. And David, too. There was this real sense that he was speaking to you through those records and, that love is the message. There were certainly things that he played that wouldn't fit in with his love, love, love message, like Love Money by Funkmasters, but the overriding message was unity and love. That was the other thing I remember feeling very drawn to. That was the manifesto.

Were there other DJs from that period who you would say were noteworthy, like Tee Scott for example?

> **"As much as disco was glitzy, there was never a sense of it being driven by celebrity culture. It was much more driven by an idea of unity"**

Another club I went to occasionally was Flamingo, which was very gay, 99%, very white for the most part, but had a great club jock there, Richie Rivera. He was really good, and also very charismatic, but in a slightly more retiring way. I'm trying to remember other people. A lot of people I would talk to on the phone and get very friendly with, like Jellybean, Tony Smith, people who I rarely heard play.

Jellybean was the first superstar DJ really wasn't he?

True, and I was surprised to see him do it, because when I first met him he was very young, very sincere and a little shy, so it seemed to me. I would never have predicted that he would be the one to break out and to be the first one to put his name on a record. He definitely upped the ante as to where you could go. He was playing at Funhouse during his most influential period. Which was only important because he was there. He really drew an interesting crowd. In a way a hip-hop crowd, very mixed, black and Puerto Rican, really young. A cute crowd. It was a great crowd for him to work on. It gave him his first real dedicated followers. He'd become successful by that point, but he really hit his stride there and was able to break records.

What do you think was the lasting impact of those early disco DJs?

There was a period, at the beginning, where they all felt like proselytisers. Not just to their audience but to each other. It was a real community. They were happy to share, and make connections with other people. They weren't jealous of each other, they weren't overly competitive. That only came later. The bigger the business, the more involved... It seemed like a small scene and they were real buddies. This was their connection. They lived and breathed music and didn't talk about anything else. It wasn't like they had a big life outside of the clubs.

Before clubs became very successful and made a lot of money, a lot of them played several nights a week at several different clubs. They lived for nothing else. This was all they had to talk about and they loved it. That was their currency: the newest record. You got a sense from them that there was a constant trawling of record stores and places where they knew they could find things. It was an active, and great, network, that was all about sharing. ✪

The best disco you never heard